The Cambridge Handbook of Creativity Across Domains

Creativity is of rising interest to scholars and laypeople alike. Creativity in the arts, however, is very different from creativity in science, business, sports, cooking, or teaching. This book brings together top experts in their fields from around the world to discuss creativity across many different domains. Each chapter includes clear definitions, intriguing research, potential measures, and suggestions for development or future directions. After a broad discussion of creativity across different domains, subsequent chapters look deeper into those individual domains (the traditional arts, the sciences, business, newer domains, and everyday life) to explore how creativity varies when expressed in different ways. Ultimately, the book offers a future-looking perspective integrating the different variations of creativity across domains.

JAMES C. KAUFMAN is Professor of Educational Psychology at the University of Connecticut. The author or editor of more than forty books (including *Creativity 101*, 2nd edition, 2016), he is a past president of APA's Division 10 and founding editor of two APA journals. Kaufman has won awards from APA (Berlyne, Arnheim, and Farnsworth), Mensa, NAGC (Torrance), and the ALA's Choice Outstanding Academic Title. He has tested Dr. Sanjay Gupta's creativity on CNN and narrated the comic book documentary *Independents*. Other work includes the book and lyrics to the musical *Discovering Magenta* and a book on bad baseball pitchers with his father, Alan. He is the president-elect of the American Creativity Association.

VLAD P. GLĂVEANU is Associate Professor at the Centre for the Science of Learning and Technology, Bergen University, Norway. He received his PhD from the London School of Economics, UK, and published over 120 articles and book chapters on creativity, imagination, art and crafts, social change and culture. He recently edited the *Palgrave Handbook of Creativity and Culture Research* (2016) and co-edited the *Oxford Handbook of Imagination and Culture* (2017). His other books include: *Thinking Through Creativity and Culture* (2014), *Distributed*

Creativity (2014), *Rethinking Creativity* (2015, co-edited), and *Creativity: A New Vocabulary* (2016, co-edited). He is also editor of *Europe's Journal of Psychology (EJOP)*, an open access peer-reviewed journal published by PsychOpen (Germany).

JOHN BAER is Professor of Educational Psychology at Rider University. He is a winner of the American Psychological Association's Berlyne Prize and the National Conference on College Teaching and Learning's Award for Innovative Excellence. His books include: *Domain Specificity of Creativity*; *Being Creative Inside and Outside the Classroom*; *Creativity and Divergent Thinking: A Task-Specific Approach*; *Creative Teachers, Creative Students*; *Creativity Across Domains: Faces of the Muse*; *Reason and Creativity in Development*; *Are We Free? Psychology and Free Will*; and *Essentials of Creativity Assessment*.

The Cambridge Handbook of Creativity Across Domains

Edited by

James C. Kaufman
University of Connecticut, USA

Vlad P. Glăveanu
University of Bergen, Norway

John Baer
Rider University, USA

CAMBRIDGE
UNIVERSITY PRESS

CAMBRIDGE
UNIVERSITY PRESS

University Printing House, Cambridge CB2 8BS, United Kingdom

One Liberty Plaza, 20th Floor, New York, NY 10006, USA

477 Williamstown Road, Port Melbourne, VIC 3207, Australia

4843/24, 2nd Floor, Ansari Road, Daryaganj, Delhi – 110002, India

79 Anson Road, #06–04/06, Singapore 079906

Cambridge University Press is part of the University of Cambridge.

It furthers the University's mission by disseminating knowledge in the pursuit of education, learning, and research at the highest international levels of excellence.

www.cambridge.org
Information on this title: www.cambridge.org/9781107110182
DOI: 10.1017/9781316274385

© Cambridge University Press 2017

First published 2017

Printed in the United States of America by Sheridan Books, Inc.

A catalogue record for this publication is available from the British Library.

Library of Congress Cataloging-in-Publication Data
Names: Kaufman, James C., editor. | Glăveanu, Vlad Petre, editor. | Baer, John, editor.
Title: The Cambridge handbook of creativity across domains / edited by James C. Kaufman, University of Connecticut, USA, Vlad P. Glaveanu, Aalborg University, Denmark, John Baer, Rider University, USA.
Description: New York : Cambridge University Press, [2017] | Includes index.
Identifiers: LCCN 2017026024 | ISBN 9781107110182
Subjects: LCSH: Creative ability.
Classification: LCC BF408 .C173 2017 | DDC 153.3/5–dc23
LC record available at https://lccn.loc.gov/2017026024

ISBN 978-1-107-11018-2 Hardback

The first book I ever did about domains was dedicated to my young bride, Allison.

Fast forward more than a decade, and we have two boys, too many pets, and a wonderful life together. This volume is notably bigger (in scope and length) than my initial offering – much as my love for her has continued to grow.

I dedicate this book to Allison Beth Katz Kaufman.

With all of my love, forever.

James

For Constance, who fills my life with joy and wonder and my parents, Corina and Petre, who guided my first steps into the many domains of creativity.

Vlad

To SKB.

John

Contents

Figures

Tables

Contributors

ÜLKÜ AYVAZ, Bolu İzzet Baysal University

JOHN BAER, Rider University

BILGE BAL-SEZEREL, Anadolu University

PAUL JOSEPH BARNETT, University of Connecticut

RONALD A. BEGHETTO, University of Connecticut

NATHALIE BONNARDEL, Aix Marseille University

CAROLE BOUCHARD, ParisTech Arts & Métiers

MARC A. BRACKETT, Yale Center for Emotional Intelligence

ELIAS CARAYANNIS, George Washington University

ARTHUR J. CROPLEY, University of Hamburg

DAVID H. CROPLEY, University of South Australia

DOUGLAS C. DERRICK, University of Nebraska at Omaha

MAJA DJIKIC, University of Toronto

STEPHEN J. DOLLINGER, Southern Illinois University at Carbondale

MARINA BAZHYDAI, Harvard University

JEANETTE G. ELSTEIN, University of Pennsylvania

GREGORY J. FEIST, San Jose State University

MARIE J. C. FORGEARD, McLean Hospital (Behavioral Health Partial Program) & Harvard Medical School

VLAD P. GLĂVEANU, University of Bergen

THALIA R. GOLDSTEIN, George Mason University

ELENA L. GRIGORENKO, University of Houston, Baylor College of Medicine

PHILLIP HARVARD, EIGSI Engineering School of La Rochelle

JESSICA D. HOFFMANN, Harvard Graduate School of Education

MOLLY HOLINGER, University of Connecticut

JEOU-SHYAN HORNG, Jinwen University of Science and Technology

RODICA IOANA DAMIAN, University of Houston

ZORANA IVCEVIC, Yale Center for Emotional Intelligence

MACIEJ KARWOWSKI, Creative Education Lab, The Maria Grzegorzewska University in Warsaw

ALLISON B. KAUFMAN, Department of Ecology and Evolutionary Biology, University of Connecticut and Department of Psychology, University of Connecticut at Avery Point

JAMES C. KAUFMAN, University of Connecticut

MARK KILGOUR, University of Waikato

AARON KOZBELT, Brooklyn College and the Graduate Center of the City University of New York

IZABELA LEBUDA, Creative Education Lab, The Maria Grzegorzewska University in Warsaw

HELMUT LEDER, University of Vienna

ANNE G. LEVY, The University of Alabama

GINA SCOTT LIGON, University of Nebraska at Omaha

LIN LIN, I-Shou University

GREGORY N. MANDEL, Temple University

DANIEL MEMMERT, Institute of Training and Computer Science in Sport, German Sport University Cologne

KEVIN MITCHELL, University of Nebraska at Omaha

KEITH OATLEY, University of Toronto

WILLIAM J. O'HEARN, Department of Ecology and Evolutionary Biology, University of Connecticut

N. NAZLI ÖZDEMIR, Anadolu University

MATTHEW PELOWSKI, University of Vienna

KYLIE PEPPLER, Indiana University

RONI REITER-PALMON, University of Nebraska at Omaha

RALF ROMEIKE, Friedrich-Alexander University Erlangen-Nürnberg

SANDRA RUSS, Case Western Reserve University

UGUR SAK, Anadolu University

BREE L. SANDWITH, University of South Australia

JOANNA SERAFIN, The Graduate Center of CUNY (primary) & Downstate Medical Center (secondary)

DEAN KEITH SIMONTON, University of California, Davis

KARYN SPORER, University of Maine

JOANNA SZEN-ZIEMIAŃSKA, University of Social Sciences and Humanities in Warsaw

MARIE TAILLARD, ESCP Europe Business School

MEI TAN, University of Houston

PAULA THOMSON, California State University, Northridge.

PABLO TINIO, Montclair State University

REESE Y.W. TOU, University of Houston

OSHIN VARTANIAN, University of Toronto

BENJAMIN G. VOYER, ESCP Europe Business School

CLAIRE WALLACE, Case Western Reserve University

Acknowledgments

The authors would like to thank David Repetto and everyone at Cambridge for their help and patience in putting this together. We would also like to thank Paul Joseph Barnett and Molly Holinger for their assistance.

PART I

Creativity and Domain

1 Creativity Across Different Domains

An Expansive Approach

James C. Kaufman
University of Connecticut

Vlad P. Glăveanu
University of Bergen

John Baer
Rider University

Abstract
Domain-generality and domain-specificity have long been debate fodder for the creativity field. As the two positions have begun to converge, the need emerges for a new reference work that both explores the general topic and offers in-depth coverage of creativity for particular domains. Our goal for this edited handbook is to offer a reference for existing research, provoke ideas for collaborations and interactions, and propel the field forward as we consider the domains that may be covered in future editions.

Creativity Across Different Domains: An Expansive Approach

Think about a computer scientist developing a new program, an artist working on a painting, and an advertising executive crafting a slogan. All three are engaging in creative endeavors, but in very different domains. Are the cognitive processes they use similar, or are they different? What about their motivations, their skills, their personalities, the way they interact with their environment? What are the particular features that distinguish them? What are the commonalities?

The question of the degree to which creativity is a general ability or domain specific is an important one in creativity research that is still being studied and discussed. The topic has grown from a dichotomy to gradually converging levels of discussion. In the only point-counterpoint, debate-style pair of articles in its history, the *Creativity Research Journal* asked two leading proponents of these competing positions to argue the case for domain specificity versus generality (Baer, 1998; Plucker, 1998).

A pair of edited books came out less than a decade later that examined the issue from different perspectives. Sternberg, Grigorenko, and Singer (2004) had top scholars write essays on the topic. Kaufman and Baer (2005a) invited researchers who studied creativity in several domains to write essays about the nuances of creativity in that domain. Both works offered essays that provided converging approaches to the topic in Plucker and Beghetto (2004) and Kaufman and Baer (2005b).

Studies have continued to examine nuances and different components of this issue. One approach that favors domain specificity but acknowledges the role of domain-general aspects is the Amusement Park Theoretical Model (Baer & Kaufman, 2005; Kaufman & Baer, 2004, 2006). We will review this theory in more detail later in this book. Just as theorists who favor domain specificity acknowledge domain-general aspects of creativity, so too do those who argue for the existence of domain-general creative-thinking skills recognize that domain-specific thinking skills play important roles in creative thinking (Sawyer, 2012).

The domain-specific approach to creativity asserts that the content matters, and that it matters very deeply. In fact, domain-specificity theorists suggest that saying that someone is creative without specifying the domain (or domains) in which they are creative is rather like saying someone is an expert without mentioning the area of that person's expertise. No one is an all-around expert, and neither is anyone universally creative across all domains. Just as someone may be an expert in Japanese literature but know nothing about quantum mechanics (or vice versa), so it is possible to be creative in one area and not at all creative in another (Baer, 2011, 2013, 2016). Of course, one may be an expert in both Japanese literature and quantum mechanics – there's no reason one can't have multiple areas of expertise – but we simply can't predict expertise in one area based on expertise in some unrelated domain. The same is true, according to domain specificity, for creativity. There are of course polymaths who are highly creative in several domains, but they are the exception, not the rule (Kaufman, Beghetto, & Baer, 2012; Kaufman, Beghetto, Baer, & Ivcevic, 2010). The underlying skills, motivations, personality traits, cognitive strengths and styles, self-beliefs, and knowledge bases that lead to creativity in different domains are different.

A domain-specific perspective has helped psychologists make sense of many troublesome and seemingly conflicting findings in the creativity literature, findings that have seemed to generate much heat but precious little light when viewed from an assumption of domain generality. For example, the highly charged question of the relationship between creativity and mental illness has long dogged creativity studies, with research pointing both toward a strong association and no association whatsoever. Recent domain-specific studies have explained past research findings that seemed contradictory by demonstrating that the mental illness–creativity connection exists in some domains and at some levels of eminence, but not others (Kaufman, 2014). So, for example, creativity in science at the highest levels is not generally associated statistically with mental illness (Simonton, 2014), but poetic creativity at such levels is more likely to show a relationship (Kaufman, 2001a, 2001b; Kaufman & Baer, 2002).

In a somewhat less-charged arena, there is similar domain-specific evidence that conscientiousness, one of the Big Five personality traits, has a significant positive impact on creativity in some domains (such as science; e.g., Feist, 1998) and a significant negative impact in others (such as creative writing or the arts; e.g., Wolfradt & Pretz, 2001). There are also differences in lower-level domains; for example, ballet dancers are more conscientious than modern/contemporary dancers (Fink & Woschnjak, 2011). These kinds of domain-based differences are allowing creativity theorists to make sense of what often seem, from a domain-general perspective, to be conflicting results.

It has been more than a decade since the two edited books (Kaufman & Baer, 2005a; Sternberg, Grigorenko, & Singer, 2004) first appeared. Since then, a great deal has happened in the world and in creativity research. Online data collection allows us to study people all over the world (Hass, 2015). We can measure creativity with applications for mobile devices (Reisman, 2017) or in a more stealthy manner using video games (Shute & Ventura, 2013). Technological advances mean we have to reconsider past creativity theory (Gangadharbatla, 2010). Creativity has been studied in text messaging (Tagg, 2013), YouTube videos (Courtois, Mechant, & De Marez, 2012), and iPad artwork (Kucirkova, & Sakr, 2015).

Considering creativity across domains means something different in the present day than in past years. We had several goals for this book, and one goal was to reflect the changing world. Some chapters are on traditional domains, whereas others are on domains that have radically expanded or entirely changed in our lifetimes. We are fully aware that many emerging domains are only cursorily addressed in the current volume and hope that future editions will be even more inclusive. Some of the most exciting potential domains, such as social networking or digital media, are slowly growing but did not offer an obvious contributor who would be well-versed both in that world and the creativity realm. Our chapters on computer science, biomedicine, educational technologies, and many others, however, do include material on creative activity that would have been unimaginable when Guilford, Barron, and Torrance were developing the field.

Another goal was to highlight important scholarship that may not quickly occur to creativity researchers as being relevant. We so often exist in silos – by discipline, department, topic, or journal – and it is easy to miss work that could influence and nurture our own approaches. Creativity studies flourish in the realms of sports, terrorism, animals, law, and cooking, and we believe that the measures, theories, and ideas discussed in these chapters will be interesting and applicable to people interested in creativity in other domains.

A third goal was to offer reflection on the ideas of creative domains themselves. In this first section, we proceed with a chapter describing the Amusement Park Theoretical Model in more detail.[1] Next come insights into cross-domain creativity[2] and the importance of considering domain-general components.[3] In the second section, we have chapters on traditional arts: literary writing,[4] visual arts,[5] architecture,[6] photography,[7] acting,[8] music,[9] and dance.[10] The third section includes essays on creativity in the sciences: physical science,[11] biomedicine,[12] psychology,[13] engineering,[14] mathematics,[15] and computer science.[16] In the fourth section are chapters on creativity in business, with wide-ranging content covering

---

[1] See Chapter 2. [2] See Chapter 3. [3] See Chapter 4. [4] See Chapter 5. [5] See Chapter 6.
[6] See Chapter 7. [7] See Chapter 8. [8] See Chapter 9. [9] See Chapter 10. [10] See Chapter 11.
[11] See Chapter 12. [12] See Chapter 13. [13] See Chapter 14. [14] See Chapter 15.
[15] See Chapter 16. [16] See Chapter 17.

advertising,[17] marketing,[18] leadership,[19] educational technologies,[20] design,[21] and entrepreneurship.[22] In the fifth section, we include the chapters on the newer domains we mentioned above (specifically law,[23] cooking,[24] sport,[25] animals,[26] and terrorism[27]). Our final full section, part six, considers creativity in many different aspects of everyday life. There are chapters on emotion,[28] teaching,[29] culture,[30] therapy,[31] play,[32] and craft.[33] Finally, we offer integrative and future-oriented thoughts in a last concluding chapter.[34]

This book has been a fascinating and gratifying experience. We were able to work with dear friends and meet new colleagues. Some of the authors you will read are the leading superstars in the field, others are rising bright lights. Some people regularly publish in creativity journals, whereas others have academic homes elsewhere. We hope that this will be an enjoyable intellectual journey for you, the reader, with some chapters reinforcing what you know about a topic and others offering pure discovery.

References

Baer, J. (1998). The case for domain specificity in creativity. *Creativity Research Journal, 11*, 173–177.

Baer, J. (2011). Why grand theories of creativity distort, distract, and disappoint. *International Journal of Creativity and Problem Solving, 21*(1), 73–100.

Baer, J. (2013). Domain specificity and the limits of creativity theory. *Journal of Creative Behavior, 46*, 16–29.

Baer, J. (2016). *Domain specificity of creativity.* San Diego: Academic Press.

Baer, J., & Kaufman, J.C. (2005). Bridging generality and specificity: The Amusement Park Theoretical (APT) model of creativity. *Roeper Review, 27*, 158–163.

Courtois, C., Mechant, P., & De Marez, L. (2012). Communicating creativity on YouTube: What and for whom?. *Cyberpsychology, Behavior, and Social Networking, 15*, 129–134.

Feist, G. J. (1998). A meta-analysis of personality in scientific and artistic creativity. *Personality and Social Psychology Review, 1998*, 290–309.

Feist, G. J. (1999). The influence of personality on artistic and scientific creativity. In R. J. Sternberg (Ed.), *Handbook of human creativity* (pp. 273–296). New York: Cambridge University Press.

Fink, A., & Woschnjak, S. (2011). Creativity and personality in professional dancers. *Personality and Individual Differences, 51*, 754–758.

Gangadharbatla, H. (2010). Technology component: a modified systems approach to creative thought. *Creativity Research Journal, 22*, 219–227.

Hass, R. W. (2015). Feasibility of online divergent thinking assessment. *Computers in Human Behavior, 46*, 85–93.

Kaufman, J. C. (2001a). Genius, lunatics, and poets: Mental illness in prize-winning authors. *Imagination, Cognition, and Personality, 20*, 305–314.

---

[17] See Chapter 18.   [18] See Chapter 19.   [19] See Chapter 20.   [20] See Chapter 21.
[21] See Chapter 22.   [22] See Chapter 23.   [23] See Chapter 24.   [24] See Chapter 25.
[25] See Chapter 26.   [26] See Chapter 27.   [27] See Chapter 28.   [28] See Chapter 29.
[29] See Chapter 30.   [30] See Chapter 31.   [31] See Chapter 32.   [32] See Chapter 33.
[33] See Chapter 34.   [34] See Chapter 35.

Kaufman, J. C. (2001b). The Sylvia Plath effect: Mental illness in eminent creative writers. *Journal of Creative Behavior, 35*, 37–50.

Kaufman, J. C. (Ed.) (2014). *Creativity and mental illness*. New York: Cambridge University Press.

Kaufman, J. C., & Baer, J. (2002). I bask in dreams of suicide: Mental illness, poetry, and women. *Review of General Psychology, 6*, 271–286.

Kaufman, J. C., & Baer, J. (2004). The Amusement Park Theoretical (APT) model of creativity. *Korean Journal of Thinking and Problem Solving, 14*, 15–25.

Kaufman, J. C., & Baer, J. (2006). Intelligent testing with Torrance. *Creativity Research Journal, 18*, 99–102.

Kaufman, J. C., & Baer, J. (Eds.). (2005a). *Creativity across domains: Faces of the muse*. Hillsdale, NJ: Lawrence Erlbaum Associates.

Kaufman, J. C., & Baer, J. (2005b). The amusement park theory of creativity. In J. C. Kaufman & J. Baer (Eds.), *Creativity across domains: Faces of the muse* (pp. 321–328). Hillsdale, NJ: Lawrence Erlbaum Associates.

Kaufman, J. C., Beghetto, R. A., & Baer, J. (2010). Finding young Paul Robesons: The search for creative polymaths. In D. D. Preiss & R. J. Sternberg (Eds.), *Innovations in educational psychology: Perspectives on learning, teaching, and human development* (pp. 141–162). New York: Springer.

Kaufman, J. C., Beghetto, R. A., Baer, J., & Ivcevic, Z. (2010). Creativity polymathy: What Benjamin Franklin can teach your kindergartener. *Learning and Individual Differences, 20*, 380–387.

Kucirkova, N., & Sakr, M. (2015). Child–father creative text-making at home with crayons, iPad collage & PC. *Thinking Skills And Creativity, 17*, 59–73.

Plucker, J. A. (1998). Beware of simple conclusions: The case for the content generality of creativity. *Creativity Research Journal, 11*, 179–182.

Plucker, J. A., & Beghetto, R. A. (2004). Why creativity is domain general, why it looks domain specific, and why the distinction does not matter. In R. J. Sternberg, E. L. Grigorenko, & J. L. Singer (Eds.), *Creativity: From potential to realization* (pp. 153–167). Washington DC: American Psychological Association.

Reisman, F. K. (2017). Please teacher, don't kill my kid's creativity: Creativity embedded into K-12 teacher preparation and beyond. In R. A. Beghetto & J. C. Kaufman (Eds.), *Nurturing creativity in the classroom* (2nd edn.) (pp. 162–189). New York: Cambridge University Press.

Sawyer, K. (2012). *Explaining creativity: The science of human innovation (2nd ed.)*. Oxford University Press.

Shute, V. J., & Ventura, M. (2013). *Measuring and supporting learning in games: Stealth assessment*. Cambridge, MA: MIT Press.

Simonton, D. K. (2014). More method in the mad-genius controversy: A historiometric study of 204 historic creators. *Psychology of Aesthetics, Creativity, and the Arts, 8*, 53–61.

Sternberg, R. J., Grigorenko, E. L., & Singer, J. L. (2004). *Creativity: From potential to realization*. Washington, DC: American Psychological Association.

Tagg, C. (2013). Scraping the barrel with a shower of social misfits: Everyday creativity in text messaging. *Applied Linguistics, 34*, 480–500.

Wolfradt, U., & Pretz, J. E. (2001). Individual differences in creativity: Personality, story writing, and hobbies. *European Journal of Personality, 15*, 297–310.

2 The Amusement Park Theoretical Model of Creativity

An Attempt to Bridge the Domain-Specificity/Generality Gap

John Baer

Rider University

James C. Kaufman

University of Connecticut

Abstract

The Amusement Park Theoretical (APT) Model of Creativity weaves together both domain-general and domain-specific factors supporting creative performance with a hierarchical structure. There are four levels of the model – Initial Requirements, General Thematic Areas, Domains, and Microdomains – that describe increasing levels of domain specificity. The APT Model reminds creativity researchers and theorists of the need to consider and to identify the differing degrees of domain generality and domain specificity in the constructs they are investigating. The APT Model also provides a useful and flexible framework for such discussions.

Is creativity domain specific, or is it domain general? Do some of the same abilities, traits, skills, motivations, habits of thought, knowledge bases, or cognitive styles underlie creative performance in all domains? Or, instead, are there different patterns that predict creative success for each domain? Does being creative when performing a task in one domain make it more likely that a person will be creative when undertaking tasks in unrelated domains? In other words, can one apply one's creativity in engineering to help write more creative sonnets, paint more creative landscapes, teach more creative history lessons, or bake more creative soufflés?

Although (by its nature) this book takes a domain-specific stance, the question is a complex one. The same broad concept underlies a recurring and fierce debate in the field of intelligence – is there a *g*, a single general factor of intelligence which accounts for most of the variance in intellectual ability? Or is intelligence comprised of distinct abilities, as conceptualized by some psychometric approaches (such as the CHC model; Horn & Cattell, 1966; McGrew, 2009) and modern theories (such as the theory of Successful Intelligence; Sternberg, 1996)? This question is quite important – there are implications for everything from best hiring practices to teaching strategies to even larger concerns about social issues – and has produced considerable vitriol.

Creativity: Domain Specificity and Domain Generality

The parallel question in creativity may provoke fewer fistfights but continues to be a hot topic after more than twenty-five years. It was the subject of *Creativity Research Journal*'s only Point-Counterpoint pair of articles in its history (Baer, 1998b; Plucker, 1998), and eleven years later the issue was at the heart of the first debate sponsored by the American Psychological Association's Division 10 (Baer, 2009; Kim, 2009; see also Baer, 2011b & 2011c and Kim, 2011a & 2011b for a follow-up written version of the same debate that was solicited by the APA journal *Psychology of Aesthetics, Creativity, and the Arts*).

When creativity research began in earnest, this issue was not debated much because there was often an implicit assumption that creativity was domain general. The early pioneers, from Wallas (1926) to Guilford (1950) to Torrance (1963), tended to approach creativity as being domain general or as being minimally different across domains. Barron (1969) was one of the few pioneers who did large bodies of research exploring creativity in different areas, studying eminent creators across several specific occupations.

Today, things are quite different (Baer, 2010, 2016). We are by no means suggesting that the tide has turned such that domain specificity is now implicitly assumed, but rather that the question of domains is often considered as a key variable (either to be studied, controlled, or included as a potential limitation) in studies. In addition, many modern theories include creativity domains as a key element or topic to be considered. There are still arguments being made for both sides, but there has been a slow movement toward the middle of the issue. Although the focus in this book is on the domain-specific components of creativity, we would not argue that there are no domain-general components. The Amusement Park Theoretical (APT) Model we will describe includes both domain-specific and domain-general aspects. Indeed, one of the purposes of this book is to gather together information on creativity across many different domains such that it can be used for many different purposes; one such purpose could be finding measures or approaches used in one domain that could then be used in more domain-general work.

Before we detail the specifics of the APT Model, we want to elaborate on some of the core principles that it is built upon. For one, abilities, skills, and traits are not seen as *either* domain specific *or* domain general. There is no clearly divided specificity-generality dichotomy, with traits and abilities falling neatly on one side or the other. Each factor related to creativity rests on its own continuum, with some being more domain specific and others more domain general. Throughout the rest of the chapter, when we say creativity-related factors, we are referring to the abilities, knowledge bases, motivational states, interests, skills, personality traits, cognitive styles, habits of mind, and individual preferences that play a role in both domain-general and domain-specific creativity.

One further issue to discuss are creativity-related factors that might be considered either broad theoretical constructs or (quite differently) actual abilities or traits. For example, think of "content knowledge." As a theoretical construct, "content knowledge" sounds very domain general, and indeed it is essential for creativity in most, if not all, domains. The need for some kind of content knowledge to be creative is so obvious that it generally goes without saying; creativity does not occur in an intellectual vacuum. But no one argues that *actual* content knowledge is a domain-general factor. Content knowledge in dance and content knowledge in chemistry and content knowledge in economics have fairly little overlap; a large database of information about the life and dance moves of Bob Fosse will probably not include much related to fluorescence microscopy. Indeed, the specific content knowledge needed to be creative in each domain is generally recognized to be domain specific. When we discuss most concepts in the model, it is usually as the specific skill or trait (i.e., being conscientious) as opposed to the larger theoretical construct (i.e., personality).

The Amusement Park Theoretical (APT) Model

Over a decade ago, the authors of this chapter edited a book about creativity across domains (which could be considered the current book's intellectual prede-cessor). As we tried to integrate the disparate ideas and studies presented throughout the book, we derived a theoretical model to explain our current thoughts (Kaufman & Baer, 2005), which we proceeded to further develop over time (Baer & Kaufman, 2006; Kaufman & Baer, 2004a, 2006).

The APT Model proposed a hierarchy with four levels — Initial Requirements, General Thematic Areas, Domains, and Micro-domains — that range from extre-mely domain general to extremely domain specific. Why is it called the Amusement Park Theoretical Model? Alas, there are no high-speed rides or parade floats to be found anywhere in the model; it serves as a central metaphor for the creative process (albeit, perhaps, one that is a bit too flippant).

Initial Requirements

The first level is the Initial Requirements. There are some things you need to enter any amusement park. You need transportation – either your own car or a friend who will give you a ride or reliable public transit. You need money; most parks aren't free and there are always souvenirs and food. You need the time to go, and perhaps someone to go with you,. Of course the importance of those things (transportation to the park, money to purchase an admission ticket, and companions to share the experience) might vary from park to park (e.g., some amusement parks are much more expensive than others).

Similarly, there are certain things one needs to be creative in any domain. In our initial model, we highlighted three key factors. First is general intelligence. Although creativity and intelligence consistently show a weak but significant corre-lation (Jung, 2014; Kim, 2006), the relationship is quite nuanced. We're not referring to the nuance (which would include both different aspects of intelligence and how some domains of creativity are more or less dependent on intelligence) here, however. Instead, intelligence is an initial requirement for creativity in that it is virtually impossible to be intentionally creative without some level of intellectual ability. There are exceptions, of course; some people with savant syndrome can be very creative (Treffert, 2014). But it is rare.

The second construct suggested by the initial model was motivation. As with intelligence, we stayed nonspecific and did not refer to intrinsic or extrinsic motivation (Deci & Ryan, 1985). We refer here to the motivation needed to get up off the couch and do something, regardless of its impetus. It might be a burning passion to change the world or the vague desire to avoid boredom, but it is motivation regardless of its expression. The third and final construct named in the original model is a supportive environment that allows one the freedom to try something (anything) new.

There are, of course, many other constructs we could have chosen. For example, repeated studies have shown that the personality factor of openness to experience is related to creativity across a wide variety of domains and activities (see review in Kaufman, 2016) and, indeed, being open to new experiences and ideas is a pretty key component of creativity. Our guess is that you could come up with a few more yourself.

General Thematic Areas

It's one thing to decide to go to an amusement park; it's another thing to decide what type of park you want to choose. Maybe you want to go on exciting roller coasters, or be in the water, or be surrounded by particular cartoon characters. Each of these different types of park represents a different theme – much as, we have argued, creativity has different General Thematic Areas.

There are many different attempts to outline the structure of creativity. Some are rooted in more broad cognitive terms. Gardner (1999) has proposed eight such "intelligences": interpersonal, intrapersonal, spatial, natural history, language, logical-mathematical, bodily-kinesthetic, and musical; he also later debated adding existential intelligence (Gardner, 2006). Hirschfeld and Gelman (1994) propose eight "domains of mind" (cognitive neuroscience, cultural anthropology, biological anthropology, developmental psychology, education, linguistics, philosophy, and psycholinguistics), whereas Feist (2004) proposes seven (art, biology, linguistics, math, music, physics, and psychology).

In creativity, Carson, Peterson, and Higgins's (2005) Creativity Achievement Questionnaire (CAQ) has two factors and ten domains. There is an arts factor (drama, writing, humor, music, visual arts, and dance) and a science factor (invention, science, and culinary). The tenth domain, architecture, did not load on a factor. In another study, Ivcevic and Mayer (2009) outlined three main factors: the creative lifestyle (e.g., crafts, self-expression, interpersonal creativity, visual arts, writing, sophisticated media use), performance arts (music, theater, and dance), and intellectual creativity (technology, science, academia).

We have conducted many studies on this topic (Kaufman, 2006, 2012; Kaufman & Baer, 2004b; Kaufman, Cole, & Baer, 2009), constructing several different self-assessment measures in the process. The number of factors has varied from three to eight; the current measure, the *Kaufman Domains of Creativity Scale* (K-DOCS; Kaufman, 2012) outlines five General Thematic Areas: everyday, scholarly, performance, math/scientific, and artistic; it has shown evidence of solid reliability and validity (McKay, Karwowski, & Kaufman, in press). Earlier incarnations included factors such as hands-on creativity, communication, problem-solving, entrepreneurship, sports, and humor.

Domains

As we descend the model we go further and further in the direction of specificity. Once you've decided on the type of amusement park you want to go to, you still have to choose the exact park. If you want roller coasters, do you choose Six Flags or the local park? If you want cartoons, do you pay up for Disneyworld or Sesame Place?

In creativity, the General Thematic Areas are only the beginning. You might begin on the path of performance creativity, but there are many possible domains, from theater acting to solo singing to group dancing. The underlying skills needed for creativity in all these areas would have many similarities, as would the traits that lead to creative performance. Many of these traits and skills may have little association with creativity in other General Thematic Areas (although there may be overlap with domains in some General Thematic Areas but not others).

It is important to note that we are using domain in a different way from how Csikszentmihalyi (1999) uses the term in his Systems Model. His "domain" is an area of expertise but can be very broad or very specific; in his model, a domain could just as easily refer to conducting research on creativity assessment or to being a psychologist. The scope is not important because the other dimensions in the model (the "field" of gatekeepers and the "person" who creates) are different categorical concepts. In our case, we use domain to refer to a particular level of specificity – not so broad as "music composition" but not so specific as "Sondheimesque musical theatre." We are not, in this instance, using it in the same way that Csikszentmihalyi (1999) uses the term in his Systems model.

Micro-domains

Once you've settled on the right park, there are still decisions to be made. If you're at an amusement park known for its roller coasters, you can go on the death-defying drop rides or the gentle ones for kids and wimps. If you're at a Disney park, there are a multitude of different worlds and lands to explore. Within creativity, there are still domains inside of domains – namely, micro-domains.

Even if you've winnowed everything down to poetry, you still have to choose between different forms, such as epic, haiku, sonnet, villanelle, elegy, sestina, abecedarian, limerick, and tanka. Many poets work with several of these forms while others concentrate on just one or two, and the underlying abilities and traits that lead to creative performance in these different micro-domains would have considerable (but far from complete) overlap. If you've settled on psychology, more decisions are still needed – Clinical? Cognitive? Social? Educational?

Table 2.1 *The Amusement Park Theory*

Level	Amusement Park examples	APT Model examples
Initial Requirements (the highest degree of domain generality)	Transportation to the park, a ticket to enter, money	Intelligence, motivation (whether intrinsic or extrinsic) to do or create something, an environment that allows some form of creativity
General Thematic Areas	What type of amusement park? Rides, animals, water, cartoon characters, etc.?	Everyday, scholarly, performance, math/scientific, or artistic creativity (among others)
Domains	Picking the actual amusement park itself	Within math/science (for example) it could be chemistry, biology, physics, psychology, economics, etc.
Micro-domains	Within the actual amusement park, where do you go?	Within psychology (for example): clinical, cognitive, social, developmental, neuroscience, educational, or organizational

Developmental? Neuroscience? Organizational? Micro-domains might seem like small distinctions to someone outside of the field but loom quite large to someone working in the field.

Table 2.1 summarizes the theory.

The specifics of the APT Model are far less important than the general ideas that (a) the skills and traits needed for creativity in any field or area of interest include both many very domain-specific factors and a few fairly domain-general ones, and (b) the more similar two fields or areas of interest are, the more similar will be the traits and skills associated with creativity in those areas.

Take-Home Points from the Amusement Park Theoretical Model

We see the importance of the model to be the way it reminds creativity researchers and theorists of the need to specify the kinds of skills and traits they are identifying. Consider motivation, which is certainly an important part of the creativity story. Without trying to settle the debate about the importance of intrinsic motivation in creative performance (or whether extrinsic motivation is a good or bad thing for creativity), we merely want to use the line of research established by Amabile and Hennessey (e.g., Amabile, 1996; Hennessey, Amabile, & Martinage, 1989; Hennessey, 2010, 2015) as a starting point. Specifically, let's begin with the idea that intrinsic motivation leads to higher levels of creativity and the more controversial idea that extrinsic motivation leads to lower levels of creativity (see, for example, Eisenberger & Shanock, 2003, as a counter argument). With this starting point, how can we demonstrate how domain-general and domain-specific factors can be easily confused? As with the term "content knowledge," "intrinsic motivation" can be taken to include all kinds of intrinsic motivation and as such it can be thought of as a possible domain-general contributor to creativity. But people's motivations are not uniformly intrinsic, and their levels of intrinsic motivation in one domain (e.g., writing poetry) may not be at all predictive of their intrinsic motivation in other domains (e.g., designing chemistry experiments). In fact, their levels of intrinsic motivation are likely different across micro-domains – the same person may love writing haikus but hate writing sonnets. There may be further layers; even within a single task there are likely some parts that are enjoyable and others that are merely tolerated.

Just as one can posit content knowledge as something that is important for creativity in all or most domains (a domain-general claim) and yet recognize that in its actual operation the effects of content knowledge on creativity are extremely domain specific, so it is with many other factors (such as intrinsic motivation) that may be considered from both domain-general and domain-specific perspectives. In these cases, the domain-general understanding of such elements can point to concepts that matter to creativity at the most general level, but these are not to be (mis)understood to mean that these traits or abilities actually operate in a domain-general way. One cannot generally take the same ability (such as content knowledge in some domain) or trait (such as interest in a particular kind of activity) and use that ability or trait productively in any unrelated domain or activity.

Studies that have claimed to show the effects of intrinsic and extrinsic motivation on creativity have not generally focused on specific domains. In a typical study of this kind, an experimental manipulation is introduced to increase subjects' intrinsic or extrinsic motivation with respect to the task at hand. Writing stories, making collages, and crafting poems are the most widely used tasks, but for the purposes of most studies the content of the task employed in the study is considered unimportant. The effects of the manipulation are reported as domain-general effects, but consider for a moment the kinds of motivations that are actually increased in these studies. A reward might be offered for writing a creative poem, or participants might be led to expect that the collages they are about to make will later be evaluated. Both interventions increase extrinsic motivation, but the extrinsic motivation they increase is very domain specific. Participants may produce less creative poems or collages under such conditions, but these manipulations – and their effects – are domain specific. So they may produce less creative poems, but this manipulation (assuming it is valid) doesn't make them less creative teachers, less creative geologists, or less creative sculptors.

It could be, of course, that things like intrinsic motivation and content knowledge have some amount of domain generality at the individual level. People who have more content knowledge in one domain may be more likely than chance to have more content knowledge in most domains. And, in fact, that is probably true, simply because people who are more intelligent (in the g, domain-general sense) are able to acquire content knowledge in most domains more readily than those with lower levels of intelligence. Highly intelligent people (as well as people who have the resources needed to spend many years as students) would be expected, therefore, to have somewhat higher levels of domain-specific knowledge in many domains than people with lower IQ scores (or fewer economic resources).

This volume looks at what abilities, traits, and other factors lead to creativity in specific domains. Most of the issues discussed are fairly domain specific, although they sometimes suggest parallel abilities or traits that might be of importance in other domains. The goals of the APT Model include producing the kinds of research that the many chapters of the volume describe and providing a framework within which we can better understand creativity in both its domain-specific and domain-general aspects.

We call for research for more information about how the different patterns of factors needed for success across the different levels of the model. In a sense, it might even be possible one day to identify strings of traits and abilities needed for success in different areas such that (theoretically) a list of algebraic formulas could be calculated to predict a person's ability in a particular micro-domain. Perhaps (in a less Orwellian manner) it could be used for guidance purposes.

As you read this book, keep the different levels of the APT Model in mind. If most chapters represent the domain level, how do they differ? How do the measurements vary by domain? What associated traits and abilities recur in their importance, and which ones seem to matter for only a select few domains? And, of course, what questions have yet to be answered – or asked?

References

Amabile, T. M. (1996). *Creativity in context: Update to "The social psychology of creativity."* Boulder, CO: Westview Press.

Baer, J. (1996). The effects of task-specific divergent-thinking training. *Journal of Creative Behavior*, *30*, 183–187.

Baer, J. (1997). Gender differences in the effects of anticipated evaluation on creativity. *Creativity Research Journal*, *10*, 25–31.

Baer, J. (1998a). Gender differences in the effects of extrinsic motivation on creativity. *Journal of Creative Behavior*, *32*, 18–37.

Baer, J. (1998b). The case for domain specificity in creativity. *Creativity Research Journal*, *11*, 173–177.

Baer, J. (2009). Are the Torrance Tests still relevant in the 21st century? Invited Address, presented at the annual meeting of the American Psychological Association, Boston, MA., August 2009.

Baer, J. (2010). Is creativity domain specific? In J. C. Kaufman & R. J. Sternberg (Eds.), *Cambridge handbook of creativity* (pp. 321–341). Cambridge: Cambridge University Press.

Baer, J. (2011a) Domains of creativity. In M.A. Runco, and S.R. Pritzker (Eds.), *Encyclopedia of creativity* (2nd edn., pp. 404–408), Vol. 1. San Diego: Academic Press.

Baer, J. (2011b). Four (more) arguments against the Torrance Tests. *Psychology of Aesthetics, Creativity, and the Arts*. *5*, 316–317.

Baer, J. (2011c). How divergent thinking tests mislead us: Are the Torrance Tests still relevant in the 21st century? *Psychology of Aesthetics, Creativity, and the Arts*, *5*, 309–313.

Baer, J. (2016). *Domain specificity of creativity*. San Diego, CA: Academic Press/Elsevier.

Baer, J., & Kaufman, J. C. (2005). Bridging generality and specificity: The Amusement Park Theoretical (APT) Model of creativity. *Roeper Review, 27*, 158–163.

Barron, F. (1969). *Creative person and creative process*. New York: Holt, Rinehart & Winston.

Carson, S. H., Peterson, J. B., & Higgins, D. M. (2005). Reliability, validity and factor structure of the Creative Achievement Questionnaire. *Creativity Research Journal, 17*, 37–50.

Csikszentmihalyi, M. (1999). Implications of a systems perspective for the study of creativity. In R. J. Sternberg (Ed.), *Handbook of creativity* (pp. 313–335). Cambridge: Cambridge University Press.

Deci, E. L., & Ryan, R. M. (1985). *Intrinsic motivation and self-determination in human behavior*. New York: Plenum.

Eisenberger, R., & Shanock, L. (2003). Rewards, intrinsic motivation, and creativity: A case study of conceptual and methodological isolation. *Creativity Research Journal, 15*, 121–130.

Feist, G. J. (2004). The evolved fluid specificity of human creative talent. In R. J. Sternberg, E. L. Grigorenko, & J. L. Singer (Eds.), *Creativity: From potential to realization* (pp. 57–82). Washington, DC: American Psychological Association.

Gardner, H. (1999). *Intelligence reframed: Multiple intelligences for the 21st century*. New York: Basic Books.

Gardner, H. (2006). *Five minds for the future*. Cambridge, MA: Harvard Business School Press.

Guilford, J. P. (1950). Creativity. *American Psychologist, 5*, 444–454.

Hennessey, B. A. (2010). Intrinsic motivation and creativity in the classroom: Have we come full circle? In R. A. Beghetto & J. C. Kaufman (Eds.), *Nurturing creativity in the classroom* (pp. 329–361). New York: Cambridge University Press.

Hennessey, B. A. (2015). If I were Secretary of Education: A focus on intrinsic motivation and creativity in the classroom. *Psychology of Aesthetics, Creativity, and the Arts, 9*, 187–192.

Hennessey, B. A., Amabile, T. M., & Martinage, M. (1989). Immunizing children against the negative effects of reward. *Contemporary Educational Psychology, 14*, 212–227.

Hirschfeld, L. A., & Gelman, S. A. (1994). *Mapping the mind: Domain specificity in cognition and culture*. New York: Cambridge University Press.

Horn, J. L., & Cattell, R. B. (1966). Refinement and test of the theory of fluid and crystallized intelligence. *Journal of Educational Psychology, 57*, 253–270.

Ivcevic, Z., & Mayer, J. D. (2009). Mapping dimensions of creativity in the life-space. *Creativity Research Journal, 21*, 152–165.

Jung, R. E. (2014). Evolution, creativity, intelligence, and madness: "Here Be Dragons." *Frontiers in Psychology, 5*, 784.

Kaufman, J. C. (2006). Self-reported differences in creativity by gender and ethnicity. *Journal of Applied Cognitive Psychology, 20*, 1065–1082.

Kaufman, J. C. (2012). Counting the muses: Development of the Kaufman-Domains of Creativity Scale (K-DOCS). *Psychology of Aesthetics, Creativity, and the Arts, 6*, 298–308.

Kaufman, J. C., & Baer, J. (2004a). The Amusement Park Theoretical (APT) Model of creativity. *Korean Journal of Thinking and Problem Solving, 14*, 15–25.

Kaufman, J. C., & Baer, J. (2004b). Sure, I'm creative – but not in mathematics!: Self-reported creativity in diverse domains. *Empirical Studies of the Arts, 22*, 143–155.

Kaufman, J. C., & Baer, J. (2005). The Amusement Park Theory of Creativity. In J. C. Kaufman & J. Baer (Eds.), *Creativity across domains* (pp. 321–328). Mahwah, NJ: Erlbaum.

Kaufman, J. C., & Baer, J. (2006). Intelligent testing with Torrance. *Creativity Research Journal, 18*, 99–102.

Kaufman, J. C., Cole, J. C., & Baer, J. (2009). The construct of creativity: A structural model for self-reported creativity ratings. *Journal of Creative Behavior, 43*, 119–134.

Kim, K. H. (2006). Can only intelligent people be creative? A meta-analysis. *Journal of Secondary Gifted Education, 16*, 57–66.

Kim, K. H. (2009). Are the Torrance tests still relevant in the 21st century?. Invited Address, presented at the annual meeting of the American Psychological Association, Boston, MA., August 2009.

Kim, K. H. (2011a). Proven reliability and validity of the Torrance Tests of Creative Thinking (TTCT). *Psychology of Aesthetics, Creativity, and the Arts, 5*, 314–315.

Kim, K. H. (2011b). The APA 2009 Division 10 debate: Are the Torrance tests still relevant in the 21st century? *Psychology of Aesthetics, Creativity, and the Arts, 5*, 302–308.

McGrew, K. S. (2009). CHC theory and the human cognitive abilities project: Standing on the shoulders of the giants of psychometric intelligence research. *Intelligence, 37*, 1–10.

McKay, A. S., Karwowski, M., & Kaufman, J. C. (in press). Measuring the muses: Validating the Kaufman Domains of Creativity Scale (K-DOCS). *Psychology of Aesthetics, Creativity, and the Arts.*

Plucker, J. A. (1998). Beware of simple conclusions: The case for the content generality of creativity. *Creativity Research Journal, 11*, 179–182.

Sternberg, R. J. (1996). *Successful intelligence.* New York: Simon & Schuster.

Torrance, E. P. (1963). *Education and the creative potential.* Minneapolis, MN: University of Minnesota Press.

Treffert, D. A. (2014). Savant syndrome: Realities, myths and misconceptions. *Journal of Autism and Developmental Disorders, 44*, 564–571.

Wallas, G. (1926). *The art of thought.* New York: Harcourt, Brace, & World.

3   Mix and Match

Opportunities, Conditions, and Limitations of Cross-Domain Creativity

Joanna Szen-Ziemiańska

University of Social Sciences and Humanities, Warsaw, Poland

Izabela Lebuda

The Maria Grzegorzewska University, Warsaw, Poland

Maciej Karwowski

The Maria Grzegorzewska University, Warsaw, Poland

Abstract

Is it possible to be creatively successful in many domains? In this chapter, we explore this question and discuss potential mechanisms of cross-domain creativity (CDC). To this end, we start with defining CDC, present its hypothetical trajectories in development, and explore the role of domain-general creative potential for CDC. We pay special attention to a creative self-concept as an important factor shaping creative activity and creative achievement in various domains. A small simulation study that estimates the number of polymaths in the world today concludes this chapter.

When science and art separated from religion, people began to seek the creative element outside the domain of mysticism and spirituality and to attribute it to humans. Polymaths received particular admiration. This recognition for individuals of versatile talents has become part of mass culture; indeed, it is still visible today in the contemporary striving for success in multiple life domains. Popular motivational slogans convince people that with enough hard work they can achieve anything and be whoever they want to be. But is it at all possible to be successful in more than one creative activity – to achieve a lot in several different domains concurrently?

In this chapter, we attempt to answer this question by determining the chances of (and identifying the important mechanisms for) cross-domain creativity (CDC). With this aim in view, we first discuss the possible meanings of CDC. Then, we discuss the importance of the domain-general creative potential for creative activity across many domains, investigate the conditions under which creative potential crystallizes, and analyze the role of individual and environmental factors that promote and/or limit cross-domain creative activity. At the end of this chapter, we briefly present the results of a pilot simulation study that aimed at estimating the number of polymaths in the world today.

Izabela Lebuda and Maciej Karwowski were supported by grants from the Polish Ministry of Science and Higher Education (Iuventus Plus Program).

Cross-Domain Creativity

CDC requires the ability to generate new and valuable artifacts in more than one domain. Still, a lot depends on what is regarded as a domain, field, or discipline of creativity. As Plucker and Zabelina (2009) rightly noted:

> If the domain is "writing," for example, then someone like Goethe does not appear to be working in multiple domains. If the domain is "poetry," then Goethe's work in criticism, novel-writing, and playwriting appears to support the view of him as a polymath who worked across disciplines. One could be forgiven for thinking that any debate that hinges on almost semantic differences in definition may not be worth one's consideration. (Plucker & Zabelina, 2009, p. 7)

Numerous classifications of such disciplines can be found in literature: from classic ones, with a demarcation line between "the two cultures" of science and art (Snow, 1964), through ones concerning human nature and evolution (psychology, physics, biology, linguistics, math, art, and music; Feist, 2004), to ones that follow factor analyses of perceived creativity (e.g., creativity in empathy/communication, "hands on" creativity, and math/science creativity; Kaufman, 2012; Kaufman & Baer, 2004). What inspires our reflection in this chapter is the Amusement Park Theoretical Model (see Chapter 2 for more details). It integrates domain-general and domain-specific approaches and takes into account the development and growth of the specialization of disciplines (Baer & Kaufman, 2005). In this model, if a person meets the initial requirements for effective activity in any domain (e.g., favorable personality profile, adequate level of intelligence, adequate strength, and right kind of motivation), she makes a choice from among *general thematic areas* (e.g., art or science), supported by her individual skills, traits, and knowledge, and only then decides on the domains to work within (e.g., dance or music in art). Finally, within the domain she selects *microdomains* with their very specialized knowledge that must be mastered. For example, within the dance domain there are microdomains such as ballet, modern, or ballroom dancing (Baer & Kaufman, 2005, 2008). We understand CDC as creative activity in at least two "core domains" – *general thematic areas* (Kaufman, Cole, & Baer, 2009). What we are interested in is, above all, activity in clearly different domains: general thematic areas where a notably different pattern of skills, abilities, or traits is needed, as opposed to domains or microdomains that may share more in common (Davis, Kaufman, & McClure, 2011; for the domain of science see Simonton, 2009). Therefore, when writing about cross-domain creators we think rather about Leonardo DaVinci (painter, engineer, mathematician, biologist, and poet, i.e., spanning multiple general thematic areas) than about Michelangelo Buonarotti, who was a painter, a sculptor, and an architect, i.e., working in in one general thematic area. Of contemporary figures, we have in mind people such as Brian May, founding member of Queen (musician and songwriter, but also astrophysicist), rather than Brian Jones of the Rolling Stones, who is a prolific multi-instrumentalist.

However, CDC is not only eminent creativity. As we demonstrate further on, it is legitimate to say that ascending to higher levels of creativity and increasing specialization decreases the chances of CDC (Kaufman, Beghetto, Baer, & Ivcevic, 2010).

In order to better understand this pattern, let us consider crystallization of the creative potential on successive levels of creativity (Kaufman & Beghetto, 2009), starting from creativity understood as a human psychological characteristic (Amabile, 1996; Runco, 1990), through creative activity having mainly personal significance (Richards, 2010; Silvia et al., 2014), to professional and eminent creativity (Simonton, 1994).

CDC and Creative Potential

Creative potential is a precondition of creativity in one or more domains (Runco, 2003). Analogous with the *g* factor, it can be assumed that this potential is involved in every creative activity, regardless of domain, which means it is domain general rather than domain specific (Baer & Kaufman, 2005; Barbot & Tinio, 2015). However, the very concept of creative potential is an umbrella term that covers a variety of characteristics (Karwowski, 2015a). It mainly comprises creative ability (divergent thinking; creative imagination; the abilities of abstraction, transformation, metaphorization, deduction, and induction) as well as personality (Feist, 1998, 2010) and motivational (Amabile, 1983, 1996) determinants of their effective use (Lubart, Zenasni, & Barbot, 2013; Runco et al., 2011). Understood as an initial requirement, potential is a predictor of future creative achievement regardless of domain (Jauk, Benedek, & Neubauer, 2013; Kim, 2008; Plucker, 1999; Runco, Millar, Acar, & Cramond, 2010). Although achievements are always domain specific, some aspects of domain-general potential may predispose a person to a specific type of expression.

Psychometric studies on creative potential have identified six profiles of potential, namely: (1) high domain-general potential; (2) low domain-general potential; (3) verbal potential (strengths in verbal tasks); (4) graphic potential (strengths in graphic tasks); (5) divergent potential (strengths in divergent tasks); and (6) integrative potential (strengths in integrative tasks) (Barbot, Besançon, & Lubart, 2015). Thus, already on the level of potential, apart from general predispositions promoting versatility, certain configurations of creative abilities are visible. They also increase the probability of specific forms of expression (e.g., graphic or verbal), thereby decreasing the chance of CDC. Differentiation of potential is also visible between individuals engaging in specific subdisciplines. For instance, higher creative potential was found among artists working in areas that require improvisation than among those working in domains based to a greater extent on tradition – for example, jazz musicians showed higher creative potential (divergent thinking ability) than classical and folk musicians (Benedek, Borovnjak, Neubauer, & Kruse-Weber, 2014), and modern/contemporary dancers exhibited higher creative potential than ballet dancers (Fink & Woschnjak, 2011). It is difficult to say whether individuals engaging in improvisation chose such work because their predispositions matched the discipline, or whether it was a result of professional activities that their creative abilities grew, or a mixture of the two. Nevertheless, it can be supposed that to create in more than one general thematic area it is necessary to have an adequate level of creative potential or an adequate level of creative metacognition (Kaufman & Beghetto, 2013) in order to use resources in a way appropriate for the requirements in the given domain or domains. We therefore consider creative ability to be a precondition of creative activity in every domain, but we also assume that different domains may require different levels of creative ability.

Similar mechanisms may be observed in the case of personality. Certain traits seem to be necessary for an individual to engage in creative activity regardless of whether the domain is artistic, scientific, or inventive. Others, by contrast, predispose a person to be active in particular domains. Two traits, sometimes even referred to as personality-driving forces of creative functioning (e.g., Acar & Runco, 2012; Feist, 1998; Karwowski & Lebuda, 2016), are of particular importance to CDC: openness to experience (McCrae, 1987; King, McKee Walker, & Broyles, 1996), and – but likely to a lesser extent – psychoticism (Eysenck, 1993, 1995; Eysenck & Furnham, 1993; Martindale & Dailey, 1996; Stavridou & Furnham, 1996).

Openness, a tendency to explore and experience what is unknown, is a consistent correlate and predictor of creative performance, hobbies, and achievement (Davis et al., 2011; Dollinger, Urban, & James, 2004; King et al., 1996; Wolfradt & Pretz, 2001). Diversity of experiences, willingness to take up new challenges, and a curiosity for novelties may limit fixation on a particular discipline and on the already possessed knowledge or skills, and consequently may be conducive to creative activity in multiple domains (Wolfradt & Pretz, 2001).

Psychoticism relates to independence and a tendency to cross boundaries (Acar & Runco, 2012; Eysenck, 1995; Karwowski, 2017; Karwowski & Jankowska, 2016), including boundaries defined by the domain. Individuals high in psychoticism have difficulties with the selection of incoming information; they are constantly "bombarded" by seemingly unimportant stimuli, and these may be used in drawing remote associations and solving problems regardless of the procedures established in the domain. The tendency for overinclusion and weakened cognitive inhibition may be conducive to going beyond the dominant domain and seeking fulfillment in CDC (see Eysenck, 1995; Runco & Acar, 2012; Woody & Claridge, 1977). Independent thinking enables not only the creation of new and original solutions, but also the defense of one's own vision and refusal to yield to pressure from the environment (Eysenck, 1993) and, in the case of mature creators, it enables independence in relation to current trends or expectations of the target audience and representatives of the field.

A specific profile of personality traits, i.e., one that matches domain requirements, plays an important role in taking up creative activities (Jauk et al., 2013) and in the formation of interests (Wolfradt & Pretz, 2001), thus eventually leading to achievements (Runco, 1990; Silvia, Nusbaum, Berg, Martin, & O'Connor, 2009a). Apart from openness and psychoticism, other personality traits appear to have more domain-specific effects and promote taking up activity in a particular general thematic area. In the case of some characteristics, it is even possible to say that those that are conducive to creativity in one domain reduce the chance of creative achievement in others. For instance, scientists are usually characterized by high conscientiousness, while artists exhibit a low level of this trait (Feist, 1998). Even in the case of openness, when intellectual, emotional, and aesthetic (imagination-related) components of this trait are analyzed, emotional involvement – using feelings, positive emotions, and empathy in making decisions – is negatively related to achievement in science, but seems to promote creative success in art (S. Kaufman, 2013). By contrast, in science the key characteristics are curiosity and intellectual commitment to complex problems (S. Kaufman, 2013; S. Kaufman et al., 2016), so if we look at the trait of Openness to experience as composed of Openness and Intellect (DeYoung, 2014), the importance of Intellect for science is clearly visible. Similarly, what can be of importance in the differentiation of achievement, even between representatives of different subdisciplines within one domain, is the level of certain personality traits – jazz and folk musicians were found to be more open to new experiences than classical musicians, and folk musicians were more extraverted than classical and jazz musicians (Benedek et al., 2014).

A particular configuration of personality traits is also associated with the direction of professional interests – extraversion correlates with enterprising and social interests, while openness dovetails with artistic and investigative interests (Larson, Rottinghaus, & Borgen, 2002). As a result, personality profiles conducive to scientific and artistic creative activity differ from each other. It is argued, however, that creators with distinguished achievements are characterized, paradoxically, by combinations of traits even from the opposing ends of the same continuum, such as introversion and extraversion (Csikszentmihályi, 1996). Perhaps the more complex the personality is (combining opposite traits), the greater the chance of CDC. There are strong reasons to believe that openness (and to a lesser extent psychoticism) are conducive to taking up creative activities in various domains, which means they increase the chance of CDC, whereas the remaining traits and their levels (or particular configurations) tend to predispose individuals to specialization.

Creative Experience: Crystallization or Diffusion of the Potential?

The transition from a potential to activity, to creative achievement may be treated as the process of "crystallization" of the creative potential. With the passage of time and with the accumulation of experience, the initially universal predispositions develop in a specific direction (Plucker & Beghetto, 2004; Plucker & Zabelina, 2009). Among others, this crystallization means that the potential becomes more visible in activities and can be noticed by parents, caregivers, or teachers (Karwowski, 2015b; Karwowski, Gralewski, & Szumski, 2015). This process takes a long time during and through creative activity (Jauk et al., 2013), and leads toward mastery in a specific domain or domains (Milgram & Hong, 1994; Perleth & Heller, 1994).

In the early stages of development and at the lowest levels of creativity (especially mini-c; Kaufman & Beghetto, 2009), CDC is relatively common and it would be quite difficult to find a creatively active person in only one general thematic area (Kaufman et al., 2010). For instance, in childhood multifaceted creative activity is visible in play (Feldman, 1989; Russ, 2014), this "explorative and curious activity which is natural and proper for every normal child may be seen as the root of creativity" (Urban, 1991; p. 178). Creativity, understood as the capacity for ideation, development of new solutions, and for processing information in a new way, seems to form the basis for learning in all domains (Beghetto, 2016; Sawyer, 2012). Therefore, it can be supposed that cross-domain creative activity is not only typical at the mini-c levels, but in fact constitutes a condition of development.

Creative behavior in the early stages of development is a predictor of subsequent creative achievement (e.g., Colangelo, Kerr, Hallowell, Huesman, & Gaeth, 1992); the broader the scope of activities taken up, the greater the chance of getting to know one's own predispositions, special abilities, and interests. Consequently, the broader one's cross-domain experience, the higher the probability of CDC at later stages of life (Kaufman et al., 2010). It is therefore important for the crystallization of creative potential to provide the child not only with support, but also with diverse challenges (Gute, Gute, Nakamura, & Csikszentmihályi, 2008) and comprehensive education (Davies et al., 2013; Mourgues, Barbot, Tan, & Grigorenko, 2014). The process of education, especially that which is based on the ideas of interdisciplinary or problem-based approaches, is precisely the kind of training that is conducive to the transfer of abilities, competencies, and knowledge (Feinstein, 2006). In the interdisciplinary model of education, combination of a variety of domains gives students a chance to get to know their predispositions, to broaden their interests, and to strengthen their intrinsic motivation to learn (Dowds, 1998; Feinstein, 2006). Problem-based education consists of blurring the boundaries between domains and disciplines: Music is combined with history, literature with science, flexibility is developed, and so is willingness to go beyond the established domains, which gives a good start for CDC.

By contrast, certain hindrances to multifaceted creative activity may lie in premature specialization, i.e., having to choose the direction of education or to focus on developing one ability (Kaufman et al., 2010) too early in life. However, development of creative ability in one domain may enhance effectiveness in other domains that require similar skills (Baer, 1996; Barbot et al., 2013; Onarheim & Friis-Olivarius, 2013), and flexible switching between generality and specificity is conducive to productivity in many domains (Plucker & Beghetto, 2004; Plucker & Zabelina, 2009). Excessive specificity may result in information from outside the domain being underestimated and unavailable, which leads to fixedness of thinking, whereas excessive generality fosters chaos, diffusion, and superficiality. Both tendencies pose a threat to the transfer of knowledge and skills between domains. What should therefore be optimal for the development of CDC is support for young people in taking up creative challenges in a specific domain and coupling it with encouragement to apply knowledge and skills in, as well as from, other domains, disciplines, and tasks (Plucker & Zabelina, 2009).

Specialization in the selected domain or domains increases as a result of systematic activity, successive educational and professional choices (Sternberg, 2002), and the impact of biological development in adolescence (Barbot & Tinio, 2015). This may be so largely due to the process of myelination, which involves an increase in the integration of distributed brain areas (Spear, 2013). It is supposed that when engaging in a specifically creative outlet, adolescents enhance the neurological connections and thus, by activating them regularly, they create the basis of key resources for a particular outlet. These processes – though hypothetical and requiring confirmation – reduce the chance of CDC. Moreover, even though it is frontal areas (DLPFC) and multicomponential neural networks that are the most important for idea generation, different creativity domains (musical, verbal, and visuo-spatial) roughly correspond to higher activation in functionally specialized brain areas (Boccia, Piccardi, Palermo, Nori, & Palmiero, 2015). On the other hand, creative activity in different areas may be stimulating for the very same brain regions (e.g., musical and verbal creativity stimulate occipital areas, see Berkowitz, 2010; Sawyer, 2012), which is not found in the case of visual creativity (Boccia et al., 2015). It can therefore be supposed that in the case of domains in which overlapping areas are activated, the chances of CDC will be greater than in the case of those in which activity occurs in different structures. When the same neural structure is being stimulated by creative activities in different domains, positive feedback likely occurs – practice in one domain enhances myelination of neural connections and thereby increases the effectiveness of activities in the other domain, and *vice versa*.

Biologically determined processes are enhanced by activity (Barbot & Tinio, 2015). Development of expertise generally appears to result from (an often enormous) time and effort commitment (Ericsson, 1996; Lubinski & Benbow, 2000; Simonton, 2002). It is estimated that the time needed for deliberate practice (e.g., Rostan, 2005), the development of expert performance, and the acquisition of task-relevant knowledge in each specific content area (Barbot, Tan, Randi, Santa-Donato, & Grigorenko, 2012; Barbot & Lubart, 2012; Barbot et al., 2015; Caroff & Lubart, 2012) that would enable paradigm-shifting, is at least ten years (Ericsson, Roring, & Nandagopal, 2007; Kaufman & Kaufman, 2007; cf. Hambrick et al., 2014). Very likely, however, an additional ten years may be necessary to achieve creative success (Kaufman & Kaufman, 2007). Usually, the longer and the more intense the practice in a given domain, the greater the achievement (Detterman & Ruthsatz, 1999; Weisberg, 1999), and the higher the level of abilities, the shorter the time of striving for it (the *better-faster* effect; Simonton, 2013). Although the time of training necessary to attain mastery ranges from a few years to a few decades (Hambrick et al., 2014), striving for professionalism in a domain usually requires many years of commitment. Members of the American National Academy of Sciences provide a good example; three-quarters of them knew that they wanted to become scientists before they turned eighteen and organized their entire activity around that goal (Feist, 2006). In artistic domains, such as music or dance, training from the earliest years is one of the best predictors of success (Ruthsatz, Detterman, Griscom, & Cirullo, 2008). Though the time needed for attaining proficiency and maintaining a high level in a domain varies (Benedek et al., 2014; Hambrick et al., 2014; Welch et al., 2008), it certainly amounts to years or even decades, and the more time one devotes to a given domain, the less of it remains for development in other fields (Barbot & Lubart, 2012). The lack of time for systematic practice in several domains is a natural barrier for professional and, to an even greater degree, eminent CDC.

With increasing lifespans and, more importantly, with the time of human intellectual and physical fitness and technological development increasing, are we going to witness a more frequent emergence of polymaths? Living longer, will people take up creative activities in multiple domains simultaneously and will they seek to master further domains after attaining mastery in one? Perhaps in reality dynamic changes, new professional categories, and new workplace challenges will be stimulators for such a course of events and will, in some way, enforce multifunctionality or multiple changes in professional career paths. Yet we have to wait at least a few decades to answer this question.

The Self-Concept of a (Cross-Domain) Creator

When taking up creative challenges in various domains, a person develops his or her self-beliefs and ideas concerning the requirements that these types of tasks involve. Of the beliefs with regards to one's own creative abilities, referred to as *creative self-beliefs* (Karwowski & Barbot, 2016) or *creative self-concept* (Karwowski & Lebuda, 2016, 2017), creative personal identity and creative self-efficacy are particularly important in determining the chances of CDC.

Creative personal identity describes the extent to which a person values creativity and the degree to which creativity is an important part of individual identity. The belief that creativity is an important element of life gives direction to a person's activities and increases the chances of taking up creative activity regardless of the domain (Karwowski & Lebuda, 2017); sometimes it is even regarded as the source of creative self-efficacy (Tierney & Farmer, 2011; but see also Karwowski, 2016). People who regard creativity as an important element of identity have a higher chance of fulfilling their potential than those who do not value creativity itself, even when they are endowed with creative potential (Karwowski & Lebuda, 2017). People who consider creativity to be important seek possibilities of using it at work or at school; they are more often intrinsically motivated (Jaussi, Randel, & Dionne, 2007) and, as a result, they obtain a higher level of creative achievement. Thus, appreciation of creativity may promote CDC.

As well as the value that a person attributes to creativity, what is equally important is the belief that one has the abilities and competencies to cope with creative challenges, i.e., creative self-efficacy (Karwowski, 2011, 2012), which is necessary to take the intellectual risk of creating something new (Beghetto, 2006). Creative self-efficacy not only predicts creative achievement (Feist & Barron, 2003; Jaussi et al., 2007; Lim & Choi, 2009; Tierney & Farmer, 2002, 2011), but also seems to mediate the relationship of creative ability and personality traits (mainly openness) with creative achievement (Karwowski & Barbot, 2016; Karwowski & Lebuda, 2017). It helps in coping with difficulties, increases perseverance in achieving creative goals (Karwowski & Lebuda, 2017), and may therefore be an important correlate of multidomain creativity.

One of the ways in which creative self-concept is formed is through comparing one's own skill and achievement in a given domain with other people's results (Lebuda & Csikszentmihályi, 2017; Karwowski, 2015b; Karwowski & Barbot, 2016). People usually engage in domains that match their abilities and predispositions (Robertson, Smeets, Lubinski, & Benbow, 2010) and tend to choose those fields in which they expect to succeed (Wigfield & Eccles, 2000). Self-beliefs concerning abilities are formed with a focus on specific domains (math, reading, music, or sports) already in elementary school students (Eccles, Wigfield, Harold, & Blumenfeld, 1993). It can therefore be supposed that the greater the successive achievements in a given domain, the greater the focus on that domain and, consequently, the smaller the chance of CDC. For instance, the Polish writer and poet Jacek Dehnel recalls in a conversation (Lebuda, 2014) that, following family tradition, he planned to become a painter, but it was his writing that was much more appreciated in the professional field. Success connected with that gradually came to require ever greater focus on writing and left little time for the development of his graphic abilities. Thus, Dehnel's paintings were assessed as works of a writer that paints, not as works of an artist aspiring to achievements in a new domain.

Achievements build a sense of self-efficacy and promote the effort associated with the development or maintenance of abilities and competencies (Bandura, 1997; Prabhu, Sutton, & Sauser, 2008). Engaging in many different creative activities in childhood (e.g., during extracurricular classes) makes it possible to discover one's own abilities and experience success in various domains. Success experienced in several domains may promote strong (both domain-general and domain-specific) creative self-efficacy and increase the chance of CDC. We tested this hypothesis in a study conducted among Polish graduate students and young scholars in the disciplines of Social Sciences and Humanities (Szen-Ziemiańska, 2015). Using the Creative Achievement Questionnaire (CAQ; Carson, Peterson, & Higgins, 2005), we added the number of domains in which participants reported creative activity or achievement, thus creating the category of versatility that ranged from zero (no activity/achievement of any kind) to 10 (at least some activity in all ten domains distinguished in CAQ). As Figure 3.1 shows, we identified quite a few young scholars with cross-domain activity.

Next, we examined if versatility assessed in this way was related to creative thinking, measured with the use of Urban and Jellen's Test of Creative Thinking-Drawing Production (TCT-DP; Urban, 2005), to creative self-beliefs (creative personal identity and creative self-efficacy, measured with the use of the Short Scale of Creative Self: Karwowski, 2012; Karwowski, Lebuda, Wisniewska, & Gralewski, 2013), as well as to the number of extracurricular activities (classes in visual arts, music, sports, or science) that the respondents had taken part in when they were children. As expected, we found positive relationships between versatility and all of the above factors: The higher the creative potential, the higher the creative self-concept, and the broader the extracurricular education – the higher the number of domains in which creative activity occurred. Additionally, knowing that successes in childhood are important to the subsequently developed creative self-efficacy, we performed the same correlational analyses for both a rewarded group (individuals

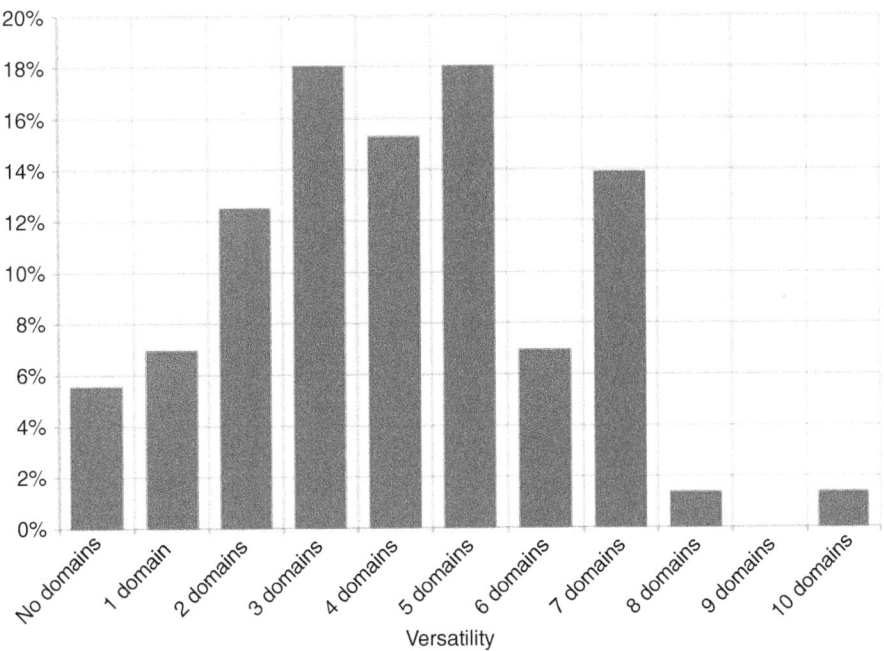

Figure 3.1 *Versatility by the number of creativity domains.*

Table 3.1 *Relations of versatility with extracurricular activities, CPI, CSE, and creative thinking in a group of doctoral students*

	Extracurricular activities	CPI	CSE	TCT-DP
Total	.30**[.07, .50]	.26*[.03, .46]	.30*[.07, .50]	.39**[.17, .57]
Unrewarded in childhood	.37**[.12, .58]	.26[−.01, .49]	.22[−.05, .46]	.39**[.14, .59]
Rewarded in childhood	.04[−.45, .51]	.33[−.18, .70]	.63**[.21, .85]	.38[−.12, .73]

Note: CPI = Creative Personal Identity; CSE = Creative Self-Efficacy; TCT-DP = Test of Creative Thinking–Drawing Production. Values in brackets are 95% confidence intervals.
* $p < .05$; **$p < .001$.

who received rewards and prizes in their school years; $N = 17$) and an unrewarded group ($N = 55$; Table 3.1). In both groups, creative thinking is associated with versatility, but in the rewarded group the correlation between versatility and creative self-efficacy is very strong, while it is much weaker and not statistically significant in the unrewarded group. This is consistent with our expectations and shows that the rewards received for creative activity in childhood played a role in developing general creative self-efficacy, which then related to the number of domains one engages in creative activity. In the unrewarded group, versatility is associated positively and to a similar degree with creative ability and with extracurricular activity. Regression analysis confirmed that creative abilities (β =.36, p <.01) and extracurricular activities at school age (β =.32, p <.05) predicted versatility in the unrewarded group, but creative personal identity or creative self-efficacy were not. In the rewarded group, creative thinking (β =.46, p <.01) and creative self-efficacy (β =.69, p <.01) were associated with versatility.

Creative self-efficacy and creative personal identity can be analyzed both at the domain-general and at the domain-specific levels. The latter is especially important at the moment of becoming a professional or expert (Baer, 2015; Karwowski & Lebuda, 2017; Lebuda & Csikszentmihályi, 2017). On the stage of professional or eminent creativity, creative-self concepts mainly refer to narrow specialization, or even micro-domains. For instance, recognized representatives of different types of media have different self-concepts and personal definitions of creativity shared with those who use the same medium in their work (Gluck, Ernst, & Unger, 2002). Professional creators think of themselves and their abilities through the lens of the work they do – a specific craft. This is illustrated by the words of a Polish cinematographer, Paweł Edelman:

> Creator is a term I don't like. That's because a creator sounds kind of proud, not humble. I also think . . . I can't imagine the people who say: I am a creator. I suppose one is a creator or an artist sometimes only, at certain moments, and usually one is an ordinary person. I believe I'm a usual person, doing some kind of job, which is partly technical and partly artistic. (Personal communication, April 12, 2015)

Although creative self-beliefs are important in all creativity domains and may promote CDC, a professional role that is too strongly focused on one domain leads to difficulties in going beyond the boundaries of that particular activity. The way of defining a particular domain and the perception of one's own role and efficiency in the specific area are strongly linked. Hence, special importance for creativity literature stems from the studies that link creative self-concept or identity with social representations of creativity in different domains (see for instance Glăveanu & Tanggaard, 2014).

CDC and Cross-Level Creativity

In the case of experienced and highly regarded creators (professional artists, scholars, and innovators), cross-disciplinary creativity, i.e., activity in multiple subdisciplines of the same domain (a musician who is an instrumentalist, a composer, and an instrument teacher, or an actor who is a script writer, a film producer, and a university teacher at a theater academy), is found much more often than CDC. Eminent creators seldom have outstanding achievements in multiple domains (Baer, 1998; Gray, 1966).

In the case of professional creators and representatives of other occupations, everyday creativity is more typical and may manifest itself during the preparation of a new signature dish, seeking an idea for a home book collection, inventing games for children, or designing a garden (Richards, 1990). Such creative activities have a common character; most people produce artifacts of personal importance in more than one life domain, often without even calling these activities creative. However, engaging in nonprofessional creative activities is obviously a different thing than outstanding creative achievement. The question arises, for example, of why Albert Einstein played the violin in his spare moments instead of constantly trying to solve the riddles of physics, or why Stravinsky took painting lessons from Pablo Picasso. What is the role played by additional creative activity for professional and eminent creativity? Does little-c serve Big-C, or is it rather a distractor and a time eater?

Members of elite societies – the National Academy of Sciences and the Royal Society – are, respectively, 1.7 and 1.9 times more likely to have an artistic or craft-based hobby than the average scientist is. Likewise, Nobel Prize–winning scientists are 2.85 times more likely than the average scientist to have an artistic or craft-based hobby (Root-Bernstein & Root-Bernstein, 2004; Root-Bernstein, Bernstein, & Garnier, 1995). Perhaps their "additional creativity" performed a relaxation function and promoted general well-being (see Silvia et al., 2014). Such activity plays an important role in looking for inspiration and crossing the boundaries of narrow specialization, thanks to which it facilitates insight and stimulates imagination (Root-Bernstein et al., 1995; Root-Bernstein & Root-Bernstein, 2004). Distinguished scientists who concurrently work on a larger number of problems pursue a larger number of passions (Root-Bernstein et al., 1995). Engaging in more than one domain of creativity may also perform a preventive function when it comes to productivity decrease in old age (Simonton, 1991), because this trend can be eliminated or reversed in the case of individuals who change their area of work (Simonton, 1998).

CDC may also be part of the tradition of the given domain or discipline. For instance, folk musicians were more cross-domain creative and achieved more in the domain of arts and crafts than representatives of other music genres. This may stem from the stronger bonds of folk musicians with traditions and related skills in arts and crafts (Benedek et al., 2014). In some domains, especially in those that require many years of deliberate practice (such as ballet), absolute concentration is expected; in others, domain boundaries are more fluid. The chances of a diversified creative "investment portfolio" (Sternberg & Lubart, 1992) are also to some extent determined by implicit theories of creativity, particularly those that concern the creator's characteristics and image (Lebuda & Karwowski, 2013). A different style of behavior and appearance is expected from a rock musician than from a scientist. Still, the case of Bryan May, who was mentioned in the beginning of this chapter, shows that image-related challenges involved in CDC can be overcome.

The Commonness of CDC

If so many factors associated with development and experience reduce the chance of CDC, is it not the case that this issue concerns only a few people in the history of the world? In a classic study (Gray, 1966) based on an analysis of 2,400 life histories of creative people, only 2 percent were found to have creative achievements in different domains, such as visual arts and literature. Another 17 percent had achievements in more than one discipline when the disciplines were related to one another (such as painting and sculpture). It appears that although creative activity in two or more domains is relatively frequent, cases of actual multidomain achievement are in fact rare. A recent study identified three latent classes with different levels of everyday creativity (von Stumm, Chung, & Furnham, 2011). They differed in terms of the level of activity rather than in terms of profile. As may be expected, the smallest one (16 percent) exhibited high cross-domain activity.

An even clearer solution has recently been obtained using a representative sample of adult Poles (Kwasnik & Karwowski, under review) – it identified three classes that differed not only in creative activity level, but also in terms of its profile. The largest class (48 percent) was characterized by an almost total lack of any kind of creative activity. Not much smaller (31 percent) was the class of everyday creativity – culinary activities or ones associated with room or flat decoration. The smallest, though still noticeable, class (21 percent) was creatively active in more professional and, importantly, multidomain areas. These people engaged in both science and art, which, of course, does not necessarily mean that in both these areas they had high achievements.

How many polymaths and individuals with high creative achievement in more than one domain are there? In a massive study (almost 800 students), Silvia, Kaufman, and Pretz (2009) demonstrated that two-thirds of the respondents had no creative achievements at all (which confirms the exclusiveness of higher levels of creativity). The remaining two classes had a higher and more varied level of achievement. Whereas the second class (17 percent) could be regarded as typically oriented towards visual arts (high achievement in this domain and low in others), the third one (17 percent) is composed of individuals with high achievements in more than one domain – characterized by a considerably high level of achievement in music, dance, creative writing, and theatrical activity. We are therefore dealing with a group – a fairly large one – that has achievements in related but not identical domains. Further studies yielded similar findings, though they gave different estimations of the sizes of classes. For example, in a large study devoted to the quality of scales that measured creativity (Silvia, Wigert, Reiter-Palmon, & Kaufman, 2012), a five-class solution was obtained: The dominant class (61 percent) had no creative achievements, smaller classes had domain-specific achievements in visual arts (12 percent), dance (14 percent), and music (9 percent), and the smallest class – the most interesting one from the point of view of this chapter – was the class of polymaths (almost 4 percent), which had high achievements in visual arts, dance, and creative writing. This shows that even though the size of the class of polymaths differs between studies, such a group can nevertheless be identified.

The fact that polymaths are few is hardly surprising. As we have demonstrated above, achievements in multiple domains depend on a number of factors. In order to get a little closer to answering the question of how many polymaths there might be in the population, we ran a small simulation analysis, developed specifically for this

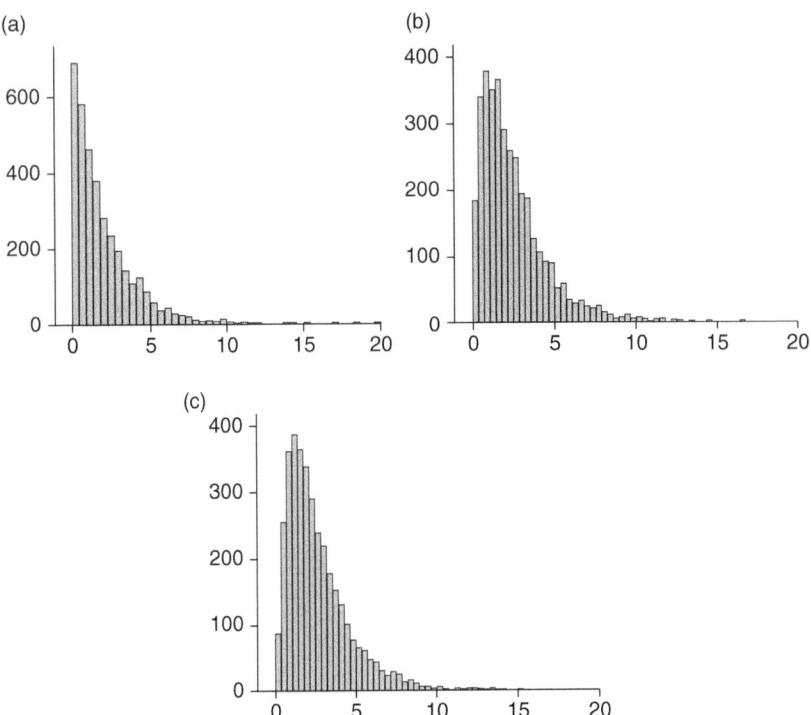

Figure 3.2 *Simulated distributions of creative achievement in three domains (A, B, and C).*

chapter. For its purposes, we simulated strongly skewed distributions of achievement in three domains of creativity (called A, B, and C, which may stand for science, art, and everyday creativity) in such a way that each of them had a Poisson distribution (Simonton, 2009, 2013, see also Simonton, this volume) (see Figure 3.2), and the correlations between these variables were assumed to be generally weak or moderate: $r = .30$ between A and B and between B and C, and $r = .10$ between A and C. In this way, we intended to test the possible consequences that stronger and weaker interrelations between domains have for the number of polymaths. Of course, sometimes – especially between domains that are close to one another – these correlations are stronger, but studies on the measurement of creative achievement usually reveal relationships of approximately that strength (Silvia et al., 2012).

For the purposes of the analyses, we simulated a data set of $N = 4,000$ and checked the percentage of people qualified as polymaths at different cut-off criteria. The key findings are presented in Table 3.2. The adopted criterion of recognizing a person as having considerable creative achievement obviously translates into the percentage of polymaths. With a fairly liberal threshold – namely, recognition of a person as a polymath when his or her creative achievement was in the top 20 percent in two of three analyzed domains – the group would amount to 14 percent, but if the requirement for a person's achievement was to be in the top 20 percent in each of the three domains, the group would constitute only 2 percent of the population. Naturally, more rigorous

Table 3.2 *Results of the simulation estimating the number of polymaths at different eminence*

Eminence criteria(%)	Two domains out of three(%)	All three domains(%)
Top 20	14.0	2.0
Top 10	4.6	0.17
Top 5	1.5	0.03
Top 3	0.5	0.00
Top 1	0.1	0.00

criteria lead to a decrease in these figures: With the requirement of falling within the tenth percentile of achievement, 4.6 percent of people have the chance to be considered successful in two out of three domains, but only 0.17 percent have that chance in all three domains. Reaching more elite levels and expecting people to be in the top 5 percent, in the top 3 percent, or even in the top one percentile results in virtually no polymaths. With a threshold of 5 percent, we could still expect to find about 1.5 percent of people whose achievement is within the top group in two domains, but there would be next to no individuals so successful in all three domains[1].

Conclusion

The well-known saying to the effect that you can achieve anything you wish for, as well as the radically egalitarian approach suggesting that anyone can be a creator in any domain or domains whatsoever, is an optimistic but not very realistic ideology. The chances of being an eminent creative polymath are infinitesimal – and they decrease with the growing number of loosely related domains that one deals with. It seems, however, that the psychological significance of CDC may be much greater and may concern not only those who have achievements in at least two different general thematic areas. Multidomain activity may have considerable significance for the comprehensive development of children and young people, as well as for acquisition of experience in numerous fields at the mini-c and little-c levels, but also as a "springboard" and a source of inspiration for creators working on the Big-C level.

As they go through life, people acquire successive abilities that make it possible or more likely for them to engage in creativity and fulfill their potential through hobby or professional activity. Multidomain creative activity at the mini-c level performs an important developmental function, increasing the chances of creative achievement but not guaranteeing that achievement. At further levels of creativity, the initial

---

[1] Of course, if our calculations were to be treated literally, it could be argued that on the global scale, with 4.8 billion adults (18+) in the world, the 0.03% that we are talking about in this case still translates into nearly 1.5 million of such people worldwide. However, what we wish to do is not literally to convert considerably error-burdened estimates into units, but to demonstrate the dynamics of the decrease in the estimated number of polymaths when various eminence criteria and different levels of interrelation between domains are assumed.

requirements and expectations grow; consequently, the chance of success in more than one field decreases. Already on the level of potential it is possible to identify predispositions for particular forms of expression, while a specific profile and level of characteristics limit the undertaken activity (Baer, 2015). Personal determinants and creative activity shape the beliefs regarding one's own abilities and give form to the expectations of success in specific domains (Karwowski, 2014). Creative achievements promote attaching great value to creativity and elevating it to an important place in self-description as well as an increase the probability of focus on the selected domain, or even on a subdiscipline or task type. As one develops, gains experiences, and makes educational and professional decisions, it is essential to strike a balance between the general, versatile character of interests and their specializations. Though extremely rare on the achievement level, creativity in more than one domain also has a more egalitarian face – that of multidomain creative activity, crucial for development and for solving everyday problems. It is therefore worth remembering the words of Maya Angelou (1982), an American author, poet, dancer, actress, and singer: "You can't use up creativity. The more you use, the more you have."

References

Acar, S., & Runco, M. A. (2012). Psychoticism and creativity: A meta-analytic review. *Psychology of Aesthetics, Creativity, and the Arts, 6,* 341–350.

Amabile, T. M. (1983). The social psychology of creativity: A componential conceptualization. *Journal of Personality and Social Psychology, 45,* 357–376.

Amabile, T. M. (1996). *Creativity in context.* Oxford: Westview Press, Inc.

Angelou, M. (1982). Creativity: It's the thought that counts (Mary Ardito, Interviewer). *Bell Telephone Magazine, 1,* 32.

Baer, J. (1996). The effects of task-specific divergent-thinking training. *Journal of Creative Behavior, 20,* 183–187.

Baer, J. (1998). The case for domain specificity of creativity. *Creativity Research Journal, 11,* 173–177.

Baer, J. (2015). The importance of domain-specific expertise in creativity. *Roeper Review, 37,* 165–178.

Baer, J., & Kaufman, J. C. (2005). Bridging generality and specificity: The Amusement Park Theoretical (APT) model of creativity. *Roeper Review, 27,* 158–163.

Baer, J., & Kaufman, J. C. (2008). Gender differences in creativity. *Journal of Creative Behavior, 42,* 75–105.

Bandura, A. (1997). *Self-efficacy: The exercise of control.* New York: Freeman.

Barbot, B., Besançon, M., & Lubart, T. (2015). Creative potential in educational settings: Its nature, measure, and nurture. *Education 3–13, 43,* 371–381.

Barbot, B., & Lubart, T. (2012). Creative thinking in music: Its nature and assessment through musical exploratory behaviors. *Psychology of Aesthetics, Creativity, and the Arts, 6,* 231–242.

Barbot, B., Randi, J., Tan, M., Levenson, C., Friedlaender, L., & Grigorenko, E. L. (2013). From perception to creative writing: A multi-method pilot study of a visual literacy instructional approach. *Learning and Individual Differences, 28,* 167–176.

Barbot, B., Tan, M., Randi, J., Santa-Donato, G., & Grigorenko, E. L. (2012). Essential skills for creative writing: Integrating multiple domain-specific perspectives. *Thinking Skills and Creativity*, *7*, 209–223.

Barbot, B., & Tinio, P. P. L. (2015). Where is the "g" in creativity? A specialization-differentiation hypothesis. *Frontiers of Human Neuroscience*, *8*, 1041.

Beghetto, R. A. (2006). Creative self-efficacy: Correlates in middle and secondary students. *Creativity Research Journal*, *18*, 447–457.

Beghetto, R. A. (2016). Creative learning: A fresh look. *Journal of Cognitive Education and Psychology*, *15*, 6–23.

Benedek, M., Borovnjak, B., Neubauer, A. C., & Kruse-Weber, S. (2014). Creativity and personality in classical, jazz and folk musicians. *Personality and Individual Differences*, *63*, 117–121.

Berkowitz, A. L. (2010). *The improvising mind: Cognition and creativity in the musical moment*. New York, NY: Oxford University Press.

Boccia, M., Piccardi, L., Palermo, L., Nori, R., & Palmiero, M. (2015). Where do bright ideas occur in our brain? Meta-analytic evidence from neuroimaging studies of domain-specific creativity. *Frontiers in Psychology*, *6*, DOI: 10.3389/fpsyg.2015.01195

Caroff, X., & Lubart, T. I. (2012). Multidimensional approach to detecting creative potential in managers. *Creativity Research Journal*, *24*, 13–20.

Carson, S. H., Peterson, J. B., & Higgins, D. M. (2005). Reliability, validity, and factor structure of the creative achievement questionnaire. *Creativity Research Journal*, *17*, 37–50.

Colangelo, N., Kerr, B., Hallowell, K., Huesman, R., & Gaeth, J. (1992). The Iowa Inventiveness Inventory: Toward a measure of mechanical inventiveness. *Creativity Research Journal*, *5*, 157–163.

Csikszentmihályi, M. (1996). *Creativity: Flow and the psychology of discovery and invention*. New York: Harper/Collins.

Davies, D., Jindal-Snape, D., Collier, C., Digby, R., Hay, P., & Howe, A. (2013). Creative learning environments in education: A systematic literature review. *Thinking Skills and Creativity*, *8*, 80–91.

Davis, C. D., Kaufman, J. C., & McClure, F. H. (2011). Non-cognitive constructs and self-reported creativity by domain. *Journal of Creative Behavior*, *45*, 188–202.

Detterman, D., & Ruthsatz, J. (1999). Toward a more comprehensive theory of exceptional abilities. *Journal for the Education of the Gifted*, *22*, 148–158.

DeYoung, C. G. (2014). Openness/intellect: A dimension of personality reflecting cognitive exploration. In M. L. Cooper & R. J. Larsen (Eds.), *APA handbook of personality and social psychology: Personality processes and individual differences* (pp. 369–399), Vol. 4. Washington, DC: American Psychological Association.

Dollinger, S. J., Urban, K. K., & James, T. A. (2004). Creativity and openness: Further validation of two creative product measures. *Creativity Research Journal*, *16*, 35–47.

Dowds, B. N. (1998). Helping students make connections across disciplines. *Creativity Research Journal*, *11*, 55–60.

Eccles, J. S., Wigfield, A., Harold, R., & Blumenfeld, P. B. (1993). Age and gender differences in children's self- and task perceptions during elementary school. *Child Development*, *64*, 830–847.

Ericsson, K. A. (1996). *The road to expert performance: empirical evidence from the arts and sciences, sports, and games*. Mahwah, NJ: Erlbaum.

Ericsson, K. A., Roring, R. W., & Nandagopal, K. (2007). Giftedness and evidence for reproducibly superior performance: An account based on the expert performance framework. *High Ability Studies*, *18*, 3–56.

Eysenck, H. J. (1993). Creativity and personality: Suggestions for a theory. *Psychological Inquiry*, *4*, 147–178.

Eysenck, H. J. (1995). *Genius: The natural history of creativity*. Cambridge, UK: Cambridge University Press.

Eysenck, H. J., & Furnham, A. (1993). Personality and the Barron-Welsh Art Scale. *Perceptual and Motor Skills*, *76*, 837–838.

Feinstein, J. S. (2006). *The nature of creative development*. Stanford, CA: Stanford University Press.

Feist, G. J. (1998). A meta-analysis of the impact of personality on scientific and artistic creativity. *Personality and Social Psychological Review*, *2*, 290–309.

Feist, G. J. (2004). The evolved fluid specificity of human creative talent. In R. J. Sternberg, E. L. Grigorenko, & J. L. Singer (Eds.), *Creativity: From potential to realization* (pp. 57–82). Washington, DC: American Psychological Association.

Feist, G. J. (2006). *The psychology of science and the origins of the scientific mind*. New Haven and London: Yale University Press.

Feist, G. J. (2010). The function of personality in creativity: The nature and nurture of the creative personality. In J. C. Kaufman & R. J. Sternberg (Eds.), *The Cambridge handbook of creativity* (pp. 113–130). New York, NY: Cambridge University Press.

Feist, G. J., & Barron, F. X. (2003). Predicting creativity from early to late adulthood: Intellect, potential, and personality. *Journal of Research in Personality*, *37*, 62–88.

Feldman, D. H. (1989). Creativity: Proof that development occurs. In W. Damon (Ed.), *Child development today and tomorrow* (pp. 240–260). San Francisco, CA: Jossey-Bass.

Fink, A., & Woschnjak, S. (2011). Creativity and personality in professional dancers. *Personality and Individual Differences*, *51*, 754–758.

Glăveanu, V. P. (2015). Creativity as a sociocultural act. *Journal of Creative Behavior*, *49*, 165–180.

Glăveanu, V. P., & Tanggaard, L. (2014). Creativity, identity, and representation: Towards a socio-cultural theory of creative identity. *New Ideas in Psychology*, *34*, 12–21.

Gluck, J., Ernst, R., & Unger, F. (2002). How creative define creativity: Definitions reflect different types of creativity. *Creativity Research Journal*, *14*, 55–67.

Gray, C. E. (1966). A measurement of creativity in western civilization. *American Anthropologist*, *68*, 1384–1417.

Gute, G., Gute, D. S., Nakamura, J., & Csikszentmihályi, M. (2008). The early lives of highly creative persons: The influence of the complex family. *Creativity Research Journal*, *20*, 343–357.

Hambrick, D. Z., Oswald, F. L., Altmann, E. M., Meinz, E. J., Gobet, F., & Campitelli, G. (2014). Deliberate practice: Is that all it takes to become an expert? *Intelligence*, *45*, 34–45.

Jauk, E., Benedek, M., & Neubauer, A. C. (2013). The road to creative achievement: A latent variable model of ability and personality predictors. *European Journal of Personality*, *28*, 95–105.

Jaussi, K. S., Randel, A. E., & Dionne, S. D. (2007). I am, I think I can, and I do: The role of personal identity, self-efficacy, and cross-application of experiences in creativity at work. *Creativity Research Journal*, *2–3*, 247–258.

Karwowski, M. (2011). It doesn't hurt to ask … But sometimes it hurts to believe: Polish students' creative self-efficacy and its predictors. *Psychology of Aesthetics, Creativity, and the Arts*, 5, 154–164.

Karwowski, M. (2012). Did curiosity kill the cat? Relationship between trait curiosity, creative self-efficacy and creative personal identity. *Europe's Journal of Psychology*, 8, 547–558.

Karwowski, M. (2014). Creative mindset: Measurement, correlates, consequences. *Psychology of Aesthetics, Creativity, and the Arts*, 8, 62–70.

Karwowski, M. (2015a). Notes on creative potential and its measurement. *Creativity: Theories – Research – Applications*, 2, 4–17.

Karwowski, M. (2015b). Peers effect on students' creative self-concept. *Journal of Creative Behavior*, 49, 211–225.

Karwowski, M. (2016). Dynamic of the creative self-concept: Changes and reciprocal relations between creative self-efficacy and creative personal identity. *Creativity Research Journal*, 28, 99–104.

Karwowski, M. (2017). Subordinated and rebellious creativity at school. In R. A. Beghetto & B. Sriraman (Eds.), *Creative Contradictions in Education* (pp. 89–114). The Netherlands: Springer.

Karwowski, M., & Barbot, B. (2016). Creative self-beliefs: Their nature, development, and correlates. In J. C. Kaufman & J. Baer (Eds.), *Cambridge companion to reason and development* (pp. 302–326). New York: Cambridge University Press.

Karwowski, M., Gralewski, J., & Szumski, G. (2015). Teachers' effect on students' creative self-concept is moderated by students' gender. *Learning and Individual Differences*, 44, 1–8.

Karwowski, M., & Jankowska, D. M. (2016). Four faces of creativity at school. In R. A. Beghetto & J. C. Kaufman (Eds.), *Nurturing creativity in the classroom* (pp. 357–354). New York: Cambridge University Press.

Karwowski, M., & Lebuda, I. (2016). The big five, the huge two and creative self-beliefs: A meta-analysis. *Psychology of Aesthetics, Creativity, and the Arts*, 10, 214–232.

Karwowski, M., & Lebuda, I. (2017). Creative self-concept: A surface characteristic of creative personality. In G. Feist, R. Reiter-Palmon & J. C. Kaufman (Eds.), *Handbook of creativity and personality* (pp. 84–101). Cambridge: Cambridge University Press.

Karwowski, M., Lebuda, I., Wisniewska, E., & Gralewski, J. (2013). Big Five personality factors as the predictors of creative self-efficacy and creative personal identity: Does gender matter? *Journal of Creative Behavior*, 47, 215–232.

Kaufman, J. C. (2012). Counting the muses: Development of the Kaufman Domains of Creativity Scale (K-DOCS). *Psychology of Aesthetics, Creativity, and the Arts*, 6, 298–308.

Kaufman, J. C., & Baer, J. (2004). Sure, I'm creative – but not in math! Self-reported creativity in diverse domains. *Empirical Studies of the Arts*, 22, 143–155.

Kaufman, J. C., & Beghetto, R. A. (2009). Beyond big and little: The four c model of creativity. *Review of General Psychology*, 13, 1–12.

Kaufman, J. C., & Beghetto, R. A. (2013). In praise of Clark Kent: Creative metacognition and the importance of teaching kids when (not) to be creative. *Roeper Review*, 35, 155–165.

Kaufman, J. C., Beghetto, R. A., Baer, J., & Ivcevic, Z. (2010). Creative polymathy: What Benjamin Franklin can teach your kindergartener. *Learning and Individual Differences*, 4, 380–387.

Kaufman, J. C., Cole, J. C., & Baer, J. (2009). The construct of creativity: Structural model for self-reported creativity ratings. *Journal of Creative Behavior, 43*, 119–134.

Kaufman, S. B. (2013). Opening up openness to experience: A four-factor model and relations to creative achievement in the arts and sciences. *Journal of Creative Behavior, 47*, 233–255.

Kaufman, S. B., & Kaufman, J. C. (2007). Ten years to expertise, many more to greatness: An investigation of modern writers. *Journal of Creative Behavior, 41*, 114–124.

Kaufman, S. B., Quilty, L. C., Grazioplene, R. G., Hirsh, J. B., Gray, J. R., Peterson, J. B., & DeYoung, C. G. (2016). Openness to experience and intellect differentially predict creative achievement in the arts and sciences. *Journal of Personality, 84*, 248–258.

Kim, K. H. (2008). Meta-analyses of the relationship of creative achievement to both IQ and divergent thinking test scores. *Journal of Creative Behavior, 42*, 106–130.

King, L. A., McKee Walker, L., & Broyles, S. J. (1996). Creativity and the five-factor model. *Journal of Research in Personality, 30*, 189–203.

Kwasnik, M., & Karwowski, M. (under review). The order matters: Asking about creative activity calibrates creative self-concept.

Larson, L. M., Rottinghaus, P. J., & Borgen, F. H. (2002). Meta-analyses of Big Six interests and Big Five personality factors. *Journal of Vocational Behavior, 61*, 217–239.

Lebuda, I. (2014). Big-C research – the big challenge? Reflections from research into eminent creativity in the light of the investment theory of creativity. *Creativity: Theories-Research-Application, 1*, 33–45.

Lebuda, I., & Csikszentmihályi, M. C. (2017). Me, myself, I, and creativity: Self-concepts of eminent creators. In M. Karwowski & J. C. Kaufman (Eds.), *The creative self: Effect of beliefs, self-efficacy, mindset, and identity*, (pp. 137–152). San Diego: Academic Press.

Lebuda, I., & Karwowski, M. (2013). Tell me your name and I'll tell you how creative your work is: Author's name and gender as factors influencing assessment of product originality in four different domains. *Creativity Research Journal*, 25, 137–142.

Lim, H. S., & Choi, J. N. (2009). Testing an alternative relationship between individual and contextual predictors of creative performance. *Social Behavior and Personality, 37*, 117–136.

Lubart, T. I., Zenasni, F., & Barbot, B. (2013). Creative potential and its measurement. *International Journal for Talent Development and Creativity, 1*, 41–51.

Lubinski, D., & Benbow, C. P. (2000). States of excellence. *American Psychologist, 55*, 137–150.

Martindale, C., & Dailey, A. (1996). Creativity, primary process cognition, and personality. *Personality and Individual Differences, 20*, 409–414.

McCrae, R. R. (1987). Creativity, divergent thinking, and openness to experience. *Journal of Personality and Social Psychology, 52*, 1258–1265.

Milgram, R. M., & Hong, E. (1994). Creative thinking and creative performance in Adolescents as predictors of creative attainments in adults. In R. F. Subotnik & K. D. Arnold (Eds.), *Beyond Terman. Contemporary longitudinal studies of giftedness and talent* (pp. 212–228). New Jersey: Ablex.

Mourgues, C., Barbot, B., Tan, M., & Grigorenko, E. L. (2014). The interaction between culture and the development of creativity. In L. A. Jensen (Ed.). *The Oxford handbook of human development and culture: An interdisciplinary perspective.* New York: Oxford University Press.

Onarheim, B., & Friis-Olivarius, M. (2013). Applying the neuroscience of creativity to creativity training. *Frontiers in Human Neuroscience, 76*, 56.

Perleth, C., & Heller, K. A. (1994). The Munich longitudinal study of giftedness. In R. F. Subotnik & K. D. Arnold (Eds.), *Beyond Terman. Contemporary longitudinal studies of giftedness and talent* (pp. 77–114). New Jersey: Ablex.

Plucker, J. A. (1999). Is the proof really in the pudding? Reanalysis of Torrance's longitudinal data. *Creativity Research Journal, 12*, 103–114.

Plucker, J. A., & Beghetto, R. A. (2004). Why creativity is domain general, why it looks domain specific, and why the distinction does not matter. In R. J. Sternberg, E. L. Grigorenko, & J. L. Singer (Eds.), *Creativity: From potential to realization* (pp. 153–167). Washington, DC: American Psychological Association.

Plucker, J. A., & Zabelina, D. (2009). Creativity and interdisciplinarity: One creativity or many creativities? *ZDM, The International Journal on Mathematics Education, 41*, 5–11.

Prabhu, V., Sutton, C., & Sauser, W. (2008). Creativity and certain personality traits: Understanding the mediating effect of intrinsic motivation. *Creativity Research Journal, 20*, 53–66.

Richards, R. (1990). Everyday creativity, eminent creativity, and health: 'Afterview' for CRJ issues on creativity and health. *Creativity Research Journal, 3*, 300–326.

Richards, R. (2010). Everyday creativity: Process and way of life—Four key issues. In J. C. Kaufman & R. J. Sternberg (Eds.), *The Cambridge handbook of creativity* (pp. 189–215). Cambridge: University Press.

Robertson, K. F., Smeets, S., Lubinski, D., & Benbow, C. P. (2010). Beyond the threshold hypothesis: Even among gifted and top math/science graduate students, cognitive abilities, vocational interests, and lifestyle preferences matter for career choice, performance, and persistence. *Current Directions in Psychological Science, 19*, 346–351.

Root-Bernstein, R. S., Bernstein, M., & Garnier, H. (1995). Correlations between avocations, scientific style, work habits, and professional impact of scientists. *Creativity Research Journal, 8*, 115–137.

Root-Bernstein, R. S., & Root-Bernstein, M. (2004). Artistic scientists and scientific artists: The link between polymathy and creativity. In R. J. Sternberg, E. L. Grigorenko, & J. L. Singer (Eds.), *Creativity: From potential to realization* (pp. 127–151). Washington: American Psychological Association.

Rostan, S. M. (2005). Educational intervention and the development of young art students' talent and creativity. *Journal of Creative Behavior, 39*, 237–261.

Runco, M. A. (1990). Implicit theories and ideational creativity. In M. A. Runco & R. S. Albert (Eds.), *Theories of creativity* (pp. 234–252). Thousand Oaks, CA, US: Sage Publications, Inc.

Runco, M. A. (2003). Education for creative potential. *Scandinavian Journal of Educational Research, 47*, 318–324.

Runco, M. A., & Acar, S. (2012). Divergent thinking as an indicator of creative potential. *Creativity Research Journal, 24*, 66–75.

Runco, M. A., Millar, G., Acar, S., & Cramond, B. (2010). Torrance tests of creative thinking as predictors of personal and public achievement: A fifty-year follow-up. *Creativity Research Journal, 22*, 361–368.

Runco, M. A., Noble, E. P., Reiter-Palmon, R., Acar, S., Ritchie, T., & Yurkovich, J. M. (2011). The genetic basis of creativity and ideational fluency. *Creativity Research Journal, 23*, 376–380.

Russ, S. (2014). *Pretend play in childhood: Foundation of adult creativity.* Washington DC: American Psychological Association.

Ruthsatz, J., Detterman, D. K., Griscom, W. S., & Cirullo, B. A. (2008). Becoming an expert in the musical domain: It takes more than just practice. *Intelligence, 36,* 330–338.

Sawyer, R. K. (2012). *Explaining creativity: The science of human innovation* (2nd edn.). New York: Oxford University Press.

Silvia, P. J., Beaty, R. E., Nusbaum, E. C., Eddington, K. M., Levin-Aspenson, H., & Kwapil, T. R. (2014). Everyday creativity in daily life: An experience-sampling study of "little c" creativity. *Psychology of Aesthetics, Creativity, and the Arts, 8,* 183–188.

Silvia, P. J., Kaufman, J. C., & Pretz, J. E. (2009b). Is creativity domain-specific? Latent class models of creative accomplishments and creative self-descriptions. *Psychology of Aesthetics, Creativity, and the Arts, 3,* 139–148.

Silvia, P. J., Nusbaum, E. C., Berg, C., Martin, C., & O'Connor, A. (2009a). Openness to experience, plasticity, and creativity: Exploring lower-order, higher-order, and interactive effects. *Journal of Research in Personality, 43,* 1087–1090.

Silvia, P. J., Wigert, B., Reiter-Palmon, R., & Kaufman, J. C. (2012). Assessing creativity with self-report scales: A review and empirical evaluation. *Psychology of Aesthetics, Creativity, and the Arts, 6,* 19–34.

Simonton, D. K. (1991). Creative productivity through the adult years. *Generations: Journal of the American Society on Aging, 15,* 13–16.

Simonton, D. K. (1994). *Greatness: Who makes history and why.* New York: The Guilford Press.

Simonton, D. K. (1998). Career paths and creative lives: A theoretical perspective on late life potential. In C. Adams-Price (Ed.), *Creativity and successful aging: Theoretical and empirical approaches* (pp. 3–18). New York: Springer.

Simonton, D. K. (2002). *Great psychologists and their times: Scientific insights into psychology's history.* Washington: American Psychological Association.

Simonton, D. K. (2009). Varieties of (scientific) creativity: A hierarchical model of domain-specific disposition, development, and achievement. *Perspectives on Psychological Science, 4,* 441–452.

Simonton, D. K. (2013). Creative performance, expertise acquisition, individual differences, and developmental antecedents: An integrative research agenda. *Intelligence, 45,* 66–73.

Snow, C. P. (1964). *The two cultures.* London: Cambridge University Press.

Spear, L. P. (2013). Adolescent neurodevelopment. *Journal of Adolescent Health, 52,* 7–13.

Stavridou, A., & Furnham, A. (1996). The relationship between psychoticism, trait creativity and the attentional mechanism of cognitive inhibition. *Personality and Individual Differences, 21,* 143–153.

Sternberg, R. J. (2002). Creativity as a decision. *American Psychologist, 57,* 376.

Sternberg, R. J., & Lubart, T. I. (1992). Buy low and sell high: An investment approach to creativity. *Current Directions in Psychological Science, 1,* 1–5.

Szen-Ziemiańska, J. (2015). *Uwarunkowania osiągnięć twórczych na wczesnych etapach kariery naukowej.* [Conditions of creative achievement in the early periods of scientific career]. Unpublished doctoral dissertation. University of Social Sciences and Humanities, Warsaw, Poland.

Tierney, P., & Farmer, S. M. (2002). Creative self-efficacy: Its potential antecedents and relationship to creative performance. *Academy of Management Journal, 45,* 1137–1148.

Tierney, P., & Farmer, S. M. (2011). Creative self-efficacy development and creative performance over time. *Journal of Applied Psychology, 96,* 277–293.

Urban, K. (2005). Assessing creativity: The test for Creative Thinking – Drawing production (TCT-DP). *International Education Journal, 6*, 272–280.

Urban, K. K. (1991). On the development of creativity in children. *Creativity Research Journal, 4*, 177–191.

von Stumm, S., Chung, A., & Furnham, A. (2011). Creative ability, creative ideation and latent classes of creative achievement: What is the role of personality? *Psychology of Aesthetics, Creativity, and the Arts, 5*, 107–114.

Weiner, E. (2016). *The geography of genius*. New York: Simon & Schuster.

Weisberg, R. W. (1999). Creativity and knowledge: A challenge to theories. In R. J. Sternberg & R. J. Sternberg (Eds.), *Handbook of creativity* (pp. 226–250). New York, NY: Cambridge University Press.

Welch, G., Papageorgi, I., Haddon, E., Creech, A., Morton, F., & de Bézanac, C. (2008). Musical genre and gender as factors in higher education learning in music. *Research Papers in Education, 23*, 203–217.

Wigfield, A., & Eccles, J. S. (2000). Expectancy–value theory of achievement motivation. *Contemporary Educational Psychology, 25*, 68–81.

Wolfradt, U., & Pretz, J. E. (2001). Individual differences in creativity: Personality, story writing, and hobbies. *European Journal of Personality, 4*, 297–310.

Woody, E., & Claridge, G. (1977). Psychoticism and thinking. *British Journal of Social and Clinical Psychology, 16*, 241–248.

4 Domain-General Creativity

On Generating Original, Useful, and Surprising Combinations

Dean Keith Simonton

University of California, Davis

Abstract

The author argues that all creative ideas, whether in the arts or the sciences, use the same set of generic processes and procedures – just as persons speaking different languages operate under the same fundamental linguistic principles. The argument begins with the basic observation that all forms of creativity are combinatorial, the generation of new combinations from given ideas. However, because not all combinations are creative, it is necessary to provide a formal definition of what can be considered such. In words, creativity is defined as the joint product of its originality, utility, and surprise. This definition then implies that combinations must be generated by a procedure or process that is blind to the utility values. However, blindness does not imply the lack of constraints on the chosen combinatorial mechanism. The chapter then closes with a discussion of the theory's explanatory scope, research applications, and theoretical syntheses.

Born just a couple of years apart, Albert Einstein and Pablo Picasso became two of the most universally acclaimed creators of the twentieth century. The former, a theoretical physicist, published his creative ideas in highly technical journal articles riddled with mathematical equations. The latter, an avant-garde artist, expressed his creative ideas in paintings and sculptures. Did they think alike when they engaged in the creative process? At first the answer might seem an emphatic "No!" Einstein could no more "paint a Picasso" than Picasso could get a manuscript accepted in *Annalen der Physik*. On further examination, however, the answer is not so straightforward. Certainly both creators were outstanding visual thinkers who could use their imaginations to create spatial-visual ideas that were initially beyond the grasp of many contemporaries. These mindboggling ideas are evident in Einstein's relativity theories and in Picasso's cubist paintings (Miller, 2001). According to Einstein's special theory of relativity, if one observer is moving relative to another observer, then two events might be absolutely simultaneous to one but quite temporally distinct to the other even when they both stand in the same spot. In Picasso's cubism, the parts of a body or face might occupy radically different spatial orientations simultaneously so that, say, the eyes might be on one side of the head but the mouth or nose on another (e.g., his 1941 *Dora Maar au Chat*). Hence, it is not impossible that they might have relied on the same basic cognitive process to visualize the world in ways that most people couldn't – to imagine a reality totally unlike what surrounds us every day.

Einstein's first language was German, Picasso's Spanish. No doubt the two contemporaries would have struggled to carry on a basic conversation about the weather, even less about their chosen domains of creativity. As someone who studied both languages in high school and college, I can appreciate how different they are in phonetics, lexicon, syntax, and pragmatics. But imagine that some afternoon in the early 1920s, the two found themselves in the same Parisian sidewalk café, at adjacent tables talking in their native languages with compatriots. Suppose, too, that both geniuses initiated their respective conversations with a brief reference to the beautiful weather – the blue sky in particular. Would what Einstein said be incommensurate with what Picasso said? Could how Picasso described the weather prove untranslatable into German? Obviously not! Both languages operate with nouns, verbs, adjectives, and other parts of speech that make direct references to the external world. Certainly both statements could be translated into, say, Mandarin, with minimal loss in meaning to a Chinese sipping espresso the next table over. An unusually bright sunny day would remain so in any language. It wouldn't be too farfetched to argue that the underlying cognitive processes behind Einstein's and Picasso's meteorological remarks might be for all practical purposes identical. Whether one says "Blau" or "azul" in response to a blue sky, the basic associative process of retrieving the appropriate adjective must be the same.

I will argue in this chapter that creativity has a generic psychological make-up that transcends the idiosyncrasies of any particular creative domain. Einstein's scientific creativity and Picasso's artistic creativity differed at a superficial level only, just like their divergent use of German and Spanish to describe the weather. The concrete content might vary, but the abstract mental structure would remain equivalent. Creativity is just creativity!

Creativity as Combinatorial

Many eminent creators have themselves claimed that creativity must entail some combinatorial process or procedure (Simonton, 2010). Einstein himself affirmed that "combinatory play seems to be the essential feature in productive thought" (Hadamard, 1945, p. 147). The mathematician Henri Poincaré (1921) provided a more elaborate affirmation when he reported how "ideas rose in crowds; I felt them collide until pairs interlocked, so to speak, making a stable combination" (p. 387). He compared these colliding images to "the hooked atoms of Epicurus" that bump against each other "like the molecules of gas in the kinematic theory of gases" so "their mutual impacts may produce new combinations" (p. 393).

Hence, it should come as no surprise that many creativity researchers have made the same claim as the creators themselves (e.g., Finke, Ward, & Smith, 1992; Martindale, 1995). For instance, Mednick's (1962) well-known theory of remote association was explicitly designed to provide a cognitive basis for combinatorial creativity. Empirical support for this position has also been published. Thus, Thagard (2012) demonstrated that 100 top discoveries and 100 top inventions can each be analyzed into combinatorial products of some kind or another (e.g., some verbal, others visual, and yet others mathematical). The same assertion can easily be made for artistic creativity. To use Picasso's *Guernica* as an illustration, detailed analyses of his sketches reveal how much the painting largely represents the arduous end product of the combination and recombination of various visual elements that can be identified in earlier work, including his famous etching *Minotauromachy* that he created a few years before (Damian & Simonton, 2011; Weisberg, 2004). If an idea were completely *de novo*, it would probably not be understood.

When we speak of creativity as combinatorial, we have by no means committed our statement to *what* is undergoing combination (i.e., the content rather than the mechanism). For Picasso and Einstein the combinations definitely involved visual elements. For instance, Einstein noted that "The words of the language, as they are written or spoken, do not seem to play any role in my mechanism of thought. The psychical entities which seem to serve as elements in thought are certain signs and more or less clear images which can be 'voluntarily' reproduced and combined" (Hadamard, 1945, p. 147). Nonetheless, other creators may depend on combining more abstract ideas (Thagard, 2012). Thus, Roe's (1953) study of sixty-four eminent scientists found that some used verbal imagery rather than visual imagery.

Indeed, the mental elements entering the combinatorial hopper can get even more diverse than what has been identified so far. Choreographers will play around kinesthetically with varied body movements, jazz pianists will manually tinker on the keyboard with chromatic notes and complex harmonies, and chefs will mix exotic flavors, aromas, and textures. As Thomas Edison observed regarding technological creativity, "To invent, you need a good imagination and a pile of junk."[1] Any entities that can undergo combination and recombination can enter into this generic process or procedure.

In fact, this openness can be quite striking in those creators whose creativity is influenced by synesthesia (cf. Dailey, Martindale, & Borkum, 1997). For example, synesthetic composers often associate tones, keys, or chords with colors and thus can combine the two modalities in a single composition. Alexander Scriabin's *Prometheus, Poem of Fire* offers a prototypical illustration. The work is scored not just for piano, orchestra, and (optional) choir, but also includes scoring for the "color organ" (aka the "Chromola" or clavier à lumières) – albeit the piece is seldom heard/seen this way in concerts because most people aren't synesthetes and even synesthetes do not always agree in their cross-modal associations!

At this point a reader may object: "Surely not all combinations are creative! Each morning I prepare breakfast using the exact same combination of elements – a bowl, a spoon, my favorite cereal, and fat-free milk. Nobody will call that creative!" Excellent observation! It now forces us to define that diminutive subset of combinatorial products that can count as creative.

---

[1] www.thomasedison.org/index.php/education/edison-quotes/.

Defining Combinatorial Creativity

Creativity researchers have been appropriately creative in creating numerous definitions of creativity (Plucker, Beghetto, & Dow, 2004). Although most may favor the two-criterion "standard definition," which imposes some version of the criteria of originality and effectiveness (Runco & Jaeger, 2012), others have argued for a three-criterion definition, such as that preferred by the United States Patent Office[2] (Simonton, 2012c; cf. Boden, 2004). To earn patent protection, an invention must be novel, useful, and nonobvious – the latter even to someone with the relevant domain-specific expertise. Recently, I have provided a quantitative and multiplicative three-criterion definition that must introduce new rigor into the discussion (Simonton, 2012a, 2013b). Although more rigorous than the norm for most creativity research, this formulation has the distinct asset that it provides the formal basis for domain-general combinatorial creativity. Here some simplifications will be imposed to present that foundation in the most elegant manner possible for our current purposes (e.g., the omission of temporal subscripts, such as required in sequential processing; cf. Simonton, 2013a).

Parameters Defined

Let us start with a set of k combinations, where $k \geq 1$ (for if $k = 0$, we have no combinations to evaluate for creativity). These k combinations can be identified as $x_1, x_2, x_3, \ldots x_i \ldots x_k$. For example, in Maier's (1931, 1940) classic experiments using the "two-strings problem," research participants were required to tie two cords together that hung from the ceiling with the lower ends resting on the floor (the last critical feature invariably depicted incorrectly in textbook graphs). One potential solution, of course, would be to grab one cord, walk over to the other cord, grasp it as well, and then complete the task. Because this combination of objects and operations would not solve the problem, given that the cords were hung too far apart given their length, the experimenter advised the participants that they could use several items in the laboratory, such as a chair, a pole, an extension cord, and a pair of pliers, using them any way that allowed them to complete the task. Although the details varied according to the specific experiment, the participants could often generate more than a half-dozen combinations of objects and operations to potentially solve the problem, so we might set $k = 7$. For instance, we could set combination x_3 = "While holding one cord the other was pulled in with a pole" (Maier, 1931, p. 183). Whatever the details, these k combinations can vary according to three parameters:

1. The *initial probability* p_i of the combination x_i, where $0 \leq p_i \leq 1$. For example, the combination with the highest initial likelihood in the two-strings problem was to try to tie the two cords directly using the hands only, the first combination that was doomed to fail. The next most common combination was to place

---

[2] www.uspto.gov/inventors/patents.jsp.

a large object, such as the chair, somewhere between the two cords, anchor one cord to that object, and then draw the remaining cord toward the anchored cord (Maier, 1931). The combination with the lowest probability was the least obvious: Shortening one cord so that it no longer hung all the way to the floor, tying the pliers at the end, setting it in motion as a pendulum, and then pulling over the other cord to get in position to catch the swinging cord. In fact, many participants were unable to spontaneously generate this combination of actions. When specifically instructed to use the pliers, some thought to use them as tongs instead – which didn't solve the problem because that combination was too short!

2. The *final utility* u_i of the combination x_i, where again $0 \leq u_i \leq 1$. In many situations, this parameter becomes a dichotomous 0–1 measure, where 0 = useless and 1 = useful. The various combinatorial responses to the two-strings problem were this way: Either a combination worked or it didn't. Nevertheless, in many other situations, the utility can be a continuous or at least ordinal variable. For example, the solution to a particular problem may be only "partial" or "incomplete." When Edison searched for a commercially viable incandescent lamp filament, he often encountered several less-than-ideal solutions, such as platinum wire. A filament might burn out too quickly, use too much electricity, be made of expensive materials, or prove too fragile to hold up to transportation and installation. I must emphasize that the term "final utility" should be taken in the broadest possible sense to include ultimate value, appropriateness, effectiveness, and so forth (cf. Runco & Jaeger, 2012). For instance, many of the ideas that Picasso came up with for his *Guernica* had to be left out because they just didn't fit (e.g., the bull with a human face, the mother climbing a ladder, the Pegasus, or the prominent up-thrust fist in the center). Such images could then be said to have a zero final utility. They ended up on the cutting room floor.

3. The *prior knowledge* v_i of the utility, where once more $0 \leq v_i \leq 1$. If $v_i = 0$, the value of u_i is not known in advance, whereas if $v_i = 1$, the utility value is already known perfectly. If the prior knowledge value falls somewhere between the two extreme values, then the person may only experience a "hunch" or a vague "feeling of knowing state" (cf. Bowers, Regehr, Balthazard, & Parker, 1990). It is critical to recognize that these two parameters are completely orthogonal: The prior knowledge of the utility is independent of the value of the utility. One may know for sure that the combination is useful or useless; or one may be completely ignorant of whether the combination is useful or useless. Even so, the specific parameter values assigned u_i and v_i taken together quite strongly constrain the most plausible parameter values for p_i, as will be demonstrated later.

It should also be emphasized that all three parameters range from zero to one, like probabilities, proportions, or response strengths. Hence, multiplying them together or subtracting any one from unity will also yield a number ranging from zero to one, with a similar potential interpretation.

Creativity Defined

Given the above three parameters, we can then define the *creativity* of combination x_i by the following three-factor product:

$$c_i = (1 - p_i)u_i(1 - v_i), \text{ where } 0 \leq c_i \leq 1$$

The first and third factors need a little more explaining, though. The first, $(1 - p_i)$, represents the *originality* of combination x_i, that is, the inverse of its probability. Highly original combinations have the lowest initial probability. The third factor, $(1 - v_i)$, represents the combination's *surprise*. Surprising combinations are those that provide us with knowledge we didn't have before. This factor can then be considered roughly the same as the "nonobvious" criterion used as the third criterion of the US Patent Office (Sawyer, 2008; Simonton, 2012c). Putting this all together, we get the assertion that creativity is the joint product of originality, utility, and surprise. Note well that according to this multiplicative definition, $c_i = 0$ whenever any of the three components equal zero. Unoriginal, useless, and/or obvious combinations cannot be creative no matter how highly the combinations might score on the remaining factors. Each holds veto power over the others.

To return to the two-strings problem, using the pliers to create a pendulum scores high in creativity by the above definition. According to Maier (1940), only this solution introduced "an element of surprise and a change in meaning since the tool changes to a weight and the string, which was too short, suddenly becomes too long and must be shortened" (p. 52). It was not ordinary thinking by any means. Even participants given prior experience using standard pendulums did not exhibit a higher probability of creating this combination of actions. Indeed, the participants usually had to receive hints from the experimenter before arriving at this combinatorial achievement (Maier, 1931). In stark contrast, using a chair to hold one string while pulling over the other string was much closer to "routine" or "reproductive" thinking. The combination was highly probable and didn't require the participant to use the chair in a radically new way: not that different from using a chair to hold a purse or coat – or blankets when the kids make a "fort" in the living room! The same definition also informs us that eating a bowl of cereal every morning cannot be considered an act of creativity.

Finding Creative Combinations

Now that creative combinations have been defined, how do we find them? This task must prove rather difficult by the very definition of creativity given earlier. In the first place, holding the utility constant at some non-zero value (i.e., $u_i > 0$), creativity c_i maximizes as $p_i \to 0$ and as $v_i \to 0$. In words, maximally creative combinations have a zero initial probability of generation and no prior basis for even having any usefulness whatsoever! Accordingly, the most highly creative ideas require an incubation period (cf. Wallas, 1926). This period often ends via a "flash of insight" or "Eureka experience" in which an initially ignored combination suddenly pops into awareness (Mandler, 1995). Many such "ah-ha!" events depend on serendipity for this "popping" to happen (Kantorovich & Ne'eman, 1989). Absolutely nothing in Alexander Fleming's exceptional expertise would have made him consider that antibiotics might be extracted from *Penicillium notatum*: That breakthrough combination required the accidental discovery that a staphylococci culture had been successfully invaded by that fungus. Speaking more generally, such highly creative combinations will often emerge through the "opportunistic assimilation" of otherwise irrelevant stimuli in the environment (Seifert, Meyer, Davidson, Patalano, & Yaniv, 1995). The most famous Eureka moment in history, that of Archimedes, was precisely of this nature.

Yet it cannot be overemphasized that such inspired moments by no means guarantee that a creative combination has been identified. Such events might only signify that the generation probability now exceeds zero while it remains true that $v_i = 0$, signifying that the actual final utility remains unknown. It was for this reason that in the classic four-stage formulation of Wallas (1926) the "illumination" stage of the creative process was followed by the "verification" stage. Generation must be followed by test, variation by selection, for trial might result in failure rather than success. After all, creators can experience "false inspirations" as well. What looked good at the time may prove far less so when subjected to extra scrutiny, yielding a "Darn, that won't work either!" moment. Hence, such failed insights often merely increase the size of k, the number of blind combinations considered by the creator.

Tellingly, whereas there is only one way a combination can be creative, there are multiple ways it can be noncreative. After all, creativity will be low when the originality is low or the utility is low or the surprise is low or any permutation of low values, including when all criteria are low. In fact, even if the values of p_i, u_i, and v_i are normally distributed in a set of k combinations, the expected distribution of c_i will be best described by an inverse power function (Simonton, 2012a). What this means is that the modal creativity for the set of combinations will be zero, with the expected frequency decreasing with the magnitude of creativity, making highly creative combinations most rare. This rarity is a necessary outcome of the multiplicative definition. Even if the three parameter values had a uniform distribution, the same result would obtain (Simonton, 2012a). Combinations that simultaneously possess originality, utility, and surprise are hard to come by. Creativity is an extremely scarce commodity.

Sightedness Defined

Formally speaking, the crucial reason why it is so challenging to find a creative combination is that such combinations cannot rate highly in a quality called *sightedness* (Simonton, 2012b, 2013b; cf. Sternberg, 1998). A combination is sighted to the extent that it is highly probable, highly useful, and highly obvious. Stated in terms of the parameters, we get

$$s_i = p_i u_i v_i, \text{ where } 0 \leq s_i \leq 1$$

Logically, it must follow from this definition that $c_i \rightarrow 0$ as $s_i \rightarrow 1$. Stated a little differently, if a combination is highly useful, and we already know that it is highly useful so that it has a high initial probability based on that prior knowledge, then it cannot be highly creative as well (i.e., as $u_i v_i \rightarrow 1$, $p_i \rightarrow 1$ and thus $c_i \rightarrow 0$). Again, such combinations result from routine or reproductive thinking rather than creative or productive thinking. Highly sighted combinations represent direct applications of what we already know rather than enlarge our knowledge – confirm, not extend. It is like that bowl of cereal for breakfast to remove those morning hunger pangs.

Monte Carlo Simulation

Given the above consequence, we might at first infer that the goal would be simply to look for combinations that are low in sightedness. Such combinations can be called *blind* instead, where clearly blindness $b_i = 1 - s_i$. In other words, blindness and sightedness define a bipolar continuum (Simonton, 2011a). Because blind combinations must be both original (low probability) and surprising (low prior knowledge of the utility), some creative combinations might hide among them. Although that conclusion is valid, there is also a catch: Blind combinations will also have a much higher likelihood of low utility. After all, many of the low-sighted ($s_i \rightarrow 0$) combinations will have the parameters $u_i \rightarrow 0$ and $v_i \rightarrow 0$ (whatever the value of p_i may be). This ambivalent consequence of looking for creative combinations among blind combinations has been demonstrated in a simple Monte Carlo simulation (Simonton, 2012a). The results are shown in Figure 4.1.

Here combinatorial creativity is plotted as a function of combinatorial sightedness. Observe right from the start that the most creative combinations are indeed exceptionally rare, occupying as they do the extreme blind (left) end of the graph. Because the upper limit of the generated scatterplot is concave downwards, the maximum possible creativity declines rapidly as we move along the blind-sighted continuum toward the sighted (right) end. Even so, as blindness increases toward the left side of the dimension, the number of combinations with low creativity also increases. Put differently, the variation in creativity increases with blindness, with the distribution becoming increasingly skewed. Hence, the resulting distribution of creativity at the extreme blind end is highly skewed, with most combinations scoring low. So to find the most creative combinations requires that the individual sift through the set of k combinations to separate the wheat from the chaff. This sifting process has been variably called "trial and error," "generate and test," "selection by consequences," "bold conjecture and refutation," and "blind variation and selective retention" or "BVSR" (Bain, 1855/1977; Campbell, 1960; Nickles, 2003; Popper, 1963; Skinner, 1981). But whatever the name for the process or procedure involved, it requires that the creator be willing and able to generate combinations without prior knowledge of whether they will actually prove useful – which brings us to the next section.

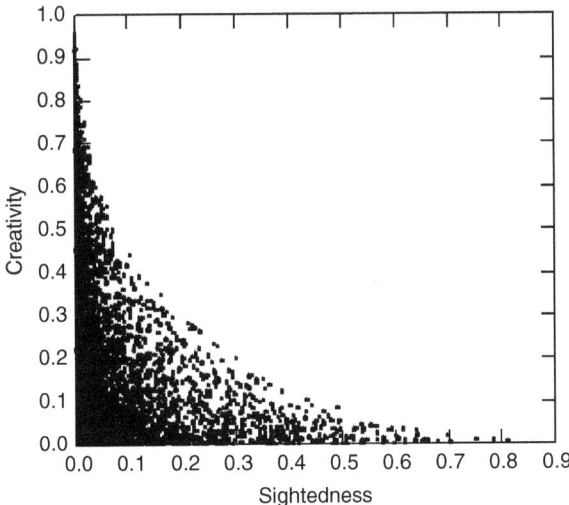

Figure 4.1 *Scatter plot showing the relation between sightedness and creativity for Monte Carlo–generated combinations, where sightedness is just the inverse of blindness (viz. $b_i = 1 - s_i$). The most creative combinations are found on the left side of the graph, where the most uncreative ideas are also located, thus requiring the implementation of BVSR, generation and test, or trial and error. The graph is adapted from Figure 4 in "Combinatorial creativity and sightedness: Monte Carlo simulations using three-criterion definitions," by D.K. Simonton, 2012,* The International Journal of Creativity & Problem Solving, 22, *pp. 5–17.*

Generating Blind Combinations

So how does one generate blind or "unsighted" combinations? Here the answer is simply, "Do anything that works!" (cf. Feyerabend, 1975). Creativity researchers have wasted too much time trying to find the single secret to creative thinking: Too often the quest concentrates on what can be considered *the* creative process as if it required only a restricted type of mental act, such as that needed for recalling a seven-digit number from working memory! Examples include remote association, divergent thinking, cognitive disinhibition (or defocused attention), primary (or primordial) process (or "regression in the service of the ego"), intuition, overinclusive (allusive) thinking, dreams and/or daydreams, analogy, conceptual reframing (frame shifting), finding the right question, broadening perspective, reversal, tinkering, play, juggling induction and deduction, dissecting the problem, etc. (e.g., Carson, 2014; Ness, 2013; Simonton & Damian, 2013). Sometimes the very names for these processes or procedures can even appear quite esoteric, such as Geneplore (Finke, Ward, & Smith, 1992) and Janusian, Homospatial, and Sep-Con Articulation thinking (Rothenberg, 2015). Alternatively, some have tried to establish that creativity involves just ordinary thought (Weisberg, 2014) or at least ordinary problem solving using an assortment of regular heuristic search techniques, such as hill-climbing, means-end analysis, working backwards, and even good old trial and error (Newell & Simon, 1972).

Guess what? All of the above processes or procedures work some of the time, but absolutely none of them work all of the time. That is precisely why so many have had to be identified. Sometimes a tried-and-true creative process will generate nothing but bad ideas (i.e., where $u_i \rightarrow 0$). For example, Edison was often inclined to use trial and error (a.k.a. BVSR; Simonton, 2015b). By generating one combination after another, and subjecting each to a set of utility criteria, he eventually ended up with the practical incandescent light bulb that not only made him rich and famous, but also provided the iconic symbol for having a "bright idea." Yet at approximately the same time, Edison applied exactly the same approach to developing a fuel cell that could power these light bulbs directly from the energy source, and dramatically failed. In short, there is no such thing as a single process or procedure that guarantees a creative combination. Instead, what we have is a toolkit of ways to generate combinations that must then be tested for utility. When one tool fails, we pull out another and hope for the best. The person with the biggest set of available tools will probably prove the most creative (cf. Ness, 2013).

The various combinatorial techniques in this toolkit can be called "weak methods" (cf. Klahr, 2000). These techniques are *weak* because they far too often fail, thus proving conclusively that they produce combinations without secure prior knowledge of the utility values. Although weak, such methods have the advantage that they can be applied to almost any domain under the sun. They are truly domain general. For instance, it is hard to imagine a creative domain where a good analogy might not prove useful from time to time. Analogical combinations permeate both the sciences and the arts, from precise mathematical models to allusive literary metaphors – even if not all models or metaphors ultimately prove effective with respect to either truth or beauty.

So-called "strong" methods or techniques (cf. Klahr, 2000), in contrast, can guarantee the production of useful combinations, but they are also far more likely to be domain specific, or at least confined to a small subset of domains. For example, when I was a chemistry student, I learned which catalysts would accelerate certain types of chemical reactions (e.g., the $2CO + O_2 \rightarrow 2CO_2$ needed for an automobile's catalytic converter). I have never found the procedures useful in anything I have done in psychology. Even platinum does not catalyze my thoughts! However, I also took calculus so that I know how to differentiate the equations that I am most likely to encounter as a psychologist (e.g., polynomials, as in Simonton, 2014). Better yet, differential calculus is absolutely essential to almost all of the mathematical sciences, such as physics and chemistry. Yet I cannot imagine that most artists would ever find differential (or integral) calculus useful. Einstein used higher mathematics all of the time, but Picasso never did.

Besides, strong methods have another problem: It is virtually impossible for them to generate creative combinations! To the extent that the method is truly strong, then the utility value of its output is already known prior to the method's application. Moreover, to the degree that the foregoing statement holds, then the probability of anything produced by that method must be very high. To give a concrete example, if at a Paris sidewalk café I find myself presented with a difficult (i.e., not easily factorable) quadratic equation and am asked to find its roots using a hand calculator, I will just plug the equation's three parameters into the quadratic formula and be done with it! I might double-check my calculations, but I have absolutely no doubt that the correct computations will yield the answer I seek (even if I end up with the square root of a negative number). In brief, the whole algorithmic procedure is 100 percent sighted and the resulting combination of the derived two roots with the given three parameters will have no creative value no matter how "original" to me. Anyone who knows the quadratic formula could do the same.

So we get back to the toolkit. Highly creative people must possess the cognitive flexibility to resort to whatever works. The larger and more diverse the set of accessible tools, and the more patient and persistent the creator's quest, the higher the odds for finding the right tool for the job. That is why "trial and error" or BVSR can be elevated to the ultimate creative technique – if by this we mean that the creator can readily generate and test multiple weak methods for producing potentially creative ideas.

Constraining Combinatorial Creativity

The theory of creativity as combination is often criticized because it would supposedly lead to a "combinatorial explosion" (e.g., Eysenck, 1995). The number of potential combinations of a given set of mental elements grows exponentially with the number of elements in that set. In theory, it would take several lifetimes to generate and test all possible combinations. This consequence is indeed true. In fact, it has been used to explain the cross-sectional distribution of creative productivity where a small number of creators account for a disproportionate number of creative products (Simonton, 2010). If the number of mental elements are normally distributed among a group of creators, then the distribution of potential combinations should be approximately lognormal, with a long upper tail (see Figure 4.1 in Simonton, 1988, p. 66).

That said, creators seldom if ever generate all possible combinations of the ideas in their heads. Many potential combinations are simply overlooked. For example, when Thomas Henry Huxley first learned about Charles Darwin's new theory of evolution by natural selection, he reportedly cried out "Why didn't I think of that?" (Wolpert, 1994, p. 68). After all, Huxley already possessed the same puzzle pieces that Darwin used in constructing the revolutionary explanation. Indeed, that prior knowledge soon rendered Huxley a highly effective "bulldog" in defending Darwin against Creationist attacks. Perhaps Huxley might have come up with the theory himself if he hadn't been preempted by his older colleague, just as Huxley's contemporary Alfred Russel Wallace managed to do in blissful isolation from Darwin's efforts. Many careers likely hide potential creative combinations that were never generated and tested. Indeed, according to one comprehensive combinatorial model, the entire scientific community regularly overlooks potential discoveries and inventions for generations if not centuries (Simonton, 2010). And with respect to the arts, many great "Tenth" symphonies have never seen the light of day because of the composer having already passed away (Simonton, 2015a).

More importantly, rather than throw every possible thought into the combinatorial mixer, most creators work with an extremely restricted subset. Poincaré (1921) expressed this reality using his chemical metaphor: "The mobilized atoms are . . . not any atoms whatsoever; they are those from which we might reasonably expect the desired solution. Then the mobilized atoms undergo impacts which make them enter into combinations among themselves or with other atoms at rest which they struck against in their course" (p. 389; viz. "spreading activation"). Accordingly, "the only combinations that have a chance of forming are those where at least one of the elements is one of those atoms freely chosen by our will" (p. 389). It is for this reason why current BVSR theory talks of "pre-selection" (Simonton, 2011b; i.e., if $u_i = 0$ and $v_i = 1$, then it necessarily follows that $p_i = 0$). For instance, when Picasso began working on his *Guernica*, which depicts a horrific war atrocity, certain visual themes in the artist's repertoire, such as his highly erotic nudes, could be omitted from the get-go. Similarly, when Einstein started developing his special theory of relativity, he automatically left out of the combinatorial mill any assumption that would violate a fundamental law of physics. Blindness does not equal stupidity.

Frequently, creativity is said to require "thinking outside the box." This statement is plain wrong. Creativity always takes place within a box – a set of constraints that increase the odds that the creator will obtain useful combinations. To offer admittedly extreme cases, Picasso could no more insert differential equations in *Guernica* than Einstein could include a figure of a mortally wounded horse in his journal article "On the Electrodynamics of Moving Bodies." Notwithstanding the originality and surprise that would be displayed by such combinations, those combinations would also have zero final utility. Hence, it is more accurate to say that the creator often needs to expand the size of the box, that is, to reduce constraints that might interfere with obtaining a creative combination.

A well-known example concerns the discovery of ring compounds in organic chemistry. Certain chemical features of benzene were not consistent with the carbon chains that had hitherto provided the usual structural interpretation for hydrocarbons. But Friedrich August Kekulé realized – supposedly in a daydream where a snake seized its own tail – that if the six-carbon chain was allowed to close upon itself to produce a ring, the observed chemical properties fell right into place. Such aromatic compounds now form a special branch of organic chemistry. Common aspirin contains one such ring.

From Weak to Strong Methods

Another constraint on combinatorial creativity is the most ironic: Weak methods that require BVSR, trial and error, or generate and tests – including the application of alternative weak methods – can sometimes yield strong methods that enable future creators to bypass the weak methods altogether. In the early history of algebra, for example, mathematicians would solve problems on a case-by-case basis using weak ad hoc procedures. But little by little, mathematicians would discover repeated patterns that permitted the strong, algorithmic solution of specific classes of problems, where those classes became increasingly inclusive over time. Thus, the solution of a complex system of linear equations today requires nothing more than the algorithmic operation of matrix inversion that even a laptop computer can do in an instant (as demonstrated every time someone performs a multiple regression analysis using standard statistical software). If the matrix cannot be inverted (because the determinant is zero), the equations cannot possibly be solved, period. An old proverb says "Give a man a fish and you feed him for a day; teach a man to fish and you feed him for a lifetime." Going from weak methods to strong methods operates in much the same way. You get more bang for your buck.

But herein arises the irony: This weak-to-strong conversion then yields routine (reproductive) combinations rather than creative (productive) combinations! If I now use matrix algebra to solve a system of linear equations, I cannot publish the solution in a mathematics journal. Mathematicians have already "been there, done that" long ago. The solution might be the means to some other end, such as new statistical method, but the latter would end up in a statistics journal, not a mathematical one. Just as importantly, the toolkit containing just strong methods has no usefulness beyond a narrow set of creative domains. In contrast, the weak methods that generated the strong methods remain universal in application forever. Both Einstein and Picasso can – and did – use trial and error, but Einstein had no use for well-established techniques for mixing paints and Picasso had no use for Maxwell's equations for explaining electromagnetism. So gains in domain-specific efficiency come at a cost in domain-general applicability and creativity (see the "No Free Lunch Theorem" discussed in Nickles, 2003).

From Strong to Weak Methods

Paradoxically, in fact, the principal way that domain-specific strong methods contribute to creativity is when they unexpectedly turn out not to be strong at all (Simonton, 2011a). In formal terms, a combination generated by a seemingly "strong" method actually has the following parameters: $p_i = 1$, $u_i = 0$, and $v_i = 0$, yielding $s_i = 0$ (rather than $p_i = u_i = v_i = s_i = 1$). In short, the combinatorial procedure that always proved useful in the past, and thus enjoys a high initial probability, is discovered to be surprisingly useless when applied in what at first seems a routine or reproductive application – like tying two strings together hanging from the ceiling.

Historic examples include the various "anomalies" that emerge in paradigmatic sciences when predictions from a well-established theory unexpectedly fail to work (Kuhn, 1970). For example, Newtonian celestial mechanics was spectacularly successful in calculating planetary orbits – even predicting the orbit of the unknown planet Neptune – until it failed to account for the observed precession of Mercury's perihelion. That surprising anomaly inspired physicists to engage in a new combinatorial enterprise that eventually led to original, useful, and surprising combinations. In particular, that predictive failure set the stage for a revolutionary theory of gravitation known as Einstein's general theory of relativity. The latter now provides a new set of strong methods that are even stronger than those provided by Newtonian theory – providing the essential basis for modern astrophysics from black holes to the Big Bang. This example helps us understand why some theoretical physicists were disappointed when the hypothesized Higgs boson or "God particle" was finally confirmed. Many had hoped that by disproving the Standard Model, the disconfirmation would lead to some "new physics" that would leave them much more creative work to do. Sometimes creators *want* to be sent back to the drawing board.

The surprising violation of expectations given by the parameters $p_i = 1$ and $u_i = v_i = 0$ can thus be taken as one formal definition of *problem finding*, a central feature of creativity (Getzels & Csikszentmihalyi, 1976; Rostan, 1994). As Einstein noted, "the formulation of a problem is often more essential than its solution, which may be merely a matter of mathematical or experimental skill. To raise new questions, new problems, to regard old problems from a new angle, requires creative imagination and marks real advances in science" (Einstein & Infeld, 1938, p. 95). Not surprisingly, Einstein was especially skilled at finding new problems.

Concluding Ideational Combinations

I have argued in this chapter that creativity does indeed have a universal psychological structure that transcends the domain in which that creativity takes place. At bottom, creativity must be combinatorial. The creator must produce at least partially "unsighted" combinations that must then be evaluated for creativity by some trial-and-error, generate-and-test, or BVSR process or procedure. Going from universals to particulars, combinatorial processes and procedures then operate on the specific content defined by a given domain. Viewing creativity as combinatorial has several critical assets for the field of creativity. These advantages may be grouped into three categories: explanatory scope, research applications, and theoretical syntheses.

Explanatory Scope

The combinatorial nature of creativity applies across the spectrum from commonplace "little-c" creativity to "Big-C" creative genius (cf. Kaufman & Beghetto, 2009; Simonton, 2013c). That smiling cook in your home kitchen using new ingredients to concoct a dish for tonight's dinner must engage in combinatorial processes or procedures just like the illustrious chef of a restaurant earning three Michelin stars. To be sure, the latter will have more domain-specific expertise acquired in culinary school and beyond, and will also be subjected to far higher standards at the instant of first taste. My spouse's newfangled chili con carne is not going to be mistaken for haute cuisine by any gourmet. Yet to the extent that the dish is creative – original, tasty, and surprising – it will be combinatorial in both cases.

Just as significantly, combinatorial theory encompasses various specialized forms of creativity, such as problem solving, problem finding, discovery, and invention (Simonton, 2010). I believe it is literally impossible to conceive a manifestation of creativity that extirpates its essential combinatorial nature. All of the solutions to

Maier's (1931, 1940) two-strings problem involved combining the cords with some object and some operation performed with that object (chair with holding, pole or extension cord with pulling, etc.), with solely one combination deemed creative (viz. pliers with swinging). And I have already pointed out Thagard's (2012) decisive demonstration with respect to 200 world-famous discoveries and inventions. Although the days when I could finger jazz improvisations on my electric guitar are long gone (and even admitting that nobody's missing out), from personal experience I am confident that improvisation is combinatorial to the degree that it is creative. That holds for improv comedy, too.

Hence, combinatorial creativity spans all levels and all domains in which creativity is manifested. Might I opine that the theory is really the only game in town?

Research Applications

Combinatorial processes and procedures have already inspired complex mathematical models that explicate a wide range of creative phenomena in the arts and sciences (Simonton, 1997, 2010). Combinatorial processes have also provided the basis for computational models of creativity and insight (e.g., Hélie & Sun, 2010; Thagard & Stewart, 2011). Genetic algorithms and genetic programming, which have provided creative solutions to real-life problems, are also inherently combinatorial (Goldberg, 1989; Koza, 1992). These diverse developments strongly suggest that combinatorial theory provides the most comprehensive and precise basis for understanding creativity.

In fact, computer programs that implement combinatorial procedures have actually generated impressive creative products in the visual arts and music (cf. Boden, 2004). For instance, Cope's (2014) EMI programs can create new musical compositions in the style of any given composer, from Antonio Vivaldi and Johann Sebastian Bach to Ludwig van Beethoven and Scott Joplin (cf. Fugues 1 and 2 in the Appendix, pp. 621–628). Even skilled listeners have difficulty distinguishing the human and computer generated works (Hofstadter, 2002).

Finally, and on the more empirical side, domain-generic theory helps explain why cognitive neuroscientists should be very wary of identifying *the* brain regions associated with creativity (cf. Dietrich & Kanso, 2010; Sawyer, 2011). Besides the crucial fact that very different modalities can contribute to the combinatorial processes or procedures, the processes and procedures themselves represent an extremely varied group of mechanisms both voluntary and involuntary, conscious and unconscious, logical and illogical. Even two creators generating the exact same combination may do so using different parts of their brain if one is a verbalizer and the other a visualizer or if one relies on defocused attention while another depends on a systematic search.

Theoretical Syntheses

As suggested at the close of the previous section, combinatorial creativity is not committed to any particular cognitive or behavioral mechanism. Anything creators can do to get new options from which to choose the optimal will suffice. Given this "anything goes" position, combinatorial creativity is necessarily inclusive rather than exclusive. It does not put forward any single mental process or behavioral procedure as the only or best means to creativity. Indeed, combinatorial creativity accepts that sometimes one approach will work, other times another, and yet other times none at all. All guises of creativity just become special cases of the generic principle. With but one exception, nobody's favorite theory is ruled out. That lone exception involves all domain-specific strong methods, which are rendered uncreative no matter what. To the degree that these methods are truly strong, they are also highly sighted. They're more like using a hammer to hammer nails than using a pair of pliers to make a pendulum bob.

The integrative power of combinatorial theory has two additional manifestations.

First, the generic conception of creativity as combinatorial permits the integration of the process and person perspectives on creativity (cf. Simonton, 2003). The creative person is obviously someone both willing and able to use a variety of weak methods to generate combinations where $p_i \rightarrow 0$ and $v_i \rightarrow 0$ in the hope of finding one where $c_i \rightarrow 1$. Certainly a tendency toward cognitive disinhibition (or defocused attention) would prove highly advantageous, especially given that such a propensity also correlates positively with divergent thinking and openness to experience (Carson, 2014). The proclivity to notice things that other persons automatically filter out would definitely support increased receptiveness to serendipitous events. Yet highly creative people must be distinguishable not just cognitively but also motivationally. After all, creative combinations are extremely rare, requiring the creator to sift through lots of useless combinations by some BVSR process or procedure. This requirement implies that highly creative persons must exhibit considerable persistence and determination even when confronted with failure after failure, and with no guarantee of success (cf. Cox, 1926; Duckworth, Peterson, Matthews, & Kelly, 2007). We must not forget that Einstein devoted the last three decades of his celebrated career to developing a unified field theory that integrated all the forces of nature – an ambitious theory that *never* worked. That great creative genius was even forced to admit that "Most of my intellectual offspring end up very young in the graveyard of disappointed hopes."[3] Yet Einstein persisted in his fruitless BVSR combinatorial endeavors right up to his final days, still trying on his death bed to finally find an integrative solution that would survive him.

Second, combinatorial theory puts creativity in the same broad class of phenomena that share one property: They all attain what may be collectively referred to as *undirected adaptive originality* (cf. Sober, 1992). These phenomena all rely on various kinds of blind (most often "random") combinatorial methods to acquire original adaptations. Examples include neurological growth in the brain, the development of antibodies by the immune system, biological evolution (both Darwinian and non-Darwinian), and Skinnerian operant conditioning (Simonton, 1999). Although the operational details must obviously depend on the specific manifestation of the phenomenon, all share the process of generating combinations from given

---

[3] www.aps.org/publications/apsnews/200512/history.cfm.

entities and then selecting those rare combinations that prove most useful (Cziko, 2001; see also Dennett, 1995). As the poet Paul Valéry described the two-stage operation, "It takes two to invent anything. The one makes up combinations; the other one chooses, recognizes what is important to him in the mass of things which the former has imparted to him" (Hadamard, 1945, p. 30). Because so many generated combinations are selected out, the combinatorial process is always to some significant degree blind – operating somewhere on the left side of Figure 4.1. If otherwise, then no selection would be necessary in the first place and the resulting combination would not qualify as an *original* adaptation. It would be too sighted, like any domain-specific strong method. The hammering, not the pliers swinging.

***

Einstein and Picasso might have observed "What a blue sky!" uttering totally different sounds, but most likely the underlying psychological processes would have been nearly identical in both minds.

References

Bain, A. (1977). *The senses and the intellect.* D. N. Robinson, Ed. Washington, DC: University Publications of America. (Original work published 1855).

Boden, M. A. (2004). *The creative mind: Myths & mechanisms* (2nd edn.). New York: Routledge.

Bowers, K. S., Regehr, G., Balthazard, C., & Parker, K. (1990). Intuition in the context of discovery. *Cognitive Psychology, 22,* 72–110.

Campbell, D. T. (1960). Blind variation and selective retention in creative thought as in other knowledge processes. *Psychological Review, 67,* 380–400.

Carson, S. H. (2014). Cognitive disinhibition, creativity, and psychopathology. In D. K. Simonton (Ed.), *The Wiley handbook of genius* (pp. 198–221). Oxford, UK: Wiley.

Cope, D. (2014). Virtual genius. In D. K. Simonton (Ed.), *The Wiley-Blackwell handbook of genius* (pp. 166–182). Oxford, UK: Wiley-Blackwell.

Cox, C. (1926). *The early mental traits of three hundred geniuses.* Stanford, CA: Stanford University Press.

Cziko, G. A. (2001). Universal selection theory and the complementarity of different types of blind variation and selective retention. In C. Heyes, & D. L. Hull (Eds.), *Selection theory and social construction: The evolutionary naturalistic epistemology of Donald T. Campbell* (pp. 15–34). Albany, NY: State University of New York Press.

Dailey, A., Martindale, C., & Borkum, J. (1997). Creativity, synesthesia, and physiognomic perception. *Creativity Research Journal, 10,* 1–8.

Damian, R. I., & Simonton, D. K. (2011). From past to future art: The creative impact of Picasso's 1935 *Minotauromachy* on his 1937 Guernica. *Psychology of Aesthetics, Creativity, and the Arts, 5,* 360–369.

Dennett, D. C. (1995). *Darwin's dangerous idea: Evolution and the meanings of life.* New York: Simon & Schuster.

Dietrich, A., & Kanso, R. (2010). A review of EEG, ERP, and neuroimaging studies of creativity and insight. *Psychological Bulletin, 136,* 822–848.

Duckworth, A. L., Peterson, C., Matthews, M. D., & Kelly, D. R. (2007). GRIT: Perseverence and passion for long-term goals. *Journal of Personality and Social Psychology, 92*, 1087–1101.

Einstein, A., & Infeld, L. (1938). *The evolution of physics: The growth of ideas from early concepts to relativity and quanta*. New York: Simon & Schuster.

Eysenck, H. J. (1995). *Genius: The natural history of creativity*. Cambridge, England: Cambridge University Press.

Feyerabend, P. K. (1975). *Against method: Outline of an anarchist theory of knowledge*. London: New Left Books.

Finke, R. A., Ward, T. B., & Smith, S. M. (1992). *Creative cognition: Theory, research, applications*. Cambridge, MA: MIT Press.

Getzels, J., & Csikszentmihalyi, M. (1976). *The creative vision: A longitudinal study of problem finding in art*. New York: Wiley.

Goldberg, D. E. (1989). *Genetic algorithms in search, optimization, and machine learning*. Reading, MA: Addison-Wesley.

Hadamard, J. (1945). *The psychology of invention in the mathematical field*. Princeton, NJ: Princeton University Press.

Hélie, S., & Sun, R. (2010). Incubation, insight, and creative problem solving: A unified theory and a connectionist model. *Psychological Review, 117*, 994–1024.

Hofstadter, D. (2002). Staring Emmy straight in the eye – and doing my best not to flinch. In T. Dartnall (Ed.), *Creativity, cognition, and knowledge: An interaction* (pp. 67–104). Westport, CT: Praeger.

Kantorovich, A., & Ne'eman, Y. (1989). Serendipity as a source of evolutionary progress in science. *Studies in History and Philosophy of Science, 20*, 505–529.

Kaufman, J. C., & Beghetto, R. A. (2009). Beyond big and little: The four c model of creativity. *Review of General Psychology, 13*, 1–13.

Klahr, D. (2000). *Exploring science: The cognition and development of discovery processes*. Cambridge, MA: MIT Press.

Koza, J. R. (1992). *Genetic programming: On the programming of computers by means of natural selection*. Cambridge, MA: MIT Press.

Kuhn, T. S. (1970). *The structure of scientific revolutions* (2nd edn.). Chicago: University of Chicago Press.

Maier, N. R. F. (1931). Reasoning in humans: II. The solution of a problem and its appearance in consciousness. *Journal of Comparative and Physiological Psychology, 12*, 181–194.

Maier, N. R. F. (1940). The behavioral mechanisms concerned with problem solving. *Psychological Review, 47*, 43–58.

Mandler, G. (1995). Origins and consequences of novelty. In S. M. Smith, T. B. Ward, & R. A. Finke (Eds.), *The creative cognition approach* (pp. 9–25). Cambridge, MA: MIT Press.

Martindale, C. (1995). Creativity and connectionism. In S. M. Smith, T. B. Ward, & R. A. Finke (Eds.), *The creative cognition approach* (pp. 249–268). Cambridge, MA: MIT Press.

Mednick, S. A. (1962). The associative basis of the creative process. *Psychological Review, 69*, 220–232.

Miller, A. I. (2001). *Einstein, Picasso: Space, time and the beauty that causes havoc*. New York: Basic Books.

Ness, R. B. (2013). *Genius unmasked*. New York: Oxford University Press.

Newell, A., & Simon, H. A. (1972). *Human problem solving*. Englewood Cliffs, NJ: Prentice-Hall.

Nickles, T. (2003). Evolutionary models of innovation and the Meno problem. In L. V. Shavinina (Ed.), *The international handbook on innovation* (pp. 54–78). New York: Elsevier Science.

Plucker, J. A., Beghetto, R. A., & Dow, G. T. (2004). Why isn't creativity more important to educational psychologists? Potentials, pitfalls, and future directions in creativity research. *Educational Psychologist, 39*, 83–96.

Poincaré, H. (1921). *The foundations of science: Science and hypothesis, the value of science, science and method* (G. B. Halstead, Trans.). New York: Science Press.

Popper, K. (1963). *Conjectures and Refutations*. London: Routledge.

Roe, A. (1953). *The making of a scientist*. New York: Dodd, Mead.

Rostan, S. M. (1994). Problem finding, problem solving, and cognitive controls: An empirical investigation of critically acclaimed productivity. *Creativity Research Journal, 7*, 97–110.

Rothenberg, A. (2015). *Flight from wonder: An investigation of scientific creativity*. Oxford, UK: Oxford University Press.

Runco, M., & Jaeger, G. J. (2012). The standard definition of creativity. *Creativity Research Journal, 21*, 92–96.

Sawyer, R. K. (2008). Creativity, innovation, and nonobviousness. *Lewis & Clark Law Review, 12*, 461–487.

Sawyer, R. K. (2011). The cognitive neuroscience of creativity: A critical review. *Creativity Research Journal, 23*, 137–154.

Seifert, C. M., Meyer, D. E., Davidson, N., Patalano, A. L., & Yaniv, I. (1995). Demystification of cognitive insight: Opportunistic assimilation and the prepared-mind perspective. In R. J. Sternberg & J. E. Davidson (Eds.), *The nature of insight* (pp. 65–124). Cambridge, MA: MIT Press.

Simonton, D. K. (1988). *Scientific genius: A psychology of science*. Cambridge: Cambridge University Press.

Simonton, D. K. (1997). Creative productivity: A predictive and explanatory model of career trajectories and landmarks. *Psychological Review, 104*, 66–89.

Simonton, D. K. (1999). *Origins of genius: Darwinian perspectives on creativity*. New York: Oxford University Press.

Simonton, D. K. (2003). Scientific creativity as constrained stochastic behavior: The integration of product, process, and person perspectives. *Psychological Bulletin, 129*, 475–494.

Simonton, D. K. (2010). Creativity as blind-variation and selective-retention: Constrained combinatorial models of exceptional creativity. *Physics of Life Reviews, 7*, 156–179.

Simonton, D. K. (2011a). Creativity and discovery as blind variation and selective retention: Multiple-variant definitions and blind-sighted integration. *Psychology of Aesthetics, Creativity, and the Arts, 5*, 222–228.

Simonton, D. K. (2011b). Creativity and discovery as blind variation: Campbell's (1960) BVSR model after the half-century mark. *Review of General Psychology, 15*, 158–174.

Simonton, D. K. (2012a). Combinatorial creativity and sightedness: Monte Carlo simulations using three-criterion definitions. *International Journal of Creativity & Problem Solving, 22*(2), 5–17.

Simonton, D. K. (2012b). Creativity, problem solving, and solution set sightedness: Radically reformulating BVSR. *Journal of Creative Behavior, 46*, 48–65.

Simonton, D. K. (2012c). Taking the US Patent Office creativity criteria seriously: A quantitative three-criterion definition and its implications. *Creativity Research Journal, 24,* 97–106.

Simonton, D. K. (2013a). Creative problem solving as sequential BVSR: Exploration (total ignorance) versus elimination (informed guess). *Thinking Skills and Creativity, 8,* 1–10.

Simonton, D. K. (2013b). Creative thought as blind variation and selective retention: Why sightedness is inversely related to creativity. *Journal of Theoretical and Philosophical Psychology, 33,* 253–266.

Simonton, D. K. (2013c). What is a creative idea? Little-c versus Big-C creativity. In J. Chan & K. Thomas (Eds.), *Handbook of research on creativity* (pp. 69–83). Cheltenham Glos, UK: Edward Elgar.

Simonton, D. K. (2014). More method in the mad-genius controversy: A historiometric study of 204 historic creators. *Psychology of Aesthetics, Creativity, and the Arts, 8,* 53–61.

Simonton, D. K. (2015a). Numerical odds and evens in Beethoven's nine symphonies: Can a computer really tell the difference? *Empirical Studies of the Arts, 33,* 18–35.

Simonton, D. K. (2015b). Thomas Alva Edison's creative career: The multilayered trajectory of trials, errors, failures, and triumphs. *Psychology of Aesthetics, Creativity, and the Arts, 9,* 2–14.

Simonton, D. K., & Damian, R. I. (2013). Creativity. In D. Reisberg (Ed.), *Oxford handbook of cognitive psychology* (pp. 795–807). New York: Oxford University Press.

Sober, E. (1992). Models of cultural evolution. In P. Griffiths (Ed.), *Trees of life: Essays in philosophy of biology* (pp. 17–39). Cambridge, MA: MIT Press.

Skinner, B. F. (1981, July 31). Selection by consequences. *Science, 213,* 5015–504.

Sternberg, R. J. (1998). Cognitive mechanisms in human creativity: Is variation blind or sighted? *Journal of Creative Behavior, 32,* 159–176.

Thagard, P. (2012). Creative combination of representations: Scientific discovery and technological invention. In R. Proctor & E. J. Capaldi (Eds.), *Psychology of science: Implicit and explicit processes.* New York: Oxford University Press.

Thagard, P., & Stewart, T. C. (2011). The AHA! experience: Creativity through emergent binding in neural networks. *Cognitive Science: A Multidisciplinary Journal, 35,* 1–33.

Wallas, G. (1926). *The art of thought.* New York: Harcourt, Brace.

Weisberg, R. W. (2004). On structure in the creative process: *A quantitative case-study of the creation of Picasso's Guernica. Empirical Studies of the Arts, 22,* 23–54.

Weisberg, R. W. (2014). Case studies of genius: Ordinary thinking, extraordinary outcomes. In D. K. Simonton (Ed.), *The Wiley-Blackwell handbook of genius* (pp. 139–165). Oxford, UK: Wiley-Blackwell.

Wolport, L. (1994). *The unnatural nature of science: Why science does not make (common) sense.* Cambridge, MA: Harvard University Press.

PART II

Creativity in the Traditional Arts

5   The Creativity of Literary Writing

Keith Oatley
University of Toronto

Maja Djikic
University of Toronto

Abstract

Literary writing involves externalization of mind onto paper or computer screen, and a process of guided exploration over a space of possibilities. Among the arts, this kind of writing may come closest in structure and content to everyday consciousness; this has enabled writers and readers to explore the workings of minds in interactions with others. Artistic writing is a kind of indirect communication in which the creativity of the writer invites the creativity of the reader. In personality, writers are higher in openness but more often depressed than other members of the population. Characteristics on which literary creativity is based make writers vulnerable to emotional disorders. With the exception of conversation, nothing may have been as important in understanding ourselves and others as works of creative writing.

Introduction

> In Xanadu did Kubla Khan
> A stately pleasure dome decree:
> Where Alph, the sacred river, ran
> Through caverns measureless to man
> Down to a sunless sea.

So begins "Kubla Khan" by Coleridge (1816/1977). He gave the idea of creative writing an influential jolt by publishing this poem with an explanatory note on how it had been written. He said had come to him in a dream "in which all the images rose up before him as *things*, with a parallel production of the correspondent expressions" (p. 156) so that, when he awoke, he had merely to write the expressions down.

"Kubla Khan" starts with a pleasure dome; this is a figure known as synecdoche, and it signifies art as a whole. Alph is the river of literature that runs through society, to make it fertile. The poem is about artistic writing, and it ends with a self-congratulatory depiction of the artist as a highly favored, extraordinary being. With its accompanying note about how the poem came unbidden as an inspiration, it could scarcely have been a better contribution to the spirit of Romanticism that was becoming influential at the beginning of the nineteenth century. As a contribution to psychology, its idea that creativity is not to be analyzed but is a property of artists of genius, it could scarcely have been worse. Although some aspects remain mysterious, some of the basic processes of creativity can be understood (see e.g., Perkins, 1981) and are open to most of us in our daily lives. In writing, too, they are open not just to geniuses but to those who are motivated to spend time, to take thought, and to practice.

The range of findings in this domain has been well covered in *The psychology of creative writing*, edited by Kaufman and Kaufman (2009). Here, we concentrate on the process of writing, treated in Kaufman and Kaufman's book by Lubart (2009), and on the personalities of creative writers, discussed in that book by Piirto (2009). We propose that the deepest insights into writing, including insights into creativity more generally, come from understanding how writers write creatively, and what kinds of personalities they need to have to do so.

Distinctiveness of Writing in Understanding Creativity

Among the arts, creative writing has been discussed in the West at least since Aristotle (330 BCE/1979) and in the East at least since Bharata Muni (200 BCE/1986). These traditions seem longer for writing than for the other arts.

Acting, music, dance, painting, dance, and other arts are popular in various ways but relatively a small number of people practice them. By contrast, across the world some 80 percent learn to read and write, and in developed countries the proportion is higher.

Reading and writing are the principal subject matters of school, and the amount of time spent in school approximates the 10,000 hours that have been found to be necessary to attain expertise in a subject (Ericsson & Lehmann, 1999). Implications for teaching creativity are well covered in Section V of Kaufman and Kaufman's (2009) book, for instance in the chapter by Baer and McKool.

Creativity as Search

In 1960, Campbell proposed that creative thought is based on what he called a Darwinian process of blind variation and selective retention. He correctly described this as search over a space of possible solutions to problems. The idea of search over such spaces, and the retention of likely candidates to serve functions in the solution to problems, was proposed by Turing (1936) and implemented by him and his colleagues in early computers. It is central to modern cognitive science (Gardner, 1985).

We agree that creativity is based on search, but we suggest that creative literary writing needs a modification to Campbell's (1960) proposal.

First, it seems to us that rather than calling search "blind variation and selective retention," it is better described in Darwin's own words from his (1859) *On the origin of species*. Darwin proposed that the creative search of evolution to generate new species was made by applying a complex of three processes. The first he called "superabundance" (members of species produce many more offspring than necessary merely to replace themselves). The second he called "variation" (members of species don't reproduce themselves exactly, but do so with essentially random variations that are passed to the next generation). The third he called "selection" (variations that fit the environment survive whereas others do not).

Creative writing depends on comparable processes, which in the same order as Darwin's processes, are as follows. First, writers produce many more word-sequences than will be used in a final text. They typically write not just one draft, but many drafts before they send their piece off to a publisher or make it public. Second, the word-sequences that writers produce are various. Paper and computer screens retain them and carry them forward. Third, some of the words and sequences are selected and make their way into a published text. Others do not.

For writing, the generative process in this search is augmented in two important ways. First, the process of producing variations of word-sequences is not random but planful. It's aimed at contributing to a set of goals, and with each word-sequence aimed to fit together with others. Second, the selection process is augmented because the writer planfully pre-selects just some specific word-sequences to go forward into subsequent drafts, before a final draft is put out for selection by editors, publishers, and readers, who decide whether a piece of writing will live or die.

Taking up Campbell's (1960) proposal, Simonton (2013) continues to argue that creativity is blind. He means (as we understand it) that innovations are essentially random (like those of Darwinian search) and that they cannot be seen in advance. The metaphor of blindness seems, however, unhelpful to understand creative writing. Of course, a published work cannot be foreseen when a writer starts it, but the augmentations of evolutionary search on which writers rely are by no means blind. The means by which words, phrases, and ideas come to writers remain mysterious. But do they come blindly? No.

In the augmented phase of production, the properties of paper or computer screen on which writing occurs mean that the writer can read what she or he has written. Production of further ideas, further word-sequences, can be guided, based on what the writer sees in the current text and what she or he knows.

In the augmented phase of pre-selection, the writer can see and read text, and decide what to retain and pass forward to future drafts. Creative writing programs, most of which lead to Master of Fine Arts (MFA) degrees, offer further guidance. Delaney (2007) wrote that in USA 20,000 people apply to these programs each year. One of their principal features is that those who attend them offer feedback to others about work they are developing; this feedback can become part of the pre-selection process before a piece goes out to publishers and the public.

Measures and Key Studies of Creative Writing

In the field of creative writing, it is possible to use measures such the verbal part of the Torrance Test of Creative Thinking (see, e.g., Runco, Millar, Acar & Cramond, 2010). The Torrance Test includes counting the number of variations produced in a piece of writing, their rarity, and the amount of detail they contain, all of which match well with the idea of creativity as an evolutionary search over a space of possibilities. Joy and Breed (2012) used this measure in their study of undergraduates who were asked to write stories in response to eight ambiguous pictures from the Thematic Apperception Test. They found that people's scores on the verbal part of the Torrance Test of Creativity correlated well with the ratings of four people who judged the creativity of the stories produced.

In much research on creative writing, rather than relying on the Torrance Test, four other kinds of measure have been given priority. One is of ratings by judges, of the kind used by Joy and Breed (2012). A second is of expertise attained by writers: the extent to which they have been through a long training, including self-training, to develop skills, in order to reach levels that are far beyond what novices can do (Ericsson & Lehmann, 1999). A third kind of measure is whether a literary work is seen by critics as original and worthwhile. The criterion of originality and public acceptance was proposed, for writing, more than two centuries ago by Johnson (1779–1781/2006), and has been taken seriously by literary critics ever since in the production of a canon of important works. Kaufman et al. (2013) compared novices, quasi-experts (who had some knowledge of creative writing), and experts (professional writers and professional literary critics) in evaluating the creativity of short stories written by college students. They found that quasi-expert raters were almost as good as the expert raters in their evaluations. By comparison quasi-expert engineers were not as good as expert engineers in evaluating the creativity of engineering designs. For writing, evaluation by critics is a measure of an important kind because it reflects not just features such as unusualness but, as Csikszentmihalyi (1996) has stressed, whether works are likely to taken up into society in a meaningful and useful way, whether they are likely to become part of Coleridge's sacred river Alph. A fourth kind of measure derives from features of recordings made of people as they think aloud while they solve a problem (Ericsson & Simon, 1980).

An example of thinking aloud while writing is to be found in the innovative study of Patrick (1935) in which she asked poets to think aloud as they composed poems in response to a picture. Patrick started with the idea of four stages of creative thought as proposed by Wallas (1926). The stages are preparation, incubation, illumination, and verification. Wallas's scheme can be seen as a version of evolutionary search in that preparation involves the production of possibilities, while illumination and verification accomplish selection and retention. The scheme adds incubation, a process described by Poincaré (1908/1952), who proposed that search (in his case, over combinations in a mathematical problem) can continue unconsciously when a problem-solver is not deliberately thinking about the issue. Patrick found some evidence for incubation in her study. She also reports that the pieces written by poets in her experiment were in the same styles as the poets' published works. She writes:

> Poets look for some deep meaning in a picture, something of emotional value or something suggestive of human life, while non-poets write more about the picture

or some idea which it immediately suggests. Poets put more imagination and meaning in their poems and are more dominated by the conventions of modern poetry. (1935, p. 35)

Expertise was central to the most important research yet published on how writing is accomplished. Expertise, here, is a proxy for established skill in creative writing. The research was conducted by Hayes and Flower (1980; 1986). They arranged for novices (students in Grade 12 or first-year university) and experts (professional writers) to come into the laboratory and think aloud as they wrote. They found that writing is aimed to accomplish a set of inter-related goals, and that it has three phases. Phase 1 is planning: Ideas and potential ways of writing them are produced. The plan develops. Sometimes it changes completely as the writing proceeds, as new ideas, new goals, and new ways of implementing them are discovered. Phase 2 is of creating sentences so a draft is produced. Phase 3 is of rewriting drafts to improve them.

Hayes and Flower found that, as compared with the novices, the experts in their study developed goals that were more elaborate in the planning phase, and that included consideration for their readers. In the phase of sentence generation, they manipulated sentence parts that were 50 percent longer than the parts manipulated by novices. In the third phase, experts made three times as many alterations of meaning. Writers develop what Ericsson and Kintch (1995) describe as a special form of long-term working memory in their writing: It has some of the properties of short-term working-memory in that large chunks of text can be accessed, cued, and manipulated so that meaning can be developed (see also Chanquoy & Almargot, 2002; see also the long-term storage and retrieval factor, "Glr," in the Cattell-Horn-Carroll model of intelligence, Schneider & McGrew, 2012). For writers, this creative ability means that as a piece of writing progresses in drafts on paper or computer screen, the specialized form of internal long-term memory of the piece being written – the writer's inner representation of the text – also changes and develops.

The term "rewriting" is used by Hayes and Flower. This, and the related term, "revising," are used also in programs and instruction books of creative writing. These terms make it seem as if, in Phase 1 and Phase 2 (in Hayes and Flower's terms), a writer may err so that corrections can be made in Phase 3. "Rewriting" and "revising" mis-describe what most artistic writers do. For such writers, externalization of words onto paper or computer screen makes it possible to think in new ways, in better ways, than by merely working within their minds. The externalization of mind onto paper or computer screen, and the reading of what one has written, and the writing again and reading again, and again, comprise an extended form of thinking (Oatley, 2003; Oatley & Djikic, 2008). Rather than "rewriting" or "revising," the concept is "exploration." In *Ulysses*, James Joyce (1922/1986) has his character Stephen Dedalus talk about Shakespeare and say this: "A man of genius makes no mistakes. His errors are volitional and are the portals of discovery" (p. 156). Joyce's Dedalus is too narrow here. With the idea of creative exploration, the volitional is open to all of us.

There are two modes of exploration in writing. One is the cycle of work on a particular piece. The other is that many writers continue to develop their style over a series of works so that, as with the poets in Patrick's (1935) experiment, it becomes distinctive. Some writers, in their work, continue to explore the same theme, or related themes. In this we see the generation and continuing exercise of expertise over a lifetime.

Concentrating on how writers work on a particular piece, Feuer (1996) describes fifteen drafts of the opening scene of Tolstoy's *War and Peace*; and these are just the ones that survived. We reviewed interviews with famous writers of fiction published in *Paris Review* (Oatley & Djikic, 2008). Of forty-five writers who mentioned the subject in their interviews, 73 percent said they wrote five or more drafts.

Collingwood (1938) has argued that art, properly so called, does not have a known object for its outcome. He says squarely that art is exploration, very often of an emotion that is pressing but not yet understood. The exploration is in a language such as words, visual art, music, dance: forms of externalization. Although it is recognized that one reason for the externalization of art is so that it can be passed to readers, viewers, and listeners, it is less recognized that this externalization is essential to the exploration of which Collingwood writes.

Writing leaves traces on paper or some other medium. At least since the nineteenth century, these traces have enabled explorations to be followed, examined, thought about, and understood. In this domain, a field of study of such developments has grown up in France: *génétique textuelle* (see, e.g., Deppman, Ferrer & Groden, 2004), and from it we can see how writers such as Flaubert created their novels and stories.

The Best Theory of Creative Writing of Prose Fiction

Although to say this is anachronistic, Flaubert's theory of writing to produce artistic prose fiction can be thought of as a development of Collingwood's theory and an improvement on Hayes and Flower's theory. The theory of Flaubert enables us to see how the augmented evolutionary process was implemented by him, and how it offers a scheme of planning that creative writers can implement for themselves. The process has five stages (derived from di Biasi, 2002, and taken from Oatley 2013, p. 454):

1. *Plan*. First conceive an idea. Flaubert called this a plan or *resumé*. You need to let the idea go round in your mind, perhaps for several weeks. Day-dream about it. You can write some notes or sketches, but don't write anything too much yet.
2. *Scenarios*. Next write what Flaubert called "scenarios." Few or none of the words written at this stage will survive into the text that will be read by others. Scenarios are notes to develop further thoughts by yourself. Explore widely and write anything you can think of about characters, situations, and events of your story. If you need to do research on locations or anything else, now is the time to do it.
3. *Expanded drafts (rough drafts)*. At this point you can start to write sentences. Explore as many possibilities as occur to you, write everything that comes into your head, in whatever form, but don't worry about how it's written.
4. *Refined drafts*. Only at this point does what Flaubert called the "labor of style" begin. Only now do the form and order of events of the story take shape. At this

point you delete or ignore most of what you have written in the expanded drafts, and choose only words and sentences that will present the characters, situations, and events you have explored in ways that will suggest how readers can imagine them.

5. *Final draft.* Write a final draft.

Oatley and Djikic (2008) draw on the analyses of Debray Genette (2004) in which she shows how Flaubert (1877/1994) implemented this plan in the writing of his 1877 short story *Un coeur simple* ("A simple heart"). Flaubert's original idea, which he had twenty years earlier, was of a woman who dies in a saintly fashion, who thought of her parrot as the holy spirit. Debray Genette describes how, in his *avant textes* (pieces of writing produced before the final published text) there survive for this story: "three plans or *résumés* . . . three scenarios, a subscenario, two [expanded] drafts, two [refined drafts], and the copyist's manuscript" (p. 72).

The protagonist of the story is a housemaid, Félicité, who lives in the village of Pont l'Evêque. During her life she has extended her love to the two children of her widowed mistress, then to her nephew who goes to sea, and then, last of all, to a parrot. All of them are taken from her by death.

Debray Genette shows how the method of guided exploration works in Flaubert's discovery of the title for his story. In the second scenario he writes: "accélération de sa poitrine de ce coeur qui n'avait battu pr rien de ignoble" (acceleration of her chest of this heart that had never beaten for anything ignoble; p. 82). At this stage, Flaubert seemed not to recognize the significance of the word "heart" (*coeur*). Debray Genette points out that only in the first expanded draft does he see (no blindness here) that this word can be part of the title for the story: "A simple heart." He sees, too, how it can be central to the story's final paragraph.

The last two pages of the story are about Félicité's death, at the feast of Corpus Christi. At this time, in Pont l'Evêque, a procession takes place in which the sacrament is carried through the village streets and stops at highly decorated altars that the villagers have constructed. One of these is outside the window of the room in which Félicité lies dying. To this altar, Félicité has donated her parrot, which she had stuffed after it died. The procession pauses outside her window. Here now is a translation by Oatley (2011, p. 150), which sticks close to Flaubert's words but draws, too, on the thoughts that Flaubert externalized in the several phases of this paragraph's composition.

> As a vapour of blue incense rose up into her room, Félicité flared her nostrils, and breathed it in with mystical sensuality; then she closed her eyes. Her lips smiled. The movements of her heart slowed down, one by one, each time more vague, more soft, like a fountain running dry, like an echo fading away; and, as she exhaled her last breath, she thought she could see, as the heavens opened to receive her,
> a gigantic parrot hovering overhead.

The thirty-eight-page story took Flaubert six months to write. The idea of a woman who thinks of the holy spirit as a parrot may seem absurd to those who look down their noses at the uneducated, but the story is beautiful, moving, with a sense of truth in it. It's of a kind that invites readers to think, and to experience their own emotions.

In its final paragraph, Flaubert guides himself to avoid clichés of literature's many death scenes, and also to avoid writing anything that might remind one of the death of Emma Bovary. The thought he has put into the scene, externalized onto paper, and worked over, and worked over again, and again, enabled him to make the death at the same time simple, physiological, sensual, and spiritual. Working on the final paragraph, in one part of the first expanded draft, he makes use of the visible layout of the page. Although these categorizations aren't consistent they include, on the left side of the page, physiological expressions such as the heart slowing down. On the right-hand side are images that include "like the vibrations of a string which has been plucked," "echo falling to the bottom of a precipice," and "as a fountain runs dry" (Debray Genette, p. 90). Flaubert would reject the image of the string that had been plucked. He would simplify the image of the echo and retain the metaphor of the fountain running dry because these were appropriate to the character of Félicité that he had developed in his explorations.

We suggest that although traces are left by architects, for instance by Brunelleschi in his construction of the dome of the Cathedral in Florence (King, 2000), and by painters such as Picasso in his sketches and photographs of *Guernica* (Arnheim, 1962), there is nothing with the kind of detail that has been left by writers in their *avant textes*. In such *avant textes*, as written for instance by Flaubert, we see a process of externalization of plans, scenarios, and drafts onto paper, the extended time that a writer needs to take in the process, and the guided way in which one exploratory thought can lead creatively to another.

Writing as Consciousness

A second aspect of how writing is distinctive for understanding creativity is that a piece of writing, be it an e-mail, a note of an event recorded in a diary, or a novel, is in a form that is the predominant mode of our reflective consciousness. (Questions of the unconscious in creative writing are discussed by Hecq, 2015).

In our view, the best psychological theory of consciousness is that of Baumeister and Masicampo (2010). They proposed that consciousness is not primarily for initiating action. It is a kind of simulation within which we inter-relate memory (in the form of general knowledge and skills together with personal knowledge of people and incidents), understandings of our current social circumstance, and our evaluations of concerns, goals, and plans. They say that:

> The influence of conscious thought on behavior can be vitally helpful but is mostly indirect. Conscious simulation processes are useful for understanding the perspectives of social interaction partners, for exploring options in complex decisions, for replaying past events (both literally and counterfactually) so as to learn, and for facilitating participation in culture in other ways. (p. 945)

Since the time of Aristotle's (330 BCE/1970) *Poetics*, there have been many elaborations of how fiction expands the consciousness of those who engage in it. With Baumeister and Masicampo's hypothesis, it becomes easier to see how this occurs. Like consciousness, fiction is a simulation (Oatley, 1999), one that inter-relates memory, current understandings, and prospects for future action. It is an externalized twin of our inner consciousness. For readers and audience members, a play, novel, short story, or film can be internalized and made part of our inner consciousness. We choose what to read and what to see, and we choose whether to make parts of such pieces of fiction our own. We like writers who are great artists, because we want to improve our own consciousness.

When we follow the intentions and actions of a fictional protagonist we use the planning ability we have for constructing actions in the day-to-day world. But as we take up a book, or prepare to watch a movie, we put aside our own concerns and plans, and enter those of the protagonist into our planning processor. We imagine the setting of the story, take in the circumstances and, using our model of how the world works, we take on the protagonist's thoughts, follow her or his actions, and experience emotions as events unfold. In the story the prota-gonist is understood to experience emotions in relation to how her or his plans turn out. We too experience emotions, but though we may empathize with the character, our emotions are not those of this character. They are our own, in the circumstances of the story.

Artistic Writing as Indirect Communication

A third aspect of how writing contributes to creativity, and to our under-standing of the importance of art in human life, is in how literary art prompts creativity in the people who engage with it.

Every fiction writer has a perspective, some have a vision. But writers of the artistic kind do not primarily seek to persuade or coerce. Artistic fiction is more delicate. Its mode of communication is what Kierkegaard called indirect:

> The indirect mode of communication makes communication an art in quite
> a different sense than when it is conceived in the usual manner . . . To stop a man on
> the street and stand still while talking to him, is not so difficult as to say something
> to a passer-by in passing, without standing still and without delaying the other,
> without attempting to persuade him to go the same way, but giving him instead an
> impulse to go precisely his own way. (1846/1968, pp. 246–247)

In a letter of 1888, Anton Chekhov took up this same theme when wrote that one must not: "mix up two ideas: *the solution of problem and the correct presentation of problem*. Only the latter is obligatory for the artist" (italics in original, Hellman, 1955, p. 57). As the letter continues Chekhov compares fiction to what goes in a court, where an advocate presents the evidence. In fiction the writer does a similar job. It's the jury or the reader who makes the judgment. This happens in Flaubert's "A simple heart."

Djikic, Oatley, Zoeterman, and Peterson (2009) found evidence of the process of indirect communication in readers of one of Chekhov's stories. The researchers first measured their participants' Big Five traits of personality (Extraversion, Emotional

Stability, Openness, Agreeableness, and Conscientiousness) and got the participants to rate how they were feeling in relation to ten emotions. Then they asked them to read either Chekhov's story "The lady with the little dog" or a control version written in non-fictional style that had the same information, length, and reading difficulty, which the readers rated just as interesting but not as artistic as Chekhov's story. After they had read the text to which they were randomly assigned, the participants' personality traits and emotions were measured again. As compared with those who read the control text, those who read Chekhov's story were found to have small variations in their personality, but not all of the same kind. Each person changed in her or his own way, and the amount of change was mediated by the intensity of emotion experienced when reading. The changes were small, and perhaps temporary, but it's possible that over a life of reading they might cumulate.

To see whether our result wasn't just peculiar to one story, we did another experiment (Djikic, Oatley & Carland, 2012) in which we asked people to read one of eight literary short stories or one of eight literary essays. We altered the essays by small amounts so that their average length and ease of reading would be the same as for the stories. We found that whether the text was fiction or non-fiction did not matter much. What mattered was that those who read a story or essay that they judged to be artistic changed their personalities more than those who judged the text they read to be less artistic. Again the changes were small, but not all in the same direction. The perturbations of people's personalities occurred in their own ways.

In these studies, we are beginning to show how artistic literature can be a form of Kierkegaard's indirect communication (Djikic & Oatley, 2014a). It is based on the writer being an artist who is creative enough to allow readers to think their own thoughts, feel their own emotions, and change in their own ways, rather than trying to persuade them to think or feel as she or he might dictate. Such art invites readers to be creative. We think of this kind of influence as democracy in art.

Personalities of Creative Writers

The question of the mad genius was raised long ago, when Aristotle at the beginning of *Problems* XXX (see Barnes, Ed., 1984, Vol II, p. 1498) asked why eminent people in philosophy, politics, poetry, and the arts are subject to melancholy. In a more day-to-day fashion, one hears publishers and editors talk about how self-absorbed many writers are. These are impressions. What is the evidence? Are creative writers especially subject to depression? Do they generally have difficult personalities?

There have been several studies in which people have read biographies to answer these questions. In 1995, for instance, Ludwig published results from biographies of 1,000 creative individuals, of whom about a quarter were writers. He found a higher prevalence of mental illness among those who were in artistic professions (writers, artists, people in the theater) than among those in non-artistic professions (business, politics, science). Following on from a number of studies of this kind, Kaufman (2001) studied biographies of 1,629 writers that ranged from a few paragraphs to a few pages in two guidebooks to writers' lives. He found that women poets were more likely to have suffered from mental illness than female writers of prose fiction, or than male writers of any genre. In a second study included in this paper, Kaufman analyzed brief biographies of 520 eminent American women who included writers, politicians, actors, and visual artists. He found that women poets were more likely than other women to have suffered mental illness. He calls this the Sylvia Plath effect. It was further investigated by Kaufman and Baer (2002).

The largest study of this issue has been by Kyaga and his colleagues (Kyaga et al. 2013; Kyaga 2015), who surveyed 1,173,763 patients in the Swedish national patient register diagnosed with psychiatric disorders. In a case-control design using longitudinal Swedish total population registries, they looked for associations with occupations; they counted creative occupations as being in science or the arts (including writing). The two most important findings relevant to the current chapter were, first, that writers were diagnosed with schizophrenia or bipolar disorder twice as often as controls. As compared with controls, writers were also more frequently diagnosed with unipolar depression, anxiety disorder, and substance abuse. They were also more likely to commit suicide. Second, Kyaga et al. (2013) found an association between people in creative professions and psychiatric diagnoses of schizophrenia or bipolar disorder in their first-degree relatives. In correspondence with other studies of the genetics of mental illness, this finding suggests that writers' tendencies to schizophrenia and bipolar disorder have a genetic component.

Overall, as may be gleaned from the book *Creativity and mental illness* edited by Kaufman (2014), whereas in daily life creativity is associated with good mental health, writers do have tendencies to mental illness. According, now, to many studies, including that of Kyaga et al. (2013), literary output is associated with vulnerability, especially to schizophrenia and depression.

This finding raises a paradox. In one of the most widely replicated findings in modern psychology, it has been found that ordinary people who, in a few sessions over a few days, write about emotional experiences that have been difficult for them in their lives received benefits in mental health (see, e.g., Pennebaker & Chung, 2011). It seems that this benefit may not extend to professional writers, or at least not to all of them.

Although reading fiction is associated with better understandings of others (see, e.g., Mar, Oatley, Djikic & Mullin, 2011; Kidd & Castano, 2013; Black & Barnes, 2015), Bischoff and Peskin (2014) found that the ability of published writers and aspiring writers to take the perspectives of others is no better than that of ordinary members of the population. Though this result may seem surprising, we think the explanation may include the fact that when one reads fiction, one samples across many societies, many types of character, many circumstances. As George Eliot (1856) put it: "Art is a means of amplifying experience" and extending our contact with others "beyond the bounds of our personal lot" (p. 193). Probably this is part of why readers of artistic fiction have better skills of perspective taking (empathy and understanding of others) than people who don't read fiction. In their own writing creative writers do not, however, sample across a wide range in this kind of way. As Djikic, Oatley and Peterson (2006) have shown, they tend to be preoccupied with negative emotions; it's their own emotions they explore. Writers tend to project themselves into their writing, and this may account for some of their self-absorption, and also for the finding that writers' ability to take the perspectives of others is no better than that of members of the ordinary population.

In terms of the Big Five measures of personality, Maslej, Rain, Fong, Oatley and Mar (2014) found that 93 aspiring writers of poetry and/or fiction were significantly higher than 114 non-writers on the trait of Openness. The writers were no lower on Emotional Stability than the non-writers, but when the trait of Emotional Stability was divided into two facets, Anxiety and Depression, they were found to be the same on the facet of Anxiety, but significantly higher on the facet of Depression. In terms of higher-level combinations of traits (the Big Two), writers were found to be significantly higher on Plasticity (Extraversion and Openness) and lower on Stability (Agreeableness, Conscientiousness and Emotional Stability).

Vulnerability of Artistic Writers

On average, then, writers who have made it into the public eye seem genetically more vulnerable to mental illness than are other members of the population. Perhaps, since genetic tendencies to mental illness can predispose people to difficult interactions with parents (see Jenkins, McGowan & Knafo-Noam, 2015), it is possible that people who become writers are likely to have had, on average, more difficult times in childhood, which continue to preoccupy them. Writing has not been therapeutic enough to lift writers (again on average) to the level of mental health of ordinary members of the population. Perhaps their experience has been such they continue to be preoccupied by it. Perhaps, too, as Kaufman and Sexton (2006) have proposed, writing poetry does not have the same therapeutic benefits as writing narrative.

On these questions we propose that literary artists do need a special set of qualities to write in a creatively artistic way (Djikic & Oatley, 2014b). Some writers do indeed suffer severe mental illness, although this does not imply that mental illness has a causal influence on creativity. Instead, we suggest that three factors are required for creative writing of an artistic kind, which also render writers more vulnerable to mental illness. In the following three paragraphs on these factors, we take as an example Virginia Woolf (see, e.g., Lee, 1996), one of the world's most creative of artistic writers, who not only was diagnosed with a condition that is now called bipolar disorder (with symptoms of elation and depression), but who committed suicide.

First, creative writers need a drive to write, something like a compulsion: a commitment that derives from their emotional lives. It carries them through the lengths of time and the amounts of detailed thought that are needed for the kind of exploration-based writing that we have discussed above. Virginia Woolf's short novel *Mrs Dalloway* took her more than two years to write at an average rate of less than half a page a day. (Some of the scenes of the novel appeared in a short story that Woolf was writing in June 1922, and she finished the novel in October 1924; Lee,

1996). Virginia Woolf wrote, and wrote, and wrote: novels, short stories, diaries, reviews. One could say she was obsessed with writing. Writers seem to need something like a compulsion, to undertake the extensive explorations necessary for literary works that come to be regarded by the public and by critics as original and worthwhile.

Second, creative writers need to be sensitive to emotional issues: to both negative and positive aspects of experience. In her biography, Lee (1996) records that Virginia Woolf wrote that sometimes she liked being Virginia, but that when she wrote she was "merely a sensibility" (Woolf Diaries, Ed. Bell & McNeillie, 1977–1984, Vol 2, p. 193). She was sensitive to subtle details of people's interactions (Wells-Jopling & Oatley, 2012). Writers are aware of issues that cause emotions. Not only do they explore such emotions, they can be thought to indulge in them; but this may also make them volatile. Woolf showed strong swings between up and down, experienced both by herself (Haviland, 1984) and by others (Lee, 1999). This characteristic reflects the lower level of Stability found by Maslej et al. (2014). So sensitivity to emotional life not only serves as a compelling driver of artists' writing, it also makes these artists more vulnerable to depression and other forms of mental illness.

Third, in order to create art, writers need to be truthful, that is to say not emotionally defended, not self-deceptive. If they are untruthful in their writing, it will not be art but a set of self-absorbed quirks, of interest only as instances of psychopathology. A person may be a very fine literary artist, truthful in her writing, but self-absorbed in day-to-day life. This seems to have been the case with Virginia Woolf. Lee records how Woolf said, happily, in her diary: "How I interest myself" (Woolf Diaries, Ed. Bell & McNeillie, 1977–1984, Vol 5, p. 75). In her life, Woolf also deceived herself and others, for instance in her crass intrusion into the marriage of her sister, Vanessa, to Clive Bell. This is described by Lee, 1996, p. 249, as a two-year "game of intimacy and intrigue." Parmar (2014) depicts the intrusion as based on envy because Virginia couldn't bear the idea of Vanessa having a satisfying marital relationship when she did not. Virginia kept from herself how destructive this intrusion was. Art is based on metaphorical depiction of truth. Artists portray human nature, and although this is often based on their own experience, in their writing (though not perhaps always in their everyday lives) they had better confront emotional life and its motivations truthfully, without deception of the self, or of others who will be their readers.

Issues for the Future

For artistic creativity, writing has been a fundamental source of our understanding. An important issue for the future is the development of conceptions of art that are not just of opinion, but of psychological theory based on evidence. Literary art, properly so called, involves guided search that is exploratory rather than having a goal of persuading readers or watchers to feel particular emotions or to draw particular conclusions. This kind of indirect communication has not been much studied; it is an important topic for the future.

Understanding the personality structures of writers has reached some substantive conclusions. For the future, questions arise of how writers might develop creative aspects of their personality, such as openness and sensitivity to subtle details of people's interactions.

Not enough is known about how writers can develop the kinds of exploration that the externalization of mind can enable. In his book *The future of creative writing*, Harper (2014) predicts that the interconnectedness of the digital world will encourage creative writers to interact with their readers as they write their stories and essays. This is already beginning to happen, though perhaps some writers will remain sufficiently self-centered to want to create on their own.

Conclusions

By means of the traces left by writing, it has been easier than with the other arts to analyze some of the processes of creativity. Creative writing takes commitment, time, and concentration to achieve. It is an exploratory act of search guided by the externalization of mind onto paper or some other medium; it is mirrored in thoughtful and emotionally engaged explorations by readers and audience members. Writers are more liable to mental illnesses than non-writers. So Coleridge, with whom we started this piece, had a serious addiction to opium, and Virginia Woolf had bipolar disorder. But the association of writing with such disorders occurs not because creativity requires one to be mad. Rather, literary art requires an emotionally based drive to write and a sensitivity to experience, which can also render writers vulnerable to depression. Overall, however peculiar some writers may be in their day-to-day lives, our writing-based society is unable to do without the wide range of circumstances and incidents they depict, which offer us glimpses of the lives of our selves and others.

References

Aristotle. (circa 330 BC). *Poetics* (G. E. Else, Trans.). Ann Arbor, MI: University of Michigan Press (1970).

Aristotle. (circa 330 BCE). Problems. In J. Barnes (Ed.), *The complete works of Artistotle: The revised Oxford translation* (pp. 1319–1527), Vol. 2. Oxford: Oxford University Press (Current publication 1984).

Arnheim, R. (1962). *Picasso's Guernica: The genesis of a painting*. Berkeley: University of California Press.

Baer, J., & McKool, S. S. (2009). How rewards and evaluations can undermine creativity (and how to prevent this). In S. B. Kaufman & J. C. Kaufman (Eds.), *The psychology of creative writing* (pp. 277–286). Cambridge: Cambridge University Press.

Baumeister, R. F., & Masicampo, E. J. (2010). Conscious thought is for facilitating social and cultural interactions: How mental simulations serve the animal-culture interface. *Psychological Review, 117*, 945–971.

Bell, A. O., & McNeillie, A. (Eds.). (1977–1984). *The diary of Virginia Woolf, Five Volumes*. London: Hogarth Press.

Bharata Muni. (200 BC). *Natyasastra; English translation with critical notes* (A. Rangacharya, Trans.). Bangalore: IBH Prakashana (Current edition 1986).

Bischoff, T., & Peskin, J. (2014). Do fiction writers have superior perspective taking ability? *Scientific Study of Literature, 4*, 125–149.

Black, J. E., & Barnes, J. L. (2015). The effects of reading material on social and non-social cognition. *Poetics, 52*, 32–43.

Campbell, D. T. (1960). Blind variation and selective retentions in creative thought as in other knowledge processes. *Psychological Review, 67*, 380–400.

Chanquoy, L., & Alamargot, D. (2002). Working memory and writing: Evolution of models and assessment of research/Mémoire de travail et rédaction de textes: évolution des modèles et bilan des premiers travaux. *L'annee Psychologique, 102*, 363–398.

Coleridge, S. T. (1977). "Kubla Khan," in *The portable Coleridge* (with explanatory note on writing the poem, pp. 156–157). Harmondsworth: Penguin (Original publication 1816).

Collingwood, R. G. (1938). *The principles of art.* Oxford: Oxford University Press.

Csikszentmihalyi, M. (1996). *Creativity: Flow and the psychology of discovery and invention.* New York: Harper Collins.

Darwin, C. (1859). *On the origin of species by means of natural selection.* London: Murray.

Debray Genette, R. (2004). Flaubert's "A simple heart," or how to make an ending: A study of manuscripts. In J. Deppman, D. Ferrer & M. Groden (Eds.), *Genetic criticism: Texts and avant-textes* (pp. 69–95). Philadelphia: University of Pennsylvania Press.

Delaney, E. J. (2007). Where great writers are made. *The Atlantic, 44* (August).

Deppman, J., Ferrer, D., & Groden, M. (Eds.). (2004). *Genetic criticism: Texts and avant-textes.* Philadelphia: University of Pennsylvania Press.

Di Biasi, PM. (2002). Flaubert: The labor of writing. In A. M. Christtin (Ed.), *A history of writing: From hieroglyph to multimedia* (pp. 340–341). Paris: Flammarion.

Djikic, M., & Oatley, K. (2014a). The art in fiction: From indirect communication to changes of the self. *Psychology of Aesthetics, Creativity, and the Arts, 8*, 498–505.

Djikic, M., & Oatley, K. (2014b). On the fragility of the artist: Art's precarious triad. In J. C. Kaufman (Ed.), *Creativity and mental illness* (pp. 281–294). New York: Cambridge University Press.

Djikic, M., Oatley, K., & Carland, M. (2012). Genre or artistic merit: The effect of literature on personality. *Scientific Study of Literature, 2*, 25.36.

Djikic, M., Oatley, K., & Peterson, J. (2006). The bitter-sweet labor of emoting: The linguistic comparison of writers and physicists. *Creativity Research Journal, 18*, 191–197.

Djikic, M., Oatley, K., Zoeterman, S., & Peterson, J. (2009). On being moved by art: How reading fiction transforms the self. *Creativity Research Journal, 21*, 24–29.

Eliot, G. (1856). The natural history of German life: Riehl. *The works of George Eliot. Standard Edition: Essays* (pp. 188–236). Edinburgh: Blackwood (this edition 1883).

Ericsson, K. A., & Kintsch, W. (1995). Long term working memory. *Psychological Review, 102*, 211–245.

Ericsson, K. A., & Lehmann, A. C. (1999). Expertise. In M. A. Runco & S. R. Pritzker (Eds.), *Encyclopaedia of Creativity, Volume 1* (pp. 695–706). San Diego: Academic Press.

Ericsson, K., & Simon, H. (1980). Verbal reports as data. *Psychological Review, 87*, 215–251.

Feuer, K. B. (1996). *Tolstoy and the genesis of War and Peace.* Ithaca, NY: Cornell University Press.

Flaubert, G. (1877). *Un coeur simple*. Paris: Livre de Poche (current edition 1994).

Gardner, H. (1985). *The mind's new science: A history of the cognitive revolution*. New York: Basic Books.

Harper, G. (2014). *The future of creative writing*. Oxford: Wiley Blackwell.

Haviland, J. M. (1984). Thinking and feeling in Woolf's writing: From childhood to adulthood. In C. E. Izard, J. Kagan & R. B. Zajonc (Eds.), *Emotions, cognition, and behavior* (pp. 515–546). Cambridge: Cambridge University Press.

Hayes, J. R., & Flower, L. S. (1980). Identifying the organization of writing processes. In L. W. Gregg & E. R. Steinberg (Eds.), *Cognitive processes in writing* (pp. 3–30). Hillsdale, NJ: Erlbaum.

Hayes, J. R., & Flower, L. S. (1986). Writing research and the writer. *American Psychologist, 41*, 1106–1113.

Hecq, D. (2015). *Towards a poetics of creative writing*. Bristol: Multilingual Matters.

Hellman, L. (1955). *The selected letters of Anton Chekhov* (S. K. Lederer, Trans.). New York: Farrar, Straus & Co.

Jenkins, J. M., McGowan, P., & Knafo-Noam, A. (2015). Parent-offspring transaction: Mechanisms and the value of within-family designs. *Hormones and Behavior, Online 2 July*. DOI: 10.1016/j.yhbeh.2015.06.018

Johnson, S. (2006). *Samuel Johnson's Lives of the poets*. Oxford: Oxford University Press (Original work published 1779–1781).

Joy, S., & Breed, K. (2012). Innovation motivation, divergent thinking, and creative story writing: Convergence and divergence across the Torrance Tests and TAT. *Imagination, Cognition and Personality, 32*, 179–185.

Joyce, J. (1986). *Ulysses*. London: Penguin and Bodley Head (Originally published 1922).

Kaufman, J. C. (2001). The Sylvia Plath effect: Mental illness in eminent creative writers. *Journal of Creative Behavior, 35*, 37–50.

Kaufman, J. C. (Ed.). (2014). *Creativity and mental illness*. New York: Cambridge University Press.

Kaufman, J. C., & Baer, J. (2002). I bask in dreams of suicide. Mental illness, poetry, and women. *Review of General Psychology, 6*, 271–286.

Kaufman, J. C., & Sexton, J., D. (2006). Why doesn't the writing cure help poets? *Review of General Psychology, 10*, 268–282.

Kaufman, S. B., & Kaufman, J. C. (Eds.). (2009). *The psychology of creative writing*. New York: Cambridge University Press.

Kaufman, J. C., Baer, J., Cropley, D. H., Reiter-Palmon, R., & Sinnett, S. (2013). Furious activity vs. understanding: How much expertise is needed to evaluate creative work? *Psychology of Aesthetics, Creativity, and the Arts, 7*, 332–340.

Kidd, D. C., & Castano, E. (2013). Reading literary fiction improves theory of mind. *Science, 342*, 377–380.

Kierkegaard, S. (1968). *Concluding unscientific postscript* (D. F. Swenson & W. Lowrie, Trans.). Princeton, NJ: Princeton University Press (Original work published 1846).

King, R. (2000). *Brunelleschi's dome: The story of the great cathedral in Florence*. London: Chatto & Windus.

Kyaga, S. (2015). *Creativity and mental illness: The mad genius in question*. New York: Palgrave Macmillan.

Kyaga, S., Landén, M., Boman, M., Hultman, C. M., Langstrom, N., & Lichtenstein, P. (2013). Mental illness, suicide and creativity: 40-Year prospective total population study. *Journal of Psychiatric Research, 47*, 1–8.

Lee, H. (1996). *Virginia Woolf*. London: Chatto & Windus.

Lubart, T. (2009). In search of the writer's creative process. In S. B. Kaufman & J. C. Kaufman (Eds.), *The psychology of creative writing* (pp. 3–22). Cambridge: Cambridge University Press.

Ludwig, A. M. (1995). *The price of greatness*. New York: Guilford.

Mar, R., Oatley, K., Djikic, M., & Mullin, J. (2011). Emotion and narrative fiction: Interactive influences before, during, and after reading. *Cognition and Emotion, 25*, 818–833.

Maslej, M., Rain, M., Fong, K., Oatley, K., & Mar, R. A. (2014). The hierarchical personality structure of aspiring creative writers. *Creativity Research Journal, 26*, 192–202.

Oatley, K. (1999). Why fiction may be twice as true as fact: Fiction as cognitive and emotional simulation. *Review of General Psychology, 3*, 101–117.

Oatley, K. (2003). Writingandreading: The future of cognitive poetics. In G.J. Steen & J. Gavins (Eds.), *Cognitive poetics in practice*. (pp. 161–173). London: Routledge.

Oatley, K. (2011). *Such stuff as dreams: The psychology of fiction*. Oxford: Wiley-Blackwell.

Oatley, K. (2013). Worlds of the possible: Abstraction, imagination, consciousness. *Pragmatics and Cognition, 21*, 448–468.

Oatley, K., & Djikic, M. (2008). Writing as thinking. *Review of General Psychology, 12*, 9–27.

Patrick, C. (1935). Creative thought in poets. *Archives of Psychology (R Woodworth, Ed.), 178*, 35–73.

Parmar, P. (2014). *Vanessa and her sister*. New York: Ballantine Books.

Pennebaker, J. W., & Chung, C. K. (2011). Expressive writing: Connections to mental and physical health. In H. S. Friedman (Ed.), *Oxford handbook of health psychology*. New York: Oxford University Press.

Perkins, D. N. (1981). *The mind's best work*. Cambridge, MA: Harvard University Press.

Piirto, J. (2009). The personalities of creative writers In S. B. Kaufman & J. C. Kaufman (Eds.), *The psychology of creative writing* (pp. 149–165). Cambridge: Cambridge University Press.

Poincaré, H. (1908). Mathematical creation (translation by G.B Halstead, of Le Raisonnement Mathematique, in *Science et Methode*, Paris: Flammarion). In B. Ghiselin (Ed.), *The creative process*. Berkeley: University of California Press (1952).

Runco, M. A., Millar, G., Acar, S., Cramond, B. (2010) Torrance tests of creative thinking as predictors of personal and public achievement: A fifty year follow-up. *Creativity Research Journal, 22*, 361–368.

Schneider, J. W., & McGrew, K. S. (2012). The Cattell-Horn-Carroll model of intelligence. In D. P. Flanagan & P. L. Harrison (Eds.), *Contemporary intellectual assessment: Theories, tests, and issues (3rd edition)* (pp. 99–144). New York: Guilford.

Simonton, D. K. (2013). Creative thought as blind variation and selective retention: Why creativity is inversely related to sightedness. *Journal of Theoretical and Philosophical Psychology, 33*, 253–266.

Turing, A. (1936). On computable numbers with an application to the Entscheidungsproblem. *Proceedings of the London Mathematical Society, Second series, 42*, 230–265.

Wallas, G. (1926). *The art of thought*. London: Cape.

Wells-Jopling, R., & Oatley, K. (2012). Metonymy and intimacy. *Journal of Literary Theory, 6*, 235–252.

Woolf, V. (1925). *Mrs Dalloway*. London: Hogarth Press.

6 Creativity in the Visual Arts

Matthew Pelowski
University of Vienna

Helmut Leder
University of Vienna

Pablo P. L. Tinio
Montclair State University

Abstract

In this chapter, we review research on creativity with visual art, and, specifically, how this has been addressed within the psychology of art. We begin with a brief review of the history of psychology of art and the unique challenges associated with studying artistic creativity and expression. We then review current creativity studies that touch on art making and that focus on techniques and methods that provide the foundation for current research. We conclude with a consideration of important questions that hold particular intrigue for future study, such as questions related to artistic development, approaches to assessing art making, and the artistic brain.

Introduction

Arguably, no domain so closely connects humans to creativity as art. Researchers suggest that art making – or visual artistic expression – dates back at least 40,000 to 75,000 years, and if one considers evidence from pigments, symbolic beads, etc., possibly much farther (Zaidel, Nadal, Flexas, & Munar, 2013). Researchers also argue that the intentional creation of art is both one of the major points of evolutionary distinction from other animals and a defining feature of modern humans. Art is ubiquitously produced in human societies, with a seemingly endless variety of expression, and thus is a major point of inter-social and cultural comparison (Dissanayake, 2000; Dutton, 2009). Art is therefore one of the more intriguing avenues for considering the development and action underlying creativity, as well as a main topic for psychology, because: (1) art is spontaneously created by almost every individual at some point in his or her lifetime; (2) art is considered a window reflecting our perception and thinking (Zaidel, 2010); and (3) art making is a unique skill involving a range of proficiencies.

This chapter was sponsored by a grant to HL by the Vienna Science and Technology Fund (WWTF), RosLed CS15-036, and by a grant to MP and HL by the Marie Skłodowska-Curie (MSCA-IF-2014-EF) Individual Fellowships, 655379.

1 A Brief Note on the Unique Challenge of Studying Creativity in Art

One only has to consider the rich history of art and the evolving range of artists and modes of visual expression to realize its importance as well as the unique challenge inherent in its study. Since the dawn of human ability to create visual images, those with a special ability in this domain have probably always held a special place of reverence. Prototypical genius creators that often come to mind when thinking about creativity are often artists. A visit to an elementary school – or a studio or museum – will also confirm that we have a special respect, and sometimes fear (Mitchell, 1987), for visual creative ability. Technically speaking, the large number of overlapping abilities that must be utilized in visual art making – perception, memory, motor control, language, spatial reasoning, not to mention imagination – also makes art one of our most complex human activities. Naturally, the question is asked: How is it possible that we can see something, or have an idea, and translate that conception through physical manipulation of materials (or our bodies) into a unique and pleasing representational, symbolic, *or even abstract* image?

Such questions related to artistic creativity comprise, in fact, some of the oldest topics of psychology. While the consideration of painting and drawing had long before been a topic of philosophy, studies on art making emerged as a branch of psychology in the late nineteenth century during a time when the field was distinguishing itself as a scientific discipline. The field's founding is often attributed to Fechner (e.g., 1876), who, among other approaches, stressed the "method of production" as a driving element in his search for general laws guiding aesthetic preferences (Westphal-Fitch, Oh, & Fitch, 2013). Art making was also subsequently taken up as a topic in the United States as well as Europe in the 1920–30s, during which there was a demand for measures of people's abilities, aptitudes, and personalities – combined with a general discourse on "creativity" – and which led to the development of several standardized drawing assessments (Holert, 2009). This was also coupled with standardized assessments of human visual memory and use of perspective or spatial arrangements (e.g., Meyers & Meyers, 1995; McManus, Chamberlain, Loo, Rankin, Riley & Brunswick, 2010). The next 100 years after Fechner also saw a slow, steady rise in research on art viewing, including landmark works by Arnheim (1956) and Berlyne (1974). This continues to the present day, when there is an obvious burgeoning of psychology of art with new empirical procedures, development of new physiological and neuroimaging measures, and robust cognitive models of art processing (Chatterjee; 2003; Leder, Belke, Oeberst & Ausgustin, 2004; Pelowski & Akiba, 2011) and dynamics between art making and viewing (Tinio, 2013).

Aesthetic reception and artistic production are at two ends of the art spectrum, with the latter being linked to the artist creating, and the former to the viewer encountering, the artwork. While studies on the aesthetic reception of art have been increasing, since Fechner there has been a disproportionate scarcity of studies on creativity as expressed within the visual arts as well as artistic production. There are several reasons for the challenging nature of such research. Amongst these is the ineffable nature of art making (Chatterjee, 2010; Lundy, 2012). Even during Fechner's time, it was already recognized that the sheer breadth of decisions and factors that go into art making, as well as its open-ended nature, make it particularly difficult to study empirically (Leder, 2014; Westphal-Fitch et al., 2013). This was coupled with a predominant focus in psychology (tied to its roots in philosophy) on top-down discussions of aesthetic judgments and reception of viewers, rather than bottom-up processes related to the making of art (Leder, 2013).

Researchers must also deal with a shifting definition of art itself. Art history has witnessed a constant evolution of conceptualizations of what it means for an object to be considered art (Becker, 1982). These include ideas, at various periods, that art might be beautiful, realistic, technically superior, contain specific styles, or even express the individuality of an artist, or challenge the prevalent conceptions held among others who make and value art (Dutton, 2009). As a consequence, it has become difficult to conceptualize what creativity in art should look like. Each of these definitions is characterized by a particular art making approach, utilizing different channels of information, and resulting in "creative" works as different as the impressionist paintings of Monet and the conceptual pieces of Rauschenberg, or the readymades of Duchamp. Approaches to art and creativity may also differ between cultures (e.g., Li, 1997, see also Section 3 below), thus introducing the danger of normalization and further challenging our understanding.

Finally, there has been minimal collaboration between scientists and artists. As put by Arrell (1997, "Teaching Aesthetics to Artists," para. 1), many individuals involved with art "are suspicious that too much analyzing of their art will harm their creativity," or "that thinking about art in this way is simply useless . . . that the issues discussed are not ones that they face as artists."

2 How Is Artistic Creativity Measured?

Even with the above challenges, there have been notable studies on creativity in art. Most of these studies are based on explorations of visual creativity in general, which is typically defined as the production of both novel and useful forms within a given context (Dake, 1991; Sternberg & Lubart, 1999). This is also considered a main counterpoint to verbal creative ability, and thus is often combined with such research. This skill is additionally considered as a primary component of drawing, painting, photography, etc. At the same time, many of the studies that we will review also directly involve the making or consideration of "art." In general, approaches can be split into four main areas (Lemons, 2011): the creative person, product, process, and environment. These will be reviewed below.

2.1 The Creative Person

One approach to studying creativity in art focuses on the creator. This involves the search for aspects of personality or behavior that might correlate to present creative achievement or future proficiency as an artist (or a visually creative person). A good body of research has shown that creative people tend to share certain characteristics, many of which have also been connected to individual skills in art (e.g., Feist, 1999 for a review). Such individuals tend to be independent, resourceful, and spontaneous (Cassandro & Simonton, 2010; Eysenck, 1997; Lemons, 2011), with tolerance for risks, conflict, or ambiguity (Feldman, 1999). They are also often confident in their abilities and have low levels of cognitive or behavioral inhibition (Eysenck, 1997; Feist, 1999). These features may be assessed through standardized personality scales or observation.

More specifically to the art domain, elements of personality such as "openness to experience" have been linked to art making and art viewing. This element of the Big Five Personality Inventory (Costa & McCrae, 1992) involves a willingness to seek out unfamiliar or novel encounters, and has been shown to correlate with an individual's ability to select "aesthetically superior" pictures (Myszkowski et al., 2014), as well as to positive ratings of both abstract and representational art (see Feist & Brady, 2004). Openness to experience has also been shown to predict creative achievement in both the arts and the sciences (Feist, 1998). Silvia, Nusbaum, Berg, Martin and O'Connor (2009) further note that openness can often be combined with "extraversion," another Big Five factor, to create a broader category of "placticity," or the ability to engage flexibly with novelty in behavior and cognition (see also DeYoung, 2006). Together, these two aspects predict scores on several creativity measures. However, see Roy, 1996, who found introversion as a key personality factor in fine artists.

2.1.1 Scales Assessing the Creative Person That Are Relevant to Art

Previous research has also used scales to identify creative persons, which can also reference or predict ability in art (see Cropley, 2000). For example, the Group Inventory for Finding Creative Talent (GIFT; Rimm & Davis, 1980) and the Group Inventory for Finding Interests (GIFFII and GIFFIII; Davis & Rimm, 1982) measure respondents' (children of different age levels) agreement to a number of Yes/No statements, which include examples such as, "I am very aware of artistic considerations." Answers are combined to yield scores for traits such as self-confidence, adventurousness, risk-taking, curiosity, humor, and artistic interest. This scale has shown moderate correlation with teacher-judged creativity of drawings (Cropley, 2000).

Similarly, the Creativity Scale for Diverse Domains (CSDD: Kaufman & Baer, 2004; see Silvia, Kaufman & Pretz, 2009 for a review) measures creative self-concepts, or people's view of themselves as creative. The scale uses nine items covering areas from mathematics and interpersonal relations to art making, and yields scores in specific domains of "math/science," "empathy/interpersonal," "hands-on creativity," as well as one global self-concept question ("How creative would you say you are in general?"). Rawlings and Locarnini (2007), for example, administered the scale to small groups of professional artists and scientists and showed that artists scored higher both on items measuring creativity in art as well as general creativity, while professional scientists scored higher only on items measuring creativity in science and mathematics, but not general creativity (Kaufman & Baer, 2004). A recent update of the scale, the Kaufman Domains of Creativity Scale (K-DOCS: Kaufman, 2012), also added visual art/aesthetic creativity as one of its five dimensions. The Rating the Behavioral Characteristics of Superior Students (SRBCSS: Renzulli, Smith, White, Callahan, & Hartman, 1976), especially its nine-item *Creative Characteristics Rating* (CCRS) subscale, also touches on art. This scale is intended for grades K–12, and is often used with teachers to rate giftedness in creativity, art, music, drama, and communication, using creative achievements or activities (however, see Chan and Zhao, 2010).

The richness of people's personal visual imagination is also argued to relate to the ability to produce artistic/creative images (Pérez-Fabello & Campos, 2007). This has been assessed by, for example, the Vividness of Visual Imagery Questionnaire (VVIQ: Marks, 1973; see McKelvie, 1995 for review), which asks participants to read a description of a scene and then rate the vividness of their resulting mental image. Kottlow, Praeg, Luethy and Jancke (2011) suggested that artists scored higher than non-artists, although not to the level of statistical significance.

2.1.2 Biographical Inventories

Art is also included as a factor in several batteries that assess life history as a means of identifying creative talent. Examples include Schaefer and Anastasi's (1968) Biographical Inventory for Identifying Creativity in Adolescents, and Taylor and Ellison's (1968) Alpha Biographical Inventory (ABI), both of which use scales that touch on a number of areas potentially connected to creative achievement (see Cropley, 2000 for a review). Schaefer and Anastasi's inventory measures, for example, family background, motivation (possession of special equipment, willingness to skip meals to work on a project), intellectual and cultural orientation (hobbies, frequency of visits to museums or art galleries), breadth of interests, and drive towards novelty/diversity (including level of interest in unusual forms of art). This inventory was shown to correlate to teacher creativity ratings of art produced by high school students (Cropley, 2000). Correlation with this inventory was also higher for art than scientific creativity, with the test correctly identifying 96 percent of students whose products were rated by teachers as artistically creative.

Similarly, the Khatena–Torrance Creative Perceptions Inventory (KTCPI: Khatena & Torrance, 1976; see Lemons, 2011 for review), intended for ages 10 and up, includes a self-rating scale assessing tendency to function creatively, based on items requiring a choice between pairs of characteristics representing high and low creativity behaviors, as well as a fifty-item self-rating scale assessing autobiographical aspects ("I have composed a dance, song, or musical piece"). The Creative Activities Checklist (Runco, 1987), developed for use with children in grades 5 to 8, also asks participants to report how frequently they recently participated in six areas of activity – literature, music, drama, crafts, science, and art. Finally, the Creative Achievement Questionnaire (CAQ: Carson, Peterson & Higgins, 2005) asks individuals to rate their own creativity in ten domains, including music, architectural design, entrepreneurial ventures, humor, inventions, theater, film, and visual art.

It also has the unique feature of asking individuals to rate specific instances of ability, which, the authors argue, may give a more objective and outwardly observable basis for measuring creative output. With visual art, this ranges from having no training to taking lessons, showing works in galleries, and being in national publications.

2.2 The Creative Art Product

Approaches to studying creativity in art have also focused on the art product. Here as well, rather than directly testing creativity, most studies have focused on assessing general creative ability using tasks such as creating figures or images that are conceptually similar to art making. In a collection of 225 creativity tests by Torrance and Goff (1989), figural image-making type tasks made up about 9 percent of the total items. Although comparatively less common than other verbal measures, the use of figural creation is valued for two reasons. First, as noted above, art is a domain in which individuals, especially children, can act in a primarily creative fashion. Thus, art making is considered a particularly ecologically valid means of inducing creative action. Second, with its emphasis on visual problem solving, art offers an alternative to verbal tests of creativity, which may also not always overlap. Considered more broadly, these studies could also shed light on the unique ability of artists.

2.2.1 Figure Completion

One such task that has seen widespread use is figure completion. This involves participants drawing from visual cues pre-printed on paper. This approach can be traced from early twentieth-century experimental psychology approaches, which sought to explore drawing ability (see Holert, 2009 for a review), later used for assessing creativity in general. Modern examples could be said to stem from the Franck Figure Completion Test of Franck and Rosen (1949; see Runco, Millar, Acar & Cramond, 2010 for updates and a review). This test provides participants with thirty-six rectangular fields, each with a simple geometric or curved figure. Participants are then asked to complete the drawing. Originally intended to test masculinity–feminity differences, it was employed by Baron (reported in Ludington, 1965) to test creativity and personality, with the completed drawings scored for novelty in terms of the extent to which they build on the cues. Similar approaches were also used by the various tests of creative thinking developed by Guilford (1967; later Meeker & Meeker, 1985). These included a drawing task, among various verbal measures, with small fields in which participants are asked to "make something different," and with drawings scored for fluency, flexibility, transformation (ability to revise something into a new form), and originality (see Lemons, 2011 for a review).

This approach was also inspiration for the Torrance Test of Creative Thinking (TTCT: Torrance, 1966; recently re-normed in 2008; see also Cropley, 2000 and Runco et al., 2010 for reviews). This is the most widely used method for assessing creativity (Cramond, Matthews-Morgan, Torrance, & Zuo, 1999) and is comprised of both a verbal and a figural section – "thinking creatively with pictures." This latter section has three activities including picture completion using a blank paper divided into ten squares, each containing a different stimulus figure. Participants are asked to sketch a novel object or design by adding lines to the figures. This is paired with a picture construction task in which participants complete a drawing and assign a title, and a lines/circles task in which participants draw as many uses for a simple image as possible. These activities yield scores for fluency (ability to create many images), originality, elaboration, abstractness of titles, and resistance to premature closure (tendancy not to quickly close off line cues). The figural tests can also be scored for thirteen creative strengths (Ball & Torrance, 1984; Kim, 2006), including: storytelling, movement and action, unusual visualization, richness of imagery, etc.

As noted by Baer (1993), the TTCT was used in 75 percent of all published creativity studies with elementary schoolchildren, and 40 percent of studies with adults or college students. This prevalence may be because the TTCT expands past verbal divergent thinking studies to integrate visual creativity and personality (Cropley, 2000). The TTCT has shown good validity for predicting creativity (Lemons, 2011). For example, a twelve-year longitudinal study of 400 primary students (originally assessed between 1958 and 1964, Torrance, 1969) comparing the TTCT, along with follow-up questionnaires on quantity/quality of creative aspirations and achievement, showed a correlation of .27–.45. The TTCT format has also been adapted for more direct assessment of drawing (e.g., Yamamoto, 1964).

Similar assessments to the TTCT include the Creativity Assessment Packet (CAP: Williams, 1980), which focuses on assessing the creativity of younger students (grades 3–12). This test includes a "divergent thinking" task that asks students to work on twelve incomplete drawings and create a title, with the end product being scored for fluency, originality, flexibility, and elaboration. The Wallach–Kogan Creativity Test (WKCT: Wallach & Kogan, 1965) also focuses on divergent thinking and assesses both visual and verbal content, including two figural subtests involving interpretation of abstract lines and patterns. It is scored for fluency (number of ideas) and uniqueness of ideas.

A more recently developed assessment, also based on art production, is the Test for Creative Thinking-Drawing Production (TCT-DP: Urban & Jellen, 1996; Urban, 2004; see Cropley, 2000 for a review). This test provides participants with two blank sheets of paper with pre-printed cues, in this case a large square with several lines inside and outside. Participants are then asked to complete a drawing, which are rated according to dimensions from a Gestalt-psychology creativity theory and which uses a standardized scoring sheet assessing factors such as continuation, completion, connections, boundary-breaking (drawing outside the large square frame), use of perspective, new elements, humor, and affectivity. Studies in a number of countries have indicated inter-rater reliability of above .90, and test-retest reliability of about .70 to .75 (Cropley, 2000). The test manual also reports correlations of up to .82 with teacher ratings of creativity.

2.2.2 Free Drawing from Imagination

Studies have also used more open-ended drawing tasks in which individuals are asked to complete a drawing from imagination. One of the most common is Clark's Drawing Abilities Test (CDAT: Clark & Zimmerman, 2004). This asks participants to make four drawings – a house, a running person, a playground, and participants' "fantasy." This test has been used with over 5,000 upper elementary, middle, and high school students in the United States and other countries, and has proven to be a reliable, standardized screening and identification measure for artistically talented students. CDAT scores have also been shown to correlate significantly with teacher rankings of student success in classes for artistically talented students (Clark & Zimmerman, 2004). As noted below, the fantasy drawing aspect has been utilized in several studies because of its ability to elicit original, free expression (Chan & Chan, 2007; Chan & Zhao, 2010).

2.2.3 Selection of Still-Life Objects, Collage

Researchers have also used paradigms in which individuals complete collages or still-life drawings based on the arrangement of predefined shapes or objects. One of the most notable was used by Getzels and Csikszentmihalyi (1976) in their study of adult art students. They presented participants with twenty-three objects and asked them to use at least two objects in an arrangement, which was then drawn. This was first developed to explore the aspect of problem finding or "ideation," referring to the initial generation and graphic representation of visual ideas (Rostan, 2010). The activity, which could be video-recorded (see Rostan, 2005), is typically scored by noting total time spent drawing, total time spent completing basic shapes, and percentage of time given to finding a problem, as well as time exploring and choosing objects, and number of erasures, as a means of exploring the creation process. Assessments can also be made of the final produced art. Similar approaches include the Test of Figural Combination (Finke, 1990), which provides participants with three images that they are asked to combine into a creative object that is then sketched, (see e.g., Palmiero et al., 2010 for recent use in a study of art making).

Amabile (1982) also offered an oft-duplicated approach in which participants create collages from predefined shapes, and which offers a more standardized, yet open-ended means of assessing creativity. Collages can be rated on several artistic dimensions including creativity, technical goodness, and aesthetic appeal, and have shown good inter-rater reliability and separation between creativity judgments and judgments of technical goodness or aesthetic appeal. This too has been used in recent studies assessing interpersonal differences (Niu & Sternberg, 2001, see also Section 3).

2.2.4 Methods for Rating Creative Art Products

The above aspect of art making also touches on the complementary approach of individuals' artistic creations being rated by peers, teachers, or experts. This approach follows from the argument that many other creativity approaches – such as those involving personality or self-introspection – tend to lack validity or reliability (Baer & McKool, 2009). In contrast, simply asking people to rate the creativity of produced art should reveal something meaningful about creativity or production, especially if there is agreement in people's ratings. The validity may be further enhanced if experts serve as raters (e.g., Cropley, 2000; Getzels & Csikszentmihalyi, 1976).

One of the most dominant approaches is the Consensual Assessment Technique (CAT: Amabile, 1982, 1983, 1996; Baer, 1993). With this method, raters (most often experts), working independently, are given a full set of created products or artworks and are asked to place the products into a number of groups representing points on a scale from non- to highly creative. Individual ratings are checked for correspondence and averaged to create a score for each product. This technique has been shown to have high inter-rater agreement (Amabile, 1983), temporal stability (Baer, 1994), and generally increasing reliability as one increases the number of raters (Baer & McKool, 2009).

This approach has had interesting use with art. Amabile (1983) reported a series of twenty-one studies of visual art making (collage), with inter-rater reliabilities ranging from .72 to .93. Amabile (1982, 1983) also found that while experts tended to agree regarding creativity, ratings often did not correlate with other attributes such as technical goodness, neatness, and expression (although it did correlate with aesthetic appeal), potentially suggesting that creativity is distinct, and that raters appear to be using the same domain specific factors for their judgments. Hennessey (1994) used this approach to assess Picasso drawings and to analyze videos of Picasso's art making process, and showed consistent ratings even among untrained undergraduates, further suggesting that even non-art-experts can agree on what they consider creative (see also Section 3 below).

The Creative Product Analysis Matrix (CPAM: Besemer & O'Quin, 1987) is another scale developed to assess creative products across disciplines, including art. This proposes three main dimensions: novelty, resolution (valuable, useful, solves a need), and synthesis or elaboration (well crafted, attractive, elegant). Raters assess the dimensions using a forty-three-item, semantic-differential scale. Besemer (1998), for example, tested the CPAM with chairs, exhibited as art, revealing that the hypothesized factors accounted for 70–80 percent of the total variance.

2.3 Perspectives on the Creative Process

Researchers have also considered the process whereby creative products are generated. This focus predominantly refers to the modeling of stages of the creative process in general. However, many of the aspects mentioned can be, and also have been, connected to creativity in art. Wallas (1926; cited in Torrance, 1988; see Niu & Sternberg, 2001 for a review), for example, proposed a four-step process of preparation, incubation, illumination, and revision, which is helpful for considering art. The work of Getzels and Csikszentmihalyi (1976) also considered the initial planning and execution of an idea during the process of drawing. Similarly, Bogousslavsky (2005) proposed three stages: perception processing, extraction and abstraction (in which major features are delineated), and final execution. Recently, Tinio (2013) proposed a model of art making, which included the three stages of initialization, expansion and adaptation, and finalizing, connecting this as well to similar stages in art viewing (see below). As noted by Acosta (2014), most of these approaches share the idea that art making must begin with a baseline knowledge of materials, techniques, and approaches. This provides a fertile setting for new insight, which must then be "codified" or recognized by the artist, and only subsequently can it be brought to fruition through art making. Models often also make explicit distinction between the roughing-out of visual ideas (e.g., initialization) and later revision/refinement, which has been argued as a way of building from the initial foundation and providing a general linear progression of art making (e.g. Tinio, 2013).

2.3.1 Ideation

A related aspect of the artwork creation process that is often considered involves "ideation," or the process of creating an initial idea or goal for the creative act, and, more specifically, the ability to compose ideas that are novel or surprising (Jackson & Messick, 1965; Kay, 1991). This type of problem solving has been cited as an essential component of the creative process in various disciplines (Mednick, 1962; Wallach & Kogan, 1965), but is also specifically important for creating new and interesting visual art. Runco and Chand (1995) offered a model stressing the interaction of processing components, motivation, and knowledge. Their first tier posited three primary controlling components – problem-finding skills and processes, ideational skills and processes, and evaluation. They suggested that it is both the ability to come up with new insight, but perhaps more importantly, the time given to problem finding and solution generation, which leads to creative products.

Empirical studies have also examined the related measure of "ideational fluency" – the propensity to generate multiple or unusual answers to problems (Barron & Harrington, 1981; Sawyers & Canestaro, 1989) – which is often a significant aspect of art. This is most often assessed through measures of original problem solving (e.g., Wallach & Kogan, 1965). Notably, the Multidimensional Stimulus Fluency Measure (Moran, Milgram, Sawyers, & Fu, 1983) combines several previous approaches, and was shown by Sawyers and Canestaro (1989) to correlate to the degree of creativity (as assessed by teachers) of university design students' projects. This ability may also relate to the unique ability of creative people to "see past" stereotypical schema or ways of depiction, or to otherwise assume the "innocent eye" of the artist (Gombrich, 1960).

Research has shown differences amongst artists in their ability to initially construct an idea visually. This was emphasized in the work of Getzels and Csikszentmihalyi (1976), who showed that time spent thinking of an idea before drawing, as well as time required to rough-out main aspects of a composition, correlated with the assessed creativity of final products. More recently, Jaarsveld and van Leeuwen (2005; see also Verstijnen, van Leeuwen, Goldschmidt, Hamel, & Hennessey, 1998) analyzed the strategies used by designers when developing visual graphics or objects. By evaluating early and intermediate sketches, the authors found that participants whose final designs received the highest ratings by art critics introduced a global structure in earlier sketches. They argued that by creating this more solid foundation, designers might have constructed a stable basis for refining their drawings during later stages. In an observational and eye-tracking study of professional artists, Miall and Tchalenko (2001) also showed that time spent looking and not drawing was significantly longer than for nonartists' (see also Cohen, 2005 for similar findings).

Studies conducted by Kozbelt and Serafin (2009), and especially Serafin, Kozbelt, Seidel and Dolese (2011), had expert and lay artists evaluate the quality of drawings at multiple points during the art-making process. Results showed that artists were able to quickly determine the quality of the emerging art, perhaps because they had in mind a gist idea, a sense of the overall structure of the work. The authors also found that for artworks rated as less creative, there was a linear, additive relationship between time and quality. In contrast, for artworks rated as highly creative, there were irregular patterns in their assessed quality during the art-making process, which suggests that ideation may only be one component in producing highly creative art.

2.4 Artistic Development and the Environment

Research has also considered artistic development, and the specific interaction of biology, culture, and/or environment (see Rostan, 1997 for a review). This is often approached via componential models that posit elements that control and influence creative individuals. Notable among these, Amabile (1983) described creativity, including creativity in art, as the result of domain-relevant skills, relating to expertise developed through education and life experience, as well as basic motivation, intelligence or talent. Urban (1991) proposed a model organized around divergent thinking, general and specific knowledge bases, task commitment, tolerance of ambiguity, and motivation. Runco and Chand (1995) proposed a two-tier model, composed of controlling components such as problem-finding skills and processes, ideational skills, and evaluation as well as contributing components such as environment and motivation.

The above models have also been coupled with empirical findings, using many of the procedures reviewed above. This has shown, for example, age-related differences in art making, often involving developments in aesthetic sensitivity, repleteness, expressivity with materials, composition, and technical ability (Gardner, 1982; Goodman, 1968; Rostan, 1997). Carothers and Gardner (1979), for example, found that children's perception of aesthetic properties increases with age, as does technical ability. Children also show a universal and increasing attraction to representing objects through graphical means (Winner, 1989), and a temporal progression from structurally simpler to more complex art (Golomb, 1992). Studies have also shown interpersonal differences regarding unique advantages of skilled artists. Milbrath (1998) analyzed and compared artworks of artistically talented and less talented children (as identified by parents and teachers). The latter acquired drawing skills at a more rapid rate, and also showed spontaneous compositional differences, such as incorporating their personal viewing position in drawings rather than general or stereotypical depictions.

Theories also consider the role of culture in creative development (Rostan, Pariser & Gruber, 2002 for review). Notably, Csikszentmihalyi (1999) proposed a model with three shaping factors: (1) a more or less stable symbol system of a culture (e.g., "art"), which can be employed by artists; (2) social institutions that both select creative products, and that could promote or develop artists; and (3) the individual artist, who is a product of training and experiences. Simonton (1984, 1996) also considered contextual effects – cultural, economic, social – on creativity in art. He used a historiometric method to study the creativity of eminent people in multiple cultures and periods, arguing that social environment can have nurturing (or inhibitory) effects on development. Lubart and Sternberg (1998) went further to propose that the effects of culture can manifest itself in four areas: the creative process; training; the extent to which people focus their creativity towards certain domains; and the "creativity" concept itself. Amabile (1996) also added specific emphasis on the role of the educational system and family structure as important facilitating/ motivating or inhibiting aspects. These theories are also supported by a number of studies (Cox, Koyasu, Hiranuma & Perara, 2001; Li, 1997; Huntsinger, Schoeneman & Ching, 1994; Toku, 2001; see Niu & Sternberg, 2001 for a review). Studies have also considered more longitudinal perspectives of creative talent over lifespans (Simonton, 1996; Csikszentmihalyi, 1988, 1999; Helson, 1999).

3 Findings and Topics for Future Research

The above approaches have provided the building blocks for a number of discussions that define important currents in research on creativity in art. They also raise intriguing questions. While not an exhaustive review, in this section we will consider some topics that we expect will define the future of research in this area.

3.1 How Is Creativity in Art Developed, and Why Do Many Become Progressively Worse at Art?

A number of issues arise from ongoing studies on artistic development, involving questions as basic as how people develop and maintain creativity in the arts. As noted above, while findings do routinely show general improvements in creativity, there is also evidence that *creativity in art* may actually peak, and then decrease, as children move from elementary to adolescence to adulthood (Barbot & Tinio, 2015). Only artistically gifted adolescents, in turn, retain or regain their artistic creativity at later stages, resulting in a "U-shaped" trajectory (Gardner & Winner, 1982; Davis, 1993). This finding is directly at the heart of artistic expression, and raises the question of whether the underlying reason has more to do with nature or culture and training.

There have been several explanations, such as those related to natural abilities that may emerge as children develop (Milbrath, 1998), or related to a link between decreasing creativity and an "inhibiting" focus on realism or practiced stereotypical popular images, as opposed to expressive drawing, both of which may reduce artistic creativity in older individuals. This latter explanation could imply either a natural "literal stage" (e.g., Rostan, 1997) in most people's development, or a social/normative impact on art making. Decreasing creativity may also be a function of the task or motivation, which may be higher in individuals interested in art (Chan & Zhao, 2010; Rostan, 1997), or even non-existent in others. It may even have to do with the judge or art perceiver and use of changing evaluation metrics for different individuals or ages (e.g., Pariser & van den Berg, 1995, 1997; Rostan et al., 2002). A better understanding of these aspects could obviously inform understanding of the unique abilities of artists, and how art making can be fostered.

Questions also arise regarding the role of training, which may play an important role in helping some individuals to smoothly develop their creativity with art. As noted above, several authors (Amabile, 1996; Csikszentmihalyi, 1999; Lubart & Sternberg, 1998) argue for the importance of supporting factors that could overcome the typical tendency to lose artistic creativity with age. Rostan et al. (2002) suggested that training might facilitate creative expression through technical ability or skill in imbuing artworks with aesthetic properties. Training could also lead to more technical improvements in finished products, such as the use of personal perspective (described above), which could increase judged creativity. This needs to be further considered.

3.1.1 What Is the Relationship Between Creativity in Art and Technical Ability with Art Media?

Another topic involves the link between creativity and the technical skill of artists. Chan and Zhao (2010) noted that technical skill and creativity are two components that have played prominent roles in the assessment of artistic quality, and how these two components interact is a major question. Such an interaction is important for two reasons. First, from a practical standpoint, assessed skill may often overlap or largely determine the judged creativity of art. For example, Rostan (1997) revealed the importance of expressivity and composition in predicting assessed novelty of drawings (see also Kozbelt, 2004; Rostan et al., 2002). Rostan (2010, p. 262) attributed this to the implicit assumptions held by many viewers, including judges, that artistically talented people are characterized by a natural technical competence, which may lead to higher assessment of creativity when they see such competence displayed in art. Kozbelt (2004) attempted to tease apart drawing skill and creativity by asking judges to rate drawings on twenty-five factors related to quality, technical skill, and originality. All three items were correlated, and skill and originality loaded highly on the same "quality" dimension (accounting for 90 percent of the variance).

Creativity may actually be facilitated via technical skill with media. Chan and Zhao (2010) suggested that skill may facilitate artistic (and creative) performance.

This was also suggested by, for example, Vinacke (1952, p. 253), who noted that "no matter how original" an idea, "it cannot result in a work of art . . . unless its originator has the requisite skills to convert it into tangible form." Gallo, Golomb, and Barroso (2002; see also Rostan, 2010 for review) also studied the drawing development of children (aged 5–9) and argued that most children's intentions exceeded their ability to express them in drawing. Rostan et al. (2002) found that the combination of skill mastery and opportunities for self-expression distinguished art students – whose artworks were also more likely to be judged as creative – from non-art students. Combining the above-discussed factors, Rostan (2005) also found differences in technical skill, creativity, and processing of visual information as a function of different amounts of art training. Rostan (1998) also showed that technical skill could nurture an artistic identity and predict both aesthetic success as well as creativity. This area needs much more research. Technical ability may also plateau as most children develop, also raising the related question of whether training would impact artistic creativity itself (e.g., Chan & Zhao, 2010).

3.1.2 Creativity and Motivation

Another interesting question involves motivation. Lemons (2011, p. 756) noted that in addition to most other context or personal abilities, there is "an often overlooked" factor – "passion" for art – which may drive creativity development and the results of many studies. This may occur to the extent that some researchers (e.g., Amabile, 2001) argue motivation to be the variable that distinguishes creative from noncreative individuals.

By merely participating in the arts – or by continuing to participate – one might further develop his or her artistic creativity beyond that accomplished by others (e.g., Eisner, 2002; Rostan, 2010). This factor may also interact with skill level. Students who initially show a certain amount of skill in art may be motivated internally, or externally by teachers/parents, to pursue more training, or may come to think of themselves as "artists," thus leading to higher levels of creativity. They may also be given more resources (e.g., attention, adult motivation), which could lead to both higher creative and technical development.

Developing creativity may also require intrinsic motivation, which could vary depending on personality or life experiences. Researchers argue that the motivation to get better, hone one's ability, or practice – with increasingly greater challenges – is necessary for both the emergence of art talent and creative performance in general, and may vary between individuals (Csikszentmihalyi, Abuhamdeh, & Nakamura, 2005; Ericsson, 1996; Feldman, 2003). Csikszentmihalyi's (1988, 1999) longitudinal study of art students found that some of the most creative children ended up pursuing occupations that had little to do with creativity or art, whereas others who had shown less potential persevered and experienced artistic or creative achievements. Amabile's (1996; Amabile & Conti, 1997) studies also showed a positive relationship between intrinsic motivation and assessed creativity, and especially argued that when one is intrinsically motivated one experiences more interest and is thus more likely to produce creative output.

Motivation may also be a major factor affecting the results of creativity assessments. Rostan (2010) compared the artistic process and the corresponding finished artworks (free drawings from imagination and life drawings following Getzels & Csikszentmihalyi, 1976) in both younger (ages 9–10) and older art students (ages 11–16). She also used the Need for Cognition assessment, which, along with the number of years spent attending arts programs, was considered a measure of motivation. Analyses revealed that technical skill explained age differences in life-drawing problem identification, creativity, and motivation. Number of years attending the art program and time spent drawing also correlated with creativity.

3.1.3 Culture and Creativity with Art?

Another major issue involves specific differences related to creativity in art that can arise as a function of culture. As noted above, several theorists have emphasized the importance of culture, to the extent that some researchers (Csikszentmihalyi, 1988, 1996; Amabile, 1982; Niu & Sternberg, 2001) have argued that creativity may be more of a cultural phenomenon than an innate/internal process. As a primary example, a series of studies have looked at differences between European/North American and Asian artists. As discussed by Niu and Sternberg (2001), in Western cultures, which is considered more independent, there is often a focus on recognizing the unique capacity of individuals and promoting individual differences. In contrast, Eastern cultures may emphasize relatedness or interdependence. Thus, with Western art, artistic exceptionality may often be characterized by expressiveness and "formal boldness" of production. Eastern art may be characterized by emphasis on technical ability or learning and using traditional art methods (Li, 1997; Rostan et al., 2002).

Such differences have been empirically shown by Jellen and Urban (1988), who employed the TCT-DP to assess children from eleven countries, and revealed that children from England, Germany, and the United States showed significantly higher art-related creativity scores than did children from China, India, and Indonesia. Niu and Sternberg (2001) compared the rated creativity of artworks – collages, (Amabile, 1982), and free drawing of an extra-terrestrial alien (Ward, 1994) – by American and Chinese college students with no artistic training. American and Chinese students (postgraduate psychology students, using CAT) served as judges. American students produced higher-rated works on scales of creativity, likeability, appropriateness, and technical quality, regardless of task or culture of rater. American judges also tended to be stricter with ratings. Regarding technical training, Cox et al. (2001) compared children's human figure drawings in the United Kingdom and Japan, and Toku (2001) compared American and Japanese children. In both cases, Japanese children produced superior drawings, possibly reflecting their school art curriculum and value placed on copying standardized comic book images (however, see Cox et al., 1998).

On the other hand, there is also evidence that interdependency within a culture could actually foster creativity in art. Rudowicz, Lok, and Kitto (1995), using the

TTCT figural circles task, found that children from Hong Kong received significantly higher creativity scores than children from the United States. The authors posited that this may be due to the character-based Chinese language, which may have given the children from Hong Kong a unique advantage. A similar study by Huntsinger et al. (1994) found that Chinese-American children were more advanced in both the technical quality and assessed creativity of their drawings and handwriting as compared to Caucasian-American children. The authors argued that this may be due to the fact that Chinese parents emphasized fine muscle activities, which may have enabled children to be more expressive of their creativity. However, once again, more work is necessary.

3.2 Judging Creativity: To What Extent Can Judges Detect Creativity in Art?

There is also the question of how and to what extent judges can detect creativity. This is especially important for creativity in art because of important repercussions from such judgments in regards to economic or educational advancement. A number of studies have found reasonable agreement using both lay and expert or quasi-expert judges (Getzels & Csikszentmihalyi, 1976; Amabile, 1982; Kozbelt, 2004; Hekkert & van Wieringen, 1996; Chan & Chan, 2007; but see Kaufman & Baer, 2012 for a discussion of issues regarding these studies). However, in more directed studies meant to specifically identify future creative talent, the results are less clear. Rostan, Pariser, and Gruber (1998) assessed whether contemporary judges trained in Western modernist art could identify juvenile works of noted artists (e.g. Picasso, Klee, Lautrec) as being exceptional. They tested such drawings mixed in with the works of students' (aged 6–11) in an after-school enrichment program. Judges did not find the masters' drawings to be consistently above average for technical skill, composition, or expressivity. Few of the masters' drawings in fact scored even among the top 25 percent (however, creativity was not directly assessed). Interestingly, a similar study by Rostan et al. (2002), which did assess creativity, found that parents showed higher interrater reliability than experts, suggesting that artists and art critics with more expert or personal experience may lead to idiosyncratic reactions that may reduce agreement. This raises the possibility that experts themselves may not always be the best judges of creativity. However, expert and lay judges may be using different factors or heuristics, with experts' ratings being less agreed upon but potentially more valid. This topic also relates to other areas of psychology of aesthetics, such as art perception, where the use of "creativity" as a factor in art judgments is often overlooked in favor of basic hedonic preference, pleasure, or liking. Rarely explored is how creativity might relate to such judgments.

3.2.1 Can Art Tests Predict Future Creative Art Achievement?

Another question involves the use of tests of creative output to predict future success in the arts. A typical finding from longitudinal studies (Lemons, 2011 for a review) is that creative children do not necessarily become highly creative adults, as assessed through their careers and activities. A review of creativity measures involving art tasks by Cropley (2000) found that most tests' ability to predict real-life creative achievements results in coefficients of around .50 (see also Plucker, 1999; Torrance, 2002 for similar findings with the TTCT). In contrast, IQ often correlates at about .70. Thus, researchers (Helson, 1999; Cropley, 2000) have suggested that creativity tests may be best thought of as tests of creative potential, not of creativity itself, with other factors also contributing to creative achievement. This highlights the need for more refined testing.

This also suggests one particular benefit that might be gleaned from creativity testing through art. For example, Cropley (2000, p. 78) suggested that one explanation for many creativity tests' lower predictive validity is that they do not resemble real-life behavior. Art may provide for a more natural activity. This is supported by the finding that personality-based tests often have lower validity than art-related studies (Schraw, 2005; Jarosewich, Pfeiffer & Morris, 2002; Lemons, 2011). However, this also begs further consideration and comparison against other performance-based measures.

3.2.2 To What Extent Is Creativity in Art Generalizable to Other Domains?

There is also the open question of what type of creativity or other abilities could be predicted by creativity within art, (see Lemons, 2011 and Silvia et al., 2009 for recent reviews). As referenced in the "Amusement Park Theory" of Kaufman and Baer (2005), some aspects of artistically creative individuals should generalize across domains. These might include many of the personality factors reviewed above (e.g., see Chen et al., 2006; Feldman, 2003; Rostan, 2010), as well as cognitive processes such as problem finding, combining, and abstracting (Palmiero et al., 2010; Simonton, 2009), and which may in fact be even more pronounced in individuals successful at art as compared to individuals showing creativity in such areas as science or math (Kaufman & Baer, 2004).

On the other hand, each domain also involves unique skills (Kaufman, Cole, & Baer, 2009; Plucker, 2005). Notably for art, these may include technical skills or expressivity (see also Han, 2003), as well as spatial skill performance, spatial manipulation, and visual memory, which have shown correlations to e.g., the Vividness of Visual Imagery Questionnaire (see review above). Myszkowski, Storme, Zenasni, and Lubart (2014) also found a relationship between figural creativity and visual aesthetic sensitivity, which was not found for verbal creativity. A study by Silvia, Kaufman, and Pretz (2009), using the CAQ and the Creativity Domain Questionnaire, also showed distinct "creative classes." These included "uncreative," as well as specific smaller classes for visual and performing arts, suggesting that art creativity may be unique. In a review of several other studies, they further noted that if a study focused on the creative product/art, then creativity often appeared domain-specific. In contrast, if a study focused on the person – typically involving divergent thinking – then creativity often appears general.

3.3 How Do People Make Art? The Need for More Nuanced Conceptions

Another area that needs attention regards how people actually create art. As noted in the above sections, there have been specific models put forth concerning basic processes in art making. These typically describe the main stages of planning, ideation, and revision. There have also been studies involving working artists. However, there has not been a significant attempt to move beyond these basic aspects of art making to the consideration of how individuals really go about constructing art that is particularly creative. Some questions that arise include: How do artists even begin to construct and shape aesthetic objects? What qualities of line, form, and concept go into art making? How do artists respond to the evolving work?

Emerging research, not necessarily dealing with creativity, has noted various elements that should be considered further. These primarily involve the ability to quickly capture the "gist" or essence of an object (e.g., Chamberlain, McManus, Riley, Rankin, & Brunswick, 2013) and the artist's unique ability to perceive and produce a gestalt or essential form (Tinio, 2013). Research on individuals skilled at realistic drawing also suggests that artists may employ a "local drawing strategy" (Drake & Winner, 2009; Chamberlain et al., 2013) that may begin with, focus on, or jump between depictions of local and global details, and which then allows better appreciation of the distinctiveness of objects. However, studies that have looked to empirically capture such elements have been inconclusive (Drake & Winner, 2009; Mottron et al., 1999). The above research should be expanded, clarified, and paired with creativity assessments. There is also the overlooked aspect of style or expressivity in artistic depiction and its impact on perception of art (Leder et al., 2004).

3.3.1 A Model of Art Production Tied to Perception?

One recent development, which we will briefly mention, involves new models that attempt to characterize specific stages of art making while simultaneously tying them to stages of art viewing. Notably, a new model by Tinio (2013) builds upon current models of art perception that have emerged in the last decade in the psychology of aesthetics (e.g., Chatterjee, 2003; Leder et al., 2004; Pelowski & Akiba, 2011). Tinio posited that art making can be considered as mirroring (perceptually and cognitively, in reverse order) the stages involved in art viewing. This model provides a theoretical foundation for considering the making of aesthetically pleasing and creative art. As can be seen in an updated version in Figure 6.1, this provides a basis for theoretically addressing how to optimize the creative aspects of artworks, with such optimization aligning closely with the initial creation of a gestalt or generation of an idea.

We also expect that the same features that individuals attend to in each processing stage should correspond to specific decisions/techniques involved in the art-making process. A recent study of art creativity (Stevenson-Taylor & Mansell, 2012), for example, which was based in part on art viewing models (Pelowski & Akiba, 2011), has shown evidence that this pursuit could be fruitful. Much work is however needed in this regard.

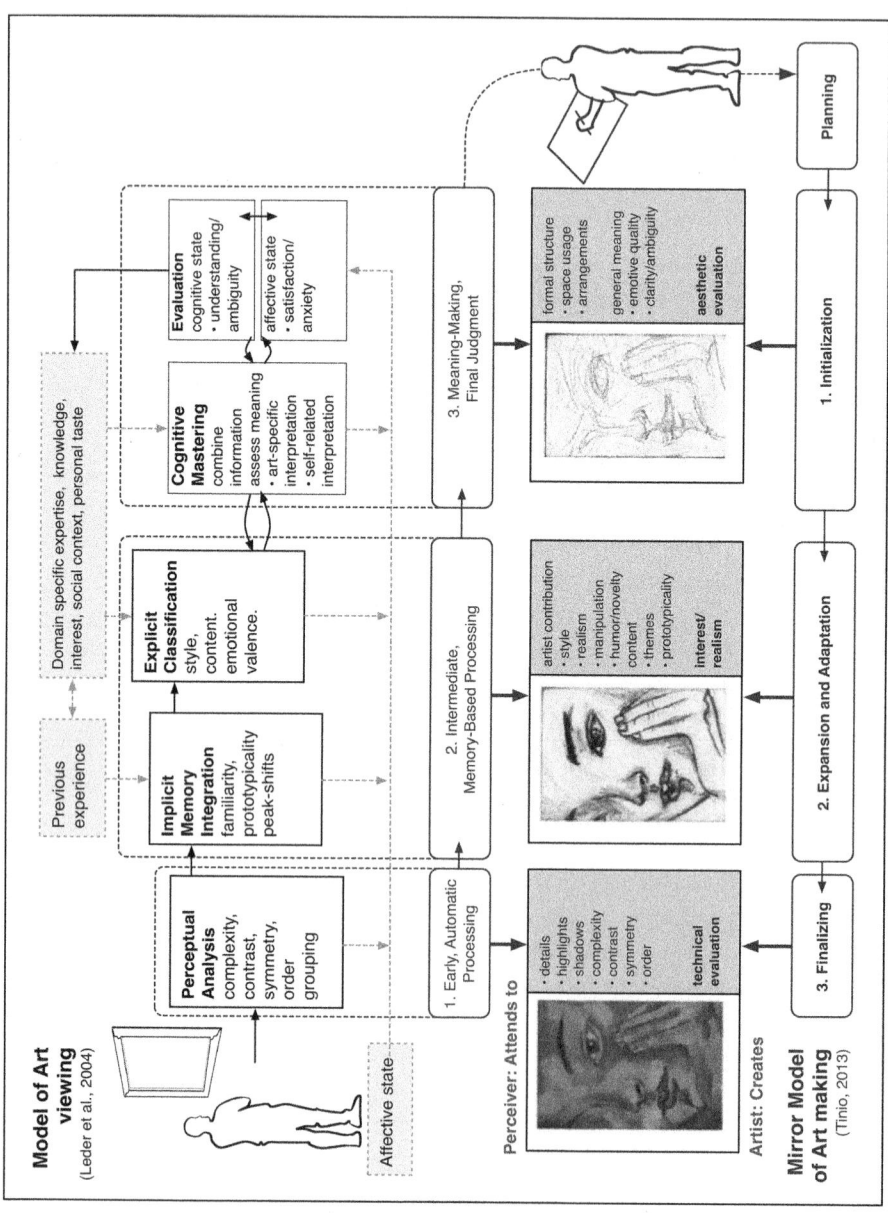

Figure 6.1 *Updated mirror model of art making and art perception: Top, model of art viewing (adapted from Leder et al., 2004). Bottom, model of art making (adapted from Tinio, 2013); Middle, posited key factors attended to in each stage. Note that stages are argued to operate in reversed order between the art making and art viewing activities.*

3.4 Creativity and the Brain

Last, an area of particular promise involves the role of the brain. This area represents a natural extension of previous empirical and cognitive approaches, connecting creative processes to their biological sources, and has grown with the rise of reliable imaging methods (fMRI, EEG). Recent research has led to the identification of a number of brain areas and neural processes that are closely associated with creative action, or are more active in creative individuals (see Palmiero, Di Giacomo, & Passafiume, 2012; Zaidel, 2014). At the same time, neuroscientific research on creativity in art has also proven to be rather challenging because of difficulty with finding appropriate art-making tasks, which must also be done under restrictive laboratory conditions. Thus, there have only been a handful of neuroscientific studies concerning creativity in art (see Aziz-Zadeh, 2013 for a review).

Nevertheless, there is evidence that such studies could be accomplished. For example, an fMRI study by Kowatari et al. (2009) asked novice and expert designers to mentally imagine designing a novel pen, which they later drew. Experts were shown to utilize a more restricted area of activation, involving only the right prefrontal cortex and parietal regions, potentially related to the processing of global aspects of the problem. Degree of creativity of finished drawings was also correlated with right prefrontal regions. Moreover, using EEG, Bhattacharya and Petsche (2005) asked artists and non-artists to mentally compose drawings while looking at a white wall. Artists had stronger delta synchronization, alpha desynchronization, and right hemispheric synchronization dominance, possibly due to long-term art memories and top-down processing.

Intriguing questions also involve hemispheric specialization, with previous studies (Solso, 2001; Kowatari et al., 2009; Bhattacharya & Petsche, 2005; Kottlow et al., 2011) finding right hemispheric lateralization in accomplished artists. Similarly, artists have also shown greater synchrony in the right (as compared to left) hemisphere during visual imagery tasks compared to non-artists (Bhattacharya & Petsche, 2005). This is potentially related to visuospatial processing, and thus may be of particular importance for creativity in art. Artists may also have less hemispheric connectivity. Moore et al. (2009), using the TTCT and fMRI, showed that higher scores on visual creativity correlated negatively with splenium size of the Corpus Callosum, which connects the two hemispheres. This suggests decreased connectivity and greater (right) hemispheric specialization. Gansler et al. (2011) further found a link between TTCT visual creativity scores and right parietal gray matter volume, which may play a role in global aspects of attention and visuospatial processing.

3.4.1 Lesion Studies, Dementia, and Creativity from the Damaged Brain

Another promising avenue for examining the neurological basis of creativity in art involves looking at the effects of damage to the brain in regard to people's ability to produce art. This too has been a growing area of study (e.g., see Chatterjee, 2004; Gretton & ffytche, 2014; Palmiero et al., 2012 for reviews), with findings showing intriguing although sometimes conflicting results. For example, Miller et al. (1996) reported several stroke patients who suffered damage to the left temporal hemisphere and dorsolateral prefrontal and parietal regions, and who developed sudden artistic abilities (see also Cela-Conde et al., 2011; Husslein-Arco & Koja, 2010; Midorikawa et al., 2008; Miller & Hou, 2004). Palmiero et al. (2012) similarly found that in fronto-temporal dementia that is restricted to the left anterior temporal regions – thus sparing frontal areas – individuals may show a "new passion" for art as well as alterations of social behaviors, which lead to wilder, freer, creative art making (also Mell, Howard, & Miller, 2003; Serrano et al. 2005).

Alzheimer's disease, which often affects frontal and temporal areas, can also have the effect of enhanced artistic creativity (Espinel, 1996), leading to surrealistic/abstract drawings – for a time – followed by progressively more schematic, less original products (Palmiero et al., 2012; Serrano et al. 2005). Parkinson's disease, which has been tied to the degeneration of the left inferior frontal cortex, has also been linked to changes in artistic creativity (see Canesi, Rusconi, Isaias, & Pezzoli 2012; Drago et al., 2009; Inzelberg, 2013 for a review), often leading individuals to create more expressive art (however, see e.g., Rankin et al., 2007 for a counterargument). Although interesting and telling, more research on the effects of brain damage or progressive brain degeneration on artistic creativity is needed.

3.4.2 Can We Increase Creativity by Changing Brain Activity?

One final area that we believe will be a major area of research involves interventions – technological or pharmaceutical – that directly impact brain functioning and thus that could increase (or reduce) creativity itself. Similar to the effects of lesion, techniques that cause disruption or excitation of brain regions, such as by using Transcranial Magnetic Stimulation (TMS) or Transcranial Direct Current Stimulation (TDCS), could impact creativity in art. Similarly, creativity changes could arise from dopamine therapy, often used as treatment for Parkinson's disease. As noted above, Parkinson's disease may be related to a malfunctioning of the left frontal regions, and tied to a deficiency in dopamine production, and which could also lead to increased right hemispheric activity. As a treatment, patients may take dopaminergic medications, such as levodopa and dopamine agonists, both of which could shift creativity to a normal level. In fact, researchers note the phenomenon of Dopamine Dysregulation Syndrome (Inzelberg, 2013; Weintraub & Nirenberg, 2012), a drug addiction-like state marked by self-medication with inappropriately high doses, which has been shown to occur among artists or other creative individuals who take the drugs to enhance creative performance, but often at the expense of other aspects of daily life such as family relations (Inzelberg, 2013; Kulisevsky, Pagonabarraga, & Martinez-Corral, 2009; Sessa, 2008).

While the specific effects of dopamine or TMS in creativity are still unclear, the use of these stimulants as possible enhancers of artistic creativity is a controversial issue (Inzelberg, 2013; see also Frecska, More, Vargha, & Luna, 2012) and lies at the crossroads of science, ethics, and art.

References

Acosta, L. M. Y. (2014). Creativity and neurological disease. *Current neurology and neuroscience reports*, *14*(8), 1–6.

Amabile, T. M. (1982). Children's artistic creativity: Detrimental effects of competition in a field setting. *Personality and Social Psychology Bulletin*, *8*, 573–578.

Amabile, T. M. (1982). Social psychology of creativity: A consensual assessment technique. *Journal of Personality and Social Psychology*, *43*, 997–1013.

Amabile, T. M. (1983). *The social psychology of creativity*. New York, NY: Springer-Verlag.

Amabile, T. M. (1996). *Creativity in context: Update to "The social psychology of creativity."* Boulder, CO: Westview Press.

Amabile, T. M. (2001). Beyond talent: John Irving and the passionate craft of creativity. *American Psychologist*, *56*, 333–336.

Arnheim, R. (1956). *Art and visual perception: A psychology of the creative eye*. London: Faber and Faber.

Amabile, T. M., & Conti, R. (1997). Environmental determinants of work motivation, creativity, and innovation: The case of R&D downsizing. *Technological innovation: Oversights and foresights*, 111–125.

Arrell, D. (1997). Teaching aesthetics to artists. *American Society for Aesthetics Newsletter*, *17*(2). Retrieved on April 10, 2017 from http://aesthetics-online.org/?page=ArrellArtists.

Aziz-Zadeh, L., Liew, S. L., & Dandekar, F. (2013). Exploring the neural correlates of visual creativity. *Social Cognitive and Affective Neuroscience*, *8*(4), 475–480.

Baer, J. (1993). *Creativity and divergent thinking: A task-specific approach*. Hillsdale, NJ: Lawrence Erlbaum.

Baer, J. (1994). Performance assessments of creativity: Do they have long-term stability? *Roeper Review*, *7*(1), 7–11.

Baer, J., & McKool, S. (2009). Assessing creativity using the consensual assessment. In C. Schreiner (Ed.), *Handbook of assessment technologies, methods, and applications in higher education*. Hershey, PA: IGI Global.

Ball, O. E., & Torrance, E. P. (1984). *Torrance tests of creative thinking: Streamlined scoring workbook: Figural and B*. Bensenville, IL: Scholastic Testing Service.

Barbot, B., & Tinio, P. P. L. (2015). Where is the "g" in creativity? A specialization-differentiation hypothesis. *Frontiers in Human Neuroscience*, *8*, 1–4.

Barron, F., & Harrington, D. M. (1981). Creativity, intelligence, and personality. *Annual Review of Psychology*, *32*(1), 439–476.

Becker, H. S. (1982). *Art worlds*. Berkeley, CA: University of California Press.

Besemer, S. (1998) Creative Product Analysis Matrix: Testing the model structure and a comparison among products-three novel chairs. *Creativity Research Journal*, *11* (4), 333–346.

Besemer, S., & O'Quin, K. (1987). Creative analysis: Testing a model by developing a judging instrument. In S. Isaksen (Ed.), *Frontiers of creativity research* (pp. 367–389). Buffalo, NY: Bearly.

Bhattacharya, J., & Petsche, H. (2005). Drawing on mind's canvas: Differences in cortical integration patterns between artists and non-artists. *Human Brain Mapping*, *26*(1), 1–14.

Bogousslavsky J. (2005). Artistic creativity, style and brain disorders. *European Journal of Neurology*, *54*(2), 103–11.

Canesi, M., Rusconi, M. L., Isaias, I. U., & Pezzoli, G. (2012). Artistic productivity and creative thinking in Parkinson's disease. *European Journal of Neurology*, *19*, 468–472.

Carothers, T., & Gardner, H. (1979). When children's drawings become art: The emergence of aesthetic production and perception. *Developmental Psychology, 15*(5), 570.

Carson, S. H., Peterson, J. B., & Higgins, D. M. (2005). Reliability, validity, and factor structure of the creative achievement questionnaire. *Creativity Research Journal, 17*(1), 37–50.

Cassandro, V., & Simonton, K. (2010). Versatility, openness to experience, and topical diversity in creative products: An exploratory historiometric analysis of scientists, philosophers, and writers. *Journal of Creative Behavior, 44*, 1–18.

Cela-Conde, C. J., Agnati, L., Huston, J. P., Mora, F., & Nadal, M. (2011). The neural foundations of aesthetic appreciation. *Progress in Neurobiology, 94*(1), 39–48.

Chamberlain, R., McManus, I. C., Riley, H., Rankin, Q., & Brunswick, N. (2013). Local processing enhancements associated with superior observational drawing are due to enhanced perceptual functioning, not weak central coherence. *The Quarterly Journal of Experimental Psychology, 66*(7), 1448–1466.

Chan, D. W., & Chan, L. (2007). Creativity and drawing abilities of Chinese students in Hong Kong: Is there a connection? *New Horizons in Education, 55*(3), 77–94.

Chan, D. W., & Zhao, Y. (2010). The relationship between drawing skill and artistic creativity: Do age and artistic involvement make a difference? *Creativity Research Journal, 22*(1), 27–36.

Chatterjee, A. (2003). Prospects for a cognitive neuroscience of visual aesthetics. *Bulletin of Psychology of the Arts, 4*(2), 55–60.

Chatterjee, A. (2004). The neuropsychology of visual artistic production. *Neuropsychologia, 42*(11), 1568–1583.

Chatterjee, A. (2010). Neuroaesthetics: A coming of age story. *Journal of Cognitive Neuroscience, 23*(1), 53–62.

Chen, C., Himsel, A., Kasof, J., Greenberger, E., & Dmitrieva, J. (2006). Boundless creativity: Evidence for the domain generality of individual differences in creativity. *Journal of Creative Behavior, 40*, 179–199.

Clark, G., & Zimmerman, E. (2004). *Teaching talented art students: Principles and practices.* New York, NY: Teachers College, Columbia University.

Cohen, D. J. (2005). Look little, look often: The influence of gaze frequency on drawing accuracy. *Perception & Psychophysics, 67*(6), 997–1009.

Costa, P. T., & McCrae, R. R. (1992). Normal personality assessment in clinical practice: The NEO Personality Inventory. *Psychological Assessment, 4*(1), 5–13.

Cox, M.V., Koyasu, M., Hiranuma, H. & Perara, J. (2001). Children's human figure drawings in the UK and Japan: The effects of age, sex, and culture. *British Journal of Developmental Psychology, 19*, 275–292.

Cropley, A. J. (2000). Defining and measuring creativity: are creativity tests worth using? *Roeper Review, 23*(2), 72–79.

Cramond, B., Matthews-Morgan, J., Torrance, E. P., & Zuo, L. (1999). Why should the Torrance tests of creative thinking be used to assess creativity? *The Korean Journal of Thinking and Problem Solving, 9*, 77–101.

Csikszentmihalyi, M. (1988). Society, culture, and person: A systems view of creativity. In R. J. Sternberg (Ed.), *The nature of creativity: Contemporary psychological perspectives* (pp. 325–339). New York, NY: Cambridge University Press.

Csikszentmihalyi, M. (1996). The creative personality. *Psychology Today, 29*(4), 36–40.

Csikszentmihalyi, M. (1999). Implications of a systems perspective for the study of creativity. In R. J. Sternberg (Ed.), *Handbook of creativity* (pp. 313–335). New York, NY: Cambridge University Press.

Csikszentmihalyi, M., Abuhamdeh, S., & Nakamura, J. (2005). Flow. A general context for a concept of mastery motivation. In Elliot, A. J. & Dweck, C. S. (Eds.), *Handbook of competence and motivation* (pp. 598–608). New York, NY: Guilford Publications.

Dake, D. M. (1991). The visual definition of visual creativity. *Journal of Visual Literacy, 1*, 99–118.

Davis, J. (1993). Drawing's demise: U-shaped development in graphic symbolization. *Studies in Art Education, 38*, 132–157.

Davis, G. A., & Rimm, S. B. (1982). Group Inventory for Finding Interests (GIFFI) I and II: Instruments for identifying creative potential in junior and senior high school. *Journal of Creative Behavior, 16*, 50–57.

DeYoung, C. G. (2006). Higher-order factors of the Big Five in a multi-informant sample. *Journal of Personality and Social Psychology, 91*(6), 1138–1151.

Dissanayake, E. (2000). *Art and intimacy: How the arts began.* Seattle, WA: University of Washington Press.

Drago, V., Foster, P. S., Okun, M. S., Haq, I., Sudhyadhom, A., Skidmore, F. M., & Heilman, K. M. (2009). Artistic creativity and DBS: a case report. *Journal of the Neurological Sciences, 276*(1), 138–142.

Drake, J. E., & Winner, E. (2009). Precocious realists: Perceptual and cognitive characteristics associated with drawing talent in non-autistic children. *Philosophical Transactions of the Royal Society B: Biological Sciences, 364*(1522), 1449–1458.

Dutton, D. (2009). *The art instinct: Beauty, pleasure & human evolution.* New York, NY: Oxford University Press.

Eisner, E. W. (2002). *The arts and the creation of mind.* New Haven, CT: Yale University Press.

Ericsson, K. A. (1996). The acquisition of expert performance: An introduction to some of the issues. In K. A. Ericsson (Ed.), *The road to excellence: The acquisition of expert performance in the arts and sciences, sports and games* (pp. 1–50). Hillsdale, NJ: Lawrence Erlbaum Associates.

Espinel, C. H. (1996) de Kooning's late colours and forms: Dementia, creativity, and the healing power of art. *Lancet, 347*, 1096–1098.

Eysenck, H. J. (1997). Creativity and personality. In M. Runco (Ed.), *The creativity research handbook* (pp. 41–66). Cresskill, NJ: Hampton Press.

Fechner, G. T. (1876). *Vorschule der aesthetik* (Vol. 1). Leipzig: Breitkopf & Härtel.

Feist, G. J. (1998). A meta-analysis of personality in scientific and artistic creativity. *Personality and Social Psychology Review, 2*(4), 290–309.

Feist, G. (1999). The influence of personality on artistic and scientific creativity. In R. J. Sternberg (Ed.), *Handbook of creativity* (pp. 273–296). Cambridge, MA: Cambridge University Press.

Feist, G. J., & Brady, T. R. (2004). Openness to experience, non-conformity, and the preference for abstract art. *Empirical Studies of the Arts, 22*(1), 77–89.

Feldman, D. H. (1999). The development of creativity. In R. J. Sternberg (Ed.), *Handbook of creativity* (pp. 169–188). Cambridge, MA: Cambridge University Press.

Feldman, D. H. (2003). Key issues in creativity and development. In R. K. Sawyer, V. John-Steiner, S. Moran, R. J. Sternberg, D. H. Feldman, J. Nakamura et al. (Eds.), *Creativity and development* (pp. 219–220). New York, NY: Oxford University Press.

Finke, R. A. (1990). *Creative imagery: Discoveries and inventions in visualization.* Hillsdale, NJ: Lawrence Erlbaum Associates.

Franck, K., & Rosen, E. (1949). A projective test of masculinity-femininity. *Journal of Consulting Psychology, 13*(4), 247.

Frecska, E., More, C. E., Vargha, A., & Luna, L. E. (2012). Enhancement of creative expression and entoptic phenomena as after-effects of repeated ayahuasca ceremonies. *Journal of Psychoactive Drugs, 44*, 191–199.

Gallo, F., Golomb, C., & Barroso, A. (2002). Compositional strategies in drawing: The effects of two-and three-dimensional media. *Visual Arts Research, 28*, 2–23.

Gansler, D. A., Moore, D. W., Susmaras, T. M., Jerram, M. W., Sousa, J., & Heilman, K. M. (2011). Cortical morphology of visual creativity. *Neuropsychologia, 49*(9), 2527–2532.

Gardner, H. (1989). The key in the slot: Creativity in a Chinese key. *Journal of Aesthetic Education, 23*, 141–158.

Gardner, H., & Winner, E. (1982). First intimations of artistry. In S. Strauss (Ed.), *U-shaped behavioral growth* (pp. 147–168). New York, NY: Academic Press.

Getzels, J., & Csikszentmihalyi, M. (1976). *The creative vision: A longitudinal study of problem-finding in art.* New York, NY: Wiley Interscience.

Golomb, C. (1992). *The child's creation of a pictorial world.* Berkley, CA: University of California Press.

Gombrich, E. H. (1960). Art and illusion: A study in the psychology of pictorial representation. *Bollingen Ser. XXXV,* (5), 9.

Goodman, N. (1968). *Languages of art: An approach to a theory of symbols.* Indianapolis, IN: Hackett Publishing.

Gretton, C., & ffytche, D. H. (2014). Art and the brain: A view from dementia. *International Journal of Geriatric Psychiatry, 29*(2), 111–126.

Guilford, J. (1967). *The nature of human intelligence.* New York, NY: McGraw-Hill.

Han, K. (2003). Domain specificity of creativity in young children: How quantitative and qualitative data support it. *Journal of Creative Behavior, 37*, 117–142.

Hekkert, P., & Van Wieringen, P. C. (1996). Beauty in the eye of expert and nonexpert beholders: A study in the appraisal of art. *The American Journal of Psychology, 109*(3), 389–407.

Helson, R. (1999). A longitudinal study of creative personality in women. *Creativity Research Journal, 12*, 89–102.

Hennessey, B. A. (1994). The consensual assessment technique: An examination of the relationships between ratings of product and process creativity. *Creativity Research Journal, 7*, 193–208.

Holert, T. (2009, Summer). A child could do it. *Cabinet,* 34. Retrieved on April 10, 2017, from http://cabinetmagazine.org/issues/34/holert.php.

Huntsinger, C. S., Schoeneman, J., & Ching, W. D. (1994). *A cross-cultural study of young children's performance on drawing and handwriting tasks.* Paper presented at the conference of the Midwestern Psychological Association, Chicago, IL.

Husslein-Arco, A., & Koja, S. (2010). *Lovis Corinth: A feast of painting.* Munich: Prestel.

Inzelberg, R. (2013). The awakening of artistic creativity and Parkinson's disease. *Behavioral Neuroscience, 127*(2), 256.

Jellen, H., and Urban, K. K. (1988). Assessing creative potential world-wide: The first cross-cultural application of the TCT-DP. *Creative Child and Adult Quarterly, 14*, 151–167.

Jaarsveld, S., & Leeuwen, C. (2005). Sketches from a design process: Creative cognition inferred from intermediate products. *Cognitive Science, 29*(1), 79–101.

Jackson, P. W., & Messick, S. (1965). The person, the product, and the response: Conceptual problems in the assessment of creativity. *Journal of Personality, 33*(3), 309–329.

Jarosewich, T., Pfeiffer, S., & Morris, J. (2002). Identifying gifted students using teacher rating scales: A review of existing instruments. *Journal of Psychoeducational Assessment, 20*, 322–336.

Kaufman, J. C. (2012). Counting the muses: Development of the Kaufman Domains of Creativity Scale (K-DOCS). *Psychology of Aesthetics, Creativity, and the Arts, 6*(4), 298.

Kaufman, J. C., & Baer, J. (2004). Sure, I'm creative – but not in mathematics!: Self-reported creativity in diverse domains. *Empirical Studies of the Arts, 22*, 143–155.

Kaufman, J. C., & Baer, J. (2005). The amusement park theory of creativity. In J. C. Kaufman & J. Baer (Eds.), *Creativity across domains: Faces of the muse* (pp. 321–328). New York, NY: Laurence Erlbaum Associates, Inc.

Kaufman, J. C., & Baer, J. (2012). Beyond new and appropriate: Who decides what is creative? *Creativity Research Journal, 24*(1), 83–91.

Kaufman, J., Cole, J., & Baer, J. (2009). The construct of creativity: Structural model for self-reported creativity ratings. *Journal of Creative Behavior, 43*, 119–134.

Kay, S. (1991). The figural problem solving and problem finding of professional and semi-professional artists and non-artists. *Creativity Research Journal, 4*, 233–252.

Khatena, J., & Torrance, E. (1976). *Khatena-Torrance Creative Perception Inventory.* Chicago, IL: Stoelting.

Kim, K. H. (2006). Can we trust creativity tests? A review of the Torrance tests of creative thinking (TTCT). *Creativity Research Journal, 18*, 3–14.

Kowatari, Y., Lee, S. H., Yamamura, H., Nagamori, Y., Levy, P., Yamane, S. et al. (2009). Neural networks involved in artistic creativity. *Human Brain Mapping, 30*, 1678–1690.

Kozbelt, A. (2004). Originality and technical skill as components of artistic quality. *Empirical Studies of the Arts, 22*, 157–170.

Kozbelt, A., & Serafin, J. (2009). Dynamic evaluation of high-and low-creativity drawings by artist and nonartist raters. *Creativity Research Journal, 21*(4), 349–360.

Kottlow, M., Praeg, E., Luethy, C., & Jancke, L. (2011). Artists' advance: Decreased upper alpha power while drawing in artists compared with non-artists. *Brain Topography, 23*(4), 392–402.

Kulisevsky, J., Pagonabarraga, J., & Martinez-Corral, M. (2009). Changes in artistic style and behaviour in Parkinson's disease: Dopamine and creativity. *Journal of Neurology, 256*, 816–819.

Leder, H. (2013). Next steps in neuroaesthetics: Which processes and processing stages to study? *Psychology of Aesthetics, Creativity, and the Arts, 7*(1), 27–37.

Leder, H. (2014). Beyond perception – Information processing approaches to art appreciation. In P. P. L. Tinio & J. K. Smith (Eds), *The Cambridge handbook of the psychology of aesthetics and the arts* (pp. 115–138). Cambridge, MA: Cambridge University Press.

Leder, H., Belke, B., Oeberst, A., & Augustin, D. (2004). A model of aesthetic appreciation and aesthetic judgments. *British Journal of Psychology, 95*, 489–508.

Lemons, G. (2011). Diverse perspectives of creativity testing controversial issues when used for inclusion into gifted programs. *Journal for the Education of the Gifted, 34*(5), 742–772.

Li, J. (1997). Creativity in horizontal and vertical domains. *Creativity Research Journal, 10*, 107–132.

Lubart, T. I., & Sternberg, R. J. (1998). Creativity across time and place: Life span and cross-cultural perspective. *High Ability Studies, 9*, 59–74.

Ludington, C. (1965). *Creativity and conformity: A problem for organizations.* Ann Arbor, MI: Foundation for Research on Human Behavior.

Lundy, D. E. (2012). Degrees of quality: A method for quantifying aesthetic impact. *Psychology Research, 2*(4), 205–221.

Marks, D. F. (1973). Visual imagery differences in the recall of pictures. *British Journal of Psychology, 64*(1), 17–24.

McKelvie, S. J. (1995). The VVIQ as a psychometric test of individual differences in visual imagery vividness: A critical quantitative review and plea for direction. *Journal of Mental Imagery, 19,* 1–106.

McManus, I. C., Chamberlain, R., Loo, P. W., Rankin, Q., Riley, H., & Brunswick, N. (2010). Art students who cannot draw: Exploring the relations between drawing ability, visual memory, accuracy of copying, and dyslexia. *Psychology of Aesthetics, Creativity, and the Arts, 4*(1), 18.

Mednick, S. A. (1962). The associative basis of the creative process. *Psychological Review, 69,* 220–232.

Meeker, M., & Meeker, R. (1985). *Structure of intellect learning abilities test.* Los Angeles, CA: Western Psychological Services.

Mell, J. C., Howard, S. M., & Miller, B. L. (2003) Art and the brain: The influence of frontotemporal dementia on an accomplished artist. *Neurology, 60,* 1707–1710.

Meyers, J. E., & Meyers, K. R. (1995). Rey Complex figure test and recognition trial. *Psychological Assessment Resources.*

Miall, R. C., & Tchalenko, J. (2001). A painter's eye movements: A study of eye and hand movement during portrait drawing. *Leonardo, 34*(1), 35–40.

Midorikawa, A., Fukutake, T., & Kawamura, M. (2008). Dementia and painting in patients from different cultural backgrounds. *European Neurology, 60*(5), 224–229.

Milbrath, C. (1998). *Patterns of artistic development in children: Comparative studies of talent.* Cambridge: Cambridge University Press.

Miller, B. L., & Hou, C. E. (2004). Portraits of artists: emergence of visual creativity in dementia. *Archives of Neurology, 61*(6), 842–844.

Miller, B. L., Ponton, M., Benson, D. F., Cummings, J. L., & Mena, I. (1996). Enhanced artistic creativity with temporal lobe degeneration. *The Lancet, 348*(9043), 1744–1745.

Mitchell, W. T. J. (1987). *Iconology; image, text, ideology.* Chicago, IL: University of Chicago Press.

Moore, D. W., Bhadelia, R., Billings, R., Fulwiler, D., Heilman, K. M., Rood, K. M. J. et al. (2009). Hemispheric connectivity and the visual-spatial divergent thinking component of creativity. *Brain and Cognition, 70*(3), 267–272.

Moran III J. D., Milgram, R. M., Sawyers, J. K., & Fu, V. R. (1983). Original thinking in preschool children. *Child Development, 54*(4), 921–926.

Mottron, L., Belleville, S., & Ménard, E. (1999). Local bias in autistic subjects as evidenced by graphic tasks: Perceptual hierarchization or working memory deficit? *Journal of Child Psychology and Psychiatry, 40*(05), 743–755.

Myszkowski, N., Storme, M., Zenasni, F., & Lubart, T. (2014). Is visual aesthetic sensitivity independent from intelligence, personality and creativity? *Personality and Individual Differences, 59,* 16–20.

Niu, W. H., & Sternberg, R. J. (2001). Cultural influences on artistic creativity and its evaluation. *International Journal of Psychology, 36,* 225–241.

Palmiero, M., Di Giacomo, D., & Passafiume, D. (2012). Creativity and dementia: A review. *Cognitive Processing, 13*(3), 193–209.

Palmiero, M., Nakatani, C., Raver, D., Belardinelli, M. O., & van Leeuwen, C. (2010). Abilities within and across visual and verbal domains: How specific is their influence on creativity? *Creativity Research Journal, 22*(4), 369–377.

Pelowski, M., & Akiba, F. (2011). A model of art perception, evaluation and emotion in transformative aesthetic experience. *New Ideas in Psychology, 29*(2), 80–97.

Pérez-Fabello, M. J., & Campos, A. (2007). The influence of imaging capacity on visual art skills. *Thinking Skills and Creativity, 2*(2), 128–135.

Plucker, J. A. (1999). Is the proof in the pudding? Reanalyses of Torrance's (1958 to present) longitudinal data. *Creativity Research Journal, 12*, 103–114.

Plucker, J. A. (2005). The (relatively) generalist view of creativity. In J. Kaufman & J. Baer (Eds.), *Creativity across domains* (pp. 307–312). Mahway, NJ: Lawrence Erlbaum.

Rankin, K. P., Liu, A. A., Howard, S., Slama, H., Hou, C. E., Shuster, K., & Miller, B. L. (2007). A case-controlled study of altered visual art production in Alzheimer's and FTLD. *Cognitive and Behavioral Neurology: Official Journal of the Society for Behavioral and Cognitive Neurology, 20*(1), 48.

Rawlings, D., & Locarnini, A. (2007). Validating the creativity scale for diverse domains using groups of artists and scientists. *Empirical Studies of the Arts, 25*(2), 163–172.

Renzulli, J. S., Smith, L., White, A., Callahan, C., & Hartman, R. (1976). *Scales for rating the behavioral characteristics of superior students.* Mansfield Center, CT: Creative Learning Press.

Rimm, S., & Davis, G. A. (1980). Five years of international research with GIFT: An instrument for the identification of creativity. *Journal of Creative Behavior, 14*, 35–46.

Rostan, S. M. (1997). A study of young artists: The development of talent and creativity. *Creativity Research Journal, 10*, 175–192.

Rostan, S. M. (1998). The development of artistic talent and creativity: An evolving systems approach. *AGATE (Journal of the Gifted and Talented Education Council of the Alberta Teachers' Association), 12*(2), 15–25.

Rostan, S. M. (2005). Educational intervention and the development of young art students' talent and creativity. *Journal of Creative Behavior, 39*, 237–283.

Rostan, S. M. (2010). Studio learning: Motivation, competence, and the development of young art students' talent and creativity. *Creativity Research Journal, 22*(3), 261–271.

Rostan, S. M., Pariser, D., & Gruber, H. E. (2002). A cross-cultural study of the development of artistic talent, creativity, and giftedness. *High Ability Studies, 13*, 125–156.

Roy, D. D. (1996). Personality model of fine artists. *Creativity Research Journal, 9*(4), 391–394.

Rudowicz, E., Lok, D., & Kitto, J. (1995). Use of the Torrance tests of creative thinking in an exploratory study of creativity in Hong Kong primary school children: A cross-cultural comparison. *International Journal of Psychology, 30*, 417–430.

Runco, M. A. (1987). Interrater agreement on a socially valid measure of students' creativity. *Psychological Reports, 61*, 1009–1010.

Runco, M. A., & Chand, I. (1995). Cognition and creativity. *Educational Psychology Review, 7*, 243–267.

Runco, M. A., Millar, G., Acar, S., & Cramond, B. (2010). Torrance tests of creative thinking as predictors of personal and public achievement: A fifty-year follow-up. *Creativity Research Journal, 22*(4), 361–368.

Sawyers, J. K., & Canestaro, N. C. (1989). Creativity and achievement in design coursework. *Creativity Research Journal, 2*(1–2), 126–133.

Schaefer, C. E., & Anastasi, A. (1968). A biographical inventory for identifying creativity in adolescent boys. *Journal of Applied Psychology, 52*, 42–48.

Schraw, G. (2005). Review of the Khatena-Torrance Creative Perception Inventory. In R. Spies & B. Plake (Eds.), *The sixteenth mental measurements yearbook* (pp. 542–543). Lincoln, NE: University of Nebraska Press.

Serafin, J., Kozbelt, A., Seidel, A., & Dolese, M. (2011). Dynamic evaluation of high-and low-creativity drawings by artist and nonartist raters: Replication and methodological extension. *Psychology of Aesthetics, Creativity, and the Arts, 5*(4), 350–359.

Serrano, C., Allegri, R. F., Martelli, M., Taragano, F., & Rinalli, P. (2005). Visual art, creativity and dementia. *Vertex 16*(64), 418–429.

Sessa, B. (2008). Is it time to revisit the role of psychedelic drugs in enhancing human creativity? *Journal of Psychopharmacology, 22,* 821–827.

Silvia, P. J., Nusbaum, E. C., Berg, C., Martin, C., & O'Connor, A. (2009). Openness to experience, plasticity, and creativity: Exploring lower-order, high-order, and interactive effects. *Journal of Research in Personality, 43*(6), 1087–1090.

Silvia, P. J., Kaufman, J. C., & Pretz, J. E. (2009). Is creativity domain-specific? Latent class models of creative accomplishments and creative self-descriptions. *Psychology of Aesthetics, Creativity, and the Arts, 3*(3), 139.

Simonton, D. K. (1984). Artistic creativity and interpersonal relationships across and within generations. *Journal of Personality and Social Psychology, 46,* 1273–1286.

Simonton, D. K. (1996). Creative expertise: A life-span developmental perspective. In K. A. Ericsson (Ed.), *The road to excellence: The acquisition of expert performance in the arts and sciences, sports, and games* (pp. 227–253). Mahwah, NJ: Lawrence Erlbaum Associates Inc.

Solso, R. L. (2001). Brain activities in an expert versus a novice artist: An fMRI study. *Leonardo, 34,* 31–34.

Sternberg, R. (2002). "Creativity as decision": Comment. *American Psychologist, 57,* 376.

Sternberg, R.J., & Lubart, T.I. (1999). The concept of creativity: Prospects and paradigms. In R. J. Sternberg (Ed.), *Handbook of creativity* (pp. 3–15). New York, NY: Cambridge University Press.

Stevenson-Taylor, A. G., & Mansell, W. (2012). Exploring the role of art-making in recovery, change, and self-understanding: An interpretative phenomenological analysis of interviews with everyday creative people. *International Journal of Psychological Studies, 4*(3), 104.

Taylor, C. W., & and Ellison, R. L. (1968). *The Alpha Biographial Inventory.* Greensboro, NC: Prediction Press.

Tinio, P. P. (2013). From artistic creation to aesthetic reception: The mirror model of art. *Psychology of Aesthetics, Creativity, and the Arts, 7*(3), 265–275.

Toku, M. (2001). Cross-cultural analysis of artistic development: Drawings by Japanese and U.S. children. *Visual Arts Research, 27,* 46–59.

Torrance, E. P. (1966). *Torrance tests of creative thinking: Norms-technical manual.* Princeton, NY: Personnel Press.

Torrance, E. P. (1969). Curiosity of gifted children and performances on timed and untimed tests of creativity. *Gifted Child Quarterly, 13,* 155–158.

Torrance, E. P. (1988). The nature of creativity as manifest in its testing. In R. J. Sternberg (Ed.), *The nature of creativity* (pp. 43–75). New York, NY: Cambridge University Press.

Torrance, E.P. (1999). *Torrance Test of Creative Thinking: Norms and technical manual.* Beaconville, IL: Scholastic Testing Services.

Torrance, E. P., & Goff, K. (1989). A quiet revolution. *Journal of Creative Behavior, 23,* 136–145.

Urban, K. K. (1991). Recent trends in creativity research and theory in Western Europe. *European Journal of High Ability, 1*(1), 99–113.

Urban, K. K. (2004). Assessing creativity: The test for creative thinking-drawing production (TCT-DP) the concept, application, evaluation, and international studies. *Psychology Science, 46*(3), 387–397.

Urban, K. K., & Jellen, H. G. (1996). *Test for Creative Thinking – Drawing Production (TCT-DP)*. Lisse: Swets and Zeitlinger.

Verstijnen, I. M., van Leeuwen, C., Goldschmidt, G., Hamel, R., & Hennessey, J. M. (1998). Creative discovery in imagery and perception: Combining is relatively easy, restructuring takes a sketch. *Acta Psychologica, 99*(2), 177–200.

Vinacke, W. E. (1952). *The psychology of thinking*. New York, NY: McGraw-Hill.

Wallach, M., & Kogan, N. (1965). *Modes of thinking in young children*. New York, NY: Holt, Rinehart & Winston.

Ward, T. B. (1994). Structured imagination: The role of category structure in exemplar generation. *Cognitive psychology, 27*(1), 1–40.

Weintraub, D., & Nirenberg, M. J. (2012). Impulse control and related disorders in Parkinson's disease. *Neurodegenerative Diseases, 11*(2), 63–71.

Westphal-Fitch, G., Oh, J., & Fitch, W. (2013). Studying aesthetics with the method of production: Effects of context and local symmetry. *Psychology of Aesthetics, Creativity, and the Arts, 7*(1), 13–26.

Williams, F. (1980). *Creativity assessment packet*. Buffalo, NY: DOK.

Winner, E. (1989). Development in the visual arts. In W. Damon (Ed.), *Child development today and tomorrow* (pp. 199–221). San Francisco, CA: Jossey Bass.

Yamamoto, K. (1964). *Experimental scoring manuals for the Minnesota test of creative thinking and writing*. OH: Kent State University.

Zaidel, D. W. (2010). Art and brain: Insights from neuropsychology, biology and evolution. *Journal of Anatomy, 216*(2), 177–183.

Zaidel, D. W. (2014). Creativity, brain, and art: Biological and neurological considerations. *Frontiers in Human Neuroscience, 8*(389), 1–9.

Zaidel, D. W., Nadal, M., Flexas, A., & Munar, E. (2013). An evolutionary approach to art and aesthetic experience. *Psychology of Aesthetics, Creativity, and the Arts, 7*(1), 100.

7 The Creation and Aesthetic Appreciation of Architecture

Oshin Vartanian

University of Toronto

Abstract

Psychologists have historically been interested in architecture as an important domain within which to study creativity. Classic studies highlighted the role of personality variables, while at the same time downplaying the contributions of some cognitive abilities (e.g., intelligence) to individual differences in architectural creativity. Recently, research in this domain has been informed by novel findings from psychology, neuropsychology, and neuroscience. Specifically, architectural creativity has been linked to the flexible interplay between associative and inferential processes, the neural systems for which are dissociable in the brain. In addition, evidence suggests that high-level creativity in architecture could in part be driven by ordinary thought processes working on exceptionally rich content. In turn, neuroimaging studies have begun to also shed light on the neural bases of our aesthetic appreciation of various basic features of architectural design such as contour, ceiling height, and perceived enclosure. Together, these various strands of research are increasing our understanding of creativity and aesthetic appreciation in the domain of architecture.

Background

People tend to perceive architects as creative types (Kirsch, Lubart, & Houssemand, 2016; MacKinnon, 1965). In some ways this is not surprising, given the ample opportunities people have to contemplate the merits of their work. For example, there is evidence to show that we spend approximately 90 percent of our lives within built spaces (Klepis et al., 2001; Ott, 1989). This high exposure rate likely affords urban dwellers many opportunities to contemplate the aesthetic aspects of built spaces, and in turn the creativity of the architects that led to their genesis. This focus has only increased recently by the media's intense reporting of the results of competitions that determine the commissioning of urban spaces of civic significance, such as art galleries, train stations, and the like. In other words, by virtue of where we spend most of our lives, we tend to have opinions about the aesthetic and creative aspects of architecture in a way that we might not have about other human activities.

In addition, the very manner in which most people think of "good architecture" also facilitates its link with creativity. Specifically, good architecture is typically perceived to fulfill two requirements: form and function. In turn, this dovetails very nicely with how we typically define creativity, as the generation of novel and useful products (Sternberg, 1999). Framed this way, it would appear that as a domain, architecture is ideally suited for the study of creative products and processes.

Indeed, early on in the history of the scientific study of creativity there was great interest among researchers to focus on architects to further our understanding of creativity. Perhaps nowhere was this more apparent than in the studies conducted at the Institute for Personality Assessment and Research (IPAR) at the University of California Berkeley beginning in the 1950s. Importantly, architects were not the singular focus for IPAR researchers, who also studied creative writers, poets, mathematicians, and space scientists, all of whom were selected because they were considered to be "effectively functioning persons." Nevertheless, IPAR's in-depth cross-sectional and longitudinal studies of architects over several decades contributed immensely to the emergence of the scientific study of creative personality (Helson, 1999).

The IPAR researchers embraced three important design principles for the study of creativity in architecture. First, they focused on bona fide creative architects. Specifically, they invited to Berkeley some of the most eminent architects of the twentieth century, including Eero Saarinen, Louis I. Kahn, Philip C. Johnson, and I. M. Pei. This ensured that the sample included highly creative people ($N = 40$). Second, the researchers also studied two control groups: age- and sex-matched architects ($N = 43$) who worked in the same firms as the highly creative architects, as well as a group of age- and sex-matched representative sample of American architects ($N = 41$) who worked in other firms throughout the United States. Third, the researchers embraced a truly holistic approach to studying creative persons, meaning that data were collected on individuals involving measures of perceptual, cognitive, and intellectual abilities, interests and values, personality, and other related characteristics. These design features enabled them to tease apart the specific variables that distinguished truly creative architects from their less creative counterparts, while also controlling for important individual and environmental factors (e.g., workplace). The outcome measures included creativity ratings conducted by editors of major professional architectural journals, an independent panel of expert judges, and ratings of each participant by every other participant in the sample, among others.

Two important findings have come to define this large corpus of work. First, the results demonstrated that personality variables play an important role in distinguishing creative architects from their less creative counterparts (MacKinnon, 1965; 1978). For example, on the California Psychological Inventory (Gough, 1956) creative architects had high scores on flexibility and achievement via independence, but low scores on self-control. Their scores on measures of values and interest reinforced this profile. For example, On the Strong Vocational Interest Blank (see Campbell, 1971) they demonstrated an interest in cognitive flexibility but lack of interest in details. In addition, Hall and MacKinnon (1969) noted that creative architects exhibited "a decided preference for openness and receptivity, both to experience and new ideas, as well as for a concern with deeper meanings and possibilities inherent in things and situations" (p. 326). Indeed, the association between creativity in architecture and intellectual openness and depth is a recurring theme, as is their coexistence with a strong drive to realize the potential of ideas (see Kirsch et al., 2016).

Second, cognitive abilities (e.g., IQ) were shown to be unrelated to variations in creativity. For example, when summarizing this work MacKinnon (1962) noted that "As for the relation between intelligence and creativity ... we have found within our creative samples essentially zero relationship between the two variables" (p. 487). Importantly, the lack of a significant correlation between cognitive ability and creativity in architecture was not due to restriction in the range of intelligence characterizing this sample. Indeed, the mean IQ as measured by the *Terman Concept Mastery Test* (Terman, 1956) was 113, with scores ranging from 39 to 179. These two findings – that creativity is related to personality but unrelated to intelligence – have had lasting reverberations on the scientific study of creativity, and are only recently undergoing revision. For example, recent studies have shown that creativity as measured by divergent thinking tasks is in fact strongly related to cognitive abilities as measured by *fluid* intelligence, executive function, and working memory tests (Gilhooly, Fiortou, Anthony, & Wynn, 2007; Nusbaum & Silvia, 2011). In a recent study involving a sample consisting mostly of students of architecture, Kirsch et al. (2016) used a structural equation modeling approach to show that fluid intelligence – measured using a test of inductive reasoning and spatial aptitudes – was a positive predictor of trait creativity – measured using the Test for Creative Thinking-Drawing Production (Urban & Jellen, 1996). More specifically, fluid intelligence exerted a positive effect on originality, which in turn exerted a positive effect on trait creativity. The results of this study extend the positive contribution of fluid intelligence to creative ability to the domain of architecture.

Rediscovering Architecture

Recently there has been a revival of interest in architecture as a domain within which to study not only the creative process but also the aesthetic appreciation of the products of architectural design. Here I will focus on three sets of contributions that have begun to enrich our understanding of the creation and aesthetic appreciation of architecture. The first set involves a reassessment of the extent to which various cognitive processes contribute to exceptional manifestations of creativity in architecture. This issue is of great interest in the scientific study of creativity, which appears to be divided between those who believe that high-level creativity necessitates outside-the-box thinking versus those who argue that even high-level creativity can be explained on the basis of ordinary inside-the-box thought processes.

The second set involves neuroimaging and neuropsychological studies that have focused on architecture and design. Neuroimaging studies are informative because they enable one to study brain function in relation to task engagement. In turn, neuropsychological studies focus on the aftereffects of focal brain lesions on task performance. This latter work is important because studies of patients allow one to test hypotheses about causation that are not possible to conduct using neuroimaging work, which by definition can provide correlational data only. In addition, to the extent that specific regions are associated with functional specialization (Poldrack, 2006), inferences can be made about the psychological processes and mechanisms related to the outcome measures of interest.

The third set of studies involves neuroimaging research on the neural bases of our aesthetic preferences for various basic physical features of built spaces, including contour, ceiling height, and perceived enclosure. Because architects regularly manipulate these features in the service of design optimization, understanding how these features affect end-users can help us understand the psychology and neurology of aesthetic appreciation of architectural design, paving the way for the design of better living, working and leisure spaces.

Cognitive Bases of Architectural Creativity

Two recent studies have contributed to our understanding of factors that underlie high-level creativity in architecture. First, Weisberg (2011) conducted a qualitative case study of Frank Lloyd Wright's development of Fallingwater – the most famous private residence in the world. What Weisberg set out to do was determine whether Frank Lloyd Wright's method resembled a stepwise, incremental progression involving past knowledge, or whether it resembled an exceptional moment of insight that signaled breaking away from the constraints of past knowledge. In essence, he tried to establish the primacy of ordinary thinking versus extraordinary thinking in the creative process leading to the creation of an exceptional architectural product. In setting up his analysis, Weisberg made an important distinction between *structure* and *content* in our efforts to understand creativity. With the former he referred to the cognitive processes that underlie creative thinking, whereas with the latter he referred to the database available in the mind of the creator that the cognitive processes are applied to. Framed as such, one can ask whether highly creative types are distinguished by the structure of their thinking, or whether the same structure is applied to a different content base.

Weisberg's detailed qualitative analysis of biographical and archival material supported the idea that Frank Lloyd Wright's development of Fallingwater was underwritten by the operation of ordinary cognitive processes operating on a rich database, rather than exceptional insight. Importantly, Frank Lloyd Wright's thinking while developing Fallingwater was strongly influenced by earlier work in two ways. First, his design appeared to be under *automatic* influences, defined as stylistic expressions that distill experiences in one's past and are henceforth reflected in one's work. His development of Fallingwater also reflected *intentional* or *strategic* influences, defined as conscious selections of earlier work as the basis for new work. Thus, Weisberg's qualitative case study of Frank Lloyd Wright's development of Fallingwater demonstrated that past knowledge can play a critical role in the creation of a highly exceptional architectural masterpiece. By extension, it suggests that when trying to understand factors that distinguish the thinking of highly creative from less creative individuals, we should pay attention to differences in content of thought rather than exclusively its structure.

Vartanian et al. (2014) conducted another recent study that was geared toward understanding the cognitive factors that underlie exceptional creativity in architecture. As noted earlier, consistent with their holistic approach, IPAR researchers collected large amounts of data in their search to isolate factors that distinguish highly creative from less creative architects. Subjects in IPAR's group of highly creative architects were administered the Alternate Uses Task (AUT). Vartanian et al. (2014) were interested in testing the hypothesis that variations in the divergent thinking ability of IPAR architects would predict the future popularity of their work fifty years later. Tackling this question was made possible in two ways. First, recent years have seen great advances in scoring methods in relation to tests of divergent thinking. Whereas previously such tests were assessed using a rather limited set of standard metrics (e.g., fluency, flexibility, originality), current subjective scoring techniques enable a much richer and deeper approach to scoring the actual creativity of generated uses (for review see Silvia et al., 2008). As such, it was possible to rescore responses using contemporary metrics. Second, rather fortuitously, in 2006–2007 the American Institute of Architects (AIA) conducted a survey to identify America's favorite architecture, first among its 2,448 members and then among 2,214 members of the general public. AIA's members' ratings led to a list of 248 favorite buildings, whereas the general public's ratings involved a subset of those 248 buildings and an eventual list of 150 favorite buildings. Given the available data, Vartanian et al. (2014) could test whether divergent thinking scores predicted the likelihood that buildings designed by any of IPAR's architects would be found on either of those lists. In addition, as noted earlier, each architect was also rated on creativity by the editors of major professional architectural journals, an independent panel of expert judges, and every other participant in the sample. This enabled Vartanian et al. (2014) to test another hypothesis, whether one's perceived creativity by the field (i.e., experts, peers) would predict the likelihood that buildings designed by any of IPAR's architects would be found on either of AIA's lists.

Vartanian et al.'s (2014) results demonstrated that divergent thinking ability – scored using traditional or more modern approaches – did not predict the likelihood that an architect's work would appear on either list of AIA's most popular buildings. In contrast, in every case (i.e., journal editors, expert panel, other architects) architectural creativity ratings predicted the likelihood that an architect's work would appear on both lists of most popular buildings. This is a remarkable finding because it is not unreasonable to assume that the expert judgments made in 1957–1961 might have been unrelated to the criteria that drove the popularity ratings collected in 2006–2007 by AIA. Nevertheless, even within a small sample of highly eminent architects, perceived creativity was predictive of future likeability among both more and less experienced viewers of the work (i.e., AIA members and laypersons, respectively).

The Story from the Brain

Our understanding of the cognitive processes that underlie architectural design has been enriched recently by brain data. Gilbert, Zamenopoulos, Alexiou, and Johnson (2009) instructed neurologically healthy subjects to position and rotate a set of objects to arrange furniture in a conference room. However, these instructions were realized under two different conditions (design vs. problem-solving) in the functional magnetic resonance imaging (fMRI) scanner. These two conditions were implemented to capture an important distinction in the problem-solving literature between well-structured and ill-structured tasks. Whereas well-structured tasks have well-defined start states, end states and transformation functions, ill-structured tasks do not. As such, they do not embody unique correct solutions. As a result, optimal performance on ill-structured tasks necessitates the generation of solution paths for navigating through poorly- defined problem spaces. In the problem-solving condition, subjects were instructed to arrange the furniture in the room to meet the following five rather concrete constraints: "(1) the two tables face each other; (2) the long table is parallel to the screen; (3) the participants can see each other; (4) one participant cannot see the screen; (5) all the furniture is used" (p. 81). In contrast, in the design condition the subjects were instructed to arrange the furniture in the room in response to a different set of five constraints: "(1) the room is spacious; (2) the room enables collaboration; (3) the participants can see each other; (4) all participants can see the screen; (5) you may use any of the furniture you like" (p. 82). As can be seen from the sets of constraints, the design condition was formulated to embody a greater degree of freedom in interpreting the requirements of the task. Importantly, whereas the problem-solving condition is an example of a well-structured task, the design condition is an example of an ill-structured task. Two important findings emerged from the study. First, the design condition took longer to complete than the problem-solving condition, suggesting that it is more effortful to solve ill-structured than well-structured tasks even when the total number of constraints is held constant. Second, the direct contrast of the design vs. problem-solving condition revealed greater activation in the right dorsolateral prefrontal cortex, consistent with the role of the right prefrontal cortex in the generation of solutions under conditions of reduced task constraints (Goel & Vartanian, 2005; Vartanian & Goel, 2005).

The idea that the right prefrontal cortex might play a critical role in ill-structured cognition in the domain of architectural design received further support from Goel and Grafman's (2000) case study of patient PF, a 57-year-old male architect who had suffered a right frontal parasagittal meningioma. Prior to this misfortune PF had been a highly accomplished and successful architect. He had earned a graduate degree in architecture from Yale University. He had scored in the 98th percentile on the Graduate Record Examination (GRE) in math and science. He was successfully self-employed prior to his injury, although at the time of testing he was involuntarily retired and lived at home with his mother. Given that he was an architect, the researchers gave him the task of redesigning their lab space. In addition, they administered the same task to an age- and sex-matched professional architect as their control condition. Importantly, to gain traction into PF's thinking in the course of the design process, Goel and Grafman (2000) employed verbal protocol analysis, which involves instructing subjects to vocalize their thoughts, which are in turn recorded and scored in relation to various indices of interest. This detailed approach can be very fruitful for revealing the types of thought that underlie various aspects of planning and problem solving (Ericsson & Simon, 1993).

Although at the time of assessment PF's intelligence and memory scores were in the excellent range, his design process was suboptimal. PF's impairment can be understood by making reference to Goel's (1995) idea, according to which the type of cognition that typically occurs in the early (preliminary) phase of the design process is markedly different than the type of cognition that typically occurs in the middle and late (refinement and detailing) phases of the design process. Specifically, the early phase of the design process is characterized by the generation and exploration of alternatives, and low commitment to generated ideas. This represents the ill-structured phase of the problem-solving process. In this early phase, lateral transformations (set shifts) are common – defined as generations of varying alternatives of an idea rather than more in-depth contemplations of the same idea. Lateral transformations widen the problem space by making more possibilities available for further examination. In turn, the later phase of the problem space is characterized by greater levels of constraint and structure on thinking, as generated ideas are pruned and executed for completion. This represents the well-structured phase of the problem-solving process. Unlike the control subject, whose performance and thinking reflected the typical pattern of progression from ill-structured to well-structured problem solving in service of the design process, PF did not engage in preliminary design until two-thirds of the way into the design process, and when he did, the preliminary designs were erratic and minimal, and left largely unexplored. These results demonstrated that PF's suboptimal design was largely due to difficulties in the preliminary phase of the design process.

Based in part on Goel and Grafman (2000) but motivated by a much larger neuropsychological and neuroimaging literature, Goel (2014) has recently proposed that creative design rests on the flexible interplay between an associative system that is specialized in handling imprecise, abstract, ambiguous, and indeterminate symbols and an inferential system that is specialized in handling precise, concrete, unambiguous, and determinate symbols. In addition, there appears to be an interesting hemispheric dissociation in the prefrontal cortex that supports these two symbol systems to varying degrees. Specifically, consistent with Gazzaniga's (1998, 2000) hypothesis regarding the "left hemisphere interpreter," the left prefrontal cortex appears to play a critical role in the manipulation of information in the service of pattern completion. Not surprisingly, the left prefrontal cortex has been implicated heavily in reasoning and decision-making tasks that necessitate inference making based on the available information. In contrast, the right prefrontal cortex has been shown to be engaged in tasks that have poorly defined constraints, do not necessarily lead to a pre-determined solution, and contain conflicting and/or misleading information (Goldberg, Podell, & Lovell, 1994). Thus, the right prefrontal cortex appears to enable the maintenance of indeterminate representations during problem solving. According to this model, PF's difficulty in the preliminary phase of the design process can be traced to his injury to the right prefrontal cortex, in turn making it difficult to engage in the thought processes necessary to navigate the early phase of an ill-structured problem space. Importantly, according to this model neither system is dominant. Rather, creative design is assumed to hinge on the flexible and judicious interplay between two cognitive engines that process different types of symbols and related mental representations.

Appreciation of Architecture

Recent research in this domain has begun to explore how people respond to specific features embodied within architecture. For example, Vartanian et al. (2013) undertook an fMRI study to explore the effect of contour on aesthetic judgments and approach-avoidance decisions in architecture. Contour was an interesting variable to focus on because there is evidence dating back to the 1920s to demonstrate that people exhibit a preference for curvilinear over rectilinear design, and that this preference is likely driven by the effect of contour on the viewers' affective systems (reviewed in Silvia & Barona, 2009). A pair of influential studies were conducted by Bar and Neta (2006, 2007) that sought to offer a putative mechanism to explain the reason for people's preference for curvilinear over rectilinear design. They were able to show that the preference pattern holds regardless of whether the viewed objects are real or imaginary. This suggested that semantic associations cannot be the sole driver of the effect. In addition, using fMRI they demonstrated that viewing rectilinear objects is correlated with greater activation in the amygdala than viewing curvilinear objects. Given the amygdala's well-established role in threat perception and the experience of negative affect, this finding was interpreted to mean that curvilinear objects are preferred over rectilinear objects because the latter might embody an evolutionarily important threat signal. In other words, people prefer curvilinear objects because they appear less threatening than rectilinear objects to them.

Vartanian et al. (2013) focused on the effect of contour on aesthetic judgments and approach-avoidance decisions in architecture for two reasons. First, behaviorally, they were interested in determining whether subjects would opt to enter spaces that they also found aesthetically more pleasing. Indeed, under "habitat theory" Appleton (1975) had argued that the spaces people find aesthetically pleasing are likely a function of the extent to which they signal environmental conditions favorable or unfavorable to survival. According to this theory, one would expect a close coupling of aesthetic judgments and approach-avoidance decisions in the domain of architecture. Second, the researchers were also interested in the neural overlap between systems that underlie aesthetic judgments versus those that underlie approach-avoidance decisions. Specifically, there is evidence to suggest that aesthetic judgments are driven by a core set of structures that include the brain's reward and emotion systems (Brown, Gao, Tisdelle, Eickhoff, & Liotti, 2011; Chatterjee & Vartanian, 2014). Given that aesthetic preference for curvilinear objects is hypothesized to be affectively driven (Silvia & Barona, 2009), then one would expect parts of this system to be activated when subjects are making beauty judgments in relation to contour in the domain of architecture. In contrast, much evidence suggests that approach and avoidance motivations in the brain are lateralized to the left and right hemispheres respectively (Rutherford & Lindell, 2011). As such, Vartanian et al. (2013) predicted that contour would modulate lateralized activations in the context of approach-avoidance decisions in relation to contour.

The behavioral results demonstrated that subjects were more likely to find curvilinear than rectilinear spaces beautiful. This finding extended this well-established effect to the domain of architecture. In addition, aesthetic preference for curvilinear spaces was correlated with activation in the anterior cingulate cortex. The anterior cingulate cortex forms part of the brain's core emotion system (Barrett, Mesquita, Ochsner, & Gross, 2007; Barrett & Wager, 2006). This finding is consistent with the notion that our aesthetic preference for curvilinear design is affectively driven. In addition, after exiting the scanner all the subjects rated all the stimuli on beauty and pleasantness – the valence dimension of the affect circumplex. Indeed, pleasantness ratings accounted for nearly 60 percent of the variance in beauty ratings. This finding too linked aesthetic preference for curvilinear design to affect.

In contrast, and contrary to expectation, contour had no effect on approach-avoidance decisions. In other words, it does not necessarily follow that people opt to enter spaces that they find aesthetically more pleasing. There could be a number of reasons for this. For example, the degree of risk involved in opting to enter a space is different than the degree of risk involved in an aesthetic judgment of that space, however hypothetical the former assessment might be. This could bring about dissociations between approach-avoidance decisions and aesthetic judgments. In addition, the setting for data collection (i.e., fMRI scanner) likely does not offer a sufficient degree of fidelity for studying approach-avoidance decisions that determine behavioral choices in real-life settings.

In a follow-up manuscript, Vartanian et al. (2015) reported the findings of the same experiment in relation to two additional variables that were also manipulated in the same design: ceiling height and perceived enclosure. Earlier behavioral research had shown that people prefer rooms with higher than lower ceilings (Baird, Cassidy, & Kurr, 1978). Vartanian et al. (2015) speculated that people might prefer spaces with higher ceilings because they offer the viewer greater opportunities for visuospatial exploration, which they might find enjoyable. The brain regions that contribute to visuospatial exploration consist of the frontal and parietal lobes in the dorsal stream that process where objects are located (Mishkin, Ungerleider, & Macko, 1983; Ungerleider & Mishkin, 1982), as well as medial temporal lobe structures involved in wayfinding and navigation (Aguirre, Detre, Alsop, & D'Esposito, 1996).

How about perceived enclosure – defined as the degree of perceived visual permeability of a space? To the extent that a space is perceived to be visually more permeable, it embodies less enclosure. We hypothesized that because open rooms offer a greater degree of perceived visual permeability, they will be found to be aesthetically more pleasing. As for the possible neural correlates of this effect, several candidate regions presented themselves, including the parahippocampal place area that responds to the presence of places (Epstein & Kanwisher, 1998), the brain's emotion and reward pathways correlated with positive affect (Barrett et al., 2007; Barrett & Wager, 2006), or indeed even frontal and parietal lobes in the dorsal stream that process the locations of objects (Mishkin et al., 1983; Ungerleider & Mishkin, 1982).

Behaviorally, as predicted, subjects were more likely to opt to enter rooms with higher ceilings. In addition, in the context of beauty judgments higher ceilings activated the precuneus and the middle frontal gyrus, two regions with well-established roles in visuospatial processing (Cavanna & Tribmle, 2006; Kravitz et al., 2011). However, as was the case with contour, the effect of ceiling height did not extend to approach-avoidance decisions.

In turn, perceived enclosure affected both aesthetic judgments as well as approach-avoidance decisions: subjects were more likely to find open rooms beautiful, and they were also more likely to opt to approach them. When judging beauty open rooms activated the middle and superior temporal gyri significantly more than enclosed rooms. These regions are involved in visuospatial attention (Nobre et al., 1997) and conceptual processing of actions (Watson, Cardillo, Ianni, & Chatterjee, 2013), suggesting that their engagement here could be due to the processing of abstract representations from visual motion information. Interestingly, enclosed spaces activated the anterior midcingulate cortex, the region within the cingulate cortex with the most direct projections from the amygdala. This finding suggests that reduced preference for enclosed spaces might be partly driven by negative emotional reactions that accompany exit decisions.

A very interesting study in this area was recently carried out by Fich and colleagues (2014) who demonstrated that people exhibit greater stress reactivity when in an enclosed compared to an open room. Specifically, the researchers used a virtual reality version of the Trier Social Stress Test (TSST) to induce stress. The standard TSST protocol induces stress by having the participant perform a series of stressful tasks (e.g., giving a presentation) in front of a committee. The advantage of using a virtual reality version of TSST consisted of the ability to manipulate the physical features of the room in systematic ways. The manipulation involved assessing participants either under the open- or enclosed-room conditions. The results demonstrated that participants in the enclosed condition exhibited greater cortisol reactivity to the stress condition and continued to show greater levels of cortisol at recovery. In other words, enclosed spaces can increase one's vulnerability to stress, possibly by not offering the potential for escape.

Summary

Building on classic work conducted on creative architects, recent research in psychology, neuropsychology, and neuroscience has highlighted the contributions of cognitive processes and the contents of cognition to exceptional creativity in architecture and design. Furthermore, we now have a better understanding of the neural bases of creative design in architecture. On the flipside, we are beginning to gain insights into how our brain and physiology respond to variations in specific design features in the domain of architecture. These findings have the potential to contribute to a deeper understanding of creativity and aesthetics in the domain of architecture.

References

Aguirre, G. K., Detre, J. A., Alsop, D. C., & D'Esposito, M. (1996). The parahippocampus subserves topographical learning in man. *Cerebral Cortex*, *6*, 823–829.

Appleton, J. (1975). *The experience of landscape*. New York: John Wiley and Sons.

Baird, J. C., Cassidy, B., & Kurr, J. (1978). Room preference as a function of architectural features and user activities. *Journal of Applied Psychology*, *63*, 719–727.

Bar, M., & Neta, M. (2006). Humans prefer curved visual objects. *Psychological Science*, *17*, 645–648.

Bar, M., & Neta, M. (2007). Visual elements of subjective preference modulate amygdala activation. *Neuropsychologia*, *45*, 2191–2200.

Barrett, L. F., Mesquita, B., Ochsner, K. N., & Gross, J. J. (2007). The experience of emotion. *Annual Review of Psychology*, *58*, 373–403.

Barrett, L. F., & Wager, T. (2006). The structure of emotion: Evidence from the neuroimaging of emotion. *Current Directions in Psychological Science*, *15*, 79–85.

Brown, S., Gao, X., Tisdelle, L., Eickhoff, S. B., & Liotti, M. (2011). Naturalizing aesthetics: Brain areas for aesthetic appraisal across sensory modalities. *Neuroimage*, *58*, 250–258.

Campbell, D. P. (1971). *Handbook for the strong vocational interest blank*. Stanford, CA: Stanford University Press.

Cavanna, A. E., & Trimble, M. R. (2006). The precuneus: A review of its functional anatomy and behavioural correlates. *Brain*, *129*, 564–583.

Chatterjee, A., & Vartanian, O. (2014). Neuroaesthetics. *Trends in Cognitive Sciences*, 18, 370–375.

Epstein, R., & Kanwisher, N. (1998). A cortical representation of the local visual environment. *Nature*, *392*, 598–601.

Ericsson, K. A., & Simon, H. A. (1993). *Protocol analysis: Verbal reports as data*. Cambridge, MA: The MIT Press.

Fich, L. B., Jönsson, P., Kirkegaard, P. H., Wallergård, Garde, A. H., & Hansen, Å. (2014). Can architectural design alter the physiological reaction to psychosocial stress? A virtual TSST experiment. *Physiology & Behavior*, *135*, 91–97.

Gazzaniga, M. S. (1998). *The mind's past*. Berkeley, CA: University of California Press.

Gazzaniga, M. S. (2000). Cerebral specialization and interhemispheric communication: does the corpus callosum enable the human condition? *Brain*, *123*, 1293–1326.

Gilbert, S. J., Zamenopoulos, T., Alexiou, K., & Johnson, J. H. (2009). Involvement of right dorsolateral prefrontal cortex in ill-structured design cognition: An fMRI study. *Brain Research*, *1312*, 79–88.

Gilhooly, K. J., Fiortou, E., Anthony, S. H., & Wynn, V. (2007). Divergent thinking: Strategies and executive involvement in generating novel uses for familiar objects. *British Journal of Psychology*, *98*, 611–625.

Goel, V. (1995). *Sketches of thought*. Cambridge, MA: MIT Press.

Goel, V. (2014). Creative brains: Designing in the real world. *Frontiers in Human Neuroscience*, 8, Article 241.

Goel, V., & Grafman, J. (2000). The role of the right prefrontal cortex in ill-structured problem solving. *Cognitive Neuropsychology*, *17*, 415–436.

Goel, V., & Vartanian, O. (2005). Dissociating the roles of right ventral lateral and dorsal lateral prefrontal cortex in generation and maintenance of hypotheses in set-shift problems. *Cerebral Cortex*, *15*, 1170–1177.

Goldberg, E., Podell, K., & Lovell, M. (1994). Lateralization of frontal lobe functions and cognitive novelty. *Journal of Neuropsychiatry*, *6*, 371–378.

Gough, H. A. (1956). *California Psychological Inventory*. Palo Alto, CA: Consulting Psychologists Press.

Hall, W. B., & MacKinnon, D. W. (1969). Personality inventory correlates of creativity among architects. *Journal of Applied Psychology*, *53*, 322–326.

Helson, R. (1999). Institute of Personality Assessment and Research. In M. A. Runco & S. R. Pritzker (Eds.), *Encyclopedia of creativity* (pp. 71–79). San Diego, CA: Academic Press.

Kirsch, C., Lubart, T., & Houssemand, C. (2016). Creativity in student architects: Multivariate approach. In G. E. Corazza & S. Agnoli (Eds.), *Multidisciplinary contributions to the science of creative thinking* (pp. 175–194). Singapore: Springer.

Klepeis, N. E., Nelson, W. C., Ott, W. R., Robinson, J. P. Tsang, A. M., Switzer, P., Behar, J. W., Hern, S. C., & Engelmann, W. H. (2001). The National Human Activity Pattern Survey (NHAPS): A resource for assessing exposure to environmental pollutants. *Journal of Exposure Analysis and Environmental Epidemiology*, *11*, 231–252.

Kravitz, D. J., Saleem, K. S., Baker, C. I., & Mishkin, M. (2011). A new neural framework for visuospatial processing. *Nature Reviews Neuroscience*, *12*, 217–230.

MacKinnon, D. W. (1962). The nature and nurture of creative talent. *American Psychologist*, *17*, 484–495.

MacKinnon, D. W. (1965). Personality and the realization of creative potential. *American Psychologist*, *20*, 273–281.

MacKinnon, D. W. (1978). *In search of human effectiveness*. Buffalo, NY: Bearly.

Mishkin, M., Ungerleider, L. G., & Macko, K. (1983). Object vision and spatial vision. *Trends in Neurosciences*, *6*, 414–417.

Nobre, A. C., Sebestyen, G. N., Gitelman, D. R., Mesulam, M. M., Frackowiak, R. S. J., & Frith, C. D. (1997). Functional localization of the system form visuospatial attention using positron emission tomography. *Brain*, *120*, 515–533.

Nusbaum, E. C., & Silvia, P. J. (2011). Are intelligence and creativity really so different?: Fluid intelligence, executive processes, and strategy use in divergent thinking. *Intelligence*, *39*, 36–45.

Ott, W. R. (1989). *Human activity patterns: A review of the literature for estimating time spent indoors, outdoors, and in transit*. Proceedings of the Research Planning Conference on Human Activity Patterns, EPA National Exposure Research Laboratory, EPA/600/4–89/004: Las Vegas, NV.

Poldrack, R. (2006). Can cognitive processes be inferred from neuroimaging data? *Trends in Cognitive Sciences*, *10*, 59–63.

Rutherford, H. J. V., & Lindell, A. K. (2011). Thriving and surviving: Approach and avoidance motivation and lateralization. *Emotion Review*, *3*, 333–343.

Silvia, P. J., & Barona, C. M. (2009). Do people prefer curved objects? Angularity, expertise, and aesthetic preference. *Empirical Studies of the Arts*, *27*, 25–42.

Silvia, P. J., Winterstein, B. P., Willse, J. T., Barona, C. M., Cram, J. T., Hess, K. I., Martinez, J. L., & Richard, C. A. (2008). Assessing creativity with divergent thinking tasks: Exploring the reliability and validity of new subjective scoring methods. *Psychology of Aesthetics, Creativity, and the Arts*, *2*, 68–85.

Sternberg, R. J. (Ed.). (1999). *Handbook of creativity*. Cambridge, MA: Cambridge University Press.

Terman, L. M. (1956). *Concept mastery test, form T manual*. New York: Psychological Corporation.

Ungerleider, L. G., & Mishkin, M. (1982). Two cortical visual systems. In D. J. Ingle, M. A. Goodale, & R. J. W. Mansfield (Eds.), *Analysis of visual behavior* (pp. 549–586). Cambridge, MA: MIT Press.

Urban, K. K., & Jellen, H. G. (1996). TCT-DP: Test for creative thinking-drawing production. Lisse, Netherlands: Swets and Zeitlinger.

Vartanian, O., & Goel, V. (2005). Task constraints modulate activation in right ventral lateral prefrontal cortex. *Neuroimage*, *27*, 927–933.

Vartanian, O., Navarrete, G., Chatterjee, A., Fich, L. B., Gonzalez-Mora, J. L., Leder, H., Modroño, C., Nadal, M., Rostrup, N., & Skov, M. (2015). Architectural design and the brain: Effects of ceiling height and perceived enclosure on beauty judgments and approach-avoidance decisions. *Journal of Environmental Psychology*, *41*, 10–18.

Vartanian, O., Navarrete, G., Chatterjee, A., Fich, L. B., Leder, H., Modroño, C., Nadal, M., Rostrup, N., & Skov, M. (2013). Impact of contour on aesthetic judgments and approach-avoidance decisions in architecture. *Proceedings of the National Academy of Sciences USA*, *110* (Suppl. 2), 10446–10453.

Vartanian, O., Vartanian, A., Beaty, R. E., Nusbaum, E. C., Silvia, P. J., Blackler, K., Lam Q, & Peele, E. (2014). Revered today, loved tomorrow: Expert creativity ratings predict popularity of architects 50 years later. In A. Kozbelt (Ed.), *Proceedings of the Twenty-third Biennial Congress of the International Association of Empirical Aesthetics* (pp. 47–51).

Watson, C. E., Cardillo, E. R., Ianni, G. R., & Chatterjee, A. (2013). Action concepts in the brain: An activation likelihood estimation meta-analysis. *Journal of Cognitive Neuroscience*, *25*, 1191–1205.

Weisberg, R. W. (2011). Frank Lloyd Wright's Fallingwater: A case study in inside-the-box creativity. *Creativity Research Journal*, *23*, 296–311.

8 Photography and Creativity

Joanna Serafin

The Graduate Center of CUNY (primary) & SUNY Downstate Medical Center (secondary)

Stephen J. Dollinger

Southern Illinois University at Carbondale

Abstract

This chapter reviews some aspects of creativity that are common to many artistic domains and particularly aspects that are distinctive about photography (e.g., the violence/entrapment metaphor, the role of timing and light, the issue of whether photography is merely a reproduction of reality with minimal creativity). Although photographers typically do not concern themselves with definitions of creativity, many have offered suggestions on how to judge photographic creativity which aids the measurement process. In this chapter we cover creativity in photography based on three different perspectives: (1) creative photographs, (2) expertise in creative photography, and (3) creative personality as studied through photographic autoportraits and photo essays. Consistent with the expansion of the literature, the rapid growth of digital technology suggests that this domain of creativity is entering its golden age.

It takes a lot of imagination to be a good photographer. You need less imagination to be a painter because you can invent things. But in photography everything is so ordinary; it takes a lot of looking before you learn to see the extraordinary.

David Bailey (Focal Power, 2009, quote 71)

What makes photography a strange invention – with unforeseeable consequences – is that its primary raw materials are light and time.

John Berger (2014, p. 55)

The simplicity of photography lies in the fact that it is very easy to make a picture. The staggering complexity of it lies in the fact that a thousand other pictures of the same subject would have been equally easy.

John Szarkowski (1973, p. 134)

Conceptual Overview

Although useful for documentary, portraiture, and fashion/advertising purposes, photography as *art* brings a wealth of new possibilities to the study of creativity, encompassing many unexplored avenues for understanding creative products, persons, processes, presses – including, in the minds of some photographers, the "pressure" to be creative. The functions of art include communication and inquiry into complex ideas, and photography is one of the artistic media that serve those important purposes (e.g., Brogowski, 1989; Cyr, 1968; Lavrentiev, 1994). As suggested by the opening quotations, photography is a new art and it brings unique philosophical or conceptual questions to the fore in a discussion of creativity. First, as noted by Sawyer (2006), a market for photographic art began to form (in the United States) in the 1960s, coinciding with "a rejection of many traditional notions of art: that it was the work of the hand, that each work was a unique creation" (Sawyer, 2006, p. 26). Moreover, in the 1970s, photography "took on the characteristics associated with art: the valuation of originality and uniqueness, the system of galleries, museums, and collectors, the supporting network of experts to evaluate value and confirm authenticity" (Sawyer, 2006, p. 26).

Second, unlike other domains, photography can involve metaphors of violence and entrapment or capturing the subject in the moment. Photographers and photographic scholars implicitly use violence metaphors in their language of "pointing and shooting" pictures (Sontag, 1977; cf. Berger, 1980). Using a similar metaphor of theft, social psychologist Stanley Milgram viewed the act of taking a photo as an unfair exchange between photographer and person photographed when the former "takes the picture" of the latter (Milgram, 1977, p. 343). He claimed that, even in photographing landmarks, "it is seizing the image through one's own act that seems uniquely satisfying" to the novice (p. 342). As a result, unlike other domains of creativity, there is a tension between subjects' privacy and the public display of photographs, particularly given the value of authenticity (Perlson, 2015, see also Milgram, 1977). However, not all scholars endorse such metaphors. Navab (2001) prefers to view the photographic act with the term *photo making*, bringing it in line with *art making* in other creative endeavors. This idea of picture making versus picture taking is also prominent in other photographers' accounts and it is related to the degree of conscious involvement, with the picture-making approach being more deliberate. Halsman (1961) asserted that there are two kinds of photographers: those who take photographs by grabbing already existing moments and those who make photographs. The former are visual reporters concerned mostly with objectivity and the latter are creators who stage and direct photography sessions and actively decide what to put in front of the camera.

The previous point leads to the third concept. Unlike other creative domains, the moment of taking a photograph is critical. Probably most artistic photographs are not created so much as discovered – requiring the photographer, as it were, to wait and then shoot the photo at the critical or *decisive moment* (Cartier-Bresson, 1999).

A fourth issue is whether photography merely reproduces reality. Susan Sontag (1977) argued that "a photograph is not only an image (as a painting is an image), an interpretation of the real; it is also a trace, something directly stenciled off the real" (p. 154). If so, is it creative? In his essay "Uses of photography," John Berger (1980) replied to Sontag by asserting that photographs are not renderings but rather traces of events and because of that photographs belong more to the event or subject photographed than to the "creator."

Fifth, modern technologies allow most people to take photographs – a feature which some view as undermining the artistic or creative status of photography (Yu,

2004). Thus, photography is unique because its technology is such an inherent part of the process as to imply that the origin of a creative photo is the equipment! This is particularly so today when everyone can use cell-phone cameras with little instruction. Hence, the role of human abstraction or rendering (and therefore credit deserved) is not immediately obvious. This rapid technological expansion also contributes to the uniqueness of the study of creativity in photography. Whereas occasionally one hears "your camera takes nice pictures," one never or very rarely hears parallel statements such as "your brushes paint nice paintings, your word processor composes insightful stories, your pots cook tasty meals, or your piano makes beautiful pieces."

Finally, in technology-heavy and fast-evolving domains like photography, the creative process plays out differently and therefore the product might not be considered as valuable. If we look at the creative process as a continuum of ideation and elaboration (Martindale, 1994; Simonton, 1997), photography appears as immediate and almost pure ideation or "illumination" (Wallas, 1926). That is, there is no laboring over a wet canvas, days on end in a studio, painting over, erasing, starting over. Although it is possible for photographers to do so, their post-capture editing is thus not always so evident. Because time and light are the raw materials, photographers must be willing to let go of the urges to elaborate, perfect, or just tinker – they do so when they take more products or shots. Perhaps that is why many people are really drawn to this immediate nature – no hassle, no pulling hair over lack of direction, quick grab and go! However, do photographers really just "grab" or "take" and go to the next? The key aspect of this medium, this "art," is the art of selection – most importantly the art of selecting the right machine, moment, and light. Photography is unique in that photographers share at least some of the credit with their tool – their photo equipment. Therefore, photography is the art of co-seeing between the human and the machine. Holleley (2009) wrote: "All photography is a process of selection. Initially the photographer goes out into the world and selects slivers of time and space. Subsequently, after the images are processed, individual images are selected from the proof sheet and printed. Finally, there comes a stage when these images accumulate to the point at which another selection process comes into play. This final stage is called editing" (p. 3; see also Simonton, 2011 for a description of the blind variation and selective retention (BVSR) model of creativity). This process of selection has continuously changed with the addition and expansion of digital photography which added versatility and tools for creators, e.g., camera LCD preview screens allow immediate review and selection, some photo-storing software packages group similar images together based on metadata (Rodden & Wood, 2003).

The preceding six distinct aspects of creativity in photography point to the role of technology and context as necessary components of creative photography in addition to the role of creative individual photographers. Nowadays, photographic technology involves digital data, meta-data, immediate sharing, and crowdsourcing, and, as the role of those elements is becoming more pronounced, the notion of meta-creativity becomes more important. The feasibility of production of vast amounts of visual renderings creates pressure for photographers to get creative about their creativity. Glăveanu (2010) described meta-creativity as involving a "multiple feed-back" social creativity process. Presumably, the same pressure can be observed in other technologically heavy domains like coding or video production.

Defining Creativity

Within psychology, most definitions of creativity focus on the dual aspects of novelty/originality and usefulness/value (Mayer, 1999). Bayles and Orland (2001) remarked: "Creativity. Readers may wish to note that *nowhere* in this book [that is, their own book] does the dreaded C-word appear. *Why should it?* Do only some people have ideas, confront problems, dream, live in a real world?" (p. 100). This indicates that artists – in this case photographers – rarely worry about *definitions*. Nevertheless, Jaeger's (2007) interviews of twenty photographers (as well as curators, gallerists, and photography editors) hint at the perspective of professional photographers. Among her interview questions, the most instructive for our purposes included these: What makes one image work (or stand out) better than another? Where do you get your inspiration? What would you like to elicit in the viewer of your photographs? Do you know beforehand whether something will be interesting?

Like classic definitions of creativity, novelty or originality came up in several interviews. For example, portraiture photographer Rineke Dijkstra desires "to show things that you might not see in normal life. I make normal things appear special. I want people to look at life in a new and different way … but … always based on reality" (in Jaeger, 2007, p. 139). Anton Corbijn similarly noted "I hope to capture something you've not seen before" (in Jaeger, 2007, p. 132).

In terms of the second aspect – value or usefulness – photographers hope that their product communicates with and elicits an emotional response in the viewer, for example when it prompts recognition of the viewer's common humanity with the subject (Zehr, 2009). Fashion/advertising photographer David LaChapelle drew an analogy to music, commenting "I think people like things that touch them … to be authentic … like soul music … you don't need the perfect voice but if someone sings with a voice that's full of emotion, people will respond to it. The same goes for photography" (in Jaeger, 2007, p. 89). As to what he hopes to capture, portraiture photographer Anton Corbijn tersely noted "Emotion – the rare element" (Jaeger, 2007, p. 132). Rankin, a portraiture photographer who frequently employs humor, hopes that the viewer "will have an emotional response" (ibid., p. 154). (Interestingly, he observed that photography is 99 percent business, connections, and politics and only 1 percent creativity.) William Eggleston, an artistic photographer, would like the viewer "to study the entire picture and everything that's in it [and] that the image would register in the viewer's mind after seeing it in print" (ibid., p. 24). Fashion photographer Mario Sorrenti claimed, "I want my pictures to ask questions. I want people to look at my pictures and have an emotional response. I want them to think: What am I seeing? What does it mean? Do I love it? Do I hate it?" (ibid., p. 103). Thus, photographers seem to focus more on the second element of classic creativity definitions, that their creative products have value or usefulness primarily by their impact on the observer's emotions; and they have a communicative function that illustrates aspects of life, individuality, or humanity.

Unlike other domains of creativity, photography raises questions about whether the product is just a simple rendering of reality, or the interaction of reality and the photographer. This is illustrated by a quote from Josef Albers, who argued that "photographs reveal the individuality of a photographer if we as spectators are able to read it . . . only a sensitive and trained eye gives us the right to judge, as it gives us a deeper reading and enjoyment" (cited by Ansel Adams (2007, p. 6), from an unpublished lecture by Albers at Black Mountain College February 24, 1943, preserved in the Josef Albers Foundation).

Although incidental to the definition of creativity, a number of the interviewees commented on the importance of *serendipity* or spontaneity and freedom or intrinsic motivation, common to the process of other creative arts. Eggleston observed that he never knows whether something will be interesting: "It just happens all at once . . . sometimes I'll leave the house with a fully loaded camera and end up with nothing. It's just about being there. Anywhere. Even the most uninteresting, ugly or boring places can for an instant become magical to me" (in Jaeger, 2007, p. 24). Stephen Shore, an artistic photographer, touched on a related theme: "I love it when I look at a work of art and it opens my eyes to something, something unexpected happens or I experience something emotional, psychological or perceptual" (ibid., p. 51). Similarly, documentary photographer Mary Ellen Mark prefers "not to think ahead about what I'm going to say with my photographs. I would rather be surprised and see what my subjects bring to the photograph" (ibid., p. 54). Tina Barney (portraiture) commented "I think that's one of the things people really like about my pictures – there are a lot of accidents" (ibid., p. 121). In a similar vein, Corbijn commented that freedom is one attraction to the profession: "I see photography as an adventure. I like to discover where my boundaries are and what I can do with each person I meet" (ibid., p. 130). Dijkstra similarly noted that the photographer draws on his or her intuition and passion and that "you have to be open for anything to happen" (ibid., p. 139). This readiness to embrace serendipity indicates photographers' masterful understanding of time, space, and working through selection of the best of many potential images (Hurn & Jay, 2008).

In sum, common themes in these interviews suggest that photographers implicitly define creativity in terms of novelty and value – especially the communicative impact on the viewer's emotions, common humanity, or understanding of life. Additionally, photographers seem to value a number of aspects of openness: intuition, absorption, aesthetic impacts, spontaneity, focus on inner meanings or hidden realities, openness to the unexpected or the surprise (Bruner, 1962; Simonton, 2012). Specifically, through mastering technical details – such as exposure, lighting, and lens choices, and composition – photographers hone their photographic instincts. That is, they develop the art of "seeing" including the ability to capture unexpected beauty, different points of view and *decisive moments* (Cartier-Bresson, 1999). Good photographers know that "it's far better to capture the right moment with the wrong settings, rather than the wrong moment with the right settings" (Carroll, 2014, p. 104).

In subsequent parts of this chapter, we will consider three strategies for research in this area. First, we briefly consider research on qualities of the photograph itself which influence its value. Second, we examine expertise of professional as compared with novice photographers. Third, we review research in Personality Psychology using the method of auto-photography (that is, Ziller's (1990/2000) technique of taking/selecting photos to answer the question "who are you?"). For these latter studies, the richness and individuality of the total photo essay can be viewed as the person's self-applied creativity.

Measurement of Photographic Creativity

One place to start a discussion of the measurement of creative photography is with the advice of curators making gallery or museum selections and experts for juried competitions. Curators act as connectors between photographers and the audience, the space, the institution, the press, and the art world at large. Ansel Adams compared a photo negative to the musical score and an exhibition to a finished performance. By analogy, photographers are composers and curators are orchestra conductors (Read, 2013). Inka Graeve Ingelmann, Head of Photography at Pinakothek der Moderne in Munich, asserted that when she curates an exhibition she needs to feel that the work grabs her emotionally, "hits a nerve," makes her think, or even makes her angry (Read, 2013). John Gill of the Brighton Photo Biennial works "organically" by selecting one or two artists and then generates the idea of the exhibition by discussing it with them and with other artists. Curators aim to show meanings and connections between photographs that photographers, in their attachment to their work, may miss. They have an extensive knowledge of photography and current trends which they apply to choose work to exhibit. Sandra Phillips, a curator at the San Francisco Museum of Modern Art, explained that photographers and photo collectors usually have idiosyncratic styles and interests while curators "try to be different, because we try to be responsible for the whole thing. Obviously our personal interests and prejudices come in, but we try and think of the larger overview of photography, it's role, it's history and all of that, and where these pieces fit into the puzzle" (PhotoWings, undated).

Several photographers have also discussed the task of judging. Jim Richardson of *National Geographic* speaks of the "rush of recognition . . . a visceral or emotional reaction" when initially scanning photographs allowing an initial sort into those that are more creative and those 'me too shots' that you've 'seen for 15 years'" (Wignall, 2009). He advises making a photo that "at its heart [has] something that offers real communication that would get to another human being." Nuhn (2011), a judge of wildlife photos, uses five criteria, including: originality, technical excellence, composition, artistic merit, and overall impact. Gampat (2014) argues that photo judging is inherently subjective and depends to some extent unfortunately on popularity but also the context or purpose of the photo. For the Professional Photographers of America, Bob Hawkins (undated) proposed twelve elements of a quality image: impact (evoking emotion), creativity, technical excellence, composition, lighting, style, print presentation, center of interest, subject matter, color balance, technique, and story telling. Of particular relevance to our purposes, he defined impact as "the sense one gets upon viewing an image for the first time. Compelling images evoke laughter, sadness, anger, pride, wonder or another intense emotion." He defined creativity as "the original, fresh, and external expression of the imagination of the maker by using the medium to convey an idea, message or thought." In general, then, competition judges' criteria often involve three things: (1) creativity; (2) photographic technical quality; and (3) genuineness or authenticity of the content. Some competitions downplay the first two but give priority to authenticity. In general, creativity is judged separately from technical quality. However, it is rare for judges to define creativity, instead operating on the implicit assumption that qualified judges will "know it when they see it."

An academic study of aesthetic judgment (Serafin, 2013) found that expert photographers have clearer criteria for judging quality of photographs and they associate overall quality with multiple characteristics such as pleasantness, appeal, content, expressiveness, composition, and *technical quality*; in contrast, non-experts' criteria are less well defined and overall quality is associated with technical quality separate from other characteristics. Professional photographers indeed seem to separate judging originality from other criteria. Hattersley (1962) provided an extensive set of criteria for evaluating photographs and photographers which include: goal, value, situation, understanding, interpretation, sensitivity, visual literacy, timeliness, control of medium, addressing audience, communication, feeling, invention, meaning, gimmicks, translatability into words, and art. Contemporary commercial photographer Ming Thein (2012a) asserted that outstanding images are products of extreme selectivity and effort and resonate with viewers on several levels: technical, compositional, cultural, psychological, and personal – the latter two being highly subjective. More systematic research is needed to pinpoint how photographic creativity is measured and the exact elements that make photographs creative.

As mentioned above, there already exist three distinct lines of research within the psychological study of creative photography. These lines use different samples and methods, and address different research questions. One line focuses on the photograph itself and experimentally dissects elements that contribute to the final product as judged by novices and/or professionals usually by presenting raters with carefully chosen sets of photographic images to represent variation in technical quality and content (e.g., Axelsson, 2007; Tinio, Leder & Strasser, 2011). Since aesthetics, creativity, and art are intimately connected, demonstrating aesthetic value in photographs points indirectly to the creative process and artistic value of such images (see also Chapter 6, cowritten by Pablo Tinio, a psychologist and former photographer, in this volume).

A second and emerging line examines the work of professional in comparison to novice or amateur photographers as well as novices and professional photographers as raters of photographic work. The latter comparison not only potentially provides a look into the differences in aesthetic judgment criteria; it also is the source of the dependent measure of quality of photographic work. For example, a study by McManus, Zhou, l'Anson, Waterfield, Stover and Cook (2011) using photographic cropping examined the effect of expertise along with other aspects like meaning and color on photo composition and as judged by separate groups of experts and non-experts. Another example was a study by Domino and Giuliani (2007), which was designed to add validation to Domino's Creativity scale for the Adjective Check List rather than explicate aspects of the photographers' creativity. Serafin's (2013) quasi-experimental studies examined novice and professional groups' ability to identify photographic flaws which addressed differences in technical skill. The four types of flaws studied were: lens, lighting, composition, and subject. A "no flaw" category was included to distinguish "correct" or technically sound photographs from the technically flawed ones. Using a cropping task, a second study explored creative expertise by asking professional photographers and novices to capture images under spatially or temporally constrained conditions and later to select their best images. The dependent measures were quality ratings of the resulting images obtained from another group of experts and non-experts. This type of dependent measure has been used for quite some time by creativity and expertise researchers (Getzels & Csikszentmihalyi, 1976; Hekkert & Van Wieringen, 1996; Kozbelt, 2006; Kozbelt & Serafin, 2009) and has yielded moderate to high interrater agreement for experts and lower or no agreement for nonexperts. In Serafin's (2013) studies the Cronbach's alpha statistics were high, ranging between .80 and .95. In addition, neuroscientific research has begun to use brain imaging techniques, such as fMRI, to examine patterns of brain activation during expert and non-expert performance (e.g., Solso, 2001; Feltovich, Prietula & Ericsson, 2006).

A third line of photography research has grown out of Robert Ziller's (1990/2000) auto-photography technique in which participants were invited to take and select photos that answer the question "who are you?"(Dollinger, Robinson & Ross, 1999; Dollinger, 2006, 2011). Initially Ziller (1977) referred to a "phenomenological use of photographs" (Ziller, 1977), or a "photographic approach to self-concept" (Combs & Ziller, 1977); in later studies he labelled the technique as auto-photography (e.g., Ziller & Lewis, 1981; Ziller & Rorer, 1985). Ziller (1990/2000) viewed the technique as "an invitation to creativity" (p. 143) and referred to the "rich revealingness" of photo essays (p. 37). Dollinger and Clancy (1993) built on that notion by rating the richness of college student photo essays. They later identified this as the quality of *individuality* (Dollinger & Clancy Dollinger, 1997), defined as "creativity applied to the self." Low-rated photo essays are almost interchangeable with one another in depicting very stereotypic lives (e.g., "self as partier"). Intermediate-level photo essays provide more differentiation to the self (e.g., including aspects of self in various roles without integration) and little focus on creative expression. Highly rated photo essays used metaphor, poetry, and aesthetics to portray complexity, depth, and uniqueness to the self. Viewing the latter style of photo essay evokes the same responses desired by the professional photographers quoted above. That is, highly rated photo essays touch the viewer emotionally and draw the viewer into spending time for more detailed study of the photos and words used. (For numerous examples and descriptions of the five levels, see the appendix in

Dollinger & Clancy Dollinger, 1997.) In this research program, photo essays were usually viewed by three or four raters; Cronbach alpha reliabilities on these individuality/richness ratings were very good (ranging from .86 to .94, Dollinger & Clancy Dollinger, 2003; Dollinger, 2011).

Key Studies on Photography and Creativity

Creative Photographs

According to Shore (2007), photographs can be viewed on three levels: physical, depictive, and mental. This means that photos exist as physical objects with specific visual grammar whose meanings vary with perceptions and mental models of viewers. In the context of visual design (*Baird's Model*, Cleveland, 2005), the *visual power* of graphic design varies depending on viewers' interest in the material – the lower the interest, the higher the need for visual power. For example, newsletters directed at a specialized audience may not need a high degree of visual power. However, consumer magazines whose aim is to appeal to a very broad audience may need a high degree of visual power to excite the reader and provide an understandable visual grammar. Perhaps there exist visual, depictive, and mental variables characteristic of photographs and the relationships between them determine viewers' responses; for example, high-content photographs like portraits would need less visual power to entice viewers. Indeed, many variables can be manipulated to achieve creative photographs: subject selection, timing, technical aspects such as composition, focal length, choice of lighting, and cropping to communicate both composition and the main idea behind a photograph (McManus, Zhou, l'Anson, Waterfield, Stover & Cook, 2011). The aesthetic appeal of photographs is influenced by viewers' familiarity with content, expressiveness, format (color vs. black/white), and pleasantness (Axelsson, 2007), technical quality associated with contrast, sharpness, and film grain (Tinio, Leder, & Strasser, 2011), content type, complexity (Tinio & Leder, 2009), and challenges to visual processing through various artistic devices such as visual abstraction, line depiction, framing, cropping, visual balance, visual continuation, peak-shift effect, sharpness of depiction, and speed of processing (Tinio & Leder, 2013). These devices challenge viewers by engaging lower levels of visual processing as well as higher-order cognition or meaning making, and this multilayered process may be responsible for the pleasure of interacting with art. The challenge of art is its power. Photographic art engages viewers in visual problem solving and their successful solutions contribute to pleasurable art viewing experience (Tinio & Leder, 2013; see also Chapter 6, this volume). In addition, photographs are produced through a process of subtraction or selection as contrasted with the additive process of painting and they necessarily appear intentional since they resemble what viewers perceive. Photographs are potent because of the human top-down tendency to close the gap between the representation and what is possible based on viewers' experience (Beilin, 1991).

Photographic Expertise

Beauty has been shown to be in the eye of the beholder and expertise level is one of the factors that affect viewer experience. Beilin (1991) asserted that the ability to process photographs is developed along with the development of knowledge about the world through construction of cognitive schemata based on perceptual information. Professional photographers have been shown to possess a better ability to process photographic information (Axelsson, 2007). Specifically, they prefer photographs that are more expressive and uncertain whereas non-experts prefer images that are familiar and pleasant. Serafin (2013) demonstrated differences in technical knowledge and creativity between experts and novices. Professional photographers were more discriminating in judging quality and more likely to detect and define photographic flaws in lighting, lens, composition, and subject (as specified by a sample of professional photographers in the preceding stimulus generation study). Creativity was assessed through photo-cropping tasks and was also higher among experts. The croppings were generated based on a still image and on a video, and all were asked to select their *best*. As compared to novices, experts' croppings were rated more highly by expert photographer raters. The selection skill is especially crucial in the multi-step process of digital photo editing: from the crude in-camera preview screen selection, through first computer screen view and selection, and the highly selective final cut that eliminates most but a small percentage of best quality images before delivery to an appropriate outlet (Thein, 2012b). The cropping tasks were designed to tap into participants' work with: (1) *space* by cropping out of a complex image, (2) capturing images at *optimal times* by pausing a video at visually interesting moments, and (3) both *space and time simultaneously* by pausing and cropping at the same time to best mimic the actual experience of taking photos. Photographers outperformed amateurs on all tasks. However, the products were rated on overall quality and *not* creativity; as shown in the same research, originality was not strongly related to overall quality (Serafin, 2013). Consequently, quality is not sufficient and potentially independent of establishing creativity; rather, establishing novelty and appropriateness to context are necessary. For example, when discussing creativity of a work of art or an invention, one must place it within specific historical context (Fleenor & Taylor, 2004). In sum, the limited work to date shows a number of differences between professional and novice photographers on photography-relevant skills.

Auto-photographic Studies of the Creative Personality

Auto-photography allows both qualitative and quantitative studies using an individual-differences approach by examining a variety of correlates of the individuality (or richness) of college student photo essays. As noted above, in this research program, individuality has been defined as "creativity applied to the self." There are a number of categories of correlates: photographic content as well as word use in the written portion of the essay, other measures of creativity, Big Five personality factors, openness-related personality traits, identity, intellectual abilities, age, and values (Dollinger, 2017). College students who devise the least individualistic photo essays tend to use their cameras in the most conventional way – that is, they take pictures of people in their social lives or families (cf. Milgram, 1977). They also include many more photos of alcohol than do their individualistic peers (i.e., photos in bars, photos showing people holding alcoholic beverages, posters depicting favorite brands). Thus, their photo content is in keeping with the lowest-level description of conveying a stereotypic partying college student.

Since photo essays are creative products, not surprisingly, the richest photo essays are devised by individuals who are creative in other ways. For example, such participants come up with more unusual word associations (Dollinger, Robinson & Ross, 1999), devise more creative drawings to an ambiguous stimulus (Dollinger, Urban & James, 2004), and report more creative accomplishments on the Creative Behavior Inventory (Dollinger et al., 2004). The correlations are usually statistically significant, albeit of a .2 to .3 magnitude.

With various Big Five personality measures, the richer more individualistic photo essays are devised by students who are higher in openness to experience (the largest and most consistent correlate; see Dollinger & Clancy, 1993). Individualistic participants also tend to score as somewhat higher on agreeableness and neuroticism and lower in extraversion, although these personality factors are not always statistically significant. In keeping with their higher openness, individualistic students have scored as having more permeable boundaries, a greater need for uniqueness, and imagined themselves involved in more culturally diverse future activities (Dollinger, 2003; Dollinger et al., 1999).

Openness to Experience is always marked by a creative aesthetic orientation but also by intellectual curiosity and cognitive complexity. Dollinger, Preston, O'Brien, and DiLalla (1996) showed that individualistic photo essayists were characterized by both higher vocabulary knowledge and higher ego development. Subsequent studies showed that individualistic photo essayists exhibited greater preference for complexity and broader interests, curiosity, need for cognition, and investigative vocational interests (Dollinger, 2003; Dollinger, Ross & Preston, 2002; Dollinger et al., 1999b). This quality of intellectual openness showed up in photographic individuality/richness ratings. Qualitative analyses of photo essays compared small groups of particularly high- and low-intellect participants. That is, the seven related scales from different measures were standardized and combined – intellectual openness to experience, breadth of interests, holding an academic philosophy of college attendance, endorsing more investigative vocational interests, higher need for cognition, higher trait curiosity, and higher scores on the adjective-based Big Five marker scale for the intellect factor (for details see Dollinger et al, 2002). From this composite, we identified the highest and lowest dozen participants (i.e., nine women and three men) and reexamined their photo essays. Within their photo essays, high-intellect participants tended to include themes about their enjoyment of books, love of learning, admiration for scientific heroes, and their appreciation for the intelligence of particular friends with whom they spend time – themes revealing their individuality! High-intellect participants also commented on their creativity, concern for nature and the environment, career explorations, nonconformity, and quest-oriented rather than traditional religiosity.

Low-intellect participants focused on the happiness of their social lives and, among women, their love of children.

We found convincing evidence that individuality/richness of photo essays predicts being a dedicated and competent student. Students who endorse a more intellectual/academic philosophy of college (learning for its own sake) scored higher on individuality/richness than those with social or vocational orientations to college (Dollinger et al., 2002). Individualists scored higher on the ACT college admissions test (Dollinger, 2011) and they devoted more of their time to study (Dollinger, 2017). The intellectual orientation of individualistic students' is also shown in their love of reading and their reading preferences, with a focus on the more academically oriented reading factors of humanities and social sciences, and fiction; more conventional (or low-individuality/richness) students' interests ran toward the news/sports and romance/sexuality factors (Dollinger, 2016).

Individualistic students' cognitive focus is evident in how they write about their photos. Burke and Dollinger (2005) applied Pennebaker's Linguistic Inquiry and Word Count (LIWC; Pennebaker, Francis, & Booth 2001) program to the words used in participants' auto-photography essays. As predicted, analyses showed that individuality/richness ratings correlated not only with word count but with the higher-order categories of cognitive word use and (negatively) with social process words. In particular, high-individuality photo essays were best characterized by specific categories of insight, tentativeness, self-discrepancy, and metaphysical words but by low-frequency usage of words referring to friends, family, or leisure. In short, individualist photo-essayists presented as unique and complex people, oriented more toward self-exploration and existential concerns and less toward peers and leisure activities.

Additional cross-sectional evidence indicates that the individuality/richness of photo essays increases with age (Dollinger & Clancy Dollinger, 2003) and with identity development in Eriksonian and other conceptual frameworks (Dollinger & Clancy Dollinger, 1997). Thus, participants who have engaged in more identity exploration depict greater auto-photographic richness. Interestingly, older participants included more black-and-white photos and photographically depict their creative activity more than do younger participants (Dollinger & Clancy Dollinger, 2003, p. 233). Older participants also included relatively more photos depicting their work, achievements, and religiosity.

Finally, individuality/richness has been correlated with social-political value orientations using the Rokeach and Schwartz paradigm of values surveys plus more direct liberal-conservative political values (Dollinger, 2007; Dollinger, Burke & Gump, 2007). For space considerations, we cannot fully describe the paradigms and measures; interested readers are referred to Dollinger (2017). Here we merely note that richer photo essays (and other creativity measures) were devised by participants who preferentially endorsed self-direction, universalism, and stimulation values but devalued power, security, conformity, and tradition values. These correlates seem to fit well with the picture that individualists live and work creatively and are less concerned about conforming to social boundaries. Moreover, based on the observation that low creativity is assumed to reflect conservative thinking in a variety of domains (clothing design, criminology, elementary education, information technology, and management), Dollinger (2007) examined the association of social-political conservatism and creative photo essays, drawings, and a creativity checklist, finding support for this connection. However, some of the variance (for drawings and photo essays) was attributable to verbal intelligence and/or openness to experience. Qualitatively, conservative participants' photo essays often depicted religious or family values and satisfaction with their lives; liberal students' photo essays conveyed boundary-crossing behaviors, creative endeavors, and exercise of their civil liberties in unconventional ways.

Values were also considered in a seven-year follow-up questionnaire study (Dollinger, 2006). Along with open-ended questions about creative accomplishments, participants rated fifteen work values (things that people might desire or value in their jobs). Individuality/richness (while in college) predicted creative involvements on average five years after college and predicted the extent to which participants valued creative opportunities in their workplaces. In short, it seems clear that individualistic persons hold to values that promote their creativity and imagination, and they oppose conservative values which they feel constrain that freedom or demand conformity to the normative. They also seem less concerned with economic reward/security but are focused on "internal" values like inner harmony and wisdom. In sum, although Ziller never directly studied creativity with his autophotography task, our research program has shown that it reveals a great deal about the personalities, values, and inner lives of creative personalities.

Other studies have focused on the question of whether photographs reflect something about the photographer – in effect whether unstructured photo making can be a kind of projective technique. Kulich and Goldberg (1978) compared the photographs of extravert and introvert college students who posed two models in a laboratory for eight photos each; they reported that, compared to introverts, the photos of extraverts were rated higher on the dimension of activity. Another early study by Henry and Solano (1983) showed many personality-by-photo category correlations although the findings were exploratory; 47 of 220 possible correlations were significant, albeit based on a sample of just 23 students taking photographs. In our own initial study of 201 college students producing 12-photo autophotography essays, Extraversion and Agreeableness were good predictors of interpersonal connectedness: In particular, these personality factors correlated with the numbers of photos depicting people touching; groups of four or more; people in the background; and self with others, parents/grandparents, and children (Dollinger & Clancy, 1993). Notably, the excitement-seeking facet of NEO-PI extraversion was a highly significant predictor of photos containing alcoholic beverages or insignia (Dollinger & Clancy, 1993; replicated in Dollinger, 1996). Other studies on specific content codes suggest that, in photo essays, "what you see *is* what you get" with respect to content like religion, achievement, alcohol, and work (Dollinger, 1996; Dollinger, 2001). In sum, based on a limited number of studies, there are hints that photographs taken might reflect the personalities of the photographers. Obviously, much more work can be done with professional and amateur photographers to study this broad question.

Future Directions

Photographs have considerable stimulus potential and thus will continue to be useful in a variety of psychological domains beyond creativity. For example, photos can be powerful stimuli for emotional and psychophysiological responses (Bernat, Patrick, Benning, & Tellegen, 2006; Ekman, 1965; Herpertz, Kunert, Schwenger, & Sass, 1999) and are very useful in studies of memory processes (Aschermann, Dannenberg, & Schulz, 1998; Garry & Wade, 2005; Schacter, Koutstaal, Johnson, Gross, & Angell, 1997). Photographs also have considerable utility in social psychological studies of person or issue perception, stereotypes, and prejudice (Mahaffey, Bryan, & Hutchison, 2005; Vidulich & Krevanick, 1966; Zebrowitz, Hall, Murphy, & Rhodes, 2002; Zillmann, Gibson, & Sargent, 1999). Moreover, therapists of a variety of orientations have reported the benefits of using photography within the treatment process (for a small sample see Ginicola, Smith & Trzaska, 2012; Kaslow & Friedman, 1977; Walker, 1991). To better understand the growth in such areas, we conducted a Google Scholar publication search including the words "creativity," "psychology," and either "photography" or "poetry." The results showed (1) a dramatic acceleration in the number of publications since the 1940s and (2) literature mentioning photography catching up with literature on poetry (see Figure 8.1). Hence we can expect continued growth of interest in integrating photography and the psychology of creativity and perhaps to exceed the trends in other artistic media. Future research should also explore the tremendous gaps in the literature on photographic expertise, creativity and psychology; e.g., to examine the extent to which creative individuals reveal their creativity and individuality via different photography modalities.

As in other arts, photographic products have been evaluated and incorporated into the domain by gatekeepers which may represent experts or scholars comprising the

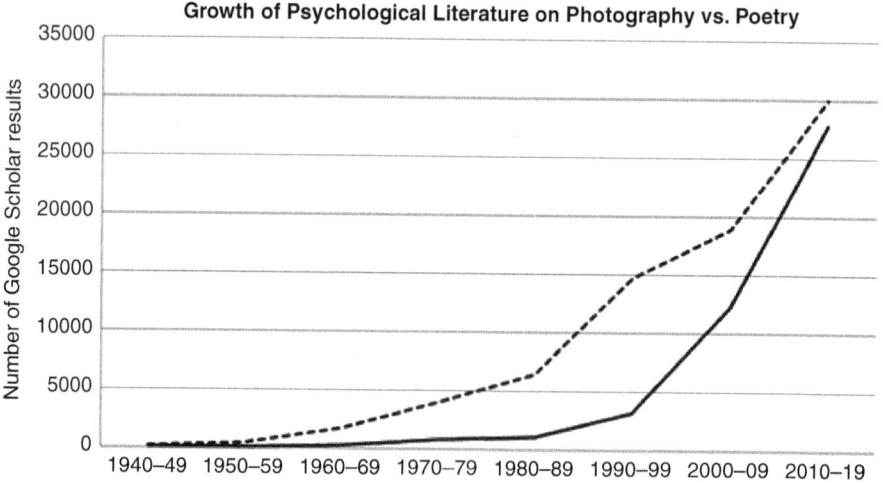

Figure 8.1 *Numbers of Google Scholar search results for combinations of the words "creativity," "psychology," and either "photography" (solid) or "poetry" (dashes) over 8 decades (2010–2019 prorated from 5.5 years).*

field component of the *system* (see Systems Model, Csikszentmihalyi, 1999). However, new technologies allow for rapid online evaluation, potentially expanding the notion of the *field* or gatekeeper. With online applications like Instagram, the process of production and selection of best artistic photographs has been greatly condensed. Juried online photography is common (1X.com, National Geographic, Nikon, World Press Photo) and allows people from all over the world to submit their work. The democratization of the medium, which was arguably the most democratic of the arts from the get-go, continues in the twenty-first century and it arguably has not affected the quality and creativity of photographs. It would be interesting to see if the sheer quantity will produce an explosion of high-quality creative products. MoMa's photo curator Quentin Bajac observed "I think that a younger generation expresses itself through the internet, though self-published books, and in very different forms, and we museums have to adapt to that" (Risch, 2014). New technological advances – such as the RED digital cameras which allow capturing high-quality still images from videos or Lytro Illum which allow refocusing a photograph after the fact – mixed with older techniques still used by some fine art photographers (e.g., platinum printing), provide a great variety of tools for photographers to express their ideas and improve their craft. Perhaps with this technological expansion, the role of photographers will expand as they will be able to see their work from capture to display through self-publishing.

An issue that deserves more research focus is how photographers *select* photos and to what extent they are supported in this task by editors or curators who oversee the coherence of photo stories, series, or exhibition themes. W. Eugene Smith, for example, resigned from *Life* magazine when he felt he was not given enough control over his own work. Subsequently, he failed at putting together a photo essay by showing too many photographs – a whopping eighty-eight images in eighty-four pages; an extreme length for any magazine (Hurn & Jay, 2008). Think-aloud methods might be informative as professional photographers – as well as college student auto-photographers – move from the photo-making to the photo-presenting stages (Fayena-Tawil, Kozbelt & Sitaras, 2011). In regard to students, it would be interesting too to modify instructions by asking auto-photographers to place their most important (creative or identity-revealing) images first in their photo essays.

Photography is likely becoming the main tool for facilitating creative behavior and shaping aesthetic sense on a large scale. How can we measure the exact process and usefulness of such an impact? Perhaps the most fruitful psychological use of photographs will be in the study of social networking sites and personal websites. Particularly for researchers with an interest in auto-photography, an obvious study should examine the similarities and differences between impressions created by auto-photographic essays and by the same participants' social network postings. Person-perception research suggests that trait inferences (e.g., extroversion) from online self-depictions are reasonably accurate (Back, Stopfer, Vazire, Gaddis, Schmukle, Egloff, & Gosling, 2010; Gosling, Augustine, Vazire, Holtzman & Gaddis, 2011; Marcus, Machilek & Schütz, 2006). Not surprisingly, social network sites and auto-photographic essays both contain information about likes and dislikes and people's social and cultural lifestyles (Ivcevic & Ambady, 2013), but occasionally both include sexualized photos or problematic depictions of substance use (Karl, Peluchette & Schlaegel, 2010). Moreover, they share similar issues regarding privacy (Christofides, Muise, & Desmarais, 2009). Of course, given the instructions to the auto-photography task, individuality would not be expected to relate to photographic excellence per se – although openness and intelligence might contribute to both. Other valuable directions include cross-cultural explorations of auto-photographic individuality and longitudinal studies of the development of family, peer, and romantic relationships of young adults who differ in individuality/richness (Dollinger, 2017). Recalling Sorrenti's comment (wanting "people to look at my pictures and have an emotional response"), another direction is to expand the base of auto-photography by considering participant-viewers' emotional responses to their own and others' photo essays. To what extent do photo essays elicit similar emotional responses in different judges?

Many psychological phenomena are being investigated at the level of brain activation, and neuroaesthetics is an emergent research area (see work of Dr. Anjan Chatterjee, 2013). The cognitive neuroscience of photo creativity and expertise will likely provide a richer explanation of the process by developing better methodology for study (e.g., use of fMRI, eye tracking) and pointing to neural mechanisms related to creative behavior in photography. Using survey and eye-tracking methods, Quinn (2015) explored factors that determine the impact value of photographs and found that viewers concentrate on faces in photos and go back and forth examining interactions between faces in a photograph; this highlights the importance of story-telling role of photography. The cognitive neuroscience of art is a young field and a recent literature search yielded no published academic studies on expert photographers' brain activation, although such a study would be obviously of interest. However, research on visuo-motor coordination (Zago, McIntyre, Senot, & Lacquaniti, 2009) and on situational awareness (Endsley, 2006) are potentially useful for understanding individual differences in creative photography. In addition, just as Kozbelt (2008; see also Chapter 10, this volume) analyzed the career trajectories of great composers and found them to be less consistent with some of the basic premises of the Darwinian principles (the importance of chance variation) and more consistent with an expertise acquisition model, a similar analysis looking at photographers' career trajectories would enrich our understanding of how highly creative photographs are made over photographers' lifespans.

At the other end of the psychological continuum, therapists of many orientations have utilized client photographs to promote the therapeutic dialogue and enhance self-understanding. The second-author's work on auto-photography provides a useful tool to enhance this process both for those whose therapy is primarily aimed at understanding (e.g., the artistic client seeking meaning in life) as well as less-thoughtful clients who are acting out in substance-abusing or other ways (Casey & Dollinger, 2007). The auto-photography tool is useful precisely because it has a number of empirical correlates for clinicians to keep in mind.

Over seventy years ago, *Popular Photography* published predictions about the future of postwar photography by nine photographers and photo enthusiasts of the time, including Bernice Abbott and Paul Strand (*The Coming World of Photography*,

1944). Many of the predictions were correct in anticipating the technological advances photographers have enjoyed since then (less grainy, faster film, ability to photograph under challenging lighting conditions). Some also predicted a burst in creativity as a result of technology making it easier for more people to practice photography. We predict that the developments in digital photography and online tools bode well for the future of the psychological study of creativity via photography, making it a fertile field for the study of eminent and everyday creativity in an art that is now virtually universal. A common adage of the past is that "a picture is worth a thousand words." In the twenty-first century, however, it seems increasingly the case that, each month, people take thousands of photos of their lives. Such prolific photo-taking suggests that photography is becoming a formative aesthetic, emotional, and mnemonic tool of everyday life for both individuals and society.

References

Adams, A. (2007). Introduction. "You don't take a photograph, you make it." In A.-C. Jaeger (Ed.) *Image makers, image takers: Interviews with today's leading curators, editors, and photographers* (pp. 6–12). New York, NY: Thames & Hudson.

Aschermann, E., Dannenberg, U., & Schulz, A.-P. (1998). Photographs as Retrieval Cues for Children. *Applied Cognitive Psychology, 12*, 55–66.

Axelsson, Ö. (2007). Towards a psychology of photography: Dimensions underlying aesthetic appeal of photographs. *Perceptual and Motor Skills, 105*, 411–434.

Back, M. D., Stopfer, J. M., Vazire, S., Gaddis, S., Schmukle, S. C., Egloff, B., & Gosling, S. D. (2010). Facebook profiles reflect actual personality, not self-idealization. *Psychological Science, 21*(3), 372–374.

Bayles, D. & Orland, T. (2001). *Art & Fear: Observations on the Perils (and Rewards) of Artmaking*. Santa Barbara, CA: Image Continuum Press.

Beilin, H. (1991). Developmental aesthetics and the psychology of photography. In R. M. Downs, L. S. Liben & D. S. Palermo (Eds.), *Visions of aesthetics, the environment and development*. Hillsdale, New Jersey: Erlbaum Assoc. Publishers.

Berger, J. (1980). Uses of photography. In J. Berger (Ed.), *About looking*. New York: Pantheon.

Berger, J. (2013). Appearances. In J. Berger (Ed.), *Understanding a photograph (1982)*. New York: Aperture.

Bernat, E., Patrick, C. J., Benning, S. D., & Tellegen, A. (2006). Effects of picture content and intensity on affective physiological response. *Psychophysiology, 43*, 93–103.

Brogowski, L. (1989). Idioms: A silent face of photography. *Leonardo, 22*(2), 159–163.

Bruner, J. S. (1962). The conditions of creativity. In H. E. Gruber, G. Terrell, & M. Wertheimer (Eds.), *Contemporary approaches to creative thinking: A symposium held at the University of Colorado. The Atherton Press behavioral science series*. New York, NY: Atherton Press.

Burke, P. A., & Dollinger, S. J. (2005). "A picture's worth a thousand words": Language use in the autophotographic essay. *Personality and Social Psychology Bulletin, 31*, 536–548.

Carroll, H. (2014). *Read this if you want to take great photographs*. London: Laurence King Publishing Ltd.

Cartier-Bresson, H. (1999). *The mind's eye writings on photography and photographers*. Millerton, N.Y: Aperture.

Casey, P. F., & Dollinger, S. J. (2007). College students' alcohol-related problems: An autophotographic approach. *Journal of Alcohol and Drug Education, 51*(2), 8–25.

Chatterjee, A. (2013). *The aesthetic brain: How we evolved to desire beauty and enjoy art 1st edition.* New York, NY: Oxford University Press.

Christofides, E., Muise, A., Desmarais, S. (2009). Information disclosure and control on Facebook: Are they two sides of the same coin or two different processes? *Cyberpsychol Behavior 12*(3):341–345.

Cleveland, P. (2005). How much visual power can a magazine take? *Design Studies, 26,* 271–317.

Combs, J. M., & Ziller, R. C. (1977). Photographic self-concept of counselees. *Journal of Counseling Psychology, 34,* 452–455.

Csikszentmihalyi, M. (1999). Implications of a systems perspective for the study of creativity. In R. J. Sternberg (Ed.), *Handbook of creativity.* New York, NY: Cambridge University Press.

Cyr, D. J. (1968). Photography: An interactive process. *Art Education, 21*(7), 40–43.

Dollinger, S. J. (1996). Autophotographic identities of young adults: With special reference to alcohol, athletics, achievement, religion and work. *Journal of Personality Assessment, 67,* 384–398.

Dollinger, S. J. (2001). Religious identity: An autophotographic study. *International Journal for the Psychology of Religion, 11,* 71–92.

Dollinger, S. J. (2003). Need for uniqueness, need for cognition, and creativity. *Journal of Creative Behavior, 37,* 99–116.

Dollinger, S. J. (2006). Autophotographic individuality predicts creativity: A seven-year follow-up. *Journal of Creative Behavior, 40,* 111–124.

Dollinger, S. J. (2007). Creativity and conservatism. *Personality and Individual Differences, 43,* 1025–1035.

Dollinger, S. J. (2011). "Standardized minds" or individuality? Admissions tests and creativity revisited. *Psychology of Aesthetics, Creativity, and the Arts, 5,* 329–341.

Dollinger, S. J. (2016). "You are as you read": Do students' reading interests contribute to their individuality? *Reading Psychology, 37,* 1–26.

Dollinger, S. J. (2017). Much more than selfies: Autophotography, individuality, and creativity. In G. J. Feist, R. Reiter-Palmon, and J. C. Kaufman (Eds.), *The Cambridge handbook of creativity and personality research* (pp. 323–354). New York: Cambridge University Press.

Dollinger, S. J., Burke, P. A., & Gump, N. (2007). Creativity and values. *Creativity Research Journal, 19,* 91–103.

Dollinger, S. J., & Clancy, S. M. (1993). Identity, self, and personality. II: Glimpses through the autophotographic eye. *Journal of Personality and Social Psychology, 64,* 1064–1071.

Dollinger, S. J., & Dollinger, S. M. C. (1997). Individuality and identity exploration: An autophotographic study. *Journal of Research in Personality, 31,* 337–354.

Dollinger, S. J., & Dollinger, S. M. C. (2003). Individuality in young and middle adulthood: An autophotographic study. *Journal of Adult Development, 10,* 227–236.

Dollinger, S. J., Preston, L. A., O'Brien, S. P., & DiLalla, D. L. (1996). Individuality and relatedness of the self: An autophotographic study. *Journal of Personality and Social Psychology, 71,* 1268–1278.

Dollinger, S. J., Robinson, N. M., & Ross, V. J. (1999). Photographic individuality, breadth of perspective, and creativity. *Journal of Personality, 67,* 623–644.

Dollinger, S. J., Ross, V. J., & Preston, L. A. (2002). Intellect and individuality. *Creativity Research Journal, 14,* 213–226.

Dollinger, S. J., Urban, K.K., & James, T. A. (2004). Creativity and openness: Further validation of two creative product measures. *Creativity Research Journal, 16,* 35–47.

Domino, G., & Giuliani, I. (2007). Creativity in three samples of photographers: A validation of the Adjective Check List Creativity scale. *Creativity Research Journal, 10,* 193–200.

Ekman, P. (1965). Differential communication of affect by head and body cues. *Journal of Personality and Social Psychology, 2,* 726–735.

Endsley, M. R. (2006). Expertise and situation awareness. In K. A. Ericsson, N. Charness, P. J. Feltovich, & R. R. Hoffman (Eds.), *The Cambridge handbook of expertise and expert performance.* New York: Cambridge University Press.

Fayena-Tawil, F., Kozbelt, A., & Sitaras, L. (2011). Think global, act local: A protocol analysis comparison of artists' and nonartists' cognitions, metacognitions, and evaluations while drawing. *Psychology of Aesthetics, Creativity, and the Arts, 5,* 135–145.

Feltovich, P. J., Prietula, M. J., Ericsson, K. A. (2006). Studies of expertise from psychological perspectives. In K. A. Ericsson, N. Charness, P. J. Feltovich, & R.R. Hoffman (Eds.), *The Cambridge handbook of expertise and expert performance* (pp. 41–67). New York: Cambridge University Press.

Fleenor, J. W., & Taylor, S. (2004). The assessment of creativity. In M. Hersen (Ed.), *Comprehensive handbook of psychological assessment* (pp. 75–84). Hoboken, NJ: John Wiley & Sons.

Focal Power (2009). The Photo Quotes Archive. Retrieved on August 10, 2009, from www .focalpower.com/app/quote/subjects/

Gampat, C. (2014, December 23). How to pick one photo out of several thousand: An inside look at how we judge photo contests. Retrieved on May 3, 2015, from www .thephoblographer.com/2014/12/23/pick-one-photo-several-thousand-inside-look -judge-photo-contests/#.VUaFB5MYPe5

Garry, M., & Wade, K. A. (2005). Actually, a picture is worth less than 45 words: Narratives produce more false memories than photographs do. *Psychonomic Bulletin & Review, 12*(2), 359–366.

Getzels, J. W., & Csikszentmihalyi, M. (1976). *The creative vision: A longitudinal study of problem finding in art.* New York: Wiley.

Ginicola, M. M., Smith, C., & Trzaska, J. (2012). Counseling through images: Using photography to guide the counseling process and achieve treatment goals. *Journal of Creativity in Mental Health, 7,* 310–329.

Glăveanu, V. P. (2010). Principles for a cultural psychology of creativity. *Culture Psychology, 16*(2), 147–163.

Gosling, S.D., Augustine, A.A., Vazire, S., Holtzman, N., and Gaddis, S. (2011). Manifestations of personality in Online Social Networks: Self-reported Facebook-related behaviors and observable profile information. *Cyberpsychology, Behavior, & Social Networking, 14*(9), 483–488.

Halsman, P. (1961). *Halsman of the creation of photographic ideas.* New York: Ziff-Davis.

Hattersley, R. (1962). A handy kit for do-it-yourself critics. In C. H. Traub, S. Heller, and A. B. Bell (Eds.), *The education of a photographer* (pp. 194–198). New York, NY: Allsworth Press.

Hawkins (undated). Elements of a merit image. Retrieved on May 3, 2015, from www
.ppa.com/article.cfm?ItemNumber=1901.

Henry, W. P., & Solano, C. H. (1983). Photographic style and personality: Developing
a coding system for photographs. *Journal of Psychology, 115*, 79–87.

Hekkert, P., & Van Wieringen, P. C. W. (1996). Beauty in the eye of expert and nonexpert
beholders: A study in the appraisal of art. *American Journal of Psychology, 109*,
389–407.

Herpertz, S. C., Kunert, H. J. Schwenger, U. B., & Sass, H. (1999). Affective responsiveness
in borderline personality disorder: A psychophysiological approach. *American
Journal of Psychiatry, 156*, 1550–1556.

Hurn, D., & Jay, B. (2008). *On being a photographer: a practical guide.* Anacortes, WA:
LensWork Publishing.

Ivcevic, Z., & Ambady, N. (2013). Face to (face)book: The two faces of social behavior?
Journal of Personality, 81(3), 290–301.

Jaeger, AC. (2007). *Image makers, image takers: Interviews with today's leading curators,
editors and photographers.* New York: NY: Thames & Hudson.

Karl, K., Peluchette, J., & Schlaegel, C. (2010). Who's posting Facebook faux pas? A cross-
cultural examination of personality differences. *International Journal of Selection
and Assessment, 18*(2), 174–186.

Kaslow, F. W., & Friedman, J. (1977). Utilization of family photos and movies in family
therapy. *Journal of Marital and Family Therapy, 3*, 19–25.

Kozbelt, A. (2006). Dynamic evaluation of Matisse's 1935 "Large Reclining Nude."
Empirical Studies of the Arts, 24, 119–137.

Kozbelt, A. (2008). Longitudinal hit ratios of classical composers: Reconciling Darwinian
and expertise acquisition perspectives on lifespan creativity. *Psychology of
Aesthetics, Creativity, and the Arts, 2*, 221–235.

Kozbelt, A., & Serafin, J. (2009). Dynamic evaluation of high- and low-creativity drawings
by artist and non-artist raters. *Creativity Research Journal, 21*, 349–360.

Kulich, R. J., & Goldberg, R.W. (1978). Differences in the production of photographs:
A potential assessment technique. *Perceptual and Motor Skills, 47*(1), 223–229.

Lavretiev, A. (1994). Inventions from photography: Light, shadow and optical transformations.
Leonardo, 27(5), 383–386.

Mahaffey, A. L., Bryan, A., & Hutchison, K. E. (2005). Using startle eye blink to measure the
affective component of anti-gay bias. *Basic and Applied Social Psychology, 27*,
37–45.

Marcus, B., Machilek, F., Schütz, A. (2006). Personality in cyberspace: Personal web sites as
media for personality expressions and impressions. *Journal of Personality and
Social Psychology, 90*(6), 1014–1031.

Martindale, C. (1994). How can we measure a society's creativity? In M. A. Boden (Ed.),
Dimensions of creativity (pp. 159–198). Cambridge, MA: MIT Press.

Mayer, R. E. (1999). Fifty years of creativity research. In R. J. Sternberg (Ed.), *Handbook of
creativity* (pp. 449–460). Cambridge: Cambridge University.

McManus, I. C., Zhou, F. A., I'Anson, S., Waterfield, L., Stover, K., & Cook, R. (2011).
The psychometrics of photographing cropping: The influence of colour, meaning,
and expertise. *Perception, 40*, 332–357.

Milgram, S. (1977). The image freezing machine. In S. Milgram (Ed.), *The individual in
a social world: Essays and experiments* (pp. 339–350). Reading, MA: Addison-
Wesley.

Navab, A. D. (2001). Re-picturing of photography: A language in the making. *Journal of Aesthetic Education, 35*(1), 69–84.

Nuhn (2011, April 25). Five factors that judges consider in reviewing photo contest entries. *National Wildlife.* Retrieved on May 3, 2015, from www.nwf.org/news-and-magazines/national-wildlife/photozone/archives/2011/5-photo-judging-factors.aspx

Pennebaker, J. W., Francis, M. E., & Booth, R. J. (2001). *Linguistic inquiry and word count (LIWC): LIWC2001 [Computer software and manual].* Mahwah, NJ: Lawrence Erlbaum.

Perlson, H. (2015, April 10). "Spying" artist wins privacy case. *Artnet News.* Retrieved on July 13, 2015, from https://news.artnet.com/art-world/arne-svenson-neighbors-photographs-supreme-court-286916.

PhotoWings (undated). Interview: Sandra Phillips, senior curator of photography at the San Francisco Museum of Modern Art. Retrieved on August 23, 2015, from http://photowings.org/interview-sandra-phillips-senior-curator-of-photography-at-the-san-francisco-museum-of-modern-art/.

Quinn, S. (2015, Jan 27). Eyetracking photojournalism: New research explores what makes a photograph memorable, shareable, and worth publishing. *NPPA The Voice of Visual Journalists.* Retrieved on August 23, 2015, from https://nppa.org/news/eyetracking-photojournalism-new-research-explores-what-makes-photograph-memorable-shareable-and.

Read, S. (2013). *Exhibiting photography: A practical guide to displaying your work, second edition.*, Burlington, MA: Focal Press.

Risch, C. (2014, February 7). MoMA's new chief photo Curator turns to studio photography for first show. Retrieved on August 23, 2015, from http://www.pdnonline.com/features/MoMAs-New-Chief-Pho-10291.shtml.

Rodden, K. & Wood, K. R. (2003). How do people manage their digital photographs? In *Proceedings of the SIGCHI Conference on Human Factors in Computing Systems*, (pp. 409–416), New York, NY: ACM.

Sawyer, R. K. (2006). *Explaining creativity. The science of human innovation.* New York: Oxford University Press.

Schacter, D. L., Koutstaal, W., Johnson, M. K., Gross, M. S., & Angell, K. E. (1997). False recollection induced by photographs: A comparison of older and younger adults. *Psychology and Aging, 12,* 203–215.

Serafin, J. (2013). Expertise in artistic photography. Dissertation submitted in partial fulfillment of the requirements for the degree Doctor of Philosophy, The Graduate Center of the City University of New York. *Dissertation Abstracts International: Section B: The Sciences and Engineering, 74*(6-B)(E), 2013. Accession number: 2013-99241-028.

Shore, S. (2007). *The nature of photographs* (2nd edn.). London: Phaidon Press Limited.

Simonton, D. K. (1997). Creative productivity: A predictive and explanatory model of career landmarks and trajectories. *Psychological Review, 104,* 66–89.

Simonton, D. K. (2011). Creativity and discovery as blind variation and selective retention: Multiple-variant definitions and blind-sighted integration. *Psychology of Aesthetics, Creativity, and the Arts, 5*(3), 222–228.

Simonton, D. K. (2012). Quantifying creativity: Can measures span the spectrum? *Dialogues in Clinical Neuroscience, 14*(1), 100–104.

Solso, R. L. (2001). Brain activities in a skilled versus a novice artist: An fMRI study. *Leonardo, 34,* 31–34.

Sontag, S. (1977). *On photography*. New York: Farrar, Straus, & Giroux.

Szarkowski, J. (1973). *Looking at photographs: 100 pictures from the Museum of Modern Art*. New York: The Museum of Modern Art.

The Coming World of Photography (1944). Popular photography. Retrieved on July 10, 2015, from https://people.rit.edu/andpph/giants/POP-PHOTO-future-1944.html.

Thein, M. (2012a). What makes an outstanding image? Retrieved on July 10, 2015, from http://blog.mingthein.com/2012/10/06/outstanding-1/.

Thein, M. (2012b). The process of editing. Retrieved on July 10, 2015, from http://blog.mingthein.com/2012/04/20/the-process-of-editing/.

Tinio, P. P. L., & Leder, H. (2013). The means to art's end: Styles, creative devices, and the challenge of art. In A. S. Bristol, J. C. Kaufman, & O. Vartanian (Eds.), *The neuroscience of creativity*. Cambridge, MA: The MIT Press.

Tinio, P. P. L., Leder, H., & Strasser, M., (2011). Image quality and the aesthetic judgment of photographs: Contrast, sharpness, and grain teased apart and put together. *Psychology of Aesthetics, Creativity, and the Arts*, *5*(2), 165–176.

Tinio, P. P. L., & Leder, H. (2009). Natural scenes are indeed preferred, but image quality might have the last word. *Psychology of Aesthetics, Creativity, and the Arts*, *3*, 52–56.

Vidulich, R. N., & Krevanick, F. W. (1966). Racial attitudes and emotional response to visual representations of the Negro. *Journal of Social Psychology*, *68*, 85–93.

Walker, J. L. (1991). Photograph as lifeline – Facing mortality. *American Journal of Psychotherapy*, *45*, 124–128.

Wallas, G. (1926). *Art of thought*. New York: Harcourt, Brace and Company.

Wignall (2009, October 12). National Geographic's Jim Richardson: How I judge photo contests. Retrieved on May 3, 2015, from http://rising.blackstar.com/national-geographics-jim-richardson-how-i-judge-photo-contests.html.

Yu, C. (2004). Aesthetics of photography: Combining the viewer's and the artist's standpoints. *Art Criticism*, *19*(1), 63–74.

Zago, M., McIntyre, J., Senot, P., & Lacquaniti, F. (2009). Visuo-motor coordination and internal models for object interception. *Experimental Brain Research*, *192*(4), 571–604.

Zehr (2009). Creating the "other" in research, photography, justice. Retrieved on July 10, 2015, from http://emu.edu/now/restorative-justice/2009/09/30/creating-the-other-in-research-photography-justice.

Zebrowitz, L. A., Hall, J. A., Murphy, N. A., & Rhodes, G. (2002). Looking smart and looking good: Facial cues to intelligence and their origins. *Personality and Social Psychology Bulletin*, *28*, 238–249.

Ziller, R. C. (1977). A phenomenological utilization of photographs. *Journal of Phenomenological Psychology*, *7*, 172–182.

Ziller, R. C., & Lewis, D. C. (1981). Orientations: Self, social, and environmental percepts through auto-photography. *Personality & Social Psychology Bulletin*, *7*, 338–343.

Ziller, R. C., & Rorer, B. A. (1985). Shyness-environment interaction: A view from the shy side through auto-photography. *Journal of Personality*, *53*, 626–639.

Ziller, R. C. (1990/2000). *Photographing the self*. Newbury Park, CA: Sage.

Zillmann, D., Gibson, R., & Sargent, S. L. (1999). Effects of photographs in news-magazine reports on issue perception. *Media Psychology*, *1*, 207–228.

9   The Constricted Muse

Acting

Thalia R. Goldstein*

Pace University

Anne G. Levy

University of Alabama

Abstract

While most laypeople and audience members would easily and quickly put acting in the "creative arts" category, what is actually creative about portraying the words of a playwright, in a recognizable manner, for many performances? Acting does not necessarily involve generation of new material – rather, most acting takes place in a collaborative environment, as an interpretation of a playwright's, director's, and designer's combined and unified vision. We therefore break down the issue of creativity in acting into three components: the process of creating a performance, the person creating the performance, and the product of the performance itself. We review the scant literature in this area, and conclude with research suggestions both for how to determine if an actor's performance is creative, and for how to define and measure the process of acting through the lens of creativity.

Lynn Fontanne, a famous stage actress of the mid-twentieth century, when asked to explain what actors do when they act, replied "We read the lines so that people can hear and understand them; we move about the stage without bumping into the furniture or each other; and, well that's it" (Lyons, 1955). And while Fontanne was speaking of certain style of acting needed for a certain style of playwriting, there may be a larger truth to the way she describes her craft. Put the way Fontanne describes, it can be easily argued that acting is not very creative. And, even if you disagree with Fontanne's assessment of what an actor does, it still raises the question: "What is essentially creative about acting?" If acting is supposed to be the authentic portrayal of the world, human emotion, behavior, and relationships, can the claim be made that acting is creative, or is it more of an interpretive practice? In the same way that one may make the claim that a photo-representational piece of art is aesthetically pleasing, engaging, or representative of talent while not being creative, it may be that acting can be powerful, moving, aesthetically pleasurable, and impressive in its virtuosic performance. Yet, because acting is necessarily representational and extends the work of the playwright, it cannot be creative.

However, as most actors and laypeople might disagree with the assessment that acting is not "creative," it is important to clarify the various aspects of acting and how each may or may not involve creativity. This requires us to look in three places:

the actor, (i.e., is a person who engages in acting creative?); the process, (i.e., as a person creates a performance, or learns how to act, are they engaged in a creative process?); and the product (i.e., is what audience members actually view, when they watch actors, be considered creative?). This can be linked back to previous findings of actors' self-reported creativity as involving three stages: general preparation (i.e., person), rehearsal (i.e., process), and performance (Nemiro, 1997).

These questions may not be unique to acting of course. Any art form, really any domain included in this volume, involves a person, a process, and a product. However, acting is unique in that the expectation of product is an expectation of heightened or reflected reality. If an actor is (to use an over-quoted phrase) "Holding the mirror up to nature," (Shakespeare, Hamlet, 3.2.) can the mirror itself be creative, or only where the actor chooses to point the mirror to create the reflection? Is acting simply interpretive? Is it merely responsive? Or is there an element of creative generation?

Likewise, can a "mirror pointing" choice be attributed solely to the single actor or must we include the group of artists collectively and collaboratively working on the play? Acting is unusual in that it is necessarily a collaborative art form. Even a solo show of monologues written by the actor requires (at the very least) someone else to run the light board and take the tickets, and it is a rare solo show that can be successfully performed without the guiding hand of a director or producer. Most acting takes place in a highly collaborative environment (Kogan, 2002): scores of other actors, the director, producers, the playwright/librettist/lyricist, the lighting, set and costume designers, and the audience with their various reactions all affect the actor's performance and must be kept in mind as the actor goes through the process of forming that performance.

One area of acting that is unquestionably creative is improvisational theatre. Theatrical (and other artistic) improvisation has been studied and discussed well and thoroughly by Keith Sawyer (2014) and is beyond the scope of this chapter, in which we are focused on creativity in acting of scripted theatre, film, and television. However, there are connections between the types of creative work done in improvisational theatre settings and the types of work done in a rehearsal room for scripted theatre. Improvisers must quickly come up with new and appropriate responses, characters, words, and actions in order to participate in an ongoing improvisation. This type of quick-thinking, in-the-moment creation is the product seen by the audience in the moment of performance. In contrast, Sawyer (2012) conceptualizes modern, scripted, European-based performance (how acting is seen by most modern American audiences) as the least open to improvisation, and therefore the least creative.

Even in scripted theatre, however, we believe that there is room for a certain type of bounded or constricted creativity. Whereas the acting experienced by most modern American audiences might appear to be less reliant on improvisation as a process, the essence of improvisation is at the core of every well-trained actor. Throughout the history of theatre, there have been influential elements of performance that relied heavily on the creative power and pleasure of improvisation. *Commedia del'Arte*, for example, was never scripted, but instead improvised from a set of known character types, including rough plots and comic "bits" known as a "lazzi" (Worthen, 1996). Commedia can trace it roots back to the Atellan Farce of ancient Rome, and forward to the Punch and Judy puppet shows of Victorian England and even to the variety shows and late-night talk shows of today. Most of these forms rely on stock characters, a series of comic encounters, and bawdy humor (Worthen, 1996), with improvisation happening in the spaces created by these outlines. In America, modern improvisation began near the Southside of Chicago in the 1930s with children's theatre workshops taught by Viola Spolin and Neva Boyed (Spolin, 1999). By leading children through a series of games (games which remain the basis for most improvisational troupes today, now called *handles* or *formats*), Spolin and Boyed saw that children, who by choice or circumstance were sworn enemies, were able to open up and connect to each other. Spolin saw the improvisation necessitated by these games as an "openness of contact with the environment and each other and a willingness to play" (Spolin, 1999, pg. 25) rather than a "clever rearranging of the known" (Schwartz, 2012, n.p.).

All acting training, improvisational or not, revolves around this idea of "willingness." Even with a written text, acting is a process of choice making that requires the practitioner to trust their instinctual response to the situation. The central metaphors of many great acting texts mirror the idea of acting training as a leap into the unknown with the faith that your choice will be supported (much like in improvisation) (Hodge, 2010). This training allows actors to feel free within its structure, nurturing the creative impulse. While the product/performance of acting may look uncreative, as it is bounded by the script and constraints of authenticity, the process by which actors train and then rehearse involves creative generation, and a level of openness and willingness to employ the kinds of trial-and-error and experimentation that many creative endeavors require.

Conceptualizing Creativity in Scripted Acting

Conceptualizing Process

The environment in which the rehearsal process takes place may be the best bet for conceptualizing creativity in scripted acting. This can include a rehearsal space where actors create characters based on scripts for performance, more improvisational spaces in which scripts or pieces are devised as they are rehearsed, and classrooms in which actors are taught to act through a variety of exercises and experiences in scene study. Directors and teachers can set the tone for either a generative and creative environment or a stifling and restrictive environment. When conceptualizing the process of directing actors, we can think of directors coming in many forms along a continuum: At one extreme, telling the actor the exact inflection of their words, and where they must stand, walk, face, etc., as they say each line, allowing for no generation or creation on the part of the actor (or, to look at it another way, requiring actors to justify choices made for them by the director – which takes creativity in connecting these choices into a believable character; Nemiro 1997). On the other extreme of the continuum, directors may provide almost no guidance for the actor, telling him or her to "trust themselves" and go with whatever type of feeling they have in any moment in the script (and in this situation, actors must individually create their own boundaries and rules in order to stay within the world of the play). The best environments, we propose, use a mixture of these two that best serves the text, with a director allowing for freedom and generation of ideas, while providing enough guidance and feedback to allow for a successful performance and allowing for interchange between actor and director (Arnold, 1991). Trying a variety of ways of expressing a thought or feeling as put in a script is how we may think of a creative process – attempting many different options, and narrowing in on which is not only true to the intentions, beliefs, desires, and emotions of the character and the plot of the story, but also is interesting for an audience to watch, and is appropriate for the performance space itself, technically (for example, one acts out a scene differently in a 2,000-seat Broadway theatre than a 50-seat black box theatre, or for film).

Training. Beyond the process of what goes into making a performance, there is also the process of what goes into becoming an actor. Ignoring the fabled story of Lana Turner's discovery in an ice cream parlor and subsequent MGM movie contract, all at the age of 16, most actors begin their career path with many years of formal training. While it may be understood that actors "get" most of the information necessary from other people (the playwright provides the words they are to say, the director tells them where to move and when), knowing how to (1) read a script, (2) receive the information contained in the script and synthesize it, (3) follow the director's direction, and (4) integrate their knowledge about themselves and broader human psychology into a character as one part of a larger story takes considerable practice.

The creative process is deeply entrenched in the training of actors – before they ever get a script and start to work on anything concrete, the entire way actor training is framed in the United States, and has been since Stanislavsky and The Group Theatre, is entrenched in creative process (Benedetti, 2007). Actors have to decide how to interpret each line, where and how to pause, how to place emphasis, and allow for how the others on stage are going to enact their characters (Sawyer, 2012). They must become fluent in the collective body of rules and conventions of their field, the domain of acting (Csikszentmihalyi, 1988; Csikszentmihalyi & Csikszentmihalyi, 1991). However, the process of achieving fluency in that domain (and it is often argued that an actor never finishes training; Dixon & Smith, 1995; Wooster, 2007) is further complicated by the number of possible techniques that an American actor may use. Anyone who remembers Diana Morales from *A Chorus Line* knows there are many different approaches to acting training, and not every one is right for everyone.

In the foundational history of American acting technique, there is Lee Strasberg and his Method, which noted that actors may get their ideas from the script, but need to create the character from themselves, their own experiences, and their knowledge of the way in which humans and the world work (Hull, 1985). Stella Adler's technique emphasized imagination, character work, and strict adherence to the given circumstances of the play and actions. Through careful and thorough script analysis, actors determine their characters' actions (what they physically do on stage), the justification of those actions (why they are performed), and their overall actions (what the character ultimately desires to accomplish) (Adler, 2000). Sanford Meisner taught that the only thing that is real is what's happening in the moment on stage – one actor responding to another in the moment. Therefore, instead of deciding *in advance* on how to act and react, moment to moment, actors must strive to experience each scene now, putting their focus on their partner so they can experience the scene as it is happening rather than be cut off from the moment by being self-conscious (Meisner & Longwell, 1987). What links these three schools of training (other than their origin in Stanislavsky) is a focus on building (and later trusting) the creative impulse in the actor. Concentrating on building this impulse enables the actor to be able to use and trust their creative impulse while rehearsing a script. Many acting training programs or schools take several years to complete, the logic being that it takes time for actors to learn to break down their own bad habits and trust themselves as creative forces (Hodge, 2000). The promise of the training is not fame or constant work, but the knowledge that they will be able to trust themselves to make good choices once they are hired.

Conceptualizing Person

There are two options when discussing the creativity of the people in acting: Are the people who are actors creative *actors*, and are the people who are actors creative in other areas of life, such as in classic cognitive creativity or in other art forms?

Given the constructed nature of most characters (either because of the necessities of the script or the necessities of time period, cultural roles, and known human nature), the room an actor has to "play" within a portrayed character may be rather minute. In 2015, Eddie Redmayne won an Oscar for his portrayal of Stephen Hawking in the biographical movie *The Theory of Everything*. The "biopic" with a highly lauded central performance is a common Oscar theme. Many other actors have been rewarded similarly: Benedict Cumberbatch (nominated) as Alan Turing in *The Imitation Game*, Reese Witherspoon as June Cash in *Walk the Line*, Daniel Day-Lewis as Christy Brown in *My Left Foot*, Robert DeNiro as Jake LaMotta in *Raging Bull*, Jamie Foxx as Ray Charles in *Ray*, Colin Firth as King George IV in *The King's Speech*, Sean Penn as Harvey Milk in *Milk*, and Helen Mirren, who has won both an Oscar and a Tony for playing Queen Elizabeth II in *The Queen* and in *The Audience*, respectively. One sees a similar theme in recent Tony awards: Bryan Cranston as Lyndon Johnson, Frank Langella as Richard Nixon, Audra McDonald as Billie Holiday, and Zoe Caldwell as Maria Callas. The list could continue. These performances are even more constricted than standard scripted theatre with fictional characters. Are these portrayals creative, even though they are, in physical and vocal performance, mimicry of a kind? Perhaps the creative actor is the person who can decide what to portray and what to hold back in such performances.

For standard measures of creativity, are actors more creative than other people? There are examples of actors who have been creative in other fields, such as Danica Keller, who is a mathematician and author, Mayim Bialik, who holds a PhD in neuroscience (Kaufman, 2009), or Johnny Depp and Dennis Hopper, who are both painters. Actors are also writers, diplomats, directors, or representatives of nonprofits. However, it is important to separate out the notion of creativity from simple fame. There is no research on whether successful actors are more likely to be successful in other creative or public domains than other kinds of artists or public figures. Perhaps the perception of creative success in one field is transferrable to another. Actors are some of the most perceived individuals in society – everyone knows their name, their personal lives, and their struggles. Perhaps they are simply *considered* more able and more creative than others, despite what the real story may be.

Conceptualizing Product

The conceptualization of creativity in acting also must be cleanly defined in the way that most of the lay public may think of acting: in the product presented in a theatre, on a television, in a film. Is there such a thing as a "creative" acting product? It is certainly easy to think of "appropriate" acting – that is, acting that is true to both real-world behavior and the world created in the play or movie. The character who is appropriately acted makes sense to an audience, reflects back to them truths about the world, and fits within the confines of the piece it is presented in. However, what is different, new, or innovative about that product? History is full of moments where the performance of theatre was ready to go in bold new directions but the audience was not ready to go with it, so what was different, new, or innovative may not be able to survive (Aronson, 2000). For example, in 1896, a Parisian audience rioted over Alfred Jarry's *Ubu Roi*, which is now considered the beginning of twentieth-century modernism (Taylor, 2007). The first production of *The Seagull* in 1896 St. Petersburg was met with jeers (Allen, 2001). Early performances of *Waiting for Godot* caused audiences to walk out of the play in frustration (Knowlson, 1996).

With a script, there is a blueprint that has been set out by the playwright that the actor must not only follow verbally, but also must remain true to the obstacles, emotional lives, plot arcs, and characterization that the playwright has written out (Noice & Noice, 1997). Of course, there are playwrights that provide more or less guidance when it comes to characterization, movement on stage, and emotionality. Tennessee Williams and Eugene O'Neil are known for their overly descriptive stage directions (Poyatos, 2002). Samuel Becket provides the details of how a role is to be performed down to the speed and vocal qualities that the actors are to use (Weiss, 2013). Some playwrights such as Charles Mee are more willing to allow for "interpretation" of their work. Mee writes that "There is no such thing as an original play … And so, whether we mean to or not, the work we do is both received and created, both an adaptation and an original, at the same time. We re-make things as we go" (Mee, 2015). However, the generation of new material in all of these cases simply does not exist. It is all already there!

There are admittedly differences between performances of any type of script – no two nights of a theatrical performance are ever the same, even with the same actors and script, because the audience reactions and the decisions the actors are making throughout the moments of the performance may change the product. But differences do not mean creativity. Many scripts are performed many times over by different casts and directors, from major revivals on Broadway, to multiple school performances of popular musicals such as "The Wizard of Oz," to the multitudes of Shakespeare productions that take place around the English-speaking world every year. These performances are never identical, even though the scripts are the same, due to both choices made by the designers, directors, and of course the actors in how they are performing the characters, the words of the script, and their interpretive and performance talent.

Important to keep in mind is that because thousands of years of theatrical scripts are so far away from real-life conversations (lacking of overlap, pauses, coughs, stops and starts, change of topics, unfulfilled thoughts and points), performing even the most realistic script could be considered creative (Sawyer, 2012). Of course, in the past forty years there are many playwrights and theatre companies dedicated to creating theatre pieces that attempt to mirror the realities of communication, but these too need to be carefully composed and rehearsed in order to authentically capture what it is to be alive right now – in other words, constructing an interpretation.

The moment of creative product also necessarily includes an audience, and perhaps that sharing of experience; the audience reacting to the performance and the performers reacting to the audience is formed performance by performance, collaboratively with the community (Bennett, 2013). The feelings of flow that occur during performance individually (Konijn, 1991), and especially between members of an ensemble, where the performance seems to be occurring naturally and cohesively, can include feelings of creative achievement, emerging from the group (Sawyer, 2012). There is also creation in the head of the audience member, filling in the gaps of what is not realistically presented on stage, ignoring the fact that they're watching an intimate scene between two lovers in the company of 2,000 other people, or not thinking it strange when a man dressed as a lion breaks into song.

Many acting coaches and theorists (McGaw, Stilson, & Clark, 2011) speak of "infecting your subconscious" with the gestation of a character, and then giving birth to a character that consumes the actor and performs on stage. Others (e.g., Brestoff, 1995) discuss acting in terms of doing as much research and work in the rehearsal process as possible, but then "leaving it alone" on stage and allowing the rehearsal to become so automatic that the actor does not think about anything on stage. In this conceptualization, rehearsal may be creative, and require conscientious preparation, but performance therefore is not creative. Instead, performance may require "task-emotions" of modulating voice, physical state, facial expression, and the conscious processes of remembering the words, blocking, etc. (Konijn, 2000). Thus, defining and further study on the "activeness" of actors while performing is necessary.

Measurement of Creativity in Acting

If the creativity inherent in acting can be divided into the subdomains of a creative process, a creative person, and a creative product, the question of how to measure creativity is bound by which aspect of acting you wish to measure. This also raises the question of whether the creativity in these subdomains can or should be intertwined. Can a "non-creative" actor come up with a creative process, or simply follow the open and creative process of his or her collaborators? Can a creative product come from a non-creative process?

Measuring Process

Measuring the creative process of acting may be the place in which the most fruitful investigations can be made. The rules of the games in improvisational theatre are not drastically different from the rehearsal structure. We can consider the words on the page and the given circumstances of the script as "rules" as they are laid out in improvisational forms.

Fully improvised theatre such as Comedysportz, improvised comedy games and devised theatrical pieces from such companies with extensive ensemble training such as SITI Company (Anne Bogart, Artistic Director, New York, NY) and Lookingglass Theatre Company (Chicago, Il) are not that dissimilar from the rehearsal or teaching process in acting. Similarly, devised theatre, as defined by Allison Oddey, one of the first scholars to formally write about devising, is "work that that has emerged from and been generated by a group of people working in collaboration" (Oddey 2013). This is theatre that does not begin with a pre-written script, but rather with either a non-textual source (such as a piece of visual art, a founding question, or simply an idea to explore), with a library of found or generated texts (news articles, poems, short stories, freewrites by actors in the ensemble) or some combination of text and no text. Devised work features an ensemble of actors who become the collaborative group working alongside a facilitator or artistic director or leader.

In both devised and improvisational theatre, a director or facilitator plays a large role in the allowance for or rejection of ideas in the process of forming a story and character, given how much freedom he or she gives to the actors in his or her stead. Measurement of this process, of the variety of newness of ways in which an actor can try out characterizations, line readings, and interpretations, and directions that the performance of a script could possibly go may be the key to measuring process. Taking cues from previous work on improvisation in comedy or jazz could also provide direction (Sawyer, 2012). To note, this is also where process in theatre differs from that of film and television; in theatre the actor has some length of time during the rehearsal process to try out different ways of playing the role without anything, such as a camera or live audience, seeing this work. In film or television, there is significantly less time to explore without compromising the continuity of the work being done.

Measuring Person

The measurement of creative persons in acting may not be any different from the measurement of creative persons whose primary domain is not acting, at least if the goal is to measure cognitive creativity in the style of standard tests. Previous work on a related topic, pretend and role-play, as engaged in naturally by young children, has found strong associations between role-play, pretend play, and measures of creativity (Russ, Robins, & Christiano, 1999). It seems likely that anyone whose main work is producing various possible responses to stimuli (that is, creating a specific interpretation of a character by trying out multiple ways of performing that character and then choosing one) may also score higher on tests of divergent thinking, although as far as we know, this study has not been conducted.

However, to measure whether someone is a creative actor, perhaps you need to look at that person's performance of an iconic character, such as Hamlet or Juliet. Multiple and different interpretations of the same character may be one way of measuring creativity in acting. Careful work would have to be done, however, to separate the performance of the character per se from the ways in which the situation of the play influences the character (for example, playing Hamlet in London in 1999 as compared to London of 1609). There is also the question of whether an internal choice, which perhaps is not seen externally or explicitly by the audience (either because it is not well performed or because it doesn't actually affect the performance) could be considered a creative choice? An actor may make an unusual or creative choice in their interpretation of lines and character, but because they are not very good at expressing those choices, or because those choices may not affect the performance in a discernable way, can the acting itself be considered creative? Or perhaps we cannot consider those choices creative because they are not appropriate – they do not affect the acting. Did the creativity "really" happen in these cases? How someone taps into his or her inner self in order to bring out the correct, appropriate, or masterful performance may be the key question into process creativity. Alternatively, how someone taps into the environment to read and synthesize what the other actors or creative forces in the room are doing may be the key to the creative process.

Measuring Product

The most standard way in which acting is measured is not creative output, but in rewards for talent and the reflection of the audience. An audience or a critic who is prompted to think or feel in response to someone's acting will reward that acting as "good." However, the connection between what is considered "good" and what is considered "creative" in acting is understudied. Is *creativity* in acting the same as *success*?

Awards and the biggest money do not necessarily reward the most creative performance (i.e., the most innovative and different from the past), but rather the most appropriate performance, the most recognizably "true" performance. As with many fields, just because something breaks the boundaries of the traditional does not mean it is worthy – although, with other art forms such as music and painting, many are the anecdotes of new styles and new forms that at first were considered too extreme, and not appropriate, such as Cubism or Atonal music, which are now considered groundbreakingly creative and a central part of the current artistic form (Dempsey, 2010). With acting, the transition has been different – styles of acting have gotten more realistic over time (Benedetti, 2007; Goldstein & Bloom, 2011), but the ultimate goal of a good actor, to be unaffected and present on stage, has not changed. Even with the first writings we have on acting, the goal is to reflect the reality of the world on stage, using the constraints of the theatres available at the time, large amphitheaters, available only to men (Cole & Chinoy, 1949). In the modern era of performance, new questions arise in the broader field of theatre and film that do not necessarily speak to the creative act of acting. For example, a show that is cast race or gender blind may be considered creative in its casting. The fact that the actors are different from the norm for a particular part may be enough to create a creative performance, but could we then say that the actual actions of the actor – the actual acting – is creative?

The gatekeepers of performances, heads of theatre festivals, Tony voters, Oscar voters, and studio heads, are not necessarily looking for creative performances to reward. Rather, they are looking for actors who will attract consumers of their product, and who will give acting performances that are recognizable and emotionally true. Rarely would you hear a virtuosic performance called "creative." In fact, looking through critical and media quotations of the winner of Best Actor, Best Actress, Supporting Actor, and Supporting Actress for the last two years, there is not a single quote that discusses the actors' creativity. Instead, the quotes use words to describe actors including "remarkable," "brilliant," "precise," "powerful," "beautiful," "towering," "crisp," "explosive," "unerring," "literally transformative," "raw," and "emotionally devastating." Not a single advertisement that we could find included the word "creative" as a descriptor for an actor's award-winning performance. It is not part of the language of judging and thinking about acting. Similarly, creative responses in schoolwork are not necessarily considered appropriate (Beghetto, 2007). We propose that creative actors may be viewed by the general audience as taking away from the most critical goal of acting: providing the representation of reality that is somehow deemed as "correct."

Key Studies of Creativity in Acting

Given all of the variables at play in acting, it is unsurprising that as far as we know there have been almost no published empirical studies that take a psychological or social science viewpoint on acting and investigate how actors, acting processes, or acting products are creative. Instead, many studies take as a given that rehearsing and performing a character is a creative act and therefore the measurement of the actor as a person *is* the measurement of someone who is creative. This is most likely not unique to acting as a domain, but rather the arts more generally. Often, when people speak about research in creativity, the assumption is that something artistic is occurring. Both for children's creativity, and in fact the term creativity is often used to simply mean engagement in the arts. The idea that there are more and less creative actors (as opposed to more and less talented) is an unanswered question. Is a more talented actor simply a more creative actor? Are talent and creativity one and the same when it comes to acting? Or is talent a handicap when it comes to creativity and vice versa? What role does intuition (as opposed to *explicit work*) play in an actor's talent and creativity?

Studies on Process

While there are also no empirical or social science studies that we know of on the process of creating a role and engaging in the rehearsal process for scripted work, again, there is a considerable body of work on improvisational acting. The main findings in this domain come from R. Keith Sawyer's (2014) book *Group Creativity: Music, Theater, Collaboration*. Sawyer focuses on how creative improvisation in theatrical forms relies on each individual listening closely to each other individual member, not paying attention to their own need to stand in a spotlight, but rather paying attention to the best needs of the group. The keys here are the interactions in both gesture and language, which each actor needs to see as highly contingent on other actors. Actors also must realize that each individual actor can independently change the collective meaning of the improvised scene or dialogue based on whether they choose to take it in a new direction, causing performances to emerge holistically. The situations and ways in which actors present scenes in improvisation start as broadly general as possible so that each subsequent actor has many options to start to narrow down into a coherent scene. But there is an art and a strategy to work broadly at first, to allow for many different possible outcomes: to allow for creativity within the form. The key to creativity in the improvisational process for acting, then, is to allow for the group to steer the direction of the outcome more than any individual decision, each minor decision narrowing down the direction, without overwhelming it. Openness for as long as possible is the preference.

This can relate to scripted acting in a few ways: While the actors begin considerably more bounded (by the words of the playwright and the ideas of a single director) they can still think through many other possibilities in the interpretation of a script, keeping themselves as open as possible to multiple interpretations, until they decide on the most appropriate response. Actors in scripted theatre can also take from the work on improvisation that creativity in performance is highly dependent on the creativity of others and using their inputs to shape their own work, without overwhelmingly preferring their own interpretation, at least in the beginning.

One of the only published studies (that we know of) that investigated the creative process in scripted actors specifically is by Nemiro (1997). In extensive qualitative interviews with three professional actors, Nemiro described the various influences that the actors reported helped their creativity. These were collaboration, unity with audience, clear direction (in performance and choices), trust with the director, freedom to develop personal interpretation, lack of evaluation, respect and recognition, and being challenged. The actors also reported on what harmed or stifled their self-reported creativity, including poor directions that were inflexible, feeling interchangeable and not special, having an evaluator or feeling judged, acting only for reward (e.g. money), when others stopped listening, and distrust. Nemiro also concluded that most of the findings on creativity for actors could be subsumed within standard social psychological theories of creativity such as Amabile (1996), again looking to group and collaborative creativity. Important to note, however, is that Nemiro and her actors did not actually take any standard measures of creative thought, nor did they particularly define what they meant by creativity. Instead, they used the word "creativity" to define their engagement with acting as a whole.

Studies on Person

There has been considerable work done on non-creativity outcomes for actors. Actors have been found to have more potential for dissociative disorders, dissociative depersonalization, and more unresolved trauma (Thomson & Jaque, 2011, 2012; Thomson, Keehn, & Gumpel, 2009) than nonactors. Acting training has also been found to be associated with social understanding. Adolescents and adults engaged in acting training have higher levels of theory of mind, empathy, and adaptive emotion regulation than adolescents and adults without acting training (Goldstein & Winner, 2010; Goldstein, Tamir, & Winner, 2013; Nettle, 2006; Schellenberg 2004). One study compared children (ages 8–10) and adolescents (ages 13–15) who signed up to take a one-year acting class with same-aged children who signed up to take one year of visual arts or music class. Participants in both arts groups were similar on socioeconomic status, IQ, gender distribution, and age. Over the course of the year, both the children and adolescents in the acting group gained in self-reported empathy, and adolescents also improved in theory of mind. An ethnographic analysis of the acting classes found that for 8–10-year-olds, classes focused on physical action and paying attention to others, while in the adolescent acting classes, teachers focused on theory of mind concepts (i.e., thinking about the mental and emotional states of the character) (Goldstein & Winner, 2012).

Actors have been found to be higher on measures of absorption into imaginative worlds, changeability through absorption into work, and depersonalization of self (Goldstein & Winner, 2009; Panero, Goldstein, Rosenberg, Hughes & Winner, 2016; Thomson & Jaque, 2011, 2012; Thomson et al., 2009). Elite actors score highly on measures of extraversion and openness to experience (both of which are highly correlated with standard measures of creativity) (Goodman & Kaufman, 2014). Taken together, this work paints a picture that perhaps actors are more able to be changed, or more malleable than individuals who generate their own work, but this does not mean they are more creative – almost, it is as if they are more responsive to engaging with others' creativity rather than coming up with their own solutions to problems they work out.

One notable in-depth study investigated what emotions and thoughts actors are having and experiencing while actually performing. Elly Konijn, a Dutch psychologist and professor of media psychology, asked what actors are actually feeling as they create characters (Konijn 2000). The main conclusion of this study was that actors are much less reliant on the emotions of their characters, or even their own personal emotions as related to their characters in the moment of performance. Instead, actors seem to focus on "task emotions" of engaging with the audience in a way in which their performance is most clearly given, and most focused on presenting the character as they would like to have the audience react. The only mention of creativity comes within the context of "spontaneous" performance; that is making highly rehearsed and highly scripted performances feel like they are occurring anew each night. In fact, the theory is that this spontaneity only comes from the development of habits and habitual performance! The more preparation, the more the "creative magic" can occur onstage. This falls in line with the "infection of the subconscious" theory of acting training (McGaw et al., 2011).

Actors themselves have of course written about their process, and there are entire media genres devoted to exploring acting and actors and their progress. Magazines are filled with long profiles of actors, and how they do what they do. Since 1994 "Inside the Actor's Studio" has plumbed the depths of what actors do and how they do it. It has become enough of a cultural touchstone that its inquiries have been satirized on Saturday Night Live. The variety of processes echo the variety of training techniques and theories – some actors spend months conducting in depth research and focusing in on the details of everything that can find out about a character. Others spend time on themselves, imagining how their own lives are echoes in the lives of the characters. Still others (e.g. Caine, 2000) simply show up and read the lines on the script in the best, most honest, and most clear way they can for that moment. All of these methods are acts of creation, and the idea of which is most creative or even best suited for performances of different types is empirically unstudied (although of course every acting coach, teacher, director, and actor has their individual opinion, based on personal experience).

Studies on Product

The performance of acting in theatre and films can often be thought of as successful in one or more of three ways: financially, critically, or through awards (Simonton, 2009). Note that "creative" success is not part of this conversation. While research has not been conducted on theatre, for film awards, acting awards tend to "cluster" with other dramatic parts of a film such as directing, writing, and editing, and separately from visuals such as art and costume direction, technical aspects such as sound editing and mixing, and the music awards for score and song (Simonton, 2004). Female Oscar winners for acting are significantly less likely to come from films that won another Oscar in any other category, while male Oscar winners for acting are more likely to come from films that also won awards for best picture (Simonton, 2004).

Otherwise, there are no studies we know of that measure creative acting products or outcomes as a result of creative process. (Perhaps because the product of acting is not considered a creative product?) One study found that undergraduate and graduate students enrolled in theatre programs reported creativity correlates – flow experiences and high levels of intrinsic motivation – when engaged in rehearsal and performance (Martin & Cutler, 2002), but without a comparison group or real-time measurement. Research on which kinds of rehearsal process are most conducive to creative and successful work, or which kinds of elements come into a creative work, from a systematic and empirical viewpoint, would be welcome. The number of variables to control, however, would be difficult, as not every acting approach would be right for every individual performer or the medium of performance.

Going Forward

The future of the study of creativity and acting is wide open. Certainly in this chapter we have raised more questions about the nature, measurement, and allowance for creativity in scripted acting than we have provided findings and conclusions. There is so small of a research base for this topic that it is almost impossible to say where research in this field should or may travel over the next years. However, we have a few recommendations. The process of acting generally is vastly understudied from a psychological viewpoint. While there are huge numbers of books telling actors how to act, and, as mentioned, the public fascination with actors' processes via magazine interviews and television programs seems to be endless, the science is limited. A systematic study of expert actors, of awarded actors, of student actors, of experimental actors, with a psychologist's eye, has never been conducted. Such a study would go a long way to answering and bringing together the three aspects of acting – the people, the process, and the product – to investigate how creativity in acting works. Clearly defining creative acting, keeping in mind other artistic forms, such as visual arts and music, as well as the distinction between generative forms, which acting is not, and interpretive forms, which acting shares with music and dance (Thomson et al., 2009), is also critical.

Finally, comparisons of how different actors process, interpret, and perform similar roles could provide much in the way of both exploratory evidence for how creativity in acting works, and help answer the question as to how bound actors actually are by the roles themselves as compared to the environments in which the roles are generated. Comparison is always going to be a reality of judgment in acting, as is personal taste. Similarly to music, audience members and expert gatekeepers can have their judgments as to who has the best interpretation of a symphony, so do acting experts have their opinions of the best Tybalt in Romeo and Juliet (besides their nephew in the local high school production, of course). The question of creativity in the performance of a role, however, is unanswered. Bring on the research!

References

Adler, S. (2000). *The art of acting*. Hal Leonard Corporation.

Allen, D. 2001. *Performing Chekhov*. London: Routledge.

Amabile, T. (1996). *Creativity in context*. Westview Press.

Arnold, N. (1991). The manipulation of the audience by the director and actor. *Psychology and Performing Arts*, 75–81.

Aronson, A. (2000). *American avant-garde theatre: A history*. New York: Routledge.

Beghetto, R. A. (2007). Does creativity have a place in classroom discussions? Prospective teachers response preferences. *Thinking Skills and Creativity*, *2*(1), 1–9.

Benedetti, J. (2007). *The art of the actor: The essential history of acting, from classical times to the present day*. New York: Theatre Arts Book.

Bennett, S. (2013). *Theatre audiences*. Routledge.

Brestoff, R. (1995). *The great acting teachers and their methods*. ERIC.

Caine, M. (2000). *Acting in film: An actor's take on movie making*. Hal Leonard Corporation.

Cole, T., & Chinoy, H. K. (1949). *Actors on acting*. Crown Publishers.

Csikszentmihalyi, M. (1988). In M. Csikszentmihalyi, & I. S., Csikszentmihalyi (Eds.), *Optimal experience: Psychological studies of flow in consciousness* (pp. 15–35). New York, NY: Cambridge University Press.

Csikszentmihalyi, M., & Csikzentmihaly, M. (1991). *Flow: The psychology of optimal experience* (Vol. 41). New York: Harper Perennial.

Dempsey, A. (2010). *Styles, schools and movements: The essential encyclopaedic guide to modern art*. Thames & Hudson.

Dixon, M. B., & Smith, J. A. (1995). *Anne Bogart: Viewpoints*. Smith & Kraus Pub Incorporated.

Goldstein, T. R., & Bloom, P. (2011). The mind onstage: Why cognitive scientists should study acting. *Trends in Cognitive Science, 15*, 141–142.

Goldstein, T. R., & Winner, E. (2009). Living in alternative and inner worlds: Early signs of acting talent. *Creativity Research Journal, 21*(1), 117–124.

Goldstein, T. R., & Winner, E. (2010). Engagement in role play, pretense, and acting classes predict advanced theory of mind skill in middle childhood. *Imagination, Cognition and Personality, 30*(3), 249–258.

Goldstein, T. R., & Winner, E. (2012). Enhancing empathy and theory of mind. *Journal of Cognition and Development, 13*(1), 19–37.

Goldstein, T. R., Tamir, M., & Winner, E. (2013). Expressive suppression and acting classes. *Psychology of Aesthetics, Creativity, and the Arts, 7*(2), 191.

Goodman, G., & Kaufman, J. C. (2014). Gremlins in my head: Predicting stage fright in elite actors. *Empirical Studies of the Arts, 32*, 133–148.

Hodge, A. (2000). *Twentieth century actor training*. Routledge.

Hodge, A. (2010). *Actor training*. Routledge.

Hull, S. L. (1985). *Strasberg's method as taught by Lorrie hull: A practical guide for actors, teachers, and directors*. Ox Bow Pub.

Kaufman, J. C. (2009). *Creativity 101*. Springer.

Knowlson, J., *Damned to fame: The life of Samuel Beckett*. London: Bloomsbury.

Kogan, N. (2002). Careers in the performing arts: A psychological perspective. *Communication Research Journal, 14*(1), 1–16.

Konijn, E. A. (1991). Empirical analysis of emotion processes in the theatre. *Psychology and Performing Arts*, 59.

Konijn, E. A. (2000). *Acting emotions: Shaping emotions on stage*. Leiden University Press.

Lyons, D. (1955). Morning Advocate, The Lyons Den by Leonard Lyons (Syndicated), Quote Page 4A, Column 2, Baton Rouge, Louisiana.

Martin, J. J., & Cutler, K. (2002). An exploratory study of flow and motivation in theater actors. *Journal of Applied Sport Psychology, 14*, 344–352.

Mee, C. (2015). Retrieved on September 15, 2015, from http://charlesmee.org/.

McGaw, C., Stilson, K., & Clark, L. (2011). *Acting is believing*. Cengage Learning.

Meisner, S., & Longwell, D. (1987). *Sanford Meisner on acting*. Vintage.

Nemiro, J. (1997). Interpretive artists: A qualitative exploration of the creative process of actors. *Creativity Research Journal, 10*(2–3), 229–239.

Nettle, D. (2006). Psychological profiles of professional actors. *Personality and Individual Differences, 40*(2), 375–383.

Noice, T., & Noice, H. (1997). *The nature of expertise in professional acting: A cognitive view*. Lawrence Erlbaum.

Oddey, A. (2013). *Devising theatre: A practical and theoretical handbook.* Routledge.

Panero, M. E., Goldstein, T. R., Rosenberg, R. Hughes, H., & Winner, E. (in press). Do actors posses traits associated with high hypnotizability? *Psychology of Aesthetics, Creativity and the Arts.*

Poyatos, F. (2002). *Nonverbal communication across disciplines: Paralanguage, kinesics, silence, personal and environmental interaction* (Vol. 2). John Benjamins Publishing.

Russ, S. W., Robins, A. L., & Christiano, B. A. (1999). Pretend play: Longitudinal prediction of creativity and affect in fantasy in children. *Creativity Research Journal, 12,* 129–139.

Sawyer, R. K. (2012). *Explaining creativity: The science of human innovation.* Oxford University Press.

Sawyer, R. K. (2014). *Group creativity: Music, theater, collaboration.* Psychology Press.

Schellenberg, E. G. (2004). Music lessons enhance IQ. *Psychological Science, 15*(8), 511.

Schwartz, G. (2012). Viola Spolin. Retrieved on September 23, 2015, from www.spolin.com/?p=864.

Shakespeare, W. (2008). *Hamlet, The Norton Shakespeare.* NY, NY. (Original work published 1699).

Simonton, D. K. (2004). Group artistic creativity: Creative clusters and cinematic success in feature films1. *Journal of Applied Social Psychology, 34*(7), 1494–1520.

Simonton, D. K. (2009). Cinematic success criteria and their predictors: The art and business of the film industry. *Psychology & Marketing, 26*(5), 400–420.

Spolin, V. (1999). *Improvisation for the theater: A handbook of teaching and directing techniques.* Northwestern University Press.

Taylor, J. (2007). *Ubu and the Truth Commission.* University of Cape Town Press.

Thomson, P., & Jaque, S. (2011). Testimonial theatre-making: Establishing or dissociating the self. *Psychology of Aesthetics, Creativity, and the Arts, 5*(3), 229.

Thomson, P., & Jaque, S. (2012). Holding a mirror up to nature: Psychological vulnerability in actors. *Psychology of Aesthetics, Creativity, and the Arts, 6,* 361–369.

Thomson, P., Keehn, E. B., & Gumpel, T. P. (2009). Generators and interpreters in a performing arts population: Dissociation, trauma, fantasy proneness, and affective states. *Creativity Research Journal, 21*(1), 72–91. DOI:10.1080/10400410802633533

Weiss, K. (2013). *The plays of Samuel Beckett.* A&C Black.

Wooster, R. (2007). *Contemporary theatre in education.* Intellect Books.

Worthen, W. B. (1996). *The Harcourt brace anthology of drama.* Houghton Mifflin Harcourt.

10 Musical Creativity

Aaron Kozbelt

Brooklyn College and the Graduate Center of the City University of New York

Abstract

Music is a paradigmatic domain of creative activity, culturally ubiquitous and manifested in a multitude of ways. Here I explore music as a domain of human creativity – both as a specific "content" domain informing *productive* aspects of musical creativity, and as a domain of mind, whose evolutionary backstory constrains the *reception* of music. In discussing the phylogenetic emergence of human musicality, I highlight possible tensions in the creative dynamic between novelty and canalized aesthetic preferences. A richer discussion of the creative process in music follows, illustrated by anecdotal and interview accounts as well as laboratory and archival studies, which collectively have shed substantial light on contemporary theories of creativity. I close by discussing the role of socio-cultural factors in musical creativity and some possible future directions for research.

Music represents a basic aspect of human experience and a culturally ubiquitous outlet of creative expression (Brown, 1991). Musicality has been identified as a fundamental domain of the mind (Feist, 2004; Gardner, 1983), emerging spontaneously in all normally developing persons. Music also figures in debates about the evolutionary origins of modern humans (Justus & Hutlser, 2005; Levitin, 2009; Miller, 2000a; Pinker, 1997; Wallin, Merker, & Brown, 2000). Archaeological evidence indicates that musical instruments were fabricated at least 42,000 years ago (Higham et al., 2012), and since singing almost certainly antedates instrumental music, *Homo sapiens* has probably engaged in music for the entirety of our existence as a species. In contemporary society, the annual worldwide revenue of the music industry is some 15 billion dollars ("Music Industry," 2015), and some surveys suggest that the average person spends some 40 percent of their waking lives listening to music (Sloboda, O'Neill, & Ivaldi, 2001). From medical and humanistic perspectives, the ability of music to entertain, inspire, and heal is well documented (Sacks, 2007). Even among aesthetic spheres of activity, music has special status, as in Pater's (1893/2010) dictum, "All art constantly aspires to the condition of music" (p. 124).

Creativity permeates human musicality. Many standard concepts in the creativity literature (see Kozbelt, Beghetto, & Runco, 2010) straightforwardly apply to the domain of music: the so-called six P's of creativity (process, product, person, place, persuasion, and potential), theoretical accounts including developmental, cognitive, and systems views, and levels of creative achievement. The latter range from so-called mini-c to Big-C creativity (Kaufman & Beghetto, 2009): the difference between someone privately humming a new tune versus enduring cultural monuments like Beethoven's symphonies.

However, creativity operates in music somewhat differently than in many domains. Music itself is evanescent, quickly passing out of personal and cultural memory unless notated or recorded. The sense of music as a fundamental, evolutionarily rooted aspect of our human nature (Levitin, 2009) differs from many other activities; for instance, chess, which seems positively artificial by comparison. Yet, while most people enjoy music, mastery of an instrument or music notation typically takes years of effort (Ericsson, Krampe, & Tesch-Römer, 1993). At the same time, individual differences in talent are at least as prominent in music as any other domain (Gardner, 1983). Manifestations of musicality often depart from the stereotype of a solitary individual producing a tangible, definitive creative production (Sawyer, 2006); thus, collaboration and distributed cognition are inherent aspects of many music-related activities. One may speak of creativity in musical composition, improvisation, performance, and even listening (Clarke, 2012; Hargreaves, Hargreaves, & North, 2012) – as in someone creating a playlist tailored for a particular mood or activity. The many modes of creativity available to contemporary musicians and listeners has made many scholars wary of understanding musical creativity in any unified sense; indeed, some have questioned the appropriateness of the term "creativity" in music, suggesting as alternatives "musical creativities" (Burnard, 2012) or "musical invention" (MacDonald, Byrne, & Carlton, 2006).

Without belaboring terminology, the goal of this chapter is to explore musical creativity from the perspective of contemporary psychological research, emphasizing the highest level of creative achievement as its clearest manifestation. I first explore the nature of the domain of music – both as a specific "content" domain, which informs *productive* aspects of musical creativity, and as a fundamental "domain of mind" (Feist, 2004), whose evolutionary backstory constrains the *reception* of music. In discussing mechanisms responsible for the phylogenetic emergence of human musicality and typical features of most human music, I highlight tensions in the creative dynamic between ambitious creators' pursuit of novelty and evolutionarily canalized aesthetic preferences. Next follows a discussion of the creative process in music, in which various methodologies have collectively illuminated contemporary theories of creativity. I close with sociocultural aspects of music and some possible future research directions.

What Is the Domain of Music?

What should be the scope for discussing creativity in music, or the domain of music in general? Many definitions of music have been offered – for instance, "the capacity to produce, perceive, and appreciate rhythmic and melodic sounds that evoke an emotional response in oneself and others" (Feist, 2004, p. 61). Most definitions emphasize the production and perception of patterns rooted in basic acoustic parameters like pitch, dynamics, tempo, timbre, rhythm, and so on. The number of ways of organizing such parameters, and musicians' potential flexibility in deploying them into small- and large-scale patterns, has produced the aesthetic riches of the world's great musical traditions. Extending notions of "music" further, composers may deliberately violate definitional sensibilities, as in John Cage's infamous *4:33*, which contains no sounds at all: A pianist sits silently for four minutes and thirty-three seconds. Such fecundity in conceptualizing and elaborating musical ideas raises the issue of how best to demarcate the 'domain' of music as a finite object of study.

Domain Generality vs. Domain Specificity

The question of how to characterize a domain of creativity is neither new nor unique to music. Among creativity researchers, a now-classic (or passé) debate concerns whether creativity is better regarded as more domain general or more domain specific (Baer, 2010). A few details of this protracted disputation are worth reviewing. Domain generalists argue that a person's creativity largely results from all-purpose cognitive mechanisms or propensities to be creative. These staples of the creativity research literature include divergent thinking (Guilford, 1950), flatter associative hierarchies (Mednick, 1962), regression into primary process cognition (Martindale, 1990), tolerance for ambiguity (Amabile, 1996), ideational abilities (Simonton, 1999), creative potential (Runco, 2007), variable attention (Vartanian, 2009), and flexible cognitive control (Zabelina & Robinson, 2010). Such mechanisms are argued to play out in many forms and disciplines, and they also inform the extent to which an individual might self-characterize as "creative." Evidence for domain-generality typically rests on psychometric or personality data, often self-report inventories (Baer, 2010). Mechanisms like divergent thinking predict creative accomplishments (Plucker, 1999), at least when creative achievement is assessed in a global way. On the domain-general account, high levels of musical creativity would emerge largely out of the confluence of such cognitive mechanisms, channeled – for whatever reason – into the domain of music.

In contrast, the domain-specific view argues that general psychological mechanisms are inadequate to explain creative accomplishment and that knowledge and skills rooted in the content and activities of a particular domain are necessary. Typically, such domain-specific knowledge and skills are thought not to transfer to creativity in other domains. One line of support for this view is the paucity of eminent polymaths like da Vinci and Leibniz (Baer, 2010); more commonly, great creators excel in only one domain. Relatedly, high achievement in complex domains invariably requires a person to dedicate enormous effort and deliberate practice (Ericsson et al., 1993; Weisberg, 1999, 2006), leaving little time to gain expertise in additional domains. Indeed, even the greatest composers typically required at least a decade of intensive study before producing original masterworks (Hayes, 1989; Simonton, 1991). Additional evidence for domain specificity involves special populations; for instance, cases of exceptional precociousness. Along these lines, Gardner (1983) asserted, "of all gifts with which individuals may be endowed, none emerges earlier than musical talent" (p. 99). Notably, the early appearance of talent is typically compartmentalized to a particular domain: Even contemporary accounts of the musically astonishing young Mozart (Barrington, 1770) emphasized his relative normalcy in non-musical contexts (see also Fisher, 1995; Kenneson, 2003).

Attempts to resolve the generality–specificity debate have taken several forms (Baer & Kaufman, 2005; Plucker & Beghetto, 2004; Silvia, Kaufman, & Pretz, 2009). Without pretending to resolve the debate, I submit that for the purposes of studying *productive* aspects of musical creativity, a domain-specific stance is more useful – particularly since most examples in this chapter involve Big-C creativity among classical composers. Such cases most clearly inform the phenomenon of creativity and appear to apply to other instances as well: See accounts of jazz saxophonist Charlie Parker's improvisations and the importance of practice for the Beatles (Weisberg, 1999), and lifespan creativity trends in American song writers (Hass & Weisberg, 2009, 2015) and cinema composers (Simonton, 2007). The extent to which such intensively domain-specific principles also inform non-Western traditions and less mainstream traditions, including contemporary practices, is an open question.

Music as a Domain of Mind

The domain-generality vs. domain-specificity controversy underscores a broader issue characterizing domains in the first place. As Sternberg (2009) noted, "The greatest challenge in understanding the domain-generality versus specificity of creativity is in understanding the concept of a domain itself" (p. 25). In music, the issue is compounded by an oft-articulated sense that music is not merely an artificial "content" domain like chess but instead is a more fundamental *domain of mind* (Feist, 2004) or one of several *multiple intelligences* (Gardner, 1983). Such accounts typically recruit several categories of evidence: Feist (2007) argued that "nothing less than the combined interdisciplinary evidence from archeology, primatology, developmental psychology, anthropology, giftedness/education, neuroscience, and genetics is required before something can be classified as a domain [of mind]" (p. 20). For instance, even quite young infants show sensitivity to many aspects of music and evince systematic musical preferences (Trehub, 2003).

Besides prodigies, some of the most provocative evidence for understanding domain specificity in music relies on other special populations. Accomplished music performers differ significantly from non-musicians in neurological, cognitive, physiological, and perceptual-motor terms (Lehmann & Gruber, 2006). Some savants (Charness, Clifton, & MacDonald, 1988) and persons with Williams syndrome (Levitin & Belluggi, 1998) show pronounced musical ability despite severe general cognitive impairments. On the less musical side is congenital amusia, leaving some individuals largely unable to process musical information (Peretz, 2008) despite otherwise normal mental functioning. I note in passing that while much of this evidence includes a strong neuroscience component, neuroscientific work on specifically creative aspects of music (Brattico & Tervaniemi, 2010) remains limited compared to other aspects of the neuroscience of music (Brattico & Pearce, 2013).

How does regarding music as a domain of mind figure into a discussion of musical *creativity*? Just as I argued for the domain-specific account of productive aspects of creativity, the domain-of-mind view is suited to understanding the *reception* of those productions. Specifically, the evolutionary backstory inherent to a domain-of-mind account suggests humans may have strong evolutionarily determined biases in how they process and respond to musical information. This process of "canalization" (Waddington, 1942; see also Wilson, 1998) would constrain the kinds of music that people find worth spending time and money on and engender culture-independent regularities in music preferences and styles around the world. Notably, combining a domain-specific view of musical creativity with a domain-of-mind view for the aesthetic reception of music introduces an inherent long-term tension into the dynamics of creativity, whereby the imperative for novelty begins to run against the grain of evolutionarily canalized aesthetic preferences – a theme taken up in the next section.

Evolutionary Roots of Musicality

Questions about the evolutionary basis of human music and musical creativity are two-tiered. One level engages our predilection for music in general: Why do we enjoy and engage in music rather than not doing so? Another level engages particular preferences in music: What specific characteristics of music appear to be intrinsically appealing, at least to large segments of humanity? I address each question in turn.

The Phylogenetic Emergence of Human Music

Several hypotheses about the purposes and functions of music (and the arts more generally) have been advanced (Dissanayake, 2007). One possibility is that music represents a genuine direct adaptation arising through Darwinian natural selection, potentially linked in some way to the origin of language (see chapters in Wallin, Merker, & Brown, 2000). In this view, musicality played an active role in promoting the differential survival and reproduction of our ancestors and was itself a basis of selection. A variant involves the use of music for social bonding, providing advantages to groups rather than individuals (Freeman, 2000) – though the viability of group selection as an evolutionary mechanism has been doubted (see Miller, 2000a). Another possibility is Darwinian sexual selection (Miller, 2000a, 2000b), whereby musical virtuosity functioned as an honest signal of high quality genes and superior cognitive ability. This perspective posits a different point of origin for our aesthetic sensibilities, evolving "as a functional part of social and sexual cognition, not as a side-effect of perceptual psychology" (Miller, 2001, p. 20), but it again affirms the idea that humans have systematic aesthetic preferences ultimately derived from evolutionary processes.

Yet another perspective views musicality as a by-product of other adaptations, rather than one that is selected for in its own right: so-called evolutionary "cheesecake" (Pinker, 1997) or exaptations (Gould & Vrba, 1982), whereby a trait or capacity is evolutionarily co-opted to some new use. Pinker (1997) noted that music draws on a variety of mental faculties for its effect – language, auditory scene analysis, emotional calls, habitat selection, and motor control, among others – and argued that the phylogenetic emergence of music resulted from selection in other cognitive domains, instead of music directly (see also Justus & Hutsler, 2005). Notably, this view suggests a greater degree of inter-cultural flexibility in human musical aesthetics, as well as a greater methodological emphasis on studying aesthetics via popular works, rather than esoteric, if revered, masterpieces. Finally, it is worth mentioning a perspective, traditionally prevalent in the humanities and dubbed the "standard social sciences model" (or SSSM) by Tooby and Cosmides (1992), that regards culture as largely independent of evolution and which thus posits few cross-cultural aesthetic or musical universals.

Apart from the last-mentioned view, proposed evolutionary mechanisms imply that human music is predicated on an underlying biological basis and should thus show substantial cross-cultural regularities. Many scholars (see, e.g., Justus & Hutsler, 2005; Trehub, 2000) have argued that human music does show such regularities – *contra* a strong SSSM view – though, alas, this does not readily discriminate among the remaining mechanisms.

Regularities and Constraints

What specific regularities are evident in human music worldwide? Justus and Hutsler (2005), synthesizing evidence from perceptual and developmental psychology with cross-cultural studies, proposed some candidate evolutionary regularities, including the importance of the octave and other simple pitch ratios like the perfect fifth, categorizing the octave into tones, unequal interval sizes in scales and the tonal hierarchies resulting from them, principles of grouping and meter, and the importance of melodic contour.

Documentation of particular musical regularities is usually achieved by archival analyses of corpuses of musical material. For instance, a long tradition of research has looked at melodic contour, that is, the ways that notes are typically arranged into melodies. Note-to-note transitions of melodies show strong consistencies, which can be computed by transposing a large population of melodies to a common tonic, then computing the proportion of melodies for which the first two notes are C-C, C-G, or any other combination, and repeating this for subsequent transitions, to yield a metric of the originality or unexpectedness of the melody. Studies using such measures (e.g., Kozbelt & Meredith, 2010; Paisley, 1964; Simonton, 1980, 1994), sometimes with samples of thousands of melodies, have produced a quantitative assessment of the typical distribution of transition probabilities and yielded findings on questions as varied as style identification, lifespan and trans-historical melodic originality trajectories, and the relation of melodic originality to composers' stressful life events – all relevant to understanding musical creativity.

Besides the overall distribution of note-to-note transition probabilities, melodies themselves show other strong structural regularities. Huron (2006) summarized four characteristics typical of melodies worldwide: pitch proximity (most note-to-note transitions involve small intervals), central pitch tendency (most melodies end on the tonic), arch phrase tendency (melodies tend to rise in pitch and then fall), and ascending leap versus descending step asymmetry (rising intervals tend to be larger than falling ones). Detailing the last example, Vos and Troost (1989) documented ascending/descending asymmetry using a corpus of 796 melodies drawn from Western classical music, Beatles songs, and folk music from around the world; in their dataset, all intervals less than or equal to a major third tended to descend in the majority of occurrences, while intervals at least as large as a perfect fourth tended to ascend.

Although available evidence amply documents systematic regularities in melodies worldwide, the evolutionary reasons they take on their specific forms are unclear. For instance, why do rising intervals tend to be larger than smaller intervals – rather than the opposite, or there being no difference – when there is no compelling adaptive reason? In considering music as a *creative* domain, evolution-derived constraints on musical expression become especially important. Musical creators work within the stylistic parameters of their domain as they inherit it from their predecessors. When creators produce significantly novel work, those parameters themselves are modified – as when Beethoven raised the stakes of writing symphonies by conceiving and composing them on a far grander scale than had his main predecessors, Haydn and Mozart, or when Wagner, in his opera *Tristan und Isolde*, introduced substantially greater chromaticism into musical tonality. If judged to be important, innovations are passed along to the next generation of creators, who take them up in turn (Csikszentmihalyi, 1988). This dynamic involving a ceaseless quest for novelty was most clearly articulated by Martindale (1990, 2009), who developed a detailed theory of stylistic evolution in the arts. The combinatorial possibilities of complex musical systems give ample scope for individual expression and stylistic development as a great musical tradition evolves.

Ultimately, however, continual striving for novelty reaches a point where the resulting creative products' characteristics begin to run against the grain of canalized preferences. A good illustration of this tension is the rise of atonal music among twentieth-century composers, particularly the iconoclastic Arnold Schoenberg. Virtually all music around the world has a tonal center and consonant, rather than dissonant, harmony. By the early twentieth century, European classical music had become progressively more chromatic. Schoenberg took the decisive step of eliminating a tonal center altogether. Despite – or because of – his many musical innovations, many find Schoenberg's music difficult or incomprehensible (Thomson, 1991). One might regard Schoenberg as monolithically rebellious, attempting to break every musical rule he could think of. This caricature overlooks the fact that some aspects of Schoenberg's music continued to obey typical constraints: For instance, in a recent study, Meredith and Kozbelt (2014) analyzed the vocal lines of ninety-seven Schoenberg compositions, finding that he preserved – indeed, exaggerated – the usual asymmetrical pattern of ascending leaps and descending steps. It is unclear if Schoenberg himself was explicitly aware of the asymmetry later documented by Vos and Troost (1989), but the fact that he retained it is notable, begging the question of the extent to which it is possible to overcome (possibly implicit) statistical regularities in music. More generally, if human aesthetics are evolutionarily canalized, what are the options for ambitious creators like Schoenberg who seek to break with an aesthetic tradition in highly novel ways, while still achieving recognition?

Such issues have not been in the forefront of psychological research on musical creativity, but understanding this tension is likely to become an increasingly important issue. Some initial empirical traction on these issues may be achieved by careful trans-historical analyses. For instance, several studies (Simonton, 1980; Kozbelt & Meredith, 2010) have documented fluctuations in melodic originality over the last few centuries of European music history, finding oscillating but generally upward-moving trends toward greater originality (see also Martindale, 1990). Rodriguez Zivic, Shifres, and Cecchi (2013) showed that distributions of note-to-note transitions, based on statistical expectancies, clearly discriminate among stylistic periods of classical music history. In other words, the statistical features of music itself provide objective metrics bearing on the development and time course of changes and consistencies in musical language. In a somewhat different vein, Gjerdingen (1988), documenting an instance of purely cultural transmission, undertook a historical study of incidence of the "1-7-4-3" idiom in Western tonal-harmonic music, finding a strong peak around 1770 and a rapid trailing-off thereafter. Applying archival methods to trans-historical questions provide a means of disentangling characteristics of music that are more canalized and thus culturally enduring, versus those arising as somewhat arbitrary conventions, like the 1-7-4-3 idiom, which may fade into obscurity and disuse.

In sum, human musicality shows deep evolutionary roots. While the specific selection pressures for its origins remain unclear, quantitative analyses of music have demonstrated numerous cross-cultural regularities, which may provide strong constraints on ambitious musicians' quest for originality. Attempts at novelty that run strongly against the evolutionary grain may be doomed either to oblivion or to approbation only by an initiated elite; alternatively, human aesthetic sensibilities may be more flexible than heretofore supposed. This is an empirical question, at the moment perhaps best addressed by careful quantitative assessments of trans-historical changes in various aspects of musical style, to distinguish those that are transient from those that stubbornly endure.

Music and the Creative Process

While the archival studies mentioned above describe many important characteristics of music, they say little about the psychological processes by which music is created or composed. The creative process has been a staple of research for decades, having been studied via multiple methodologies; in the domain of music, these have collectively drawn a rich picture of the composer at work (see also Schmidt, 2016). Sloboda (1985) delineated three approaches to gaining psychological insight into music composition: examining written manuscripts (including sketches), composers' own comments about their compositional process, and observation during a session of composition. These, plus historiometric archival studies of composers' outputs, which have also greatly informed issues in musical creativity, are now reviewed.

Sketches, First-Person Accounts, and Observational Studies

Musicologists have long examined composers' sketches and notebooks as a way of understanding their methods and goals. Such approaches have been useful for establishing the complexity of the creative process and have debunked myths like Mozart's supposed invariably revisionless fluency (Konrad, 1992). However, understanding sketches – even at the level of deciphering the notes – demands enormous domain-specific and contextual knowledge, and scholars' conclusions are always open to interpretation. Moreover, while some composers sketched prolifically (e.g., some 8,000 pages of Beethoven's sketches survive: Cooper, 1990), in other instances they are much rarer. Indeed, questions about the representativeness of the sketches for a composer's working methods as well as the completeness and chronological sequence of the paper trail can rarely be fully resolved.

Besides sketches and scores, many composers have also left provocative descriptive accounts of their own creative processes. These often show a suspicious Romantic veneer (see Perkins, 1981). For example: Richard Wagner, having written the text for his monumental four-opera *Ring* cycle but at a loss for how to begin the music, fell into a reverie and imagined hearing the low roll of a river, which became – naturally, in short order – the sustained, slowly unfolding E-flat major chord comprising the prelude to *Das Rheingold*, whose first scene takes place underwater (Millington, 1992). Other composers have described their creative struggles: Claude Debussy once remarked, "it sometimes takes me weeks to choose between two chords" (Vallas, 1973, p. 224). However interesting, such anecdotes suffer from clear methodological limitations, most notably questionable representativeness and veracity: For instance, a famous letter attributed to Mozart and detailing his own creative process continues to be cited as such (Cook, 2012), despite having been proved a forgery (Solomon, 1980). Moreover, anecdotes can be cherry-picked to support virtually any theoretical position (Kozbelt, 2007). Such limitations can sometimes be overcome, but usually research questions are better served by other methods, particularly when the goal is to conduct strong tests of psychological theories of creativity.

Along such qualitative methodological lines, some researchers have investigated the nature of composers' creative processes by more systematic interview and/or observational methods, sometimes supplemented with analyses of sketches and works-in-progress. For instance, Sigmund Koch conducted extensive interviews with noted composers like Virgil Thompson and Milton Babbitt (see Franklin, 2001), attempting to understand something of their creative processes. More recently, Katz and Gardner (2012) conducted in-depth interviews of twenty-four contemporary "New Music" composers, detailing accounts of their creative processes and finding two distinct prototypical compositional strategies: Within Domain and Beyond Domain. Within-Domain processes are inspired predominantly by musical materials themselves, and Beyond-Domain processes are influenced by metaphors and associations beyond the discipline of music – an intriguing wrinkle in the classic domain-generality vs. domain-specificity debate. Katz and Gardner also argued that much of the activity of composers roughly follows classic 'stage theories' of the creative process. Indeed, many characterizations of creativity have drawn on Wallas's (1926) venerable four-stage model of creative insight: preparation (initial active work on a problem), incubation (a subsequent period of not working on a problem), illumination (the sudden appearance into consciousness of a viable solution), and verification (the act of working through the details and implications of that solution). More recent stage theories (e.g., Bennett, 1976; Burnard & Younker, 2002) have often modified Wallas's original account, allowing recursion and cycling through the various steps at both global and local levels (e.g., Bamberger, 1977; Davidson & Welsh, 1988).

Other models of creative thinking in music have emphasized particular cognitive processes, like the interplay between divergent and convergent thinking (e.g., Webster, 1987) or concurrent streams of thought (Aranosian, 1981). More recently, Schubert (2012) proposed a mechanism for musical creativity rooted in spreading activation and the principle of dissociation, involving the activation of a large number of nodes in a semantic network while inhibiting pain nodes, which is thought to maximize overall pleasure and permit profound aesthetic experience (see also other associative theories of creativity: e.g., Mednick, 1962; Gabora, 2000).

Yet another methodology in laboratory studies involves having composers verbalize their thoughts while writing music. This technique of verbal protocol analysis (Ericsson & Simon, 1984) can reveal a great deal about a composer's concerns and goals, particularly when supplemented by other sources of data. For instance, Reitman (1965) conducted a pioneering case study of a professional composer writing a fugue, with the aim of establishing whether or not it would provide adequate material for computer modelling. Another notable investigation is that of McAdams's (2004) case study of Pulitzer Prize-winning composer Roger Reynolds, using his notebooks, sketches, diagrams, recorded interviews, and the final score to document and understand the process by which a new work for piano, chamber orchestra, and computer-processed sound was created – in particular, addressing how several significant compositional problems were solved. Collins (2005) engaged in a similar three-year case study of a composer, using converging methods and data sources, finding evidence for chunking of processes and strategies at both micro and macro levels, and suggesting a generative process of problem proliferation and successive solution implementation, both linearly and recursively. Donin (2012), summarizing several of his studies of composer Philippe Leroux, argued for ongoing cross-fertilization of different methodologies in studying musical creativity and articulated several emerging issues in the study of compositional cognition, notably synoptic planning vs. heuristic ideation, generating rules in the course of music writing, cycle development and concern of coherence, and creative borrowing as a crucial part of creative cognition.

In sum, a great deal of research has advanced a number of concepts and cognitive processes that are potentially useful for a psychological understanding of the nature of the creative process in music. These varied approaches largely have in common a view of music as a form of ill-defined problem solving (Reitman, 1965), in which there is no single "correct" answer or "best" solution. To achieve a good-enough solution, composers must make many decisions, generating musical ideas, evaluating them on aesthetic and pragmatic criteria, assembling them into a coherent structure, working out scoring, voice-leading, and counterpoint, gauging the piece's likely emotional impact, and so on, until it is deemed finished. Composers organize and structure their behavior to transform nascent ideas into a performable product. Composers' domain-specific means of structuring their creative problem-solving behavior can be regarded as schemas, which may be defined as mental structures used "to perceive or act effectively by anticipating the organization of what the person apprehends or does, so the person needn't function as much from scratch" (Perkins, 1981, p. 173). Professional composers' schemas represent probably the clearest example of domain-specific musical knowledge enabling high-level creativity, and musicians have long recognized their utility: As composer Aaron Copland (1939) noted, "every well-trained composer has, as his stock in trade, certain normal structural molds on which to lean for the basic framework of his compositions" (p. 31). Indeed, in line with the importance of schemas and other expertise accounts of creativity (e.g., Weisberg, 1999, 2006), the composition process itself is often regarded as highly rational (Konečni, 2012; Kozbelt, 2008a). This supposition has strong implications for issues like the extent to which Big-C creators could learn to control the creative process and become more creative with experience – questions that have been informed by archival studies of great composers.

Archival Studies of Lifespan Creativity

Archival studies of classical composers use creators' outputs and pragmatic assessment of that output (e.g., recording counts or citations in music history books) to test hypotheses about how, for instance, output changes with age (Simonton, 1997). Psychologists have developed two major perspectives on lifespan creativity: the expertise acquisition view (Ericsson, 1999; Weisberg, 1999, 2006) and the blind variation and selective retention (BVSR) view (Simonton, 1997, 2011). The two theories make different assumptions and predictions about how creativity unfolds throughout creators' lives. The expertise view emphasizes domain-specific knowledge and logical problem-solving processes and is thus optimistic about creative control and longitudinal improvement; however, the view of expertise as superior reproducible performance does not necessarily translate into creative productivity (Simonton, 2000). In contrast, the classic BVSR perspective emphasizes serendipity and a quantity-drives-quality dynamic and has traditionally been more pessimistic about creative control and agewise improvement.

The most direct evidence bearing on these two views comes from empirical studies in which aspects of creators' outputs are quantitatively operationalized. One operationalization is career landmarks: the ages at which individual composers began studying music, composing, wrote their earliest acknowledged masterwork, greatest work, and final masterwork, and stopped composing altogether. Some results on career landmarks support the expertise acquisition perspective, particularly the so-called "ten-year rule" (Hayes, 1989; Kozbelt, 2008a) mentioned earlier, but others do not. For instance, the very greatest composers began studying and writing music – and masterpieces – earlier, and wrote their last masterpiece later than their less eminent counterparts (Simonton, 1991). This suggests the acquisition of expertise and its translation into creative productivity is modulated by talent.

Many findings on career landmarks can be understood via the BVSR account (Simonton, 1997, 2011), which takes individual differences in creative potential as a starting point and which models typical agewise output in a way consistent with observed results: Productivity starts low, rapidly climbs, peaks around age 40, and gradually declines. Varying parameters of the model changes the trajectory's shape; for instance, greater potential increases overall output and broadens the age span encompassing the career landmarks described above, although with no change of predicted age at best work – all consistent with empirical findings. Intriguingly, the classic BVSR view (Simonton, 1997) explicitly posited an inability of creators to control the creative process or systematically improve with age. This construct is often operationalized via a "hit ratio," an index of masterworks to total works that are produced within each age interval of a creator's career. On the BVSR account, hit ratio should not systematically change with age, consistent with earlier research (e.g., Dennis, 1966; Simonton, 1977), albeit using fairly small samples.

Notably, more recent research on lifespan creativity in classical composers (e.g., Kozbelt, 2008a, 2011), using much larger samples and different statistical approaches, has revised this view. Case studies of Mozart's lifespan creativity (Kozbelt, 2005) and of the acumen of Beethoven's self-critical assessments (Kozbelt, 2007) yielded results inconsistent with the classic BVSR view (see also Weisberg, 2006). In perhaps the most extensive study of composers' longitudinal hit ratios (Kozbelt, 2008a), sixty-five great composers' complete works were tabulated; each work's masterpiece status was determined by expert ratings, citation in music history books, and recording counts. Multi-level modeling showed hit ratio robustly followed a single-peaked function with a maximum around age 50, inconsistent with the classic BVSR model. Individual differences in trajectories were also notable – specifically, composers who wrote their best work later in their careers showed stronger overall agewise increases in hit ratio. Similar results have been found for expert ratings of masterwork quality (Kozbelt, 2011), implying that some composers continually improve, while others fizzle out (see also Kozbelt, 2008b). Kozbelt (2008a) also found that late-peaking composers evinced a reliably weaker quantity-drives-quality dynamic than early-peaking composers.

Such strong individual differences suggest nomothetic views creativity may be misguided. An alternative is to prioritize inter-creator variability, which may be organized into typological categories, as in Galenson's (2006) framework of "finders" and "seekers." Kozbelt (2012, 2014) applied Galenson's typology to music, coupling quantitative findings on variability in composers' career trajectories with qualitative accounts of their compositional concerns and processes. In brief, "seekers," like Haydn, Brahms, Verdi, Franck, Bruckner, Dvořák, and Bartók, showed longitudinal improvement and late career peaks. They also habitually worked in traditional forms highlighting craftsmanship and the development of musical ideas, extended themselves to new compositional problems only incrementally, deliberately sought longitudinal improvement within the context of tradition, and distrusted preconceived theories of composition. In contrast, prototypical "finders," like Stravinsky, Schumann, Wagner, Liszt, Schoenberg, and Richard Strauss, often produced their best-known work early in their careers, and this work dominates their later reputation. They also prioritized novel ideas, frequently pioneered new musical forms, could clearly articulate their compositional goals via clear-cut theoretical criteria, and showed great certainty while creating and confidence in their self-evaluations. Such distinctions highlight the fact that there are many pathways to greatness in music (see also Katz & Gardner, 2012) and that variability at one level of analysis (like the creative process) can predict outcomes at a very different level (like career trajectories).

A final aspect of archival research relevant to music concerns composers' ultimate reputations, operationalized by differential space allotment in music history books. Murray (2003) has amply demonstrated high concordance among varied sources in music (and other domains) and an invariably strongly positively skewed distribution of achievement, with the supremely eminent Beethoven, Mozart, Bach, and Wagner significantly outdistancing their nearest competitors. Such findings beg the question of how social judgments of the relative importance of different creators' contributions are formed.

Socio-cultural Aspects of Musical Creativity

Characterizing the nature of creativity in music requires moving beyond domain-specific characterizations of acts of musical creativity to the social reception of creative products (see Csikszentmihalyi, 1988) – a complex, multi-disciplinary topic pervaded with unanswered questions. A central issue, related to themes developed above, is the extent to which musical preferences and systems may be arbitrarily modulated by cultural convention (and how this happens). Note that intercultural modulations are not inconsistent with an undercurrent of strong cross-cultural regularities, since the combinatorics quality of musical parameters permits an enormous number of culturally specific and individual musical styles, even given evolutionary canalized constraints on music appreciation.

The social dynamics of musical creation and appreciation are central in the domain of music. The details of these dynamics have been much debated by scholars interested in how aesthetic choices may reinforce class distinctions (e.g., Bourdieu, 1979/1984), in understanding the social context and situated cultural practice of creative music making (e.g., Folkestad, 2012), in characterizing the plurality of contemporary approaches to music making (e.g., Burnard, 2012) and in how collaborative, improvisatory aspects of creativity function (e.g., Sawyer, 2006). Within psychology, such approaches continue to gain momentum. A key challenge is in how to integrate the often-qualitative data and emphasis on social factors with a more traditional view of creativity emphasizing quantitative measurement and psychological factors, not to mention recent advances in the neuroscience of music.

Future Directions

The study of musical creativity is a rich and vibrant scientific enterprise. Considerable progress has been made in conceptualizing key issues and in devising theoretical and empirical approaches to understanding them. Much current research benefits from a convergence of multiple methodologies, as in some case studies of the creative process reviewed above (e.g., Collins, 2005; Donin, 2012; McAdams, 2004). Productive future research is likely to partake of the best of the many methods now available, coupled with powerful analytic tools, such as the "Humdrum" software toolkit ("Humdrum," 2015), which allows sophisticated computer-based analyses of large corpuses of music to test well-defined hypotheses about the psychology of music. Such analyses have great potential, not only for descriptive musical characterizations, but for trans-historical analyses exploring the relative permanence versus transience of specific musical regularities and for addressing cross-cultural questions. Such approaches would inform key evolutionary and socio-cultural questions, which, together with a comprehensive understanding of the creative process, remain central in considering the very nature of the domain of music as a fundamental arena for human creativity.

References

Amabile, T. M. (1996). *Creativity in context.* Boulder, CO: Westview.

Aranosian, C. M. (1981). Musical creativity: The stream of consciousness in composition, improvisation and education. *Imagination, Cognition and Personality, 1,* 67–88.

Baer, J. (2010). Is creativity domain specific? In J. C. Kaufman & R. J. Sternberg (Eds.), *The Cambridge handbook of creativity* (pp. 321–341). New York: Cambridge University Press.

Baer, J., & Kaufman, J. C. (2005). Bridging generality and specificity: The Amusement Park Theoretical (APT) model of creativity. *Roeper Review, 27,* 158–163.

Bamberger, J. (1977) In search of a tune. In D. Perkins and B. Leondar (Eds.), *The arts and cognition* (pp. 284–389). Baltimore, MD: Johns Hopkins University Press.

Barrington, D. (1770). Account of a very remarkable young musician. *Philosophical Transactions of the Royal Society of London, 60,* 4–64.

Bennett, S. (1976). The process of musical creation: interviews with eight composers. *Journal of Research in Music Education, 24,* 3–13.

Bourdieu, P. (1979/1984). *Distinction: A social critique of the judgement of taste.* Cambridge, MA: Harvard University Press. (Originally published in 1979 by Les Éditions de Minuit, Paris, as *La Distinction: Critique sociale du jugement.*

Brattico, E., & Pearce, M. (2013). The neuroaesthetics of music. *Psychology of Aesthetics, Creativity and the Arts, 7,* 48–61.

Brattico, E., & Tervaniemi, M. (2010). Creativity in musicians: Evidence from cognitive neuroscience. In R. Bader, C. Neuhaus, & U. Morgenstern (Eds.), *Concepts, experiments and fieldwork: Studies in systematic musicology and ethnomusicology* (pp. 233–244). Frankfurt: Peter Lang.

Brown, D. (1991) *Human universals.* New York: McGraw-Hill.

Burnard, P., & Younker, B.A. (2002). Mapping pathways: Fostering creativity in composition. *Music Education Research, 4,* 245–261.

Burnard, P. (2012). *Musical creativities in practice*. New York: Oxford University Press.

Campbell, D.T. (1960). Blind generation and selective retention in creative thought as in other thought processes. *Psychological Review, 67*, 380–400.

Charness, N., Clifton, J., & MacDonald, L. (1988). Case study of a mono-musical savant. In L. K. Obler & D. A. Fein (Eds.), *The exceptional brain: Neuropsychology of talent and special abilities* (pp. 277–293). New York: Guilford Press.

Clarke, E. (2012). Creativity in performance. In D. J. Hargreaves, D. E. Miell, & R. A. R. MacDonald (Eds.), *Musical imaginations: Multidisciplinary perspectives on creativity, performance, and reception* (pp. 17–30). New York: Oxford University Press.

Collins, D. (2005). A synthesis process model of creative thinking in music composition. *Psychology of Music, 33*, 193–216.

Collins, D. (2007). Real-time tracking of the creative music composition process. *Digital Creativity Journal, 18*, 239–256.

Collins, D. (Ed.). (2012). *The act of musical composition: Studies in the creative process*. Farnham, UK: Ashgate.

Cook, N. (2012). Beyond creativity? In D. J. Hargreaves, D. E. Miell, & R. A. R. MacDonald (Eds.), *Musical imaginations: Multidisciplinary perspectives on creativity, performance, and perception* (pp. 452–459). New York: Oxford University Press.

Cooper, B. (1990). *Beethoven and the creative process*. New York: Oxford University Press.

Csikszentmihalyi, M. (1988). Society, culture, and person: A systems view of creativity. In R. J. Sternberg (Ed.), *The nature of creativity: Contemporary psychological perspectives* (pp. 325–228). New York: Cambridge University Press.

Davidson, L., & Welsh, P. (1988). From collections to structure: The developmental path of tonal thinking. In J. A. Sloboda (Ed.), *Generative processes in music: The psychology of performance, improvisation and composition* (pp. 260–285). Oxford: Oxford Science Publications.

Dennis, W. (1966). Creative productivity between the ages of 20 and 80 years. *Journal of Gerontology, 9*, 175–178.

Dissanayake, E. (2007). What art is and what art does: An overview of contemporary evolutionary hypotheses. In C. Martindale, P. Locher, & V. M. Petrov (Eds.), *Evolutionary and neurocognitive approaches to aesthetics, creativity, and the arts* (pp. 1–14). Amityville, NY: Baywood.

Donin, N. (2012). Empirical and historical musicologies of compositional processes: Towards a cross-fertilisation. In D. Collins (Ed.), *The act of musical composition: Studies in the creative process* (pp. 1–26). Farnham, UK: Ashgate.

Ericsson, K. A. (1999). Creative expertise as superior reproducible performance: Innovative and flexible aspects of expert performance. *Psychological Inquiry, 10*, 329–333.

Ericssson, K. A., Krampe, R. T., & Tesch-Römer, C. (1993). The role of deliberate practice in the acquisition of expert performance. *Psychological Review, 100*, 363–406.

Ericsson, K. A., & Simon, H. A. (1984). *Protocol analysis: Verbal reports as data*. Cambridge, MA: MIT Press.

Feist, G. J. (2004). The evolved fluid specificity of human creative talent. In R. J. Sternberg, E. L. Grigorenko, & J. L. Singer (Eds.), *Creativity: From potential to realization* (pp. 57–82). Washington, DC: American Psychological Association.

Feist, G. J. (2007). An evolutionary model of artistic and musical creativity. In C. Martindale, P. Locher, & V. M. Petrov (Eds.), *Evolutionary and neurocognitive approaches to aesthetics, creativity, and the arts* (pp. 15–30). Amityville, NY, Baywood.

Fisher, R. B. (1995). *Musical prodigies: Masters at an early age.* New York: Association Press.

Folkestad, G. (2012). Digital tools and discourse in music: The ecology of composition. In D. J. Hargreaves, D. E. Miell, & R. A. R. MacDonald (Eds.), *Musical imaginations: Multidisciplinary perspectives on creativity, performance, and reception* (pp. 193–205). New York: Oxford University Press.

Franklin, M. B. (2001). The artist speaks: Sigmund Koch on aesthetics and creative work. *American Psychologist, 56,* 445–452.

Freeman, W. (2000). A neurobiological role of music in social bonding. In N. L. Wallin, S. Merkur, & S. Brown (Eds.), *The origins of music* (pp. 411–424). Cambridge, MA: MIT Press.

Gabora, L. (2000). Toward a theory of creative inklings. In R. Ascott (Ed.), *Art, technology, and consciousness* (pp. 159–164). Bristol, UK: Intellect Press.

Galenson, D. W. (2006). *Old masters and young geniuses: The two life cycles of artistic creativity.* Princeton, NJ: Princeton University Press.

Gardner, H. (1983). *Frames of mind.* New York: Basic Books.

Gjerdingen, R. O. (1988). *A classic turn of phrase: Music and the psychology of convention.* Philadelphia: University of Pennsylvania Press.

Gould, S. J., & Vrba, E. S. (1982). Exaptation: A missing term in the science of form. *Paleobiology, 8,* 4–15.

Guilford, J. P. (1950). Creativity. *American Psychologist, 5,* 444–454.

Hargreaves, D. J., Hargreaves, J. J., & North, A. C. (2012). Imagination and creativity in music listening. In D. J. Hargreaves, D. E. Miell, & R. A. R. MacDonald (Eds.), *Musical imaginations: Multidisciplinary perspectives on creativity, performance, and perception* (pp. 156–172). New York: Oxford University Press.

Hass, R. W., & Weisberg, R. W. (2009). Career development in two seminal American songwriters: A test of the equal odds rule. *Creativity Research Journal, 21,* 183–190.

Hass, R. W., & Weisberg, R. W. (2015). Revisiting the 10-year rule for composers from the *Great American Songbook*: On the validity of two measures of creative production. *Psychology of Aesthetics, Creativity, and the Arts, 9,* 471–479.

Hayes, J. R. (1989). Cognitive processes in creativity. In J. A. Glover, R. R. Roning, & C. R. Reynolds (Eds.), *Handbook of creativity* (pp. 202–219). New York: Plenum Press.

Higham, T., Basell, L., Jacobi, R., Wood, R., Ramsey, C. B., & Conard, N. J. (2012). Testing models for the beginnings of the Aurignacian and the advent of figurative art and music: The radiocarbon chronology of Geißenklösterle. *Journal of Human Evolution, 62,* 664–676.

Humdrum (2015, November 9). Retrieved on November 9, 2015, from http://www.humdrum.org/

Huron, D. (2006). *Sweet anticipation: Music and the psychology of expectation.* Cambridge, MA: MIT Press.

Justus, T., & Hutsler, J. J. (2005). Fundamental issues in the evolutionary psychology of music: Assessing innateness and domain specificity. *Music Perception, 23,* 1–27.

Katz, S. L., & Gardner, H. (2012). Musical materials or metaphorical models? A psychological investigation of what inspires composers. In D. J. Hargreaves, D. E. Miell, & R. A. R. Macdonald (Eds.), *Musical imaginations: Multidisciplinary perspectives on creativity, performance, and perception* (pp. 107–123). New York: Oxford University Press.

Kenneson, C. (2003). *Musical prodigies: Perilous journeys, remarkable lives*. Portland, OR: Amadeus Press.

Konečni, V. J. (2012). Composers' creative processes: The role of life-events, emotion and reason. In D. J. Hargreaves, D. E. Miell, & R. A. R. Macdonald (Eds.), *Musical imaginations: Multidisciplinary perspectives on creativity, performance, and perception* (pp. 141–155). New York: Oxford University Press.

Konrad, U. (1992). Mozart's sketches. *Early Music, 20*, 119–130.

Kozbelt, A. (2005). Factors affecting aesthetic success and improvement in creativity: A case study of the musical genres of Mozart. *Psychology of Music, 33*, 235–255.

Kozbelt, A. (2007). A quantitative analysis of Beethoven as self-critic: Implications for psychological theories of musical creativity. *Psychology of Music, 35*, 147–172.

Kozbelt, A. (2008a). Longitudinal hit ratios of classical composers: Reconciling "Darwinian" and expertise acquisition perspectives on lifespan creativity. *Psychology of Aesthetics, Creativity, and the Arts, 2*, 221–235.

Kozbelt, A. (2008b). One-hit wonders in classical music: Evidence and (partial) explanations for an early career peak. *Creativity Research Journal, 20*, 179–195.

Kozbelt, A. (2011). Age and aesthetic significance in classical music: A multi-level reanalysis of Halsey's (1976) ratings. *Empirical Studies of the Arts, 29*, 129–148.

Kozbelt, A. (2012). Process, self-evaluation, and lifespan creativity trajectories in eminent composers. In D. Collins (Ed.), *The act of musical composition: Studies in the creative process* (pp. 27–51). Farnham, UK: Ashgate Press.

Kozbelt, A. (2014). Musical creativity across the lifespan. In D. K. Simonton (Ed.), *Handbook of genius* (pp. 451–472). Hoboken, NJ: Wiley-Blackwell.

Kozbelt, A., Beghetto, R., & Runco, M. A. (2010). Theories of creativity. In J. C Kaufman & R. J. Sternberg (Eds.), *The Cambridge handbook of creativity* (pp. 20–47). New York: Cambridge University Press.

Kozbelt, A., & Meredith, D. (2010). A note on trans-historical melodic originality trends in classical music. *International Journal of Creativity and Problem Solving, 20*, 109–125.

Lehmann, A. C., & Gruber, H. (2006). Music. In K. A. Ericsson, N. Charness, P. J. Feltovich, & R. R. Hoffman (Eds.), *The Cambridge handbook of expertise and expert performance* (pp. 457–470). New York: Cambridge University Press.

Levitin, D. J. (2009). *The world in six songs: How the musical brain created human nature*. London: Plume.

Levitin, D. J., & Bellugi, U. (1998). Musical abilities in individuals with Williams syndrome. *Music Perception, 15*, 357–389.

MacDonald, R. A. R., Byrne, C., & Carlton, L. (2006). Creativity and flow in music composition: An empirical investigation. *Psychology of Music, 34*, 292–307.

Martindale, C. (1990). *The clockwork muse: The predictability of artistic change*. New York: Basic Books.

Martindale, C. (2009). The evolution and end of art as Hegelian tragedy. *Empirical Studies of the Arts, 27*, 133–140.

McAdams, S. (2004). Problem-solving strategies in music composition: A case study. *Music Perception, 21*, 391–429.

Mednick, S. A. (1962). The associative basis of the creative process. *Psychological Review, 69*, 220–232.

Meredith, D., & Kozbelt, A. (2014). Ascending/descending melodic interval asymmetry in Arnold Schoenberg's vocal music: Implications for trans-historical creativity.

In A. Kozbelt (Ed.), *Proceedings of the Twenty-Third Biennial Congress of the International Association of Empirical Aesthetics* [CD-ROM] (pp. 505–509). New York, NY: IAEA.

Miller, G. F. (2000a). Evolution of human music through sexual selection. In N. L. Wallin, B. Merker, & S. Brown (Eds.), *The origins of music* (pp. 329–360). Cambridge, MA: MIT Press.

Miller, G. F. (2000b). *The mating mind*. New York: Basic Books.

Miller, G. F. (2001). Aesthetic fitness: How sexual selection shaped artistic virtuosity as a fitness indicator and aesthetic preferences as mate choice criteria. *Bulletin of Psychology and the Arts, 2*, 20–25.

Millington, B. (1992). *The Wagner compendium*. New York: Schirmer Books.

Murray, C. (2003). *Human accomplishment: The pursuit of excellence in the arts and sciences, 800 B.C. to 1950*. New York: HarperCollins.

Music Industry. (2015, November 9). Retrieved on November 9, 2015, from https://en .wikipedia.org/wiki/Music_industry#Total_revenue_by_year.

Paisley, W. J. (1964). Identifying the unknown communicator in painting, literature, and music: The significance of minor encoding habits. *Journal of Communication, 14*, 219–237.

Pater, W. (1893/2010). *Studies in the history of the Renaissance* (4th edn.). New York: Oxford University Press.

Peretz, I. (2008). Musical disorders: From behavior to genes. *Current Directions in Psychological Science, 17*, 329–333.

Perkins, D. N. (1981). *The mind's best work*. Cambridge, MA: Harvard University Press.

Pinker, S. (1997). *How the mind works*. New York: Norton.

Plucker, J. A. (1999). Is the proof in the pudding? Reanalyses of Torrance's (1958 to present) longitudinal data. *Creativity Research Journal, 12*, 103–114.

Reitman, W. R. (1965). *Cognition and thought*. New York: Wiley.

Rodriguez Zivic, P. H., Shifres, F., & Cecchi, G. A. (2013). Perceptual basis of evolving Western musical styles. *Proceedings of the National Academy of Sciences of the United States of America, 110*, 10034–10038.

Runco, M. A. (2007). *Creativity*. Amsterdam: Elsevier.

Sacks, O. (2007). *Musicophilia: Tales of music and the brain*. New York: Vintage.

Sawyer, R. K. (2006). *Explaining creativity: The science of human innovation*. New York: Oxford University Press.

Schmidt, S. (2016). *Musical extrapolations: Creative processes involved while music is being listened to and composed*. Wiesbaden: Springer VS.

Schubert, E. (2012). Spreading activation and dissociation: A cognitive mechanism for creative processing in music. In D. J. Hargreaves, D. E. Miell, & R. A. R. MacDonald (Eds.), *Musical imaginations: Multidisciplinary perspectives on creativity, performance, and reception* (pp. 124–140). New York: Oxford University Press.

Simonton, D. K. (1977). Creative productivity, age, and stress: A biographical time-series analysis of 10 classical composers. *Journal of Personality and Social Psychology, 35*, 791–804.

Simonton, D. K. (1980). Thematic fame, melodic originality, and musical zeitgeist: A biographical and transhistorical content analysis. *Journal of Personality and Social Psychology, 38*, 972–983.

Simonton, D. K. (1991). Emergence and realization of genius: The lives and works of 120 classical composers. *Journal of Personality and Social Psychology, 61*, 829–840.

Simonton, D. K. (1994). Computer content analysis of melodic structure: Classical composers and their compositions. *Psychology of Music, 22*, 31–43.

Simonton, D. K. (1997). Creative productivity: A predictive and explanatory model of career landmarks and trajectories. *Psychological Review, 104*, 66–89.

Simonton, D. K. (1999). *Origins of genius: Darwinian perspectives on creativity.* New York: Oxford University Press.

Simonton, D. K. (2000). Creative development as acquired expertise: Theoretical issues and an empirical test. *Developmental Review, 20*, 283–318.

Simonton, D. K. (2007). Cinema composers: Career trajectories for creative productivity in film music. *Psychology of Aesthetics, Creativity, and the Arts, 1*, 160–169.

Simonton, D. K. (2011). Creativity and discovery as blind variation: Campbell's (1960) BVSR model after the half-century mark. *Review of General Psychology, 15*, 158–174.

Sloboda, J. A. (1985). *The musical mind.* New York: Oxford University Press

Sloboda, J. A., O'Neill, S. A., & Ivaldi, A. (2001). Functions of music in everyday life: An exploratory study using the experience sampling method. *Musicae Scientiae, 5*, 9–32.

Solomon, M. (1980). On Beethoven's creative process: A two-part invention. *Music and Letters, 61*, 272–283.

Sternberg, R. J. (2009). Domain-generality versus domain-specificity of creativity. In P. Meusburger, J. Funke, & E. Wunder (Eds.), *Milieus of creativity: An interdisciplinary approach to spatiality of creativity* (pp. 25–38). Dordrecht, Netherlands: Springer.

Thomson, W. (1991). *Schoenberg's error.* Philadelphia: University of Pennsylvania Press.

Tooby, J. & Cosmides, L. (1992). The psychological foundations of culture. In J. Barkow, L. Cosmides, & J. Tooby (Eds.), *The adapted mind: Evolutionary psychology and the generation of culture* (pp. 19–136). New York: Oxford University Press.

Trehub, S. E. (2000). Human processing predispositions and musical universals. In N. L. Wallin, B. Merker, & S. Brown (Eds.), *The origins of music* (pp. 427–448). Cambridge, MA: MIT Press.

Trehub, S. E. (2003). The developmental origins of musicality. *Nature Neuroscience, 6*, 669–673.

Vallas, L. (1973). *Claude Debussy: His life and works*, trans. Marie O'Brien and Grace O'Brien. New York: Dover.

Vartanian, O. (2009). Variable attention facilitates creative problem solving. *Psychology of Aesthetics, Creativity, and the Arts, 3*, 57–59.

Vos, P. G., & Troost, J. M. (1989). Ascending and descending melodic intervals: Statistical findings and their perceptual relevance. *Music Perception, 6*, 383–396.

Waddington, C. H. (1942). Canalization of development and the inheritance of acquired characters. *Nature, 150*, 563–565.

Wallin, N. L., Merker, B., & Brown, S. (Eds.). (2000). *The origins of music.* Cambridge, MA: MIT Press.

Webster, P. R. (1987). Conceptual bases for creative thinking in music. In J. C. Peery, I. C. Peery, & T. W. Draper (Eds.), *Music and child development* (pp. 158–174). New York: Springer-Verlag.

Weisberg, R. W. (1999). Creativity and knowledge: A challenge to theories. In R. J. Sternberg (Ed.), *Handbook of creativity* (pp. 226–250). New York: Cambridge University Press.

Weisberg, R. W. (2006). *Creativity: Understanding innovation in problem solving, science, invention, and the arts*. Hoboken, NJ: Wiley.

Wilson, E. O. (1998). *Consilience: The unity of knowledge*. New York: Vintage.

Younker, B. A., & Smith, W.H. (1996). Comparing and modelling musical thought processes of expert and novice composers. *Bulletin of the Council for Research in Music Education, 128*, 25–35.

Zabelina, D., & Robinson, M. D. (2010). Creativity as flexible cognitive control. *Psychology of Aesthetics, Creativity, and the Arts, 4*, 136–143.

11 Dance

The Challenges of Measuring Embodied Creativity

Paula Thomson

PsyD, Professor, California State University, Northridge,
Co-Director, Performance Psychophysiology Laboratory,
Professor Emeritus, York University, and Choreographer
and Dance Educator

Abstract

The human body and movement are the locus of dance and the intention is aesthetic appeal, whether it is expressions of exquisite beauty or ugliness. Creative research in dance includes the practical demands of a dance career and the imaginative potential embodied in the dancer. Dancers rely on their kinesthetic sense, also described as a somatic feeling, when they are creating. The creative experience is a merging of aesthetic awareness, imaginative engagement, and physical knowing. These are related to an affective experience that manifests in the dancers' kinesthetic sensations and perceptions. Measuring creativity in dance necessitates an interdisciplinary approach, along with study designs that are qualitative and quantitative. Motor creativity encompasses neuroscience, physiology, and psychology; all offer insight into the complexity of non-verbal creative movement.

> I am a dancer. I believe that we learn by practice. Whether it means to learn to dance
> by practicing or to learn to live by practicing living, the principles are the same.
> In each it is the performance of a dedicated precise set of acts, physical or
> intellectual, from which comes shape of achievement, a sense of one's being,
> a satisfaction of spirit. One becomes in some area an athlete of God.
>
> Martha Graham (1991, p. 3)

Dance as a Unique Creative Form

Dance is movement and the human body is the expressive instrument. Ultimately, dance is an embodied activity that exists in time and space. What makes dance a unique creative art form is that its medium, human movement, is at the center of human expression. Dance is perhaps the most immediate of all creative forms of expression; it "is a living language which speaks of man" (Wigman, 1966, p. 10). Whether it is embraced and welcomed or vilified and rejected, dance persists.

Acknowledgments are extended to my research colleague, Dr. S. Victoria Jaque, Co-Director, Performance Psychophysiology Laboratory, California State University, Northridge, and to Mr. Maurice Godin, Actor, Director, and Lecturer, California State University, Northridge.

181

For example, religious groups such as the Shakers embraced dance as the ultimate expression in their worship of God, whereas extreme Christian and Muslim fundamentalist groups often banish it.

The reality that dance resides within the human body is impossible to deny. The human body and movement are the locus of dance and the intention is aesthetic appeal, whether it is expressions of exquisite beauty or ugliness (Christensen & Calvo-Merino, 2013; Thomson, 2011). Individual, societal, and cultural identities can be shaped during aesthetic experiences; dancers and their audience are influenced by these experiences and also inform them (Sullivan & McCarthy, 2009). Because dance is a non-verbal expressive art form it transcends the limits of language. Cultural context and educational backgrounds also influence the recognition of dance talent, dance styles, and aesthetic appreciation (Matare, 2009). "The dance is the mother of the arts. Music and poetry exist in time; painting and architecture in space. But dance lives at once in time and space" (Sachs, 1937/ 1965. p. 3).

Dance is rooted in our biological nature. Neuroscientists speculate that cognition is embodied in action and that the motor system is also deeply linked to higher order mental functioning such as social interactions and meaning making (Jackson & Decety, 2004). Our brains can mobilize intentional actions and recognize and respond to the actions of others; it is this biological reality that allows us to appreciate the immediacy of actions found in dance. This ability is embedded in feed forward and backward cycles of perception and action; these neural cycles are foundational to all adaptive functioning and are directed by our nervous systems. In order to survive, we can readily identify actions generated by self versus others, and yet we can also sense or feel movements generated by others. When we observe the movements of others our mirror neurons evoke a similar motor firing pattern, even it if is smaller and unseen by others (Jackson & Decety, 2004; Leube, Knoblich, Erb, Grodd, Bartels, & Kircher, 2003). Speech and gesture share the same neural network communication systems in our brains and we implicitly understand these verbal and non-verbal symbolic expressions (Bernardis & Gentilucci, 2006). In all cultures, language and gestures are integrally linked and reinforce each other to consolidate communication and meaning. Furthermore, linguistic meanings are commonly expressed as embodied experiences (Gibbs, 2003); we inherently understand emotional content based on movement quality (dynamics and range) (Freedberg & Gallese, 2007; Saarikallio, Luck, Burger, Thompson, & Toivianinen, 2013; Sheets-Johnstone, 1999). By adopting specific body postures, whether directly, imaginally, or vicariously, autobiographical memories can be retrieved. In fact, autobiographical memories are stored in the perceptual and motor pathways that were involved in the original processing of an event (Dijkstra, Kaschak, & Zwaan, 2007). Autobiographical memories are a form of embodied simulation that includes visual, kinesthetic, spatial, and affective aspects of the original experience.

These scientific findings support the primacy of dance as a creative art form. This line of neuroscience investigation supports what dancers and dance researchers have speculated for years. Not only do the audiences who witness dance have kinesthetic empathy, but also so do the dancers and choreographers who give life to the dance.

The kinesthetic sense is enlivened in the dance artist and communicated to the audience (Krasnow, 1994). Dancers rely on their kinesthetic sense, also described as a somatic feeling, when they are creating. The creative experience is a merging of aesthetic awareness, imaginative engagement, and physical knowing. These are related to an affective experience that manifests in the dancers' kinesthetic sensations and perceptions (Lussier-Ley & Durand-Bush, 2009).

Measuring Creativity in Dance

There are many methods and instruments to measure creativity and a diverse range of methods and instruments have been administered to dancers; however, fully assessing creativity in dancers remains somewhat elusive. Often it is only audience members who can truly determine the depth of creativity revealed in a dance performance. If they were profoundly moved by the experience of witnessing a dance artist or dance work, then they may describe the experience as creative and significant (Piirto, 1998). Dance artists such as Martha Graham, George Balanchine, Fred Astaire, and Michael Jackson captured our imagination. How did we know they were creative? Perhaps the ability to recognize the charismatic force of these dance artists is instantaneous? We respond with a visceral and emotional knowing. The experience often leaves us speechless, may move us to tears, and reverberates long after the performance ended. Although these are some of the giants of the dance world, when we witness dance, especially when we are physically present in a theater or concert hall, our embodied self participates. The experience touches us on multiple levels. Consequently, when investigating creativity in dance, the role of "feel" should be included; this is perhaps the most primary response when experiencing dance.

Who becomes a dancer? Like an athlete they usually possess talents in psychomotor expression (Chang & Kuo, 2009). Dancers frequently acknowledge their early interest in dance, and experienced dance teachers readily recognize young dancers who are endowed with talent (Chang & Kuo, 2009). To be talented as a dancer usually includes a combination of musicality, kinesthetic ability, and imagination. These same variables are also essential ingredients in dance training. Ultimately it is long hours and years of practice coupled with a deep intrinsic desire to dance that shapes the dance artist. The resulting performances that move audiences are the product of years of training, coupled with innate talents.

The challenge for researchers is to understand and describe how these dance artists affect us. Earlier, it was the dance artists themselves who wrote detailed accounts of their creative process. With the beginnings of modern dance, dance shifted from the more formalized structure of ballet and ballroom performances (Hagood & Kahlich, 2007) to more individual artistic expressions (Press & Warburton, 2007). Along with the growth of modern dance, dance education expanded into schools, including universities. Educators participated in creative dance workshops and pedagogical dance curriculum grew and became more structured. Assessment tools were developed during this educational explosion. Not only were the dance artists writing about their artistic process, but also so were the teachers, who described ways to enhance creative dance in children and adults. This trend moved into the burgeoning new healing arts of dance therapy and somatic practices. Until the early 1980s, this anecdotal reporting was the norm in dance research (Hagood & Kahlich, 2007; Press & Warburton, 2007); however, large questions still loomed and empirical analyses were needed. Today, questions such as the following remain the subject of investigation. Are dancers creative? Is their creativity the compelling force in their performance? How do we nurture their creative potential? How do we articulate and operationalize that which is unique to dance? Are the choreographers, the generators of new works, more creative than the dancers who interpret the choreographers' vision? Are they mutually interdependent in the creative process? Is the creative process different in dance compared to the other art forms? What makes expert judges and professional critics different in their ability to appraise creativity in dance? Are teachers able to promote creativity in their students? How do they know if they have met their curricular goal of teaching creative dance? How is technology changing the once ephemeral nature of dance?

In the last two decades, qualitative studies have tended to dominate the field of dance and creativity (Hagood & Kahlich, 2007). They address the choreographic process (Hagood & Kahlich, 2007), the dancers' phenomenological experiences (Lussier-Ley & Durand-Bush, 2009; Walker & Nordin-Bates, 2010), the capacity and type of imagery produced (Hefferon & Ollis, 2006; Hanrahan & Vergeer, 2000–2001; Nordin & Cumming, 2006a), and the somatic practices that are embraced by choreographers and dancers (Stinson, 2004). Improvisational explorations were analyzed qualitatively within pedagogical research studies, especially in the field of creative dance for children (Chappell, 2007). Common qualitative research methods in dance include phenomenological, case study, and ethnographic designs (Chappell, 2007; Hagood & Kahlich, 2007).

Recently, the Resonance Performance Model was applied; it is a "person-centered approach to performance and living" that investigates the creative and felt experiences of dancers (Lussier-Ley & Durand-Bush, 2009, p. 203). This individual reflective approach was conducted to assess the physical and emotional felt experience of space and time both between dancers and within the dancer. In this study, awareness and ability to feel and regulate sensations and perceptions increased within a group of dancers, and within each individual dancer. In a different study investigating felt sense, expert dance teachers participated in a qualitative interpretive study that included semi-structured interviews, video analysis, photography, collected documentations, and reflective diaries. Again, an embodied way of knowing was described as "sensing," "thinking body-mind," "whole self-awareness," and "reciprocity." These were regarded as layered experiences that frame dance educators expertise (Chappell, 2007).

The use of expert judges to evaluate the creative product has been integrated into research studies examining professional choreography and student-based classroom work. This research method, although not fully conforming to Amabile's Consensual Assessment Technique (Amabile, 1996), is a common practice amongst dance educators (Hagood & Kahlich, 2007), especially when these educators are trained to embody their aesthetic appraisals (Stinson, 2004). Krasnow created a training tool for expert judges in order to evaluate the effect of imagery on performance practice in dancers (Krasnow, Chatfield, Barr, Jensen, & Dufek, 1997). In this study, the expert judges were also given inter-rater reliability scores, a practice that is not typical in many of the studies in the dance field. Recently, a study examined constraint influences on performers engaged in contact improvisation (Martin, Ric, & Hristovski, 2015). Expert observers analyzed the movement based on observational methodology that organized movement responses into a temporal binary matrix. This was then statistically analyzed in a series of calculations that included a principal component analysis. This study moved beyond the expert appraisal into a complex statistical analysis to determine the emergence of dance movements initiated by instructional constraint, such as requiring dancers to execute lifts or to move within small or large performing areas.

When measuring creative cognitive processes related to dance, several quantitative measurements have been implemented. For example, the Torrance Tests of Creative Thinking (TTCT), both verbal and figural, were used to determine divergent thinking outcome results between children who participated in improvised and non-improvised dance classes, with results indicating that improvisational dance classes enhanced divergent thinking in primary school children (Sowden, Clements, Redlich & Lewis, 2015). These tests have been used in other studies such as that conducted by Mary Brennan (1982) to determine creative ability in dancers. She recommended that creativity be considered multifactorial, dancers' originality and flexibility were separate factors, and creativity needed to be explored in dancers' movements. The researchers in these studies generally found that the TTCT only demonstrated general patterns of divergent thinking but was not necessarily a good measurement to discriminate dance creativity.

To assess cognitive processes as motor creativity several tests exist, although they are not commonly referenced. The Wyrick Motor Creativity Test is designed for children to measure responses in problem-solving tasks of a motor nature. The children perform four different tasks but during the time-limited performance of these simple motor tasks they are asked to use as many different possible ways to perform them. Fluency was calculated as the total completed motor possibilities and frequency of occurrence was related to originality (Bournelli, Makri, & Mylonas, 2009; Wyrick, 1968). Brennan created a more specific Dance Creativity Measure to assess dance (1983, 1985). Following Guilford's Structure of Intellect theory that explains creative ability, she followed the three large categories (operations, content, and product). In her test, she examined divergent thinking (operation), tactile-kinesthetic figures (content) and units, systems, and transformations (products). In the position test to assess fluency she had dancers assume as many imaginative body positions as possible within a 90-second time limit. The composition test required the dancer to replicate four body positions that were modeled prior to beginning the test and they were asked to compose an imaginative movement sequence (system) in the order that the body positions were demonstrated. After this was completed the dancers were asked to compose a different sequence still incorporating the same body positions in the same order (transformation).

An expert(s) rated originality and response flexibility for each of the two sequences. In the third test, improvisation, the dancer was asked to imaginatively improvise for 90 seconds. In this test the dancer must maintain one foot in the same spot; this improvisation was rated for originality. The researchers conducted a replication study to determine reliability. The consistency in rater evaluation over two testing situations was shown to be high, with overall reliability values of (COl = .96, C02 = .94. IT = .99), to moderate (PT = .88); they reflect the relative stability of these measures over time (Brennan, 1985).

There are multiple quantitative studies, and some that are mixed-method designs. The quantitative measurements are primarily self-report instruments and are included in cross-sectional, experimental, and longitudinal designs. Like the majority of creativity studies, these measurements are implemented to gain insight into the person (Alter, 1984), the process, and the product (Ma, 2009); however, the majority of the studies examined the person. Some of the studies on dancers included self-report instruments that measured both positive and negative effects in dancers compared to non-dancers. The positive variables included increased empathy, self-esteem (Kalliopuska, 1989), and flow experiences (Thomson & Jaque, 2012). The negative psychological variables included greater perfectionism (Cumming & Duda, 2012; Eusanio, Thomson, & Jaque, 2014), poorer body image (Heiland, Murray & Edley, 2008), increased body objectification, negative stereotypes (Clabaugh & Morling, 2004; Tiggermann & Slater, 2003), increased eating disorders (Tseng, Fang, Lee, Chie, Liu, & Chen, 2007), anxiety (Lench, Levine, & Roe, 2010; Monsma & Overby, 2004; Thomson & Jaque, 2011–2012), and shame (Thomson & Jaque, 2013, 2015). Motivation (Lacaille, Koestner, & Gaudreau, 2007) and passion (Padham & Aujla, 2014; Rip, Fortin, & Vallerand, 2006) were assessed in dancers with clear indications that they had high intrinsic and passionate motivation in comparison to non-dancers. These studies generally suggested that dancers had good self-esteem, empathy, and flow-like experiences, although they also had more difficulty with anxiety, shame, body image, and eating disorders. Like the motor tests for creativity, a specific instrument to assess dance imagery was designed – the Dance Imagery Development Questionnaire (Nordin & Cumming, 2006b, 2006c). Again, dancers effectively employed imagery (kinesthetic and mental images) to augment performance. General imagery self-report instruments were used to demonstrate that expert dancers engaged multiple imagery types and strategies compared to novice dancers (Fish, Hall, Cumming, 2004; Overby, Hall, & Haslam, 1997–1998). In the studies listed above, none of the major creative self-report instruments were used, such as the Creative Achievement Questionnaire, the Biographical Inventory of Creative Behavior, the revised Creative Behavior Inventory, or the Creative Domain Questionnaire (Silvia, Wigert, Reiter-Palmon, & Kaufman, 2012). However, the Experience of Creativity Questionnaire (Nelson & Rawlings, 2009) was recently used to determine group differences between dancers with and without PTSD, how they were able to cope under stress, and how PTSD affected their creativity (Thomson & Jaque, 2016).

Lastly, outcome studies and repeated measures studies have been conducted. Many studies examined the effect of instructor or experimental feedback or changes in environment on dancers' self-esteem (Dantas & Quested, 2015), frequency of imagery (Karageorghis, Smith, & Priest, 2012), self-perceptions (Price & Pettijohn, 2006), motivation and performance anxiety (Nordin-Bates, Quested, Walker, & Redding, 2012), theory of mind (Chaplin & Norton, 2014), and movement intention (Couillandre, Lewton-Brain, & Portero, 2008). All these studies involved experimental changes in condition. In another series of studies, neurofeedback was used to alter anxiety in dancers (Singer, 2004) and to increase creativity and decrease anxiety (Gruzelier, Thompson, Redding, Brandt, & Steffert, 2014). Video dance games were used to alter arousal, generate emotional responses, and enhance creativity (Hutton & Sundar, 2010).

Key Studies

It is difficult to determine key creativity studies in dance, although there are many excellent studies that cross multiple fields of investigation, in particular, biomechanics (Kulig, Oki, Chang, & Bashford, 2014), dance injuries (Liederbach, Schanfein, & Kremenic, 2013), and nutrition (Brown & Wyon, 2014a, 2014b). Psychological distress and injury has received substantial attention with findings indicating that dancers have high levels of psychological distress while injured (Air, 2013), and they tend to have difficulty differentiating between injury and performance pain (Anderson & Hanrahan, 2008). Dance education is a strong field of research with several journals dedicated to this topic (e.g., *Journal of Dance Education, Journal of Physical Education, Recreation and Dance, Dance Research Journal*). As listed above, many studies have investigated dance imagery, anxiety, perfectionism, passion, motivation, shame, and flow.

A study that directly assessed creativity in professional dancers revealed that the group with the highest level of creativity was contemporary/modern dancers, followed by jazz/musical theater and then ballet dancers (Fink & Woschnjak, 2011). These results reflect the degree of training and performance constraints in each dance domain. This finding reinforces the need to increase improvisational or exploratory dance in pre-vocational dance training (Watson, Nordin-Bates, & Chappell, 2012).

Results from one study that examined creative potential and exercise demonstrated that greater creativity followed moderate aerobic exercise (Blanchette, Ramocki, O'del, & Casey, 2005). This study used the Torrance Test of Creative Thinking and did not examine dancers per se. Because dance is generally regarded as a low to moderate aerobic activity, perhaps dancers receive the added benefit of augmenting their creativity simply by virtue of dancing. Along this line of investigation, improved cognitive performance and cognitive flexibility in elderly individuals is robustly associated with dance, especially in those individuals who engaged in dance for long periods of time (Coubard, Duretz, Lefebvre, Lapalus, & Ferrufino, 2011; Kattenstroth, Kolankoswka, Kalisch, & Dinse, 2010; Verghese, 2006).

Distributed creativity has been studied directly in the creation of theatrical productions (Sawyer & DeZutter, 2009); this line of investigation has been indirectly supported by many dance researchers (Press & Warburton, 2007). Dance is an interactive art form that involves socially distributed development, including engagement with musicians, designers, dance educators, choreographers, and rehearsal directors. Today dance is also technologically distributed (Press & Warburton, 2007), in part, because memory is not only distributed amongst dance artists and the ephemeral memory of an audience but it is now stored on multiple digital media servers such as YouTube. Dance is now recorded and can be viewed repeatedly and immediately around the world. Technology has also enabled human movement to expand beyond what the physical limits of the human body can produce. These new video tools have altered how we perceive and understand dance. Research studies have just begun to investigate this terrain (Hutton & Sundar, 2010).

Studies designed to investigate how dancers respond in work environments have the potential to extend the careers of dancers and support their ongoing creativity. These studies examine work conditions and hazards. For example, Wanke and colleagues (2014) demonstrated that transitioning from the familiar environment of rehearsal studios to theatrical stages increased risk for injury, especially because theatrical stages often have different floor surfaces, temperature regulations, and lighting. Added to these environmental risks, dancers usually have much less time acclimating to the theatrical stage, primarily because of theater costs. Although intrinsic factors such as performance anxiety may have increased their potential for injury, most seasoned dancers do not find the actual experience of performing to be significantly stressful (Wanke, Arendt, Mill, Koch, Davenport, Fischer, & Groneberg, 2014). Another study examined dancer daily workload. Dancers varied in the degree of workload demands, depending on their rank as a principal dancer, soloist, or chorus member (Twitchett, Angioi, Koutedakis, & Wyon, 2010), but all dancers experienced substantial stressors managing training, rehearsing, and performing, with often insufficient time for recovery (Grove, Main, & Sharp, 2013). These studies increase awareness about the external stressors that dancers face in their profession.

Marchant-Haycox and Wilson (1992) suggested that dancers were the most physically and psychologically vulnerable of all the performing artists, plus their work stress compromised their mental health (Wilhelm, Kovess, Rios-Seidel, & Finch, 2004). Despite these challenges, dancers maintained strong connections to their artistry and to the belief that their work was valued and important (Barker, Soklaridis, Waters, Herr, & Cassidy, 2009). Given these very real challenges, academic training programs need to include curriculum to educate students about the rigors of real-world dance careers and help them prepare for these challenges (Bennett, 2009).

Future Recommendations

When investigating dance as a creative activity, it is not adequate to only examine the scientific elements of movement, a common investigation in kinesiology, because dance is not just movement (Reid, 2008). Feeling and intent need to be integrated when studying dance as an expressive art form (Dale, Hyatt, & Hollerman, 2007); they must also be included in future creativity research studies.

To date, creative research seldom includes the motor-action cycle as creative cognition and it is this avenue that will help expand our understanding of dance as a creative process, including how these motor-action cycles develop throughout the lifespan.

Interdisciplinary approaches are critical to fully examine dance performance (Kennedy, 2009). For example, when examining creativity in the workplace (James, Brodersen, & Eisenberg, 2004), integrating individual affective states and traits can inform organizational workplace needs. This is even more pertinent when considering the diverse workplace structures of most dance companies, including the freelance work of the majority of dance artists. Recommendations by Hamilton and Robinson (2006) include the need for performing arts consultants that are regarded as domain-specific experts. Application of this recommendation will increase performer confidence and address specific performer needs. Hopefully this will also enhance creative performance. Despite this excellent recommendation, Hamilton, Solomon, and Solomon (2006) created a standardized psychological screener for dancers and did not include any of the positive psychological variables that can enhance creativity. By measures to assess creativity (person and process), the whole dancer can be assessed, rather than only exploring the dancer's potential psychological distress and physical vulnerability to injury.

Twyla Tharp, a highly esteemed dance artist, stated, "dancers are totally governed by ritual. . . . What makes it a ritual is that they do it (daily dance class) without questioning the need" (2003, p. 16). She described one of the most consistent features of a dancer. They need to dance and they need to do it daily. They are trained to be self-disciplined artists. Creativity in dance is rooted in the reality of the body and the imagination of the artist. Mary Wigman, one of the leading European pioneers of modern dance, stated that "creative ability belongs to the sphere of reality as much as the realm of fantasy" (1966, p. 12). Creative research in dance is essential, especially if it includes the practical reality of a dance career and the imaginative potential embodied in the dancer. Understanding this ancient art form has the potential to capture embodied creativity.

References

Air, M. E. (2013). Psychological distress among dancers seeking outpatient treatment for musculoskeletal injury. *Journal of Dance Medicine and Science, 17*(3), 115–125. DOI: 10.12678/1089.313X.17.3.115

Alter, J. B. (1984). Creativity profile of university and conservatory dance students. *Journal of Personality Assessment, 48*(2), 153–158. DOI: 10.1207/s15327752jpa4802_8

Amabile, T. M. (1996). *Creativity in context.* Boulder, Colorado: Westview Press.

Anderson, R., & Hanrahan, S. J. (2008). Dancing in pain: Pain appraisal and coping in dancers. *Journal of Dance Medicine and Science, 12*(1), 9–16.

Barker, K. K., Soklaridis, S., Waters, I., Herr, G., & Cassiday, J. D. (2009). Occupational strain and professional artists: A qualitative study of an underemployed group. *Arts and Health: An International Journal for Research Policy and Practice, 1*(2), 136–150.

Bennett, D. (2009). Academy and the real world: Developing realistic notions of career in the performing arts. *Arts and Humanities in Higher Education, 8*(3), 309–327. DOI: 10.1177/1474022209339953

Bernardis, P., & Gentilucci, M. (2006). Speech and gesture share the same communication system. *Neuropsychologia, 44*, 178–190. DOI: 10.1016/j.neuropsychologia.2005.05.007

Blanchette, D. M., Ramocki, S. P., O'del, J. N., & Casey, M. S. (2005). Aerobic exercise and creative potential: Immediate and residual effects. *Creativity Research Journal, 17* (2 & 3), 257–264.

Bournelli, P., Makri, A., & Mylonas, K. (2009). Motor creativity and self-concept. *Creativity Research Journal, 21*(1), 104–110. DOI: 10.1080/10400410802633657

Brennan, M. A. (1982). Relationship between creative ability in dance and selected creative attributes. *Perceptual and Motor Skills, 55*, 47–56.

Brennan, M. A. (1983). Dance creativity measures: A reliability study. *Research Quarterly for Exercise and Sport, 54*(3), 293–295. DOI: 10.1080/02701367.1983.10605308

Brennan, M. A. (1985). Dance creativity tests and the structure-of-intellect model. *Journal of Creative Behavior, 19*(3), 185–190. DOI: 10.1002/j.2162–6057.1985.tb00657.x

Brown, D., & Wyon, M. (2014a). The effect of moderate glycemic energy bar consumption on blood glucose and mood in dancers. *Medical Problems of Performing Artists, 29*(1), 27–31.

Brown, D., & Wyon, M. (2014b). An international study on dietary supplementation use in dancers. *Medical Problems of Performing Artists, 29*(4), 229–234.

Chang, H. J., & Kuo, C. C. (2009). Overexcitabilities of gifted and talented students and its related research in Taiwan. *Asia-Pacific Journal of Gifted and Talented Education, 1*(1), 41–74.

Chaplin, L. N., & Norton, M. I. (2014). Why we think we can't dance: Theory of mind and children's desire to perform. *Child Development, 86*(2), 651–658. DOI: 10.1111/cdev.12314

Chappell, K. (2007). The dilemmas of teaching for creativity: Insights from expert specialist dance teachers. *Thinking Skills and Creativity, 2*, 39–56. DOI: 10.1016/j.tsc.2007.01.001

Clabaugh, A., & Morling, B. (2004). Stereotype accuracy of ballet and modern dancers. *Journal of Social Psychology, 144*(1), 31–48.

Coubard, O. A., Duretz, S., Lefebrve, V., Lapalus, P., & Ferrufino, L. (2011). Practice of contemporary dance improves cognitive flexibility in aging. *Frontiers in Aging Neuroscience, 3*(13), 1–12. DOI: 10.3389/fnagi.2011.000013

Couillandre, A., Lewton-Brian, P., & Portero, P. (2008), Exploring the effects of kinesiological awareness and mental imagery on movement intention in the performance demi-plie. *Journal of Dance Medicine and Science, 12*(3), 91–98.

Christensen, J. F., & Calvo-Merino, B. (2013). Dance as a subject for empirical aesthetics. *Psychology of Aesthetics, Creativity, and the Arts, 7*(1), 76–88. DOI: 10.1037/a0031827

Cumming, J., & Duda, J. L. (2012). Profiles of perfectionism, body-related concerns, and indicators of psychological health in vocational dance students: An investigation of the 2 x 2 model of perfectionism. *Psychology of Sport and Exercise, 13*(6), 729–738. DOI: 10.1016/j.psychsport.2012.05.004

Dale, J. A., Hyatt, J., & Hollerman, J. (2007). The neuroscience of dance and the dance of neuroscience: Defining a path of inquiry. *Journal of Aesthetic Education, 41*(3), 89–110.

Dantas, A. G., & Quested, E. (2015). The effect of manipulated and accurate assessment feedback on the self-efficacy of dance students. *Journal of Dance Medicine and Science, 19*(1), 22–30.

Dijkstra, K., Kaschak, M. P., & Zwaan, R. A. (2007). Body posture facilitates retrieval of autobiographical memories. *Cognition, 102*(1), 139–149. DOI: 10.1016/j.cognition.2005.12.009

Eusanio, J., Thomson, P., & Jaque, S. V. (2014). Perfectionism, shame, and self-concept in dancers: A mediation analysis. *Journal of Dance Medicine and Science, 18*(3), 106–114.

Fink, A., & Woschnjak, S. (2011). Creativity and personality in professional dancers. *Personality and Individual Differences, 51*, 754–758. DOI: 10.1016/j.paid.2011.06.024

Fish, L., Hall, C., & Cumming, J. (2004). Investigating the use of imagery by elite ballet dancers. *Avante, 10*(3), 25–39.

Freedberg, D., & Gallese, V. (2007). Motion, emotion and empathy in esthetic experience. *Trends in Cognitive Science, 11*(5), 197–205. DOI: 10.1016/j.tics.2007.02.003

Gibbs, R. W. (2003). Embodied experience and linguistic meaning. *Brain and Language, 84*, 1–15.

Graham, M. (1991). *Blood memory: An autobiography*. New York: Doubleday.

Grove, J. R., Main, L. C., & Sharp, L. (2013). Stressors, recovery processes, and manifestations of training distress in dance. *Journal of Dance Medicine and Science, 17*(2), 70–78. DOI: 10.12678/1089.313X.17.2.70

Gruzelier, J. H., Thompson, T., Redding, E., Brandt, R., & Steffert, T. (2014). Application of alpha/theta neurofeedback and heart rate variability training to young contemporary dancers: State anxiety and creativity. *International Journal of Psychophysiology, 93*, 105–111. DOI: 10.1016/j.ijpsycho.2013.05.004

Hagood, T. K., & Kahlich, L. C. (2007). Research in choreography. In L. Bresler (Ed.), *International handbook of research in arts education* (pp. 517–531), Vol. 16. The Netherlands: Springer.

Hamilton, L. H., & Robson, B. (2006). Performing arts consultation: Developing expertise in this domain. *Professional Psychology: Research and Practice, 37*(3), 254–259. DOI: 10.1037/0735–7028.37.3.254

Hamilton, L. H., Solomon, R., & Solomon, J. (2006). A proposal for standardized psychological screening of dancers. *Journal of Dance Medicine and Science, 10*(1 & 2), 40–45.

Hanrahan, C. & Vergeer, I. (2000–2001). Multiple uses of mental imagery by professional modern dancers. *Imagination, Cognition and Personality, 20*(3), 231–255.

Hefferon, K. M. & Ollis, S. (2006). 'Just clicks': An interpretive phenomenological analysis of professional dancers' experience of flow. *Research in Dance Education, 7*(2), 141–159.

Heiland, T. L., Murray, D. S., & Edley, P. P. (2008). Body image of dancers in Los Angeles: The cult of slenderness and media influence among dance students. *Research in Dance Education, 9*(3), 257–275. DOI: 10.1080/14647890802386932

Hutton, E., & Sundar, S. S. (2010). Can video games enhance creativity? Effects of emotion generated by Dance Dance Revolution. *Creativity Research Journal, 22*(3), 294–303. DOI: 10.1080/10400419.2010.503540

Jackson, P. L., & Decety, J. (2004). Motor cognition: A new paradigm to study self-other interactions. *Current Opinion in Neurobiology, 14*, 259–263.

James, K., Brodersen, M., & Eisenberg, J. (2004). Workplace affect and workplace creativity: A review and preliminary model. *Human Performance, 17*(2), 160–194.

Kalliopuska, M. (1989). Empathy, self-esteem and creativity among junior ballet dancers. *Perceptual and Motor Skills, 69*, 1227–1234.

Karageorghis, C. I., Smith, D. L., & Priest, D-L. (2012). Effects of voice enhancement technology and relaxing music on the frequency of imagery among break dancers. *Journal of Dance Medicine and Science, 16*(1), 8–16.

Kattenstroth, J-C., Kolankowska, I., Kalisch, T., & Dinse, H. R. (2010). Superior sensory, motor, and cognitive performance in elderly individuals with multi-year dancing activities. *Frontiers in Aging Neuroscience, 2*(31), 1–9. DOI: 10.3389/fnagi2010.00031

Kennedy, M. (2009). An examination of critical approaches to interdisciplinary dance performance. *Research in Dance Education, 10*(1), 63–74. DOI: 10.1080/14647890802697221

Krasnow, D. (1994). Performance, movement and kinesthesia. *Impulse, 2*, 16–23.

Krasnow, D. H., Chatfield, S. J., Barr, S., Jensen, J. L., & Dufek, J. S. (1997). Imagery and conditioning practices for dancers. *Dance Research Journal, 29*(1), 43–64.

Kulig, K., Oki, K. C., Chang, Y-J., & Bashford, G. R. (2014). Achilles and patellar tendon morphology in dancers with and without tendon pain. *Medical Problems of Performing Artists, 29*(4), 221–228.

Lacaille, N., Koestner, R., & Gaudreau, P. (2007). On the value of intrinsic rather than traditional achievement goals for performing artists: A short-term prospective study. *International Journal of Music Education, 25*(3), 245–257.

Lench, H. C., Levine, L. J., & Roe, E. (2010). Trait anxiety and achievement goals as predictors of self-reported health in dancers. *Journal of Dance Medicine and Science, 14*(4), 163–170.

Leube, D. T., Knoblich, G., Erb, M., Grodd, W., Bartels, M. & Kircher, T. T. J. (2003). The neural correlates of perceiving one's own movements. *Neuroimage, 20*, 2084–2090. DOI: 10.1016/j.neuroimage.2003.07.033

Liederbach, M., Schanfein, L., & Kremenic, I. J. (2013). What is known about the effect of fatigue on injury occurrence among dancers. *Journal of Dance Medicine and Science, 17*(3), 101–108. DOI: 10. 12678/1089-313X.17.3.101

Lussier-Ley, C., & Durand-Bush, N. (2009). Exploring the role of feel in the creative experience of modern dancers: A realistic tale. *Research in Dance Education, 10*(3), 199–217. DOI: 10.1080/14647890993324154

Ma, H-H. (2009). The effect size of variables associated with creativity: A meta-analysis. *Creativity Research Journal, 21*(1), 30–42. DOI: 10.1080/10400410802633400

Marchant-Haycox, S. E., & Wilson, G. D. (1992). Personality and stress in performing artists. *Personality and Individual Differences, 13*(10), 1061–1068.

Martin, C. T., Ric, A., & Hristovski, R. (2015). Creativity and emergence of specific dance movements using instructional constraints. *Psychology of Aesthetics, Creativity, and the Arts, 9*(1), 65–74. DOI: 10.1037/a0038706

Matare, J. (2009). Creativity or musical intelligence? A comparative study of improvisation/ improvisation performance by European and African musicians. *Thinking Skills and Creativity, 4*, 194–203. DOI: 10.1016/j.tsc.2009.09.005

Monsma, E. V., & Overby, L. Y. (2004). The relationship between imagery and competitive anxiety in ballet auditions. *Journal of Dance Medicine and Science, 8*(1), 11–18.

Nelson, B., & Rawlings, D. (2009). How does it feel? The development of the Experience of Creativity Questionnaire. *Creativity Research Journal, 21*(1), 43–53. DOI: 10.1080/10400410802633442

Nordin, S. M., & Cumming, J. (2006a). The development of imagery in dance: Part I: Qualitative findings from professional dancers. *Journal of Dance Medicine and Science, 10*(1 & 2), 28–34.

Nordin, S. M., & Cumming, J. (2006b). The development of imagery in dance: Part II: Quantitative findings from a mixed sample of dancers. *Journal of Dance Medicine and Science, 10*(1 & 2), 21–27.

Nordin, S. M., & Cumming, J. (2006c). Measuring the content of dancers' images development of the dance imagery questionnaire (DIQ). *Journal of Dance Medicine and Science, 10*(3 & 4), 85–98.

Nordin-Bates, S. M., Quested, E., Walker, I. J., & Redding, E. (2012). Climate change in the dance studio: Findings from the UK centres for advanced training. *Sport Exercise and Performance Psychology, 1*(1), 3–16. DOI: 10.1037/a0025316

Overby, L. Y., Hall, C., & Haslam, I. (1997–98). A comparison of imagery used by dance teachers, figure skating coaches, and soccer coaches. *Imagination, Cognition and Personality, 17*(4), 323–337.

Padham, M., & Aujla, I. (2014). The relationship between passion and the psychological well-being of professional dancers. *Journal of Dance Medicine and Science, 18*(1), 37–44.

Piirto, J. (1998). *Understanding those who create. 2nd edition.* Scottsdale, AZ: Great Potential Press, Inc.

Press, C. M., & Warburton, E. C. (2007). Creativity research in dance. In L. Bresler (Ed.), *International handbook of research in arts education, Vol. 16* (pp. 1273–1290). The Netherlands: Springer.

Price, B. R., & Pettijohn, T. F. (2006). The effect of ballet dance attire on body and self-perceptions of female dancers. *Social Behavior and Personality: An International Journal, 34*(8), 991–998. DOI: 10.2224/sbp.2006.34.8.991

Reid, L. A. (2008). Aesthetics and education. *Research in Dance Education, 9*(3), 295–304. DOI: 10. 1080/j.4647890802416713

Rip, B., Fortin, S., & Vallerand, R. J. (2006). The relationship between passion and injury in dance students. *Journal of Dance Medicine and Science, 10*(1 & 2), 14–20.

Saarikallio, S., Luck, G., Burger, B., Thompson, M., & Toivianinen, P. (2013). Dance moves reflect current affective state illustrative of approach-avoidance motivation. *Psychology of Aesthetics, Creativity and the Arts, 7*(3), 296–305. DOI: 10.1037/a0032589

Sachs, C. (1937/1965). *World history of the dance.* New York: W.W. Norton & Company, Inc.

Sawyer, R. K., & DeZutter, S. (2009). Distributed creativity: How collective creations emerge from collaboration. *Psychology of Aesthetics, Creativity, and the Arts, 3*(2), 81–92. DOI: 10.1037/a0013282

Sheets-Johnstone, M. (1999). Emotion and movement: A beginning empirical-phenomenological analysis of their relationship. In R. Nunez & W. J. Freeman (Eds.), *Reclaiming cognition: The primacy of action, intention and emotion* (pp. 259–277). Bowling Green, OH:, Imprint Academic.

Silvia, P. J., Wigert, B., Reiter-Palmon, R., & Kaufman, J. C. (2012). Assessing creativity with self-report scales: A review and empirical evaluation. *Psychology of Aesthetics, Creativity and the Arts, 6*(1), 19–34. DOI: 10.1037/a0024071

Singer, K. (2004). The effect of neurofeedback on performance anxiety in dancers. *Journal of Dance Medicine and Science, 8*(3), 78–81.

Sowden, P. T., Clements, L., Redlich, C., & Lewis, C. (2015). Improvisation facilitates divergent thinking and creativity: Realizing a benefit of primary school arts education. *Psychology of Aesthetics, Creativity, and the Arts*, 9(2), 128–138. DOI: 10.1037/aca0000018

Stinson, S. W. (2004). My body/myself: Lessons from dance education. In L. Bresler (Ed.), *Knowing bodies, moving minds: Towards embodied teaching and learning* (pp. 153–168). London: Kluwer Academic.

Sullivan, P., & McCarthy, J. (2009). An experimental account of the psychology of art. *Psychology of Aesthetics, Creativity and the Arts*, 3(3), 181–187. DOI: 10.1037/a0014292

Tharp, T. (2003). *The creative habit: Learn and use it for life: A practical guide*. New York: Simon & Schuster.

Thomson, P., & Jaque, S. V. (2011–2012). Anxiety and the influences of flow, trauma, and fantasy experiences on dancers. *Cognition, Imagination and Personality*, 32(2), 165–178.

Thomson, P., & Jaque, S. V. (2012). Dancing with the Muses: Dissociation and flow. *Journal of Trauma and Dissociation*, 13(4), 478–489.

Thomson, P., & Jaque, S.V. (2013). Exposing shame in dancers and athletes: Shame, trauma, and dissociation in a non-clinical population. *Journal of Trauma and Dissociation*, 141, 1–16. DOI: 10.1080/ 15299732.2012.757714

Thomson. P., & Jaque, S. V. (2015). Shame and fantasy in athletes and dancers. *Cognition, Imagination and Personality*, 34(3), 291–305.

Thomson, P., & Jaque, S. V. (2016). Visiting the Muses: Creativity and trauma in talented dancers and athletes. *American Journal of Play*, 8(3), 363–378.

Thomson, P. (2011). Dance and Creativity. In M. A. Runco & S. R. Pritzker (Eds.), *Encyclopaedia of creativity, 2nd edition, Vol. 1* (pp. 343–350). London: Elsevier Publishing Company.

Tiggermann, M., & Slater, A. (2001). Test of objectification theory in former dancers and non-dancers. *Psychology of Women Quarterly*, 25(1), 57–64. DOI: 10.1111/1471–6402.00007

Tseng, M. M-C., Fang, D., Lee, M. B., Chie, W-C., Liu, J-P., & Chen, W. J. (2007). Two-phase survey of eating disorders in gifted dance and non-dance high-school students in Taiwan. *Psychological Medicine*, 37, 1085–1096. DOI: 10.1017/S0033291707000323

Twitchett, E., Angioi, M., Koutedakis, Y., & Wyon, M. (2010). The demands of a working day among female professional ballet dancers. *Journal of Dance Medicine and Science*, 14(4), 127–132.

Verghese, J. (2006). Cognitive and mobility profile in older social dancers. *Journal of American Geriatric Society*, 54(8), 1241–1244. DOI: 10.1111/,.1532–5415.2006.00808.x

Walker, I. J. & Nordin-Bates, S. M. (2010). Performance anxiety experiences of professional ballet dancers: The importance of control. *Journal of Dance Medicine and Science*, 14(4), 133–145.

Wanke, E. M., Arendt, M., Mill, H., Koch, F., Davenport, J., Fischer, A., & Groneberg, D. A. (2014). The theatrical stage as accident site in professional dancers. *Medical Problems of Performing Artists*, 29(1), 32–36.

Watson, D. E., Nordin-Bates, S. M., & Chappell, K. A. (2012). Facilitating and nurturing creativity in pre-vocational dancers: Findings from the UK centers for advanced training. *Research in Dance Education*, 13(2), 153–173.

Wigman, M. (1966). *Mary Wigman: The language of dance*. Middletown, CT: Wesleyan University Press.

Wilhelm, K., Kovess, V., Rios-Seidel, C., & Finch, A. (2004). Work and mental health. *Social Psychiatry and Psychiatric Epidemiology, 39*, 866–873. DOI: 10.1007/s00127.004. 0869-7

Wyrick, W. (1968). The development of a test of motor creativity. *Research Quarterly, 39(3)*, 756–765. DOI: 10.1080/10671188.1968.10616608

PART III

Creativity in the Sciences

12 Creativity in the Physical Sciences

Gregory J. Feist

San Jose State University

Abstract

It is not uncommon for people to gloss over the high degree of creativity involved in science. The physical sciences (physics, chemistry, geology, and astronomy) would not be where they are today without extremely creative insights and solutions to both experimental and theoretical problems. In this chapter I review the vast and growing psychological literature on creativity in the physical sciences. I do so by organizing the studies by their overarching methodology, namely psychometric, experimental, biographical, historiometric, and biometric. I begin, however, by first defining creativity and how it is measured in the physical sciences. I end by pointing out some of the important gaps in our understanding of creativity in the physical sciences, such as the biological, genetic, epigenetic, and neuroscientific foundations of creative talent in the physical sciences, why still so few women are entering the profession, and whether personality traits distinguish those who are interested in and have talent for the physical sciences compared to the social and biological sciences.

More often than not, people not familiar with creativity research believe creativity to be a trait reserved mostly for artists, writers, poets, musicians, and playwrights – but not for scientists. Indeed, this is ironic given the person most synonymous with creative genius is a physicist – Albert Einstein. That creativity is reserved for artists, writers, and musicians is of course not true. A major quality that distinguishes everyday scientists from truly great ones is her or his level of creative problem solving. My task in this chapter is to demonstrate the existence of creativity in the physical sciences and to review a representative sample of the vast literature on the topic.

Creativity and Its Measurement in Physical Science

The two major concepts of this chapter are creativity and physical science so I shall begin by being clear on what I mean by each of these terms. In addition, the problem of how we measure creativity in general and in science in particular is of crucial importance and hence I will devote some attention to that as well.

Defining Creativity

First, a nearly universal definition by creativity researchers is that creativity requires two things: thought and behavior that is both novel/original and useful/adaptive (Amabile, 1996; Feist, 2006a; Guilford, 1950; Kaufman & Baer, 2004; MacKinnon, 1970; Runco, 2004; Simonton, 2008; Sternberg, 1988). Simonton has recently added a third criterion, namely surprisingness, to originality and usefulness (Simonton, 2013). Although I fundamentally agree with the standard two-fold definition, I believe there is value to slightly modifying it – rather than useful/adaptive thought and behavior it would be better to say the thought and behavior must be "meaningful" to be creative. Useful/adaptive implies utilitarian and although technological and even scientific advances can be useful, it is always a bit awkward to refer to art, music, and literature as "useful" or even "adaptive." Hence, I argue for the term "meaningful," which carries all the connotations of useful/adaptive but without the awkwardness and seemingly irrelevance for the arts.

Secondly, let me define what I mean by physical science in its broadest, most psychological sense. Physical knowledge concerns the inanimate world of physical objects (including tools), their movement, positioning, and causal relations in space, and their inner workings (machines). Because the tool-use element is a large component of physical knowledge, some archeologists refer to this domain as "technical intelligence" (cf. Byrne 2001; Mithen 1996). An "implicit physics" is also seen in children's automatic sense that physical objects obey different rules than living things (inanimate vs animate rules). Inanimate objects fall to the ground and do not get up. Understanding the physical world has been a crucial component to our species' survival, especially as it is involved in our tool-making abilities and spatial and geographic understanding. As I argued in more depth in *The Psychology of Science and the Origins of the Scientific Mind* (Feist, 2006c), the physical sciences (astronomy, physics, chemistry, geology) as well as applied science, technology, and engineering stem from our evolved capacity to understand and solve problems dealing with the physical objects.

Additionally, along with various other scholars, I argue that intelligence of the physical, inanimate world is one of many specific domains of intelligence, an argument that I base on seven different criteria: archeological, comparative, developmental, universality, precocity, neuroscientific, and genetic. Developmental criterion simply means there is a natural development of the intelligence starting at birth (or before) and there is a systematic growth or change over time. Precocity is related in that there are in rare cases extremely precocious signs of the intelligence in certain individuals. Universality requires that the form of the intelligence be expressed in all people, the world over. Now is not the time or place to detail these criteria but suffice it to say that physical intelligence is not just theoretical or arbitrary (see Feist, 2006c, ch. 8 for more detail). A summary of the distinct domains of intelligence that various psychologists have argued for is presented in Table 12.1.

Specifically, I argue that the focus of science as either "thing oriented" (physical objects) or "people oriented" attracts different kinds of people to the profession and therefore these two groups should have distinct psychological profiles (Baron-

Table 12.1 *Domains of mind proposed by different theorists*

Domain	Author								
	Geary and Huffman	Gopnik, Meltzhoff, andKuhl	Parker and McKinney	Carey and Spelke	Mithen	Karmiloff-Smith	Feist	Gardner	Pinker
Psychology	x	x	x	x	x	x	x	x	x
Physics	x	x	x	x	x	x	x	x	x
Linguistics		x	x	x	x	x	x	x	x
Mathematics			x	x		x	x	x	x
Biology	x				x		x	x	x
Art						x	x		
Music							x	x	
Kinesthetics								x	
Economics									x

Note: Information is from the following sources: Carey and Spelke 1994, Feist 2001, 2004a, Gardner, 1983, 1999, Geary and Huffman 2002, Gopnik et al. 1999, Karmiloff-Smith 1992, Mithen 1996, Parker and McKinney 1999, and Pinker 2002. Pinker, in fact, argues for ten separate domains (psychology, physics, engineering, spatial, language, biology, math, probability, logic, and economics), but I have combined certain categories in this table; for example, physics, engineering, and spatial are combined and math, probability and logic are combined.
Reprinted with permission, Yale University Press.

Cohen, Wheelwright, Stott, & Goodyer, 1997; Baron-Cohen, Bolton, Wheelwright, Short, Mead, Smith, & Scahill, 1998; Billington, Baron-Cohen, & Wheelwright, 2007; Feist 2006a, 2006c, 2011; Thomson, Wurtzburg, & Centifanti, 2015). Elsewhere I argued that different kinds of intelligence and problem-solving skills underpin career paths in the physical sciences or the social sciences (Feist, 2006b). Thing-oriented individuals tend to be more introverted and interested in molecules, numbers, and other inanimate objects, whereas those who are people-oriented, not surprisingly, are drawn towards social stimuli and tend to be more extraverted (Feist, 2006b; Lippa, 1998; Mount, Barrick, Scullen, & Rounds, 2005; Prediger, 1982).

Now is neither time nor place to delve deeply into the nature of science and the distinction between "hard" (physical) and "soft" (social) sciences. However, a few words are in order concerning the differences between the physical and social sciences, since this chapter focuses on the former rather than the latter. For centuries, Science was synonymous with the physical sciences – physics, chemistry, astronomy, geology. We now refer these to the STEM (Science, Technology, Engineering, Math). Dean Keith Simonton (2009) has quantified these heretofore conceptual differences between the physical and social sciences. Compared to the social sciences, the physical sciences do indeed have more agreement on what a contribution is and have greater consensus as to what the most important work is. Moreover, the latter have contributions made by younger scientists and are more likely to use visual/graphical means of communicating findings. Finally, the physical sciences have more laws compared to theories.

Measuring Creativity

Closely associated to clearly defining creativity is the problem of measuring it reliably and validly. How is creativity assessed? One long-standing approach in empirical research of creativity is to argue that creativity really has four distinct components: Person, Product, Process, and (Environmental) Press – the four Ps as they are sometimes referred to. The question that each asks then is how creative is the person, product, process, or press? Creativity of the person is assessed most directly via personality, such as the Creative Personality Scale (CPS) of the California Psychological Inventory Gough, 1987). Products are works of art, literature, music, science, innovation etc. that can be evaluated independently of the creator. Amabile (1996), for example, developed the Consensual Assessment Technique where outside raters (often "experts") would assess the level of creativity of a product. The product approach is one of the most common in the assessment of creativity in physical science. The idea is simple: In science the outcome of creative work is most often a publication and the creativity of these publications is assessed by impact. Impact is most directly assessed via citation counts or more recently a variation on citation, namely the h-index (Feist, 1993, 1997; Grosul & Feist, 2014; Hirsch, 2005; Soler, 2007). In turn, publications and citations lead to recognition and awards by one's peers and these become an index of creativity (Feist, 1993; Simonton, 2000). Publication and citation counts follow the very real non-normal positively skewed distribution found in many areas of life, such as income or number views on YouTube sites. Indeed, this well-known law goes back to at least the 1920s, when Lotka (1926) proposed the law taking the form $1/n^c$, where n is the number of articles and c is a constant (most commonly being around 2.0). This law in effect describes the phenomenon that fewer and fewer people publish more and more articles. For example, if c is 2, then 1/100th the number of scientists will produce ten articles in a given time period compared to the number who produce one article during that time period; 1/25th the number of scientists will produce five articles in a given time period compared to the number who produce one article; and 1/16th as many scientists will publish four articles compared to one. Numerous studies have validated the general nature of this law (Chung & Cox, 1990; Gupta, 1987; Huang & Yang, 2012; Price, 1963; Simonton, 1988a, 1988b).

Assessing the creative process in science often takes a cognitive approach by measuring creative problem solving and thinking directly. For example, scientists who are creative and/or experts are more likely to use analogy and metaphor in their solutions to problems than less creative and/or novice scientists (Clement, 1991; Dunbar, 1995; Gentner & Jeziorski, 1989) Measurement of creativity in these studies generally consists of assigning a prescribed problem to different groups of scientists and then analyzing the cognitive strategies and products of their solutions.

Findings from Five Research Traditions on Creativity in Physical Science

Plucker and Renzulli (1999) argued for five distinct approaches to studying creativity: psychometric, experimental, biographical, historiometric, and biometric. Briefly, the psychometric approach consists of directly measuring creativity and its correlates. The experimental approach is in some ways a subset of the psychometric approach in that it involves only experimental or quasi-experimental designs, such as laboratory manipulation of independent variables and random assignment to conditions (or at least manipulation of an independent variable). Biographical approaches tend to be qualitative case study assessments of the lives of eminently creative individuals. Historiometric studies cull quantitative data from the historical record and analyze patterns, correlations, and trends. Finally, the biometric approach investigates physiological and biological aspects of creative achievements such as genetic influence and neuroscientific correlates of creative thought. In science in general and in physical science in particular, creativity has been assessed with all five approaches (Simonton, 1999; Tweney, 1998).

Psychometric Studies of Physical Science Ability and Creativity

Empirically but non-experimentally assessing creativity along with other non-manipulated traits, such as personality, intelligence, or Autism-spectrum, is the essence of the psychometric approach and it is fair to say that the majority of studies on creativity in the physical sciences utilize this methodology. Physical science by definition involves the study of inanimate objects or things and hence it is not surprising that people with talent in understanding things gravitate toward the physical sciences.

Developmental Influences

The people–thing distinction maps not only onto social and physical science interest and talent but also onto what other researchers refer to as "empathizing" and "systemizing " (E-S; Lawson, Baron-Cohen, & Wheelwright, 2004; Thomson et al., 2015). Moreover, they argue that E-S is a model or theory of autism (Lawson et al. 2004). Empathizing consists of the ability and drive to know what other people are thinking and feeling and to behave accordingly. Systemizing consists of the ability and drive to understand and build systems and to understand and predict events without agents (i.e., people). Most commonly these systems are technical or natural, as in understanding machines or natural processes such as chemical responses. They can also involve motor skills seen in musical performance or abstract-logical skills as expressed in mathematics.

One of the most fascinating and baffling examples of ability with things and patterns comes from a certain kind of savantism, a rare condition often but not always associated with autism. Savants are people who have an island of extreme and mostly unlearned talent in a sea of severe cognitive disability (Treffert, 2006). A typical savant, for example, may not be able to hold a utensil but can play a piano piece by Tchaikovsky after hearing it once! Some savants have shown incredible ability with making and manipulating things, such as building and repairing objects (e.g., wood carvings, clocks, computers, clay structures, machines, guitars) (Brink, 1980; Robinson, 2008; Treffert, 2006). Brink, for example, described a "Mr. A" who had acquired savantism as a result of a gunshot wound to the head at age 9. After his accident, he could not read or write, but he could take a bicycle apart and completely put it back together again, was a gifted carpenter, and could reproduce complex drawings extremely accurately. Another example of mechanical savantism is John Robinson (2008), who in his memoir described his odd social habits, inability to look people in the eye (high-functioning Asperger's), but also how he developed an uncanny ability in electronics and went on to be the genius behind the "exploding guitars" of the rock band KISS.

Various lines of evidence, sometimes direct and sometimes indirect, converge on the conclusion that physical scientists from very early in life have temperaments and personalities that are more thing-oriented rather than people-oriented or system-atizing rather than empathizing (Rasoal, Danielsson, & Jungert, 2012; Rawlings & Locarnini, 2008). For instance, indirect evidence comes from Simon Baron-Cohen and his colleagues who have demonstrated a thing- versus people-orientation as early as thirty-six hours after birth, with male neonates showing a slight preference for things over people and females showing no real preference one way or the other (Lawson et al., 2004). Whether this effect, assuming it can be replicated, has an influence on interest in science has yet to be demonstrated, but it is an intriguing hypothesis since males, as reported by the National Science Foundation (NSF, 2015), are still disproportionately represented in the physical sciences and math. Recent research has demonstrated that this systematizing bias in students in the physical sciences holds even after controlling for gender (Thomson, Wurtzburg, & Centifanti, 2015). In addition, Baron-Cohen and his colleagues have shown that engineers, mathematicians, and physical scientists score much higher on measures of high-functioning autism and Asperger's syndrome than non-scientists, and that physical scientists, mathematicians, and engineers are higher on a non-clinical measure of autism than social scientists. Lastly, autistic children are more than twice as likely as non-autistic children to have a father or grandfather who was an engineer.

Another psychometric approach to the study of scientific creativity is a giftedness perspective. How and when does scientific talent in youth flourish into scientific creativity and achievement in adulthood? In general, longitudinal investigations find that adolescent precocity in math and science does translate into adult scientific achievement (Berger, 1994; Brody & Mills, 2005; Csikszentihalyi, Rathunde, & Whalen, 1997; Feist, 2006b; Lubinski, & Benbow, 2005; Subotnik & Steiner, 1994; Subotnik, Duschl, & Selmon, 1993; Wai, Webb, Lubinski, & Benbow, 2002). That is, an inordinately high percentage of precocious students (compared to the general population) goes on to earn their doctorate degrees in math or science and some produce scientific findings that earn them membership in the National Academy of Science or even the Nobel Prize at rates much higher than the base rates of other scientists. Wai et al. (2005), for instance, divided precocious youth (top 1 percent) into their top and bottom quartiles. That is, the top quartile represents intellectual talent at the rate of 1 in 1,000 in the general population, whereas the bottom quartile represents a rate of 1 in 100. The former compared to the latter were more likely to earn a PhD, have a higher income, acquire more patents, and obtain tenure at a top-fifty research university. In addition to precocious quantitative ability, these talented youths in math and science also possess unusually high levels of spatial ability (Wai, Lubinski, & Benbow, 2009). Similarly, Roberston, Smeets, Lubinski, and Benbow (2010) challenge the "threshold theory" of cognitive aptitude and career/creative achievement. The top 1 percent of 13-year-olds in mathematical ability were divided into quartiles, and compared to the bottom quartile the top quartile was 2.7 times more likely to earn a doctorate, 4.5 times more likely to publish a peer-review article, 18 times more likely to obtain a STEM (science, technology, engineering, technology) doctorate, and 3.3 times more likely to be in the top 95th percentile in income.

And yet gender appears to be a demographic developmental that can affect how and to what extent talented teenagers in science go on to achieve at high levels as adults. For example, the most talented scientific high school youths in the country are the forty finalists of the annual Westinghouse/Intel Science Talent Search going back to the 1940s. Although it has only been since the 1980s that girls were approximately as likely to be chosen a finalist as boys, reaching parity or near parity by the late 1990s, longitudinal investigations still show these talented girls are more likely to leave science by the time they reach adulthood than boy finalists (Berger, 1994; Feist, 2006b; Subotnik et al., 1993; Webb et al., 2002). For example, 43 percent of the finalist girls compared to 11 percent of the finalist boys left the science profession as adults (although many of the women went on to very successful careers in medicine; Feist, 2006b). Moreover, talented women are more likely to choose careers that allow them more balance between career and family obligations (Robertson et al., 2010).

The extreme imbalance of males to females in the very top end of the distribution in math ability seems to be declining. Benbow and Stanley (1983) famously reported in *Science* a ratio of 13 to 1 (males to females) in extreme mathematical precocity (scores above 700 on the SAT before one's 13th birthday). In a more detailed, current, and extensive analysis of over 500,000 boys and 500,000 girls who took the SAT (and ACT), Wai, Cacchio, Putallaz, and Makel (2010) found evidence for a decline in gender imbalance, but not its disappearance: the male–female ratio of perfect SAT scores during 2006–2010 was 6.58 to 1. The same analysis on perfect scores on the math portion of the ACT found a ratio of 3.87 to 1 in 2006–2010. Also of note was the 5.13 male/female ratio on perfect Science scores of the ACT in 2006–2010 compared to 4.27 in 1990–1995. It should also be pointed out that in general, extreme verbal scores tend to favor females: ratios of .83 for perfect SATs (800) in 2006–2010 and .58 for perfect scores (≥32) on the ACT English (Wai et al., 2010). Results from representative samples on IQ report similar math and verbal sex differences (Deary, Strand, Smith, & Fernandes, 2007; Deary, Thorpe, Wilson, Starr, & Whalley, 2003; Hedges & Nowell, 1995; Strand, Deary, & Smith, 2006). To be clear, the evidence also shows males are over-represented on the very lowest ends of the distribution on math and IQ as well (Deary et al., 2003).

The problem with research on gender differences is it does not directly uncover causes and reasons for the differences. Needless to say, the literature on this topic is large and contentious with no overall agreement on the extent to which gender differences in cognitive ability exist and what their causes may be (Ceci & Williams, 2007, 2010; *Edge, The Third Culture*, 2005; Gallagher & DeLisi, 1994; Gallahger & Kaufman, 2005; Kumar, 2012; Pinker, 2002).

Another developmental-demographic influence that affects scientific achievement is immigrant status. One of the more interesting findings predicting scientific interest and talent has been immigrant status, specifically being from a family that is within two generations of immigrating to the United States. A disproportionate number of science majors, scientists, and elite scientists had at least one parent who was new to this country. By disproportionate I mean upwards of 35% when only about 20% of the US population in 2000 are first- or second-generation American (Berger, 1994; Feist, 1993; 2006b; Helson & Crutchfield, 1970; Portes & Rumbaut, 2001; Simonton, 1988a). For instance, in a study of elite scientists, Feist (2006b) reported that 20 out of 55 (36%) Westinghouse Science Fair finalists had a father and 22 out of 55 (40%) had a mother either born elsewhere or was a first-generation American. Similarly, in a sample of members of the National Academy of Sciences, 28 of 85 (33%) had fathers and 29 (34%) had mothers who were immigrants or first-generation Americans (Feist, 2006b).

Families who recently come to the shores of the United States may well foster a particular set of values that encourages and maybe even demands high-level achievement, whether it be in science, medicine, or business. As suggested by classic work in the sociology of science, an interesting speculation on this phenomenon is that science may be more meritocratic than most other career paths and therefore talent and achievement in and of itself is more likely to be recognized and rewarded (see Cole & Cole, 1973; Merton, 1973). A significant scientific finding is perhaps more likely to be evaluated on its own merits than novel business or political ideas. Immigrant families may realize this, and given that fluency in the native language may not be as critical as it is in other careers, parents may therefore encourage their children to go into math, science, or engineering careers.

Simonton (1988b) offers another possible explanation: "Individuals raised in one culture, but living in another are blessed with a heterogeneous array of mental elements, permitting combinatory variations unavailable to those who reside solely in on cultural world" (p. 126). Having been an exchange student myself, I can personally attest to the power of simultaneously having two cultural lenses through which to compare experiences. By being exposed to a different way of doing things and a different way of thinking, one's own implicit assumptions are more explicit and one takes less for granted, that is, without reflection. By being aware of multiple perspectives simultaneously, one has a wider associative network from which to tackle problems creatively.

The connection between scientific productivity and age has a long and distinguished history. Since the 1950s, researchers in psychology and sociology have systematically examined the association between age and productivity and have determined that the relationship is an inverted-U (Bayer & Dutton, 1977; S. Cole, 1979; Dennis, 1956; Diamond, 1986; Feist, 2006b; Horner, Rushton, & Vernon, 1986; Lehman, 1953, 1960, 1966; Levin & Stephan, 1991; Over, 1982, 1989; Simonton, 1988a, b, 1991; Zuckerman, 1996). More specifically, the curve peaks around twenty years into one's career, usually in one's early 40s. To graphically model this relationship, Simonton has developed one of his better-known differential equations, with the peak occurring roughly twenty years into one's career and thereafter slowly declining (Simonton, 1988b). However, it does peak somewhat differently for various disciplines (earlier in math and physics, later in biology and geology). Stroebe (2010) argues that motivation, availability of resources, and compulsory retirement are more important than cognitive decline in explaining the general decline in productivity with age after age 45 or 50. In fact, Stroebe presents evidence that calls into question the general decline in scientific productivity during the last decades of life. Similarly, Feist (2006b) reported a significant uptick in publications among members of the National Academy of Sciences at the very end of their careers.

A related question concerns whether producing works early in life predicts later levels of productivity. The empirical consensus is that early levels of high productivity do regularly predict continued levels of high productivity across one's lifetime (S. Cole, 1979; Dennis, 1966; Feist, 2006b; Helson & Crutchfield, 1970; Horner et al., 1986; Lehman, 1953; Over, 1982; Reskin, 1977; Roe, 1965; Simonton, 1988a, 1991). Those who are prolific early in their careers also tend to continue to be productive for the longest periods of time. Simonton (1991), however, reported some interesting disciplinary differences in science by examining the ages of first, best, and last works in nearly 500 historically eminent scientists (math, astronomy, physics, chemistry, biology, medicine, technology, and earth science). He found that mathematicians, biologists, and physicists were the only scientists with the mean age of first publication under age 30. In general, the disciplines with the oldest age of first publication (Medicine $M = 32.3$, Astronomy, $M = 30.5$; and Earth Science $M = 30.9$) had the oldest age of last work published (Ms of 54.5, 56.0, and 58.2 respectively). The only exception was biologists, who started young (29.4) and ended late (57.8).

Feist (2006b) reported in a sample of members of the National Academy of Science (NAS) that the younger they were when they and others knew they had talent for science, the younger they were to publish their first paper, which in turn predicts greater lifetime productivity (publications).

Personality Correlates

The research that has been conducted explicitly on the personality traits of scientists has confirmed a personality constellation that is relatively introverted, asocial, and thing-oriented. For instance, in summarizing the results from twenty-six studies (and forty-one samples), I reported the median effect size (Cohen's d) for introversion comparing scientists to non-scientists was .26, or about a quarter of a standard deviation higher in scientists – a small but non-zero effect size (Feist, 1998). More specifically, the cluster of social traits (i.e., introversion, independence, arrogance, dominance, hostility, and self-confidence) suggests a relatively low threshold for social stimulation in physical scientists, meaning that physical scientists are more likely than others to be overstimulated by social activities. They regulate this over-stimulation by preferring to be in non-social or fewer social situations, such as working with things rather than people.

For example, using the Eysenck Personality Questionnaire (EPQ), Wilson and Jackson (1994) examined personality traits in physicists and reported that compared to controls, male and female physicists were more introverted, controlled, cautious, and unsociable. More systematically, Feist (1998) conducted a meta-analysis of twenty-six studies reporting effect sizes on the relation between personality and scientific interest showed that scientists compared to non-scientists were moderately higher in conscientiousness and lower on openness to experience. Conscientiousness is characterized by being cautious, careful, fastidious, and self-controlled, and low openness is characterized by being conventional, socialized, and rigid. Similarly, a meta-analysis of twenty-eight studies comparing personality in creative to less-creative scientists found that, compared to their less-creative peers, creative scientists are more confident and open to experience and are less conscientious (Feist, 1998). In short, the personality traits that make scientific interest more likely are high conscientiousness and low openness, whereas the traits that make scientific creativity more likely are high openness, low conscientiousness, and high confidence and hostility.

Beginning with Eysenck's research and theory (1993, 1995), psychoticism has been a basic personality dimension associated with creative thought and behavior. Yet various scholars have criticized the dimension of psychoticism as too multi-factored and not internally coherent enough and therefore began to tease apart some of its components. Schizotypy is one of those and is defined as milder psychosis proneness and consists of traits such as magical thinking and unusual perceptual experiences. Schizotypy is another personality quality generally associated with creative people (Nettle, 2006; Schuldberg, 2000). The question, however, is whether this is also true of creative scientists. The answer seems to that it is not. For instance, Rawlings and Locarnini (2000) found that compared to artists and musicians, physical scientists score lower on schizotypic subscales of "unusual experiences" and "cognitive disorganization."

Social/Environmental Influences

Science in general, but physical science in particular, is more and more conducted in teams – large teams. This is not to say the individual does not matter, but rather that scientific thought and behavior is increasingly taking place in networked groups (Falk-Krzesinski et al., 2010; Hemlin & Olsson, 2013; National Research Council, 2015; Paletz & Schunn, 2010). There is much interest, therefore, in which kinds of groups, teams, and labs are most productive. A recent report by the National Research Council (2015) found that the structure of teams, institutions, and leadership have significant positive and negative effects on team science. For example, team interaction, climate, psychological safety, cohesion, and conflict all impact the overall effectiveness of team science output (cf. Paletz & Schunn, 2010). Similarly, Hemlin and Olsson (2013) reported that, although the findings are mixed, medium-sized research groups may be optimally productive and that productive research teams require sufficient resources and social networking, but most importantly leadership structures that facilitate creative and innovative thinking. Specifically, the kinds of leadership styles that facilitate creativity in research groups include leaders being open, secure, and using pleasant communication. These styles tend to strike a balance between being competitive and cooperative (see also Schulze & Seuffert, 2013).

In another attempt to examine the social context of scientific productivity, creativity, and innovation, psychologists of science have recently taken to observing real-world, naturalistic laboratory behavior (Falk-Krzesinski et al., 2010; Hemlin & Olsson, 2013; National Research Council, 2015; Nersessian, 2009; Paletz & Schunn, 2010). Among others, Gorman and Dunbar refer to these studies as "in-vivo" or naturalistic investigations into the psychology of science (Dunbar, 1995; Gorman, 2013). In her work with scientists and engineers in their labs, for instance, Nancy Nersessian (2009) argued that naturalistic scientific thinking can only be understood in the context of "distributed cognition" – that is, knowledge systems that are distributed among members of a social group.

Videotaping and audiotaping laboratory scientists, Dunbar and Blanchette (2001) reported that scientists use different kinds of analogies (superficial or structural) depending on which phase of problem solving they were engaged in. Hypothesis testing, for instance, fostered the most structural (deep) analogies compared to designing an experiment or explaining a phenomenon Moreover, they conducted simulated laboratory research (in vitro) in order to manipulate tasks and to see whether analogies changed in a similar way to their in vivo studies. They found that they did. In short, Dunbar and Blanchette argued that combining in vivo and in vitro (experimental) techniques offered a fuller and more complete picture of scientific thinking than either technique alone (cf., Dunbar, 1995).

In an in vivo study of engineers, Christensen and Schunn (2007) reported that the greater the "analogical distance" (i.e., space from source to target of the analogy), the more original and novel the solutions. In addition, scientists and engineers use analogies to identify and solve problems as well as explain concepts. Other aspects of laboratory behavior, such verbal and non-verbal behavior, have also been examined and analyzed. Schunn and Trafton (2013), for instance, report a series of studies that coded videotaped speech and gesture signs of uncertainty of earth scientists at Jet Propulsion Lab working on the Mars Rover project. Uncertainty was demonstrated verbally with hedgewords (e.g., "possibly," "maybe," "sort of") and gesturally with shoulder shrugs. Knowing the antecedents and consequences of uncertainty in labs is a necessary first step in knowing there are problems that need to be solved. Finally, knowledge diversity of research teams (that is, the number of different domains of expert knowledge in a group) was associated with greater team innovation (Paletz & Schunn, 2010).

Team science is not only becoming more common but also more funded. Not surprisingly, both public and private funding agencies have a vested interest in knowing which teams are most productive and why. Indeed, a new program at the National Science Foundation (NSF) program, Science of Science and Innovation Policy (SciSIP) began to examine just this question (*Science of Science and Innovation Policy*, n.d.).

Intelligence/Cognitive Style (Curiosity)

Science is inherently a cognitive act, and there are many studies on problem solving strategies of novices and experts, implicit cognition, heuristics, hypothesis testing, confirmation bias, and analogy and metaphor in science (Carruthers, Stich, & Siegal, 2002; Feist & Gorman, 1998; Klahr, 2000; Klahr & Simon, 1999; Proctor & Capaldi, 2012; Tweney, 1989, 1998; Tweney, Doherty, & Mynatt, 1981). I review some of this literature in the next section on "Experimental Studies." In this section, I focus instead on cognitive ability and style, namely intelligence and need for cognition.

Cultural stereotypes of scientists have them pegged for being "smart," "nerdy," "brains," or, to use the British term, "boffin" – a disheveled, brilliant, but socially isolated and clueless egg-head or scientist (Francis, Skelton, & Read, 2012; Jones, 1997). There is, however, surprisingly little direct research on the overall IQ of scientists and even less on physical scientists. One of the first to make estimates of the IQ levels of world-class historical creative geniuses, including 39 scientists, was Catherine Cox (1926) in the 1920s. Her team, led by Lewis Terman, compared abilities of each person to the norms and estimate IQ based on estimated "mental age" over chronological age. The estimated mean IQ of 39 scientific geniuses was 140–155. To pick a few of the most well-known: Sir Isaac Newton's and Charles Darwin's estimated IQs were between 130 and 140, Kepler's and Galileo's between

140 and 150 and Leibnitz between 180 and 190, but Copernicus' was estimated to be only between 100 and 110.

Cox's estimates are not very different from more direct and recent assessments. The few studies reporting on the IQ of scientists find them to be two to three standard deviations above the mean (i.e., around 130–140). For example, Anne Roe (1952) assessed IQ more directly in a group of 64 physical, biological, and social scientists and reported median verbal IQs of around 165, mathematical of around 155, and median spatial of around 140. Similarly, Gibson and Light (1967) reported slightly higher (but statistically so) IQs in chemists and physicists than in social scientists (130, 128, and 122 respectively). Harmon (1961) examined the school IQ tests of more than 6,000 PhD students in the United States in the late 1950s and reported functional IQ scores of 130 for physicists, 128 for mathematicians, and 124 for social scientists. When Herrnstein and Murray (1994) refer to "high IQ professions" they include natural scientists, social scientists, computer scientists, engineers, and mathematicians and argue the mean IQ of these professions is about 120. These scores are in line with PhDs in general.

The need for cognition should also predict who is interested in and has talent for science. Cohen, Stotland, and Wolfe (1955, p. 291) first described need for cognition as "a need to structure relevant situations in meaningful, integrated ways. It is a need to understand and make reasonable the experiential world." Science in general involves understanding and making reasonable our experience of our world. More recently, Cacioppo and colleagues defined the need for cognition as "an individual's tendency to engage in and enjoy effortful cognitive endeavors." (Cacioppo, Petty, Kao, 1984, p. 306). Need for cognition, therefore, should be associated with interest in science, because the latter begins with wonder, questioning, and curiosity about how the world operates (Feist, 2006a). Science, almost everyone would agree, involves "effortful cognitive activity" and hence people disposed toward such activity would also tend toward a life of science, or at least be interested in it, which is precisely what Feist (2012) found. Moreover, need for cognition explained variance in scientific interest even once variance due to personality was held constant. This implies that need for cognition is not merely a personality dimension, but rather also a unique cognitive style construct.

Experimental Studies

Experimental research that randomly assigns participants to conditions and manipulates an independent variable is, for ethical, practical, and methodological reasons, often constrained to cognitive or social investigations. I will also review a few quasi-experimental studies here that manipulate independent variables but that have naturally formed groupings.

Experimental studies on scientific thinking and problem solving are too numerous to summarize in this chapter. Suffice it to say that cognitive psychologists of science have found scientific thought and problem solving a goldmine for explicating the cognitive basis of science (Carruthers, Stich, & Siegal, 2002; Gick & Holyoak,

1983; Gorman, 1992, 2013; Nersessian, 2009; Novick, 1988; Proctor & Capaldi, 2012; Tweney et al. 1981).

I can only give a hint of some of the main findings from in vivo research on scientific thinking. In general, visualization, superior memory, and analogical and metaphorical reasoning are important cognitive elements of scientific problem solving (Feist, 2006b; Feist & Gorman, 1998; Gick & Holyoak, 1983; Gorman, 1992). For example, Gick and Holyoak (1983) had participants solve a problem in which a patient has a stomach tumor. The problem is to use a laser to kill the tumor without killing healthy tissue. In one condition, participants are given information about soldiers who split up and then converge on a fortress. In general, only when participants are given hints that the soldier information is relevant do they come up with an analogous "convergence" solution for the tumor – a process known as "analogical transfer."

Gorman (1992) summarized much of the research on falsification and confirmation bias, inspired by Popper's demarcation problem. For instance, there is the classic work on Wason's four-card selection task, in which participants must guess a rule the experimenter has in mind that explains a three-digit sequence, for example "2–4–6." Most participants only choose confirming strategies (such as 8–10–12) and ignore the more necessary disconfirming solution to test their hypotheses (such as 1–2–3) (Wason, 1966). As it turns out, both of these guesses are correct, because the rule is simply "any three digits in increasing order" but the correct rule can only be surmised once one tries to disconfirm it. The surprising finding from this early work was that even scientists and statisticians fall prey to confirmation bias, albeit at a somewhat lower rate than novices (cf. Einhorn & Hogarth, 1978; Mahoney & Kimper, 1976). Further research by Tweney and colleagues (1981) uncovered a more nuanced rule used by experts: confirm early, disconfirm late. That is, when first testing an idea, follow a confirmation strategy that is biased toward information and evidence that confirms the hypothesis. Once it is established, then switch over to a disconfirmation strategy where evidence is sought to tear down the original hypothesis (falsification strategy). Strong hypotheses withstand attempts at falsification. Moreover, in non-scientists, being asked to discover more than one rule, being low in dispositional trust, or even being primed with a distrusting face each improved the likelihood that participants would search for disconfirming rules in the Wason 2–4–6 task (Gorman, Stafford, & Gorman, 1987; Mayo, Alfasi, & Schwarz, 2014).

Some cognitive research on scientific thinking is more quasi-experimental than experimental in that it manipulates an independent variable (often a scientific, math, or engineering problem), but then gives these problems to two or more naturally-occurring groups (often experts and novices) and analyses different strategies. Larkin and colleagues (1980), for example, reviewed much of the quasi-experimental research on the specific cognitive strategies and skills used "intuitively" by expert but not novice scientists by examining verbal "thinking out loud" accounts from both groups as they solved chess, physics, or engineering problems. In short, they report that experts have superior perceptual knowledge and memory (chunking) and have built up large patterned knowledge stores (pattern-indexed schemata) to solve problems very quickly – what some call "intuitively." One surprising finding is that experts work forward on easier problems whereas novices work backwards (and more slowly).

Biographical Studies

Recall that biographical approaches are qualitative case study assessments of the lives of eminently creative individuals. There have been numerous biographical studies of famous scientists: Einstein alone has dozens of biographies written about him (e.g., Isaacson, 2008, 2014; Neffe & Frische, 2007). Other famous physicists have had multiple biographies written about their lives, such as Newton (Gleick, 2003), Oppenheimer (Goodchild, 1980; Hecht, 2015), Feynman (Gleick, 1992), and Sagan (Davidson, 1999), just to name a few. The advantage of biographical portrayals is they allow great idiographic depth and analysis of the scientists' entire life and personality. Moreover, the psychobiographic approach of William McKinley Runyan (2006, 2013) has been a very fruitful application of the detailed study of lives to the scientific process and development of scientific theories and discoveries. Similarly, Simonton has applied biographical analysis in answering questions of genius, especially in the sciences. For example, he asked the question of whether "Darwin was a genius?" and using historical record concludes "no" by a psychometric definition of genius (IQ > 140), but "yes" by a Galtonian definition of creative achievement (Simonton, 1999).

A more purely cognitive offshoot of the biographical and historical approach examines historical records of individual scientists and attempts most often to unravel the cognitive processes used to make some important discovery (Gorman, 1992; Miller, 1986; Nersessian, 1984, 1986, 2008; Tweney, 2013). In short, this method combines history and cognitive psychology. Typically, in this cognitive-historical method, psychologists will comb the diaries, logs, or lab notes of a famous scientist and dissect the problem and solution strategies in an attempt to gain insight into the development of scientific solutions and ideas. This can only be done with scientists and inventors who left detailed notes. A few of the more well-studied cases involve Michael Faraday's discovery of electromagnetism (Tweney, 1991, 2013), Bell's discovery of the telephone (Gorman, 1992), and Edison's development of the carbon transmitter (Gorman, 1992). The cognitive-historical approach can be used to supplement and extend the experimental or psychometric approaches. Tweney (2013), for instance, began his historical analysis of Faraday as an attempt to confirm (or disconfirm) theories of cognitive psychology of science reported in experimental studies. By doing so with Faraday, Tweney uncovered his well-known "confirm early, disconfirm late" principle (Tweney & Hoffner, 1987).

The Historiometric Approach

Historiometric studies of creativity and genius gather quantitative data from the historical record and analyze patterns, correlations, and trends. Catherine Cox's (1926) investigations, for instance, into genius were among the first to use the historical record to assess the psychology of creative genius. She collected data from eminent scientists (and others) over the course of centuries and estimated their IQ, among other things. Scholars during the 1950s and 1960s continued to make use of historical records of scientists' lives and examined various psychological forces – such as personality and motivation – in their creative accomplishments (Cattell, 1963, Roe, 1952).

The person, however, almost single-handedly responsible for the historiometric study of creative and eminent achievement is Dean Keith Simonton. One key question Simonton (1979, 1986, 1988b) has addressed historiometrically is that of "multiple discoveries," namely the extent to which particular discoveries were inevitable or not. Sociologists often cite historical instances of multiple discoveries – e.g., calculus, natural selection, telephone – as evidence of the superiority of cultural, sociological, and *zeitgeist* influences over individual cognitive and personality traits. Simonton, however, presents historiometric evidence that cognitive processes of blind variation and selective retention (BVSR) explain more of the variance in multiples than *zeitgeist* explanations. BVSR stipulates that idea generation is a blind process, whereas the selection of ideas is a guided or sighted process. Moreover, Simonton argues that environmental *zeitgeist* conditions only make the discovery potential, but specific cognitive, combinatorial qualities of the individual make the discovery actual (Simonton, 2010).

More generally, Simonton demonstrates the importance of the BVSR process in historically creative scientific discoveries as a whole and not just in terms of multiples (1988b, 2010, 2012) For example, Simonton (2012) recently used the case of Galileo's discoveries to test his theory of blind-variation and selective retention. Specifically, he argues that foresight, insight, oversight, and hindsight all played important roles in Galileo's astronomical sightings and discoveries. In addition, Simonton proposes that current evaluations of Galileo's discoveries and contributions are shadowed by our own current conceptions and we tend to apply hindsight bias to Galileo's "hits" and successes but oversight in ignoring his "misses" or failures. Such a tendency tends to downplay the blinded elements in the creative process.

One standard technique for historiometrically operationalizing eminence is the count entries in major references books in that field. The idea is simple: the most eminent/creative people will receive the most discussion. For example, Murray (2003) did this for more than 4,000 important artists and scientists throughout history (from 800 BC to AD 1950) – not just in the West but also in the Middle East and Asia.

Another major contribution to historiometric studies of scientific achievement comes from Frank Sulloway's *Born to Rebel* (1995). The crux of the book is a thorough investigation into the effect that birth-order plays in whether or not scientists accept or reject revolutionary new theories in science. Sulloway's signature finding was that first-born scientists were much more likely to fall on the conservative side of scientific revolutions, whereas latter-born scientists were much more likely to accept new, revolutionary ideas. This finding generalized to political revolutions as well. He explains this as a learned trait of latter-borns to challenge and question the established order of things, given they are smaller and less powerful than their siblings for the first parts of their lives.

Biometric Studies

There are relatively few biometric studies with physical scientists per se, but there are some with non-scientists while performing tasks of physical causality or understanding of the physical world (e.g., Green, Kraemer, Fugelsang, Gray, & Dunbar, 2010; Roser, Fugelsang, Dunbar, Corballis, & Gazzaniga, 2005; Vartanian, Bristol, & Kaufman, 2013). For instance, in split-brain (severed corpus callosum) patients, different aspects of perceptual physical causality appear to require both right and left hemisphere functioning. In general, the right hemisphere was better at understanding perceptual causality, whereas the left hemisphere excelled at simple causal inference. Moreover, the medial frontal cortex is most active when people are instructed to physical causality between two events (balls colliding) (Fonlupt, 2003). Other indirect brain research on physical science capacities come from the neuroscience of mathematical and quantitative reasoning (Rivera, Reiss, Eckert, & Menon, 2005). Transcranial direct current stimulation (TDCS) to the parietal lobe during numerical learning facilitated acquisition of number processing (Kadosh, Soski, Iuculano, Kanai, & Walsh, 2010). Similarly, the left frontopolar cortex is most active during semantic analogical reasoning, an essential task in scientific reasoning (e.g., A is B and C is to D; Bunge, Wendelken, Badre, & Wagner, 2005; Green et al., 2010). Finally, Simonton (2008) has recently presented a genetic analysis of the personality and intellectual foundations of scientific talent and reported small but robust genetic effects.

Conclusions and Future Research

In this review of the literature, we see that talent and creativity in the physical sciences develops uniquely in some people and not others. The disposition to be interested in and have a talent for understanding the physical and inanimate world is shaped by developmental, personality, cognitive, and social factors, just to focus on the most obvious and most widely studied. In that sense we all have some implicit capacity for physical knowledge. Only some of us, however, take these implicit capacities and develop a real talent for formal and explicit skill in understanding the physical world. Like interest and talent in the other domains (psychology, biology, math, linguistics, art, and music), physical science talent stems from and is built upon the implicit, evolved constraints, capacities, and first principles. These constraints and implicit first principles sometimes facilitate the development of explicit formal physical knowledge and sometimes hinder such knowledge.

The most compelling needs for the future of this field would be more biometric investigations into scientific thought and behavior. Brain development in high-functioning autism is one possibility. People with high functioning autism may exist in a sweetspot for being prone to recognizing patterns and mathematical-technical thinking, but also having enough verbal and social skills to interact with others. Scientists are just now uncovering some of the brain processes behind autism. For example, there is fascinating and suggestive evidence from neuroscience that people with autism have dysfunctional synaptic pruning during development and this results in hyper-connectivity of neural networks (Koyama & Ikegaya, 2015; Tang et al., 2014). This neural hyper-connectivity is consistent with the uncanny ability and disability seen in savants, such as calculation and pattern recognition at the expense of verbal and social skills. Although speculative, this line of research into the neural and brain development processes might suggest that people with less extreme "thing-oriented" numeric and spatial abilities may also have some kind of unusual neuro-developmental history. Additionally, research into epigenetic influences on intellectual and mathematical ability is in its infancy and has the potential for unlocking many questions of the mechanisms beyond talent and achievement in science.

Whether gender differences are the product of nature, nurture, or some interaction between the two has been an ongoing debate in social science and as this difference affects interest in and talent for science it still has a long way to go before we grasp its underlying causes. What is clear, however, is that men still are opting for careers in the physical sciences at higher rates than women and so the questions are: Is this difference lessening over time?; why does it exist to begin with?; and is there anything we can do to ameliorate this gender gap?

A relatively untapped line of research for the personality psychology of science is to explore differences in personality between physical, biological, and social scientists. My hunch is that the physical scientists as a group will be more introverted and thing-oriented (i.e., have more developed implicit physical domain knowledge) than the social scientists. Another fascinating and difficult to answer question about personality and science is the extent to which personality traits are causes or effects of scientific interest and ability.

In the end, scientific interest and talent in general is a function of many psychological processes (development, cognition, personality, and social influences, to name just the most obvious), and the explication and analysis of these processes is a central task for the psychology of science. Physical knowledge and physical science is a perfect place for the psychology of science to focus its attention. Understanding the physical and inanimate world is indeed part of what humans do intuitively and implicitly and sometimes explicitly, and understanding those who understand the physical world is part of what psychologists of science do. Indeed, it takes much creativity to solve the mysteries of the physical world – just as it takes much creativity to understand those who solve the mysteries of the physical world.

References

Amabile, T. (1996). *Creativity in context*. Boulder, CO: Westview.
Baron-Cohen, S., Wheelwright, S., Stott, C., Bolton, P., & Goodyer, I. (1997). Is there a link between engineering and autism? *Autism, 1*, 101–109.

Baron-Cohen, S., Bolton, P., Wheelwright, S., Short, L., Mead, G., Smith, A., & Scahill, V. (1998). Autism occurs more often in families of physicists, engineers, and mathematicians, *Autism*, *2*, 296–301.

Baron-Cohen, S., Wheelwright, S., Skinner, R., Martin, J., & Clubley, E. (2001). The Autism-Spectrum Quotient (AQ): Evidence from Asperger Syndrome/ High-Functioning Autism, males and females, scientists and mathematicians, *Journal of Autism & Developmental Disorders*, *31*, 5–17.

Bayer, A. E., & Dutton, J. E. (1977). Career age and research–professional activities of academic scientists: Tests of alternative non-linear models and some implications for higher education faculty policies. *Journal of Higher Education*, *48*, 259–282.

Benbow, C. P., & Stanley, J. C. (1983). Sex differences in mathematical reasoning ability: More facts. *Science*, *222*, 1029−1031.

Berger, J. (1994). *The young scientists: America's future and the winning of the Westinghouse.* Reading, MA: Addison-Wesley.

Billington, J., Baron-Cohen, S., & Wheelwright, S. (2007). Cognitive style predicts entry into physical sciences and humanities: Questionnaire and performance tests of empathy and systemizing. *Learning and Individual Differences*, *17*, 260–268.

Brink, T. L. (1980). Idiot savant with unusual mechanical ability: An organic explanation. *The American Journal of Psychiatry*, *137*(2), 250–251.

Brody, L. E., & Mills, C. J. (2005). Talent search research: What have we learned? *High Ability Studies*, *16*, 97–111.

Bunge, S. A., Wendelken, C., Badre, D., & Wagner, A. D. (2005). Analogical reasoning and prefrontal cortex: Evidence for separable retrieval and integration mechanisms. *Cerebral Cortex*, *15*, 239–249.

Byrne, R. W. (2001). Social and technical forms of primate intelligence. In F. B. M. deWaal (Ed.), *Tree of origin: What primate behavior can tell us about human social evolution* (pp. 145–172). Cambridge: Harvard University Press.

Cacioppo, J. T., Petty, R. E., & Kao, C. F. (1984). The efficient assessment of need for cognition. *Journal of Personality Assessment*, *48*, 306–307.

Carey, S., & Spelke, E. (1994). Domain specific knowledge and conceptual change. In L. A Hirschfeld and S. A. Gelman (Eds.). *Mapping the mind: Domain specificity in cognition and culture*, (pp. 169–200). Cambridge, England: Cambridge University Press.

Carruthers, P., Stich, S., & Siegal, M. (Eds.). (2002). *The cognitive basis of science.* Cambridge, England: Cambridge University Press.

Cattell, R. B. (1963). The personality and motivation of the researcher from measurements of contemporaries and from biography. In C. W. Taylor & F. X. Barron (Eds.). *Scientific creativity* (pp. 119–131). New York: Wiley.

Ceci, S. J., & Williams, W. (Eds.). (2007). *Why aren't more women in science? Top researchers debate the evidence.* Washington, DC: American Psychological Association Books.

Ceci, S. J., & Williams, W. (2010). *The mathematics of sex: How biology and society conspire to limit talented women and girls.* Oxford, England: Oxford University Press.

Christensen, B. T., & Schunn, C. D. (2007). The relationship of analogical distance to analogical function and preinventive structure: The case of engineering design. *Memory & Cognition*, *35*(1), 29–38. DOI:10.3758/BF03195939

Chung, K. H., & Cox, R. A. K. (1990). Patterns of productivity in the finance literature: A study of the bibliometric distributions. *Journal of Finance*, *45*, 301–309. DOI:10.1111/j.1540–6261.1990.tb05095.x

Clement, J. (1991). Experts and science students: The use of analogies, extreme cases, and physical intuition. In J. E Voss, D. N. Perkins, & J. W. Segal (Eds.), *Informal reasoning and education* (pp. 345–362). Hillsdale, NJ: Erlbaum.

Cohen, A. R., Stotland, E., & Wolfe, D. M. (1955). An experimental investigation of need for cognition. *Journal of Abnormal and Social Psychology, 51,* 291–294.

Cole, J. R., & Cole, S. (1973). *Social stratification in science.* Chicago: University of Chicago Press.

Cole, J. R., & Zuckerman, H. (1987). Marriage, motherhood, and research performance in science. *Scientific American, 256,* 119–125.

Cole, S. (1979). Age and scientific performance. *American Journal of Sociology, 84,* 958–977.

Cox, C. (1926). *Genetic studies of genius: Volume II – The early mental traits of 300 geniuses.* Stanford, CA: Stanford University Press.

Csikszentihalyi, M., Rathunde, K., & Whalen, S. (1997). *Talented teenagers: The roots of success and failure.* New York: Cambridge University Press.

Davidson, K. (1999). *Carl Sagan: A life.* New York: Wiley & Sons.

Deary, I. J., Strand, S., Smith, P., & Fernandes, C. (2007). Intelligence and educational achievement. *Intelligence, 35,* 13–21.

Deary, I. J., Thorpe, G., Wilson, V., Starr, J.M., & Whalley, L. J. (2003). Population sex differences in IQ at age 11: The Scottish mental survey 1932. *Intelligence, 31,* 533–542. DOI: 10.1016/S0160-2896(03)00053–9.

Dennis, W. (1956). Age and productivity among scientists. *Science, 123,* 724–725.

Dennis, W. (1966). Creative productivity between the ages of 20 and 80 years. *Journal of Gerontology, 21,* 1–8.

Diamond, A. M. (1986). The life-cycle research productivity of mathematicians and scientist. *Journal of Gerontology, 41,* 520–525.

Dunbar, K. (1995). How scientists really reason: Scientific reasoning in real-world laboratories. In R. J. Sternberg & J. E. Davidson (Eds.), *The nature of insight* (pp. 365–395). Cambridge, MA: MIT Press.

Dunbar, K., & Blanchette, I. (2001). The in vivo/in vitro approach to cognition: The case of analogy. *TRENDS in Cognitive Science, 5,* 334–339.

Edge, The Third Culture (2005) The science of gender and science: Pinker vs. Spelke, a debate, May 16. Retrieved on September 24, 2015, from http://edge.org/3rd_cul ture/debate05/debate05_index.html.

Einhorn, H. J., & Hogarth, R. M. (1978). Confidence in judgment: Persistence of the illusion of validity. *Psychological Review, 85,* 395–416.

Eysenck, H. J. (1993). Word association, origence and psychoticism. *Creativity Research Journal, 7,* 209–216.

Eysenck, H. J. (1995). *Genius: The natural history of creativity.* Cambridge, UK: Cambridge University Press.

Falk-Krzesinski, H. J., Börner, K., Contractor, N., Fiore, S. M., Hall, K. L., Keyton, J., & Uzzi, B. (2010). Advancing the science of team science. *Clinical and Translational Science, 3,* 263–266.

Feist, G. J. (1993). A structural model of scientific eminence. *Psychological Science, 4,* 366–371.

Feist, G. J. (1997). Quantity, quality, and depth of research as influences on scientific eminence: Is quantity most important? *Creativity Research Journal, 10,* 325–335. DOI:10.1207/s15326934crj1004_4

Feist, G. J. (1998). A meta-analysis of the impact of personality on scientific and artistic creativity. *Personality and Social Psychological Review, 2*, 290–309.

Feist, G. J. (2001). Three perspectives on evolution, creativity, and aesthetics. *Bulletin of Psychology and the Arts, 2*, 3.

Feist, G. J. (2006a). How development and personality influence scientific thought, interest, and achievement. *Review of General Psychology, 10*, 163–182.

Feist, G. J. (2006b). The development of scientific talent in Westinghouse finalists and members of the National Academy of Sciences. *Journal of Adult Development, 13*, 23–35. DOI: 10.1007/s10804-006–9002-3.

Feist, G. J. (2006c). *The psychology of science and the origins of the scientific mind.* New Haven, CT: Yale University Press.

Feist, G. J. (2011). Psychology of science as a new subdiscipline in psychology. *Current Directions in Psychological Science, 20*, 330–334. DOI: 10.1177/0963721411418471

Feist, G. J. (2012). Predicting interest in and attitudes toward science from personality and need for cognition. *Personality and Individual Differences, 52*, 771–775. DOI:10.1016/j.paid.2012.01.005

Fonlupt, P. (2003). Perception and judgment of physical causality involve different brain structures. *Cognitive Brain Research, 17*, 248–254.

Francis, B., Skelton, C., & Read, B. (2012). *The identities and practices of high achieving pupils: Negotiating achievement and peer cultures.* London: Continuum International Publishing Group.

Gallagher, A. M., & DeLisi, R. (1994). Gender differences in Scholastic Aptitude Test – Mathematics problem solving among high ability students. *Journal of Educational Psychology, 86*, 204–211.

Gallagher, A. M., & Kaufman, J. C. (Eds.). (2005). *Gender differences in mathematics: An integrative psychological approach.* New York: Cambridge University Press.

Gardner, H. (1983). *Frames of mind: The theory of multiple intelligences.* New York: Basic Books.

Gardner, H. (1999). *Intelligence reframed: Multiple intelligences for the 21st century.* New York: Basic Books.

Geary, D. C., & Huffman, K. J. (2002). Brain and cognitive evolution: Forms of modularity and functions of mind. *Psychological Bulletin, 128*, 667–698.

Gentner, D., & Jeriorski, M. (1989). Historical shifts in the use of analogy in science. In B. Gholson, W. R. Shadish, R. A. Neimeyer, & A. C. Houts (Eds.), *Psychology of science: Contributions to metascience* (pp. 296–325). Cambridge, England: Cambridge University Press.

Gibson, J., & Light, P. (1967). Intelligence among university scientists. *Nature, 213*(5075), 441–443. DOI:10.1038/213441a0

Gick, M. L., & Holyoak, K. J. (1983). Schema induction and analogical transfer. *Cognitive Psychology, 15*, 1–38.

Gleick, J. (1992). *Genius: The life and science of Richard Feynman.* New York: Pantheon.

Gleick, J. (2003). *Isaac Newton.* New York: Pantheon.

Goodchild, P. (1980). *J. Robert Oppenheimer: Shatterer of worlds.* Boston: Houghton Mifflin.

Gopnik, A., Meltzoff, A. N., & Kuhl, P. K. (1999). *The scientist in the crib: Minds, brains, and how children learn.* New York: William Morrow and Co.

Gorman, M. E. (1992). *Simulating science: Heuristics, mental models, and technoscientific thinking.* Bloomington, IN: Indiana University Press.

Gorman, M. E. (2013). The psychology of technological invention. In G. J. Feist & M. E. Gorman (Eds.), *Handbook of the psychology of science* (pp. 383–396). New York, NY: Springer Publishing Co.

Gough, H. G. (1987). *California Psychological Inventory: Administrators guide.* Palo Alto, CA: Consulting Psychologists Press.

Green, A. E., Kraemer, D. J. M., Fugelsang, J. A., Gray, J. R., & Dunbar, K. N. (2010). Connecting long distance: Semantic distance in analogical reasoning modulates frontopolar cortex activity. *Cerebral Cortex, 20*, 70–76. DOI: 10.1093/cercor/bhp081.

Gorman, M. E., Stafford, A., & Gorman, M. E. (1987). Disconfirmation and dual hypotheses on a more difficult version of Wason's 2–4–6 task. *The Quarterly Journal of Experimental Psychology, Section A, 39*, 1–28.

Grosul, M., & Feist, G. J. (2014). The creative person in science. *Psychology of Aesthetics, Creativity, and the Arts*, 30–43. DOI:10.1037/a0034828.

Guilford, J. P. (1950). Creativity. *American Psychologist, 5*, 444–454.

Gupta, D. K. (1987). Lotka's law and productivity patterns of entomological research in Nigeria for the period, 1900–1973. *Scientometrics, 12*, 33–46. DOI:10.1007/BF02016688

Harmon, L. R. (1961). The High School background of science doctorates: A survey reveals the influence of class size, region of origin, as well as ability, in PhD production. *Science, 133*, 679–688.

Hecht, D. K. (2015). *Storytelling and science: Rewriting Oppenheimer in the Nuclear Age.* Amherst, MA: University of Massachusetts Press.

Hedges, L. V., & Nowell, A. (1995). Sex differences in mental test scores, variability, and numbers of high-scoring individuals. *Science, 269*, 41–45.

Helson, R., & Crutchfield, R. S. (1970). Mathematicians: The creative researcher and the average PhD. *Journal of Consulting and Clinical Psychology, 34*, 250–257.

Hemlin, S., & Olsson, L. (2013). The psychology of research groups: Creativity and performance. In G. J. Feist & M. E. Gorman (Eds.), *Handbook of the psychology of science* (pp. 397–418). New York: Springer Publishing.

Herrnstein, R. J., & Murray, C. (1994). *The bell-curve: Intelligence and class structure in American life.* New York: Free Press.

Hirsch, J. E. (2005). An index to quantify an individual's scientific research output. *PNAS: Proceedings of the National Academy of Science, 102*, 16569–16572. DOI:10.1073/pnas.0507655102

Horner, K. L., Rushton, J. P., & Vernon, P. A. (1986). Relation between aging and research productivity of academic psychologists. *Psychology and Aging, 4*, 319–324.

Huang, S. H., & Yang, JM. (2012). A study on the productivity review for management of performance using bibliometric methodology. *Eleventh Wuhan International Conference on e-Business*. Paper 4. Abstract retrieved on October 20, 2015, from http://aisel.aisnet.org/whiceb2011/4

Isaacson, W. (2008). *Einstein: His life and universe.* New York: Simon & Shuster.

Isaacson, W. (2014). *Einstein: The life of a genius.* London: Carlton Publishing.

Jones, R. A. (1997). The Boffin: A stereotype of scientists in post-war British films (1945–1970). *Public Understanding of Science, 6*, 31–48.

Kadosh, R. C., Soski, S., Iuculano, T., Kanai, R., & Walsh, V. (2010). Modulating neuronal activity produces specific and long-lasting changes in numerical competence. *Current Biology, 20*, 2016–2020. Doi: 10.1016/j.cub.2010.10.007

Karmiloff-Smith, A. (1992). *Beyond modularity: A developmental perspective on cognitive science*. Cambridge: MIT Press.

Kaufman, J. C., & Baer, J. (2004). Hawking's haiku, Madonna's math: Why it is hard to be creative in every room of the house. In R. J. Sternberg, E. L. Grigorenko, & J. L. Singer (Eds.), *Creativity: From potential to realization*. Washington, DC: APA Books.

Klahr, D. (2000). *Exploring science: The cognition and development of discovery processes*. Cambridge: MIT Press.

Klahr, D., & Simon, H. (1999). Studies of scientific discovery: Complementary approaches and convergent findings. *Psychological Bulletin, 125*, 524–543.

Kokosh, J. (1969). MMPI personality characteristics of physical and social science students. *Psychological Reports, 24*, 883–893.

Koyama, R., & Ikegaya, Y. (2015). Microglia in the pathogenesis of autism spectrum disorders. *Neuroscience Research*. Retrieved on October 23, 2015, from http://dx .doi.org/10.1016/j.neures.2015.06.005

Kumar, N. (Ed.). (2012). *Gender and science: Studies across cultures*. Delhi, India: Foundation Books.

Larkin, J., McDermott, J., Simon, D. P., & Simon, H. A. (1980). Expert and novice performance in solving physics problems. *Science, 208*(4450), 1335–1342. DOI:10.1126/ science.208.4450.1335z

Lawson, J., Baron-Cohen, S., & Wheelwright, S. (2004). Empathizing and systemizing in adults with and without Asperger Syndrome. *Journal of Autism and Developmental Disorders, 34*, 301–310.

Le, H., Robbins, S. B., & Westrick, P. (2014). Predicting student enrollment and persistence in college STEM fields using an expanded PE fit framework: A large-scale multilevel study. *Journal of Applied Psychology, 99*(5), 915–947.

Lehman, H. C. (1953). *Age and achievement*. Princeton, NJ: Princeton University Press.

Lehman, H. C. (1960). The age decrement in outstanding scientific creativity. *American Psychologist, 15*, 128–134.

Lehman, H. C. (1966). The psychologist's most creative years. *American Psychologist, 21*, 363–369.

Levin, S. G., & Stephan, P. E. (1991). Research productivity over the life cycle: Evidence for academic scientists. *The American Economic Review, 81*, 114–132.

Lippa, R. (1998). Gender-related individual differences and the structure of vocational interests: The importance of the people-things dimension. *Journal of Personality and Social Psychology, 74*, 996–1009.

Lotka, A. J. (1926). The frequency distribution of scientific productivity. *Journal of the Washington Academy of Sciences, 16*(12), 317–324.

Lounsbury, J. W., Foster, N., Patel, H., Carmody, P., Gibson, L. W., & Stairs, D. R. (2012). An investigation of the personality traits of scientists versus nonscientists and their relationship with career satisfaction. *R&D Management, 42*(1), 47–59.

MacKinnon, D. W. (1970). Creativity: A multi-faceted phenomenon. In J. Roslansky (Ed.), *Creativity* (pp. 19–32). Amsterdam: North-Holland Publishing.

Mahoney, M. J., & Kimper, T. P. (1976). From ethics to logic: A survey of scientists. In M. J. Mahoney (Ed.), *Science as subject: The psychological imperative* (pp. 187–193). Cambridge, MA: Ballinger.

Mayo, R., Alfasi, D., & Schwarz, N. (2014). Distrust and the positive test heuristic: Dispositional and situated social distrust improves performance on the Wason

Rule Discovery Task. *Journal of Experimental Psychology: General, 143*(3), 985–990. DOI:10.1037/a0035127

Merton, R. K. (1973). *The sociology of science: Theoretical and empirical investigations.* Chicago: Chicago University Press.

Miller, A. I. (1996). *Insights of genius: Imagery and creativity in science and art.* New York: Springer Verlag.

Mithen, S. (1996). *The prehistory of the mind: The cognitive origins of art and science.* London: Thames and Hudson.

Mount, M. K., Barrick, M. R., Scullen, S. M., & Rounds, J. (2005). Higher-order dimensions of the big five personality traits and the big six vocational interest types. *Personnel Psychology, 58,* 447–478.

Murray, C. (2003). *Human accomplishment: The pursuit of excellence in the arts and sciences, 800 B. C. to 1950.* New York: HarperCollins.

National Research Council (2015). *Enhancing the effectiveness of team science.* Committee on the Science of Team Science. N. J. Cooke & M. L. Hilton (Eds.). Washington, DC: The National Academies Press.

National Science Foundation, National Center for Science and Engineering Statistics. (2015). *Women, Minorities, and Persons with Disabilities in Science and Engineering: 2015.* Special Report NSF 15–311. Arlington, VA. Retrieved on September 25, 2015 at www.nsf.gov/statistics/wmpd/.

Neffe, J., & Frische, S. (2007). *Einstein: A biography.* New York: Macmillan.

Nersessian, N. J. (1984). *Faraday to Einstein: Constructing meaning in scientific theories.* Dordrecht, Holland: Nijhoff.

Nersessian, N. J. (1986). How do scientists think? Capturing the dynamics of conceptual change in science. In R. N. Giere (Ed.), *Cognitive models of science* (pp. 3–44). Minneapolis, MN: University of Minnesota Press.

Nersessian, N. J. (2008). *Creating scientific concepts.* Cambridge, MA: MIT Press.

Nersessian, N. J. (2009). How do engineering scientists think? Model-based simulation in biomedical engineering research laboratories. *Topics in Cognitive Science, 1*(4), 730–757. doi:10.1111/j.1756–8765.2009.01032.x

Nettle, D. (2006). Schizotypy and mental health amongst poets, visual artists, and mathematicians. *Journal of Research in Personality, 40,* 876–890.

Novick, L. R. (1988). Analogical transfer, problem similarity, and expertise. *Journal of Experimental Psychology: Learning, Memory & Cognition, 14,* 510–520.

Over, R. (1982). Is age a good predictor of research productivity? *Australian Psychologist, 17,* 129–139.

Over, R. (1989). Age and scholarly impact. *Psychology and Aging, 4,* 222–225.

Paletz, S. B. F., & Schunn, C. D. (2010). A social-cognitive framework of multidisciplinary team innovation. *Topics in Cognitive Science, 2,* 73–95. DOI: 10.1111/j.1756–8765.2009.01029.x

Parker, S. T., and McKinney, M. L. (1999). *Origins of intelligence.* Baltimore, MD: Johns Hopkins University Press.

Pinker, S. (2002). *The blank slate: The modern denial of human nature.* New York: Viking.

Plucker, J. A., & Renzulli, J. S. (1999). Psychometric approaches to the study of human creativity. In R.J. Sternberg (Ed.), *Handbook of creativity* (pp. 35–61). Cambridge, England: Cambridge University Press.

Portes, A., & Rumbaut, R. G. (2001). *Legacies: The story of the immigrant second generation.* Berkeley, CA: University of California Press.

Proctor, E. J., & Capaldi, R. W. (Eds.), (2012). *Psychology of science: Implicit and explicit processes*. New York: Oxford University Press.

Prediger, D. J. (1982). Dimensions underlying Holland's hexagon: Missing link between interests and occupations? *Journal of Vocational Behavior, 21*, 259–287.

Price, D. (1963). *Little science, big science*. New York, NY: Columbia University Press

Rasoal, C., Danielsson, H., & Jungert, T. (2012). Empathy among students in engineering programmes. *European Journal of Engineering Education, 37*(5), 427–435.

Rawlings, D., & Locarnini, A. (2008). Dimensional schizotypy, autism, and unusual word associations in artists and scientists. *Journal of Research in Personality, 42*, 465–471.

Rivera, S. M., Reiss, A. L., Eckert, M. A., & Menon, V. (2005). Developmental changes in mental arithmetic: Evidence for increased functional specialization in the left inferior parietal cortex. *Cerebral Cortex, 15*, 1779–1790. DOI: 10.1093/cercor/bhi055

Robertson, K. F., Smeets, S., Lubinski, D., & Benbow, C. P. (2010). Beyond the threshold hypothesis: Even among the gifted and top math/science graduate students, cognitive abilities, vocational interests and lifestyle preferences matter for career choice, performance and persistence. *Current Directions in Psychological Science, 19*, 346–351. DOI: 10.1177/0963721410391442.

Robinson, J. E. (2008). *Look me in the eye: My life with Asperger's*. New York: Three Rivers Press.

Roe, A. (1952). *The making of a scientist*. Westport, CT: Greenwood Press.

Roe. A. (1953). A psychological study of eminent psychologists and anthropologists, and a comparison with biological and physical scientists. *Psychological Monographs: General and Applied, 67*, 1–55.

Roe, A. (1965). Changes in scientific activities with age. *Science, 150*, 313–318.

Roser, M. E., Fugelsang, J. A., Dunbar, K. N., Corballis, P. M., & Gazzaniga, M. S. (2005). Dissociating processes supporting causal perception and causal inference in the brain. *Neuropsychology, 19*, 591–602. DOI: 10.1037/0894–4105.19.5.591.

Rubinstein, G. (2005). The big five among male and female students of different faculties. *Personality and Individual Differences, 38*(7), 1495–1503.

Runco, M. (2004). Everyone has creative potential. In R. J. Sternberg, E. L. Grigorenko, & J. L. Singer (Eds.), *Creativity: From potential to realization* (pp. 21–30). Washington, DC: APA Books.

Runyan, W. M. (2006). Psychobiography and the psychology of science: Understanding the relations between the live and work of individual psychologists. *Review of General Psychology, 10*, 147–162.

Runyan, W. M. (2013). Psychobiography and the psychology of science: Encounters with psychology, philosophy, and statistics. In G. J. Feist & M. E. Gorman, (Eds.), *Handbook of the psychology of science* (pp. 353–379). New York, NY: Springer Publishing Co.

Science of Science and Innovation Policy. (n.d.). Retrieved on September 25, 2015 from www .nsf.gov/funding/pgm_summ.jsp?pims_id=501084.

Schuldberg, D. (2000). Six subclinical spectrum traits in normal creativity. *Creativity Research Journal, 13*(1), 5–16.

Schulze, A. D., & Seuffert, V. (2013). Conflicts, cooperation, and competition in the field of science and technology. In G. J. Feist & M. E. Gorman (Eds.), *Handbook of the psychology of science* (pp. 303–330). New York, NY: Springer Publishing Co.

Schunn, C. D., & Trafton, J. G. (2013). The psychology of uncertainty in scientific data analysis. In G. J. Feist & M. E. Gorman, (Eds.), *Handbook of the psychology of science* (pp. 461–483). New York, NY: Springer Publishing Co.

Simonton, D. K. (1979). Multiple discovery and invention: Zeitgeist, genius, or chance? *Journal of Personality and Social Psychology, 37*, 1603–1616.

Simonton, D. K. (1986). Multiple discovery: Some Monte Carlo simulations and Gedanken experiments. *Scientometrics, 9*, 269–280.

Simonton, D. K. (1988a). Age and outstanding achievement: What do we know after a century of research? *Psychological Bulletin, 104*, 251–267.

Simonton, D. K. (1988b). *Scientific genius: A psychology of science*. Cambridge, England: Cambridge University Press.

Simonton, D. K. (1991). Career landmarks in science: Individual differences and interdisciplinary contrasts. *Developmental Psychology, 27*, 119–130.

Simonton, D. K. (1999). Significant samples: The psychological study of eminent individuals. *Psychological Methods, 4*, 425–451.

Simonton, D. K. (2000). Methodological and theoretical orientation and the long-term disciplinary impact of 54 eminent psychologists. *Review of General Psychology, 4*(1), 13–24.

Simonton, D. K. (2008). Scientific talent, training, and performance: Intellect, personality, and genetic endowment. *Review of General Psychology, 12*, 28–46. DOI: 10.1037/1089–2680.12.1.28.

Simonton, D. K. (2009). Varieties of (scientific) creativity: A hierarchical model of domain-specific disposition, development, and achievement. *Perspectives on Psychological Science, 4*, 441–452.

Simonton, D. K. (2010). Creative thought as blind-variation and selective-retention: Combinatorial models of exceptional creativity. *Physics of Life Reviews, 7*, 156–179. DOI: 10.1016/j.plrev.2010.02.002

Simonton, D. K. (2012). Foresight, insight, oversight, and hindsight in scientific discovery: How sighted were Galileo's telescopic sightings? *Psychology of Aesthetics, Creativity, and the Arts, 6*(3), 243–254. http://dx.doi.org/10.1037/a0027058.

Simonton, D. K. (2013). Creative thoughts as acts of free will: A two-stage formal integration. *Review of General Psychology, 17*(4), 374.

Soler, J. M. (2007). A rational indicator of scientific creativity. *Journal of Infometrics, 1*, 123–130. doi:10.1016/j.joi.2006.10.004

Spelke, E. S. (2005). Sex differences in intrinsic aptitude for mathematics and science? A critical review. *American Psychologist, 60*, 950–958.

Sternberg, R. J. (1988). A three-facet model of creativity. In R. J. Sternberg (Ed.), *The nature of creativity* (pp. 125–147). Cambridge, England: Cambridge University Press.

Strand, S., Deary, I. J., & Smith, P. (2006). Sex differences in cognitive abilities test scores: A UK national picture. *British Journal of Educational Psychology, 76*, 463–480.

Stroebe, W. (2010). The graying of academia: Will it reduce scientific productivity? *American Psychologist, 65*, 660–673. DOI: 10.1037/a0021086

Subotnik, R. F., & Steiner, C. L. (1994). Adult manifestations of adolescent talent in science: A longitudinal study of 1983 Westinghouse Science Talent Search winners. In R. Subotnik & K. D. Arnold (Eds.), *Beyond Terman: Contemporary longitudinal studies of giftedness and talent. Creativity research* (pp. 52–76). Norwood, NJ: Ablex Publishing Corp.

Subotnik, R. F., Duschl, R. A., & Selmon, E. H. (1993). Retention and attrition of science talent: A longitudinal study of Westinghouse Science Talent Search winners. *International Journal of Science Education, 15*, 61–72.

Sulloway, F. (1995). *Born to Rebel: Birth order, family dynamics and creative lives*. New York: Pantheon Books.

Tang, G., Gudsnuk, K., Kuo, S-H., Cotrina, M. L., Rosoklija, G. Sosunov, A., & Sulzer, D. (2014). Loss of mTOR-dependent macroautophagy causes autistic-like synaptic pruning deficits. *Neuron, 83*, 1131–1143. DOI: 10.1016/j.neuron.2014.07.040.

Terman, L. M. (1954). Scientists and nonscientists in a group of 800 gifted men. *Psychological Monographs: General and Applied, 68*(7), 1–44. DOI:10.1037/h0093672.

Thomson, N. D., Wurtzburg, S. J., & Centifanti, L. C. M. (2015). Empathy or science? Empathy explains physical science enrollment for men and women. *Learning and Individual Differences, 40*, 115–120. http://dx.doi.org/10.1016/j.lindif.2015.04.003

Treffert, D. A. (2006). *Extraordinary people: Understanding savant syndrome (updated version)*. Lincoln, NE: iUniverse.

Tweney, R. D. (1989). A framework for the cognitive psychology of science. In B. Gholson, W. R. Shadish, Jr., R. A. Neimeyer, & A. C. Houts (Eds.), *Psychology of science: Contributions to metascience* (pp. 342–366). Cambridge, MA: Cambridge University Press.

Tweney, R. D. (1991). Faraday's notebooks: The active organization of creative science. *Physics Education, 26*, 301–306.

Tweney, R. D. (1998). Toward a cognitive psychology of science: Recent research and its implications. *Current Directions in Psychological Science, 7*, 150–154.

Tweney, R. D. (2013). Cognitive-historical approaches to the understanding of science. In G. J. Feist & M. E. Gorman (Eds.), *Handbook of the psychology of science* (pp. 71–93). New York, NY: Springer Publishing.

Tweney, R. D. & Hoffner, C. E. (1987). Understanding the microstructure of science: An example. In *Program of the ninth annual conference of the cognitive science society* (pp. 677–681). Hillsdale, NJ: Lawrence Erlbaum.

Tweney, R. D., Doherty, M. E., & Mynatt, C. R. (Eds.), (1981). *On scientific thinking*. New York: Columbia University Press.

Vartanian, O., Bristol, A. S., & Kaufman, J. C. (Eds.), (2013). *Neuroscience of creativity*. Cambridge, MA: MIT Press.

Wai, J., Lubinski, D., & Benbow, C. P. (2005). Creativity and occupational accomplishments among intellectually precocious youths: An age 13 to Age 33 longitudinal study. *Journal of Educational Psychology, 97*, 484–492.

Wai, J., Lubinski, D., & Benbow, C. P. (2009). Spatial ability for STEM domains: Aligning over 50 years of cumulative psychological knowledge solidifies its importance. *Journal of Educational Psychology, 101*, 817–835.

Wai, J., Cacchio, M., Putallaz, M., & Makel, M. C. (2010). Sex differences in the right tail of cognitive abilities: A 30-year examination. *Intelligence, 38*, 412–423. DOI: 10.1016/j.intell.2010.04.006

Wason, P. C. (1966). Reasoning. In B. Foss (Ed.), *New horizons in psychology: I.* (pp. 135–151). Baltimore, MD: Penguin.

Webb, R. M., Lubinski, D., & Benbow, C. P. (2002). Mathematically facile adolescents with math-science aspirations: New perspectives on their educational and vocational development. *Journal of Educational Psychology, 94*, 785–794.

Wilson, G. D., & Jackson, C. (1994). The personality of physicists. *Personality and Individual Differences, 16*, 187–189.

Zuckerman, H. (1996). *Scientific elite* (2nd edn.). New York: Free Press.

13 Biomedicine, Creativity, and the Story of AIDS

Mei Tan

University of Houston

Elena L. Grigorenko

University of Houston

Abstract

Far from being a static entity, creativity may be observed to evolve over time as the contexts that require it shift and change. This principle is illustrated in the thirty-plus years of biomedicine since the advent of AIDS and the discovery of its viral cause, HIV. This constituted a time period of dramatic changes in the field of biomedical research, particularly with respect to the patient–researcher relationship and the ways that characteristics of a patient population must be understood to effectively shape research practices. The essentially social nature of creativity, usually obscured in this domain, is shown to now play a central role in the field of biomedicine.

To consider the nature of creativity in the field of biomedicine, we begin with a story.

In June of 1981, a surveillance report from a health department in California to the US Center for Disease Control (CDC) noted that in the past eight months, five cases of an extremely rare type of pneumonia caused by *Pneumocystis carinii*, a fungus, had been diagnosed in the Los Angeles area. At about the same time, the CDC also received reports that, within a period of thirty months, twenty-six cases of a rare and often fatal form of cancer, Kaposi's sarcoma, had been diagnosed among young homosexual men in both New York and California (Heyward & Curran, 1988). These were the first patients of what would become known as acquired immunodeficiency syndrome, or AIDS. By March of 1983, although much more was known about the disease, the count of diagnosed was 1,112 and the death toll 418 – 195 dead in New York City alone. The cause of the epidemic was still unknown (Kramer, 2003). Adding to the tension, popular news magazines were sensationalizing the situation, with one referring to an unknown "killer" pathogen and an accompanying

The authors would like to acknowledge the generous support of Karen Jensen Neff and Charlie Neff for the writing of this chapter. Although focused on creativity, the content of the chapter was inspired and shaped by work carried out under R01 HD085836 (PI: Grigorenko) from the US National Institutes of Health. Grantees undertaking such projects are encouraged to express freely their professional judgment. The chapter does not necessarily reflect the position or policies of the abovementioned funding agencies, and no official endorsement should be inferred.

"AIDS hysteria" (Isaacson, 1983). Theories about what was causing the disease included unknown viruses, chemicals, and overstimulation from sex (A. Park, 2014).

Later that same year, two labs working in parallel – one in France and the other in the United States – were finally able to identify the causal retrovirus (retroviruses contain RNA rather than DNA as their genetic material), which they called the human immunodeficiency virus, or HIV (Gallo, 2002; Gallo & Montagnier, 2003; Montagnier, 2002). This was a pivotal finding that would lead to a long-awaited blood test for early diagnosis and an HIV-free donor blood supply. Countless lives would be saved.

The story of AIDS could be ended here with a satisfactory sense of resolution. A biomedical mystery of great import had been solved, and many lives would now be saved. With respect to creativity, however, this is only a fragment of the tale. The larger picture of the story surrounding AIDS and now HIV illustrates the changeability of creativity as an essentially social construct – that is, an entity not only generated by people, but generated between people, received by people, and validated by people's valuation of its products. Drastic changes in the world of biomedicine have changed the nature of creativity in that domain. One of the drivers of this change was the emergence of AIDS and HIV, which brought about, vividly and undeniably, the public's entry into the sphere of basic medical science in a way that changed the world of research by demanding more from it, including, ultimately, new forms of creativity. In the pages that follow, we will look at the cognitive and social traits and dispositions that have traditionally been associated with creativity, particularly in the biological sciences. We will then descend more deeply into the scientific, social, and political events of the AIDS story that contributed to the re-shaping of creativity in the field of biomedicine. We will close the chapter with a look at how creativity has been assessed in this field, and where it might blossom in the future.

Traits and Dispositions of Creative Biomedical Scientists

Scientific creativity in itself is not a new subject of study. It has been held up and scrutinized, and its character questioned, since the days of Francis Bacon and René Descartes, who, in the sixteenth century, argued that the cognitive engine of scientific discovery must be logic. Others who followed, though, demurred. Most convincing were the scientists themselves, Nobel Laureates who credited the power of the imagination and intuition for their ability to seize upon new ideas and perspectives (Simonton, 2003). Since the 1950s, psychologists have taken up the issue and debated scientific creativity's essential cognitive texture (associative and divergent versus logical) and its differences from other types of creativity with respect to process, product, and person. It is mostly in the latter inquiry, using biographical studies to identify the traits and dispositions that lead an individual to develop eminent scientific creativity, where the examination of possible domain differences has arisen.

In a meta-analytic review of which personality traits make interest and creativity in science more likely, Feist (1998; 2006; see also this volume) looked at twenty-six studies carried out in 1950–1998 on the quantitative effects of personality in scientists versus non-scientists. Based on these studies, he parsed several factors contributing to interest and achievement in science. Concerning domain interest, for want of any finer metric, he distinguished between a scientific interest in people (social science oriented) and a scientific interest in things (physical science oriented), distinctions he borrowed from the vocational interest literature (Holland, 1992; Prediger, 1982). He also drew upon the work of Baron-Cohen and colleagues on the occurrence of high-functioning autism in engineers, mathematicians, and physical scientists (Baron-Cohen et al., 1998; Baron-Cohen, Wheelwright, Skinner, Martin, & Clubley, 2001). Feist then predicted that physical scientists will be more introverted and have a more developed implicit physical intelligence than those in the biological sciences. The biological scientists, in turn, will be less sociable and extraverted than the social scientists (Feist, 2006). Concerning scientific creativity, Feist considered three categories of traits – cognitive, motivational, and social – but did not attempt a domain-specific analysis. Briefly, consistent across studies, more-creative scientists tend to be more tolerant and flexible in their thinking and behavior than less-creative scientists. These conclusions are based largely upon data collected using the Tolerance and Flexibility scales of the California Psychology Inventory (CPI; Feist & Barron, 2003; Garwood, 1964; Gough, 1961; Helson, 1971; Helson & Crutchfield, 1970; McAllister, 1996). Motivational traits included ambition, achievement-orientation, and competition.

In a study of the personality characteristics of biologists, chemists, and physicists, commitment to work was found to be the highest predictor of productivity in terms of number of publications (Busse & Mansfield, 1984). A similar study of 196 academic psychologists showed that while intrinsic motivators (such as commitment to work) were positively related to both publication and citation numbers, the extrinsic motivator (i.e., competition) was positively related to publications but negatively to citations, suggesting that extrinsic motivation might lead to more quantity, but not necessarily quality (Helmreich, Spence, Beane, Lucker, & Matthews, 1980). Finally, the social traits that seemed to support scientific creativity were related to competitiveness and confidence. This conclusion is based on the self-descriptions of 514 technical and scientific personnel at a research foundation and university, such as "argumentative," "assertive," and "self-confident" (van Zelst & Kerr, 1954). A study of female scientists versus non-scientists differed in dominance as well as self-confidence (Bachtold & Werner, 1972). In a structure equation model, the path between observer-rated hostility and eminence was direct and significant; the path between arrogant working style and eminence was indirect but significant (Feist, 1993). Cognitive and motivational traits likely do cross domains. Social traits, as suggested by the Baron-Cohen studies, might vary across domains depending upon the amount of social interaction required by the field. In sum, according to the results of Feist's meta-analysis, the eminently creative scientific elite tend to be open, tolerant, and flexible (cognitive traits); dominant, arrogant, and hostile (social traits); and intrinsically motivated or driven (motivational traits).

Using a different approach to domain specific creativity in the sciences, Simonton has played with the balance of opposing dispositions in creativity, first ranking the scientific disciplines in the following hierarchy based on a proposal by French philosopher Auguste Comte: physics, chemistry, biology, psychology, and sociology (Comte, 1855). He then explored whether this hierarchy of disciplines had any foundation in psychology by looking at the incidence and severity of psychopathology across creative domains, from scientists to artists (Ludwig, 1992, 1995, 1998). It turned out that scientists appeared to be less prone to mental illness than artists, a finding observed by other researchers as well (Post, 1994; Raskin, 1936). Within the sciences alone, pathological dispositions seemed to follow a similar gradient, with creative psychologists scoring higher than creative chemists on the abstractedness factor of the 16 Personality Factors test (Cattell & Drevdahl, 1955; Cattell, Eber, & Tatsuoka, 1970), indicating higher tendencies for imaginativeness, absentmindedness, impracticality, and absorbedness by the former (Chambers, 1964). A similar study of sixty-four eminent scientists, physicists, and chemists appeared to be more factual, less emotional, and less rebellious than psychologists and anthropologists, according to their performance on the Thematic Apperception Test (TAT; Murray, 1973; Roe, 1953). Simonton then created a corresponding scale of dispositional variables: logical, objective, conventional, formal, intuitive, subjective, individualistic, and emotional. Juxtaposing this scale with his ranking of disciplines, in their respective orders, Simonton posited that the more a scientist accesses a disposition nearer the opposite or "lower" end of the spectrum (i.e., a statistician who tends toward individualism or emotion), the more her creativity will be increased. Simonton referred to this phenomenon as the "domain-regressive creator" (Simonton, 2009). According to this model, encompassing opposite or extreme dispositions may lead to greater creativity in one's field. These trait and dispositional scale assignments presented by Feist and Simonton have been informative and provocative, but are they still wholly relevant?

To answer this question, we consider some of the storylines around the emergence of AIDS and the subsequent struggle to discover and manage its cause, HIV. Specifically highlighted are how activated social contexts and the competitive atmosphere of the research affected both the scientists and their work. This tale, roughly told, is meant to illustrate the evolution of unforeseen trends in the field of biomedical research, involving new roles for both patients and researchers that may define the new traits, dispositions, and skills needed for creativity in the context of contemporary medical research.

Hidden Challenges in the Discovery of HIV

In the laboratory, creativity and innovation still require, as in other fields, the intrinsic motivation fueled by passionate interest and the motivational traits of drive and ambition. When asked what makes a creative scientist, Jack Hirsh, former professor of hematology and thromboembolism and winner of the Canada Gairdner International Award (in 2000, for excellence in biomedical research) was adamant:

Energy for excellent research is driven by curiosity and a real passion to identify the important questions of the field and devise innovative ways to answer them (Collier, 2014). Creative scientists have a *need* to find answers to the questions that interest them (Amabile, 1998). This was no different in the case of Robert Gallo and Luc Montagnier, the two researchers who hotly pursued and later identified, in separate laboratories, the virus that caused AIDS. In a retrospective account, Gallo and Montagnier describe explicitly the excitement of contemplating the very unique challenge presented by AIDS:

> because unlike other viral diseases responsible for past epidemics ... AIDS was characterized by clinical signs that developed years after the infection had occurred, and by then, patients usually had numerous other infections. Thus, an exceptional linkage of agent to disease had to be established. (Gallo & Montagnier, 2003, p. 2284)

Gallo vividly recalls being drawn in when Jim Curran of the CDC, speaking of the players in the search for the cause of AIDS, asked, "Where are the virologists?" (Gallo, 2002). Gallo had heard about AIDS back in 1981, in newspaper reports, but was moved only when he realized his part in this scientific challenge. Like many creative scientists before them, Gallo and Montagnier then defied the current dominant school of thought that held that diseases caused by microbes and viruses no longer posed a threat in industrialized countries, that viruses did not cause any human cancers, and that there were no retroviruses that infected humans (Gallo & Montagnier, 2003). Instead, these two scientists persisted in their investigations of cancer-causing retroviruses. This can be contrasted with the actions of Alexander Fleming, who dismissed the significance of the *Penicillium* mold's effect on staphylococcus because it did not fit into the larger picture that he and many others thought likely, that outside agents such as mold would be toxic to the human system (Goldsworthy & McFarlane, 2002). The subsequent discovery by Gallo and Montagnier of the leukemia-causing retroviruses (HTLV-1 and HTLV-2) provided an analogue or model of what the AIDS-causing virus could be. This hunch eventually led them to the discovery of HIV (Gallo & Montagnier, 2003), the putative cause of AIDS. A general disquiet about the disease, however, persisted. Why?

In part, it was the timing. For almost a century already, the American public had been learning to speak out – from the suffragist movement, to civil rights marches, to the protests of the Vietnam War and the feminist movement. Now, a large, politicized (and terrified) population was affected. AIDS Network members began studying civil disobedience with people who had worked and marched with Dr. Martin Luther King, Jr. Others began to use the press and write, exhorting the gay community to get angry and fight for the medical attention warranted by such an extreme public-health threat (Kramer, 2003). While Howard Florey, the scientist who carried forward Fleming's work on both lysozyme and *Penicillin*, was certainly subjected to the pressure of war to quicken his research (in 1939, more men were being killed by delayed infection than by bullet wounds), he was able to shun the media, which he found contemptible for inaccuracies that created false expectations (Goldsworthy &

McFarlane, 2002). For Gallo and Montagnier there was no such possibility of escape. Gallo especially was unable to ignore a relentless press, the involvements of governments, and the intrusion of activists into his life and work, which he struggled to cope with calmly. This drama, which played out over the years both before and after the discovery of HIV, seemed to reveal two things: the ability of the patient to approach and "get to" researchers; and a seeming Achilles heel of some researchers, previously protected within institution walls, in their inability to cope with the emotional fallout that sometimes surrounds disease. After all, whether proximally (as, for example, medical doctors or epidemiologists) or more distally (as, say, virologists), the research of biomedical scientists takes place within a larger human story that may be fraught with emotions as various as terror and suffering, prejudice and anger, pain and confusion. All of these emerged as powerful entities in the course of the AIDS epidemic (Fan, Conner, & Villarreal, 2007).

A profile published in 1987, just a few years after the discovery of HIV, described the hate mail, protests, and public accusations that Gallo suffered, which ostensibly blamed him for the delay in finding the cause and subsequent cure for AIDS. These came in the form of published attacks from the gay community that he was a thief, a fraud, a homophobe, a schizophrenic (Remnick, 1987), among other accusations. Gallo was ill-equipped to handle the press. Before AIDS, he had simply been a brilliant scientist, secure in the admiration of his peers; after AIDS he was haunted and punished by the public's anxiety and despair. Gallo had "no genius at all for public relations ... He cares deeply about AIDS, but he does little to hide his ambitions, his hurts, his envy, his disdain. He says what he is thinking at the moment" (Remnick, 1987, p. 2). Gallo was and is still more the scientific genius described by Feist – arrogant, ambitious, and sure enough of his scientific acumen to take the imaginative leaps required for breakthrough discoveries – but he was made uneasy by the strength of the emotional wave that had managed to breach the bastions of science around AIDS research. Although the years of 1982 to 1985 were a period of intense and exciting discovery, Gallo looked back and saw a time that was more bitter than sweet.

> these were also years of disquiet and frustration; years in which we would encounter in an unprecedented manner the negative face of politics, the media, patient activists, and legal issues. For myself and others trained in science and disciplined by the rigor and analysis that are the essence of scientific endeavor, the rough and tumble of the outside world provided harsh and bitter lessons. (Gallo, 2002, p. 1730)

What Gallo describes is perhaps the end of an era of science protected from a "rough and tumble," demanding, critical, outside world. In a piece written jointly with Montagnier the following year, the two admitted being humbled by the experience: "Many lessons can be drawn from this early intense period, and most suggest that science requires greater modesty" (Gallo & Montagnier, 2003, p. 2285). Inexplicable to Gallo was that he was somehow perceived as having fallen short and failed the constituency he intended to help. An online opinion piece from 1996 exemplifies the activist public's new (confused and confusing) demands on science:

> Critical work on the science of AIDS must take two forms: one, a critique conducted within the discourse of current biomedical science, aimed at expanding, refining and expediting research programs; the other, less talked about but no less necessary, a critique of the ways by which the science of AIDS is formulated within a broader techno-scientific and social milieu. In this essay, I show how this milieu produced the formulation of HIV as a cause for AIDS, how such a formulation effectively erased other possible ways of formulating the cause(s) of AIDS, and some hitherto neglected reasons for this drive towards a single "cause of AIDS." I hope this paper contributes in some way to the formulation of a science that is more responsive to the needs of people. (Boon, 1996)

How much more responsive, Gallo and Montagnier might have wondered, were they expected to be? Whether taken rhetorically or literally, this commentary expresses new demands on scientists: that they be aware of the people whom their work would ultimately affect; that they recognize the complex social contexts of their work; and that they somehow be more human or more humane.

Beyond the social turmoil going on outside the walls of research, a second issue highlighted by the story of AIDS was the complications caused by the tensions of competition and collaboration that are necessarily a part of solving a highly complex picture of disease. Limited funding and the very public nature of the products of this domain of creativity raise the stakes, making it a highly competitive, and sometimes highly political, environment. Yet, at the same time, the investigation of complex human health conditions usually requires a great deal of collaboration with others in the same or related fields. This balance between competition and collaboration must be struck carefully if creativity in the field is to be preserved. Indeed, some cite a "dark side" of competition (Fang & Casadevall, 2015), suggesting that scientists in competition often duplicate efforts, yet hide information from each other, and may even sabotage each others' work. Others refer to a detrimental "hypercompetitive" environment that threatens to stifle scientific curiosity (Alberts, Kirschner, Tilghman, & Varmus, 2014; McDowell et al., 2014). Recent studies in business (the latest field clamoring for creativity), have explored the positive and negative effects of extrinsic motivation (incentives and challenge) and competition versus collaboration. One found that neither piecemeal nor competitive types of incentive, while leading to greater effort, led to greater creativity compared to baseline levels, even when subjects knew that they were being evaluated for creativity. Further, competitive incentives (rewards for doing better relative to others) reduced creativity (Erat & Gneezy, 2016). These are in line with previous research that extrinsic motivation and competition can be detrimental to creativity (Amabile, 1996). In her admonishment to business organizations on how to kill creativity, Amabile (1998) talks about how managers need to carefully dole out time and resources to control the elements of pressure and collaboration. Time pressure can promote creativity by increasing the intrinsic motivation stimulated by meaningful challenges, but creativity also requires time for people to explore the pieces of the puzzle in front of them and see non-obvious connections. In terms of personnel, says Amabile, teams should be mutually supportive rather than competitive, and include a variety of perspective and backgrounds to enhance collaboration. Cooperative conditions have been found to foster significantly more creativity than conditions of conflict (Bittner & Heidemeier, 2013; Carnevale & Probst, 1998).

Unlike a managed business environment, however, the world of biomedical research is subject to multiple sources of competition and tension, with little oversight or control. Individual researchers know when the work that they are doing may be worthy of world-wide recognition, such as the receipt of the Nobel Prize. That is one level of competition. Yet, the governments funding the research are also hungry for recognition, as well as the patent rights to newly discovered procedures. Several tales, relayed outside of academic papers, reveal the thinly veiled hostility and strong emotions that can underlie professional competition. Recently recovered letters between Francis Crick and Maurice Wilkins reveal the strain of trying to remain collegial while maintaining a competitive stance (Hsu, 2010). At the highest levels of work in any field, it seems, an incredible tension between competition and collaboration must be negotiated.

The details of the working relationship (or rivalry) between the Gallo and Montagnier groups are not well known to the public at large (although bits and pieces have been shared in interviews and professional anecdotes; Bass, 1994; Remnick, 1987; Varmus, 2009), but the very competitive atmosphere in which they carried out their high-stakes research was highlighted by several very public events: the first US press conference announcing Gallo's group's discovery of the virus that caused AIDS, at which Luc Montagnier was not present; the French and US governments' disputes over the patent rights to the blood test, leading to the French government suing the United States in 1985; and the awarding of the Nobel Prize for Physiology or Medicine in 2008 to Luc Montagnier and his French colleague, Francoise Barre-Sinoussi, for their discovery of HIV, with no mention of Robert Gallo at all (A. Park, 2014). These events suggest the great tension between and surrounding both groups. Yet retrospective publications on the work that preceded the discovery of HIV suggest an at least cordial relationship, in which they spoke, mutually built upon each other's discoveries, and exchanged samples (Gallo, 2002; Gallo & Montagnier, 2003; Montagnier, 2002). Publicized events emphasize the story of a negative, contentious relationship, but this perhaps overshadowed the reality of something more like negotiated competition. Such balancing acts and negotiations suggest that scientists, especially those who work in what can be such public domains as medicine, need to exert their social and professional skills creatively to manage their competitive/collaborative relationships for optimal progress. Jack Hirsh termed it "entrepreneurial": the need to simultaneously collaborate, negotiate, and inspire. "No single scientist or institute has all the skills needed to answer big questions" (Collier, 2014, p. 821). In short, the field of biomedicine was transforming, facing many of the challenges of discovery it had always faced, but in an increasingly public and publicized global arena now penetrated by the voices of those most invested in the outcomes of biomedical research – patients.

New Contexts for Creativity

In the ongoing work on HIV and AIDS, the field of biomedicine evolved, encountering new problems necessitating new kinds of creative solutions – medical and non-medical – and new kinds of collaborations. This is because, like no other disease, AIDS has proven to be one of the most socially complex medical conditions. It occurs prominently in marginalized, stigmatized, and therefore highly politicized populations, and its transmission is embedded in sociocultural practices (e.g., needle sharing of drug users, unprotected anal sex) and economic circumstances (e.g., of sex workers and sex trafficking) not well understood by many, often punished, and sometimes willfully ignored. Thus, the effective prevention, treatment, and care of HIV patients has required (and requires still; Villarosa, 2017) a nuanced and multi-faceted approach that includes both social and biomedical understandings of HIV (Kippax, Holt, & Friedman, 2011). When the first HIV vaccine preparatory studies were being devised in cities around the United States in 1993, the teams included experts in the fields of epidemiology, medicine, psychology, sociology, anthropology, public health, and social work (MacQueen, 2011). Their initial concerns were how to successfully recruit and retain large samples of individuals whose social, psychological, and health conditions were often not conducive to the consistent behaviors required by clinical trials. AIDS stigma might deter them from participating. They may not feel comfortable answering honestly questions about sexual and drug-use behavior in the screening process. They may, as a vulnerable population, harbor strong distrust of government-funded research. In a twenty-year retrospective on working with HIV–related clinical trials, MacQueen describes the slow process of integrating social and biomedical research approaches to address some of these difficulties. Over the years, they progressed from a majority of trials showing flat or negative outcomes to some trials finally demonstrating limited effectiveness in some specific populations (MacQueen, 2011). What has been realized over the years is that HIV/AIDS takes place in particular social ecologies, and therefore preventative measures must be contextualized in order to work; approaches to encouraging protected sex in one population may need to be different from those encouraged in a different population, based on the beliefs and usual sexual practices of that population. Several examples from the current literature concerning stigma, adherence, and differences between populations illustrate how the interactions between these factors may vary between cultures in complex ways that require creative or novel approaches for each one.

Internalized stigma occurs when persons living with HIV (PLWH) adopt the stigmatizing beliefs of others, experiencing self-hatred, shame, and inferiority. It has been linked to negative effects on physical and psychosocial aspects of health and well-being. In a cross-country analysis of Demographic and Health Surveys (DHS) data of 4,314 PLWH in Africa, internalized stigma was found to occur in about one-fifth of the survey respondents along gradients of SES. That is, regression models fitted to variables related to SES – educational attainment, professional occupation, and household asset wealth – showed that those individuals of lower

education levels and lower quintiles of wealth (ARR = 0.70, 95% CI: 0.56–0.86***
and 0.84, 95% CI: 0.68–1.03***) were more likely to report internalized stigma than
those of higher education and wealth (ARR = 0.24, 95% CI: 0.12–0.47*** and 0.33,
95% CI: 0.25–0.42***, respectively, *** indicating $P < 0.0001$). These gradients
were consistent in both cross-country and country-specific analyses (Tsai, 2015).
Internalized stigma, in turn, may affect treatment adherence in different ways.

For example, in a multi-state, multi-site study carried out in the United
States on women's adherence to ART, internalized stigma was found to be
a significant predictor of non-optimal ART adherence (AOR = 0.76, $P = 0.042$,
95% CI: 0.58–0.99), with racial/ethnic minority group status exacerbating the
effect (AOR = 0.69, $P = 0.009$, 95% CI: 0.52–0.91). Serial mediation analyses
showed that depression (B = 20.21, SE = 0.05, 95% CI: 20.32–20.11), low
levels of social support (B = 20.098, SE = 0.042, 95% CI: 20.195–20.030), and
loneliness (B = 20.12, SE = 0.05, 95% CI: 20.23–0.02) were significant
mediators between internalized stigma and lower ART adherence (Turan,
Smith, Cohen, Wilson, & Adimora, 2016). In contrast, in Birmingham, AL,
an area in the United States' Deep South characterized by high incidence and
fatality rates of HIV but lower tolerance of the disease (Baunach & Burgess,
2013; Reif et al., 2014;Villarosa, 2017), other mediators of internalized stigma
and adherence were examined. Results suggested that such stigma led to
attachment-related anxiety, which caused concern about being seen taking
HIV medication, ultimately affecting adherence (B = −0.10, SE =.07, 95%
CI: −0.26–0.004) (Helms et al., 2016). These few examples illustrate how the
cultural, social, and psychosocial complexities of how HIV is acquired, transmitted, and treated compel biomedical scientists and clinicians to work creatively with social scientists to develop population-appropriate approaches to
preventative intervention.

It's no wonder that Gallo, who continues to work on retroviruses, has expressed
skepticism at stemming the AIDS epidemic without a vaccine (A. Park, 2014)
despite the effectiveness of antiretroviral treatments in preventing the progress of
the virus and its transmission. Why the grim view? Perhaps Gallo does not think that
the behavior changes needed to wholly prevent the spread of HIV are possible, so for
him, the vaccine is the only answer. Right or wrong, his feelings reflect the
challenges facing those who are working on containment and prevention until
a vaccine can be developed; they might also reflect a personal reluctance on his
own part to deeply engage with the social and behavioral aspects of the disease, even
while caring deeply about it. Innovative methods have emerged, however, from
grappling with these problems.

One recent study (Garcia, Colson, Parker, & Hirsch, 2015) conducted in
New York City describes the successful systematic incorporation of ethnographic
work to promote acceptance and adherence in clinical trials, exemplifying innovative and effective approaches made possible through the collaboration of ethnographic and clinical teams. Before running a clinical trial of Pre-exposure
prophylaxis (PrEP) medication with black men who have sex with men (BMSM),
an ethnographic study was carried out to better define and understand the barriers

and vulnerabilities experienced by that population that might pose obstacles to their full engagement with the health services available to them. The factors considered included individual factors (behaviors, attitudes), social factors (social risk, life goals, social networks), and institutional factors (community services, health systems, the labor market). These were explored with the target population using participant observation (eleven months) in public spaces, virtual spaces, and private spaces, such as informal gatherings at homes; key informant interviews (seventeen hour-long interviews); and in-depth interviews (three 90-minute interview sessions per participant). The data were analyzed in collaboration with community advisory board members, who validated the veracity and applicability of the identified themes. The interview data and field notes, coded by two researchers with inter-coder agreement greater than 80 percent, revealed six main themes related to health care engagement by BMSM: (1) a lack of services, such as those pertaining to employment, housing, and other benefits; (2) life goals related to adherence; (3) a lack of social support from close individuals and communities (e.g., relatives, the black community, or church); (4) avoidance of stigmatizing situations (e.g., being seen with other men in public) leading to risky behavior; (5) felt stigma and racism leading to poor risk-reduction behaviors (e.g., condomless sex, multiple partners, sex while taking drugs or alcohol); and (6) suspicion of medical institutions, reluctance to take medication, lack of knowledge of PrEP (Garcia et al., 2015). These findings were discussed with the community advisory board, as well as in joint discussions with the ethnography team, the clinical team, and the clinic where the participants for the clinical trials would be recruited. Together, these teams formulated four intervention components: (1) peer navigators, to help find information and overcome barriers to basic services, and to provide social and moral support; (2) study-specific face-to-face support groups, for emotional and other support, but also to provide opportunities for social learning and discussion of ways to confront stigma; (3) social networking via an online discussion group, for connectedness to a larger group and information sharing; and (4) SMS texting to participants, to deliver reminders and calls to action. Each of these components addressed at least two of the themes cited above, supporting access to information, the development of new adherence-supportive attitudes and habits, re-framing PrEP to align with BMSM values, and providing safe spaces to protect against social risks. They were implemented concurrently with the clinical trial.

To underscore the importance and novel nature of this work, it should be noted that BMSM are disproportionately affected by HIV in the United States, having the highest HIV prevalence and incidence compared to any other US subpopulation (Maulsby et al., 2013; Mayer et al., 2014; Millett, Flores, Peterson, & Bakeman, 2007; van Griensven & Stall, 2014). Thus, it has been investigated, yet the reasons for this situation are still not well understood. Notably, most studies have relied on information collected via survey or structured interview, resulting in descriptive associations of HIV diagnoses with diagnoses of sexually transmitted disease, lack of knowledge of HIV status, and limited access to health services and treatment (Maulsby et al., 2013; Mayer et al., 2014). Relatively few studies have been qualitative, in-depth, and preceding RCT in order to inform implementation

(Garcia et al., 2015). In a literature review on the topic carried out in 2013 (Maulsby et al.), of the thirty-nine papers included, only three were qualitative rather than quantitative. Thus, the ethnographically based tailoring of RCT to address the cultural or population-specific barriers to treatment adherence reflects functional collaborations between interdisciplinary teams working with diverse communities. It also constitutes one of the more successful forms – born of necessity in the arena of HIV/AIDS – of translational research, using ethnography to effectively connect the outputs of basic science to successfully implemented clinical trials. New problems demand new approaches, generating opportunities for new forms of creativity to emerge.

The Challenges of Translational Science

Thus, the field of biomedicine is evolving, not in small part because of a new focus on the process that takes a discovery in basic science, such as the discovery of HIV as the cause of AIDS, to the implementation of an intervention that has a public-health impact (Drolet & Lorenzi, 2011), such as the actual usage of PrEP (beyond mere distribution of the drug) by the vulnerable population that needs it. However, translation, a continuum that has traditionally been understood as comprising two (combining T1 and T2) or three different stages (T1, basic research to new methods for diagnosis, therapy, or prevention; T2, new method to proven clinical efficacy; T3, efficacy to health care delivery; Drolet & Lorenzi, 2011; Woolf, 2008), or even as many as six stages (Fishbein, Ridenour, Stahl, & Sussman, 2016) can be a frustratingly long process (Collins, 2011). The actual translation of scientific discoveries into human health benefits is still a major challenge that takes ten–twenty years, if not longer (Fishbein et al., 2016; Ioannidis, 2015), with the gaps generally occurring between stages. The changes and new ways of working required at all levels of biomedicine to effect translation have not been easy. Back in the early 2000s, the director of the National Institutes of Health (NIH) and author of the new NIH Roadmap (Zerhouni, 2003) wrote urgently and convincingly of the need for a revolutionary period of rapid change in the life sciences, instigated by scientific, but also social and economic, forces, such as the rising costs of health care, new technology in genetics, and emerging health challenges, such as obesity, chronic disease, and novel infectious diseases (Zerhouni, 2005). He called for an increased understanding of the complexity of biological systems and attention to strategies to effectively contribute to the translational and clinical sciences, requiring "unconventional forms of collaboration across disciplines and within and across scientific teams" and "closer working relationships among basic, translational and clinical scientists" (Zerhouni, 2005, p. 1355). The obstacles to realizing this vision have revealed basic research to be a synergistic complex, connected to global issues, ethical issues, public opinion, and policy making, each of which may pop up at any point to effectively delay the process of basic research to patient care (Fishbein et al., 2016). In addition, both structural and cultural contexts, such as university systems that more readily support individual or intra-departmental over collaborative or cross-departmental work, or opposing work cultures in hospitals and universities attempting to collaborate, can either hinder or help translational processes (Fishbein et al., 2016). Yet more fundamental aspects such as communication between the disciplines of research and practice, including the attitudes of scientists and clinicians toward translation, have also been cited as problematic and obstructive to the process of translation.

Basic researchers have often been portrayed as resistant to engaging with the translational connection between the bench and bedside. For example, in interviews with seven biomedical scientists engaged in stem cell research to contribute to the treatment of diabetes, themes of wariness or distance due to the expectations of outcomes by others (i.e., funders and practitioners) were prevalent, indicating these scientists' interpretation of expectation as pressure for outcomes beyond their purview, and their desire to avoid it. There was also the perception of scientists that their goals and agendas were wholly distinct from those of clinicians (Wainwright, Williams, Michael, Farsides, & Cribb, 2006).

Similarly, in a study of response to translational priorities, as represented by the employment of a research translator (whose role was to promote Type 1 translation – guide the results of basic research into the development of new methods for diagnosis, therapy, and prevention and their first testing in humans) in an academic/practical (university/hospital) site in the United Kingdom, basic researchers in a variety of biomedical fields and clinicians held distinct attitudes and views toward translational research, expressed in several interviews. Basic researchers generally regarded the goals of the translational model as opposed to their main concern, which was discovery over application. It has been hypothesized that this may be because the rewards and recognition in their fields are garnered through grants, publications, and awards, as opposed to things like patents (Morgan et al., 2011). These scientists, in turn, were regarded by the Research Translator as "dogged, egocentric," and opposed to change (p. 949). Clinical scientists, on the other hand, were more positive and receptive toward both translational research and the research translator, and saw them as more supportive of their overall objectives of improved healthcare.

In a recent systematic review of twenty-six papers reporting the views of scientists' and clinicians' on the factors affecting translational research, five factors were found, one of which highlighted the processes of research, such as ethics approvals or patient recruitment. The others, however, were more related to individuals' attitudes, feelings, or behaviors: differing concepts or definitions of translational research and their role in it; perceptions of the relationship between basic research and clinical care; social aspects of interdisciplinary collaboration; and discomfort with engaging entrepreneurial aspects of science (Fudge et al., 2016). That is to say, translation is heavily dependent not only upon adequate systems but also individual factors, which highly influence both how much individuals or groups of individuals may inject into the processes of discovery, translation, and implementation, and how much creativity is needed to move the field forward. That being said, creativity in the field of biomedicine has traditionally been difficult to gauge, as its effects are not often immediately apparent.

Measuring Creativity in the Biomedical Sciences

In 2013, Dean Keith Simonton, one of the premier researchers of scientific genius and creativity (Simonton, 2003, 2004, 2009) commented that scientific genius – what he considers the highest form of scientific creativity – appeared to be endangered (Simonton, 2013). He explained the rather high bar: While creative scientists generate ideas that are original and useful, the discoveries of creative geniuses in the sciences revolutionize and create whole new domains of expertise, such as Einstein's field of relativity and Darwin's evolution. While Simonton's comments may have been intended in part to be a bit of a challenge to the field, they serve to point out that the meaningfulness of science, the fruition of its originality and its usefulness to a field/society/the world, take time to eke out. How long does it take for a revolution in science to occur? Or how long before we recognize it as such? As John Ioannidis more recently asked, "Is it possible to recognize a major scientific discovery?" (Ioannidis, 2015).

Measuring creativity within the sciences has proved to be quite challenging. In the particular field of biomedicine, there is no specific or sanctioned measure of such. General approaches that could be applied as indicators in this domain include the number of citations of publications (Philipson, 2005; Piffer, 2012; Segal, Busse, & Mansfield, 1980; Simonton, 2002), or professional goal attainment, such as earning a doctorate, earning tenure at a top-fifty US university, securing a patent, or publishing a novel. These last were all considered aspects of creativity in a longitudinal study looking at SAT scores as predictors of creativity after twenty-five years (G. Park, Lubinski, & Benbow, 2007; Piffer, 2012). These are questionable in not being directly concerned with creativity per se, but more productivity and predictivity. More direct indicators might be actual awards or grants, for example, securing one of the NIH Director's Awards for high-risk research – a Pioneer Award, New Innovator Award, or Transformative Research Project Award (NIH, 2011). These awardees are scrutinized and recognized specifically for originality of ideas and the capability of moving the field forward more than incrementally, and therefore this honor might be a more believable indicator of creativity and innovation than mere degrees or citations. However, one scientist being awarded over another cannot tell us anything about their relative creativity, nor the general state of the field; not all creative scientists apply, and many creative scientists who do are not awarded. It might be reasonable to say, only, that those who gain that honor may be considered creative.

Even more rarefied indicators might be the Lasker and Nobel Prize awards. The Lasker Award is given to scientists, physicians, and public servants who have contributed significantly, with "creativity, persistence, and passion," to the fight against disease and the improvement of human health (Pomeroy, 2015, p. 1117). Nominated by their peers, those considered are then selected by an international jury of leading biomedical scientists. In 2016, Evelyn Witkin was awarded the Albert Lasker Basic Medical Research Award for work she carried out in the 1970s on bacteria that exhibited sophisticated mechanisms of DNA repair in response to ultraviolet light (Witkin, 1976). Her work contributed to advances in understanding familial and sporadic types of cancers. By the time of the award, she had already retired from the faculty at Rutgers University in New Jersey in 1991, at the age of 70, which at the time was the mandatory age of retirement (Gitschier, 2012). Similarly, the Nobel Prize for Physiology or Medicine is awarded for major discoveries that have proved to be of significant benefit to humanity. Candidates are chosen from among nominations from the field by the Nobel Committee for Physiology or Medicine. These candidates are then recommended to the Nobel Assembly at the Karolinska Institutet, which selects the Nobel Laureate (Nobel Media AB, 2014). Notably, though, as in Evelyn Witkins' case with the Lasker, the award may be bestowed many years after the major work actually happened. Luc Montaigne and his colleague, Francoise Barré-Sinoussi, were given the Nobel Prize for their 1983 work on AIDS in 2008, twenty-five years after they first published their discovery. Which is to say that, according to all methods of recognition, creativity in the biomedical sciences is a long game.

Due to the nature of this game, key creativity studies in biomedicine are retrospective, for example, Csikszentmihalyi on Linus Pauling (Csikszentmihalyi & Nakamura, 2014), in addition to Feist's and Simonton's work. Few of these studies, in fact, focus solely on the biomedical field, and few biographies of biomedical researchers focus solely on creativity. One notable study has examined the optimal environment for creativity and major discoveries in biomedicine, as exemplified by the Rockefeller Institute (Hollingsworth, 2002; Hollingsworth & Hollingsworth, 2000). In most if not all cases, though, the creative biomedical scientists working today will not be recognized or characterized for decades to come.

New Forms of Creativity in Biomedicine

In looking to the future, we return to Feist's exploration of the cognitive traits that lend themselves to interest in biological sciences and the development of scientific creativity. We might predict that in the current contexts, focusing on collaborative and translational research that the range of traits leading to scientific creativity might broaden. That is, there will always need to be brilliant scientists like Gallo who, while falling short in social skills, are capable of making the cognitive leaps necessary for breakthrough scientific discovery. However, there may be more room in the field now for the creative success of those with stronger social traits of agreeableness (McCrae & John, 1992), such as sympathy, warmth, and the ability to soothe more often than antagonize. Agreeableness has been linked with the ability to positively respond to and manage interpersonal conflict. Such skills may smooth the way for successful innovative collaborations and peer and patient interactions (Graziano, Jensen-Campbell, & Hair, 1996; Jensen-Campbell & Graziano, 2001). In addition, it is worth noting here that one of the cognitive traits found by Feist and Barron (2003) to explain Lifetime Creativity in a longitudinal predictive study was Psychological Mindedness, as measured using the California Psychological Inventory (McAllister, 1996), which is described as being interested in and responsive to the inner needs, motives, and experiences of others. With respect to

Simonton's conception of the domain-regressive creator, according to which the most creative scientists in a given domain share dispositional traits with those who are "lower" in the disciplinary hierarchy (Simonton, 2009), a new model might need to recognize that modern creators are less often scientists working singly (the Nobel shared prizes in science and economics already acknowledge this) than in small groups. Therefore, the genius creators, such as the emotional logician found in Gallo, may become small clusters of scientists who incorporate such extremes, with the whole being greater than the sum of its parts, and the parts including the opposing elements Simonton has identified in eminently creative scientists.

We close this chapter now with a brief glimpse into the newest arena of medical science, the internet, in which even more unexplored manifestations of creative genius may play an important role in overcoming obstinate medical conundrums, including the continued spread of HIV.

And They Lived

Crowdsourcing, the outsourcing of a certain job or task to a veritable crowd, is one of the latest innovative uses of the internet. Its possibilities for research were first realized in Amazon's Mechanical Turk, where researchers can collect large amounts of data from people willing to respond to surveys or questionnaires for a small payment. Since then, crowdsourcing has evolved more generally into a huge collaborative arena of exchange, connecting crowds to professional endeavors through common interests. There are many recent examples in the field of biomedicine. Transparency Life Sciences, a drug company co-founded by Stanford University researcher Lawrence Steinman, constructed a website to coordinate patient-researcher–designed clinical trials. In 2012, the FDA approved the first protocol developed using such crowdsourcing. As of 2013, PatientsLikeMe, a clinical research platform, also has an online patient network of more than 220,000 members sharing their health data on more than 2,000 diseases and conditions. It has published more than forty studies in peer-reviewed journals since 2004. Similarly, 75 percent of consumers who have used the genetic testing services of 23andMe are willing to participate in the company's studies. Findings from their crowd-sourced studies have also been published in peer-reviewed papers. Online platforms are being refined to curate better, more monitored, ethically sound, and rigorous clinical trials (Morton, 2014). A more recently developed platform, CrowdMed, invites individuals with undiagnosed illnesses to share their relevant medical information and test results anonymously online so that medical and non-medical "case-solvers" can contribute suggestions and participate in discussions to come up with possible diagnoses (Meyer, Longhurst, & Singh, 2016). MIT's Hacking Medicine events ("hackathons," twenty-four- to forty-eight-hour intensive global forums on specific, difficult problems), have resulted in worldwide collaborations involving technicians, patients, doctors, and researchers to produce innovative ideas, and even piloted prototypes (Celi, Ippolito, Montgomery, Moses, & Stone, 2014). The list of such mechanisms will only continue to get longer.

And so the story of AIDS was really just a prologue. A patient revolution began with HIV, when people affected by the disease began protesting the slow progress of basic research to effective clinical trials, and began hammering at the silence of researchers working mysteriously behind their institution walls. Today, in a more peaceful manner, patients can direct their energies online to organize their own clinical trials, donate data, and contribute to the development of outcome measures, interventions, and diagnoses. In a way, the field of biomedicine has been changed by patients determined to save their own lives. As this new and complex partnership between patient, doctor, and researcher will no doubt continue to evolve, and carry the field of biomedicine into the future, the forms of creativity needed by the field's scientists will continue to evolve as well. As life changes, so does creativity, which is why, in fact, the story never ends.

References

Alberts, B., Kirschner, M. W., Tilghman, S., & Varmus, H. (2014). Rescuing US biomedical research from its systemic flaws. *Proceedings of the National Academy of Sciences*, *111*(16), 5773–5777.

Amabile, T. M. (1996). *Creativity in context*. Boulder, CO: Westview Press.

Amabile, T. M. (1998). *How to kill creativity*. Boston, MA.: Harvard Business School Publishing .

Bachtold, L. M., & Werner, E. E. (1972). Personality characteristics of women scientists. *Psychological Reports*, *31*, 391–396.

Baron-Cohen, S., Bolton, P., Wheelwright, S., Scahill, V., Short, L., Mead, G., & Smith, A. (1998). Autism occurs more often in families of physicists, engineers, and mathematicians. *Autism*, *2*(3), 296–301.

Baron-Cohen, S., Wheelwright, S., Skinner, R., Martin, J., & Clubley, E. (2001). The autism-spectrum quotient (AQ): Evidence from asperger syndrome/high-functioning autism, males and females, scientists and mathematicians. *Journal of Autism and Developmental Disorders*, *31*(1), 5–17.

Bass, T. A. (1994). *Reinventing the future: Conversations with the world's leading scientists*. Reading, MA: Addison Wesley Publishing Company.

Baunach, D. M., & Burgess, E. O. (2013). HIV/AIDS prejudice in the American deep south. *Sociological Spectrum*, *33*(2), 175–195.

Bittner, J. V., & Heidemeier, H. (2013). Competitive mindsets, creativity, and the role of regulatory focus. *Thinking Skills and Creativity*, *9*, 59–68.

Boon, M. (1996). Naming the enemy: AIDS research, contagion, and the discovery of HIV. 4. Retrieved on from http://cultronix.eserver.org/boon/

Busse, T. V., & Mansfield, R. S. (1984). Selected personality traits and achievement in male scientists. *The Journal of Psychology*, *116*, 117–131.

Carnevale, P. J., & Probst, T. M. (1998). Social values and social conflict in creative problem solving and categorization. *Journal of Personality and Social Psychology*, *41*, 210–219.

Cattell, R. B., & Drevdahl, J. E. (1955). A comparison of the personality profile (16PF) of eminent researchers with that of eminent teachers and administrators, and of the general population. *British Journal of Psychology*, *46*, 248–261.

Cattell, R. B., Eber, H. W., & Tatsuoka, M. M. (1970). *Handbook for the 16 Personality Factor Questionaire (16PF) in Clinical Educational Industrial and Research Psychology*. Savoy, IL: Institute for Personality, Ability Testing.

Celi, L. A., Ippolito, A., Montgomery, R. A., Moses, C., & Stone, D. J. (2014). Crowdsourcing knowledge discovery and innovations in medicine. *Journal of Medical Internet Research*, *16*(9), e216.

Chambers, J. A. (1964). Relating personality and biographical factors to scientific creativity. *Psychological Monographs: General and Applied*, *78*(7, whole no. 584).

Collier, R. (2014). A blueprint for medical research stardom. *Canadian Medical Association. Journal*, *186*(11), 821.

Collins, F. S. (2011). Reengineering translational science: The time is right. *Science Translational Medicine*, *3*(90), 90cm17–90cm17.

Comte, A. (1855). *The positive philosophy of Auguste Comte* (Trans. H. Martineau). New York: Blanchard.

Csikszentmihalyi, M., & Nakamura, J. (2014). Catalytic Creativity: The case of Linus Pauling *The systems model of creativity* (pp. 185–194): Netherlands: Springer.

Drolet, B. C., & Lorenzi, N. M. (2011). Translational research: Understanding the continuum from bench to bedside. *Translational Research*, *157*(1), 1–5.

Erat, S., & Gneezy, U. (2016). Incentives for creativity. *Experimental Economics*, *19*(2), 269–280. DOI:10.1007/s10683-015-9440-5

Fan, H. Y., Conner, R. F., & Villarreal, L. P. (2007). *AIDS: Science and society*. Sudbury, MA: Jones and Bartlett Publishers.

Fang, F. C., & Casadevall, A. (2015). Competitive science: Is competition ruining science? *Infection and Immunity*, *83*(4), 1229–1233. DOI:10.1128/iai.02939-14

Feist, G. J. (1993). A structural model of scientific eminence. *Psychological Science*, *4*, 366–371.

Feist, G. J. (1998). A meta-analysis of the impact of personality on scientific and artistic creativity. *Personality and Social Psychological Review*, *2*, 290–309.

Feist, G. J. (2006). How development and personality influence scientific thought, interest, and achievement. *Review of General Psychology*, *10*(2), 163.

Feist, G. J., & Barron, F. X. (2003). Predicting creativity from early to late adulthood: Intellect, potential, and personality. *Journal of Research in Personality*, *37*(2), 62–88.

Fishbein, D. H., Ridenour, T. A., Stahl, M., & Sussman, S. (2016). The full translational spectrum of prevention science: facilitating the transfer of knowledge to practices and policies that prevent behavioral health problems. *Translational Behavioral Medicine*, *6*(1), 5–16.

Fudge, N., Sadler, E., Fisher, H. R., Maher, J., Wolfe, C. D., & McKevitt, C. (2016). Optimising translational research opportunities: A systematic review and narrative synthesis of basic and clinician scientists' perspectives of factors which enable or hinder translational research. *Plos One*, *11*(8), e0160475.

Gallo, R. C. (2002). The early years of HIV/AIDS. *Science*, *298*(5599), 1728–1730.

Gallo, R. C., & Montagnier, L. (2003). The discovery of HIV as the cause of AIDS. *New England Journal of Medicine*, *349*(24), 2283–2285.

Garcia, J., Colson, P. W., Parker, C., & Hirsch, J. S. (2015). Passing the baton: Community-based ethnography to design a randomized clinical trial on the effectiveness of oral pre-exposure prophylaxis for HIV prevention among black men who have sex with men. *Contemporary Clinical Trials*, *45*, 244–251.

Garwood, D. S. (1964). Personality factors related to creativity in young scientists. *Journal of Abnormal and Social Psychology*, *68*(413–419).

Gitschier, J. (2012). It was heaven: An interview with Evelyn Witkin. *PLOS Genetics*, *8*(10), 1–6.

Goldsworthy, P., & McFarlane, A. C. (2002). Howard Florey, Alexander Fleming and the fairy tale of penicillin. *Medical Journal of Australia*, *176*(4), 178–180.

Gough, H. G. (1961). *A personality sketch of the creative research scientist*. Paper presented at the 5th Annual Conference on Personnel and Industrial Relations Research, UCLA, Los Angeles, CA.

Graziano, W. G., Jensen-Campbell, L. A., & Hair, E. C. (1996). Perceiving interpersonal conflict and reacting to it: the case for agreeableness. *Journal of Personality and Social Psychology*, *70*(4), 820.

Helmreich, R. L., Spence, J. T., Beane, W. E., Lucker, G. W., & Matthews, K. A. (1980). Making it in academic psychology: Demographic and personality correlates of attainment. *Journal of Personality and Social Psychology*, *39*(5), 896–908.

Helms, C. B., Turan, J. M., Atkins, G., Kempf, M.-C., Clay, O. J., Raper, J. L., & Turan, B. (2016). Interpersonal mechanisms contributing to the association between hiv-related internalized stigma and medication adherence. *AIDS and Behavior*, 1–10.

Helson, R. (1971). Women mathematicians and the creative personality. *Journal of Consulting and Clinical Psychology*, *36*, 210–220.

Helson, R., & Crutchfield, R. (1970). Mathematicians: The creative researcher and the average PhD. *Journal of Consulting and Clinical Psychology*, *34*, 250–257.

Heyward, W. L., & Curran, J. W. (1988). The epidemiology of AIDS in the U.S. *Scientific American*, 72–81.

Holland, J. L. (1992). *Making vocational choices*, 2nd ed. Odessa, FL: Psychologica Assessment Resources.

Hollingsworth, J. R. (2002). *Research organizations and major discoveries in twentieth-century science: A case study of excellence in biomedical research*. WZB.

Hollingsworth, J. R., & Hollingsworth, E. J. (2000). Major discoveries and biomedical research organizations: perspectives on interdisciplinarity, nurturing leadership, and integrated structure and cultures. *Practising Interdisciplinarity*, 215–244.

Hsu, J. (2010). History: 'Lost' letters reveal twists in discovery of double helix. *livescience*.

Ioannidis, J. P. (2015). Is it possible to recognize a major scientific discovery? *JAMA*, *314*(11), 1135–1137.

Isaacson, W. (1983). Hunting for the hidden killers: AIDS. *Time*, 50–55.

Jensen-Campbell, L. A., & Graziano, W. G. (2001). Agreeableness as a moderator of interpersonal conflict. *Journal of Personality*, *69*(2), 323–362.

Kippax, S. C., Holt, M., & Friedman, S. R. (2011). Bridging the social and the biomedical: engaging the social and political sciences in HIV research. *Journal of the International AIDS Society*, *14*(Supp. 2), S1.

Kramer, L. (2003). 1,112 and counting. In C. Bull (Ed.), *While the world sleeps: Writings from the first twenty years of the global AIDS plague* (pp. 7–20). New York, NY: Thunder's Mouth Press.

Ludwig, A. M. (1992). Creative achievement and psychopathology: Comparison across professions. *American Journal of Psychopathology*, *46*(330–356).

Ludwig, A. M. (1995). *The price of greatness: Resolving the creativity and madness controversy*. New York, NY: Guilford Press.

Ludwig, A. M. (1998). Method and madness in the arts and sciences. *Creativity Research Journal*, *11*, 93–101.

MacQueen, K. (2011). Framing the social in biomedical HIV prevention trials: A 20-year retrospective. *Journal of the International AIDS Society, 14* (Supp. 2), S3.

Maulsby, C., Millett, G., Lindsey, K., Kelley, R., Johnson, K., Montoya, D., & Holtgrave, D. (2013). HIV among black men who have sex with men (MSM) in the United States: A review of the literature. *AIDS and Behavior, 18*(1), 10–25.

Mayer, K. H., Wang, L., Koblin, B., Mannheimer, S., Magnus, M., Del Rio, C., & Watson, C. C. (2014). Concomitant socioeconomic, behavioral, and biological factors associated with the disproportionate HIV infection burden among Black men who have sex with men in 6 US cities. *PloS One, 9*(1), e87298.

McAllister, L. (1996). *CPI interpretation,* 3rd ed. Palo Alto, CA: Consulting Psychologists Press, Inc.

McCrae, R. R., & John, O. P. (1992). An introduction to the five-factor model and its applications. *Journal of Personality, 60*(2), 175–215.

McDowell, G. S., Gunsalus, K. T., MacKellar, D. C., Mazzilli, S. A., Pai, V. P., Goodwin, P. R., & Kraemer, J. (2014). Shaping the Future of Research: a perspective from junior scientists. *F1000Research, 3*.

Meyer, A. N., Longhurst, C. A., & Singh, H. (2016). Crowdsourcing diagnosis for patients with undiagnosed illnesses: an evaluation of CrowdMed. *Journal of Medical Internet Research, 18*(1).

Millett, G. A., Flores, S. A., Peterson, J. L., & Bakeman, R. (2007). Explaining disparities in HIV infection among black and white men who have sex with men: A meta-analysis of HIV risk behaviors. *AIDS, 21*(15), 2083–2091.

Montagnier, L. (2002). A history of HIV discovery. *Science, 298*(5599), 1727–1728.

Morgan, M., Barry, C. A., Donovan, J. L., Sandall, J., Wolfe, C. D., & Boaz, A. (2011). Implementing 'translational' biomedical research: Convergence and divergence among clinical and basic scientists. *Social Science & Medicine, 73*(7), 945–952.

Morton, C. C. (2014). Innovating openly: Researchers and patients turn to crowdsourcing to collaborate on clinical trials, drug discovery, and more. *IEEE Pulse,* 63–67.

Murray, H. A. (1973). *Thematic apperception test.* San Antonio, TX: Pearson Education.

NIH. (2011). NIH announces 79 awards to encourage creative ideas in science. Retrieved on from https://www.nih.gov/news-events/news-releases/nih-announces-79-awards-encourage-creative-ideas-science

Nobel Media AB. (2014). The Nobel Assembly at Karolinska Institutet – Nobel Prize awarder for the Nobel Prize in Physiology or Medicine. Retrieved on from http://www.nobelprize.org/nobel_prizes/medicine/prize_awarder/

Park, A. (2014). The man who co-discovered HIV 30 years ago on why there won't be a cure for AIDS. *Time.*

Park, G., Lubinski, D., & Benbow, C. P. (2007). Contrasting intellectual patterns predict creativity in the arts and in the sciences: Tracking intellectually precocious youth over 25 years. *Psychological Science, 18,* 948–952.

Philipson, L. (2005). Medical research activities, funding, and creativity in Europe. *Journal of the American Medical Association, 294*(11), 1394–1398.

Piffer, D. (2012). Can creativity be measured? An attempt to clarify the notion of creativity and general directions for future research. *Thinking Skills and Creativity, 7,* 258–264.

Pomeroy, C. (2015). THe lasker awards at 70. *JAMA, 314*(11), 1117–1118. DOI:10.1001/jama.2015.10116.

Post, F. (1994). Creativity and psychopathology: A stud of 291 world famous men. *British Journal of Psychiatry, 165*, 22–34.

Prediger, D. J. (1982). Dimensions underlying Holland's hexagon: Missing link between interest and occupations? *Journal of Vocational Behavior, 21*, 259–287.

Raskin, E. A. (1936). Comparison of scientific and literary ability: A biographical study of eminent scientists and men of letters of the nineteenth century. *Journal of Abnormal and Social Psychology, 168*, 20–35.

Reif, S. S., Whetten, K., Wilson, E. R., McAllaster, C., Pence, B. W., Legrand, S., & Gong, W. (2014). HIV/AIDS in the Southern USA: A disproportionate epidemic. *AIDS Care, 26*(3), 351–359.

Remnick, D. (1987, August 9, 1987). Robert Gallo goes to war. *Washington Post.*

Roe, A. (1953). *The making of a scientist.* New York, NY: Dodd, Mead.

Segal, S. M., Busse, T. V., & Mansfield, R. S. (1980). The relationship of scientific creativity in the biological sciences to predoctoral accomplishments and experiences. *American Educational Research Association, 17*(4), 491–502.

Simonton, D. K. (2002). *Great psychologists and their times: Scientific insights into psychology's history.* Washington, D. C.: APA Books.

Simonton, D. K. (2003). Scientific creativity as constrained stochastic behavior: The integration of product, person, and process perspectives. *Psychological Bulletin, 129*(4), 475–494. DOI:10.1037/0033-2909.129.4.475.

Simonton, D. K. (2004). *Creativity in science: Chance, logic, genius, and zeitgeist.* New York, NY: Cambridge University Press.

Simonton, D. K. (2009). Varieties of (scientific) creativity: a hierarchical model of domain-specific disposition, development, and achievement. *Perspectives on Psychological Science, 4*(5), 441–452.

Simonton, D. K. (2013). Scientific genius is extinct. *Nature, 493*, 602.

Tsai, A. C. (2015). Socioeconomic gradients in internalized stigma among 4,314 persons with HIV in sub-Saharan Africa. *AIDS and Behavior, 19*(2), 270–282. DOI:10.1007/s10461-014-0993-7.

Turan, B., Smith, W., Cohen, M. H., Wilson, T. E., & Adimora, A. A. (2016). Depression and social isolation mediate effect of hiv stigma on women's art adherence. *Age (years), 49*, 8.59.

van Griensven, F., & Stall, R. D. (2014). Racial disparity in HIV incidence in MSM in the United States: How can it be reduced? *AIDS, 28*(1), 129–130.

van Zelst, R. H., & Kerr, W. A. (1954). Personality self-assessment of scientific and technical personnel. *Journal of Applied Psychology, 38*, 145–147.

Varmus, H. (2009). *The art and politics of science.* New York, NY: W. W. Norton & Company.

Villarosa, L. (2017). America's hidden H.I.V. epidemic. *The New York Times Magazine*, 38–49.

Wainwright, S. P., Williams, C., Michael, M., Farsides, B., & Cribb, A. (2006). From bench to bedside? Biomedical scientists' expectations of stem cell science as a future therapy for diabetes. *Social Science & Medicine, 63*(8), 2052–2064.

Witkin, E. M. (1976). Ultraviolet mutagenesis and inducible DNA repair in Escherischia coli. *Bacteriological Reviews, 40*(4), 869–907.

Woolf, S. H. (2008). The meaning of translational research and why it matters. *JAMA, 299*(2), 211–213.

Zerhouni, E. A. (2003). The NIH roadmap. *Science, 302*(5642), 63–72.

Zerhouni, E. A. (2005). US biomedical research: basic, translational, and clinical sciences. *JAMA, 294*(11), 1352–1358.

14 Creativity in Psychology

Finding Its Niche in the Sciences

Dean Keith Simonton

University of California, Davis

Abstract

Although creativity in psychology involves the same processes and procedures discussed in the earlier chapter on domain-general creativity, sufficient differences arise in their application that it becomes important to distinguish psychology's various subdisciplines as well as discern the discipline's overall placement in the hierarchy of the sciences, a placement that determines the amount of field consensus regarding the most creative contributors to the domain. Discussion then turns to the four major ways of assessing creativity in the domain, namely, peer evaluations, research citations, professional recognition, and historical eminence. This then sets the stage for reviewing key creativity studies regarding individual differences (including both general personality characteristics and specific theoretical and methodological orientation) and longitudinal changes (viz. early development and career trajectories). The chapter closes with recommendations regarding future research on creativity in the domain of psychology.

Writing this chapter was not very easy. Like probably most of the chapter authors for this edited volume, I am a psychologist by training. This comes as no surprise because the majority of creativity researchers are likely psychologists of one kind or another, whether they be cognitive, developmental, personality, social, educational, or organizational psychologists. Hence, I am implicitly writing about the creativity of most creativity researchers as well as the creativity of most chapter authors, including myself. I suppose, too, that many readers of the present chapter will also be psychologists who think themselves creative – or desire to be so – and perhaps have already developed their own views about what it takes to be creative in psychology. Hence, right from the start I may have a delicate task at hand. So, please, let nobody take offense! My profile of the creative psychologist reflects statistical averages only, not a deterministic equation. You, my reader, may be an outlier, and in a positive sense!

I start by defining creativity in the domain of psychology. From there, I discuss how creativity is measured within the domain and then illustrate this discussion by describing key findings from representative studies of creativity in the domain. I close with speculations about where future researchers might go in understanding creativity within the domain of psychology.

Defining Creativity in the Domain

Because in Chapter 4 of this volume I have already argued that all creativity adopts the same generic form regardless of domain, I am not about to repudiate that argument here. So, indeed, all creativity in the domain of psychology involves the contribution of original, useful, and surprising combinations. Moreover, the "weak methods" discussed in Chapter 4 can be easily documented in the creativity of psychologists (see ch. 6 in Simonton, 2002). The only modification on this general assertion is relatively minor: The combinatorial products in psychology are almost without exception ideational. Psychologists work with psychological ideas rather than improvise at the piano or choreograph new dance movements. In line with this restriction, creative ideas in psychology are almost invariably communicated via the publication of journal articles and books. It is largely by reading these documents that other psychologists decide whether the ideas contained therein are creative or not (cf. Kaufman & Beghetto, 2009; Simonton, 2013). Admittedly, some creative psychologists may opt for alternative ways to communicate their ideas, such as offering workshops or posting presentations on YouTube. But for the most part, the communication of creative ideas in psychology still adheres closely to the Gutenberg Era, whether actual paper in print journals, electronic files (especially in Portable Document Format), or web pages in online journals (particular those that are open access). Even eminent therapists from Sigmund Freud to Carl Rogers published such articles. So creativity in psychology differs not one iota from that in physics, chemistry, biology, sociology, etc.

At this point, however, the discussion must get more complex. Once a potentially creative idea is communicated to the field, *who* decides on its creativity? It is certainly not the entire field of psychologists but rather that subset who represent the same general specialty area. The size of this field varies according to the specialty, but Wray (2010) has estimated that for scientific specialties in general the figure ranges from 205 to 600 colleagues or peers (as in "peer review"). These are the actual persons most often responsible for judging a psychologist's creativity. These colleagues both subscribe to and publish in the same journals. Hence, it is perfectly possible for a psychologist to become well-known in one field while remaining virtually unknown in other fields. As a consequence, the field as a whole may not exhibit any consensus on the creativity of the ideas that psychologists are contributing to the domain.

To be sure, almost all creative domains can be partitioned into specialties that undermine the overall consensus. An astrophysicist could not easily judge a solid-state physicist's work. Nonetheless, the consensus problem is much more severe in psychology than in the natural sciences, especially physics, chemistry, and biology (Simonton, 2004, 2015; cf. Cole, 1983). Psychologists appear to be much more divided than physicists, chemists, and biologists. The relative degree of domain consensus is suggested by Figure 14.1, which shows the hierarchical arrangement for the three natural sciences, psychology, and sociology (which falls even lower).

Although this configuration incorporated other features of the five domains besides field consensus, the same overall pattern results when only consensus

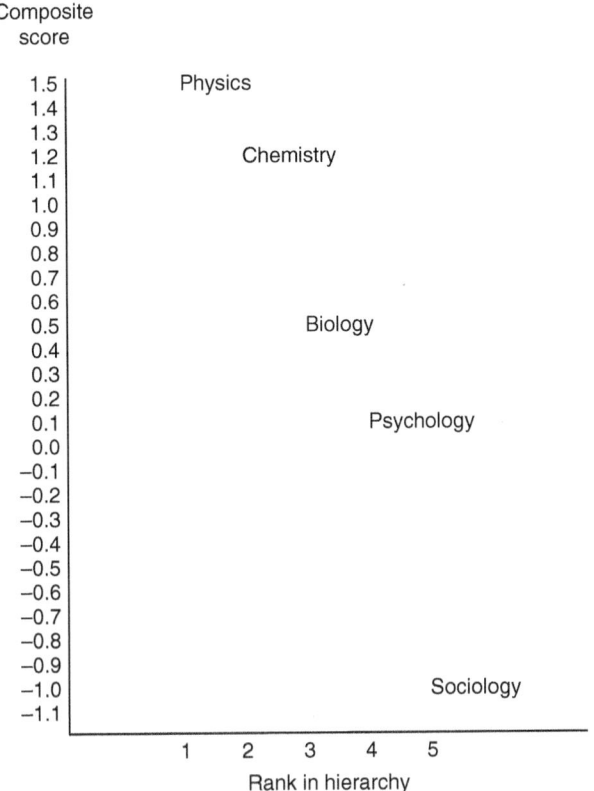

Composite
score

Figure 14.1 *The disciplines of physics, chemistry, biology, psychology, and sociology placed in a Comtean hierarchy of the sciences. Figure taken from Simonton (2004).*

measures are used (Simonton, 2004, 2015; cf. Fanelli, 2010; Fanelli & Glänzel, 2013).

It is not difficult to understand why psychologists differ so much in their appraisals of the creativity of other psychologists. Psychologists represent a very diverse group. The most obvious and often divisive split is that between research psychologists (scientists) and clinical psychologists (practitioners). When Kimble (1984) surveyed members of the American Psychological Association (APA) just a few years before many scientists broke away to form the American Psychological Society (now the Association for Psychological Science), he found that psychologists who belonged exclusively to Division 3 (experimental psychologists) differed from those who belonged exclusively to Division 29 (psychotherapists). The former were far more strongly committed to scientific rather than human values, determinism rather than free will, objectivism rather than intuitionism, laboratory investigations rather than field studies, nomothetic rather than idiographic explanations, and elementism rather than holism (cf. Simonton, 2000). Even psychologists who consider themselves scientists rather than clinicians can disagree dramatically along theoretical and methodological lines. A classic example is Cronbach's (1957) "two disciplines of scientific psychology," namely, the experimental versus correlational researchers.

Even research psychologists belonging to closely related specialties might as well belong to totally different fields. For instance, personality and social psychologists share a major APA publication (the *Journal of Personality and Social Psychology*, or *JPSP*) as well as an APA division (viz. Eight) with its own two journals (*Personality and Social Psychology Bulletin* and *Personality and Social Psychology Review*), yet in theory and methodology they might be considered to define different disciplines (Tracy, Robins, & Sherman, 2009). So great have been the tensions between these two groups that *JPSP* ended up splitting so that the personality psychologists could have their own section on *Personality Processes and Individual Differences*, plus in 2001 the personality psychologists founded the Association for Research in Personality that in 2009 held its own standalone conference separate from the Society for Personality and Social Psychology. Hairs are split ever thinner.

Nor can such within-domain differences be simply attributed to divergent areas of expertise. The conflicting views of psychology often reflect deep-rooted personality differences. For instance, psychologists who favor mechanistic approaches differ from those who prefer organismic approaches with respect to cognitive and inter-personal style, personality, and occupational interests (Johnson, Germer, Efran, & Overton, 1988). In a comparable fashion, scientists and practitioners have distin-guishable personalities (Zachar & Leong, 1992; see also Conway, 1988). As people, psychologists may represent a psychologically more heterogeneous group than do physicists, chemists, or biologists (cf. Chambers, 1964; Roe, 1953; Suedfeld, 1985). Perhaps there are almost as many psychologies as there are psychologists.

Assessing Creativity in the Domain

Typically, research on psychologists does not explicitly measure creativity. Instead, researchers focus on various indicators of a psychologist's impact on the domain of psychology. These measures are also used in scientometric and historio-metric studies in general and thus are not unique to research on psychology. In any case, these indicators can be assigned to the following four categories:

1. Peer Evaluations – One approach to creativity assessment is to survey fellow psychologists with the inquiry about who are the top contributors to the discipline (e.g., Annin, Boring, & Watson, 1968). The targets of these judgments may involve either living contemporaries or deceased figures of the past or even both simulta-neously (e.g., Coan & Zagona, 1962; Davis, Thomas, & Weaver, 1982). Occasionally, too, the peer evaluations will be applied to individual creative pro-ducts rather than the creators themselves (e.g., Heyduk & Fenigstein, 1984). Sometimes these peer evaluations are more properly called "superior" evaluations, as when a future psychologist's creativity is assessed by supervisors at research institutes or mentors at graduate schools (e.g., Kuncel, Hezlett, & Ones, 2004).

2. Research Citations – Even more widespread than the above are citations that psychologists receive in the research literature (Rushton, 1984; e.g., Simonton,

2000). Again, these citation counts may be applied to either the researcher's collective publications or single publications (e.g., Lee, Vicente, Cassano, & Shearer, 2003; Shadish, 1989). These citation counts can adopt a wide variety of forms as well (Ruscio, Seaman, D'Oriano, Stremlo, & Mahalchik, 2012). Probably the most popular citation measure recently is the h-index, where h indicates the highest number of publications that have been cited at least h times (Hirsch, 2005). This indicator has the advantage that it combines both quantity and quality of creative output (cf. Platz & Blakelock, 1960). One-hit wonders who staked their reputations on a single publication (most often the doctoral dissertation) cannot have an h greater than one no matter how often it is cited, while a mass-producer whose work is seldom if ever cited by others will also have a low h, especially if self-citations are excluded from the calculations (but see Ruscio et al., 2012).

3. Professional Recognition – Presumably psychologists who receive strong peer recognition and high citation rates will also earn more conspicuous forms of validation, including various awards and honors (e.g., Lyons, 1968; Over, 1981; Simonton, 1992). Most professional organizations feature prestigious prizes, from early career awards to awards for career contributions. Again, prizes are often accorded to individual creative products as well, such as various "best article" and "best book" awards (e.g., Lee, Vicente, Cassano, & Shearer, 2003).

4. Historical Eminence – The culmination of the preceding three assessments would correspond closely with a psychologist's posthumous reputation, as gauged by reference works such as encyclopedias, biographical dictionaries, disciplinary histories, and introductory textbooks (e.g., Simonton, 1992; Zusne, 1985, 1987; Zusne & Dailey, 1982). However, historical eminence provides the ultimate measure, based as it is on the assessment of posterity, not just contemporaries. Although it is rare, sometimes the "test of time" does not agree with a psychologist's standing in his or her own time (cf. Over, 1982a).

Ideally, research on creativity in psychology should use all four sets of measures (see, e.g., Simonton, 1992). But often methodological considerations cause research to rely on just one or two (cf. Diener, Oishi, & Park, 2014; Haggbloom et al., 2002). For instance, personality assessment is most often applied to living psychologists (e.g., Helmreich, Spence, Beane, Lucker, & Matthews, 1980; Wispé, 1963), an application that is far more easy to execute than to use at-a-distance measurements on deceased luminaries (e.g., Overskeid, Grønnerød, & Simonton, 2012; see Song & Simonton, 2007). In contrast, historical eminence often becomes a useful criterion when the goal is to examine the entire life and work of creative psychologist, a goal that necessarily requires that the individual be deceased anyway (e.g., Simonton, 1992; Zusne, 1976). A career may not end until a life ends.

Key Creativity Studies in the Domain

Because the biggest, most ambitious book I have ever written was devoted to what it takes to exert a major impact on psychological science (Simonton, 2002), I cannot hope to review that extensive literature here (see

Table 14.1 *Complete contents for* Great Psychologists and Their Times *(Simonton, 2002)*

Part I: The Scientific History of Psychology
    Chapter 1: Eminence in Psychology
    Chapter 2: History and Science
Part II: Lifetime Output of Psychologists and Their Impact on the Field
    Chapter 3: Individual Differences in Productivity and Eminence
    Chapter 4: Longitudinal Changes in Creativity
    Chapter 5: The Creative Product in Psychology
Part III: Personal Characteristics that Contribute to Greatness as a Psychologist
    Chapter 6: Cognition
    Chapter 7: Disposition
    Chapter 8: Worldview
Part IV: Life-Span Development of Great Psychologists
    Chapter 9: Family Background
    Chapter 10: Career Training
    Chapter 11: Maturity and Aging
    Chapter 12: Nature versus Nurture
Part V: Sociocultural Context of Psychological Science
    Chapter 13: Internal Milieu
    Chapter 14: External Milieu
    Chapter 15: Genius versus Zeitgeist
Part VI: Implications for the Field of Psychology
    Chapter 16: Research and Teaching

Note: Also includes a preface, 48 pages of references, and 19 pages of index entrees.

also Simonton, 2005). May it suffice to just provide the complete contents outline in Table 14.1 and then offer the mere highlights in the current chapter. Furthermore, because the literature is so vast, I must focus on creative psychologists. Readers interested in detailed comparisons between psychologists and creators in other domains, whether the arts or sciences, should consult Simonton (2002; also see Simonton, 2009, 2014a). By the same token, I will necessarily ignore creativity in pure practitioners – primarily psychotherapists whose impact seldom goes beyond their clients.

    I start with a look at individual differences associated with creative contributions in psychology, and then turn to longitudinal changes across the life and career.

Individual Differences

The goal is to examine the creativity of psychologists from the standpoint of differential psychology: Do the most creative differ from the less creative regarding some variables or factors on which people vary? Here such variables can be assigned to two major groupings – those applicable to all people and those that are only relevant to creative psychologists.

General Personality Characteristics. Not surprisingly, creative achievement as psychology requires a high degree of motivation (Wispé, 1963). For example, both the number of publications and the number of citations those publications receive are positively correlated with assessed achievement strivings (Helmreich, Spence, & Pred, 1988) and with orientations toward work and mastery (Helmreich et al., 1980). Although achievement has been associated with the coronary-prone Type A personality, it is the achievement, mastery, job involvement, and self-efficacy components that are relevant, not the competitiveness, irritability, and impatience (Helmreich, Spence, & Pred, 1988; Matthews, Helmreich, Beane, & Lucker, 1980; Taylor, Locke, Lee, & Gist, 1984). Predictably, given these motives, creative psychologists enjoy their research activities far more than holds for less creative psychologists (Chambers, 1964). Somewhat related to this achievement drive are certain personality traits (Cattell & Drevdahl, 1955). Notable psychologists tend to be highly dominant, self-sufficient, and schizothymic, where the latter indicates the tendency to "withdrawn, skeptical, internally preoccupied, precise, and critical" (Cattell, 1963, p. 121).

Unlike dominance and self-sufficiency, schizothymia sounds somewhat pathological, and indeed can very well be at extreme levels. So do creative psychologists have any inclinations toward mental illness, or at least subclinical traits shared with mental illness? Some empirical evidence suggests a connection. In the first place, the rates at which psychologists tend to seek psychotherapy are comparable to those seen in creative writers and artists, groups that are highly prone to need therapeutic interventions (Wispé & Parloff, 1965). Although this particular investigation did not find that the rates correlated with productivity, a second inquiry using two different samples, and defining the criterion in two different ways, found that a psychologist's research creativity was positively correlated with the score received on psychoticism, a measure of subclinical levels of psychopathology (Rushton, 1990). Highly creative psychologists are not necessarily mentally ill, but they are not totally normal either (cf. Grosul & Feist, 2014).

Specific Theoretical and Methodological Orientation. Because psychology is such a heterogeneous domain of creativity, psychologists differ immensely in their theoretical and methodological orientations (Coan, 1968, 1973). Of special importance is the distinction between psychologists who view the domain as a natural science and those who see it as a human science (Simonton, 2000; cf. Coan, 1979). These alternative perspectives differ on the following six bipolar dimensions: (1) Objectivistic versus Subjectivistic (emphasis on observable behavior versus emphasis on subjective experience); (2) Elementaristic versus Holistic (emphasis on molecular or atomistic analysis versus emphasis on molar analysis); (3) Impersonal versus Personal (emphasis on the nomothetic, deterministic, abstract, and tightly controlled versus emphasis on the idiographic, emotional, and the unconscious); (4) Quantitative versus Qualitative (emphasis on mathematics, statistics, and precision versus emphasis on qualitative attributes and processes); (5) Static versus Dynamic (emphasis on the normative and stable versus emphasis on motivation, emotion, and the self); (6) Exogenist versus Endogenist (emphasis on environmental determinants and social influences versus emphasis on biological determinants and heredity).

Interestingly, psychologists with the highest long-term citation rates represent the extremes on this general bipolar factor (Simonton, 2000). In contrast, those who attempt to balance the two – such as by integrating both nature and nurture – tend to suffer in influence. Even more interesting, perhaps, psychologists who advocate psychology as a human science boast higher citation rates than those who advocate psychology as a natural science (cf. Campbell, 1965; Suedfeld, 1985). The work of the former is probably more broadly accessible.

Longitudinal Changes

Here the research concentrates on lifespan development rather than individual differences, albeit sometimes the two perspectives are connected. Once more, the literature can be divided into two parts, the first dealing with early development and the second with career trajectories.

Early Development. Some researchers have focused on the family experiences of highly creative psychologists. An example is the research showing that high-impact researchers in psychology tend to be first-born children (Helmreich et al., 1980; Simonton, 2008; Terry, 1989). In addition, eminent psychologists tend to grow up in professional homes where one or both parents had higher than average formal education (Chambers, 1964; Simonton, 2017; Wispé, 1965).

Other investigators have concentrated on the formal education and training necessary to acquire the appropriate domain-specific expertise. For instance, not only are highly creative psychologists more likely to have earned their doctoral (or medical) degrees at highly prestigious universities (Kinnier, Metha, Buki, & Rawa, 1994; Rodgers & Maranto, 1989; Simonton, 1992; Wispé & Ritter, 1964), but they are also more likely to have studied under one or more mentors who were themselves highly creative (Boring & Boring, 1948; Simonton, 1992).

All told, highly creative psychologists tend to emerge from very propitious circumstances, albeit these circumstances are often of their own making, such as performing very well scholastically in college and thus getting into a high-quality graduate program (Rodgers & Maranto, 1989). Future high-impact psychologists usually got superlative grades and received scholastic honors upon graduation.

Career Trajectories. Consistent with the foregoing findings, high-impact psychologists earn their highest degree at earlier ages than the average, typically in the mid- to late 20s (Lyons, 1968; Simonton, 1992) in contrast to the general mean in the early 30s (Clark, 1954; Vance & MacPhail, 1964; but see Kuncel, Hezlett, & Ones, 2004). Just as expected, too, their productive output begins early and their first highly cited articles appear early as well, usually around age 30 (Simonton, 1992; cf. Horner, Rushton, & Vernon, 1986). Moreover, they maintain a prolific level of productivity throughout their careers, not ceasing after receiving tenure and still producing cited publications well into their 60s (Bridgwater, Walsh, & Walkenbach, 1982; Horner, Rushton, & Vernon, 1986; Simonton, 1992; see also Helmreich, Spence, & Thorbecke, 1981). Because highly creative psychologists start early, end late, and maintain high output and citation rates throughout, they define a productive elite, a small percentage accounting for the bulk of the research literature: Those in the top decile in lifetime output usually account for between 36 and 47 percent of all research (Dennis, 1954; White & White, 1978). Needless to say, the cross-sectional distribution of output is highly skewed (Platz, 1965; Simon, 1954), as is the corresponding distribution of eminence in the field (Zusne, 1985). The link connecting productivity and eminence is defined almost entirely by the citations received (Myers, 1970; Simonton, 1992).

A more complex issue concerns the peak of the career trajectory: When do creative psychologists produce their best work? In general, the career peak appears in the late 30s and early 40s (Cole, 1979; Dennis & Girden, 1954; Horner, Rushton, & Vernon, 1986; Lehman, 1966). However, a more accurate answer to this question requires that we more precisely define what we mean by the career peak. Are we talking about the age for the highest output rate, the highest level of citations, the single most-cited journal article, the most-cited publication of any kind, or the contribution that has received a "best book" or "best article" award? Although psychologists publish mostly journal articles, books often receive the most citations (Heyduk & Fenigstein, 1984; Simonton, 1992), where the latter appear about a decade later in the career (Christensen & Jacomb, 1992; Simonton, 1992). Complicating matters all the more, we have to consider whether the career peak should be defined in terms of chronological age or career age (e.g., Lyons, 1968; Simonton, 1992). Hence, the safest conclusion is simply that a psychologist's most creative work tends to appear about mid-career (see also Zusne, 1976). Seldom is the best saved for last.

Finally, it should be manifest that those psychologists who have the biggest impact on the domain in terms of the quantity and quality of their work will start to earn recognition in the form of awards and honors (Simonton, 1992). Not counting early career awards, which by definition must occur early, this disciplinary endorsement begins about a quarter century into their careers, or when the psychologists are in their 50s in chronological age (Lyons, 1968; Wispé & Ritter, 1964). Various lifetime achievement honors will appear about a decade later, in the 60s or even 70s. Most critically, recognition most likely occurs after the psychologist has produced their single most important contribution to the domain, thereby providing the maximally valid foundation for bestowing suitable honors.

Future Research on the Domain

One final reminder: I've only skimmed along the surface of a vast literature on the subject of this chapter. Back in 2002 I was able write a book more than 500 pages long, but were a new edition that same book to come out more than a dozen years later, it would have to be about 100 pages longer! Furthermore, many research questions remain so that, if suitably addressed, a third edition a decade or so from now should easily reach 700 pages. Although I'm not particularly inclined to make forecasts, I am willing to venture two main suggestions.

First, future research should deal with a fundamental shift in the discipline of psychology: Female researchers have gone from being a tiny minority to rapidly approaching the majority of all creative psychologists (cf. Simonton, 2002). Although some investigations have examined the creative contributions of women to the field, these are very few and far between (e.g., Bachtold & Werner, 1970; Guyter & Fidell, 1973; Over, 1982b; Simonton, 2008, 2017; Stevens & Gardner, 1985). Moreover, we already have reason to expect gender differences to emerge. For example, although the prominence of first-born children among eminent psychologists has been well established, that prominence becomes even more conspicuous for eminent female psychologists (Simonton, 2008). Apparently, women need special status in the home to provide support for overcoming any sexist obstacles that might be thrown in their path (see also Simonton, 2017). A first-born daughter is more likely to become an "honorary son."

Second, additional research should be devoted to filling out the details regarding psychology's placement in the hierarchy of the sciences depicted in Figure 14.1. This placement concerns more than just contrasts in consensus between the natural and social sciences (Simonton, 2015). We already have sufficient empirical evidence that scientists creating at different locations on this hierarchy will also tend to differ with respect to both dispositional traits and developmental experiences (Simonton, 2009, 2014a). Additionally, we already have some empirical rationale for extending this hierarchy beyond the social sciences into the humanities and arts (Simonton, 2009). For instance, placement closely reflects the likelihood that a creative contributor will exhibit some traits associated with subclinical levels of psychopathology (Ludwig, 1998; Simonton, 2014b). That said, we need more empirical data to fill in the details of what now can only be considered a highly schematic sketch.

The upshot of these future studies should be a better understanding of what makes psychologists creative. We might even learn how to become more creative. Who among us would not want that?

References

Annin, E. L., Boring, E. G., & Watson, R. I. (1968). Important psychologists, 1600–1967. *Journal of the History of the Behavioral Sciences, 4*, 303–315.

Bachtold, L. M., & Werner, E. E. (1970). Personality profiles of gifted women: Psychologists. *American Psychologist, 25*, 234–243.

Boring, M. D., & Boring, E. G. (1948). Masters and pupils among the American psychologists. *American Journal of Psychology, 61*, 527–534.

Bridgwater, C. A., Walsh, J. A., & Walkenbach, J. (1982). Pretenure and posttenure productivity trends of academic psychologists. *American Psychologist, 37*, 236–238.

Campbell, D. P. (1965). The vocational interests of American Psychological Association presidents. *American Psychologist, 20*, 636–644.

Cattell, R. B. (1963). The personality and motivation of the researcher from measurements of contemporaries and from biography. In C. W. Taylor & F. Barron (Eds.), *Scientific creativity: Its recognition and development* (pp. 119–131). New York: Wiley.

Cattell, R. B., & Drevdahl, J. E. (1955). A comparison of the personality profile (16 P. F.) of eminent researchers with that of eminent teachers and administrators, and of the general population. *British Journal of Psychology, 46,* 248–261.

Chambers, J. A. (1964). Relating personality and biographical factors to scientific creativity. *Psychological Monographs: General and Applied, 78* (7, whole no. 584).

Christensen, H., & Jacomb, P. A. (1992). The lifetime productivity of eminent Australian academics. *International Journal of Geriatric Psychiatry, 7,* 681–686.

Clark, K. E. (1954). The APA study of psychologists. *American Psychologist, 9,* 117–120.

Coan, R. W. (1968). Dimensions of psychological theory. *American Psychologist, 23,* 715–722.

Coan, R. W. (1973). Toward a psychological interpretation of psychology. *Journal of the History of the Behavioral Sciences, 9,* 313–327.

Coan, R. W. (1979). *Psychologists: Personal and theoretical pathways.* New York: Irvington Publishers.

Coan, R. W., & Zagona, S. V. (1962). Contemporary ratings of psychological theorists. *Psychological Record, 12,* 315–322.

Cole, S. (1979). Age and scientific performance. *American Journal of Sociology, 84,* 958–977.

Cole, S. (1983). The hierarchy of the sciences? *American Journal of Sociology, 89,* 111–139.

Conway, J. B. (1988). Differences among clinical psychologists: Scientists, practitioners, and scientist-practitioners. *Professional Psychology: Research and Practice, 19,* 642–655.

Cronbach, L. J. (1957). The two disciplines of scientific psychology. *American Psychologist, 12,* 671–684.

Davis, S. F., Thomas, R. L., & Weaver, M. S. (1982). Psychology's contemporary and all-time notables: Student, faculty, and chairperson viewpoints. *Bulletin of the Psychonomic Society, 20,* 3–6.

Dennis, W. (1954). Productivity among American psychologists. *American Psychologist, 9,* 191–194.

Dennis, W., & Girden, E. (1954). Current scientific activities of psychologists as a function of age. *Journal of Gerontology, 9,* 175–178.

Diener, E., Oishi, S., & Park, J. (2014). An incomplete list of eminent psychologists of the modern era. *Archives of Scientific Psychology, 2,* 20–32.

Fanelli, D. (2010). "Positive" results increase down the hierarchy of the sciences. *PLoS ONE 5*(4): e10068. DOI:10.1371/journal.pone.0010068.

Fanelli, D., & Glänzel, W. (2013). Bibliometric evidence for a hierarchy of the sciences. *PLoS ONE, 8*(6): e66938. DOI:10.1371/journal.pone.0066938

Grosul, M., & Feist, G. J. (2014). The creative person in science. *Psychology of Aesthetics, Creativity, and the Arts, 8,* 30–43.

Guyter, L., & Fidell, L. (1973). Publications of men and women psychologists. *American Psychologist, 28,* 157–160.

Haggbloom, S. J., Warnick, R., Warnick, J. E., Jones, V. K., Yarbrough, G. L., Russell, T. M., & Monte, E. (2002). The 100 most eminent psychologists of the 20th Century. *Review of General Psychology, 6,* 139–152.

Helmreich, R. L., Spence, J. T., Beane, W. E., Lucker, G. W., & Matthews, K. A. (1980). Making it in academic psychology: Demographic and personality correlates of attainment. *Journal of Personality and Social Psychology, 39,* 896–908.

Helmreich, R. L., Spence, J. T., & Pred, R. S. (1988). Making it without losing it: Type A, achievement motivation, and scientific attainment revisited. *Personality and Social Psychology Bulletin, 14,* 495–504.

Helmreich, R. L., Spence, J. T., & Thorbecke, W. L. (1981). On the stability of productivity and recognition. *Personality and Social Psychology Bulletin, 7*, 516–522.

Heyduk, R. G., & Fenigstein, A. (1984). Influential works and authors in psychology: A survey of eminent psychologists. *American Psychologist, 39*, 556–559.

Hirsch, J. E. (2005). An index to quantify an individual's scientific research output. *Proceedings of the National Academy of Sciences, 102*, 16569–16572.

Horner, K. L., Rushton, J. P., & Vernon, P. A. (1986). Relation between aging and research productivity of academic psychologists. *Psychology and Aging, 1*, 319–324.

Johnson, J. A., Germer, C. K., Efran, J. S., & Overton, W. F. (1988). Personality as the basis for theoretical predilections. *Journal of Personality and Social Psychology, 55*, 824–835.

Kaufman, J. C., & Beghetto, R. A. (2009). Beyond big and little: The four c model of creativity. *Review of General Psychology, 13*, 1–13.

Kimble, G. A. (1984). Psychology's two cultures. *American Psychologist, 39*, 833–839.

Kinnier, R. T., Metha, A. T., Buki, L. P., & Rawa, P. M. (1994). Manifest value of eminent psychologists: A content analysis of their obituaries. *Current Psychology: Developmental, Learning, Personality, Social, 13*, 88–94.

Kuncel, N. R., Hezlett, S. A., & Ones, D. S. (2004). Academic performance, career potential, creativity, and job performance: Can one construct predict them all? *Journal of Personality & Social Psychology, 86*, 148–161.

Lee, J. D., Vicente, K. J., Cassano, A., & Shearer, A. (2003). Can scientific impact be judged prospectively? A bibliometric test of Simonton's model of creative productivity. *Scientometrics, 56*, 223–232.

Lehman, H. C. (1966). The psychologist's most creative years. *American Psychologist, 21*, 363–369.

Ludwig, A. M. (1998). Method and madness in the arts and sciences. *Creativity Research Journal, 11*, 93–101.

Lyons, J. (1968). Chronological age, professional age, and eminence in psychology. *American Psychologist, 23*, 371–374.

Matthews, K. A., Helmreich, R. L., Beane, W. E., & Lucker, G. W. (1980). Pattern A, achievement striving, and scientific merit: Does Pattern A help or hinder? *Journal of Personality and Social Psychology, 39*, 962–967.

Myers, C. R. (1970). Journal citations and scientific eminence in contemporary psychology. *American Psychologist, 25*, 1041–1048.

Overskeid, G., Grønnerød, C., & Simonton, D. K. (2012). The personality of a nonperson: Gauging the inner Skinner. *Perspectives on Psychological Science, 7*, 187–197.

Over, R. (1981). Affiliations of psychologists elected to the National Academy of Sciences. *American Psychologist, 36*, 744–752.

Over, R. (1982a). The durability of scientific reputation. *Journal of the History of the Behavioral Sciences, 18*, 53–61.

Over, R. (1982b). Research productivity and impact of male and female psychologists. *American Psychologist, 37*, 24–31.

Platz, A. (1965). Psychology of the scientist: XI. Lotka's law and research visibility. *Psychological Reports, 16*, 566–568.

Platz, A., & Blakelock, E. (1960). Productivity of American psychologists: Quantity versus quality. *American Psychologist, 15*, 310–312.

Roe, A. (1953). *The making of a scientist.* New York: Dodd, Mead.

Rodgers, R. C., & Maranto, C. L. (1989). Causal models of publishing productivity in psychology. *Journal of Applied Psychology, 74*, 636–649.

Ruscio, J., Seaman, F., D'Oriano, C., Stremlo, E., & Mahalchik, K. (2012). Measuring scholarly impact using modern citation-based indices. *Measurement: Interdisciplinary Research and Perspectives*, *10*, 123–146.

Rushton, J. P. (1984). Evaluating research eminence in psychology: The construct validity of citation counts. *Bulletin of the British Psychological Society*, *37*, 33–36.

Rushton, J. P. (1990). Creativity, intelligence, and psychoticism. *Personality and Individual Differences*, *11*, 1291–1298.

Shadish, W. R., Jr. (1989). The perception and evaluation of quality in science. In B. Gholson, W. R. Shadish, Jr., R. A. Neimeyer, & A. C. Houts (Eds.), *The psychology of science: Contributions to metascience* (pp. 383–426). Cambridge: Cambridge University Press.

Simon, H. A. (1954). Productivity among American psychologists: An explanation. *American Psychologist*, *9*, 804–805.

Simonton, D. K. (1992). Leaders of American psychology, 1879–1967: Career development, creative output, and professional achievement. *Journal of Personality and Social Psychology*, *62*, 5–17.

Simonton, D. K. (2000). Methodological and theoretical orientation and the long-term disciplinary impact of 54 eminent psychologists. *Review of General Psychology*, *4*, 13–24.

Simonton, D. K. (2002). *Great psychologists and their times: Scientific insights into psychology's history*. Washington, DC: APA Books.

Simonton, D. K. (2004). Psychology's status as a scientific discipline: Its empirical placement within an implicit hierarchy of the sciences. *Review of General Psychology*, *8*, 59–67.

Simonton, D. K. (2005). Creativity in psychology: On becoming and being a great psychologist. In J. C. Kaufman & J. Baer (Eds.), *Faces of the muse: How people think, work, and act creatively in diverse domains* (pp. 139–151). Mahwah, NJ: Erlbaum.

Simonton, D. K. (2008). Gender differences in birth order and family size among 186 eminent psychologists. *Journal of Psychology of Science and Technology*, *1*, 15–22.

Simonton, D. K. (2009). Varieties of (scientific) creativity: A hierarchical model of disposition, development, and achievement. *Perspectives on Psychological Science*, *4*, 441–452.

Simonton, D. K. (2013). What is a creative idea? Little-c versus Big-C creativity. In J. Chan & K. Thomas (Eds.), *Handbook of research on creativity* (pp. 69–83). Cheltenham Glos, UK: Edward Elgar.

Simonton, D. K. (2014a). Hierarchies of creative domains: Disciplinary constraints on blind-variation and selective-retention. In E. S. Paul & S. B. Kaufman (Eds.), *The philosophy of creativity: New essays* (pp. 247–261). New York: Oxford University Press.

Simonton, D. K. (2014b). More method in the mad-genius controversy: A historiometric study of 204 historic creators. *Psychology of Aesthetics, Creativity, and the Arts*, *8*, 53–61.

Simonton, D. K. (2015). Psychology as a science within Comte's hypothesized hierarchy: Empirical investigations and conceptual implications. *Review of General Psychology*, *9*, 334–344.

Simonton, D. K. (2017). Eminent female psychologists in family context: Historical trends for 80 women born 1847–1950. *Journal of Genius and Eminence*, *1*(2), 15–25.

Song, A. V., & Simonton, D. K. (2007). Personality assessment at a distance: Quantitative methods. In R. W. Robins, R. C. Fraley, & R. F. Krueger (Eds.), *Handbook of research methods in personality psychology* (pp. 308–321). New York: Guilford Press.

Stevens, G., & Gardner, S. (1985). Psychology of the scientist: LIV. Permission to excel: A preliminary report of influences on eminent women psychologists. *Psychological Reports, 57*, 1023–1026.

Suedfeld, P. (1985). APA presidential addresses: The relation of integrative complexity to historical, professional, and personal factors. *Journal of Personality and Social Psychology, 47*, 848–852.

Taylor, M. S., Locke, E. A., Lee, C., & Gist, M. E. (1984). Type A behavior and faculty research productivity: What are the mechanisms? *Organizational Behavior and Human Performance, 34*, 402–418.

Tracy, J. L., Robins, R. W., & Sherman, J. W. (2009). The practice of psychological science: Searching for Cronbach's two streams in social-personality psychology. *Journal of Personality and Social Psychology, 96*, 1206–1225.

Terry, W. S. (1989). Birth order and prominence in the history of psychology. *Psychological Record, 39*, 333–337.

Vance, F. L., & MacPhail, S. L. (1964). APA membership trends and fields of specialization of psychologists earning doctoral degrees between 1959 and 1962. *American Psychologist, 9*, 654–658.

White, K. G., & White, M. J. (1978). On the relation between productivity and impact. *Australian Psychologist, 13*, 369–374.

Wispé, L. G. (1963, September 27). Traits of eminent American psychologists. *Science, 141*, 1256–1261.

Wispé, L. G. (1965). Some social and psychological correlates of eminence in psychology. *Journal of the History of the Behavioral Sciences, 7*, 88–98.

Wispé, L. G., & Parloff, M. B. (1965). Impact of psychotherapy on the productivity of psychologists. *Journal of Abnormal Psychology, 70*, 188–193.

Wispé, L. G., & Ritter, J. H. (1964). Where America's recognized psychologists received their doctorates. *American Psychologist, 19*, 634–644.

Wray, K. B. (2010). Rethinking the size of scientific specialties: Correcting Price's estimate. *Scientometrics, 83*, 471–476.

Zachar, P., & Leong, F. T. L. (1992). A problem of personality: Scientist and practitioner differences in psychology. *Journal of Personality, 60*, 665–677.

Zusne, L. (1976). Age and achievement in psychology: The harmonic mean as a model. *American Psychologist, 31*, 805–807.

Zusne, L. (1985). Contributions to the history of psychology: XXXVIII. The hyperbolic structure of eminence. *Psychological Reports, 57*, 1213–1214.

Zusne, L. (1987). Contributions to the history of psychology: XLIV. Coverage of contributors in histories of psychology. *Psychological Reports, 61*, 343–350.

Zusne, L., & Dailey, D. P. (1982). History of psychology texts as measuring instruments of eminence in psychology. *Revista de Historia de la Psicología, 3*, 7–42.

15 Creativity in the Engineering Domain

David H. Cropley
University of South Australia

Arthur J. Cropley
University of Hamburg

Bree L. Sandwith
University of South Australia

Abstract

Engineering can claim an important association with the birth of the modern creativity era. The Sputnik Shock of 1957 led to the identification of creativity not only as a valuable quality in general, but also as a vital element of practical, successful problem solving. The engineering domain epitomizes the interdependence of the Four Ps of creativity – Person, Product, Process, and Press – highlighting the necessity of each as a component of generating effective and novel solutions to problems.

In this chapter, we discuss both what makes engineering unique as a domain of creativity, and also how important the core, psychological constructs of creativity are to this domain. We discuss, in particular, two facets of creativity – the characteristics of creative products, and the measurement of divergent thinking – where insights from the domain of engineering add value to the understanding of creativity as a *systems* phenomenon.

The Sputnik Shock – the reaction to the launch of the Soviet satellite in 1957 – launched the modern creativity era. As Western nations – most notably, the United States – sought to explain their failure in the first leg of the Space Race, two domains were linked, possibly for the first time. The deficiency was seen as stemming from both a *quantitative* source – simply, a shortage of engineers – and a *qualitative* source – a shortage of *creative* engineers (Cropley, 2015). The former was addressed, in the United States, through programs such as the National Defense Education Act of 1958 that provided a funding boost to STEM education, and the establishment of organizations like the Defense Advanced Research Projects Agency (DARPA). However, the latter required a connection to be made between the psychology of creativity and domain of engineering. Despite this obvious connection, creativity has not always figured prominently in engineering in the years since Sputnik, despite the fact that the core activity in engineering – design – is, in essence, a process of generating novel and effective solutions to problems.

In this chapter, we explore some key questions surrounding creativity and engineering. Are there any aspects of creativity that are unique in this domain? How is creativity defined in engineering? How is creativity measured in the engineering domain, and is there anything we can learn from creativity placed in this practical, problem-solving context? We also ask what is required to define key studies in engineering creativity, and conclude by examining a contribution that the engineering domain may make to developing a better understanding of the core divergent-thinking process.

Understanding Creativity in the Engineering Domain

What Is Unique about Creativity in Engineering?

It is tempting to think that creativity in the domain of engineering is unique because it is focused largely, if not exclusively, on creating real, tangible solutions to problems. This means that it seems natural to focus on the "product" in any study of engineering creativity. However, this is deceptive, because creativity in the context of engineering is far more a question of how personal, psychological factors, cognitive processes, and organizational conditions *combine* to bring about a specific, novel outcome or product. Therefore, what may be unique, and we say this cautiously and provocatively, is that engineering may be the only domain in which each of Rhodes's (1961) "Four Ps" (4Ps) – Person, Process, Press, and Product – plays an *equally important* role in the generation of effective and novel outcomes. In other contexts, it may be sufficient to look only at what makes a person creative, or what cognitive processes favor the generation of ideas, but in a highly pragmatic and solution-focused domain such as engineering, all four Ps contribute to the successful development of the outcome. Indeed, the domain of engineering may be unique in that creativity cannot exist – or cannot be understood properly – without the framework of the 4Ps. In other words, the domain of engineering can only be characterized by a *systems model* in which creativity *emerges* as a result of the interaction of the 4Ps (Figure 15.1).

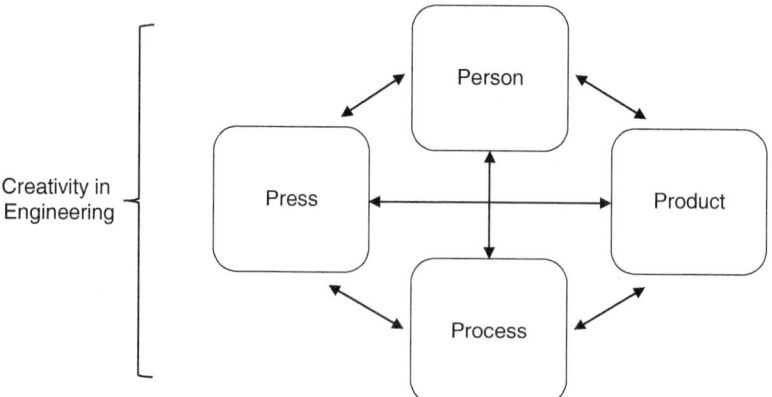

Figure 15.1 *Creativity in engineering: a* systems *phenomenon.*

Claiming that engineering is unique in this respect, however, is fraught with danger! Not only is it likely that other domains will make similar, and valid, claims, but *Systems theories* of creativity have been considered for some time (see Kozbelt, Beghetto, & Runco, 2010, for a summary) and the concept of creativity "emerging from a complex system with interacting subcomponents" (p. 38) is *not new*. However, where previous systems models, such as Gruber and Wallace's (1999) *evolving systems* concept or Csikszentmihalyi's (1988, 1999) *systems perspective* of creativity, take a particular focus – asking, for example, "what is creativity?" or "where is creativity?" (Kozbelt, Beghetto, & Runco, 2010) – a systems concept of creativity in engineering asks "how?" in the broadest sense. How do all four Ps *interact* to deliver creative outcomes?

How Is Creativity Defined in Engineering?

As important as it is to articulate a unique perspective on creativity in engineering, it is also important to recognize how much is *not* different. Too many forays into creativity in specific domains make the mistake of assuming that either *nothing* is known about creativity, or that the current body of knowledge does not apply to a domain like engineering. It is all too common to see articles on creativity in STEM disciplines begin by stating, for example, that "it is imperative that we move … towards a more precise definition" (Mishra & Henriksen, 2013, p. 10) or to "leave it up to the readers to think about their own definition of creativity in engineering" (Ihsen & Brandt, 1998, p. 3). While minor differences in how creativity is defined in psychology may remain, there is nothing to suggest that the definition by Plucker, Beghetto and Dow (2004) – "the interaction among *aptitude, process and environment* by which an individual or group produces a *perceptible product* that is both *novel and useful* as defined within a *social context*" (p. 90) – fails to capture the essence of creativity in engineering. Indeed, this definition is an excellent description of the systems concept of creativity illustrated in Figure 15.1. If there is one distinguishing feature of creativity in engineering, both in the definition and in the systems concept, it is the primacy of *the outcome* – the perceptible product. Engineering, after all, is about *making* things, not just *thinking about* making things!

What Other Constructs Are Important in Engineering Creativity?

Even articles in the engineering domain that fail to draw adequately on the body of knowledge of creativity (e.g., Badran, 2007) usually do a good job in one important, and related, aspect – that of articulating the *importance of creativity* (and innovation) in engineering. The practical, outcome-focused character of a *systems* model of creativity in engineering naturally demands an explanation of "why?" – why is creativity so important in this domain? What value does creativity confer on the process of developing technological solutions to practical problems? Why is creativity *necessary* in engineering?

Mokyr (1990) explains that creativity is the key driver of economic and social progress, providing technological solutions to problems of nutrition, shelter, transport, health, and more. Buhl (1960) recognized that the essence of engineering design is the ability to "create *new* products and processes" (p. 9) in response to new needs and problems – creative solutions, in other words. Cropley (2015) explained that without an injection of novelty in problem-solving processes we are limited, at best, to replication and, at worst, to stagnation. With creativity, engineering problem solving equips society with the means to move forward, finding solutions to the new problems that arise as a result of constant change.

Measuring Creativity in the Engineering Domain

If creativity – the ability to generate new and effective ideas, defined in a universal sense by Plucker, Beghetto and Dow (2004) – is the same whether we are engaging in engineering or in musical composition, then it seems axiomatic that creativity will be *measured* in exactly the same way, using the same instruments. Questions of domain differences – engineering versus art, for example – do not change the underlying definition, even if they lead to different interpretations of the measurements obtained. While this may hold true in a general sense, is it true, as we drill down into the detail of person, process, product, and press, as they are manifest in the engineering domain?

Measuring Person and Press

With respect to the Person, the question of measurement is unaffected by the domain. We measure the Person – or *personality*, more specifically, in the sense of the Big Five (Costa & McCrae, 1992) – in engineering creativity in exactly the same way that we measure the Person in artistic domains of creativity. Where differences are thought to exist – conscientiousness, for example (see Baer, 2010, for a discussion) – it is not a question of the *means of* measurement, but a question of *interpretation*. Conscientiousness is not *measured* differently in engineers – they answer the same subset of questions as anyone else – rather, it is the question of how the measured values are associated with creativity that may differ. Even extending measures in this area to include other personality constructs – for example, the Dark Triad of psychopathy, narcissism, and Machiavellianism (e.g., Paulhus, 2002) – any argument over domain differences is a question of the interpretation of the measurement, not the means of measurement (i.e. the instrument). Similarly, the question of the means of measurement and the Press, or climate, is also not affected by the domain. The interpretation of data may differ, and the way those data are associated with creativity may also differ, but the underlying construct, and therefore the instrument that operationalizes that construct, remains the same.

Measuring Process

Turning to the cognitive Process, it appears that the same issue is at play for this dimension of creativity. Creativity, while not exclusively defined in terms of divergent thinking (e.g., Cropley, 2006), is nevertheless strongly linked to divergent production in the realm of testing and measurement (e.g., Plucker and Makel, 2010). The ability of an individual to generate many (fluency) ideas in different categories (flexibility) that are unusual (originality) and that are developed in some way (elaboration) remains the foundation of creativity tests, whether part of the *Torrance Tests* (Torrance, 1966) or Urban and Jellen's (1996) *Test of Creative Thinking – Drawing Production*. Like Person and Press, there is no disputing the relevance of the construct divergent thinking to engineering. However, unlike Person and Press, there is something intuitively unsatisfactory, from the point of view of engineering, about the way that divergent thinking is measured. It would appear that the issue is not simply one of differences in interpretation. To understand what this might be consider how engineers themselves define the difference between convergent and divergent thinking. Horenstein (2002) does this by contrasting two key activities in engineering design:

> If only one answer to a problem exists, and finding it merely involved putting together the pieces of the puzzle, then the activity is probably analysis ... if more than one solution exists, and if deciding upon a suitable path demands being creative, making choices, performing tests, iterating and evaluating, then the activity is most certainly design. Design can include analysis, but it must also involve at least one of these latter elements. (p. 23)

What this means is that, in engineering problem-solving processes (i.e., design), there is, in effect, a *directionality* to the process. This flow typically proceeds in what is referred to as a *top-down* manner, first defining (Blanchard & Fabrycky, 2006) "*what* needs to be accomplished" and not "*how* it is to be done." Engineering creativity (design) therefore proceeds by defining first a *function*, and then seeks to finds a variety of ways (*forms*) in which this function could be satisfied. This is notably different from the typical format of divergent-thinking tests which, for example, ask the test subject to consider a *form* (e.g., a shoe) and generate possible *functions* that could be satisfied by this solution (see Cropley, 2014, for a discussion). Put simply, divergent thinking in the engineering domain is characterized by *function-first problems*, in contrast to typical divergent-thinking tests that are structured in a *form-first* manner. The underlying constructs remain the same – fluency, flexibility, originality, and elaboration; however, the stimulus in traditional form-first tests is unrepresentative of the way that problems are solved (not just in engineering, but probably in *all* practical problem-solving contexts). This raises at least some questions about the validity of traditional divergent-thinking tests in the engineering creativity domain.

There is other evidence that this may be more than merely a definitional problem. The ability to generate many different, original, and elaborate ideas in response to a function-first problem has real value. This is because engineers seek not simply *any* solution to the problem, but *the best* solution to the problem. They do so also under conditions of constraint (e.g., Cropley, 2014), meaning that the ability to find the most diverse set of possible solutions to a problem increases the likelihood of finding a *good* solution.

A second benefit of defining divergent thinking in engineering in a manner that is congruent with problem solving in this domain is that we see the importance of how the problem is defined. Not only are engineering problems defined in terms that are *function-first*, but the way that function is stated may have an impact on the quality of the subsequent divergent thinking. Dieter and Schmidt (2012) captured this when they discussed the fact that "The modelling of a mechanical product in a form-independent and solution-neutral way will allow for more abstract thinking about the problem and enhance the possibility of more creative solutions" (p. 225). Both how divergent thinking is defined in the engineering domain, and how it is measured, may matter a great deal. We will explore this a little further later in this chapter.

Measuring Product

If Person and Press highlight differences in the interpretation of creativity measurements in the engineering domain, and Process highlights differences in the way that creativity is measured, Product draws attention to both facets.

Previous research has developed a broad consensus – the essence of creativity in the *perceptible product* includes usefulness, appropriateness, and similar functional constructs that seem to relate to the ability of the product to do what it is intended to do (see Cropley & Cropley, 2005 for a discussion) to which must be added, as a minimum, novelty. The characteristics of creative products have been explored by many researchers (Amabile & Tighe, 1993; Cattell & Butcher, 1968), and with variations in the higher-order characteristics (e.g., Besemer & O'Quin, 1987; Cropley & Kaufman, 2012; Miller, 1992; Taylor, 1975;), but it is perhaps a perspective uniquely expressed in engineering that suggests that the characteristics exist in a *hierarchy* (Cropley & Cropley, 2005; Cropley, 2015).

The rationale for such a hierarchy is simple. Creativity in the engineering domain is concerned with solving problems. The value that creativity offers is to improve that problem-solving process by generating a wide range of possible solutions. New problems demand new – i.e., creative – solutions. While novelty seems to be vital, the problem-solving focus should not draw attention away from the fact that effectiveness is the key. If a product does not solve the problem for which it was developed, then it is not a *solution*. In fact, both Heinelt (1974) and Cattell and Butcher (1968) recognized this, respectively defining quasi-creativity and pseudo-creativity to differentiate novel and effective solutions from those that are merely surprising, unusual, or different.

For engineering, if not all creative problem-solving domains, a solution must, as a pre-requisite, be relevant and effective. Once this condition is satisfied, then the addition of novelty defines a *creative* product. While this is easily said and may be logical, is this hypothesis supported by any empirical evidence?

In two studies of product creativity, Cropley, Kaufman, and Cropley (2011) and Cropley and Kaufman (2012) examined the utility of various product creativity rating scales. Participants evaluated a range of products (five different designs of mousetraps) both in terms of a single measure of *Overall Creativity* – much like a Consensual Assessment (Amabile, 1982) rating of creativity – as well as in terms

Table 15.1 *Hierarchical multiple regression output*

Product	R Square (R&E)(%)	R Square (novelty)(%)	R Square (elegance)(%)	R Square (genesis)(%)	Mean creativity
A	11.7	17.5	11.8	20.7	2.78
B	25.0	31.0	31.1	26.2	3.56
C	4.3	16.6	20.8	19.7	2.67
D	36.9	34.4	15.4	27.3	4.22
E	14.6	30.6	24.6	29.2	3.39

All values were significant at $p<.01$.

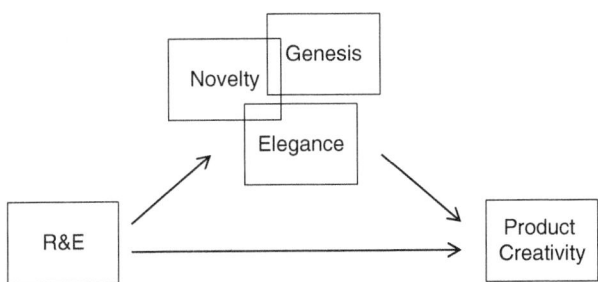

Figure 15.2 *Generic mediation model: product creativity.*

of individual items: Relevance and Effectiveness; Novelty; Elegance; and Genesis. These data were used in the evaluation of a more detailed, thirty-item product scale. However, they also provide an opportunity to explore the question of the hierarchy of product characteristics. Is there any empirical evidence to support the claim that effectiveness and novelty *are* pre-requisites for product creativity?

To test this hypothesis we re-analyzed data from the two previous studies of product creativity and applied hierarchical multiple regression to the ratings of mean creativity for the five different products. This technique allowed us to examine the amount of overall creativity predicted by each product characteristic, across a sample of n = 266, with *five different* products. Each product characteristic (e.g., novelty) was entered, in turn, at Step 1, with the remaining characteristics entered together at Step 2. In each case, the percentage of variance (R Square) explained by the single product characteristic at Step 1 was recorded (Table 15.1) with the dependent variable set as the mean creativity of the product.

Individually, each hierarchical multiple regression test tells us, not surprisingly, that the four characteristics all contribute to overall creativity. More formally, each test, with each characteristic entered in turn at Step 1, tests a mediation model such as that shown in Figure 15.2.

To test the hypothesis of interest – effectiveness and novelty are pre-requisites for product creativity – it was necessary to combine the results of the separate hierarchical regression tests across the five products. The values of R Square for each

Table 15.2 *Correlation coefficients for R Square values and product creativity*

	Mean creativity
R Square (R&E)	.962**
R Square (novelty)	.943*
R Square (elegance)	.297
R Square (genesis)	.798

** $p<.01$, * $p<.05$

product characteristic were tested for correlations with mean product creativity. The correlation coefficients for this test are shown in Table 15.2.

These results suggest, for the first time, that there is empirical support for the assertion that effectiveness and novelty are *pre-requisite* characteristics of creativity. The correlation coefficients in Table 15.2 suggest that *the more creative the product, the more its creativity is predicted by relevance and effectiveness, and to a slightly lesser extent, by novelty.* In other words, this supports the hypothesis that for a product to be judged creative, it must, as a pre-requisite, be relevant and effective, and novel.

At the same time, elegance and genesis are *not* unimportant – the individual hierarchical regression models (each row in Table 15.1) show that these also play a role in predicting creativity; however, that role is more complex and is the subject of ongoing research. What seems to be emerging from the work reported here is that the characteristics of a creative product are both systematic and hierarchical. Different characteristics contribute to creativity in different ways, and some characteristics matter more than others.

Key Creativity Studies in the Engineering Domain

The question of key studies in the domain of engineering creativity is overlaid with many conditions. Is a *key study* characterized by an underpinning theoretical framework that is specific to engineering? Is it characterized by a sample that is uniquely representative of the wider population of "engineers"? Is it defined by a focus on engineering products? Would it be one that used a test of divergent thinking that better reflected the manner in which engineers actually generate ideas?

In terms of their utility as a basis for expanding the body of knowledge – regardless of any specific 4Ps focus – those studies that are firmly grounded in the psychology of creativity are frontrunners for the status of key studies. The work of Buhl (1960) – his book *Creative Engineering Design* – is a rather obscure and little-cited work that, nevertheless, is remarkably prescient. Written early in the modern creativity era, this book is surprisingly germane to the discussions of engineering design, problem solving and the role of creativity. Charyton (2008) is one of the few examples of studies published in mainstream creativity literature that is built on the creativity body of knowledge in psychology, but is specific to the engineering domain. Similarly, Cropley and Cropley (2000) has emerged as a frequently cited study of a domain-specific sample, utilizing constructs and tests from the psychology of creativity. More recently, we see other engineering studies emerging that are building on established concepts in the psychology of creativity (e.g., Berger et al, 2014), and applying these to the engineering domain. Finally, and most recently, studies of engineers and other domains are emerging (e.g., Agogué et al., 2015) that are drilling into more specific issues of creativity – product measurement, personal qualities, and process characteristics – with a much stronger grounding in the literature of the psychology of creativity.

The Future of Creativity in Engineering

The earlier discussion of Process and the validity of current tests of divergent thinking opens up an exciting area of investigation in the domain of engineering creativity. In fact, the unique perspectives of the engineering domain may assist in developing a better understanding of what it means to be creative across all domains. The core question is one of form-first versus function-first problems and their relationship to creativity.

The first issue is that traditional divergent-thinking tests – the Alternate Uses Test, for example – present the test subject with a *solution*, and fluency, flexibility, etc., are measured for a range of possible *problems* that could be satisfied in this *form-first task* (Figure 15.3). Thus, a shoe (the Form) might be associated with "paperweight" (Function A), "doorstop" (Function B), and "pencil case" (Function C).

Not only is this unrepresentative of the way that engineers solve problems, but it may also place an unwitting constraint on the individual's creativity. Specifically, the *functional fixedness*[1] inherent in form-first tasks may place a constraint on creativity by

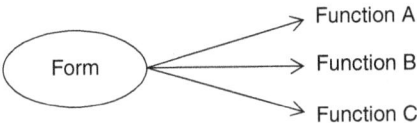

Figure 15.3 *Form-first problems.*

[1] Functional fixedness was first discussed in detail by Duncker (1945). He used it to refer to the tendency of people to use objects only in ways that are customary in their experience, which usually means in socially defined ways; a hammer, for example, is regarded as useful only for hammering in nails and is not regarded as providing a weight for the pendulum of a grandfather clock. The divergent thinker has to break this functional fixedness. However, function is also fixed by other factors apart from social convention such as the laws of biology or physics. Even for a divergent thinker the function of a tin can remains fixed: The criterion of relevance and effectiveness means, for instance, that it cannot be used as food for a starving baby or burned in a campfire to provide warmth. Asking people being tested for divergent thinking how many ways they can think of to use a tin can thus involves giving them a solution (the tin can) and asking them to find problems it could be used to solve from within the fixed functionality of tin cans.

Table 15.3 *Task types, structure, and creativity*

Task type	Structure	Creativity
Form-first	HI	LO
Function-first	LO	HI

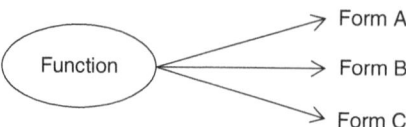

Figure 15.4 *Function-first problems.*

reinforcing conventional associations – between form and function – making it harder for the test subject to find and articulate the remote associations (see Mednick, 1962, for the classic discussion of remote associates) that are beneficial to divergent thinking.

In contrast to form-first tasks, *function-first* tasks present the test subject with a more open-ended problem statement and measure fluency, flexibility, originality, and elaboration across the range of solutions that are generated in response (Figure 15.4). In this case, "how to store baked beans?" (a Function) might be satisfied by "a ziplock bag" (Form A), "a paper cup" (Form B), or "a tin can" (Form C).

One way to explain the difference between these two problem types is that they represent different forms of externally imposed *structure* – i.e. rules and limits inherent in the Press – that impact on individual creativity. Cropley (2014) described this in terms of the tension between freedom and constraint, and the so-called *design space*. If constraint limits the available design space, then it would seem that high structure must be bad for creativity, and form-first tasks cannot generate the same variability as low-structure, function-first problems (Table 15.3).

There is domain-specific evidence in engineering to support our assertions about the impact of externally imposed structure on creativity. For example, in a task where participants were asked to design a new toy (in general terms, a function-first task), Moreau and Dahl (2005) found that participants who were told that they had to include a specific number of design features (in effect, more explicit function-first tasks) had a higher degree of creative thought processes, and hence came up with toy designs that were judged as more novel, than those who were left to choose whether or not they incorporated those features. Similarly, research conducted by Goldenberg, Mazursky, and Solmon (1999) found that suggestions for improving existing products (once again, in general, a function-first task) were rated as more original and practical when participants were given instructions to think about those products in terms of specific features and functions, and then asked to change or modify these components (again, highlighting more specific function-first problems).

More recently, Sandwith (2015) found further evidence supporting the beneficial impact of low structure on product creativity. In her study, product creativity scores

Table 15.4 *Restrictive and expansive function-first tasks*

Task type	Structure	Creativity
Form-first	HI	LO
Function-first (restrictive)	HI?	LO?
Function-first (expansive)	LO	HI

on a form-first, high-structure task were uncorrelated with individual participants' creativity, while product creativity and individual creativity were positively correlated on a function-first, low-structure task.

However, in contrast to these findings, Sagiv, Arieli, Goldenberg, and Goldschmidt (2010) have also found evidence suggesting that a high-structure task can have a *positive* influence on creativity. Two factors explain why this might be the case. First, harking back to the statement by Dieter and Schmidt (2012), the manner in which the function is stated may have a strong impact on the apparent structure of the problem. Engineers know that the most concise way to state a function is as a verb-noun pair, e.g., move (verb) a load (noun). Function-first problem statements then take the form of the question "how to verb-noun?," e.g., how to move a load? A form-*dependent* and solution-*specific* function is one in which the verb-noun pair is highly specific, for example, "how to screw screws?" In this example, another form of fixation may constrain thinking to the point that the only possible solution that can be imagined is a screwdriver. Conversely, a form-*independent* and solution-*neutral* function would state the verb-noun pair in the most abstract terms possible, minimizing fixation and maximizing the range of solutions that can be imagined. "How to apply torque?" is therefore likely to lead to greater creativity, inviting solutions like "knife blade," "fingers," "coin," and "paper clip," as well as the more conventional "screwdriver." The explanation for the finding of Sagiv et al. (2010) is that there are, in fact, *three* generic task types: form-first, function-first (restrictive), and function-first (expansive) – see Table 15.4.

While expansive, abstract, function-first tasks and low structure in general seem likely to support higher creativity, a question remains over the relative impact of different forms of more structured task types. This also begs a very important question – are current form-first, divergent-thinking tests really the best way to measure individual creativity?

The second factor that explains why some findings (Sagiv et al., 2010) suggest that high structure may be associated with creativity concerns a second form of *imposed structure*. Personal Need for Structure (PNS) can be thought of as a form of internally imposed structure, in contrast to the externally imposed structure, of constraints, rules, and problem type. Individuals with a high Personal Need for Structure are predisposed to think convergently (Goclowska, Baas, Crisp, & De Dreu, 2014), and thus the solutions they produce are constrained by both externally imposed convergent thought (as prompted by the task type) and internally imposed convergent thought (an intrinsic preference to do so). This is supported by the finding (Sagiv et al., 2010) that the greatest difference between *systematic* and *intuitive* thinkers (similar to high and low PNS) was found on the function-first (low structure) task, with the intuitive thinkers (low PNS) producing ideas that were more novel and creative than the systematic (high PNS) thinkers.

It is also important here to note the research of, for example, Stokes (2008), Haught and Johnson-Laird (2003), and also Onarheim (2012), concerning the positive effects of constraints on creativity. Structure, limitations, and constraints may impact on creativity in a variety of ways, both in terms of absolute size of the search, or design, space, and also in terms of where, within that design space the engineer is able to look for solutions.

Conclusions

The engineering domain represents a very practical expression of creativity. The outcome, or Product, is of special significance, although it is clear that Person, Process, and Press are necessary contributing factors. This means that creativity in the engineering domain is very much a systems phenomenon, representing the result of the *interaction* of the 4Ps.

Although there is much that should be shared across engineering and other domains of creativity, one aspect that is put into a new perspective is the manner in which creativity in measured – both in the Process and in the Product. The engineering domain highlights the fact that practical real-world problems, which require divergent thinking for their solution, are usually expressed as *functions* for which an appropriate *form* is sought. This is distinctly different from the traditional test of divergent thinking that places the form first, calling into question the appropriateness, if not the validity, of divergent-thinking tests for studying engineering creativity. The engineering domain further highlights the importance of the characteristics of the creative product. While a number of characteristics matter as far as product creativity is concerned, some matter more than others. To an engineer, it is self-evident that a product can only be creative if it is both effective *and* novel, and evidence is emerging to support this hierarchical view of product creativity.

The interest – in a formal sense – for creativity in the engineering domain is growing. More studies and literature are emerging that build on the body of knowledge of creativity research, and it seems likely that this will continue to grow as more engineering researchers, interested in the factors that contribute to engineering problem solving, continue to tap into the psychology of creativity. A particular area of interest for future research concerns developing a better understanding of the impact of *problem type* (i.e., form-first or function-first) and a range of different manifestations of *constraint* (e.g., limitations on the absolute size of a given design space, versus limitations imposed within a given design space) on creativity. Coupled with a growing understanding of the domain-specific elements of personality and press on engineering creativity, this holds out the prospect of far more efficient methods for finding and developing novel and effective solutions to technological problems.

References

Agogué, M., Le Masson, P., Dalmasso, C., Houdé, O., & Cassotti, M. (2015). Resisting classical solutions: The creative mind of industrial designers and engineers. *Psychology of Aesthetics, Creativity, and the Arts, 9*(3), 313–318.

Amabile, T. M. (1982). Social psychology of creativity: A consensual assessment technique. *Journal of Personality and Social Psychology, 43*, 997–1013.

Amabile, T. M., & Tighe, E. (1993). Questions of creativity. In J. Brockman (Ed.), *Creativity. The Reality Club* (Vol. 4, pp. 7–27). New York: Simon and Schuster.

Badran, I. (2007). Enhancing creativity and innovation in engineering education. *European Journal of Engineering Education, 32*(5), 573–585.

Baer, J. M. (2010). Is creativity domain specific? In J. C. Kaufman & R. J. Sternberg (Eds.), *The Cambridge handbook of creativity* (pp. 321–341). New York: Cambridge University Press.

Berger, K., Surovek, A., Jensen, D., & Cropley, D. (2014). *Individual creativity and team engineering design: A taxonomy for team composition.* Paper presented at the Proceedings of the Frontiers in Education Conference, Madrid, Spain.

Besemer, S. P., & O'Quin, K. (1987). Creative product analysis: Testing a model by developing a judging instrument. In S. G. Isaksen (Ed.), *Frontiers of creativity research: Beyond the basics* (pp. 367–389). Buffalo: Brady.

Blanchard, B. S., & Fabrycky, W. J. (2006). *Systems engineering and analysis* (4th ed.). Upper Saddle River, NJ: Pearson Prentice Hall.

Buhl, H. R. (1960). *Creative engineering design.* Iowa State University Press.

Cattell, R. B., & Butcher, H. J. (1968). *The prediction of achievement and creativity.* New York: Bobbs-Merrill.

Charyton, C., Jagacinski, R. J., & Merrill, J. A. (2008). CEDA: A research instrument for creative engineering design assessment. *Psychology of Aesthetics, Creativity, and the Arts, 2*(3), 147–154.

Costa Jr, P. T., & McCrae, R. R. (1992). Four ways five factors are basic. *Personality and Individual Differences, 13*(6), 653–665.

Cropley, A. J. (2006). In praise of convergent thinking. *Creativity Research Journal, 18*(3), 391–404.

Cropley, D. H. (2014). Engineering, ethics and creativity: N'er the twain shall meet? In S. Moran, D. H. Cropley, & J. C. Kaufman (Eds.), *The ethics of creativity* (pp. 152–169). Basingstoke, UK: Palgrave MacMillan Ltd.

Cropley, D. H. (2015). *Creativity in engineering: Novel solutions to complex problems.* San Diego: Academic Press.

Cropley, D. H., & Cropley, A. J. (2000). Fostering creativity in engineering undergraduates. *High Ability Studies, 11*(2), 207–219.

Cropley, D. H., & Cropley, A. J. (2005). Engineering creativity: A systems concept of functional creativity. In J. C. Kaufman & J. Baer (Eds.), *Faces of the muse: How people think, work and act creatively in diverse domains* (pp. 169–185). Hillsdale: NJ: Lawrence Erlbaum.

Cropley, D. H., & Kaufman, J. C. (2012). Measuring functional creativity: Non-expert raters and the creative solution diagnosis scale. *The Journal of Creative Behavior, 46*(2), 119–137.

Cropley, D. H., Kaufman, J. C., & Cropley, A. J. (2011). Measuring creativity for innovation management. *Journal of Technology Management & Innovation, 6*(3), 13–30.

Csikszentmihalyi, M. (1988). Society, culture, and person: A systems view of creativity. In R. J. Sternberg (Ed.), *The nature of creativity* (pp. 325–339). New York: Cambridge University Press.

Csikszentmihalyi, M. (1999). Implications of a systems perspective for the study of creativity. In R. J. Sternberg (Ed.), *Handbook of creativity* (pp. 313–335). Cambridge, UK: Cambridge University Press.

Dieter, G. E., & Schmidt, L. C. (2012). *Engineering design* (5th ed.). New York: McGraw-Hill Higher Education.

Duncker, K. (1945). *On problem-solving* (J. F. Dashiell, Ed., Vol. 58). Washington DC: The American Psychological Association Inc.

Goclowska, M. A., Baas, M., Crisp, R. J., & De Dreu, C. K. W. (2014). Whether social schema violations help or hurt creativity depends on need for structure. *Personality and Social Psychology Bulletin, 40*(8), 959–971.

Goldenberg, J., Mazursky, D., & Solmon, S. (1999). Toward identifying the inventive templates of new products: A channeled ideation approach. *Journal of Marketing Research, 36*, 200–210.

Gruber, H. E., & Wallace, D. B. (1999). The case study method and evolving systems approach for understanding unique creative people at work. In R. Sternberg (Ed.), *Handbook of creativity* (pp. 93–115). New York, NY: Cambridge University Press.

Haught, C., & Johnson-Laird, P. N. (2003). *Creativity and constraints: The production of novel sentences.* Paper presented at the Proceedings of the 25th Annual Meeting of the Cognitive Science Society.

Heinelt, G. (1974). *Kreative Lehrer/kreative Schüler [Creative Teachers/Creative Students].* Freiburg: Herder.

Horenstein, M. N. (2002). *Design concepts for engineers* (2nd ed.). Upper Saddle River, NJ: Prentice-Hall, Inc.

Ihsen, S., & Brandt, D. (1998). Editorial: Creativity: How to educate and train innovative engineers. *European Journal of Engineering Education, 23*(1), 3–4.

Kozbelt, A., Beghetto, R. A., & Runco, M. A. (2010). Theories of creativity. In J. C. Kaufman & R. J. Sternberg (Eds.), *The Cambridge handbook of creativity* (pp. 20–47). New York, NY: Cambridge University Press.

Mednick, S. A. (1962). The associative basis of creativity. *Psychological Review, 69*, 220–232.

Miller, A. I. (1992). Scientific creativity: A comparative study of Henri Poincare and Albert Einstein. *Creativity Research Journal, 5*(4), 385–414.

Mishra, P., & Henriksen, D. (2013). A NEW approach to defining and measuring creativity: Rethinking technology & creativity in the 21st century. *TechTrends, 57*(5), 10–13.

Mokyr, J. (1990). *The lever of riches: Technological creativity and economic progress.* New York, NY: Oxford University Press.

Moreau, P., & Dahl, D. W. (2005). The impact of constraints on consumers' creativity. *Journal of Consumer Research, 32*(1), 13–22.

Onarheim, B. (2012). Creativity from constraints in engineering design: Lessons learned at Coloplast. *Journal of Engineering Design, 23*(4), 323–336.

Paulhus, D. L., & Williams, K. M. (2002). The dark triad of personality: Narcissism, Machiavellianism, and psychopathy. *Journal of Research in Personality, 36*(6), 556–563.

Plucker, J. A., Beghetto, R. A., & Dow, G. T. (2004). Why isn't creativity more important to educational psychologists? Potentials, pitfalls, and future directions in creativity research. *Educational Psychologist, 39*(2), 83–96.

Plucker, J. A., & Makel, M. C. (2010). Assessment of creativity. In J. C. Kaufman & R. J. Sternberg (Eds.), *The Cambridge handbook of creativity* (pp. 48–73). New York: Cambridge University Press.

Rhodes, M. (1961). An analysis of creativity. *The Phi Delta Kappan, 42*(7), 305–310.

Sagiv, L., Arieli, S., Goldenberg, J., & Goldschmidt, A. (2010). Structure and freedom in creativity: The interplay between externally imposed structure and personal cognitive style. *Journal of Organizational Behavior, 31*(8), 1086–1110.

Sandwith, B. L. (2015). *The influence of structure and personality on creativity in a military context*. University of South Australia, Adelaide, Australia.

Stokes, P. D. (2008). Creativity from constraints: What can we learn from Motherwell? From Modrian? From Klee? *The Journal of Creative Behavior, 42*(4), 223–236.

Taylor, I. A. (1975). An emerging view of creative actions. In I. A. Taylor & J. W. Getzels (Eds.), *Perspectives in creativity* (pp. 297–325). Chicago: Aldine.

Torrance, E. P. (1966). *Torrance tests of creative thinking: Technical norms manual*. Lexington, MA: Personnel Press.

Urban, K. K., & Jellen, H. G. (1996). *Test for Creative Thinking – Drawing Production (TCT-DP)*. Lisse, Netherlands: Swets and Zeitlinger.

16 Creativity in the Domain of Mathematics

Ugur Sak

Center for Research and Practice for High Ability Education, Anadolu University, Turkey

Ülkü Ayvaz

Abant Izzet Baysal University, Turkey

Bilge Bal-Sezerel

Center for Research and Practice for High Ability Education, Anadolu University, Turkey

N. Nazli Özdemir

Center for Research and Practice for High Ability Education, Anadolu University, Turkey

Abstract

In this chapter, we first review mathematical creativity with an emphasis on the nature of novelty in mathematics. We compare mathematical creativity to creativity in other domains, provide examples of novelty, and contrast these to novelty in other domains and explain types of creativity in mathematics based on perspectives in philosophy. All the theoretical perspectives we reviewed led us to synthesize that mathematical creativity involves knowledge production which is either discovery or invention. The chapter also covers pioneers and their contributions to the study of mathematical creativity, such as Polya and Krutetskii. The last part of the chapter includes a review and critique of the assessment of mathematical creativity, such as paper and pencil assessments, observations and interviews, and self-assessment.

Introduction

One of the primary principles of science is to ask the right questions to understand complex phenomena or to discover something unknown. Asking the right question about mathematical creativity will be our first step in this chapter. Is it possible to define creativity before defining and explaining its domain? Let's assume the commonly accepted definition of creativity to be absolutely true. The consensus definition of creativity suggests that creativity is the generation of novel and useful or appropriate ideas or products. Most leading researchers in the field of creativity more or less agree with this definition (e.g., Kaufman, 2016; Runco, 1996, 2004; Sawyer, 2006; Sternberg & Lubart, 1995; Sternberg & Kaufman, 2010; Weisberg, 1993). Indeed, Runco and Jaeger (2012) wrote an article about the standard definition of creativity that has been adopted by many researchers and theorists, a definition that is in accord with the suggested definition above.

However, the nature of the discipline itself and knowledge construction in this discipline can require additional criteria for ideas or products to be considered creative. Indeed, creativity itself is a domain-specific production resulting from domain-specific processes and field-specific expert evaluations (Baer, 1998; Chamberlin & Moon, 2005; Han & Marvin, 2002; Weisberg, 1999). Therefore, any piece of creative production must belong at least to one domain. A creative novel belongs to literature, a creative painting belongs to arts, the invention of a new energy source belongs to science, and a new theory of numbers belongs to mathematics. Undoubtedly, some particular inventions or discoveries require multi-domain-specific work, such as the ones in mathematical physics, genetics, or business. In this chapter, first we describe and discuss mathematical creativity, with an emphasis on the role of domain-specific knowledge in mathematics from the philosophical point of view. Then, we review pioneer studies that have contributed to the study of mathematical creativity. Lastly, we examine assessment methods and strategies used in the measurement of mathematical creativity.

The Nature of Mathematical Creativity

Mathematical creativity is a prime example of domain-specific creativity, just like creativity in the arts, science, and the literature, which includes the joint operation of the domain of mathematics and the creativity process required for it (Peng, Cherng, & Chen, 2013). Thus, defining creativity without describing and defining its domain-specific knowledge can result in incomplete definitions. An understanding of how mathematical knowledge is constructed is essential to understanding mathematical creativity. While many creativity criteria and processes might be the same or similar in most disciplines, how mathematical knowledge is constructed makes mathematical creativity different from creativity in other disciplines.

The construction of mathematical knowledge is influenced by the philosophy of mathematics (Handal, 2009). According to the philosophy of mathematics, absolutism and fallibilism are accepted to be influential paradigms related to knowledge construction in mathematics. These paradigms' views about how mathematical knowledge is constructed differ substantially. Because they differ in their views of knowledge construction, they inevitably diverge in their beliefs about mathematical creativity. For example, absolutists view creativity in mathematics as discovery, whereas fallibilists consider it as invention. Both types of creativity can produce relatively equally important results and essentially new knowledge for us as we do not know or are not aware of the invented or discovered knowledge before. Yet it is important to point out the difference between an invention and a discovery to fully understand the creative process in mathematics. Invention means constructing something new, whereas discovery means finding or uncovering something that already exists but is unknown to us.

According to absolutists, for example, mathematical knowledge is independent of time, place, or people (Ernest, 2002). Mathematical knowledge already exists. What a mathematician does is the discovery of already existing knowledge. This discovery process is not different from some other discoveries, such as the discovery of America, which already existed on Earth before it was "discovered." Even though America was not known by people outside of America, it was of course known by others who made it home for themselves long before Europeans found it. Similarly, as mathematical facts already exist according to absolutists, creativity in mathematics can be considered merely as "discovery" and there is no such thing in mathematics as inventing new knowledge. Mathematical facts and knowledge that are unknown by people on Earth may be well known by others who live on other places and in different times, just like the people of America who found it long before the Europeans.

In contrast to absolutists, fallibilists reason differently about how new knowledge is constructed in mathematics. According to them, mathematical knowledge is not absolute or independent of people, time, or place; rather, it can be changed or improved through building new knowledge (Stanley, 2005). According to this point of view, the construction of mathematical knowledge means inventing further knowledge that did not exist before through the use of existing knowledge. This invention process is continuous and advances mathematics. It is analogous to some inventions in science or technology, such as the invention of telephone by Alexander Graham Bell, who used existing knowledge to invent something unknown before.

Mathematical creativity substantially differs from other types of domain-specific creativity if the construction of mathematical knowledge is accepted as discovery as absolutists claimed (Devlin, 2000). Devlin argued that Euclid's proof of the infinity of prime numbers, which is thought to be one of the highest creative successes in mathematics, is a perfect example of discovery in mathematics rather than invention. Someone else absolutely would have discovered the proof of the infinity of prime numbers if Euclid had not found it; because, as absolutists claimed, knowledge is independent of people and time. That is, the proof already exists in the world of mathematics and just needs to be discovered by a prepared mind; hence, there is nothing new to be invented.

In contrast to mathematics, some domains of creativity do not have to-be-discovered knowledge or products. Consider literature and the arts, for example. Hamlet would not have been written if Shakespeare had not lived (Devlin, 2000). Indeed, even if Shakespeare lived but a century earlier or later, Hamlet still would not have existed because the creation of Hamlet depends not only on the existence of Shakespeare (person) but also on time and place of the creation. Likewise, consider Frida Kahlo, who was a creative visual artist. Her famous works (*The Wounded Deer, Henry Ford Hospital*, and many more) would not have existed if she had not lived. Obviously, someone else could not create these works because the inspiration behind her works was Frida's own life. She explained her work as her own reality (Kettenmann, 1993). A number of her most-acclaimed paintings, such as the

Henry Ford Hospital, portray reproduction failures because Kahlo could not have her own children due to an accident she had had (Herrera, 2002).

If the construction of mathematical knowledge is accepted to be invention, on the other hand, as fallibilists argued, not discovery as absolutists claimed, mathematical creativity would depend to a great extent on person, place, and time and therefore be very much like other types of domain-specific creativity in terms of new knowledge construction or novelty production. This acceptance would also refute our argument so far about mathematical creativity from the absolutists' point of view. Let's consider the proof of Fermat's Last Theorem as an example to carry out an argument whether mathematical creativity is invention or not. In the sixteenth century, Pierre de Fermat wrote a conjecture without its proof on the edge of a page of the book, *Arithmetica*. He also wrote on the page that he knew the proof, but he did not write it because the proof was so long that it could not fit on the page. This conjecture was accepted as Fermat's Last Theorem after it was proved centuries later. Many mathematicians, amazed by Fermat's conjecture, attempted to prove it for three and a half centuries, but they all failed. Selecting, relating, and combining mathematical theorems and knowledge produced after Fermat's time to the late twentieth century, the British mathematician Andrew Wiles came up with the brilliant proof (Kilic, 2012). It included many theorems closely or distantly related to Fermat's conjecture and the entire proof took over 250 pages (Wiles, 1995). Could the theorem have been proved if Wiles did not live? It could have been, undoubtedly, but perhaps not in Wiles's time. That is, the proof of Fermat's Last Theorem was dependent upon the existence of Wiles (person), at least in his time and knowledge construction necessary for the proof that took more than three hundred years of collective work. Both Fermat and Wiles are believed to be geniuses of mathematics. Fermat discovered a mathematical theorem whereas Wiles constructed or invented the proof of Fermat's theorem. That is, mathematical creativity has two faces; one is the discovery of mathematical facts, the other face is the invention of proofs of mathematical facts. These two processes result in the construction of new knowledge in mathematics.

The work and ideas of the famous mathematician Poincare also support the claim that mathematical creativity is inventing. Poincare (1951) emphasized the process of "selection" in his definition of mathematical creativity. His definition emerged as his own observation of his creative process (Haylock, 1984). Because mathematics is a quite comprehensive discipline with lots of theorems, conjectures, proofs, and lemmas, numerous combinations can be created for the production of new knowledge. Combining many theorems and conjectures and choosing useful ones among all these combinations actually means constructing or inventing something new.

Turning back to the comparison of mathematical creativity to domain-specific creativity in other domains, such as literature or the arts, creativity in mathematics is dependent upon person, but in a particular time and place. Without the time restriction, creativity in mathematics would be independent of person. Any particular discovery or invention in mathematics can definitely be made by someone else in a different time period as long as problem-specific knowledge necessary for the discovery is constructed by other mathematicians before the discovery. Nevertheless, it is implausible to claim that any particular creation in literature or the arts can be absolutely made by someone else rather than its original creator, because creation in literature and the arts involve personal emotions, feelings, or beliefs as well that someone else cannot experience the way the original creator did. Mathematical creativity is not necessarily influenced by emotions and feelings. Unquestionably, a young mathematician can admire a genius mathematician; but this admiration cannot be an ingredient of his creative outputs, but only an inspiration to work hard. Therefore, it is a reasonable hypothesis that Fermat's Last Theorem could be proved by someone else even if Wiles did not live or prove it; however, *Henry Ford Hospital* could not be created by someone else rather than Frida Kahlo.

Another fundamental difference between mathematical creativity and other types of creativity refers to the attribute of creative outputs. An invention or discovery in mathematics is not accepted to be a theorem or creative contribution unless it is proved and generalizable. That is why mathematicians always seek formal proofs for their inventions (Davis, Hersh, & Marchisotto, 1995; Poincare, 1958; Schoenfeld, 1994; Sriraman, 2004). However, a theory in the sciences, for example, does not necessarily have to be proven. The essential attribute of a scientific output is falsifiability through experimentation, observation, and data collection. The proof of a mathematical theorem does not necessarily need experimentation or empirical evidence; rather, it is a plausible argument using axioms or established theorems (Polya, 1954b). Likewise, proofs and generalizations are not necessary conditions for creativity in literature, arts, and even some domains of social sciences. A creative poet does not need to use proofs and generalizations for themes or issues in her poems to be acknowledged as a creative writer. A creative use of analogies can be a sufficient condition for poems to be an acclaimed work. Proofs and generalizations in the arts are even more meaningless and less valuable. Undoubtedly, an artist creatively can portray causes and consequences of some circumstances and abstractly present proofs of a cause-effect relationship in her paintings, and this work even might receive high recognition in the world of the arts. As a matter of fact, the proof she uses in her paintings can be a sufficient ingredient for the work to be acknowledged as creative; yet no expert in the arts would claim the use of proofs of ideas in the arts is a necessary condition for a particular piece of art to be evaluated as an acclaimed work. Nevertheless, the use of proofs and generalizations in mathematics is a necessary condition but might be insufficient for creativity. Other conditions might be necessary as well.

Our discussion about creativity in mathematics so far implies that the definition of mathematical creativity is influenced by not only the definition of general creativity but also the relative nature and attribute of mathematical knowledge. Based on our discussion, we simply define Big-C mathematical creativity as the discovery or invention of mathematical conjectures or proofs that are generalizable.

Pioneer Studies in Mathematical Creativity

The history of scientific studies in mathematical creativity could be examined in two episodes like the history of research in general creativity. Guilford's speech at the American Psychological Association in 1950 is widely accepted as the starting point of a new era for creativity research (Urban, 1991). The number of studies on creativity dramatically increased after the 1950s (Piirto, 2004). Influenced by studies in general creativity, scientific studies on mathematical creativity also began to rise in the late 1950s.

Henri Poincare's speech in 1908 is considered to mark the beginning of the first part of the history of studying mathematical creativity. In his speech, Poincare addressed mathematical creation at the French Psychological Society. This speech is one of the most influential talks in mathematical creativity because it is considered to be the first attempt to define and explain the discovery and invention part of mathematical creativity (Liljedahl, 2008). Mathematicians like Henri Poincare and Jacques Hadamard of this period made great contributions to the understanding of mathematical creativity (Pelczer & Rodriguez, 2011; Sriraman, 2004). However, this period is said to be marked mostly by pure mathematicians' views on mathematical creativity (Münz, 2013) and characterized by their retrospections and assumptions. They generally focused on the processes of invention and discovery in mathematics to explore the nature of mathematical creativity, which was believed to be based on inductive reasoning, resulting in discoveries or inventions.

The second period included researchers in education and psychology who began to take part in the study of mathematical creativity. They interlinked creativity, education, psychology, and mathematics with a focus on a number of components of mathematical creativity (e.g., Sheffield, 2009; Silver, 1997; Sriraman & Lee, 2011), its assessment (e.g., Getzels & Jackson, 1961, 1962; Haylock, 1984, 1987; Kim, Cho, & Ahn, 2003; Leikin & Lev, 2013) and its nurturance (e.g., Fetterly, 2010; Nadjafikhah, Yaftian, & Bakhshalizadeh, 2012; Prabhu & Czarnocha, 2013; Shriki, 2010). Among all the researchers of both the first and second periods, Hadamard (1945), Polya (1954a, 1957, 1962), and Krutetskii (1976) made seemingly the most influential pioneering contributions to the study of mathematical creativity. It is rather interesting to note that Hadamard was a pure mathematician of the first period, Polya was both a mathematician and an educator of the first and second periods, and Krutettskii was a psychologist who wrote on mathematical ability and mathematical creativity in the second period.

The Work of Jacques Hadamard

Hadamard's book *The psychology of invention in the mathematical field* (1945) has become one of the most influential works in the history of mathematical creativity (Pelczer & Rodriguez, 2011; Sriraman, 2004). Hadamard's thoughts on mathematical creativity were shaped by not only his own experience but also by Poincare's retrospections and Gestalt psychology. Influenced by Poincare, Hadamard thought mathematical inventions as judgment and selection and further postulated two different kinds of mathematical minds as analysts and creators. The notion of different mathematical minds also has influenced researchers in creativity. Using this model, for example, Sak (2009) developed a test of mathematical ability and found strong evidence for the two kinds of mathematical minds.

Influenced by Gestalt psychology, Hadamard used Wallas's (1926) four-stage model of creativity (preparation, incubation, illumination, and verification) to explain the origin of mathematical inventions. He is the first person who applied Wallas's model in theorizing mathematical creativity. By using both Poincare's ideas and Wallas's model, he elaborated on the role of the conscious and unconscious processes in mathematical creativity. His unique synthesis and amalgamation of Poincare's retrospections and Gestalt psychology together in explaining mathematical creativity is remarkable. According to Hadamard's analysis of the processes that result in mathematical inventions, the first stage of the invention is the preparation during which numerous ideas are examined and various combinations of these ideas are constructed. However, only a few of these combinations can be useful. A mathematician's choice is important to select the most useful combination. Sometimes, mathematical inventions can arise from unconsciousness or insight; yet conscious work for correct choices is required in the first stage. Correct choices may result from judgment, but chance may also be as useful as judgment because a fruitful combination of numerous mathematical elements may be a result of chance. That is, according to Hadamard, chance plays a vital role in inventions in mathematics but mathematical inventions depend mostly on desire and planned efforts.

The incubation, illumination, and verification stages of mathematical discovery put forward by Hadamard are similar to those of Wallas's (1926) four-stage model. Hadamard states that "also there is an unconscious work, could we not admit that nothing at all occurs" (1945, p. 33). Through the analysis of Poincare's discoveries and retrospections, Hadamard claimed that the illumination stage is a bridge between unconscious and conscious mind, because creativity arises in this stage after unconscious works.

Hadamard put forward a conceptual framework to explain the processes of mathematical inventions. His model has inspired researchers to define mathematical creativity (Aiken, 1973; Sheffield, 2013). The model also was supported and validated by research (Cohen, 2002; Liljedahl, 2008; Sriraman, 2004; Vivona, 1998; Wertheimer, 1945). For example, Sriraman (2004) conducted research on the process of mathematical creativity by interviewing mathematicians. His results showed that the processes mathematicians used in a sequential order from viewing a problem for the first time to coming up with a creative solution were similar to those suggested by Hadamard. That is, real creativity in mathematics follows through a number of sequential processes from preparation to verification.

The Work of George Polya

Being a mathematician, Polya (1954a, 1957, 1962) devoted most of his career to the teaching of mathematics. His works focused both on the nature of mathematical creativity and how to foster creative ability in mathematics. He did not conduct any empirical research on mathematical creativity, but his views and models have inspired researchers to develop problem-solving models that could be used not only in mathematics but also in other fields (Bal-Sezerel & Sak, 2013; Leiken,

2009; Sak, 2005, 2011). His views also have become a foundation for definitions and research in mathematical creativity (e.g., Balka, 1974; Sriraman, 2004).

What makes Polya a special case in the study of mathematical creativity are his unique approaches and views on plausible reasoning, demonstrative reasoning, and the use of analogy in creative problem solving in mathematics. Polya (1957) suggested that mathematics has two facets. One is the deductive facet and it is the rigorous side of it. The second facet is more related to the making of mathematics as an inductive science. Similar to his views on the structure of mathematics as a discipline, Polya (1954a, 1954b) proposed two kinds of reasoning. One is demonstrative reasoning. This type of thinking belongs to analysts. The principal function of demonstrative reasoning is to distinguish a proof from a conjecture or a valid argument from an invalid argument. The other type of reasoning is plausible reasoning, which includes induction, analogy, and insight. Polya considered these particular reasoning tools as particular cases of plausible reasoning. The primary function of plausible reasoning is to differentiate a more reasonable conjecture from a less reasonable conjecture by providing logical evidences. This mode of thinking belongs to creators. Indeed, to point out the importance of plausible reasoning in mathematical creativity, Polya (1954a) stated that analogy has the lion's share in many mathematical discoveries. According to him, if a conjecture contains an analogy, the conjecture becomes more valuable.

Another important work of Polya is his model of creative problem solving in mathematics, reviewed in detail in his book *How to solve it* (1957). Polya's problem-solving model consists of four stages: understanding problems, devising plans, carrying out plans, and looking back. Using his model, a problem solver employs plausible reasoning, demonstrative reasoning, and analogies during the solution of a problem. This model is accepted as one of the most influential models of problem solving in mathematics (Lopez-Real, 2006) and has provided a strong framework for both researchers and educators to develop additional problem-solving models that could be used in teaching mathematics. For example, the Selective Problem Solving Model (SPS) that is used to foster creativity in mathematics and other disciplines was developed based on Polya's model (Bal-Sezerel & Sak, 2013; Sak, 2011). Further, Polya's model has influenced researchers to develop instruments to assess mathematical creativity. For example, Kim et al. (2003) used Polya's four stages as a framework to develop mathematical creativity tasks to identify mathematically creative students. They argued that throughout the four stages, students used mathematical thinking, mathematical creativity, mathematical task commitment, and mathematical knowledge to solve problems. In conclusion, it is safe to claim that Polya's ideas on mathematical reasoning and mathematical creativity have become a framework for scientific studies in mathematics.

The Work of Krutetskii

Krutetskii, a Russian psychologist, is well known for his book *The psychology of mathematical abilities in school children* (1976). Krutetskii's research on school children has received recognition because of its originality (Dowker, 2005; Mason &

Johnston-Wilder, 2007). Kilpatrick and Wirszup (1976) suggested two reasons for the high credibility of Krutetskii's research. First, Krutetskii used the Soviet view on mathematical creativity to conduct research for twelve years on individual differences in mathematical ability. Second, Krutetskii used ingenious and varied problems in his studies and led research on problem posing.

Krutetskii believed that ability is a dynamic construct and therefore suggested different methods of assessment in long periods, such as observation and think aloud. He conducted a longitudinal study beginning in 1955 and ending in 1966 to investigate the nature and development of mathematical ability. This study included both experimental and nonexperimental research. During the experimental study, he worked with 201 pupils who solved different problems by thinking out loud to make their thinking observable. Students included very capable, relatively capable, average, and relatively incapable pupils in mathematics as classified by Krutetskii. He found that mathematically promising students used different problem-solving methods and suggested that gifted students see the world through a mathematical lens, "a mathematical cast of life" (pp. 302). Based on his observations, he proposed the observation of problem-solving processes to be used to screen or identify students with high potential in mathematics.

In the qualitative part of the study, Krutetskii surveyed teachers and mathematicians to uncover their views on characteristics of mathematical ability. His research showed that mathematical ability included the ability to generalize, reasoning, keenness of wit, resourcefulness, mathematical memory, ability for abstracting, flexibility of thinking, support by visual means, presence of spatial concepts, ability to transfer from a direct to reverse train of thought, striving for economy of one's mental power, curtailment of reasoning process, and reduced fatigue during mathematical tasks. Based on the results of his research, Krutetskii proposed a number of variables that were thought to be related to creative mathematical ability, such as independent creative mastery, independent formulation of uncompleted mathematical problems, solving problems, invention proofs, and finding original solutions.

Krutetskii (1976) put forward two types of mathematical ability: creative ability and school ability. According to him, there is a strong relationship between mathematical creativity and mathematical ability and this relationship was supported in his twelve-year study. In this study, for example, mathematically gifted students had more creative solutions as measured by Krutetskii for mathematical problems compared to students who had lower performance in mathematics. In conclusion, Krutetskii's work on mathematical creativity is important because his research uncovered essential facets of mathematical ability. Indeed, Kilpatrick and Wirszup (1976) made a comparison between Krutetskii and Piaget to emphasize Krutetskii's contribution to our understanding of mathematical creativity and further argued that Piaget and Krutetskii had the same kind of impact on mathematics education. They maintained that "just as Piaget's notions of intellectual growth have made mathematics educators aware of difference in children's thinking at various ages, so Krutetskii's notions on the structure of mathematical abilities could make them aware of different components of ability and how they might function together" (p. xv).

Assessment of Mathematical Creativity

Consider famous mathematicians such as Carl Friedrich Gauss, the prince of mathematicians[1] (Gindikin, 2007, p. 263) When 20 years old, he wrote the *Disquisitions Arithmeticae* (Gauss, 1966), which still is accepted as a remarkable textbook of the number theory. Further, consider Evariste Galois, who, before the age of 20, discovered that all polynomial equations of the fifth or higher degree could not be solved in radicals (Bewersdorff, 2006; Rothman, 1982). Such biographies show that potential for mathematical creativity can be discovered before adulthood. Research also shows that mathematical geniuses can emerge at early ages. For example, Simonton did historiometric studies on scientists, composers, and mathematicians (1988, 1991, 2004). His findings showed that the creative career at the youngest age is seen in mathematics. Mathematicians begin their creative productivity in their the late 20s and make their best contribution in their the late 30s. Thus, it is easy to identify mathematical prodigies, such as Gauss, by observation and subjective evaluations at early ages. No objective measurement other than expert evaluations might be necessary to identify their prodigious talent. Although a number of mathematical talents emerge at early ages (Balka, 1974), not all creative mathematicians demonstrate their potential for mathematical creativity in childhood. Clearly, non-prodigies need different methods of assessment to be discovered because some mathematical potential at early ages does not transform into visible talents.

Various forms of assessment, including objective and subjective methods, have been used to measure mathematical creativity both at the childhood and adulthood level. The type of assessment, however, slightly differs by age. For example, paper and pencil tests of mathematical creativity have often been used in childhood whereas interview has been the dominant approach in the assessment at the adulthood level. In this section, assessment methods of mathematical creativity are grouped into four categories: paper and pencil assessment, assessment by observation, assessment by interviews, and assessment by self/others.

Assessment by Paper and Pencil

Paper and pencil assessment of mathematical creativity is used most frequently. Assessment of mathematical creativity is usually traditional but there also have been novel approaches. There were only a few studies on the paper-pencil assessment of mathematical creativity before the 1970s (Evans, 1964; Prouse, 1967; Suydam, & Weaver, 1971). After the 1970s, the number of paper-pencil assessments increased gradually. This increase largely comes from studies on general creativity. Balka (1974) initiated the use of divergent-convergent thinking approaches. These approaches were seen as particularly novel and well accepted by researchers in mathematical creativity.

---

[1] "In January 1855, Gauss agreed to pose for a medallion by the artist Heinrich Hesemann. After the scientist's death in February 1855, a medal was prepared from the medallion, by order of the Hannover court. Beneath a bas-relief of Gauss, these words were written: Mathematicorum princeps (Prince of Mathematicians)" (Gindikin, 2007, p. 263).

The fundamental questions of the paper-pencil assessment of mathematical creativity have been which constructs are essential and have predictive potential. Besides divergent and convergent thinking, the skills of problem solving, problem posing, and problem redefinition have been found to be fundamental (Haylock, 1984, 1985, 1987; Mayer, 2013; Pelczer & Rodriguez, 2011). Divergent and convergent thinking can be used as two aspects of creativity, but, in fact, they are not specific mathematical skills required for mathematical creativity. Rather, they can be considered approaches to measure some fundamental skills involved in mathematical creativity. Fluency, for example, can be accepted as the production of many ideas in problem-construction tasks in mathematics. Balka (1974) developed an instrument consisting of six items (four open items and two closed items) to measure mathematical creativity. The instrument included formulation of mathematical hypotheses, determination of patterns, breaking from established mind sets, consideration and evaluation of mathematical ideas, sensing missing parts of situations, and filling in the missing mathematical information and splitting mathematical problems into specific problems, which were determined based on experts' views in order to examine the nature of mathematical creativity. Close-ended items were scored for convergent thinking whereas open-ended problems were scored for fluency.

Similar to Balka's work, Kim et al. (2003) developed the Mathematical Creative Problem Solving Ability Test (MCPSAT) to identify mathematically gifted students from grades 2 to 11. The authors proposed that divergent thinking and convergent thinking are concurrently used in creative problem solving; and therefore they used both divergent and convergent thinking in the construction of the instrument. The MCPSAT is composed of two parts. The first part measures fluency, flexibility, and originality as components of divergent thinking. The second part includes the measurement of intuitive insight, organization of knowledge, space perception and visualization, abstraction, reasoning, generalization and application, and reflective thinking. All the problems in the second part have one correct answer only; therefore, they are supposed to measure convergent thinking. The researchers did a series of studies on the psychometric qualities of the test with over ten thousand students. They found strong evidence of validity and reliability.

Another important skill used by researchers in the assessment of mathematical creativity is problem posing. It is defined as the formation of a new problem (Mamona-Downs, 1993; Van den Heuvel-Panhuizen, Middleton, & Streefland, 1995). Some researchers propose that there is a direct relationship between problem posing and mathematical creativity (Haylock, 1984; Silver 1994, 1997; Singer, Pelczer, & Voica, 2011; Sriraman & Lee, 2011). Having such importance, problem-posing tasks are frequently used in a number of assessments of mathematical creativity. For example, Stoyanova (1997) proposed three frameworks for problem-posing situations defined as ill-structured problems. The first one is the unstructured situation; the problem is ill defined. The second is semi-structured problem posing situations that involve discovery and formulation of a problem proceeded from previous mathematical experience. The last one is structured problem-posing situations in which students pose problems for specific problems or solutions. Stoyanova (1997) developed a problem-posing test based on this model to assess students' problem-posing outputs. The problem-posing tests included three items: structured, semi-structured, and free situations. Five aspects of problem are measured: accuracy, correctness, originality, level of difficulty, and type of the problem. Stoyanova proposed that although the test is a scheme for problem-posing abilities, it could be used for problem-solving abilities as well because problem-posing activities are inseparable parts of problem-solving abilities.

Pittalis, Christou, Mousoulides, and Pitta-Pantazi (2004) proposed a structure model for problem-posing assessment. The model includes four cognitive processes: the editing of problems based on iconic or symbolic stimuli, the filtering of important and critical information, the comprehending of the structural relations in quantitative information, and the translating the quantitative information from one mode to another. Editing problems involves posing problems using information, stories, or prompts provided for students. Filtering information requires students to identify information necessary for posing problems. Comprehending quantitative information is related to the understanding of the structure of problem's quantitative information such as mathematical equations and calculations. Translating quantitative information involves posing problems using diagrams or tables. Researchers tested this model through structural equation modeling and found that the four cognitive processes contribute to students' ability to pose problems, but the filtering and editing cognitive processes were found to be more essential.

Some of mathematical creativity tests include both problem-solving and problem-posing items together. For example, Haylock's (1984) work on mathematical creativity consists of both types. Indeed, Haylock offered a new approach to the assessment of mathematical creativity, using process and product aspects of mathematical creativity. The process aspect is associated with overcoming fixation construct. This includes algorithmic fixation and content universe fixation. The product aspect is associated with divergent production construct. The process (algorithmic fixation, content universe fixation, problem solving, problem posing, and redefinition) and product aspects are measured through the use of numeric and spatial items. Fixation items are evaluated whether students' responses are true or not. Divergent production aspects are evaluated with respect to fluency, flexibility, and originality. In Haylock's study, the fixation component and the divergent component were found to be moderately correlated, meaning that they measure somehow different aspects of mathematical creativity.

Mann (2006, 2009) criticized frequently used assessment approaches of mathematical ability by claiming that they mostly use speed and accuracy of computation. He asserted that mathematical ability includes creativity in problem solving. He believed that mathematical creativity can be efficiently assessed using several instruments. He proposed a regression model to assess mathematical creativity. It was composed of mathematical achievement, attitude towards mathematics, self-perception of creative ability, gender, and teacher perception of mathematical talent and creative ability. He used several instruments in his research with students to measure these variables. He found that all the variables included in the regression accounted for 35 percent of the variance in mathematical creativity. Mathematical achievement was the best predictor of mathematical creativity followed by attitudes towards mathematics, self-perception of creative ability, and gender. He suggested that objective tests of mathematical creativity should be supported with supplementary instruments, such as attitudes and self-perception, in the assessment of mathematical creativity.

Assessment by Observation

Assessment by observation focuses on the behavior of an individual or a group of individuals while they actively engage in mathematical tasks in natural settings, such as classrooms. This type of assessment can include observation of students' problem-solving behaviors and interactions as well as think aloud procedures. Through observations, students' influence on each other and their collective or group creativity could be examined (Leikin & Stanger, 2011), and problem-solving and problem-posing skills, strategies, and reasoning could be directly monitored.

Individual and group observations. A number of attempts have been made to assess mathematical creativity using individual and group observations in school settings. For example, Meyer (1969) observed first-grade students to assess their mathematical creativity using certain criteria determined based on characteristics of creative processes and creative persons identified by mathematicians. These included introducing a goal, identifying a property, seeking a relationship, seeking a generalization, reaching a mathematically elegant product, and modifying the task to assess mathematical creativity. In the study, trained observers monitored and videotaped students' problem-solving processes using the six criteria. The results showed the effectiveness of the six criteria as measure of students' creativity and that mathematical creativity could be assessed through the use of observations.

In another study, Levenson (2011) observed a group of students' problem-solving behaviors during their mathematics courses to assess their mathematical creativity. In this study, group mathematical creativity was analyzed in terms of both the process and the product. Group mathematical creativity included behaviors of both students and teachers and the relationship between individual creativity and group creativity. During observations, closed-ended and open-ended problems were asked and students' interactions with materials, other students, and teachers were recorded and their problem-solving processes and products analyzed. Students' solutions were analyzed for fluency, flexibility, and originality. The number of correct solutions was accepted as a collective fluency score for the group. Although each individual had original ideas to some extent, it was obvious that individual solutions in the group might be the product of a collective process. For instance, when one student put forward an idea, another student expanded it. One of the students evaluated whether the idea was correct or wrong and the teacher clarified the boundaries. That is, collective creativity promoted individual creativity and vice versa. Observations as an assessment of creativity in natural settings can be an excellent tool to monitor the process of creativity as well as the creative products.

The think aloud method consists of asking someone to think out loud when solving a problem (Ericsson & Simon, 1993). As individuals are solving problems while thinking aloud, everything is recorded. Based on transcriptions, experts assess the process and their evaluations are compared. Finally, an extensive analysis is done for each individual (Charters, 2003). The think-aloud method has its roots in introspection. Although introspection methods have had strong critics as being unscientific, the think-aloud method includes a simple verbalization process which Ericsson and Simon (1983) consider as a scientific tool. The use of the think-aloud method in psychological studies has been applied from the 1940s until today. For example, Duncker (1945) examined the problem-solving processes in terms of memory via the think-aloud method. After the 1960s, interest in human cognitive process increased so the number of studies using the think-aloud method also increased (Van Someren, Barnard, & Sandberg, 1994). De Groot (1965) searched chess players' thinking processes using the think-aloud method. Additionally, in the Soviet Union, the Central Committee of the Communist Party prohibited the use of any mental test in 1936 and thereafter. In order to evaluate students' mental processes, Soviet educational psychologists asked students to think aloud while they were solving problems. If they did not respond to it, they got hints and probes. Krutetskii (1976) is one of those who pioneered think-aloud methods in the Soviet Union.

As discussed before, Krutetskii's research (1976) using the think-aloud method revealed essential attributes that lead to mathematical creativity. Krutetskii analyzed the nature and structure of students' mathematical ability based on the observation of students' mental process with the think-aloud method. Krutetskii's research findings showed that there were basic stages of the mental process for mathematical problem solving. Capable students comprehend the essence of problems more easily than less-capable students do. In addition, capable students solve problems in heuristic and elegant ways and they remember the principles of the solution, whereas less-capable students remember only specific details. Krurtetskii's study shows that the think-aloud method is an effective method to figure out the mental activities of students while they are producing creative solutions for problems.

Koichu and Berman (2005) used the think-aloud method to investigate gifted students' conceptions of effectiveness and elegance in problem solving in mathematics. Problem solving is accepted as effective if a solution is obtained easily without an unnecessary effort. Problem solving is considered to be elegant if it is clear, simple, parsimonious, and ingenious. Their research revealed that appreciation of elegance in problem solving comes with particular problem-solving experiences, and that students' appreciation can be developed by engaging in such experiences. They argued that natural observation was the best way to analyze cognitive processes because more and deeper information about the intrinsic part of problem-solving processes can be obtained through observations.

Although many researchers have preferred the think-aloud method, just like other types of observations, it is criticized for being subjective, unreliable, and time consuming (Van Someren et al., 1994). However, if scoring criteria are structured well, the subjectivity of analysis might be reduced (Kantowski, 1977). Triangulation also can be used to increase the validity of the think-aloud assessment (Charters, 2003). Ericsson and Simon (1983, 1993) state that if the items are asked clearly, individuals' cognitive processes can be evaluated objectively. In summary, although a think-aloud approach has certain limitations, it is one of the most effective ways to assess higher-order thinking processes such as mathematical creativity.

Assessment by Interviews

The interview method enables us to obtain both quantitative and qualitative information about one's mathematical creativity. In interviews, whether they are structured or semi-structured, people are asked questions about their problem-solving processes, strategies, thinking, and attitudes and so on (Van Someren et al., 1994). The introspection method is similar to the think-aloud one. People are asked to solve problems with different methods during interviews. Interviewers direct interviewees to creative solutions by giving them hints (Levav-Waynberg & Leikin, 2012). Retrospections and introspections are used as information sources to explore their experiences. In the retrospection method, individuals disclose their experiences with problems they solved before (e.g., Tjoe, 2011) or they evaluate generalizations, abstractions, or problem-finding abilities by adding new parameters to problems they solved before (e.g., Singer et al., 2011). People's characteristics and dispositions for mathematical creativity can be discovered through the use of retrospections (Singer et al., 2011; Sriraman, 2004). For example, the famous mathematician Poincare's retrospections were used extensively to conceptualize mathematical creativity (Hadamard, 1945; Sak, 2009). However, this method could be unreliable in many cases because it is not easy to remember what exactly an inventor does during the solution of a problem in the past.

An example of research using the interview method grounded in retrospection to assess mathematical creativity is a study carried out by Sriraman (2004). He interviewed five mathematicians to explore the nature of mathematical creativity and problem-solving processes. He developed a structured interview instrument by modifying *L'Enseigement Mathematique*. The interviews included how mathematicians create mathematics. In this study, Sriraman used analytic induction to analyze transcriptions of interviews. As mentioned previously, the findings showed that the process of mathematical creativity followed the preparation, incubation, illumination, and verification processes. That is, it was possible to assess the cognitive processes of mathematical inventions through retrospective interviews. Also revealed in the study were social interaction, imagery, heuristics, intuition, and proof as the common characteristics of mathematical creativity. In conclusion, interviews are an effective method to answer how an individual invents or comes up with creative solutions in mathematics.

Self-Assessment and Assessment by Others

People can be assessed by themselves or others regarding their mathematical creativity. Indeed, self-assessment and assessment by others have been used to assess creativity since the early 1970s (Casakin & Kreitler, 2006). Since then, researchers (e.g., Khatena & Torrance, 1976; Schaefer & Bridges, 1970) developed different tools to assess self-perception of creativity. Rating scales, checklists, and questionnaires are the most frequently used instruments to assess people's perceptions of their own or others' creativity. These types of assessment of creativity can range from one question to a variety of questions (Kaufman, Plucker, & Baer, 2008). These instruments measure either creativity characteristics, behaviors, habits, and attitudes of the person or characteristics of the product.

Sheffield (2000) developed a rubric to assess children's mathematical creativity. It can be used by teachers and students to evaluate students' or their peers' mathematical creativity. The instrument included such items as depth of understanding (the extent to which core concepts are explored and developed); fluency (number of different correct answers, methods of solution, or new questions formulated); flexibility (the number of different categories of answers, methods, or questions); originality (solutions, methods, or questions are unique and show insight); quality of expression of thinking (including charts, graphs, drawings, models, equations, and words); generalizations and reasoning (patterns that are noted, hypothesized about, and verified); and extension (related questions to be explored, involving why and what if) (p. 419). Each item is scored by awarding 1 to 4 points. Sheffield states that mathematicians use this type of criteria when they compare and contrast their peers' creativity in mathematics, and further claims that young children's mathematical creativity also can be assessed using these aspects of mathematical creativity.

Modifying Carlton's work (1959) on the assessment of mathematical creativity, Leu and Chiu (2015) developed the Creative Behaviors in Mathematics Questionnaire (CBMQ). The original CBMQ was developed by Carlton in 1959 using characteristics of creative mathematicians in history and potentially creative thinkers and gifted children in mathematics. Carlton identified twenty-one characteristics of creative behaviors in mathematics and included each characteristic as an item in the questionnaire. Leu and Chiu (2015) carried out research on the validity of the questionnaire and found five behaviors to be key behaviors for mathematical creativity: representation invention, component association, outcome improvement, alternative curiosity, and space imagination.

Livne and Milgram (2000) developed a questionnaire of out-of-school activities to assess creative ability in mathematics. Firstly, they developed a mapping sentence to define the conceptual components of creative ability in mathematics at four hierarchical levels. The questionnaire consisted of sixty-one self-report items in a random order, with each item representing one level out of the four levels of creative talent in nonacademic activities and accomplishments in mathematics. The first level is related to unchallenging activities in mathematics. The second, or mild, level includes partly unchallenging activities in mathematics. It represents convergent thinking and results in a popular and high quality product. It is more extrinsically than intrinsically motivated, reflects mild task commitment and mild initiative, and is performed with a mild degree of intensity. The third, or moderate, level includes partly challenging activities in mathematics. It uses more unusual but low-quality divergent thinking and results in an unusual but low-quality product. However, the low quality of products probably comes from the nature of activities. It is more intrinsically than extrinsically motivated, and reflects a moderate level of task commitment, initiative, and intensity. The fourth or profound level consists of challenging activities in mathematics. It uses mainly unusual and high-quality divergent thinking and results in an unusual and high-quality product. Livne and Milgram carried out research on the questionnaire and found evidence for its validity and reliability. Further research about the questionnaire has not been reported yet.

Self-assessment of creativity and assessment by others have been criticized because they are rather subjective measurements. They might possess high levels of reliability but are questioned for lacking strong validity evidence. This mode of assessment is believed to be influenced by beliefs, stereotypes, bias, and expectations (Siegle & Powell, 2004). Although self-assessments are criticized for being subjective, they frequently have been used in research and will continue to contribute to the assessment of creativity because creativity itself is a subjective construct. In other words, it is contextual. For example, a new product or an idea does not have the same value for all people or cultures.

Conclusions

Mathematical creativity can be studied from multiple perspectives as mathematics is a highly domain-specific discipline. Although mathematical creativity differs from other types of creativity, it is not different from most scientific disciplines in the making of knowledge. For example, a mathematician has to make conjectures about a mathematical theorem before he proves it, just like a scientist who hypothesizes about some scientific phenomenon. Then, he conjectures the method of proof before he works out the details (Polya, 1962). In the sciences, a scientist finds or develops methods for data collection, such as experimentation. The result of a mathematical discovery or invention is a generalization. That is, a mathematical invention should be applicable to a wide range of problems. Similarly, a scientific theory must be generalizable for a variety of cases.

One of the most shared traits among creative mathematicians is the use of analogous problems that simulate new insights in their problem solving (Sriraman, 2004). However, most assessments of mathematical creativity lack this component of mathematical creativity. Laplace expressed that the principal instruments for discoveries in mathematics are induction and analogy (as cited in Polya, 1954a). According to Polya's point of view, there are almost no problems unrelated to previously solved problems in mathematics because mathematical knowledge is stored in the form of formerly proven theorems. When people encounter a new problem, they use experience they gain while they solve a similar problem. They can use the results or the methods of the formerly solved problem. In the case of problems to relate to a problem, people usually seek for relations by analogy. Although analogical thinking is frequently used in many multiple-choice tests to measure mathematical ability or reasoning (McCallum & Bracken, 2005; Preckel, Goez, Pekrun, & Kleine, 2008; Sternberg, Kaufman, & Grigorenko, 2008), creativity researchers have not made use of analogical thinking in their design of creativity tests. Indeed, most paper and pencil tests of mathematical creativity have focused on divergent thinking only. However, analogical thinking in mathematics can be measured within the framework of divergent thinking as well. For example, people can generate many analogies for a mathematical problem. The number of analogies generated could be accepted as fluency, the conceptual categories of analogies could be considered flexibility, and the rarity of analogies could represent originality.

Retrospections and introspections of creative mathematicians are invaluable sources for understanding the creativity process in mathematics (Leikin & Lev, 2013; Sriraman, 2004; Tjoe, 2011). There is definitely a need for more qualitative research on mathematicians' experiences about their discoveries to understand the underlying processes of mathematical creativity. Creativity researchers in mathematics have stressed problem solving and problem construction in the process of creativity but overlooked other important processes of mathematical creativity. Among such processes repeatedly pointed out by creative mathematicians are selection and selective attention (Hadamard, 1945; Poincare, 1952; Polya, 1954a). Indeed, Poincare (1952) asserted that discovery is *discernment* or *choice*. These processes can be the critical components of problem solving in mathematics, particularly in the case of ill-structured problems (Sak, 2009). As creativity researchers, we need to scrutinize how selection contributes to the creativity process and subsequently develop instruments to measure the selection process or ability as a component of creativity.

References

Aiken, L. R. (1973). Ability and creativity in mathematics. *Review of Educational Research, 43*(4), 405–432.

Baer, J. (1998). The case for domain specificity of creativity. *Creativity Research Journal, 11*, 173–177.

Bal-Sezerel, B., & Sak, U. (2013). The Selective Problem Solving Model (SPS) and its social validity in solving mathematical problems. *International Journal of Problem Solving and Creativity, 23*(1), 71–86.

Balka, D. S. (1974). *The development of an instrument to measure creative ability in mathematics.* (Unpublished doctoral dissertation). Edith University of Missouri, USA.

Bewersdorff, J. (2006). *Galois theory for beginners: A historical perspective.* Rhode Island: American Mathematical Society.

Carlton, L. V. (1959). *An analysis of the educational concepts of fourteen outstanding mathematicians, 1790–1940, in the areas of mental growth and development, creative thinking and symbolism and meaning.* (Unpublished doctoral dissertation). IL: Northwestern University, USA.

Casakin, H., & Kreitler, S. (2006). Self-assessment of creativity: Implications for design education. In *DS 38: Proceedings of E&DPE 2006, The 8th International Conference on Engineering and Product Design Education* (pp. 1–6). Salzburg, Austria.

Chamberlin, S. A., & Moon, S. M. (2005). Model-eliciting activities as tool to develop and identify creativity gifted mathematicians. *Journal of Secondary Gifted Education, 17*(1), 37–47.

Charters, E. (2003). The use of think-aloud methods in qualitative research an introduction to think-aloud methods. *Brock Education, 12*(2), 68–82.

Cohen, P. (2002). The discovery of forcing. *Rocky Mountain Journal of Mathematics, 32*(4), 1071–1100.

Davis, P. J., Hersh, R., & Marchisotto, E. A. (1995). *The mathematical experience: Study edition*. Boston: Birkhäuser.

De Groot, A. D. (1965). *Thought and choice in chess*. The Hague: Mouton Publishers.

Devlin, K. (2000). *The math gene: How mathematical thinking evolved and why numbers are like gossip*. New York: Basic Books.

Dowker, A. (2005). *Individual differences in arithmetic: Implications for psychology, neuroscience and education*. New York: Psychology Press.

Duncker, K. (1945). On problem solving. *Psychological Monographs, 58*(5), 1–113.

Ericsson, K. A., & Simon, H. A. (1983). *Verbal protocol analysis*. Cambridge: The MIT Press.

Ericsson, K. A., & Simon, H. A. (1993). *Protocol analysis*. Cambridge: The MIT Press.

Ernest, P. (2002). *The philosophy of mathematics education*. Briston, PA: The Falmer Press.

Evans, E. W. (1964). *Measuring the ability of students to respond in creative mathematical situations at the late elementary and early junior high school level*. (Unpublished doctoral dissertation). University of Michigan, USA.

Fetterly, J. M. (2010). *An exploratory study of the use of a problem-posing approach on pre-service elementary education teachers' mathematical creativity, beliefs, and anxiety*. (Unpublished doctoral dissertation). Florida State University, USA.

Gauss, C. F. (1966). *Disquisitiones arithmeticae* (Vol. 157). US: Yale University Press.

Getzels, J. W., & Jackson, P. W. (1961). Family environment and cognitive style: A study of the sources of highly intelligent and of highly creative adolescents. *American Sociological Review, 26*(3), 351–359.

Getzels, J. W., & Jackson, P. W. (1962). Creativity and intelligence: Explorations with gifted students. *American Journal of Sociology, 68*(2), 278–279.

Gindikin, S. (2007). *Tales of mathematicians and physicists*. NY: Springer Science & Business Media.

Hadamard, J. (1945). *The psychology of invention in the mathematical field*. New York: Dover Publications.

Han, K. S., & Marvin, C. (2002). Multiple creativities? Investigating domain specificity of creativity in young children. *Gifted Child Quarterly, 46*(2), 98–109.

Handal, B. (2009). Philosophies and pedagogies of mathematics. *Elementary Education Online, 8*(1), 1–6.

Haylock, D. W. (1984). *Aspects of mathematical creativity in children aged 11–12*. (Unpublished doctoral dissertation). Chelsea Collage, University of London, England.

Haylock, D. W. (1985). Conflicts in the assessment and encouragement of mathematical creativity in schoolchildren. *International Journal of Mathematical Education in Science and Technology, 16*(4), 547–553.

Haylock, D. W. (1987). A framework for assessing mathematical creativity in school children. *Educational Studies in Mathematics, 18*,1, 59–74.

Herrera, H. (2002). *Frida: A biography of Frida Kahlo*. New York: HarperCollins.

Kantowski, M. G. (1977). Processes involved in mathematical problem solving. *Journal for Research in Mathematics Education, 8*(3), 163–180.

Kaufman, J. C., Plucker, J. A., & Baer, J. (2008). *Essentials of creativity assessment*. New Jersey: John Wiley & Sons.

Kaufman, J. C. (2016). *Creativity 101* (2nd edn.). New York: Springer Publishing Company.

Kettenmann, A. (1993). *Frida Kahlo: Pain and passion*. Köln: Taschen GmbH.

Khatena, J., & Torrance, E. P. (1976). *Manual for Khatena-Torrance creative perception inventory*. Chicago: Stoelting Company.

Kilic, S. (2012). Scientific art/artistic science. *The Journal of Academic Social Science Studies, 5*(1), 193–203.

Kilpatrick, J., & Wirszup, I. (1976). *The psychology of mathematical abilities in schoolchildren*. London: The University of Chicago Press.

Kim, H., Cho, S., & Ahn, C. (2003). Development of mathematical creative problem solving ability test for identification of the gifted in math. *Gifted Education International, 18*(2), 164–174.

Koichu, B., & Berman, A. (2005). When do gifted high school students use geometry to solve geometry problems? *The Journal of Secondary Gifted Education, 16*(4), 168–179.

Krutetskii, V. A. (1976). *The psychology of mathematical abilities in school children*. London: The University of Chicago Press.

Leikin, R. (2009). Exploring mathematical creativity using multiple solution tasks. In R. Leikin, A. Berman, & B. Koichu (Eds.), *Creativity in mathematics and the education of gifted students* (pp. 129–145). Rotterdam: Sense Publishers.

Leikin, R., & Stanger, O. (2011). Teachers' images of gifted students and the roles assigned to them in heterogeneous mathematics classes. In B. Sriraman & K. E. Lee (Eds.), *The elements of creativity and giftedness in mathematics* (pp. 1–4). Rotterdam: Sense Publishers.

Leikin, R., & Lev, M. (2013). Mathematical creativity in generally gifted and mathematically excelling adolescents: What makes the difference? *ZDM Mathematics Education, 45*(2), 183–197.

Leu, Y. C., & Chiu, M. S. (2015). Creative behaviours in mathematics: Relationships with abilities, demographics, affects and gifted behaviours. *Thinking Skills and Creativity, 16*, 40–50.

Levav-Waynberg, A., & Leikin, R. (2012). The role of multiple solution tasks in developing knowledge and creativity in geometry. *Journal of Mathematical Behavior, 31*, 73–90.

Levenson, E. (2011). Exploring collective mathematical creativity in elementary school. *Journal of Creative Behavior, 45*(3), 215–234.

Liljedahl, P. (2008). *Mathematical creativity: In the words of the creators*. In Proceedings of the 5th International Conference on Creativity in Mathematics and the Education of Gifted Students, Israel, 24–28 February 2008 (pp. 153–159).

Livne, N. L., & Milgram, R. M. (2000). Assessing four levels of creative mathematical ability in Israeli adolescents utilizing out-of-school activities: A circular three-stage technique. *Roeper Review, 22*(2), 111–116.

Lopez-Real, F. (2006). A new look at a Polya problem. *Mathematics Teaching, 196*, 12–16.

Mamona-Downs, J. (1993). On analyzing problem posing. In *Proceedings of the 17th International Conference for the Psychology of Mathematics Education, Tsukuba, Japan, 18–23 July 1993* (Vol. 3, pp. 41–47).

Mann, E. L. (2006). Creativity: The essence of mathematics. *Journal for the Education of the Gifted, 30*(2), 236–260.

Mann, E. L. (2009). The search for mathematical creativity: Identifying creative potential in middle school students. *Creativity Research Journal, 21*(4), 338–348.

Mason, J., & Johnston-Wilder, S. (2007). *Designing and using mathematical tasks*. London: Tarquin Pubns.

Mayer, R. E. (2013). Implications of cognitive psychology for instruction in mathematical problem solving. In E. A. Silver (Ed.), *Teaching and learning mathematical problem solving: Multiple research perspectives* (pp. 123–138). New York: Routledge.

McCallum, R. S., & Bracken, B. (2005). The universal nonverbal intelligence test: A multidimensional measure of intelligence. In D. P. Flanagan & P. L. Harrison (Eds.), *Contemporary intellectual assessment: Theories, test, and assessment* (pp. 425–440). New York: The Guilford Press.

Meyer, R. W. (1969). *The identification and encouragement of mathematical creativity in first grade students.* (Unpublished doctoral dissertation). University of Wisconsin, Madison.

Münz, M. (2013). The elements of mathematical creativity and the function of the attachment style in early childhood. In *Online proceedings of the POEM conference,* (pp. 1–11).

Nadjafikhah, M., Yaftian, N., & Bakhshalizadeh, S. (2012). Mathematical creativity: Some definitions and characteristics. *Procedia-Social and Behavioral Sciences, 31,* 285–291.

Pelczer, I., & Rodriguez F. G. (2011). Creativity assessment in school settings through problem posing tasks. *The Montana Mathematics Enthusiast, 8,* 383–398.

Peng, S. L., Cherng, B. L., & Chen, H. C. (2013). The effects of classroom goal structures on the creativity of junior high school students. *Educational Psychology, 33*(5), 540–560.

Piirto, J. (2004). *Understanding creativity.* Scottsdale: Great Potential Press.

Pittalis, M., Christou, C., Mousoulides, N., & Pitta-Pantazi, D. (2004). A structural model for problem posing. In *Proceedings of the 28th Conference of the International Group for the Psychology of Mathematics Education* (Vol. 4, pp. 49–56). Bergen, Norway.

Polya, D. (1954a). *Induction and analogy in mathematics.* Princeton, NJ: Princeton University Press.

Polya, D. (1954b). *Patterns of plausible inference.* Princeton, NJ: Princeton University Press.

Polya, D. (1957). *How to solve it* (2nd ed.). NJ: Princeton University Press.

Polya, D. (1962). *Mathematical discovery.* New York: John Wiley & Sons, Inc.

Poincare, H. (1951). *Bilim ve metot [Science and method].* (H. R. Atademir & S. Ölçen, Trans.). İstanbul: Milli Eğitim Basımevi.

Poincare, H. (1952). *Science and hypothesis.* New York: The Modern Library.

Poincare, H. (1958). *The value of science.* New York: The Modern Library.

Prabhu, V., & Czarnocha, B. (2013). Democratizing mathematical creativity through Koestler's Bisociation Theory. *Mathematics Teaching-Research Journal Online, 6*(2), 33–46.

Preckel, F., Goez, T., Pekrun, R., & Kleine, M. (2008). Self-concept, interest, and motivation in mathematics gender differences in gifted and average-ability students: Comparing girls' and boys' achievement. *Gifted Child Quarterly, 52*(2), 146–159.

Prouse, H. L. (1967). Creativity in school mathematics. *The Mathematics Teacher, 60,* 876–879.

Rothman, T. (1982). Genius and biographers: The fictionalization of Evariste Galois. *American Mathematical Monthly, 89*(2), 84–106.

Runco, M. A. (1996). Personal creativity: Definition and developmental issues. *New Directions for Child Development, 72,* 3–30

Runco, M. A. (2004). Creativity. *Annual Review of Psychology, 55,* 657–687.

Runco, M. A., & Jaeger, G. J. (2012). The standard definition of creativity. *Creativity Research Journal, 24*(1), 92–96.

Sak, U. (2005). *M³: The three-mathematical minds model for the identification of mathematically gifted students.* (Unpublished doctoral dissertation). University of Arizona, USA.

Sak, U. (2009). Test of the three-mathematical minds (M^3) for the identification of mathematically gifted students. *Roeper Review, 31*, 53–67.

Sak, U. (2011). Selective Problem Solving (SPS): A model for teaching creative problem solving. *Gifted Education International, 27*(3), 349–357.

Sawyer, R. K. (2006). *Explaining creativity.* New York: Oxford University Press.

Schaefer, C. E., & Bridges, C. I. (1970). Development of a creativity attitude survey for children. *Perceptual and Motor Skills, 31*(3), 861–862.

Schoenfeld, A. H. (1994). What do we know about mathematics curricula? *Journal of Mathematical Behavior, 13*, 55–80.

Sheffield, L. J. (2000). Creating and developing promising young mathematicians. *Teaching Children Mathematics, 6*(6), 416–419.

Sheffield, L. J. (2009). Developing mathematical creativity – questions may be the answer. In R. Leikin, A. Berman, & B. Koichu (Eds.), *Creativity in mathematics and the education of gifted students* (pp. 87–100). Rotterdam: Sense Publishers.

Sheffield, L. J. (2013). Creativity and school mathematics: Some modest observations. *ZDM Mathematics Education, 45*(2), 325–332.

Shriki, A. (2010). Working like real mathematicians: Developing prospective teachers' awareness of mathematical creativity through generating new concepts. *Educational Studies in Mathematics, 73*(2), 159–179.

Siegle, D., & Powell, T. (2004). Exploring teacher biases when nominating students for gifted programs. *Gifted Child Quarterly, 48*(1), 21–29.

Silver, E. A. (1994). On mathematical problem solving. *For the Learning of Mathematics, 14*(1), 19–28.

Silver, E. A. (1997). Fostering creativity through instruction rich in mathematical problem solving and problem posing. *ZDM Mathematics Education, 29*(3), 75–80.

Simonton, D. K. (1988). Age and outstanding achievement: What do we know after a century of research? *Psychological Bulletin, 104*(2), 251–267.

Simonton, D. K. (1991). Career landmarks in science: Individual differences and interdisciplinary contrasts. *Developmental Psychology, 27*(1), 119–130.

Simonton, D. K. (2004). *Creativity in science: Chance, logic, genius, and zeitgeist.* New York: Cambridge University Press.

Singer, F. M., Pelczer, I., & Voica, C. (2011). Problem posing and modification as a criterion of mathematical creativity. In *Proceedings of the 7th Conference of the European Society for Research in Mathematics Education (CERME 7)* (pp. 1133–1142). Rzeszow, Poland.

Sriraman, B. (2004). The characteristics of mathematical creativity. *The Mathematics Educator, 14*, 19–24.

Sriraman, B., & Lee, K. E. (2011). What are the elements of giftedness and creativity in mathematics? In B. Sriraman & K. E. Lee (Eds.), *The elements of creativity and giftedness in mathematics* (pp. 1–4). Rotterdam: Sense Publishers.

Stanley, J. (2005). Fallibilism and concessive knowledge attributions. *Analysis, 65*(2), 126–131.

Sternberg, R. J., & Lubart, T. I. (1995). *Defying the crowd: Cultivating creativity in a culture of conformity.* New York: The Free Press.

Sternberg, R. J., Kaufman, J. C., & Grigorenko, E. L. (2008). *Applied intelligence*. New York: Cambridge University Press.

Sternberg, R. J., & Kaufman, J. C. (2010). Constrains on creativity: Obvious and not so obvious. In J. C. Kaufman & R. J. Sternberg (Eds.), *The Cambridge handbook of creativity* (pp. 467–482). New York: Cambridge University Press.

Stoyanova, E. N. (1997). *Extending and exploring students' problem solving via problem posing: A study of years 8 and 9 students involved in Mathematics Challenge and Enrichment Stages of Euler Enrichment Program for Young Australians.* (Unpublished doctoral dissertation). Edith Cowan University, Australia.

Suydam, M. N., & Weaver, J. F. (1971). Research on mathematics education (K-12) reported in 1970. *Journal for Research in Mathematics Education, 2*(4), pp. 257–298.

Tjoe, H. H. (2011). *Which approaches do students prefer? Analyzing the mathematical problem solving behavior of mathematically gifted students.* (Unpublished doctoral dissertation). Columbia University, USA.

Urban, K. K. (1991). Recent trends in creativity research and theory in Western Europe. *European Journal of High Ability, 1*(1), 99–113.

Van den Heuvel-Panhuizen, M., Middleton, J. A., & Streefland, L. (1995). Student-generated problems: Easy and difficult problems on percentage. *For the Learning of Mathematics, 15*(3), 21–27.

Van Someren, M. W., Barnard, Y. F., & Sandberg, J. A. (1994). *The think aloud method: A practical guide to modelling cognitive processes*. London: Academic Press.

Vivona, R. F. (1998). *Toward a theory of mathematical creativity.* (Unpublished doctoral dissertation). Union Institute, USA.

Wallas, G. (1926). *The art of thought*. New York: Harcourt, Brace and Company.

Weisberg, R. W. (1993). *Creativity: Understanding innovation in problem solving, science, invention, and the arts*. New Jersey: Wiley.

Weisberg, R. W. (1999). Creativity and knowledge: A challenge to theories. In R. J. Sternberg (Ed.), *Handbook of creativity* (pp. 226–250). New York: Cambridge University Press.

Wiles, A. (1995). Modular eliptic curves and Fermat's last theorem. *Annals of Mathematics, 142*, 443–551.

Wertheimer, M. (1945). *Productive thinking*. New York: Harper.

17 Creativity Within Computer Science

Paul Joseph Barnett

Neag School of Education University of Connecticut

Ralf Romeike

Friedrich-Alexander University Erlangen-Nürnberg

Abstract

This chapter focuses on creativity within computer science. We examine what those within the field have said about creativity and how it relates to computer science and to computer scientists. We also look at the results of creativity in the form of products of computer science. We often reference programing both directly and indirectly, but we also address areas of computer science beyond programing whenever possible. We address creativity from the perspective of those within the field. We discuss examples of how creativity in computer science is implemented in areas such as coding, open-source projects, video games, augmented reality, and artificial intelligence. We look at creativity in computer science education as both a method of instruction as well as a desired outcome. We then look at malevolent creativity and how different types of hackers use creativity with either malevolent or benevolent intent.

In this chapter our focus is on creativity within computer science. Our goal is to address creativity in as many areas of computer science as is feasible for a book chapter. We will take a direct approach, examining what those within the field have said about creativity and how it relates to computer science and to computer scientists. At times, however, it is necessary to look at the results of creativity. We acknowledge that there is a difference between creativity in the process and creativity in the product (Rhodes, 1961). There is much creativity in the process of computer science that has yet to be studied in detail or may remain unknown to anyone other than those who were participants. It is common when discussing computer science to use a narrow focus and emphasize programing. We will often reference programing both directly and indirectly, but we also address areas of computer science beyond programing whenever possible.

We start with an overview of the field of computer science and clarify the areas we will and will not be addressing in the chapter. We then define the terms most pertinent to this chapter including computer science, creativity, and creativity within computer science. We address creativity from the perspective of those within the field. We discuss examples of how creativity in computer science is implemented in current and developing areas such as coding, open-source projects, video games, augmented reality, and artificial intelligence. Then we shift focus slightly toward creativity in computer science education as both a method of instruction as well as a desired outcome. We conclude the chapter by looking at malevolent creativity and how different types of hackers use creativity with either malevolent or benevolent intent.

Overview

Computer science is a broad field, and it would be foolhardy to attempt to address all of its areas and how creativity relates to each in a chapter of a single book. For example, an entire edited book recently came out devoted solely to the interaction of video games and creativity (Green & Kaufman, 2015). Instead, the goal of this chapter is to focus on creativity within computer science itself. The purpose of this chapter is *not*, therefore, to address how computer science affects creativity or the creative process, or how computers and technology have changed, advanced, or otherwise affected creativity or creative endeavors such as graphic arts, movies, or music.

We will also not be addressing how creativity from areas outside of computer sciences has had an effect, either directly or indirectly, on the advancement of technology. For example, the genre of science fiction has provided the inspiration for advancements and innovations in computer science, often attributable to a specific book or film such as the tablet devices on *2001: A Space Odyssey*, or one of the founders of the augmented reality movement being inspired by the *Terminator* (London, 2013). Our intent for this chapter is to give readers the opportunity to see how prevalent creativity is within computer science and how incredibly vital it is to the continued growth and development of the field.

Defining Creativity in Computer Science

Computer Science: Art? Science? Both

The first undertaking in this chapter should be to define the main terms we intend to address, namely *computer science* and *creativity*. On the surface this seems a modest task that requires little more than a glance at a dictionary. Unfortunately, it is not that simple. Just as creativity papers often do not actually define the topic (Plucker, Beghetto, & Dow, 2004), many works on computer science do not provide explicit definitions. The question is broader, however: *Is computer science a science or an art?* Although this chapter appears in the Sciences part of the book, our question is not as straightforward as it may appear.

In 1959, the editorial board of the Association for Computing Machinery (ACM) encouraged its members to submit papers that were reflective of the diversity and rapid growth in the computing field. In doing so they made a point to state, "It is realized that if computer programming is to become an important part of computer research and development a transition of programming from an art to a disciplined science must be effected" (Bauer, Juncosa, & Perlis, 1959, p. 122). Art and programing are not two terms that someone outside the field might consider related, yet within the field of computer science they are inextricably linked. Fifteen years later, renowned computer scientist Donald Knuth addressed the issue as he accepted the A.M. Turing Award. He first explained the origins of the two words, "art" and "science" and how their meanings have evolved and shifted throughout history, even overlapping at times until

> the words took on more and more independent meaning, "science" being used to stand for knowledge, and "art" for the application of knowledge. Thus, the science of astronomy was the basis for the art of navigation. The situation was almost exactly like the way in which we now distinguish between "science" and "engineering." ... Computer programming is by now *both* a science and an art, and that the two aspects nicely complement each other. (Knuth, 1974, pp. 668–669)

Of course, not all computer scientists see the distinction as being complementary sides of the same world. For some it serves as a clear demarcation between the mathematical and engineering sides (Denning, 2005). In his book *Hackers & painters: Big ideas from the Computer Age*, Paul Graham succinctly expressed his objections:

> I've never liked the term "computer science." The main reason I don't like it is that there's no such thing. Computer science is a grab bag of tenuously related areas thrown together by an accident of history ... It's as if mathematicians, physicists, and architects all had to be in the same department. ... Bundling all these different types of work together in one department may be convenient administratively, but it's confusing intellectually. (2004, pp. 18–19)

In 1989, an ACM task force on the core of computer science curricula, in cooperation with the Institute of Electrical and Electronics Engineers (IEEE) Computer Society, issued a report where the division of the field was not only addressed, but embraced:

> As ACM enters its 42nd year, an old debate continues. Is computer science a science? ... We immediately extend our task to encompass both computer science and computer engineering ... computer science focuses on analysis and abstraction, computer engineering on abstraction and design. We use the phrase 'discipline of computing' here to embrace all of computer science and engineering. (Comer et al. 1989, p. 64)

The report goes on to define three paradigms of computer science: theory, abstraction (modeling), and engineering. Establishing the three paradigms may seem like an endorsement for further separation of the field, but the authors of the report acknowledge the individuals that work under each paradigm and how they approach their work. For each paradigm, the authors outline a separate, though similar, workflow process derived from the scientific method (hypothesis, tests, analysis). They then argue that computer science is a unified field. "Many debates about the relative merits of mathematics, science, and engineering implicitly rely on an assumption that one of the three processes (theory, abstraction, or design) is the most fundamental. However, a closer examination reveals that, in computing, the three processes so intricately intertwine that it is irrational to say that any one is the most fundamental" (Comer et al. 1989, p. 64).

There are subtle lines of division in every industry and distinctions between concentrations may be lost to laypeople. The disagreement within the field illustrates the complexity of the topic, even for experts. Addressing the debate doesn't change the field of computer science, nor does it help resolve the disagreement. Despite its remarkable growth and tremendous success, the field is relatively young; like creativity (Guilford, 1950), it was established as a full discipline in the 1950s (Fein, 1959). Even in such a short time, it encompasses multiple concentrations that range from theoretical to applied; each one has its own nuanced relationship with creativity.

Because of the general public's lack of exposure to and knowledge or understanding of computer science, the layperson may not realize the extent to which creativity is utilized. Indeed, most people gravitate toward the arts when thinking of a creative person (Glăveanu, 2014; Kaufman & Baer, 2004). Yet a recurring pattern in the computer science literature is the assertion that creativity is vital to every possible aspect of the discipline (Gu & Tong, 2004; Leach & Ayers, 2005; Saunders & Thagard, 2005). Creativity is not limited to one type of computer scientist or one area; it permeates every part of the field.

Defining Computer Science

> The fundamental question underlying all of computing is, "What can be (efficiently) automated?"
>
> (Comer et al. 1989, p. 65)

The diversity within the field of computer science makes it challenging to define. Placing it within the hierarchical structure of the other major scientific disciplines based on its perceived "hardness" or "softness" (Simonton, 2009) seems equally problematic (Tang, Baer, & Kaufman, 2015). There are many definitions for the field of computer science, such as, "the science that deals with the theory and methods of processing information in digital computers" (Dictionary.com, n.d.); "the study of computing, programing, and computation in correspondence with computer systems" (BusinessDictionary.com, n.d.); and, perhaps most succinctly, computer science is the study of computers and the phenomena surrounding computers (Newell, Perlis, & Simon, 1967).

When Newell et al. proposed their definition in 1967, computers were nowhere near as common as they are today (Anderson, 2015). Listing all the computers and devices many of us use on a daily basis seems unnecessary at first, but computers are so integrated into our daily lives that they can become invisible. In a typical day, a person may interact with a desktop, a laptop, a tablet, a smart phone; she may even wear a computer, such as a watch. Some readers might be viewing this chapter on an electronic book that turns pages automatically; some will even read to you out loud

(Carmody, 2013). Consider, further, the miscellaneous other components that our devices interact with on a daily basis, such as wireless routers, modems, cellular towers, printers, cloud drives, flash drives, backup drives, gaming consoles, or smart televisions. The level of interaction with computers is far more extensive and complex than it seems at first glance. In 1965, future Intel co-founder Gordon Moore predicted that computing power would double every year (Moore, 1965/2006). In a 1975 speech, he revised his prediction to doubling every two years (Moore, 1975) and his prediction has held up (Fieldman, 2015; Sneed, 2015). Although there are some claims that what became known as Moore's law will eventually fail or plateau, it is safe to say that computers and the phenomena surrounding computers now encompasses a great deal more than it once did.

Computers represent only part of the field of computer science. A larger and more encompassing element is the particular way in which computer scientists think. Their method of thought is fundamental to the field and supersedes all other areas. Without it no aspect of the field would exist, including computers and their associated phenomena. "Computer science is no more about computers than astronomy is about telescopes ... Science is not about tools, it is about how we use them and what we find out when we do" (Fellows & Parberry, 1993, p. 7). Seymour Papert (1980) coined the term "computational thinking," which was later elaborated on by Janet Wing as the, "thought process involved in formulating a problem and expressing its solution(s) in such a way that a computer – human or machine – can effectively carry out" (Wing, 2014). Problem formulation is as important as problem solving; the work of humans is more important than that of the machine. Indeed, in creative problem solving, Reiter-Palmon and Robinson (2009) argue that the initial stage of problem construction is a crucial yet underappreciated component.

Denning (2010) describes computing as an agent of thought and discovery that is integral to science in general and emphasizes the fundamental principles that empower and constrain the technologies emerging from computer science. Such principles fall into the categories computation, communication, coordination, recollection, automation, evaluation, and design. "Computing is now seen as a broad field that studies information processes, natural and artificial" (Denning, 2010 p. 372).

Defining Computer Science Creativity

In order to be considered creative, the two most fundamental requirements are that something is both novel and task appropriate or useful (Kaufman, 2016). Further, a product needs to be evaluated by members of a relevant community before it can be judged as creative (Kaufman & Baer, 2012; Plucker et al., 2004). Computer science encompasses everything from theory to application and opportunities for creativity are manifold. Although each discipline within computer science is focused on the creation of a new or adapted "perceptible product" (Plucker et al., 2004, p. 91), the product may take the form of ideas, solutions, insights, techniques, interactive systems, machines, mechanisms, hardware, or software (Kaufman & Baer, 2002; Kaufman & Sternberg, 2007; Saunders & Thagard, 2005). Regarding software, computer scientists are not limited by natural laws like in physics or chemistry, which clearly limit the space of possibilities. In computer science, the limit is one's imagination! The processes by which computer scientists produce these products varies widely depending on the requirements of the specific discipline, but every concentration employs ideation (the creation of new ideas) and elaboration (the development and refinement of existing ideas; Dexter & Kozbelt, 2013).

Elaboration (sometimes called incrementation; Sternberg, Kaufman, & Pretz, 2001; the term does not refer to Torrance's (2008) use of the word) is not unique to computer science. History is littered with examples of inventions built on the foundation work of others (such as the light bulb or telephone; H. R. Res. 269, 2002; Palermo, 2014). Some elaborations are little more than replications with slight improvements (Sternberg, Kaufman, & Pretz, 2004). In computer science, however, elaboration is not only common but vital to continued progress in the field (Comer et al. 1989, Dexter & Kozbelt, 2013, Graham, 2004; Leach & Ayers, 2005; Saunders & Thagard, 2005). Part of the reason that elaboration is so common is that the systems within which many computer scientists work are immense; rebuilding from scratch is unfeasible and unnecessary. Often there are components of a system that are stable, successful, and have no reason to be replaced. Software developers can make use of comprehensive libraries that provide collections of resources some-times referred to as objects for integration in the software. This component approach, a paradigm know as object-oriented programming, is the most common approach to programming, and one of the most common forms of formalized reuse and elaboration. One would no more expect a computer scientist to start from scratch than expect a car designer to (literally) reinvent the wheel. Computer science is particularly receptive to elaboration because, unlike the natural sciences where there may be a single correct answer to an empirical question, there can be many different possible solutions (Saunders & Thagard, 2005). The development of a project can shift as a result of numerous contributing factors including time, budget, resources, and even the mood of the scientist (Graziotin, Wang, & Abrahamsson, 2014). Each point at which a choice was made represents an opportunity for an alternative path, and possibly an alternate result (Kozbelt, 2009). Accordingly, many innovative software companies today use methodologies such as an agile approach of software development, where the systems are changed incrementally instead of trying to accomplish everything in one comprehensive release. Revisiting an old, broken, or incomplete project with the intent of improving, repairing, or completing it still requires problem solving and creativity. The ACM considered the task of completing or altering existing code so important that it was included in the model for laboratory work practices (Comer et al. 1989).

Creative Computer Science Doesn't Need to be Possible

The difference between creativity and innovation has its own implications for computer science. Innovation is creativity with the added requirement of implemen-tation (Amabile, 1988). It is important to distinguish, therefore, that creativity in computer science does not necessarily need to have been implemented. Something can be creative without even being technically possible. To clarify, we are referring to possibility as it relates to current or available resources or technology. There are instances in computer science, referred to as undecidable problems, where an algorithmic solution is not mathematically or logically possible regardless of technology or available resources. Between the extremes on the possibility spectrum there are problems that are technically possible to solve, but it is very ineffective and hence practically impossible to do so in a straightforward way. For example, the problem of finding an optimal route for visiting a given number of cities and returning to the place of origin is known as the travelling salesman problem. This type of problem where there is no known efficient way of finding the solution, but once found the solution can be quickly verified, is known as NP-complete. It is part of what is known as the P versus NP problem: Can a problem with a solution that is easily verified (NP) also be easily solved (P)? The answer to this question is considered so important that it is one of the seven Clay Mathematics Institute's Millennium Problems; a correct solution for any of which will receive a $1,000,000 award from the institute (Clay Mathematics Institute, n.d.).

One of the principal concerns of computer science is the future. That can manifest as things that do not yet exist, or even things that are currently incapable of existing. An idea, a design, or a concept can be novel, task appropriate, and judged by the community of practice to be creative – all without being actualized. Simply put, creativity does not require possibility. In the 1830s, the English mathematician and computer pioneer Charles Babbage described the design for a general-purpose computer that he called the Analytical Engine. Though he was never able to complete its construction, it can be seen as the first successful attempt of describing the structure that computers still rely on today (Bromley, 1982). If an idea was impossible to realize when first conceived, it is just as creative as when the technology eventually exists to allow it to work in the real world. Creativity can emerge from excelling within a system or through changing and challenging the system (Kozbelt, 2009).

The Creative Process in Computer Science

Creativity is considered a necessary component of all areas in computer science (Leach & Ayers, 2005; Saunders & Thagard, 2005). With respect to software development, the importance of creativity is stressed in all phases of the process (Glass & DeMarco, 2006; Gu & Tong, 2004). Creativity is seen as essential in designing, constructing, testing, and implementing, as well as in the phases of maintaining the product and in project management. A lack of flexibility in strictly regulated top-down-approaches of software development has been found to restrain software developers from creative work. Approaches such as the agile framework for software development allow more flexibility for engaging in a creative process. Though creativity in the process is considered paramount, very few studies examine the creative process in computer science; most papers focus on the end product.

Yet there is much to be gained by studying the process and the incremental stages and choices that led to the final result. Unlike most creative endeavors, much of the process in computer science is lost if it is not intentionally documented. Software is a particularly apt example. There may be a historical record left for hardware in the form of prototypes and models; if any such trace exists for software, it is far less accessible. Studying the process would not only promote a better understanding of how creativity relates to computer science, it would also offer exemplars for study and practice (Graham, 2004). Much as aspiring painters study the works of the masters, aspiring computer scientists could have the ability to reference the creative process of experts across multiple stages. There is a great deal to learn from evaluating a painting from sketch to final product (Kozbelt, 2006) and the same holds true for computer science.

Within the software development community, there is a category of software, often developed by groups of volunteers, for which the source code is available for anyone. The software itself is freely distributed for anyone to use without charge. This system is called free and open-source software (FOSS) and includes nearly any type of software needed, from operating systems (e.g., Linux) and applications (e.g., Firefox) to artificial intelligence (e.g., TensorFlow). A survey of 684 software developers who contributed to FOSS projects revealed that a feeling of being creative is one of the chief motivating factors for contributors to continue work (Lakhani & Wolf, 2003). One of the unique artifacts of the FOSS development process as opposed to many commercial software projects is a publicly available record of the progression of the project, as well as the communication among members of the development group. Very little research has been done on this extensive documentation, but it may provide insight regarding the nature of creativity within the process, particularly regarding the importance of ideation and elaboration discussed earlier (Dexter & Kozbelt, 2013).

Implicit Beliefs about Computer Science Creativity

The literature examining computer scientists' beliefs about creativity is also sparse. One study asked graduate students in psychology and graduate students and professionals in computer science in the United States and mainland China about their implicit concepts of creativity (Tang, Baer, & Kaufman, 2015). First, graduate students in computer sciences and industry professionals were asked to list characteristics of a creative computer scientist; 1,480 words were generated across 308 participants. Words that were similar or repeated were eliminated, leaving 261 unique words that were then categorized and reduced to 65 adjectives. Included in the list were artistic, innovative, lonely, unique, logical, imaginative, lazy, intelligent, romantic, and diligent. Participants of the main study then ranked the words based on how well they described a creative person in the field of computer science. Four factors emerged: smart/effective, outgoing, creative thinking, and having a dark side.

Some of the descriptors generated by the pilot study may seem more appropriate for a musician or a painter, but words such as art, beautiful, elegant, and graceful are, indeed, found within the computer science literature (Graham, 2004; Knuth, 1974; Kozbelt, Dexter, Dolese & Seidel, 2012). "Another important way for a production program to be good is for it to interact grace-fully with its users, especially when recovering from human errors in the input data. It's a real art to compose meaningful error messages" (Knuth, 1974, p. 671). References to beauty of both form and function are common, as is the importance of empathy: "You need to have empathy not just for your users, but for your readers. It's in your interest, because you'll be one of them. Many a hacker has written a program only to find on returning to it six months later that he has no idea how it works" (Graham, 2004, p. 32).

The Aesthetics of Code

Although the art of code may be appreciated mostly by people inside the field, it is a core part of the industry. Programmers developed aesthetical standards for "beau-tiful code" and "proper software design" (Bond, 2005). Such programming aes-thetics can focus on the act of programming as well as on the program itself. Knuth (2001) describes program texts which show elegance and even humor on one side, and programs which are a horror to read on the other side. According to Bond (2005) there is mutual agreement between software practitioners about program aesthetics, which is mainly determined by the following attributes as described by Knuth in 1974: correctness, maintainability, readability, lucidity, grace of interaction with users, and efficiency. These properties may inspire pleasure, or pain, in (the soft-ware's) readers. These considerations finally led to the philosophy of "literate programming," which calls for good readability of program text.

Kozbelt, Dexter, Dolese, and Seidel (2012) found that programmers with experi-ence ranging from undergraduate student to expert correlate highly in their criteria for aesthetic judgment of code and the majority responded that it was easier to write correct code than to write beautiful code. Unfortunately, many layperson users never get to see the code that makes their devices function. Most consumers can dismantle any appliance they own and become more familiar with its component parts and how it works. Though they may lack the knowledge or skill to reassemble them, there are very few barriers impeding access to the inner workings. With a screwdriver, a socket set, and a pair of pliers one can gain access to the component parts of an appliance and develop a better understanding of how each part contributes to the whole. Code, however, is virtually impossible to see, often on purpose. There is no way to know if the code that powers your device is the equivalent of a precision-tuned sports car or a rickety box car racer cobbled together from spare parts. A programmer once remarked that if users could see code the way they could see a bridge on a highway, some code is so ugly that most people would be looking for alternate routes. (Barnett, personal communication, January 2005). Knuth observed, "[I]t is especially nice when the things we regard as beautiful are also regarded by other people as useful" (1974, p. 671). Code is not required to be beautiful to work. Further, beautiful code may not be correct. Yet there is a whole subculture that has developed around the artistry of beautiful code. This subculture is one of the rare science-art collaborations, as noted by Pelowski, Leder, and Tinio in Chapter 6 of this volume.

Applied Creativity in Computer Science

Code Poetry and Esoteric Programing Language

Because code is so foreign to the average person, it is easy to forget that computer code is a type of language and therefore can often be used in the same manner as many other languages, though with notably more stringent rules. Code literature has various forms. For example, code poetry is poetry written in programming language. There are code versions of haiku and sonnets. Shakespeare programing language is an esoteric programing language, not intended for conventional or even practical use, in which the program appears to be written in the form of a Shakespearean play (Hasselström & Åslund, 2001). Obfuscated code competitions involve purposefully concealing the operation of a program through overly complex and intentionally convoluted means (Broukhis, Cooper, & Noll, n.d.).

Programming Art

Programming to create artwork is another dimension of the connection of programming and art. It is the goal in such artworks to master an artistic challenge (Knuth, 2001). As such, challenges for programmers include one-line programs, demos (small, self-contained computer programs that produce audio-visual presentations), and programs that reproduce a copy of themselves. Such software generally does not have a purpose other than artistic expression or demonstration of technical mastery. However, such artwork generally receives appreciation only by peers or people involved in the scene. Hopkins (1995) demonstrated the poetic potential of code. The syntactically correct Perl program entitled *Listen* received appreciation even outside of programming communities. Being creative does not necessarily need to serve a purpose other than enjoyment. As an example, live coding programming of laptop music is described as a fascinating possibility of end-user programming (Blackwell & Collins, 2005).

Hidden Messages in Code

One of the easier ways for a layperson to look at code is in the source code of websites. If one right clicks on a website and selects "inspect" or "inspect element," a developer tool will open. Items on the page will highlight when the mouse is moved over the corresponding source code. The code can be temporarily altered and the changes will then preview in real time. It can be educational and occasionally entertaining. The photo sharing website Flickr once hid a posting for jobs within its source code. A clever user could find a tagged comment that read, "You're reading. We're hiring." It then provided the web address for the company job page (Kiefaber, 2013). These hidden messages, called steganography, are not uncommon (Germ, 2013; Hewitt, 2013; Kemps, 2013). Different websites have their own variation on the technique. At one time, a search for certain programing language-related terms through Google would trigger a secret prompt to appear and give the searcher the opportunity to complete a coding challenge that could end with a job offer (Rosett, 2015). Such recruiting techniques may well be the future of the industry; they not only identify possible candidates but also filter out less-qualified individuals (Hong, 2013).

Video Games and Creativity

Most studies of video games and creativity focus on how playing video games can increase creativity (Green & Kaufman, 2015). For the purposes of this chapter, however, it is the creativity of the video game designer that is of interest.

Procedural generation is one method game developers use to generate game content. Components of the game are generated algorithmically and according to rules established by the developer creating a virtually infinite number of combinations. This technique has been used in games for almost forty years (King, 2015) but some more recent games have started to use it on a more extensive level. Exploration-based games such as *No Man's Sky* and *Elite: Dangerous* use procedural generation to create massive galaxies for players to explore. *Elite: Dangerous* has created 400 billion star systems and the planets are generated using scientific principles to determine features such as topography, tectonics, and elemental composition (McKeand, 2015). *No Man's Sky* is set in an open universe that currently has 18 quintillion planets, each of which was generated using algorithms to determine orbit, atmospheric composition, atmosphere, weather, flora, and fauna (Khatchadourlan, 2015). How players interact with the environment is determined by game physics. A physics engine is software used to simulate the laws of physics in the game environment, making items behave in a way that appears real. *Physics Playground* uses game physics to teach basic physics and the fundamentals of simple machines (Empirical Games, n.d.). Shute, Ventura, and Kim found that playing the game increased student qualitative and conceptual physics understanding over time (2013). Stealth assessments are evidence-based assessments that are built into the action of the game and involve gathering and evaluating gameplay performance data (Shute and Ventura, 2013). Shute et al. found that specific achievements within the game were useful for assessment purposes (2013). Stealth assessment in video games could become a standard method to measure student learning without the students being aware it is happening.

Virtual Reality and Augmented Reality

The concept of virtual or augmented reality is not new (Brockwell, 2016; "How did virtual reality begin?," n.d.), but it is only recently that it has become more common. To avoid confusion, for the purposes of this chapter we will use the concepts and terms as outlined by Milgram and Kishino (1994) about what they termed the "reality-virtuality continuum." At one end is the actual world with no digital manipulation, and at the other is a completely virtual world with no interaction or relation to one's immediate physical surroundings. Between these two extremes is what Milgram and Kishino refer to as "mixed reality" (1994). The distinctions between types of mixed reality depend on such aspects as the type of display used (monitor, screen, eyepiece) or whether the real environment is observed directly or indirectly (such as using the camera on a mobile device to display the actual environment; Milgram & Kishino, 1994).

The mixed reality field has two primary areas: augmented reality and hybrid reality. Augmented reality has been part of everyday life in some form for years, albeit with different terminology. Augmented reality happens any time that the real environment is observed with the addition of a synthetic element. Examples can be as banal as driving a car that projects the speed on the bottom of the windshield or watching a football game on television in which computer graphics are used to note the line of scrimmage or first down. More complex instances are the head up display (HUD) a pilot uses in a cockpit or a vein illuminator that uses near-field infrared light to scan and project images of veins in real time on a patient's skin ("Vein illumination," n.d.). In augmented reality, the user cannot interact directly with the computer graphics. Hybrid reality, on the other hand, is when the user observes the real environment with the addition of synthetic elements and is also able to interact with these added elements.

Mixed realty is a relatively new area but is growing rapidly. Numerous companies have projects in development, such as a device no more obtrusive than a pair of glasses that would eliminate the need for physical computer monitors (Edwards, 2016). The device could allow users to interact with virtual monitors that would seem to float mid-air. Another possible future device could translate any written or spoken words in real time (Lomas, 2015).

Artificial Intelligence (AI)

Some of the advancements of artificial intelligence, like natural language recognition, have already made their way to the mainstream world. Programs such as Apple's Siri, Google Now, or Amazon's Alexa use natural-language processing to interact with users. They can perform tasks such as getting directions, ordering products, making phone calls, sending texts, playing music, or even interacting with home automation to control devices from the television to the thermostat. The internet of things (IoT) is an expanding infrastructure of network-connected items including everyday objects such as a refrigerator or washing machine as well as whole communities or entire cities ("Internet of things global standards initiative," n.d.).

One of the best-known examples of current AI is IBM's Watson. Watson is famous for many different accomplishments. It beat two Jeopardy champions in 2011 (Zimmer, 2011) and collaborated on a published cookbook with the Institute of Culinary Education in 2015 (O'Brien, 2015); it also diagnosed a rare form of leukemia in approximately ten minutes (Fingas, 2016). Although Watson is a remarkable example of state of the art artificial intelligence, it is not a single super computer. Watson is a cognitive system that learns through a process known as deep learning. Its success lies in its ability to process unstructured data, such as natural spoken language, and then suggest an answer that is most probably true based on its confidence in its correctness. Each Watson machine serves as an expert advisor in its specific field. The Watson that won at Jeopardy was an expert in trivia and had been studying 15 terabytes of information, including all of Wikipedia (though it did not use the internet during the game) (Zimmer, 2011). The Watson that diagnosed the case of leukemia had studied over 20 million cancer research papers (Fingas, 2016).

Computational Creativity

Although computational creativity is generally outside the scope of this chapter, it does raise fascinating philosophical questions. The exact definition of computational creativity is still a matter of debate, but in very broad terms it is the idea that a computer can produce something that is creative through the use of artificial intelligence (Jordanous, 2014). Is a computer capable of being creative? Should the creative products of a machine be attributed to the software or to the programmer? Will humans ever consider a product produced by a machine truly creative? It is possible that the future will bring such advances that computers may need to be considered a distinct population to be studied, much as workers or students are currently considered separately. Programs such as The Painting Fool or AARON produce works of art that are comparable to artworks created by human artists. It may seem strange to imagine a machine being creative since it can only produce something it was programmed to do. Hofstadter (1996) describes the drawings of AARON as having a charming naiveté and recognizable style. However, Harold Cohen, the artist who created AARON, does not claim that the program is "creative" and, in fact, prefers to avoid even using the word (Cohen, 1999a, 1999b).

Creativity in CS Education

> Companies are seeing the need for techs that go beyond problem solving and think like artists.
>
> (McCormack & d'Inverno, 2012, p. 434)

In 2016, Japan announced a six-year plan to add computer programming as a required subject in primary, middle, and high schools as a step to foster creativity (Verma, 2016). At the same time, computer science lessons are introduced in schools all around the world, in some countries starting in the age of 6, in order to foster creativity related skills such as problem solving, computational thinking, and reflection.

The ubiquity of computers has inspired many to study computer science. There are myriad first steps for a novice to begin the journey of discovery, from books and websites to hands-on exploration. Knobelsdorf and Romeike (2008) found in an empirical study that analyzed biographical data of freshman computer science majors and non-majors that, for a large number of the former, creativity served as a pathway leading them to the field. But many people have their interest first piqued by a class taken in middle school, high school, or even college. These initial contact points in computer science education can inspire those with no previous experience and motivate those already interested. Some instructors have employed creativity as a factor for raising motivation and interest in computer science lessons, e.g. by encouraging creative, hands-on-learning and exploration (Lewandowski et al., 2005) or by allowing programming as personal creative expression (e.g., Peppler and Kafai, 2009; Resnick, 2008). Such a creative expression may follow a "creative thinking spiral" helping people to become creative thinkers:

> In this process, people *imagine* what they want to do, *create* a project based on their ideas, *play* with their creations, *share* their ideas and creations with others, and *reflect* on their experiences – all of which leads them to *imagine* new ideas and new projects. As students go through this process, over and over, they learn to develop their own ideas, try them out, test the boundaries, experiment with alternatives, get input from others, and generate new ideas based on their experiences. (Resnick, 2008, p. 18)

Conversely, such early interactions, if handled poorly by an instructor, can alienate newcomers and suppress aspiring computer scientists (Beghetto, 2014).

Introducing students to a subject such as programing in a low-risk environment can increase engagement and interest. Visual programing languages such as Scratch or Alice use a building-block approach that teaches foundational concepts and provides immediate feedback. Students can experiment, create, and solve problems without confronting the difficulties associated with formal programming languages such as syntax errors. Visual programing tools allow students to cultivate a basic understanding of how software functions and an appreciation of the potential capabilities of higher-level programing languages (Brusilovsky,1997; Romeike, 2008b). These type of positive interactions increase student perceptions of creativity in themselves, in the process (programming), and in the environment (computer science; Romeike, 2007b). Simply getting students to see the field of computer science as being creative allows them to understand how creativity is present in a wide variety of lesson types, from programming to physical computing (Przybylla & Romeike, 2014).

The intentional implementation of creativity in the computer science classroom, beyond helping student engagement (Howard et al. 2009), also encourages a mastery-based mindset in which the process becomes more important to the student than the product (Knobelsdorf & Romeike, 2008). Cennamo et al. (2011) found that establishing a human-computer interaction class using the format of a design studio with traditional critiques helped develop designer introspection and empathy for the user. Students asked to reflect on the relationship between creativity and computer science were better able to understand that the interaction between the two is complex and multifaceted (Romeike, 2008a).

In addition, emphasizing the creativity present in computer science can help address issues of equity. This is consistent with past arguments that creativity can increase general inequity in college admissions (Kaufman, 2010) or gifted admissions (Luria, O'Brien, & Kaufman, 2016) based on empirical studies (Kaufman, Baer, & Gentile, 2004; Kaufman, 2006). Romeike (2007a) compared traditional high school computer science classes taught with a problem-solving method with classes taught emphasizing creativity. He found that females performed notably better in classes that focused on creativity.

Malevolent Creativity

When addressing the subject of creativity there is often a tacit assumption of benevolence, or at least neutrality (Cropley, Kaufman, White, & Chiera, 2014). Although creativity is neither inherently good or bad, there are instances where it is used for malicious purposes, such as Leonardo Da Vinci designing weapons for the military or terrorists developing plans of attack. When creativity is used with the intent to cause harm or damage it is known as malevolent creativity (Cropley, Cropley, Kaufman, & Runco, 2010; Cropley, Kaufman, & Cropley, 2008).

Hackers: Black Hats vs. White Hats

There are numerous instances of malevolent creativity in computer science, but the most infamous and prominent of examples is the hacker. Hackers are most associated with criminal acts by the lay public, likely because hackers operate in a world that is largely misunderstood or completely unknown to most. Further, many people believe hackers have wildly exaggerated capabilities, such as being able to order a nuclear missile launch with a whistle and a payphone (Sirius, 2000). These different factors combine to create the image of the mythical hacker.

The evil, all-powerful hacker of popular culture bears as much resemblance to the typical hacker as Keyser Soze or Hannibal Lecter represent the typical criminal. In the world of computer scientists, a hacker is an expert programmer (Graham, 2004) who wants to explore and test the possibilities of a system. Some hackers do so for profit (Vollmer, 2016). Others hack for fun or to prove something is possible. Consider, for example, hacking NASA or the Department of Defense and leaving a message that says, "Your security is crap" (Bowcott, 2012; Palande, 2014). Hacking isn't always about material gain. "The game, the rush, the power was the hack itself" (Skibell, 2002, p. 341).

Hackers interested in more nefarious activities (sometimes called black hats) rely heavily on their creativity. If creativity means being new and task appropriate, however, a hacker's approach to the task-appropriate part may be circuitous. Some hackers take a Rube Goldbergesque approach, with wild leaps and indirect connections like using a Microsoft Word document to infect a computer (Ducklin, 2015) or using web cams, DVRs, internet routers, and other IoT connected devices to temporarily shut down websites such as Amazon, PayPal, Twitter, Spotify, and dozens more (Blue, 2016). There is still a specific task to be accomplished, however, even amidst such demonstrations of talent or self-expression.

Novelty is of paramount importance to criminal hackers and is often the most important factor in their success. Criminal hackers often exploit "zero-day vulnerability" to gain access to a system. Zero-day vulnerabilities are unknown to the software company (Park, 2015), meaning that criminal hackers must be especially novel to succeed; they must find paths that are entirely unknown. Once a zero-day vulnerability has been identified, warnings are often issued so software users are aware of the vulnerability. The software company will start creating a patch to correct the problem. In the interim between the identification of the vulnerability and the issuance of the software patch to fix the problem, the effectiveness of the exploit will begin to decrease. Once the patch has been released, effectiveness will drop to almost zero. This process is what Cropley et al. (2008) call creativity decay. The value that was added by the novelty of the exploit begins to decline once others become aware of its existence; therefore, its effectiveness as a means for accomplishing a desired task is drastically reduced or eliminated. The creativity of the exploit had decayed to the point of no longer being an effective solution. Once the criminal hacker reaches this point, they must discover a new method. This cycle of malevolent creativity and creative decay is continuous as new software is released on a regular basis.

Malware

The malevolently creative product is most readily observable in the form of malicious software (also known as malware). Malware includes worms, viruses, spyware, and many invasive programs designed to force a system to execute operations without user consent or, often, awareness. The creativity of malware is difficult to study because by design it is meant to be undetected. Any malware that has been discovered becomes the subject of intense study. A piece of spyware called Project Sauron, also known as Remsec, operated for at least five years without being detected because it was designed to behave in a way inconsistent with the patterns used by security experts to detect malware (GReAT, 2016). Flame or Flamer, which remained undiscovered for at least two years, was referred to by a security expert as "fantastic and incredible in complexity" (Zetter, 2012, para. 9). One of the most creative aspects of the software was that it had a kill module that, when sent, would delete and overwrite any files associated with the program, thereby removing any trace of its presence. Security software developers use files left by malware to create tools that can detect a breach and remove the offending program. By eliminating any proof that it had infected a system, the makers of Flame made its discovery difficult. Determining if a computer had been infected at some point in the past was virtually impossible. Some malware comes from individual criminal hackers, but others are so advanced and complex that the development of such software would be virtually impossible for any group other than a government or other large, well-funded organization. For example, a piece of malware called Duqu contained high-level code initially believed to be from an unidentified programing language (Soumenkov, 2012a). Ultimately it was determined that the code had been compiled using techniques indicative of professional developers making Duqu, "a 'one of a kind' piece of malware which stands out like a gem from the large mass of 'dumb' malicious program[sic] we normally see" (Soumenkov, 2012b).

Computer Forensics

The opposite of criminal hackers (black hats) are the hackers who use their skills for positive, benevolent purposes (often called white hats). These individuals may be security professionals or private individuals working in a realm of ethical hacking. Cropley et al. (2008) point out the importance of not just problem solving, but also problem finding. There are experts working for benevolent and malevolent purposes who are constantly probing for any way into a system. Some hackers test systems and look for vulnerabilities to exploit and then inform the software company so a patch can be developed. Others work as hacker specialists in the world of computer forensics. Computer forensics holds an interesting place within the world of computer science because the goal is often to discover what someone else has done, and how it has been done. Computer forensics are more similar to natural sciences in that respect; an empirical question is asked, investigated, and has a specific right answer (Saunders & Thagard, 2005). However, even a task as straightforward as generating a list of search terms to apply to a population of documents requires skill and creativity. "An effective search that results in responsive items being identified begins with the intangible creativity that forms a bond between knowledge of the law and technology" (Garrie, 2012, p. 401).

We have only briefly touched on a few of the many ways in which creativity plays a role in computer science. The field is diverse, complex, and expansive. Creativity is a major component of all parts from education to practice, yet has been studied very little. Future studies of creativity in computer science that concentrate on the process and the person will help develop a deeper understanding of the field. Increasing creativity in all areas of computer science education has the potential to diversify the population, and consequently the creative perspectives of future computer scientists. The field is growing rapidly and expanding to encompass more aspects of daily life. Exposing new students to the opportunities for creativity in computer science will attract the eclectic mix of professionals that will be needed in the future while at the same time creating more informed users who will see computer science for the creative field that it is.

References

Amabile, T. M. (1988). A model of creativity and innovation in organizations. *Research in Organizational Behavior, 10*(1), 123–167.

Anderson, M. (2015). *Technology device ownership: 2015.* Pew Research Center. Retrieved on August 14, 2016, from www.pewinternet.org/2015/10/29/technology-device-ownership-2015/

Bauer, W. F., Juncosa, M. L., & Perlis, A. J. (1959). ACM publication policies and plans. *Journal of the ACM (JACM), 6*(2), 121–122.

Beghetto, R. A. (2014). Creative mortification: An initial exploration. *Psychology of Aesthetics, Creativity, and the Arts, 8*(3), 266.

Blackwell, A., & Collins, N. (2005). The programing language as a musical instrument. In P. Romero, J. Good, E. Acosta Chaparro, & S. Bryant (Eds.), *Proceedings of Psychology of Programming Interest Group (PPIG), 17*, pp. 120–130.

Blue, V. (2016, October 28). That time your smart toaster broke the internet [Blog post]. *Engadget*. Retrieved on October 29, 2016, from www.engadget.com/2016/10/28/that-time-your-smart-toaster-broke-the-internet/

Bond, G. W. (2005). Software as art. *Communications of the ACM, 48*(8), 118–125. DOI:10.1145/1076211.1076215.

Bowcott, O. (2012, October 16). Gary McKinnon: How unknown hacker sparked political and diplomatic storm. *The Guardian*. Retrieved on September 21, 2016, from www .theguardian.com/world/2012/oct/16/gary-mckinnon-hacker-sparked-storm

Brockwell, H. (2016, April 3). Forgotten genius: The man who made a working VR machine in 1957. *TechRadar*. Retrieved on September 21, 2016, from www.techradar.com/ news/wearables/forgotten-genius-the-man-who-made-a-working-vr-machine-in-1957-1318253

Bromley, A. G. (1982). Charles Babbage's analytical engine, 1838. *Annals of the History of Computing, 4*(3), 196–217.

Broukhis, L., Cooper, S., and Noll, L. (n.d.). The international obfuscated C code contest. Retrieved on September 21, 2016 from http://www.ioccc.org/index.html

Brusilovsky, P., Calabrese, E., Hvorecky, J., Kouchnirenko, A., & Miller, P. (1997). Mini-languages: A way to learn programming principles. *Education and Information Technologies, 2*(1), 65–83.

BusinessDictionary.com. (n.d.). Computer science Retrieved October 21, 2016, from www .businessdictionary.com/definition/computer-science.html

Carmody, T. (2013, January 24). Amazon acquires Kindle Fire text-to-speech provider, but this isn't about Siri. *The Verge*. Retrieved on October 21, 2016 from www.theverge .com/2013/1/24/3911056/amazon-acquires-kindle-fire-text-to-speech-provider-but-this-isnt

Cennamo, K., Douglas, S. A., Vernon, M., Brandt, C., Scott, B., Reimer, Y., & McGrath, M. (2011). Promoting creativity in the computer science design studio. *Proceedings of the 42nd ACM Technical Symposium on Computer Science Education*, 649–654.

Cohen, H. (1999a). Colouring without seeing: A problem in machine creativity. *AISB Quarterly, 102*, 26–35.

Cohen, H. (1999b). A self-defining game for one player. *Proceedings of the 3rd conference on Creativity & Cognition, 14*. DOI: 10.1145/317561.317564

Comer, D. E., Gries, D., Mulder, M. C., Tucker, A., Turner, A. J., Young, P. R., & Denning, P. J. (1989). Computing as a discipline. *Communications of the ACM, 32*(1), 9–23.

Cropley, D. H., Cropley, A. J., Kaufman, J. C., & Runco, M. A. (Eds.). (2010). *The dark side of creativity*. New York, NY: Cambridge University Press.

Cropley, D. H., Kaufman, J. C., & Cropley, A. J. (2008). Malevolent creativity: A functional model of creativity in terrorism and crime. *Creativity Research Journal, 20*(2), 105–115.

Cropley, D. H., Kaufman, J. C., White, A. E., & Chiera, B. A. (2014). Layperson perceptions of malevolent creativity: The good, the bad, and the ambiguous. *Psychology of Aesthetics, Creativity, and the Arts, 8*(4), 400.

Denning, P. J. (2005). Is computer science science? *Communications of the ACM, 48*(4), 27–31. DOI:10.1145/1053291.1053309

Denning, P. J. (2010). The great principles of computing: Computing may be the fourth great domain of science along with the physical, life and social sciences. *American Scientist, 98*(5), 369.

Dexter, S., & Kozbelt, A. (2013). Free and open source software (FOSS) as a model domain for answering big questions about creativity. *Mind & Society, 12*(1), 113–123.

Dictionary.com Unabridged. (n.d.). Computer science. Retrieved on August 7, 2016, from http://www.dictionary.com/browse/computer-science

Ducklin, P. (2015, September 28). Why Word "macro malware" is back, and what you can do about it … [Blog post] *Naked Security by Sophos*. Retrieved September 22, 2016 from https://nakedsecurity.sophos.com/2015/09/28/why-word-macro-malware-is-back-and-what-you-can-do-about-it/

Edwards, L. (2016, June 16). What is Magic Leap and why might it kill all screens? *Pocket-lint*. Retrieved on October 30, 2016, from http://www.pocket-lint.com/news/135688-what-is-magic-leap-and-why-might-it-kill-all-screens

Empirical Games (n.d.). http://www.empiricalgames.org/games/

Fein, L. (1959). The role of the university in computers, data processing, and related fields. *Communications of the ACM, 2*(9), 7–14. DOI:10.1145/368424.368427

Fellows, M., & Parberry, I. (1993). SIGACT trying to get children excited about CS. *Computing Research News, 5*(1), 7.

Fieldman, T. (2015, May 13). Moore's law turns 50. *The New York Times*. Retrieved on August 6, 2016 from http://nyti.ms/1IAnBxP

Fingas, J. (2016, August 7). IBM's Watson AI saved a woman from leukemia. *Engadget*. Retrieved on September 21, 2016, from www.engadget.com/2016/08/07/ibms-watson-ai-saved-a-woman-from-leukemia/

Garrie, D. B. (2012). Effective keyword selection requires a mastery of storage technology and the law. *Pace Law Review, 32*(2), pp. 400–406.

Germ, E. (2013, January 15). 6 Awesome Easter eggs hidden in programs you use every day. *Cracked*. Retrieved on October 21, 2016, from www.cracked.com/article_20174_6-awesome-easter-eggs-hidden-in-programs-you-use-every-day.html

Glass, R. L., & DeMarco, T. (2006). *Software creativity 2.0.* developer.* Books.

Glăveanu, V. P. (2014). *Distributed creativity: Thinking outside the box of the creative individual.* New York: Springer International Publishing.

Graham, P. (2004). *Hackers & painters: Big ideas from the computer age.* Sebastopol, CA: O'Reilly Media, Inc.

Graziotin, D., Wang, X., & Abrahamsson, P. (2014). Software developers, moods, emotions, and performance. *IEEE Software, 31*(4), 24–27.

GReAT. (2016, August 9). *The Project Sauron APT.* Global Research and Analysis Team Kaspersky Lab. Retrieved September 21, 2016, from https://kas.pr/a9sn

Green, G., & Kaufman, J. C. (Eds.). (2015). *Video games and creativity.* Academic Press.

Gu, M., & Tong, X. (2004). Towards hypotheses on creativity in software development. *International Conference on Product Focused Software Process Improvement*, 47–61.

Guilford, J. P. (1950). Creativity. *American Psychologist, 5*(9), 444–454. DOI:10.1037/h0063487

Hasselström, K., & Åslund, J. (2001, August 21). The Shakespeare programming language. Retrieved on August 16, 2016, from http://shakespearelang.sourceforge.net/report/shakespeare/

Hewitt, A. (2013, July 3). Discover the coded message hidden in campus floor tiles. *UCLA Newsroom*. Retrieved on October 17, 2016, from http://newsroom.ucla.edu/stories/a-coded-message-hidden-in-floor-247232

Hofstadter, D. R. (1996). *Fluid concepts & creative analogies: Computer models of the fundamental mechanisms of thought.* New York: Basic Books.

Hong, L. (2013, May 30). The 5 most creative 'developer job ads.' [Blog post]*Smart Recruiters*. Retrieved on October 23, 2016, from https://www.smartrecruiters .com/blog/the-5-most-creative-developer-job-ads/

Hopkins, S. (1995). Listen. In *The Princeton Encyclopedia of Poetry and Poetics*, 2012, 396–397.

H. Res. 269, 107th Cong., 148 Cong. Rec. H3308 (2002).

Virtual Reality Society (n.d.). How did virtual reality begin? Retrieved on September 21, 2016. from www.vrs.org.uk/virtual-reality/beginning.html

Howard, E. V., Bulach, T. M., Carver, L. A., Creekbaum, C. R., Parker, R. J., & Shockley, L. G. (2009). Perceptions of using creativity in an IT ethics course–A case study of students and instructor. *Proceedings of the Information Systems Education Conference, 26*.

International Telecommunication Union (ITU) (n.d.). Internet of things global standards initiative. Retrieved on September 21, 2016. from www.itu.int/en/ITU-T/gsi/iot/ Pages/default.aspx

Jordanous, A. (2014, April 10). What is computational creativity? [Blog post]. *The Creativity Post*. Retrieved on September 5, 2016. from www.creativitypost.com/science/ what_is_computational_creativity

Kaufman, J. C. (2006). Self-reported differences in creativity by ethnicity and gender. *Applied Cognitive Psychology, 20*(8), 1065–1082.

Kaufman, J. C. (2010). Using creativity to reduce ethnic bias in college admissions. *Review of General Psychology, 14*(3), 189.

Kaufman, J. C. (2016). *Creativity 101*. New York: Springer Publishing Company.

Kaufman, J. C., & Baer, J. (2004). Sure, I'm creative—but not in mathematics!: Self-reported creativity in diverse domains. *Empirical Studies of the Arts, 22*(2), 143–155.

Kaufman, J. C., & Baer, J. (2002). Could Steven Spielberg manage the Yankees?: Creative thinking in different domains. *Korean Journal of Thinking and Problem Solving, 12*(2), 5–14.

Kaufman, J. C., & Baer, J. (2012). Beyond new and appropriate: Who decides what is creative? *Creativity Research Journal, 24*(1), 83–91.

Kaufman, J. C., Baer, J., & Gentile, C. A. (2004). Differences in gender and ethnicity as measured by ratings of three writing tasks. *The Journal of Creative Behavior, 38*(1), 56–69.

Kaufman, J. C., & Sternberg, R. J. (2007). Resource review: Creativity. *Change, 39*(4), 55–58.

Kemps, H. (2013, May 22). The funny, occasionally dirty, hidden messages in your favorite games. *WIRED*. Retrieved on October 21, 2016. from https://www.wired.com /2013/05/hidden-messages/

Khatchadourlan, R. (2015, May 18). World without end. *The New Yorker*. Retrieved on September 21, 2016. from www.newyorker.com/magazine/2015/05/18/world-without-end-raffi-khatchadourian

Kiefaber, D. (2013, May 28) Flickr recruits coders with ads hidden in its website's source code. *Adweek*. Retrieved on August 16, 2016. from www.adweek.com/adfreak/ flickr-recruits-coders-ads-hidden-its-websites-source-code-149818

King, A. (2015, April 10). The key design elements of Roguelikes. *Envato*. Retrieved on September 21, 2016. from https://gamedevelopment.tutsplus.com/articles/the-key-design-elements-of-roguelikes–cms–23510

Knobelsdorf, M., & Romeike, R. (2008). Creativity as a pathway to computer science. *ACM SIGCSE Bulletin, 40*(3) 286–290.

Knuth, D. E. (2001). *Things a computer scientist rarely talks about*. Stanford, CA: CSLI Publications.

Knuth, D. E. (1974). Computer programming as an art. *Communications of the ACM, 17*(12), 667–673. DOI:10.1145/361604.361612

Kozbelt, A. (2006). Dynamic evaluation of Matisse's 1935 large reclining nude. *Empirical Studies of the Arts, 24*(2), 119–137.

Kozbelt, A. (2009). Ontogenetic heterochrony and the creative process in visual art: A précis. *Psychology of Aesthetics, Creativity, and the Arts, 3*(1), 35–37.

Kozbelt, A., Dexter, S., Dolese, M., & Seidel, A. (2012). The aesthetics of software code: A quantitative exploration. *Psychology of Aesthetics, Creativity, and the Arts, 6*(1), 57.

Lakhani, K., & Wolf, R. G. (2003). Why hackers do what they do: Understanding motivation and effort in free/open source software projects. *Social Science Research Network (SSRN) Journal*. DOI: 10.2139/ssrn.443040

Leach, R. J., & Ayers, C. A. (2005). The psychology of invention in computer science. In P. Romero, J. Good, E. Acosta Chaparro, & S. Bryant (Eds), *Proceedings of Psychology of Programming Interest Group (PPIG), 17*, pp. 131–144.

Lewandowski, G., Johnson, E., & Goldweber, M. (2005). Fostering a creative interest in computer science. *ACM SIGCSE Bulletin, 37*(1), pp. 535–539.

Lomas, N. (2015, March 2). Google's Pichai talks up Magic Leap's AR but says "It'll take some time." *Tech Crunch*. Retrieved on October 29, 2016, from https://techcrunch.com/2015/03/02/pichai-magic-leap/

London, E. (2013, May 30). Google Glass: inspired by Terminator [Blog post] *Slice of MIT*. Retrieved on September 18, 2016 from https://slice.mit.edu/2013/05/30/google-glass-inspired-by-terminator/

Luria, S. R., O'Brien, R. L., & Kaufman, J. C. (2016). Creativity in gifted identification: Increasing accuracy and diversity. *Annals of the New York Academy of Sciences, 1377*(1), 44–52.

McCormack, J., & d'Inverno, M. (2012). Computers and creativity: The road ahead. In J. McCormack & M. d'Inverno (Eds.), *Computers and creativity* (pp. 421–424) New York: Springer.

McKeand, K. (2015, October 10). Elite: Dangerous shows us the science and technology behind creating realistic planets [Blog post]. *PCGamesN.com*. Retrieved on September 21, 2016 from http://www.pcgamesn.com/elite-dangerous/elite-dangerous-shows-us-the-science-and-technology-behind-creating-realistic-planets

Milgram, P., & Kishino, F. (1994). A taxonomy of mixed reality visual displays. *IEICE Transactions on Information and Systems, 77*(12), 1321–1329.

Clay Mathematics Institute, (n.d.). Millennium Prize Problems. Retrieved on October 28, 2016 from www.claymath.org/millennium-problems/millennium-prize-problems.

Moore, G. E. (1975). Progress in digital integrated electronics. *International Electron Devices Meeting Tech Digest, IEEE*, 11–13.

Moore, G. E. (2006). Cramming more components onto integrated circuits. *Solid-State Circuits Newsletter, IEEE, 20*(3), 33–35. (Reprinted from *Electronics, 38*(8), April 19, 1965, p. 114). DOI:10.1109/N-SSC.2006.4785860

Newell, A., Perlis, A. J., & Simon, H. A. (1967). Computer science. *Science, 157*(3795), 1373–1374.

O'Brien, T. (2015, June 20). Watson's South American spin on a Canadian classic. *Engadget*. Retrieved on September 21, 2016, from www.engadget.com/2015/06/20/cooking-with-watson-peruvian-potato-poutine/

Palande, S. (2014, June 23). 10 Best hackers the world has ever known. *Thought Catalog*. Retrieved August 16, 2016, from http://tcat.tc/1sA0fm6

Palermo, E. (2014, February 15) Who invented the light bulb? [Blog post]. *Live Science*. Retrieved on September 22, 2016, from www.livescience.com/43424-who-invented-the-light-bulb.html

Papert, S. (1980). *Mindstorms: Children, computers, and powerful ideas*. New York: Basic Books, Inc.

Park, R. (2015, November 9). Guide to zero-day exploits [Blog post] *Symantec*. Retrieved on October 21, 2016, from www.symantec.com/connect/blogs/guide-zero-day-exploits

Peppler, K. and Kafai, Y. (2009): Creative coding: Programming for personal expression. *Proceedings of the 9th International Conference on Computer Supported Collaborative Learning (CSCL), Rhodes, Greece*.

Plucker, J. A., Beghetto, R. A., & Dow, G. T. (2004). Why isn't creativity more important to educational psychologists? Potentials, pitfalls, and future directions in creativity research. *Educational Psychologist, 39*(2), 83–96.

Przybylla, M., & Romeike, R. (2014) Overcoming issues with students' perceptions of informatics in everyday life and education with physical computing. *Proceedings of the 7th International Conference on Informatics in Schools: Situation, Evolution and Perspectives (ISSEP)*, (pp. 9–20).

Reiter-Palmon, R., & Robinson, E. J. (2009). Problem identification and construction: What do we know, what is the future? *Psychology of Aesthetics, Creativity, and the Arts, 3*(1), 43.

Resnick, M. (2008). Sowing the seeds for a more creative society. *Learning & Leading with Technology, 35*(4), 18–22.

Rhodes, M. (1961). An analysis of creativity. *The Phi Delta Kappan, 42*(7), 305–310.

Romeike, R. (2007). Applying creativity in CS high school education: Criteria, teaching example and evaluation. *Proceedings of the Seventh Baltic Sea Conference on Computing Education Research-Volume 88*, 87–96.

Romeike, R. (2007). Three drivers for creativity in computer science education. *Proceedings of the IFIP-Conference on "Informatics, Mathematics and ICT: a golden triangle."* Boston, USA.

Romeike, R. (2008). Workshop: A creative introduction to programming with scratch. In *Learning to live in the knowledge society, 281* (pp. 341–344). New York: Springer. DOI: 10.1007/978-0-387-09729-9_49

Romeike, R. (2008). What's my challenge? The forgotten part of problem solving in computer science education. In *Informatics Education – Supporting Computational Thinking, 5090* (pp. 122–133). DOI:10.1007/978–3–540–69924-8_11

Rosett, M. (2015, August 24). Google has a secret interview process ... and it landed me a job. [Blog post]. *The Hustle*. Retrieved on August 16, 2016 from http://thehustle.co/the-secret-google-interview-that-landed-me-a-job

Saunders, D., & Thagard, P. (2005). Creativity in computer science. In J. C. Kaufman & J. Baer (Eds.), *Creativity across domains: Faces of the muse* (pp. 153–167). Psychology Press.

Shute, V. J., Ventura, M., & Kim, Y. J. (2013). Assessment and learning of qualitative physics in newton's playground. *The Journal of Educational Research, 106*(6), 423–430.

Shute, V., & Ventura, M. (2013). *Stealth assessment: Measuring and supporting learning in video games*. MIT Press.

Simonton, D. K. (2009). Varieties of (scientific) creativity: A hierarchical model of domain-specific disposition, development, and achievement. *Perspectives on Psychological Science : A Journal of the Association for Psychological Science*, *4*(5), 441–452. DOI:10.1111/j.1745–6924.2009.01152.x

Sirius, R. U. (2000). Superhacker Kevin Mitnick: Menace to fear or rogue to love? *Village Voice, 22*

Skibell, R. (2002). The myth of the computer hacker. *Information, Communication & Society*, *5*(3), 336–356.

Sneed, A. (2015, May 19). Moore's law keeps going, defying expectations. *Scientific America*. Retrieved on August 6, 2016, from www.scientificamerican.com/article/moore-s-law-keeps-going-defying-expectations/

Somenkov, I. (2012a, March 7). The mstery of the Duqu framework [Blog post]. *Securelist Kasperky Lab*. Retrieved on October 21, 2016, from https://securelist.com/blog/research/32086/the-mystery-of-the-duqu-framework–6/

Somenkov, I. (2012b, March 19). The mystery of the Duqu framework solved [Blog post]. *Securelist Kasperky Lab*. Retrieved on October 21, 2016, from https://securelist.com/blog/research/32354/the-mystery-of-duqu-framework-solved–7/

Sternberg, R. J., Kaufman, J. C., & Pretz, J. E. (2001). The propulsion model of creative contributions applied to the arts and letters. *Journal of Creative Behavior*, *35*(2), 75–101.

Sternberg, R. J., Kaufman, J. C., & Pretz, J. E. (2004). A propulsion model of creative leadership. *Creativity and Innovation Management*, *13*(3), 145–153.

Tang, C., Baer, J., & Kaufman, J. C. (2015). Implicit theories of creativity in computer science in the United States and China. *Journal of Creative Behavior*, *49*(2), 137–156. doi:10.1002/jocb.61

Torrance, E. P. (2008). *The Torrance Tests of Creative Thinking Norms-Technical Manual Figural (Streamlined) Forms A & B*. Bensenville, IL: Scholastic Testing Service

Christie Medical Holdings, Inc (n.d.). Vein illumination. Retrieved on September 21, 2016, from www.christiemed.com/vein-illumination

Verma, A. (2016, May 24). Japan just made computer programming a compulsory subject in its schools [Blog post]. *fossBytes*. Retrieved on November 4, 2016, from https://fossbytes.com/japan-computer-programming-compulsory-subject-schools/

Vollmer, J. (2016, July 14). The biggest hacker whodunit of the summer [Blog post]. *Motherboard*. Retrieved on September 22, 2016, from http://motherboard.vice.com/read/the-biggest-hacker-whodunnit-of-the-summer

Wing, J. (2014, January 10). Computational thinking benefits society [Blog post]. *Social Issues in Computing*. Retrieved on October 29, 2016, from http://socialissues.cs.toronto.edu/2014/01/computational-thinking/

Zetter, K. (2012, May 28). Meet 'Flame,' the massive spy malware infiltrating Iranian computers. *WIRED*. Retrieved on September 21, 2016, from www.wired.com/2012/05/flame/

Zimmer, B. (2011, February 17). Is it time to welcome our new computer overlords? *The Atlantic*. Retrieved on September 21, 2016, from www.theatlantic.com/technology/archive/2011/02/is-it-time-to-welcome-our-new-computer-overlords/71388/

PART IV

Creativity in Business

18 Studying Creativity across Different Domains

Advertising

Mark Kilgour

University of Waikato, New Zealand

Abstract

Creativity is the heart of advertising. The advertising industry provides a unique research setting with a range of highly specialized roles. These roles range from undertaking creative ideation processes through to idea refinement and expression, evaluation, and relationship management roles. Like all creative ideas, great creativity in advertising requires ideas that are both original and appropriate, but also well presented. Numerous constraints exist to achieving great creative advertising including time, medium, and evaluation pressures. Evaluative pressures result from the difficulty in accurately assessing the effects of an advertising campaign prior to vast expenditures being made. This increases the potential for conflict and the need for structures and processes to be established to manage relationships. For the privileged few who have been fortunate to research in this industry, their insights have assisted our understanding of a range of complex interactions and constraints that influence the full range of creative processes and outcomes. While this research has provided many practical findings, there is still much to learn from this dynamic field.

Research into advertising creativity provides a distinctive setting, affording an opportunity to look in detail at the full range of factors that influence the creative thinking process, from the individual, or team, that develops the idea, to the medium through which the creative idea is expressed, through to the external gatekeepers and evaluation systems that accept or deny the progress of the creative idea. All of this in a highly dynamic, albeit constrained, environment.

The industry attracts and assists in the development of creative individuals, providing a basis for analyzing the characteristics, development, and work, of extremely creative people. Group dynamics and their effect on creative processes can be observed and these are multifaceted, interrelated, complex, and multilevel. They include: (1) the Agency-Client relationship, which provides both resources and constraints to the process; (2) the internal agency account team, which can vary significantly in terms of size and expertise, depending upon the client; (3) the

I would like to thank my friends and colleagues Sheila Sasser, Huw O'Connor, Scott Koslow and Roy Larke for their comments and insights.

creative team, which is focused on creative ideation; and (4) the creative director and other people involved in evaluation processes.

Within the advertising agency there are a variety of key roles. Three of these have attracted significant research attention. The first of these are the creative personnel, or "creatives," who are focused on creative ideation processes. Next there are account roles, which are part of what Kover (1963) referred to as the client-centered system. This is the system established to ensure the objectives of the client are understood, and the agency-client relationship maintained. Account personnel are primarily involved in idea refinement, relationship building, and idea expression processes. The other key role to attract significant research attention is the creative director. They have a complex boundary spanning role, tasked with supporting and protecting the creatives, while also ensuring the client's brand requirements are met.

It is important to understand the dynamics within each of these groups and their interrelationships with the client. In addition, the interactions, structures, and relative power of these groups and individuals provides the basis for understanding creative processes and the resultant quality of the outcomes. The interplay between these groups, and the internal goals and motivations of individuals within the process, can also be observed. The manner in which creative ideas are assessed and rewarded by different groups within the industry then provides the basis for understanding different motivational drivers.

Creativity in Advertising

So what is creative advertising? While creative advertising contains the commonly accepted components of originality and appropriateness (Ford, 1996; Guilford, 1968; Runco & Jaeger, 2012; Sternberg & Lubart, 1996; Torrance, 1974), different groups within the industry put different weight on these two elements. Early research definitions of creative advertising, while not ignoring the need for advertisements to include a brand's selling proposition, emphasized the attention-grabbing, originality component. This reflected the fact that a number of these early research articles came from creatives in advertising agencies (Bogart, Tolley, & Orenstein, 1970; Gibson, 1996; Jones, 1995) and creatives place greater weight on originality (Csikszentmihalyi, 1999; Gambetti, Biraghi, Schultz, & Graffigna, 2015; Kilgour, Sasser, & Koslow, 2013; Koslow, Sasser, & Riordan, 2006; Kover, Goldberg, & James, 1995). There are a number of potential reasons for this.

First, advertising creatives' primary focus is creative idea generation, and it is important that this process is not constrained by a preponderance of appropriateness criteria (Nyilasy & Reid, 2009; Osborn, 1953). Second, as highlighted by a quote from a creative in research by Kover (1995), advertising creatives view the consumer as a tired and exhausted viewer who after returning home at the end of the day drops in front of the TV to be entertained and to relax. Third, there are strong motivational forces driving the focus on originality. Highly original ads grab attention, are talked about, and draw attention to the creative person, or team, which developed them (Helgesen, 1994). Further reinforcement comes in the form of

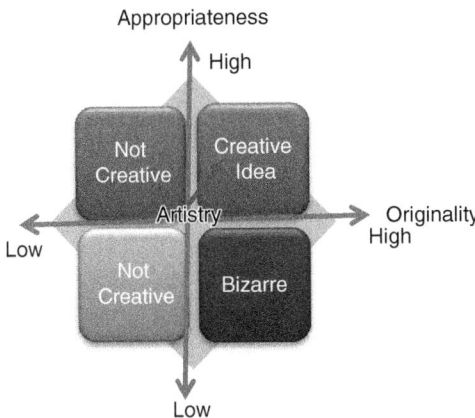

Figure 18.1 *Creative combination diagram.*

industry awards that focus on novel elements. Winning awards has positive effects on morale and brings publicity and visibility to the creative team (El-Murad & West, 2003; Morrison & Haley, 2003, Pratt, 2006; Verbeke, Franses, Blanc, & van Ruiten, 2008; West, 1999). Finally, there are intrinsic rewards that come from making the distant leaps that generate novel outcomes (Sasser & Koslow, 2012; White, 1972).

In recent times, advertising researchers have focused more on appropriateness elements, or meeting the brand strategy of the client. This is perhaps in response to criticism from clients that agency creatives are too novelty focused, and do not put enough emphasis on achieving their brand objectives (Heath, Nairn, & Bottomley, 2009; Jones, 2009; Lehnert, Till, & Ospina, 2014; Rothenberg, 1994). Hence most current advertising researchers define creative advertising as containing the components of originality and appropriateness (Amabile, 1996; Ford, 1996; Kasof, 1995; Kilgour & Koslow, 2009; Mumford & Gustafson, 1988; Mumford & Simonton, 1997; Runco, 2004; Runco & Charles, 1992).

In addition, some researchers have added a third element – artistry or expression (see Figure 18.1). Likewise, advertising industry award shows include the quality of the execution as one of the criteria for judges to focus on (West, Caruana, & Leelapanyelert, 2013). Execution quality, or artistry, is a reflection of the need for an ad to be attractive in order to elicit attention and ease processing. It may also work as a substitute for originality when highly original ads are difficult to achieve, or hard to sell to a client.

This substitute contention is supported by agency-based research. Koslow, Sasser, and Riordan (2003) found that account executives viewed artistry as an acceptable substitute for originality, although this substitution was not acceptable to creatives. Presumably account people think clients will accept non-original but well-presented work, as long as it is on strategy. In advertising, "on strategy" refers to the appropriateness of the creative idea in meeting the client's brand objectives (Hirschman, 1989; Kilgour & Koslow, 2009; Koslow et al., 2003; Sasser & Koslow, 2008; Vanden Bergh, Smith, & Wicks, 1986). One possible explanation for this difference in views is that work that is both high in originality and appropriateness is difficult to evaluate in an advertising setting.

Gaining acceptance of any creative advertisement requires that the target audience perceives it as original and appropriate. However, an idea that is poorly expressed, or executed, increases processing requirements, and in a constrained advertising environment with (1) high levels of clutter, (2) low levels of attention toward ads, (3) generally low motivation to process, and (4) limited time to get the message across, artistry or expression becomes crucial.

A viewer may be able to make sense of highly creative ideas over time with additional processing, or greater explanation of how the ideas are related, but in an advertising environment these conditions are rarely met. The importance of artistry is emphasized in this constrained environment. However, irrespective of the exact definition of creativity a researcher chooses to use, measurement is still complex (El-Murad & West, 2004; Ford, 1996; Guilford, 1968; Kasof, 1995; Koslow et al., 2003; Kover et al., 1995; Michell, 1984; Runco, 2004; Torrance, 1974; West, Kover, & Caruana, 2008).

Measuring Advertising Creativity

In the advertising industry there are numerous award shows that have been set up to recognize and reward creative work. The most famous of these is the Cannes Lions International Festival of Creativity. At Cannes, Gold, Silver, Bronze and Grand Prix Lions are awarded to what are deemed by seasoned advertising professionals as the most deserving entries. These creativity awards appear to have a bias toward the originality component (Kilgour et al., 2013). This is not surprising given the focus on originality by creative personnel in the industry. However, in recent times there has been a growth in effectiveness awards, which focus on measurable outcomes for the client rather than awareness-grabbing components.

In line with these changes, academic researchers have become more focused on using a balance of originality and appropriateness in their measures. Measurement from an academic perspective poses a number of interesting problems, and creativity measurement in particular is fraught with difficulties. Advertising creativity researchers have tended to use three main means of determining the creativity of an advertisement: (1) using award-winning ads as proxy measures, (2) assessment of an ad's creativity by participants in the study, or (3) using panels of external judges to evaluate the ads used in their research.

Each of these methods has weaknesses. Award show results provide an industry-backed standard, but creativity awards appear to be focused on originality, and there is limited assurance that those campaigns were effective. Effectiveness awards are difficult to objectively assess as they tend to evaluate campaign effects, and success is based upon a range of additional factors beyond the advertisement itself. In addition, as noted by Dahlen, Rosengren, and Torn (2008), the use of award-winning ads classifies ads as an absolute, either creative or not, while researchers are increasingly looking at the degree of creativity of advertisements based upon a combination of their levels of originality and appropriateness (Kilgour & Koslow, 2009; Sasser, Koslow, & Kilgour, 2013; Sasser, Koslow, & Riordan, 2007).

Assessments by study participants reflect the reality that evaluations of creative ads are dependent upon the knowledge of the viewer (Koslow et al., 2006). However, unless the study participants are also the target audience, these assessments may not be reflective of effective ads. Selection of the ads used in the research also becomes a crucial consideration. If the assessments are self-assessments by agency personnel of their own work, or that of their agency, this also provides a number of biases. Not least of these is the tendency to overrate work that has already proven successful, irrespective of its true creativity. In addition, as noted, creative personnel tend to have a focus on the originality component.

To overcome these limits some researchers have used Amabile's (1983) consensual definition of creativity. This method essentially states that if enough judges, with appropriate domain knowledge in the field within which the idea was created, view the idea as being creative, then it is (Amabile, 1983; 1996). Subsequently using advertising professionals to assess the ads used by the researchers, on both originality and appropriateness elements, is increasingly being used (Baack, Wilson, & Till 2008; Stuhlfaut & Windels, 2012; West et al., 2008).

However, this method depends upon the definition of the field, as advertising research has found that judges from quite similar areas of expertise have very different opinions when it comes to ratings of appropriateness (Koslow et al., 2003; Kover et al., 1995; Mitchell, 1984; West et al., 2008; Young, 2000). Ideally, creative directors who are the same judges used in agencies, and in award shows, would be used through providing them with set measurement criteria based on the two, or three, main constructs. This method provides a more balanced measure than using award-winning ads, but is difficult to achieve given the high cost and time limits of creative directors. A final issue with all of these measures is that originality and appropriateness are dependent upon the audience, and presumably the most important audience is the target market for the brand itself.

Surprisingly few researchers have used the target market as judges in their measures of creativity (Dahlen, Rosengren, & Torn, 2008). This begs the question, "to whom are the ads appropriate and original?" What is new to a novice in a domain may be old information to an expert, and the same applies for appropriateness. Researchers have found that judgments differ between ad professionals and the general public (White & Smith, 2002) and that professional judgments are no guarantee of success (Kover, James, & Sonner, 1997). This suggests that creative advertising should be defined by the target market consumer, as it is the target audience that ultimately determines the effectiveness of advertising.

Creative vs. Effective Advertising

So is creative advertising effective? Given that advertising has the clear purpose of communicating a brand message to a target audience (White, 1972; Zinkhan, 1993), effective ads require two central elements: (1) the ability to attract attention and (2) the ability to achieve the brand's objective; or being on strategy with the brief. These two elements primarily depend upon the originality and appropriateness of the ad. However, while both elements are important, their relative emphasis within an effective ad depends upon a range of factors, and these factors have changed over time as the advertising environment has evolved (Ashley & Oliver, 2010).

Factors include: (1) the motivation of the person listening to the message, which in turn depends upon their level of involvement and risk in the product category; (2) their previous knowledge and experience of the product category; and (3) a range of situational factors. Changes in the advertising environment, including the amount of clutter, new media, and changing lifestyles, has also changed the relative effect of the two components.

In the golden age of advertising, the 1960s, ads were less common and less intrusive. People did not live in an age where they were constantly bombarded with information, and many product categories were still new to many consumers. Fast forward to today, and advertisers face a very different consumer and advertising environment. Consumers live in a world of information overload, they often view advertising with cynicism and distrust, they do not accept advertising as the price they must pay for content, and they have easy access to social sources of information. Hence, not surprisingly, what it takes for advertising to be effective has also changed.

The advertising client determines effectiveness, often in conjunction with the agency, which is in turn determined by the client's brand objectives and the consumer response. For well-established brands in mature oligopolistic markets, the objective of advertising may be on reinforcement of an existing brand position. In contrast, new product categories in dynamic growth markets, or challenger brands with limited brand presence, will need to focus on novel stimuli to break through the clutter and grab attention.

In addition, advertising is rarely the entirety of an organization's promotional program, and the objective of an advertisement may be to achieve awareness with more in-depth affective and behavioral changes to be achieved through other promotional components (Naik & Raman, 2003; Sasser et al., 2007). Increasingly in the era of social media, digital engagement, and interaction, advertising is only one portion of a brand's integrated marketing communication mix.

This all makes for an interesting research environment, as while an effective ad must be both original and appropriate, creativity researchers are having to grapple with the fact that the relative weights of the two primary components will vary depending upon objectives, target market, and environmental characteristics (Li, Dou, Wang, & Zhou, 2008). Understanding creative and effective advertising therefore requires researchers to look at what drives the relative weight of the appropriateness and originality of the advertisement.

Of course, if an ad is both highly original and appropriate – i.e., "Big C" creative – then this overcomes the need for a trade-off. For an ad to be true Big C it is not enough that both components are present separately within the ad; the ad needs to provide a novel combination which incorporates the brand message into that combination. In this way, the ad both captures attention and instils the brand message. True Big C advertising has huge value for an organization and the results can be literally world changing. Big C ads can catapult little known brands from obscurity to global awareness, or take huge chunks out of a competitor's market share.

If an organization can project their message in an attention-grabbing way, making that creative combination part of the message, then the results can be dramatic. Indeed, this is what more recent research has indicated. Advertisements that contain novelty result in awareness and attention (Lee & Mason, 1999; Till & Baack, 2005), but those advertisements also need to be relevant to achieve the higher-order effects of recall and recognition (Ang, Lee, & Leong, 2007; Ang, Leong, Lee, & Lou, 2014; Pieter, Warlop, & Wedel, 2002; Smith, MacKenzie, Yang, Buchholz, & Darley, 2007). These Big C ads also reduce costs, as frequency of exposure can be reduced, and in a connected world great creative advertising can result in significant engagement, diffusion, and publicity.

However, Big C advertisements are rare, and given the problems with researching small datasets, rarely researched at all. Great advertisements are ones in which the divergent combination, or originality component, reflects the key brand message. For example, the ad for Nolan Cheese that shows a mouse using a trap for push-ups as the brand of cheese has made it so strong.[1] Similarly, an advertisement by Nestle uses emotive reflections from a mother's diary to trigger an affective response and reinforce the need for good food.[2] More often there is a trade-off between these two components and this compromise is something that has only recently become of interest to the advertising creativity field.

But why is the trade-off an issue at all? Why not just produce advertisements that are both original and appropriate? What makes this so difficult? To understand this requires an analysis of the advertising environment and the myriad of constraints that the environment imposes on the creative process from idea generation to evaluation.

Understanding Advertising Creativity: Key Studies

In the vast majority of cases advertising creativity is not Big C, and yet this is what clients purport to want from their agencies. Developing creative ideas is complex and requires the right balance of people, organizational processes, risk tolerance, and motivation. When these factors are not aligned then it is difficult for true Big C creativity to occur. Understanding what contributes to this alignment is a key focus of advertising research. While researchers have made great strides in this area, the interrelationships and interplay of factors means the field is still far from providing a total solution.

Factors that need to be understood are many and include:

1) The medium
2) The creative personnel
3) Structural elements
4) The client.

---

[1] See www.youtube.com/watch?v=-L6UWk6-Hg8, last accessed on April 12, 2017.
[2] See www.youtube.com/watch?v=P4oB8Mxdv7k, last accessed on April 12, 2017.

The Medium

The medium through which advertising is presented places a number of constraints on what is creatively possible. Developing an attention-grabbing ad that gets a brand's positioning message across in a limited number of thirty-second time slots is hard enough on the television. Constrain that further by only allowing a verbal message, or a static visual, all in combination with extremely low levels of audience desire to process, and it becomes a very difficult proposition to achieve highly creative advertisements. Meeting brand objectives can be achieved by increasing the frequency of exposure through repetition, or using multiple media and different promotional techniques, but at a significant cost (Lehnert, Till, & Carlson, 2013).

At the same time, the apparent constraint of the medium provides opportunities for real creative talent to shine (Dahlen, 2005). The anti-smoking advertisement that uses the exhaust pipe of the bus to look like a cigarette giving off black smoke, or the billboard with people hanging from it playing a game of horizontal football, are examples.

New media necessarily means "original creative," as any use of a new media will be a new combination (Sasser et al., 2007). The HBO Voyeur campaign[3] that utilized social and mobile media to great effect, creating an engaging story that was then diffused through blogs and other social media platforms, or the Sydney Metro "Dumb ways to die" campaign,[4] which won an unprecedented eighteen Gold Lions at Cannes after making use of Youtube and gaming applications to great effect, are good examples.

Of course, these first mover advantages quickly wear off, leaving later entrants to the media wondering why their success has not been as great. So, like any new area, early use provides novelty. If that media has been properly understood and effectively used, then any late mover will find it harder to find novel ways to use the medium successfully. Later entrants face an environment where increased clutter reduces the propensity of the target audience to process.

In sum, while the medium undoubtedly has the potential to constrain creativity, it also provides opportunities (Sasser, 2008). The biggest constraining effect is arguably not the medium itself, but the restrictive time and perceptual limits of that medium. Big C creative ideas mean distant domain connections, and it is more difficult to make sense of distant connections. In an advertising setting the creative rarely has the opportunity to explain in detail how those ideas actually connect. This limits how big a leap they can actually make. Undoubtedly media restrictions mean creatives learn to constrain their creativity over time. Creative ads may be very clever, but they cannot be too clever.

The Creative Personnel

Ideas depend upon people, and their abilities and skills are the single most important consideration in relation to the quality of the output (Osborn, 1953; Reid & Rotfeld,

---

[3] See www.youtube.com/watch?v=lupyD3a9d_E.
[4] See www.youtube.com/watch?v=IJNR2EpS0jw.

1976). The creative in an agency generates the idea and one central question is the extent to which these individuals rely on inherent associative ability or make use of learned techniques. Undoubtedly, it is a combination of both. Creative people possess a greater ability to associate more unusual ideas than other people. This is referred to as possessing a flatter associative hierarchy (Mednick, 1962). However, early research across a range of disciplines would suggest that creative-thinking techniques can be used to improve the ability of respondents to develop more creative ideas – at least with student samples (Baer, 1988; 1996; Scott, Leritz, & Mumford, 2004).

One stream of research has focused on identifying a structure, or template, for highly creative advertisements. If there are certain structural elements common to creative ads then, presumably, we can teach these to people and increase the likelihood that they will produce creative ads. Probably the best known of these is the templates approach (Goldenberg, Mazursky, & Solomon, 1999).

The template approach analyzed award- and non-award-winning ads to determine if there was a common structure used by the winners. They identified six templates that were commonly used in award-winning ads. They then taught these templates to a group of study participants and found that they were significantly better at improving their ability to develop creative ads, relative to the other methods tested. Other researchers have identified similar structures in creative ads; such as the Remote Conveyor Model (Rossiter, 1994; 2008; Rossiter & Bellman, 2005; Rossiter & Percy, 1997).

These findings illustrate the use of common structures that assist in demonstrating a brand's unique selling proposition in a novel way. In one version of a template, extreme consequences of using the brand are used to illustrate the brand's key message. For example, the ad might show polar bears freezing to death because everyone has switched to a new brand of electric car and the effects are so great that global warming has become global cooling. This illustrates the environmental credentials of the new car in a novel way.

These structural approaches provide simple techniques that people can follow. This allows them to focus on undertaking the core idea-generation process, which is the combination of unusual domains of knowledge. At the same time, the technique ensures that the combination illustrates the key brand message. These structural formulas assist people by providing useful linking mechanisms, but the person developing the idea still has to come up with the divergent combination. This divergent thinking depends upon the associative ability and domain knowledge of the idea generator (Reid, 1978).

The value of these techniques for experienced agency creatives is probably limited. Experienced creatives already understand the need to combine the brand message within the divergent thinking process. What is probably more important is whether divergent thinking, or associative techniques, can be taught to enhance a creative's expertise.

Divergent thinking techniques are essentially associative techniques that train respondents to combine very different domains of knowledge. More complex techniques encourage the connection of more distant domains than simpler techniques. In addition, some techniques may provide alternative benefits, such as with brainstorming, which encourages divergent cues from the ideas of others in a group setting as the basis for idea generation processes. These group processes may also increase the motivation levels of respondents and enhance commitment to the process and solution.

To what extent these associative techniques work on actual creatives requires research. A review of creativity techniques by Scott, Leritz, and Mumford (2004) supported the effectiveness of creativity training, but very few of the studies available for their review were from organizational studies. One experimental study undertaken on both advertising professionals and students (Kilgour & Koslow, 2009) tested the differing effect of providing priming cues and divergent-thinking techniques to three sample groups: creative personnel, account executives, and undergraduate students.

In the experiment, half of the participants received a convergent-thinking prime (priming cues) and the other half received a random word-associative technique (divergent-thinking technique). It was found that the associative technique increased the originality of responses in account executives, but reduced the originality of the creatives. This is probably due to creatives possessing internalized divergent-thinking associative techniques that are superior to those used in their experiment.

These divergent associative techniques encourage distant domain combinations, which increase originality, but usually at the cost of a decrease in appropriateness. As creative personnel already have a tendency toward originality it may be better to place more emphasis on improving their appropriateness. The experiment found that providing creatives with appropriateness-based cues resulted in a large increase in the appropriateness of their ideas, with a much smaller negative trade off effect on originality. Many of the evaluation processes set up within agencies are focused on ensuring creatives' ideas are on strategy – i.e., appropriate. The creative brief is one example of an information cue that assists creatives to keep their ideas on strategy. Other processes, such as consumer research and copy testing, are also used.

The key finding of this research was the contrasting effects found for these techniques on the various groups. What this reinforces is the importance of a person's existing domain knowledge and associative expertise (Reid, 1978). Essentially a base level of knowledge in an area, or domain, is needed before divergent-thinking techniques will be effective. However, more research in this area is needed.

While it is clear that creatives are good at producing highly original ideas, these creative ideas must be developed and presented, and make it through multiple levels of evaluation (Csikszentmihalyi, 1999; Vanden Bergh & Stuhlfaut, 2006). The first evaluation process is the self-evaluation of creative ideas by the idea generator. There has been a surprising dearth of research into self-evaluation processes (Higgins, Harris, & Kuehn, 1994; Kousoulas, 2010; Runco, 1995), given that if the idea generator does not decide to express their idea then it never has a chance. Additionally, if the idea generator's internal evaluation processes are poor, then good ideas may be erroneously discarded.

The next evaluation process is usually the evaluation of the idea by other creatives. Other creatives provide additional insights and angles for generating and refining creative ideas. However, a disadvantage of using other creatives is their similar disposition toward originality, and hence other external evaluation is needed. Agencies have therefore developed structures to manage creative idea evaluation and refinement processes.

The Structure

Although identified as a key area almost half a century ago (Kover, 1970), structural elements and their effect on creativity have been under researched. Advertising agencies have developed structures and systems over time to assist creativity. These structures are necessary for any outsourcing process, as it is crucial that the client and the agency have effective systems of communication and evaluation. These allow any conflicts that may occur from differences in expectations to be managed (Barry, Peterson, & Bradford-Todd, 1987; Kover & Goldberg, 1995; West, 1999).

Developing highly original and highly appropriate ads is a difficult process given that the focus of clients and creative personnel often differ (Gambetti et al., 2015; Kover & Goldberg, 1995; West, 1999; West & Berthon, 1997; West et al., 2008). Creative personnel need a lack of constraints in order to develop creative ideas (Kilgour, 2008; Nyilasy & Reid, 2009; Wiley, 1998), and are usually focused on developing highly original solutions from which they receive both intrinsic and extrinsic rewards. In contrast, clients are often more focused on the appropriateness of the creative idea given their intimate knowledge of brand objectives (Hackley & Kover, 2007; Hirschman, 1989; Hurman, 2011; Kover et al., 1997; Michell, 1984). Hence there is an underlying conflict that must be managed.

In terms of evaluation, problems occur if various parties have different view-points, motivations, and objectives (Amabile, 1996; El-Murad & West, 2004; Ford, 1996; Guilford, 1968; Koslow et al., 2003; Kasof, 1995; Kover et al., 1995; Michell, 1984; Murphy & Maynard, 1996; Runco, 2004; Sasser & Koslow, 2008; Sasser et al., 2013; Torrance, 1974; West et al., 2008). It is often the view of the client that agencies get too focused on doing something original and lose sight of their brand needs. In contrast, creatives lament that their best work does not make it out of their bottom draw, and that copy testing and other rigid objective measures kill really good creative ideas (Sasser et al., 2013). These issues are compounded by the problem that Big C creative ideas are difficult to evaluate, and there are large differences between judges from different domains.

Creatives are very good creative thinkers with the ability to connect distant, seemingly dissimilar, domains. Rather than a linear thought approach, this involves leaps of insight (Schilling, 2005), and hence other people often have trouble following along. The issue is therefore getting others to see the appropriateness of their creative ideas. While the originality part of a creative idea is easy for others to see, appropriateness is much more problematic. Research has shown that groups of judges across a wide range of areas have significantly different views of appropri-ateness. These differences have been shown between account executives and creatives (Koslow et al., 2003), clients and agency personnel (Michell, 1984), industry award judges and consumers (Kover et al., 1995), practitioners and the target market (West et al., 2008), and even between copy-writers and art directors (Young, 2000).

The evaluation of the appropriateness of Big C creative ads requires that the viewer makes sense of the distant combinations and this would normally take time and effort. Time and effort are not normally something afforded to a few thirty-second time slots. Therefore it is crucial that creative ads are evaluated by external judges in order to identify creative ideas that people other than the creative personnel are likely to understand. Subsequently, ideas with potential need to be refined to fit in with the appropriateness criteria used by key external evaluators. The most important of these external evaluators is the client, who must achieve legitimacy in their own organizational context (Kover, 1971), but agencies also use a number of internal systems of evaluation.

Given the difficulty in evaluating highly creative advertisements and their outcomes (Cagley, 1986; Cagley & Roberts, 1984; Hurman, 2011; Weilbacher, 1983), systems of evaluation are especially important in the advertising setting (Kover & Little, 1980; Levinthal, 1988; Nilakant & Rao, 1994; Spake, D'Souza, Crutchfield, & Morgan, 1999; West, 1999; West & Ford, 2001; West et al., 2008; Zhou, 2005). Most agencies have evolved internal structures of evaluation and development that create a safety net before any ad ever reaches the client. These systems have many names and organizational structures, but they often involve a combination of skilled collaborators who review creative campaigns at different stages in the development process. One of the structural elements that helps overcome the evaluation problem is the use of the account executive.

Account executives, in their role of client liaison, are in a strong position to understand the client-appropriateness criteria. The account executive has a key role in providing relevant appropriateness criteria information to creatives from the client, as well as through research (Hackley, 2003). They also assist to sell good creative work to clients using the strength of their client relationship (Haytko, 2004).

The role of the creative director is also crucial in enabling and supporting creativity (Mallia, Windels, & Broyles, 2013). They act as an evaluation and refinement mechanism to assist in matching client needs to creative ideas. As creative directors are experienced creatives, they have learnt the importance of appropriateness criteria and what clients are likely to accept. In addition, the creative director is likely to recognize Big C combinations and can champion these creative ideas, using their position and knowledge, to risk-averse clients.

Creative ideas may also be evaluated using systems of external testing, such as copy testing. David Stewart, one of the most prominent researchers in the field, has worked extensively on models of advertising effects and how copy testing can be used to promote effective ads (Stewart, 1996; Stewart & Furse, 1986; Stewart & Koslow, 1989). Methods of testing finished versions of advertisements have developed significantly in recent years with improvements in technologies. Even with all these levels of evaluation, ideas must be presented, evaluated, and accepted by the client.

The Client

The client provides arguably the biggest constraint to the creativity of advertising, especially when it comes to originality (Beverland, Farrelly, & Woodhatch, 2007; Gambetti et al., 2015; Haytko, 2004). While the work in this area is limited, risk-averse clients, or clients who view themselves as highly knowledgeable of the advertising process (Koslow et al., 2006), appear to constrain agency creativity. This may be a result of three factors: (1) that they put too many evaluative criteria in place that focus on appropriateness elements (Hackley & Kover, 2007; Hirschman, 1989; Hurman, 2011; Kover et al., 1997; Michell, 1984); (2) that creative personnel are not motivated to present highly creative work if they perceive that the client is unlikely to accept it (Dewett, 2006; Feldman, 1999; Sternberg, 2006; West, 1999; West & Ford, 2001); and (3) that clients take a parity position that affords little room for improvement on either appropriateness or originality (Ashley & Oliver, 2010; Budner, 1994; Tapiero, 1978).

Developing highly creative ideas may be intrinsically rewarding but if you know the client is not open to these ideas, then why bother expressing or even generating those ideas? Essentially, the risk-intolerant or sophisticated client does not allow the creative to do their part in the process. Therefore, the client gets the advertising they are willing to accept. All of this of course is not without inputs from the various actors in the process. However, in some cases it may be that the client is getting not only what they want, but also what they need when they ask for creativity that is focused on appropriateness.

Clients with products at different stages of that product category's life cycle, or in different positions within a market, will require different effects from their advertisements. Creative personnel often state that smaller clients allow them to do more creative work (West, 1999). At least some of this is due to the requirements of those clients. For smaller clients with less-dominant positions in a market, or for new products trying to overcome the inertia of markets and gain awareness of their new products, their focus may well be on advertising that is concentrated more toward originality.

In contrast, for dominant brands with a long-established brand-positioning strategy, it may be detrimental to push for highly original advertisements as it may muddy their brand message and create confusion among their loyal customer base (Kilgour et al., 2013). This is because any new idea moves them away from that existing position. The idea must be novel and hence different from what has been done before. This creates risk for the brand manager, as why would anyone want to change a winning formula? Indeed, researchers have found that clients usually stick with their agency unless there are major environmental changes that mean their brand is losing marketing share (Beverland et al., 2007; Buchanan & Michell, 1992; Oster, 1982; Sasser et al., 2013; West, 1999).

Summary

While great creative ads are the ideal, there are numerous constraints. The biggest of these is an issue not unique to advertising – the difficulty in evaluating creative ideas. The problem lies within the appropriateness dimensions and it is to ensure appropriateness that many of the systems have been set up which constrain Big C creativity.

Being an advertising creative is challenging. They strive for highly original breakthrough ideas and distant domain connections, but these new creative combinations by their very nature are harder to get others to appreciate. They have limited time to present complex combinations and do so to clients, who often have a different perspective in terms of what is appropriate. The advertising field has made huge strides in terms of understanding these differences but more research is needed to narrow down how to overcome these differences amongst a confluence of factors.

Where to from Here?

There is unlimited scope for research in relation to the ever-changing effects of new technology and media on what makes ads effective, and the subsequent effects on the creative process. Social media has changed the way ads are delivered, viewed, and responded to, with massive changes in terms of interactivity and diffusion. This in turn has changed the emphasis on different media and the ways in which consumers respond to content.

Another related area of significant growth and interest is the crowdsourcing of creative ideas. Harnessing the power of consumers around the world to develop creative ideas, rather than relying on agencies, has appeal to many clients. Research has indicated that quantity leads to quality in terms of creative-ideation processes. With the potential to access creative thinkers throughout the world, a number of companies have already begun to change the traditional advertising agency model.

More research is needed to develop better target-audience-based measures of creativity. It is somewhat surprising that relatively few studies use the target audience as judges of creative ideas. More work is needed to determine just how different the judgments of agency personnel, and in particular creative directors, are relative to the final target audience. Such research may significantly change how advertising creativity is measured and give us new insights into advertising effectiveness.

Another difficulty with measures of advertising creativity is that of replicating real-world conditions. In trying to determine the effectiveness of creativity, any treatment or measurement conditions that result in increased attention levels from the consumer has obvious negative impacts on the relative importance of originality. These issues mean the question of whether creative advertising is effective advertising still requires further work.

More work is needed to understand the complex interactions on how structural elements influence creativity. From a better review of agency theory and its implications to the advertising industry, through to internal structural processes and constraints, there is significant scope for research. While this area was touched upon by Kover (1970), and structural processes and constraints were the focus on Kover's work until the first research journals in advertising (Kover, 1963; 1970), it is an area that has been largely neglected in the advertising creativity domain since then.

While there is some good work in relation to motivational influences on creative processes (Sasser & Koslow, 2012; Torr, 2008), given the importance of motivation in an industry where creative personnel face constant evaluative pressures from multiple sources and at many different levels, this is an area of importance. Finally, expression is an area that is surprisingly under researched. In a field that is all about telling a good story about brands, there is surprisingly little research looking into expression processes.

Advertising creativity may best be described as constrained creativity. For advertising creatives it may be their ability to overcome these constraints and provide truly Big C advertisements that is the true measure of their success. Creative personnel must be as much salespeople as they are idea generators. They have to overcome multiple rounds and layers of evaluation in order to get their ideas developed. Constant evaluative pressure and a need to compromise to meet different evaluation criteria from different external judges makes the process a minefield. Creative personnel must possess a range of exceptional talents at multiple levels and we have much still to learn from them.

References

Amabile, T. M. (1983). *The social psychology of creativity*. New York: Springer-Verlag.

Amabile, T. M. (1996). *Creativity in context*. New York: Westview.

Ang, S. H., Lee, Y. H., & Leong, S. M. (2007). The ad creativity cube: Conceptualization and initial validation. *Journal of the Academy of Marketing Science, 35*(2), 220–232.

Ang, S. H., Leong, S. M., Lee, Y. H., & Lou, S. L. (2014). Necessary but not sufficient: Beyond novelty in advertising creativity. *Journal of Marketing Communications, 20*(3), 214–230.

Ashley, C., & Oliver, J. D. (2010). Creative Leaders. *Journal of Advertising, 39*(1), 115–130.

Baack, D. W., Wilson, R. T., & Till, B. D. (2008). Creativity and memory effects: Recall, recognition, and an exploration of non-traditional media. *Journal of Advertising, 37*(4), 85–94.

Baer, J. M. (1988). Long-term effects of creativity training with middle school students. *The Journal of Early Adolescence, 8*(2), 183–193.

Baer, J. (1996). The effects of task-specific divergent-thinking training. *The Journal of Creative Behavior, 30*(3), 183–187.

Barry, T. E., Peterson, R. L., & Bradford-Todd, W. B. (1987). The role of account planning in the future of advertising agency research. *Journal of Advertising Research, 27*(1), 15–21.

Beverland, M., Farrelly, F., & Woodhatch, Z. (2007). Exploring the dimensions of proactivity within advertising agency-client relationships. *Journal of Advertising, 36*(4), 49–60.

Bogart, L., Tolley, B. S., & Orenstein, F. (1970). What one little ad can do. *Journal of Advertising Research, 10*(4), 3–13.

Buchanan, B., & Michell, P. C. (1991). Using structural factors to assess the risk of failure in agency-client relations. *Journal of Advertising Research, 31*(4), 68–75.

Budner D. M. (1994). Increasing the odds for marketplace success – Advertising development at FCB/LKP. *Journal of Advertising Research, 34*(3), 112–115.

Cagley, J. W. (1986). A comparison of advertising agency selection factors: Advertiser and agency perceptions. *Journal of Advertising Research, 26*(3), 39–44.

Cagley, J. W., & Roberts, C. R. (1984). Criteria for advertising agency selection: an objective appraisal. *Journal of Advertising Research, 24*(2), 27–31.

Csikszentmihalyi, M. (1999). 16 Implications of a Systems Perspective for the Study of Creativity. In Sternberg R. J. (Ed.), *Handbook of creativity* (p. 313). Cambridge: Cambridge University Press.

Dahlén, M. (2005). The medium as a contextual cue: Effects of creative media choice. *Journal of Advertising, 34*(3), 89–98.

Dahlén, M., Rosengren, S., & Torn, F. (2008). Advertising creativity matters. *Journal of Advertising Research, 48*(3), 392–403.

Dewett, T. (2006). Exploring the role of risk in employee creativity. *Journal of Creative Behaviour, 40*(1), 27–41.

El-Murad, J., & West, D. C. (2003). Risk and creativity in advertising. *Journal of Marketing Management, 19*(5–6), 657–673.

El-Murad, J., & West, D. C. (2004). The definition and measurement of creativity: What do we know? *Journal of Advertising Research, 44*(2), 188–201.

Feldman, D. H. (1999). The development of creativity. In Sternberg R. J. (Ed.), *Handbook of creativity* (169–186), Cambridge: Cambridge University Press.

Ford, C. (1996). A theory of individual creative action in multiple social domains. *Academy of Management Review, 21*(4), 1112–1142.

Gambetti, R., Biraghi, S., Schultz, D. E., & Graffigna, G. (2015). Brand wars: Consumer–brand engagement beyond client–agency fights. *Journal of Strategic Marketing, 24*(2), 1–14.

Gibson, L. D. (1996). What can one TV exposure do. *Journal of Advertising Research, 36*(2), 9–18.

Goldenberg, J., Mazursky, D., & Solomon, S. (1999). The fundamental templates of quality ads. *Marketing Science, 18*(3), 333–351.

Guilford, J. P. (1968). *Intelligence, creativity, and their educational implications.* San Diego: RR Knapp.

Hackley, C. (2003). From consumer insight to advertising strategy: the account planner's integrative role in creative advertising development. *Marketing Intelligence & Planning, 21*(7), 446–452.

Hackley, C., & Kover A. (2007). The trouble with creatives: Negotiating creative identity in advertising agencies. *International Journal of Advertising, 26*(1), 63–78.

Haytko, D. L. (2004). Firm-to-firm and interpersonal relationships: Perspectives from advertising agency account managers. *Journal of the Academy of Marketing Science, 32*(3), 312–328.

Heath, R. G., Nairn, A. C., & Bottomley, P. A. (2009). How effective is creativity? *Journal of Advertising Research, 49*(4), 450–463.

Helgesen, T. (1994). Advertising awards and advertising agency performance criteria. *Journal of Advertising, 34*(4), 43–53.

Higgins, K. M., Harris, N. A., & Kuehn, L. L. (1994). Placing assessment into the hands of young children: A study of student-generated criteria and self-assessment. *Educational Assessment, 2*(4), 309–324.

Hirschman, E. C. (1989). Role-based models of advertising creation and production. *Journal of Advertising, 18*(4), 42–53.

Hurman, J. (2011). *The case for creativity*. Auckland, NZ: AUT Press

Jones, M. (2009, March 20). Pitch secret: How clients really think. *Campaign*. Retrieved on April 12, 2017, from: www.campaignlive.co.uk/news/892385.

Jones, J. P. (1995). Single-source research begins to fulfil its promise. *Journal of Advertising Research* (May/June), 9–16.

Kasof, J. (1995). Explaining creativity: The attributional perspective. *Creativity Research Journal, 8*(4), 311–366.

Kilgour, M., (2008). *Understanding creativity: The creative thinking process and how to improve it*, VDM Verlag, Germany.

Kilgour, M., & Koslow, S. (2009). Why and how do creative thinking techniques work?: Trading off originality and appropriateness to make more creative advertising. *Journal of the Academy of Marketing Science, 37*(3), 298–309.

Kilgour, M., Sasser, S., & Koslow, S. (2013). Creativity awards: Great expectations? *Creativity Research Journal, 25*(2), 163–171.

Koslow, S., Sasser, S. L., & Riordan, E. A. (2003). What is creative to whom and why?: Perceptions in advertising agencies. *Journal of Advertising Research, 43*(1), 96–110.

Koslow, S., Sasser, S. L., & Riordan, E. A. (2006). Do marketers get the advertising they need or the advertising they deserve? Agency views of how clients influence creativity. *Journal of Advertising, 35*(3), 85–105.

Kousoulas, F. (2010). The interplay of creative behavior, divergent thinking, and knowledge base in students' creative expression during learning activity. *Creativity Research Journal, 22*(4), 387–396.

Kover, A. J. (1963). Reorganization in an advertising agency: A case study of a decrease in integration. *Human Organization, 22*(4), 252–259.

Kover, A. J. (1970). *Creativity and Structure in Advertising Agencies*. PhD Dissertation. New Haven, CT: Yale University.

Kover, A. J. (1971) Marketing research and two kinds of legitimacy. *The American Sociologist 6*, (supplementary): 69–72.

Kover, A. J. (1995). Copywriters' implicit theories of communication: An exploration. *Journal of Consumer Research, 21*(4), 596–611.

Kover, A. J., Goldberg, S. M., & James, W. L. (1995). Creativity vs. effectiveness?: An integrative classification for advertising. *Journal of Advertising Research, 35*(6), 29–38.

Kover, A. J., James, W. L., & Sonner, B. S. (1997). To whom do advertising creatives write? An inferential answer. *Journal of Advertising Research, 37*(1), 41–53.

Kover, A. J., & Little, C. H. (1980). Crises in copy testing. *Journal of Advertising Research, 20*(4), 65–71.

Lee, Y. H., & Mason, C. (1999). Responses to information incongruency in advertising: The role of expectancy, relevancy, and humor. *Journal of Consumer Research, 26*(2), 156–169.

Lehnert, K., Till, B. D., & Carlson, B. D. (2013). Advertising creativity and repetition: Recall, wearout and wearin effects. *International Journal of Advertising, 32*(2), 211–231.

Lehnert, K., Till, B. D., & Ospina, J. M. (2014). Advertising creativity: The role of divergence versus meaningfulness. *Journal of Advertising, 43*(3), 274–285.

Levinthal, D. (1988). A survey of agency models of organizations. *Journal of Economic Behavior & Organization, 9*(2), 153–185.

Li, H., Dou, W., Wang, G., & Zhou, N. (2008). The effect of agency creativity on campaign outcomes: The moderating role of market conditions. *Journal of Advertising, 37*(4), 109–120.

Mallia, K. L., Windels, K., & Broyles, S. J. (2013). An examination of successful leadership traits for the advertising-agency Creative Director. *Journal of Advertising Research, 53*(3), 339–353.

Mednick, S. (1962). The associative basis of the creative process. *Psychological Review, 69*(3), 220.

Michell, P. C. (1984). Accord and discord in agency-client perceptions of creativity. *Journal of Advertising Research, 24*(5), 9–24.

Morrison, M. A., & Haley, E. (2003). Account planners' views on how their work is and should be evaluated. *Journal of Advertising, 32*(2), 7–16.

Mumford, M. D., & Gustafson, S. B. (1988). Creativity syndrome: Integration, application, and innovation. *Psychological Bulletin, 103*(1), 27–43.

Mumford, M. D., & Simonton, D. K. (1997). Creativity in the workplace: People, problems and structures. *Journal of Creative Behaviour, 31*(1), 1–6.

Murphy P., & Maynard M. L (1996) Using judgment profiles to compare advertising agencies' and clients' campaign values. *Journal of Advertising Research,* 36 (2): 19–27.

Naik, P. A., & Raman, K. (2003). Understanding the impact of synergy in multimedia communications. *Journal of Marketing Research, 40*(4), 375–388.

Nilakant, V. & Rao, H. (1994). Agency Theory and uncertainty in organizations: An evaluation. *Organization Studies, 15*(5), 649–672.

Nyilasy, G. & Reid, L. N. (2009). Agency practitioner theories of how advertising works. *Journal of Advertising, 38*(2), 81–96.

Osborn, A. F. (1953), *Applied Imagination* (Rev edn.) New York: Charles Scribner's Sons.

Oster, S. (1982). Intra-industry structure and the ease of strategic change. *The Review of Economics and Statistics, 64*(3), 276–383.

Pieters, F. G. M., Warlop, L., & Wedel, M. (2002). Breaking through the clutter: Benefits of advertisement originality and familiarity for brand attention and memory. *Management Science, 48*(6), 765–781.

Pratt, A. C. (2006). Advertising and creativity, a governance approach: a case study of creative agencies in London. *Environment and Planning A, 38*(10), 1883–1899.

Reid, L. N. (1978). Factors affecting creativity in generation of advertising. *Journalism Quarterly, 55*(4), 781–85.

Reid, L. N., & Rotfeld, H.J. (1976). Toward an associative model of advertising creativity. *Journal of Advertising, 5*(4), 24–29.

Rossiter, J. R. (1994). The RAM-Conveyor theory of creative strengtheners in ads. *Forschungsgruppe Konsum und Verhalten, Konsumentenforschung, Munich:* Vahlen.

Rossiter, J. R. (2008). Defining the necessary components of creative, effective ads. *Journal of Advertising, 37*(4), 139–144.

Rossiter, J. R., & Bellman, S. (2005). *Marketing communications: Theory and applications.* Upper Saddle River, NJ: Prentice-Hall.

Percy, L., & Rossiter, J. R. (1987). *Advertising communication and promotion management.* New York: McGraw-Hill Book Company.

Rothenberg, R. (1994). *Where the suckers moon: An advertising story.* New York: Alfred A.

Runco, M. A. (1995). Insight for creativity, expression for impact. *Creativity Research Journal, 8*(4), 377–390.

Runco, M. (2004). Personal creativity and culture. *Creativity: When East Meets West,* 9–22.

Runco, M. A., & Charles, R. (1992). Judgements of originality and appropriateness as predictors of creativity. *Personality, Individual Differences, 15*(5), 537–546.

Runco, M. A., & Jaeger, G. J. (2012). The standard definition of creativity. *Creativity Research Journal*, *24*(1), 92–96.

Sasser, S. L. (2008). Creating passion to engage versus enrage consumer co-creators with agency co-conspirators: Unleashing creativity. *Journal of Consumer Marketing*, *25*(3), 183–186.

Sasser, S., & Koslow, S. (2012). Passion, expertise, politics, and support. *Journal of Advertising*, *41*(3), 5–17.

Sasser, S., Koslow, S., & Kilgour, M. (2013). Matching creative agencies with results-driven clients? *Journal of Advertising Research*, *53*(3), 297–312.

Sasser, S. L., Koslow, S., & Riordan, E. A. (2007). Creative and interactive media use by agencies: Engaging an IMC media palette for implementing advertising campaigns. *Journal of Advertising Research*, *47*(3), 237–256.

Schilling, M. A. (2005). A" small-world" network model of cognitive insight. *Creativity Research Journal*, *17*(2–3), 131–154.

Scott, G., Leritz, L. E., & Mumford, M. D. (2004). The effectiveness of creativity training: A quantitative review. *Creativity Research Journal*, *16*(4), 361–388.

Smith, R. E., MacKenzie, S. B., Yang, X., Buchholz, L. M., & Darley, W. K. (2007). Modeling the determinants and effects of creativity in advertising. *Marketing Science*, *26*(6), 819–833.

Spake, D. R., D'Souza, G., Crutchfield, T. N., & Morgan, R. M. (1999). Advertising agency compensation: An agency theory explanation. *Journal of Advertising*, *28*(3), 53–72.

Sternberg, R. J. (2006). The nature of creativity. *Creative Research Journal*, *18*(1), 87–98.

Sternberg, R. J., & Lubart, T. I. (1996). Investing in creativity. *American Psychologist*, *51*(7), 677.

Stewart, D. W. (1996). Market-back approach to the design of integrated communications programs: A change in the paradigm and a focus on determinants of success. *Journal of Business Research*, *37*(3), 147–153.

Stewart, D. W., & Furse, D. (1986). *Effective television advertising: A study of 1000 commercials*. Lexington, MA: Lexington Books.

Stewart, D. W., & Koslow, S. (1989). Executional factors and advertising effectiveness: A replication. *Journal of Advertising*, *18*(3), 21–32.

Stuhlfaut, M. W., & Windels, K. (2012). Measuring the organisational impact on creativity: The creative code intensity scale. *International Journal of Advertising*, *31*(4), 795–818.

Tapiero C. S. (1978). Optimum advertising and goodwill under uncertainty. *Operations Research*, *26*(3), 450–463.

Torr, G. (2011). *Managing creative people: Lessons in leadership for the ideas economy*. John Wiley & Sons.

Till, B. D., & Baack, D. W. (2005). Recall and persuasion: Does creative advertising matter? *Journal of Advertising*, *34*(3), 47–57.

Torrance, E. P. (1974). *Torrance tests of creative thinking*. Lexington, MA: Personnel Press.

Verbeke, W., Franses, P. H., Blanc, A. L., & van Ruiten, N. (2008). Finding the keys to creativity in ad agencies: Using climate, dispersion, and size to examine award performance. *Journal of Advertising*, *37*(4), 121–130.

Weilbacher, W. M. (1983). *Choosing an advertising agency*, NTC Business Books. New York: McGraw-Hill Book Company

West, D. C. (1999). 360° of creative risk. *Journal of Advertising Research*, *39*(1), 39–50.

West, D. C., & Berthon, P. (1997). Antecedents of risk-taking behaviour by advertisers: Empirical evidence and management implications. *Journal of Advertising Research*, *37*(5), 27–40.

West, D., Caruana, A., & Leelapanyalert, K. (2013). Judging creativity in advertising at award shows. *Journal of Advertising Research*, *53*(*3*), 324–338.

West, D. C., & Ford, J. (2001). Advertising agency philosophies and employee risk taking. *Journal of Advertising*, *30*(1), 77–91.

West, D. C., Kover, A. J., & Caruana, A. (2008). Practitioner and customer views of advertising creativity: same concept, different meaning? *Journal of Advertising*, *37*(4), 35–45.

White, G. E. (1972). Creativity: The X factor in advertising theory. *Journal of Advertising*, *1*, 28–32.

White, A., Shen, F., & Smith, B. L. (2002). Judging advertising creativity using the creative product semantic scale. *The Journal of Creative Behavior*, *36*(4), 241–253.

Wiley, J. (1998). Expertise as mental set: The effects of domain knowledge in creative problem solving. *Memory and Cognition*, *26*(4), 716–730.

Young, C. E. (2000). Creative differences between copywriters and art directors. *Journal of Advertising Research*, *40*(3), 19–26.

Vanden Bergh, B. G., Smith, S. J., & Wicks, J. L. (1986). Internal agency relationships: Account services and creative personnel. *Journal of Advertising*, *15*(2), 55–60.

Vanden Bergh, B., & Stuhlfaut, M. (2006). Is advertising creativity primarily an individual or a social process? *Mass Communication & Society*, *9*(4), 373–397.

Zhao, H. (2005). Incentive-based compensation to advertising agencies: A principal–agent approach. *International Journal of Research in Marketing*, *22*(3), 255–275.

Zinkhan, G. M. (1993). From the Editor. *Journal of Advertising*, *22*(2), 1–3.

19 The Relationship Between Marketing and Creativity

It's Complicated

Marie Taillard

and

Benjamin G. Voyer

ESCP Europe Business School

Abstract

In this chapter, we explore the role of creativity in marketing, and suggest that a better understanding of creativity in the marketing domain can yield unique insights for research in both creativity and marketing. We first discuss the definitions of the concept of creativity in marketing and marketing research, and its relation to other associated constructs. Second, we focus on three core domains of application for creativity in marketing: operational, strategic, and organizational. Third, we shift to consumer creativity and offer a critical overview of some of the methodological aspects of creativity research in marketing. Finally we discuss our findings and introduce key questions to be addressed in future research in the field.

Marketing is often seen as a fertile ground for creativity, mainly because its most visible aspect, advertising, is deeply woven into our cultures and into our everyday lives – from thought-provoking campaigns like Benetton's in the 1980s and 1990s,[1] often using nudity or famous personalities to communicate about its brand, to iconic Super Bowl spots such as Apple's Big Brother commercial,[2] narrating a world inspired from Orwell's 1984, or the Coca Cola Hilltop commercial[3] gathering young men and women from around the world on the top of a hill in Italy to sing "I'd Like to Buy the World a Coke," and whose status was recently enhanced with a cameo appearance in the finale of the Mad Men television series.

Less clearly associated with marketing in the public's mind, but no less transformative, are innovative strategies such as the real-time pricing adjustments practiced by budget airlines in Europe. In fact, the technological advances of the last couple of decades have greatly accelerated both the need and the opportunities for greater creativity in marketing and have helped resolve a fundamental tension for marketers

---

[1] See www.ibtimes.co.uk/benetton-history-shocking-ad-campaigns-pictures-252087, retrieved on December 1, 2015

[2] See www.youtube.com/watch?v=2zfqw8nhUwA, retrieved on December 1 2015

[3] See www.coca-colacompany.com/stories/coke-lore-hilltop-story/, retrieved on December 1, 2015.

between an analytical and rigorous approach to marketing (indeed, one talks of "marketing science"), and a much more intuitive, creative, and artistic approach. Finally, another lens in which to think of creativity in marketing is that of the different stakeholders that make up the marketing landscape or ecosystem: from the consumer, to the company as an organization, its employees, and other actors in the so-called value chain such as suppliers, distributors, and retailers, to the brand itself. The present chapter offers a broad panorama of creativity across these different dimensions: from definitions and classical creativity studies in marketing, to a review of the role and effects of creativity across the different elements of the so-called marketing mix and the principal aspects of marketing strategy and marketing organizations, to finally exploring the future of creativity research and upcoming challenges in the area of marketing.

Defining Creativity from a Marketing Perspective

Marketing is both an organizational function and an academic discipline. Studying creativity in marketing means exploring the implications of adopting a creative approach to the practice of marketing, as well as understanding how marketing scholars approach the notion of creativity, and its implications for marketing theory. An important particularity of studying creativity in marketing is that its effects can be evaluated in terms of performance for the firm. In this way, marketing provides an excellent research ground for the two commonly accepted dimensions of creativity: novelty and value (Hennessey & Amabile, 2010). It is for customers to judge with their wallets whether messages, products, services, and other offerings are novel enough and valuable enough. Marketers should adjust their creative thinking to their market performance and assess how much creativity they need to inject into their marketing practices in order to reach their performance goals.

Creativity can be evaluated for its effectiveness within the same firm or in relation to a particular sector (Campbell 2011). With the exponential acceleration of information, marketers find it increasingly difficult to "break through the clutter," whether with their promotional messages or their products. Organizations that do not raise their creative bar simply can no longer compete. In the words of Jeremy Bullmore, a former chairman of the worldwide leading advertising agency J. Walter Thompson and a veritable advertising industry icon, "Creativity is the means, effectiveness is the end" (Campbell 2011). The organizational aspect of creativity in marketing is key, as outlined by Knox (1990), who suggests that marketing managers using creativity at the idea stage can foster durable innovation. Several frameworks have been offered to study organizational creativity, including that of Woodman, Sawyer, and Griffin (1993).

The domain of marketing remains a rich field of exploration for creativity researchers interested in linking creativity to valuable outcomes, but also in investigating creative planning processes, how creativity is communicated and perceived, the structures of creative organizations, and, finally, the fascinating question of the longevity of creative outcomes: Does a creative product remain creative after it has been copied? We will explore these questions as we review creative practices in marketing, discovering a number of best practice cases along the way.

1 Creativity in the Marketing Mix

1.1 Creativity in Product Development

Im and Workman (2004) suggest that a firm's ability to identify and market creative new products is key to the long-term success of a company. Recent years have seen the introduction of a huge range of creative products into the market, mostly technology-based, or enhanced. The most creative products constitute a new "category" altogether. Oft-cited examples include Cirque du Soleil, which is not a circus but a new form of entertainment; Swatch watches, which revolutionized the very definition of a watch from expensive jewelry item to fashion accessory; and in the service sector, Uber, AirBnB, and other "new economy" offerings. These category innovations are very different from more common product innovation, which consists mostly of adding features to existing products or "stretching" product ranges by adding different formulations, container sizes, etc. In fact, recent research indicates that the overall effect of these creative exercises is increasing commoditization, or lack of differentiation. In other words, much of what passes as creative product development actually results in remarkably uncreative outcomes (Moon, 2010) and is often not recognized as creative by consumers.

These questionable effects of creative endeavors raise an interesting question familiar to scholars teaching marketing as well as to marketing and strategic innovation practitioners: What serves as the best source of inspiration for the creative development of new products? Whereas the traditional view has been to identify so-called market gaps, or failures to meet consumer needs, the resounding success of products such as Apple's iPad, which certainly did not address explicitly stated needs, led Steve Jobs, the celebrated founder of Apple, to state that: "A lot of times, people don't know what they want until you show it to them." Recent research methodologies emphasize observation of consumer behavior patterns, creative and unusual uses of certain products (e.g., using woolen socks as handwarmers), as more promising than the time-honored questioning of consumers about their needs. Observing consumers buying milkshakes early in the morning before they set off for a long commute allowed consultants to a leading fast food chain to understand that milkshakes were being used as a convenient and nutritious breakfast alternative for long-distance commuters, thus opening up new opportunities for product innovation in the milkshake category around the breakfast theme (Christensen, Cook & Hall, 2005).

The importance for marketers to identify consumers' creativity in their use of conventional products is discussed by Taillard and Voyer (2016), with their example of the myriad of ways consumers can craft their coffee purchasing and drinking experience in cafés. Marketers can of course foster creativity in the consumption of products, for instance by delivering recipes and creative use of products (e.g., Philadelphia cream cheese or Oreo cookies). Often, it comes down to a company's ability to manage a creative team and generate positive dynamics (Im, Montoya, & Workman, 2013) or their adoption of a market orientation (Kohli, & Jaworski, 1990; Jaworski, & Kohli, 1993). Others have suggested that much can be learned from how the cultural industries work and innovate (e.g., Lampel, Lant, & Shamsie, 2000).

1.2 Creativity in Communications and Promotion

Communications and promotions are the areas in which creativity is most commonly applied and recognized. Yet again, here there are significant variations in approaches to creativity and effectiveness assessment. For instance, a television commercial can be very creative in its style or in its message while relying on a very conventional communication channel. A recent example is an IBM commercial for Watson, its artificial intelligence system. The product is highly innovative and its applications very creative. The communication strategy of introducing such a highly specialized business-to-business product to mainstream audiences is itself very creative. And the format and content of the commercial are also very creative: It features a short and fast conversation between Watson and musician Bob Dylan, in which Watson shows its appreciation for Dylan's creativity. The viewer is left with an image of Watson as a quirkily human and likeable persona, rather than as a cold, analytical set of algorithms. In recent years, marketers have talked about "media as the new creative," recognizing that the large range of channels available to marketers constitutes an opportunity for creativity. Combining channels expertly and adapting them to different contexts can lead to highly creative results. Luxury brand Burberry live-streams its fashion shows to the whole world on social networks, thereby flying in the face of conventional wisdom according to which such events were reserved for the crème de la crème of the fashion industry.

Another example of creativity in the advertising field is the new practice of programmatic marketing. As consumers unwittingly generate huge amounts of data by communicating traces of information about their every move, advertisers are able to address them at a very granular, personalized level, with messages and via channels that are contextually relevant. Digital advertising clearinghouses can fulfill advertisers' buying orders by matching them up with publishers' inventories dynamically and in real time. These new advertising models are becoming more and more prevalent and will soon migrate beyond purely digital channels to television and other media. This domain is interesting as it highlights a disparity between highly innovative technology (in the form of granular data and resulting analytics and real-time personalized delivery mechanisms) and lagging creative practices. Anyone who is seeing the same ad for the shoes they almost bought a week ago for the umpteenth time will testify to this disparity. In spite of the huge creativity behind the technological advances that permit real-time buying and selling, the creative ability to deliver the shoe customer a more novel and valuable message has simply not yet materialized.

Other striking signs of creativity in promotion and communications include content marketing, in which brands unleash all manners of branded stories, games, and other highly shareable bits of content to crowds of consumers eager to engage with friends and often with the world at large via these nuggets. Content marketing is about the creative and strategic development and diffusion of content emanating from the entire ecosystem around a brand: marketers and other employees, consumers, fans, retailers, media and other observers, and more. Here again, media is a big element of the creativity equation: Owned media (e.g., brand website or social network page) are blended with paid (e.g., advertising on other sites or networks) and earned (e.g., influencers' blogs, fan tweets) to derive maximum effectiveness without compromising credibility or trust.

As mentioned earlier, the big unknown, particularly with newer communication channels, is often return on investment. While activities such as online advertising, facilitated or not via programmatic buying, are evaluated using standard metrics such as cost per thousand impressions (the cost for a given message to be delivered to 1,000 users or viewers), or click-through rates (the percentage of users who click on an ad after having viewed it on their screen), there is still plenty of room for interpretation, for instance around the percentage of impressions that are actually seen or read, or the count of "unique" first-time visitors vs. repeat visitors using different devices. Social media and content marketing efforts are notoriously difficult to evaluate and to build reliable metrics for, making this yet another field in which analytical and creative approaches must be reconciled.

More traditionally, so-called branding campaigns, such as the ones cited in our introduction (Benetton, Apple, Coca Cola), were evaluated in terms of an increase on metrics such as "brand recall," the ability of consumers to recall having seen the ad and associating it with the brand itself, either spontaneously ("unprompted recall"), or by identifying the name among a short list of competitors ("prompted recall"). More promotional campaigns, aimed at driving traffic into a store or increasing sales, are evaluated in the same way as other costs of doing business, by calculating return on investment (a percentage of revenue to cost.) Creative campaigns are also evaluated internally within the advertising industry, for instance via awards and critical reviews. This constitutes an interesting application of the so-called consensual assessment of experts, a standard creativity assessment tool widely discussed in the creativity literature (Hennessey & Amabile, 2010, 573). However, some research suggests that winning a creative advertising award may not translate into financial benefit for a brand (Tippins & Kunkel, 2006), highlighting the distinction between creativity, as evaluated by experts, and effectiveness, as evidenced by revenue.

1.3 Creativity in Distribution

Distribution channels are another opportunity for creative marketing. Technological advances have drastically revolutionized most distribution channels, and the ability to find new channels to connect with customers clearly constitutes an opportunity to create value and break through the clutter. The online retailer Zappos is an interesting example here, as it was built on the highly risky and paradoxical premise that shoes (in particular women's shoes, an accessory for which perfect fit is notoriously difficult to find) could be successfully sold online. In order to deliver on this promise, Zappos built a large customer service call center, something highly unusual among online retailers who typically seek to avoid speaking to customers "live" in order to keep operational costs down. Every single decision that was taken early on at Zappos rested on this risky and paradoxical foundation of the business but delivered time and time again. In fact, Zappos was one of the leaders in adopting a so-called omnichannel retailing strategy by carefully integrating its distribution channels to deliver a "seamless" experience to its customers. Working with its suppliers and shipping companies, Zappos has crafted a highly reliable service for its customers, often delivering a day before they are expected. By allowing free returns, Zappos also makes online purchasing risk and hassle free. And the in-store experience is replaced with the more rewarding experience of trying shoes on in one's own bedroom with the outfits they are meant to complement. Any size or other type of advice about the shoes is provided in real time on the phone by highly trained customer service agents who are not tied to pre-written scripts or call duration metrics. In fact, Zappos located its headquarters in Nevada to take advantage of the availability of highly trained customer service employees coming from the hospitality sector in Las Vegas. All of these details, while they have now been emulated by other online retailers, constituted at first a truly creative distribution strategy at the very core of Zappos' business model.

Also inherent to Zappos' model is the ability to collect huge amounts of data about customers, both individually and as groups. Understanding what styles are popular in what regions, for instance, can help improve sales forecasting, as well as optimize inventory, thus reducing operating costs. At the more granular level, consumers' individual preferences and shopping styles can be analyzed to better tailor the messages that will be sent to them.

New opportunities for creativity in distribution come from "omnichannel experience" strategies in which distribution channels are no longer seen as a one-size-fits-all, but rather tailored to individual customers. Accommodating consumers' personal preferences such as comparing eyewear frames online, shopping for prescription glasses in traditional brick-and-mortar brand-owned stores, and ordering them online so as to get them in time for a special event, has been a recipe for success for Warby Parker. Again in this case, being able to analyze large amounts of individual data allows creative marketers to meet their customers where they want to be and tell them what they want to hear.

In a similar way, Amazon has set new standards in terms of delivery, and used creativity to turn a disadvantage – the absence of brick and mortar locations – into an advantage. The company has pioneered the use of alternative ways of distributing products, for instance creating Amazon Lockers in cities to allow consumers to access their parcels 24/7 and return unwanted products. More recently, the company has been working on a form of anticipatory shipping, which would rely on the use of big data and consumer information to predict when a consumer might be interested in buying a product (for instance the newest release of their favorite artist). The company has also regularly captured the attention of the media with creative delivery ideas, such as using drones, for instance.

1.4 Creativity in Pricing

Pricing represents a huge but often unheeded opportunity for creativity. In addition to its central role in enabling revenues, price is also a very potent communication tool for brands and can be used creatively to convey important features. From the original outrageously high pricing of a cup of coffee at Starbucks (particularly in the United States, where the de facto price of a cup of coffee was close to zero thanks to free refills), to the newly announced no-tipping policy of New York celebrity restaurateur Danny Meyer, pricing can be manipulated to grab the attention of customers. For Starbucks, the clear message was that "this is not your average cup of coffee, it is a new kind of experience." For Danny Meyer, the message is also transparent: His restaurants deliver a fundamentally human and social experience. In order to do so, they must balance the interests of all of the actors that participate in the experience, not just customers, but also the employees who make it possible.

Pricing can become especially creative when combined with operational data. This allows, for instance, companies to adjust prices to real-time supply and demand, as is the case with transportation company Uber, who adjusts its prices on the basis of the number of cars available in a given local zone, and live demand from consumers. Called "surge" prices, these can reach twice the standard rate, or more.

Examples of creative uses of customer data for pricing purposes include pricing according to the "job done" for the customer, or so-called value pricing. In the industrial sector, for instance, aircraft engine manufacturers sell their engines by the number of hours flown. In effect, this creative pricing strategy means that they are redefining their offering: They no longer offer their customers (airlines) a straight off-the-shelf product, but rather a solution or a "job done," an hour of flight with all the required operational elements such as pre- and post-flight checks and maintenance customized to each airline's operations and requirements.

In the consumer sector, some health insurance companies are experimenting with discounts to consumers who are willing to share lifestyle and health data, by wearing bracelets that track and communicate their level of activity and fitness, or by joining health clubs or making other healthy living choices.

2 Creativity in Marketing Strategy

At the macro, or company, level, creative marketing strategies are ones which defy conventional wisdom. Andrews and Smith (1996) find that establishing a creative marketing program is a function of the marketing manager's personal problem-solving skills, as well as situational and motivational factors. And according to Slater, Hult, and Olson (2010), the creativity of a marketing strategy, combined with the effectiveness of its implementation, leads to organizations achieving their objectives. Implementation is key, and, in fact, Levitt (2002) even argued that poorly implemented creativity can be dangerous for companies. As noted by Sok and O'Cass (2015), it often takes "ambidextrous" research and development managers, that is, people can display both creativity and attention to detail, to go from a new product development idea to market success. One of the main pillars of a brand's strategy is referred to as the triptych "segmentation, targeting, and positioning." Segmentation is the carving out of a single market into "segments" of more or less desirable customers against which different types and amounts of resources are invested. Segments are typically defined according to demographic variables (age, gender, socio-economic category, etc.), or psychographic variables (attitude towards environmental issues, attitude towards change, tolerance for ambiguity, etc.). More creative segmentation variables are based on more relevant criteria such as, for instance, the jobs that customers seek to get done (Christensen et al., 2005) and how they fulfill these jobs. Taiwanese bicycle manufacturer Giant opened up new stores for women customers based on research that showed that women sought different outcomes from bike riding and were underserved in traditional bike stores. In other words, although there was no reason to believe that women would value their own stores simply because of their gender, intuition and observational research convinced the CEO that women did indeed have a different "job to be done" when buying bikes and accessories than men. In fact, for most Taiwanese women, the entire cycling experience had a different meaning than for their male counterparts and required a completely different retail approach. It is the segmentation strategy that we identify as creative in this instance: a novel and valuable way of thinking about how to carve out a seemingly homogeneous market.

Targeting highly specialized markets can also be a creative marketing strategy. India-based Aravind Eye Care System specializes in delivering low-cost eye care, mostly cataract operations, to the rural population of India. Inspired by the efficient processes of fast-food chains, the founder of Aravind was able to scale up his surgical procedures to perform high-quality operations very fast and very reliably. He also adopted a creative pricing strategy by allowing patients to pay only what they could afford, in effect subsidizing the care provided to the poorest patients with fees collected from the better off. While it can be debated whether this approach would work in the West, the result is a model of efficiency and profitability that outperforms traditional Western models and has revolutionized eye care in India (Rosenberg, 2013). The prescription here combines creativity, audacity, and focus.

Positioning is another aspect of marketing strategy in which creativity can make its mark by defining the unique place a brand or product will occupy in consumers' minds. The non-profit Mozilla Foundation markets a web browser that competes effectively with competitors such as Windows and Chrome thanks to its mission to "promote openness, innovation and opportunity on the Web."[4] As brands attempt to compete with each other, creativity is necessary to establish unassailable points of differentiation. Warby Parker established itself creatively not just as an online eyewear brand selling its own affordable yet trendy designs by bypassing conventional middlemen, but also as a socially minded firm that distributes a free pair of glasses to customers in the developing world for every pair it sells. Its creative strategy reinforces and defends this positioning in everything the company does.

---

[4] See www.mozilla.org/en-US/mission/, retrieved on December 1, 2015

As mentioned above, the ability to collect customer data, analyze it, and draw value from it also requires high doses of creativity. How to generate data, what data to extract, how to combine different sources of data, what questions to ask of the data, how to interpret and contextualize the data, and how to communicate insights and embed them into decision-making processes are all questions whose more or less creative answers will result in different levels of effectiveness and long-term performance. The lines between a firm's technology, information, and marketing departments are increasingly blurry and creative, as forward-thinking organizations are designing new governance and management models to address these new realities.

Another important domain for creativity in strategy is the development of ecosystems around a brand. Technological advances have broken down most barriers to information sharing and communication. A customer can easily reach out to the CEO of a brand by tweeting to her, or share ideas on new uses of a particular product with other customers around the world. Similarly, brands can communicate new and exciting features virally through creative content marketing, using a variety of different channels. The result as mentioned earlier is a brand ecosystem, a self-adjusting, highly productive, and efficient system in which all of the stakeholders who interact in some way with a brand can contribute as actors. Creative opportunities exist for marketers to manage these ecosystems openly and transparently, with benefits for all involved. Examples include forums on Epicurious.com, the cooking and entertainment website owned by Condé Nast publishers, which enables consumers to share cooking tips and answer each other's questions (Taillard et al., 2014). In the industrial sector, GE Aviation's use of software that permits customers (sometimes from competing firms), and sales and marketing staff to communicate with each other and collaborate in real time is an example of one piece of technology enabling an entire ecosystem. The creative aspects of these examples are manifold: Opening up communication channels between different stakeholders is certainly novel and valuable; doing so openly and collaboratively without concerns about information being used competitively (particularly in the industrial sector) requires vision and creative thinking on the part of all participants, conceptualizing the ecosystem as a common ground for all participants to meet and collaborate also requires a creative mindset. Finally, and most importantly, ecosystem thinking enables collective creativity and its valuable outcomes. In the Epicurious.com example, consumers who contribute to the forum benefit from each other's experience and from the social interaction, and together develop new ideas, recipes, or technique. The publisher benefits from enormous amounts of spontaneously generated ideas for new recipes and other new content; it can also extract highly valuable customer data (both granular and collective) that can be used for ongoing targeting, personalization, and product development. Professional chefs who contribute their recipes benefit from customer feedback and build their reputation and brand image. Finally, and certainly most lucrative, the publisher sells advertising space to advertisers who value not just the "eyeballs" but also the rich data that comes with them.

In all of these instances, creativity is clearly at work when novel solutions are introduced that provide clear value to all ecosystem participants as well, of course, as to the creative companies that foster ecosystem strategies. Note, however, that creativity occupies a space at the very edge of these strategies: It is in claiming a new opportunity that brands or firms are creative. Once the strategy has been imitated it loses its creative edge. The highly successful investor and businessman Warren Buffett once commented on how good new ideas go wrong. He called this progression the "three I's." First come the *innovators*, who see opportunities that others don't. Then come the *imitators*, who copy what the innovators have done. And then come the *idiots*, whose avarice undoes the very innovations they are trying to use to get rich (Taylor, 2008). Creative strategies are both pervasive and ephemeral.

3 Creativity in Marketing Organizations

Some management and organization scholars have explored the links between organizational features (culture, structure, hierarchy, decision-making processes) and creativity. While a review of creativity in organizations is beyond the scope of this chapter, we will mention some of the work pertaining specifically to marketing organizations. Recent work conducted in a fast-growing retail environment, for instance, indicates that creativity was fostered by adjusting both the level of resources available to store employees (capital and knowledge resources, physical resources such as merchandising fixtures and products, and human resources) and the degree of autonomy or ownership they were given (Sonenshein, 2014). In general, higher levels of creativity were achieved under greater autonomy and restricted resources: Managers who were made to feel ownership for their stores and given limited budgets and means exhibited more creativity than the ones who were managed more closely and offered more resources. Prior work had sought to identify the features of a marketing organization that were most likely to result in creative marketing programs for mature products (i.e., products requiring a high degree of creativity to compete with newer, better differentiated products). Planning and prior experience were found to be conducive to creative outcomes. Although teamwork was linked to creativity, some individual autonomy was necessary to avoid group-think and generate new ideas. Time pressure was found to be a strong hindrance to creative marketing programs, suggesting that marketing teams should be given both the time and the levels of staffing necessary to produce creative outcomes (Andrews & Smith, 1996). Another study suggests that managing team dynamics can be an important tool to build competitive advantage resulting from the development of creative products and marketing programs (Im and Workman 2006). Team dynamics include such internal factors as cohesion and shared identity, and external factors such as market-based performance incentives, formal planning processes, and senior management encouragement to take risks.

Beyond academic research, we find examples of interesting practices linking creative strategy to creative organizational structure and sustained solid market performance. Polymer maker W.L. Gore and Associates, best known for Gore-Tex fabrics, is a privately held multinational that has been consistently profitable since it was founded in 1958. Thanks in no small part to its long-term perspective on product development and marketing strategy, an increasingly uncommon orientation in the consumer goods sector, Gore's positioning as an innovative and reliable brand is reflected in the unusual culture and structure of the firm's organization (Deutschman, 2004). From its very beginning, Gore has rejected the traditional hierarchical model common amongst product manufacturers in favor of one in which employees choose the projects and teams they want to contribute to. Leadership is earned and awarded to individuals whom others want to follow. Gore was one of the first adopters of the holacracy management model in which superior performance is achieved by letting employees manage themselves. What is remarkable in the case of Gore is how its creative organizational structure and culture is a reflection of its creative strategy of innovation, both aspects resulting in outstanding market performance over time in a very competitive sector. In sum, what defines and drives creativity in the domains of operational, strategic, and organizational marketing is that it challenges existing and established practices and uses at times counter-intuitive strategies to generate value for both the organization and its different stakeholders.

Studying Creativity in Marketing Research: Understanding and Harnessing Consumer Creativity

Among a firm's stakeholders, consumers play an important, though often unrecognized, creative role (Taillard et al., 2014). This is in part because scholars have mainly focused their research on the outcome of consumption rather than on the process of consumption itself (Xie, Bagozzi, and Troye 2008), and as a result failed to recognize the creative input of consumers in their everyday lives. However, the literature is starting to catch up with a two-decade-old trend of inviting consumers to customize or co-produce their products or services. In many cases, services, especially those which are experienced intensely by consumers (e.g., transformative haircuts) tend to make consumers happier than simple products (Van Boven & Gilovich, 2003). Atakan, Bagozzi, and Yoon (2014), for instance, showed that positive (but not negative) experiences of co-production (e.g. customizing a t-shirt) enhance the perception of self-made vs. other-made products.

Marketing research offers different ways to understand creativity and the role of creativity in a marketing context. Quantitative research, often using experimental methods, has shown that consumers value their own creativity, although creativity is not actually measured, but rather manipulated in experimental designs. Looking at the creative consumer, Burroughs and Mick (2004, p. 402) suggest that the main factors which affect creative consumption are situational factors, such as involvement in the consumption process or time pressure, as well as personal ones, such as consumers' locus of control. In a set of studies, Norton, Mochon, and Ariely (2012) showed that consumers valued the amount of work and creativity displayed as part of a consumption activity. Across four experiments, the researchers found that consumers who created products such as origami or Lego objects before being asked to purchase them would value these at a higher price, compared with simply being offered the same items without having created them. According to the authors, consumers value their own creative work in the consumption process. This higher perceived value of co-created items, however, disappears if the items are destroyed or if the creation process is not finished.

Shapiro (2004) suggests that consumer creativity needs to be genuinely valued by marketers for it to generate product satisfaction. Citing the example of a cake mix marketed in the 1950s, Shapiro suggested that initial dissatisfaction with the product came from the fact that its consumers' creativity was insufficiently valued as the product only required the addition of liquid. Later, when manufacturers added extra steps, therefore requiring more user creativity, or giving them the illusion that their creativity was needed, consumers adopted the product more readily.

Buechel and Janiszewski (2014) showed that, depending on when consumers' creativity is solicited in the creation process, it can affect their enjoyment and outcome of the consumption process. Their first study shows that, in the context of a product-assembly task, making simultaneous customization decisions and assembly tasks increases the perceived creativity of the task and the value generated by it. In their second study, they showed that when customization decisions and assembly tasks were coupled together, more effort increased the perceived value of the product to be assembled. Finally, their third study showed that consumer mindset was instrumental in generating a positive effect of effort on perceived value. When consumers were primed to be in a positive mindset, effort would increase the perceived value of customized and to-be-assembled products, whereas the opposite would happen when consumers were in a negative mindset.

Soliciting consumer creativity, or co-creation, can also backfire for companies, as marketing research suggests (Heidenreich, Wittkowski, Handrich, & Falk 2015). Despite stimulating consumer creativity, co-production can also lead to more problematic situations of product failure. When a co-produced item fails, consumers can experience a sense of guilt and take part of the blame for the product failure. The dissatisfaction in the consumption experience comes from the heightened hopes of a better consumption experience and the actual outcome, and requires that companies offer a form of service recovery, ideally a co-created one. In the service industry, pre-service encounters play an important role in determining how consumers react to a co-creation failure (HsiuJu Rebecca, Gwinner, & Wanru, 2004).

The role played by creativity in shaping consumers preferences could also be attributed to what Fuchs, Schreier, and van Osselaer (2015) refer to as the "handmade effect" (p. 98). Fuchs et al. (2015) suggest that handmade products, which are paradoxically less perfect than machine-made products, can be preferred by consumers, who will infer that these products have been made "with love." This opens up interesting questions around the perception of human vs. industrial creativity, and its role in consumer decision-making and satisfaction. Altogether, quantitative approaches to studying creativity in consumer behavior have mainly focused on manipulating consumers' level of creativity rather than measuring it. This suggests a large scope for future research on the topic.

Consumer creativity in marketing is also studied from a more constructivist perspective. Taillard, Voyer, Glăveanu, and Gritzali (2014) argue that all acts of consumptions involve a certain degree of consumer creativity. In their study, the authors look at value generation on cooking forums. They found that consumer creativity, in the form of conversations on forums, and internalization and externalization of knowledge and shared practices contribute to the creation of value. Value created in consumers' sharing of cooking tips and experience benefits all range of actors on the forum. Consumer creativity generates value for consumers who receive advice on how to solve their cooking problem or dilemma; for those who give advice and become reference points; for readers of the forum, who can incorporate all the advice in their own cooking; and finally for the hosting platform, which generates traffic and therefore advertising revenues.

Finally, research methods in marketing are fast opening novel domains for creativity research. From the growing use of neurosciences to that of netnography, creativity research in marketing is in its infancy. Taillard et al. (2014) use conversation analysis (CA), a social sciences research method widely used in linguistics and anthropology (Goodwin & Heritage, 1990). CA enables researchers to capture the process of collective creativity by analyzing the successive contributions of the different participants in a conversation (Levinson, 1983, 321). Another research method which can be useful to understand and capture creativity netnography (Kozinets, 2002). According to Kozinets, "netnography uses the information that is publicly available in online forums to identify and understand the needs and decision influences of relevant online consumer groups" (Kozinets 2002, p. 62). Netnography allows to understand the emergence of creativity both at an individual and collective level, by looking at how communities of consumption organize the sharing of resources, and how each individual member internalizes and externalizes these. Emerging market research techniques such as neurosciences or "neuromarketing" can also bring a nice addition to the understanding of creativity in marketing. Lee, Broderick, and Chamberlain (2007) highlight that several marketing areas, especially those related to pricing, could benefit from neuroscience insights. For instance, it could be interesting to better understand how consumers react to discounts, and the types of discounts, which are the most effective. Haller (2014) also highlighted the need for a neuroscience of creativity, which will help to understand the complexity and multiple facets of creativity (from social to cognitive or personality aspects).

Discussion

Our overview of the role of creativity in marketing has uncovered a number of different questions of interest to creativity scholars looking beyond the marketing domain. We now turn to a discussion of these questions using Glăveanu's (2013) "5-A's" model of socio-cultural creativity as a framework for our discussion. Taillard et al. (2014) adopt this model of creativity encompassing actors, actions, affordances, audiences, and artifacts in their study on consumer creativity and value creation on online forums. Throughout our discussion, we have shown how the relationships between marketers and their customers (actors and audiences), and the actions they take within these relationships, define creative outcomes, or artifacts, such as product innovations, distribution, pricing, or communications strategies, or even broader strategic aspects such as segmentation or positioning. The affordances here are the different resources that contribute to the creative processes and outcomes: the use of the product, its features, the brand, the knowledge that goes into creating the product, or any other material or socio-cultural element that is manipulated by actors to craft a creative outcome.

We will now consider four of these questions in hope that they can bring value to the field of creativity research

(1) One first area of interest is that of the *evaluation* of creativity. Marketing is one of the rare creative domains in which performance can be used as a proxy to test the effect of creativity. More specifically, how well a product or brand differentiates itself from its competitors can be attributed to creativity. From there, some or all of the performance of this product or brand can be seen as a reflection of the degree of creativity it brings to the market, and offers a measure of the effectiveness and perceived value of its creativity. This type of evaluation challenges the generally accepted consensual method discussed earlier. If we accept that creativity is part novelty, part relevance, it seems reasonable to assume that assessing both of these dimensions should be left to the users of creative outcomes, such as customers who will "vote with their feet." This would in turn suggest that rather than experts, one should consider beneficiaries, or users, as the best judges of creative outcomes. However, this more democratic approach to creativity is also inherently destructive. Once the novel aspect has disappeared, at least within a particular segment of the market, the creative effect is lessened. This leads us to ask another interesting question: Can consumers understand groundbreaking innovation – and do they perhaps prefer smaller increments? The field of marketing is full of occurrences of successful groundbreaking innovations (e.g., Apple's iPhone), but also failed ones (e.g., Apple's Newton Personal Digital Assistant).

(2) Our discussion of creative *processes* in organizations also opens up interesting avenues for creativity researchers. Because of the structured approaches to creativity often found in companies and the resources poured into understanding consumer creativity, marketing constitutes a fertile ground from which to extract insights into the most favorable creativity processes and contexts. Insights such as the ones gained from research into the organization of marketing departments can be useful in this regard. One particularly promising area is the increased complementarity in marketing between analytical and creativity approaches. As marketers access increasing amounts of hard data and analytics, it seems that valuable results can be obtained from combining analytical and creative approaches as discussed above. Processes based on such blended approaches have been used in other domains such as design (e.g., design thinking), and could be applied to other domains in which creativity is prized such as

education, policy making, etc. A focus on how to blend the two approaches, possibly in different domains, would be particularly illuminating.

(3) One aspect of creativity which does not get much attention in creativity research is how to *communicate* creative outcomes. Interestingly, whereas products that lack in creative features must rely on highly creative communications strategies in order to stand out in the market, many creative brands in fashion and other such sectors lack often fail to distinguish themselves in their communications efforts. One might argue that creative products speak for themselves and do not require the additional artifices of a creative communications campaign. It is also possible that a very creative communications campaign might in fact over-shadow or taint the creative features of a product.

(4) This last question is also related to the longevity of creative outcomes: Does a creative product remain creative after it has been thoroughly adopted in a market, and possibly been copied by competitors? Brands clearly feel that they must keep developing innovative products in order to remain competitive and continue to perform at a high level. This suggests that consumers consider that a product's creativity fades as it reaches a critical mass. The same is observed with advertisements and other creative marketing activities. In fact, marketers know that the points of differentiation which they work hard to develop for their products will sooner or later turn into points of parity. The answer to this quandary is what some have called "disruptive innovation," in which new markets are created, or "Blue Ocean Strategies," in which a product is designed to compete in an "uncontested" part of the market. With these strategies, marketers reach so far beyond existing parameters that they buy themselves additional time and breathing space before their creative outcomes are desecrated.

This discussion confirms the perspective of creativity as a socio-cultural process and outcome.

Conclusion

Almost two decades ago, Day and Montgomery (1999) outlined the future of marketing research and emerging problems to address. To date, although market-ing provides one of the most fertile grounds for the study of creativity, research on the topic has only recently started to build up. This new interest can be attributed to several factors: Digital channels have accelerated the access to information and the need for brands to be able to stand out or be heard; customer empowerment has given rise to the increased prevalence of product, or more accurately, solution customiza-tion; and the globalization and commoditization of products have increased the pressure on marketers to find untapped opportunities in the markets in which they compete. Finally, the barriers between stakeholders, whether they be customers, suppliers, retailers, or marketers, are becoming increasingly irrelevant. This has led marketing practitioners as well as scholars to consider ecosystems as relevant models for marketing organizations. As these new models are invented, in which exchanges take place between all parties interested in contributing value-creating activities to the common good, creativity itself becomes part of the energy that flows back and forth. This reality is recognized in the Service Dominant Logic (SDL) paradigm of academic research (Vargo & Lusch, 2004). SDL postulates that marketing should break free of its "goods dominant logic" which distinguishes between producers and customers, to consider a new logic of service exchanges between "actors" seeking to create value for themselves and others by fulfilling their needs.

This growing interest in creativity related topics offers exciting areas for future research in marketing. Marketing is sometimes seen as a field which mainly borrows from other social science and humanities disciplines. Yet, the specificity of creativity in marketing, and the fact that its role is increasingly recognized as central to the consumption and value-creation process, means that marketing scholars have the possibility to theorize the field of creativity marketing and develop original and discipline-specific theories. It would be especially interesting to understand the role played by creativity in novel forms of consumption, for instance sharing products (e.g., car sharing) or access-based consumption (Bardhi & Eckhardt, 2012). Creativity, both at its micro (consumer or employee) or macro (corporate, community, or market) level can undoubtedly help improve these novel types of consumption experiences and generate value. Finally, as pointed out in our discussion, marketing offers a most propitious domain for creativity scholars to observe and test creativity at work in highly social and cultural contexts.

References

Andrews, J., & Smith, D. C. (1996). In search of the marketing imagination: Factors affecting the creativity of marketing programs for mature products. *Journal of Marketing Research*, 174–187.

Atakan, S. S., Bagozzi, R. P., & Yoon, C. (2014). Make it your own: How process valence and self-construal affect evaluation of self-made products. *Psychology & Marketing*, *31*(6), 451–468. DOI:10.1002/mar.20707

Bardhi, F., & Eckhardt, G. M. (2012). Access-based consumption: The case of car sharing. *Journal of Consumer Research*, *39*(4), 881–898. DOI:10.1086/666376

Buechel, E. C., & Janiszewski, C. (2014). A lot of work or a work of art: How the structure of a customized assembly task determines the utility derived from assembly effort. *Journal of Consumer Research*, *40*(5), 960–972. DOI:10.1086/673846

Burroughs, J. E., & Mick, D. G. (2004). Exploring antecedents and consequences of consumer creativity in a problem-solving context. *Journal of Consumer Research*, *31*(2), 402–411

Campbell, E. (2011). Evidence proves the future is now: Why great creative needs great research. *Journal of Advertising Research* (*March*).

Christensen, C.M., Cook, S., & Hall, T. (2005). Marketing malpractice: The cause and the cure. *Harvard Business Review* (*December*).

Day, G. S., & Montgomery, D. B. (1999). Charting new directions for marketing. *Journal of Marketing*, 3–13.

Deutschman, A. (2004). The fabric of creativity. *Fast Company*. Retrieved on October 18, 2015, at www.fastcompany.com/51733/fabric-creativity.

Fuchs, C., Schreier, M., & van Osselaer, S. M. J. (2015). The handmade effect: What's love got to do with it? *Journal of Marketing*, *79*(2), 98–110. DOI:10.1509/jm.14.0018

Glăveanu, V. P. (2013). Rewriting the language of creativity: The Five A's framework. *Review of General Psychology*, *17*(1), 69.

Goodwin, C. and Heritage, J. (1990), Conversation analysis. *Annual Review of Anthropology*, 19: 283–307.

Haller, C. S. (2014). Neuroscience needs creativity: The implications of reliable instruments that fail to measure a loosely defined latent variable. *Frontiers in Human Neuroscience*, 8.

Heidenreich, S., Wittkowski, K., Handrich, M., & Falk, T. (2015). The dark side of customer co-creation: exploring the consequences of failed co-created services. *Journal of the Academy of Marketing Science*, 43(3), 279–296. DOI:10.1007/s11747-014-0387-4.

Hennessey, B.A. & Amabile, T. M. (2010). Creativity. *Annual Review of Psychology*, *61*, 569–598.

Im, S., Montoya, M. M., & Workman, J. P. (2013). Antecedents and consequences of creativity in product innovation teams. *Journal of Product Innovation Management*, *30*(1), 170–185.

Im, S., & Workman Jr, J. P. (2004). Market orientation, creativity, and new product performance in high-technology firms. *Journal of Marketing*, *68*(2), 114–132.

Jaworski, B. J., & Kohli, A. K. (1993). Market orientation: Antecedents and consequences. *Journal of Marketing*, 53–70.

Kohli, A. K., & Jaworski, B. J. (1990). Market orientation: The construct, research propositions, and managerial implications. *Journal of Marketing*, 1–18.

Kozinets, R. V. (2002). The field behind the screen: Using netnography for marketing research in online communities. *Journal of Marketing Research*, *39*(1), 61–72.

Knox, S. (1990). Creativity in marketing management – A unified approach. *Journal of Marketing Management*, *5*(3), 245–257.

Lampel, J., Lant, T., & Shamsie, J. (2000). Balancing act: Learning from organizing practices in cultural industries. *Organization Science*, *11*(3), 263–269.

Lee, N., Broderick, A. J., & Chamberlain, L. (2007). What is 'neuromarketing'? A discussion and agenda for future research. *International Journal of Psychophysiology*, *63*(2), 199–204.

Levinson, S. C. (1983) *Pragmatics*. Cambridge: Cambridge University Press.

Levitt, T. (2002). Creativity is not enough. *Harvard Business Review*, *80*(8), 137–145.

Moon, Y. (2010). *Different: Escaping the competitive herd*. New York: Crown.

Norton, M. I., Mochon, D., & Ariely, D. (2012). The IKEA effect: When labor leads to love. *Journal of Consumer Psychology*, *22*, 453–460.

Rosenberg, T. (2013). A Hospital network with a vision. *New York Times*, January 16, 2013.

Shapiro, L. (2004). *Something from the oven: Reinventing dinner in 1950s America*. New York: Viking.

Slater, S. F., Hult, G. T. M., & Olson, E. M. (2010). Factors influencing the relative importance of marketing strategy creativity and marketing strategy implementation effectiveness. *Industrial Marketing Management*, *39*(4), 551–559.

Sok, P., & O'Cass, A. (2015). Examining the new product innovation–performance relationship: Optimizing the role of individual-level creativity and attention-to-detail. *Industrial Marketing Management*, *47*, 156–165.

Sonenshein, S. (2014). How organizations foster the creative use of resources. *Academy of Management Journal*, *57*(3), 814–848.

Taillard, M., Voyer, B., Glăveanu, V. P., & Gritzali, A. (2014). Value creation and consumption: When consumer creativity generates value in online forums. *Advances in Consumer Research*, *42*, 381–386.

Taillard, M., & Voyer, B.G. (2016). Giving creative credit where credit is due: A sociocultural approach to consumer creativity. In V. P. Glăveanu (Ed.), *The Palgrave handbook of creativity and culture research*. London: Palgrave Macmillan.

Taylor, B., (2008). Wisdom of Warren Buffett: On innovators, imitators and idiots. *Harvard Business Review*, October 9, 2008. Retrieved on December 27, 2015, from https://hbr.org/2008/10/wisdom-of-warren-buffet-on-imi.

Tippins, M. J., & Kunkel, R. A. (2006). Winning a Clio advertising award and its relationship to firm profitability. *Journal of Marketing Communications*, *12*(1), 1–14.

Van Boven, L., & Gilovich, T. (2003). To do or to have: That is the question. *Journal of Personality and Social Psychology*, *85*, 1193–1202.

Vargo, S. L., & Lusch, R. F. (2004). Evolving to a new dominant logic for marketing. *Journal of Marketing*, *68*(1), 1–17.

Woodman, R. W., Sawyer, J. E., & Griffin, R. W. (1993). Toward a theory of organizational creativity. *Academy of Management Review*, *18*(2), 293–321.

Xie, C., Bagozzi, R. P., & Troye, S. V. (2008). Trying to pro-sume: Toward a theory of consumers as co-creators of value. *Journal of the Academy of Marketing Science*, *36*, 109–122.

Yen, H.R., Gwinner, K.P. & Wanru, S. (2004). The impact of customer participation and service expectation on Locus attributions following service failure. *International Journal of Service Industry Management*, *15*(1), 7–26. DOI: 10.1108/09564233410523312.

20 Creative Leadership

How Problem Solving, Decision Making, and Organizational Context Influence Leadership Creativity

Kevin Mitchell

and

Roni Reiter-Palmon

University of Nebraska at Omaha

Abstract

Leadership and creativity are broad, complex domains. Creativity in the leadership domain is often examined in terms of how the leaders influence the creativity of their subordinates, but there is less focus on how the leaders are creative themselves. This chapter examines a range of individual differences, managerial decision making, and organizational factors that could influence a leader's creativity. Individual differences such as personality traits, emotional intelligence, creative cognitions, and expertise could be important factors that influence the leader's creativity. Further, we integrate research on decision-making styles and information processing to further explore potential influences on leader creativity. Although the individual differences and managerial decision-making factors are important, leadership and creativity in an organization do not happen without the influence of environmental factors. We explore how resources, organizational strategy, and differing levels of leadership (e.g., the leader-follower dynamics) influence leader creativity. By combining multiple research lines, we hope to offer a more robust examination of a perceived scarcity of research into how leaders can be creative.

As markets and organizations become increasingly complex, leaders are faced with a myriad of ambiguous and complicated problems. The creative problem-solving ability of these leaders becomes crucial to ensure continued organizational success. In a study including 1,541 chief executive officers (CEOs), IBM (2010) found that "creativity is the most important leadership quality, according to CEOs" (p. 8). This report also concludes that creative leaders encourage change, take risks, and are open-minded in their management and communication styles. In this chapter, we examine research on creativity in leadership and explore the relationship between decision making, creativity, and organizational contexts to better understand how creativity manifests in the leadership domain.

When leaders are faced with ambiguous and complex problems, they may engage in creative problem-solving to generate a solution (Mumford, 1986; Mumford,

Connelly, & Gaddis, 2003; Urabe, 1988). To assist in our understanding of how leaders develop creative solutions to organizational problems, this chapter will explore both research on creative problem-solving as well as research on managerial decision making. The pairing of managerial decision-making literature with creative problem-solving allows a more robust lens through which we can examine cognition and individual differences of leaders during the creative process. However, these individual differences do not operate in a vacuum, and the increasing complexity of organizations must be accounted for when examining leadership and creativity (Mainemelis, Kark, & Epitropaki, 2015).

Leadership is a broad, complex domain. For the purpose of this chapter, we conceptualize leadership as a process between the cognitions, traits of the leader, and the interaction between leaders, followers, and the organizational context (Bass & Bass, 2008). Leader cognition is examined in terms of decision-making styles, creative cognition, and individual propensities that lead to greater creativity. Leader traits can cover a wide breadth of constructs, but this current chapter focuses on emotional intelligence, expertise, and the "Big Five" personality factors as they relate to leadership and creativity. Finally, the organizational context influences how a leader makes decisions, interacts with creative individuals, and produces creative solutions to organizational problems.

Creativity is conceptualized as the production of a useful and novel solution, idea, or product (Mumford & Gustafson, 1988). Similar to leadership, creativity can be examined in terms of the individual, interactions between individuals (e.g., team creativity), and the interplay between individuals and contextual factors. Much of the current research on leadership and creativity focuses on leaders as more passive actors in the creative process and places greater emphasis on resource allocation or idea evaluation (Mumford, Connelly, & Gaddis, 2003; Redmond, Mumford, & Teach, 1993), that is, how leaders can facilitate creativity in their followers or employees. The focus of this chapter, though, is on how leaders themselves solve problems creatively.

Measures of Creative Leadership

One important issue that must be addressed is how leadership, creativity, and of course creative leadership are measured. In the domain of business, in which creative leadership resides, creativity can be measured using more objective measures such as productivity (number of patents, awards, publications). These measures are more appropriate for organizations and units within an organization that directly engage in the creation of new knowledge and products. In addition, these measures of creativity only evaluate those ideas that have been fully developed and progressed enough such that a patent could be filed, an article published, or awards be given, a process that may take years, resulting in a low base rate (Hunter, Cushenbery, & Friedrich, 2012; Keller, 2012; Mumford, Hester, & Robledo, 2011). This may be further compounded by the fact that leaders may not be directly involved in product generation.

Other approaches use an evaluation of the creativity of an idea or solution to a problem using the Consensual Assessment Technique (Amabile, 1996). Many researchers have used supervisory ratings of creativity (George & Zhou, 2001). This can be done using a scenario-based approach, where leaders provide a solution to a business problem presented to them. This approach allows for standardization such that all leaders are responding to the same stimulus. Alternatively, solutions to existing problems can be evaluated. However, in this case, different leaders will respond to different problems and therefore comparisons between solutions will be more difficult. Ratings, however, allow for measurement that is more objective in the sense that it is outside of the person being studied.

Finally, supervisory evaluation is also important from the perspective of the organization. Supervisory evaluations are not without problems. While managers are used to providing supervisory evaluations of performance, evaluation of creativity may not be always a part of the job and may be more difficult for the manager to recognize, or managers may have different understanding of what creativity is (Reiter-Palmon, Beghetto, & Kaufman, 2014). Overall, measures of creative leadership focus on more observable outcomes, which is appropriate given the domain.

Leaders as Creative Individuals

Creativity researchers have long been fascinated with identifying personality traits of creative individuals (Barron & Harrington, 1981). More recently, personality has been conceptualized in terms of the Big Five framework (Feist, 1998). In a meta-analysis on leadership emergence, Judge, Bono, Ilies, and Gerhardt (2002) found that four of the Big Five traits were positively associated with leadership: Emotional stability, Extraversion, Openness, and Conscientiousness. Only Agreeableness was unrelated to leadership emergence.

Similarly, the research on creativity and personality also has focused on the Big Five. This research suggests that openness to experience is consistently related to creative performance (Hornberg & Reiter-Palmon, in press). The relationship with other personality variables seems to be more inconsistent, and depends on the specific measure of creativity, or criterion, being evaluated. Extraversion has been linked to performance measures of creativity, specifically those requiring interactions with others such as drama or musical performance. Similarly, conscientiousness seems to be important when creativity is evaluated in areas where following some rules is critical, such as in science (Feist, 1998; Hornberg & Reiter-Palmon, in press). There should be no surprise that conscientiousness, extraversion, and openness also emerge as important variables in the leadership literature. Openness directly relates to creativity in all its forms, so should be related to leader creative problem solving. Extraversion seems to be an important personality variable when creativity is associated with others, as it for leaders. Finally, leaders must operate within organizational constraints and rules, so it was expected that conscientiousness emerges as an important factor.

Emotional intelligence is an additional individual difference variable that impacts leadership and creative outcomes. Emotional intelligence is the ability to recognize and manage emotions (Goleman, 1995; Goleman, Boyatzis, & McKee, 2002, Mayer, Salovey, & Caruso, 2000; Salovey & Mayer, 1990). A leader who is better able to recognize the emotions in his/her subordinates should be able to influence the outcome of those subordinates. Likewise, a leader who is better able to understand their own emotions given the situation should be able to produce better outcomes that are accepted by the organizational stakeholders. Creativity and leadership literature typically treat emotional intelligence as a predictor to subsequent creativity or employee performance (Barczak, Lassk, & Mulki, 2010; Carmeli, McKay, & Kaufman, 2014; Castro, Gomes, & de Sousa, 2012; Harris, Reiter-Palmon, & Kaufman, 2013; Parke, Seo, & Sherf, 2015; Sanchez-Ruiz, Hernandez-Torrano, Perez-Gonzalez, Batey, & Petrides, 2011). Using responses from a single organization, Castro et al. (2012) examined the relationship between leader emotional intelligence, organizational climate, and followers' creativity. The authors found support that leader emotional intelligence was positively related to follower creativity. Further, research has found support for management emotional regulation and creativity (Parke, Seo, & Sherf, 2015). The pattern of results indicates that emotional intelligence is important in a leadership context when examining creative performance; however, there is a lack of research explicitly examining creative leaders and emotional intelligence. Leaders who can understand and manage their own emotions should be able to use this skill to better grapple with ambiguous problems as well as forecast how their subordinates and other stakeholders in the organization will react to their proposed creative solution. In this way, leaders higher in emotional intelligence should follow the same pattern as non-leaders in having more creative outcomes.

Another important individual difference variable that has been linked to creative problem solving is that of expertise (Mumford, Blair, Dailey, Leritz, & Osburn, 2006). As individuals gain more knowledge and experience within a given domain, they build their expertise. Traditionally, expertise refers to knowledge in a narrow, well-defined field; however, some researchers argue that leadership should be considered a single domain when researching expertise (Goldring, Huff, Spillane, & Barnes, 2009; McCall & Hollenbeck, 2008; Okpala, Hopson, Chapman, & Fort, 2011). However, it is important to point out that the nature of expertise in the leadership domain is multifaceted (Hunter, Thoroughgood, Myer, & Ligon, 2011; McCall & Hollenbeck, 2008; Mumford, Bedell, & Hunter, 2008; Yukl, 2007). That is, leaders must have technical expertise in the domain that they are working in. For example, a leader of a marketing unit must have expertise in marketing, while a leader of an engineering team must have expertise in engineering. However, expertise in the technical domain is not sufficient. Leaders must also possess expertise in the social domain, such as knowing how to provide feedback to employees, guide performance, manage conflict and so on. Leaders, in their role as boundary spanners, or those that connect the work unit with the broader organization, must also have political expertise such as knowing who to turn to for support and advice, who has the necessary knowledge within the organization, and how to garner political capital. As leaders are faced with ambiguous organizational problems, they will gain knowledge and experience in how to respond to these types of problems. This expertise in leadership ultimately influences how the leader produces a creative solution.

In creativity research, expertise is examined in terms of how it influences the creative process. Research suggests that there may be a double-edged sword with expertise in terms of creativity. Expertise is considered a requirement for creative performance (Mumford, Blair, Dailey, Leritz, & Osburn, 2006). However, even though experts are more aware that there are multiple solutions and solution paths, too much expertise can lead to routinization (Basadur, 1994; Hoover & Feldhusen, 1994). Experts typically spend more time defining and identifying the problem before proceeding any further in the problem-solving process (Selnes & Troye, 1989). Task-relevant knowledge influences the experts' ability to effectively find and synthesize information needed to solve the problem (Barrick & Spilker, 2003; Mumford et al., 2006; Selnes & Troye, 1989). Experts are typically controlled and deliberate when searching for information, which cause a search for more relevant information, thus generating higher quality and more original solutions (Moxley, Ericsson, Charness, & Krampe, 2012). An individual who has expertise in the leadership domain will likely have more task-relevant knowledge and skills to solve organizational problems. When faced with an ambiguous organizational problem, experts in leadership will deliberately use the available information as well as their experience to formulate a higher quality and a more original solution. In addition, the technical expertise available to the leader is likely to be utilized.

That said, it is important that leaders recognize the limits of their expertise. Leaders may lead interdisciplinary teams, and therefore may not be experts in all the technical domains that are represented on the team. Further, as suggested, expertise may limit the leader's ability to conceptualize the problem in a new way or steer him or her to a tried and true solution. Therefore, leaders must be aware of this possibility and recognize that they may be following a routine solution when a creative solution is called for.

Leaders as Creative Problem-Solvers

Leaders may engage in some form of creative decision making or creative problem solving when faced with ambiguous problems. Problems can range from highly routinized to ill-defined (Allaire & Marsiske, 2002; Schraw, Dunkle, & Bendixen, 1995; Reed, 2015; Reitman, 1964). A highly routinized problem has a clearly defined solution path and solution and therefore requires knowledge, experience, and the application of cognitive processes in a prescribed way (Dillon, 1982; Reitman, 1964; Wakefield, 1992). Conversely, an ill-defined problem has multiple solutions with multiple paths to reach that solution and therefore may require more complex application of cognitive processes (Kitchener, 1983; Reitman, 1964; Wakefield, 1992). Leaders are often faced with ambiguous or ill-defined problems that are novel, and have important organizational consequences.

As these problems typically do not have a standard solution, they may require creative solutions.

Creative problem-solving skills have been identified as important for leaders in order to solve complex organizational problems (Mumford, Hunter, Eubanks, Bedell, & Murphy, 2007; Mumford, Zaccaro, Harding, Jacobs, & Fleishman, 2000; Zaccaro, Mumford, Connelly, Marks, & Gilbert, 2000). These skills encompass the leader's ability to identify the problem, formulate solutions, and ultimately produce a creative solution to be implemented. Similar skills appear in the leadership innovation literature. Innovation is the implementation of a new product or process (Baregheh, Rowley, & Sambrook, 2009; Damanpour, 1996; Harmancioglu, Droge, & Calantone, 2009; Urabe, 1988). The notion of innovation, which focuses on the implementation of a new idea, is of particular importance for organizations (West, 2002). While generating novel ideas is important, ideas that cannot be implemented are of little use to the organization. As with the importance of creative problem-solving skills, the proper implementation of an innovative process depends on the leaders' ability to identify opportunities, align organizational resources, and get buy-in for the implementation of the new product or process (Bassett & Shandas, 2010; Duarte, Goodson, & Dougherty, 2014; Stenmark, Shipman, & Mumford, 2011).

Creativity researchers developed cognitive process models to examine how individuals engage in creative problem solving. Mumford et al. (1991) outlined an eight-component model of the creative process. This process model contained the following steps: problem construction, information encoding, category search, specification of best-fitting categories, combination and reorganization of best fitting categories, idea evaluation, implementation, and monitoring. Empirical work supports the relationship between creativity and problem construction (Csikszentmihalyi & Getzels, 1988; Okuda, Runco, & Berger, 1991; Reiter-Palmon, Mumford, & Threlfall, 1998), information search (Bettman & Park, 1980; Karlins, Lee, & Schroder, 1967; Mumford, Baughman, Supinski, & Maher, 1996), and conceptual combination (Kohn, Paulus, & Korde, 2011; Mobley, Doares, & Mumford, 1992, Mumford et al., 1997; Scott, Lonergan, & Mumford, 2005). Leaders who supported and facilitated engagement in these creative processes tended to positively influence employee creative production (Mumford, Scott, Gaddis, & Strange, 2002; Redmond et al., 1993). The research on the cognitive process models largely examines employees rather than those in leadership positions. This pattern is not surprising given the more passive role ascribed to leaders in previous creativity research. However, Mumford et al. (2003) proposed a modified cognitive model to account for a less passive leader role in the creative process.

Mumford et al. (2003) argued that idea proposal by a follower generates the creative process for leaders. The model outlines an interactive relationship between leader and follower in the production of creative solutions. In this model, the leader is not necessarily a driver of creativity, but plays an integral organizational role as an idea evaluator. This role makes sense based on the leader's position in an organization, and the leader's goals change to weighing the consequences of ideas that are posed by others (Mumford, 1986; Mumford et al., 2007). Further, there may be a challenge to obtain organizational information as well as determining the relevance of that information (Mumford & Connelly, 1991), and this interactive model facilitates better information exchange for eventually structuring and evaluating the problem. Although the role of evaluating ideas and acting as that repository for employees is important, we argue that leaders can be active in the creative process.

When we examine the cognitions and skills that are important to creative problem solving and compare them to the cognitions and skills important to leadership, there are overlaps. This pattern leads us to believe that leaders can be creative problem-solvers, and not just creative facilitators. One avenue into further exploration of the creative leader is the research on decision making. Differences in how leaders come to decisions can influence the effectiveness and quality of those decisions. Because creativity is the union of novelty and quality, the addition of decision-making research allows for a more comprehensive view of how a leader may be creative.

Leaders as Decision-Makers

Good decision making is a key component of leadership (Crooke, Csikszentmihalyi, & Kikel, 2015; Hadley, Pittinsky, Sommer, & Zhu, 2011; Yukl, 1989). Decision making and problem solving are linked, as the process of problem solving typically results in a decision (a solution to the problem). Further, decisions typically result in implementation – an important aspect of innovation. As a result, leaders may have to come up with creative solutions as part of the decision-making process.

Van Knippenberg (2013) suggests that leadership decision making can be evaluated using one of three distinct perspectives: a shared decision-making perspective, follower decision-making perspective, and leader decision-making perspective. The follower decision-making perspective refers to the leader's influences on the followers' decision making. The shared decision-making perspective refers to the collective decision making between followers and leaders. Both the follower and shared decision making are not relevant to the current chapter. We therefore will focus our discussion on the leader decision-making perspective.

The leader decision-making perspective examines those decisions that are uniquely tied to leadership (van Knippenberg, 2013). One main area leader decision-making may be important is in how the leader allocates organizational resources (Giessner & van Knippenberg, 2007; Rus, van Knippenberg, & Wisse, 2010; van Knippenberg, 2013). Leaders may be faced with a paradox of exploring or exploiting organizational resources in the course of making a decision (Smith, 2014). Paradoxes are coexisting, ongoing tensions that have competing demands and are typically not solved with a one-time solution (Lewis, 2000; Smith & Lewis, 2011). Through exploring, the leader uses resources for innovation for long-term sustainability; whereas, the leader may exploit resources by using current products to find short-term sustainability by increasing efficiency (Smith, 2014). The exploring or exploiting paradox is only one example of the strategic decisions leaders are faced with. The balance of these two approaches, or engaging in both, can be important for creativity. Exploiting allows for short-term sustainability, but also typically involves more incremental creativity, whereas exploration allows for longer term and more radical creativity (Gilson & Madjar, 2011). The combination of both has been termed ambidextrous leadership, and it has been found to be related to innovation (Zacher & Rosing, 2015; Zacher, Rosing, & Rosing, 2014). Leaders also typically have significant latitude about making decisions about work priorities, which in turn can influence creativity. Those leaders that focus on more mundane or routine problems will tend to be less creative than those leaders that tackle more complex, ill-defined, and less routine problems which allow for creativity (Mumford & Hunter, 2005).

Another way in which leadership decision making has been examined is through decision-making styles. Decision-making styles are the learned, habitual patterns individuals use to make decisions (Scott & Bruce, 1995). Scott and Bruce (1995) proposed five types of decision-making styles: rational, intuitive, dependent, avoidant, and spontaneous. Rational decision-makers are more deliberate, logical, and have greater confidence in approaching a problem. Intuitive decision-makers rely on hunches and are less deliberate in the decision-making process. Dependent decision-makers approach problems with little confidence and project decision responsibility to others; relying on the advice of others to make the decision. Avoidant decision-makers attempt to avoid making a decision. Spontaneous decision-makers attempt to get through the decision-making process as quickly as possible and feel a sense of immediacy in their decisions. Research has examined these decision-making styles in relation to leadership styles in educational administrators (Jabeen, Akhtar & Muhammad, 2013), bank employees (Rehman & Waheed, 2012), and service-industry employees (Riaz & Khalili, 2014). This research displays a pattern of positive relationships between decision-making styles and leadership styles. An understanding of how the leadership and decision-making styles interact allows researchers to better understand which leader (based on their leadership and decision-making styles) will more likely engage ambiguous problems in a creative way or produce creative solutions. For example, Andersen (2000) proposed that an intuitive decision-making style can lead to a creative-innovative decision-making style. These stylistic differences for a creative leader also extend to how the leader processes information when faced with a problem.

A closely related construct to decision-making styles are information-processing styles. These processing styles play a role in the quality of leadership decisions and refer to how a decision-making situation is processed by the individual. These information-processing styles are typically classified as deliberate or intuitive. Deliberate processing styles are more effortful and slower, whereas the intuitive processing styles are quicker, unconscious, and more error-prone (Ayal, Rusou, Zakay, & Hochman, 2015). The type of processing style can influence the decision outcome. Ayal et al. (2015) integrated the information-processing styles with situational factors and decision-making styles. The authors proposed that both deliberate and intuitive information processing could lead to optimal decisions, but the optimal decision would be dependent upon the matching between the processing style and the situation factor (i.e., the task at hand). The authors found that when participants are encouraged to use a more intuitive thought pattern and processing style, optimal decisions were made when also presented with an intuitive task rather than a more deliberate task. Likewise, this matching pattern of information processing style, decision-making style, and task was found when a deliberate thought process was encouraged. Thus, decision quality is influenced by the flexibility and compatibility between the processing style, decision-making style, and the task at hand. Information processing can be a key factor in examining the cognitive processes of creative leaders. A central process of the creative process is the information search. To better understand this component, the information-processing style of a leader can shed light on what cognitive differences could elucidate the information search beyond the current creativity and leadership literature. Returning to the discussion on experts, individuals with more expertise are more deliberate with their information searches and will examine more relevant information (Moxley, Ericsson, Charness, & Krampe, 2012; Selnes & Troye, 1989). Creative leaders with the aforementioned information-processing styles should be akin to experts, with more deliberate information searches and examining more relevant information to produce higher-quality solutions.

Decision-making differences have implications when examining creative leaders. A leader who is better able to exploit or explore resources, utilize multiple decision-making styles, and effectively process information should produce higher-quality decisions. When paired with creative problem solving, leaders who make good decisions when faced with an ambiguous problem have a better opportunity to produce creative solutions. These solutions, however, are influenced by the larger organizational structure. To properly understand the creative outcomes of the creative leader, the organizational factors must also be taken into consideration.

Organizational Context for Creative Leaders

Leaders do not operate in a vacuum. Because leaders operate within an organizational setting, any decision made must also take into account the goals of their immediate workgroup and the broader organizational goals. Leaders must also attend to restrictions posed by the organization, such as resources, time, as well as political issues within and outside the organization (Hogan & Hogan, 2002). In addition, leaders serve as the connection between their team to the larger organization and to the environment external to the organization such as customers, suppliers, and competitors (Mumford et al., 2002). Therefore, it is not surprising the organizational context has an effect on leaders' creative problem solving.

A significant amount of research exists on the contextual factors that influence creativity in organizations (Amabile, Conti, Coon, Lazenby, & Herron, 1996; Anderson, Potocnik, & Zhou, 2014; Hunter, Bedell, & Mumford, 2007). While not specific to leaders, these factors nevertheless are relevant when leaders need to solve problems creatively. One of the most influential contextual factors that has been studied has been that of the leader. Even in the context of discussing creativity of leaders, it is important to remember that most leaders also have a leader (Sy &

Reiter-Palmon, 2015). The leader of the team reports to the department leader, the department leader may report to the vice president, and so on. As such, leaders can also be influenced by their own leaders. Specifically, research on the effect of leadership on creativity indicates that leaders that are supportive in general and of new and creative ideas specifically are non-controlling and provide psychological safety encourage their employees to share new and creative ideas and be more creative (Carmeli, Reiter-Palmon, & Ziv, 2010; Carmeli, Sheaffer, Binyamin, Reiter-Palmon, & Sihmoni, 2014; Hunter et al., 2007). In addition, research indicates that when leaders expect creativity from their subordinates, those subordinates indeed perform more creatively (Carmeli & Schaubroeck, 2007; Tierney & Farmer, 2004). Therefore, the behavior of the superior to the leader has important implications for leader creativity.

Another important contextual factor that has emerged is that of organizational strategy. Organizational strategy that incorporates or stresses creativity and innovation signals to the leader that creativity is important and worth pursuing. Research on the role of organizational strategy has focused on the effect of strategy on firm level innovation (Ettlie, 1983; Mumford & Hunter, 2005). However, organizational strategy should also be effectively tied to organizational climate that stresses the importance of creativity and the rewards that are provided (Galbraith, 1982). Further, goals should reflect the organizational strategy, and as such, if the strategy is one that focuses on creativity and innovation, then organizational goals should reflect that. Research on the effect of goals found that creativity goals or instructions to be creative have elicited more creative ideas compared to "do your best" goals, instructions to generate many ideas or the best solution (Shalley, 1991; 1995). It is therefore suggested that it is the consistency of these factors that seems to matter in setting expectations for creativity and innovation. If various contextual factors seem to be conflicting, such that organizational goals seem to stress creativity, however, rewards seem to be directed toward tried and true solutions, organizational leaders are less likely to be creative. As creativity is resource intensive and risky (Crowe & Higgins, 1996; Friedman & Forster, 2001), leaders are more likely to be creative when they perceive the environment to be conducive to these creative ideas. Mixed messages are therefore likely to actually send a signal that creativity may not be desirable.

Resources have been suggested as an important organizational issue that may facilitate or inhibit creativity and innovation. Organizational leaders are viewed as those that are responsible for resource availability. That is, the leader of the team or department is responsible for obtaining any needed resource and then controls how that resource is used. A number of studies have found that slack resources, or the availability of resources, are linked to creativity and innovation (Dougherty & Hardy, 1996; Greve, 2003). It has been suggested that the availability of resources allows creativity due to the ability to free time and energy towards experimentation and innovation (Amabile et al., 1996; Sonenshein, 2014). For leaders, this may be of particular importance. Not only do resources allow the leader to be creative, but the availability of resources may facilitate team creativity as well. However, other researchers argue that limited resources can foster creativity. Organizations with limited resources tend to be newer organizations and allow for flexibility, which in turn facilitates creativity (Kanter, 1985). Limited resources are also viewed as a challenge or crisis, which may require creativity (Ohly & Fritz, 2010; Scott & Bruce, 1994). Others have suggested more nuanced approaches. Mumford and Hunter (2005) indicated that a curvilinear relationship may exist. While access to some degree of resources is necessary for creativity, having too many resources may facilitate less selective choosing of projects and investment in more risky ideas that are likely to fail. Another study suggested that resources themselves can be acquired and used creatively (Sonenshein, 2014). Leaders can be important in knowing what organizational resources are available, and how to then transform and use these resources for maximum capacity, potentially in a creative way. Thus a creative leader is one that is able to find creative ways to obtain and use resources for his or her team.

Conclusion

In this chapter we have provided a review of the research that can inform us how leaders can be creative. Although past work has focused mostly on leaders as facilitators of creativity in their subordinates, our goal was to discuss leaders as creative problem-solvers. Much of the work that leaders do requires creative problem solving, as organizational problems are not routine and tend to be ill defined. We have noted some important parallels in terms of individual differences between leaders and creative individuals, factors that facilitate both leadership and creativity. Further, research from decision making as well as creative problem solving provides support for the creative problem-solving framework in which leaders must make decisions. Finally, we have discussed organizational context that supports leader creative problem solving.

It is important to understand how these various approaches can be integrated. For example, how do individual differences in emotional intelligence influence decision making or creative problem solving? Do decision-making styles interact with other individual difference variables such as expertise or openness to influence creative problem solving? Are certain individual differences more influential or result in increased creativity for certain environmental factors? In addition, these research teams suggest that an important consideration of creative leadership is the multi-level nature of this phenomenon. That is, factors that affect creative leadership exists at the individual, team, and organizational levels. Further, the demands placed by each may not be compatible (Hunter et al., 2011).

References

Allaire, J. C., & Marsiske, M. (2002). Well- and ill-defined measures of everyday cognition: Relationship to older adults' intellectual ability and functional status. *Psychology and Aging, 17*, 101–115. DOI:10.1037/0882–7974.17.1.101

Amabile, T. M. (1996). *Creativity in context: Update to the social psychology of creativity.* Boulder, CO: Westview Press.

Amabie, T. M., Conti, R., Coon, H., Lazenby, J., Herron, M. (1996). Assessing the work environment for creativity. *The Academy of Management Journal, 39*, 1154–1184. DOI:10.2307/256995

Andersen, J. A. (2000). Intuition in managers: Are intuitive managers more effective? *Journal of Managerial Psychology, 15*, 46–67. DOI:10.1108/02683940010305298

Anderson, N., Potocnik, K., & Zhou, J. (2014). Innovation and creativity in organizations: A state-of-the-science review, prospective commentary, and guiding framework. *Journal of Management, 40*, 1297–1333. DOI:10.1177/0149206314527128

Ayal, S., Rusou, Z., Zakay, D., & Hochman, G. (2015). Determinants of judgments and decision making quality: The interplay between information processing style and situational factors. *Frontiers in Psychology, 6*, 1088. DOI:10.3389/fpsyg.2015.01088

Barczak, G., Lassk, F., Mulki, J. (2010). Antecedents of team creativity: An examination of team emotional intelligence, team trust, and collaborative culture. *Creativity and Innovation Management, 19*, 332–345. DOI:10.1111/j.1467–8691.2010.00574.x

Barrick, J. A., & Spilker, B. C. (2003). The relations between knowledge, search strategy, and performance in unaided and aided information search. *Organizational Behavior and Human Decision Making Processing, 90*, 1–18. DOI:10.1016/S0749-5978(03)00002-5

Barron, F., & Harrington, D. M. (1981). Creativity, intelligence, and personality. *Annual Review of Psychology, 32*, 432–476. DOI:10.1146/annurev.ps.32.020181.002255

Baregheh, A., Rowley, J., & Sambrook, S. (2009). Towards a multidisciplinary definition of innovation. *Management Decision, 47*, 1323–1339. DOI:10.1108/00251740910984578

Basadur, M. S. (1994). Managing the creative process in organizations. In M. A. Runco (Ed.), *Problem finding, problem solving, and creativity* (pp. 237–268). New York: Ablex.

Bass, B. M. & Bass R. (2008). *The Bass handbook of leadership: Theory, research, and managerial applications* (4th ed.). New York: Free Press.

Bassett, E., & Shandas, V. (2010). Innovation and climate action planning: perspectives from municipal plans. *Journal of the American Planning Association, 76*, 435–450.

Bettman, J. R., & Park, C. W. (1980). Effects of prior knowledge and experience and phase of the choice process on consumer decision processes: A protocol analysis. *Journal of Consumer Research*, 234–248.

Carmeli, A., McKay, A. S., Kaufman, J. C. (2014). Emotional intelligence and creativity: The mediating role of generosity and vigor. *The Journal of Creative Behavior, 48*, 290–309. DOI:10.1002/jocb.53

Carmeli, A., Reiter-Palmon, R., & Ziv, E. (2010). Inclusive leadership and employee involvement in creative tasks in the workplace: The mediating role of psychological safety. *Creativity Research Journal, 22*, 250–260. DOI:10.1080/10400419.2010.504654

Carmeli, A., & Schaubroeck, J. (2007). The influence of leaders' and other referents' normative expectations on individual involvement in creative work. *The Leadership Quarterly, 18*, 35–48. DOI:10.1016/j.leaqua.2006.11.001

Carmeli, A., Sheaffer, Z., Binyamin, G., Reiter-Palmon, R., & Shimoni, T. (2014). Transformational leadership and creative problem-solving: The mediating role of psychological safety and reflexivity. *The Journal of Creative Behavior, 48*, 115–135. DOI:10.1002/jocb.43

Castro, F., Gomes, J., & de Sousa, F. C. (2012). Do intelligent leaders make a difference? The effect of a leader's emotional intelligence on followers' creativity. *Creativity and Innovation Management, 21*, 171–182. DOI:10.1111/j.1467–8691.2012.00636.x

Crooke, M., Csikszentmihalyi, M., & Kikel, R. (2015). Leadership in a complex world: How to manage "the tragedy of choice." *Organizational Dynamics*, *44*, 146–155. DOI:10.1016/j.orgdyn.2015.02.009

Crowe, E., & Higgins, E. T. (1997). Regulatory focus and strategic inclinations: Promotion and prevention in decision-making. *Organizational Behavior and Human Decision Processes*, *69*, 117–132. DOI:10.1006/obhd.1996.2675

Csikszentmihalyi, M., & Gretzels, J. W. (1988). Creativity and problem finding in art. In F. H. Farley & R. W. Neperud (Eds.), *The foundations of aesthetics, arts, & art education* (pp. 91–116). New York: Praeger.

Damanpour, F. (1996). Organizational complexity and innovation: Developing and testing multiple contingency models. *Management Science*, *42*(5), 693–713.

Dillon, J. T. (1982). Problem finding and solving. *Journal of Creative Behavior*, *16*, 97–111.

Dougherty, D., & Hardy, C. (1996). Sustained product innovation in large, mature organizations: Overcoming innovation-to-organization problems. *Academy of Management Journal*, *39*, 1120–1153. DOI:10.2307/256994

Duarte, N. T., Goodson, J. R., & Dougherty, T. M. P. (2014). Managing innovation in hospitals and health systems: Lessons from the Malcolm Baldrige national quality award winners. *International Journal of Healthcare Management*, *7*, 21–34.

Ettlie, J. E. (1983). Organizational policy and innovation among suppliers to the food processing sector. *Academy of Management Journal*, *26*, 27–44. DOI:10.2307/256133

Feist, G. J. (1998). A meta-analysis of personality in scientific and artistic creativity. *Personality and Social Psychology Review*, *2*, 290–309. DOI:10.1207/s15327957pspr0204_5

Friedman, R. S., & Forster, J. (2001). *The effects of promotion and prevention cues on creativity. Journal of Personality and Social Psychology*, 81, 1001–1013. DOI:10.1037/0022–3514.81.6.1001

Galbraith, J. R. (1982). Designing the innovating organization. *Organizational Dynamics*, *10*, 5–25. DOI:10.1016/0090–2616(82)90033-X

George, J. M., & Zhou, J. (2001). When openness to experience and conscientiousness are related to creative behavior: An interactional approach. *Journal of Applied Psychology*, *86*, 513–524. DOI:10.1037/0021–9010.86.3.513

Giessner, S. R., & van Knippenberg, D. (2007). *Leading FOR the team: Situational determinants of team-oriented leader behavior*. Paper presented at the 2007 Annual Meeting of the Society of Industrial and Organizational Psychology, New York, April.

Gilson, L. L., & Madjar, N. (2011). Radical and incremental creativity: Antecedents and processes. *Psychology of Aesthetics, Creativity, and the Arts*, *5*, 21–28. DOI:10.1037/a0017863

Goldring, E., Huff, J., Spillane, J. P., & Barnes, C. (2009). Measuring the learning centered leadership expertise of school principals. *Leadership & Policy in Schools*, *8*, 197–228. DOI:10.1080/15700760902737170

Goleman, D. (1995). *Emotional intelligence*. New York: Bantam Books.

Goleman, D., Boyatzis, R., & McKee, A. (2002). *Primal leadership: Realizing the power of emotional intelligence*. Boston, MA: Harvard Business School Press.

Greve, H. R. (2003). A behavioral theory of R&D expenditures and innovations: Evidence from shipbuilding. *Academy of Management Journal*, *46*, 685–702. DOI:10.2307/30040661

Hadley, C. N., Pittinsky, T. L., Sommer, S. A., & Zhu, W. (2011). Measuring the efficacy of leaders to assess information and make decision in a crisis: The C-LEAD scale. *The Leadership Quarterly, 22*, 633–648. DOI:10.1016/j.leaqua.2011.05.005

Harmancioglu, N., Droge, C., & Calantone, R. J. (2009). Theoretical lenses and domain definitions in innovation research. *European Journal of Market, 43*, 229–263. DOI:10.1108/03090560910923319

Harris, D. J., Reiter-Palmon, R., & Kaufman, J. C. (2013). The effect of emotional intelligence and task type on malevolent creativity. *Psychology of Aesthetics, Creativity, and the Arts, 7*, 237–244. DOI:10.1037/a0032139

Hogan, J., & Hogan, R. (2002). Leadership and sociopolitical intelligence. In R. E. Riggio, S. E. Murphy, & F. J. Pirozzolo (Eds.), *Multiple intelligences and leadership* (pp. 75–88). Mahwah, NJ: Lawrence Erlbaum Associates Publishers.

Hoover, S. M., & Feldhusen, J. F. (1994). Scientific problem solving and problem finding: A theoretical model. In M. A. Runco (Ed.), *Problem finding, problem, and creativity* (pp. 201–219). New York: Ablex.

Hornberg, J. & Reiter-Palmon, R. (in press). Creativity and the Big Five personality traits: Is the relationship dependent on the creativity measure? In G. Feist, R. Reiter-Palmon, & J. Kaufman (Eds.), *Handbook of personality and creativity.* Cambridge Press.

Hunter, S. T., Cushenbery, L., & Friedrich, T. (2012). Hiring an innovative workforce: A necessary yet uniquely challenging endeavor. *Human Resource Management Review.* DOI:10.1016/j.hrmr.2012.01.001

Hunter, S. T., Bedell, K. E., & Mumford, M. D. (2007). Climate for creativity: A quantitative review. *Creativity Research Journal, 19*, 69–90. DOI:10.1080/10400410709336883

Hunter, S. T., Thoroughgood, C. N., Myer, A. T., & Ligon, G. S. (2011). Paradoxes of leading innovative endeavors: Summary, solutions, and future directions. *Psychology of Aesthetics, Creativity, and the Arts, 5*, 54–66. DOI:10.1037/a0017776

IBM. (2010). *Capitalizing on complexity.* Retrieved on April 20, 2017, from www-935.ibm.com/services/c-suite/series-download.html

Jabeen, S., Akhtar, S., & Muhammad, M. (2013). Decision making styles of university leadership. *Dialogue, 8*, 273–284.

Judge, T. A., Bono, J. E., Illies, R., & Gerhardt, M. W. (2002). Personality and leadership: A qualitative and quantitative review. *Journal of Applied Psychology, 87*, 765–780. DOI:10.1037/0021–9010.87.4.765

Kanter, R. (1985). Supporting innovation and venture development in established companies. *Journal of Business Venturing, 1*, 47–60. DOI:10.1016/0883–9026(85)90006–0

Karlins, M., Lee, R. E., & Schroder, H. M. (1967). Creativity and information search in a problem-solving context. *Psychonomic Science, 8*, 165–166.

Keller, R. T. (2012). Predicting the performance and innovativeness of scientists and engineers. *Journal of Applied Psychology, 97*, 225–233. DOI: 10.1037/a0025332

Kitchener, K. S. (1983). Cognition, metacognition, and epistemic cognition: A three-level model of cognitive processing. *Human Development, 26*, 222–232. DOI:10.1159/000272885

Kohn, N. W., Paulus, P. B., & Korde, R. M. (2011). Conceptual combinations and subsequent creativity. *Creativity Research Journal, 23*, 203–210. DOI:0.1080/10400419.2011.595659

Lewis, M. W. (2000). Exploring paradox: Toward a more comprehensive guide. *Academy of Management Review, 25*, 760–776. DOI:10.2307/259204

Mainemelis, C., Kark, R., & Epitropaki, O. (2015). Creative leadership: A multi-context conceptualization. *The Academy of Management Annals*, *9*, 393–482. DOI:10.1080/19416520.2015.1024502

Mayer, J. D., Salovey, P., & Caruso, D. R. (2000). Models of emotional intelligence. In R. J. Sternberg (Ed.), *Handbook of intelligence* (pp. 396–420). New York: Cambridge University Press

McCall, M. W., Jr., & Hollenbeck, G. P. (2008). Developing the expert leader. *People & Strategy*, *31*(1), 20–28.

Mobley, M. I., Doares, L. M., & Mumford, M. D. (1992). Process analytic models of creative capacities: Evidence for the combination and reorganization process. *Creativity Research Journal*, *5*, 125–155. DOI:10.1080/10400419209534428

Moxley, J. H., Ericsson, K. A., Charness, N., & Krampe, R. T. (2012). The role of intuition and deliberative thinking in experts' superior tactical decision-making. *Cognition*, *124*, 72–78. DOI:10.1016/j.cognition.2012.03.005

Mumford, M. D. (1986). Leadership in the organizational context: A conceptual approach and its applications. *Journal of Applied Social Psychology*, *16*, 508–531. DOI:10.1111/j.1559–1816.1986.tb01156.x</doi>

Mumford, M. D., Baughman, W. A., Maher, M. A., Costanza, D. P., & Supinski, E. P. (1997). Process-based measures of creative problem-solving skills: IV. Category combination. *Creativity Research Journal*, *10*, 59–71. DOI:10.1207/s15326934crj1001_7

Mumford, M. D., Baughman, W. A., Supinski, E. P., & Maher, M. A. (1996). Process-based measures of creative problem-solving skills: II. Information encoding. *Creativity Research Journal*, *9*, 77–88. DOI:10.1207/s15326934crj0901_7

Mumford, M. D., Bedell, K. E., & Hunter, S. T. (2008). Planning for innovation: A multi-level perspective. In M. D. Mumford, S. T. Hunter, & K. E. Bedell (Eds.), *Research in multi-level issues: Vol. VII*. Oxford, England: Elsevier.

Mumford, M. D., Blair, C., Dailey, L. Leritz, L. E., & Osburn, H. K. (2006). Errors in creative thought? Cognitive biases in a complex processing activity. *The Journal of Creative Behavior*, *40*, 75–109.

Mumford, M. D., & Connelly, M. S. (1991). Leaders as creators: Leader performance and problem solving in ill-defined domains. *Leadership Quarterly*, *2*, 289–315. DOI:10.1016/1048-9843(91)90017-V

Mumford, M. D., Connelly, S., & Gaddis, B. (2003). How creative leaders think: Experimental findings and cases. *The Leadership Quarterly*, *14*, 411–432. DOI:10.1016/S1048-9843(03)00045-6

Mumford, M. D., & Gustafson, S. B. (1988). Creativity syndrome: Integration, application and innovation. *Psychological Bulletin*, *103*, 27–43. DOI:10.1037/0033–2909.103.1.27

Mumford, D., Hester, K. S., & Robledo, I. C. (2011). Creativity in organizations: Importance and approaches. In M. D. Mumford (Ed.), *Handbook of organizational creativity* (pp. 3–16). San Diego, CA: Academic Press.

Mumford, M. D., & Hunter, S. T. (2005). Innovation in organizations: A multi-level perspective on creativity. In F. Dansereau & F. J. Yammarino (Eds.), *Multi-level issues in strategy and methods* (pp. 9–73). Emerald Group Publishing Limited.

Mumford, M. D., Hunter, S. T., Eubanks, D. L., Bedell, K. E., & Murphy, S. T. (2007). Developing leaders for creative efforts: A domain-based approach to leadership development. *Human Resource Management Review*, *17*, 402–417. DOI:10.1016/j.hrmr.2007.08.002

Mumford, M. D., Mobley, M. I., Reiter-Palmon, R., Uhlman, C. E., & Doares, L. M. (1991). Process analytic models of creative capacities. *Creativity Research Journal, 4,* 91–122. doi:10.1080/10400419109534380

Mumford, M. D., Scott, G. M., Gaddis, B., & Strange, J. M. (2002). Leading creative people: Orchestrating expertise and relationships. *Leadership Quarterly, 13,* 705–750. DOI:10.1016/S1048-9843(02)00158-3

Mumford, M. D., Zaccaro, S. J., Harding, F. D., Jacobs, T. O., & Fleishman, E. A. (2000). Leadership skills for a changing world: Solving complex social problems. *The Leadership Quarterly, 11,* 11–35. DOI:10.1016/S1048-9843(99)00041-7

Ohly, S., & Fritz, C. (2010). Work characteristics, challenge appraisal, creativity, and proactive behavior: A multi-level study. *Journal of Organizational Behavior, 31,* 543–565. DOI:10.1002/job.633

Okpala, C. O., Hopson, L. B., Chapman, B., & Fort, E. (2011). Leadership development expertise: A mixed-method analysis. *Journal of Instructional Psychology, 38,* 133–137.

Okuda, S. M., Runco, M. A., & Berger, D. E. (1991). Creativity and the finding and solving of real-world problems. *Journal of Psychoeducational Assessment, 9,* 145–153. DOI:10.1177/073428299100900104

Parke, M. R., Seo, M., & Sherf, E. N. (2015). Regulating and facilitating: The role of emotional intelligence in maintaining and using positive affect for creativity. *Journal of Applied Psychology, 100,* 917–934. DOI:10.1037/a0038452

Redmond, R. R., Mumford, M. D., & Teach, R. (1993). Putting creativity to work: Effects of leader behavior on subordinate creativity. *Organizational Behavior and Human Decision Processes, 55,* 120–151. DOI:10.1006/obhd.1993.1027

Reed, S. K. (2015). The structure of ill-structured (and well-structured) problems revisited. *Educational Psychology Review.* DOI:10.1007/s10648-015-9343-1

Reiter-Palmon, R., Beghetto, R., & Kaufman, J. C. (2014). Looking at creativity through the Business-Psychology-Education (BPE) lens: The challenge and benefits of listening to each other. In E. Shiu (Ed.), *Creativity research: An interdisciplinary and multidisciplinary research handbook* (pp. 9–30). Routledge.

Reiter-Palmon, R., Mumford, M. D., & Threlfall, K. V. (1998). Solving everyday problems creatively: The role of problem construction and personality type. *Creativity Research Journal, 11,* 187–197. DOI:10.1207/s15326934crj1103_1

Reitman, W. R. (1964). Heuristic decision procedures, open constraints, and the structure of ill-defined problems. In M. W. Shelly, & G. L. Bryan (Eds.), *Human judgments and optimality* (pp. 282–315). New York: Wiley & Sons.

Rehman, R. R., & Waheed, A. (2012). Individual's leadership and decision making styles: A study of banking sector of Pakistan. *Journal of Behavioral Sciences, 22,* 79–89.

Riaz, M. N., & Khalili, M. T. (2014). Transformational, transactional leadership and rational decision making in services providing organizations: Moderating role of knowledge management processes. *Pakistan Journal of Commerce and Social Science, 8,* 355–364.

Rus, D., van Knippenberg, D., & Wisse, B. (2010). Leader self-definition and leader self-serving behavior. *The Leadership Quarterly, 21,* 509–529. DOI:10.1016/j.leaqua.2010.03.013

Salovey, P., & Mayer, J. D. (1990). Emotional intelligence. *Imagination, Cognition and Personality, 9,* 185–211.

Sanchez-Ruiz, M. J., Hernandez-Torrano, D., Perez-Gonzalez, J. C., Batey, M., & Petrides, K. V. (2011). The relationship between trait emotional intelligence and creativity across subject domains. *Motivation and Emotion*, *35*, 461–473. DOI:10.1007/s11031-011-9227-8

Schraw, G., Dunkle, M. E., Bendixen, L. D. (1995). Cognitive processes in well-defined and ill-defined problem solving. *Applied Cognitive Psychology*, *9*, 523–538. DOI:10.1002/acp.2350090605

Scott, G. M., Lonergan, D. C., Mumford, M. D. (2005). Conceptual combination: Alternative knowledge structures, alternative heuristics. *Creativity Research Journal*, *17*, 79–98. DOI:10.1207/s15326934crj1701_7

Scott, S. G., & Bruce, R. A. (1995). Decision-making style: The development and assessment of a new measure. *Educational and Psychological Measurement*, *55*, 818–831.

Selnes, F., & Troye, S. V. (1989). Buying expertise, information search, and problem solving. *Journal of Economic Psychology*, *10*, 411–428. DOI:10.1016/0167–4870(89)90032–9

Shalley, C. E. (1991). Effects of productivity goals, creativity goals, and personal discretion on individual creativity. *Journal of Applied Psychology*, *76*, 179–185. DOI:10.1037/0021–9010.76.2.179

Shalley, C. E. (1995). Effects of coaction, expected evaluation, and goal setting on creativity and productivity. *Academy of Management Journal*, *38*, 483–503. DOI:10.2307/256689

Smith, W. K. (2014). Dynamic decision making: A model of senior leaders managing strategic paradoxes. *Academy of Management Journal*, *57*, 1592–1623. DOI:10.5465/amj.2011.0932

Smith, W. K., & Lewis, M. W. (2011). Toward a theory of paradox: A dynamic equilibrium model of organizing. *Academy of Management Review*, *36*: 381–403.

Sonenshein, S. (2014). How organizations foster the creative use of resources. *Academy of Management Journal*, *57*, 814–848. DOI:10.5465/10.5465/amj.2012.0048

Stenmark, C. K., Shipman, A. S., & Mumford, M. D. (2011). Managing the innovative process: The dynamic role of leaders. *Psychology of Aesthetics, Creativity, and the Arts*, *5*, 67–80. DOI:10.1037/a0018588

Sy, T., & Reiter-Palmon, R. (2015). *Follower-leader identity integration*. Unpublished paper.

Tierney, P., & Farmer, S. M. (2004). The Pygmalion process and employee creativity. *Journal of Management*, *30*, 413–432. DOI:10.1016/j.jm.2002.12.001

Urabe, K. (1988). *Innovation and the Japanese management system: Innovation and management international comparisons*. Berlin: Walter de Gruyter.

Van Knippenberg, D. (2013). Leadership and decision making: Defining a field. In S. Highhouse, R. S. Dalal, & E. Salas (Eds.), *Judgment and decision making at work* (pp. 140–158). New York: Routledge.

Wakefield, J. F. (1992). *Creative thinking: Problem-solving skills and the arts orientation*. Norwood, NJ: Ablex.

West, M. A. (2002). Sparkling fountains or stagnant ponds: An integrative model of creativity and innovation implementation in work groups. *Applied Psychology*, *51*, 355–387. DOI:10.1111/1464–0597.00951

Yukl, G. (1989). Managerial leadership: A review of theory and research. *Journal of Management*, *15*, 251–289.

Yukl, G. (2007). Best practices in the use of proactive influence tactics by leaders. In J.A. Conger & R. E. Riggio (Eds.), *The practice of leadership: Developing the next generation of leaders* (pp. 109–128). San Franscisco: Jossey-Bass.

Zaccaro, S. J., Mumford, M. D., Connelly, M. S., Marks, M. A., & Gilbert, J. A. (2000). Assessment of leader problem-solving capabilities. *Leadership Quarterly, 11*, 37–64.

Zacher, H., Robinson, A. J., & Rosing, K. (2014). Ambidextrous leadership and employees' self-reported innovative performance: The role of exploration and exploitation behaviors. *The Journal of Creative Behavior.* DOI:10.1002/jocb.66

Zacher, H., & Rosing, K. (2015). Ambidextrous leadership and team innovation. *Leadership & Organization Development Journal, 36*, 54–68. DOI:10.1108/LODJ-11–2012-0141

21 Creativity in Business and Technology

Educational Technologies

Kylie Peppler

Indiana University

Abstract

Ever since the introduction of desktop computers in schools, the degree to which technology constrains or enables students' creativity has been explored in a number of guises and continues to color our understanding of the current trends in education. Because a central objective of educational technology is to redesign our tools and environments to enable new forms of teaching that make learning more efficacious, educational technologies offer new ways to think about and to measure creativity, teach creative thinking, and deepen creative expression. This chapter offers a broad survey of creativity research within this domain, presenting the definitions and constructs that are most important to the conceptualization of creativity with educational technologies and suggesting future considerations for the study of creativity in this area.

Introduction

With new tools come new opportunities for individuals to experience creativity. Ranging from new materials to new visual programming environments, virtual reality, apps, social media, online learning, robotics and more, technology is rapidly opening up new areas of study in the creativity literature. Ever since the introduction of desktop computers in schools, the degree to which technology constrains or enables students' creativity has been explored in a number of guises and continues to color our understanding of the current trends in education, including tinkering (Resnick & Rosenbaum, 2013), social networking (Donath & boyd, 2004), and computational flexibility (Smith, 2006).

The integration of digital technologies into educational domains is widely varied but far-reaching, spanning from pre-school to professional settings. Such integrations introduce new forms of creative expression to students, resulting in artifacts and practices that sit at the nexus of different forms of play, creative exploration, and

Special thanks to Sophia Bender and Tony Phonethibsavads for compiling the literature review that informed the writing of this chapter. Additional financial support was provided from the National Science Foundation to Kylie Peppler (IIS-1324047).

disciplinary learning. For instance, prior research demonstrates how pre-school students playing with Squishy Circuits – a circuitry toolkit that includes playdough, LEDs, and other electrical components – transforms simple, sculptural-artistic play into a new activity that integrates the arts, technology, and other domains (Wohlwend, Keune, & Peppler, 2016):

> With rolled up sleeves, 4-year old Nate plunges star-shaped cookie cutters into flattened playdough. Calling each playdough star "rocket ships," he picks up a star and waves his arms across his body from left to right and up and down. He then grabs a Dora the Explorer keychain, casually flings Dora around his index finger and places her next to the star.
>
> Across the table, 5-year-old Suparna, fairy wings strapped to her back and cinnamon across her face, holds an LED light in front of 4-year-old Aamir. Carefully, Suparna takes one of the leads into one hand while pulling on the other by tightly squeezing her thumb and index finger together. She looks up at Aamir, explaining "you have to spread them apart." Suparna sticks one lead of LED into Aamir's playdough snowman and the other into her own. Both figures are connected to a battery pack and the LED flickers, shining a dim glimmer upon the connected characters. Aamir squeezes the playdough tightly around the leads. The light brightens.
>
> All at the same time, Nate, Suparna, and Aamir are crafting, playing, collaborating, and debugging with Squishy Circuits, an electronic toolkit and educational technology with creative potential. It builds on the conductive properties of salty playdough to invite colorful LEDs, humming motors, squeaking buzzers along their technological practices, to join the playful crafting with ordinary playdough.

The domain of educational technologies spans work in computer science and the arts, resting at the intersection of these two fields. Though researchers have argued that the construct of creativity differs between these two fields (Salgian et al., 2013), we can assert that a focus on educational technologies gets us to think more widely about how a tool or learning environment is designed to teach and cultivate creativity. Because a central objective of educational technology is to redesign our tools and environments to enable new forms of teaching that make learning more efficacious, educational technologies offer new ways to think about and to measure creativity, new ways to teach creative thinking, and new ways to deepen creative expression.

This is a vast area, not least because the boundary between educational technology and educational uses of commercial technology is hard to define. Because it would be impossible to review everything, this chapter focuses particularly on aspects of educational technology that include social media, robotics, online learning, and software, as well as new-media art platforms that allow for programming and other aspects of digital production. In the process, I will present a broad survey of creativity research within this domain, and present the definitions and constructs that are most important to the conceptualization of creativity, as well as how creativity is commonly measured, and offer future considerations for the study of creativity in this area.

Defining Creativity Within Educational Technology

Novelty and Usefulness

Like many other domains, research on creativity within the domain of educational technology has a pervasive focus on defining creativity in terms of novelty, flexible thinking, and usefulness (e.g., Baumer, Tomlinson, Richland, & Hansen, 2009; Jahnke, 2011). As Plucker and colleagues argue, creativity is "the interaction among *aptitude, process, and environment* by which an individual or group produces a *perceptible product* that is both *novel and useful* as defined within a *social context*" (Plucker, Beghetto, & Dow, 2004, p. 90, original emphasis). Mishra and Henriksen (2013) have further operationalized this definition by defining creativity for educational technology as a measurement along three independent axes – *novel, effective,* and *whole* – arguing that "creative products (be they artifacts or ideas) are not just new or interesting, they are useful, and they have a certain aesthetic sensibility, which is connected to and evaluated within a specific context – the whole!" (p. 11). This work provides a basis for rubrics and other ways of evaluating creative products that the authors argue is particularly useful in the field of educational technology (and is further described later in this chapter).

Ecological Nature of Creativity

Scholarship on creativity has also recognized the genesis and development of creative ideas as being part of a broader, socially determined process (Sternberg, 2003; Sawyer, 2006, 2007). Consistent with Csikszentmihalyi's (1996) model, creativity is becoming increasingly understood as a system, composed of individuals, knowledge domains, and a field of informed experts. Given the pervasiveness of Internet-enabled devices in youths lives, the acts of information acquisition and product sharing are largely done in a communal (at least virtually) context, placing a stronger role of the environment in shaping youths creativity. Peppler and Solomou (2011), for example, examined how environmental creativity is uniquely shaped by the kinds of networks afforded in today's online culture. This study explored the design of a social media environment to foster collaborative learning and creativity. The researchers designed two parallel virtual worlds where participants were encouraged to engage in 3D architectural construction. Despite offering users the same toolset for construction, the two worlds emphasized very different cultural values – one designed for high levels of creativity (i.e., players were encouraged to design highly original buildings, regardless of fiscal viability) and the other for low (i.e., players were encouraged to follow formulaic design practices as befitting in-game market demand). The resulting work within these environments reflected the cultural values designed into the system, indicating that the way in which we design our social media environments has implications for the creativity of the products users produce. Using chat and archival data of the 3D virtual environment, the researchers explored how architectural ideas spread within the online space (i.e., other users referencing or emulating a design), ultimately defining creativity in this domain as *a spreadable idea that is taken up by others* in the field, and that this lineage of ideas can be traced back to a single individual, the origin of the idea. Implications for measuring creativity as the spread of ideas taken up by others in the field offers a way of measuring creativity through an embedded assessment, utilizing embedded data metrics. Another possibility is to look at how the ideas transform and become appropriated through the spread of a creative idea and to examine the larger patterns or iterative evolutions of the ideas. These ways of defining creativity emphasize the importance of social networks in determining whether a creative idea is taken up by the larger field, contributing to the domain.

Designing Creativity-Enhancing Tools and Environments

The design of the technology itself plays a large role in shaping these outcomes. Several scholars have provided new frameworks for conceptualizing creativity within the domain of educational technology, paying particular attention to aspects of human-computer interaction and the types of creative activities they precipitate. For example, Shneiderman (2000) advances a proposal for a *genex (generator of excellence) framework*, which is a four-phase integrative framework for designing powerful technologies that enable users to produce creative work. Technologies that adhere to the framework enable users to collect (i.e., learn from prior works), relate (i.e., consult with peers and mentors at all stages), create (i.e., explore, compose, and evaluate possible solutions) and donate (i.e., publish and share results) in the production of creative work. Shneiderman further proposes eight activities that can be incorporated into the design of an environment to facilitate creativity, including users' ability to (1) search and browse digital libraries, (2) consult with peers and mentors, (3) visualize data and processes, (4) think by free association, (5) explore solutions, (6) compose artifacts and performances, (7) review and replay session histories, and ultimately (8) disseminate results (2000). Shneiderman's framework clarifies a future research agenda for the designers of human-computer interaction as well as the researchers who evaluate the creative expressions of individuals who engage with these technologies (cf. Albors-Garrigos & Carrasco, 2011).

Constructs Informing the Conceptualization of Creativity in Educational Technology

Creativity researchers have drawn upon a breadth of constructs important to the conceptualization of creativity in their analysis of educational technology, including surprise, problem solving, human agency, improvisation, and social capital. Several researchers have drawn on *surprise*, for example, as a central construct to the design and study of creativity within new educational technologies (e.g., Zheng, Bromage, Adam, & Scrivener, 2007; Rosen, Schmidt, & Kim, 2013). Educational technologies can promote surprise through the random presentation of materials as well as by users coming up with a new valuable idea. Researchers have dubbed this as p-creativity (for "psychological" creativity," which describes a surprising or valuable idea that is new to the person coming up with it, regardless if others had come up with the idea before. This is opposed to h-creativity (for "historical" creativity), which relates to surprising ideas not known to be had by anyone else in human history (Boden, 2004). Though not referred to as "surprise," Clements speaks of a similar phenomenon in terms of *mental reorganization* fostered through early educational technologies, arguing that such technologies necessitate "continuous reformations and modifications within a context of the invention and construction of one's own graphic projects" (1986, p. 310).

Another focus of work on creativity within educational technologies is the creativity that emerges through the *problem-solving* process, including "deciding on the nature of the problem, choosing performance components (lower-order components not as critical to creative thought) relevant to the solution of the problem, combining these performance components, selecting a mental representation, and monitoring" (Clements, 1995, p. 144). This is likely because educational technologies are frequently utilized in an intervention format, where challenges are posed and addressed through the introduction of the technology.

The interactive elements of new technologies have brought the role of *human agency* in our conceptualizations of creativity to the fore. Researchers like Charles and Shumar have grappled with the relationship between humans and computers, asserting that "much of social life is constrained structures that themselves are the product of past action both conscious and habitual and that these constraints are something that social actors must indeed face" (2007, p. 120). This draws on the earlier work of Emirbayer and Mische (1998), who emphasize the creative dimensions of human agency have a future focus and are tied to *imagination* and *improvisation* (as cited in Charles & Shumar, 2007). Linder and colleagues (2015) also recognize the importance of improvisation in the conceptualization of creativity, applying Fisher and Amabile's (2009) notion of improvisational creativity to the study of educational technology. In their view, technology brings about opportunities for improvisational creativity by allowing for free-form, spontaneous, and unrestricted thinking (Linder et al., 2015). Linder and colleagues define *free-form thinking* as involving: "(1) improvisational exploration of associations; (2) the emergence of new ideas, generated through building on previously known associations; (3) divergent wanderings to unexpected places; and (4) spontaneous synthesis of new understandings, relationships, and ideas" (2015, p. 285).

Furthermore, educational technology, particularly social media, has accentuated the role of social networks in youths' learning and creativity. As such, several scholars have placed an increased emphasis on social capital and have even gone so far as to define creativity as a form of social capital needed for productive participation in a knowledge society (Dawson, Tan, & McWilliam, 2011; Lai & Hwang, 2014). In a way, these various constructs coordinate, helping us to understand how educational technology pushes our prior conceptualizations of creativity in new directions.

Measuring Creativity Within the Domain of Educational Technology

Since educational technologies can range from alternative modes of content delivery and engagement (e.g., video games) to new tools and materials for production (e.g., graphic design, computational textiles, robotics), a variety of research approaches have been applied to better understand the creativity of the user of the technology as well as the artifacts they create with it. The former body of research has focused primarily on traditional cognitive measures of creativity, such as the Torrance Test of Creative Thinking (TTCT; Torrance, 1972) and Guilford's Alternative Uses Task (1967), described in detail below. Such assessments have often been employed using traditional means: as pre- and post-test measures around an intervention using educational technologies (e.g., the students engage with a technology product, or they respond to each other or stimuli in a technology-filled environment) to measure the effects of the intervention on students' creative thinking.

Alternatively, several researchers have sought to assess the creativity of the products created with educational technologies using measures like the Amabile Consensual Assessment Technique (CAT) (Amabile, 1982). Many of these studies inherently emphasize that creativity can be exemplified in a variety of products, regardless of the nature of the technology in the educational intervention. Asserting that creativity can be expressed uniquely through technological means, recent scholarship has adapted rubrics like the CAT for technology-specific applications (Besemer, 1998; Besemer & O'Quin, 1999; Michael, 2001), or developed new methods of assessing creative expression in online environments that rely less on the development of products and more on creative actions and behaviors. Similarly, some research has sought to measure the impact of online networks on a person's creativity (Yang & Cheng, 2010; Dawson, Tan & McWilliam, 2011).

Some researchers have also sought to employ technology as an impartial assessor of youths' creativity, extending traditional assessment techniques with computational assessments that mine data for patterns of creative behavior (Baumer et al., 2009). Computational assessments open up new ways to quantitatively measure creativity as well as create more fluid ways for assessment to become integrated with students' play with technology, potentially fostering, as well as measuring, growth in student creativity. Below, three different approaches to the measurement of creativity are presented that vary by theoretical perspective and toolsets employed, including a survey of cognitive, artifact-based, and computational measures of creativity.

Cognitive Measures of Creativity

Researchers of educational technologies have long been interested in how students' creative thinking is shaped through the use of alternative modes of teaching and learning. The earliest uses of the computer in educational settings was met with both high expectations and skepticism. The first research to explore the efficacy of these technological interventions on students' creativity is documented in Douglas Clements's comprehensive review of how creativity was taught with computers (Clements, 1995). This review focused mostly on studies that had used educational technologies like the Logo programming environment (Papert, 1980) as well as some considerations of other programs, like Scardamalia and Bereiter's CSILE (1996) and LEGO/Logo (Resnick, Ocko & Papert, 1988). Pervasive across all the articles reviewed was the assessment of creativity using the TTCT (Torrance, 1972). Assessing verbal and/or non-verbal measures of creative thinking, these studies examined students' cognitive expressions of creativity as a result of the technologies used. Looking across these studies, Clements noted that the technologies that seemed to have the greatest impact on creativity included design features that encouraged higher-order thinking, control, and mastery. Beyond the software itself, the meta-review noted how the teacher's facilitation style in coordination with the educational technology can impact student creativity. Furthermore, this meta-review provided evidence that children were having the opportunity to express creativity across content areas – through knowledge-building in mathematics, through design or artistic expression, or through computer science.

The programming language Logo (Papert, 1980) was among the first educational technologies to be used in creativity studies. This early work examined Logo using the TTCT (cf. Clements, 1986; Horton & Ryba, 1986). The Logo programming language, which enabled users to control the path of a mechanical turtle (or, later, a graphic turtle on the screen) was designed to engage students in conceptually different ways of learning mathematics and science through computer programming and meta-reflection. Soon after Logo was introduced to schools, several researchers began a series of studies where they investigated the impacts of the Logo programming language on children's creativity and cognition. Early reports noted significant gains in creativity, noting that students using Logo more fully developed their graphic compositions in completeness, originality, and drawing style than students not doing Logo programming (Horton & Ryba, 1986). Around the same time, Clements compared computer-assisted instruction (i.e., instructional mediation presented on a computer) to Logo programming and to a control group, measuring the impacts of these approaches on first- and third-graders' creativity, operational competence, metacognitive skills, and achievement (1986). Children in the two treatment conditions took time out of class to either program with Logo or participate in computer-assisted instruction over the course of twenty-two weeks. To measure creativity, Clements used the Figural TTCT (1972), which assesses several mental characteristics (including fluency, flexibility, originality, and elaboration) through picture-based exercises. Findings indicated that the Logo programming group had higher posttest gains than the other groups on almost all measures. Gains were particularly prominent in the originality and elaboration dimensions.

A follow-up study compared third graders working in Logo to students engaging in a prescribed, computer-supported creativity enhancement process – which included brainstorming, composing, revising, and editing – as they composed writings with a word processor and illustrated using with a graphics program (Clements, 1991). The students who used Logo were encouraged to use procedural thinking and cognitive componential processes thought to be crucial to creativity. These processes were conveyed through "homunculi" – characters that used these processes, including "Detective Selective," "Problem Decider," "Representer," and "Strategy Planner" – and were often called upon to help remind students of what they could do to help them accomplish their goals. Clements again measured creativity using the Figural TTCT as well as the Verbal TTCT, a test that employs word-based exercises to assess three mental characteristics (i.e., fluency, flexibility, and originality). The Logo group's total score on the figural posttest was significantly higher than the other two groups' scores, and both the Logo and creativity comparison group scored significantly higher on the verbal test than the control group.

Despite the tremendous development in educational uses of technology, many of today's studies continue to use derivations of the TTCT to measure creativity. Lewis (2009), for example, measured the impact of educational technologies that support design and intention activities on children's problem-solving ability, divergent thinking, combination thinking, and metaphorical thinking.

In addition, studies have used other time-honored cognitive measures of creativity (or a mix of cognitive measures), including the Guilford Alternative Uses Test (Guilford, 1967). In this test, examinees are asked to list as many uses for a common household item as possible. Scoring comprises four components: originality, fluency, flexibility, and elaboration. In a 2007 study, Zheng and colleagues used both the Guilford Alternative Uses Test as well as the TTCT to examine a new model, based on research on the value of "surprise," to help generate greater creativity in children. Based on constructivist theory, the researchers asserted that surprising outcomes challenge previously held beliefs (i.e., disequilibration), thus engaging people's curiosity to explain what caused the surprising outcome and changing their schema. Zheng and colleagues applied this model to the design of an interactive artifact called EYE-JUMP (i.e., a jump rope with LEDs that produces persistence-of-vision images) that would produce surprising outcomes in children. They tested the interactions with this artifact to measure its effects on surprise and on creative idea generation. In this study, the TTCT was used to measure creativity/ divergent thinking before and after playing with the technology. Guilford's Alternative Uses Test (1967) was used to ask youth to come up with alternate uses for a beaker (pre-test) and a towel (post-test). Answers were scored using four categories from Torrance: Fluency, Flexibility, Originality, and Elaboration. Results indicated that children who played with EYE-JUMP came up with ideas that were significantly more creative, but only in the Originality dimension.

Accumulatively, this work helps to dispel popular notions – especially those that emerged when the first technologies were introduced in schools – that technology has a negative impact on creativity (Cordes & Miller, 2000). While this may be true for some technologies, particular design features have been shown to have a significantly positive impact on students' creativity over time.

Measuring the Creativity of Technology-Produced Artifacts

Several educational technologies are designed to foster learning through production, whether it be circuitry-enhanced electronic textiles or interactive digital stories. In these instances, many researchers have sought to measure creativity through an examination of the artifacts youth produce. A foundational assessment of the creativity of artifacts used in the field of educational technology is the CAT developed by Amabile (1982). This test measures creativity using an assortment of (typically) expert judges, who assess creative works individually and in isolation. Their views are then collected and collated so that an overall rating or measure can be established.

Within the field of educational technology, Amabile's work has guided many examinations of youths' creative productions. For example, in an early study on the potential extrinsic constraints of the computer on children's creativity, Hennessey tasked a set of expert judges to use the CAT to measure the creativity of geometric shapes produced by children (Hennessey, 1989). Similarly, Peppler and colleagues (2011) employed the CAT in the examination of youths' e-textile (e.g., fabric artifacts that make use of computation and electronic circuitry through microcomputing and conductive thread) creations. The researchers tasked novices and experts to sort and assess the creativity of those artifacts. These investigations sought to determine the extent to which expertise was necessary to assess creativity. The study determined that expertise was not needed within the emerging domain of e-textiles and that novices and experts bear a great deal of resemblance when judging the creativity of e-textile artifacts. Given the range of new emerging technology domains, this study affirms the usefulness of the CAT for assessing the creativity of products created using new educational technologies.

Researchers have also developed rubrics to guide the measurement of creative artifacts, which have over time been adapted for technology-specific applications. Besemer's Creative Product Semantic Scale (CPSS), for instance, offers a framework based on three dimensions: Novelty (i.e., the product is original, surprising, and germinal), Resolution (i.e., the product is valuable, logical, useful, and understandable), and Elaboration and Synthesis (i.e., the product is organic, elegant, complex, and well-crafted). The CPSS involves 55 adjectives applied to some aspect of the creativity of a product. Raters, who do not have to be experts, use a Likert-like scale to rate products along all 55 adjective dimensions using a semantic-differential rating scale (e.g., "surprising – unsurprising," "logical – illogical," or "elegant – inelegant") (Besemer, 1998; Besemer & O'Quin, 1999). Researchers have applied these scales toward the assessment of products in technology-rich environments. For instance, Michael (2001) used the CPSS to examine creativity in problem-solving, which is one of the main goals of educational technology. This study compared the effect of computer simulation on product creativity versus a hands-on activity. Sub-scales "Original" and "Useful" from the CPSS were chosen to be consistent with Moss's (1966) theoretical model, which characterizes creativity as a combination of unusualness/originality and usefulness. They found that those who utilized computer simulations generated more creative solutions than those using hands-on solutions. The low cost of computer simulations has implications for efficaciously scaling approaches to creativity across settings.

The CPSS was later adapted by Mishra and colleagues, resulting in the NEW (Novel, Effective, Whole) measure of creative artifacts, to be used for providing a structure to "guide judgement and give each project or artifact a fair, systematic, consistent and comprehensive assessment" (Mishra & Henriksen, 2013, p. 13; Mishra & Koehler, 2008). Undergirding this framework is the understanding that creative solutions are – or creativity is – a goal-driven process of developing solutions that are Novel (i.e., the product must be something that did not exist prior, and it often has the quality of being surprising or original), Effective (i.e., purposeful or useful), and Whole (i.e., the aesthetic dimensions of the work, such as attractiveness, understandability, and order, must be valued by the domain). Mishra advocated for this rubric to apply generally to the measurement of creativity in technology-rich settings (Mishra & Henriksen, 2013).

Researchers have also used both the CAT and the CPSS to triangulate their findings. In their study of creativity in educational technology interventions, Thang and colleagues (2008) asked children (ages 8–12) to either brainstorm or prototype solutions for a child with a broken limb who needs to attend classes online. The researchers engaged design experts (i.e., industrial design Masters students) to rate the creativity of the student's solutions using a combination of the CAT and the CPSS, and were later interviewed about the designs that were rated as most and least creative. Results demonstrated that brainstorming led to higher ratings of designs, though both methods generally led to creative designs. Brainstorming produced more designs that were rated as surprising and novel, while prototypes were rated more relevant and workable.

Computational Assessments of Creativity

Moreover, the study of creativity within the domain of educational technology opens up new possibilities for the measurements of creativity using computational assessments. One early example is derived from the use of Computational Metaphor Identification (CMI; Baumer et al., 2009), which is a computer program that searches a corpus of text and generates a list of categories of words that tend to appear together. This approach uses technology to draw potential conceptual metaphors to users' attention and encourage critical thinking, creativity, and reflection about metaphor. Baumer and colleagues used this technique to help students think of creative metaphors about cells. In the treatment condition, the researchers presented three metaphors gleaned from a CMI analysis of various relevant Wikipedia articles, while in the control condition they had students watch a video on cells. They then asked both groups to generate a new metaphor about cells and map as many organelles as they could using this new metaphor. Notably, the creativity (operationalized as novelty, uniqueness, and aptness) of the students' new metaphors was assessed quantitatively. Researchers used a mathematical formula to compare a metaphor's uniqueness to all other metaphors students identified. The metaphors were also coded for aptness based on whether all the mappings of the organelles fit in with the overall metaphor, and whether the metaphors were based on featural/surface similarities or functional similarities (more apt). Scores for uniqueness and aptness were combined into an overall creativity score by averaging the two scores and giving them equal weight.

Technology has also expanded the range of artifacts that can be mined for expressions of creativity. For instance, Jain and colleagues (2015) evaluated exploratory browsing (an alternative to search-bar-driven Internet browsing) as a unique way to express and cultivate creativity in the digital age. Examining a Twitter plug-in called TweetBubble – which opens up contextual info on usernames and hashtags without users having to leave the page they are currently browsing – the researchers measured whether users' search behaviors led to more exploratory browsing, a technique similar to "fortuitous searching" identified by Ito and colleagues (2009). Being able to explore in a creative way for new information is an educationally relevant "Mini-C" creativity practice that allows people to encounter and learn about new perspectives. The researchers modified Kerne et al.'s (2014) ideation metrics to evaluate TweetBubble users' fluency, flexibility, and novelty, as compared to users browsing with ordinary Twitter. Fluency was measured by total number of feeds browsed, Flexibility was measured by total number of distinct feeds browsed, and Novelty was measured by the relative uniqueness of feeds browsed compared to everyone else in the sample. Results showed that TweetBubble users' ideation metrics were much higher than those of users without access to the browser extension.

A separate study utilized data-mining techniques to create a personalized creativity learning system (PCLS), which is an adaptive, game-based approach to teaching creativity among college students (Lin, Yeh, Hung, & Chang, 2013). The experimental study found that when a hybrid decision-tree was employed, learners have above a 90 percent likelihood of attaining an above-average creativity score, further suggesting that technologies can be created to not only encourage greater creativity but also teach creativity. While just emerging, approaches like these are among several promising avenues of computational assessments of creativity to be able to track and measure creative output over time, as well as provide immediate data for prototyping tools and online environments.

Studying Creativity across Educational Technologies

How we understand creativity in this area is tightly tied to the technology itself and how it's designed. As mentioned earlier, the field of educational technology is a broad collection of studies across several genres of digital media, spanning social media, software applications, virtual environments, wikis, and intelligent tutors. Since the expression of creativity varies by genre just as it does by domain, we stand to benefit from a review of the technologies not addressed above and the areas of creativity that they are shown to engender. Furthermore, understanding the notable gaps in this emergent field is also something that can help guide our future efforts in fostering and understanding creativity through the use of technology.

The Internet, Online Interaction, and Social Media

There is a group of scholars who have theorized that the Internet resembles many of the core characteristics of creative individuals, and that extended use of the Internet may inspire creativity in users by proxy (cf. Shoshani & Hazi, 2007). This work posits that the extended networks enabled through Web 2.0, social media, and the Internet may actually be democratizing creativity by exposing users to a wealth of information beyond what they would have access to in their local sites, as well as extended sets of digital tools. With access to a broad range of information upon which to inform innovation, users can jump off the ideas of others, become familiar with new connections, and build on the legacy of an idea in their own work. This theory plays out in microcosm through the educational use of digital scrapbooking (Swan, Tanase, & Taylor, 2010), interfaces/websites where users showcase aggregated content from across the Internet. It emerged in practice as not only a way to assess students, but also to demonstrate the processional nature of their creative process and to inspire other students who viewed it. While the researchers did not assess creativity per se, the tool was viewed as a way to demonstrate creative leaps in thinking that occurred as students followed new lines of inspiration.

Web 2.0 has also substantially changed the ways in which people interact and communicate online. With the rise of online and hybrid classroom models, some researchers have examined how these online interactions, ranging from synchronous to asynchronous communication, can be possible purveyors of creativity. For some, online interactions engender a new way of approaching societal structure and traditional means of communication. Charles and Shumar (2007), for instance, view creativity as a form of emancipatory agency, as something that helps people think outside of the predetermined structures of society, or that helps people engage with these structures in new ways. The researchers qualitatively report on two cases from students working on math problems within a synchronous chat environment. The structures of the chat environment, such as anonymity, equality, and a chat setting that is reminiscent of social instant messaging, seemed to allow students in these two cases to exercise creative agency in ways that would be unlikely within the structures of a classroom.

Furthermore, scholars have investigated how the use of social media in higher education can facilitate creativity in instruction. Allen and colleagues (Allen, Caple, Coleman, & Nguyen, 2012), for example, worked with university professors on the integration of Wikis, Ning, and Facebook into the classroom, asking the instructors to assess when they felt the most creative. Findings suggested that creativity was inherent in the teaching process when there was an emphasis on designing the learning activity and the environment, when instructors could be creative in the roles that they play in their teaching, and when providing and participating in social communities. Furthermore, the researchers believe that the social media tools themselves promoted the creative process by tasking instructors to experiment with unfamiliar modes of communication and participation. Through these studies, we see that creativity is not just enabled through the introduction of the technology but through subsequent shifts in our social practices.

Crowdsourcing Education

Educators today are often interested in individualized education, and crowdsourcing offers promising leads for that direction. Weld and colleagues (2012) explain potentials for crowdsourcing in education, and they claim that (1) crowd techniques will be required in order to deliver quality education in some areas; (2) existing techniques are ready for application to this new area; and (3) online education represents a new, relatively unexplored way of creating crowds. They discuss crowdsource peer-grading, and they argue that it may lead to more accurate assessments because it combines different people's opinions and expertise, and the high overlap would account for high reliability. They believe that there is great potential for crowdsourcing education, but they also argue that there are challenges at the level of the curriculum (e.g., deciding on the content to be learned), the personalization/engagement (e.g., sustaining long-term involvement with the forum), and providing rich feedback to students (e.g., implementing a system of votes/rewards to promote good academic performance). In spite of these challenges, a study by Duveger and Steffes (2012) demonstrates the reliability of crowdsourced grading in a marketing course. In their study, they prompted marketing students to create videos that explained the Millennial generation to the Baby Boomer generation, and they crowdsourced the grading to 60 external marketing students (i.e., the "crowd") and four external marketing professors. This composition of judges simulates the composition of crowdsourced judges in expanded online communities, and use of the CAT to evaluate the creativity of the videos replicates the rating process in the communities. The grading proved to be reliable because both groups rated the videos similarly in both content and creativity, and both were reliable with each other. Unlike previous studies comparing educators' grades to fellow students', the students were not harsher in their grading. This advances our understanding of creativity because it shows that a group of people with limited "special training" (e.g., students in a field who have not yet mastered that field) can rate creativity just as reliably and with just as much strictness/leeway as a group of educators.

Re-Envisioning Art Domains Through Educational Technology

The introduction of technology into the classroom in some cases radically changes established domains of creativity. For example, tools enable novices to compose original music without using traditional instruments as well as enable painters to mix virtual paint without paying for materials or gaining prior experience in art class. To a certain extent, the evolution of every domain is inevitable whenever new media is introduced. Conversely, not every form of new technology ruptures paradigms; some technology actually reinvigorates interest in traditional domains and translates them into new digitally mediated forms (Peppler, 2014).

The frequent source of disruption in the arts domains is the introduction of new multimodal expressions made possible through the use of technology. For example, digital technology has extended print-based creative writing into new forms that synthesize art and multimedia components, including digital storytelling, animated stories, hypertext, kinetic poetry, computer-generated animation, digital visual poetry, and code poetry, among others (Rasula, 2009; Richey & Kratzert, 2006; Zervos, 2007). Creativity researchers have investigated how multimodal forms of communication can stimulate a broad spectrum of creativity through the incorporation of additional modes of expression (cf. Ohler, 2013), including increased divergent thinking (Wilburg, 1987) and free-form thinking (Linder et al., 2015).

Similar trends have emerged through the incorporation of technology into music education, as new applications are expanding the channels through which people perform and learn about music. The music education community has long lamented that many youths fail to connect the repertoire, instruments, and skills embodied in informal music activities to formal music education. In the past decade, rhythmic video games – the hugely successful Guitar Hero, DJ Hero, and Rock Band franchises by Harmonix are especially salient examples – have dominated this informal music space for teens. A 2011 study demonstrated that extended play in Rock Band positively correlated with the assessment results of youths' traditional music abilities, providing evidence that youths playing rhythmic video games see a connection between the two ways of notating music (Peppler et al., 2011). Although there are obvious differences between learning to play a guitar and learning to use a peripheral device shaped like a guitar, Brown University ethnomusicologist Kiri Miller (2009) argues that performing a song in a game environment such as Guitar Hero or Rock Band is an authentic music performance. Furthermore, creativity researchers have lauded computer-based tools for their ability to immerse non-trained music students in the creative process (Rosen, Schmidt, & Kim, 2013).

Similarly, new domains unique to the medium of the computer – including video - game design, media arts (the blurring of computation, media, and Information Communication Technologies), and Do-It-Yourself (DIY) fusions of sculpture, robotics and crafts – are changing the nature of creative expression through educational technology. Work on the popular Scratch online community, a visual programing community for sharing interactive stories and games online, has looked at fostering social and collective creativity in the online environment (Aragon et al, 2009), providing a framework for successful creative collaborations. Specifically, systems that support social creativity must facilitate sharing and play, and their design must consider the effects of repurposing, augmentation, and behavior adaptation.

There is also a growing body of work examining the creative use of computation that extends between the screen and the physical world. Salgian and colleagues reported on the measurement of creativity in an interdisciplinary undergraduate computer science class, where students from diverse fields had to collaboratively design a robot that could conduct an orchestra (Salgian, Nakra, Ault, & Wang, 2013). Quantitatively, the researchers administered the Abbreviated Torrance Test for Adults (ATTA), Amabile's CAT, and a self-assessment based on creative activities and accomplishments, adapted from Hocevar (1981). Survey reports on perceptions of creativity from the students before and after the class showed that the collaborative design activity helped students appreciate how diverse ideas from a multidisciplinary group can stimulate creativity.

Other researchers have similarly studied collaborative robotics design activities as a source of creativity, but have brought the design principles of tools and activities that support critical and creative thinking to the fore in their analysis. DiSalvo and colleagues (DiSalvo, Louw, Coupland & Steiner, 2009) systematically compared the role of custom-built creativity support tools and associated activities in the process of enabling imaginative and resourceful robotic designs. Although the domain of robotics can become a powerful form of creativity in its own right, the researchers outline a series of general design principles for encouraging creativity in robotics, such as keeping activities open and allowing for speculation. They further argue, "as makers of technological fluency, we look to group processes that demonstrate social creativity around robotic and sensing technologies and the facility to imagine and translate non-technical goals into technical solutions" (DiSalvo, Louw, Coupland, & Steiner, 2009, p. 246).

Across this work, particularly in the arts, there is a review of creative work without much attention paid to expanding the literature on creativity. Furthermore, the research on creativity has overlooked many of the burgeoning areas of educational technology, including the new digital and media art forms. Considering the amount of transformation occurring in these fields, this area is ripe for more exploration.

Future Considerations Within This Domain

Educational technologies offer new opportunities to shape and design learning environments and to enable new forms of teaching that enhance creative outcomes. As such, educational technology offers a multitude of new directions for the field of creativity research. For example, the ability to create novel and immersive contexts – such as augmented reality, social media applications, new computational tools, and video games – allow the field to design and test the impact of the environment on creative behavior (Amabile et al., 1996; Kerne et al., 2014). For each of these designs, researchers can investigate the design features of the environment that enable, or conversely constrain, creativity. Findings from such investigations can, at a more global level, inform how we (re)design our everyday online experiences, tools, and learning environments (e.g., apps, mobile platforms, social media tools) to encourage greater creativity in and out of school.

Because the domain of educational technologies places a heavy emphasis on the design of the environment, a new emphasis is placed on how we can design new educational technologies to embody and further refine how an individual engages in the creative process. A number of researchers are currently investigating this possibility. For example, engineers are designing new technologies to encourage convergent and divergent thinking, to present an array of similar solutions to push novel thoughts, and to leverage peer review and iterative refinement, among other processes with known impacts on creative outcomes (Benjamin et al., 2014; Zhao et al., 2014). Although to some extent we can leverage design in all domains to better encourage creativity, educational technologies make the role of the designer more visible in the process, affording the learner opportunities for critical reflection on how technology design decisions are made (Kafai & Peppler, 2011; Resnick & Siegel, 2015).

The design of educational technologies also reflects the cultural, historical, and social values of its creators and enables and constrains creativity through the communication of these values. In this way, creativity can be seen as a cultural endeavor, shaped and persisted through the actions and values of many people (Peppler & Solomou, 2011). The design of social media or online environments can serve as a public manifestation of the creative values of a community, and innovations that happen within those communities (or not) are inextricably linked to and confined by the values that the community holds. The educational use of Web 2.0 capabilities – embodied in gaming environments, Twitter, and YouTube, among others – is moving greater areas of the Internet beyond transmission-only spaces and into dynamic environments that thrive on the thought transactions and contributions of a community of participants.

Furthermore, social technologies allow us to investigate the systemic nature of creativity, extending what recent scholarship asserts about the development of creative ideas as being part of a broader, socially determined process (Sternberg, 2003; Sawyer, 2006, 2007). This view builds upon Csikszentmihalyi's systems model of creativity, where individuals build on culturally valued practices to produce new modifications of the domain, which, if prized by the community, becomes part of what constitutes the ever-adapting domain. Social technologies alter the relationship between the various components of this system, given that many are designed to sidestep the panel of experts as a proxy for the "field," instead giving individuals themselves the power to rate, promote, and give cultural heft to the contributions of other individuals. In this way, creative contributions within the community are not determined by experts (Kaufman et al., 2008) but are crowd-sourced (e.g., through ratings on Amazon.com). This fundamentally changes the nature of how we view and assess "creativity," calling into question who constitutes the "field," and expands the methodologies that we can use to investigate creativity. It also raises key questions about whether a YouTube video that receives the most views is indeed the most "creative" of contributions to the community.

Sometimes the environments in which the learning takes place can be quite expansive, changing the nature of how learners' creativity is incentivized and assessed. With the rise of Massive Open Online Courses (MOOCs) and Big Open Online Courses (BOOCs), peer-based assessment of quality and creativity is becoming an increasingly prominent part of some students' educational experience. Much of our understanding about the role of crowdsourced knowledge in academia is informed by the work of researchers who have examined the collective intelligence of online crowds in determining creativity. Crowdsourcing is a method of collaboration in which organizations can leverage the activity level of outside users and expanded communities for the purpose of completing tasks, such as generating new content or evaluating existing goods. While crowdsourcing ratings and user-generated content is commonplace in online commerce, its applicability to educational settings is becoming increasingly explored (cf. Duverger & Steffes, 2012; Kittur, 2010).

As the field of educational technologies continues to expand, new genres are emerging that expand beyond video games and app-based kinds of technologies and engagement. While the arts, for example, have had several centuries to cement emerging traditions into the established visual and performing art forms, the new media arts enable types and genres of educational technologies that often defy categorization and are interdisciplinary in nature. This will pose some difficulties moving ahead for all research, but particularly for the fields of creativity research. This review, for example, was challenging in many respects to pull together as the field of "educational technologies" is actually an umbrella of several types of technologies that don't yet have their own genre. Future research should not only aim to help determine how creativity is being defined and conceptualized within these novel contexts as well as tools used to measure creativity in this landscape, but also to further our understanding of this diverse landscape. As the field of educational technology continues to evolve, how do we define the boundaries of the domain between commercial and educational use? Furthermore, are there clusters of technologies that bear more similarities than others? This is particularly important as we begin to think about how social media and online networks are transforming this domain, in addition to the blurring boundaries between in- and out-of-school learning. Particularly problematic is the fact that many studies in this area come from the leveraging of commercial technologies, where we have little to no control over systematically testing the design features in order to inform our emerging theories.

It is also interesting to note that the field of educational technologies (and others involving newer forms of technology that are now ubiquitous, like film) seems to suggest that we need to further consider history in this domain, and perhaps more so than other domains. For example, research using the Consensual Assessment Technique has started to fairly consistently document that novices and experts don't demonstrate the same kinds of consistent differences of opinion than in domains that have longer histories (Plucker, Holden & Neustadter, 2008; Plucker, Kaufman, Temple & Qian, 2009; Peppler, Fields, Kafai & Glosson, 2011). Might this be an artifact of the short history of technology-rich fields, or the expansiveness of technology (for example, more people see movies than read poetry)? Further, longitudinal studies are needed to establish the extent to which this will change over time, as the technologies themselves become less novel, as large corporations begin to control this landscape, and as the technologies themselves evolve.

References

Albors-Garrigos, J., & Carrasco, J. C. R. (2011). New learning paradigms: Open course versus traditional strategies. the current paradox of learning and developing creative ideas. In B. White, I. King, & P. Tsang (Eds.), *Social media tools and platforms in learning environments* (pp. 53–79). Heidelberg, Berlin: Springer. Retrieved on April 18, 2017, from https://link.springer.com/chapter/10.1007/978-3-642-20392-3_4

Allen, B., Caple, H., Coleman, K., & Nguyen, T. (2012). Creativity in practice: Social media in higher education. Future challenges, sustainable futures. In *Proceedings ascilite Wellington*, 15–20.

Amabile, T. M. (1982). Social psychology of creativity: A consensual assessment technique. *Journal of Personality and Social Psychology, 43*, 997–1013.

Aragon, C. R., Poon, S. S., Monroy-Hernández, A., & Aragon, D. (2009). A tale of two online communities: Fostering collaboration and creativity in scientists and children. In *Proceedings of the seventh ACM conference on Creativity and cognition* (pp. 9–18). ACM.

Baumer, E. P. S., Tomlinson, B., Richland, L. E., & Hansen, J. (2009). Fostering metaphorical creativity using computational metaphor identification. In *Proceedings of the Seventh ACM Conference on Creativity and Cognition* (pp. 315–324). New York, NY: ACM. Retrieved on April 18, 2017 from http://doi.org/10.1145/1640233.1640280

Benjamin, W., Chandrasegaran, S., Ramanujan, D., Elmqvist, N., Vishwanathan, S., & Ramani, K. (2014). Juxtapoze: Supporting serendipity and creative expression in clipart compositions. In the *Proceedings of the ACM Conference on Human Factors in Computing Systems*, April 26–May 1, Toronto, Canada. pp. 341–350.

Boden, M. A. (2004). *The creative mind: myths and mechanisms*. London: Routledge.

Burnap, A., Ren, Y., Papalambros, P. Y., Gonzalez, R., & Gerth, R. (2013, August). A simulation based estimation of crowd ability and its influence on crowdsourced evaluation of design concepts. In *ASME 2013 International Design Engineering Technical Conferences and Computers and Information in Engineering Conference* (pp. V03BT03A004–V03BT03A004). American Society of Mechanical Engineers.

Burningham, C., & West, M. A. (1995). Individual, climate and group interaction processes as predictors of work team innovation. *Small Group Research, 26*, 106–118. doi:10.1177/1046496495261006

Charles, E. S. & Shumar, W. (2007). Creativity, collaboration and competence: agency in online synchronous chat environment. In *Proceedings of the 8th International Conference on Computer Supported Collaborative Learning* (pp. 118–126). New Brunswick, New Jersey, USA: International Society of the Learning Sciences. Retrieved on April 18, 2017, from http://dl.acm.org/citation.cfm?id=1599600.1599621

Clements, D. H. (1986). Effects of Logo and CAI environments on cognition and creativity. *Journal of Educational Psychology, 78*(4), 309.

Clements, D. H. (1991). Enhancement of creativity in computer environments. *American Educational Research Journal, 28*(1), 173–187. Retrieved on April 18, 2017, from http://doi.org/10.2307/1162883

Clements, D. H. (1995). Teaching creativity with computers. *Educational Psychology Review, 7*(2), 141–161.

Cordes, C. & Miller, E. (Eds.). (2000). *Fool's gold: A critical look at computers in childhood*. College Park, MD: Alliance for Childhood.

Csikszentmihalyi, M. (1996). *Creativity: Flow and the psychology of discovery and invention*. New York: Harper/Collins.

Dawson, S., Tan, J. P. L., & McWilliam, E. (2011). Measuring creative potential: Using social network analysis to monitor a learners' creative capacity. *Australasian Journal of Educational Technology, 27*(6), 924–942. Retrieved on April 18, 2017, from http://doi.org/10.14742/ajet. 921

Donath, J. & Boyd, D. (2004). Public displays of connection. *bt technology Journal, 22*(4), 71–82.

DiSalvo, C., Louw, M., Coupland, J., & Steiner, M. (2009). Local issues, local uses: Tools for robotics and sensing in community contexts. In *Proceedings of the Seventh ACM Conference on Creativity and Cognition* (pp. 245–254). New York, NY, USA: ACM. Retrieved on April 18, 2017, from http://doi.org/10.1145/1640233.1640271.

Duverger, P., & Steffes, E. M. (2012). The reliability of crowdsource grading in a creative marketing project context. *Journal for Advancement of Marketing Education, 20*(2), 39

Emirbayer, M. and Mische, A. (1998). What is agency? *American Journal of Sociology, 103*(4), 962–1023.

Fisher, C. M., & Amabile, T. (2009). Creativity, improvisation and organizations. In *The Routledge companion to creativity*, 13–24. Abingdon, UK: Routledge.

Guilford, J. P. (1967). *The nature of human intelligence*. New York: McGraw-Hill.

Hennessey, B. A. (1989). The effects of extrinsic constraints on children's creativity while using a computer. *Creativity Research Journal, 2*, 151–168.

Hill, W., Stead, L., Rosenstein, M., & Furnas, G. (1995, May). Recommending and evaluating choices in a virtual community of use. In *Proceedings of the SIGCHI conference on Human factors in computing systems* (pp. 194–201). ACM Press/Addison-Wesley Publishing Co. Retrieved on April 18, 2017, from http://www.sigchi.org/chi95/proceedings/papers/wch_bdy.htm

Hocevar, D. (1981). Measurement of creativity: Review and critique. *Journal of Personality Assessment, 45*, 450–464.

Horton, J., & Ryba, K. (1986). Assessing learning with Logo: A pilot study. *Computing Teacher, 14*(1), 24–28.

Ito, M., Horikoshi, M., & Kodama, M. (2009) A cross-sectional survey of age and sense of authenticity among Japanese. *Psychological Reports, 105*, 575–581.

Jahnke, I. (2011). How to foster creativity in technology enhanced learning? In *Social media tools and platforms in learning environments* (pp. 95–116). Heildelberg, Berlin: Springer.

Jain, A., Lupfer, N., Qu, Y., Linder, R., Kerne, A., & Smith, S. M. (2015). Evaluating TweetBubble with ideation metrics of exploratory browsing. In *Proceedings of the 2015 ACM SIGCHI Conference on Creativity and Cognition* (pp. 53–62). New York, NY: ACM.

Kafai, Y. & Peppler, K. (2011). Youth, technology, and DIY: Developing participatory competencies in creative media production. In V. L. Gadsden, S. Wortham, and R. Lukose (Eds.), *Youth cultures, language and literacy. Review of Research in Education, 35*(1), pp. 89–119.

Kaufman, J. C., Baer, J., Cole, J. C., & Sexton, J. D. (2008). A comparison of expert and nonexpert raters using the consensual assessment technique. *Creativity Research Journal, 20*, 171–178. doi:10.1080/ 10400410802059929

Kerne, A., Webb, A. M., Smith, S. M., Linder, R., Lupfer, N., Qu, Y., Moeller, J., Damaraju, S. (2014). Using metrics of curation to evaluate information-based ideation, *ACM Transactions on Computer-Human Interaction* (ToCHI), *21*(3).

Kittur, A. (2010). Crowdsourcing, collaboration and creativity. *XRDS: Crossroads, The ACM Magazine for Students*, *17*(2), 22–26. Retrieved on April 18, 2017, from http://xrds .acm.org/article.cfm?aid=1869096

Lai, C. L. & Hwang, G. J. (2014). Effects of mobile learning time on students' conception of collaboration, communication, complex problem–solving, meta–cognitive awareness and creativity. *International Journal of Mobile Learning and Organization*, *8*(3/4), 276–291.

Lewis, T. (2009). Creativity in technology education: Providing children with glimpses of their inventive potential. *International Journal of Technology and Design Education*, *19*(3), 255–268.

Lin, C. F., Yeh, Y. C., Hung, Y. H., & Chang, R. I. (2013). Data mining for providing a personalized learning path in creativity: An application of decision trees. *Computers & Education*, *68*, 199–210.

Linder, R., Lupfer, N., Kerne, A., Webb, A. M., Hill, C., Qu, Y., & Kellogg, E. (2015). Beyond slideware: How a free-form presentation medium stimulates free-form thinking in the classroom. In *Proceedings of the 2015 ACM SIGCHI Conference on Creativity and Cognition* (pp. 285–294). New York, NY: ACM. Retrieved on April 18, 2017, from http://doi.org/10.1145/2757226.2757251

Loveless, A. (2002). *Literature review in creativity, new technologies and learning*. A NESTA Futurelab Research report - report 4. 2002. Retrieved on April 18, 2017. from https://hal.archives-ouvertes.fr/hal-00190439/document

Michael, K. Y. (2001). The effect of a computer simulation activity versus a hands-on activity on product creativity in technology education. *Journal of Technology Education*, *13*(1), 31–43.

Miller, K. (2009) Schizophrenic performance: Guitar Hero, Rock Band, and virtual virtuosity. *Journal of the Society for American Music*, *4*, 395–429.

Mishra, P. & Koehler, M. J. (2006). Technological pedagogical content knowledge: A new framework for teacher knowledge. *Teachers College Record*, *108*(6), 1017–1054.

Mishra, P. & Henriksen, D. (2013). A new approach to defining and measuring creativity: Rethinking technology & creativity in the 21st century. *TechTrends*, *57*(5), 10.

Moss J. (1966). *Measuring creative abilities in junior high school industrial arts*. Washington, DC: American Council on Industrial Arts Teacher Education.

Ohler, J. B. (2013). *Digital storytelling in the classroom: New media pathways to literacy, learning, and creativity*. Thousand Oaks, CA: Corwin Press.

Papert, S. (1980). *Mindstorms: Children, computers, and powerful ideas*. New York: Basic Books.

Peppler, K. (2014). *New creativity paradigms: Arts learning in the digital age*. New York: Peter Lang Publishing.

Peppler, K., Downton, M., Lindsay, E., & Hay, K. (2011). The nirvana effect: Tapping video games to mediate music learning and interest. *International Journal of Learning and Media*, *3*(1), 41–59.

Peppler, K., Fields, D., Kafai, Y., & Glosson, D. (2011). Articulating creativity in a new domain: Expert insights from the field of e-textiles. Published in the *ACM Cognition & Creativity Conference Proceedings*. ACM: Atlanta, GA.

Peppler, K., & Solomou, M. (2011). Building creativity: Collaborative learning and creativity in social media environments. *On the Horizon*, *19*(1), 13–23.

Plucker, J. A., Beghetto, R. A., & Dow, G. (2004). Why isn't creativity more important to educational psychologists? Potential, pitfalls, and future directions in creativity research. *Educational Psychologist*, *39*, 83–96.

Plucker, J. A., Holden, J., & Neustadter, D. (2008). The criterion problem and creativity in film: Psychometric characteristics of various measures. *Psychology of Aesthetics, Creativity, and the Arts, 2*, 190–196. doi: 10.1037/a0012839

Plucker, J. A., Kaufman, J. C., Temple, J. S., & Qian, M. (2009). Do experts and novices evaluate movies the same way? *Psychology & Marketing, 26*, 470–478. doi:10.1002/mar.20283

Rasula, J. (2009). From corset to podcast: The question of poetry now. *American Literary History, 21*, 660–673.

Resnick, M., Ocko, S., & Papert, S. (1988). LEGO, Logo, and design. *Children's Environments Quarterly*, 14–18.

Resnick, M. & Rosenbaum, E. (2013). Designing for tinkerability. In M. Honey & D. Kanter (Eds.), *Design, make, play: Growing the next generation of STEM innovators* (pp. 163–181). New York: Routledge.

Resnick, M. & Siegel, D. (2015). A different approach to coding: How kids are making and remaking themselves from Scratch. *Bright*. Retrieved on April 18, 2017, from https://medium.com/bright/a-different-approach-to-coding-d679b06d83a#.uzibrebuu

Richey, D., and Kratzert, M. (2006). "I Too Dislike It": The Evolving Presence of Poetry on the Internet. *Evolving Internet Reference Resources, 41*. New York: Routledge.

Riedl, C., Blohm, I., Leimeister, J. M., & Krcmar, H. (2013). The effect of rating scales on decision quality and user attitudes in online innovation communities. *International Journal of Electronic Commerce, 17*(3), 7–36.

Rosen, D., Schmidt, E. M., & Kim, Y. E. (2013). Utilizing music technology as a model for creativity development in K-12 education. In *Proceedings of the 9th ACM Conference on Creativity & Cognition* (pp. 341–344). New York, NY, USA: ACM. Retrieved on April 18, 2017, from http://doi.org/10.1145/2466627.2466670

Salgian, A., Nakra, T. M., Ault, C., & Wang, Y. (2013). Teaching creativity in computer science. In *Proceeding of the 44th ACM Technical Symposium on Computer Science Education* (pp. 123–128). New York, NY: ACM. Retrieved on April 18, 2017, from http://doi.org/10.1145/2445196.2445238

Sawyer, R. K. (2006). *Explaining creativity: The science of human innovation*. Oxford: Oxford University Press.

Sawyer, R. K. (2007). *Group genius: The creative power of collaboration*. New York: BasicBooks.

Scardamalia, M., & Bereiter, C. (1996). Student communities for the advancement of knowledge. *Communications of the ACM, 39*(4), 36–37.

Sefton-Green, J. & Sinker, R. (2005). *Evaluating creativity: Making and learning by young people*. Routledge.

Shneiderman, B. (2000). Creating creativity: User interfaces for supporting innovation. *ACM Transactions on Computer-Human Interactions, 7*(1), 114–138.

Shoshani, Y., & Hazi, R. B. (2007). The use of the internet environment for enhancing creativity. *Educational Media International, 44*(1), 17–32.

Smith, B. K. (2006). Design and computational flexibility. *Digital Creativity, 17*(2), 65–72.

Sternberg, R. J. (2003). WICS: A theory of wisdom, intelligence, and creativity, synthesized. New York: Cambridge University Press.

Swan, L., Tanase, D., & Taylor, A. S. (2010). Design's processional character. In *Proceedings of the 8th ACM Conference on Designing Interactive Systems* (pp. 65–74). New York, NY: ACM. Retrieved on April 18, 2017, from http://doi.org/10.1145/1858171.1858186

Thang, B., Sluis-Thiescheffer, W., Bekker, T., Eggen, B., Vermeeren, A., & de Ridder, H. (2008). Comparing the creativity of children's design solutions based on expert assessment. In *Proceedings of the 7th International Conference on Interaction Design and Children* (pp. 266–273). New York: ACM. Retrieved on April 18, 2017, from http://doi.org/10.1145/1463689.1463765

Torrance, E. P. (1972). Predictive validity of the Torrance tests of creative thinking. *Journal of Creative Behavior*, 6(4), 236–252.

Weld, D. S., Adar, E., Chilton, L., Hoffmann, R., Horvitz, E., Koch, M., & Mausam, M. (2012). Personalized online education – a crowdsourcing challenge. In *Workshops at the Twenty-Sixth AAAI Conference on Artificial Intelligence* (pp. 1–31). Retrieved on April 18, 2017, from http://homes.cs.washington.edu/~weld/papers/weld-hcomp12.pdf

Wiburg, K. M. (1987). *The effect of different computer-based learning environments on fourth grade students' cognitive abilities (Educat.D.)*. United States International University, United States – California. Retrieved on April 18, 2017, from http://search.proquest.com/docview/303495976/abstract

Yang, H L. & Cheng, H H. (2010). Creativity of student information system projects: From the perspective of network embeddedness. *Computers & Education*, *54*(1), 209–221. Retrieved on April 18, 2017 from http://doi.org/10.1016/j.compedu.2009.08.004.

Zervos, K. (2007). The virtualization of poetry and self. *epoetry.paragraphe.info*, 1–16.

Zhao, Z., Badam, S. K., Chandrasegaran, S., Park, D. G., Elmqvist, N., Kisselburgh, L., & Ramani, K. (2014). skWiki: A multimedia sketching system for collaborative creativity. In *Proceedings of the ACM Conference on Human Factors in Computing Systems*, April 26–May 1, Toronto, Canada. pp. 1235–1244.

Zheng, S., Bromage, A., Adam, M., & Scrivener, S. A. (2007). Surprising creativity: A cognitive framework for interactive exhibits designed for children. In *Proceedings of the 6th ACM SIGCHI Conference on Creativity & Cognition* (pp. 17–26). New York, NY: ACM. Retrieved on April 18, 2017, from http://doi.org/10.1145/1254960.1254964

22 Creativity in Design

Nathalie Bonnardel

Aix Marseille Univ, PSYCLE, Aix-en-Provence, France

Carole Bouchard

ParisTech Arts & Métiers, LCPI, Paris, France

Abstract

This chapter aims at characterizing creativity in design and, thus, creativity that occurs in an area in which there is an increasing need for innovations in our society. Indeed, designers have to satisfy the demand for new products that differ from existing ones. To help designers come up with new ideas leading to new products, it is necessary both to understand the creative process that underlays design activities and to determine appropriate ways to support it. To contribute to these goals, first, we characterize creativity in design and present descriptive models of both creativity and design processes. Then, we describe series of studies that focused on creativity in design, and we discuss ways of assessing creativity in design areas. Finally, we suggest potential orientations for future research in this domain and, especially, methods and computational systems to support creativity in design.

1 Creativity in Design: Main Characteristics

1.1 Design Activities and Creativity

Whatever the design areas, designers' activities require a degree of creativity since they have to face the challenge of coming up with products that are both *new* and *adapted* to the characteristics of the situation or context, including future users and usages (Bonnardel, 2006, 2012a). These characteristics are in line with definitions of creativity since it is commonly defined as the ability to produce work that is both novel and appropriate (e.g., Sternberg & Lubart, 1999; Isaksen et al., 2000; Lubart et al., 2003; Runco, 2007). Especially, according to Bonnardel (2002), creativity corresponds to a "capacity to produce an idea that can be expressed under a viewable form or to realize a production ... that is both new, adapted to the situation and considered as having some value" (p. 95). Thus, we can highlight the fact that, in design, the creative product is expected to be not only original and aesthetic but also useful, functional, and valuable (Christiaans, 2002). Therefore, creativity in design

We thank all students (especially Ph.D students) who were involved in the research that were mentioned as well as CREAPRO, CREATIVENESS, T'nD, TRENDS, GENIUS and SKIPPI consortium partners for their contribution to the mentioned projects as well as the AMU Foundation, the European Commission (CEE) and the National French Agency of Research (ANR) for supporting these projects.

may present specificities by comparison with other domains of creativity, although it is also in line with certain approaches of creativity, which consider that creativity is dependent on the individual who creates the new products and the environment or society in which these products are created (Csíkszentmihályi, 1996; Lubart et al., 2003).

To define design activities, we first refer to Herbert Simon's seminal work (1973, 1995), which aims at better understanding design sciences and, especially, the invention of artifacts. According to this author, "design ... means conceiving of objects, processes or ideas for accomplishing goals, and showing how these objects, processes or ideas can be realized" (Simon, 1995, p. 246). More precisely, a distinction has been established between routine and non-routine design activities (Brown & Chandrasekaran, 1989; Gero & Maher, 1993). In the first case, the product to be designed is not really different from products developed before; thus, the designer can adapt a predefined frame (or schemata) to solve the design problem at hand. In the second case, no predefined frame can be reused and the designer has to manifest a certain level of creativity often in using analogical reasoning. In this chapter, we are interested in this last kind of design activities, which correspond to non-routine and *creative* design activities.

From a cognitive point of view, design activities can be regarded as problem-solving activities. In accordance with Treffinger (1995), we consider that a *problem* corresponds to any "important, open-ended, and ambiguous situation for which one wants and needs new options and a plan for carrying a solution successfully" (p. 304). In line with this definition, design problems are regarded as *ill structured* or *ill defined* (Eastman, 1969; Simon, 1995), insofar as designers' mental representations are initially incomplete and imprecise, and *open-ended* since they admit a large number of possible solutions (Rittel & Webber, 1984). Thus, design activities carry out a process in which the problem space (based initially on the design brief) is gradually transformed into the solution space (see Figure 22.1), through a series of iterations that progressively aim to realize the design solution (Bouchard & Aoussat, 2002, 2003). In addition, Dorst and Cross (2001) described a coevolution of problem and solution spaces. It is only through the problem-solving process itself that designers can complete their mental representations by imagining, generating, and choosing design options. The mental representation evolves until the designer reaches a design solution that is considered satisfying. In the case of a creative design solution, it has both to be new and to respect certain constraints and criteria (Bonnardel, 2000). Therefore, designers have to assimilate and deal with a large volume of information without losing sight of objectives.

According to Bouchard and Aoussat (2002), design activities correspond to a process of "conceptualization" (Wang, 1994), where: (1) the selection of a solution or partial solutions enable(s) the limitation of uncertainty, while keeping in mind the necessary level of vagueness for modifications during subsequent phases (Lebahar, 1986), (2) the addition of new constraints is led in preserving global shape and initial ideas; and (3) new physical representations are produced, generating new ideas and new solutions. In this way, intangible information is transformed step-by-step into tangible information by way of mental and physical representations.

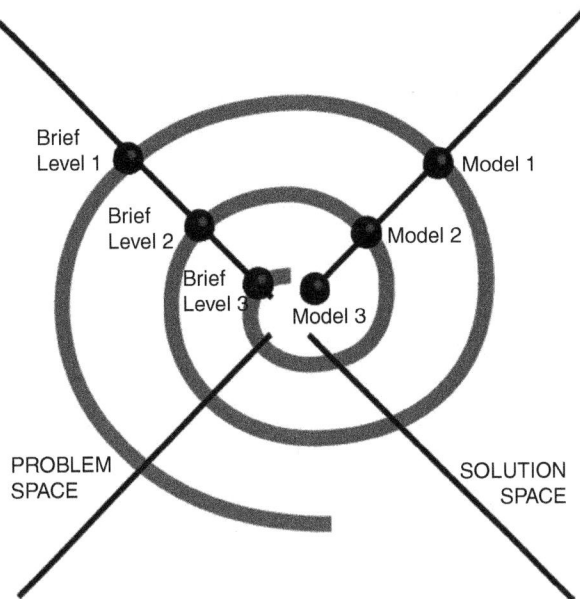

Figure 22.1 *Design seen as the iterative transformation of a problem space into a solution space.*

The solution space is made explicit by external representations, also called "intermediate objects" (Tichkiewitch, 2010), progressing from first sketches to final product. As the design process progresses, abstraction is reduced through successive representations, each integrating numerous design constraints. The external representations may also be considered as systems of signs, which supply the external memory and modify the perception in a decisive way (Bouchard & Aoussat, 2002; Goldschmidt, 1991). The design activity is thus also described as based on both top-down and bottom-up processes. So when designers try to reach a design solution, they frequently engage in an *opportunistic process*, where each new decision is motivated by the one before (Hayes-Roth & Hays-Roth, 1979; Visser, 1994).

Therefore, the task of imagining and conceiving new products is particularly complex for designers. In order to meet the constant challenge of producing creative solutions in each design project they work on, designers can develop individual strategies but they can also use the levers of social interaction, possibly associating individual and collective situations. In this process, it is essential to first produce some explicit individual constructs that will support the cooperation between the participants. Those individual cognitive constructs will then be progressively enriched and merged with the more or less developed constructs from the partners (Bouchard, & Omhover 2016). So the best ideas may result from the adoption of various points of views, before being merged into a single concept (see Bonnardel, 2012a; Bongard-Blanchy et al, 2015; Bonnardel, Forens, & Lefevre, 2016). Thus, the complexity here is due to the consideration of a whole system, including the individual, the environment, and the social context (Bila-Deroussy et al, 2015).

1.2 Macroprocess and Microprocesses of Creative Design

In line with proposals by Botella, Nelson, and Zenasni (2016), Bonnardel et al (2016) described the creative design processes as based on different stages, or *macroprocesses*, as well as resulting from different mechanisms, or *microprocesses*, involved in the generation of ideas.

1.2.1 Macroprocess of Creative Design

At the macro level of the design process, early models described it as being based on *a sequence of stages*. For instance, Asimov (1962) identified three stages: analysis, synthesis, and evaluation. *Analysis* corresponds to gathering the relevant information (or preparing the problem) and framing (or (re)formulating) the problem, *synthesis* is associated with the search for an appropriate solution, and *evaluation* leads to the validation of the proposed solution. If at the end of the evaluation stage, the design solution is judged unsatisfactory, the whole process is repeated. This model was reinterpreted by McNeil, Gero, and Warren (1998), who showed that there is more than one possible sequence for these stages: After evaluation, for instance, the designer can proceed to either the analysis or the synthesis stage. Bonnardel (2009) compared these models of the design process with models of the creative process, such as those developed by Wallas (1926) and Amabile (1996), and pointed out similarities between the design process and the creative process. The initial models of the design process were also completed by Bouchard and Aoussat (2002), who pointed out the importance of the information phase in design activities – previously called "analysis," but also called "inspiration" or "exploration." Such findings, formalized through a macro-model including *information*, *generation*, and *evaluation* phases (see Figure 22.2) (Bouchard & Aoussat, 2002), are in line with the ones of Ansburg and Hill (2003). The latter found that creative thinkers tend to use more peripherical cues, i.e. data not directly linked to the problem at hand.

Information gathering is therefore an emerging area for study in the discipline of *design science* (see e.g. Eckert & Stacey, 2000; Büsher et al., 2000; Bouchard & Aoussat, 2003; McDonagh et al., 2005; Keller, 2005; Restrepo et al., 2004). Access to inspirational materials is important since it constitutes a basis for design thinking

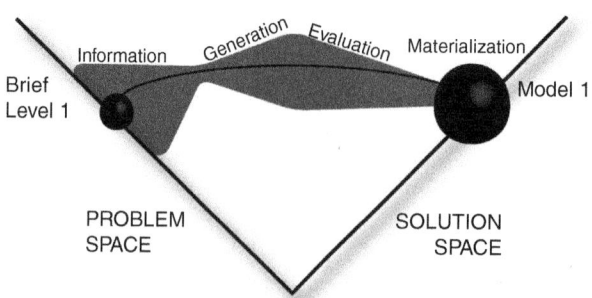

Figure 22.2 *Cycles of information-generation-evaluation-materialization.*

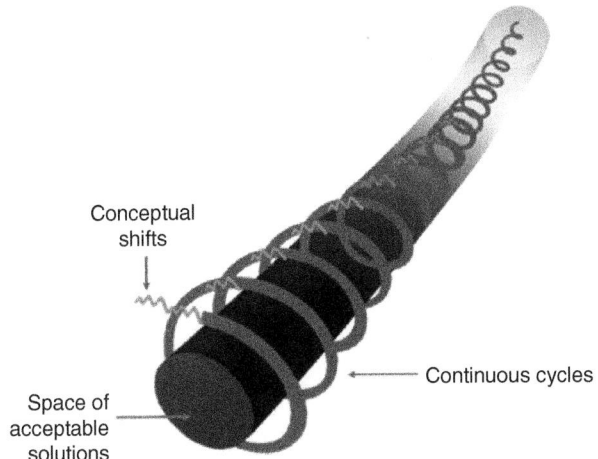

Conceptual
shifts

Continuous cycles

Space of
acceptable
solutions

Figure 22.3 *Adaptation of Zeisel's spiral (1981).*

and even more for analogical thinking, helping designers to define context, establishing constraints, supporting idea generation (Bonnardel & Rech, 1998;
Bonnardel, 2000; Eckert & Stacey, 2000; Bonnardel & Marmèche, 2004, 2005),
and providing structure for designers' mental representations of design alternatives.
Informational materials also provide designers with support when communicating
design ideas to others. Information gathering activities are prioritized during the
early stages of the design process, and the outcome of the related stage forms the
basis against which potential design solutions will be evaluated. However, information requirements may also be re-evaluated as the design process progresses.
Moreover, although designers typically access information relating to specific
design projects, as part of their professional activities, they also maintain a more
or less systematic watch of relevant sources, as part of their natural inspirational
process (Bouchard & Aoussat, 2003). Such information can be memorized and
potentially evocated in future design contexts.

   However, it is important to highlight that designers' activities are not viewed as
a linear succession of stages, but as based on an iterative process (Simon, 1973,
1995). Zeisel (1981)'s metaphor of a spiral is a good illustration of the dynamics of
the design problem-solving process (see Figure 22.3).

   For his part, Schön (1983) talked about a *reflective conversation* between the
designer and external representations of the object to be designed. During this
process, designers make unexpected discoveries, which can be positive (results
perfectly meeting requirements), negative (emergence of problems interfering
with the goals being pursued), or innovative (perception of new directions for
creative search). Other models of the design activity include components related
to situated cognition. This is especially the case of the Function-Behaviour-Structure
(FBS) model (Gero, 1998), the description of design put forward by Tan and Melles
(2010), in line with the opportunistic nature of design activities, and the Analogy and
Constraint Management (A-CM) model (Bonnardel, 2000).

1.2.2 Microprocesses Involved in Creative Design Activities

According to the A-CM model (Bonnardel, 2000, 2006), two main processes contribute to both divergent and convergent thinking in design:

- **Analogical thinking**, and more generally associations, can in certain circumstances lead designers to open up or extend their search space to new ideas, in line with divergent thinking (see, for instance, Bonnardel & Marmèche, 2004, 2005, as well as Section 2.2). Although other forms of creative thought have been described (see, for instance, Mumford, 2003), we consider that it is useful for designers to establish relationships between the design domain (e.g., a mechanical device) and other domain(s) that can provide them with inspiration (e.g., a biological system). In this case, the originality of the design ideas or solutions may come from the creative distance between the conceptual domain of the object to be designed (or *reference sector*) and conceptual domains (or *sectors of influence*) from which analogies are extracted. Studies by Bouchard (1997) and Mougenot (2008), investigating the information sources of car designers, have enabled to make explicit the designers' sectors of influence. These studies also confirmed that these sectors are long-term indicators. In design contexts, *sectors of influence* correspond to discrete semantic domains that bear analogical reference to the target domain (e.g., arts, nature, industrial design, transportation, furniture design). Designers are so able to select relevant information more or less consciously, considering also different levels of information abstraction: high-middle (e.g., semantic adjectives, consumer values, concepts) or low-level information (e.g., shape, color, or texture) (Bouchard, Kim & Aoussat, 2009; Kim et al., 2010). In order to do this, designers bring analogical references to the target domain. In this regard, *sectors of influence* play a major role in providing some relevant analogies in which designers will filter the useful information. For instance, they can use the similarity of shape features between a snake in the analogical sector and the front side of a car in the reference sector. This may provide an aggressive expression to a sporty vehicle, which will then provoke particular emotions to the observer or user. Analogical thought so allows designers to transfer the features of one or more sources of inspiration to the design solution being constructed (Bonnardel, 2000; Bonnardel & Marmèche, 2004, 2005). Associations can also enable designers to propose solutions whose features are similar to or, on the contrary, different from the source of inspiration (Bonnardel, Didierjean, & Marmèche, 2003). Although this brings potential benefits, there is also a risk of *design fixation* if designers are too focused on certain pre-existing design solutions or examples (Jansson & Smith, 1991; Chrysikou & Weisberg, 2005). Therefore, it is important to determine conditions that allow designers to benefit from analogical thinking and associations during the process of design thinking (see Section 2.2).
- **Constraint management** allows designers to orient their search for ideas. We consider that a variety of constraints govern designers' choices and decisions (e.g. Bonnardel, 1999, 2000). Some of these constraints, external to the designers, are derived from the design brief (*"prescribed" constraints*). Others are internal to

the designers and based on their previous experience and preferences ("*constructed*" constraints). Other constraints are inferred by designers from an analysis of the current state of the design problem or from the implications of previously defined constraints ("*deduced*" constraints). These different kinds of constraints can contribute to divergent thinking when they stimulate designers to look for ideas in a conceptual domain other than the one of the design product being conceived. They can also lead to convergent thinking, insofar as they help designers to assess ideas or solutions, and gradually delimit their search space until they reach a solution that is both new and meets all the various constraints. Therefore, we believe that creative design activities cannot take place – or at least only with considerable difficulty – unless constraints are taken into account (see Bonnardel, 2000), be they internal or external. We also consider that analogical thinking (and, more generally, associations) and constraint management interact throughout the design process, and influence other cognitive processes, such as constructing mental representations, evaluating solutions, and adopting different perspectives.

Our views are consistent with proposals made by authors such as Ward (1994), Stokes (2007), and Kelsey et al. (2014). According to Ward (1994), creativity is based on the activation of previous knowledge elements and on their re-combination to generate new outputs. Indeed, the GENEPLORE (GENErate and exPLORE) model (Finke, Ward, & Smith, 1992; Ward, Smith, & Vaid, 1997; Ward, Smith, & Finke, 1999) describes a combination between a generative phase, in which mental representations or *preinventive* structures are constructed, and an exploratory phase, in which these structures are explored in ways that lead to insights and discoveries (Finke, Ward, & Smith, 1992). According to Stokes (2007), implementing constraints reframes the problem and induces a new one for designers to solve. It is also in line with Kelsey, Medeiros, Partlow, and Mumford (2014), who argue that constraints can generate creative solutions to problems. This brings the question of the format of the constraints that are given in the design project. Indeed, there may be an important difference in the creative process between using a constraint as a key word or a playful card, thereby communicating some pieces or chunks of information in an open way, or the use of verbal or analytic tables in a more detailed brief. In the first case, the constraint may probably play the role of a stimulator for divergence, whereas, in the second case, the same information could become a vector of quick fixation.

2 Some Studies on Creativity in Design

Numerous researchers contributed to a better understanding of creativity in design activities (see, for instance, Bonnardel, 2000, 2006, 2012a; Casakin, 2007, 2010; Casakin & Kreitler, 2011; Dorst & Cross, 2001; Fischer, 2011; Fischer et al., 2005; Gero, 1996, 2000; Gero & Bonnardel, 2005; Gero & Maher, 1993; Goldschmidt & Tatsa, 2005; Maher, Kim & Bonnardel, 2010; Sarkar &

Chakrabarti, 2008, 2011). Our objectives are here, first, to describe the designers' perception of their own creative process (section 2.1), and then to present studies that contribute to identify conditions that can favor or inhibit creativity in design (section 2.2). In addition, we will discuss the assessment of creative productions in design (section 2.3).

2.1 Designers' Perception of Their Creative Process of Design Thinking

In order to contribute to understand designers' perceptions of both their creativity and the stages in their design process, interviews and questionnaires were conducted with professional designers (see Bonnardel et al, in press). The research protocol, developed during the CREAPRO ANR research contract, was based on the multivariate approach to creativity (Sternberg & Lubart, 1999; Lubart et al., 2003), which presents the interest of taking into account both the individual's characteristics and the environmental conditions. Thus, we considered a variety of factors that can influence the development of creative potential: cognitive (e.g., intelligence, knowledge), conative (e.g., personality, motivation), emotional, and environmental factors.

The first results we obtained indicated that professional designers considered the cognitive factors to be the most important for their creative process (these factors were followed by conative, environmental, and emotional factors). Therefore, we then focused on such cognitive factors and identified different stages in creative design. Five steps were pointed out by professional designers about their own process of creative design thinking (Bonnardel et al., in press): (1) *idea building* (or *generation*), based on documentation as well as impregnation and analysis of the stimuli present in the environment; (2) *idea developing*, based on sketching and both divergent and convergent thinking; (3) *idea materializing* through mock-ups; (4) *realization or finalizing*, with regard to final constraints; and (5) *presentation to the relevant audience*, such as customers. More precisely, during *idea building* or *generation*, designers reflect about how to build their own ideas, they evoke previous experiences in order to find sources of inspiration, and they choose one or more ideas to be developed. This process appears to be based on both analogies and the generation (or management) of constraints, in accordance with the A-CM model (Bonnardel, 2000, 2006). Professional designers are therefore engaged in both problem framing and problem solving, which is also in line with proposals by Dorst and Cross (2001). During *idea developing, materializing*, and *finalizing*, the designers externalize their ideas in the form of sketches, mock-ups, or prototypes, which allow them to experiment, rectify, and finalize their design solutions. As the design process integrates more and more the interaction dimension, some new representations appeared more recently from this field, such as story-boards or video cards. These video cards play the role of inspiration sources under the form of very short sequences showing some interaction technologies in use or domain-related information. An example is provided in a study from Halskov and Dalsgaard (2007), where the authors used short video clips to inspire the creativity sessions. This is in accordance with the exploration phase described in the GENEPLORE model (Finke, Ward, & Smith, 1992; Ward, Smith, & Vaid, 1997; Ward, Smith, & Finke, 1999). Finally, validated design solutions can be communicated to other people, which is also in accordance with Simon (1995)'s characterization of design and Amabile (1996)'s model.

A complementary analysis, associating interviews and questionnaires, allowed us to also identify three general stages that the professional designers regarded as particularly important in their process of creative design thinking (Bonnardel et al., in press): (1) *definition and redefinition of the creative problem*, for which designers explained that they initially consider the constraints provided in the design brief (or schedule of conditions) and later supplement them with others (because a deep understanding of the problem leads to the best solutions), (2) *openness to new experiences, new ideas, and aesthetic dimensions*, for which designers explained that they draw ideas from other domains and that these ideas can be useful both for understanding the object to be designed and for dealing with the design problem at hand, (3) *self-assessment* or *"reflexive evaluation,"* when designers evaluate their own creative productions (see Bonnardel, 1999), which can be supplemented by external evaluations performed by other persons. These findings will underlay suggestions about how to support creativity in design (in Section 3 of this chapter).

To conclude, this study allowed us to highlight sequences that take place throughout the design process, which is in line with models of the design process, such as McNeill et al. (1998)'s model, as well as general descriptions of creativity, such as the GENEPLORE model (Finke et al., 1992; Smith et al., 1995; Ward et al., 1999) or those developed by Amabile (1996) and Mumford et al. (1991).

2.2 Conditions That Influence Creativity in Design

In order to deepen cognitive factors that intervene in creative design, and especially factors that exert an influence on the generation of ideas or design solutions, we describe several experimental studies that were conducted in order to determine conditions that contribute to inhibit or favor creativity in design.

2.2.1 Some Conditions That Inhibit Creativity in Design

- First, we refer to the seminal work by Jansson and Smith (1991) that showed what these authors called an effect of *"design fixation,"* in line with the fixation effect that was described by the Gestalt psychologists (Duncker, 1935/1945; Scheerer, 1963; see also Weisberg & Alba, 1981). Jansson and Smith (1991) conducted several experiments with engineering design students, which allowed them to analyze the effect of the presentation of examples – more precisely pictorial examples – on the solving of design problems consisting, for instance, in conceiving a new kind of bike rack or a new kind of coffee cup offering different new functionalities (e.g., to prevent coffee overflowing or to insulate the cup). More precisely, the participants had to propose as many design solutions as possible to solve the design problem at hand. In each experiment, a "fixation" group was provided with the design brief (or design instructions) accompanied *with a design example*, whereas a "control" group was provided with the design brief *without any example*. Participants' performances were scored with regard to the total number of solutions generated as well as similarities with the design example provided to the fixation group (although this last kind of measure can be considered as arbitrary for the control group, it allowed the authors to have a common basis for analyzing the participants' sketches). Results showed that, although the mean number of design solutions (or sketches) was not significantly different in the groups, participants who were in the fixation group included in their solutions significantly more components from the example than did participants in the control group. It appears also important to point out that the same results were obtained when the example was provided with descriptions highlighting its negative characteristics (even negative features were included in the participants' solutions) as well as when participants were explicitly instructed to avoid using the problematic features from the examples. Moreover, such a "design fixation" effect was also observed with professional engineers, which suggests that even years of professional experience did not allow a diminution of the fixation effect.

- Purcell et al. (1993, 1996) extended Jansson and Smith (1991)'s research by analyzing the occurrence of the fixation effect according to different design disciplines and levels of experience. Participants in their studies were students engaged in different specialties related to design (mechanical engineering, industrial design, and interior design). The results showed a fixation effect for the students in mechanical engineering, but only marginally significant fixation effects were observed for the students in industrial and interior design. The authors suggested that the complexity of the design example imposes attentional constraints on the design process, which could play a role in the occurrence of the fixation effect: A more precise pictorial example would draw on the cognitive resources of participants and thus participants would rely more on features of the example for elaborating their design solution.

- Chrysikou and Weisberg (2005) conducted two complementary experiments in order to examine the negative effects of pictorial examples with participants naïve to design tasks (participants who were following an introductory psychology class). These authors combined both quantitative analyses, including various fixation measures used in previous experiments, and qualitative ones based on an analysis of verbal protocols (participants in one of their studies had to think aloud). Their experiments comprised three conditions: "control" (participants being only provided with the design instructions), "fixation" (participants being provided with the design instructions accompanied with a problematic example and including a description of its problematic elements), and "defixation" (participants being provided with the design instructions as well as the same problematic example as in "fixation" condition but also with specific instructions to avoid the problematic elements). A negative transfer or "fixation" effect due to examples was again identified by Chrysikou and Weisberg (2005), both in an experiment with participants who had to think aloud and in a similar experiment with nonverbalizing participants. These authors concluded that (1) participants having no experience in design tended to follow the examples even when they included inappropriate elements, and (2) the fixation effects can be diminished with the use of defixating instructions.

2.2.2 Some Conditions That Favor Creativity in Design

- Bonnardel and Rech (1998) and, later, Bonnardel and Marmèche (2004, 2005), and Bonnardel (2009) proposed new experimental conditions in addition to the ones used in the studies we just described. Indeed, all the previous experiments we evoked were based on the presentation of pictorial examples that were directly related to the design problem at hand (although they included inappropriate elements). In our experiments, we wished to provide participants, whether professionals in design or students, with complementary kinds of examples:
  - first, not only pictorial examples but also verbal examples, the latter kind of examples might allow participants both to be less focused on a specific instance of a design example and to evoke a potentially larger category of design examples;
  - second, not only examples directly related to the design problem at hand (referred to as "intradomain" examples) but also examples that are *a priori* far from the design problem at hand (referred to as "interdomain" – or "cross-domain" examples) although they could be possibly exploited as sources of inspiration; the latter kind of examples might lead participants to open up their research space of ideas.
- In accordance with the A-CM model (Bonnardel, 2000, 2006), our general hypothesis was that, contrary to the design fixation effect that was observed in previous studies, some specific examples – and especially interdomain examples – could stimulate designers to open up their research space of ideas, which would favor creativity in design activities. As it was the case in Chrysikou and Weisberg (2005)'s research, we asked participants to solve a design problem while thinking aloud. These participants were both professionals in design and students, which allowed us to analyze the impact of professional experience in design. Moreover, according to the experimental conditions, our participants were either in "control" groups, which were provided only with the design brief, or in "guided" groups, which were provided with examples. More precisely, according to the "guided" conditions, participants were provided with either intradomain pictorial examples, interdomain pictorial examples, intradomain verbal examples, or interdomain verbal examples. In these studies, the analyses were focused on (1) the number of ideas evoked by the participants, and (2) the nature of the ideas (or sources of inspiration evoked by participants). To determine whether the evoked ideas were intradomain or interdomain, three analysts conducted separately the analysis and we then compared their findings and reached a high level of agreement.
- The results we obtained first showed that professional designers evoke significantly more ideas than novices (Bonnardel & Marmèche, 2004; Bonnardel, 2009). We also observed differentiated effects depending on the nature of the examples. Only marginally significant differences were due to the pictorial vs. verbal nature of the examples but highly significant differences were due to the intra- vs. interdomain nature of examples, when the participants were *professional designers* but not

students (the latter evoked less ideas than professionals and mainly intradomain ideas, whatever the experimental conditions). Indeed, when professional designers were provided with *intradomain examples* (directly related to the design problem at hand), we observed a design fixation effect, in accordance with previous studies, insofar that these participants evoked less ideas and these ideas were mainly intradomain. In contrast, when professional designers were provided with interdomain examples, these examples led them to evoke significantly more numerous ideas and these ideas were mainly interdomain, which showed both a stimulation of the evocation process and an extension of the designers' research space of ideas. Consistent with these results, Mougenot (2008) confirmed through *a posteriori* sketches analysis that creativity increases with the distance related to the "sector source" or conceptual domain of the object to be designed. The sketches considered as the most creative were inspired from source images coming from close interdomain sectors. However, the images sources far distant sectors inspired concepts sketches considered as less. creative since the newness evolved at the opposite of feasibility.

- Further research by Bonnardel (2012b) as well as Bonnardel and Moscardini (2012) added another component to the examples that were suggested to participants: In addition to providing them with intra- or inter-domain examples, these authors took into consideration an emotional component insofar that the examples were selected in order to have a positive or a negative valence (pictorial examples were pre-selected as conveying positive vs. negative emotions). The results we obtained again with professional designers showed a significant effect of the valence of the examples: The examples with a positive valence appeared to stimulate designers' evocation process and the "best" condition we observed was the one consisting in proposing *interdomain examples with a positive valence*.

- Moreover, authors such as Bouchard et al. (2005) and Bila-Deroussy et al. (2015) demonstrated the power of analogical reasoning for obtaining creative outputs in *collaborative design contexts* by using idea associations through brainstorming or brainwriting. The use of analogies appeared to provide more ideas, which were also more original (Bila-Deroussy et al., 2015). In addition, again in collaborative design contexts, we recently analyzed the influence of the communication mode used by participants, being either in "face-to-face" groups or working in a virtual environment, on the fluency – or number of ideas – and their originality – with regard to the frequency of occurrence of ideas in the groups of participants (Forens, Bonnardel & Barbier, 2015; Forens, Barbier, & Bonnardel, 2015). Therefore, it appears possible to identify conditions that favor creativity in design both in individual situations and in collective situations.

2.3 Assessment of Creativity in Design

In the experiments we just presented, different ways were used to assess or measure features related to creativity:

- in the first part of the studies we described, the authors took into account the number of common features between the participants' productions (or sketches) and the example design; thus, the participants' productions could be considered as more creative when they comprised less common features with the example;

- in the second part of the studies, we took into account (1) the number of ideas, which is in line with measurements of creativity (based on the fluency), as it is the case in divergent creative tasks, and (2) the nature of the ideas, in order to determine whether the participants remained focused on the conceptual domain of the object to be design or if they extended their search for ideas to other conceptual domains. In this last case, and in accordance with the A-CM model (Bonnardel, 2000, 2006), we considered that sources of inspiration related to interdomains (or cross-domains) would allow participants to evoke more innovative ideas;
- in the last part of the studies, we also evoked the originality of ideas but it was, in this case, related to the "statistical originality" of ideas. It is based on the frequency of occurrence of an idea with regard to ideas expressed by all the participants. Therefore, the less an idea is expressed, the more it is considered as original.

To complement our reflexion on how to measure creativity in design, we are going to evoke other studies in which designers had the opportunity to concretize their ideas through the development of design projects. Indeed, one advantage of analyzing creativity in design is that when designers, either professionals or students in design, can participate in longer studies (during several hours or days), it becomes possible to analyze not only the number and nature of their ideas or the components of their sketches, but also to ask judges to assess the level of creativity of the designers' productions. Indeed, even if there is no a single design solution, some designs do seem to be better than others. Thus, one complementary way of assessing the quality of design solutions is to ask experts in the field for their opinion but some questions have to be considered: What kinds of externalization of creative ideas are possible? Who should we regard as an expert in this matter? What kinds of criteria should be considered during the assessment process?

2.3.1 Externalization of the Design Ideas and Presentation of Design Projects

In several studies we – and other researchers – performed, the participants' ideas were "externalized," that is to say represented through the creation or modification of external representations (such as sketches). Externalizing allows designers to engage in a dialogue, or "reflective conversation" with their project, which serves as a basis for reasoning and exploring, as well as for criticizing their ideas (Schön, 1983). It also allows them to communicate these ideas to other people.

In some of the studies we conducted, the design projects were presented under different forms, such as (1) final graphical representations produced with paper and pencils (Bonnardel & Didier, 2016; Wojtczuk & Bonnardel, 2012), (2) digital mock-ups of the future artifacts corresponding to 3D virtual representations produced with a CAD (computer-aided design) system (e.g., Wojtczuk & Bonnardel, 2011), and (3) physical mock-ups developed, for instance, in polyurethane through manual modelling (Wojtczuk & Bonnardel, 2011).

In the early stages of design, it is acknowledged that the external representations should be abstract, ambiguous, and imprecise (Tversky, 2003), to allow the designer to maintain a large number of possible interpretations. Indeed, by keeping their externalizations imprecise, designers avoid having to make some decisions too early in the design process and new ideas frequently emerge from ambiguous representations. However, when the objective is to ask judges to assess creative productions, the ideas can be more developed and their external representations can be both complete and precise. Therefore, we consider that various kinds of external representations can be considered for an assessment of the creative productions by judges. Nevertheless, it may be necessary to standardize the presentations in order to avoid biases in judges' assessments. For example, in Wojtczuk & Bonnardel (2011)'s research, one of our objectives was to determine whether the use of different externalization tools (one group working with a CAD system and the other carrying out manual modelling) affected the assessment of final designs. All the participants' productions were gathered in order to be submitted to judges. Since it was not possible, in our research, to turn the CAD designs into physical mock-ups, we choose to present 2D images of all the designs. This approach yielded more comparable data. We could not control all the visual differences between photos and screenshots but, to make them as similar as possible, all the representations were shown from the same viewpoint and the images were printed in black and white (in order to avoid biases due to the color).

2.3.2 Background of the Judges

As pointed out by Norman (1988), people may have different expectations about the same object or system depending on their background. For instance, a given system and its affordances will be differently interpreted, depending on whether they are viewed by the designer or by the user: The designer's perception could be more heavily influenced by the structure and functioning of the system, while the user could rely instead on his or her own experience of the system, as well as on that of colleagues. Glăveanu (2010) also argued that the creativity assessment depends on the social and cultural context of the judge, such as his/her professional experience or status in the society. In design areas, inside the social and cultural context, we could also point to the brand identity, the culture of the company, and its intrinsic level of innovation. These proposals are in line with the systemic approach of creativity described by Csikszentmihalyi (1996). For this author, in order for it to be regarded as creative, an artifact must gain the approval of the domain gate-keepers – specialists whose opinions are acknowledged as being important within a particular field.

Therefore, depending on the studies we performed, the judges were teachers specialized in creative activities (Bonnardel & Didier, 2016), or professional designers, teachers in design, and, depending on the domain of the object to be designed, either future users of the artifacts and commercials (or retailers) specialized in selling these artifacts, or art directors (Wojtczuk & Bonnardel, 2011, 2012).

2.3.3 Criteria to Assess Creativity in Design

As the assessment of design products can be highly subjective, some authors have tried to find out which criteria are the most relevant for people assessing design objects (see, for instance, Kruger & Cross, 2001; Casakin & Kreitler, 2005; Sarkar & Chakrabarti, 2008, 2011).

In the studies we conducted, we first asked the judges to express their overall satisfaction about these participants' productions. Then, depending on the studies, either the judges were free to assess the creative productions with regard to criteria that they spontaneously considered as important or we provided them with pre-defined specific criteria for assessing the participants' design productions (Wojtczuk, 2014). If we consider the criteria that were provided to judges, we can observe differences in these criteria. For instance, in Bonnardel and Didier (2016)'s study, after an assessment of the overall satisfaction of the productions, the judges had to take into account four criteria: (1) adaptation to or compliance with the design brief, (2) feasibility of the design project, (3) innovative dimension, and (4) unexpected nature of the project. In Wojtczuk and Bonnardel (2011)'s study, the judges were also provided with four specific criteria but they were different due to the nature of the object to be designed: (1) aesthetics, (2) originality, (3) functionality, and (4) marketability. In Wojtczuk and Bonnardel (2012)'s study, after an assessment of the overall creativity of the participants' productions, the judges had to take into account four criteria, which consisted in (1) originality, (2) appropriateness to the design brief, (3) aesthetics, (4) audience appropriateness. Therefore, the criteria that were taken into consideration were different according to the specific design areas.

2.3.4 Complementary Reflexions on the Assessment of Creativity in Design

If we base our reflexion on our own studies, although the precise results we obtained depend on the design areas, our findings allowed us to point out significant differences according to the design conditions in which the participants had to perform the design task (e.g., Bonnardel & Didier, 2016) but we did not observe a significant effect of the judges' backgrounds on the overall assessments. Such findings are in favor of Amabile's Consensual Assessment Technique or CAT (Amabile, 1982, 1996). Indeed, this technique is based on the assumption that judges give similar scores for creativity. According to this author, "A product or response is creative to the extent that appropriate observers independently agree it is creative. Appropriate observers are those familiar with the domain in which the product was created or the response articulated" (p. 1001). By taking this as a basis for the CAT, Amabile moved away from the notion of objectivity in creativity assessment and allowed for *correlated* subjectivity. The reliability of the CAT approach has been examined in numerous studies. Owing to its simplicity and the high levels of inter-judge agreement, it has become a popular methodology in many areas of creativity.

A survey of numerous scientific journals revealed that the number of CAT citations in design journals was limited compared to other journals specializing in creativity (Jeffries, 2012), even if inter-judge reliability in design creativity studies using the CAT is above the standard 0.7 level (Christiaans & Venselaar, 2005). Moreover, in other studies we conducted, we observed significant differences, due to the judges' background, in the assessments conducted with regard to certain specific criteria. In addition, these analyses allowed us to determine which specific criteria contribute the most to the judgment of overall creativity or overall satisfaction (for more information, see Wojtczuk & Bonnardel, 2011, 2012).

3 Future Research on Creativity in Design

Our general objective in this chapter was to contribute to a better understanding of creativity in design and to exploit some of our findings to suggest orientations for future research. To this end, we began by setting out the characteristics of design activities and presenting descriptive models of creativity and design activities. We then supplemented these descriptions with the results of several studies conducted with both professional designers and students. The first research we presented allowed us to identify general stages in the creative design process (Section 2.1) and the series of studies we then described allowed us to point out conditions that can inhibit but also enhance the designers' evocation processes (Section 2.2). At this stage, we argue that future research on creativity in design should concretely aim at favoring both *individual and collective designers' creative activities*. To illustrate this objective, we propose examples of methods and computational systems for supporting different aspects of designers' creative activities.

3.1 Examples of Methods for Supporting Creative Design

Some pedagogical methods, such as the ones proposed by Bonnardel and Didier (2016), aim at supporting divergent thinking and convergent thinking during *individual* creative design activities. In particular, we developed two design-oriented methods to be used in *individual* situations of design problem solving (Bonnardel & Didier, 2016; Bonnardel, Mazon & Wojtczuk, 2013): (1) the first one aims at stimulating designers (or students in design) to adopt an approach favoring the emergence of ideas – in line with the classical brainstorming technique (Osborn, 1963), and (2) the second one was specifically elaborated to stimulate designers to take into account, analyze, and hierarchize constraints related to the design problem at hand. These methods were tested with classes of design students and the students' productions were then submitted to teachers specialized in creative activities in order to identify their impact on the assessment of the creative productions.

Another example of method is "*user centered*" and it can be used in professional contexts. It is inspired by the "personas method" (Bornet & Brangier, 2013; Cooper, 1999; Grudin & Pruitt, 2002), which aims at favoring the adoption by the designers of future users' viewpoints. In particular, personalized information elements about future users (e.g., name, photo, age, hobbies) are usually provided to the designers on the basis of written information (e.g., presented on a sheet). Thus, we qualified this classical method of "static." It is supposed to favor an empathy process from the designers towards future users. Bonnardel, Forens and Lefevre (2016) proposed a new kind of method called "*dynamic persona*". It is derived from the "personas method," but the information elements related to future users are delivered by an avatar during *collective* design activities that occur in a virtual collaborative environment. An exploratory study allowed us to compare the impact of the use of these two kinds of methods (Bonnardel et al., 2016). The "dynamic persona" method appeared to stimulate the proposal of more ideas and, especially, more original ones. In addition, it seemed to slightly favor empathy from designers towards the dynamic persona than the static persona.

3.2 Examples of Computational Systems for Supporting Creative Design Thinking

Due to the variety of functionalities that are allowed by computational systems and their frequent use by professional designers and students in design, we consider that it is – and will be – particularly useful to develop computational ways to support creative design activities. Indeed, complementary modalities of human-computer interaction and cooperation have been described (see, for instance, Hewett, 2005; Lubart, 2005; Bonnardel & Zenasni, 2010; Burkhardt, & Lubart, 2010; Bonnardel, 2016). In particular, we contributed to the development and evaluation of several computational systems aiming to support designers' activities.

In order to elaborate new computer support tools dedicated to the generative phases of design, the following factors structure the research from the needs definition to software development (Bouchard et al., 2008):

(1) formalization of the cognitive design processes and related emotional designers' state (Rieuf & Bouchard, 2017), with the extraction of design knowledge, rules, and skills;
(2) translation of design rules into design algorithms;
(3) development of software tools to be used by the designers themselves or by other professionals involved in the early collaborative design process.

In view of the difficulties that designers can encounter (Bonnardel, 2012a), Bonnardel and Zenasni (2010) described several computational systems that can favor different design stages, such as the ones we identified in Section 2.1 of this chapter: (1) definition and redefinition of the design problem definition, (2) generation of design solutions based on the evocation of new ideas (as pointed out in Section 2.2), and (3) evaluation of design solutions.

3.2.1 Definition and Redefinition of the Design Problem

Some of the tools aim at favoring the definition and redefinition of both the design problem and solution, such as the *T'nD (Touch and Design) system* (Bonnardel & Cugini, 2007; Cugini & Bordegoni, 2007). This system has been developed to allow designers to create new products and to represent them in 3D on a computer, without requiring complex classical human-computer interactions. Indeed, interactions with this system are intended to mimic physical manual activities and gestures performed by designers (and modelers) when they develop mock-ups of the products. Therefore, T'nD aims at exploiting the existing skills of designers as well as taking advantage of computational functionalities, for instance, by allowing users to easily delete and modify what they previously developed or to access to complementary views of the product they are creating.

3.2.2 Evocation of New Ideas

Other systems can favor the openness to new ideas and the evocation of new ideas, such as TRENDS, GENIUS, or SKIPPI. These three computer support tools have been designed and developed following the model of Bouchard (2002, with the implementation of the *information-generation-evaluation* phases), to progressively complete a digital chain of early design. For the *information* phase, the TRENDS system provides designers with possible sources of inspiration in the form of images from the web in real time (Bouchard et al, 2008; Setchi et al, 2010; Bonnardel & Bouchard, 2011; Bouchard & Omhover, 2016). This flexible tool, adapted to various users' profiles such as design, marketing, and ergonomics, enables image retrieval from semantic descriptors or from image example. It is able to link different levels of abstraction of information and to propose, through the digital transformation, new types of processing for this information. Image processing enables automatic image grouping by color harmonies and the automatic generation of pallets of color harmonies. Semantic processing applied to the website's content supports the semi-automatic production of semantic mapping. A statistic function examines in real time the level of representativeness of a word or an image in the inspiration sectors. For the *generation* phase, the GENIUS system allows semi-automatic shape generation, with the possible regulation of different levels of serendipity by the end-users (Kim et al, 2010). This serendipity level goes from completely random shapes, through semantic regulation of shapes and source and target morphing, to silhouettes and contours extracted from existing images held in the image database. Finally, the SKIPPI system provides designers with sources of inspiration in word form (Bonnardel & Bouchard, 2014, Bouchard et al, 2016). This tool is more transverse across the *information-generation-evaluation* phases, and it opens with a live lexical database. It calls for a collaborative use by displaying in a playful way a graph of words implementing heterogeneous knowledge of the different profiles (design, marketing, ergonomics).

3.2.3 Evaluation of Design Solutions

Other systems again can facilitate the evaluation of design solutions. It is especially the case of "critiquing expert systems" that help designers to more completely assess their own design solutions by providing them with "critics" (or critiquing messages) which point out solutions' limitations when features of these solutions do not respect constraints that are in the system's knowledge basis (see, for instance, Bonnardel & Zenasni, 2010).

To conclude, the design process consists in answering to the brief by exploring several conceptual alternatives, which will be evaluated and selected in part through a series of presentations and discussions. Consistent with this, some models have been formalized, which cover the generative phase of early design, including ideas and concepts generation in individual or collective configurations. Thus, we believe that future research on creativity in design will associate both individual and collaborative processes and will be supported by human-computer cooperation.

References

Amabile, T. M. (1996). *Creativity in context*. Boulder, CO: Westview Press.

Ansburg, P., & Hill, K. (2003). Creative and analytic thinkers differ in their use of attentional resources. *Personality and Individual Differences, 34*(7), 1141–1152.

Asimov, M. (1962). *Introduction to design*. Englewood Cliffs, NJ: Prentice-Hall.

Bongard-Blanchy, K., Bouchard, C., Bonnardel, N., Lockner, D., & Aoussat, A. (2015). User experience dimensions in product design: A consolidation of what academic researchers know and what design practitioners do. *Journal of Design Research, 13*(2), 107–124.

Bila-Deroussy, P., Bouchard, C., & Diakite, S. (2015). Addressing complexity in design: a systemic model of creativity and guidelines for tools and methods. *International journal of Design and Creativity, 5*(1–2), 60–77.

Bonnardel, N. (1999). L'évaluation réflexive dans la dynamique de l'activité du concepteur [Reflexive evaluation in the dynamics of the designer's activity]. In J. Perrin (Ed.), *Pilotage et évaluation des activités de conception* (pp. 87–105). Paris: L'Harmattan.

Bonnardel, N. (2000). Towards understanding and supporting creativity in design: Analogies in a constrained cognitive environment. *Knowledge-Based Systems, 13*, 505–513.

Bonnardel, N. (2002). Entrée : Créativité [Creativity]. In G. Tiberghien, (Ed.), *Dictionnaire des Sciences Cognitives [Dictionary of Cognitive Sciences]*, (pp. 95–97), Paris: Armand Colin/VUEF.

Bonnardel, N. (2006). *Créativité et conception: Approches cognitives et ergonomiques [Creativity and design: Cognitive and ergonomic approaches]*. Marseille: Solal.

Bonnardel, N. (2009). Activités de conception et créativité: De l'analyse des facteurs cognitifs à l'assistance aux activités de conception créatives [Design activities and creativity: From an analysis of cognitive factors to creative design support]. *Le Travail Humain, 72*, 5–22.

Bonnardel, N. (2012a). Designing future products: What difficulties do designers encounter and how can their creative process be supported? *Work, A Journal of Prevention, Assessment & Rehabilitation, 41*, 5296–5303.

Bonnardel, N. (2012b). Cognition and emotion in creative design. In S. Masmoudi, D. Yun Dai & A. Naceur (Eds.). *Attention, Representation, and Human Performance: Integration of Cognition, Emotion, and Motivation* (pp. 187–200), New York: Psychology Press (Taylor & Francis Group).

Bonnardel, N. (2016). Propositions de méthodes d'analyse et de modalités d'assistances pédagogique et informatique aux activités créatives. Illustrations dans le domaine du design [Proposals of analysis methods as well as pedagogical and computational ways to support creative activities]. In I. Capron-Puozzo (Ed.), *La créativité en éducation et en formation. Perspectives théoriques et pratiques* (pp. 167–180). Bruxelles: De Boeck.

Bonnardel, N., & Bouchard, C. (2011). Towards supporting creative design: Analysis of the use of the TRENDS system according to designers' expertise. *Proceedings of the 8th ACM Conference on Creativity and Cognition – C&C 2011* (pp. 315–316), Atlanta. New York: ACM Press.

Bonnardel, N., & Bouchard, C. (2014). Design, ergonomie et IHM: Etudes complémentaires pour favoriser les activités de conception créatives [Design, ergonomics, and HCI: Complementary studies to favour creative design activities]. In N. Couture, C. Bastien, & T. Dorta (Eds.), *Quelle articulation pour la co-conception de l'interaction? Proceedings of the international conference 2014 Ergonomie et Informatique Avancée Conference – ErgoIA'2014* (pp. 33–40), Toulouse, New York: ACM Press.

Bonnardel, N., & Cugini, U. (2007). *Test Case Evaluation Report. Deliverable 14.* Research contract FP6-IST–2002–001996.

Bonnardel, N., & Didier, J. (2016). Enhancing creativity in the educational design context: An exploration of the effects of design project-oriented methods on students' evocation processes and creative output. *Journal of Cognitive Education and Psychology, 15*(1), 80–101.

Bonnardel, N., Didierjean, A., & Marmèche, E. (2003). Analogie et résolution de problèmes [Analogy and problem solving]. In C. Tijus (Ed.), *Métaphores et analogies* (pp. 115–149). Paris: Hermès.

Bonnardel, N., Forens, M., & Lefevre, M. (2016). Enhancing collective creative design: An exploratory study on the influence of static and dynamic personas in a virtual environment. *Design Journal, 19*(2), 189–203.

Bonnardel, N., & Marmèche, E. (2004). Evocation processes by novice and expert designers: Towards stimulating analogical thinking. *Creativity and Innovation Management, 13*(3), 176–186.

Bonnardel, N., & Marmèche, E. (2005). Towards supporting evocation process in creative design: A cognitive approach. *International Journal of Human-Computer Studies, 63*, 442–435.

Bonnardel, N., Mazon, S., Wojtczuk, A. (2013). Impact of project-oriented educational methods on creative design *Proceedings of the 31st annual Conference of the European Association of Cognitive – ECCE 2013.* Toulouse, France.

Bonnardel, N., & Rech, M. (1998). Les sources d'inspiration en conception [Inspiration sources in design]. *Sciences et Techniques de la Conception / International Journal of Design Sciences & Technology, 6*(1), 37–53.

Bonnardel, N., Wojtczuk, A., Gilles, P.-Y., & Mazon, S. (in press). The creative process in design. In T. Lubart (Ed.), *The creative process: Perspectives from multiple domains.* New York: Palgrave Macmillan.

Bonnardel, N., & Zenasni, F. (2010). The impact of technology on creativity in design: An enhancement? *Creativity and Innovation Management, 19*(2), 180–191.

Botella, M., Nelson, J., & Zenasni, F. (2016). Les macro et microprocessus créatifs. In I. Capron-Puozzo (Ed.), *La créativité en éducation et en formation. Perspectives théoriques et pratiques* (pp. 31–44). Bruxelles: De Boeck.

Bouchard, C. (1997), *Modelling the car design process.* ENSAM Thesis, Paris: ENSAM.

Bouchard, C., & Aoussat A. (2002). Design process perceived as an information process to enhance the introduction of new tools. *International Journal of Vehicle Design, 31*(2), 162–175.

Bouchard, C., Lim, D., & Aoussat, A. (2003). Development of a Kansei Engineering System for Industrial design – Identification of input data for KES, *6th Asian Design International Conference*, Tsukuba University.

Bouchard, C., & Aoussat, A. (2003). Modelling the car design process, *International Journal of Vehicle Design, 31*(1), 1–10.

Bouchard, C., Camous, R., Aoussat, A. (2005). Nature and role of intermediate representation (IR) in the design process: Case studies in car design. *International Journal of Vehicle Design, 38*(1), 1–25.

Bouchard, C., Omhover, J.-F., Mougenot, C., Aoussat, A., & Westerman S. (2008). Trends: A content-based information retrieval system for designers, *Third International Conference on Design Computing and Cognition* (DCC'08). Georgia Institute of Technology, Atlanta, USA.

Bouchard, C., Kim, J., Aoussat, A. (2009). Kansei Information Processing in Design. *Proceeding of IASDR'2009*. Séoul.

Bouchard, C. Omhover, J.-F. (2016). Supporting early design through conjoint trends analysis methods and the TRENDS system. In P. Markopoulos, J. B. Martens, J. Malins, K. Coninx, & A. Liapis (Eds.), *Collaboration in creative design, methods and tools* (pp. 53–72). Switzerland. Springerlink, International Publishing.

Bouchard, C., Omhover J.-F., Bongard-Blanchy, K., Bonnardel, N., Lockner, D., Dubois, P, & Amaral, E. (2016). Mixing and structuring design-product-process knowledge: Towards a design product process formalism, Submitted to *Journal of Engineering Design*.

Büsher, M., Frielaender, V., Hodgson, E., Rank, S., & Shapiro, D. (2000). Design on objects: imaginative practice, aesthetic categorisation, and the design of multimedia archiving support. *Digital Creativity, 11*(3), 161–172.

Bornet, C. & Brangier, E. (2013). La méthode des personas: principes, intérêts et limites. *Bulletin de Psychologie, 66*(524), 115–134.

Brown, D. C., & Chandrasekaran, B. (1989). *Design problem solving. Knowledge structures and control strategies*. London: Pitman.

Burkhardt, J.-M., & Lubart, T. (2010). Creativity in the age of emerging technology. *Creativity and Innovation Management, 19*, 160–166.

Casakin, H. (2007). Metaphors in design problem-solving: Implications for creativity. *The International Journal of Design, 1*, 23–35.

Casakin, H. (2010). Visual analogy, visual displays, and the nature of design problems: The effect of expertise. *Environmental Planning and Design: Design B, 37*, 170–188.

Casakin, H., & Kreitler, S. (2005). The nature of creativity in design. In J. S. Gero & N. Bonnardel (Eds.), *Studying Designers'05* (pp. 87–100). University of Sydney, Sydney.

Casakin, H., & Kreitler, S. (2011). The cognitive profile of creativity in design. *Thinking Skills and Creativity, 6*, 159–168.

Christiaans, H. (2002). Creativity as a design criterion. *Creativity Research Journal, 14*, 41–45.

Christiaans, H., & Venselaar, K. (2005). Creativity in design engineering and the role of knowledge: Modeling the expert. *International Journal of Technology and Design Education, 15*, 217–236.

Chrysikou, E. G., & Weisberg, R. W. (2005). Following the wrong footsteps: Fixation effects of pictorial examples in a design problem-solving task. *Journal of Experimental Psychology: Learning, Memory and Cognition, 31*, 1134–1148.

Csíkszentmihályi, M. (1996). *Creativity: Flow and the psychology of discovery and invention*. New York: Harper Collins.

Cugini, U., & Bordegoni, M. (2007). Touch and design: Novel haptic interfaces for the generation of high quality surfaces for industrial design. *The Visual Computer, 23*(4), 233–246.

Cooper, A. (1999). *The inmates are running the asylum*. Indianapolis, IN: Macmillan.

Dorst, K., & Cross, N. (2001). Creativity in the design process: Co-evolution of problem-solution. *Design Studies, 22*, 425–437.

Duncker, K. (1945). On problem-solving. *Psychological Monographs, 58*(5), 113. (Original work published in 1935).

Eastman, C. M. (1969). Cognitive processes and ill-defined problems: A case study from design. *Proceedings of the 1st International Joint Conference on Artificial Intelligence* (pp. 669–690). Washington, DC.

Eckert, C. M., & Stacey, M. K. (2000). Sources of inspiration: A language of design. *Design Studies, 21*(5), 523–538.

Fischer, G. (2011). Understanding, fostering, and supporting cultures of participation. *ACM Interactions, XVIII*(3), 42–53.

Fischer, G., Giaccardi, E., Eden, H., Sugimoto, M., & Ye, Y. (2005). Beyond binary choices: Integrating individual and social creativity. *International Journal of Human-Computer Studies, 63*, 482–512.

Finke, R. A., Ward, T. B., & Smith, S.M. (1992). *Creative cognition: Theory, research, and applications*. Cambridge, MA: MIT Press.

Forens, M., Bonnardel, N., & Barbier, M.-L. (2015). How communication modalities can impact group creativity in multi-user virtual environment. *Proceedings of the 33rd European Conference on Cognitive Ergonomics – ECCE 2015* (pp. 25–28). Warsaw, Poland. New-York: ACM Press.

Forens, M., Barbier, M.-L., & Bonnardel, N. (2015). Modalités de communication et créativité en environnement virtuel collaboratif. In N. Bonnardel, L. Pellegrin, & H. Chaudet (Eds.), *Actes du 8ème Colloque de Psychologie Ergonomique – EPIQUE' 2015* (pp. 175–181). Paris, France: Arpege Science Publishing.

Gero, J. S. (1996). Creativity, emergence and evolution in design: Concepts and framework. *Knowledge-Based Systems, 9*, 435–448.

Gero, J. S. (1998). Towards a model of designing which includes its situatedness. In H. Grabowski, S. Rude, & G. Grein (Eds.), *Universal design theory* (pp. 47–56). Aachen: Shaker Verlag.

Gero, J. S. (2000). Computational models of innovative and creative design processes. *Technological Forecasting and Social Change, 64*, 183–196.

Gero, J. S., & Bonnardel, N. (Eds.). (2005). *Studying designers'05*. Sydney: University of Sydney.

Gero, J. S., & Maher, M. L. (1993). Introduction. In J. S. Gero & M. L. Maher (Eds.), *Modeling creativity and knowledge-based design* (pp. 1–6). Hillsdale, N.J.: Lawrence Erlbaum.

Glăveanu, V. P. (2010). Creativity in context: The ecology of creativity evaluations and practices in an artistic craft. *Psychology Studies, 55*, 339–350.

Goldschmidt, G. (1991). The dialectics of sketching. *Creativity Research Journal, 4*, 123–143.

Goldschmidt, G., & Tatsa, D. (2005). How good are good ideas: Correlates of design creativity. *Design Studies, 26*, 593–611.

Hayes-Roth, B., & Hayes-Roth, F. (1979). A cognitive model of planning. *Cognitive Science*, *3*, 275–310.

Halskov, K., & Dalsgaard, P. (2007). The emergence of ideas: the interplay between sources of inspiration and emerging design concepts. *CoDesign*, *3*(4), 185–211.

Hewett, T. T. (2005). Informing the design of computer-based environments to support creativity. *International Journal of Human-Computer Studies*, *63*, 383–405.

Isaksen, S. G., Dorval, K. B., & Treffinger, D. J. (2000). *Creative approaches to problem solving: A framework for change*. Buffalo, CPSB.

Jansson, D. G., & Smith, S. M. (1991). Design fixation. *Design Studies*, *12*, 3–11.

Jeffries, K. K. (2012). Amabile's consensual assessment technique: Why has it not been used more in design creativity research? *Proceedings of the 2nd International Conference on Design Creativity* (pp. 211–220). Glasgow.

Keller, A. I. (2005). *For inspiration only – Designer interaction with informal collections of visual material*, Ph.D. thesis, Delft University of Technology, The Netherlands.

Kelsey, E., Medeiros, P., Partlow, J. P., & Mumford, M. D. (2014). Not too much, not too little: The influence of constraints on creative problem solving. *Psychology of Aesthetics, Creativity, and the Arts*, *8*, 198210.

Kim, J., Bouchard, C., Omhover J.-F., & Aoussat A. (2010). Towards a model of how designers mentally categorize design information. *CIRP – Journal of Manufacturing Science and Technology*, *3*(3), 218–226.

Kruger, C., & Cross, N. (2001). Modelling creative strategies in creative design. In J. S. Gero & M. L. Mahler (Eds.), *Computational and cognitive models of creative design V* (pp. 205–226), Sydney: University of Sydney.

Lebahar, J.-C. (1986). Le travail de conception en architecture, contraintes et perspectives apportées par la CAO. *Le Travail Humain*, *49*(1), 17–30.

Lubart, T. (2005). How can computers be partners in the creative process? *International Journal of Human Computer Studies*, *63*, 365–369.

Lubart, T., Mouchiroud, C., Tordjman, S., & Zenasni, F. (2003). *Psychologie de la créativité*. Paris: Armand Colin.

McNeill, T., Gero, J. S., & Warren, J. (1998). Understanding conceptual electronic design using protocol analysis. *Research in Engineering Design*, *10*, 129–140.

Maher, M. L., Kim, Y. S., & Bonnardel, N. (Eds.). (2010). *Special issue of AIEDAM – Artificial Intelligence for Engineering Design, Analysis and Manufacturing on "Creativity: Simulation, Stimulation and Studies,"* *24*(2).

McDonagh, D., & Denton, H. (2005). Exploring the degree to which individual students share a common perception of specific trend boards: observations relating to teaching, learning and team-based design. *Design Studies*, *26*, 35–53.

Mougenot, C. (2008). *Modélisation de la phase d'exploration du processus de conception de produits, pour une créativité augmentée*. Ph.D. Thesis. Paris: ENSAM.

Mumford, M. D. (2003). Where have we been, when are we going? Taking stock in creativity research. *Creativity Research Journal*, *15*(2–3), 107–120.

Mumford, M. D., Mobley, M. I., Reiter-Palmon, R., Uhlman, C. E., & Doares, L. M. (1991). Process analytic models of creative capacities. *Creativity Research Journal*, *4*, 91–122.

Norman, D.A. (1988). *The design of everyday things*. London: MIT Press.

Osborn, A.F. (1963). *Applied imagination: Principles and procedures of creativity thinking*. New York: Charles Scribner's Sons.

Pruitt, J., & Grudin, J. (2003). Personas: Practice and theory. *Proceedings of the conference on designing for user experiences* (pp. 1–15). New York: ACM.

Purcell, A. T., Williams, P., Gero, J. S., & Colbron, B. (1993). Fixation effects: Do they exist in design problem-solving? *Environment and Planning B: Planning and Design*, *20*, 333–345.

Purcell, A. T., & Gero, J. S. (1996). Design and other types of fixation. *Design Studies, 17*, 363–383.

Rieuf, V., & Bouchard, C. (2017). Emotional activity in early immersive design: Sketches and moodboards in virtual reality, *Design Studies, 48*, 43–75.

Rittel, H., & Webber, M. M. (1984). Planning problems are wicked problems. In N. Cross (Ed.), *Developments in design methodology* (pp. 135–144). New York: John Wiley & Sons.

Restrepo, J., Christiaans, H., & Green, W. S. (2004). Give me an example: supporting the creative designer. In M. Agger Eriksen., L. Malmborg, & J. Nielsen (Eds.), *Proceedings of Computers in Art and Design Education Conference – CADE2004*. Copenhagen Business School, Denmark and Malmö University, Sweden.

Runco, M. A. (2007). *Creativity. theories and themes: Research development, and practice.* Burlington, MA: Elsevier.

Sarkar, P., & Chakrabarti, A. (2008). Studying engineering design creativity – Developing a common definition and associated measures. In J. Gero (Ed.), *Studying design creativity* (pp. 2–20). Springer Verlag.

Sarkar, P., & Chakrabarti, A. (2011). Assessing design creativity. *Design Studies, 32*, 348–383.

Scheerer, M. (1963). Problem-solving. *Scientific American, 208*, 118–128.

Schön, D. A. (1983). *The reflective practitioner: How professionals think in action.* New York: Basic Books.

Setchi, R., & Bouchard, C. (2010). In search of design inspiration: A semantic-based approach, *Journal of Computing and Information Science and Engineering, 10*(3). DOI:10.1115/1.3482061.

Simon, H. A. (1973). The structure of ill-structured problems. *Artificial Intelligence, 4*, 181–201.

Simon, H. A. (1995). Problem forming, problem finding and problem solving in design. In A. Collen & W. Gasparski (Eds.), *Design & systems* (pp. 245–257). New Brunswick: Transaction Publishers.

Stappers, P. J., & Pasman, G. (2001). ProductWorld: An interactive environment for classifying and retrieving product samples. *Proceedings of the 5th Asian Design Conference* (pp. 1–11). Seoul, Korea.

Stokes, D. (2007). Incubated cognition and creativity. *Journal of Consciousness Studies, 14*, 83–100.

Sternberg, R. J., & Lubart, T. (1999). The concept of creativity: Prospects and paradigms. In R. J. Sternberg (Ed.), *Handbook of creativity* (pp. 3–15). New York: Cambridge University Press.

Tan, S., & Melles, G. (2010). An activity theory focused case study of graphic designers' tool-mediated activities during the conceptual design phase. *Design Studies, 31*, 461–478.

Tichkiewitch, S. (2010). Method and tools for the effective knowledge management in product life cycle. *20th CIRP Design Conference*. Nantes.

Treffinger, D. J. (1995). Creative problem solving: Overview and educational implications. *Educational Psychology Review, 7*, 301–311.

Tversky, B. (2003). Sketching for design and design of sketches. In U. Lindemann (Ed.), *Human behaviour in design* (pp. 79–86). Berlin: Springer.

Visser, W. (1994). Organisation of design activities: Opportunistic, with hierarchical episodes. *Interacting with Computers, 6*, 235–238.

Wallas, G. (1926). *The art of thought*. New York: Harcourt-Brace.

Wang, H. (1994). An approach to computer-aided styling: Form creation techniques for automotive CAD. *Design Studies, 15*(1), 85–114.

Ward, T. B. (1994). Structured imagination: The role of category structure in exemplar generation. *Cognitive Psychology, 27*, 1–40.

Ward, T. B., Smith, S. M., & Vaid, J. (1997). Conceptual structures and processes in creative thought. In T. B. Ward, S. M. Smith, & J. Vaid (Eds.), *Creative thought: An investigation of conceptual structures and processes* (pp. 1–27). Washington, DC: American Psychological Association.

Ward, T. B., Smith, S. M., & Finke, R. A. (1999). Cognition. In R. Sternberg (Ed.), *Handbook of creativity* (pp. 189–212). Cambridge: Cambridge University Press.

Weisberg, R. W., & Alba, J. W. (1981). An examination of the alleged role of "fixation" in the solution of several "insight" problems. *Journal of Experimental Psychology: General, 110*, 169–192.

Wojtczuk, A. (2014). *Creative product assessment in design: Influence of judges backgrounds and levels of experience in design*. Ph.D. thesis. Aix-en-Provence: Aix-Marseille University.

Wojtczuk, A., & Bonnardel, N. (2011). Designing and assessing everyday objects: Impact of externalisation tools and judges' backgrounds. *Interacting with Computers, 23*(4), 337–345.

Wojtczuk, A., & Bonnardel, N. (2012). Differences in creative design assessment. *Proceedings of the 2nd International Conference on Design Creativity – ICDC' 2012*. Glasgow, U.K.

Zeisel, J. (1981). *Inquiry by design: Tools for environmental behavior research*. Cambridge, MA: Cambridge University Press.

23 A Minimalist Model for Measuring Entrepreneurial Creativity

Elias Carayannis

George Washington University

Phillip Harvard

EIGSI Engineering School of La Rochelle

Abstract

This *esquisse* of entrepreneurial creativity begins and ends with two Irishman: Richard Cantillon of the eighteenth century and Tony Ryan of the twenty-first century. "Entrepreneur," a twentieth-century buzzword, has interesting etymological origins, including Anglo-Franco-Greek roots which contribute richly to better explain, understand, and define entrepreneurial creativity. A very succinct survey of some pertinent research literature highlights the great theoretical complexity when attempting to measure, in order to better define, entrepreneurial creativity. The theoretical complexity is found in the vast number of variations of indicators, aspects, parameters, and criteria proposed by experts and organizations, foundations and institutes. Most agree upon the imminent, even desperate, need for more universalism when conceiving models to better compare, understand, and define entrepreneurial creativity. There seems to be one thing everyone agrees upon – a distinct link between the creative behavior of entrepreneurs and their resulting success. Adopting a more French Cartesian approach means taking into consideration opposites when trying to understand something comprehensively. Is empirical simplicity the opposite of theoretical complexity? A daring attempt is made by the authors to propose a more universal model, hence simplistic and minimalist, for measuring and defining entrepreneurial creativity based on empirical experiences lived by real entrepreneurs. The authors propose a *Minimalist Model* respecting three criteria for measuring entrepreneurial creativity and applying it to the careers of three entrepreneurs from the British Commonwealth: Roy Thomson (Scottish-Canadian), Tony Ryan (Irish), and Richard Branson (English). The three criteria of the *Minimalist Model* are: Timing, Cognitive capacity, and Quantifiable changes.

This presentation is an *esquisse* of entrepreneurial creativity beginning and ending with Irishmen. To begin with we shall refer to an eighteenth-century

Irish banker in France, Richard Cantillon, who was one of the first to define the theoretical importance of the role of entrepreneurs (Ewing Marion Kauffman Foundation [EMKF], 2009; Wikipedia, n.d.-b). We shall also later refer again to the lucky Irish when examining some pertinent empirical experiences from the life of a more recent twenty-first century Irishman and entrepreneur, Tony Ryan of Ryanair (Aldous, 2013). Cantillon referred to entrepreneurs as sources of new wealth or new "money" circulating in the economy, thus contributing to economic development. His idea of new money or new sources of wealth as an integral part of economic growth is "the Cantillon effect" (E.M.K.F., 2009; Wikipedia, n.d.-b). The OCED (Office of Commercial and Economic Development) claims it was not until the 1990s that "entrepreneurship" became a worldwide economic buzzword (E.M.K.F., 2009) Since definitions are always formulated with words, whether key words or buzzwords, it seems only logical to take a moment to examine the importance of words chosen to define, in our case, entrepreneurial creativity. Researchers give great importance to semantics. In this light, it is only logical to take the time for a very brief etymological study comparing pertinent interesting words when defining entrepreneurial creativity. For example, the etymological origin of the English word "pirate" is the Greek word *peirates* ("Pirates and Privateers Definitions," n.d.). But the root of *peirates* is *peiran* and is translated in French as meaning *celui qui entreprend*, or "he who undertakes" ("Pirates and Privateers Definitions," n.d.). French for "undertake" is *entreprendre*, and *entreprendre* is the root of entrepreneurship in English. The French used *entreprandre* (another form of the same word) in the Middle Ages to mean to seize, surprise attack, and aggress ("Pirates and Privateers Definitions," n.d.). This French connection between Greek and English can help explain why adventure and risk are so often associated with entrepreneurship. The French word *entreprendre* is actually two words combined into one word: *entre* and *prendre*. In French *entre* means "between" and *prendre* means "to take." This is why, in French, *entreprendre* means successfully taking on or achieving specific objectives over time. So is this why entrepreneurs can see tomorrow today? In short, entrepreneurship is a pattern of pre-planned intermediary or in-between actions leading to foreseen and hoped-for results.

Considering the French connection, one could say entrepreneurship is a point of view of what to do between two points in time – today and tomorrow – thus offering

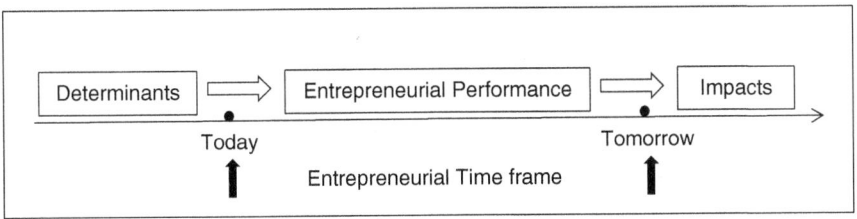

Figure 23.1 *Entrepreneurship is what to do between two points in time.*

a more creative vision of future potential. These two points can be situated between the three main phases of OCED's model for measuring entrepreneurship based on reference points or criteria called Entrepreneurial Indicators: Determinants/ Entrepreneurial performance/Impacts (see Figure 23.1). These three phases are composed of indicators such as regulatory authorities, R&D and technology, culture, capabilities, market conditions (the Determinants) plus action, firms, employment, wealth (the Performance), and finally monetary or non-monetary value, job creation, economic growth, and poverty reduction (the Impacts). According to the OCED, entrepreneurship must create wealth, increase employment, reduce inequalities, and help answer environmental questions. The OCED see entrepreneurs as generating value through creativity and expansion with new products, processes, or markets (E.M.K.F., 2009). The OCED, together with Eurostart, contributes richly to measuring entrepreneurship through research carried-out in their member countries.[1]

The OCED leads international efforts around the world in proclaiming how much measuring to define entrepreneurship requires going beyond just measuring self-owned and medium-sized companies. This is why the authors choose to examine later on a trio of world-wide entrepreneurs and some of their empirical global experiences.

Leaving behind a brief etymological word search, we now move on to culture. Like language, creativity, in almost all professional fields of activity, is influenced by culture. A comparative analysis of how different cultures can color entrepreneurial performance, and hence entrepreneurial creativity, offers some very interesting considerations. The second of our two authors, Harvard, an American, has been working and researching in France, his adopted culture, for over thirty years (Harvard, 2005, 2015–16a). His analysis of some determinants compares entrepreneurial performance in American and French work cultures (see Figure 23.2).

At this point it is important to expand our very brief survey of research literature, beyond the OCED, to include other known prominent experts and researchers. For example, experts like Justo, De Castro, and Maydeu-Olivares reinforce the need for better measuring because of difficulties encountered in cross-country comparisons. They promote the GEM (Global Entrepreneurship Monitor) model for more homogeneous cross-country measuring. Their approach measures the likelihood of someone engaging in entrepreneurial activities and focuses on criterion 1. entrepreneurial behavior (for example: What is his or her current job?), as well as criterion 2. social environment of the entrepreneur (for example: Does he or she know any business angels?) (Justo et al., 2008) The OCED literature refers to young high-growth, high-tech dynamic entrepreneurs as gazelles and an entrepreneurial timeframe where these gazelles have a lower survival rate in their second year of doing business compared to their first year of doing business (E.M.K.F., 2009).

The Kauffman Foundation's research model focuses on two indicators or criteria for measuring entrepreneurial creativity: *Vibrancy* and *Outcomes*, which offer a very

---

[1] Australia, Austria, Belgium, Canada, Czech Republic, Denmark, Finland, France, Germany, Greece, Hungary, Iceland, Italy, Japan, Korea, Luxembourg, Mexico, Netherlands, New Zealand, Norway, Portugal, Slovak Republic, Spain, Sweden, Switzerland, Turkey, United Kingdom and the United States (E.M.K.F., 2009).

American entrepreneurhship:	French entrepreneurship:
pioneer heritage / self-reliance / D-Y-I	Latin heritage / *patronus* & *pater* / guilds / specialists / *système D*
wealth is Heaven's blessing for hard work	rich are selfish and dishonest / rich are mean & poor are good
no taxes to anybody (Boston Tea party)	Republican princes replace Royal princes (French Revolution)
overview from top down / American eagle symbol	details from bottom up / French rooster symbol
American freedom = financial autonomy	French *noblesse oblige* = civic responsibilities & duties
take risks	analyze risk
for / positive	against / criticize
We can - so why not?	Because of......
material progress improves life	social progress for all
private financing through tax deductions	government financing through high taxes
management by objectives for profit	paternalistic management / legal strikes / employee rights
admire winners / want to be the best	admire survivors / being #2 is less pretentious & more authentic
Bill Gate's 70 hour work week	Martine Aubry's 35 hour work week
$10+ registration fee to create a company	required capital to create a company (≈ 7500–30000 Euros)
< $50 Copyright fee / ≤ $500 patent fee (lifetime + 50 years)	≥ 30000 Euros patent fee (+ fees to renew patents annually)
competitive	cooperative
team players & team spirit to create together	isolated individual creative excellence

Figure 23.2 *Some cultural determinants coloring American & French entrepreneurial performance & creativity.*

rich, almost universal, framework to examine four various aspects of profiles and skills of entrepreneurs. The first is *density*, which is more present in certain sectors of activity, etc. The second is *fluidity*, including population, market, labor market, relocating, etc. The third is *connectivity*, meaning high-tech networking, mobility, etc., and the fourth is *diversity*, or spin offs, deal-making, etc. (Strangler & Bell-Masterson, 2015). According to experts like Jonathan Ortmans (2010), there are many other foundations and institutions acting as information-gathering databanks about entrepreneurship such as GEDI (Global Entrepreneurship and Development Index). The writings of Carayannis, the senior author, along with his colleague Dubina, reinforce the importance of understanding innovation and entrepreneurial behavior of entrepreneurs who are engaged economic actors (Carayannis, 2014). Basadur, Pringle, Speranzani, and Bacot also contribute to the understanding of entrepreneurial creative behavior and roles of entrepreneurs as actors but on various economic levels. Their collaboration resulted in giving priority to a collaborative win-win model that increased creativity and innovation between heterogeneous cognitive styles for greater employee satisfaction in team-related performance (Basadur et al., 2000).

In the *International Handbook of Innovation*, Carayannis and Gonzales contribute to the defining of entrepreneurial creativity by suggesting creativity is a cognitive capacity to imagine the future beyond the "box" limits of daily work habits and thinking (Carayannis et al., 2003). Basadur et al.'s model of entrepreneurial behavior goes further and defines four main roles of creative behavior: the *implementer*, the *generator*, the *optimizer*, and the *conceptualizer*. All four gravitate between two opposing poles of creativity: experiencing-thinking vs. evaluation-ideation (Basadur et al., 2000). They attribute a great deal of importance to problem defining, emphasizing this as a key element of entrepreneurial creativity as well as the nurturing of tools in a given work place favoring creativity going out of and beyond the corporate work box structure (Basadur et al, 2000). In short, entrepreneurs can be either short-term corporate creativity stars shining in a stormy crisis or long-term low-key innovators providing a strong stable presence in highly competitive markets. Whichever of the myriads of models chosen to measure and define entrepreneurship, it is necessary to understand what to measure.

Murphy, Traiter, and Hill further highlight the existence of an enormous diversity of models and measures plus the overly numerous performance variables being proposed as essential to consider when defining entrepreneurial creativity. Carayannis et al (2003) prefer to zoom in on one essential element – knowledge – and even propose the superiority of imagination over knowledge.

Knowledge reshapes, increases, and changes the limits of one's work box structure because knowledge is organized information put into action through decisions (Carayannis et al., 2003). When raw data is put into a logical order it becomes usable information that is later transformed into decision-making knowledge, and includes both social and cultural knowledge as well as semantics. According to Dell'Era, Buganza, Speranzani and Bacot (2011), knowledge can make almost any work box structure (a company's organization, work environment, and working conditions) evolve technologically and therefore become commercially and economically more competitive on the market. Carayannis and Gonzalez describe sources of creativity as originating from a personal view point or vision, seeing things from product-oriented or process-oriented points of view and, finally, being empirically inspired by particularities of a given environment or work culture (Carayannis et al., 2003); see again Figure 23.2. Carayannis, Hens, and Nicolopoulon-Stamati (2015) elaborated ideas about creativity in regards to the work box structure syndrome. They explain evolutionary differences between just thinking outside the box to thinking beyond the box and even transdisciplinary thinking out of the box. Here, it is possible to imagine a new vision of Maslowian progressive evolution from lower to higher levels (Harvard, 2010). Just as in the different levels on Maslow's pyramid of employee needs, for Carayannis and his colleagues (2015), the issue is not a judgmental one of better or worse/superior or inferior, but rather progressing and evolving to improve and development employee competencies to be more creative in his/her given work box structure. Going back to the 1990s, research literature clearly demonstrates laudable efforts to propose models of measuring cognitive behavioral capacities of entrepreneurs. Stormer, Kline and Goldenberg (1999), proposed the GET (General Enterprising Tendency) Test with a fifty-four-item questionnaire to measure the capacity of being an entrepreneur ("GET2," n.d.). Still in the 1990s, Buttner and Moore focused on the motivation of women to succeed as entrepreneurs (1997).

More recently, McAfee and Brynjolfsson (2012) propose a second "machine age" of digital technologies, as opposed to the first machine age of mechanical technologies during the Industrial revolution, and the resulting disruptive decoupling. Such a disruptive differentiating gulf between previously statistically coupled measurements now separates the statistical measuring of productivity from that of income and employment. McAfee and Brynjolfsson (2012) are convinced that more entrepreneurship is needed. They emphasize a more pertinent and very decisive role of creativity in future work box structures because more creativity is needed more than ever before for marketplace value to be assured. Therefore the importance of creativity for entrepreneurs has an even greater importance in the twenty-first century than ever before. In other words it seems Carayannis and Gonzales are right because imagination is superior to knowledge (Caryannis et al., 2003). Winter and Govindarajan (2015) offer a pristine empirical example of true entrepreneurial imagination explaining the dilemma of the long-term advantage or utility of the PlayPump Project. It was viable only on a short-term basis. It consisted of African children playing and pushing a merry-go-round, in isolated desert regions, creating energy to pump needed water from a source in the ground up into an elevated storage tank for a nearby village. Unfortunately, it has been abandoned since 2010 because it does not offer long-term feasibility. It would require up to 200 children playing 10 minutes a day to provide 3,000 liters of water for a village of 1,000 people. Gatewood (1995) gave great importance to, even a priority to, the vital importance of timeframes (foreseen beginning and ending dates) being directly related to the sustainability (duration) of entrepreneurial actions. In the case of PlayPump, entrepreneurial creativity was very timely but only during a too-short specific period of time before the timeframe expired. In other words, entrepreneurs must be able to see, size-up, then seize chances to create within a timeframe.

The preceding, but all too succinct, survey of some entrepreneurship literature paves the way for the authors' audacious attempt to propose their *Minimalist Model* of three criteria for measuring, hence better defining, entrepreneurial creativity. But it is important to clarify two very pertinent concepts: measuring and defining. Often when doing surveys or analysis or research, links between concepts and ideas seem to occur as if in a pattern of cycles. Since cyclic linking of ideas surface regularly in most research pursuits it seems appropriate to link up "measuring" with efforts to better "define." It is only logical that the outcomes of models for measuring entrepreneurship can enrich and contribute to updating and revising a definition of entrepreneurial creativity. In fact, in order to define entrepreneurial creativity, it is necessary to establish criteria or indicators (such as OCED/Eurostart) as reference points. Thus, there is some degree of measuring inherent in any attempt at definitions. We can hence surmise definitions that may seem theoretical, can be based upon empirical measurements and provide criteria reference points regarding how to measure. We can also say the non-universality of existing measurement models is due to their complexity. This complexity can be attributed to the fact they seek to conform to the measuring of a vast number of overly theoretical variables rather than empirical constants experienced and lived by real entrepreneurs. Whatever the research criteria, indicators, variables, or standard, the purpose of any measurement (theoretical or empirical) is to offer a better definition of entrepreneurial creative behavior. The second author, Harvard, suggests no matter how numerous or how varying are the definitions of creativity, entrepreneurial creativity behavior is an empirical constant influencing success (Harvard, 2013). Once success has been achieved, the intermediary creative behavior typical of entrepreneurs taking action must be replaced by permanent more structured behaviors to guarantee ongoing long-term success. Entrepreneurs carrying out successful intermediate actions often have a hard time adapting their intermediary creative behavior and transform themselves into managers with the more day-to-day vision needed for long-term stability. The spontaneous high energy level behavior feeding the entrepreneur's risk-taking creative vision of the future is not always transformable into continuous ongoing day-to-day behavior on the lower energy level needed to manage and maintain the initial structure. Therefore it is very important to realize spontaneity, so typical of entrepreneurial creative behavior, is usually short term, or intermediary, and not easily integrated into long-term management behavior. The failure to make the needed career change, from short- to long-term entrepreneurial behavior, between two points in time (today and tomorrow), can perhaps help explain the overly dramatic dilemma of Dickens' fictitious, yet famous, entrepreneur named Ebenezer Scrooge (1843). Though fictitious from literary and historical points of view, the *personnage* symbolized by Scrooge is a not-so-fictitious example of the need for a long-term career vision. The lack of long-term vision allows for end-of-career regrets by entrepreneurs and the possibility of them being haunted by the ghosts of bad short-term decisions.

Storybooks aside, creativity remains a very important guiding "North Star" among the key ideas of the OCED/Eurostart's research about entrepreneurship. This means no matter which work box structure, or company, where one finds himself/herself as an employee on OCED's structural scale of companies (micro, small, medium-sized or large companies), entrepreneurial creativity can exist! A few poignant examples from various professional activities, like education or the music industry or the medical industry, clearly demonstrate a unique aspect of entrepreneurial creativity: a high-risk survival factor. As has already been mentioned, this risky pirate syndrome of entrepreneurs goes back to the Greek *peirates* origins of the French word *entreprendre*. If we consider a university lecturer in higher education, such as Harvard, his pedagogical creativity to redo a module and put it online does not necessarily change his salary yet he might receive a bonus or other employee incentives to be more creative in his teaching responsibilities or tasks. For him there is relatively little chance of a risky pirate syndrome threatening his present stability for future actions. When it comes to the music industry, we can consider the well-known examples of Michael Jackson and Madonna, who contributed richly and creatively to the music industry markets over decades. Their professional creativity benefited from a comfortable safety net called "fame" due to acquired client loyalty and repeated client purchase of music they produced. The risk factor for similar famous entertainers is diluted and reduced by the saving grace of a celebrity status framework favoring creativity which defines, even initiates, the creation of new music market trends. This kind of exponential creativity stabilizes, hence minimalizes, the risk factor, almost eliminating entirely the risky pirate syndrome. Medical researchers in global pharmaceutical companies, such as Harvard's oldest daughter,

Astrid, a recent med school grad, benefit from a creative comfort zone of a global work box stability. Consequently, for her too, the presence of any risky pirate syndrome is relatively non-existent in a global corporate multi-choice career path scheme. In this light, we propose the following about entrepreneurial creativity: It includes a high-risk survival factor, not only because of a high-level energy so typical of entrepreneurs, but also because of a high level of spontaneity.

Hence from a minimalist point of view, there are to be at least three reoccurring elements in the research literature considered about measuring entrepreneurship to better define entrepreneurial creativity. Above of all, we propose that the first criterion of the *Minimalist Model* for entrepreneurial creativity is the importance of *Timing*, which means giving priority to detecting and foreseeing opportunities where others only see risks. This means organizing risk taking into a profitable pattern of actions at the right time and place. Or in other words, being able to see what to do between two points in time, today and tomorrow, in order to accomplish a future objective during a foreseen timeframe (see Figure 23.1). This, the first criterion of a more universal model, provides a common working ground to put into harmony ideas proposed by some of the researchers, institutes, and experts cited. Secondly, we propose considering the fact that entrepreneurial creativity requires a *Cognitive capacity* to come up with what is different and new. Creative ideas can include taking even further risks like judging, choosing, deciding how to think out of and beyond a work box structure or even on a transdisciplinary level, all the while taking into consideration social and cultural knowledge and semantics of in-house innovation processes. These different thinking levels of entrepreneurial creativity provide the insight and foresight to discern what needs to be done now to open doors to feasible future changes. This, the second criteria of a more universal model, also tries to put into harmony concepts of the experts and researchers cited. Thirdly, we propose a final criterion for the *Minimalist Model* to be that of *Quantifiable changes*, which can be likened to a red carpet of ideas across a bridge through time leading up to results, impact, and hopefully success. Such quantifying requires statistics in order to numerically analyze and interpret the long-term viability of changes resulting from entrepreneurial actions. This, the third criterion of a more universal model, also opens doors for harmonizing principles researched by certain experts and institutes cited.

So the question now to ask is: How can we measure, in order to better define, entrepreneurial creativity? Here we adopt the more Cartesian approach of the French based upon Descartes' (1595–1650) idea that everything in the universe has its opposite to consider when trying to understand it more completely (Harvard, 2007; Wikipedia, n.d.-a). We dare offer an approach to measuring entrepreneurial creativity by taking into consideration the opposite of the myriad of theoretical complex models traced by researchers, institutes, and experts. We dare give priority to a more minimalist model based on empirical experiences lived by real entrepreneurs. In other words, we dare propose a more empirically based *Minimalist Model* articulating around the aforementioned three criteria: (1) *Timing*, including timeliness and timeframe, (2) engaged entrepreneurial creative behavior favoring a *Cognitive capacity* to think outside existing work box structures, and

In...	His creative project was...	In...	His creative project was...
1966	student magazine	1996	second record label
1969	mail order-company	2004	space travel launchers
1971	record shop	2006	cable, broadband, telephone
1972	recording studio	2007	health bank
1973	1st artist on his record label	2008	health care
1980	travel agency	2009	Formula One
1983	radio station and Mega Virgin Stores	2010	hot air balloons
1984	airline	2012	test launch of a spaceship
1992	financial difficulties (He cried when he sold Mega Virgin Stores for $1 billion.)		
1993	railways	2014	drones

Figure 23.3 *Branson's entrepreneurial creativity.*

(3) *Quantifiable changes* resulting from entrepreneurial impacts over time. A probable application can be attempted by comparing the careers of three entrepreneurs of the British Commonwealth: a savvy Scotsman, Roy Thomson (1894–1976); an impossible Irishman, Tony Ryan (1934–2007); and an eccentric Englishman, Richard Branson (1950–). Their combined careers span an accumulated hundred years of entrepreneurship between the three of them. Here we adhere to Carayannis and Gonzalez, previously cited, who express the same preference as OCED to examine aspects of entrepreneurship in an empirical business and industrial context and not examine "artists, scientists, entrepreneurs as obsessed manias and clairvoyant oracles" (Carayannis et al., 2003; E.M.K.F., 2009).

The following very short keyhole retrospectives of Thomson and Ryan and Branson as entrepreneurs offer empirical sources as constants with critical information to consider when attempting to measure, hence better define, entrepreneurial creativity. How would Bassadur attribute his Cognitive Profiles of entrepreneurial creative behavior? Would Thomson be more of a creative *implementer* or Ryan a creative *generator* or Branson a creative *conceptualizer*? Would Bassadur categorize all three as *optimizers*? And what about Carayannis and Gonzalez's first level of creativity, meaning being capable of thinking outside the limits of a given work box structure to see new work box structures? Thomson was capable of going from one box to another and Ryan certainly did see beyond a certain airline service work box structure to see market potential for another work box structure. Branson's vivacious zest for diversity certainly puts him in the transdisciplinary thinking-out-of-the-box category (see Figure 23.3). Measuring by quantifiable changes of empirical entrepreneurial behavior can include changes in production cost, market price, profit margin, job creation, and employee performance, as well as unemployment rates, different kinds of income like employee salaries as well as work box structure company turnover. Quantifying changes in company turnover as outcome may seem a cruel crude common sense approach, perhaps too empirically primitive or overly simplistic, even very materialistic, for certain researchers, institutes, and experts.

Out of all the models considered, it is evident that the simplicity of the Kauffman model puts it first on the list of candidates for being the most universal model. Simplicity is universality (Strangler & Bell-Masterson, 2015). The Kauffman model's first indicator, or criterion, for measuring entrepreneurial creativity is *Vibrancy*, corresponding to *Cognitive capacity* or the second criterion of the *Minimalist Model* (Strangler & Bell-Masterson, 2015). *Outcome* is the second indicator, or criterion, for measuring in the Kauffman model and corresponds to *Quantifiable changes*, which is the third indicator of the *Minimalist Model*. Outcomes change things, but what makes changes or impacts measurable is quantifying numbers. After all, when it comes to outcome, one cannot ignore the hard, cold economic and commercial fact that in industry, engineers do not consider inventions to be an innovation until if, and when, they generate quantifiable profits within a specific timeframe. Was it not the entrepreneur's new wealth or new money contributing to economic growth that made "Cantillon's effect" famous for centuries? (E.M.K.F., 2009; Wikipedia, n.d.-b). The following, though limited, career excerpts considered here are empirical constants, meaning real-life experiences, from the lives of Thomson, Ryan, and Branson. They are timely but non-exhaustive, and therefore indicative, not representative, of the importance of *Timeliness*, which is the first criteria of the *Minimalist Model*.

A Savvy Scotsman

One of Roy Thomson's first newspapers was *The Scotsman* (Köhler & Kingston, 2006; Wikipedia, n.d.-d). We respect his ferocious fidelity to his origins and present him as Scottish because his hereditary peerage as a Baron attributed in 1962 costed him his Canadian citizenship. The son of a barber, this Canadian-born entrepreneur was a prominent twentieth-century newspaper magnate and media entrepreneur. His family was among the first settlers of Scarborough. He tried to follow the tenant farmer family tradition of his Scottish ancestors of Wester Kirk, Dumfriesshires, but he failed at farming in Manitoba, Ontario. During World War I, he attended a business college and was later rejected by the army due to his poor eyesight. After the war, he returned to the big city of Toronto and tried different jobs until he finally ended up selling radios in Northern Ontario. Early on in his career, his entrepreneur mind-set allowed him to see, size-up, then seize the chance to buy the rights to a radio frequency and set up in 1931 a radio station so his customers would have something to listen to in North Bay, Ontario. His creativity gave him the insight to understand and know what needed to be done. In 1934 he made a down payment to purchase a newspaper, the *Timmins Daily Press* in Ontario (Köhler & Kingston, 2006; Wikipedia, n.d.-d). By 1949 his entrepreneurial creativity had expanded to include fitted-kitchen manufacturing, ice cream cones, and ladies hairstyling shops. He was not afraid of what was new or different and was cognitively capable of thinking outside one box to invest in another one (criterion 2 of the *Minimalist Model*). He returned to his ancestral country, purchasing *The Scotsman* in 1952 and Scottish Television in 1957. In 1959 he purchased a group of British newspapers including *The Sunday Times* and later bought the legendary *The Times* in 1966. Roy Thomson could see an opportunity where others only saw a risk. He even had some joint projects with John Paul Getty in North Sea oil ventures (Köhler & Kingston, 2006; Wikipedia, n.d.-d).

The joking and teasing between certain members of the Thomson family about being descendants of Scottish pirates may or may not confirm the Anglo-Franco-Greek etymological origins of the word "entrepreneur." At the same time, it goes without saying Roy Thomson did have the entrepreneurial savvy to organize his risk-taking profitable actions into a chronological timeframe with a pattern of pre-calculated, but at the same time very creative, approach to risk management. For example, chronologically speaking, there was a three-year period between his creating his radio in North Bay, Ontario, and purchasing the *Timmins Daily Press*, a two-year period between *The Scotsman* and Scottish Television, another two-year period between Scottish Television and *The Sunday Times*, but a nine-year period before acquiring *The Times*. Thomson's pre-planned entrepreneurial timeframe (criterion 1 of the *Minimalist Model*) was a pattern of intermediary actions which lead to foreseen and hoped-for results. Thomson understood that the spontaneity of creative behavior typical of entrepreneurs is usually short term, or intermediary, thus difficult to transform into long-term management behavior.

One might say the crowning act of Roy Thomson's entrepreneurial creativity was expressed for his posterity in his last will and testament requiring (male) heirs to assume their entrepreneurial responsibility in the running of family affairs. His son, Kenneth Thomson (1923–2006) followed in his father's footsteps. Ken's paternal, gentlemanly entrepreneur-style probably explains his kind coaching and exchanges with Harvard through personal correspondence and telephone conversations. At crucial career-path moments, Harvard had trouble thinking beyond his work box structure. When Harvard asked advice about solutions, Ken Thomson warned that it is easier to find solutions on "familiar territory, so to speak" (June 8, 1982) and "one has to specialize and this usually takes a great deal of time and effort." (September 6, 1982). Thomson's advice to Harvard refers to the second criterion of the *Minimalist Model* of cognitive capacities. When Harvard encountered critical ethical conflict about trust management of client funds with California friends, who were also partners, Ken Thomson's advice proved providential and Harvard eventually left Laguna Beach, California, for La Rochelle, France, where he began a second career in higher education as a university lecturer and researcher. In their last telephone conversation, Thomson reassured Harvard that what seems to be the thing to do at a given moment under pressure or stress, when doing business with friends, seldom is in the long run. (November 2005). Today, the Thomson legacy continues to become more global in the capable hands of Ken's son, David (1957–), who began assuming his Thomson heritage of an entrepreneur role at the head of the family enterprises well before Ken's death. David's sister has also followed the family entrepreneur traditional behavior by trying out her own entrepreneurial creativity in Hollywood's Entertainment Industry arenas. Today the Thomson Organization is a multi-faceted global structure worth over 27 billion dollars, making them one of the planet's wealthiest families (criterion 3 of the *Minimalist Model*) (Köhler & Kingston, 2006; Wikipedia, n.d.-d).

An Impossible Irishman

The historian Richard Aldous in his writings says that Tony Ryan is the epitome of what an entrepreneur is about and claims Ryan to be the Irish Great Gatsby (Aldous, 2013; Wikipedia, n.d.-e). Tony Ryan was as proud of being Irish as Thomson was of being Scottish. Ryan's life was the cold hard reality of a working man's self-made dream come true, not an impossible Gatsby-style fantasy. But how did the impossible dream become possible for this lucky Irishman? Did he see clear enough between points in time; today's risks and tomorrow's results? Ryan was born in Ireland in a railway man's cottage in Thurles, County Temporary, and died in Ireland of Pancreatic cancer in Elbridge, County Kildare (Aldous, 2013; Wikipedia, n.d.-e.) His entrepreneurial creativity survived the loss of one fortune (Guinness Peat Aviation) to participate in the building of another (Ryanair). But why did he invest millions in a Georgian version of Scarlett's O'Hara's Tara? Had fictitious dreams become Tony Ryan's reality? What about foresight and creative vision? After Ryan's success was achieved it seems his intermediary creative entrepreneur behavior was not completely replaced by permanent, more structured ones. Although he and Roy Thomson shared the same do-or-die work ethic mind-set, unfortunately, in comparison to Thomson and his heirs, Ryan's entrepreneurial creativity was not transformed into continuous ongoing day-to-day energy to maintain the structure he set up and put into place. He and his heirs did not adapt to being managers. Hence his spontaneous high-level energy necessary for his risk-taking creative vision of the future was short term and never converted into long-term management actions by himself or his heirs, as was the case with the Thomson family.

It is also interesting to consider and compare further information researched about Tony Ryan as an entrepreneur. His company GPA (Guinness Peat Aviation) ordered very expensive new aircraft in 1992, the same year he tried to go public, but it turned into a disaster. He mismanaged his entrepreneurial timeframe (criterion 1 of the *Minimalist Model*). He owed Merrill Lynch millions, and even though his properties in both Mexico and Spain plus his art, antiques, bank accounts were worth millions, his GPA shares, once estimated at 234 million dollars, were now worthless (Aldous, 2013; Wikipedia, n.d.-e). But Ryan had his way out! With the luck of the Irish, he had foreseen a very creative approach to risk-taking. With a friend from Air Lingus, he creatively participated in the setting up of a renegade, ruthless Ryanair as a no-thrills airlines (Aldous, 2013; Wikipedia, n.d.-e). Here we see his entrepreneurial creativity at its best when he was inspired to list his interest in Ryanair under the names of his three children; Cathal, Declan, and Shane. He made the impossible possible (Aldous, 2013; Wikipedia, n.d.-e). Was Ryanair a safety exit out of his GPA crisis?

Ryanair corresponds to a growing need of low-cost transportation systems and networks in the twenty-first-century global knowledge-based economy for no-collar creative yuppies in their cozy comfy suburbs and burbs as opposed to the overly stressed competitive getting-old-when-young traditional white and blue collar employees. The New York/London/Tokyo trio of mega-cities no longer dominates banks and industries as they did at the end of the twentieth century. Low-cost transportation gave birth to "burbs" (beyond the suburbs) favoring an even more affordable, low-key "country" life style far from the world's raging mega-cities like London. Even more than before, websites and e-mails have enabled the new offices of Internet start-ups and e-commerce companies to be located far away from the stressful corporate lifestyle of mega-cities (Harvard, 2015-16b). Ryan could detect an opportunity where others only feared risk. He saw beyond the work box of traditional airline service (criterion2 of the *Minimalist Model*). His entrepreneurial creative behavior definitely still matches the global economy's low-cost transportation needs and favors a formerly unimaginable lifestyle for skilled professionals. The story of Harvard's fellow Ryanair passenger, Nicolas Long, is a charming testimony about how Ryan's vision of low-cost air travel makes a previously unimaginable life-style far from a mega-city (like London) become a reality. Long, an English engineer (who works on the Tube in London) flew from London Stansted to La Rochelle on Ryanair every weekend to be with his wife and daughters in their French seventeenth-century *Saintoge Logis* Manor he restored in the village of *La Jarne* near the *Château de Buzay* just outside of La Rochelle. Thanks to Ryan's entrepreneurial creativity, living in La Rochelle while working in London became an imaginable reality for Long. God bless Tony Ryan! His entrepreneurial creativity of different ideas was his red carpet leading up to, and consequently the opening up of, future airline service markets. Ryanair went public in 1997, becoming a multi-million pound airline venture. The impossible dream of Ryan's partners became their reality. Ryanair is today Europe's largest airline, worth over 10 billion euros. It is important to note his multi-millionaire protégés, Denis O'Brien and Michael O'Neal, attribute their own success to Ryan's hard-nosed coaching style (Aldous, 2013; Wikipedia, n.d.-e). At his death Tony Ryan was worth 1.5 billion euros and considered to be one of the wealthiest Irishmen to have ever lived. (criterion 3 of the *Minimalist Model*) (Aldous, 2013; Wikipedia, n.d.-e).

An Eccentric Englishman

Richard Branson was born in London, resides in the Virgin Islands, and is a multimedia/website/blog/Twitter/Facebook/LinkedIn/e-mail connected entrepreneur. He founded the 5 billion dollar Virgin Group (criterion 3 of the *Minimalist*

Model) (Branson, 2005; Wikipedia, n.d.-b). His global business empire, spanning more than thirty countries, is governed by a complex structure of offshore trusts. His father was a barrister and his grandfather was a judge of the High Court Justice. Dyslexic, he attended different schools until the age of sixteen (Branson, 2005; Wikipedia, n.d.-b). A headmaster once told him he would end up either in a prison or be a millionaire. He believes in the decriminalization of drugs, is pro-European, is anti-nuclear, is a minister of the Universal Life Church Monastery, has already written his own autobiography, was married two times, and has had three children. Her Majesty the Queen named him Knight Bachelor for "services to entrepreneurship" (Branson, 2005; Wikipedia, n.d.-b). It was the fund-raising, fun-loving Solihull dinner party friends of the late Austrian Baroness Notburga Tilt Van Hann (one of Schindler's World War II Austrian resistance courier/party girls) who tried to convince Harvard, but failed to make him an ardent fan of Sir Richard (Tilt, 1972). They portrayed Sir Richard as a sincere philanthropist, not just another big city carpetbagger.

It is true he is involved in a myriad of humanitarian causes such as "The Elders" (to resolve global conflicts) as well as admirable efforts for missing and exploited children, or his own school of entrepreneurship plus Virgin Unite, his non-profit foundation. His charismatic career clearly reflects an entrepreneurial timeframe (criterion 1 of the *Minimalist Model*) with logical year-to-year astounding creative behavior, highlighted in the a very impressive, yet incomplete, listing of his projects (see Figure 23.3) (Branson, 2005; Wikipedia, n.d.-b). To sum up, Sir Richard is an enigmatic transdisciplinary entrepreneur who became a celebrity media star. Without a doubt, he incarnates the entrepreneur who creatively undertook a wide range of projects demonstrating strong cogntive capcities (criterion 2 of the *Minimalist Model*). He was not afraid of new ideas leading to the opening of future markets by perceiving opportunities where others were overwhelmed by risks. We can say without hesitation he successfully replaced his intermediary entrepreneurial creative behavior by a permanent more structured one, which guaranteed his ongoing long-term success and stability. Sir Richard's track record proves his capability to adapt and transform his spontaneous behavior on a high-energy level as an entrepreneur into continuous, stable, ongoing day-to-day managerial behavior on a lower energy level, thus maintaining structures he set up and put into place. The spontaneity of his creativity has lasted for over a half a century since 1966. There are those who claim Sir Richard is the entrepreneur's entrepreneur (Branson, 2005; Wikipedia, n.d.-b).

In conclusion, a very brief analysis, limited to the information cited, reveals things in common between our trio of Sottish, Irish, and English British Commonwealth entrepreneurs through empirical experiences from the careers of Roy Thomson, Tony Ryan, and Richard Branson. Indeed, what they have in common contributes to a better empirical understanding of entrepreneurial creativity. They offer us some down-to-earth criteria to help define a more practical approach to measuring entrepreneurial creativity (see Figure 23.4).

These three empirical elements, *Timing, Cognitive capacity*, and *Quantifiable changes* seem to be plausible universal measurements that not only indicate, but

Criteria #1: **_Timing_**
All three carried out a successful pattern of entrepreneurial actions within a specific timeframe.

Criteria #2 : **_Cognitive capacity_**
All three possessed a cognitive capacity to think outside and beyond their own boxes and become Involved in different new entrepreneurial actions.

Criteria #3 : **_Quantifiable changes_**
All three experienced evolutionary profitable changes numerically quantifiable on a long term basis.

Figure 23.4 *The Minimalist Model for measuring entrepreneurial creativity.*

help define and determine, what is entrepreneurial creativity. Certainly, one can well imagine Dickens would not have hesitated to say a final word or two about such non-Scrooge, non-gazelle entrepreneurial creative behavior: God bless everyone, especially creative entrepreneurs (Dickens, 1843)!

References

Aldous, R. (2013). *Tony Ryan: Ireland's aviator.* Dublin, Ireland: Gill & Macmillan.

Basadur, M., Pringle, P., Speranzini, G., & Bacot, M. (2000), Collaborative problem solving through creativity in problem definition: Expanding the pie. *Creativity and Innovation Management, 9*(1), 54–76.

Branson, R. (2005). *Losing my virginity: How I survived, had fun, and made a fortune doing business my way* (2nd edn.). London, UK: Virgin Books.

Buttner, E. H., & Moore, D. P. (1997). Women's organizational exodus to entrepreneurship: Self-reported motivations and correlates with success. *Journal of Small Business Management, 35*(51), 34.

Carayannis, E., Gonzalez, E., & Wetter, J. (2003) The nature and dynamics of discontinuous and disruptive innovation from a learning knowledge management perspective. In L. V. Shavinina (Ed.), *The international handbook on innovation* (pp. 115–138). London, UK: Elsevier Science.

Carayannis, E. & Dubina, I. (2014) Thinking beyond the box; Game-theoretic living lab approaches to innovation policy and practice improvement. *Journal of the Knowledge Economy, 5*(3), 427–439.

Carayannis, E., Hens, L., & Nicolopoulou-Stamati, P. (2015, September 19). Transdisciplinary and growth: Nature and characteristics of transdisciplinary training programs in the human-environment interphase. *Journal of the Knowledge Economy,* 1–22. DOI: 10.1007/s13132-015-0294-z

Dell'Era, C., Buganza, T., Fecchio, C., & Verganti, R. (2011). Language brokering: Stimulating creativity during the concept development phase. *Creativity and Innovation Management, 20*(1), 6–48.

Dickens, C. (1843/2009). *A Christmas carol.* New York: Barnes & Noble.

Ewing Marion Kauffman Foundation. (2009). *Co-operation and development, organisation for economic, measuring entrepreneurship: A collection of indicators, 2009 Edition.*

Gatewood, E. J., Shater, K. G., & Gartner, W. B. (1995) A longitudinal study of cognitive factors influencing start-up behaviors and success at venture creation. *Journal of Business Venturing*, *10*(5), 371–391.

GET2 (n.d.) *General measure of enterprising tendency v2*. Retrieved on March 30, 2015, from www.get2test.net

Harvard, P. (2005) Team culture communicating = semantics + semiology. In E. Carayannis, Y. H. Kwak, & F. T. Anbari (Eds.), *The story of managing projects: an interdisciplinary approach* (pp. 72–88). Westport, CT: Praeger.

Harvard, P. (2007). Descartes + mayoism + confucius + taoism = ideas about managing creative employees. In E. Carayannis & J. J. Chanaron (Eds.), *Leading and managing creators, inventors, and innovators: The art, science, and craft of fostering creativity, triggering invention, and catalyzing innovation* (pp. 217–232). Westport, CT: Praeger.

Harvard, P. (2010) Maslow, mazes, minotaurs: Updating employee needs and behavior patterns in a knowledge-based global economy. *Journal of the Knowledge Economy*, *1*(2), 117–127.

Harvard, P. (2013). Two Hs from harvard to hapsburg or creative semantics about creativity: A prelude to creativity. In E. Carayannis (Ed.), *Encyclopedia of creativity, invention, innovation, and entrepreneurship* (pp. 1861–1868). New York: Springer.

Harvard, P. (2015–16a). *Franco-American cultural differences in entrepreneurship, leadership and teamwork*. (Unpublished manuscript). Department of Organizing and Managing Enterprises, EIGSI General Engineering School, La Rochelle, France.

Harvard, P. (2015–16b). *The new global engineer*. (Unpublished manuscript). Department of Organizing and Managing Enterprises, EIGSI General Engineering School, La Rochelle, France.

Justo, R., De Castro, J. O., & Maydeu-Olivares, A. (2008) Indicators of entrepreneurship activity: Some methodological contributions. *International Journal of Entrepreneurship and Small Business*, *6*(4), 604–621.

Köhler, N. & Kingston, A. R. (2006). Canada's rich, troubled Thomson family. In *The Canadian encyclopedia*.

McAfee, A., Brynjolfsson, E. (2012). Big data: The management revolution. *Harvard Business Review*, *90*(10), 61–67.

Murphy, G. B., Trailer, J. W., & Hill, R. C. (1996). Measuring performance in entrepreneurship research, *Journal of Business Research*, *36*(1), 15–23.

Ortmans, J. (2010, October 11). Measuring entrepreneurship around the world. *Global Entrepreneurship Week USA*, Retrieved on from http://genglobal.org/united-states/measuring-entrepreneurship-around-world.

Pirates-Corsaires (n.d.). "Pirates" and "Privateers" definitions. Retrieved on March 30, 2015, from www.pirates-corsaires.com

Stormer, F., Kline, T., & Goldenberg, S. (1999). Measuring entrepreneurship with the general enterprising tendency (GET) test: Criterion-related validity and reliability. *Human Systems Management*, *18*(1), 47–52.

Strangler, D. & Bell-Masterson, J. (2015) Kauffman foundation series on city, metro, and regional entrepreneurship: Measuring an entrepreneurial ecosystem. Ewing Marion Kauffman Foundation. Retrieved on from: http://www.kauffman.org/what-we-do/research/2015/03/measuring-an-entrepreneurial-ecosystem

Tilt, N. (1972) *The strongest weapon*. Devon: Arthur H. Stockwell Ltd.

Wikipedia, The Free Encyclopedia. (n.d.-a). "René Descartes." Retrieved on March 30, 2015, from https://en.wikipedia.org/w/index.php?title=Ren%C3%A9_Descartes&oldid=731477708

Wikipedia, The Free Encyclopedia. (n.d.-b). "Richard Branson." Retrieved on March 30, 2015, from https://en.wikipedia.org/w/index.php?title=Richard_Branson&oldid=731858382

Wikipedia, The Free Encyclopedia (n.d.-c). "Richard Cantillon." Retrieved on March 30, 2015, from https://en.wikipedia.org/w/index.php?title=Richard_Cantillon&oldid=725841122

Wikipedia, The Free Encyclopedia. (n.d.-d). "Roy Thomson, 1st Baron of Fleet." Retrieved on July 14, 2016, from https://en.wikipedia.org/w/index.php?title=Roy_Thomson,_1st_Baron_Thomson_of_Fleet&oldid=732546886

Wikipedia, The Free Encyclopedia. (n.d.-e). "Tony Ryan." Retrieved on March 30, 2015, from https://en.wikipedia.org/w/index.php?title=Tony_Ryan&oldid=706338511

Winter, A. & Govindarajan, V. (2015) Engineering reverse innovations. *Harvard Business Review, 93*, 80–89.

PART V

Newer Domains for Creativity Research

24 Intellectual Property

Does the Law Influence Creativity?

Gregory N. Mandel[*]

Temple University–Beasley School of Law

Abstract

Legal research on creativity centers on intellectual property law, a field of law that regulates rights in creations of the mind. Recent studies in this area explore how creativity is evaluated for purposes of awarding intellectual property rights, how the prospect of legal rights affects creativity, whether creativity impacts the valuation of subject works, and how the public conceptualizes creativity in relation to intellectual property rights. This body of research speaks to creativity studies in many domains and to the ability of intellectual property law to function as designed.

The primary manner in which legal studies interact with creativity research concerns intellectual property law. Intellectual property law comprises several fields of law that regulate private property rights in creations of the human mind. Two prominent areas of intellectual property law, patent law and copyright law, exist in order to promote and reward creativity. Though other fields of law intersect with creativity research in a variety of tangential manners, the success of patent and copyright law depend significantly on how they interact with the human creative process (Mandel, 2011).

The study of creativity implicates intellectual property law issues on several fronts. Creativity research can help elucidate how the law influences creativity, how creativity is evaluated under the law, how creativity is conceptualized with respect to legal rights, and how creativity influences perceptions of legal rights.[1] This chapter surveys legal research about creativity as it relates to intellectual property law. In order to situate this research, it is necessary to first provide a brief introduction to intellectual property law and policy.

Intellectual Property Law

Every country provides for intellectual property rights for the creators of certain types of new intellectual works. Though the particular rights vary somewhat

---

[*] Dean & Peter J. Liacouras Professor of Law, Temple University–Beasley School of Law. J.D., Stanford Law School; B.A., Wesleyan University. Email: gmandel@temple.edu. I am grateful to Stephanie Bair and Christopher Buccafusco for their valuable feedback on a draft of this chapter and to Shannon Daniels for her outstanding research assistance.
[1] Though various authors have discussed the value of creativity for successful lawyers (Menkel-Meadow, 1999; Brest & Kreiger, 1999), there do not appear to have been any studies of creativity in lawyers per se.

depending on the jurisdiction, nearly all countries have ratified a number of international intellectual property treaties, producing substantial harmonization across the world's intellectual property regimes. The discussion of intellectual property law that follows is generally accurate in most jurisdictions.

There are four primary areas of intellectual property law: patent, copyright, trademark, and trade secret. Patent law and copyright law both have objectives that relate to promoting, rewarding, or supporting creativity and are discussed in greater detail below. Trademark law provides protection for marks that identify the source of goods or services for a consumer. Trademark law is focused on establishing more efficient markets by reducing potential consumer confusion and allowing producers to protect their goodwill. The United States Supreme Court has noted that trademark law is not designed to reward creativity (Dastar v. Twentieth Century Fox, 2003). Trade secret law provides protection for valuable business information that is not commonly known. Trade secret protection depends significantly on acceptable business practices. Trademark and trade secret law do not significantly intersect with creativity and are not discussed further here.

Both patent and copyright law provide a creativity threshold that a new work must meet in order to merit intellectual property protection. Patent law enables the inventor of a useful, new, and nonobvious invention to obtain a patent on the subject matter of the invention (these requirements are referred equivalently to as "industrially applicable," new, and "inventive step" in certain jurisdictions). In most jurisdictions, obtaining a patent requires filing a patent application with a national patent office. The patent office reviews the invention described in the application to determine whether it meets the applicable patent validity requirements. If the patent office grants a patent, the owner obtains the right to exclude anyone else from making, using, selling, or importing the patented subject matter for a fixed period of time. An inventor who obtains a patent on an invention thus acquires exclusive rights to the invention, and can leverage those rights to profit by selling or licensing the invention. A patent generally lasts for twenty years from the date the inventor applied for protection. After the patent lapses, the subject matter enters the public domain and anyone is free to make the patented invention.

Copyright law provides protection for a wide range of literary and artistic expression, including books, music, dance, dramas, computer programs, movies, and fine arts. A work is protected by copyright the moment an original work of authorship is fixed in a tangible medium of expression. Thus, copyright protection cannot cover an idea, but covers a particular form or manner in which an idea is expressed. In most countries and contexts, no application or registration is required. The owner of a copyright possesses the exclusive rights to reproduce the work, prepare derivative works, distribute copies, and to perform or display the work. Similar to patent protection, the owner of a copyright can exercise the exclusive rights over the subject matter to profit from the subject intellectual creation. Copyright protection lasts substantially longer than patent protection, generally running for the duration of the author's life plus fifty to ninety-nine additional years, depending on the jurisdiction. As with patent protection, once the copyright term ends a work enters the public domain and is freely available for anyone to copy.

Given the length of copyright protection, however, works are slow to enter the public domain.

As even this briefest of introductions to intellectual property law makes evident, the law conceptualizes creativity as falling into two distinct fields: artistic creativity and inventive creativity. Copyright law and patent law differ starkly in their subject matter, the means of acquiring intellectual property rights, requirements for obtaining protection, and the scope and duration of rights. This division maps somewhat loosely onto a tripartite division of human creativity that has been proposed by several experts in the field. Though it is still a matter of debate, certain analyses indicate three thematic areas of creativity: arts, empathy/communication, and math/science (Baer & Kaufman, 2005). Creativity in the arts would loosely overlap with copyright protection, and creativity in math and science would loosely overlap with patent protection. In general, there is no intellectual property protection available for creative achievement in empathy/communication.

Beyond this division between fields of creativity at the broadest echelon, however, copyright and patent law each generally take a one-size-fits-all approach to intellectual property protection (Mandel, 2012; Carroll, 2009). Stated in the language of creativity research, intellectual property law tends not to differentiate at a domain-specific level of creativity. The same patent law generally applies whether one patents a better mousetrap, component of a cell phone, or new nanobiotechnological process. The same copyright law generally applies to literary works, musical compositions, and artistic creations.

This broad brush approach to intellectual property protection has been criticized by several experts for failing to recognize that the context and process of innovation in different fields varies greatly (Burk & Lemley, 2009; Carroll, 2009). Creativity research supports these concerns to some extent. Though there are likely some common features of creativity across the patentable and copyrightable domains (Plucker, 2005), it also appears that human modes and methods of creativity differ greatly between these fields as well (Baer & Kaufman, 2005). This may be particularly troubling because intellectual property rights attach to real-world creative endpoints, and it is precisely in real-world application where creativity may be most domain specific (Plucker, 2005).

How intellectual property law conceptualizes creativity has been criticized in other regards as well. Several legal scholars have taken issue with patent and copyright law's apparent bias towards a romantic view of individual authors and inventors achieving creative works (Sibley, 2008; Kwall, 2001; Jaszi, 1991). This critique finds support among creativity psychologists who have long challenged such individualistic perceptions of creative achievement (Glăveanu, 2010; Amabile, 1996). Social and cultural theories of creativity now recognize that creativity takes place within a complex milieu of social relations and cultural practices; creativity is not simply the result of individual, internal dispositions (Glăveanu, 2010; Hennessey, 2003). Intellectual property law's simplistic views of solitary authors and inventors have been debunked by several scholars, but the law changes slowly and these misperceptions have significant staying power in legal doctrine (Sawyer, 2008; Jaszi, 1991).

Differences across the artistic versus innovation fields can also play out in the policy objectives of patent and copyright law.[2] One prominent view holds that the purpose of intellectual property law is to incentivize creative and innovative activity (Fromer, 2012; Burk & Lemley, 2003). Under this perspective, patent and copyright protection exist based on the rationale that providing authors and inventors with the potential for intellectual property rights will induce them to engage in greater innovative activity than they would otherwise. Absent intellectual property law, an inventor might not build a better mousetrap or a director might not produce the next blockbuster motion picture because anyone would be free to copy the creation and the inventor or director would not be able to profit from it. With patent or copyright rights, on the other hand, the inventor or author can secure protection for his or her creation and therefore is incentivized to create and commercialize the work to a greater degree in the first instance. This utilitarian incentive perspective of intellectual property rights is particularly dominant in the United States, where it has a basis in the United States Constitution and has been repeatedly affirmed by the United States Supreme Court (U.S. Const.; Mayo Collaborative Servs. v. Prometheus Labs, 2012; Feist Publications v. Rural Telephone Services, 1991).

An alternative intellectual property rights policy perspective derives from John Locke's labor theory of property rights and similar concepts to reason that authors and inventors should hold natural rights in their creative works (Merges, 2011; Gordon, 1993). This equitable perspective views individuals as automatically entitled to the fruits of their efforts. Natural rights theory supports intellectual property protection on the basis that a creator is morally entitled to control the copying and distribution of inventions or artistic creations produced as a result of the creator's own labor and effort.

A third school of intellectual property policy contends, based on reasoning from Kant and Hegel, that intellectual property rights can advance an expressive function for creators (Fromer, 2012; Radin, 1987). Intellectual property rights should be protected under this rationale to promote greater personal freedom, human flourishing, and cultural development. Just as individuals use physical property, such as homes or clothing, to express their personality, an individual's intellectual creations can achieve similar objectives.

Consistent with the natural rights and expressive perspectives of intellectual property rights, several European countries and other jurisdictions endow authors with significant "moral rights" in copyrighted works (Ginsburg, 2010). These moral rights can include a right of attribution (requiring that an author of a work be identified), a right to publish a work anonymously or pseudonymously, and a right of integrity (permitting the author of a work to prevent others from distorting the work in a way that would injure the author's reputation). Even if an author assigns her or his copyright in a work to another party, the author still retains moral rights in the work.

---

[2] The following discussion on the policy objectives of intellectual property law is drawn from Mandel (2014).

Though the varying justifications for intellectual property law differ in their import for a number of law and policy matters, each interacts with creativity in several regards. The natural rights perspective recognizes intellectual property law as necessary to protect the fruits of creators' labor, while expressive rights proponents view intellectual property law as advancing people's ability to enrich their lives through creative expression. Under each of these perspectives, how people evaluate creativity is an important component of the intellectual property system. The incentive theory views the primary objective of intellectual property law as promoting creativity. Understanding how the law can (and cannot) incentivize creativity is necessary to achieving successful intellectual property law under this perspective.

Despite the central role that creativity plays in intellectual property law, legal research has been slow to investigate how the law actually interacts with creativity. Recently, a number of experimental studies have begun to fill this void, exploring people's ability to measure creativity pursuant to intellectual property law, how intellectual property law may affect creative activity and effort, the effect of creativity on perceptions of intellectual property rights, and how individuals conceptualize intellectual property law and creativity in relation to it. The following sections explore current research in each of these areas.

Measuring Creativity

In order to obtain a patent, an applicant must demonstrate that the subject invention is useful, new, and nonobvious. The utility standard simply mandates that the invention does what the inventor claims it does and that what the invention does is useful to society in some way. The novelty requirement requires that the subject matter of the invention itself has not been patented, published, or otherwise made available to the public before. The nonobviousness standard goes further; it states that a patent shall not issue for an invention "if the differences between the claimed invention and the prior art are such that the claimed invention as a whole would have been obvious ... to a person having ordinary skill in the art to which the claimed invention pertains" (35 U.S.C. §103).

The nonobviousness requirement thus sets out a creativity threshold for patentability. Patents are not available for trivial advances over the prior state of the technological art, but only for advances that are "nonobvious" to those skilled in the field. The nonobviousness requirement is the most critical, core patent validity standard. It is the requirement that is both the most commonly litigated patent validity issue and is the validity requirement most likely to result in a patent being held invalid.

Setting a creativity threshold for patentability presents a number of theoretical and practical challenges. Creativity researchers generally do not recognize any such thresholds in creativity (Sawyer, 2008). Creativity experts do distinguish between what is creative and what is not creative (Sawyer, 2008; Simonton, 1999), but this is different from the nonobviousness requirement, which recognizes some inventions as possessing creativity, but not enough creativity to merit patent protection.[3] The Supreme Court's most recent decision on the nonobviousness standard postulates a distinction between "ordinary creativity" on the one hand and creativity that satisfies the nonobviousness threshold on the other (KSR v. Teleflex, 2007). This differentiation does not appear to have a basis in creativity theory or research. Exacerbating this challenge, the Patent Act does not define the term "obvious," and neither the Supreme Court nor the Federal Circuit – the federal appeals court with jurisdiction over most patent appeals – has done so either.

In part because of the perceived challenge of measuring creativity, copyright law has a minimalist creativity threshold for protection. In order to obtain a copyright, an author must demonstrate that a work is original. Originality simply requires that the work was not copied and was the product of some minimal degree of creativity on the part of the author (Feist Publications v. Rural Telephone, 1991). Originality thus only requires a decision-maker to evaluate that at least some modicum of creativity is present, but not to evaluate that creativity quantitatively. This copyright standard for creativity is akin to how creativity researchers conceptualize the "novelty" requirement for creativity (Sawyer, 2008; Amabile, 1996). In explaining why the originality standard presents a low bar for creativity, Supreme Court Justice Oliver Wendell Holmes, Jr. famously wrote, "It would be a dangerous undertaking for persons trained only to the law to constitute themselves final judges of the worth of pictorial illustrations" (Bleistein v. Donaldson Lithographing, 1903).

The reasons for the divergence between the creativity thresholds in copyright and patent law lie in a combination of differing historical development, different mediums of creative endeavor, differing public perceptions of the fields, and possibly differing policy objectives (Buccafusco et al. 2014; Mandel, 2010). Several commentators have argued for changing the creativity thresholds in copyright or patent law in order to achieve various policy objectives (Parchomovsky & Stein, 2009; Miller, 2009; Jaffe & Lerner, 2004). The thresholds have become so ingrained throughout each field's doctrine, however, that any change is extremely unlikely.

The challenge of evaluating nonobviousness in patent law does not end with the difficulty of measuring the creativity of an invention. The nonobviousness standard also requires the decision-maker to make an historical judgment: whether the invention would have been obvious at the time the patent application on the invention was filed in the past. To reach a proper nonobviousness conclusion, the decision-maker must step backward in time to a moment just before the invention was achieved. Evaluating nonobviousness thus requires decision-makers to make a judgment about creativity in hindsight. Though the Supreme Court recognized the potential risk of hindsight bias in nonobviousness decisions in the Court's first

---

[3] Intriguingly, this "threshold" concept of creativity bears some resemblance to pre-psychological notions of creativity from the eighteenth and nineteenth centuries and before. Creative geniuses in those eras were viewed as unique individuals, chosen by God or their biology, that stood apart from ordinary people (Glăveanu, 2010). These perspectives distinguished genius creativity from ordinary person creativity, and, it was during the mid-nineteenth century that the concept of nonobviousness began to emerge (Mandel, 2006; Hotchkiss v. Greenwood, 1850).

decision on the matter (Graham v. John Deere, 1966), the existence and scope of the hindsight bias in patent decisions had never been tested until recently.

Because the nonobviousness validity standard requires a decision-maker to make an *ex ante* judgment (whether the invention was obvious at the time of filing) after having received *ex post* information (the invention), hindsight bias is expected to impact the analysis. I conducted a series of experiments to test this hypothesis (Mandel, 2007; Mandel, 2006). Participant mock jurors were provided with hypothetical fact scenarios concerning an invention, either involving a new fishing lure or a new baseball instruction product. The scenarios included background information about the field of art of the invention, a variety of prior art reference information, a description of the problem that a person cast in the role of the inventor was working on, and a questionnaire. The scenarios were selected for inventions that would be easy for mock jurors to comprehend, based on the facts of actual issued patents that were challenged on nonobviousness validity grounds in litigation.

To assess the impact of the hindsight effect without biasing individual responses, a between-subjects experimental design was used. The foresight (control) condition included all of the lead-up information and ended with the scenario character trying to solve the identified problem. The hindsight condition was identical to the foresight condition except that it had one additional sentence at its end which stated that the character had come up with a solution, and stated what the solution was.

Participants rated inventions as nonobvious significantly more frequently in foresight than in hindsight in both the baseball scenario ($X^2=25.203$, Fisher's $p<.001$) and the fishing lure scenario ($X^2=10.623$, Fisher's $p<.01$). For the baseball scenario, 24 percent of participants in the foresight condition thought that a solution to the problem was obvious, while 76 percent of participants in the hindsight condition thought that a solution was obvious at a time before the invention was achieved. Results were similar for the fishing lure scenario: 23 percent of participants in the foresight condition thought that a solution to the problem was obvious, while 59 percent of those in the hindsight condition thought that a solution was obvious (Mandel, 2006).

The judiciary has developed various rules in an effort to combat the hindsight bias in patent law. These include Model Patent Jury Instructions (Federal Circuit Bar Association, 2010; American Intellectual Property Law Association, 2015); Supreme Court doctrine on how to analyze nonobviousness decisions (KSR v. Teleflex, 2007; Graham v. John Deere, 1966); and Federal Circuit Court of Appeals doctrine concerning how a decision-maker should analyze nonobviousness cases, which was subsequently overturned by the Supreme Court (KSR v. Teleflex, 2007). Follow-up studies analyzed whether any of these attempted debiasing practices are effective at mitigating the hindsight bias in nonobviousness decisions. None of the instructions or doctrine were found to have a statistically significant effect on reducing the hindsight effect (Mandel, 2006; Mandel, 2007).

These studies indicate a significant limitation on people's ability to judge creativity in hindsight. Once a person knows the solution to a problem, that person tends to evaluate the solution as more obvious than they would have prior to the solution knowledge. These results raise a substantial challenge for patent law, which at its heart requires decision-makers to evaluate whether a historic creative achievement was obvious to people of ordinary skill in the art at the time the patentee filed the patent application. More broadly, the results raise concerns regarding judgments about creativity in any context once an evaluator knows what the creative output is.

Motivating Creativity

The dominant view of patent law and copyright law in the United States is that such intellectual property rights exist to serve incentivization objectives. These incentive goals include inspiring inventors and authors to invent or create an intellectual work in the first instance, to distribute and commercialize their works, and to disclose an invention in the context of patent law (Eisenberg, 1989). Whether the potential grant of an intellectual property right actually motivates creativity is therefore a central question for intellectual property law.

Creativity research indicates that intrinsically motivated work (i.e., doing something for its own sake) often produces more creative output than extrinsically motivated work (i.e., work motivated by an external goal) (Amabile, 1996; Hennessey, 2003). Though these effects are context-dependent (Eisenberger & Cameron, 1996), the results raise a potential challenge for intellectual property law because the law's ability to promote creativity may be limited, or even detrimental, to the extent it turns an artist's or inventor's internally motivated activity into one conducted primarily for a copyright or patent prize (Mandel, 2011).

Trying to study the effect of intellectual property law on creativity presents numerous hurdles. Studies conducted in real-world contexts contain so many exogenous variables that it is rarely possible to pin any particular effects on intellectual property rights, and controlled experiments can never capture all the factors that go into real-world innovation efforts. Nevertheless, several researchers have tried to investigate how intellectual property law may, or may not, influence creativity.

Jessica Silbey has studied how intellectual property law interacts with creativity through qualitative field research involving real-world creators (Silbey, 2015). Silbey conducted a series of in-depth interviews with more than fifty people involved in the creative process in a wide range of arts and sciences. She found that intellectual property rights tend to play a relatively small role in the interviewee's self-identified reasons that they create and innovate. Rather, many creators spoke to motivation inspired by reputational goals, the challenges of creativity and innovation, collaboration, and audience appreciation.

Other researchers have tried to study the interaction between intellectual property rights and creativity through laboratory experiments. Andrew Torrance and Bill Tomlinson attempted to examine the relationship between patent protection and creativity by designing a computer-simulated patenting game (Torrance and Tomlinson, 2009). Their simulation provides a networked multi-user environment in which participants piece together conceptual elements into imaginary "inventions" that are valued based on a preset database. In this context, the experiment actually involves a "search" task, rather than what is commonly understood to be creativity, but may be relevant to some forms of innovation. The participants could license, assign, buy, infringe, or enforce patents on their inventions in the simulation, analogous to the real-world context. The study was run in conditions that approximated a pure patenting environment, an environment that allowed participants to either patent their inventions or make them available as open source, and a pure open commons environment in which the inventions received no protection and would be freely available.

The researchers found that there was not a significant difference in the number of unique inventions achieved (as defined within the context of the study) between the pure patent and the hybrid or commons environment, but that participants in the pure commons system achieved more inventions than participants in the hybrid system. Thus, a simulated system that combined patent and open source options, as do actual patent systems, produced fewer different inventions than the commons environment (Torrance & Tomlinson, 2009).

Torrance and Tomlinson used the same patent-simulation model to test the effect of different remedy rules for patent infringement on innovation behavior. They designed conditions that varied based on whether a patent owner could obtain both monetary payment and an injunction for infringement, only one of these options, or neither (Torrance & Tomlinson, 2011). This study found that rates of innovation were lowest in the model that simulated the availability of both damages and injunctions (which is similar to current law), and greatest in the model where no remedy for patent infringement was available.

Another set of researchers have explored how intellectual property law may influence creativity in a very different way. Christopher Buccafusco, Zachary Burns, Jeanne Fromer, and Christopher Sprigman designed an experiment to try to test whether the disparate creativity thresholds for copyright versus patent protection might have differing effects on creative efforts (Buccafusco et al., 2014). As discussed above, the creativity threshold for copyright protection is minimal. In the Supreme Court's words, the requisite level "is extremely low; even a slight amount will suffice" (Feist Publications v. Rural Telephone Service, 1991). Patent protection, on the other hand, requires the inventor to achieve an elevated "nonobvious" innovation (KSR v. Teleflex, 2007).

Buccafusco et al. designed a series of experiments in which the participants were invited to complete a variety of creative tasks in exchange for an opportunity to win a $500 prize. The authors varied how the prize would be awarded in an effort to simulate differing creativity thresholds. In the "no incentive" condition, subjects were told that although their performance would be scored, the creativity of their performance would not affect their chance to win a prize. In a "copyright" condition, subjects were told that for each point they received, they would receive one lottery ticket for the prize, so a higher score would increase the odds of winning a prize. Finally, in "patent" conditions subjects were told that only subjects whose performance exceeded a certain relative threshold, such as being in the top 25 percent of performances, would receive one lottery ticket for each point they received. Thus, in the patent condition, higher scores would increase one's odds of winning a prize, but only if the score was sufficiently high to place the participant above the threshold.

The results of the experiments were mixed. For a computational creativity task requiring convergent thinking, the authors found that participants in the patent conditions performed significantly better than participants in the other conditions, and that there was no difference in performance between subjects in the copyright and no incentive conditions. Based on participants' answers to a series of questions, it appears that the subjects in the copyright condition were less motivated and paid less attention to the task than subjects in the patent condition. A separate verbal creativity task that required divergent thinking produced roughly similar results. For an experiment involving creativity analysis of a spatial figure, on the other hand, there were no significant differences across the conditions (Buccafusco et al., 2014).

The results of these studies suggest that a nontrivial creativity threshold for intellectual property protection may motivate work of greater creativity. The effects may vary depending on the type of creativity or task involved. The results do not support concerns about the extrinsic motivation of intellectual property rights dampening creativity. In the studies, the heightened threshold of the patent condition did not appear to result in any lesser creativity, such as by crowding out subjects' intrinsic motivation. That being said, all subjects were taking part in an experiment, so none were purely intrinsically motivated.

As noted above, the research findings concerning the effects on creativity of intrinsic versus extrinsic motivation are context dependent. Some research indicates that extrinsic rewards specifically contingent on creativity or high performance can increase task interest and self-determination, which in turn can lead to heightened creativity (Eisenberger & Rhoades, 2001). Buccafusco et al.'s results are partially consistent with this line of research as participants' rewards in the copyright and patent conditions were dependent on high performance. However, it was only the patent condition that sometimes produced greater creativity. In sum, the outcomes indicate that effects of extrinsic motivation on creativity are quite complex, particularly when layered on top of varying creativity thresholds, and still in need of further research.

In a related vein, Stefan Bechtold, Christopher Buccafusco, and Christopher Jon Sprigman explored how creators decide whether to borrow from existing information or to innovate around it (Bechtold et al., 2016). Most innovation is sequential: Innovators build upon the inventions and achievements of those who came before them. In the context of intellectual property protection, this means that creators must decide whether to pay to license prior patented subject matter that may enable further innovation or find a way to design around existing patents. Using a computational creativity task, subjects were shown a prior player's solution to a task, and told that the subject's payout would be modified based on how much they borrowed from the prior solution. The results were somewhat perplexing: About two-thirds of the subjects chose to innovate on their own rather than to borrow from the prior solution, but this ratio was almost entirely unaffected by the bonus the subjects received for innovating, even to the point where subjects could not have received a higher payment from innovating instead of borrowing. The authors hypothesize that there may be a fundamental personality difference between "pioneers" and "tweakers," and that these personality preferences had a greater effect on subjects' decisions about whether to borrow or innovate than did the potential payouts (Bechtold et al., 2016). Consistent with this reasoning, the results may speak to preferences related to the intrinsic motivation of a challenge, as opposed to being extrinsically motivated solely by the highest expected payout.

As the authors of all the studies note, though the results provide intriguing information about how the intellectual property system may or may not motivate creativity, it is hard to know how the experimental outcomes translate in the real world. All of the experiments involved highly abstracted contexts with relatively rapid creative tasks performed by nonprofessional, nonexpert creators. The ecological validity of this research is therefore somewhat unclear.

Valuing Creativity

Another line of intellectual property research examines the effect of creativity on how intellectual property works are valued. The endowment effect is one of best-known effects identified in behavioral economics. The endowment effect refers to the fact that people value property much more highly if they own the property than if someone else owns the property. This effect has been demonstrated in a wide variety of contexts for many types of property (Korobkin, 2003).

For intellectual property, there appears to be an equivalent "creativity effect." Individuals value a creative work more when they are the one who created it (Buccafusco & Sprigman, 2009). In one experiment, painters were invited to enter a painting into a contest for a $100 prize. The painters' valuation of the amount required for them to part with their opportunity to win the prize was much greater than individuals who were placed in the role of simply owning the same paintings, which in turn was much greater than the amount individuals placed in the role of buyers were willing to offer for the opportunity to win the prize. Creators valued their works much more than noncreator owners and potential buyers.

In follow-up questions, the researchers explored what psychological mechanisms might be causing the creativity effect. Creators appeared to have wildly overoptimistic perceptions of their probability of winning the prize. In contests involving ten paintings, where each creator averaged a ten percent chance of winning the contest, creators' mean estimate of their chance of winning was 53 percent. Creators' ratings of emotional attachment to their works and the amount of time that they reported putting into their works did not correlate with their valuations. Similarly, creators did not report any significantly greater likelihood of regret than owners or buyers. Thus, the creativity effect appears to derive from creators perceiving their works to be substantially more valuable relative to other works than appears economically rational, an effect that does not appear to relate to the amount of labor that went into the work or emotional attachment to the work. This effect could arise from an attachment that the creator feels to his or her creative work, from an overconfidence effect in judging the merit of the work, or from some combination of these two or other factors. As the authors point out, the creativity effect could mean that otherwise efficient licensing and sale of intellectual property rights may not take place (Buccafusco & Sprigman, 2009).

Conceptualizing Creativity and Intellectual Property

A final manner in which the law interacts with creativity research concerns lay understandings of intellectual property law. As discussed above, intellectual property experts and scholars generally perceive policy bases for intellectual property law that lie in incentives, natural rights, or expressive theories. It turns out that the general public understands the law quite differently.

In a series of experiments, Kristina Olson, Annie Fast, and I found that the most common perception of intellectual property law among American adults is that intellectual property law is designed to prevent plagiarism (Mandel et al., in press). These results were consistent across a wide variety of media tested, including creativity and innovation involving writing, music, painting, medicine, electronics, and software. The majority of subjects consistently reported that copying of creative material without the creator's permission should be permissible so long as the copier simply provides proper attribution to the original creator. These results generally did not differ between contexts involving inventive creativity that would be the subject of patent protection and artistic creativity that would be protected by copyright law. This study was consistent with the research by Silbey discussed above, who found that concerns about proper attribution and credit were pervasive among the creators that she interviewed (Silbey, 2015).

These studies are also consistent with psychological research on plagiarism itself, which indicate that one of the norms adults endorse concerning plagiarism is disapproval for taking credit for ideas that have been put forth by others (Park, 2003). Research on the psychology of property indicates that these norms develop at an early age. Children as young as five years old develop a dislike of people who deliberately copy the work of others (Olson & Shaw, 2011). This dislike appears to relate to the potential negative influence of copying on one's reputation (Shaw & Olson, 2014).

In the public's mind, the ethical wrong in intellectual property infringement involves taking credit for another person's creativity, not in a failure to reward the creator with intellectual property rights. This fallacy concerning the legal purpose and rule of intellectual property law likely helps to explain pervasive illegal infringing activity on the Internet, common dismissal of copyright warnings, and other infringing consumer behavior (Mandel et al., 2015). Prior to these studies, the received wisdom was that the public is ethically dismissive or indifferent towards intellectual property rights. This research indicates instead that experts may have failed to comprehend what the public's conception of intellectual property law actually is.

The studies identify several additional intellectual property law findings that pertain to how individuals tend to view creativity and intellectual property rights. For example, the majority of respondents perceived that intellectual property rights were too broad and too strong, knowledge of intellectual property law did not affect opinions about what the law should be, and there were significant demographic and cultural divides concerning preferences for the strength of intellectual property rights, particularly concerning individuals' gender, age, political identity, and income. On the latter finding, in general, women, older individuals, conservatives, and wealthier individuals tended to prefer stronger intellectual property protection.

Conclusion

The study of creativity in law is still at a relatively nascent stage, but has been progressing rapidly. Twenty years ago, legal studies in most areas of law tended to ignore the teachings of psychological and other research on creativity. Over the past decade, legal scholars have not only made rapid advances in integrating lessons from other disciplines, but have also implemented a variety of original creativity research with direct application in law. This legal research on creativity has been most prevalent in intellectual property law where studies have begun to explore how creativity is evaluated under the law, how the law motivates creativity, and public perceptions of creativity and the law.

These studies, however, represent only a start. There are still significant avenues for further research concerning whether and how intellectual property law influences creativity, how creativity can be measured for intellectual property purposes, and how intellectual property rights interact with creators in the real-world environment.

References

35 U.S.C. §103 (2012).

Amabile, T. M. (1996). *Creativity in context*. Boulder, CO: Westview Press.

American Intellectual Property Law Association (2015). *Model Patent Jury Instructions*. AIPLA.

Baer, J., & Kaufman, J. C. (2005). Bridging generality and specificity: The Amusement Park Theoretical (APT) model of creativity. *Roeper Review, 27*(3), 158–163.

Bechtold, S., Buccafusco, C., & Sprigman, C. J. (2016). Innovation heuristics: Experiments on sequential creativity in intellectual property. *Indiana Law Review, 91*, 1251–1307.

Bleistein v. Donaldson Lithographing Co., 188 U.S. 239 (1903).

Brest, P., & Kreiger, L. H. (1999). Lawyers as problem solvers. *Temple Law Review, 72*(4), 811–832.

Buccafusco, C., & Sprigman, C. J. (2009). The creativity effect. *University of Chicago Law Review, 78*(1), 31–52.

Buccafusco, C., Burns, Z. C., Fromer, J. C., & Sprigman, C. J. (2014). Experimental tests of intellectual property laws' creativity thresholds. *Texas Law Review, 92*(7), 1921–1980.

Burk, D. L., & Lemley, M. A. (2003). Policy levers in patent law. *Virginia Law Review, 89*(7), 1575–2003.

Burk, D. L., & Lemley, M. A. (2009). *The patent crisis and how the courts can solve it.* Chicago, IL: University of Chicago Press.

Carroll, M. (2009). One size does not fit all: A framework for tailoring intellectual property rights. *Ohio State Law Journal, 70*(6), 1361–1434.

Dastar Corporation v. Twentieth Century Fox Film Corporation, 539 U.S. 23 (2003).

Eisenberg, R. (1989). Patents and the progress of science: Exclusive rights and experimental use. *University of Chicago Law Review, 56*(3), 1017–1086.

Eisenberger, R., & Cameron, J. (1996). Detrimental effects of reward: Reality or myth? *American Psychologist, 51*(11), 1153–1166.

Eisenberger, R., & Rhoades, L. (2001). Incremental effects of reward on creativity. *Journal of Personality and Social Psychology, 81*(4), 728.

Federal Circuit Bar Association (2010). *Model Patent Jury Instructions.* Federal Circuit Bar Association.

Feist Publications, Inc., v. Rural Telephone Service Co., 499 U.S. 340 (1991).

Fromer, J. C. (2012). Expressive incentives in intellectual property. *Virginia Law Review, 98*(8), 1745–1824.

Ginsburg, J. C. (2010). "European Copyright Code" – Back to first principles (with some additional detail). *Journal of the Copyright Society of the U.S.A., 58*(2), 265–300.

Glăveanu, V. P. (2010). Paradigms in the study of creativity: Introducing the perspective of cultural psychology. *New Ideas in Psychology, 28*(1), 79–93.

Gordon, W. J. (1993). A property right in self-expression: Equality and individualism in the natural law of intellectual property. *Yale Law Journal, 102*(7), 1533–1609.

Graham v. John Deere Co., 383 U.S. 1 (1966)

Hennessey, B. (2003). Is the social psychology of creativity really social? Moving beyond a focus on the individual. In P. Paulus & B. Nijstad (Eds.), *Group creativity: Innovation through collaboration* (pp. 181–201). New York, NY: Oxford University Press.

Hotchkiss v. Greenwood, 52 U.S. 248 (1850).

Jaffe, A.B., & Lerner, J. (2004). *Innovation and its discontents. How our broken patent system is endangering innovation and progress, and what to do about it.* Princeton, NJ: Princeton University Press.

Jaszi, P. (1991). Towards a theory of copyright: The metamorphoses of "authorship." *Duke Law Journal, 40*(2), 455–502.

Korobkin, R. B. (2003). The endowment effect and legal analysis. *Northwestern Law Review, 97*(3), 1227–1291.

KSR Int'l Co. v. Teleflex, Inc., 550 U.S. 398 (2007).

Kwall, R. (2001). "Author-Stories:" Narrative's implications for moral rights and copyright's joint authorship doctrine, *Southern California Law Review, 75*(1), 1–64.

Mandel, G. N. (2006). Patently non-obvious: Empirical demonstration that the hindsight bias renders patent decisions irrational. *Ohio State Law Journal, 67*(1), 1391–1463.

Mandel, G. N. (2007). Patently non-obvious II: Experimental study on the hindsight bias issue before the Supreme Court in KSR v. Teleflex. *Yale Journal of Law & Technology, 9*(1), 1–43.

Mandel, G. N. (2010). Left brain v. right brain: Competing conceptions of creativity in intellectual property law. *University of California Law Review, 44*(1), 283–361.

Mandel, G. N. (2011). To promote the creative progress: Intellectual property law and the psychology of creativity. *Notre Dame Law Review, 86*(5), 1999–2026.

Mandel, G. N. (2012). Proxy signals: Capturing private information for public benefit. *Washington University Law Review, 90*(1), 1–25.

Mandel, G. N. (2014). The public perception of intellectual property. *Florida Law Review, 66*(1), 261–312.

Mandel, G. N. Fast, A. A., & Olson, K. R. (2016). Intellectual property law's plagiarism fallacy. *BYU Law Review* 2015, 915–984.

Mayo Collaborative Services v. Prometheus Laboratories, Inc., 132 S. Ct. 1289 (2012).

Menkel-Meadow, C. (1999). Lawyer as problem solver and third-party neutral: Creativity and nonpartisanship in lawyering, *Temple Law Review, 72*(4), 785–810.

Merges, R. (2011). *Justifying intellectual property.* Cambridge, MA: Harvard University Press.

Miller, J. S. (2009). Hoisting originality. *Cardozo Law Review, 31*(2), 451–496.

Olson, K. R., & Shaw, A. (2011). "No fair, copycat!": What children's response to plagiarism tells us about their understanding of ideas. *Developmental Science, 14*(2), 431–439.

Parchomovsky, G., & Stein, A. (2009). Originality. *Virginia Law Review, 95*(6), 1505–1550.

Park, C. (2003). In (other) people's words: Plagiarism by students – literature and lessons. *Assessment & Evaluation in Higher Education, 28*(5), 471–488.

Plucker, J. A. (2005). The (relatively) generalist view of creativity. In J. C. Kaufman & J. Baer (Eds.), *Creativity across domains: Faces of the muse* (pp. 307–312). Mahweh, NJ: Lawrence Erlbaum Associates.

Sawyer, R. K. (2008). Creativity, innovation, and obviousness. *Lewis & Clark Law Review, 12*(2), 461–488.

Shaw, A., & Olson, K. (2014). Whose idea is it anyway? The importance of reputation in acknowledgement. *Developmental Science, 18*(3), 502–509.

Silbey, J. (2008). The mythical beginnings of intellectual property, *George Mason Law Review, 15*(2), 319–382.

Silbey, J. M. (2015). *The eureka myth: Creators, innovators and everyday intellectual property.* Stanford, CA: Stanford University Press.

Simonton, D. K. (1999). *Origins of genius: Darwinian perspectives on creativity.* New York: Oxford University Press.

Radin, M. J. (1987). Market-inalienability. *Harvard Law Review, 100*(8), 1849–1889.

Torrance, A. W., & Tomlinson, B. (2009). Patents and the regress of the useful arts. *Columbia Science & Technology Law Review, 10*, 130–168.

Torrance, A. W., & Tomlinson, B. (2011). Property rules, liability rules, and patents: One experimental view of the cathedral. *Yale Journal of Law & Technology, 14*(1), 138–161.

US Constitution art. I, § 8, cl. 8.

25 Gastronomy and Culinary Creativity

Jeou-Shyan Horng

Department of Food and Beverage Management, Jinwen University of Science and Technology

Lin Lin

Department of Culinary Arts, I-Shou University

Abstract

Development of creativity and innovation in culinary art is a continuous process which brought us the diversity of current food and cuisines. From the nouvelle cuisine in the 1970s to fusion cuisine and molecular cuisine, various innovations suggested that culinary creativity is closely integrated with culture, art, science, and technology. This chapter is going to review the characteristics and evaluation principles of the Four Ps of culinary creativity (creative culinary person, creative culinary process, creative culinary products, and environmental factors (places)) affecting culinary creativity. Also, this chapter points out trends of culinary creativity to serve as references for chefs now and in the future. Such trends include green gastronomy, health-improved culinary, new technology application, and culinary localization and globalization.

1 Development of Culinary Creativity

The phrase "culinary arts" is the combination of culinary and arts, which has been widely acknowledged as a discipline that mixes food science, food preparation, cooking skills, aesthetics, and culinary culture. In modern times, a culinary professional should have specialized knowledge and skills in food as well as cultural and artistic knowledge. Hegarty & O'Mahony (2001) suggest that "gastronomy" is an artistic activity, and all the preparations for food are not only for consumption, but also contain status, ritual, and art. Balazs (2002) believes that culinary arts, like film, drama, and fashion industries, essentially belong to the creative industry. A creative chef is an artist with food who has the ability to free his/her mind from any set norms and give greater meaning to food by handling the materials in a different way (Hegarty & O'Mahony, 2001). Creativity is the essence of the development of culinary arts from the perspectives of skill, art, or knowledge. The aforementioned studies also point out the diversity of culinary arts. The development and cultivation of higher-order ability of culinary are more and more valued by the catering industry, academic research, and education.

Due to the fact that people have more and more dining choices and expectations, competition in the food industry has become increasingly intense. It is important for a restaurant to change the menu or offer new dishes in order to meet the constantly changing needs of customers. Menu development is one of the business strategies to ensure the long-term success of a restaurant business, and effective development could satisfy customer's needs (The Culinary of Institute of American, 2011. From the fast-food restaurant chains to the high-end restaurants, it is necessary for all the chefs and managers to maintain popularity. The chefs would lose competitiveness if they couldn't meet the requirements of the consumers (Perlik, 2002). Therefore, the role of a chef has changed from a craftsman to a creative inventor who constantly thinks of improving the culinary quality through re-designing the restaurant's menu to appeal to the consumers. Creative dishes could attract more consumers, enhance competitiveness of the restaurant, and make the restaurant unique.

There are many food programs, cooking shows, and cooking competitions on television. Food magazines and online food news are also very abundant and popular. The spread of knowledge greatly stimulates consumer's diverse demands for food (Andersson & Mossberg, 2004; Santich, 2004). The more the consumers learn about food, the more their expectations grow. Moreover, gastronomy tourism becomes more and more popular, and gourmet food plays an important role in the marketing strategies for tourist attractions (Horng & Tsai, 2010). It could promote the local culture and increase the attractiveness of the city (Okumus et al., 2007). Tourists look forward to experiencing the traditional cuisine and food specialties; therefore, the creativity and improvement in food products could maximize the beneficial effects of local gourmet and increase tourists' acceptance of and preference for exotic food.

From a historical perspective, the development of creativity and innovation in culinary art is a continuous process. We have grown accustomed to taking food for granted, such as bread, cheese, and wine, which have been developed and improved over hundreds, even thousands, of years, and finally evolved into the delicacy that we know today. The creativity and originality of the chef has made today's dietary life and culinary culture. Culinary arts has become a global topic with profound historic meaning and which touches every aspect of life. Hence, this chapter will introduce three contemporary issues of creativity in culinary arts: nouvelle cuisine, fusion cuisine, and molecular cuisine.

1.1 Nouvelle Cuisine

Food plays a major role in French culture, and French celebrity chefs have long been role models for those interested in learning culinary skills. The development of food culture in France can be roughly divided into haute cuisine, cuisine bourgeois, and nouvelle cuisine. Haute cuisine developed from the kitchens of French aristocracy during the seventeenth century. It is widely agreed that haute cuisine laid the foundation for French cuisine and represents the soul of French cooking (Petruzzaelli & Savino, 2014). Cuisine bourgeois is a style of French traditional rural cuisine that is popular among the middle class. However, the word "luxury" has been labeled as a political slogan for social injustice since 1960, when the new value of healthy diet began to emerge. A slender figure became the symbol of social position, which was considered as a means of compensation for unrestrained development.

The term "nouvelle cuisine" can be traced back to the cookbooks of the 1970s. The French food writers Henri Gault and Christian Millau used the term "nouvelle cuisine" for the first time in the *Gault Millau* magazine, which focused on four values: truth, lightness, simplicity, and imagination. Nouvelle cuisine focuses on more healthy cooking methods by using natural flavor and ingredients, and encourages creativity and innovation in the kitchen (Mennell, 1985).

Rao, Monin, and Durand (2003) point out that the nouvelle cuisine movement sought to turn chefs into inventors rather than mere technicians. The advocates of nouvelle cuisine celebrated their differences with classical cuisine but also exploited the foundations of classical cuisine for their project. Bocuse and Chapel, two of the most famous chefs in France, suggested that chefs should create and invent new recipes rather than simply following Escoffier's techniques.[1] Therefore, nouvelle cuisine chefs were conceptualist avant-gardes and customers often went to their restaurant to enjoy the shock of the new.

Rao, Monin, and Durand (2003) distinguish between haute cuisine and nouvelle cuisine taking into account the following six aspects: culinary rhetoric, cooking methods, choice of ingredients, role of the chef, organization of the menu, and food presentation. The culinary rhetoric (names of dishes) of nouvelle cuisine emphasizes innovation and imagination; the rules of nouvelle cuisine are basically cross-cultural, combining cooking techniques in various ways, or using exotic foreign cuisine techniques; the ingredients of nouvelle cuisine are known for health and diversity, which reduce the traditional use of butter in French cuisine; the chefs of nouvelle cuisine play the role of an innovator or creator; the nouvelle cuisine menu is short and simple because it requires low inventories and fresh ingredients. Symmetry and luxury are vital to the food presentation of haute cuisine, while nouvelle cuisine combines innovation with inspiration from rural cuisine and Japanese cuisine by using aesthetic concepts of asymmetrical balance and white space in food design. Nouvelle cuisine still makes up a large proportion of the restaurants listed in the *Michelin Guide*. It can be foreseen that the nouvelle style of cooking, which is simple, fresh, healthy, and creative, will continue to affect the development of culinary arts and its values.

1.2 Fusion Cuisine

In recent years, fusion cuisine or cross-cultural cuisine has become popular in many countries. These terms first appeared in some US states with large Asian populations such as California or Hawaii, but they can now be seen everywhere. There are many factors that contribute to the development of the globalization of

[1] Georges Auguste Escoffier (1846–1935) was a legendary French chef who popularized traditional French cooking method, and he also simplified and modernized French cuisine. His *Le Guide Culinaire* was a major textbook and reference book for both the industry and academia.

cuisine. Similar food materials are available in the supermarkets or bazaars all over the world because of European colonization and global capitalism. Cuisine associated with a specific culture or geographic region began to take root in other places along with the transfer of migrants or industries to foreign countries. It is important for new immigrants to keep themselves within the cultural boundaries regarding "how to cook" or "what to eat." They are more likely to choose accustomed tastes, though they may also conform to the dominant culture, which could create new foods through cultural communication and promote gastronomic globalization (Kittler & Sucher, 2004). Richard Wilk (1999) points out that the identities of national and local cuisines are actually in a constant state of flux and change. In today's crisis of global capitalism, cultural contact, fusion, and change occur almost everywhere through foreign media, marketing, tourism, and migration.

Cwiertka (1999) mentioned the influence and impact of culinary globalization on the development of culinary arts. Culinary globalization is known as an international melting pot in which various culinary arts combine and blend into each other. Both exquisite nouvelle cuisine and daily home cooking are included in culinary globalization. The chef either uses old cooking methods with new and unfamiliar ingredients, or uses new cooking methods with old ingredients. Therefore, the invented dishes appear to be unprecedented, which blend different ingredients across geographic regions, cooking methods, dietary habits, and some other historical factors. Japanese cuisine has been influenced by Western cuisine. Rice is frequently used in Japanese-Western fusion cuisine because it could be served along with Western cuisine, topped with a pork cutlet, or made into a rice burger. On the other hand, Japanese cuisine also affected Western cuisine. Many famous Western chefs began to learn Japanese cooking methods and use Japanese food ingredients. For instance, raw fish is not easy to find in some Western countries and some people are not used to it. Therefore, Western chefs make sushi with smoked salmon and avocado instead of raw fish. This is how the famous California roll was invented (Cwiertka, 1999).

The globalization of food ingredients and cuisine has been the main trend in culinary arts since the end of the twentieth century. New combinations are created during the process of localization. Cross-cultural combinations have also been applied in the food industry to create a wide variety of products. The creolization of food ingredients, cooking techniques, tastes, and food habits will bring more excitement to culinary arts (Cwiertka, 1999). It should also be noted that the ideas of renowned chefs always come from their cross-cultural experience and their open-minded attitude; in short, appreciation of foreign food ingredients, cooking methods, and food cultures gave birth to the invention of new dishes.

1.3 Molecular Cuisine

Creativity in the art of food also includes the whole dining experience of customers, which is a unique stimulus for our five senses. For instance, a customer orders a solid cocktail at the bar counter which looks like a small table tennis ball. It melts as soon as he puts it into his mouth, and leaves a lingering taste of wine in the throat and nasal cavity. In this case, the texture and composition of the drink has been transformed in order to release a new flavor. The term "molecular gastronomy" was initially coined by the French chemist Hervé This and Hungarian physicist Nicholas Kurti in the 1980s. The basis of the theoretical framework is to investigate every little detail during the cooking process, such as the texture of the food, the changes of the temperature, the length of cooking time, and the physical and chemical transformations of food when adding different ingredients. Based on these research results, the chefs could overturn and deconstruct the traditional cooking methods and the morphological structure of a dish, and reconstruct and create new flavors, tastes, and dining experiences. For example, ice cream made with liquid nitrogen tastes richer, smoother, and creamier because it contains smaller ice crystals; espuma can be created with the use of a siphon bottle and nitrogen canister; and sodium alginate is added to juice or soup to produce the formation of gelatin substance. In other words, molecular gastronomy not only explores food by using technology; it also brings new excitement to our senses of sight, taste, and even touch.

Molecular gastronomy has also caused a lot of controversy. Many critics argued that molecular gastronomy is too pretentious and a cause of food waste, while some critics worry about food safety. However, there are also many advocates of molecular gastronomy that believe in the potential of food science to explore the chemistry of food and cooking. For example, Fat Duck, the famous molecular gastronomy restaurant in England, has been awarded three Michelin stars and was voted one of the world's best restaurants by *Restaurant Magazine*. Chef Heston Blumenthal of the Fat Duck claims that molecular gastronomy is actually a derivation of traditional cooking. Some dishes are created by applying the basic chemical reactions in cooking, like caramelization and the Maillard reaction, which fully reflect the essence of food science.

2 Culinary Creativity Research and Literature Review

Rhodes (1961) proposes that there are four Ps in creativity: Person, Process, Product, and Place (4P). In fact, many creativity researches were based on Rhodes' 4P framework. Simonton (1988) adds a fifth P, Persuasion, emphasizing that a creative idea or product must persuade and be accepted by the public, especially achieving recognition by experts. The original 4P model subsequently has evolved into a 5P model. This chapter will illustrate culinary creativity from perspectives of person, process, product, and place factors based on previous studies.

2.1 Creative Culinary Person

A previous study on Michelin chefs investigated the personal characteristics of creative chefs. The results indicate that excellent culinary professionals have played multiple roles in the workplace, including that of inventor, leader, entrepreneur, and businessman, as well as spokesman for the French culture (Balazs, 2002). Because of their great talent and creativity, they raised culinary art work to a higher level. These chefs have been found to possess special characteristics, including professional knowledge, a thirst for new knowledge, ambition, planning ability, curiosity, confidence, a risk-taking tendency, decisiveness, charisma, and courage to trust their employees (Gazzoli, 1995; Balazs, 2002). Birdir and Pearson (2000) explore the basic competencies of chefs and point out that research-focused chefs and management-focused chefs differ in their basic competencies. The research-focused chefs mainly develop new products and create new recipes based on a strong knowledge of food ingredients, sauces and stocks, and various cuisines. The management-focused chefs, on the other hand, mainly report to the employer, take care of presentation, and sell products. They often play the role of strategic planners who carry out the goals and objectives of the organization and work closely with customers.

Horng and Lee (2006) identified thirteen significant personality traits shared by creative chefs, which constitute an integrated combination of art and science essentials. Creative chefs seem to exhibit the traits of both artists and scientists, including being imaginative, curious, sensitive, open to a broad array of interests, having a huge appetite for art, passionate, self-confident, ambitious, taking reasonable risks, achievement-oriented, and perseverant, and possessing a sense of mission and honor. Creative chefs also show strong intrinsic and extrinsic motivation. They are willing to sacrifice time and money to learn and improve, and eventually get a sense of achievement and achieve self-realization with their strong interests and passion for cooking. Extrinsic motivation is also one of the important factors for creative chefs. Offering rewards can increase motivation, whether it is tangible reward like money, or a psychological reward like praise.

This result differs from previous studies on creativity. For example, studies on art suggested that an individual's creativity is more related to intrinsic motivations (Amabile, 1979). A possible reason for this difference is that culinary creativity is more closely related to product commercialization, and extrinsic rewards are the most definite and affirmative encouragement for creative chefs.

Moreover, creative chefs tend to think positively, independently, and freely. They explore other people's work, reconsider their own limitations, learn from others, and jump out of traditional frameworks. It is important for creative chefs to have a solid foundation of cooking knowledge and skills. They know not only the "facts," but also the "reasons." The skillful and flexible use of knowledge of cooking and food preparation leads to culinary creativity. Many creative chefs have multicultural experiences and living experiences in different countries, which heighten the senses and enhance experiences. They can combine the new things that they had seen and heard with their existing knowledge, and then turn their multicultural experience into inspirations for creative thinking.

2.2 Creative Culinary Process

Creativity in cuisine and culinary arts originates from continuing professional development and continuous accumulation of experiences. Beghetto, Kaufman, and Hatcher (2015) applied the 4C model of creativity to discuss the creative process of famous chefs, suggesting that culinary creativity comes from accumulating everyday creativity, and develops from mini-c to big-C. Many chefs try to expand their culinary knowledge and heighten their sensitivity to food by traveling, tasting, and reading. Traveling can provoke new thoughts and ideas and help chefs learn about local culinary traditions and foodstuffs; many chefs would like to visit other restaurants while on vacation and find out what other chefs are doing. Reading can provide innovative ideas and reinterpret old ones; therefore, many chefs are inspired from reading cookbooks, food and cookery magazines, and so on. Moreover, chefs often find their inspiration from customers' reviews (Birdir & Pearson, 2000; Dornenburg & Page, 2003).

Horng and Hu (2008) explored the process of culinary creation and propose that "preparation" is the first and hardest step during the creative process. Creative chefs have to collect more information to match or illustrate the theme of a cooking competition in order to develop their creative potential. They also learn and make breakthroughs from past failures and successes, and classify new ideas and information. The next step, "incubation and transformation," is the most important phase of the creative process. Creative chefs might have to put aside an idea that does not look promising and seek a new one instead, which is incubated and evaluated repeatedly, and make a decision after careful consideration. Sometimes a different perspective may yield new solutions. "Concretizing ideas" is also a necessary step during the creative process. Creative chefs have to improve, illustrate, or draw new ideas in different ways by applying a function of multiple transformations. Finally, the representation of the creative culinary process as well as its sub-processes is given in Figure 25.1, which shows that "idea development" contains four key phases: discovering new ideas, concretizing ideas, discussion and compromise, and clarification. It is important to discover new ideas during the creative process. Creative chefs could watch cooking competitions, use new ways to connect old ideas, or seek out a particular ingredient and cooking technique. However, the final creative work is always generated after many discussions and compromises in both individual competition and team competition. They need to discuss their ideas with other chefs and brainstorm to get new and better ideas. They also have to manage and accumulate culinary knowledge in order to help make compromises and reach a final agreement. "Clarification" is a sub-process to clarify concepts and find the final solution to a problem in a flash of insight. During this phase, abstract ideas are incubated and concretized, problems are discussed and solved, and various ideas are evaluated and applied. Finally, the sub-process of "idea evaluation" includes the following steps: find available ideas by searching memory or data, discuss and solve problems in a flash of insight, and keep looking for the best possible combination.

Ottenbacher and Harrington's (2007) innovation process model can be broken down into seven main steps based on an analysis of the Michelin-starred chefs' innovation. The major sources of inspiration are dining in colleagues' restaurants, cooking literature, and new cooking technology. The main concept screening criteria are the use of seasonal ingredients, high-quality ingredients, and compatibility with the cooking style. Chefs often use a recipe-date file and photographing concept to formulate their concept, and their market research techniques include: dining at

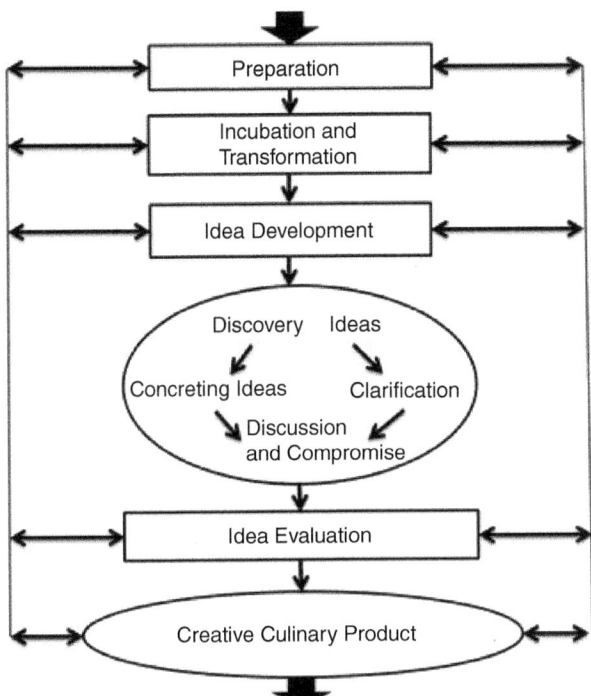

Figure 25.1 *The Creative Culinary Process Development. Adapted from Horng J. S & Hu, M. L., 2008, The mystery in the kitchen: Culinary creativity. Creativity Research Journal, 20(2), p. 225. Used with permission.*

other Michelin-starred restaurants, cooking trends used by competitors, and competitors' pricing policies.

2.3 Creative Culinary Products

Creating successful dishes is one of the most important issues for restaurant managers and chefs. The qualities needed to make a successful dish have been described and analyzed academically. Klosse, Riga, Cramwinckel, and Saris (2004) proposed six characteristics found in at least 80 percent of the described dishes from Michelin-starred restaurants, which are also called culinary success factors (CSFs), including:

(1) Name and presentation fit the expectation.
(2) Appetizing smell that fits the food.
(3) Good balance of flavor components in relation to the food.
(4) Presence of umami, also called the fifth basic taste.
(5) A mix of hard and soft textures and mouthfeel.
(6) High flavor richness.

Ottenbacher and Harrington (2007) listed the criteria Michelin-starred chefs use when developing new dishes, including seasonality of products, quality of products, fit with cooking style, cost and profitability, menu pricing considerations, fit with menu style, customer acceptance, operational factors, and so on. Kawasaki, Kasamatsu, and Nonaka (2015) summarized the following CSFs: texture, flavor, umami, main, good pairings, not too rich, good balance, cuisine style, elegance, and surprise. After an analysis of the factors, and a comparison of the dishes from Michelin-starred restaurants in Japan with that in France, they concluded that umami is used to describe the taste of glutamates and nucleotides, which has been widely recognized as the fifth basic taste, after sour, sweet, bitter, and salty.

Brunon (2007) investigated the food quality described by TV food networks and proposes five categories: functional, aesthetic, ethical, political, and ecological. From the functional perspective, "taste" is used to describe flavors of food, including sour, sweet, bitter, spicy, and so on; "texture" refers to those qualities of food that can be felt in mouth, such as crispy, firm, soft, and flexible; "freshness" refers to freshly picked, freshly made, or seasonal food; "health" is considered nutritional, medicinal, and beneficial to health; "feeling" is always used to describe experiences such as contented, happy, glad, pleasantly surprised, and yearning; "innovation" under the aesthetic category refers to new ideas or new techniques used in cooking; "distinction" is used to describe the unique species of food, seasonal products, local products, and rare products; "art" refers to the aesthetic feelings arising by sight, for example, white and beautiful could be used to describe the colors and shapes on the plate; "authenticity" under the ethical category refers to terms used to describe history or family inheritance, such as traditional, nostalgic, hundred-year-old, three generations; "care" is used to describe the effort, time, and money spent to grow, breed, or make food products, including labor-consuming, time-consuming, patience; "ecology" refers to food products without additives or natural farming. The five categories used to describe food products reflect consumers' expectations about gourmet and the values of food in our present society, which are also used by restaurant managers in menu description.

Horng and Lin (2009) proposed five properties of creative culinary products, which are described as follows:

(1) **Cooking techniques**: First of all, basic cooking techniques are required in order to produce creative culinary products. The creative chefs have to use advanced skills to make perfect products. The realization of a great creative culinary idea relies on the solid foundation of cooking techniques.
(2) **Flavor and seasoning**: All flavors should be matched and in balance. Thus, the subversion of the traditional flavor should be a pleasant surprise to customers. Moreover, it should also highlight the natural flavors of food ingredients.
(3) **Modeling and arrangement**: The arrangement of the dishes also plays an important role in creative culinary products. The shapes and decorations of the traditional dishes have been changed.
(4) **Handling of ingredients**: First, chefs must have good understanding of the special features of ingredients and basic theories of food science. Then, they could present their creative idea by applying the features of ingredients ingeniously during cooking, arrangement of the dishes, and color pairings.

The combination of various ingredients should be meaningful, logical, and well balanced in taste and sight. Creative culinary products could also integrate different cultures by combining exotic ingredients with seasonal ingredients.

(5) **Conception**: Creative culinary products must produce new ideas and introduce fresh energy into traditional cuisine. On the other hand, the food served in restaurant must take cost, consistency, and efficiency into consideration from a practical point of view (Fine, 1992).

2.4 Environmental Factors Affecting Culinary Creativity

Because of the booming food industry, as well as the diversification and popularization of culinary education, becoming a professional chef is now easier than ever before. However, the road to becoming a famous chef or be on top is still difficult, and new trainees will have to overcome many environmental obstacles. Pratten (2003) points out the environmental challenges faced by chefs today:

(1) **Training**: Training, both for food preparation and hygiene, is seen to be essential. A chef must be able to work quickly and effectively under pressure and have excellent skills and techniques. If he/she lacks practical experience from schools, the chef has to receive more on-the-job training.

(2) **Work environment**: Kitchens are hot, uncomfortable, and extremely noisy and crowded. There exists a long tradition of culinary authoritarianism. Some people give up the idea of becoming a chef because they cannot cope with the conditions.

(3) **Gender roles**: The food industry is always male dominated. In the *Michelin Guide* of 2000, of over 100 restaurants awarded a star in Paris, none had a female senior chef. Nowadays, although there are more excellent female chefs in the food industry, people still tend to question and distrust their competency.

(4) **Working hours**: Restaurants normally serve breakfast, lunch, and dinner from early in the morning till late at night. Therefore, chefs have to work long hours, and the weekends are usually the busiest. Their work schedule is contrary to normal working hours, which also puts a great deal of stress on them.

Horng and Lee (2009) identify the environmental factors that have a positive impact on culinary creativity of creative chefs, including family, school, and workplace:

(1) **Family**: Many creative chefs' initial interests in the culinary field came from their family. Those with a family background in the food industry are able to work in the culinary field much more easily. Support from family is a great motivation for creative chefs to concentrate on the development of culinary creativity.

(2) **School**: The culinary arts must integrate relevant courses and knowledge that would improve students' self-directed learning skills, explore the science and psychology behind food and cooking, enhance students' professional techniques and independent research skills, and train their abilities to design culinary creative products.

(3) **Workplace**: The hard and difficult work experiences are a driving force for the advance of creative chefs. Chefs must be very creative and innovative in order to meet the special needs of customers and markets, and to make their restaurants stay competitive and become more appealing. Moreover, they would find it very inspiring and encouraging if their managers could keep an open mind and take a positive attitude towards their creativity.

However, the traditional culinary environment and culture might also hold back the development of creativity. In a hierarchical system, low-level chefs have no freedom to present their creative ideas or products; in the traditional mentor system, the culinary mentors used to "hold back tricks" or only teach their own disciples, which is a great hindrance to passing down the creative culinary arts. Furthermore, there is an old Chinese saying, "One must excel in a scholastic field in order to acquire a good job and a good future." In a negative environment, chefs may have to defy the objections from family and stick to their beliefs (Horng & Lee, 2009).

The development of creativity in food and culinary arts could be discussed from four aspects, that is, person, process, product, and press. The 4P framework has been extended in recent studies. Peng, Lin, and Baum (2013) compared creativity in general with culinary creativity, and proposed five main principles based on the nature of culinary creativity: time limitation, professional skill, market acceptance, practical experience, and culture. They established a model of culinary creativity through a modified 5P model using the intermediary factor of education and training. Their study showed a unique factor: the principle of the 5P, which doesn't appear in creativity in general, and thus shows that culinary creativity is commercially driven.

3 Assessment of Culinary Creativity

It is very important for the culinary industry to develop an effective scale for evaluating creative culinary products. The marketability of new products could be measured by using proper evaluative tools (Im & Workman, 2004). Analyzing creative products could help the market positioning, find out the basic needs of new products (Goldenberg & Mazursky, 2002), and help improve the design of new products (O'Quin & Besemer, 2006). Restaurant managers and chefs should carefully evaluate whether the properties of new creative products have reached the ideal standards in order to enhance the marketability and competitiveness of new products. Horng and Lin (2009) developed a creative culinary product criteria matrix (Table 25.1), which assumes that the creative culinary products are comprised of multiple elements, such as smell, taste, color, modeling, and conception. All the elements of culinary products have to be included in order to measure or evaluate creativity.

Using a content analysis method, Lin and Mao (2015) analyzed the attributes of successful food specialties and provide suggestions for the development of food specialties based on the analysis of 192 Gold Award winners from 2008 to 2013.

Table 25.1 *Creative culinary product criteria matrix*

Dimension	Criteria
Professional technique	Non-traditional techniques
	Excellent skills
	Preparation, cutting technique, size of portions, cooking method and garnish in
	balance
Aroma; taste and texture	Unique aroma, taste, and texture
	Match customers' favor expectations
	Natural flavor
	All flavors matched and balanced
Color	Unique use of colors
	Appetizing colors
	Natural colors
Modeling; arrangement	Unique modeling, arrangement, and shapes
	Amount, size, and position are appropriate
	Graceful modeling
Garnish	Unique garnish
	Adds the finishing touch
Dishware	Non-traditional dishware
	Using transitional dishware in a creative new way
	Highlights the product
	Product and dishware are matched
Handling of ingredients	New and extraordinary ingredients
	Seasonal and fresh ingredients
	Healthy and nutritional
	Full understanding of the features of ingredients
	Good quality of ingredients
	Good balance of food ingredients
Overall assessment	Original interpretation of traditional cuisine; Introduction of different culture
	Attractive and surprising
	Commercial potential; tells interesting stories; hygienic and safe, natural flavors
	Creative name of culinary product

After reviewing the previous literature, this study summarizes three dimensions of food specialties, including sensory, utility, and symbol. Within these three dimensions, fifteen attributes were identified. The sensory-related descriptions could be classified into four attributes: flavor versatility, texture modification, procedural innovation, and visual appreciation. The utility-related descriptions could be classified into six attributes: natural and organic, environmentally sustainable, healthy, understandable, high quality, and market feasible. The symbolism-related sentences could be classified into five attributes: authentic and indigenous, traditional, craftsmanship, possessing a story and reminiscent, and modern and fun. The results of the

Table 25.2 *Evaluation criteria for food specialties*

	Dimension	Criteria
Creative food specialty	1. Sensory	1.1 Flavor versatility
		1.2 Texture modification
		1.3 Procedure innovation
		1.4 Visual appreciation
	2. Utility	2.1 Natural & organic
		2.2 Environmental sustainability
		2.3 Healthy
		2.4 Understandable
		2.5 High quality
		2.6 Market feasibility
	3. Symbolic	3.1 Authentic & indigenous
		3.2 Traditionality
		3.3 Craftsmanship
		3.4 Story-telling & reminiscent
		3.5 Modern & fun

analysis are summarized in Table 25.2. Generally, the most frequently emphasized five attributes are natural and organic, flavor versatility, convenience, authentic and indigenous, and craftsmanship.

4 Trends Driving the Future of Gastronomy

4.1 Green and Environmental-Friendly Gastronomy

Few studies have examined or discussed the responsibilities of chefs in relation to environmental protection. Nowadays, with the rise of environmental awareness, increasing attention has been given to corporate social responsibility; therefore, the concept of eco-culinology or green culinology has emerged. Now chefs must have a comprehensive understanding of how ingredients (and seasoning), cooking oils, heat control, and cooking techniques could influence the cuisine, people's health, air quality, water, and heat energy, as well as noise, oil, air, and water pollution. The chefs of the future should have faith in the concept of ecological gastronomy. For example, when selecting ingredients such as poultry, meat, seafood, vegetables, and fruits, chefs should choose natural and seasonal ones, so as to reduce inhuman farming methods and illegal farms that might cause mudslides or sandstorms. These methods are environmentally friendly and could reduce the amount of air pollution associated with transportation (Hsu, 2010). In terms of cooking, many energy-consuming dishes (e.g., stews) might be creatively modified with carbon-reduced cooking methods; besides, some ingredients which are eatable but not preferred were often simply thrown away (e.g., internal organs and tough vegetable stems), but with creative designs, these ingredients can also be made into dishes, reducing unnecessary waste.

Restaurant managers should attempt to enhance environmental protection in the whole manufacturing process, including producing, processing, delivering, and consuming, so as to support the sustainable development of food and environment. Recent studies point out that the most important evaluation activities are the use of local food ingredients, an emphasis on food miles, and reducing energy consumption during the food delivery process. Restaurant managers and staff should also use seasonal and organic food, apply simple and environmentally friendly cooking methods, reduce unnecessary decorations, and avoid the use of processed food. Moreover, they are required to provide more vegetables and less meat items in the menu (Hu, Horng, Teng, & Chou, 2013). Although there are still many difficulties to realize eco-culinology or green culinology, the sustainable development of food and environment is inevitable (Stein, Dern, & Hinds, 2004).

4.2 Health-Improving Gastronomy

Although concern with health is not a new issue in the culinary industry, it continues to attract attention. Chefs today often seek to combine new and popular methods of healthy dieting with basic knowledge of food nutrition to create new culinary products. Many chefs attempt to find new natural flavors from exotic ingredients, such as Brazilian camu fruit, Australian breadfruit, lyceum, pomegranate white tea with acai, mangosteen, and lime; or they blend the functional ingredients into cooking techniques, including high-fiber foods, seeds, catechin, red yeast, chitin, lycopene, and probiotics. Many traditional cuisine and food products can be revised and improved by reducing oil and sugar, using organic and natural ingredients, and increasing functional ingredients.

4.3 New Technological Applications

"Culinary arts" is a discipline that has developed within the chemical, physical, and biological sciences. Culinology, food science, and food products are all based on the application of scientific knowledge (Hegarty, 2006). Creativity in culinary technology requires chefs to understand the properties of ingredients and changes that might take place during food preparation. Moreover, chefs of the future should be able to use high-tech kitchen equipment to help improve cooking. They should also learn various theories of food science and the physical and chemical changes of food that occur during cooking. Molecular gastronomy is actually based on the physical and chemical transformations of food and created by using technology. Hu (2010) proposed nine technological skills necessary for chefs to provide unique products and service.

(1) Understand the properties of ingredients and the physical and chemical changes of food that occur during cooking.
(2) Learn the theories of food science.

(3) Be able to maintain the freshness of food by using technology.
(4) Be able to prolong the food preservation time by using technology.
(5) Be able to ensure food hygiene by using technology.
(6) Be able to use high-tech kitchen equipment (e.g., steam ovens).
(7) Be able to pack the products by using new technology.
(8) Be able to communicate with customers by using technology.
(9) Be able to improve food quality by using technology.

4.4 Culinary Localization and Globalization

In response to the trend of culinary globalization, the issue of "authenticity" of foreign cuisine has been heatedly discussed within the academic field (Sims, 2009; Timothy, & Ron, 2013). At the same time, the sameness of large restaurant chains is also a widely considered issue. In order to maintain the authenticity of local cuisine cultural heritages and protect the sense of place that local people cherished, it has become the primary task for many chefs to intensify the unique and regional features of food and culinary arts.

Many famous chefs and restaurants are dedicated to the creativity of regional food and cuisine. For example, Paul Bocuse focused on improving French cuisine and invented "nouvelle cuisine," which is known to make sauces less rich than traditional French cuisine, put small portions on big plates, and integrate Japanese ingredients and cooking techniques to promote international acceptance. However, many chefs found that the once-innovative and exquisite French cuisine has eventually become a form of local cuisine that highlights the freshness and the quality of ingredients. The traditional concept has the power to move people. Later, Paul Bocuse returned to the origins of the French cuisine style of cooking.

Another example is the D.O.M., a Brazilian cuisine restaurant in São Paulo, which is also one of the best restaurants in South America. The head chef, Alex Atala, is known for his use of native Brazilian ingredients such as the Amazonian fruits of tapioca and tucupi juice to create unique flavors. Furthermore, the Danish restaurant Noma has been ranked the best restaurant in the world three times and has helped make the cuisine of Northern Europe world famous. The food served in Noma is Nordic cuisine, which uses the local and seasonal ingredients from the seashore and forest, such as dandelion and papyrus. The restaurant managers have consulted biologists and nutritionists about the properties of plants in order to blend the local elements into the creativity of cuisine. The success of these two restaurants comes from giving the most traditional regional food brand-new styles and looks, attracting from diners all over the world. It also shows that the best creative culinary ideas often come from the oldest elements of dining.

In conclusion, culinary creativity has multiple dimensions including professional skills, knowledge, culture, art and science technology, and it is an important factor in the diversification of culinary life and competitiveness of the food industry. Culinary creativity was largely neglected by the academic circle until about ten years ago, but recent research on creativity has been mostly focused on the Four Ps in creativity and the development of some theoretical models and tools for assessment using the Four Ps, so as to serve as a foundation and point of reference for culinary creativity practice, education, and research in the future.

References

Amabile, T. M. (1979). Effects of external evaluation on artistic creativity. *Journal of personality and Social Psychology*, *37*(2), 221.

Anderson, T., & Mossberg, L. (2004). The dining experience: Do restaurants satisfy customer needs. *Food Service Technology*, *4*(4), 171–177.

Balazs, K. (2002). Take one entrepreneur: The recipe for success of France's great chefs. *European Management Journal*, *20*(3), 247–259.

Beghetto, R. A., Kaufman, J. C., & Hatcher, R. (2015). Applying creativity research to cooking. *The Journal of Creative Behavior*.

Birdir, K., & Pearson, T. E. (2000). Research chefs' competencies: A Delphi approach. *International Journal of Contemporary Hospitality Management*, *12*(3), 205–209.

Brunori, G. (2007). Local food and alternative food networks: a communication perspective. *Anthropology of food*, (S2).

Culinary Institute of America. (2011). *The professional chef*. John Wiley & Sons.

Cwiertka, K. (1999). Culinary globalization and Japan. *Japan Echo*, *26*, 52–58.

Dornenburg, A., & Page, K. (2003). *Becoming a chef*. Wiley.

Fine, G. A. (1992). The culture of production: Aesthetic choices and constraints in culinary work. *American Journal of Sociology*, 1268–1294.

Gazzoli, J. J. (1995). The recipe for" three star" management success. *Trusts and Estates-Atlanta*, *134*, 8–15.

Goldenberg, J., & Mazursky, D. (2002). *Creativity in product innovation*. Cambridge University Press.

Hegarty, J. A. (2006). Developing "subject fields" in culinary arts, science, and gastronomy. *Journal of Culinary Science & Technology*, *4*(1), 5–13.

Hegarty, J. A., & O'Mahony, G. B. (2001). Gastronomy: A phenomenon of cultural expressionism and an aesthetic for living. *International Journal of Hospitality Management*, *20*(1), 3–13.

Horng, J. S., & Lee, Y. C. (2006). What does it take to be a creative culinary artist? *Journal of Culinary Science and Technology*, *5*(2/3), 5–22.

Horng J. S., & Hu, M. L. (2008). The mystery in the kitchen: Culinary creativity. *Creativity Research Journal*, *20*(2). 221–230.

Horng, J. S., & Lin, L. (2009). The development of a scale for evaluating creative culinary products. *Creativity Research Journal*, *21*(1), 54–63.

Horng, J. S., & Tsai, C. T. S. (2010). Government websites for promoting East Asian culinary tourism: A cross-national analysis. *Tourism Management*, *31*(1), 74–85.

Hsu, M. R. (2010). A modified delphi study to identify chefs' green competencies. *Journal of Tourism and Leisure Studies*, *16*(1). 67–88.

Hu, M. L. M. (2010). Developing a core competency model of innovative culinary development. *International Journal of Hospitality Management*, *29*(4), 582–590.

Hu, M. L., Horng, J. S., Teng, C. C., & Chou, S. F. (2013). A criteria model of restaurant energy conservation and carbon reduction in Taiwan. *Journal of Sustainable Tourism*, *21*(5), 765–779.

Im, S., & Workman Jr, J. P. (2004). Market orientation, creativity, and new product performance in high-technology firms. *Journal of Marketing, 68*(2), 114–132.

Kawasaki, H., Kasamatsu, C., & Nonaka, M. (2015). Cognitive structures based on culinary success factors in the development of new dishes by Japanese chefs at fine dining restaurants. *Flavour, 4*(1), 1.

Kittler, P. G., & Sucher, K. P. (2004). *Cultural foods: Traditions and trends.* EC LINK LTD.

Klosse, P. R., Riga, J., Cramwinckel, A. B., & Saris, W. H. (2004). The formulation and evaluation of culinary success factors (CSFs) that determine the palatability of food. *Food Service Technology, 4*(3), 107–115.

Lin, L., & Mao, P. C. (2015). Food for memories and culture: A content analysis study of food specialties and souvenirs. *Journal of Hospitality and Tourism Management, 22,* 19–29.

Mennell, S. (1985). *All manner of foods.* Oxford: Blackwell.

Okumus, B., Okumus, F., & McKercher, B. (2007). Incorporating local and international cuisines in the marketing of tourism destinations: The cases of Hong Kong and Turkey. *Tourism Management, 28*(1), 253–261.

O'Quin, K., & Besemer, S. P. (2006). Using the creative product semantic scale as a metric for results-oriented business. *Creativity and Innovation Management, 15*(1), 34–44.

Ottenbacher, M., & Harrington, R. J. (2007). The innovation development process of Michelin-starred chefs. *International Journal of Contemporary Hospitality Management, 19*(6), 444–460.

Peng, K. L., Lin, M. C., & Baum, T. (2013). The constructing model of culinary creativity: an approach of mixed methods. *Quality & Quantity, 47*(5), 2687–2707.

Perlik, A. (2002). Chefs a la mode. *Restaurant & Institution, 15,* 40–52.

Petruzzelli, A. M., & Savino, T. (2014). Search, recombination, and innovation: Lessons from haute cuisine. *Long Range Planning, 47*(4), 224–238.

Pratten, J. D. (2003). What makes a great chef? *British Food Journal, 105*(7), 454–459.

Rao, H., Monin, P., & Durand, R. (2003). Institutional change in Toque Ville: Nouvelle cuisine as an identity movement in French gastronomy1. *American Journal of Sociology, 108*(4), 795–843.

Rhodes, M. (1961). An analysis of creativity. *Phi Delta Kappan, 42*(7), 305–310.

Santich, B. (2004). The study of gastronomy and its relevance to hospitality education and training. *International Journal of Hospitality Management, 23*(1), 15–24.

Sims, R. (2009). Food, place and authenticity: Local food and the sustainable tourism experience. *Journal of Sustainable Tourism, 17*(3), 321–336.

Simonton, D. K. (1988). 16 Creativity, leadership, and chance. *The Nature of Creativity: Contemporary Psychological Perspectives,* 386.

Stein, S., Hinds, M., & Dern, J. H. (2004). *Sustainable kitchen.* New Society Publishers.

Timothy, D. J., & Ron, A. S. (2013). Understanding heritage cuisines and tourism: Identity, image, authenticity, and change. *Journal of Heritage Tourism, 8*(2–3), 99–104.

Wilk, R. R. (1999). "Real Belizean food": Building local identity in the transnational Caribbean. *American Anthropologist,* 244–255.

26 Tactical Creativity in Sport

Daniel Memmert

Institute of Training and Computer Science in Sport,
German Sport University Cologne, Germany

Abstract

The objective of this chapter is to give an overview of literature on tactical creativity in team sports. After stressing the relevance and definitions of tactical creativity in team sports, the advantages and disadvantages of different tests (video tests, game test situations, and game observation) to measure tactical creativity are compared with one another. The main focus lies on the introduction of the tactical creativity approach (TCA) for team sports, which summarizes seven methodological principles fostering tactical creativity. All these principles (1-dimension games, diversification, deliberate practice, deliberate play, deliberate coaching, deliberate memory, and deliberate motivation) are discussed following an overview of their empirical background. This chapter is enclosed by directions for potential further research with links to other research topics.

Before winning the Soccer World Cup 2014 in Brazil, the national head coach of the German team, Jogi Löw, substantiated the special meaning of creativity in soccer: "Creativity and playful class should be the new German virtues" (Memmert, 2015a). Additionally, Matthias Sammer, the former sports director of the Champions League winners of 2013, FC Bayern Munich, emphasizes the meaning of creativity in sports: "The first initiative to increase the flexibility in your own team always stems from the coach ... We just had the feeling that our game had to become more creative and unpredictable ... Only then was our way of playing unpredictable and modern – extremely creative" (KICKER, 2013).

Creative solutions are of crucial importance not only in soccer but also in other team sports like handball, basketball, field hockey, or volleyball, but are less important in individual sports like swimming, track and field sport, or triathlon (Memmert, 2011). The reason is that clear basic conditions (e.g., run 100 meters as quickly as possible) and optimal solutions (e.g., run directly from the start to the finish line) exist in these individual sports, in which athletes try to achieve different performances with a clearly described system of rules, in the majority of cases on their own. Nevertheless, coaches and officials like managers or sport directors should also be aware of the need to create better solutions for given tasks (e.g., the Fosbury Flop in the high jump).

Players in basketball, field hockey, soccer, or handball, for example, use original actions to prepare and secure their teammates' shots on target. One example is that of one of the world's best soccer players, Lionel Messi, who is able to make decisions in specific soccer situations that are unexpected and therefore less likely to be anticipated by opponents. Another one is Kobe Bryant, who is able to prepare his teammates' closing options under the basket by using creative solutions.

Because of the relevance of original solutions in team sports, the term "tactical creativity" describes a sport-specific thinking style in team sports and is based on the theoretical framework of divergent thinking by Guilford (1967, but see also Runco, 2007; Sternberg & Lubart, 1995). Tactical creativity in team and racket sports can be defined as the generation of several solutions for problems in specific individual groups or in team tactical game situations, which can be denoted as surprising, seldom, and original, but also useful (Memmert, 2015a). Thereby, this ability differs from tactical intelligence, game sense, or game ability (Memmert & Roth, 2007). The main task of tactical intelligence is the production of the best solution for specific individual, group, or team tactic match situations. The paradigm of tactical creativity and intelligence also corresponds to the agreement of sports coaching textbooks in advocating the difference between improvised creative behavior and planned behavior (Reilly, 1996; Smith & Cushion, 2006). Empirical data from a longitudinal study in team sports show (for an overview see Memmert, 2015a) that greater tactical creativity seems to correlate with a greater tactical intelligence.

Additional empirical support for the relevance of tactical creativity, especially in soccer, comes from a recent study by Kempe and Memmert (2017). In this study, all goals scored by thirty-two nations of the six continental associations were qualitatively analyzed in the soccer World Cup 2014 in Brazil. The data record covers fifty-five of the sixty-four games played in total, due to the fact that nine games ended goalless (except for goals scored in penalty shoot-outs). Overall 171 goals were scored in these games, whereas twelve of them were scored during penalty-shootouts. The last eight actions (e.g., passes and movement of players) in front of a goal were evaluated by soccer experts using a creativity scale from 0–10 (0 = not creative, 10 = highly creative). They found out that the actions were rated as more creative when they occurred closer to the goal. At least one of the eight actions in the high creative area was included in 85 percent of all goals.

This chapter touches upon a variety of issues of tactical creativity in the area of team sports, including theoretical, methodological, and empirical considerations. The evaluation possibilities to measure tactical creativity are discussed by comparing the advantages and disadvantages of video tests, game test situations, and game observation with one another. Some of the key creativity studies in team sports will be introduced and structured by the Tactical Creativity Approach (TCA; Memmert, 2015a). These investigations are based on different sports (soccer, handball, basketball, field hockey, and others) and were conducted using groups of different ages (children, youth, adolescents, and adults) and expertise (amateurs, semi-professionals, and professionals).

Evaluation of Tactical Creativity in Team and Racket Sports

The operationalization of tactical creativity is often assessed in relation to the factor analytical characteristics such as originality, flexibility, and fluency identified by the research group from Guilford (1967). These observation criteria are also usually used to evaluate athletes' creative performances (Memmert, 2013). This means that: (a) the unusualness of tactical decision-making actions (see also Kaufman, Baer, Cropley, Reiter-Palmon, & Sinnett, 2013 and Kaufman & Baer, 2012 for product evaluation in business) or – as is common in creativity research – the rarity of tactical responses (i.e., originality) are rated by soccer experts; (b) the variety of tactical decision-making actions (e.g., performing a one-on-one action, shooting at goal with jump throw, performing a no-look-pass, and passing with a feint) is determined by the action and response diversity of the players (flexibility); and (c) the number of appropriate tactical decision-making actions are counted, which identifies which players perform certain situational constellations (fluency). All these factors are important in the area of team sports. For example, it is possible that a basketball player may display a wealth of appropriate solutions, each of which, however, is based on feinting a pass only (high fluency and low flexibility value). Another player may only demonstrate one solution, but uses different feint versions like body or shot feints.

The most common forms to evaluate tactical creativity in team sports are video tests, game test situations, and game observations (see Figure 26.1; adapted from Memmert, 2013).

Video test scenarios evaluate the tactical creativity of players by watching different game scenes and therefore recording individual creative behaviors under highly standardized conditions (e.g., Memmert, 2010a). Players have to view brief sport-specific videos (e.g., basketball, soccer) in which, for example, attacking players play against defending players. They usually watch them in a laboratory setting scenario on a computer monitor or in front of a large display. The participants have to imagine themselves as the acting player with the ball and report all possibilities that might lead to a goal after the final frozen image. The included motor skills

(a)   (b)   (c)

Figure 26.1 *Evaluating tactical creativity with (a) a standardized video test in a laboratory setting in front of a large display, (b) a game test situation under representative task design conditions with real motor skills, and (c) game observations from video footage of competitive matches.*

(e.g., passing with the non-dominant hand, indirect pass) could also be mentioned here. Two independent soccer experts with high-level trainer certifications judge the originality of the responses for each scene (1 = not original at all, up to 5 = very original). Flexibility is measured via diversity of solution. All answers suggested by the participants were sorted into different categories (e.g., shot on goal, feint followed by a pass, dribble, short pass). Fluency is defined as the number of adequate solutions produced by a participant. This is a standard procedure in creativity research in sport (Memmert & Roth, 2007, Memmert, 2015a).

In contrast, game test situations have a high validity regarding contextual, complex game situations, in which human behavior can be studied in natural and ecologically valid conditions of team sports. In a comparable tactical environment, these real-world representations evoke reliable and repeated creative behavior in specific match situations (Memmert, 2007, 2010b). These kinds of games involve simple forms of game play with clearly defined environmental conditions and rules, skill execution (e.g., the use of hands), as well as specified numbers of players. In order to analyze creative solutions, a video of the recorded tactical behavior is rated with regard to specific concepts by several independent expert evaluators using a specific checklist (Memmert, 2007; Memmert & Roth, 2007). This approach guarantees a high inter-rater reliability.

Finally, the present standard is to assess tactical performance during game play by means of the method of game observation of real matches (Franks, 1985), which are performed under field conditions and therefore have very high ecological validity. Quantitative game observations proceed very objectively by using predefined observation schedules (category systems) to collect the data, in this case, game behavior (e.g., Palao & Morante, 2013). In contrast, qualitative game observations are objective (if you have more coders you can calculate inter-rater-reliability coefficients) and systematic (e.g., structured and comprehensive), but could also include the subjective impressions of the observers and take advantage of the experiences and know-how of experts. Subsequently, both quantitative and qualitative data is evaluated and indices are calculated to value all of the players' performances (Sampaio & Leite, 2013), individual performance components (O'Donoghue, 2013), or group/team performances (Gréhaigne & Godbout, 2013).

Table 26.1 gives an overview of the specific advantages and disadvantages as well as the possibilities and limitations of all three approaches (see also Memmert, 2015a). Video tasks are definitely less complex (e.g., stimuli, response options) than the game test situations or game observations. The distinct advantages of the video tasks are the clear test situations in the video sequences so that almost no confounding variables (e.g., conditional or technical factors) appear. In contrast, the performances in game test situations or game observations are always confounded with partial performances of the participants. Motor skills, for example, interact with tactical solutions. The identification of tactical actions by using motor actions is technically possible in videos as well, however, this is seldom used and is only applicable to a certain extent. In game test situations or game observations, the motor-action coupling (meaning the integration of the motor answer in the cognitive solution) is naturally obvious.

Table 26.1 *Advantages and disadvantages of different tests (video tests, game test situations, and game observation) to measure tactical creativity (Memmert, 2015a, with permission from Taylor & Francis)*

	Video tests	Game test situations	Game observation
Complexity of the situation/task	Low	High	High
Confounders (team mate, etc.)	Low	Middle to high	High
Motor-action coupling	Middle	High	High
Interaction between players	Low	Middle	High
Authenticity of situations	Low	Middle	High
Transferability in practice	Low	High	High
One-dimensional structure of tasks	Given	Nearly given	Not given
Density of relevant actions	High	Middle to high	Middle to less
Relative consistency of conditions	High	Middle	Less

Currently, the interactivity between offensive and defensive players is always given in game test situations and game observations. However, the interaction using the medium of the large screen has been quite low in most of the published approaches. Despite the fact that game test situations or game observations hold a high authenticity regarding complex match situations, it is less the case for video tests due to their artificial setup in a laboratory setting. An advantage of video tests is that the selected video sequences can be chosen and adjusted to specific tactical decision performances. In game test situations or game observations, it is more difficult to provoke tactical actions of the test persons which only lead to one isolated tactical partial performance. Another advantage of video tests is that the test participants are forced to react to many different comparable situations through tactical responses. By showing several different video sequences ($N=30$), a high consistency and thus reliability of the examined material can be guaranteed. An additional advantage of the video tests is that further manipulation stimuli in video sequences (e.g., inducing motivational focus, or attention-directing instructions) can easily be installed. This is technically not possible for game observations; however, in this case for game test situations it is harder to control.

Empirical Studies of Tactical Creativity in Sport

In this chapter, some of the key creativity studies in sport will be introduced and structured by the Tactical Creativity Approach (TCA, Figure 26.2) by Memmert (2015a). The theoretical framework of the TCA is based on the Investment Theory of Creativity by Sternberg and Lubart (1995) which postulates six resources (intelligence, knowledge, personality, motivation, intellectual styles, and environment).

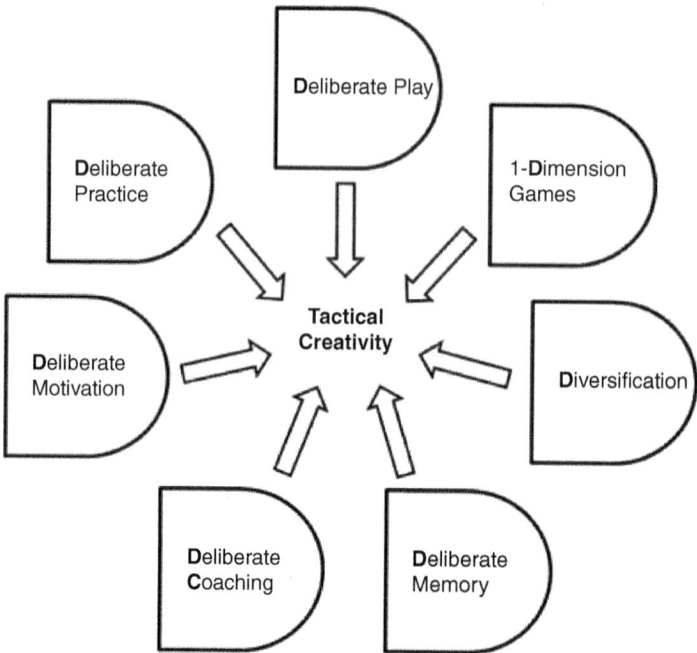

Figure 26.2 *The 7 Ds fostering tactical creativity in team and racket sports (see Tactical Creativity Approach by Memmert, 2015a).*

The following will present evidence from the area of team sports with a focus on resources intelligence (working memory, attention), knowledge (expertise), motivation, and environment in sport-relevant contexts.

According to the TCA (see Figure 26.2), different factors could foster the development of tactical creativity during training sessions of team and racket sports via PE lessons at school. Theoretically connected to the Sternberg and Lubart (1995) model, the seven methodological principles of tactical creativity, namely dimension games, diversification, deliberate practice, deliberate play, deliberate coaching, deliberate memory, and deliberate motivation, emerged as a result of numerous empirical studies in sports. The order of the seven training principles indicates a chronological order from children training to adult training. Although the first six principles (starting with deliberate play and then moving clockwise) are more suited for younger age groups, all of the principles are useful for older age groups. Coaches and teachers should integrate tasks in training units which concentrate on the development of these seven principles as early as possible (Ashby, Valentin, & Turken, 2002; Huttenlocher, 1990; Memmert, 2010a; Milgram, 1990). After childhood, the effect of training activities for tactical creativity probably becomes weaker and weaker, but is still possible (Memmert, 2010b). The empirical evidence fostering tactical creativity in team sports are presented in more depth below, following the structure of the seven Ds.

Deliberate Play: Game play that is uninstructed, a more natural game setting, and/or unstructured situations are denoted as "deliberate play" (Côté, Baker, & Abernethy, 2007). Deliberate play is expected to have influenced the creative thinking of current national players during their youth, based on exercise biography studies (Memmert, Baker, & Bertsch, 2010). Therefore, the examination of response behavior variations can be the result of uninstructed play. Greco, Memmert, and Morales (2010) also introduce this outcome in a field-based investigation in basketball. Within this study, youth basketball players performed two different kinds of basketball training tasks: one, under the terms of the deliberate play approach, and the other one in accordance with structured game forms and specific routines of a traditional basketball approach. This way the authors could demonstrate that greater improvements of tactical creativity can rather be achieved through a training program that includes deliberate play than by the training of the placebo group (see Russ in this volume for more information on play).

1-Dimension Games: General or sport-specific tactical skills can be developed by 1-dimension games in soccer (for a review, see Memmert, 2015a), where games are progressively used to enhance technical skills or aerobic fitness components (see Hill-Haas, Dawson, Impellizzeri, & Coutts, 2011; Clemente, Couceiro, Martins, & Mendes, 2012). 1-dimension games were found to foster the development of tactical creativity in recent research (Memmert, 2007; Memmert & Roth, 2007). Learning divergent tactical thinking in complex and dynamic situations represents the main goal of 1-dimension games, meaning that children practice single basic tactical elements by constantly repeating comparable complex tactical constellations (cf. "representative learning design," Pinder, Davids, Renshaw, & Araújo, 2011). Another aspect of 1-dimension games is that they have strictly determined game ideas, steady numbers of players, and specified rules and environmental conditions. With regard to team and racket sports, non-specific 1-dimension games were created, acknowledged, and validated (cf. Griffin, Mitchell, & Oslin, 1997; Memmert & Harvey, 2010), and by using them, basic tactics – which are important in various different team and racket sports – can be practiced.

Diversification: The perception and handling of many different sport game situations have a positive effect on the transferability of cognitive skills like pattern recognition (Abernethey, Baker, & Côté, 2005) and on the progress of tactical creativity (Memmert & Roth, 2007). The fact that, in contrast to less original ball game athletes, creative players were able to try different sports and collect their movement experience in various sport-oriented situations is emphasized by movement biography studies of highly creative sport game artists (Memmert, Baker, & Bertsch, 2010). These are based on questionnaires designed to measure sport experiences across the sport careers of the participants.

In order to produce solutions that include original ideas, it is useful if children and adolescents are brought into contact with different balls as early as possible in their "ball-game life" and, furthermore, learn to additionally use their hand, foot, and tennis/hockey racket in order to think of situations differently or in a new way. Therefore, clubs and associations should be the ones to encourage their coaches at an early stage to practice tactical creativity with various ways of training that overlaps many sport games letting children solve tasks with hands, feet, and hockey sticks. During the training of beginners and within talent promotion this is particularly important.

Deliberate Memory. In the center of conscious information processing lies the Working Memory (WM), in which a limited amount of information can be processed that is relevant for the current activity (for an overview see Baddeley, 2007). The capacity and the general function of WM (for an overview see Furley & Memmert, 2010) are of special importance for tactical training in team and racket sports. Even though an athlete's individual WM capacity does not seem to have an influence on divergent performance in team and racket sports (Furley & Memmert, 2015), it is nevertheless advisable that a trainer does not deliver too much information simultaneously when imparting tactical orders or instructions or during team meetings because of the limited capacity of WM (Cowan, 2001, 2005). Furthermore, it needs to be considered that especially during the stage of learning something for the first time (whether tactical, cognitively, or motoric), even more is demanded of WM than in later stages of expertise (Maxwell, Masters, & Eves, 2003; Schmidt & Wrisberg, 2004). In contrast to novices, experts do not store specific events (e.g., routes of certain players, tactic constellations) as single information chunks, but as tactic patterns of all players ("Chunking Processes"). On the one hand, this simplifies and especially improves early anticipation of meaningful game constellations (Williams & Ericsson, 2005). On the other hand, the limited capacity of the expert's WM is not used up as quickly as the capacity of the novice's WM. Thus, the expert's WM can be used for the perception of further situation constellations or deeper tactical decision processes (Williams, Hodges, North, & Barton, 2006).

The general functioning of WM (i.e., the fact that information in the WM are worked on, manipulated, and structured on short notice; Conway et al., 2007), has important consequences for decision training in team and racket sports. Recent studies demonstrated that the activated contents of WM guide an athlete's focus of attention (Furley & Memmert, 2013) by biasing attention towards objects in the visual field that are related to the recent contents of WM. In addition, WM has been shown to be predictive of controlling attention in a goal-directed manner and avoiding distraction and interference amongst athletes (Furley & Memmert, 2012). Therefore, in a positive case, this implies that instructions of the trainer can guide the attentional focus of athletes and thus make the tactical decisions easier. In a negative case, athletes refer to irrelevant information from the trainer, which prevents them from making optimal decisions through unfavorable attentional control in a specific situation.

Deliberate Coaching: Many sport psychological studies have revealed that sport-specific attention processes (for an overview, see Memmert, 2015b, c) play an important role in the development of creative thoughts. It is necessary to have a wide focus of attention, for example, in order to also perceive unexpected objects like freestanding teammates, which could therefore be the beginning of an original solution (Memmert & Furley, 2007). When the coach provides less instructions, children and adolescents are better able to develop original solution possibilities with many variations – due to the induction of a wider focus of attention – than children and adolescents constantly confronted with attention-leading hints during practice (Memmert, 2007). Hence, the coach should not continuously stop the game during practice and constantly give tactical advice to players (Furley, Memmert, & Heller, 2010).

In general, there are two possibilities with which coaches can influence their players' scope of attention: first directly, with instructions, and second indirectly, by inventing game forms that provoke a wider focus of the players' attention. Attention-focusing can be controlled in a specific way (Memmert & Furley, 2007), especially by certain instruction possibilities and external (implicit) stimuli. The aim of a coach or a teacher should be to offer the possibility to perceive and search for unexpected and potentially better solution variations by giving reduced instructions to children alongside his or her own solution demands (Memmert, 2015b).

Deliberate Motivation: The simplest instructions that are, for example, able to manipulate the emotional conditions of a person can have a direct influence on creative performance, which is demonstrated by current theory models and empirical results from social psychology (Hirt, Levine, McDonald, Melton, & Martin, 1997; Isen, 2000; Isen, Daubman, & Nowicki, 1987). Thereby, a promotion focus, regulating pleasure as the achievement of positive results of action and suffering as the absence of those positive results, is shown by the clear pattern of results (cf. Higgins, 1997). It facilitates the handling of creative solutions as a prevention focus, expressed by the successful avoidance of unpleasant, negative results and their arrival as suffering.

Memmert, Hüttermann, and Orliczek (2013) demonstrated that divergent performances of decision making also benefit from a promotion focus in sports. In a standardized video soccer test, soccer players had to name as many decision options as possible per video sequences. Similar to the work of Friedman and Förster (2001), identical labyrinths with different framing in the run-up were presented to them: One half of the players were given the task to find the way in which a mouse would reach the cheese (promotion-focus), while the other half had to solve the labyrinth with the task that a mouse needs to escape from an owl (prevention-focus). The results show that the soccer players were able to develop more original and flexible solutions in the promotion condition than in the prevention condition. All in all, the results demonstrate that better results can be achieved when coaches and teachers try to enhance their athletes' divergent thinking with suitable promotion-focus instructions.

Deliberate Practice: The aim to actually improve specific individual performance criteria in exercise-centered and structured situations is called "deliberate practice" (Côté, Baker, & Abernethy, 2007). Top professional experts have spent more than ten years researching the acquisition of decision-making and skill execution in their sport. The theory of deliberate practice (see Ericsson, Krampe, & Tesch-Römer, 1993; but see Macnamara, Hambrick, & Oswald, 2014) states that specialized knowledge in a given sport (such as soccer and basketball) provides the final result of extended engagement in high-quality training. Memmert and colleagues (2010) demonstrated that creative athletes have practiced their main in a sport a goal-oriented way much longer than less-creative athletes. The difference between more-

and less-creative team sport players is characterized by the quantity of hours of deliberate practice, particularly for top team players on professional teams. On average, national league athletes started to practice their specific sport later in life than players in the next highest level of competition. This leads to the fact that deliberate practice plays an important role for the promotion of tactical creativity in late childhood and the beginning of adolescence.

Conclusion

Training units and learning environments in team sports use the outstanding relevance of tactical optimum (Williams, 2013) and creative solutions (Memmert, 2015a) as their main components. For example, Kobe Bryant, Lionel Messi, Sidney Crosby, and Wayne Gretzky have provided us with unexpected and surprising solutions for their opponents, fans, audiences, television commentators, and sometimes even their teammates and, furthermore, delighted us with their creative imagination. Since nowadays more information on the opposing team and its players is known before the competition, the coaches can perfectly prepare their teams according the merits and limitations of the opposing team. Therefore, the players are the ones to develop creative responses in the game situations during the match, and the coaches have to search for new things in order to find creative plans and strategies. Research concerning tactical creativity in sport is certainly at an early stage. However, further research activity is necessary to extend the theoretical framework, to create and acknowledge new sport specific-creativity tests (Moraru, Memmert, & van der Kamp, 2016), and to study policies that support tactical creativity in sports in an experimental way (Memmert, 2015a). It is possible to find several ways in which research is going to develop in the future.

The outline of neural mechanisms involved in the development of creative solutions in more complex ecologically valid creativity tasks could be another fruitful road to study neuronal correlates of tactical creativity. The domain of sports facilitates the investigation of creative performance in an ecologically valid way and could therefore be considered as a "worthwhile field to study behavior in a complex context" (Memmert, 2011, p. 373). Additionally, creative solutions in sport situations seem to require domain-specific knowledge, manifold attentional processes, or memory-related demands. These processes are known as important ingredients of tactical creativity in team sports. During the development of creative solutions in video test scenarios (see Memmert et al., 2013), functional patterns of brain activity could be measured during the solution processes in fMRI studies.

Last but not least, one has to undergo a process of rethinking traditional training concepts in order to accept the fact that tactical creativity can also be respected and recorded as a talent indicator at an early stage. This certainly cannot be regarded as an easy step; however, it is possible and certainly desirable. In the highest German national league, currently one of the strongest soccer leagues in the world, the best young German players are sampled and rewarded in certain rankings. Nevertheless, it is surprising that only 35 percent of these early star players are able to achieve a permanent place in one of the eighteen national league clubs and, consequently, manage high levels of achievement in adult soccer. The fact that the selection is mainly made through the evaluation of physical and technical factors and less through the evaluation of individual tactical criteria like creativity could be one of the reasons.

References

Kaufman, J. C., Baer, J., Cropley, D. H., Reiter-Palmon, R., & Sinnett, S. (2013). Furious activity vs. understanding: How much expertise is needed to evaluate creative work?. *Psychology of Aesthetics, Creativity, and the Arts*, *7*, 332–340.

Kaufman, J. C., & Baer, J. (2012). Beyond new and appropriate: Who decides what is creative? *Creativity Research Journal*, *24*, 83–91.

Abernethy, B., Baker, J., & Coté, J. (2005). Transfer of pattern recall skills may contribute to the development of sport expertise. *Applied Cognitive Psychology*, *19*, 705–718.

Ashby, F. G., Valentin, V. V., & Turken, A. U. (2002). The effects of positive affect and arousal on working memory and executive attention: Neurobiology and computational models. In S. Moore & M. Oaksford (Eds.), *Emotional cognition: From brain to behaviour* (pp. 245–287). Amsterdam: John Benjamins.

Baddeley, A. D. (2007). *Working memory, thought, and action*. Oxford: Oxford University Press. DOI: 10.1093/acprof:oso/9780198528012.001.0001

Clemente, F., Couceiro, M., Martins, F. M. L., & Mendes, R. (2012). The usefulness of small-sided games on soccer training. *Journal of Physical Education and Sport*, *12*, 93–102.

Conway, A. R. A., Jarrold, C., Kane, M. J., Miyake, A., & Towse, J. N. (2007). *Variation in working memory*. New York: Oxford University Press.

Côté, J., Baker, J., & Abernethy, B. (2007). Play and practice in the development of sport expertise. In G. Tenenbaum & R.C. Eklund (Eds.), *Handbook of sport psychology* (pp. 184–202), Hoboken, NJ: John Wiley & Sons.

Cowan, N. (2001). The magical number 4 in short-term memory: A reconsideration of mental storage capacity. *Behavioral and Brain Sciences 24*, 87–185. DOI:10.1017/S0140525X01003922.

Cowan, N. (2005). *Working memory capacity*. Hove, East Sussex, UK: Psychology Press.

Ericsson, K. A., Krampe, R. T., & Tesch-Römer, C. (1993). The role of deliberative practice in the acquisition of expert performance. *Psychological Review*, *100*, 363–406.

Franks, I. (1985). Qualitative and quantitative analysis. *Coaching Review 8*, 48–50.

Friedman, R. S., & Förster, J. (2001). The effects of promotion and prevention cues on creativity. *Journal of Personality and Social Psychology*, *81*, 1001–1013.

Furley, P., & Memmert, D. (2010). The role of working memory in sports. *International Review of Sport and Exercise Psychology*, *3*, 171–194.

Furley, P., & Memmert, D. (2012). Working memory capacity as controlled attention in tactical decision making. *Journal of Sport and Exercise Psychology*, *34*, 322–344.

Furley, P., & Memmert, D. (2013). "Whom should I pass to?" The more options the more attentional guidance from working. *PLOS ONE 8*(5): e62278. DOI: 10.1371/journal.pone.0062278

Furley, P., & Memmert, D. (2015). Creativity and working memory capacity in sports: Working memory capacity is not a limiting factor in creative decision making amongst skilled performers. *Frontiers in Psychology*, *6*:1361. DOI: 10.3389/fpsyg.2015.01361.

Furley, P., Memmert, D., & Heller, C. (2010). The dark side of visual awareness in sport – Inattentional blindness in a real-world basketball task. *Attention, Perception, & Psychophysics*, *72*, 1327–1337.

Greco, P., Memmert, D., & Morales, J. C. P. (2010). The effect of deliberate play on tactical performance in basketball. *Perceptual & Motor Skills*, 110, 849–856.

Gréhaigne, J. F., & Godbout, P. (2013). Collective variables for analysing performance in team sports. In T. McGarry, P. O'Donoghue, & J. Sampaio (Eds.), *Routledge Handbook of Sports Performance Analysis* (pp. 101–114), Abingdon: Routledge.

Griffin, L. A., Mitchell, S. A., & Oslin, J. L. (1997). *Teaching sport concepts and skills: a tactical games approach.* Champaign: Human Kinetics.

Guilford, J. P. (1967). *The nature of human intelligence.* New York: McGraw-Hill.

Higgins, E. T. (1997). Beyond pleasure and pain. *American Psychologist*, *52*, 1280–1013.

Hill-Haas, S. V., Dawson, B., Impellizzeri, F. M., & Coutts, A. J. (2011). Physiology of small-sided games training in football. A systematic review. *Sports Medicine*, *41*, 199–220.

Hirt, E. R., Levine, G. M., McDonald, H. E., Melton, R. J., & Martin, L. L. (1997). The role of mood in quantitative and qualitative aspects of performance: Single or multiple mechanisms? *Journal of Experimental Social Psychology*, *33*, 602–629.

Huttenlocher, P. R. (1990). Morphometric study of human cerebral cortex development. *Neuropsychologia*, *28*, 517–527.

Isen, A. M. (2000). Positive affect and decision making. In M. Lewis & J. Haviland-Jones (Eds.), *Handbook of emotions* (2nd edn., pp. 417–435). New York: Guilford.

Isen, A. M., Daubman, K. A., & Nowicki, G. P. (1987). Positive affect facilitates creative problem solving. *Journal of Personality and Social Psychology*, *52*, 1122–1131.

Kempe, M., & Memmert, D. (2017). Good, better, creative! The relevance of tactical creativity in world class soccer. Manuscript submitted for publication.

KICKER (2013). *German Soccer Magazine.* Issue from 22.01.2013.

Macnamara, B. N., Hambrick, D. Z., & Oswald, F. L. (2014). Deliberate practice and performance in music, games, sports, education, and professions: A meta-analysis. *Psychological Science*, *25*, 1608–1618.

Maxwell, J. P., Masters, R. S., & Eves, F. F. (2003). The role of working memory in motor learning and performance. *Consciousness and Cognition*, *12*, 376–402.

Memmert, D. (2007). Can creativity be improved by an attention-broadening training program? – An exploratory study focusing on team sports. *Creativity Research Journal*, *19*, 281–292.

Memmert, D. (2010a). Creativity, expertise, and attention: Exploring their development and their relationships. *Journal of Sport Science*, *29*, 93–104.

Memmert, D. (2010b). Testing of tactical performance in youth elite soccer. *Journal of Sports Science and Medicine*, *9*, 199–205.

Memmert, D. (2011). Sports and creativity. M. A. Runco & S. R. Pritzker (Eds.), *Encyclopedia of creativity* (pp. 373–378). San Diego: Academic Press.

Memmert, D. (2013). Tactical creativity. In T. McGarry, P. O'Donoghue, & J. Sampaio (Eds.), *Routledge handbook of sports performance analysis* (pp. 297–308). Abingdon: Routledge.

Memmert, D. (2015a). *Teaching tactical creativity in team and racket sports: Research and practice.* Abingdon: Routledge.

Memmert, D. (2015b). Attention in sports. J. Fawcett, E. F. Risko, & A. Kingstone (Eds.), *The handbook of attention*. Cambridge: MIT Press.

Memmert, D. (2015c). Development of tactical creativity in sports. J. Baker, & D. Farrow (Eds.), *The handbook of sport expertise* (pp. 363–372). Abingdon: Routledge.

Memmert, D., & Furley, P. (2007). "I spy with my little eye!" – Breadth of attention, inattentional blindness, and tactical decision making in team sports. *Journal of Sport & Exercise Psychology, 29*, 365–347.

Memmert, D., & Harvey, S. (2010). Identification of non-specific tactical problems in invasion games. *Physical Education and Sport Pedagogy, 15*, 287–305.

Memmert, D., & Roth, K. (2007). The effects of non-specific and specific concepts on tactical creativity in team ball sports. *Journal of Sport Science, 25*, 1423–1432.

Memmert, D., Baker, J., & Bertsch, C. (2010). Play and practice in the development of sport-specific creativity in team ball sports. *High Ability Studies, 21*, 3–18.

Memmert, D., Hüttermann, S., & Orliczek, J. (2013). Decide like Lionel Messi! The impact of regulatory focus on divergent thinking in sports. *Journal of Applied Social Psychology, 43*, 2163–2167.

Milgram, R. M. (1990). Creativity: An idea whose time has come and gone. In M. A. Runco & R. S. Albert (Eds.), *Theory of creativity* (pp. 215–233). Newbury Park: Sage.

Moraru, A., Memmert, D., & van der Kamp, J. (2016). Motor creativity: The roles of attention breadth and working memory in a divergent doing task. *Journal of Cognitive Psychology, 28*. DOI: 10.1080/20445911.2016.1201084

O'Donoghue, P. (2013). Sports performance profiling. In T. McGarry, P. O'Donoghue, & J. Sampaio (Eds.), *Routledge handbook of sports performance analysis* (pp. 127–139). Abingdon: Routledge.

Palao, J. M., & Morante, J. C. (2013). Technical effectiveness. In T. McGarry, P. O'Donoghue, & J. Sampaio (Eds.), *Routledge handbook of sports performance analysis* (pp. 213–225). Abingdon: Routledge.

Pinder, R. A., Davids, K. W., Renshaw, I., & Araújo, D. (2011). Representative learning design and functionality of research and practice in sport. *Journal of Sport and Exercise Psychology, 33*, 146–155.

Reilly, T. (1996). *Science and soccer*. London: E & FN Spon.

Runco, M. A. (2007). *Creativity – theories and themes: Research, development, and practice*. Burlington: Elsevier Academic Press.

Sampaio, J., & Leite, N. (2013). Performance indicators in game sports. In T. McGarry, P. O'Donoghue, & J. Sampaio (Eds.), *Routledge handbook of sports performance analysis* (pp. 115–126). Abingdon: Routledge.

Schmidt, R. A., & Wrisberg, C. A. (2004). *Motor learning and performance. A problem-based learning approach* (3rd edn.). Champaign: Human Kinetics.

Smith, M., & Cushion, C. J. (2006). An investigation of the in-game of professional, top level youth soccer coaches. *Journal of Sport Sciences 24*(4), 355–366.

Sternberg, R. J., & Lubart, T. I. (1995). *Defying the crowd*. New York: Free Press.

Williams, A. M., & Ericsson, K. A. (2005). Some considerations when applying the expert performance approach in sport. *Human Movement Science, 24*, 283–307.

Williams, A.M., Hodges, N.J., North, J.S., & Barton, G. (2006). Perceiving patterns of play in dynamic sport tasks: identifying the essential information underlying skilled performance. *Perception, 35*, 317–332.

Williams, M. (Ed.). (2013). *Science and soccer: Developing elite performance*. Abingdon: Routledge.

27 Creativity in Non-Human Animals

Allison B. Kaufman

and

William J. O'Hearn

Department of Ecology and Evolutionary Biology, University of Connecticut

Abstract

While they are not traditionally associated with creativity, non-human animals often use creative behaviors, innovative tools, and social learning to increase evolutionary fitness. This creativity can result in better foraging, higher mating success, increased social standing, better problem-solving abilities, or any number of other adaptive traits. This chapter discusses some general subcategories of creativity and innovation in non-human animals, along with key studies in the area.

Introduction

As recently as the last half a century, scientists have begun to acknowledge both that non-human animals have the ability to create and innovate, and that the study of this ability may enable us to learn about the development of our own creative abilities. Initially, interest in the creative abilities of non-human animals (henceforth "animals") focused on apes – with their human-like behavior; however, it soon became apparent that creativity extended far beyond the primates to a variety of other species in the animal kingdom (Menzel, Davenport, & Rogers, 1961; Boogert, Reader, Hoppitt, & Laland, 2008; Lefebvre, 1995). The resulting publications have come from various disciplines, including ethology, psychology, evolutionary biology, neuroscience, molecular biology, and ecology. This percolation of multiple fields and increase in collaboration and cooperation has led to not only answers, but a myriad of new questions. This chapter will provide a brief overview of the study of innovation and creativity in animals, discuss some of the unique issues facing researchers in the area, and highlight key studies which have shaped the field thus far.

The Vocabulary Problem

Human creativity researchers have long debated the exact way to define terms such as "creativity," "innovation," and "invention" (J. Kaufman, 2009), so it should come as no surprise that the issue of inconsistent definitions extends to animal research. In addition, because animal researchers are constantly worried about anthropomorphism (Mitchell, Thompson, & Miles, 1997; Wynne, 2004), terms become even more convoluted – for example, the human trait of "personality" is often referred to as "individual differences in behavior" or by use of other similarly complicated descriptions. Human researchers can – and do – focus on mental processes associated with creativity; however, being that animals cannot explain what they are thinking, animal researchers do not. This means that a term used by human researchers may have additional levels of depth or imply further cognitive abilities than what is meant by an animal researcher using the same term. In addition, it makes for logistical difficulties when comparing across studies.

The Scale of Study

One of the largest differences between the study of creativity in animals and humans is one of scale. Animals are not to be expected to produce Picasso-like paintings or spectacular inventions – indeed, some may never even reach the level of "mini-c," or personal creativity (Kaufman & Beghetto, 2009). Instead, the focus is on the very basis for creativity, what Glăveanu (2015) terms "proto-c," in addition to the building blocks of creativity – neophobia and neophilia (fear of or affinity for creativity), risk taking, and observational learning and teaching. The creative product is important and measurable, but many species which do not possess higher cognitive abilities have measurable preferences or variations in behavior which are innovative but do not yield actual products (and, as previously mentioned, the process itself is difficult to study).

Subtopics of Creativity

As mentioned previously, the study of creativity in animals focuses far less on the creative process than studies of human creativity, due to the communication barrier between humans and animals (A. Kaufman & J. Kaufman, 2014). While the creative process is nearly impossible to study in animals, the creative product is challenging as well, often taking the form of a behavior or temporary object, gone after it has been used. As a result of these challenges, when creativity in animals is studied it is usually done via "subtopics" which are used as a proxy for creativity, such as social learning, behavioral transmission, neophilia, play, and personality. The majority of this chapter will focus on these areas, as opposed to directly discussing "creativity." Additionally, innovations or creative products will be discussed within the context of the particular subtopics in which they come about (for example, learning to use tools via observation).

The overall story combining the subtopics can be told in different forms or models. J. Kaufman and A. Kaufman (2004) use a three-level model to discuss creativity in animals, breaking it down into recognition of novelty, observational learning, and innovation. Ramsey et al. (2007) use specific criteria for creative behavior, including originality within a geographic area, social properties, change over time, and occurrence (or lack thereof) of the behavior in captivity. However, the field is so new that models or measurements are far from standard or commonplace.

Neophobia, Neophilia, and Risk Taking

Neophobia, neophilia, and risk taking are precursors to creativity and can be viewed in a lens similar to the Openness to Experience personality trait (a measure of the tendancy toward cognitive exploration; DeYoung, Peterson, & Higgins, 2005; A. Kaufman & J. Kaufman, 2014). They require a delicate balance for survival, both within individuals and within cohorts. Animals which live or feed in groups, such as ants or birds, have been shown to thrive with very specific ratios of risk takers to non-risk takers; enough risk takers to find new food sources, but not enough to gamble the well-being of the group or colony (Griffin, Lermite, Perea, & Guez, 2013; Heck & Ghosh, 2000, 2002; Stöwe, Bugnyar, Heinrich, Kotrschal, & Stowe, 2006; Stöwe & Kotrschal, 2007). Behavioral flexibility is vital for the evolution of complex behaviors, like manipulative foraging (foraging using complex manipulations with hands/digits) and is predicated upon contact with novel environmental stimuli (Reader & Laland, 2001). Mery and Burns (2010) hypothesize that novel stimuli play a key role in the development of new adaptive behaviors, and animals that seek out such interactions, termed neophilic species, will more rapidly develop novel behaviors. Researchers have found that species relying on manipulative and explorative foraging in the wild were more likely to approach novel foods and were more successful at exploiting the food (Ashe, Heithaus, & Marshall, 2003; Day, Coe, Kendal, & Laland, 2003). Other studies have found a correlation between neophilia and innovation in a wide variety of species (Day et al., 2003; Krueger, Farmer, & Heinze, 2014; Kuczaj, Gory, & Xitco Jr, 2009). Boogert et al (2006) showed a relationship between social rank and neophilia in starlings, wherein individuals who readily approached novel food sources occupied high competitive social ranks, indicating a correlation between novelty-seeking behavior and social rank. Conversely, other studies have observed more exploratory behavior and higher innovation frequencies in low-ranking males, who are not spending time defending females and who have little to lose from risky investments (Krueger et al., 2014; Reader & Laland, 2001). Finally, some studies have hypothesized that personality or temperament may account for variation in exploratory behavior between individuals (Bell, 2007; Reale et al., 2007). Brosnan and Hopper (2014) identify five specific traits which limit novel behavior – neophobia, conservativism, conformity, functional fixedness, and the endowment effect (the tendency to value what is already in one's possession). None of these is particularly surprising and all have been shown to be limiting factors on creativity in humans to one extent or another (J. Kaufman, 2009).

Recognition of novelty is most often investigated using tests of neophilia and neophobia. Traditionally, these involve mice, rats, or other small mammals being introduced to new situations, new foods, or new objects. Open field tests, for example, place a subject in a new, open environment and track the number and location of "rearing" behaviors (Belzung, 2010). Rearing in this context involves standing on the hind feet and is useful for animals to get a better look at the immediate area. It is, however, potentially dangerous due to exposure to predators. Strains of rats have been engineered as "high responders" (HR) and "low responders" (LR); HR rats are more attracted to novelty, more likely to engage in risky behaviors like rearing, and tend toward sensation seeking; traits akin to the human "Openness to Experience," which is highly correlated with creativity (Dellu, Mayo, Piazza, Le Moal, & Simon, 1993; A. Kaufman, Butt, J. Kaufman, & Colbert-White, 2011). These animals make excellent subjects for in-lab experimental protocols.

Evolutionary Advantage

A second major emphasis in the study of creativity in animals is on the benefits of creative abilities from an evolutionary perspective. We currently cannot speculate on any intrinsic value of creativity for animals, so we must focus on benefits to survival. In humans, this is mirrored to some extent in the field of evolutionary psychology. However, true evolutionary change occurs at the level of the species and over vast amount of time, so the benefit of any creative ability must be examined from the perspective of the survival of the entire species as opposed to the individual.

Invasive species are an excellent example of creativity in the form of behavioral flexibility being used to enhance survivorship. In order to succeed in a foreign environment, a new species must find adequate food sources, proper housing, and develop strategies for evading predator species. Creative abilities are a distinct benefit.

Here the stipulation of "appropriateness" in the traditional definition of creativity also becomes more significant than it might otherwise be in human situations. Inappropriate creativity in the animal kingdom is far more likely to get one killed. For example, many species are far more likely to approach or eat a novel food item after having witnessed a conspecific do so (Rymer, Schradin, & Pillay, 2008; Thornton & Malapert, 2009). Overly creative behavior in courtship might result in a courtship display which is more frightening than it is impressive, thus scaring away a potential mate (Patricelli, Coleman, & Borgia, 2006). Humans, with their higher cognitive abilities, can label faux pas as such – but in animals these mistakes are evidence of poor fitness, and thus damning.

Innovation frequency, a measure of the number of observed innovations a given species has performed (Lefebvre, Whittle, Lascaris, & Finklestein, 1997), can also be used to estimate the potential for creativity to increase an organism's evolutionary success – for example, by measuring the benefits or adaptations offered by the innovation. As a measure, innovation frequency is fairly easy to work with – it can often be measured for a particular species simply by reviewing published anecdotes or examples of behavior, and was first developed by conducting an exhaustive search of existing literature for terms such as "novel" or "innovative" and tallying repeated observations of these behaviors in birds (Lefebvre, Timmermans, & Rosza, 1998;

Lefebvre et al., 1997). In addition, innovation frequency has a number of advantages as a measure of holistic intelligence. It focuses on general cognitive abilities rather than specialized ones, as well as large brain areas rather than smaller ones. Innovation frequency allows comparison across different species in the wild and hence improves our abilities to determine trends and make generalizations about the evolution of the brain (Lefebvre, Reader, & Sol, 2004, 2013). Finally, innovation frequency can be used as a direct empirical measure of cognition in the field (Lefebvre et al., 2004). This last benefit is particularly salient given later studies in the lab, which found that innovation frequency is correlated with species' forebrain size (Reader & Laland, 2003). This relationship between innovation frequency and forebrain size appears to be pervasive across multiple taxa, including non-human primates (Overington, Morand-Ferron, Boogert, & Lefebvre, 2009; Reader & Laland, 2002).

Using the relationship between avian brain size and innovation frequency, Sol and Lefebvre (2000) found that innovation frequency is positively correlated with invasion success (measured as survival in non-native habitat) in New Zealand bird species – validating the idea mentioned previously that creative abilities are a boon to invasive species. Their findings led to a "behavioral flexibility" hypothesis, which proposed a relationship between innovation frequency and the ability of a species to adapt to a novel environment (Sol, Timmermans, & Lefebvre, 2002). Work in non-human primates has provided additional support for this hypothesis by demonstrating directed selection for increased executive brain function through development of specific brain regions (Reader & Laland, 2002). Similar findings in New Caledonian crows link their immense innovative behavioral repertoire with rapid encephalization (Cnotka, Gunturkun, Rehkämpera, Gray, & Hunt, 2008).

Social or Observational Learning

Social learning, or the spread of information within a population, can also be used to measure the spread of creativity when a creative behavior becomes incorporated into the larger behavioral tradition of a population (Auersperg et al., 2014).

Reader and Laland (2003) found that social learning had a greater impact when inducing intake of an unfamiliar food, rather than a familiar food. Based on this, they proposed the hypothesis that social learning can be used to introduce novel behavioral patterns into a population. A similar supporting hypothesis has been posited by Sol and Lefebvre (2000), stating that social learning acts as one of the key forces for the spread of innovative behavior, be it a novel foraging behavior (for example, the population of birds which learned to open milk bottles left on doorsteps; Lefebvre, 1995), or an unexplored ecological niche (Krützen et al., 2014). Similar supporting evidence for behavioral transmission has been observed in most, if not all, species of primates (Burkart, Strasser, & Foglia, 2009; Huebner & Fichtel, 2015; Ottoni, de Resende, Izar, & Resende, 2005; Reader & Laland, 2001), cetaceans (Allen, Bejder, & Krützen, 2010), crocodilians (Dinets & Brueggen, 2013), horses (Krueger et al., 2014), bears (Mazur & Seher, 2008), and many species of birds (Boogert et al., 2008; Kenward, Weir, Rutz, & Kacelnik, 2005; Morand-Ferron, Lefebvre, Reader, Sol, & Elvin, 2004), to name a few. In addition to short-term survival benefits, Huffman and Hirata (2003) demonstrated the long-term diffusion of an innovative behavior within and between populations.

In a slight contrast, Heyes (2012) concludes that social learning is not social by virtue of using distinctly social learning mechanisms; it is social by virtue of a conspecific individual playing some role in providing the information to be learned. This suggests that social learning, defined as information acquired from watching conspecifics, is not evolutionarily distinct from asocial learning, defined as information gained from direct manipulation. This idea is supported by a comparative study of primate innovation and executive brain size conducted by Reader and Laland (2002), which found that the two forms of learning may be rooted in the same neurological processes. The hypothesis presented by Heyes (2012) lends credibility to the theory that many behaviors associated with larger relative brain size and higher cognition may have evolved simultaneously (Lefebvre et al., 2013).

Behavioral transmission, as concerned with the larger movement of behaviors between different populations of the same species (Huffman & Hirata, 2003), has been identified as a distinct process in animals. However, much like work on creativity across cultures (J. Kaufman, 2009), studies of behavioral transmission are concerned with the patterns of transmission and variation in behavioral repertoires between similar populations. Krutzen et al (2005) determined that the proliferation of sponging behavior (see below) observed in the bottlenose dolphin (*Tursiops truncates*) population of Shark Bay, Western Australia, could not be explained by genetic inheritance and fit the criteria of behavioral transmission. Other studies have demonstrated strong evidence of variation of foraging tactics along social boundaries (Sargeant & Mann, 2009). Similarly, repertoire size and similarity between populations could be determined by the stimuli individuals are exposed to in their environment (Huffman & Hirata, 2003).

Cantor and Whitehead (2013) proposed that this process of behavioral transmission occurs not by random observations of the behavior but along predetermined and predictable social avenues as dictated by the social network of the species. There is observational evidence supporting social-network-linked transmission in cases such as humpback whale (*Megaptera noveangeliae*) songs in the North and South Pacific (Rendell & Whitehead, 2001), and in sperm whale (*Physeter macrocephalus*) clans (Rendell, Mesnick, Dalebout, Burtenshaw, & Whitehead, 2011). Evidence of social-network-linked transmission has also been observed in non-human primates living in social hierarchal communities (Brydson, 2014). Conversely, researchers have found that transmission of certain foraging tactics is linked to ecological availability of resources (Sargeant & Mann, 2009).

However, while the proliferation of a new behavior cannot be explained by genetic inheritance, it can sometimes be tracked by genetics. There are several cases where social transmissions such as the ones above can be followed across groups of individuals using mitochondrial DNA (mtDNA). mtDNA is inherited matrilineally and thus serves as a distinct marker for family lines. Sponging behavior in dolphins, which appears to be taught by mothers to offspring, has been traced this way (Kopps et al., 2014; Kruetzen et al., 2005), as have some types of marine mammal vocalizations (Rendell et al., 2011).

Play

The more informal transmission of behaviors via play must also be considered. Play holds a key role in early social learning and group development (Kuczaj et al., 2009). For example, Kuczaj et al (2006) observed that juvenile dolphins are more likely to learn behaviors from conspecifics within their own cohort, and proposed that this served to both create social cohesiveness and transmit behaviors. Similar behaviors in a group, in turn, would again lead to further cohesiveness, completing the "circle." Researchers conducting primate studies have observed that juveniles play for longer periods of time and more frequently when in larger groups (Monteiro de Almeida Rocha, Pedreira dos Reis, & de Carvalho Oliveira, 2014). Interaction between an animal and the environment can also be characterized as play. Montgomery (2014) proposed that this interaction is key during development. His finding is supported by Kuczaj (2006), who hypothesized that play may create events which are a mix of novel and familiar stimuli, and which facilitate the development of adaptive behaviors and flexible problem-solving skills (Kuczaj et al., 2006).

In addition, the type of creative play an animal engages in appears to be directly related to ecological niche – for example, birds known to be good at problem solving show intricate combinations of objects in their play, while those which cache food in holes tend to play more often by inserting objects into things (Auersperg et al., 2015). This type of practicing and modeling of creative behavior is very reminiscent of the creative modeling and accumulation of expertise found while studying creativity in humans (S. Kaufman & J. Kaufman, 2007; Yi, Plucker, & Guo, 2015).

Planning and Intention

Innovation of an actual creative product generally requires planning and intention. Recent studies have found evidence of that ability in several species of primates (Beran & Parrish, 2012; Bourjade, Call, Pelé, Maumy, & Dufour, 2014; Sirianni, Mundry, & Boesch, 2015), dolphins (Kuczaj, Xitco Jr, & Gory, 2010) and corvids (Wimpenny, Weir, Clayton, Rutz, & Kacelnik, 2009) when selecting appropriate tools or solving problems which required using tools in a specific order. In captivity, animals are often trained to provide new or different behaviors upon request (see below), and are generally able to do this with high levels success (Kuczaj & Eskelinen, 2014).

Personality

The personality trait Openness to Experience is highly correlated with creativity in humans (S. Kaufman, 2003; McCrae, 1987). As the measurement of personality (often called "individual differences") in animals becomes more and more common, similar constructs can be seen in animal tests, and can be measured in conjunction with creative results.

Highfill and Kuczaj (2007) were among the first to make a direct comparison of personality between humans and animals. Their attempt to measure personality in dolphins used the human Five Factor scale on a group of dolphins which had been washed out to sea during Hurricane Katrina; trainers were asked to fill out questionnaires based on the animals' behavior before and after the hurricane. They later modified the personality constructs to include contextual sensitivity (Kuczaj, Highfill, & Byerly, 2012). Freeman et al (2013) performed a comprehensive review and exploratory analysis of published scales (both top-down and bottom-up) developed for chimpanzees. They produced a final measurement test which includes five to six constructs – Reactivity, Openness, Agreeableness, Dominance, and Extraversion (the sixth, Methodical, required further investigation before it could be formally included or excluded). Interestingly, the items which were predicted to load on a Neuroticism factor instead loaded on Reactivity and Dominance. Conscientiousness appeared as a factor in some of the studies the group reviewed, but did not show as a final factor. Other, less formal, assessments of personality have also been conducted in conjunction with cognitive experiments (Herrmann & Call, 2012). In humans, these tests – which are often done via self-report – are standardized with large groups of people and use complex measures to confirm reliability and validity. This may not be the case for tests of personality in non-humans (A. Kaufman & Rosenthal, 2009). As a result, while these tests can and do provide some method by which success at creative or novel tasks can be predicted, the open field trial or novelty trials discussed previously may be more reliable for obtaining empirical results.

Key Studies

Pryor et al. (1969) were among the first to demonstrate that animals (particularly marine mammals) had the ability to plan innovations on demand. This 1969 paper explained how a group of dolphins at Sea Life Park in Hawaii were trained to "innovate," or provide a behavior which they had not done for the trainers previously. By requesting the behavior several times in succession, the group was able to elicit increasingly complex behavior (i.e., multiple back or front flips), including tandem behaviors when more than one animal was presented with the hand signal. This type of training for creativity is still used in many training programs today in zoos, aquariums, and with pets (Pryor, 2014).

Lefebvre, Reader, and Sol unified and synthesized many of their findings over the past two decades (Lefebvre et al., 2013). Using innovation frequency and related measures of behavioral flexibility, they demonstrated evidence for convergent cognitive evolution in birds and primates. The paper posits that when literature on innovation in birds and primates are compared, the data show similar convergent relationships between innovation frequency and relative forebrain volume, innovation frequency and tool use, and innovation frequency and individual learning (see also Reader & MacDonald, 2003). They hypothesize that the similar relationship between numerous measures of behavioral flexibility and forebrain size is indicative of a selective force affecting the evolution of animal cognition (Lefebvre et al., 2013; Reader & MacDonald, 2003; Sol et al., 2002).

Several key studies have specifically highlighted innovative abilities in particular animals. The first time social transmission of a behavior – the opening of milk bottles on doorsteps by small birds in London – was tracked and recorded was in 1949 (Fisher & Hinde). Fifteen years later another extraordinary case was documented – that of Imo the Japanese macaque (*Macaca fuscata*). Imo was a female who developed an unusual custom of washing the dirt off her sweet potatoes before eating them. Not only did this innovation spread amongst Imo's conspecifics, but Imo continued to innovate – when scientists left piles of rice mixed with sand on the beach, Imo tossed handfuls into the water, causing the rice to float and the sand to sink – and others continued to adopt her creative behaviors (Kawai, 1965).

Over the years, there have been several other landmark innovators or groups of innovators which have become the subject of scientific study. In 2008, a group of dolphins was found to have developed a behavior dubbed "sponging"; these dolphins liked to eat small animals buried in the sediment, but often cut their rostrums on the jagged rocks and corals there. To alleviate this, the group took to carrying sponges, deliberately placed over the rostrum, to protect the area during foraging (Mann et al., 2008). More recently, and in yet another taxa, birds such as Betty the Crow (Weir, Chappell, & Kacelnik, 2002) and Figaro the Cockatoo (Auersperg, Szabo, von Bayern, & Kacelnik, 2012) have shown remarkable abilities to use tools and, particularly in the case of Betty, to plan a series of actions needed to obtain appropriate tools for a job (Wimpenny et al., 2009).

Conclusion

Animals are not traditionally what one would call a "discipline" in which to study creativity. Nevertheless, non-human creativity is becoming an area of study that is not just considered relevant, but which may also have broader implications for how creativity evolved in humans, and what specific components of creativity are adaptive. By looking at smaller subsets of overall creativity such as risk taking, tool use, play, social learning, and personality, it becomes possible to distill what is a very complex concept in humans to a level of study appropriate for non-human animals.

The relative newness of the study of typically human constructs in animals means there are an abundance of future directions available. As of now, no standard or models have been established to unify the work, so it is difficult to synthesize – and the lack of common terminology is the largest obstacle research in the area currently faces. Once this is complete, it will be easier to determine what we know about which species, and from there to trace abilities via evolutionary lineages. Theoretically, this would allow us to predict which species possess what degree of creative abilities. Lastly, relationships between creativity and other constructs such as intelligence are also in need of exploration.

References

Allen, S. J., Bejder, L., & Krützen, M. (2010). Why do Indo-Pacific bottlenose dolphins (Tursiops sp.) carry conch shells (Turbinella sp.) in Shark Bay, Western Australia? *Marine Mammal Science, 27*(2), 449–454. http://doi.org/10.1111/j.1748–7692 .2010.00409.x

Ashe, E. E., Heithaus, M. R., & Marshall, G. J. (2003). Studies of foraging in "southern resident" killer whales during July 2002: Dive depths, bursts in speed, and the use of a "Crittercam" system for examining sub-surface behavior. *National Marine Fisheries Service, National Marine Mammal Laboratory.*

Auersperg, A. M. I., Szabo, B., von Bayern, A. M. P., & Kacelnik, A. (2012). Spontaneous innovation in tool manufacture and use in a Goffin's cockatoo. *Current Biology, 22*(21), R903–904. http://doi.org/10.1016/j.cub.2012.09.002

Auersperg, A. M. I., van Horik, J. O., Bugnyar, T., Kacelnik, A., Emery, N. J., & von Bayern, A. M. P. (2015). Combinatory actions during object play in parrots (Psittacus erithacus) and corvids (Corvus). *Journal of Comparative Psychology, 1*, 62–71.

Auersperg, A. M. I., von Bayern, A. M. I., Weber, S., Szabadvari, A., Bugnyar, T., & Kacelnik, A. (2014). Social transmission of tool use and tool manufacture in Goffin cockatoos (Cacatua goffini). *Proceedings of the Royal Society B: Biological Sciences, 281*(1793), 20140972–20140972. http://doi.org/10.1098/rspb .2014.0972

Bell, A. M. (2007). Evolutionary biology: Animal personalities. *Nature, 447*, 539–540.

Belzung, C. (2010). Open-field test. In I. P. Stolerman (Ed.), *Encyclopedia of psychopharmacology* (pp. 920–926). New York: Springer.

Beran, M. J., & Parrish, A. E. (2012). Sequential responding and planning in capuchin monkeys (Cebus apella). *Animal Cognition, 15*(6), 1085–1094.

Boogert, N. J., Reader, S. M., Hoppitt, W., & Laland, K. N. (2008). The origin and spread of innovations in starlings. *Animal Behaviour, 75*(4), 1509–1518. http://doi.org/10 .1016/j.anbehav.2007.09.033

Boogert, N. J., Reader, S. M., & Laland, K. N. (2006). The relation between social rank, neophobia and individual learning in starlings. *Animal Behaviour, 72*(6), 1229–1239. Retrieved on November 10, 2016, from www.sciencedirect.com/ science/article/B6W9 W-4M1DB4 C-1/2/a54cdd8d1e495ece5335553bc0a6b1d8

Bourjade, M., Call, J., Pelé, M., Maumy, M., & Dufour, V. (2014). Bonobos and orangutans, but not chimpanzees, flexibly plan for the future in a token-exchange task. *Animal Cognition.* http://doi.org/10.1007/s10071-014–0768-6

Brosnan, S., & Hopper, L. (2014). Psychological limits on animal innovation. *Animal Behaviour.* http://doi.org/10.1016/j.anbehav.2014.02.026

Brydson, R. (2014). Incipient tradition in wild chimpanzees. *Physical Sciences, 12*, 9–10.

Burkart, J. M., Strasser, A., & Foglia, M. (2009). Trade-offs between social learning and individual innovativeness in common marmosets, Callithrix jacchus. *Animal Behaviour, 77*(5), 1291–1301. Retrieved on November 15, 2016, from www.sciencedirect.com/science/ article/B6W9 W-4VW4VC9-3/2/b5a6092d93262e59736d231c16d00926

Cantor, M., & Whitehead, H. (2013). The interplay between social networks and culture: theoretically and among whales and dolphins. *Philosophical Transactions of the Royal Society of London. Series B, Biological Sciences, 368*(1618), 20120340. http://doi.org/10.1098/rstb.2012.0340

Cnotka, J., Gunturkun, O., Rehkämpera, G., Gray, R. D., & Hunt, G. R. (2008). Extraordinary large brains in tool-using New Caledonian crows. *Neuroscience Letters*, *433*, 241–245.

Day, R. L., Coe, R. L., Kendal, J. R., & Laland, K. N. (2003). Neophilia, innovation and social learning: A study of intergeneric differences in callitrichid monkeys. *Animal Behavior*, *65*(3), 559–572.

Dellu, F., Mayo, W., Piazza, P. V. V, Le Moal, M., & Simon, H. (1993). Individual differences in behavioral responses to novelty in rats. Possible relationship with the sensation-seeking trait in man. *Personality and Individual Differences*, *15*(4), 411–418. http://doi.org/10.1016/0191–8869(93)90069-F

DeYoung, C. G., Peterson, J. B., & Higgins, D. M. (2005). Sources of openness/intellect: cognitive and neuropsychological correlates of the fifth factor of personality. *Journal of Personality*, *73*(4), 825–858.

Dinets, V., & Brueggen, J. C. J. D. (2013). Crocodilians use tools for hunting. *Ethology Ecology & Evolution*, *27*(1), 1–5. http://doi.org/10.1080/03949370.2013.858276

Fisher, J., & Hinde, R. A. (1949). The opening of milk bottles by birds. *British Birds*, *42*, 347–357.

Freeman, H. D., Brosnan, S. F., Hopper, L. M., Lambeth, S. P., Schapiro, S. J., & Gosling, S. D. (2013). Developing a comprehensive and comparative questionnaire for measuring personality in chimpanzees using a simultaneous top-down/bottom-up design. *American Journal of Primatology*. http://doi.org/10.1002/ajp.22168

Glăveanu, V. (2015). Proto-c creativity? In A. B. Kaufman & J. C. Kaufman (Eds.), *Animal creativity and innovation* (pp. 120–128). Waltham, MA: Academic Press.

Griffin, A. S., Lermite, F., Perea, M., & Guez, D. (2013). To innovate or not: contrasting effects of social groupings on safe and risky foraging in Indian mynahs. *Animal Behaviour*. Retrieved on October 29, 2016 from www.sciencedirect.com/science/article/pii/S0003347213004399

Heck, P. S., & Ghosh, S. (2000). A study of synthetic creativity: Behavior modeling and simulation of an ant colony. *IEEE Expert Intelligent Systems and Their Applications*, *15*(6), 58–67. http://doi.org/10.1109/5254.895863

Heck, P. S., & Ghosh, S. (2002). The design and role of synthetic creative traits in artificial ant colonies. *Journal of Intelligent & Robotic Systems*, *33*(4), 343–370. Retrieved on November 15, 2015 from https://link.springer.com/article/10.1023/A:10155526 02374 <Go to ISI>://000175751000001

Herrmann, E., & Call, J. (2012). Are there geniuses among the apes? *Philosophical Transactions of the Royal Society of London. Series B, Biological Sciences*, *367*(1603), 2753–61. http://doi.org/10.1098/rstb.2012.0191

Heyes, C. M. (2012). What's social about social learning? *Journal of Comparative Psychology*, *126*, 193–202.

Highfill, L. E., & Kuczaj, S. A. (2007). Do bottlenose dolphins (Tursiops truncatus) have distinct and stable personalities? *Aquatic Mammals*, *33*(3), 380–389.

Huebner, F., & Fichtel, C. (2015). Innovation and behavioral flexibility in wild redfronted lemurs (Eulemur rufifrons). *Animal Cognition*, *18*(3), 777–787. http://doi.org/10.1007/s10071-015-0844-6

Huffman, M., & Hirata, S. (2003). Biological and ecological foundations of primate behavioral traditions. The biology of traditions: Models and evidence. In Dorothy M. Fragaszy and Susan Perry (Eds.), *The Biology of Traditions* (pp. 267–296). Cambridge: Cambridge University Press.

Kaufman, J. C., & Beghetto, R. A. (2009). Beyond big and little: The four C model of creativity. *Review of General Psychology*, *13*, 1–12.

Kaufman, A. B., Butt, A. E., Kaufman, J. C., & Colbert-White, E. N. (2011). Towards a neurobiology of creativity in nonhuman animals. *Journal of Comparative Psychology*, *125*(3), 255–272.

Kaufman, A. B., & Kaufman, J. C. (2014). Applying theoretical models on human creativity to animal studies. *Animal Behavior and Cognition*, *1*(1), 78–90. http://doi.org/10.12966/abc.02.01.2014

Kaufman, A. B., & Rosenthal, R. (2009). Can you believe my eyes? The importance of interobserver reliability statistics in observations of animal behaviour. *Animal Behaviour*, *78*(6), 1487–1491. http://doi.org/10.1016/j.anbehav.2009.09.014

Kaufman, J. C. (2009). *Creativity 101*. New York: Springer.

Kaufman, J. C., & Kaufman, A. B. (2004). Applying a creativity framework to animal cognition. *New Ideas in Psychology*, *22*(2), 143–155. http://doi.org/10.1016/j.newideapsych.2004.09.006

Kaufman, S. B. (2013). Opening up openness to experience: A four-factor model and relations to creative achievement in the arts and sciences. *Journal of Creative Behavior*, *47*, 233–255.

Kaufman, S. B., & Kaufman, J. C. (2007). Ten years to expertise, many more to greatness: An investigation of modern writers. *Journal of Creative Behavior*, *41*(2), 114–124.

Kawai, M. (1965). Newly-acquired pre-cultural behavior of the natural troop of Japanese monkeys on Koshima islet. *Primates*, *6*(1), 1–30.

Kenward, B., Weir, A. A. S., Rutz, C., & Kacelnik, A. (2005). Behavioural ecology: Tool manufacture by naive juvenile crows. *Nature*, *433*(7022), 121.

Kopps, A. M., Ackermann, C. Y., Sherwin, W. B., Allen, S. J., Bejder, L., Krutzen, M., & Krützen, M. (2014). Cultural transmission of tool use combined with habitat specializations leads to fine-scale genetic structure in bottlenose dolphins. *Proceedings of the Royal Society B: Biological Sciences*, *281*(1782), 20133245–20133245. http://doi.org/10.1098/rspb.2013.3245

Krueger, K., Farmer, K., & Heinze, J. (2014). The effects of age, rank and neophobia on social learning in horses. *Animal Cognition*, *17*(3), 645–55. http://doi.org/10.1007/s10071-013–0696-x

Kruetzen, M., Mann, J., Heithaus, M. R., Connor, R. C., Bejder, L., Sherwin, W. B., & Sherman, W. B. (2005). Cultural Transmission of Tool Use in Bottlenose Dolphins. *Proceedings of the National Academy of Sciences*, *102*(25), 8939–8943. http://doi.org/10.1073/pnas.0500232102

Krützen, M., Kreicker, S., Macleod, C. D., Learmonth, J., Kopps, A. M., Walsham, P., & Allen, S. J. (2014). Cultural transmission of tool use by Indo-Pacific bottlenose dolphins (Tursiops sp.) provides access to a novel foraging niche. *Proceedings. Biological Sciences / The Royal Society*, *281*(1784), 20140374. http://doi.org/10.1098/rspb.2014.0374

Kuczaj, S. A., & Eskelinen, H. C. (2014). The "Creative Dolphin" revisited: What do dolphins do when asked to vary their behavior? *Animal Behavior and Cognition*, *1*(1), 66–77. http://doi.org/10.12966/abc.02.05.2014

Kuczaj, S. A., Gory, J. D., & Xitco Jr, M. J. (2009). How intelligent are dolphins? A partial answer based on their ability to plan their behavior when confronted with novel problems. *Japanese Journal of Animal Psychology*, *59*(1), 99–115.

Kuczaj, S. A., Highfill, L., & Byerly, H. (2012). The importance of considering context in the assessment of personality characteristics: Evidence from ratings of dolphin personality. *International Journal of Comparative Psychology, 25*(4), 309–329. Retrieved from http://escholarship.org/uc/item/4hg0p6cq.pdf

Kuczaj, S. A., Makecha, R., Trone, M., Paulos, R. D. R. D., & Ramos, J. A. A. J. A. (2006). Role of peers in cultural innovation and cultural transmission: Evidence from the play of dolphin calves. *International Journal of Comparative Psychology, 19*(2), 223–240. Retrieved on October 25, 2016 from http://escholarship.org/uc/item/4pn1t50s.pdf

Kuczaj, S. A., Xitco Jr, M. J., & Gory, J. D. (2010). Can dolphins plan their behavior? *International Journal of Comparative Psychology, 23*(4), 664–670. Retrieved on November 15, 2016, from http://comparativepsychology.org/ijcp-2010–4/07 .Kuczaj_etal_Final.pdf

Lefebvre, L. (1995). The opening of milk bottles by birds: Evidence for accelerating learning rates, but against the wave-of-advance model of cultural transmission. *Behavioral Processes, 34*, 43–54.

Lefebvre, L., Reader, S. M., & Sol, D. (2004). Brains, innovations, and evolution in birds and primates. *Brain, Behavior, and Evolution, 63*(4), 233–246. http://doi.org/10.1159 /000076784

Lefebvre, L., Reader, S. M., & Sol, D. (2013). Innovating innovation rate and its relationship with brains, ecology and general intelligence. *Brain, Behavior and Evolution, 81*(3), 143–5. http://doi.org/10.1159/000348485

Lefebvre, L., Timmermans, S., & Rosza, L. (1998). Feeding Innovations and forebrain size in Australasian birds. *Behaviour, 135*, 1007–1097.

Lefebvre, L., Whittle, P., Lascaris, E., & Finklestein, A. (1997). Feeding innovations and forebrain size in birds. *Animal Behavior, 53*, 549–560.

Mann, J., Sargeant, B. L., Watson-Capps, J. J., Gibson, Q. A., Heithaus, M. R., Connor, R. C., & Patterson, E. (2008). Why do dolphins carry sponges? *PloS One, 3*(12), e3868. http://doi.org/10.1371/journal.pone.0003868

Mazur, R., & Seher, V. (2008). Socially learned foraging behaviour in wild black bears, Ursus americanus. *Animal Behaviour, 75*(4), 1503–1508. http://doi.org/10.1016/j .anbehav.2007.10.027

McCrae, R. R. (1987). Creativity, divergent thinking, and openness to experience. *Journal of Personality and Social Psychology, 52*, 1258–1265.

Menzel, E. W., Davenport, R. K., & Rogers, C. M. (1961). Some aspects of behavior toward novelty in young chimpanzees. *Journal of Comparative and Physiological Psychology, 54*, 16–19.

Mery, F., & Burns, J. (2010). Behavioral plasticity: An interaction between evolution and experience. *Evolutionary Ecology, 24*, 571–583.

Mitchell, R. W., Thompson, N. S., & Miles, H. L. (1997). Taking anthropomorphism and anecdotes seriously. In R. W. Mitchell, N. S. Thompson, & H. L. Miles (Eds.), *Anthropomorphism, anecdotes, and animals.* Albany, New York: State University of New York Press.

Monteiro de Almeida Rocha, J., Pedreira dos Reis, P., & de Carvalho Oliveira, L. (2014). Play behavior of the golden-headed lion tamarin in Brazilian cocoa agroforests. *Folia Primatologica, 85*(3), 192–199. http://doi.org/10.1159/10.1159/000362813

Montgomery, S. H. (2014). The relationship between play, brain growth and behavioural flexibility in primates. *Animal Behaviour, 90*, 281–286. http://doi.org/10.1016/j .anbehav.2014.02.004

Morand-Ferron, J., Lefebvre, L., Reader, S. M., Sol, D., & Elvin, S. (2004). Dunking behaviour in Carib grackles. *Animal Behaviour*, *68*(6), 1267–1274.

Ottoni, E. B., de Resende, B. D., Izar, P., & Resende, B. D. (2005). Watching the best nutcrackers: What capuchin monkeys (Cebus apella) know about others' tool-using skills. *Animal Cognition*, *24*(4), 215–219. http://doi.org/10.1007/s10071-004-0245-8

Overington, S. E., Morand-Ferron, J., Boogert, N. J., & Lefebvre, L. (2009). Technical innovations drive the relationship between innovativeness and residual brain size in birds. *Animal Behaviour*, *78*(4), 1001–1010. http://doi.org/10.1016/j.anbehav.2009.06.033

Patricelli, G. L., Coleman, S. W., & Borgia, G. (2006). Male satin bowerbirds, Ptilonorhunchus violaceus, adjust their display intensity in response to female startling: An experiment with robotic females. *Animal Behavior*, *71*(1), 49–59. http://doi.org/10.1016/j.anbehav.2005.03.029

Pryor, K. W. (2014). Historical perspectives: A dolphin journey. *Aquatic Mammals*, *40*(1), 104–114.

Pryor, K. W., Haag, R., & O'Reilly, J. (1969). The creative porpoise: Training for novel behavior. *Journal of the Experimental Analysis of Behavior*, *12*(4), 653. Retrieved on November 30, 2016, from www.ncbi.nlm.nih.gov/pmc/articles/PMC1338662/

Ramsey, G., Bastian, M. L., & van Schaik, C. (2007). Animal innovation defined and operationalized. *The Behavioral and Brain Sciences*, *30*(4), 393–407; discussion 407–32. http://doi.org/10.1017/S0140525X07002373

Reader, S. M., & Laland, K. N. (2002). Social intelligence, innovation, and enhanced brain size in primates. *Proceedings of the National Academy of Sciences*, *99*(7), 4436–4441. http://doi.org/10.1073/pnas.062041299

Reader, S. M., & Laland, K. N. (Eds.). (2003). *Animal innovation: An introduction*. Oxford: Oxford University Press.

Reader, S. M., & Laland, K. N. N. (2001). Primate innovation: Sex, age and social rank differences. *International Journal of Primatology*, *22*(5), 787–805. Retrieved on October 15, 2015, from www.springerlink.com/index/ln47117526184421.pdf

Reader, S. M., & MacDonald, K. (2003). Environmental variability and primate flexibility. In S. M. Reader & K. N. Laland (Eds.), *Animal innovation* (pp. 83–116). Oxford: Oxford Univ Press.

Reale, D., Reader, S. M., Sol, D., McDougall, P. T., Dingemanse, N. J., & Réale, D. (2007). Integrating animal temperament within ecology and evolution. *Biological Reviews*, *82*(2), 291–318. http://doi.org/10.1111/j.1469-185X.2007.00010.x

Rendell, L. E., Mesnick, S. L., Dalebout, M. L., Burtenshaw, J., & Whitehead, H. (2011). Can genetic differences explain vocal dialect variation in sperm whales, Physetermacrocephalus? *Behavior Genetics*, *42*(2), 332–43. http://doi.org/10.1007/s10519-011-9513-y

Rendell, L. E., & Whitehead, H. (2001). Culture in whales and dolphins. *Behavioral and Brain Sciences*, *24*(2), 309–382. Retrieved on November 25, 2016, from https://www.ncbi.nlm.nih.gov/pubmed/11530544 <Go to ISI>://000170177900061

Rymer, T., Schradin, C., & Pillay, N. (2008). Social transmission of information about novel food in two populations of the African striped mouse, Rhabdomys pumilio. *Animal Behaviour*, *76*(4), 1297–1304. Retrieved on November 15, 2016, from www.sciencedirect.com/science/article/B6W9W-4T1SKGD-1/2/05b77926cd3356c318 53a5e8e5f24c39

Sargeant, B. L., & Mann, J. (2009). Developmental evidence for foraging traditions in wild bottlenose dolphins. *Animal Behaviour, 78*(3), 715–721. Retrieved on November 24, 2016, from www.sciencedirect.com/science/article/B6W9W-4WWPFWR-2/2/c599b183fc722418d061b4c8005b81a2

Sedley, D. (2003). *The Cambridge companion to Greek and Roman philosophy.* Cambridge, UK: Cambridge University Press.

Sirianni, G., Mundry, R., & Boesch, C. (2015). When to choose which tool: Multidimensional and conditional selection of nut-cracking hammers in wild chimpanzees. *Animal Behaviour, 100*, 152–165. http://doi.org/10.1016/j.anbehav.2014.11.022

Sol, D., & Lefebvre, L. (2000). Behavioral flexibility predicts invasion success in birds introduced to New Zealand. *Oikos, 90*, 599–615.

Sol, D., Timmermans, S., & Lefebvre, L. (2002). Behavioral flexibility and invasion success in birds. *Animal Behavior, 60*, 495–502.

Sternberg, R. J. (1999). *Handbook of creativity.* Cambridge, England: Cambridge University Press.

Stöwe, M., Bugnyar, T., Heinrich, B., Kotrschal, K., & Stowe, M. (2006). Effects of group size on approach to novel objects in ravens (Corvus corax). *Ethology, 112*(11), 1079–1088. http://doi.org/doi:10.1111/j.1439–0310.2006.01273.x

Stöwe, M., & Kotrschal, K. (2007). Behavioural phenotypes may determine whether social context facilitates or delays novel object exploration in ravens (Corvus corax). *Journal of Ornithology, 148*(S2), 179–184. http://doi.org/10.1007/s10336-007-0145-1

Thornton, A., & Malapert, A. (2009). Experimental evidence for social transmission of food acquisition techniques in wild meerkats. *Animal Behaviour, 78*(2), 255–264. Retrieved on October 30, 2016, from www.sciencedirect.com/science/article/B6W9W-4WKJ5GC-1/2/12eb7df91fb86724be45a89cce069b1e

Weir, A. A. S., Chappell, J., & Kacelnik, A. (2002). Shaping of hooks in New Caledonian crows. *Science (New York, N.Y.), 297*(5583), 981. http://doi.org/10.1126/science.1073433

Wimpenny, J. H., Weir, A. A. S., Clayton, L., Rutz, C., & Kacelnik, A. (2009). Cognitive processes associated with sequential tool use in New Caledonian crows. *PloS One, 4*(8), e6471. http://doi.org/10.1371/journal.pone.0006471

Wynne, C. D. L. (2004). The perils of anthropomorphism. *Nature, 428*(6983), 606.

Yi, X., Plucker, J. A., & Guo, J. (2015). Modeling influences on divergent thinking and artistic creativity. *Thinking Skills and Creativity, 16*, 62–68. http://doi.org/10.1016/j.tsc.2015.02.002

28 Violent Innovation

Creativity in the Domain of Terrorism

Gina Scott Ligon
University of Nebraska at Omaha

Karyn Sporer
University of Maine

Douglas C. Derrick
University of Nebraska at Omaha

Abstract

Terrorism provides a rich yet understudied domain to examine creativity. Because violent ideological organizations must continue to generate covert and novel ways to recruit members, raise finances, and plan attacks, theories of creativity typically applied to more conventional organizations can also apply to terrorist organizations. The present effort reviews the extant literature on malevolent creativity, examining commonalities and differences about studying creativity in the domain of terrorism. Reviewing both lab-based and field-based research on terrorist creativity, we present a call for research to measure creativity in this domain.

Terrorism provides an archetype context for examining creativity, as the need for survival and innovation pervades these destructive and malevolent groups. Violent extremist organizations (VEOs) operate in a turbulent environment with an ill-defined problem set (Lubart, 2001) and work toward creative goals (Shalley, 1995) that are both ideologically and organizationally motivated. Perhaps most importantly, terrorists must maintain the element of novelty and surprise due to the clandestine nature of their operations and the requirement to shock their targets. Despite this potentially rich context for exploration, relatively little systematic analysis exists to examine how conventional models for creativity operate in this domain. The exceptions are a handful of researchers trained in the examination of the creative process (Cropley, Kaufman, & Cropley, 2008; Gill, Horgan, Hunter, & Cushenberry, 2013; Mumford, Espejo, Hunter, Bedell-Avers, Eubanks, & Connelly, 2007), as well as political scientists and international relations researchers who have applied traditional

This material is based upon work supported by the U.S. Department of Homeland Security under Grant Award Number 2012-ST-061-CS0001, Principal Investigator G.S. Ligon. The views and conclusions contained in this document are those of the authors and should not be interpreted as necessarily representing the official policies, either expressed or implied, of the U.S. Department of Homeland Security creativity models to explain violent, ideologically motivated behavior from lone wolves and groups (Ackerman, 2015; Dolnick, 2007, 2015; Horowtiz, 2010; Sinai, 2015). Thus, in this chapter, we examine violent innovation in the domain of terrorism. We begin by providing a brief overview of the nature of violent ideological organizations to demonstrate their unique operating domain. We then explore key studies from other researchers as well as our own longitudinal work on terrorism to illustrate how creativity is measured in this field. Next, we describe constructs that are most important to studying terrorism and creativity. Finally, we present a set of propositions to shape future research about violent innovation in terrorism.

The Context: The Nature of Violent Ideological Organizations

VEOs are both similar to and different from more conventional organizations in how they solve problems (Ligon, Simi, Harms, & Harris, 2013). A model developed by Ligon and Derrick (2015) describes the three interacting goals that shape VEO pursuits as: (1) ideological, (2) violent, and (3) organizational forces (see Figure 28.1).

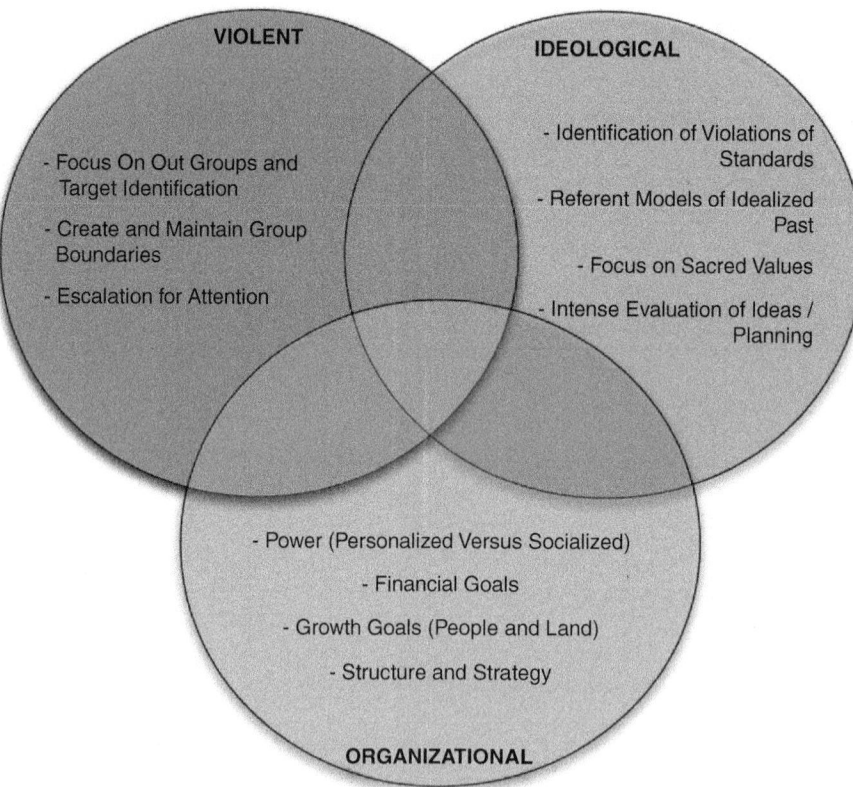

VIOLENT

- Focus On Out Groups and
  Target Identification

- Create and Maintain Group
  Boundaries

- Escalation for Attention

IDEOLOGICAL

- Identification of Violations of
  Standards

- Referent Models of Idealized
  Past

- Focus on Sacred Values

- Intense Evaluation of Ideas /
  Planning

- Power (Personalized Versus Socialized)

- Financial Goals

- Growth Goals (People and Land)

- Structure and Strategy

ORGANIZATIONAL

Figure 28.1 *Forces in VEO problem solving, adapted from Ligon & Derrick, 2015.*

First, VEOs operate under an overarching ideology, which creates a framework through which decisions are made and/or decisions are framed to followers. Second, VEOs operate in dangerous, crisis-laden environments. Environmental danger and illicit activities are related to VEOs' use and pursuit of violence in the name of their ideological and group-maintenance goals. Moreover, VEOs' target characteristics dictate the nature of violence they pursue (Drake, 1998). For example, groups whose targets' have no possibility of being conscripted into the terrorist organization (e.g., groups with "Strong Othering" of the out-group based on strong, observable differences in ethnicity, religion, and other measurable characteristics) are more violent, lethal, and destructive when planning attacks on their targets (Asal & Rethemeyer, 2008). Finally, the need to grow and maintain an organization in the context of their ideological goals creates a powerful shaping mechanism for VEOs, and is perhaps where the most parallels to conventional organizations can be made. For example, VEOs have organizational boundaries, hierarchy, leadership structures, succession planning, financial portfolios, and recruiting functions (Ligon et al, 2013; Shapiro, 2013). In a recent profile of the Islamic State in Iraq and Syria (ISIS), we identified that this organization has a defined organizational structure comprised of media relations, military operations, and public administration/governance (Ligon, Harms, Crowe, Simi, & Lundmark, 2014). ISIS also recruits a cadre of technical experts who focus on the development of cyber operations, weaponry, and oversee maintenance of critical oil and water resources (Weiss & Hassan, 2015).

According to internal documents found from the group, it is evident that ISIS is intent on developing increasingly *novel* and *effective* ways to procure resources, generate revenue, recruit foreign fighters, and execute strategic missions (Stern & Berger, 2015). Thus, VEOs, while different from conventional organizations given their focus on ideology and violence, are similar to conventional organizations in their structures, operations, and growth objectives. We argue that, given the ill-defined domain in which they operate coupled with the expressed intent to increase the novelty and effectiveness of activities, VEOs provide a perfect context to study creativity. What is less clear, however, is which creativity constructs operate as expected in the terrorism domain and which may manifest differently.

Conceptualizing Creativity in the Domain of Terrorism: Key Studies

Cropley, Kaufman, and Cropley (2008) argued that malevolent creativity is the use of creativity for undesirable ends.[1] Given that terrorists engage in novel attacks to bring damage to people, processes, property, and/or symbols of their target group (Ligon, 2010), it seems that the definition of malevolent or negative creativity

---

[1] While outside the scope of the current chapter, we can still question who and how do we determine if an outcome is desirable vs. undesirable? Certainly one can argue that malevolent innovation and undesirable ends are, in fact, desirable for the violent ideological/terrorist organizations (Cropley, Kaufman, & Cropley, 2008). In the current chapter, however, we assume that terrorism and destructive outcomes are undesirable.

can be applied to this domain. Why, then, are there not more studies from creativity scholars in this domain? We identified at least three reasons for less attention from our fellow creativity researchers.

First, malevolent creativity is historically under-studied in a laboratory environment. While some studies have examined the underlying psychological processes of malevolent creativity (e.g., Cropley, Kaufman, White, & Chiera, 2014; Harris, Reiter-Palmon, & Kaufman, 2013), approximating conditions similar to those in real-world ideological groups can be challenging. This is exacerbated by the fact that few creativity researchers have interest in pursuing investigations of creative problem solving with participants who may have engaged in violent activities in the name of an ideological purpose.

Second, it is difficult to assess research and development (R&D) and its requisite experimentation that happens organizationally in VEOs with ethnographic or field research methodologies. This is partly because VEOs face budget constraints that prevent them from investing in infrastructure required for larger organizational innovation. In addition, due to the clandestine nature of these organizations, any element of a formal R&D arm is likely to operate in secrecy that prevents outside examination. However, there is some evidence that VEOs and other criminals value innovation and the scientific processes. For example, ISIS recently put out a recruitment message in their *Dabiq* magazine asking for engineers and persons with specialized technical training to join the organization, where they can use their skills to create destruction. There is some evidence that the recruits are then placed into specialized jobs or positions (Gates & Podder, 2015). Thus, it is likely that more sophisticated, organized VEOs have R&D elements (Ligon, 2013). Nonetheless, it is difficult to identify which VEOs these may be, as well as engage in field methods to study them relative to other organizational innovation where databases exist that facilitate field research (e.g., Patent rates).

Third, and related to the above impediment to the examination of creativity in terrorist groups, it is difficult to measure a VEO's organizational capacity for innovation (Horowitz, 2010). For example, larger VEOs may have the munificence required to invest in innovation, but they may also be larger and more bureaucratic – which can make it more difficult for them to adopt radical innovation (Crenshaw, 1981). VEOs, like other organizations, tend to invest human and political capital into successful tactics (e.g., suicide bombings), and when they do this at the cost of investing in broader goals, it can be difficult for them to switch practices and generate new tactics. Thus, some terrorism scholars have argued that the older, more established VEOs may be more likely to engage in incremental innovation rather than broad, sweeping campaigns (Rasmussen & Hafez, 2010). These inconsistencies may impede researchers from adequately assessing this domain for creativity.

Research from Creativity Scholars

Despite these barriers to studying creativity in the domain of terrorism, there have been four important lines of research from creativity scholars about violent innovation. First, Cropley et al (2008) outlined eleven principles of malevolent creativity by examining the products of creativity for destructive ends (e.g., the work of criminals, competitors, and terrorists). They suggested that even negative or destructive creativity should be evaluated against the criteria of relevance, effectiveness, novelty, elegance, and generalizability – similar to how we evaluate the products of other types of benevolent creativity. Their work has profiled criminals, competitors, and terrorists to draw parallels between productive and destructive creativity (Cropley, Cropley, Kaufman, & Runco, 2010).

Harris et al (2013) examined antecedents of malevolently creative products in a lab setting across two studies. Here they found that even when controlling for situational factors, individuals who were lower in Emotional Intelligence were more likely to generate malevolently creative solutions. While their study was based on individuals, it stands to reason that such individuals may not work as cohesively when placed in a team; thus, destructive teams may suffer from within group conflict and a lack of synchronicity that may detract from accomplishing objectives. It is therefore unclear how group dynamics relate to creativity in VEO teams. However, the notion of ideology in VEOs may serve as a unifying contextual factor that can reduce in-group conflict among such individuals by focusing aggression on the out-group rather than internal to the team (McCauley, 1998; McCauley & Moskalenko, 2008).

Finally, Gill et al (2013) developed a model of malevolent creativity with a particular emphasis on case studies of terrorist attacks.[2] In their model, they emphasized the process nature of creativity and innovation, and they described both endogenous (e.g., inside the organization such as creative individuals, resources) and exogenous (e.g., environmental conditions) variables that could be examined in the context of terrorist organizations. Gill and colleagues reviewed conventional creativity literature to identify well-established trends in other types of organizations, and then they used compelling case examples (e.g., the 2006 Transatlantic Liquid Bomb plot) to illustrate how these concepts may operate in the planning and execution of attacks. For example, they identified how resources (Tushman & O'Reilly, 1996), exposure to novel problems (Lubart, 2001), and processes (Mumford et al., 1991) might have been related to the terrorist team's capacity for creativity; the researchers pointed out that the terrorist team stopped short of implementing the attack due to counter-terrorism laws, however (Gill et al., 2013).

While the examinations from Cropley and colleagues (2008), Harris and colleagues (2013), and Gill and colleagues (2013) are important and groundbreaking in the development of malevolent creativity as a construct, a fourth line of research we have pursued seeks to examine creativity in actual terrorist groups. Our research, funded primarily by University Programs at the Department of Homeland Security, Science and Technology Directorate (Ligon, 2010), sought to accomplish three objectives. First, to apply our models of creativity to VEOs, we need to understand the unique context of the violent ideological group, with particular focus on how different organizational structures lead to different performance outcomes

---

[2] See also Gill et al (2011) for a discussion on the use of improvised explosive devises in terrorist attacks.

(Ligon et al., 2013). Second, although it may seem intuitive that we can apply what we know in creativity literature to understand VEO innovation in teams, unless we have empirically grounded findings about actual terrorist groups, our generalizations are much less certain and more tenuous. Given the intent of this broader book is to examine how creativity varies across domains, it makes sense that findings about malevolent creativity, particularly in the context of terrorism, may also vary. Finally, like the study of innovation in conventional organizations, a broad range of performance variables was required to capture the whole range of potential innovation in VEOs. While many past studies primarily used attacks and lethality as outcome measures, we use additional measures of performance. In short, we attempted to fill in these gaps with a longitudinal examination of creativity and innovation in a sample of fifty VEOs across multiple performance measures.

As seen in recent advancements by ISIS in terms of their use of social media, innovation from VEOs can also occur in recruiting/marketing campaigns and fundraising efforts. Thus, when examining creativity in the domain of terrorism, we argue that it is important to examine the full range of where creativity may manifest rather than only examining attacks. Figure 28.2 depicts our model, which describes links between the operating environment (e.g., environmental catalysts such as Failed States, fragile governments, perceived population grievances), VEO characteristics (e.g., violence, organizational, and ideological influences), team creativity processes (e.g., divergent and convergent activities), creativity components that underlie innovative products (e.g., fluency and flexibility of weapons, recruiting strategies), and the full spectrum of terrorism innovative performance in an organizational setting (attacks, fundraising, and recruiting).

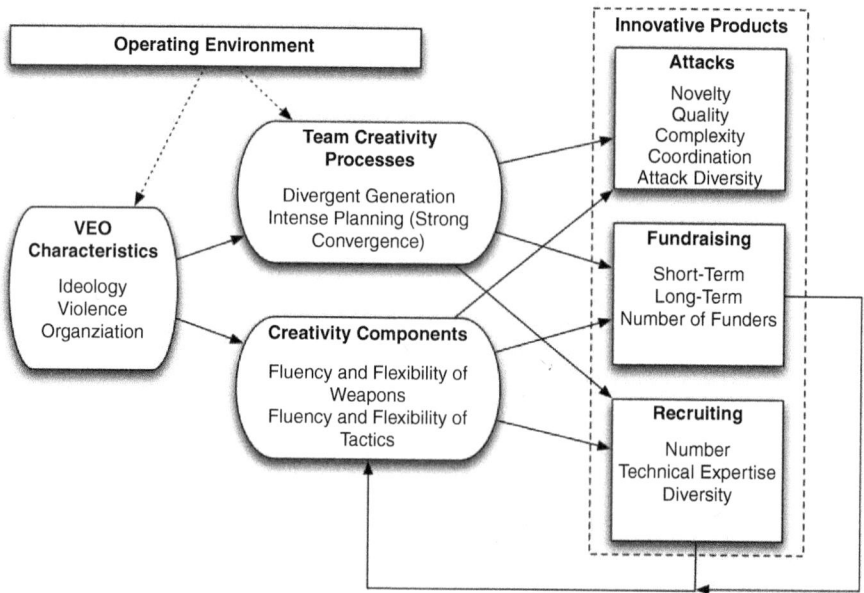

Figure 28.2 *Creativity and innovation in VEO teams, as printed in Ligon, Derrick, & Harms (2015).*

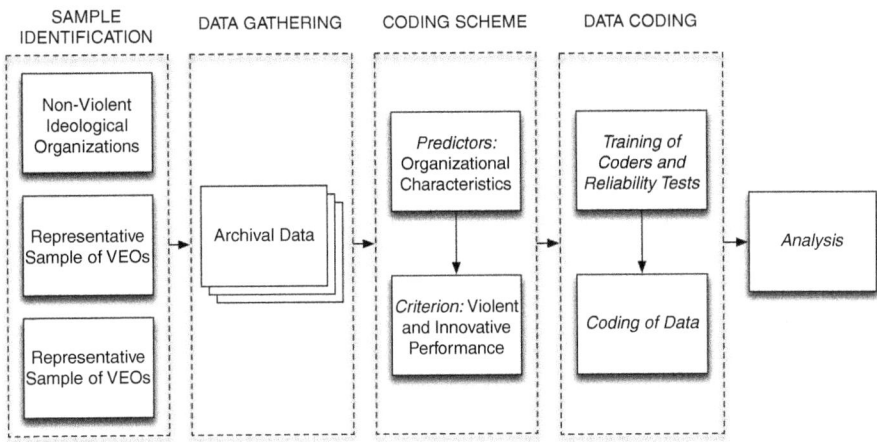

SAMPLE IDENTIFICATION   DATA GATHERING   CODING SCHEME   DATA CODING

Figure 28.3 *Overview of methodology to construct the LEADIR project to examine VEO performance.*

Over the past five years, we have developed a unique dataset, Leadership of the Extreme and the Dangerous for Innovative Results (LEADIR), to examine how organizational features (e.g., leadership style, team structures) predict both violence and innovation in ideological groups. Figure 28.3 provides an overview of the multiple methods and data sources we have used to examine VEO performance (Ligon, Harms, & Harris, 2014).

The LEADIR project was designed to examine violent organizations using theory and methods typically applied to more conventional organizations' innovation. Similar to the methodology that other creativity researchers use examine organizational phenomena as it relates to creative output (e.g., Simonton, 1990), we examined precursors such as organizational structure, leadership style, norms and processes, and other organizational-level characteristics as they related to multiple indices of VEO innovation over time (e.g., yearly lethality, attacks methods, weaponry choice, fundraising tactics, and recruiting strategies).

As it relates to violent innovation, this work has highlighted at least three important findings. First, hierarchically structured organizations tend to have more complex, novel, and effective attacks (Ligon, Harms, & Derrick 2015). This is likely due to more sophisticated command and control mechanisms that allow for independent cells to coordinate attacks and pool resources effectively. Second, a factor analysis revealed that attacks are characterized by two unique factors: (1) unique proficiency (i.e., novelty), and (2) cultural potency (i.e., effectiveness at achieving group objectives) (Ligon, Harms & Harris, 2014). After examining characteristics of 1,402 attacks of the fifty VEOs in our sample, we found that the factor of unique proficiency taps into the constructs of originality and complexity, as it was comprised of (1) weapon uniqueness, (2) level of expertise required to carry out attack, and (3) attack uniqueness. In other words, this factor described attacks that were sophisticated and varied from prior attacks in terms of weapons used and methods employed. These three findings are seen in Aum Shinrikyo's use of Sarin gas agents to attack a Tokyo subway system in 1995.

Aum, which was hierarchical and rule-laden, had both novel and organized financial strategies. They sold personalized artifacts from Asahara, Aum's leader, which were said to evoke "enlightenment," such as his used bath water and blood. But they also had an intricate accounting system to track the effectiveness of their financial diversity. Despite the several areas of Aum's organizational capabilities that hindered their weapons of mass destruction attack planning and execution, several aspects of the organization were highly successful relative to other organizations. For instance, while Asahara was a poor decision maker as a leader, his highly charismatic rhetoric and belief in his own enlightenment contributed to a large and highly radicalized group of followers. Many of these followers believed so strongly in Asahara's vision that they donated their life's savings to the organization. In addition, Asahara was creative in his fundraising and recruitment tactics. These tactics led Aum to be one of the largest and most financially secure extremist organizations in the world, allowing them to avoid reliance on external sources for material or financial support. This may be because some degree of hierarchy is needed to coordinate and manage resources associated with innovation; structure can provide feedback and guidance needed to move creative ideas to innovative products (Gill et al., 2013). This in the end led to their successful attack on the subway system.

Conversely, cultural potency tapped into both effectiveness and destructiveness facets of malevolent innovation. This factor loaded onto how the attack centered on (1) importance of process targeted, (2) scope of damage, (3) symbolic nature of the target to the group's ideology, and (4) expectancy of the attack. For example, ISIS attacks on ancient relics in Palmyra impacted transportation processes that were important for Syrian troops, as well as imposed massive damage on important symbols to their target "apostate" groups. Thus, when examining how "effective" of a target this city was for achieving ISIS strategic objectives, we argue that Palmyra's capture is an example of a culturally potent attack for their stakeholders.

Performance in VEOs is not limited to the nature of their attacks. Thus, we examined VEO performance at two levels of analysis using a nested approach: (1) attack level (e.g., characteristics of each attack such as degree of sophistication, novelty, and destructiveness), and (2) organizational level (e.g., novelty of recruiting campaigns for new members, diversity of fundraising strategies). The organizational-level performance of fundraising was assessed using two long-term studies of terrorist fundraising (Financial Crimes Enforcement Network, 2002; United States Institutes of Peace, 2006). We assessed coding scales such as diversity of sources, sustainability of sources, legality of sources, and effectiveness of sources. Recruiting campaigns were assessed using open-source descriptions of recruitment methods as well as examination of the VEOs' public-facing websites (Derrick, Ligon, Harms, Mahoney, & Crowe, 2015). Recruitment was evaluated based on novelty, diversity, and quality of methods, as well as the quality and originality of the recruitment pool (e.g., deep level diversity in terms of skills and knowledge of recruits). In this study, we found that more novel recruitment methods resulted in attacks, financial resources, and organizational membership (Ligon, Harms, & Derrick, 2015).

Research from Terrorism Studies and Security Scholars

While the above four lines of effort represent scholars in the field of creativity research investigating violent innovation in VEOs, scholars who have expertise in the domain of terrorism and political science have also applied models to understand creativity. For example, Dolnik (2015) argued that terrorist groups are innovative despite the generally limited and static scope of their tactics and technologies over the last sixty years. He outlined eleven factors and conditions that best predict future innovation in terrorist groups and their applicability across four terrorist organizations: Aum Shinrikyo, Popular Front for the Liberation of Palestine – General command, Riyadus Shaliheen Suicide Batalion, and November 17th. Some factors were better predictors of tactical and technological innovation than others. Symbolic attachment to weaponry (e.g., sacred scripture citing "strike their necks") was the strongest predictor of innovation. On the other hand, and contrary to what he hypothesized, durability – or the ability of terrorist organizations to survive over time – was only somewhat related to an organization's decision to innovate. He also found innovation to emerge either gradually or quickly across different terrorist organizations. Dolnik concluded that terrorist innovation is in fact a highly complex process that occurs only when the organization determines it has the capacity to be successful.

Ackerman (2015) examined differences and similarities in the early stages of the innovation decision-making process across terrorist and non-terrorist organizations (e.g., business sector, state militaries). He concluded that the innovation decision-making process is generally comparable across these organizations. Specifically, an organization often makes a decision to adopt an innovation when it has clear or expected advantages over existing methods, and that the novel method is compatible with the organization's mission or ethos. Second, both terrorist and non-terrorist organizations ground their logic and ultimate decisions in the social, ideological, and organizational biases of the greater organization. In general, all organizations must adapt and evolve in order to survive, regardless of whether the mission is benevolent or malevolent. In contrast to these similarities, Ackerman noted two differences between terrorist and non-terrorist organizations and the innovation decision-making process. First, terrorist organizations are far more dispersed and less bureaucratic than conventional organizations. For example, the broad scope of a terrorist organization (e.g., hierarchical vs. cell-based; rigid vs. flexible leadership) and conservative leadership can potentially interrupt the organization's adoption of a novel tactic; the lack of progress or change might result in organizational inertia. Second, the goals of terrorist organizations are generally more complex than maximizing profits in more conventional organizations. Terrorism is a highly dynamic phenomenon and, as such, the terrorist innovation process constantly changes as technical capabilities and resources ebb and flow.

Terrorist organizations must deploy innovative strategies to circumvent surveillance and scrutiny posed by adversaries. In general, governments are constantly surveying and monitoring terrorist operatives, training facilities, and other activities in an attempt either to foil any planned terror attack before it occurs (e.g., identify indicators of an impending attack) or to respond quickly after a successful terror attack (e.g., apprehend perpetrators and locate their associated networks). Sinai (2015) offered insight on how physical and electronic surveillance tactics implemented for terrorist deterrence have inadvertently led to highly innovative counter-surveillance tactics among terrorist groups. He outlined twelve physical and electronic counter-surveillance tactics, including the use of training manuals and instruction. Sinai looked specifically at the effectiveness of the strategies during pre-incident attack planning and preparations for al-Qaeda's 9/11 attack and London Airliner plot.

In regard to 9/11, al-Qaeda successfully combatted issues related to identification and credentialing, and internet and telephone communications. For example, operatives elicited no suspicion during flight school training or at fitness clubs, or even during international travel. They meticulously disguised their identities and plans by the use of different name spellings and nationalities, and implemented different purchasing methods for airline tickets (e.g., cash, internet sites). 9/11 operatives also used complex code schemes during internet and telephone communications. For example, they assigned code names for each attack site, such as the World Trade Center as "The Faculty of Town Planning" and the Pentagon as "The Faculty of Fine Arts." These tactics essentially secured a successful attack.

In contrast to the 9/11 hijackings, al-Qaeda's London airliners plot was unsuccessful despite the successful implementation of counter-surveillance tactics. In general, the operatives' use of internet and telephone counter-surveillance tactics made detection difficult for outside agencies and governments. They used coded messaging in all communication. For example, the operatives travelled hundreds of miles to send emails at internet cafes and made cultural or behavioral references in the emails that are "inappropriate" for those of Islamic faith (e.g., sexual references). Relatedly, the al-Qaeda operatives rarely used cellphones; this tactic suppressed potential issues related to geographical location data that are available in cellphones. During the pre-planning stages, operatives also met in parks and reservoirs, thus making eavesdropping virtually impossible. However, the sloppiness of a single al-Qaeda operative – Ahmed Ali – foiled their plan to detonate liquid explosives on board airliners traveling from the United Kingdom to North America.

Horowitz (2010) focused his study on innovation in suicide attacks and how organizational capital and group interlinkages relate to innovation and the adoption of new tactics. Horowitz made three conclusions that support the notion that organizational capital does relate to the use of suicide bombing. First, religious groups are more likely to adopt suicide attacks; this finding indicates religion to be a predictor in the diffusion of innovation. Second, Horowitz found that non-religious groups had very little probability of adopting suicide attacks at any age and the chances these groups would eventually adopt such tactics further decreased with age. This might be due to the lack of direct network connections among different groups and, as such, minimizes potential recognition of new tactics, which in this research were suicide-bombing strategies. Third, Horowitz demonstrated how various groups that rely on suicide attacks tend to be directly or indirectly connected to one another. As such, inter-group relationships and connections strongly predict the diffusion of innovation. Horowitz highlighted the importance of looking at ideological motivations; instead, counter-terrorism measures ought to focus on organizational constraints and capabilities that influence terrorist behavior and innovation.

Measurement of Creativity in the Domain of Terrorism

Based on work from creativity scholars and security studies scholars, creativity is measured by its precursors and output across a variety of criteria. In addition, environmental processes such as diffusion are also examined at a macro level. In the following sections, we categorize some commonalities across these studies to inform measurement. However, it is of note that most of this work is done by political scientists who do not share the same methodology used in studies of creativity research (e.g., experiments, content coding). Instead, these scholars tend to apply the following variables in a case study method that is more descriptive rather than empirical.

Precursors. Similar to other studies of creativity, precursor studies examined the person and organizational characteristics that are predictive of creativity. For example, expertise is a common characteristic found in a variety of studies that predicts creativity in violent domains (Ackerman, 2015; Gill et al., 2013). In addition, organizational factors outlined for innovation (Damanapour, 1991) are less often directly examined, but certainly are alluded to by political science and terrorism scholars. For example, in Crenshaw's (1981) seminal work on terrorist innovation, she described the notion of incremental problem solving versus radical innovation as the mode for organizational adaptation among violent groups. In addition, Ackerman's work highlights organizational features such as leadership acceptance of technology adoption as a central element for technology emergence among terrorist groups.

Creative Performance. Because surprise is a central tenet of most terrorist campaigns, assessing creativity typically revolves around attack novelty and success at achieving desired effects. Thus, most scholars of both terrorism and creativity research tend to focus on the attack as the unit of analysis for estimating VEO creativity and innovation. However, it is our hope that through this work and others (e.g., Ligon, Harms, & Derrick, 2015), we can draw attention to other elements of terrorist innovation such as use of social media, fundraising mechanisms, and other components of organizational performance that may give rise to the expression of creativity – albeit malevolent creativity.

Conclusions and Implications for Future Research

This chapter has reviewed the extant literature on malevolent creativity and examined commonalities and differences in how scholars have studied creativity in the terrorism domain. One primary theme has emerged from our review: Terrorist organizations need to be creative in order to pursue their ideological goals and to ensure success. Terrorist organizations are creative in how they procure resources, generate revenue, and recruit members. ISIS, for example, would face defeat if lacking in money, weapons, or fighters. However, these components do not alone ensure success. Innovative tools and tactics that allow these organizations to thwart adversaries and avoid surveillance are imperative to their success and execution of strategic missions.

Despite the innovation used by counter-terrorism organizations, such as drones or cyber warfare, we can be almost certain that terrorist organizations will continue to find ways to evade their adversaries, whether their innovation is in the use of recycled or novel tactics. Styszyński (2014) explained how changing political forces and the death or elimination of leaders forced strategic change across jihadi organizations in the post-Arab Spring. He examined these changes in locations most affected by violent extremism: Iraq and Syria, the Arabian Peninsula, North Africa and Sahel, West Africa, and Somalia. Of significance is the use of enculturation – when a group immerses their norms or ideology with the dominant culture – in terrorist organizations. For example, Boko Haram can lend some of its success in West Africa to its merging of traditional jihadist rhetoric with the clannish/Africa ethnic autonomy. Their marketing campaign, which used propaganda similar to that in Rwanda and the Congo, was strategically developed and implemented in a way that all but ensured the locals' allegiance to their ideology. Extremist groups also have taken advantage of social conflict in places like Iraq and Syria. For example, displaced soldiers and officers found refuge within the Sunni communities after the collapse of Saddam Hussein's regime. The soldiers offered the marginalized Sunnis weapon- and war-related expertise, which enabled conditions favorable to a jihadist regime (Styszyński, 2014). Sectarian violence and failed peace talks combined with ideological rhetoric strengthened ISIS's stronghold on the region.

Stories like these remind us why we need a vigilant and systematic research agenda that will offer insight into how to predict terrorist innovation and attacks. Given what we know about terrorist innovation, key areas for future research in the creativity and counter-terrorism arena might include a multi-level approach similar to innovation research in other domains. First, understanding the context where innovation is likely to occur is important. Similar to Florida's research on creative environments, is there a set of preconditions that lead to a VEOs' strategic choice to use and successful implementation of an innovation strategy? We know from Asal and Rethemeyer (2008) that allied groups are more lethal, but are they also more creative in how they achieve that lethality? In addition, in a VEO environment with multiple competition groups, how do groups strategically differentiate themselves from each other (Ligon, Harms, & Derrick, 2015)? How might the diffusion of innovation literature inform the terrorism literature about alliance relationships across a given region or type of VEO community (e.g., all groups in the Global Jihad "Industry")?

Next, at the organizational level, what factors are most predictive of sustained innovation in VEOs? How does specificity of organizational mission relate to organizational innovation in the name of that mission? There is limited research on how issue-specific groups such as the Animal Liberation Front (A.L.F.) engage in innovation when compared to religious groups (e.g., al-Qaida in the Arabian Peninsula or AQAP). Related, these groups have differing command and control mechanisms that result in greater or lesser autonomy in decision making from members as to how to innovate. Thus, another organizational-level question to answer is how organizational structure characteristics (e.g., degree of centralization) impede or facilitate innovation in VEOs.

Third, at the individual level, it is less clear what, beyond expertise, leads to more or less innovation toward destructive ends. While Harris and colleagues' (2013) study showed that the interaction between the situation and the individual characteristics of aggression led to more malevolently innovative products, it is less clear how these characteristics differentiate performance in an organization with likely significant range restriction (i.e., more aggressive individuals are attracted to and remain in violent organizations). Thus, field research such as that conducted by Horgan (2009) and Simi (Simi & Futrell, 2009) that examine characteristics of actual extremists might need to incorporate an examination of characteristics required for innovation in their samples.

Fourth, in terms of terrorism performance, it is our hope that the examination of innovation moves beyond that of attacks in terrorism research. As recruitment of personnel with specialized skills is likely related to subsequent lethality and destruction (Hunter, Shortland, Crayne, & Ligon, under review), examining the innovative methods used to attract, recruit, and select members for various roles in a terrorist organization can also help with counter-terrorism goals and operations. Moreover, in identifying scientists with expertise in biology, Aum Shinrkyo perused academic journals and sent cold call–type letters as a precursor to recruiting scientists. Understanding this effective, novel approach to recruiting experts can also help law enforcement identify interdiction points to stop recruitment from occurring. Thus, research on other domains of VEO terrorism innovation – such as that found in fundraising, marketing, and recruiting – should be conducted to broaden our understanding of this malevolent creativity.

In closing, we also argue for a time series approach to understanding terrorist organizations' innovation. As external influences such as sanctions to funders, coalition attacks on headquarters, and counter-recruitment campaigns unfold, these VEOs are likely pressed to develop novel, effective ways of doing business. Thus, examining how VEOs move in and out of innovation can also be telling as to the effectiveness of different interventions on them. For example, after Executive Order 13224 was passed, which required the seizure of funds for anyone donating to a terrorist group, a significant source of at least United States–based backers to various violent groups was lessened. Whether this also led to a reduction in the innovative output of VEOs is less clear; using a time-series, longitudinal approach may provide some initial data about the efficacy of such interventions. It is our hope that through this publication and recent advancements in innovation from terrorists groups such as ISIL, we are able to encourage more of our peers who research creativity systematically to turn their attention to this unique problem set.

References

Ackerman, G. (2015). The theoretical underpinnings of terrorist innovation decisions. In M. Ranstorp and M. Normack (Eds.), *Understanding terrorism innovation and learning learning: Al-Qaeda and Beyond* (pp. 19–52). New York: Routledge.

Asal, V., & Rethemeyer, R. K. (2008). The nature of the beast: Organizational structures and the lethality of terrorist attacks. *The Journal of Politics, 70,* 437–449. DOI: 10.1017/S0022381608080419

Crenshaw, M. (1981). The causes of terrorism. *Comparative Politics, 13*(4), 379–399. DOI: 10.2307/421717

Cropley, D. H., Cropley, A. J., Kaufman, J., & Runco, M. A. (2010). *The dark side of creativity.* New York: Cambridge University Press.

Cropley, D. H., Kaufman, J., & Cropley, A. J. (2008). Malevolent creativity: A functional model of creativity in terrorism and crime. *Creativity Research Journal, 20*(2), 105–115. DOI: 10.1080/10400410802059424

Cropley, D. H., Kaufman, J. C., White, A. E., & Chiera, B. A. (2014). Layperson perceptions of malevolent creativity: The good, the bad, and the ambiguous. *Psychology of Aesthetics, Creativity, and the Arts, 8,* 400.

Damanpour, F. (1991). Organizational innovation: Meta-analysis of effects of determinants and moderators. *Academy of Management Journal, 26,* 555–590.

Derrick, D. C., Ligon, G., Harms, M., Mahoney, W., & Crowe, J. (2015). Cyber sophistication assessment methodology for public facing terrorist websites. Manuscript submitted for publication.

Dolnik, A. (2007). *Understanding terrorist innovation: Technology, tactics and global trends.* New York: Routledge.

Dolnik, A. (2015). "The dynamics of terrorist innovation." In M. Ranstorp and M. Normack (Eds.), *Understanding terrorism innovation and learning learning: Al-Qaeda and Beyond* (pp. 76–95). New York: Routledge.

Drake, C. J. (1998). The role of ideology in terrorists' target selection. *Terrorism and Political Violence, 10*(2), 53–85. DOI: 10.1080/09546559808427457

Eisenman, R. (1991). *From crime to creativity: Psychological and social factors in deviance.* Kendall/Hunt Publishing Company.

Financial Crimes Enforcement Network (2002). *FinCEN Portal and Query System.* The United States Department of the Treasury. Retrieved on April 11, 2017, from www.fincen.gov/

Gates, S., & Podder, S. (2015). Social media, recruitment, allegiance, and the Islamic State. *Perspectives on Terrorism, 9*(4), 2334–3745. Retrieved on April 11, 2017, from www.terrorismanalysts.com/pt/index.php/pot/article/view/446/html

Gill, P., Horgan, J., & Lovelace, J. (2011). Improvised explosive device: The problem of definition. *Studies in Conflict & Terrorism, 34*(9), 732–748. DOI: 10.1080/1057610X.2011.594946

Gill, P., Horgan, J., Hunter, S. T., & Cushenbery, L. D. (2013). Malevolent creativity in terrorist organizations. *Journal of Creative Behavior, 47*(2), 125–151. DOI: 10.1002/jocb.28

Harris, D. J., Reiter-Palmon, R., & Kaufman, J. C. (2013). The effect of emotional intelligence and task type on malevolent creativity. *Psychology of Aesthetics, Creativity, and the Arts, 7*(3), 237–244. DOI: 10.1037/a0032139

Horgan, J. (2009). *Walking away from terrorism: Accounts of disengagement from radical and extremist movement.* New York: Routeledge.

Horowitz, M. C. (2010). Nonstate actors and the diffusion of innovations: The case of suicide terrorism. *International Organization, 64,* 33–64. DOI: 10.1017/S0020818309990233

Hunter, S. T., Shortland, N., Crayne, M., & Ligon, G. S. (2015). Recruitment and selection in violent extremist organizations: Viewing through an industrial and organizational psychology lens. Manuscript submitted for publication to the *American Psychologist.*

Ligon, G. S. (2010). *Organizational determinants of violence.* College Park, MD: Study of Terrorism and Responses to Terrorism.

Ligon, G. S. (2013). *Organizational determinants of violence: Research Brief.* National Consortium for Studies of Terrorism and Responses to Terrorism (START), August 2013 Newsletter.

Ligon, G. S., & Derrick, D. C. (2015). Violent extremist organizations decision making. *The science of decision making across the span of human activity.* A Strategic Multi-Layer (SMA) Periodic Publication. May 2015.

Ligon, G. S., Harms, M., Crowe, J., Simi, P., & Lundmark, L. (2014). *ISIL: Branding, leadership culture and lethal attraction.* College Park, MD: Study of Terrorism and Responses to Terrorism.

Ligon, G. S., Harms, M., & Derrick, D. C. (2015). Lethal brands: How VEOs build reputations. *Journal of Strategic Security, 8,* 27.

Ligon, G. S., Harms, M., & Harris, D. J. (2014). *Organizational determinants of violence and performance: The L.E.A.D.I.R. study and dataset.* College Park, MD: Study of Terrorism and Responses to Terrorism.

Ligon, G. S., Simi, P., Harms, M., & Harris, D. J. (2013). Putting the 'O' in VEO: What makes an organization. *Dynamics of Asymmetric Conflict: Pathways toward Terrorism and Genocide, 6*(1–3), 110–134. DOI: 10.1080/17467586.2013.814069

Lubart, T. I. (2001). Models of the creative process: Past, present and future. *Creativity Research Journal, 13*(3–4), 295–308. DOI: 10.1207/S15326934CRJ1334_07

McCauley, C. (1998). Group dynamics in Janis's theory of groupthink: Backward and forward. *Organizational Behavior and Human Decision Processes, 73*(2–3), 142–162. DOI: 10.1006/obhd.1998.2759

McCauley, C., & Moskalenko, S. (2008). Mechanisms of political radicalization: Pathways toward terrorism. *Terrorism and Political Violence, 20*(3), 415–433. DOI: 10.1080/09546550802073367

Mumford, M. D., Espejo, J., Hunter, S. T., Bedell-Avers, K. E., Eubanks, D. L., & Connelly, S. (2007). The sources of leader violence: A comparison of ideological and non-ideological leaders. *The Leadership Quarterly, 18*(3), 217–235. DOI: 10.1016/j.leaqua.2007.03.005

Mumford, M. D., Mobley, M. I., Reiter-Palmon, R., Uhlman, C. E., & Doares, L. M. (1991). Process analytic models of creative capacities. *Creativity Research Journal, 4*(2), 91–122. DOI: 10.1080/10400419109534380

Rasmussen, M. J., & Hafez, M. M. (2010). Terrorist innovations in weapons of mass effect: Preconditions, causes, and predictive indicators (Report Number ASCO 2010–019). Retrieved on April 11, 2017 from: http://calhoun.nps.edu/bitstream/handle/10945/25358/2010_019_Terrorist_WME.pdf?sequence=1

Shalley, C. E. (1995). Effects of coaction, expected evaluation, and goal setting on creativity and productivity. *Academy of Management Journal, 38*(2), 483–503.

Shapiro, J. N. (2013). *The terrorist's dilemma: Managing violent covert organizations.* Princeton, NJ: Princeton University Press.

Simi, P., & Futrell, R. (2009). Negotiating white power activist stigma. *Social Problems, 56,* 89–110.

Simonton, D. K. (1990). *Psychology, science, and history: An introduction to historiometry.* New Haven, CT: Yale University Press.

Sinai, J. (2015). Innovation in terrorists' counter-surveillance: The case of al-Qaeda and its affiliates. In M. Ranstorp and M. Normack (Eds.), *Understanding terrorism innovation and learning: Al-Qaeda and Beyond* (pp. 196–210). New York: Routledge.

Stern, J., & Berger, J. M. (2015). *ISIS: The state of terror.* New York: Harper Collins Publishers.

Styszyński, M. (2014). Present trends among jihadists after the Arab Spring. *Krakowskie Studia Międzynarodowe, 3,* 25–49. Retrieved on April 11, 2017, from http://ksm.ka .edu.pl/tresc/KSM-3–2014-Styszynski.pdf

Tushman, M., & O'Reilly, C. (1996). *Evolution and revolution: Mastering the dynamics of innovation and change.* Cambridge: Harvard Business School Press.

United States Institutes of Peace (2006). *How modern terrorism uses the internet.* Washington, DC: United States Institute of Peace. Retrieved on April 11, 2017, from www.usip.org

Weiss, M., & Hassan, H. (2015). *ISIS: Inside the army of terror.* New York: Regan Arts.

PART VI

Creativity in Everyday Life

29 Creativity in the Domain of Emotions

Zorana Ivcevic
Yale Center for Emotional Intelligence

Marina Bazhydai
Harvard Graduate School of Education

Jessica D. Hoffmann
Yale Center for Emotional Intelligence

Marc A. Brackett
Yale Center for Emotional Intelligence

Abstract
The role of emotions in the creative process is well documented. In this chapter, we distinguish emotional processes in creativity from creativity in the domain of emotions. Creativity in the domain of emotions exists when people are creative with emotions – emotions are the *object* of the creative process. We describe three kinds of creativity in the domain of emotions – emotional creativity (experience of unique emotions), creative communication of emotions, and creative emotion regulation. Furthermore, we present a model in which we argue that creativity in the domain of emotions is less likely to have the same impact on society and culture as creativity in other domains that are more defined by education and formal gate keepers (e.g., art or science), but that it is crucial for psychological health and well-being.

The creative process is filled with emotion – from the emotional decision of whether to attempt being creative (e.g., *Do I dare? Will I anger the field?*) to the role of different emotional states across the process of creation (e.g., happiness facilitating initial idea generation; Baas et al., 2008) and the role of emotion-regulation ability in maintaining passion and persistence for creative activities (Ivcevic & Brackett, 2015). Emotions play a significant role in the creative process across domains, from the arts and sciences (Feist, 1998, 1999), to engineering and technology

The work on this chapter was funded and supported through a collaboration between the Yale Center for Emotional Intelligence and the Botin Foundation, Santander, Spain (*Emotions, Creativity and the Arts* grant; Principal investigators: Zorana Ivcevic and Marc Brackett).

The authors also gratefully acknowledge the contributions of Nadine Maliakkal who has assisted with the preparation of the manuscript.

(Cropley, 2015) and to entrepreneurship (Cardon, Wincent, Singh, & Drnovsek, 2009). In this chapter, we first briefly review research on the role of emotions in the creative process. Next, we ask a different question and one that is at the core of this volume – How can we describe creativity in the domain of emotions? Here, emotions are the *object* of the creative process – people are creative with emotions. We argue that there are at least three aspects of creativity in the domain of emotions – experiencing unique combinations of emotions, communicating emotions creatively, and creative regulation of emotion. Furthermore, we argue that creativity in the domain of emotions is less likely to have the same visible impact on society and change culture in the same way a new scientific discovery or a new technology might, but that it is crucial for psychological health and well-being.

After defining the term "emotion," we divide this chapter into three sections. First, we review the role of emotions in creativity and define creativity in the domain of emotions. We compare this domain to other creativity domains and describe what is unique about creativity in the domain of emotions. Next, we review emerging research on creativity in the domain of emotions, including emotional creativity, creative communication of emotion, and creative emotion regulation. Finally, we describe a model that positions creativity in the domain of emotions in relation to other domains of creativity.

What Are Emotions?

We define emotions as psychological syndromes including physiological, experiential, cognitive, and behavioral aspects that arise in response to external and/or internal events and that are adaptive in nature (Salovey & Mayer, 1990). We focus on three major aspects of emotions: (1) subjective experience of emotions, (2) managing or regulating emotions, and (3) communicating emotions effectively.

Experience of emotions varies along the axes of valence (from unpleasant/negative to pleasant/positive) and arousal or activation (from low to high activation) (Russell, 1980). For instance, sadness is an unpleasant low activation emotion, joy is a pleasant high activation emotion, and serenity is a pleasant low activation emotion. Furthermore, individual differences exist in the tendency to experience different emotions, as well as in the intensity of emotion experiences (Diener, Larsen, Levine, & Emmons, 1985; Larsen & Diener, 1987; Watson & Clark, 1992).

The experience of emotion goes beyond distinct states, such as anger, anxiety, or happiness; rather, it also includes emotion management processes (Mayer, Salovey, Gomberg-Kaufman, & Blainey, 1991). These processes involve thoughts and actions that influence and modify emotion states. Both emotion states and emotion management are to a large extent culturally and socially constructed (Averill, 2002). Individual-level emotion processes are influenced both by cultural beliefs about the nature and meaning of emotions (e.g., *Are emotions valuable? Should one pay attention to emotions?*) and beliefs about how one should express emotions (e.g., *When and how is it appropriate to show anger?*).

Emotions are signals to individuals (e.g., fear when encountering a rattle snake warns a person to avoid the animal and steers her away from danger) and they help manage social interactions (e.g., lack of interest communicated by a date signals to change a conversation topic). The function of emotions is acutely visible in the social context, which becomes dramatically obvious when emotion processing is impaired because of an injury or illness (Niedenthal & Brauer, 2012). Emotions are communicated through relatively automatic processes (e.g., facial expressions) and also more deliberate ways of communication (e.g., verbal descriptions). Emotion states can be communicated using adjective labels, such as guilt or elation when an experience corresponds to a schema or prototype of these emotions. However, situations that elicit emotions (i.e., physical and social context, personal circumstances) vary sufficiently that even within the same individual no two emotion episodes will be identical (Averill, 2002). Because anxiety in one circumstance will be different from another experience of anxiety, it is important to communicate emotions successfully (and possibly, creatively) beyond using emotion adjective labels.

Creativity and Emotions vs. Creativity in the Domain of Emotions

Emotion processes related to creativity have been examined for as long as psychologists have been studying creativity. Freud (1958/1925) believed that regulating potentially overwhelming emotions can lead to creativity through the process of sublimation. In this process, socially unacceptable impulses and associated emotions are expressed through socially desirable behavior, such as when everyday sexual or aggressive motives are expressed through art. Almost one hundred years after it was originally formulated, Freud's idea received empirical support in a series of laboratory studies that induced unacceptable sexual desire or required participants to suppress anger. Compared to those in the control condition, those primed with guilt produced more creative sculptures, collages, poems, and cartoon captions (Kim, Zeppenfeld, & Cohen, 2013).

Modern research on emotion and creativity primarily asked how positive versus negative emotion states impact the creative process. After more than three decades of research, it is well documented that creativity benefits from positive affect based both on mood induction studies in the lab (for a meta-analysis see Baas, De Dreu, & Nijstad, 2008) and multi-method studies in the workplace (Amabile, Barsade, Mueller, & Staw, 2005). Although this effect is reliable, it appears to be limited to the initial few minutes of idea generation and is relatively small in size (Baas et al., 2008).

Negative moods too can be beneficial for creativity, especially when criteria for creativity are broader than short divergent thinking tasks. Research by Kaufmann and Vosburg (2002) replicated that positive mood led to greater creativity in early idea generation, but also found that neutral and negative moods resulted in greater creativity during later stages of work on a creative task. Research outside of the laboratory shows that distress-related variables, such as job dissatisfaction, group conflicts, or budget shortages, could stimulate innovation (Anderson, De Dreu, &

Nijstad, 2004). Certain levels of dissatisfaction or frustration might inspire exploration and problem finding (Berrone, Fosfuri, Gelabert, & Gomez-Mejia, 2013; Runco, 1994), which are crucial to the creative process (Csikszentmihalyi & Getzels, 1971; Runco, 1994).

Personality psychologists examined the role of emotion traits in creativity. The Big Five model provides a way to systematize research on a large number of traits. Openness to experience emerged as the most reliable and strongest predictor of creativity, as measured by divergent thinking test scores (e.g., McCrae, 1987; Silvia, Martin, & Nusbaum, 2009), laboratory writing and art tasks (e.g., Ivcevic, Brackett, & Mayer, 2007; Wolfradt & Pretz, 2001), self-reported creative behavior (e.g., Carson, Peterson, & Higgins, 2005; Ivcevic & Mayer, 2009), and professional creative achievement (e.g., Feist & Barron, 2003; Helson, Roberts, & Agronick, 1995), leading personality theorists to define it as a personality disposition for creativity (McCrae, 1994, 1996). While openness to experience includes some lower-level emotion traits, such as curiosity and receptiveness to a wide range of emotions, extraversion and neuroticism primarily concern affective tendencies (toward positive and negative affect, respectively).

Affective traits of extraversion and neuroticism are not unequivocally related to creativity. Neuroticism is largely unrelated to creativity measured by divergent thinking tests administered in the laboratory, whereas the results for extraversion are mixed (positive correlations: Batey, Chamorro-Premuzic, & Furnham, 2009; Furnham & Bachtiar, 2008; Furnham, Batey, Anand, & Manfield, 2008; Furnham, Crump, Batey, & Chamorro-Premuzic, 2009; Martindale, 2007; non-significant correlations: Batey, Furnham, & Safiullina, 2010; Burch, Hemsley, Pavelis, & Corr, 2006; Ivcevic et al., 2007; Silvia, Martin, & Nusbaum, 2009; Silvia, Nusbaum, Berg, Martin, & O'Connor, 2009).

Neuroticism and extraversion appear to be associated with creativity measured in terms of everyday behavior and achievement, but this association depends on the creativity domain. Neuroticism correlates with creativity in the arts – artists have higher neuroticism-related traits than non-artists (Feist, 1998), advanced art students have higher negative emotionality traits than science students (Sheldon, 1994), and dancers have higher shame-proneness than athletes (Thomson & Jaque, 2013). Extraversion is related to creativity in a limited set of domains, including everyday creativity (e.g., self-expressive creativity, interpersonal creativity; Ivcevic, 2007; Ivcevic & Mayer, 2009) and entrepreneurial creativity (Lee & Tsang, 2001; Marcati, Guido, & Peluso, 2008; Zhao, Seiberg, & Lumpkiin, 2010). Positive emotions can broaden thinking and help create surprising connections that contribute to everyday creativity (e.g., telling a joke and making people laugh in social situations, coming up with a funny nickname for someone; Ivcevic, 2007) and they can facilitate the development of large networks of business contacts, which is associated with entrepreneurial performance and venture growth (Lee & Tsang, 2001; Marcati, Guido, & Peluso, 2008; meta-analysis: Zhao, Seibert, & Lumpkin, 2010).

Other emotion-related variables, often operationalized as relatively narrow traits, have also been related to creativity. Intrinsic motivation – which includes enjoyment and perceived challenge – predicts engagement in creative activities and rated creativity of products (Amabile, 1996). Conceptually similar to intrinsic motivation is the construct of passion. In addition to enjoying an activity, passionate individuals integrate the activity into their sense of personal identity (i.e., someone who enjoys science defines themselves as a scientist; Vallerand et al., 2003). Emerging research points to the important role of passion in commitment and persistence on tasks that predict creativity (Grohman, 2015; Vallerand et al., 2007).

Collectively, existing research on emotions and creativity shows that general positive mood helps initial idea generation, suggests that negative moods might play a role in problem finding and critical evaluation of generated ideas, and points to the important role of task-specific emotions of enjoyment and passion. In the research reviewed so far, emotion states or traits are inputs into the creative process. Outputs are creative ideas studied in the context of relatively domain-general laboratory tasks (e.g., Baas et al., 2008) or behaviors and products in various domains, from everyday activities and interactions (e.g., Ivcevic, 2007; Ivcevic & Mayer, 2009), to the arts and sciences (e.g., Feist, 1998), and business (e.g., Zhao et al., 2010). When we speak about creativity in the domain of emotions, the outputs of the creative process – whether ideas, behaviors, or products – pertain to emotions.

What does creativity in the domain of emotions look like? Plucker, Beghetto, and Dow (2004) defined creativity as "the interaction among aptitude, process, and environment by which an individual or group produces a perceptible product that is both novel and useful as defined within a social context" (p. 90). Novel and useful products pertaining to emotions can include emotional experiences, communication of emotions, and regulation of emotions.

To illustrate the concept of creativity in the domain of emotions we can consider an analogy with intelligence. Traditional conceptions of intelligence primarily consider convergent thinking processes – analysis and reasoning directed toward reaching a single best answer, while traditional conceptions of creative thinking primarily consider divergent thinking processes – a broad search resulting in multiple ideas to open-ended problems (Guilford, 1975; Torrance, 1988). Creativity in the domain of emotions can be conceptualized as the counterpart to intelligence in the domain of emotions – emotional intelligence.

Emotional intelligence is an ability to reason with and about emotions (Mayer & Salovey, 1997). Emotional intelligence is comprised of four component abilities: accurately perceiving emotions in oneself and others, using emotions to aid thinking and problem solving, understanding emotions, and managing emotions. Ability tests have been developed where responses are evaluated for their quality, correctness, or effectiveness and emotional intelligence has been shown to develop with age, modestly correlate with general intelligence, and predict relevant behavioral criteria (Mayer, Roberts, & Barsade, 2008; Mayer, Salovey, Caruso, & Sitarenios, 2001, 2003). These tests ask respondents to identify labels for emotion states or evaluate effectiveness of different emotion and regulation strategies. For instance, an item assessing understanding emotions asks: "When you feel pleased and content, you feel. . ." [response options: brave, proud, happiness, surprise, challenge]. A problem assessing emotion regulation first describes an emotionally charged situation – "Someone who often says mean things approaches you and says a very insulting thing to you in front of others. You want to make him feel guilt and regret this behavior" – and then asks test-takers to evaluate helpfulness of presented regulation strategies for the stated goal (example strategy: "You ask him how he would feel if someone talked to him that way, and tell him he should be ashamed").

We propose that in order to assess creativity in the domain of emotions, these and similar questions should be asked in an open-ended format and people should be invited to creatively respond with multiple possible ideas. The emotion state where one is pleased and content can be described as happiness (emotionally intelligent, correct and appropriate response), but it can also be described as luminous (original and appropriate response). If we accept that the multiple determinants of emotions, from the physical environment, social relationships, and personal circumstances of the individual, create experiences in which no two emotion episodes are the same (Averill, 2002), the value of richer and more nuanced emotion descriptions is more apparent. The description of an experience as luminous conveys more closely the unique nature of the experience than the commonly used "happy." Such open-ended responses can be evaluated similarly to responses to divergent thinking tests (e.g., Silvia et al., 2008).

Breaking New Ground: Creativity in the Domain of Emotions

Creativity in the domain of emotions has received much less theoretical and empirical attention than emotional intelligence. Here, we argue that creativity in the domain of emotions has at least three components: emotional creativity (experiencing novel, but appropriate, combinations of emotions), creativity in communicating emotions (using symbolic language to describe nuances and richness of emotional experience), and creative emotion regulation (generating original and effective strategies to influence emotions). In the following sections, we will discuss each of the three potential components of creativity in the domain of emotions.

Emotional Creativity

Emotional creativity is the ability to experience and express emotions that are original, appropriate, and authentic (Averill & Thomas-Knowles, 1991). The conceptualization of emotional creativity is based on a social-constructionist view of emotion, which maintains that people not only regulate their emotions based on social expectations but also create and experience their emotions following social rules, thus creating differences across cultures and individuals (Averill, 1999). The idea that people create their emotional experience rather than being at the mercy of their feelings is key to emotional creativity; it means that individuals possess the freedom to both shape their emotional experience and decide how to express it.

People differ in their ability to shape and construct their emotional experiences creatively (Averill, 1999). People who are emotionally creative diverge from the common emotional reaction to a situation and generate a novel emotional experience, often by experiencing multiple feelings simultaneously (Averill & Thomas-Knowles, 1991).

Creativity requires that a person come up with ideas, behaviors, or products that are both novel and appropriate (Lubart, 1994). The same is true for emotional creativity: the emotional experience should be different from the norm (original or novel), be of some value to the person (appropriate or effective), and be authentic and genuine to the person (Averill, 2004). Novelty alone is not enough for something to be creative; nonconforming emotional responses are more often reflective of psychopathology than creativity (e.g., Gutbezahl & Averill, 1996; Lovejoy & Steurwald, 1992). A novel emotional experience could be effective or appropriate if it resolves an issue, enhances an individual's sense of self or a relationship, or opens up new possibilities for action (Gutbezahl & Averill, 1996). Finally, a creative emotional response should be authentic as opposed to a disingenuous display to fit the circumstances (Morgan & Averill, 1992). In other words, emotional creativity involves being genuine and sincere, where one's reaction accurately reflects one's inner feelings.

Thinking of emotional creativity as an ability implies that there are measurable individual differences in this ability. Averill (1999) outlined what different levels of emotional creativity might look like, from effective applications of an existing emotion, through modifications of emotions to meet the needs of an individual or group, to the development of new blends of emotions (e.g., being at the same time serene, bewildered, and impulsive). Furthermore, Averill (1999) proposed that a person's emotional creativity might differ across emotions, the way that cognitive creativity differs across domains.

There are several measures currently available to assess emotional creativity, including both self-report trait scales and ability tests. The Emotional Creativity Inventory (ECI; Averill, 1999) is a thirty-item, self-report measure that assesses emotional preparedness, as well as novelty, effectiveness, and authenticity criteria for emotional creativity. Emotional preparedness concerns the degree to which people consider emotions to be an important part of their lives and therefore spend time thinking about and trying to understand their feelings (e.g., "I believe people should work on their emotional development as hard as they work on their intellectual development"). Novelty refers to uniqueness of one's experience and behavior compared to either one's own past or in relation to others (e.g., "I have felt combinations of emotions that other people probably have never experienced"). Effectiveness concerns a potential benefit of emotions, as opposed to emotions that are bizarre or eccentric (e.g., "The way I experience and express my emotions helps me in my relationships with others"). Lastly, authenticity addresses whether a person's emotional reactions reflect their values, beliefs, and true self (e.g., "My emotions are almost always an authentic expression of my true thoughts and feelings").

Emotional creativity has also been measured with two performance tests – Emotional Consequences and Emotional Triads (Averill & Thomas-Knowles, 1991). In the Emotional Consequences test, participants are presented with emotionally salient hypothetical situations and are asked to produce multiple possible consequences, such as "What would happen if people fell in love with a different person every day?" Participants are explicitly asked to be creative, and their answers are scored for fluency (the total number answers), and originality (novelty or uniqueness of responses). In the Emotional Triads test, participants are given four sets of three dissimilar emotions (e.g., serene, bewildered, impulsive), and are asked to imagine a situation in which all three feelings would be experienced simultaneously. Responses are then scored for creativity using the Consensual Assessment Technique.

Ivcevic, Brackett, and Mayer (2007) administered all three measures of emotional creativity – the self-report Emotional Creativity Inventory and performance-based Emotional Consequences and Emotional Triads – and examined the structure of emotional creativity. Confirmatory factor analyses supported three correlated factors: (1) experience of unusual combinations of emotions (loading Emotional Triad items); (2) emotional ideation (loading Emotional Consequences items); and, (3) self-perceived preparedness, novelty and effectiveness (loading scales from the Emotional Creativity Inventory). Emotional creativity has thus been shown as multifactorial, similar to other broad abilities, such as personal or emotional intelligence (Mayer, Panter & Caruso, 2012; Mayer, Salovey & Caruso, 2004; Mayer, Salovey, Caruso & Sitarenios, 2001).

Averill (1999) found that self-reported emotional creativity was most closely associated with the personality trait of openness to experience and was largely independent of neuroticism, extraversion, and conscientiousness. Averill theorized that people who score high on neuroticism may have uncommon emotional responses but that they are often ineffective, whereas people high on conscientiousness are likely to be effective, but conventional. People high on agreeableness also tend to think about their feelings (preparedness) and be effective, but are not more original than less agreeable people. Supporting these theoretical propositions, Ivcevic and colleagues (2007) found that novelty correlated with neuroticism and openness, effectiveness correlated with agreeableness, conscientiousness and openness, and the total self-reported emotional creativity significantly correlated only with openness. Ability tests of emotional creativity (Emotional Consequences and Emotional Triads) showed no significant correlations with personality traits. Beyond Big Five traits, self-reported emotional creativity positively correlated with mysticism (religious orientation characterized by an individual asking existential questions openly and honestly) and self-esteem, and negatively correlated with authoritarianism (defined as unquestioning adherence to authority).

Considering the development of emotional creativity, Averill (1999) reported findings regarding childhood traumatic experiences. The number and severity of prior traumatic events before age 18 significantly positively correlated with emotional creativity, specifically preparedness and novelty. Reported hassles and disappointments in childhood showed a similar pattern of relationships with self-reported emotional creativity, suggesting that such events inspire a person to think about their emotional responses in novel yet appropriate or effective ways. Moreover, those who reported being better off because of their prior unpleasant experiences had higher scores of the effectiveness/authenticity component of self-reported emotional creativity (Averill, 1999). These findings mirror research showing that early traumatic experiences can predict to novel thinking when approaching problems (e.g., Runco & Albert, 1986; Forgeard, 2013). For instance, Forgeard (2013) showed that when people perceived that traumatic experiences made them stronger, they showed increased breadth of creativity.

It is also important to establish what emotional creativity is not. Significant relationships were not found between emotional creativity and SAT verbal or math scores (Gutbezahl & Averill, 1996), or between emotional creativity and locus of control (Averill, 1999). Emotional creativity is also different from emotional intelligence. Confirmatory factor analyses showed distinct emotional creativity and emotional intelligence factors (Ivcevic et al., 2007). The understanding emotions branch of emotional intelligence correlates significantly, but modestly, with self-reported preparedness (Ivcevic et al., 2007). Both emotional intelligence and emotional creativity include a sensitivity to and knowledge of emotions; however, emotional creativity refers to the potential for novel responses whereas emotional intelligence does not. This means that while those who are emotionally creative should have some degree of emotional intelligence, the reverse is not true (Averill, 2004). Stated another way, emotional creativity is to emotional intelligence what cognitive creativity is to cognitive intelligence. Although a certain degree of intelligence is necessary for creativity, intelligence is no guarantee of creativity.

Predictive validity studies showed that emotional creativity measures predicted relevant creativity criteria, especially on tasks requiring emotion expression. In one study, emotional preparedness, novelty, and the total self-reported emotional creativity score predicted creative performance on a Haiku task beyond what was predicted by openness to experience (Ivcevic et al., 2007). This study also found correlations between self-reported emotional creativity and self-initiated artistic activity (e.g., painting and exhibiting art in public), as well as interest in the arts (e.g., seeing a play or visiting a musuem). Emotional creativity also related to behavioral creativity that involves expressing emotion, such as writing a love poem (Gutbezahl & Averill, 1996). The authors gave participants a series of tasks, including writing narratives about emotionally charged situations, drawing pictures of different feelings, writing the ending of a story that was emotionally charged, and creating a collage that expressed joy, anger, and despair. People who scored higher on self-reported emotional creativity were also more creative at expressing emotions in both the narrative and pictorial tasks, with the strongest correlations for the verbal tasks.

Although emotional creativity is the aspect of creativity in the domain of emotions that received most theoretical and empirical attention, many questions remain unanswered. How does emotional creativity relate to creativity in other domains? What are the psychological effects or the potential consequences of emotional creativity? Richer and more complex emotional experiences at the core of emotional creativity should be related to multiple aspects of psychological well-being such as personal growth and meaning in life. Future research will have to explicitly address these questions.

Creative Communication of Emotion

Emotions can be described creatively. To describe a good day, we could use general and unspecific words like "wonderful" or "amazing," or specific emotion words like "blissful" or "elated." We could also describe feeling alight, which would success-fully communicate the feeling, yet be semantically innovative.

Writers, poets, and philosophers have long been using metaphorical expressions to describe feelings (Aitchison, 2012; Lakoff & Johnson, 1980; Ricoeur, 2003). Shakespeare is credited as being the first to describe jealousy as a green-eyed monster. Or consider, for example, the following passage written by William Wordsworth in 1884 (p. 15):

> There was a time when meadow, grove, and stream,
> The earth, and every common sight,
> To me did seem
> Apparelled in celestial light,
> The glory and the freshness of a dream.

Here, the emotionally laden memory is described in metaphorical terms, evoking the "freshness of a dream" and the "celestial light." Instead of an array of metaphorical expressions, we could use one emotion word to describe it – awe (Keltner & Haidt, 2003). Both approaches to communicating emotion are valid. Yet, Wordsworth's description is more vivid and communicates details and images in the way that a single word cannot.

Communicating emotions by generating emotion-descriptive metaphors is an inherently creative process and a prominent example of creativity in the domain of emotions (Beaty & Silvia, 2013; Benedek et al., 2014; Smith, Gerkens, Shah, & Vargas-Hernandez, 2006; Silvia & Beaty, 2013). Generation of metaphors is related to fluid intelligence in ways similar to how performance on divergent thinking tests relates to fluid intelligence (Beaty & Silvia, 2013; Silvia & Beaty, 2012), and metaphor production engages brain areas associated with divergent idea production (Benedek et al., 2014). Others have specifically pointed to the important role of metaphorical language in the development of emotions (Kövecses, 1998, 2003; Lakoff & Johnson, 1980).

We conducted a study to examine the emotion vocabulary in early adolescents and examined whether they spontaneously use metaphors to describe emotions (Ebert, Ivcevic, Widen, & Brackett, 2016). We asked middle school students (n = 230) to describe the feelings of someone who is happy, calm, angry, nervous, and sad. No time restrictions were posed on students, and they could list as many or as few descriptors as they wished.

To analyze the responses, we created a list containing all unique terms generated by the students (n = 1,472). A two-step procedure was used to code the responses. In Step 1, two independent coders categorized each response into one of the five target categories (happy, sad, nervous, angry, and relaxed) and five additional, closely associated categories (love, pride, disappointment, embarrassment, and surprise; feelings of embarrassment, for instance, may accompany the feeling of nervousness; 84% inter-rater agreement).

In Step 2, the terms which did not fit the above target and closely related emotion categories were assigned to one of six categories: physical reactions (e.g., "crying"; 86 terms, 5.8% of unique responses), social experiences that cause or are associated with emotional experiences (e.g., "underappreciated"; 157 terms, 10.7%), personality traits (e.g., "shy"; 113 terms, 7.7%), activities (e.g., "daydreaming"; 49 terms, 3.3%), metaphors (e.g., "frozen"; 201 terms, 13.7%), and other emotion words (e.g., "bored"; 145 terms, 9.8%). Two independent coders reached an overall 69% agreement for this exploratory coding.

Adolescents readily used metaphors to describe emotions, such as saying "wobbly bridge" or "caged in" to describe the feeling of anxiety or describing anger as being "zestful" or "alight." Metaphorical descriptors were numerous and accounted for almost identical proportions of responses (13.7% of unique responses; 201 terms) as target emotion words (e.g., describing someone who is happy as joyous or cheerful; 13.1% of unique responses; 194 terms), showing that metaphorical descriptions of emotions are salient and spontaneously used. Adolescents generated a total of 1.63 metaphors, ranging from $M = .53$ for the "relaxed" category to $M = .25$ for the "happy" category.

Metaphors provide an effective medium for expressing the mental states and personal meanings (e.g., Fainsilber & Ortony, 1987; Lubart & Getz, 1997). Metaphorical understanding of language emerges early and is evident in children's spontaneous speech (Billow, 1981; Winner, 1997). Some metaphors ("enactive metaphors") grow out of tendency for symbolic play, (e.g., pretending an object is something else). Another kind of metaphor is based on perceptual similarities, such as saying that a dripping faucet is "drooling." The ability to generate spontaneous metaphors also helps children derive meaning and learn about complex concepts, such as those forming part of scientific knowledge (Jakobson & Wickman, 2007). Analyses of classroom investigations with 6–8 year-old students revealed that student-generated metaphors often helped make the distant scientific content personally salient and meaningful. For example, while observing salt using a magnifying glass, children related to it as "little diamonds." Rich meaning achieved through metaphoric means in turn enhances complex conceptual learning. Collectively, theoretical and empirical work suggest that emotions can be communicated creatively and that generation of metaphors could be a useful tool in teaching emotion skills, such as understanding and expressing emotions.

Creative Emotion Regulation

Emotions can be managed or regulated creatively. While research on the appropriateness and effectiveness of emotion-regulation strategies has been extensive and fruitful (Aldao, Sheppes, & Gross, 2015; Gross, 2015; Mayer, Roberts, & Barsade, 2008; Mayer, Salovey, Caruso, & Sitarenios, 2001; Webb, Miles, & Sheeran, 2012), little attention has been paid to the role of creativity in this domain. Strategies such as reappraisal, acceptance, problem solving, and suppression of the expression of emotion are more effective in general than strategies that have to do with rumination, avoidance, suppressing the experience of emotion, and concentration (Aldao, Nolen-Hoeksema, & Schweizer, 2010; Gross, 2002; Webb, Miles, & Sheeran, 2012). Yet there is a virtually infinite number of actions that can be used to regulate emotions. Here, we offer evidence that originality of the strategies adds another layer to the ability to effectively regulate emotions.

To test this, we presented early adolescents with five vignettes describing everyday situations requiring emotion regulation. Students were asked to list as many strategies as they could think of that help change the emotional state of the story protagonist (making them feel less angry, less nervous, less excited, more relaxed and calm, or less disappointed). For example, one of the stories read as follows: "Arturo and Tong are walking to school together. Arturo asks Tong if she is ready for the math test that afternoon. Tong realized suddenly that she completely forgot about the test. Tong has not been doing well in math and needs to do well on this test. Tong is now really nervous." Students were then asked: "Imagine you were Tong, what would you think about or do to help you feel less nervous" and prompted to generate multiple emotion-regulation strategies.

Two research assistants rated the originality and effectiveness of the responses produced for each of the scenarios, using a five-point Likert scale (each set of responses given a single rating; rating strategy developed and tested by Silvia, Martin, & Nusbaum, 2009), with $\alpha = .73$ for originality and .70 for effectiveness. Highly original strategies were defined as uncommon ways to manage the emotion and reach the stated goal. Effectiveness was conceptualized as usability and appropriateness of the strategy in influencing the emotions towards a stated goal.

Students came up with the most emotion-regulation strategies for the goals of reducing anxiety ($M = 3.79$ strategies) and feeling relaxed ($M = 3.49$ strategies). The most effective strategies were produced for reducing anxiety ($M = 3.81$) and for relaxing ($M = 3.67$). Students produced the most original strategies for situations calling for reduction of excitement ($M = 2.92$) and disappointment ($M = 2.93$). Effectiveness ratings were significantly higher than originality ratings (t (220) = -28.76, $p < .001$), but originality and effectiveness ratings were significantly positively correlated ($r = .63$, $p < .001$).

A subset of responses was rated as both original and effective and can thus be considered examples of creative emotion regulation (see Table 29.1).

Taking a deep breath or doing breathing exercises are potentially effective strategies commonly mentioned across emotion-regulation goals and different situations. Such exercises can reduce bodily activation that accompanies strong emotions and can thus help an individual successfully manage their emotions. The original and creative strategies, on the other hand, are situation and goal specific. Feelings of anger caused by a school dance being cancelled can be creatively managed by holding a party in a park and disappointment after not getting a part in a play can be creatively managed by writing and performing in one's own play. While this study is only a proof of concept – we demonstrated that adolescents can produce

Table 29.1 *Creativity in emotion regulation*

Vignette	Effective, not original responses	Creative regulation strategies: Effective and original responses
Sam heard that someone had damaged one of the bathrooms at school. At lunch that day, an announcement is made that if no one claims responsibility for the damage, the school dance that evening will be cancelled. Sam is really excited to go to the dance with friends, but finds out that afternoon that the dance is cancelled. Sam feels angry. Emotion-regulation goal: Feel less angry	• Breathe • Punch a punching bag • Do something fun with your friends instead	• Start a protest • Play Super Mario and spend the whole time pretending that the goomas are the school admin and the toilet damager • In compensation, hold a party in the park and invite the entire school
Arturo and Tong are walking to school together. Arturo asks Tong if she is ready for the math test that afternoon. Tong realized suddenly that she completely forgot about the test. Tong has not been doing well in math and needs to do well on this test. Tong is now really nervous. Emotion-regulation goal: Feel less nervous	• Take deep breaths • Study as much as possible before the test • Ask teacher to retake the test another time	• Think about the things in math that you remember, like, or are good at • Get a planner so she will not have this experience in the future • Fail the test, then make it up with a bunch of extra-credit
It's Friday morning and Jesse is excited about his family vacation. He is leaving for the airport as soon as school is over. Jesse has an important test that afternoon, but he can't concentrate because he is so excited about going on vacation. Jesse needs to lessen his excitement so he can focus and do well on the test. Emotion-regulation goal: Feel less excited	• Do breathing exercises • Concentrate on the test • Think of something calming	• Think if I fail this I might get held and miss the plane • Make up a quick relaxing song, sing it three times and continue on the test • Pretend reward himself if he does well (like, if I do well on this test, then I will allow myself to do. . .)
Masa had a really busy week. He plays several sports and either had games or practice every night. It also was a busy week at school. It's now Friday afternoon and Masa really wants to relax and feel calm. Emotion-regulation goal: Feel relaxed and calm	• Take deep breaths • Watch TV • Read a book	• I would lie outside and look at the sky • Interpretive dance like a boss! • Lie down with a dog

Table 29.1 (*cont.*)

Vignette	Effective, not original responses	Creative regulation strategies: Effective and original responses
Chis has been in the drama club for two years. She's excited about auditioning for the next school play. She's trying out for a lead role. After what she thought was a great audition, she finds out that she was not chosen for the part. Chris is really disappointed. Emotion-regulation goal: Feel less disappointed	• Deep breaths • Try out for a different role • Join another drama group	• Try and find out if you can help out with the production in a different way • Get feedback from the director and learn what you need to do to improve, then work on it and try again next year • Write my own play and invite friends over to perform it to the grown ups

emotion-regulation strategies in response to a range of emotionally charged situations that are reliably rated as both original and effective – much remains to be learned about creative emotion regulation. We present these results as an invitation for new research to creativity scholars and educators, especially those working in the area of social and emotional learning (Elbertson, Brackett, & Weissberg, 2009). In order to fully understand the nature of emotion regulation and the impact of different emotion-regulation strategies on individuals, educators and scholars alike should acknowledge the role of creativity and explicitly encourage people to think outside of common strategies, such as taking a deep breath or reappraising the situation.

Suggestions for Future Research: Predictors and Consequences of Creativity across Domains

We defined creativity in the domain of emotions as ideas or behaviors that involve a novel and appropriate or meaningful experience of emotions (emotional creativity), as well as original and appropriate communication of emotion and regulation of emotion. We reviewed research on emotional creativity and presented data that illustrate creative communication of emotions and emotion regulation. In this section we discuss what is unique about creativity in the domain of emotions when compared to creativity in other domains.

Creativity in the domain of emotions differs from creativity in other domains in two major ways: in relation to the levels of creativity and the outcomes of the creative process. Kaufman and Beghetto (2009) described four levels of creativity, from creativity in the learning process (mini-c), to everyday creativity (little-c), professional creativity (Pro-c), and finally eminent creativity (Big-C; see also Necka, Grohman, & Słabosz, 2006). A child who creates an imaginative picture of a dinosaur exemplifies mini-c, a person creating a collage of their photographs as a birthday gift for a friend shows little-c, an artist having a solo show in a gallery demonstrates Pro-c, and a creator who pioneers a new art style and enters art history books is an example of Big-C. We can think of similar examples in other creativity domains, from the sciences, technology, and business, to domains of human interaction, such as teaching or therapy, as this book demonstrates. The outcomes of creative thinking and work range from enriching one's life and solving everyday problems (Richards, Kinney, Benet, & Merzel, 1988) to influencing or changing the culture as a whole (Csikszentmihalyi, 1999). Creativity in the domain of emotions, by contrast, is largely confined to mini-c and little-c levels. Experiencing creative combinations of emotions, communicating emotions creatively, or creatively regulating emotions will not be included in people's job descriptions and it is not likely to establish new cultural practices. Emotional creativity and creative communication of emotions can be helpful in creative writing or visual arts, for instance. Creativity in the domain of emotions might even contribute to Pro-c or Big-C creativity in some domains (e.g., creative

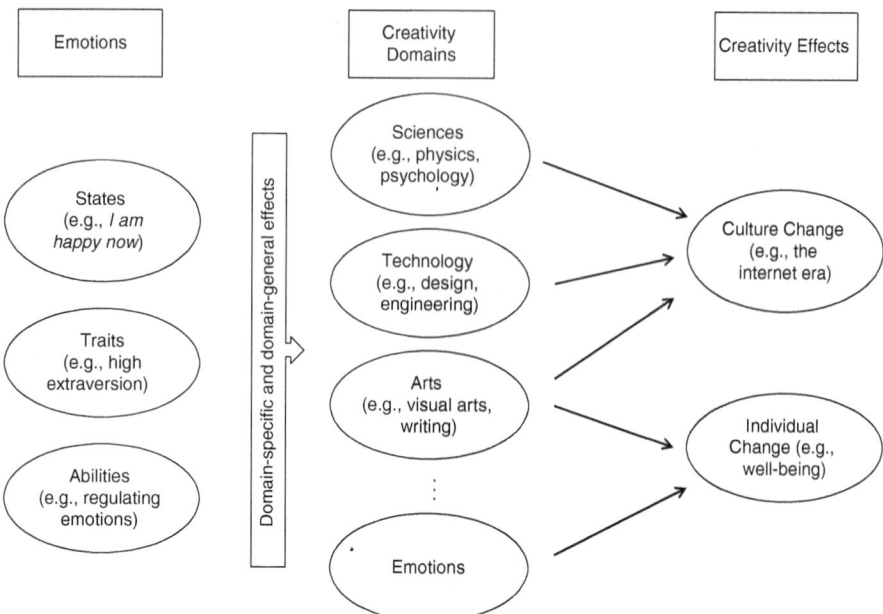

Figure 29.1 *The relationship between creativity in the domain of emotions and other creativity domains.*

writing). However, creativity in the domain of emotions is not essential for creativity in these domains.

Another major difference between creativity in the domain of emotions and creativity in other domains involves effects of creativity. Figure 29.1 depicts the relationship of creativity across different domains with their antecedents and outcomes. Emotion states, personality traits, and abilities are inputs in this model (in addition to domain-general and domain-specific skills and traits; Amabile, 1996). These predictors of creativity often show domain-specific relationships with creativity (e.g., trait negative emotionality is high in artists, but not creative scientists; Feist, 1998).

Outcomes of the creative process have different effects or consequences on the individual or society at large, depending on the creative domain. Creativity in the domains defined by educational and professional institutions primarily has consequences outside of the individual, such as when creative teaching benefits students or when smartphones change the way we communicate with others and manage daily schedules. These influences range from interpersonal to making contributions to the domain or even changing the culture or society. Creativity can also have consequences for individual well-being. For instance, perceived organizational creativity is related to individual well-being (Rasulzada & Dackert, 2009). It remains unclear whether these effects are limited to the work contexts or they generalize to a sense of well-being across people's professional and personal lives. Everyday creativity – self-expression through arts and crafts or other avocational pursuits – is more clearly and reliably related to psychological well-being (Cropley, 1990; Flach, 1990; Ivcevic, 2007; Richards & Kinney, 1990).

By contrast, creativity in the domain of emotions primarily influences the person, such as when creative emotion regulation strategies help an individual successfully manage feelings of frustration or disappointment. Creativity in the domain of emotions can also have interpersonal consequences, such as in instances when creative emotion regulation involves relationships with others or emotions are creatively communicated. However, even in those instances, the reach of creativity in the domain of emotions is relatively limited to personal well-being or quality of interpersonal relationships.

Emotional creativity, creative communication of emotions, and creative emotion regulation provide novel ways to experience and react in situations in which common experiences or actions are not sufficient. As such, creativity in the domain of emotions should be beneficial for personal problem solving and emotional well-being. Although the effects of creativity in the domain of emotions have not been explicitly studied, several lines of research strongly suggest that creative expression of emotions is related to psychological well-being. People who are better able to describe their emotions (i.e., have higher emotion clarity) are likely to engage in active coping and reappraisal of challenging events (Gohm & Clore, 2002), which are associated with well-being (Gross & John, 2003). Research on the effects of art therapy – a therapeutic approach based on creative expression – shows that it enhances people's ability to express emotions and enhances productive coping skills (Geue et al., 2010). Similarly, music hobbyists who play for purposes of self-expression show lower levels of stress than professional music therapists, who play for the more instrumental reasons (Nicol & Long, 1996). When adolescents use artistic outlets to express their emotions, they report that these activities help them to productively cope with everyday challenges (Kyzer, 2001).

Creativity in the Domain of Emotions: Looking Forward

In this chapter, we defined creativity in the domain of emotions as novel and useful or meaningful products – ideas or behaviors – pertaining to emotional experiences (emotional creativity), communication of emotions, and managing emotions. Creativity in the domain of emotions differs from other domains of creativity in being limited to mini-c (personal creativity or creativity in the learning process) and little-c (everyday creativity) and in effecting primarily the individual or their immediate interpersonal environment. While we reviewed extant research on emotional creativity and presented preliminary data examining creativity in communicating emotions and regulating emotions, many questions about creativity in the domain of emotions remain to be empirically examined. Does creativity in the domain of emotions relate to emotion states and personality traits in similar ways to creativity in other domains? We know that this is the case for emotional creativity (Averill, 1999), but empirical research still has to examine other facets of creativity in the domain of emotions. Research should also examine the relationship between this and other domains of creativity. We could hypothesize that creativity in the domain of emotions is associated with artistic, but not scientific creativity, for instance. Even within the artistic domain, it is likely that creativity in the domain of emotions is more strongly related to some styles than others (e.g., expressive vs. conceptual). Finally, future research should examine the effects or consequences of creativity in the domain of emotions. Is this form of creativity present when significant relationships between creativity and psychological well-being are found? Answering these and similar questions will not only clarify the nature of creativity in the domain of emotions, but also enrich our understanding of the interplay among the various domains of creativity and their distinct effects on individuals and society.

References

Aitchison, J. (2012). *Words in the mind: An introduction to the mental lexicon.* Chichester: John Wiley & Sons.

Aldao, A., Nolen-Hoeksema, S., & Schweizer, S. (2010). Emotion-regulation strategies across psychopathology: A meta-analytic review. *Clinical Psychology Review*, *30*(2), 217–237. DOI:10.1016/j.cpr.2009.11.004.

Aldao, A., Sheppes, G., & Gross, J. J. (2015). Emotion regulation flexibility. *Cognitive Therapy and Research*, *39*(3), 263–278. DOI:10.1007/s10608-014-9662-4

Amabile, T. M. (1996). *Creativity in context.* Boulder, CO: Westview Press.

Amabile, T. M., Barsade, S. G., Mueller, J. S., & Staw, B. M. (2005). Affect and creativity at work. *Administrative Science Quarterly*, *50*(3), 367–403. DOI:10.2189/asqu.2005.50.3.367

Anderson, N., De Dreu, C. K., & Nijstad, B. A. (2004). The routinization of innovation research: A constructively critical review of the state-of-the-science. *Journal of Organizational Behavior*, *25*(2), 147–173. DOI:10.1002/job.236

Averill, J. R. (1999). Individual differences in emotional creativity: Structure and correlates. *Journal of Personality*, *67*(2), 331–371. DOI:10.1111/1467-6494.00058

Averill, J. R. (2002). Emotional creativity: Toward "spiritualizing the passions." In C. R. Snyder & S. J. Lopez (Eds.), *Handbook of positive psychology* (pp. 172–185). New York: Oxford University Press.

Averill, J. R. (2004). A tale of two snarks: Emotional intelligence and emotional creativity compared. *Psychological Inquiry*, *15*(3), 228–233. Retrieved from www.jstor.org/stable/20447232

Averill, J. R., & Thomas-Knowles, C. (1991). Emotional creativity. In K. T. Strongman (Ed.), *International review of studies on emotion* (Vol. 1, pp. 269–299). London: Wiley.

Baas, M., De Dreu, C. K. W., & Nijstad, B. A. (2008). A meta-analysis of 25 years of mood-creativity research: Hedonic tone, activation, or regulatory focus? *Psychological Bulletin*, *134*(6), 779–806. DOI:10.1037/a0012815

Batey, M., Chamorro-Premuzic, T., & Furnham, A. (2009). Intelligence and personality as predictors of divergent thinking: The role of general, fluid and crystallised intelligence. *Thinking Skills and Creativity*, *4*(1), 60–69. DOI:10.1016/j.tsc.2009.01.002

Batey, M., Furnham, A., & Safiullina, X. (2010). Intelligence, general knowledge and personality as predictors of creativity. *Learning and Individual Differences*, *20*(5), 532–535. DOI:10.1016/j.lindif.2010.04.008

Beaty, R. E., & Silvia, P. J. (2013). Metaphorically speaking: Cognitive abilities and the production of figurative language. *Memory & Cognition*, *41*(2), 255–267. DOI:10.3758/s13421-012-0258-5

Benedek, M., Beaty, R.E., Jauk, E., Koschutnig, K., Fink, A., Silvia, P. J., . . . Neubauer, A. C. (2014). Creating metaphors: The neural basis of figurative language production. *NeuroImage*, *90*(100), 99–106. DOI:10.1016/j.neuroimage.2013.12.046

Berrone, P., Fosfuri, A., Gelabert, L., & Gomez-Mejia, L. R. (2013). Necessity as the mother of "green" inventions: Institutional pressures and environmental innovations. *Strategic Management Journal*, *34*(8), 891–909. DOI:10.1002/smj.2041.

Billow, R. M. (1981). Observing spontaneous metaphor in children. *Journal of Experimental Child Psychology*, *31*(3), 430–445. DOI:10.1016/0022–0965(81)90028-x

Burch, G. S. J., Hemsley, D. R., Pavelis, C., & Corr, P. J. (2006). Personality, creativity and latent inhibition. *European Journal of Personality*, *20*(2), 107–122. DOI:10.1002/per.572

Cardon, M. S., Wincent, J., Singh, J., & Drnovsek, M. (2009). The nature and experience of entrepreneurial passion. *Academy of Management Review*, *34*(3), 511–532. DOI:10.5465/amr.2009.40633190

Carson, S. H., Peterson, J. B., & Higgins, D. M. (2005). Reliability, validity, and factor structure of the Creative Achievement Questionnaire. *Creativity Research Journal*, *17*(1), 37–50. DOI:10.1207/s15326934crj1701_4

Cropley, A. J. (1990). Creativity and mental health in everyday life. *Creativity Research Journal*, *3*(3), 167–178. DOI:10.1080/10400419009534351

Cropley, D. H. (2015). *Creativity in engineering: Novel solutions to complex problems*. San Diego, CA: Academic Press.

Csikszentmihalyi, M. (1999). Implications of a systems perspective for the study of creativity. In R. Sternberg (Ed.), *Handbook of creativity* (pp. 313–328). New York: Cambridge University Press.

Csikszentmihalyi, M., & Getzels, J. W. (1971). Discovery-oriented behavior and the originality of creative products: A study with artists. *Journal of Personality and Social Psychology*, *19*(1), 47–52. DOI:10.1037/h0031106

Diener, E., Larsen, R. J., Levine, S., & Emmons, R. A. (1985). Intensity and frequency: Dimensions underlying positive and negative affect. *Journal of Personality and Social Psychology*, *48*, 1253–1265.

Ebert, M., Ivcevic, Z., Widen, S. C., & Brackett, M. A. (2016). Breadth of emotion vocabulary in middle school students. *Unpublished manuscript*.

Elbertson, N. A., Brackett, M. A., & Weissberg, R. P. (2009). School-based social and emotional learning (SEL) programming: Current perspectives. In A. Hargreaves, M. Fullan, D. Hopkins, & A. Lieberman (Eds.), *The second international handbook of educational change* (pp. 1017–1032). Netherlands: Springer. DOI:10.1007/978–90-481–2660-6_57

Fainsilber, L., & Ortony, A. (1987). Metaphorical uses of language in the expression of emotions. *Metaphor and Symbolic Activity*, *2*(4), 239–250. DOI:10.1207/s15327868ms0204_2

Feist, G. J. (1998). A meta-analysis of personality in scientific and artistic creativity. *Personality and Social Psychology Review*, *2*(4), 290–309. DOI:10.1207/s15327957pspr0204_5

Feist, G. J. (1999). The influence of personality on artistic and scientific creativity. In R. J. Sternberg (Ed.), *Handbook of creativity* (pp. 273–296). New York: Cambridge University Press.

Feist, G. J., & Barron, F. X. (2003). Predicting creativity from early to late adulthood: Intellect, potential, and personality. *Journal of Research in Personality, 37*(2), 62–88. DOI:10.1016/S0092-6566(02)00536-6

Flach, F. (1990). Disorders of the pathways involved in the creative process. *Creativity Research Journal, 3*(2), 158–165. DOI:10.1080/10400419009534349

Forgeard, M. J. C. (2013). Perceiving benefits after adversity: The relationship between self-reported posttraumatic growth and creativity. *Psychology of Aesthetics, Creativity, and the Arts, 7*(3), 245–264. DOI:10.1037/a0031223

Freud, S. (1958). *On creativity and the unconscious ("Papers on Applied Psychoanalysis" [Vol. 4] Collected Works of Sigmund Freud)*. New York: Harper. (Original work published in 1925).

Furnham, A., & Bachtiar, V. (2008). Personality and intelligence as predictors of creativity. *Personality and Individual Differences, 45*(7), 613–617. DOI:10.1016/j.paid.2008.06.023

Furnham, A., Batey, M., Anand, K., & Manfield, J. (2008). Personality, hypomania, intelligence and creativity. *Personality and Individual Differences, 44*(5), 1060–1069. DOI:10.1016/j.paid.2007.10.035

Furnham, A., Crump, J., Batey, M., & Chamorro-Premuzic, T. (2009). Personality and ability predictors of the "Consequences" Test of divergent thinking in a large non-student sample. *Personality and Individual Differences, 46*(4), 536–540. DOI:10.1016/j.paid.2008.12.007

Geue, K., Goetze, H., Buttstaedt, M., Kleinert, E., Richter, D., & Singer, S. (2010). An overview of art therapy interventions for cancer patients and the results of research. *Complementary Therapies in Medicine, 18*(3–4), 160–170. DOI:10.1016/j.ctim.2010.04.001

Gohm, C. L., & Clore, G. L. (2002). Affect as information: An individual differences approach. In L. F. Barrett & P. Salovey (Eds.), *The wisdom in feeling: Psychological processes in emotional intelligence* (pp. 89–113). New York: Guilford Press.

Grohman, M. G. (2015, August). Grit, passion, and persistence in creative achievements. *Paper presented at Annual Convention of the American Psychological Association.* Toronto, Canada.

Gross, J. J. (2002). Emotion regulation: Affective, cognitive, and social consequences. *Psychophysiology, 39*(3), 281–291. DOI:10.1017/s0048577201393198

Gross, J. J. (2015). Emotion regulation: Current status and future prospects. *Psychological Inquiry, 26*(1), 1–26. DOI:10.1080/1047840x.2014.940781

Gross, J. J., & John, O. P. (2003). Individual differences in two emotion regulation processes: Implications for affect, relationships, and well-being. *Journal of Personality and Social Psychology, 85*(2), 348–362. DOI: 10.1037/0022–3514.85.2.348.

Guilford, J. P. (1975). Creativity: A quarter of century of progress. In I. A. Taylor & J. W. Getzels (Eds.), *Perspectives in creativity* (pp. 37–59). Chicago: Aldine Publishing Company.

Gutbezahl, J., & Averill, J. R. (1996). Individual differences in emotional creativity as manifested in words and pictures. *Creativity Research Journal, 9*(4), 327–337. DOI:10.1207/s15326934crj0904_4

Helson, R., Roberts, B., & Agronick, G. (1995). Enduringness and change in creative personality and the prediction of occupational creativity. *Journal of Personality and Social Psychology, 69*(6), 1173–1183. DOI:10.1037/0022–3514.69.6.1173

Ivcevic, Z. (2007). Artistic and everyday creativity: An act-frequency approach. *The Journal of Creative Behavior, 41*(4), 271–290. DOI:10.1002/j.2162–6057.2007.tb01074.x

Ivcevic, Z., & Brackett, M. A. (2015). Predicting creativity: Interactive effects of openness to experience and emotion regulation ability. *Psychology of Aesthetics, Creativity, and the Arts, 9*(4), 480–487. DOI:10.1037/a0039826

Ivcevic, Z., Brackett, M. A., & Mayer, J. D. (2007). Emotional intelligence and emotional creativity. *Journal of Personality, 75*(2), 199–235. DOI:10.1111/j.1467–6494.2007.00437.x

Ivcevic, Z., & Mayer, J. D. (2009). Mapping dimensions of creativity in the life-space. *Creativity Research Journal, 21*(2–3), 152–165. DOI:10.1080/10400410902855259

Jakobson, B., & Wickman, P.O. (2007). Transformation through language use: Children's spontaneous metaphors in elementary school science. *Science & Education, 16*(3–5), 267–289. DOI:10.1007/s11191-006–9018-x

Kaufman, J. C., & Beghetto, R. A. (2009). Beyond big and little: The four c model of creativity. *Review of General Psychology, 13*(1), 1–12. DOI:10.1037/a0013688

Kaufmann, G., & Vosburg, S. K. (2002). The effects of mood on early and late idea production. *Creativity Research Journal, 14*(3–4), 317–330. DOI:10.1207/S15326934CRJ1434_3

Keltner, D., & Haidt, J. (2003). Approaching awe, a moral, spiritual, and aesthetic emotion. *Cognition & Emotion, 17*(2), 297–314. DOI:10.1080/02699930302297

Kim, E., Zeppenfeld, V., & Cohen, D. (2013). Sublimation, culture, and creativity. *Journal of Personality and Social Psychology, 105*(4), 639–666. DOI:10.1037/a0033487

Kövecses, Z. (1998). Are there any emotion-specific metaphors? In A. Athanasiadou & E. Tabakowska (Eds.), *Speaking of emotions: Conceptualisation and expression* (pp. 127–152). Berlin: Mouton de Gruyter.

Kövecses, Z. (2003). *Metaphor and emotion: Language, culture, and body in human feeling.* New York: Cambridge University Press.

Kyzer, M. L. (2001). *Empathy, creativity, and conflict resolution in adolescents (Unpublished doctoral dissertation).* University of Georgia, Athens, GA.

Lakoff, G., & Johnson, M. (1980). *Metaphors we live by.* Chicago: University of Chicago Press.

Larsen, R. J., & Diener, E. (1987). Affect intensity as an individual difference characteristic: A review. *Journal of Research in Personality, 21*, 1–39.

Lee, D. Y., & Tsang, E. W. (2001). The effects of entrepreneurial personality, background and network activities on venture growth. *Journal of Management Studies, 38*(4), 583–602. DOI:10.1111/1467–6486.00250

Lovejoy, M. C., & Steuerwald, B. L. (1992). Psychological characteristics associated with subsyndromal affective disorder. *Personality and Individual Differences, 13*(3), 303–308. DOI:10.1016/0191–8869(92)90106-y

Lubart, T. I. (1994). Creativity. In R. J. Sternberg (Ed.), *Thinking and problem solving* (pp. 289–332). San Diego, CA: Academic Press.

Lubart, T. I., & Getz, I. (1997). Emotion, metaphor and the creative process. *Creativity Research Journal, 10*(4), 285–301. DOI:10.1207/s15326934crj1004_1

Marcati, A., Guido, G., & Peluso, A. M. (2008). The role of SME entrepreneurs' innovativeness and personality in the adoption of innovations. *Research Policy*, *37*(9), 1579–1590. DOI:10.1016/j.respol.2008.06.004

Martindale, C. (2007). Creativity, primordial cognition, and personality. *Personality and Individual Differences*, *43*(7), 1777–1785. DOI:10.1016/j.paid.2007.05.014

Mayer, J. D., Panter, A. T., & Caruso, & D. R. (2012). Does personal intelligence exist? Evidence from a new ability-based measure. *Journal of Personality Assessment*, *94* (2), 124–140. DOI:10.1080/00223891.2011.646108

Mayer, J. D., Roberts, R. D., & Barsade, S. G. (2008). Human abilities: Emotional intelligence. *Annual Review of Psychology*, *59*(1), 507–536. DOI:10.1146/annurev.psych.59.103006.093646

Mayer, J. D., & Salovey P. (1997). What is emotional intelligence? In P. Salovey & D. Sluyter (Eds.), *Emotional development and emotional intelligence: Educational implications* (pp. 3–31). New York: Basic Books.

Mayer, J. D., Salovey, P., & Caruso, D. R. (2004). Emotional intelligence: Theory, findings, and implications. *Psychological Inquiry*, *15*(3), 197–215. DOI:10.1207/s15327965pli1503_02

Mayer, J. D., Salovey, P., Caruso, D. R., & Sitarenios, G. (2001). Emotional intelligence as a standard intelligence. *Emotion*, *1*(3), 232–242. DOI:10.1037/1528–3542.1.3.232

Mayer, J. D., Salovey, P., Caruso, D. R., & Sitarenios, G. (2003). Measuring emotional intelligence with the MSCEIT V2.0. *Emotion*, *3*(1), 97–105. DOI:10.1037/1528–3542.3.1.97

Mayer, J. D., Salovey, P., Gomberg-Kaufman, S., & Blainey, K. (1991). A broader conception of mood experience. *Journal of Personality and Social Psychology*, *60*, 100–111.

McCrae, R. R. (1987). Creativity, divergent thinking, and openness to experience. *Journal of Personality and Social Psychology*, *52*(6), 1258–1265. DOI:10.1037/0022–3514.52.6.1258

McCrae, R. R. (1994). Openness to experience: Expanding the boundaries of factor V. *European Journal of Personality*, *8*(4), 251–272. DOI:10.1002/per.2410080404

McCrae, R. R. (1996). Social consequences of experiential openness. *Psychological Bulletin*, *120*(3), 323–337. DOI:10.1037/0033–2909.120.3.323

Morgan, C., & Averill, J. R. (1992). True feelings, the self, and authenticity: A psychosocial perspective. In D. D. Franks & V. Gecas (Eds.), *Social perspectives on emotion* (Vol. 1, pp. 95–124). Greenwich, CT: JAI Press.

Nęcka, E., Grohman M., Słabosz, A. (2006). Creativity studies in Poland. In J. C. Kaufman, R. J. Sternberg (Eds.), *International handbook of creativity* (pp. 270–306). Cambridge, UK: Cambridge University Press.

Nicol, J. J., & Long, B. C. (1996). Creativity and perceived stress of female music therapists and hobbyists. *Creativity Research Journal*, *9*(1), 1–10. DOI:10.1207/s15326934crj0901_1

Niedenthal, P. M., & Brauer, M. (2012). Social functionality of human emotion. *Annual Review of Psychology*, *63*, 259–285. DOI: 10.1146/annurev.psych.121208.131605

Plucker, J. A., Beghetto, R. A., & Dow, G. T. (2004). Why isn't creativity more important to educational psychologists? Potentials, pitfalls, and future directions in creativity research. *Educational Psychologist*, *39*(2), 83–96. DOI:10.1207/s15326985ep3902_1

Rasulzada, F., & Dackert, I. (2009). Organizational creativity and innovation in relation to psychological well-being and organizational factors. *Creativity Research Journal*, *21*(2–3), 191–198. DOI:10.1080/10400410902855283

Richards, R., & Kinney, D. K. (1990). Mood swings and creativity. *Creativity Research Journal*, *3*(3), 202–217. DOI:10.1080/10400419009534353

Richards, R., Kinney, D. K., Benet, M., & Merzel, A. P. (1988). Assessing everyday creativity: Characteristics of the lifetime creativity scales and validation with three large samples. *Journal of Personality and Social Psychology*, *54*(3), 476. DOI:10.1037/0022–3514.54.3.476

Ricoeur, P. (2003). *The rule of metaphor: The creation of meaning in language*. Abingdon: Psychology Press.

Runco, M. A. (1994). *Problem finding, problem solving, and creativity*. Norwood, NJ: Ablex.

Runco, M. A., & Albert, R. S. (1986). The threshold theory regarding creativity and intelligence: An empirical test with gifted and nongifted children. *The Creative Child and Adult Quarterly*, *11*(4), 212–218.

Russell, J. A. (1980). A circumplex model of affect. *Journal of Personality and Social Psychology*, *39*, 1161–1178.

Salovey, P., & Mayer, J. D. (1990). Emotional intelligence. *Imagination, Cognition, and Personality*, *9*(3), 185–211.

Sheldon, K. M. (1994). Emotionality differences between artists and scientists. *Journal of Research in Personality*, *28*(4), 481–491. DOI:10.1006/jrpe.1994.1034

Silvia, P. J., & Beaty, R. E. (2012). Making creative metaphors: The importance of fluid intelligence for creative thought. *Intelligence*, *40*(4), 343–351. DOI:10.1016/j.intell.2012.02.005

Silvia, P. J., Martin, C., & Nusbaum, E. C. (2009). A snapshot of creativity: Evaluating a quick and simple method for assessing divergent thinking. *Thinking Skills and Creativity*, *4*(2), 79–85. DOI:10.1016/j.tsc.2009.06.005

Silvia, P. J., Nusbaum, E. C., Berg, C., Martin, C., & O'Connor, A. (2009). Openness to experience, plasticity, and creativity: Exploring lower-order, high-order, and interactive effects. *Journal of Research in Personality*, *43*(6), 1087–1090. DOI:10.1016/j.jrp.2009.04.015

Silvia, P. J., Winterstein, B. P., Willse, J. T., Barona, C. M., Cram, J. T., Hess, K. I., . . . & Richard, C. A. (2008). Assessing creativity with divergent thinking tasks: Exploring the reliability and validity of new subjective scoring methods. *Psychology of Aesthetics, Creativity, and the Arts*, *2*(2), 65–85. DOI:10.1037/1931–3896.2.2.68

Smith, S. M., Gerkens, D. R., Shah, J. J., & Vargas-Hernandez, N. (2006). Empirical studies of creative cognition in idea generation. In A. L. L. Thompson & H.S Choi (Eds.), *Creativity and innovation in organizational teams* (pp. 3–20). Mahwah, NJ: Lawrence Erlbaum Associates, Inc.

Thomson, P., & Jaque, S. V. (2013). Exposing shame in dancers and athletes: Shame, trauma, and dissociation in a nonclinical population. *Journal of Trauma & Dissociation*, *14*(4), 439–454. DOI:10.1080/15299732.2012.757714

Torrance, E. P. (1988). The nature of creativity as manifest in its testing. In R. J. Sternberg (Eds.), *The nature of creativity: Contemporary psychological perspectives* (pp. 43–75). Cambridge, UK: Cambridge University Press.

Vallerand, R. J., Blanchard, C., Mageau, G. A., Koestner, R., Ratelle, C., Léonard, M., . . . & Marsolais, J. (2003). Les passions de l'ame: On obsessive and harmonious passion.

Journal of Personality and Social Psychology, 85(4), 756–767. DOI:10.1037/0022–3514.85.4.756

Vallerand, R. J., Salvy, S. J., Mageau, G. A., Elliot, A. J., Denis, P. L., Grouzet, F. M., & Blanchard, C. (2007). On the role of passion in performance. *Journal of Personality, 75*(3), 505–534. DOI:10.1111/j.1467–6494.2007.00447.x

Watson, D., & Clark, L. A. (1992). On traits and temperament: General and specific factors of emotional experience and their relation to the Five-Factor Model. *Journal of Personality, 60*(2), 441–476. DOI: 10.1111/j.1467–6494.1992.tb00980.x

Webb, T. L., Miles, E., & Sheeran, P. (2012). Dealing with feeling: A meta-analysis of the effectiveness of strategies derived from the process model of emotion regulation. *Psychological Bulletin, 138*(4), 775. DOI:10.1037/a0027600

Winner, E. (1997). *The point of words: Children's understanding of metaphor and irony.* Cambridge, MA: Harvard University Press.

Wolfradt, U., & Pretz, J. E. (2001). Individual differences in creativity: Personality, story writing, and hobbies. *European Journal of Personality, 15*(4), 297–310. DOI:10.1002/per.409

Wordsworth, W. (1884). *Ode: Intimations of immortality from recollections of early childhood.* Boston: D. Lothrop and Company.

Zhao, H., Seibert, S. E., & Lumpkin, G. T. (2010). The relationship of personality to entrepreneurial intentions and performance: A meta-analytic review. *Journal of Management, 36*(2), 381–404. DOI:10.1177/0149206309335187

30 Creativity in Teaching

Ronald A. Beghetto

University of Connecticut

Abstract

Creative teaching, like all forms of teaching, is a polymorphous act. It can take multiple forms and have different pedagogical aims. The purpose of this chapter is to describe creativity in the domain of teaching and clarify three forms of creative teaching: teaching *about* creativity, teaching *for* creativity, and teaching *with* creativity. The chapter will describe each of these types of creative teaching, including their different aims, previous work on each type, and the knowledge base necessary for each type of creative teaching. Directions for future research will also be discussed.

It is the supreme art of the teacher to awaken joy in creative expression and knowledge.

Albert Einstein

Introduction

How might researchers think about creativity in the domain of teaching? An important first step is to recognize that creative teaching, like all forms of teaching, is a polymorphous act (Hirst, 1971). Researchers, therefore, need to distinguish between different forms of creative teaching based on differing pedagogical aims. Elsewhere (Beghetto, 2013a), I have outlined three different but interrelated forms of creative teaching: teaching *about* creativity, teaching *for* creativity, and teaching *with* creativity. These different forms of creative teaching have different pedagogical aims.

Whereas teaching *about* creativity is aimed at increasing knowledge about creativity and the field of creativity studies, teaching *for* creativity is aimed at cultivating creative thinking and creative actions in students. Finally, teaching *with* creativity is aimed at teaching any subject matter (be it biology, mathematics, or even creativity itself) creatively. In addition to having different aims, each of these forms of creative teaching also draws from a different knowledge base.[1] Consequently, just because

---

[1] Three decades ago, Lee Shulman (1987) stressed the importance of recognizing distinct yet interrelated types of knowledge necessary for knowing how to teach academic subject-matter. In the intervening decades, scholars from various fields of study (e.g., technology, engineering) have elaborated on Shulman's ideas. Following along these same lines, the field of creativity studies might benefit from elaborating on Shulman's pioneering work and applying it to creative teaching. I therefore introduce three types of knowledge necessary for creative teaching: Pedagogical Creative-Domain Knowledge (PCdK), Pedagogical Creativity Enhancement Knowledge (PCeK), and Creative Pedagogical Domain Knowledge (CPDK). My hope is that introducing these different types of pedagogical knowledge can

someone knows how to teach about creativity or even teach for creativity, it does not mean that person would know how to teach creatively. Indeed, Simonton (2012), who has taught courses on creativity for more than two decades, notes that teaching creativity creatively is "a far more difficult goal to achieve" (p. 220).

The purpose of this chapter is to explore creativity in the domain of teaching by describing three different forms of creative teaching. This includes highlighting the different aims, the knowledge base necessary for each form of creative teaching, previous work on each form, and directions for future research.

Three Forms of Creative Teaching

As already noted, creative teaching can take at least three different forms: teaching *about* creativity, teaching *for* creativity, and teaching *with* creativity. Table 30.1 provides a summary of these three forms of creative teaching.

As displayed in Table 30.1, each of the three forms of creative teaching is differentiated by its pedagogical aim and specific knowledge base. In the sections that follow, I elaborate on each of the three forms of creative teaching.

Teaching About Creativity

Teaching about creativity refers to teaching students about creative phenomena, including the individual and contextual factors that influence the development and expression of creativity. This starts with helping students understand how creativity is defined (e.g., Plucker, Beghetto, & Dow, 2004) and also helping students understand different ways it can be expressed (Rhodes, 1961; Glăveanu, 2013; Sternberg, Kaufman, & Pretz, 2002), what it looks like in various domains (Kaufman, Beghetto, Baer, & Ivcevic, 2010), how it develops (Beghetto & Dilley, 2016; Beghetto & Kaufman, 2007; Kaufman & Beghetto, 2009), what environmental factors influence creativity (Amabile, 1996; Beghetto & Kaufman, 2014; Hennessey, 2010), and understanding key theories (e.g., Kozbelt, Beghetto, & Runco, 2010), research findings (Kaufman, 2016; Runco, 2007), and controversies in the field (Simonton, 2012). In short, teaching about creativity has the aim of promoting students' understanding of creative phenomena in its many manifestations by introducing students to findings and insights from the field of creativity studies.

Prior Work on "Teaching About Creativity." There are a small but growing number of scholarly works on how to teach about creativity (Beghetto, 2013a; Plucker & Dow, 2010; Simonton, 2012). Some of this work (e.g., Beghetto, 2013a) has focused on how to teach about creativity in the context of other academic subject areas (e.g., math, science, history, and literature). Some examples include:

clarify the knowledge necessary for creative teaching and, in turn, help researchers start empirically examining how such knowledge develops and the impact that this knowledge has on creative teaching, student learning, and even student creativity.

Table 30.1 *Three forms of creative teaching*

Form of teaching	Pedagogical aim	Knowledge necessary	Examples of prior work
Teaching *about* creativity	Develop students' awareness of creativity by introducing them to key theories and findings in the creativity studies literature and helping them develop and understand creative phenomena in its many manifestations. This can occur in the context of subject matter teaching (e.g., teaching about creativity in a writing class or a class devoted specifically to creativity).	Pedagogical Creative-Domain Knowledge (PCdK)	Beghetto (2013a); Beghetto & Kaufman (2010); Plucker & Dow (2010); Simonton (2012)
Teaching *for* creativity	Nurturing students' creativity in the context of specific subject areas (e.g., creative expression in science) or nurturing creativity itself in training programs (e.g., develop creative problem-solving skills, promoting positive self-beliefs, attitudes, and behaviors about creativity).	Pedagogical Creativity Enhancement Knowledge (PCeK)	Baer & Garrett (2010); Beghetto (2013a, 2016a, 2016b); Beghetto et al. (2015); Craft et al. (2013); Grohman & Szmidt (2013); Halpern (2010) Isaksen & Treffinger (2004); Nickerson (1999); Scott et al. (2004); Sternberg (2010)
Teaching *with* creativity	Teaching creatively by applying principles and techniques of creativity to subject matter teaching (e.g., creatively teaching math, creatively teaching educational psychology) or the teaching of creativity itself (e.g., teaching creativity creatively).	Creative Pedagogical Domain Knowledge (CPDK)	Beghetto (2013a, 2013b); Gregerson et. al (2013); Jeffrey & Craft (2004); Sawyer (2004)

(a) Identifying and discussing domain-specific examples of everyday and highly accomplished creators (e.g., Who has made creative contributions in this domain? Who were some of the key progenitors of the ideas, concepts, events and accomplishments we are studying about in this course?);

(b) Exploring specific kinds of creative accomplishments in the domain (e.g., What are some of the legendary or key contributions that have been made in this domain? What kinds of creative contributions are still being made in this domain? What additional contributions are needed or might be on the horizon?),

(c) Learning about the kinds of domain-specific and domain-general creative processes involved in making contributions in subject area (e.g., What role does the creative imagination play in mathematical thinking and reasoning? How do poets use language and grammar in new and highly original ways? How do engineers find problems to address, develop designs, and test out and refine those designs? How are creative processes similar or different in this domain as compared to others?), and

(d) Discussing circumstances that support and impede accomplishments in the domain (e.g., Who decides what counts as a creative contribution in this domain? How are accomplishments recognized in this domain? How do some creative accomplishments in this domain stand the test of time, whereas others fade away? What types of chance opportunities, access to resources, and socio-cultural and historical supports allowed for these accomplishments? What kinds of setbacks did creators face and how did they overcome such setbacks? How many years of sustained effort are, on average, needed to make a contribution to this domain? Who historically has had the access and opportunities to make contributions in this domain? Who has been excluded? Has this changed in recent years? If so, how? If not, why not and what can be done about it?)

In addition to work that has focused on teaching about creativity in the context of other academic topics, there is also a line of work that has focused on standalone creativity courses (Plucker & Dow, 2010; Simonton, 2012). This work tends to focus on college-level courses, although this trend may be changing (see Zhao, 2012).

When teaching standalone creativity courses, instructors can use standard pedagogical techniques to teach students about the topic of creativity. Indeed, as Simonton (2012) has explained, "teaching creativity is not different than teaching any other subject in psychology" (p. 220). Given that the topic is creativity, however, instructors often recognize that there is a tacit (if not explicit) expectation to try to approach the topic somewhat creatively. Indeed, it is easy to imagine such courses being criticized on course evaluations as being ironically uncreative. Such a criticism, however, fails to recognize that teaching about creativity is very different from teaching creativity creatively. Still, there are opportunities for the creative teaching of creativity.

Plucker and Dow (2010), for instance, describe several creative teaching activities that they have used to help students learn about creativity and have also helped students develop more positive attitudes about creativity. Simonton (2012) has also described such opportunities, such as when teaching students about divergent thinking tests. In such cases, the instructor and students can complete sample test items together (e.g., unusual uses for a brick or paper clip) and thereby experience the double benefit of introducing students to "measurement issues in the context of a direct experience that [they] all share" (Simonton, 2012, p. 220). In this way, teaching about creativity can (and sometimes does) involve teaching with and for creativity. As will be discussed in later sections, however, teaching with and for creativity requires more than having students try out a few sample items on a divergent thinking test. Still, such an example does illustrate how these three forms of teaching can be interrelated.

Pedagogical Knowledge Necessary for "Teaching About Creativity." It is easy to assume that teaching about a topic, like creativity, simply requires knowing something about it. Such an assumption oversimplifies the act of teaching. Although it is true that domain knowledge (i.e., knowledge of the key concepts, theories, and research about creativity) is necessary, it is not sufficient. A simple reflection on one's own experiences learning from top experts in a particular domain (e.g., physics, mathematics, philosophy, literature) can make this readily evident. Although you may have been fortunate enough to learn from a brilliant scholar who was also a brilliant teacher, chances are you have also experienced subpar instruction from top scholars in their field.

Scholars of teaching have endeavored to document, over the past thirty years, that teaching any subject matter requires more than just having deep domain knowledge. Lee Shulman (1987), for instance, highlighted three types of knowledge necessary for successful instruction in any domain: *content knowledge* (i.e., knowledge of the subject matter you are teaching), *pedagogical knowledge* (i.e., general knowledge of teaching, including general strategies and techniques), and *pedagogical content knowledge* (i.e., more specific knowledge of how to teach particular subject matter topics to a particular set of students in a particular context).

With respect to teaching *about* creativity, these three forms of knowledge can be combined into what I call Pedagogical Creative-Domain Knowledge (PCdK). PCdK refers to a combination of creative domain knowledge (i.e., knowledge of key creativity concepts, theories, and studies from the field) and the pedagogical knowledge (i.e., knowing how to teach a particular population of students about creativity in a particular context). The importance of PCdK can be illustrated by considering what one would need to know if teaching an introductory undergraduate creativity course to undergraduates versus teaching sixth graders about creativity in the context of their science class. The former would require knowledge of creativity and knowledge of how to make the subject matter relevant and accessible to undergraduate students. The latter would also require knowledge about the domain of creativity, but also knowledge of how it is represented in the domain of science and knowledge of how to make it accessible for young students. Recognizing, assessing, and developing this unique type of pedagogical knowledge is an area of research that has gone largely unnoticed by creativity researchers. As such, subsequent work aimed at understanding this form of pedagogical knowledge serves as a potentially fruitful line of future research for scholars interested in creative teaching.

How Teaching About Creativity Can Be Measured. Given that teaching about creativity treats creativity as a subject-matter topic or focus of a course, researchers interested in studying the impact of teaching about creativity would need to use (or develop) measures that focus on potential changes in students' knowledge, attitudes, and beliefs about creativity. This would include more traditional measures used by instructors, such as student performance on assignments, exams, projects, and course grades. It could also include measures that pertain more directly to the aims of a particular course (e.g., changes in beliefs and attitudes about creativity, see Plucker & Dow, 2004).

Research on teaching about creativity is a small but promising area of inquiry for creativity researchers. Indeed, as more courses focus on or include teaching about creativity, researchers will have opportunities to explore how pedagogical creativity-domain knowledge impacts instructors' ability to teach about creativity more effectively and perhaps even how it influences instructors' ability to teach for and with creativity.

Teaching for Creativity

Teaching for creativity refers to efforts aimed at enhancing students' creativity. As with teaching *about* creativity, teaching for creativity can occur in the context of other academic subject areas (Beghetto, 2013a; 2015; Beghetto, Kaufman, & Baer, 2015; Halpern, 2010). Teaching for creativity can also focus more directly on nurturing or training creativity itself, most commonly in creativity training programs (Isaksen & Treffinger, 2004; Nickerson, 1999; Scott et al., 2004).

Prior Work on "Teaching for Creativity." With respect to teaching for creativity in the context of other subject-areas, prior work has highlighted how instructors can blend students' original ideas, examples, and insights within the context of pre-existing academic subject-matter constraints. Some researchers have highlighted how teaching for creativity in the context of academic learning can simultaneously promote student learning and students' creative capacity (see Craft et al. 2013; Beghetto, 2013a, 2016a; Niu & Zhou, 2010). Others have focused on developing habits of creative thinking in the context of teaching other academic subject areas (e.g., Sternberg, 2010). Still others have focused on teaching for creativity in the context of external content standards and accountability mandates (e.g., Baer & Garret, 2010; Beghetto et al. 2015). In all cases, this line of work has attempted to demonstrate how creativity can not only co-exist, but thrive, in the context of academic subject-matter constraints.

Consider, for example, teaching for creativity within the context of teaching elements of a narrative (adapted from Beghetto et al. 2015). In such a case, the teacher might list out the various required elements for students on the top of a matrix, including *setting, main characters, conflict*, and *point of view*. Next, the teacher would invite students to offer several examples under each column representing a particular element of narrative (e.g., setting = remote island, abandoned building; main characters = group of friends, group of teachers; conflict = zombie apocalypse, mistaken identity; and point of view = third person; naïve narrator).

Finally, in an effort to provide students with an opportunity to express their creativity in the context of a narrative, the teacher could have students randomly select examples from each category and then write a unique story based on those elements. In this way, students are being encouraged to develop and express their creativity in the context of learning about specific academic subject matter. Doing so meets the typical definition of creativity (Beghetto, 2016c; Beghetto & Kaufman, 2014; Simonton & Damian, 2013): *Creativity (C) = Originality (O) x Meeting Task Constraints (TC) as defined within a particular context)*. In the case of this particular example, a creative narrative (C) = students' unique examples of narrative (O) x meeting the criteria of each narrative element (TC) as defined within the context of this particular lesson.

In addition to teaching for creativity in the context of academic subject-matter learning, there are also standalone creativity training programs aimed at promoting skills and strategies of creative thinking and problem solving (for reviews see Isaksen & Treffinger, 2004; Nickerson, 1999; Scott, Leritz, & Mumford, 2004). Although programs that focus on promoting "general creativity" or "instant creativity" have long been criticized for being nothing more than a bag of decontextualized tricks and tips (Baron, 1969; Baer & Garrett, 2010), researchers have identified several features of creativity-enhancement programs that seem to lead to positive outcomes (e.g., Scott et al., 2004).

More specifically, programs that have demonstrated the most promising results tend to be lengthy, challenging, and engage participants in cognitive activities related to creativity. Moreover, they include examples of how principles and strategies that are taught to participants can be applied to the relevant domain of interest and also provide ample opportunities to apply those strategies in realistic contexts (Scott et al., 2004).

There are several longstanding and well-developed training programs that include features found to be successful for promoting gains in creative thinking and problem solving. One example is the Creative Problem Solving (CPS) programs described by Isaksen and Treffinger (2004). CPS (and programs like CPS) teach participants how to solve realistic and ill-defined problems using a combination of strategies and thinking skills aimed at generating (e.g., problem finding, using analogies and metaphors) and evaluating ideas (e.g., idea evaluation, solution monitoring, convergent and critical thinking).

In sum, teaching people key principles and practices of creative thinking and problem solving, as documented in the creative studies literature, can help them develop their capacity to more creatively address the kinds of ill-defined problems and complex real-world challenges they face in their personal and professional lives (see Cropley & Cropley, 2010; Beghetto, 2016d; Sawyer, 2012).

Teaching for creativity (as compared to teaching about and teaching with creativity) has received the most attention in the scholarly literature. Still, much work is needed in this area. Historically, a key hurdle in this line of work has been finding teachers who actually know how to teach for creativity (Schacter, Thum, & Zifkin, 2006; Torrance & Safter, 1986). With increased interest in promoting creativity in K12 and higher-education settings, there likely will be more opportunities for researchers to explore what instructional factors are most supportive of student creativity in and across various academic domains.

Understanding how creative thinking and problem solving differs across domains will go a long way in helping clarify principles of how to best nurture creativity in specific academic subject areas. Such work may yield insights that can help instructors move away from reaching for general or "ready-made" techniques that lack relevance for a particular problem or situation (e.g., come up with a hundred uses for a pencil) and move toward understanding the principles of creative thinking and problem solving that can be used to development more effective "tailor-made" approaches (e.g., come up with novel and meaningful solutions to ill-defined domain-specific problems).

Pedagogical Knowledge Necessary for "Teaching for Creativity." Knowing how to teach for creativity requires a blend of creativity-domain knowledge and pedagogical knowledge about how to enhance creativity. I call this specialized form of pedagogical knowledge Pedagogical Creativity-Enhancement Knowledge (PCeK). PCeK refers to knowing how to enhance students' creative attitudes, beliefs, thoughts, and actions in the context of other academic subject areas or in standalone creativity enhancement trainings or workshops. As with pedagogical creativity-domain knowledge, the importance of recognizing that specialized pedagogical knowledge is necessary to teach for creativity is often overlooked by instructors and scholars. However, anyone who has attempted to enhance creativity – either in a standalone seminar or in the context of another academic domain – recognizes that there is more to teaching for creativity than knowing an array of creativity techniques, activities, or tricks (Beghetto, 2010, 2013a). Knowledge of one's audience, potential barriers, affordances, and constraints, and how creativity can be applied in specific contexts, are also critically important.

At present, this knowledge has only been indirectly recognized by virtue of identifying features of more or less "successful" creativity training programs (Scott et al., 2004; Isaksen & Treffinger, 2004) and other instructional practices believed to be linked with supporting creativity (e.g., Beghetto & Kaufman, 2014; Schacter et al. 2006). Much additional work is needed to explore how PCeK can be developed, assessed, and applied in efforts aimed at enhancing creativity both in standalone trainings and in the context of other subject areas (e.g., teaching for creativity in the context of a mathematics classroom).

How Teaching for Creativity Can Be Measured. There are various ways that teaching for creativity can be measured. When teaching for creativity in the context of other academic subject areas, researchers have described methods for simultaneously assessing students' subject matter learning and ability to think creatively in specific subject areas (Beghetto, 2013a; Grigorenko, Jarvin, Tan, & Sternberg, 2008). This includes developing and using rubrics that can help assess growing levels of academic and creative competence within specific subject areas (see Beghetto, 2013a; Beghetto et al. 2015 for examples).

With respect to assessing the effectiveness of creativity enhancement, researchers can also draw on the full array of existing creativity measures (see Kaufman, Plucker, & Baer, 2008 for an overview). Examples of such measures include everything from more subjective measures of self-beliefs (e.g., Beghetto & Karwowski, 2017) to performance on divergent thinking tests (e.g., Torrance, 1966) and the assessment of actual creative products (e.g., Amabile, 1996; Besemer & O'Quinn, 1989).

Although existing measures are useful, there is also need for the development of more nuanced and dynamic assessments of teaching for creativity (see Beghetto, 2016; Beghetto & Tanggard, 2015). Developing more sensitive and dynamic methods for measuring teaching for creativity (e.g., simultaneously assessing the confluence of teacher, student, and environmental factors on domain-specific creativity enhancement) is an important and much needed area of future inquiry for researchers interested in understanding how teachers might support students' creative thinking and action.

Teaching with Creativity

Teaching with creativity refers to approaching teaching creatively. It is therefore most readily signified by the terms "creative teaching" or "teaching creatively." Teaching with creativity locates creativity in the act of teaching itself, rather than positioning it as the subject matter (i.e., teaching about creativity) or an instructional outcome (i.e., teaching for creativity). Teaching creatively can also occur when teaching *for* or *about* creativity. Consequently, teaching with creativity can occur in the context of teaching almost any subject matter in an effort to promote almost any instructional goal.

Pedagogical Knowledge Necessary for "Teaching with Creativity." Knowing how to teach creatively requires a blend of creativity-domain knowledge and creative pedagogical knowledge. I call this specialized form of pedagogical knowledge Creative Pedagogical Domain Knowledge (CPDK). CPDK refers to the knowledge necessary for creatively teaching specific subject matter (e.g., mathematics, science, and even creativity itself) to a particular population of students. Consequently, just because someone might know how to creatively teach 8th grade students mathematics does not mean they would know how to creatively teach 1st grade students mathematics or how to creatively teach 8th grade students social studies. CPDK is specialized knowledge that varies across subject-matter topics, populations of students, and contexts.

Prior Work on Teaching with Creativity. In the creativity studies literature, teaching creatively is typically described in the context of teaching for creativity (e.g., Beghetto, 2013a; Gregerson, Snyder, & Kaufman, 2013; Jeffrey & Craft, 2004). One reason is because researchers who have focused on teaching for creativity often highlight how teaching creatively can establish a classroom context conducive to supporting student creativity. Lilly & Bramwell-Rejskind (2004) have, for instance, asserted that creative teaching "provides a safe climate where students can [take intellectual risks] and push boundaries" (p. 104).

Central to the claim of the influence that creative teaching has on student creativity is the phenomenon of social-behavioral modeling. Specifically, the key assertion is: If teachers model behaviors associated with creativity, then they can help establish classroom conditions whereby students feel encouraged and supported in exhibiting the similar behaviors (Bandura, 1997; Beghetto, 2016c; Jeffery & Craft, 2004). More specifically, teaching with creativity is thought to model key behaviors such as the willingness to: take risks (such as trying to learn or do something new); learn from (rather than avoid) mistakes; accept uncertainty; seek out complexity; approach teaching and learning with flexible thinking and open-mindedness; seek out and explore diverse ideas, perspectives, and experiences; and demonstrate a deep commitment to and enjoyment of one's own learning process (Beghetto, 2013a; Jeffrey & Craft, 2004; Lilly & Bramwell-Rejskind, 2004).

Although the link between teaching with creativity and teaching for creativity makes sense conceptually, it can obscure what exactly is involved in teaching creatively. Indeed, beyond describing creative teaching as using behaviors associated with creativity more generally (e.g., openness, flexibility, risk-taking), there has been scant theoretical, conceptual, and thereby empirical work focused on clarifying what exactly teaching creatively entails, how it develops, and what impact it can have on teachers and students.

One way creativity researchers have conceptualized creative teaching is by using the metaphor of "disciplined improvisation" (Beghetto & Kaufman, 2011; Sawyer, 2004), likening it to a performance that blends specific knowledge and skills with more emergent actions and behaviors. Such a view recognizes that creative teaching includes more than a set of ready-made strategies and techniques and, instead, has its basis in knowing how to approach instructional planning and the actual moment-to-moment decision making of teaching (Beghetto, 2013a, 2013b). In short, there is a knowledge base of teaching creatively. Unfortunately, only a few creativity researchers have attempted to understand and document this knowledge base (e.g., Niu & Zhou, 2010; Sawyer, 2011). As such, much additional work is needed to clarify what exactly teaching creatively entails, outcomes of doing so, and how it can be developed. This includes exploring the relationship between creative teaching and what educators might describe as successful teaching (or simply teaching well).

How Can Teaching with Creativity Be Measured? Given that teaching creatively has received little attention in the literature, there are few studies or descriptions of how it might be measured (e.g., Beghetto, 2016a; Beghetto & Tanggard, 2015; Niu & Zhou, 2010; Sawyer, 2011). One of the difficulties in measuring teaching creatively is that it is a dynamic act or performance. As such, traditional survey methods, checklists, and other static outcomes measures are not sufficiently dynamic to capture the act of teaching creatively. Fortunately, creativity researchers have started using and developing more dynamic techniques that might be adapted for measuring teaching with creativity, including experience sampling (Silvia, Beaty, Nusbaum, Eddington, Levin-Aspenson, & Kwapil, 2014), Consensual Assessment Technique (Kaufman & Baer, 2012), and trajectory mapping (Beghetto, 2017; Gajda, Beghetto, & Karwowski, 2016; Tanggaard & Beghetto, 2015).

In addition to such methods, researchers will need to modify or develop methods that allow them to zoom-in on idiosyncratic and micro-dynamic features of creative teaching (e.g., moment-to-moment instructional moves used when teaching in particular contexts) and zoom-out to identify features of creative teaching that may generalize across domains and contexts (Beghetto, 2014). Doing so likely will yield new insights into how creative teaching influences (and is influenced by) students' emerging creative ideations and actions. This is a fertile ground for additional research. Indeed, there is a great need for researchers to carefully consider how to best measure teaching for creativity. This includes developing new methods and measures and also exploring whether and how existing methods and measures used in other domains might be adapted for educational settings (see Reiter-Palmon, Beghetto, & Kaufman, 2014, and other chapters in this volume).

Conclusion and Future Directions

In this chapter, I attempted to provide an introduction to what I see as key themes in research on creativity in the domain of teaching. This is an emerging and exciting line of inquiry for current and future creativity researchers. Indeed, there are numerous promising directions for research on creative teaching. As has been discussed, the vast majority of previous work has focused on the impact of creativity training (or teaching *for* creativity). Although this work is important, it represents a narrow slice of the full domain of creative teaching.

Given that there are at least three ways to classify creative teaching, including numerous aims, knowledge bases, and processes and outcomes that can be explored, there is a need to broaden the scope of research on creative teaching. Moreover, with increased interest and attention being paid to creativity in K12 and higher education settings, there is a growing need to understand how teachers and instructors can teach for, with, and about creativity. In what follows, I close by highlighting a few promising areas for future research on creative teaching.

Measures of Creative Pedagogical Knowledge

The types of pedagogical knowledge introduced herein (e.g., pedagogical creativity-domain knowledge, pedagogical creativity-enhancement knowledge, and creative pedagogical domain knowledge) require further theoretical elaboration and empirical exploration. Specifically, measures and methods for assessing these forms of knowledge need to be developed. Doing so will go a long way to understanding how these specific forms of pedagogical knowledge influence creative teaching. Moreover, such work can also provide a window into how these specific forms of creative teaching knowledge might be systematically developed in K12 teachers and college-level instructors.

Creative teaching, like all teaching, is an embodied activity. As such, the kinds of methods and measures for assessing the knowledge necessary for creative teaching would require the development of measures that take into account both the espoused situational knowledge of teaching (e.g., knowing how to plan and deliver lessons based on particular situations, with specific instructional aims, and with particular populations of students) and the more dynamic-enacted knowledge (i.e., actual teaching behaviors and instructional moves used when teaching for and with creativity).

Curriculum-Based Measures of Creativity

Given that teaching about, for, and with creativity can occur in the context of a course on any topic or subject matter (including creativity itself), the development of curriculum-based measures are necessary to assess the impact of different forms of creative teaching on domain-specific student outcomes. The typical kinds of measures used by creativity researchers to assess the impact of instruction on creativity (e.g., divergent thinking tasks) and learning (course grades, GPA), likely lack the sensitivity to detect potentially meaningful changes resulting from creative teaching (Gajda, Karwowski, Beghetto, 2016). Consequently, more sensitive and multifaceted measures are needed. Such measures would need to be sensitive enough to assess changes in the target content being taught (e.g., knowledge about creativity, mathematical reasoning, understanding of scientific concepts, and so on), creative expression situated in that particular subject matter (e.g., creative expression in mathematics versus science or some other domain), and the targeted area of learning and engagement in particular populations of students (e.g., creative expression in 4th grade mathematics versus 8th grade math or college calculus).

Developing such curriculum-based measures is an ambitious undertaking. The vast array of measures that could be developed is overwhelming (and likely one reason why we tend to reach for existing, albeit far less sensitive measures). However, if researchers start by focusing on a few specific subject areas and populations, then the work becomes more manageable. There are examples of such work being done to help teachers and researchers assess creativity in the context of academic domains (e.g., Beghetto, 2013a; Beghetto et al. 2015; Grigorenko et al, 2008), but additional efforts are needed. Researchers who put the time and effort into this work will likely yield benefits by way of greater understanding of how creative teaching influences student creativity and student learning.

Classroom-Situated and Multidisciplinary Efforts

Developing more than a cursory understanding of creative teaching will require more detailed and in-depth studies in classrooms representing different age levels and different domains. Although the field of creativity studies has a history of research situated in classrooms (e.g., Torrance, 1959), such work is scant. One reason why there are not more classroom-based research projects is because such research is resource intensive – especially with respect to time invested (e.g., establishing school contacts, obtaining permissions, time spent traveling to and from school sites, observing classrooms, and so on). It is therefore not surprising that so few researchers have engaged in more intensive, classroom-based studies of creative teaching.

With the availability of various free and effective digital video, communications, and research technologies, it seems like a good time for researchers to revisit how such technology might make such projects more feasible. Working in teams, alongside teachers, creativity researchers can make important and much needed contributions to the literature on the various forms and outcomes of creative teaching. Such efforts would benefit from cross-cultural and interdisciplinary approaches to studying creativity (Hennessey & Amabile, 2010; Reiter-Palmon et al, 2014; Kaufman & Sternberg, 2006; Sawyer, 2012; Tan, 2007).

Curating Cases of Creative Teaching

Creative teaching tends to be an ephemeral phenomenon. That is, once a lesson has been taught there is no record of it other than fragments of the teacher's planning notes and possible students' in-class notes. Whatever "wisdom of practice" (Shulman, 1987) that can be learned from highly skilled creative teachers is lost. Although it is true that there are outlets, such as edited volumes and books that focus on teaching for and with creativity (e.g., Beghetto, 2013a; Beghetto & Kaufman, 2010; Gregerson et al. 2013; Tan, 2007), there is no repository of frequently updated and detailed cases of creative teaching (providing lessons, materials, videos, and reflections).

Such repositories of academic subject matter teaching do exist for K12 teachers and college-level teachers[2] and may serve as a good model for developing creativity-specific versions. As such, a promising area of future work would be to develop ways to curate and share detailed case-based examples of teaching for, with, and about creativity across domains and grade levels. These data not only could help improve the practice of creative teaching, but serve as a data warehouse for researchers interested in exploring the processes and outcomes of creative teaching.

References

Amabile, T. M. (1996). *Creativity in context: Update to the social psychology of creativity.* Boulder, CO: Westview.

Baer, J., & Garrett, T. (2010). Teaching for creativity in an era of content standards and accountability. In R. A. Beghetto & J. C. Kaufman (Eds.), *Nurturing creativity in the classroom.* New York, NY: Cambridge University Press.

Bandura, A. (1997). *Self-efficacy: The exercise of control.* New York, NY: Freeman.

Barron, F. (1969). *Creative person and creative process.* New York: Holt, Rinehart, & Winston.

Beghetto, R. A. (2010). Creativity in the classroom. In J. C. Kaufman & R. J. Sternberg (Eds.), *Cambridge handbook of creativity.* New York: Cambridge University Press.

Beghetto, R. A. (2013a). *Killing ideas softly? The promise and perils of creativity in the classroom.* Charlotte, NC: Information Age.

Beghetto, R. A. (2013b). Expect the unexpected: Teaching for creativity in the micromoments. In M. Gregerson, J. C. Kaufman, & H. Snyder (Eds.), *Teaching creatively and teaching creativity.* New York: Springer Science.

Beghetto, R. A. (2014). Is the sky falling or expanding? A promising turning point in the psychology of creativity. *Creativity: Theories-Research-Applications, 1,* 206–212.

---

[2] Examples include www.learner.org; http://gallery.carnegiefoundation.org

Beghetto, R. A. (2015). Teaching creative thinking. In R. Wegerif, L. Li, & J. C. Kaufman (Eds.), *The Routledge international handbook of research on teaching thinking*. New York: Routledge.

Beghetto, R. A. (2016a). Creative learning: A fresh look. *Journal of Cognitive Education and Psychology, 15*, 6–23.

Beghetto, R. A. (2016b). Learning as a creative act. In T. Kettler (Ed.), *Modern curriculum for gifted and advanced academic students*. Waco, TX: Prufrock.

Beghetto, R. A. (2016c). *Big wins, small steps: How to lead for and with creativity*. Thousand Oaks, CA: Corwin.

Beghetto, R. A. (2016d). Creative openings in the social interactions of teaching. *Creativity: Theories-Research-Applications, 3*, 261–273.

Beghetto, R. A., & Dilley, A. E. (2016). Creative aspirations or pipe dreams? Toward understanding creative mortification in children and adolescents. In B. Barbot (Ed.), *Perspectives on creativity development. New Directions for Child and Adolescent Development, 151*, 79–89.

Beghetto, R. A., & Karwowski, M. (2017). Toward untangling creative self-beliefs. In M. Karwowski & J. C. Kaufman (Eds.), *The creative self: Effect of beliefs, self-efficacy, mindsets, and identity* (pp. 4–22). London: Academic Press.

Beghetto, R. A., & Kaufman, J. C. (2007). Toward a broader conception of creativity: A case for mini-c creativity. *Psychology of Aesthetics, Creativity, and the Arts, 1*, 73–79.

Beghetto, R. A., & Kaufman, J. C. (2010). Broadening conceptions of creativity in the classroom. In R. A. Beghetto & J. C. Kaufman (Eds.), *Nurturing creativity in the classroom*. Cambridge, UK: Cambridge University Press.

Beghetto, R. A., & Kaufman, J. C. (2011). Teaching for creativity with disciplined improvisation. In R. K. Sawyer (Ed.), *Structure and improvisation in creative teaching*. Cambridge: Cambridge University Press.

Beghetto, R. A., & Kaufman, J. C. (2014) Classroom contexts for creativity. *High Ability Studies, 25*, 53–69.

Beghetto, R. A., Kaufman, J. C., & Baer, J. (2015). *Teaching for creativity in the common core classroom*. New York: Teachers College Press.

Besemer, S. P., & O'Quin, K. (1999). Confirming the three-factor Creative Product Analysis Matrix model in an American sample. *Creativity Research Journal, 12*, 287–296.

Craft, A., Cremin, T., Burnard, P., Dragovic, T., & Chappell, K. (2013). Possibility thinking: Culminative studies of an evidence-based concept driving creativity? *Education 3–13: International Journal of Primary, Elementary, and Early Years of Education, 41*, 538–556.

Cropley, D. H., & Cropley, A. J. (2010), Functional creativity: Products and the generation of effective novelty. In J. C. Kaufman & R. J. Sternberg (Eds.), *Cambridge handbook of creativity* (pp. 301–320). New York: Cambridge University Press.

Gajda, A., Beghetto, R. A., & Karwowski, M. (in press). Exploring creative learning in the classroom: A multi-method approach. *Thinking Skills and Creativity*.

Gajda, A., Karwowski, M., & Beghetto, R. A. (2016). Creativity and school achievement: A meta-analysis. *Journal of Educational Psychology, 109*, 269–299.

Glăveanu, V. P. (2013). Rewriting the language of creativity: The five A's framework. *Review of General Psychology, 17*, 69–81.

Gregerson M., Kaufman J. C., & Snyder H. (Eds.). (2013). *Teaching creatively and teaching creativity*. New York: Springer Science.

Grigorenko, E. L., Jarvin, L., Tan, M., & Sternberg, R. J. (2008). Something new in the garden: Assessing creativity in academic domains. *Psychology Science Quarterly*, *50*, 295–307.

Grohman, M. G., & Szmidt, K. J. (2013). Teaching for creativity: How to shape creative attitudes in teachers and in students. In M. B. Gregerson, H. T. Snyder, & J. C. Kaufman (Eds.), *Teaching creatively and teaching creativity*. New York: Springer.

Halpern, D. F. (2010). Creativity in the college classroom. In R. A. Beghetto & J. C. Kaufman (Eds.), *Nurturing creativity in the classroom*. New York, NY: Cambridge University Press.

Hennessey, B. A. (2010). Intrinsic motivation and creativity in the classroom: Have we come full circle? In R. A. Beghetto & J. C. Kaufman (Eds.), *Nurturing creativity in the classroom*. New York: Cambridge University Press.

Hirst, P. H. (1971). What is teaching? *Journal of Curriculum Studies*, *3*, 5–18.

Isaksen, S. G., & Treffinger, D. J. (2004). Celebrating 50 years of reflective practice: Versions of creative problem solving. *Journal of Creative Behavior*, *38*, 75–101.

Jeffrey, B., & Craft, A. (2004). Teaching creatively and teaching for creativity: Distinctions and relationships. *Educational Studies*, *30*, 77–87.

Lilly, F. R., & Bramwell-Rejskind, G. (2004). The dynamics of creative teaching. *Journal of Creative Behavior*, *38*, 102–124

Kaufman, J. C. (2016). *Creativity 101* (2nd edn.). New York, NY: Springer.

Kaufman, J. C., & Beghetto, R. A. (2009). Beyond big and little: The four C model of creativity. *Review of General Psychology*, *13*, 1–12.

Kaufman, J. C., Beghetto, R. A., Baer, J. & Ivcevic, Z. (2010). Creative polymathy: What Benjamin Franklin can teach your kindergartener. *Learning & Individual Difference*, *20*, 380–387.

Kaufman, J. C., Plucker, J. A., & Baer, J. (2008). *Essentials of creativity assessment*. New York, NY: Wiley.

Kaufman, J. C., & Sternberg, R. J. (Eds.). (2006). *The international handbook of creativity*. New York: Cambridge University Press.

Kozbelt, A., Beghetto, R. A., & Runco, M. A. (2010). Theories of creativity. In J. C. Kaufman & R. J. Sternberg (Eds.), *Cambridge handbook of creativity*. New York: Cambridge University Press.

Plucker, J., Beghetto, R. A., & Dow, G. (2004). Why isn't creativity more important to educational psychologists? Potential, pitfalls, and future directions in creativity research. *Educational Psychologist*, *39*, 83–96.

Plucker, J. A., & Dow, G. T. (2010). Attitude change as the precursor to creativity enhancement. In R. A. Beghetto & J. C. Kaufman (Eds.), *Nurturing creativity in the classroom*. New York, NY: Cambridge University Press.

Nickerson, R. S. (1999). Enhancing creativity. In R. J. Sternberg (Ed.), *Handbook of human creativity*. New York: Cambridge University Press.

Niu, W., & Zhou, Z. (2010). Creativity in mathematics teaching: A Chinese perspective. In R. A. Beghetto & J. C. Kaufman (Eds.), *Nurturing creativity in the classroom*. New York, NY: Cambridge University Press.

Reiter-Palmon, R., Beghetto, R. A., & Kaufman, J. C. (2014). Looking at creativity through a business-psychology-education (BPE) lens: The challenge and benefits of listening to each other. In E. Shiu (Ed.), *Creativity research: An interdisciplinary and multidisciplinary research handbook*. New York: Routledge.

Rhodes, M. (1961). An analysis of creativity. *Phi Delta Kappan, 42*, 305–310.

Runco, M. A. (2007). *Creativity. Theories and themes: Research, development, and practice.* Burlington, MA: Elsevier Academic Press.

Sawyer, R. K. (2004). Creative teaching: Collaborative discussion as disciplined improvisation. *Educational Researcher, 33*, 12–20.

Sawyer, R. K. (Ed.). (2011). *Structure and improvisation in creative teaching.* New York, NY: Cambridge University Press.

Sawyer, R. K. (2012). *Explaining creativity: The science of human innovation* (2nd edn.). New York, NY: Oxford University Press.

Schacter, J., Thum, Y. M., & Zifkin, D. (2006). How much does creative teaching enhance elementary school students' achievement? *The Journal of Creative Behavior, 40*, 47–72.

Scott, G., Leritz, L. E., & Mumford, M. D. (2004). The effectiveness of creativity training: A quantitative review. *Creativity Research Journal, 16*, 361–388.

Shulman, L. S. (1987). Knowledge and teaching: Foundations of the new reform. *Harvard Educational Review, 57*, 1–22.

Silvia, P. J., Beaty, R. E., Nusbaum, E. C., Eddington, K. M., Levin-Aspenson, H., & Kwapil, T. R. (2014). Everyday creativity in daily life: An experience-sampling study of "little c" creativity. *Psychology of Aesthetics, Creativity, and the Arts, 8*(2), 183–188.

Simonton, D. K. (2012). Teaching creativity: Current findings, trends, and controversies in the psychology of creativity. *Teaching of Psychology, 39*, 217–222.

Simonton, D. K., & Damian, R. I. (2013). Creativity. In D. Reisberg (Ed.), *Oxford handbook of cognitive psychology* (pp. 795–807). New York: Oxford University Press.

Sternberg, R. J., Kaufman, J. C., & Pretz, J. E. (2002). *The creativity conundrum.* Philadelphia, PA: Psychology Press.

Tanggaard, L., & Beghetto, R. A. (2015). Ideational pathways: Toward a new approach for studying the life of ideas. *Creativity: Theories-Research-Applications, 2*, 129–144.

Tan, A. G. (Ed.). (2007). *Creativity: A handbook for teachers.* Singapore: World Scientific.

Torrance, E. P. (1959). Current research on the nature of creative talent. *Journal of Counseling Psychology, 6*, 309–316.

Torrance, E. P. (1966). *Torrance tests of creative thinking: Norms technical manual.* Princeton, NJ: Personnel.

Torrance, E. P., & Safter, H. T. (1986). Are children becoming more creative? *Journal of Creative Behavior, 20*, 1–13.

Zhao, Y. (2012). *World class learners: Education creative and entrepreneurial students.* Thousand Oaks, CA: Corwin.

31 Culture and Creativity

Rodica Ioana Damian

University of Houston

Reese Y.W. Tou

University of Houston

Abstract

We present research on creativity in the culture domain through the lens of four broad guiding questions: unique features, constructs and measurements, empirical findings, and future directions. Regarding unique features, we note that (a) creativity and culture are naturally intertwined concepts and it is difficult to imagine one without the other; (b) the meaning of creativity may differ across cultures; (c) creativity and culture can be studied taking a broad variety of theoretical perspectives; and (d) culture does not exist in isolation, so it is essential to consider the role of multiculturalism on creativity. Regarding constructs and measurements, we describe both historiometric and psychometric methodological approaches. Historiometric approaches have mainly focused on creative products and have explored the link between culture and creativity both at the aggregate and individual level, whereas psychometric approaches have focused on the creative product, person, and process, conducting both correlational and experimental studies. We introduce the most common constructs and measurements from each methodological approach. The empirical findings section is structured based on two broad research questions that are typical of creativity in the culture domain: (a) Does creativity differ across cultures (especially across East vs. West), and (b) How does multiculturalism affect creativity? Findings pertaining to each of these two sections are further differentiated based on the methodology employed (historiometric vs. psychometric). In the last section of the chapter, we discuss future directions relevant to each of the different streams of research traditions.

Culture represents the shared meaning systems that a collection of interconnected people use as their standards for perceiving, believing, evaluating, communicating, and acting; these networks of knowledge can be both procedural (learned sequences of responses to specific cues) and declarative (representations of norms, events, people), and they are produced, distributed, and reproduced among people who share a language, a historic period, a geographic location, or any other feature that renders a cohesive group (Triandis, 1996;

Chiu & Hong, 2007).[1] Thus, culture can vary by broad geographical location (e.g., Eastern vs. Western culture), by country (e.g., Germany vs. Singapore), by region within a country (e.g., East Coast vs. West Coast in the United States), or even by profession (e.g., academics vs. investment bankers). For the purpose of this chapter, we will focus on culture defined by broad geographical location or country. We chose this focus because the vast majority of past research on culture and creativity has concentrated on Eastern versus Western cross-cultural comparisons of creativity. In this context, when researchers refer to the "Eastern" culture, they include countries from the Far East (e.g., China, Japan, and Korea), and when they refer to the "Western" culture, they include countries from Western Europe (e.g., Germany, the United Kingdom, Italy) and its cultural offshoots following the Age of Exploration (e.g., the United States, Australia, and Canada). Notably, large cultural groups (e.g., from Central Asia, the Indian sub-continent, South America, Africa, or the Middle-East) are excluded from these comparisons. There are several reasons past research has focused on Eastern versus Western cross-cultural comparisons (Simonton & Ting, 2010): (a) cross-cultural comparisons of creativity could be especially striking and produce the largest effects when the civilizations evaluated are farthest apart geographically and have evolved in parallel, with little historical interaction and cross-pollination, as is the case with the opposites ends of Eurasia; (b) both Eastern and Western civilizations can claim creative achievements extending over at least three millennia and these achievements have occurred largely independently, as trade or exchanges only started in modern times; and (c) compared to other regions of the world, these two regions consist of wealthier countries that invest more in research and that have better historical records of their creative achievements. This cross-cultural research typically asks questions such as: How can we measure creativity across cultures? Does creativity differ across Western versus Eastern cultures (i.e., are some cultures more creative than others), and if so, how and why? In addition, we will also review the rich literature that investigates the role of multiculturalism (i.e., belonging to, identifying with, or having been immersed in two or more distinct cultures) on creativity, as multiculturalism is increasingly common in today's globalizing world. Research on multiculturalism and creativity focuses on questions such as: What is the role of multiculturalism on creative thinking and achievement? Does exposure to multiple cultures increase creativity, and if so, when and why? Furthermore, the chapter is structured around four broad guiding questions: (a) What is unique to studying creativity within the culture domain?; (b) What are the constructs and measurements typically used when studying

---

[1] We used this definition for the present chapter because this is the most common view among social-personality psychologists and because it applies to the vast majority of the research reviewed here. However, it is important to note that this is a psychological view of culture that is biased towards a focus on the individual and on cognition. From a more interdisciplinary perspective, culture goes beyond meanings and includes material artifacts, institutions, etc. Furthermore, the notion that culture represents "shared meanings" can be problematic because it implies that culture represents only what is similar across people; this clashes with theory that conceptualizes unique meanings to be part of culture as well, because they emerge from and contribute to a cultural basis (see Glăveanu, 2010; 2011).

creativity and culture?; (c) What are some key empirical findings?; and (d) What are some possible avenues for future research? Before we begin, however, we must define creativity.

Creativity is the process by which creative ideas are generated, selected, and successfully implemented. The majority of the research reviewed in this chapter has used either two or three criteria to define creative ideas, and has considered different levels of magnitude of creativity. The "two criteria" definition includes *originality* and *usefulness* (Runco & Jaeger, 2012). The "three criteria" definition includes *originality, usefulness*, and *surprise* (Simonton, 2012; 2016). To be original, an idea must be novel and unique, and it must have a low probability of being generated. To be useful, an idea should work and should solve a problem of interest. To be surprising, an idea must be nonobvious; for instance, if a solution were a simple derivation based on previous expertise, it might be considered original but not surprising. Each of these three criteria is necessary but not sufficient to render an idea creative. Additionally, each of these criteria is quantitative rather than qualitative and is theorized to have a zero point (Simonton, 2016). Hence, the creativity of an idea can be conceptualized as the product of these three criteria. If an idea has zero originality (a reinvented wheel), zero usefulness (a plane made of bricks), or zero surprise (an incremental derivation of an existing scientific finding), it can also be said to have zero creativity. The higher the level of each of the three criteria, the more creativity there is. Thus, the level of creativity can vary, on a continuum, from the smallest creative acts that are part of everyday life to the biggest most historically impactful acts. To distinguish between different levels of magnitude of creativity, researchers have proposed four guiding categories: (a) "mini-c" creativity, which includes subjective acts of personal everyday creativity (e.g., finding a creative solution to an emotional problem); (b) "little-c" creativity, which includes more objective acts of everyday creativity (e.g., improving a home recipe by adding a new spice); (c) "Pro-c" creativity, which includes professional creativity in a domain (e.g., publishing a journal article) that has not received worldwide acclaim; and (d) "Big-C" creativity, which includes ideas of a broad impact that go down in history (e.g., discovering and manufacturing antibiotics) (Beghetto & Kaufman, 2007; Kaufman & Beghetto, 2009).

Unique Aspects

There are several unique aspects to studying creativity within the culture domain. First, culture and creativity are naturally intertwined concepts because we cannot have culture without creativity or creativity without culture (Csikszentmihalyi, 2014; Glăveanu, 2010). Culture, defined as the body of knowledge, beliefs, and behaviors that humanity passes down across generations, is constantly updating to incorporate acts of individual creativity. For example, social behavior has changed dramatically in the past years as the result of the social media revolution spearheaded by Mark Zuckerberg's Facebook. However, individuals create within a cultural context (e.g., Facebook appeared as a natural continuation of previous social media platforms such as MySpace and could not have happened without the Internet, which was an older innovation that had been integrated already within cultural practices). What's more, this bidirectional process likely happens at many different levels of magnitude of creativity (Glăveanu, 2010). The Facebook example is conceived around an act of high level of creativity, but we can also think of smaller acts of creativity, performed by regular people as a part of social participation within culture, that can subsequently change culture, such as the evolution of human language, which was the result of thousands of years of creative tweaking by groups of people. Although creativity happens within culture and culture incorporates creative ideas, or some even argue that creativity is a form of cultural participation (Glăveanu, 2011), if we go back to the definition of creativity, where a creative idea must be original, useful, and surprising, it follows that idea must represent something that no one has thought of before, so it is necessarily outside culture.[2] This leads to a fine boundary that each creative idea must balance on: One the one hand it has to be outside culture in order to be original and surprising, but on the other hand it cannot be too far off outside the boundaries of culture, or it may not be fully appreciated and perceived as useful. This idea has received extensive support when it comes to major creative contributions, where the cultural Zeitgeist is one of the main predictors of whether a creative idea will be successful or not at the time it is produced (Simonton, 2004). In other words, a creative idea must be original, useful, and surprising, but not to the extent to which it falls outside of the cultural Zeitgeist, because it is essential that the culture is ready for that idea in order to recognize its value and incorporate it. The examples given so far pertain to "little-c," "Pro-c," and "Big-C" creativity, all of which involve some degree of appreciation from other people, which makes for an easy argument that culture must play an essential role, given that other people operate within the cultural context. But a similar argument can be applied to "mini-c" or "personal creativity." According to Simonton (2016), we can conceive the originality, useful-ness, and surprise criteria of creativity in the personal context (e.g., originality is defined as $(1-p)$, where p represents the initial probability of generating an idea when an individual first starts thinking about a problem); even in this context, culture cannot be said to not play a role, because the structure of goals and knowledge of the individual are likely to drive all processes, and these can be seen as internalized aspects of the culture in which the individual is immersed. In sum, whether we conceptualize creativity as personal or public, "mini-c" or "Big-C," creative acts are uniquely intertwined with culture.

Second, and related to the point above, when researchers ask "How does creativity vary across cultures?" the immediate next question is "Does creativity mean the

---

[2] Note that in the systems view of creativity, original ideas are not considered to be outside the boundaries of culture, because in that view, culture is not limited to "shared meanings," but it includes "unique meanings" or ideas that emerge from and contribute to the cultural basis (see Csikszentmihalyi, 2014; Glăveanu, 2010; 2011). The reasoning behind incorporating "unique mean-ings" within culture is that even unique ideas emerge from existing ideas and from interacting with cultural groups and communities, and all new ideas are expressed with the means of culture (e.g., language or other symbolic systems). This is the core of conceptual difficulty and unique aspect in studying culture and creativity: the two concepts are highly intertwined.

same thing across cultures?" If we consider the two-part definition described earlier, whereby a product or an idea can be considered creative if it is perceived as both original and useful, it is clear that culture can significantly alter the very meaning of creativity in two ways (De Dreu, 2010; Lubart, 2010): (a) culture may influence the criteria used by "gate-keepers" (i.e., the community of experts tasked with evaluating and endorsing creative outputs) to assess originality, usefulness, or both; and (b) culture may influence the relative weight placed on originality and usefulness (i.e., which of the two characteristics the field deems more important in defining creativity may vary across cultures). Indeed, there is now mounting evidence that Eastern (as opposed to Western) cultures may value usefulness more than originality when assessing creativity (Morris & Leung, 2010).

Third, to study creativity within the culture domain, researchers have used multiple theories of creativity, as well as novel mixtures of these theories. For example, developmental theories of creativity (e.g., Goertzel, Goertzel, & Goertzel, 1978) posit that creativity develops over time as a result of dynamic transactions between person and environment. As we will see later, culture and cultural diversity are some of the transformative early life experiences that are essential for understanding the development of the creative person and predict their level of accomplishment or quality of their creative products. Cognitive theories of creativity (e.g., Guilford, 1968) posit that certain cognitive styles or thought processes underlie the creative person and product; in other words, regardless of the level or domain of accomplishment, any creative ideation should be characterized by a similar basic thinking style, which involves a high "cognitive flexibility" or "divergent thinking" or the ability to "break set" and shift from one set of ideas to another. Cognitive theories of creativity propose that this type of thinking (i.e., flexible or "divergent") is a necessary but not sufficient component of any level of creativity, including Big-C creativity, whereby highly creative geniuses need the ability to think flexibly, but in addition to that, they also need the motivation and expertise to make a valuable contribution (Amabile, 1996; Simonton & Damian, 2013). A great deal of experimental research, which I will summarize below, has focused on investigating the role of culture and multiculturalism on creative thinking. More recently, developmental and cognitive theories of creativity have been integrated and have inspired new avenues for research. Specifically, the diversifying experiences theory of creativity (e.g., Damian & Simonton, 2015) suggests that certain life experiences, including cultural diversity, may have the potential to influence development and ultimately the creative personality and product, precisely because they may change the way people think about the world or their cognitive style. Systems theories of creativity (e.g., Csikszentmihalyi, 2014) take an even broader and integrating approach, focusing on the creative product as it is received and appreciated within society; therefore, in these models, culture plays the role of transmitting information to new recruits from any field, then these people, based on their genetics and environment, produce novel ideas, which in turn are selected for quality by fields and gatekeepers; if highly successful, the novel ideas eventually enter the realm of culture thus changing it.

Fourth, culture is most often not isolated, but part of a larger system of cultures that sometimes interact, especially in today's globalizing world. Migration has always been an integral part of human existence. The United States of America are a great example of a nation that has had a constant and steady stream of immigrants, with foreign-born immigrants constituting about 13 percent of its population for the past sixty years (Peri, 2012). Furthermore, civil wars, political unrest, and tyranny have always led to massive numbers of refugees in search for safety. Finally, advances in transportation and information technology have led to world-wide globalization, which has made migration even easier and more appealing than before. Thus, human societies have always been shaped by migration and this tendency has skyrocketed in recent times. Multiculturalism or cultural diversity is the natural consequence of migration: the new comers are different from the locals; they often speak a different language, have different cultural customs, look different, and have different religions. The natural question that arises is: How does multiculturalism or cultural diversity affect individuals and societies at large? Does multiculturalism show any benefits in terms of creativity, innovation, and economic growth, or does it harm local economies and communities? As it turns out, decades of psychological and economic research show that multiculturalism may have great positive consequences by stimulating creativity at both the individual and aggregate level. In doing so, multiculturalism increases human capital and is thus likely to lead to economic growth and prosperity (Peri, 2012).

In sum, studying creativity in the culture domain is unique because (a) creativity and culture are naturally intertwined concepts and it is difficult if not impossible to imagine one without the other; (b) the meaning of creativity may differ across cultures; (c) creativity and culture can be studied taking a broad variety of theoretical perspectives; and (d) culture does not exist in isolation, especially in today's globalizing world, and therefore it is essential to consider the role of multiculturalism (a.k.a., cultural diversity) on creativity.

Constructs and Measurements

To study creativity within the culture domain, researchers have used multiple methodological approaches, both quantitative and qualitative. The quantitative methods include historiometric and psychometric approaches. The qualitative methods include case studies, biographical research, and interviews. The diversity of methodological approaches in the study of culture and creativity is a direct consequence of the various theories and perspectives on creativity and it influences the variety of constructs and measurements employed. In this chapter, we will focus on quantitative methods only, that is, the historiometric and psychometric approaches, and we will describe characteristic constructs and measurements. In the historiometric method, biographical and historical information is first quantified and then subjected to statistical analysis (Simonton, 2009). This method is ideal for the study of genius-level creative achievement, because geniuses are often dead or otherwise unavailable to visit psychological laboratories for psychometric measures, and it can be used to study genius-level creativity at the aggregate (e.g., national) level, as well as at the individual level. Eminent creativity can be objectively measured by counting, at the aggregate level, the number of internationally acclaimed scientists or artists, the total number of patents approved in a certain country, and so on. At the individual level, eminent creativity can be measured by counting the total number of publications or artworks of a particular scientist or artist. Regarding measurements and constructs related to culture, the historiometric method can be a fairly cost-effective method of comparing creativity at the aggregate level across cultures, by simply counting creative products from different countries that represent different cultures. Furthermore, at the aggregate level, broad societal factors can be assessed (e.g., political system, immigration trends) and correlated with national-level creative achievement to identify which broad socio-cultural factors promote or inhibit creativity. At the individual level, biographical and historical information can be coded to identify developmental influences in the lives of the great (e.g., socio-economic, age, and education, or for research on multiculturalism, having lived abroad or having experienced cultural diversity), and thus measures of individual differences can be obtained and correlated with the level of creative achievement of each subject. Because this method uses historical archives that have recorded acts of creativity, it follows that this method primarily focuses on assessing creative products at the "Pro-c" or "Big-C" levels of magnitude (because a certain level of public appreciation is necessary for any creative idea to be recorded and archived).

Unlike historiometric research, psychometric research collects direct individual measures from participants or groups of participants. The advantage of such research is that it allows us to delve more deeply into the social, cognitive, and developmental processes underlying creativity. Regarding relevant creativity constructs, the psychometric method can investigate: (a) the creative product, asking which individual differences or situational factors lead to creative products; (b) the creative person, asking how creative people differ from their less creative counterparts; and (c) the creative process, asking which cognitive and motivational processes promote or inhibit creative thinking and performance. Psychometric research includes both correlational and experimental studies. The Creative Achievement Questionnaire (Carson et al., 2005) is an example of a product-based creativity measure, where participants are asked about their creative contributions to various domains of achievement (e.g., number of scientific publications or musical pieces composed). Other product-based measures of creativity that have been used in research on culture and creativity include subjective evaluations by independent raters of creative products and desire to purchase these products (Paletz & Peng, 2008), and self-reported team creativity at the end of a group task (Lee et al., 2015). Person-based measures of creativity include Adjective Check Lists which consist of sets of personality trait descriptions that are assessed either through self- or other-report (e.g., Gough, 1979). Measures of the creative process or creative thinking (i.e., the cognitive processes underlying creative ideation) include the Unusual Uses Test (Guilford, 1968), which involves coming up with creative uses for a household object under a time limit (the list of uses is then coded for cognitive flexibility by counting the number of different categories of uses, which serves a proxy for the participant's ability to "break set" or "think outside the box"). Other tasks used to measure creative problem solving are insight tasks, that is, tasks that have a correct pre-defined solution that is not immediately obvious, such as the Remote Associate Test where participants have to find a word that fits conceptually with a set of three other words (e.g., Mednick, 1962). Another measure widely used in the context of culture and creativity is the Torrance Test of Creative Thinking (e.g., Torrance, 1998), which includes several verbal and figural test batteries that are norm-referenced and scored for fluency (i.e., number of relevant ideas), originality (i.e., the number of statistically infrequent ideas), elaboration (i.e., the number of ideas added), abstractness of titles, and resistance to premature closure (i.e., degree of psychological openness). Generally, in the experimental realm, measurements of creativity focus on divergent- and convergent-thinking tasks, that is, tasks that either do not have a pre-defined solution and where cognitive flexibility can be scored (such as the Unusual Uses Test) or tasks that have a pre-defined solution that requires an insight (such as the RAT), respectively. Typically, the measures used in psychometric research on culture and creativity assess everyday "little-c" creativity, rather than "Big-C" real-world creative achievement at the genius level, and that is mainly the case because it is nearly impossible to bring bona fide geniuses into the laboratory. Regarding constructs related to culture or cultural diversity, the psychometric method uses a wide variety of instruments. As seen in the context of historiometric work, one way to vary culture within the data sample is to simply collect data from different cultures (e.g., Eastern vs. Western), using the same instruments. In order to measure the effects of cultural diversity, studies can look at people who are bicultural (i.e., identify with more than one culture, such as, Chinese-Americans) or at people who lived or traveled abroad (e.g., Saad et al., 2013; Fee et al., 2013); one construct that is particularly relevant in the context of biculturals is Bicultural Identity Integration (BII; Benet-Martinez & Haritatos, 2005). The BII scale measures variations in people's success at integrating their potentially competing cultural orientations and sets of norms and values within their self-concept. The BII measure can be seen as a measure of adaptation to cultural diversity (Damian & Simonton, 2014). Another way to make culture salient experimentally is to prime participants with cultural symbols (e.g., ask them to write about a Chinese vs. an American cultural symbol, such as the Great Wall of China vs. the Statue of Liberty; or ask them to write about both symbols in the cultural diversity condition; Saad et al., 2013). Other ways to manipulate cultural diversity are by comparing multicultural versus monocultural teams. Finally, a large portion of research on culture and creativity has centered on three constructs: individualism-collectivism, uncertainty avoidance, and power distance (Hofstede, 2001; Rank et al., 2004). The individualism-collectivism dimension refers to the strength and cohesion of bonds between people. Specifically, in societies that are higher in individualism, people tend to look after themselves, they experience lower power distance (i.e., power hierarchies are not that prominent), and they are lower in uncertainty avoidance (i.e., they are more tolerant to risk, change, and making mistakes). These individualistic norms are consistent with a cultural environment that encourages self-expression, which is the case in most Western cultures according to the World Values Survey (Inglehart & Baker, 2000), as well as exploration of new ways of doing things and expressing one's unique ideas (Brewer & Chen, 2007;

Brewer & Gardner, 1996; Kim & Markus, 1999). In contrast, in societies that are higher in collectivism, people tend to look after the group more than after themselves, and they experience higher power distance and higher uncertainty avoidance; these collectivistic norms are consistent with a cultural environment that emphasizes conformity to social norms and that discourages self-expression, which is the case in most Eastern cultures (Inglehart & Baker, 2000; Harzing & Hofstede, 1996; Westwood & Low, 2003).

One complication with constructs and measurements in the context of research on culture and creativity is their source. Specifically, there are two approaches for developing theory, constructs, and measurements in cross-cultural research. The emic (i.e., indigenous) approach allows for the emergence of theory, constructs, and instruments within each culture; this approach posits that behaviors cannot be separated from their cultural contexts (Markus & Kitayama, 1998). In contrast, the etic (i.e., imported) approach takes theory, constructs, and instruments that were developed primarily in Western cultures, translates them, and applies them to Eastern cultures; this approach posits that culture has an external role on behavior (Triandis, 1996). The main reason for using the etic approach is because direct cross-cultural comparisons require for the measurement instrument to be kept constant so that any differences can be attributed to cultural differences; measurements using the etic approach are also much more cost-effective and their development requires less time and effort. The vast majority of past research has chosen an etic approach (Kaufman & Sternberg, 2006). Thus, most of the research discussed in this chapter also follows the etic approach to define constructs and measurements from a Western perspective and then compare and contrast findings across cultures or test the role of cultural diversity. Despite this, many of the studies presented here are sensitive to possible cultural differences in how people define creativity and test this hypothesis. Furthermore, the historiometric method could be seen as pertaining more to the emic approach given that "Big-C" creative products are defined within a specific cultural context and have passed the test of time in that culture (i.e., each culture defines itself which creative accomplishments will be included in historical records); on the other hand, researchers often decide which types of creative products to focus on and which ideas to test using etic approaches. One challenge of future research on culture and creativity will be to increase the use of emic approaches.

Empirical Findings

Across methodological approaches (historiometric or psychometric) and across measurement levels of creativity (aggregate or individual), two broad categories of research questions have been driving research on culture and creativity: (a) Does creativity differ across cultures (especially across Eastern vs. Western cultures)?; and (b) How does multiculturalism (or cultural diversity) affect creativity? As economies around the world shift towards innovation economies, and as globalization and immigration increase, both these questions have been in the focus of the public eye in recent years, as they have deep policy implications. Regarding the first question, if it turns out that some cultures are less creative than others, then the former will need to devote significant resources to the development of creativity if they wish to stay competitive in the future global market. Indeed, in recent years, some scientists have taken the scarcity of science Nobel prizes in Asia as an indication that Eastern cultures stunt creativity (Kanazawa, 2006). Some have suggested that this difference may occur because ideographic languages such as Chinese do not promote abstract thinking as much as alphabetic languages (Hannas, 2003) or because Asian education emphasizes holistic (rather than analytic) thinking (Nisbett, 2003). However, historical records do not support the idea that Eastern cultures are less creative than Western cultures due to some inherent national character or ability. If we investigate creative accomplishments across longer historical time-spans we find that many of the world's breakthroughs (e.g., gunpowder, paper, and printing) were first developed in the Far East (Murray, 2003). One possible explanation for the recent differences observed in aggregate level creativity between Eastern and Western cultures could be that more recent socio-political context experienced in some of the Eastern cultures (e.g., the anti-intellectualist Cultural Revolution that took place in China) may have stunted creativity. Another possible explanation is that creativity per se does not differ between Eastern and Western cultures, but that the definition of creativity differs. In other words, creativity may be evaluated differently and different aspects may be more appreciated in Eastern versus Western cultures. Beyond differences in creative products or assessments, it is also possible that the differences between East and West (if any) may be due to differences in the traits of the creative person or in the creative process. The research reviewed below addresses each of these possibilities. Regarding the second question, whether multiculturalism affects creativity, most research has found a positive impact on creativity and economic growth, which is highly relevant for immigration policies around the world. We will review the studies that have produced these findings and discuss possible explanations for the purported link.

In sum, this empirical review is split into two sections that each address one of the two main research questions described earlier: (a) creativity across cultures and (b) multiculturalism and creativity. Additionally, each section is split into two subsections, depending on the type of methodology employed, that is, historiometric or psychometric.

Creativity Across Cultures

Historiometric Research

Simonton and Ting (2010) conducted an extensive review and systematic comparison of historiometric findings on the correlates of creative achievement ("Big-C" creative products) from Western and Eastern cultures. The authors ensured that the reviewed studies shared the same methodology (e.g., statistical techniques and measurements), and thus the only plausible explanation for the differences in findings could be found in cross-cultural differences, and similar results implied similarities across cultures. The research reviewed can be split based on the type of creative achievement measured, that is, either aggregate or individual level creativity, and the authors found both convergence and divergence at both levels of analysis. At the aggregate level, the typical research question is "Which broad societal factors are related to creativity in the East and (/versus) the West?" Regarding common factors, Simonton and Ting (2010) found that across many studies, role model availability (e.g., a "golden age," where many creative people live in the same space and historical time) had a positive effect on aggregate level creativity both in Eastern and Western cultures, whereas political instability had a negative effect in both cultures when it comes to scientific creativity. Regarding divergence at the aggregate level, the reviewers found that political fragmentation (i.e., the existence of many independent states vs. one empire) and civil disturbances (i.e., revolts and rebellions) were positively associated with increased creativity a generation later in Western cultures, but not in Eastern cultures. At the individual level, the typical research question is "Which individual differences in demographics, traits, and abilities are related to creativity in individuals coming from Eastern and (/versus) Western cultures?" Following their extensive review, Simonton and Ting (2010) found that precocity is related to more creativity in both Eastern and Western cultures, that is, the earlier the individual makes his or her first contribution, the more successful they end up being. Another common factor in both cultures is productivity – the more works one produces, the higher their level of creative achievement. The positive link between versatility and creativity, that is, more creative people tend to have been creative in more than one domain, also seems to be a cultural universal. In addition to the above convergent results across the East and West, Simonton and Ting (2010) also note a few divergent results. Specifically, the level of formal education achieved by an individual is positively related to versatility, productivity, and creative achievement among Eastern cultures, but not among Western cultures, where the relation between education and creativity seems to follow an inverted U-shaped curve, whereby the highest levels of education may be detrimental (though this is mainly the case for the arts, not the sciences). Mental illness is also a point of divergence, being a positive correlate of creative achievement in the West, but not in the East.

In sum, historiometric research suggests that there are many commonalities in the way creativity operates across cultures, at both the aggregate and the individual level, but there are also a few discrepancies. At the aggregate level, these discrepancies could be explained by the fact that in Eastern cultures political fragmentation is decoupled from cultural diversity (i.e., more political fragmentation in China did not mean increased cultural diversity, unlike in Europe). As we will see later, cultural diversity is associated with more creativity in both the East and the West, so it is possible that the positive effects of political fragmentation found in the West are merely due to increased cultural diversity. In other words, the aggregate-level discrepancies may be more apparent than real. Analogously, at the individual level, discrepancies may not represent genuine contradictions. Instead, they might point to differences in the way creativity is defined across Eastern and Western cultures. For instance, it would make sense that if Eastern cultures placed a higher emphasis on usefulness as opposed to originality (compared to Western cultures where the reverse might be the case), then more education and less psychopathology would be conducive to more creativity (these individual differences might still be related to more originality, but that might not be the main focus in Eastern cultures).

Psychometric Research

Psychometric research has investigated cross-cultural comparisons of creativity in Eastern versus Western cultures by taking three different kinds of creativity constructs: the creative person, the creative product, and the creative process.

Regarding the creative person, the typical research question has been "Are there personality dimensions that are cultural universals when it comes to characterizing a creative person or are there systematic differences?" One way to test this question is by measuring laypeople's implicit theories of what personality dimensions they think are characteristic of creative people, and compare Western and Eastern views. Research has found that there are some cultural universals regarding cognitive skills (e.g., ability to think flexibly, make connections, and ask questions), personality traits (e.g., self-confidence, independence, and assertiveness), and motivation (e.g., ambition, high energy, enthusiasm). These characteristics are mentioned with respect to creative adults and creative children, and the findings replicate across various samples of evaluators and they hold across Eastern and Western cultures (see Kaufman & Sternberg, 2006; Rudowicz, 2003). Another individual difference that seems to be a cultural universal is openness to experience (Heine & Buchtel, 2009). These cultural universals regarding characteristics of the creative person seem to mirror the findings from historiometric research that we discussed earlier (Simonton & Ting, 2010). In other words, precocity, productivity, and versatility could reasonably be the result of increased ambition, enthusiasm, self-confidence, independence, and ability to think flexibly. Furthermore, as was the case for historiometric research, psychometric research has also found some points of divergence. Specifically, "sense of humor," "aesthetic," or "artistic orientation" were deemed characteristic of creative people in the West but not in the East, whereas "inspires people," "makes a contribution to society," and "is appreciated by others" were deemed characteristic of creative people in the East but not in the West (Rudowicz, 2003). Moreover, some of the characteristics that were deemed part of the creative personality across cultures, such as assertiveness, nonconformity, and expressiveness, were seen negatively in Eastern cultures (Chan & Chan, 1999; Lim & Plucker, 2001). Evaluators from Eastern cultures also had a more difficult time distinguishing between creativity and intelligence (Chan & Chan, 1999), which was not the case in the West. These findings support the results from historiometric research where education was associated with more creative achievement in the East but not in the West; it follows naturally that if Eastern cultures indeed value intelligence, conformity, and contributing to society when they define a creative person, then people who embody these characteristics, which are likely to be related to educational attainment, are more likely to end up as genius-level creative achievers in that culture.

These findings may also explain why mental illness is related to more creative achievement in the West but not in the East, given that Eastern cultures seem to be less tolerant of nonconformity. In sum, psychometric research on the creative person indicates that, although there are some cultural universals, Western cultures tend to value more nonconformity and assertiveness, whereas Eastern cultures tend to value more "making a contribution to society." This raises the question whether the creative product and process also differ across cultures.

Regarding the creative product, the typical research question has been "Are there differences across cultures in creative products and productivity?" After initial studies suggesting that Eastern cultures might be less creative (Kanazawa, 2006), the focus has been primarily on understanding how and why creative products and processes might differ across cultures. One possibility is that people's implicit theories of what counts as creative might differ and these implicit theories might be the result of internalized social norms that might differ between individualistic and collectivistic cultures. Supporting these ideas, one study (Bechtoldt et al., 2010) found that when participants in a brainstorming session were Dutch (i.e., individualistic culture) and were asked to do their best, their ideas increased in originality, whereas when the participants were Korean (i.e., collectivistic culture) their ideas increased in usefulness. Moreover, these cultural groups were able to shift their performance styles when they were explicitly primed with originality versus usefulness goals. These ideas were further supported in a study on East Asian-Americans who were either primed with East Asian or American symbols to activate the respective processing styles, and who varied on Bicultural Identity Integration (Mok & Morris, 2010). When participants were high in BII, they produced more original ideas in the American context, indicating that the two cultural systems may have different social norms that dictate what counts as creative and how people go about being creative. When people were low in BII, a contrast effect was observed, presumably because people who have not integrated their two cultures well may see them as conflicting. Extending this research to other social norms, one study (Nouri et al., 2014) showed that people from cultures high in power distance, such as China (i.e., cultures where there is a strong emphasis on power hierarchies), produced less original ideas when in the presence of a supervisor (as opposed to when working alone), which was not the case in cultures low in power distance, such as the United States. Another study comparing Chinese and American task groups working on the same project supported the idea that high power distance might hinder creativity by showing that Chinese team-members spoke up less and interacted less with other team-members when in the presence of a supervisor (Conyne et al., 1999). In sum, it does not appear to be the case that Eastern cultures are less creative than Western cultures; instead, it seems that Western individualistic social norms (e.g., low uncertainty avoidance and low power distance) prioritize originality over usefulness in deciding which products count as creative, whereas Eastern collectivistic social norms (e.g., high uncertainty avoidance and high power distance) prioritize usefulness over originality (Erez & Nouri, 2010).

Multiculturalism and Creativity

Historiometric Research

Historiometric research has addressed the role of cultural diversity on creativity at two different levels of analysis: aggregate and individual. At the aggregate level, Simonton (1997) showed the repercussions of cultural diversity on eminent creativity using generational time-series analysis. He selected the Japanese civilization because its history has shown an unusual variation in the degree to which the country was open or not to foreign influences. A total of 1,803 eminent Japanese were included in the sample, across sixty-eight consecutive twenty-year intervals from 580 to 1939 CE. Openness to foreign influence (or cultural heterogeneity) was assessed using three measures: (1) the number of foreign immigrants who left a mark on Japanese history, (2) the number of eminent Japanese who travelled abroad, and (3) outside influences in which native Japanese studied under foreigners, studied abroad, or admired, developed, or imitated the style or ideas of foreigners. Across many of the fourteen domains of national achievement, significant cross-lagged correlations emerged, showing that cultural heterogeneity at generation $g - 2$ positively predicted eminent creativity at generation g. In other words, cultural diversity helps creativity, but it must first be assimilated by the previous two generations. At the individual level, several studies have shown the preponderance of cultural diversity among highly creative people. One study of twentieth-century eminent personalities found that one-fifth were either first- or second-generation immigrants (Goertzel, Goertzel, & Goertzel, 1978). Another study found that 25 percent of highly eminent scientists were second-generation immigrants (Eiduson, 1962). Among distinguished mathematicians, 32 percent were foreign born (Visher, 1947), and 52 percent were either foreign born or second-generation Americans (Helson & Crutchfield, 1970). In case you are wondering whether these figures are still true today, a recent economic study conducted in the United States over a ten-year period, from 2000 to 2010 (Peri, 2012), showed that foreign-born immigrants stimulate economic growth with their disproportionate degrees of eminent creativity and innovation. Although foreign-born immigrants represent only 13 percent of the US population, they account for 30 percent of all the patents granted and for 25 percent of all the US Nobel Laureates. Further supporting the idea that cultural diversity is relevant for creativity, historiometric research has shown that highly creative people tend to have experienced extensive traveling (including traveling and living abroad), and that their families show high geographical mobility (Simonton, 2004). In line with these results, a recent study found that the foreign experience of influential executives had a curvilinear link with the creative output of their businesses, that is, moderate levels of multiculturalism were associated with the highest level of creativity. In this latter study, creativity was measured by looking at the industry ratings of all major fashion houses over eleven years (Godart et al., 2015). These findings mirror the aggregate-level results, supporting the idea that being exposed to cultural heterogeneity is related to more creativity.

Psychometric Research

Psychometric research has also shown a positive link between cultural diversity and creativity, and provides us with some insight into the underlying cognitive processes. For example, Tadmor, Galinksy, and Maddux (2012) showed that bicultural people (i.e., people who identify as pertaining to two different cultures) achieve higher levels of creativity and professional success. Moreover, they found that this effect was driven by biculturals' higher level of integrative complexity (i.e., the information-processing capacity that involves considering and combining multiple perspectives). In other words, biculturals who are creative are only so to the extent to which they can benefit from the ideological and cultural diversity they are exposed to by integrating it into their thinking. A recent experiment by Saad and colleagues (2013) supports the idea that biculturalism can predict higher levels of creativity under certain circumstances. Specifically, the authors found that Chinese-Americans were more creative when they were reminded of both their identities (i.e., bicultural context), as opposed to just one of their identities (i.e., monocultural context), but this was only the case when the participants were high in bicultural identity integration, that is, they chronically experienced their two cultural identities as compatible (or blended) versus oppositional (or in conflict).

In addition to showing that a bicultural background may be conducive to more creativity, research has also shown that living in a foreign country for a significant amount of time (but not brief travels abroad) is linked to more creative thinking and cognitive flexibility, as measured in the laboratory (Leung, Maddux, Galinsky, & Chiu, 2008; Maddux, Adam, & Galinsky, 2010; Lee et al., 2012). Furthermore, Fee and Grey (2012) and Fee and colleagues (2013) showed in a longitudinal study that people who had lived abroad had increased cognitive flexibility and creativity relative to both other people who had not lived abroad, and to their own pre-departure scores. Notably, however, Leung and Chiu (2008) found that the positive link between multiculturalism and creativity thinking holds only for people who are high in openness to experience. Supplementing research on adults, a recent study conducted on 700 Taiwanese adolescents showed that children belonging to bicultural families performed better on laboratory creativity tasks compared to children belonging to monocultural families, and this link persisted when parental socio-economic status and children's personality were statistically controlled (Chang et al., 2014).

Beyond research on cultural diversity and creativity at the individual level, there is also extensive psychometric research looking at the role of cultural diversity on team creativity. Specifically, some researchers found that group creativity increased significantly when group membership was diverse, owing to the increased heterogeneity of perspectives and ideas (Nemeth & Nemeth-Brown, 2003; Page, 2007). Other researchers, however, have noted that the literature on group diversity and creativity has produced mixed findings (for a review, see van Knippenberg & Schippers, 2007). Furthermore, a meta-analysis by Stahl and colleagues (2010) showed that cultural diversity had both costs and benefits in teams; specifically, more culturally diverse teams had low social integration, such as low cohesion, trust, morale, and attraction, but they also had more creativity. In an attempt to resolve the inconsistencies in this literature, several studies have proposed moderator effects of the link between group diversity and creativity. One experiment (Homan, van Knippenberg, Van Kleef, & De Dreu, 2007) showed that diverse groups performed better only when they were persuaded to value group diversity. In other words, diverse groups only performed better when they held pro-diversity rather than pro-similarity beliefs, whereas the performance of homogeneous groups was unaffected by diversity beliefs. Another laboratory experiment (Hoever, van Knippenberg, van Ginkel, & Barkema, 2012) showed that the effect of a team's diversity on its creativity was moderated by the degree to which team members were instructed to engage in perspective taking, that is, when people placed themselves in their team member's shoes. In line with these findings, more recent studies that investigated the role of cultural diversity on team creativity found that the link was only positive when the team members were also high in diversity mindsets (Pluut & Curseu, 2013), when they received diversity training if they initially had low positive views towards diversity (Homan et al., 2015), or when they were high in cultural metacognition, which measures cultural consciousness and awareness during social interaction (Crotty & Brett, 2012). A recent review on cultural diversity and team creativity (Leung & Wang, 2015) proposed additional moderators of the link between creativity and cultural diversity in teams. According to the authors, the main impediments to creativity in culturally diverse teams are identity threat (when the presence of other cultural groups is seen as threatening to one's cultural identity), identity fragmentation (i.e., a lack of common cultural identity among the team members), and intercultural obstacles (i.e., conflicting assumptions, ideas, and views). These cultural identity obstacles tend to cause conflict, withdrawal, and disengagement from team activities, thus lowering sharing and integration of diverse ideas, which lowers creativity. Thus, any factors that enhance information sharing and promote a focus on the task at hand, such as task interdependence (where team members must rely on each other for different kinds of expertise) and task complexity, will buffer the negative effects of cultural identity obstacles and will render a positive link between cultural diversity and team creativity (Leung & Wang, 2015).

Future Directions

We have shown so far that the study of creativity across cultures (especially Eastern vs. Western cultures) has resulted in both convergent and divergent findings. In the realm of historiometric research, future studies could refine our understanding of similarities and differences in creativity and the predictors of creativity by extending current research to more Eastern cultures (most historiometric research to date, with the few exceptions cited earlier, has focused on Western cultures). Another important future direction for historiometric research is to carefully study the evolution of creativity across cultures across the centuries, because both Western and Eastern cultures have undergone significant cultural shifts over time, so the discrepancies found for creative achievements from 500 years ago may not hold today, and we may see greater convergence as a result of globalization. In the realm of psychometric research, scientists could employ more emic methods to discover culturally appropriate measurements of creativity. Future research could also use more cross-cultural longitudinal studies to study the development of creativity over time, which would help us better understand which personality factors, cognitive skills, and life experiences predict creative achievement in different cultures. Another promising future direction is asking why people create in the first place and whether culture influences preferences towards certain domains of creativity (De Dreu, 2010). Addressing these questions could help us better understand the underlying motivational processes behind creativity and why it might differ across cultures.

We have also shown that the link between cultural diversity is a complex one, so the key to understanding that link lies in our ability to explain the underlying processes: Why does cultural diversity affect creativity? The answer may lie in taking a broader view and considering research on multiculturalism and creativity from the perspective of research on diversifying experiences and creativity. Diversifying experiences are unusual and unexpected experiences that "push people outside of normality." In other words, they are transformational developmental experiences that are likely to trigger flexible thinking styles that can promote creativity (Simonton, 1999; Damian & Simonton, 2014). Multiculturalism or cultural diversity can be considered one type of diversifying experience (Damian & Simonton, 2014; Gocłowska et al., in press). Other diversifying experiences include familial instability and trauma (e.g., early parental death or economic instability), physical illness, psychopathology, and enrichment (e.g., access to books or diverse ideologies) (Damian, 2017). All these experiences are in some way non-normative, and thus press the individual for accommodation and change. Although these experiences are over-represented among geniuses, they might not always be conducive to creativity among the general population. Extensive research on various types of diversifying experiences, including multiculturalism, suggests that the link between diversifying experiences and creativity might depend on certain moderators (e.g., adaptive resources, such as certain personality traits, intelligence, or coping skills) and mediators (e.g., challenge vs. threat appraisals) (Gocłowska et al., in press). By considering the link between multiculturalism and creativity through the lens of diversifying experiences, we can take new research avenues, as we can pose more diverse research questions and benefit from multiple research tools, some of which may be outside traditional research on culture and creativity. For example, we may ask if past successful coping with other kinds of diversifying experiences might enhance creative benefits drawn from cultural diversity. Or we may ask if a developmental history rich in diversifying experiences enhances cultural competence and creativity. We may also investigate which individual differences are more likely to promote the perception of cultural diversity as a challenge rather than as a threat, thus enhancing creativity; and we may investigate whether the same individual differences apply to coping with cultural diversity and other diversifying experiences, or whether there is more content specificity involved. By addressing such questions, we may better understand the cognitive and developmental processes that are specific to cultural diversity and creativity, versus those that are common across multiple kinds of diversifying experiences. This could help us better characterize the role of cultural diversity as a transformational developmental experience.

Conclusion

Studying creativity in the culture domain is unique because (a) creativity and culture are naturally intertwined concepts; (b) the meaning of creativity may differ across cultures; (c) creativity and culture can be studied taking a broad variety of theoretical perspectives; and (d) culture does not exist in isolation. To study creativity within the culture domain, researchers have used multiple methodological approaches, both quantitative and qualitative. We reviewed here the constructs and measurements typical of quantitative approaches, both historiometric and psychometric. Across these two methodological approaches, two broad categories of research questions have been driving research on culture and creativity: (a) Does creativity differ across cultures (especially across Eastern vs. Western cultures), and (b) How does multiculturalism (or cultural diversity) affect creativity? Regarding the first question, it does not appear to be the case that Eastern cultures are less creative than Western cultures; instead, it seems that Western cultures prioritize originality over usefulness in deciding which products count as creative, whereas Eastern cultures prioritize usefulness over originality (Erez & Nouri, 2010). Regarding the second question, there is mounting evidence across methods that multiculturalism may be beneficial to creativity at both the aggregate (e.g., national) and individual level. Future research may extend these findings by adopting more emic (i.e., local) approaches, by better understanding the underlying motivational processes behind creativity, and by understanding when and why diversity increases creativity. Creativity will become increasingly essential for success and growth, as economies around the world shift towards innovation economies. According to a recent study (Frey & Osborne, 2013), about 47 percent of total US employment is at high risk for computerization, that is, these jobs are expected to be automated relatively soon, within the next decade or two. The main characteristic of non-computerizable jobs is creativity. By studying how creativity differs across cultures and how multiculturalism impacts creativity, we can offer solutions to enhance creativity around the world, which will in turn promote prosperity.

References

Amabile, T. M. (1996). *Creativity in context: Update to "The social psychology of creativity."* Boulder, CO: Westview Press.

Bechtoldt, M. N., De Dreu, C. K., Nijstad, B. A., & Choi, H. S. (2010). Motivated information processing, social tuning, and group creativity. *Journal of Personality and Social Psychology, 99*, 622–637.

Beghetto, R. A., & Kaufman, J. C. (2007). Toward a broader conception of creativity: A case for" mini-c" creativity. *Psychology of Aesthetics, Creativity, and the Arts*, *1*(2), 73–79.

Benet-Martínez, V., & Haritatos, J. (2005). Bicultural identity integration (BII): Components and psychosocial antecedents. *Journal of Personality*, *73*(4), 1015–1050.

Brewer, M. B., & Chen, Y. R. (2007). Where (who) are collectives in collectivism? Toward conceptual clarification of individualism and collectivism. *Psychological Review*, *114*(1), 133–151.

Brewer, M. B., & Gardner, W. (1996). Who is this" We"? Levels of collective identity and self-representations. *Journal of Personality and Social Psychology*, *71*(1), 83–93.

Carson, S. H., Peterson, J. B., & Higgins, D. M. (2005). Reliability, validity, and factor structure of the creative achievement questionnaire. *Creativity Research Journal*, *17*(1), 37–50.

Chan, D. W., & Chan, L. K. (1999). Implicit theories of creativity: Teachers' perception of student characteristics in Hong Kong. *Creativity Research Journal*, *12*(3), 185–195.

Chang, J. H., Hsu, C. C., Shih, N. H., & Chen, H. C. (2014). Multicultural families and creative children. *Journal of Cross-Cultural Psychology*, *45*(8), 1288–1296.

Chiu, C. Y., & Hong, Y. Y. (2007). Cultural processes: Basic principles. In A. W. Kruglanski & E. T. Higgins (Eds.), *Social psychology: Handbook of basic principles* (2nd edn., pp. 785–804). New York: Guilford Press.

Conyne, R. K., Wilson, F. R., Tang, M., & Shi, K. (1999). Cultural similarities and differences in group work: Pilot study of a US–Chinese group comparison. *Group Dynamics: Theory, Research, and Practice*, *3*(1), 40.

Crotty, S. K., & Brett, J. M. (2012). Fusing creativity: Cultural metacognition and teamwork in multicultural teams. *Negotiation and Conflict Management Research*, *5*(2), 210–234.

Csikszentmihalyi, M. (2014). Society, culture, and person: A systems view of creativity. *The systems model of creativity* (pp. 47–61). Dordrecht, Netherlands: Springer Netherlands.

Damian, R. I. (in press). Where do diversifying experiences fit in the study of personality, creativity, and career success? In G. Feist, R. Reiter-Palmon, & J. C. Kaufman (Eds.), *Handbook of creativity and personality research* (pp. 102–124). New York: Cambridge University Press.

Damian, R. I., & Simonton, D. K. (2014). Diversifying experiences in the development of genius and their impact on creative cognition. In D. K. Simonton (Ed.), *The Wiley handbook of genius* (pp. 375–393). Hoboken, NJ: Wiley-Blackwell.

Damian, R. I., & Simonton, D. K. (2015). Psychopathology, adversity, and creativity: Diversifying experiences in the development of eminent African Americans. *Journal of Personality and Social Psychology*, *108*(4), 623–636.

De Dreu, C. K. (2010). Human creativity: Reflections on the role of culture. *Management and Organization Review*, *6*(3), 437–446.

Eiduson, B. (1962). *Scientists: Their psychological world*. New York, NY: Basic Books.

Erez, M., & Nouri, R. (2010). Creativity: The influence of cultural, social, and work contexts. *Management and Organization Review*, *6*(3), 351–370.

Fee, A., & Gray, S. J. (2012). The expatriate-creativity hypothesis: A longitudinal field test. *Human Relations*, *65*(12), 1515–1538.

Fee, A., Gray, S. J., & Lu, S. (2013). Developing cognitive complexity from the expatriate experience: Evidence from a longitudinal field study. *International Journal of Cross Cultural Management*, *13*(3), 299–318.

Frey, C. B., & Osborne, M. A. (2013). The future of employment: how susceptible are jobs to computerization? *Technological Forecasting and Social Change, 114*: 254–280.

Glăveanu, V. P. (2010). Paradigms in the study of creativity: Introducing the perspective of cultural psychology. *New Ideas in Psychology, 28*(1), 79–93.

Glăveanu, V. P. (2011). Creativity as cultural participation. *Journal for the Theory of Social Behaviour, 41*(1), 48–67.

Goclowska, M., Damian, R. I., & Mor, S. (in press). The diversifying experience-creativity model: Taking a broader conceptual view of the multiculturalism-creativity link. *Journal of Cross-Cultural Psychology.*

Godart, F. C., Maddux, W. W., Shipilov, A. V., & Galinsky, A. D. (2015). Fashion with a foreign flair: Professional experiences abroad facilitate the creative innovations of organizations. *Academy Of Management Journal, 58*, 195–220.

Goertzel, M. G., Goertzel, V., & Goertzel, T. G. (1978). *Three hundred eminent personalities.* San Francisco: Jossey-Bass.

Goertzel, V., & Goertzel, M. G. (1962). *Cradles of eminence.* Boston, MA: Little, Brown.

Gough, H. G. (1979). A creative personality scale for the Adjective Check List. *Journal of Personality and Social Psychology, 37*(8), 1398–1405.

Guilford, J. P. (1968). *Intelligence, creativity, and their educational implications.* San Diego: RR Knapp.

Hannas, W. C. (2003). *The writing on the wall: How Asian orthography curbs creativity.* Philadelphia, PA: University of Pennsylvania Press.

Harzing, A. W., & Hofstede, G. (1996). Planned change in organizations: The influence of national culture. *Research in the Sociology of Organizations, 14*(1), 297–340.

Heine, S. J., & Buchtel, E. E. 2009. Personality: The universal and the culturally specific. *Annual Review of Psychology, 60*, 369–394.

Helson, R., & Crutchfield, R. S. (1970). Mathematicians: The creative researcher and the average PhD. *Journal of Consulting and Clinical Psychology, 34*(2), 250–257.

Hoever, I. J., Van Knippenberg, D., van Ginkel, W. P., & Barkema, H. G. (2012). Fostering team creativity: Perspective taking as key to unlocking diversity's potential. *Journal of Applied Psychology, 97*(5), 982–996.

Hofstede, G. (2001). *Culture's consequences: Comparing values, behaviors, institutions and organizations across nations.* Thousand Oaks, CA: Sage Publications.

Homan, A. C., Buengeler, C., Eckhoff, R. A., van Ginkel, W. P., & Voelpel, S. C. (2015). The interplay of diversity training and diversity beliefs on team creativity in nationality diverse teams. *Journal of Applied Psychology, 100*(5), 1456–1467.

Homan, A. C., Van Knippenberg, D., Van Kleef, G. A., & De Dreu, C. K. (2007). Bridging faultlines by valuing diversity: Diversity beliefs, information elaboration, and performance in diverse work groups. *Journal of Applied Psychology, 92*(5), 1189–1199.

Inglehart, R., & Baker, W. E. (2000). Modernization, cultural change, and the persistence of traditional values. *American Sociological Review*, 19–51.

Kanazawa, S. (2006). No, It ain't gonna be like that. *Evolutionary Psychology, 4*, 120–128.

Kaufman, J. C., & Beghetto, R. A. (2009). Beyond big and little: The four c model of creativity. *Review of General Psychology, 13*(1), 1–12.

Kaufman, J. C., & Sternberg, R. J. (Eds.). (2006). *The international handbook of creativity.* Cambridge, UK: Cambridge University Press.

Kim, H., & Markus, H. R. (1999). Deviance or uniqueness, harmony or conformity? A cultural analysis. *Journal of Personality and Social Psychology, 77*(4), 785–800.

Van Knippenberg, D., & Schippers, M. C. (2007). Work group diversity. *Annual Reviews of Psychology, 58*, 515–541.

Lee, C. S., Therriault, D. J., & Linderholm, T. (2012). On the cognitive benefits of cultural experience: Exploring the relationship between studying abroad and creative thinking. *Applied Cognitive Psychology, 26*(5), 768–778.

Lee, D. S., Lee, K. C., & Seo, Y. W. (2015). An analysis of shared leadership, diversity, and team creativity in an e-learning environment. *Computers in Human Behavior, 42*, 47–56.

Leung, K., & Wang, J. (2015). Social processes and team creativity in multicultural teams: A socio-technical framework. *Journal of Organizational Behavior, 36*(7), 1008–1025.

Leung, K., & Chiu, C. Y. (2008). Interactive effects of multicultural experiences and openness to experience on creative potential. *Creativity Research Journal, 20*(4), 376–382.

Leung, K., Maddux, W. W., Galinsky, A. D., & Chiu, C. Y. (2008). Multicultural experience enhances creativity: The when and how. *American Psychologist, 63*(3), 169–181.

Lim, W., & Plucker, J. A. (2001). Creativity through a lens of social responsibility: Implicit theories of creativity with Korean samples. *The Journal of Creative Behavior, 35* (2), 115–130.

Lopez, E. C., Esquivel, G. B., & Houtz, J. C. (1993). The creative skills of culturally and linguistically diverse gifted students. *Creativity Research Journal, 6*(4), 401–412.

Lubart, T. (2010). Cross-cultural perspectives on creativity. In J. C Kaufman. & R. J. Sternberg (Eds.), *The Cambridge handbook of creativity* (pp. 265–278). Cambridge, UK: Cambridge University Press.

Maddux, W. W., Adam, H., & Galinsky, A. D. (2010). When in Rome ... Learn why the Romans do what they do: How multicultural learning experiences facilitate creativity. *Personality and Social Psychology Bulletin, 36*(6), 731–741.

Markus, H. R., & Kitayama, S. (1998). The cultural psychology of personality. *Journal of Cross-Cultural Psychology, 29*(1), 63–87.

Mednick, S. (1962). The associative basis of the creative process. *Psychological Review, 69*(3), 220–232.

Morris, M. W., & Leung, K. (2010). Creativity east and west: Perspectives and parallels. *Management and Organization Review, 6*(3), 313–327.

Murray, C. (2003). *Human accomplishment: The pursuit of excellence in the arts and sciences, 800 BC to 1950.* New York: HarperCollins.

Nemeth, C., & Nemeth-Brown, B. (2003). Better than individuals. *Group Creativity: Innovation Through Collaboration*, 63–84.

Nisbett, R. E. (2003). *The geography of thought: How Asians and Westerners think differently ... and why.* New York: Free Press.

Nouri, R., Erez, M., Lee, C., Liang, J., Bannister, B. D., & Chiu, W. (2014). Social context: Key to understanding culture's effects on creativity. *Journal of Organizational Behavior, 36*, 899–918.

Page, S. E. (2007). *Difference: How the power of diversity creates better groups, firms, schools, and societies.* Princeton, NJ: Princeton University Press.

Paletz, S. B., & Peng, K. (2008). Implicit theories of creativity across cultures: Novelty and appropriateness in two product domains. *Journal of Cross-Cultural Psychology, 39*(3), 286–302.

Peri, G. (2012). The effect of immigration on productivity: Evidence from U.S. states. *Review of Economics and Statistics, 94*(1), 348–358.

Pluut, H., & Curşeu, P. L. (2013). The role of diversity of life experiences in fostering collaborative creativity in demographically diverse student groups. *Thinking Skills and Creativity, 9*, 16–23.

Rank, J., Pace, V. L., & Frese, M. (2004). Three avenues for future research on creativity, innovation, and initiative. *Applied Psychology, 53*(4), 518–528.

Rudowicz, E. (2003). Creativity and culture: A two-way interaction. *Scandinavian Journal of Educational Research, 47*(3), 273–290.

Runco, M. A., & Jaeger, G. J. (2012). The standard definition of creativity. *Creativity Research Journal, 24*(1), 92–96.

Saad, C. S., Damian, R. I., Benet-Martínez, V., Moons, W. G., & Robins, R. W. (2013). Multiculturalism and creativity effects of cultural context, bicultural identity, and ideational fluency. *Social Psychological and Personality Science, 4*(3), 369–375.

Simonton, D. K. (1997). Foreign influence and national achievement: The impact of open milieus on Japanese civilization. *Journal of Personality and Social Psychology, 72*, 86–94.

Simonton, D. K. (1999). *Origins of genius: Darwinian perspectives on creativity.* Oxford University Press.

Simonton, D. K. (2004). *Creativity in science: Chance, logic, genius, and zeitgeist.* Cambridge, UK: Cambridge University Press.

Simonton, D. K. (2009). *Genius 101.* New York: Springer.

Simonton, D. K. (2012). Taking the US Patent Office creativity criteria seriously: A quantitative three-criterion definition and its implications. *Creativity Research Journal, 24*, 97–106.

Simonton, D. K. (2016). Defining creativity: Don't we also need to define what is not creative? *Journal of Creative Behavior.* Early view.

Simonton, D. K., & Damian, R. I. (2013). Creativity. In D. Reisberg (Ed.), *Oxford handbook of cognitive psychology* (pp. 795–807). New York: Oxford University Press.

Simonton, D. K., & Ting, S. S. (2010). Creativity in Eastern and Western civilizations: The lessons of historiometry. *Management and Organization Review, 6*(3), 329–350.

Stahl, G. K., Maznevski, M. L., Voigt, A., & Jonsen, K. (2010). Unraveling the effects of cultural diversity in teams: A meta-analysis of research on multicultural work groups. *Journal of International Business Studies, 41*(4), 690–709.

Tadmor, C. T., Galinsky, A. D., & Maddux, W. W. (2012). Getting the most out of living abroad: Biculturalism and integrative complexity as key drivers of creative and professional success. *Journal of Personality and Social Psychology, 103*, 520–542.

Torrance, E. P. (1998). *The Torrance tests of creative thinking norm–technical manual figural (streamlined) forms A & B.* Bensenville, IL: Scholastic Testing Service, Inc.

Triandis, H. C. (1996). The psychological measurement of cultural syndromes. *American Psychologist, 51*(4), 407–415.

Visher, S. (1947). Starred scientists: A study of their ages. *American Scientist, 35*, 543, 570, 572, 574, 576, 578, 580.

Westwood, R., & Low, D. R. (2003). The multicultural muse culture, creativity and innovation. *International Journal of Cross Cultural Management, 3*(2), 235–259.

32 The Benefits of Creativity in Therapy

Current Evidence and Future Directions

Marie J. C. Forgeard

Department of Psychiatry, McLean Hospital, Belmont MA
Department of Psychiatry, Harvard Medical School, Boston MA

Jeanette G. Elstein

Department of Psychology, University of Pennsylvania

Abstract

Eminent creators have often anecdotally suggested that their creative work contributes positively to their well-being. In this chapter, we provide a brief review of the literature investigating the therapeutic benefits of creative activities. Specifically, we review *what* creative activities have been shown to be beneficial. To do so, we describe findings related to the study of art therapy, which has produced a rich body of empirical evidence. We also discuss research methods used to investigate the benefits of creative activities. Next, we review existing research examining *how* creative activities benefit those who engage in them, focusing on potential underlying processes – such as changes in affect or growth through adversity. Finally, we describe gaps in existing knowledge and recommend directions for future scholarship.

Many eminent creators throughout history have commented on the benefits of creative work or activities for their well-being. While staying in a psychiatric hospital in the South of France, Van Gogh (1889) famously wrote in a letter to his brother: "Work distracts me infinitely better than anything else, and if I could once really throw myself into it with all my energy that might possibly be the best remedy." These words have been echoed by others, who similarly reported finding relief in the act of creation. Observing that many individuals suffering from psychological difficulties were drawn to expressing themselves creatively, clinicians and institutions provided opportunities for them to do so. Soon, scientists became interested in understanding whether, when, and how creative behavior – defined as the generation or ideas and/or products that are both novel and useful (Stein, 1953; Sternberg & Lubart, 1995) – can help address symptoms of mental illness and increase psychological well-being (Cropley, 1990, 1997; Richards, 2007).

This chapter provides a brief review of existing scholarship investigating the benefits of creativity in therapy. To do so, we begin by describing research examining *what* creative activities have documented benefits, focusing specifically on findings related to art therapy, the discipline which has most thoroughly and formally used creative tools for therapeutic purposes. Second, we describe research that more specifically explores *how* creative activities and creative thinking may have an impact on those who engage in them. To that end, we highlight different underlying processes examined in creative arts therapies and other forms of treatment that incorporate creativity less formally, as well as nonclinical research that has produced relevant findings.

"What": Articulating Therapy around Creative Content

We offer art therapy as the main example of a form of treatment articulated around creative content (and, as detailed later on, creative processes) as a way to promote psychological health. Given the wide variety of existing approaches to art therapy, we here only describe some common features shared by these approaches. Art therapy is typically (but not always) delivered by individuals who are training or are trained in this discipline (often through a master's level program), and generally have an extensive background in the medium or media they employ (e.g., drawing, painting, sculpting, printmaking, crafts, photography, digital media). The American Art Therapy Association (AATA; 2017 p. 4) defines art therapy as

> an integrative mental health profession that combines knowledge and understanding of human development and psychological theories and techniques with visual arts and the creative process to provide a unique approach for helping clients improve psychological health, cognitive abilities, and sensory-motor functions. Art therapists use art media, and often the verbal processing of produced imagery, to help people resolve conflicts and problems, develop interpersonal skills, manage behavior, reduce stress, increase self-esteem and self-awareness, and achieve insight.

Art therapy is often (but not always) adjunctive, offered in addition to other kinds of treatment. Much like traditional psychotherapy, the specific activities and nature of the interactions and work between therapist and patient depends on the approach used, which can (among others) encompass psychoanalytic, humanistic, gestalt, cognitive-behavioral, solution-focused, narrative, or eclectic approaches, with individuals, groups, or families. Thus, the reader is referred to existing comprehensive manuals presenting different approaches for a description of goals, processes, procedures, and mindsets adopted by art therapists (Brooke, 2006; Case & Dalley, 2014; Gussak & Rosal, 2015; Malchiodi, 2011; McNiff, 2009, 2013; Rubin, 2009, 2011; Wadeson, 2010).

Evidence. An increasing number of studies have documented that art therapy confers a variety of benefits across a diverse set of populations spanning many ages and diagnoses. Art therapy appears to be helpful for individuals suffering from mood disorders (Thyme et al., 2007) and psychotic disorders (Meng et al., 2005; Richardson, Jones, Evans, Stevens, & Rowe, 2007). It has also been shown to improve psychological health for cancer patients (Bar-Sela, Atid, Danos, Gabay,

& Epelbaum, 2007; Geue et al., 2010; Monti et al., 2006; Puig, Lee, Goodwin, & Sherrard, 2006; Svensk et al., 2008) and their caregivers (Walsh, Radcliffe, Castillo, Kumar, & Broschard, 2007), though the durability of these benefits is unclear (Öster et al., 2014). In a series of studies, Gussak (2006, 2007, 2009) demonstrated art therapy's effectiveness in reducing depressive symptoms for individuals currently in prison. In addition, children and adolescents may be especially receptive to art therapy (Malchiodi, 2003), including those who have experienced a trauma (Eaton, Doherty, & Widrick, 2007; Lyshak-Stelzer, Singer, St John, & Chemtob, 2007; Ottarsdottir, 2010; Steele & Raider, 2001) or health challenges such as asthma (Beebe, Gelfand, & Bender, 2010). Art therapy may also be beneficial for older adults (Levine-Madori, 2013; Kim, 2013; Rusted, Sheppard, & Waller, 2006). It should be noted that the research has not unequivocally provided positive results, as some studies have found either minimal or no effect of art therapy on outcomes, especially when compared to standard care (e.g., Crawford et al., 2012).

Methods. Researchers have debated which kinds of methods are most appropriate to assess patients' progress, as well as to establish the efficacy of art therapy in general. Regardless of the research methods different researchers prefer, all agree that further scholarship is needed in this area, and advocate for the continued growth of art therapy research (Gilroy, 2006; Junge, 2010; Kapitan, 2010; Kaplan, 2000; McNiff, 1998). Gilroy (1996, 2006) proposed that art therapy should base its efficacy on its "own kind of evidence" (1996, p. 59), as a rebuttal to the notion that Randomized Controlled Studies (RCTs) are the preferred method for establishing empirical support for treatments (Chambless & Hollon, 1998). In keeping with this, Gilroy proposed the use of a broader range of both qualitative (e.g., ethnographic approaches) and quantitative (e.g., single-case experimental designs) research methods to examine the usefulness of art therapy. Similarly, McNiff (1998) suggested that qualitative research should be on par with quantitative research in the quest to support art therapy. Kaplan (2000) insisted that qualitative research alone cannot provide evidence of efficacy because it is more subject to biases. Quoting Slavin (1992), Kaplan explained that both qualitative and quantitative research designs are useful, depending on the goals of research: "To ask which [type of research] is better is like asking whether a car or a boat is better. The answer, obviously, is that it depends where you are going." (p. 72). Although qualitative research provides valuable information about the therapy process and the subjective experience of participants, quantitative data provides invaluable information in order to evaluate treatment outcomes. Thus, a comprehensive approach in which different forms of research are valued, and researchers are able to work together to meaningfully recognize the strengths and limitations of each kind of design, and to integrate results of different studies, appears most promising.

For example, researchers often use uncontrolled designs in which participants are assessed before and after an intervention on variables of interest (e.g. depressive symptoms, quality of life). In this type of design, researchers cannot determine whether the change was due to the intervention or to some other factor. Improved outcomes could be due to time passing, other external factors, or to common factors of therapy – intervention processes that are not specific to an intervention, but rather shared across all therapies, such as the therapist/client relationship, or expectations for positive outcomes, among others (Asay & Lambert, 1999). Thus, although uncontrolled studies are useful to document what changes are seen with treatment, other designs are needed to more carefully assess the causal factors explaining these changes. Many studies are able to compare groups of participants, but not always to randomize assignment to conditions. For example, Bar-Sela et al. (2007) compared levels of anxiety, depression, and fatigue among adult chemotherapy patients before and after art therapy treatment in two non-randomized groups (one group of participants elected to participate in four or more art therapy sessions, while the other participated in one to three). Results showed that participants in the first group had greater gains in well-being, but the lack of randomization could not eliminate the possibility of selection bias (e.g., patients in that group may have differed on other important variables such as motivation, expectations regarding art therapy). These studies are nonetheless quite informative given the need to describe the usefulness of creativity-based interventions in a variety of clinical settings.

In addition to such studies, RCTs can be particularly helpful in addressing the limitations of uncontrolled and/or non-randomized studies and more formally establish the efficacy of treatments (Chambless & Hollon, 1998). However, it is also important to acknowledge some of the possible limitations of RCTs, such as the need to exclude some participants to obtain the sample with desired criteria, the prescribed length/dosage of treatment delivered, or the (sometimes) less naturalistic settings in which treatment takes place (among others). In addition, there is always the possibility of selection bias: Individuals who are willing to participate in clinical trials and be randomized to experimental conditions may differ in crucial ways from those who choose not to participate, and these differences may affect the generalizability of findings. Nonetheless, research studies examining the efficacy of art therapy using randomized controlled designs have consistently found small but significant improvements on a range of psychological measures (Maujean, Pepping, & Kendall, 2014; Reynolds, Nabors, & Quinlan, 2000; Slayton, D'Archer, & Kaplan, 2010). Future research can continue to strengthen the existing body of evidence documenting what creativity-based interventions work by combining different designs, using larger sample sizes, using statistical methods that can account for attrition, and providing clear descriptions of procedures and interventions used (given the heterogeneity in intervention content) (Maujean et al., 2014).

"How": Processes Involved in the Therapeutic Benefits of Creativity

In addition to establishing what kinds of interventions may benefit participants, researchers also examine *how* these interventions (or creative activities in general) might work – in other words, the processes, mechanisms, or "active ingredients" responsible for the benefits of creative activities. More empirical studies are needed to determine whether these processes account for the observed effects. In particular, process research using mediational designs (Kazdin, 2007) can ascertain the mechanisms underlying the benefits of creative therapies. Importantly, such research can help scientists understand whether creative activities affect participants through general mechanisms or through creativity-specific mechanisms (Forgeard & Elstein, 2014). We review relevant research studies below and discuss how they may help inform future work in this area.

Affective Processes. Most of the empirical work documenting changes in affect and emotions related to creative behavior comes from experimental studies conducted with non-clinical populations. Such studies have shown that creative activities are most helpful when they provide opportunities for experiencing positive emotions and being distracted from negative ones (Dalebroux et al., 2008; Drake et al., 2011). These results stand in contrast with the psychodynamic idea that catharsis, the venting of negative emotions, is helpful (De Petrillo & Winner, 2005). In addition, one study examining pretend play in children suggested that creative thinking is linked to emotion-regulation processes (Hoffmann & Russ, 2012).

Designs using intensive longitudinal measurement strategies such as daily diary or experience sampling methods may be particularly helpful to gain a better understanding of the relationship between creative activities and affective processes. Such research can help assess the therapeutic potential of creative activities throughout people's lives, and test hypotheses regarding the causal mechanisms underlying therapeutic change (if the timing of measurements allows it). In another nonclinical study that demonstrated the potential of such methods, Silvia et al. (2014) found using experience sampling that young adult art students were more likely to be engaged in creative activities when they reported feeling happy and active. In another study, Conner and Silvia (2015) asked a large sample of young adults to complete daily diary reports in which they rated their creativity and their emotions every day for a period of almost two weeks. Results again showed that creativity was most closely linked to positive and activated emotions (e.g., excitement). In addition, the emotion-creativity link was strongest for individuals high in the personality trait of openness to experience, suggesting that individual differences in personality must be taken into account when trying to understand the relationship between creativity and well-being. Personality may therefore determine who decides to engage in creative activities and who benefits from them.

Growth through Adversity. Another line of research suggests that involvement in creative activities, or perceived increases in creativity, may be part of growth following adversity (Aldwin & Sutton, 1998; Bloom, 1998; Zausner, 1998, 2007). In other words, individuals that have gone through highly stressful experiences may be especially interested in creative activities as a way to grow from their experience. This phenomenon is also known as posttraumatic growth, stress-related growth, or benefit finding, among other terms (Jayawickreme & Blackie, 2014; Joseph & Linley, 2005; Tedeschi & Calhoun, 2004). Researchers have identified five domains of growth following adverse life experiences: interpersonal relations, the identification of new possibilities for one's life, personal strength, spirituality, and appreciation of life (Tedeschi & Calhoun, 2004). Growth may happen because people have a natural tendency to try to integrate their experiences into their worldviews, or because they need to rebuild shattered assumptions about themselves and their lives through deliberate cognitive processing (Cann et al., 2011; Janoff-Bulman, 1992, 2006; Joseph & Linley, 2005; Tedeschi & Calhoun, 2004). One correlational study conducted by Forgeard (2013) asked participants to identify the past adverse experience that had had the biggest impact in their lives. Results suggested that distress during those events was associated with subjectively experiencing more creative growth, measured by a brief scale designed for the purpose of the study. This finding was explained by the specific domains of posttraumatic growth reported: Specifically, changes in the perception of possibilities for one's life and in relationships following adversity predicted perceived creative growth. In another related study, Garland, Carlson, Cook, Lansdell, and Speca (2007) compared mindfulness-based stress reduction (MBSR) and a healing arts program for facilitating posttraumatic growth among cancer patients. Participants in both programs showed an increase in posttraumatic growth (though the MBSR group showed the greatest improvements). These results suggest that the arts may help participants perceive opportunities for growth during or after adversity.

Thus, providing opportunities for finding meaning in difficult experiences (which may include precipitants for psychological distress such as trauma, other life events, and stress, but also the experience of psychological distress and psychological disorder itself) may explain why creative activities are healing. In keeping with this, an important line of research examining changes in cognitions following adversity has looked at the benefits of expressive writing, during which participants write about difficult experiences (Sexton & Pennebaker, 2009). Participants appear to particularly benefit from writing when they use words connected to meaning making such as "understanding" or "knowing" (Pennebaker & Seagal, 1999). Such writing has the potential to be done creatively (though participants are not explicitly asked to engage in "creative" writing).

Additional research is needed to verify whether the experience of adversity is reliably associated with changes in creativity (and what the nature of these changes are), and whether interventions that use creativity can be helpful to help individuals make meaning out of challenges. For example, more research using prospective designs (that can rule out biases inherent to retrospective reports) as well as behavioral measures of creativity (that can distinguish subjective vs. objective changes in creativity) would help shed light on the relationship between adversity, creativity, growth, and healing (Jayawickreme & Blackie, 2014).

Other Mechanisms. Many other possible mechanisms may underlie the benefits of creative activities. These include the experience of flow and mastery (Csikszentmihalyi, 1990, 1996; Forgeard & Eichner, 2014), defined as engagement in activities in which the level of challenge provided by the activity matches or only slightly exceeds the participant's skills, resulting in feelings of competence and control over the activity at hand. Other mechanisms include increased psychological flexibility (Kashdan & Rottenberg, 2010), behavioral activation (Jacobson et al., 2001), and self-efficacy (Bandura, 1997). Additional research is needed to determine the degree to which the therapeutic effects of creative activities may rely on these ingredients.

Processes in Psychotherapy. Creativity may also play an important role in psychotherapy, even if treatment does not rely on creative activities with predefined creative content (such as art therapy). Traditional psychotherapy also involves helping patients come up with new and effective ways to understand their experiences and take action in their lives. Learning to do so could be important across a wide range of disorders and life problems, suggesting that creative thinking may potentially constitute a beneficial transdiagnostic process fostered in therapy (Forgeard & Elstein, 2014). Creative thinking is closely related to, but distinct from, future-oriented thinking as well as psychological flexibility, two processes which appear to be impaired in various forms of psychopathology (Kashdan & Rottenberg, 2010; Miloyan et al., 2014; Miranda & Mennin, 2007; Roepke & Seligman, 2015). More research is needed to examine whether and how changes in creative thinking during treatment may benefit recovery, and if certain limits apply to such potential benefits (e.g., excessive creative thinking or creative thinking at inappropriate times may not be beneficial) (Kaufman & Beghetto, 2013).

Creativity in Therapists. In addition to potentially being useful for individuals engaged in therapy, creativity might also be needed on the part of the therapist (Carson & Becker, 2003; Kottler & Hecker, 2002). The need for creativity is often described (yet more rarely studied) in many widely used manuals from varying orientations. Describing cognitive behavior therapy, Beck (2011) suggested that working with challenging patients can help "promote your flexibility and creativity, and to gain new understandings and expertise in helping other patients" (p. 346) (see also Kuehlwein, 2000). In Acceptance and Commitment Therapy, Hayes, Strosahl, and Wilson (2012) emphasized the importance of fostering a "creative sense of hopelessness": by helping individuals recognize and accept the ways in which previous attempts at coping have not worked and may even have backfired (a step which may at least initially produce some degree of hopelessness forcing individuals to reconsider their approach), therapists can then guide patients towards finding and committing to implementing truly new and more effective solutions. In Dialectical Behavior Therapy, therapists teaching skills often encourage patients to allow themselves to consider creative ideas; group leaders "often have to be creative in demonstrating how particular sets of skills apply to particular problems" (Linehan, 2015, p. 56). In group therapy, Yalom and Leszcz (2008) suggested that "trainees should aspire to be creative and compassionate therapists with conceptual depth, not laborers with little vision and less morale" (p. xiv). Finally, in brief psychodynamic psychotherapy, proficiency requires "the capacity for flexibility and creativity in responding to the inevitable unanticipated exigencies of the therapeutic encounter" (Binder & Betan, 2013, p. 130). Thus, thinkers from a wide range of therapeutic orientations agree on the importance of the therapist's creativity for effective treatment.

To date, little research has examined predictors and outcomes of therapist creativity. With regard to the well-being of mental health providers, Nicol and Long (1996) found that creative thinking skills were not related to the stress levels reported by a group of music therapists. With regard to the psychotherapy process, Carson, Becker, Vance, and North (2003) found in a survey of couples' and family therapists that their participants perceived creativity to be an important part of their work. Participants identified the following components/examples of creativity in therapy: applying traditional modalities to new clients and situations, taking risks and using improvisation, "thinking on one's feet," and connecting with the intuitive parts of themselves and their clients. Participants described creative therapists as flexible, willing to take risk, and being able to use humor effectively. Thus, participants suggested that creativity is a key skill therapists use to adapt to new situations, address challenges, and tailor treatment to each client. Similarly, Duffey, Haberstroh, and Trepal (2009) surveyed members of the Association for Creativity in Counseling and found that the majority of therapists interviewed believed their creativity facilitated deeper connection, understanding, and communication with clients (see also Rouse, Armstrong, & McLeod, 2015). Although there appears to be consensus among therapists that creativity is important for effective treatment, further research is needed to understand how therapists develop their own creative thinking skills, and whether these affect other therapeutic processes as well as therapy outcomes.

The use of creativity in therapy might be becoming increasingly important, as the widespread use of manuals has raised concerns that treatment may not be tailored for the unique individuals who present for treatment (Kendall, 1998; Westen et al., 2004). Yet, recent research suggests that being able to find creative solutions to appropriately adapt empirically supported therapeutic principles to suit the needs and circumstances of specific patients may be a key skill: "Flexibility within fidelity" (Kendall & Beidas, 2007, p. 13) can allow therapists to continue to faithfully use specific treatments even as they make modifications and find the right examples, exercises, or sequences of steps to fit the needs of their present patients (Kendall & Beidas, 2007; Kendall, Chu, Gifford, Hayes, & Nauta, 1998; Peterman, Read, Wei, & Kendall, 2015). Deacon (2000), for example, reported that supervisors may be able to bolster trainees' competence in delivering psychotherapy by using divergent-thinking exercises to enhance their ability to problem-solve with clients.

Conclusions

This chapter provided a brief review of research suggesting that creative activities have the potential to heal and to foster well-being in those who participate in them, and that creativity constitutes an important process at play in various forms of therapy. The exciting and accumulating body of evidence produced by researchers examining the benefits of art therapy has shown that creative activities used in therapeutic settings likely have a positive impact on participants, though more research using randomized controlled designs are needed in order to understand how the effects of therapies using creative content compare to those of other interventions (or control conditions). In addition, clinical and nonclinical research studies have begun to examine the mechanisms that may account for these benefits such as providing opportunities to regulate emotions, or make meaning and growing from difficult experiences (among others). Such research can also help clinicians, researchers, and participants better understand the circumstances under which creative activities may not be beneficial – if they are not set up in a way that allows for the provision of the "active" therapeutic ingredients. Findings from psychotherapy also highlight the importance of creative processes even in treatments that do not employ a creative activity as content. An increasing amount of research suggests that cultivating tools for creative, flexible thinking might be a key to maximizing the benefits of psychotherapy. Thus, creative activities may help individuals learn thinking skills that could then be transferred to other domains of their lives (though more research is needed to explore this hypothesis).

In addition to describing the strengths and limitations of past research, we also highlighted that future research using intensive longitudinal methods might prove fruitful to continue building and strengthening the body of evidence attesting to the benefits of creativity. The rise of digital technology may help researchers both find ways to engage participants in meaningful creative activities multiple times throughout the day, and test the benefits of such repeated interventions in a fine-grained manner. Expressive Digital Imagery (EDI; Koppel, Byers, Sklar, De Angelis et al. 2015) provides an example of how technology can be harnessed to provide creative tools accessible at any moment, in real time, for therapeutic purposes. In EDI, participants use an application (through a smartphone or a tablet) to capture and creatively shape a picture employing easy-to-use digital imagery tools. Pilot studies of EDI recruiting from patient populations also provided participants with opportunities to discuss the meaning of images created as they relate to the recovery process in small groups. This discussion may include both the creator's explanation of their intentions in creating and composing the photograph, their reflections on the creative process, as well as other participants' reactions and insights into what might be conveyed by the image. More research is needed in order to understand whether and how participants' experiences of technology-based interventions such as EDI differ from more traditional creative self-expression media. Complementing such interventions with multiple timely longitudinal assessments could help researchers make important advancements in understanding how repeated engagement in creative activities benefits well-being. Qualitative feedback from EDI pilot participants suggests that the high accessibility of this medium may be especially useful, as participants can conveniently both create images and share them with others at any time. Thus, recent increases in the availability of technology may help advance the scientific understanding of the benefits of creativity.

These are exciting times for researchers interested in better understanding the role of creativity in therapy, in recovery, and in well-being more broadly. Researchers can both aim to deepen their examination of the benefits of creativity-based interventions (such as art therapy), and to broaden their awareness and understanding of the existence of creative processes in other interventions (such as other forms of psychotherapy). The literature reviewed here suggests that in addition to short-term emotional gains, creativity in therapy can have more profound effects by helping individuals work through challenges and find meaning. In keeping with this, best-selling author Elizabeth Gilbert (2015) recently proposed that "creative living" leads to individual fulfillment. Recognizing that creativity involves choosing and accepting challenges with courage and persistence, Gilbert emphasized that creative living will take on different forms for different people, but may lead to enhanced purpose and well-being:

> While the path and outcomes of creative living will vary wildly from person to person, I can guarantee you this: A creative life is an amplified life. It's a bigger life, a happier life, and a hell of a lot more interesting life. (p. 12)

Researchers and clinicians can help individuals find an amplified, bigger, and happier life by continuing to carefully document, research, and invent new ways to harness the benefits of creativity.

References

Aldwin, C. M., & Sutton, K. J. (1998). A developmental perspective on posttraumatic growth. In R. G. Tedeschi, C. L. Park, & L. G. Calhoun (Eds.), *Posttraumatic growth: Positive changes in the aftermath of crisis* (pp. 43–64). Mahwah, NJ: Erlbaum.

American Art Therapy Association . (2017). What is art therapy? Retrieved on April 20, 2017, from www.arttherapy.org/aata-aboutus/

Asay, T. P., & Lambert, M. J. (1999). The empirical case for the common factors in therapy: Quantitative findings. In M. A. Hubble, B. L. Duncan, & S. D. Miller (Eds.), *The heart and soul of change: What works in therapy* (pp. 23–55). Washington, DC: American Psychological Association.

Bandura, A. (1997). *Self-efficacy: The exercise of control*. New York, NY: Freeman.

Bar-Sela, G., Atid, L., Danos, S., Gabay, N., & Epelbaum, R. (2007). Art therapy improved depression and influenced fatigue levels in cancer patients on chemotherapy. *Psycho-Oncology, 16*, 980–984.

Beck, J. S. (2011). *Cognitive behavior therapy: Basics and beyond*. New York, NY: Guilford.

Beebe, A., Gelfand, E. W., & Bender, B. (2010). A randomized trial to test the effectiveness of art therapy for children with asthma. *Journal of Allergy and Clinical Immunology, 126*, 263–266.

Binder, J. L., & Betan, E. J. (2013). *Core competencies in brief dynamic psychotherapy: becoming a highly effective and competent brief dynamic psychotherapist*. New York, NY: Routledge.

Bloom, S. L. (1998). By the crowd they have been broken, by the crowd they shall be healed: The social transformation of trauma. In R. G. Tedeschi, C. L. Park, & L. G. Calhoun (Eds.), *Posttraumatic growth: Positive changes in the aftermath of crisis* (pp. 173–208). Mahwah, NJ: Erlbaum.

Brooke, S. L. (2006). *Creative arts therapies manual: A guide to the history, theoretical approaches, assessment, and work with special populations of art, play, dance, music, drama, and poetry therapies*. Springfield, IL: Charles C Thomas.

Cann, A., Calhoun, L. G., Tedeschi, R. G., Triplett, K. N., Vishnevsky, T., & Lindstrom, C. M. (2011). Assessing posttraumatic cognitive processes: The Event Related Rumination Inventory. *Anxiety, Stress, & Coping, 24*, 137–156.

Carson, D. K., & Becker, K. W. (2003). *Creativity in psychotherapy: Reaching new heights with individuals, couples, and families*. Binghamton, NY: Haworth Clinical Practice Press.

Carson, D. K., Becker, K. W., Vance, K. E., & Forth, N. L. (2003). The role of creativity in marriage and family therapy practice: A national online study. *Contemporary Family Therapy, 25*, 89–109.

Case, C., & Dalley, T. (2014). *The handbook of art therapy*. East Sussex, UK: Routledge.

Chambless, D., & Hollon, S. (1998). Defining empirically supported therapies. *Journal of Consulting and Clinical Psychology, 66*, 7–18.

Chapman, L., Morabito, D., Ladakakos, C., Schreier, H., & Knudson, M. M. (2001). The effectiveness of art therapy interventions in reducing posttraumatic stress disorder symptoms in pediatric trauma patients. *Art Therapy: Journal of the American Art Therapy Association, 18*, 100–104.

Conner, T. S., & Silvia, P. J. (2015). Creative days: A daily diary study of emotion, personality, and everyday creativity. *Psychology of Aesthetics, Creativity, and the Arts, 9*, 463–470.

Crawford, M. J., Killaspy, H., Barnes, T. R., Barrett, B., Byford, S., Clayton, K.,. . . Waller, D. (2012). Group art therapy as an adjunctive treatment for people with schizophrenia: Multicentre pragmatic randomised controlled trial. *BMJ, 344*, e846.

Cropley, A. J. (1990). Creativity and mental health in everyday life. *Creativity Research Journal, 3*, 167–178.

Cropley, A. J. (1997) Creativity and mental health in everyday life. In M. A. Runco & R. Richards (Eds.), *Eminent creativity, everyday creativity, and health*. Greenwich, CT: Ablex Publishing Corporation.

Csikszentmihalyi, M. (1990). *Flow: The psychology of optimal experience*. New York, NY: Harper & Row.

Csikszentmihalyi, M. (1996). *Creativity: Flow and the psychology of discovery and invention*. New York, NY: HarperCollins.

Dalebroux, A., Goldstein, T. R., & Winner, E. (2008). Short-term mood repair through art-making: Positive emotion is more effective than venting. *Motivation and Emotion, 32*, 288–295.

Deacon, S. A. (2000). Using divergent thinking exercises within supervision to enhance therapist creativity. *Journal of Family Psychotherapy, 11*, 67–73.

De Petrillo, L., & Winner, E. (2005). Does art improve mood? A test of a key assumption underlying art therapy. *Art Therapy: Journal of the American Art Therapy Association, 22*, 205–212.

Drake, J. E., Coleman, K., & Winner, E. (2011). Short-term mood repair through art: Effects of medium and strategy. *Art Therapy, 28*, 26–30.

Duffey, T., Haberstroh, S., & Trepal, H. (2009). A grounded theory of relational competencies and creativity in counseling: Beginning the dialogue. *Journal of Creativity in Mental Health, 4*, 89–112.

Eaton, L. G., Doherty, K. L., & Widrick, R. M. (2007). A review of research and methods used to establish art therapy as an effective treatment method for traumatized children. *The Arts in Psychotherapy, 34*, 256–262.

Forgeard, M. J. C. (2013). Finding benefits after adversity: Perceived creativity constitutes a manifestation of posttraumatic growth. *Psychology of Aesthetics, Creativity, and the Arts, 7*, 245–264.

Forgeard, M. J. C., & Eichner, K. V. (2014). Creativity as a target and tool for positive interventions. In A. C. Parks (Ed.), *Handbook of positive psychological interventions* (pp. 137–154). Oxford, UK: Wiley-Blackwell.

Forgeard, M. J., & Elstein, J. G. (2014). Advancing the clinical science of creativity. *Frontiers in Psychology*, *5*. Retrieved on April 20, 2017, from www.ncbi.nlm.nih.gov/pmc/articles/PMC4063272/

Garland, S. N., Carlson, L. E., Cook, S., Lansdell, L., & Speca, M. (2007). A non-randomized comparison of mindfulness-based stress reduction and healing arts programs for facilitating post-traumatic growth and spirituality in cancer outpatients. *Supportive Care in Cancer*, *15*, 949–961.

Geue, K., Goetze, H., Buttstaedt, M., Kleinert, E., Richter, D., & Singer, S. (2010). An overview of art therapy interventions for cancer patients and the results of research. *Complementary Therapies in Medicine*, *18*, 160–170.

Gilbert, E. (2015). *Big magic: Creative living beyond fear*. New York, NY: Riverhead.

Gilroy, A. (1996). Our own kind of evidence. *Inscape: The Journal of the British Association of Art Therapists*, *1*, 52–60.

Gilroy, A. (2006). *Art therapy, research, and evidence-based practice*. London, UK: Sage.

Gussak, D. (2006). Effects of art therapy with prison inmates: A follow-up study. *The Arts in Psychotherapy*, *33*, 188–198.

Gussak, D. (2007). The effectiveness of art therapy in reducing depression in prison populations. *International Journal of Offender Therapy and Comparative Criminology*, *51*, 444–460.

Gussak, D. (2009). The effects of art therapy on male and female inmates: Advancing the research base. *The Arts in Psychotherapy*, *36*, 5–12.

Gussak, D. E., & Rosal, M. L. (Eds.). (2015). *The Wiley handbook of art therapy*. West Sussex, UK: Wiley.

Hayes, S. C., Strosahl, K. D., & Wilson, K. G. (2012). *Acceptance and commitment therapy: The process and practice of mindful change* (2nd ed.). New York, NY: Guilford.

Hoffmann, J., & Russ, S. (2012). Pretend play, creativity, and emotion regulation in children. *Psychology of Aesthetics, Creativity, and the Arts*, *6*, 175–184.

Jacobson, N. S., Martell, C. R., & Dimidjian, S. (2001). Behavioral activation treatment for depression: Returning to contextual roots. *Clinical Psychology: Science and Practice*, *8*, 255–270.

Janoff-Bulman, R. (1992). *Shattered assumptions*. New York, NY: Free Press.

Janoff-Bulman, R. (2006). Schema-change perspectives on posttraumatic growth. In L.G. Calhoun & R. G. Tedeschi (Eds.), *Handbook of posttraumatic growth* (pp. 81–99). Mahwah, NJ: Erlbaum.

Jayawickreme, E., & Blackie, L. E. R. (2014). Post-traumatic growth as positive personality change: Evidence, controversies and future directions. *European Journal of Personality*, *28*, 312–331.

Joseph, S., & Linley, A. P. (2005). Positive adjustment to threatening events: An organismic valuing theory of growth through adversity. *Review of General Psychology*, *9*, 262–280.

Junge, M. B. (2010). *The modern history of art therapy in the United States*. Springfield, IL: Charles C Thomas.

Kapitan, L. (2010). *Introduction to art therapy research*. New York, NY: Routledge.

Kaplan, F. F. (2000). *Art, science, and art therapy*. London, UK: Jessica Kingsley.

Kashdan, T. B., & Rottenberg, J. (2010). Psychological flexibility as a fundamental aspect of health. *Clinical Psychology Review*, *30*, 865–878.

Kaufman, J. C., & Beghetto, R. A. (2013). In praise of Clark Kent: Creative metacognition and the importance of teaching kids when (not) to be creative. *Roeper Review, 35*, 155–165.

Kazdin, A. E. (2007). Mediators and mechanisms of change in psychotherapy research. *Annual Review of Clinical Psychology, 3*, 1–27.

Kendall, P. C. (1998). Empirically supported psychological therapies. *Journal of Consulting and Clinical Psychology, 66*, 3–6.

Kendall, P. C., & Beidas, R. S. (2007). Smoothing the trail for dissemination of evidence-based practices for youth: Flexibility within fidelity. *Professional Psychology: Research and Practice, 38*, 13–20.

Kendall, P. C., Chu, B., Gifford, A., Hayes, C., & Nauta, M. (1999). Breathing life into a manual: Flexibility and creativity with manual-based treatments. *Cognitive and Behavioral Practice, 5*, 177–198.

Kim, S. K. (2013). A randomized, controlled study of the effects of art therapy on older Korean-Americans' healthy aging. *The Arts in Psychotherapy, 40*, 158–164.

Koppel, S., Byers, J., Sklar, K., DeAngelis, I. et al. (2015). Expressive Digital Imagery (EDI). Retrieved on April 20, 2017, from www.ediinstitute.org

Kottler, J. A., & Hecker, L. L. (2002). Creativity in therapy: Being struck by lightning and guided by thunderstorms. *Journal of Clinical Activities, Assignments & Handouts in Psychotherapy Practice, 2*, 5–21.

Kuehlwein, K. T. (2000). Enhancing creativity in cognitive therapy. *Journal of Cognitive Psychotherapy, 14*, 175–187.

Levine-Madori, L. (2013). Utilizing a thematic approach to art therapy with seniors: Enhancing cognitive abilities and social interactions. In P. Howie, S. Prasad, & J. Kristel (Eds.), *Using art therapy with diverse populations: Crossing cultures and abilities* (pp. 317–327). Philadelphia, PA: Jessica Kingsley.

Linehan, M. M. (2015). *DBT skills training manual* (2nd ed.). New York, NY: Guilford.

Lyshak-Stelzer, F., Singer, P., St John, P., & Chemtob, C. M. (2007). Art therapy for adolescents with posttraumatic stress disorder symptoms: A pilot study. *Art Therapy: Journal of the American Art Therapy Association, 24*, 163–169.

Malchiodi, C. A. (Ed.). (2003). *Handbook of art therapy.* New York, NY: Guilford.

Malchiodi, C. A. (Ed.). (2011). *Handbook of art therapy* (2nd ed.). New York, NY: Guilford.

Maujean, A., Pepping, C. A., & Kendall, E. (2014). A systematic review of randomized controlled studies of art therapy. *Art Therapy, 31*, 37–44.

McNiff, S. (1998). *Art-based research.* London, UK. Jessica Kingsley.

McNiff, S. (2009). *Integrating the arts in therapy: History, theory, and practice.* Springfield, IL: Charles C Thomas.

McNiff, S. (2013). *Art as medicine: Creating a therapy of the imagination.* Boston, MA: Shambhala.

Meng, P., Zheng, R., Cai, Z., Cao, D., Ma, L., Liu, J., & Liu, Y. (2005). Group intervention for schizophrenia inpatient with art as medium (Article written in Chinese). *Acta Psychologica Sinica, 37*, 403–412.

Miloyan, B., Pachana, N. A., & Suddendorf, T. (2014). The future is here: A review of foresight systems in anxiety and depression. *Cognition & Emotion, 28*, 795–810.

Miranda, R., & Mennin, D. S. (2007). Depression, generalized anxiety disorder, and certainty in pessimistic predictions about the future. *Cognitive Therapy and Research, 31*, 71–82.

Monti, D. A., Peterson, C., Kunkel, E. J. S., Hauck, W. W., Pequignot, E., Rhodes, L., & Brainard, G. C. (2006). A randomized, controlled trial of mindfulness-based art therapy (MBAT) for women with cancer. *Psycho-Oncology, 15*, 363–373.

Nicol, J. J., & Long, B. C. (1996). Creativity and perceived stress of female music therapists and hobbyists. *Creativity Research Journal, 9*, 1–10.

Öster, I., Tavelin, B., Thyme, K. E., Magnusson, E., Isaksson, U., Lindh, J., & Åström, S. (2014). Art therapy during radiotherapy: A five-year follow-up study with women diagnosed with breast cancer. *The Arts in Psychotherapy, 41*, 36–40.

Ottarsdottir, U. (2010). Art therapy in education for children with specific learning difficulties who have experienced stress and/or trauma. In V. Karkou (Ed.), *Arts therapies in schools: Research and practice* (pp. 145–160). Philadelphia, PA: Jessica Kingsley.

Pennebaker, J. W., & Seagal, J. D. (1999). Forming a story: The health benefits of narrative. *Journal of Clinical Psychology, 55*, 1243–1254.

Peterman, J. S., Read, K. L., Wei, C., & Kendall, P. C. (2015). The art of exposure: Putting science into practice. *Cognitive and Behavioral Practice, 22*, 379–392.

Puig, A., Lee, S. M., Goodwin, L., & Sherrard, P. A. (2006). The efficacy of creative arts therapies to enhance emotional expression, spirituality, and psychological well-being of newly diagnosed Stage I and Stage II breast cancer patients: A preliminary study. *The Arts in Psychotherapy, 33*, 218–228.

Reynolds, M. W., Nabors, L., & Quinlan, A. (2000). The effectiveness of art therapy: Does it work? *Art Therapy, 17*, 207–213.

Richards, R. R. (2007). *Everyday creativity and new views of human nature.* Washington, DC: American Psychological Association.

Richardson, P., Jones, K., Evans, C., Stevens, P., & Rowe, A. (2007). Exploratory RCT of art therapy as an adjunctive treatment in schizophrenia. *Journal of Mental Health, 16*, 483–491.

Roepke, A. M., & Seligman, M. E. P. (2015). Depression and prospection. *British Journal of Clinical Psychology, 55*, 23–48.

Rouse, A., Armstrong, J., & McLeod, J. (2015). Enabling connections: Counsellor creativity and therapeutic practice. *Counselling and Psychotherapy Research, 15*, 171–179.

Rubin, J. A. (2009). *Introduction to art therapy: Sources & resources.* New York, NY: Routledge.

Rubin, J. A. (2011). *The art of art therapy: What every art therapist needs to know.* New York, NY: Routledge.

Rusted, J., Sheppard, L., & Waller, D. (2006). A multi-centre randomized control group trial on the use of art therapy for older people with dementia. *Group Analysis, 39*, 517–536.

Sexton, J. D., & Pennebaker, J. W. (2009). The healing powers of expressive writing. In S. B. Kaufman & J. C. Kaufman (Eds.), *The psychology of creative writing* (pp. 264–273). New York, NY: Cambridge University Press.

Silvia, P. J., Beaty, R. E., Nusbaum, E. C., Eddington, K. M., Levin-Aspenson, H., & Kwapil, T. R. (2014). Everyday creativity in daily life: An experience-sampling study of "little c" creativity. *Psychology of Aesthetics, Creativity, and the Arts, 8*, 183–188.

Slavin, R. (1992). *Research methods in education* (2nd ed.). Boston, MA: Allyn & Bacon.

Slayton, S. C., D'Archer, J., & Kaplan, F. (2010). Outcome studies on the efficacy of art therapy: A review of findings. *Art Therapy: Journal of the American Art Therapy Association, 27*, 108–119.

Steele, W., & Raider, M. (2001). *Structured sensory intervention for traumatized children, adolescents, and parents: Strategies to alleviate trauma* (Vol. 1). Lewiston, NY: Edwin Mellen Press.

Stein, M. I. (1953). Creativity and culture. *The Journal of Psychology, 36*, 311–322.

Sternberg, R. J., & Lubart, T. I. (1995). *Defying the crowd: Cultivating creativity in a culture of conformity.* New York, NY: Free Press.

Svensk, A. C., Oster, I., Thyme, K. E., Magnusson, E., Sjodin, M., Eisemann, M., & Lindh, J. (2008). Art therapy improves experienced quality of life among women undergoing treatment for breast cancer: A randomized controlled study. *European Journal of Cancer Care, 18,* 69–77.

Tedeschi, R. G., & Calhoun, L. G. (2004). Posttraumatic growth: Conceptual foundations and empirical evidence. *Psychological Inquiry, 15,* 1–18.

Thyme, K. E., Sundin, E. C., Stahlberg, G., Lindstrom, B., Eklof, H., & Wiberg, B. (2007). The outcome of short-term psychodynamic art therapy compared to short-term psychodynamic verbal therapy for depressed women. *Psychoanalytic Psychotherapy, 21,* 250–264.

Van Gogh, V. (1889). *Letter to Theo.* Retrieved on April 20, 2017, from http://vangoghletters .org/vg/letters/let798/letter.html

Wadeson, H. (2010). *Art psychotherapy.* Hoboken, NJ: Wiley.

Walsh, S. M., Radcliffe, S., Castillo, L. C., Kumar, A. M., & Broschard, D. M. (2007). A pilot study to test the effects of art-making classes for family caregivers of patients with cancer. *Oncology Nursing Forum, 34,* 1–8.

Westen, D., Novotny, C. M., & Thompson-Brenner, H. (2004). The empirical status of empirically supported psychotherapies: Assumptions, findings, and reporting in controlled clinical trials. *Psychological Bulletin, 130,* 631–663.

Yalom, I. D., & Leszcz, M. (2008). *The theory and practice of group psychotherapy* (5th ed.). New York, NY: Basic Books.

Zausner, T. (1998). When walls become doorways: Creativity, chaos theory, and physical illness. *Creativity Research Journal, 11,* 21–28.

Zausner, T. (2007). Artist and audience: Everyday creativity and visual art. In R. Richards (Ed.), *Everyday creativity and new views of human nature: Psychological, social, and spiritual perspectives* (pp. 75–89). Washington, DC: American Psychological Association.

33 Creativity in the Domain of Play

Product and Processes

Sandra Russ

and

Claire Wallace

Case Western Reserve University

Abstract

Pretend play is both a creative product and a reflection of creative processes. Pretend play is unique in that it is an open-ended activity that the child must begin from scratch; it is self-reinforcing, in that it is fun; it reflects many processes important in creativity and involves practice with those processes; it is a vehicle that can be tailored to the talents and interests of the child; it includes processes important in different domains of creativity; it is universal, it involves the whole child; and it is a safe space for the child to express themselves without being judged. Because so many processes important in creativity occur in pretend play, measures of play can indicate creative potential in children. Key studies in the area of pretend play and creativity are reviewed and suggestions for future research are offered.

Pretend play – the ability to transform objects, make-up story events, use imagination and fantasy, ignore reality, represent people, and express emotion – is an activity for all children in all cultures. There is a wealth of information in pretend play about child development and creativity, if we can learn to mine it to the fullest. Although studying play has many challenges, it is worth the effort – and besides, it is fun to do research in the area of children's play.

What Is Unique in Pretend Play?

There are a number of ways in which pretend play is unique. Pretend play is a creative product within which a number of processes important in creative production can also be identified and measured. This is a unique combination.

Looking first at the creative processes in pretend play, children are making things up from scratch. Even though they may be taking bits from TV, daily life, long-term memory, or books, they are choosing the bits and recombining these elements into new forms. As the neuroscientists say, this is self-generated thought that is independent of external stimuli (Andrews-Hanna, Smallwood, & Spreng, 2014). Children are practicing self-generated thinking in pretend play and are experiencing joy in the process. Many other childhood activities start with external stimuli, such as video-games or model building, and the child builds on what is given, whether prompts or specific directions. In pretend play, the child provides the starting point. It is this generation of ideas by the child in an unstructured space that is so unique to the pretend play activity. The play can go in any direction. Free drawing may come close to self-generated thought, but enjoying the drawing process is not as universal as is enjoying pretend play.

Universality of pretend play is another unique feature. Children in all cultures engage in pretend play. Gaskins, Haight, and Lancy (2007) concluded that there are qualitative and qualitative differences in play across cultures. Symbolism in play seems to be universal but it is valued differently in different cultures. Diamond (2012) observed pretend play in traditional cultures such as New Guinea. He was struck by the self -invented play of these children that involved tribal war games with pretend bows and arrows. In contrast, Nani children in the Sudan built pretend cattle enclosures out of sand and mud and played at herding cattle. The pretend play content was relevant to what was important to the culture. Diamond speculated that play is an educational activity that prepares children for adult life.

For typically developing children, play is fun. It is self-reinforcing, so children go back to playing and experiencing positive affect. Play activities may have evolu-tionary roots in animal behavior. Some animal behaviorists propose that human play is continuous with animal play in many ways (Burghardt, 2005). In animals, pretend play such as pretend fighting in bears is preparation for adult activities. There are advantages of practicing through play in preparation for adult behaviors (Mitchell, 2007). If so, children may be genetically "wired" to play.

Pretend play can also be broken down into its components. One can observe and measure divergent thinking (number and variety of ideas), transformations of objects, flexibility of thinking, access to affect in ideation, expression of emotion, and joy in the activity. All of these are processes that have been found to be important in many domains of creativity (Runco, 2007; Russ, 2014). For example, as children play, they transform objects from one thing into another (e.g., a block becomes a telephone). They create stories that contain both imagination and emotion, shifting from one idea to the next in their narrative. Divergent thinking, cognitive flexibility, and affect in fantasy are all parallel processes that occur simultaneously as children play and can be measured as distinct entities in the broader construct of creativity. There is no other childhood activity that can reflect so many different creative processes. Because of the potential of pretend play to encompass so many different processes, it is also a vehicle that can be tailored to the individual child. The child who loves to make up stories can do so in the playhouse. The child who likes to build can make complex forts before charging the castle or can make interesting mechan-ical toys. The child who wants to put on plays can engage in role-play with her friends. Because play is an open-ended activity, the child can take it in many directions based upon his talents and interests. It is one of the most open-ended activities of childhood.

Another unique feature of pretend play, probably because so many creative processes are involved, is that pretend play reflects processes that cut across different domains of creativity. For example, divergent thinking and cognitive flexibility are thought to be important in many areas of science, dance, literature, and engineering (Feist, 2011; Russ, 2014). Access to affect in memories and to emotion in general is especially important in the many of the arts (Boyd, 2009). The beginnings of the creative processes important in adult creative production can be seen in early pretend play. In that sense, play can be a general vehicle in which children develop those skills that they can then use in later creative activities. Of course, other characteristics of talent, preference, motivation, and opportunity also determine adult creative achievement. Perhaps one creative process important in all domains of creativity is joy in creative production. That intrinsic motivation – love of the activity – is a natural part of pretend play. The experience of joy in a creative activity can develop the motivation to experience this positive affect in later creative pursuits.

Pretend play involves the whole child more than other activities such as sports, board games, or playing an instrument. Play involves motoric action, language, imagination, interpersonal representations of other people, and emotional expression. The child is "all in." Pretend play is a creative act that involves all of the child and is accompanied by positive emotions and, at times, joy.

An important construct to consider in the domain of play is that of verbal intelligence. Because measurement of creativity in play relies heavily on children's verbalizations, researchers regularly measure children's verbal IQ in order to control for its possible influence in measuring a child's creativity. Most studies have found minimal correlations between IQ and creative processes in play (Russ, 2014). However, the relationship between play skills and intellectual and language abilities may be stronger for younger children and for children with developmental delays (Kaugars, 2011).

Another construct vital to conceptualizing creativity in play is that of child development. Developmental domains such as object permanence, perspective taking, and social interaction are all relevant to pretend play. A child's development in all of these areas can influence the quality of the creative product in play. As children progress developmentally, their play moves from reacting to objects, to exploring properties of objects, to using objects as symbols (Belsky & Most, 1981). Symbolic representation is a hallmark feature of pretend play, and one measure of creativity in play is the number and quality of symbolic representations. As children develop greater perspective-taking skills, their play can take on more complexity (Ashaibi, 2007; Shirk & Russell, 1996). For example, children may be able to create more interesting stories by playing as multiple characters in the story. Perspective taking allows characters in the story to communicate unique ideas, express preference, and even create and resolve conflict. Various studies have also linked pretend play to interpersonal skills such as empathy (Hughes, 1999; Seja & Russ, 1999), development of relational schemas (Fromberg, 2002), and prosocial behavior (Fehr & Russ, 2013). Of course, it is probable that there is a bi-directional quality to these associations – each ability influences the other.

Pretend play itself can be considered to be a creative product. Play can be evaluated as a creative product using the standard criteria of creativity. Criteria of originality, quality, and appropriateness to the task (Sternberg, Kaufman, & Pretz, 2002) can be applied to play. Play can be evaluated for quality of story, fantasy and imagination, and originality. On the other hand, play is distinct from domains of art or science or music in that the product is not concretely documented or preserved. It does not contribute to society or to a field. Play is a universal creative activity of childhood that involves, as Sawyer (1997) has theorized, improvisation. Pretend play is an example of mini-c creativity and little-c creativity (Russ, 2014). Little-c creativity involves novel and task-appropriate creative events that occur on a daily basis (Plucker & Beghetto, 2004). In pretend play, children can practice with creative activities, have fun, and – uniquely – not be judging or censoring what they are doing. There is no way to fail in play. Play is a safe area for children in many ways.

In summary, pretend play is unique because it can be defined as both a creative product and as a reflection of creative processes; it is an open-ended activity that the child must begin from scratch; it is self-reinforcing, in that it is fun; it reflects many processes important in creativity and involves practice with those processes; it is a vehicle that can be tailored to the talents and interests of the child; it includes processes important in different domains of creativity; it is universal, it involves the whole child; and it is a safe space for the child to express themselves without being judged.

Measuring Creative Potential in Pretend Play

Because there are so many creative processes that can be observed in pretend play, play is an ideal activity in which to measure these processes. Most researchers in the play area have developed their own measures of play. There are a few measures that have been used in a number of studies in different research programs. Lillard et al. (2013) and Russ (1993) have stressed the importance of using uniform measures across studies so results can be compared.

Russ developed the Affect in Play Scale (1993) in order to fill the need for a comprehensive standardized measure that assessed both cognitive and affective processes and could be used in many research programs. She followed the guidelines that Singer had outlined in 1973. Singer stressed the need to focus on specific variables, identify specific behavior samples, stay with observable behaviors, and train raters carefully. He emphasized systematic measurement of play samples.

The Affect in Play Scale (APS; Russ 1993;)is a comprehensive measure of the processes important in creativity in the domain of play. It is a standardized five-minute play task developed to measure different processes in pretend play that are involved in creativity. The APS is a well-validated measure of imagination and affect expression in pretend play (Russ, 2004;2014). Children receive two puppets and three blocks and are given the following instructions:

> I'm here to learn about how children play. I have here two puppets and would like you to play with them any way you would like for five minutes. For example, you can have the puppets do something together. I also have some blocks that you can use. Be sure to have the puppets talk out loud. The video camera will be on so that I can remember what you say and do. I'll tell you when to stop. (Russ, 2014, p. 177)

The child is informed when there is one minute left. If the child stops playing during the five-minute period, the child receives the prompt, "There's still time left, keep playing." The task is discontinued if the child cannot play after a two-minute period.

The child's play is scored from the videotape using a criterion-based rating scale. There are five main scores: (1) Organization, the quality of the plot and the complexity of the story, scored from 1–5; (2) Imagination, the novelty and uniqueness of the play and ability to pretend and transform the blocks, scored from 1–5; (3) Comfort, a global rating of the child's comfort engaging in play and their level of enjoyment, scored from 1–5; (4) Frequency of Affect, a total count of affect units expressed within the play narrative (e.g. A child might have the puppets say "Yikes, a monster!" (fear) or "Whee! This slide is fun!" (happy) and (5) Variety of Affect, a total count of the number of affect categories out of eleven possible categories, expressed during the play.

A detailed scoring manual for the APS has been developed (Russ, 2004, 2014). Past studies have reported the interrater reliability of the APS to be high, consistently in the .80s and .90s. Internal consistency for the affect scores on the APS using the Spearman-Brown split-half reliability is also high (.85; Seja & Russ, 1999). The APS has a large body of validity studies demonstrating associations with theoretically relevant criteria in different research programs and countries (Russ, 2014).

The APS as a measure of creative processes in play has been validated by relating it to other measures of creativity. The imagination and affect expression scores on the APS significantly relate to creativity measures in a number of studies (Russ, 2014). The APS itself might be considered one measure of creativity in children. For example, the APS captures the child's enjoyment and engagement in the task, an important quality of creative production. It also measures affect in fantasy and cognition, an important component of imagination. It measures imagination and the ability to make up a story with unstructured toys (puppets and blocks). Further, it measures affect expression in fantasy. Affect is often left out of creativity and play measures, a phenomenon referred to as the "cognification of play" (Rubin, Fein, & Vandenberg, 1983). The APS was developed to fill this gap in the literature and provides a standardized play task and a detailed coding system that measures *both* imagination and affect in play and enjoyment of the task.

A preschool version of the scale that uses a variety of toys with more structured instructions has also found associations between play and creativity (Kaugars & Russ, 2009; Fehr & Russ, 2016).

Examples of Pretend Play from the APS

Below are examples of play segments from different children from 6–10 years old. These examples are from children who participated in a study of play and creativity (Hoffmann & Russ, 2012). These are brief samples of play using two puppets and three blocks. Affect coding is in parentheses. The following are examples of affect expression in a well-organized segment.

Child 1

I wonder what to build. Let's see, we could build a tower.
Put this one on top of this one . . . ah! It's a tower. How are we going to climb it?
I don't know, maybe we shouldn't climb it; it could be dangerous . . . (FEAR)
Maybe we could climb it.
First we have to get a ladder.
Okay. Here it is. Climb up.
I'm on top of a mountain. Whee! Wow Silvia this is fun. (HAPPY)
Yeah!
Let's go down because I am afraid of heights. (FEAR)

This child (Child 1) expressed a variety of affect units in the story – fear and happiness. This child is also using imagination in using blocks to be a ladder and then a mountain. Children who engage in this type of play tend to score higher on creativity measures.

Child 2

Do you want to go on the stepping stones?
Ok (uses blocks as stepping stones) . . . Maybe we should, but they're above the
    river, it is kind of dangerous to skip. *(FEAR)
But I want to skip. (BICKERING AGGRESSION)
It is very dangerous to skip! (FEAR)
But I want. (BICKERING AGGRESSION)
No. (BICKERING AGGRESSION)
Well I am.
Okay, I will watch you.
Ahhh! (SADNESS/HURT)
Oh, my. Dive in, whee!
Okay, thank goodness you saved me. Maybe you were right. (AFFECTION)
Yeah, mm hmm.
How about . . . we better go home.
We should?
Yeah. My mom is cooking something really nice for dinner she said. (NURTURANCE)

For Child 2, there is a very wide range of affect in this story segment – from bickering to affection to hurt. There are many story elements as well – dangerous action on a river with a good dinner at the end.

Child 3

Hi. What should we do today?
Uh, we could build a little tower.
Ok. Whoopsies. (It fell) (FRUSTRATION)
That kind of looks like a tent, with a big chimney thing.

Let's make another one. It's a truck!

Yeah. And I'm driving it.

That's cool. (NURTURANCE)

Let's make another one. Hmm, this looks like a farm. We could be animals who live on the farm.

Ok, I'll be a rooster.

And I'll be a chicken who just laid eggs. (ORAL)

And I'll come get your eggs and I'll bring them to my mommy in the house.

Child 4

What's that?

Well I don't know. It could be a little design for a tree house.

Oh that is awesome! (HAPPY)

Like this could be the tree with all the leaves and then the triangle could be the house.

Yeah that's good! Can I come in? (NURTURANCE)

Yeah just knock. Come in!

Hi. Wanna play hair?

Sure you can do my hair.

The following examples (Child 5 and 6) show good imagination, divergent thinking, and transformations of the blocks. There is little affect expressed in the play. These children would have a high imagination and low affect profile in the play.

Child 5

Do you know what we could do? If we take a green block, we could make a tower. Ta-da!

I wonder who could live in it.

Maybe a princess with long hair or a cat.

A cat in a castle?

It's a tower! Anything can live there . . . Um we could – they could be chairs and we could have a tea party.

Hmm you're right we could. Sit on the yellow block and I'll sit on the green block.

Here's your cup of tea.

Thank you, here is your cup of tea.

Child 6

"I wonder where my dog is.

You have a dog?

I wish. (FRUSTRATION)

We could pretend that I have a dog and the yellow block could be my puppy.

Um, I've always wanted a horse. We could pretend that the green one was my horse.

How about the red one?

Hm. The red one. The red one can be your food station.

That's right.

Or you can put it on top of the green one and make it look more like a horse. And if you put the yellow block on top it could look like a horse with a head.

You're right!
I've also wanted a horse.
We could pretend it is a horse.
What should we name it?
How about Mary?
How about Sunshine?
How about Rainbow?
Oh yeah that's perfect – Rainbow. It has all different colors.
I think Rainbow's hungry, let's feed it. (ORAL)

Possible profiles on the APS are children with high affect and imagination in well-organized play; children with high imagination and low affect; children with high affect and low imagination and organization; children with average scores in all areas; children low in both imagination and affect expression.

The Test of Pretend Play (ToPP; Lewis, Boucher, Lupton, & Watson, 2000) is a standardized, structured test of children's ability to imitate and initiate symbolic play. It has been used in a number of studies of children's play and evaluates levels of play. It is also recommended by Lillard et al. (2013). It yields an overall performance score that has largely been used to evaluate children with developmental delays and to assess the effectiveness of interventions (e.g. Sherratt, 2002).

Evaluating pretend play in natural settings is important to do. For evaluating young children in the classroom, Lillard et al. (2013) recommends combining Parten's (1932) system with Smilansky's approach (1968). One of the methodological problems with evaluating play in groups of children is that personality characteristics of children can cloud the picture. A shy child in a group of more dominant children may not express their natural level of play ability. This issue should be considered when evaluating children's pretend play in a group situation.

While there exist other measures of children's pretend play (See Kaugars, 2011, for a review), additional research is needed to determine whether they might be used to assess children's creativity as well. The Child-Initiated Pretend Play Assessment (ChIPPA; Stagnitti, Unsworth, & Rodger, 2000) is a standardized assessment of how well children are able to initiate and sustain pretend play. Children's play is assessed first with conventional toys and next with symbolic toys, resulting in scores for elaborateness, complexity, and organization of play; number of object substitutions; and number of imitated actions. The ChIPPA has potential for use with measuring creativity, but to date it has been primarily utilized in clinical populations for purposes such as occupational therapy evaluations (Stagnitti & Unsworth, 2000). Similarly, the Structured Play Assessment (Ungerer & Sigman, 1981) includes a measure of functional versus symbolic play, but it has been used primarily with children with autism to describe play typology and to develop treatment goals (Kasari, Freeman, & Paparella, 2006).

There is a need for additional standardized and well-validated measures of creative potential in young children. Standardized observational measures may prove particularly useful, but developing standardized measures that capture children's play as it occurs naturally is difficult. In order to understand how creativity develops over the lifetime, assessments must meet individuals at their developmental level. Examining children's pretend play provides a window into their creative capacities, but additional standardized measures are needed to gain a fuller understanding of, and appreciation for, creativity in early childhood.

Key Studies in Play and Creativity

In 1983, Kogan stated that the research in the play-creativity relationship was a promising set of findings. The research since that time has supported that promise. Fisher's (1992) meta-analysis of the research found that the effect size for the play and divergent-thinking studies was .387. Singer and Singer's (1990) book, *The house of make-believe*, is one of the best discussions of play and creativity and exactly how these areas overlap. Singer and Singer conceptualize play as practice with divergent thinking and the research supports this link. Two early classic studies were that of Lieberman (1977) and Fein (1987). Lieberman focused on "playfulness" which included affective components of spontaneity and joy. She found that playful kindergarten children did better on divergent-thinking tasks than nonplayful children. Fein studied fifteen children who were excellent at pretend play. Fein referred to them as master players. From observing their play, she developed a theory of the role of affect in play. One important component of her system was an affective symbol system that represented real or imagined affect-laden experiences. In play, these symbols are manipulated and recombined. Fein theorized that this affective symbol system was important in creativity.

Another classic study was that of Russ and Grossman-McKee (1990), which was the first study with the APS that found that both cognitive and affective processes in play significantly related to divergent thinking, independent of IQ. This finding has been replicated a number of times with different populations of children, different examiners, and different ages – preschool as well as elementary school.

Theory proposes affect as a facilitator of creative expression, where openness to emotion broadens associative networks (Isen, Daube, & Nowicke, 1987). While positive affect in play is most frequently associated with creative production, negative affect in the play narrative also related to creativity. For example, Russ and Schafer (2006) found that negative affect in play related to divergent thinking.

Longitudinal studies have found a stable association between play on the APS and later creativity. Two studies with different child populations have found that early play was significantly associated with divergent thinking four years later (Russ, Robins, & Christiano, 1999; Wallace & Russ, 2015), independent of verbal intelligence.

Recently, Lee and Russ (2016) followed up the girls in the Wallace & Russ study and found that the association between early pretend play and divergent thinking was stable and independent of intelligence. These longitudinal studies are important because they suggest that pretend play ability can be an indicator of creative potential independent of intelligence. Assessing pretend play could be an important addition to measures evaluating creative potential in children.

Some experimental studies have shown that play facilitates the development of divergent-thinking skills (Dansky, 1980; Dansky & Silverman, 1973). There is mixed evidence in this area of research, and some researchers have proposed the existence of some third variable that accounts for the relation between play and divergent thinking. In a recent review, Lillard et al. (2013) criticized some of these studies for having the same individual administer both the play task and the divergent-thinking task, which raises the possibility of experimenter bias. However, Russ & Wallace (2013) concluded that there are some rigorous studies that have found that play sessions increased imagination in play and on creativity tasks. For example, Hoffmann and Russ (2016) found that a six-session pretend play small group intervention resulted in significant improvement in play skills for the play group when compared with a control group. For below average players, improvement on a divergent-thinking task also occurred in comparison with the control group.

In conclusion, rigorous research evidence exists to support the association between pretend play and creativity, and some research suggests that pretend play may facilitate the development of divergent thinking over time (Russ & Wallace, 2013). However, the Lillard et al. (2013) review clearly articulates the need for rigorous research design and need for caution in inferring causation between play and creativity.

Future Possibilities in Play and Creativity Research

The important role of play in child development has been well demonstrated. Pretend play is related to many domains of adaptive functioning that impact creativity, such as emotion regulation (Hoffman & Russ, 2012), coping (Fiorelli & Russ, 2012), and divergent thinking (Wallace & Russ, 2015). Future research should examine both how these associations persist over time and what other areas of adaptive functioning might be impacted by creative expression, measured with pretend play. For example, various studies have linked pretend play to perspective taking (Ashaibi, 2007; Shirk & Russell, 1996), empathy (Hughes, 1999; Seja & Russ, 1999), insight (Russ, Fiorelli, & Spannagel, 2011) and mood (Fiorelli & Russ, 2012), all of which may impact creativity as children develop.

Research has demonstrated that a child's intelligence is far from the sole determinant of creative potential or even academic achievement. A longitudinal study of pretend play skills over time showed that the combination of positive affect in play and divergent thinking significantly predicted math achievement four years later, over and above verbal ability (Wallace & Russ, 2015). These results carry implications for how parents and teachers view the role of play in child development. They may be able to promote academic achievement in a way that does not rely so heavily on IQ. A study of upper elementary school students and teachers showed that in classrooms where eachers elicited student creativity, students showed the largest gains in academic achievement (Schacter, Thum, & Zifkin, 2006). Shifting teachers' approach to education can promote the development of creativity by giving children opportunities for pretend play and can even utilize students' creativity to improve their learning. Future research should investigate specifically how regular opportunities for pretend play in curriculum can improve students' creativity and achievement over time.

Another approach to research would be to return to studying individual children closely and observe their play and other creative activities. Fein (1987) learned a great deal from her creative players. Individual case studies should remain part of our research programs.

Neuroimaging studies of children's imaginative activities could lend insight into neurological correlates of imagination and the development of imagination. The important role of affect in fantasy and imagination could also be investigated in this way.

We need to find ways to integrate growing technology with pretend play experiences. For example, apps that facilitate imagination, play, and self-generated thought could be the way of the future. Videogames and apps could be developed that are very loosely structured to leave much room for the child to develop the story or to play-out the story.

Finally, we must translate research into practice. As we develop techniques that facilitate imaginative play, we need to disseminate this information to parents and teachers. Through brochures, videos, and apps, we could encourage adults to develop the creative potential within each child.

References

Andrews-Hanna, J., Smallwood, J., & Spring, R. (2014) The default network and self-generated thought. *Annals of the New York Academy of Sciences, 1316*, 29–52.

Ashiabi, G. S. (2007). Play in the preschool classroom: Its socioemotional significance and the teacher's role in play. *Early Childhood Education Journal, 35*, 199–207.

Belsky, J., & Most, J. (1981). From exploration to play: A cross-sectional study of infant free play behavior. *Developmental Psychology, 17*, 630–639.

Boyd, B. (2009) *On the origin of stories.* Cambridge, MA: Harvard University Press.

Burghardt, G. (2005) *The genesis of animal play.* Cambridge, MA: MIT Press.

Dansky, J. (1980). Make-believe: A mediator of the relationship between play and associative fluency. *Child Development, 51*, 576–579.

Dansky, J., & Silverman, F. (1973). Effects of play on associative fluency in preschool-aged children. *Developmental Psychology, 9*, 38–43.

Diamond, J. (2012). *The world until yesterday.* New York: Viking.

Fehr, K. K., & Russ, S. W. (2013). Aggression in pretend play and aggressive behavior in the classroom. *Early Education & Development, 24*, 332–345.

Fehr, K. & Russ, S. (2016) Pretend play and creativity in preschool-aged children: Associations and brief intervention. *Psychology of Aesthetics, Creativity and the Arts*, 296–308.

Fein, G. G. (1987). Pretend play: Creativity and consciousness. In P. Gorlitz & J. Wohlwill (Eds.), *Curiosity, imagination, and play: On the development of spontaneous cognitive motivational processes* (pp. 281–304). Hillsdale, NJ: Lawrence Erlbaum Associates, Inc.

Feist, G. (2011). Creativity in science. In M. Runco & S. Pritzker (Eds.), *Encyclopedia of creativity* (Vol. 1, pp. 296–302). San Diego: Academic Press.

Fiorelli, J. A. & Russ, S. W. (2012). Pretend play, coping, and subjective well-being in children: A follow-up study. *American Journal of Play*, *5*, 81–103.

Fisher, E. P. (1992). The impact of play on development: A meta-analysis. *Play and Culture*, *5*, 159–181.

Fromberg, D. P. (2002). *Play and meaning in early childhood education*. Boston: Allyn & Bacon.

Gaskins, S., Haight, W., & Lancy, D. (2007). The cultural construction of play. In A. Goncu & S. Gaskins (Eds.), *Play and development* (pp. 179–202). New York: Taylor & Francis.

Hoffmann, J., & Russ, S. W. (2012). Pretend play, creativity, and emotion regulation in children. *Psychology of Aesthetics, Creativity, and the Arts*, *6*, 175–184.

Hoffmann, J. & Russ, S. (2016) Fostering pretend play skills and creativity in elementary school girls: A group play intervention. *Psychology of Aesthetics, Creativity, and the Arts*. 114–125.

Hughes, F. P. (1999). *Children, play, and development* (3rd edn.). Needham Heights, MA: Allyn & Bacon.

Isen, A., & Daubman, K., & Nowicki, G. (1987). Positive affect facilitates creative problem solving. *Journal of Personality and Social Psychology*, *52*, 1122–1131.

Kasari, C., Freeman, S., & Paparella, T. (2006). Joint attention and symbolic play in young children with autism: A randomized controlled intervention study. *Journal of Child Psychology and Psychiatry*, *47*, 611–620.

Kaugars, A. (2011). Assessment of pretend play. In S. Russ & L. Niec (Eds.), *Play in clinical practice: Evidence-based approaches* (pp. 51–82). New York: Guilford Press.

Kaugars, A. S., & Russ, S. W. (2009). Assessing preschool children's pretend play: Preliminary validation of the affect in play scale-preschool version. *Early Education and Development*, *20*, 733–755.

Kogan, N. (1983). Stylistic variation in childhood and adolescence: Creativity, metaphor, and cognitive styles. In P. Mussen (Ed.), *Handbook of child psychology*, Vol 3 (pp. 631–706). New York: Wiley.

Krasnor, L., & Pepler, D. (1980). The study of children's play: Some suggested future directions. *New Directions for Child Development*, *9*, 85–94.

Lee, A., & Russ, S. (2016, August) Early pretend play as a predictor of later creativity: A seven-year follow-up. Paper presented at the American Psychological Association, Denver.

Lewis, V., Boucher, J., Lupton, L., & Watson, S. (2000). Relationships between symbolic play, functional play, verbal and non-verbal ability in young children. *International Journal of Language & Communication Disorders*, *35*, 117–127.

Lieberman, J. N. (1977). *Playfulness: Its relationship to imagination and creativity*. New York: Academic Press.

Lillard, A. S., Lerner, M. D., Hopkins, E. J., Dore, R. A., Smith, E. D., & Palmquist, C. M. (2013). The impact of pretend play on children's development: A review of the evidence. *Psychological Bulletin*, *139*, 1–34.

Mitchell, R. (2007) Pretense in animals: The continuing relevance of children's pretense. In A. Goncu & S. Gaskins (Eds.), *Play and development* (pp. 51–75). New York: Taylor & Francis.

Parten, M. (1932). Social participation among pre-school children. *Journal of Abnormal and Social Psychology, 27*, 243–269.

Plucker, J., & Beghetto, R. (2004). Why creativity is domain general, why it looks domain specific, and why the distinction does not matter. In R. Sternberg, E. Grigorenko, & J. Singer (Eds.), *Creativity: From potential to realization* (pp. 153–167). Washington, DC: APA Books.

Rubin, K. H., Fein, G. G., & Vandenberg, B. (1983). Play. In Mussen, (Ed.), *Handbook of child psychology, 4* (pp. 693–774). New York: Wiley.

Runco, M. (2007). *Creativity.* San Diego: Elsevier.

Russ, S. W. (1993). *Affect and creativity: The role of affect and play in the creative process.* Hillsdale, NJ: Erlbaum.

Russ, S. W. (2004). *Play in child development and psychotherapy: Toward empirically supported practice.* Mahwah, NJ: Erlbaum.

Russ, S. W. (2014) *Pretend play in childhood: Foundation for adult creativity.* Washington, DC. : American Psychological Ass.

Russ, S. W., Fiorelli, J., & Spannagel, S. C. (2011). Cognitive and affective processes in play. In S. W. Russ & L. N. Niec (Eds.), *Play in clinical practice: Evidence-based approaches.* New York: Guilford Press.

Russ, S. W., & Grossman-McKee, A. (1990). Affective expression in children's fantasy play, primary process thinking on the Rorschach, and divergent thinking. *Journal of Personality Assessment, 54*, 756–771.

Russ, S. W., Robins, D., & Christiano, B. (1999). Pretend play: Longitudinal prediction of creativity and affect in fantasy in children. *Creativity Research Journal, 12*, 129–139.

Russ, S., & Schafer, E. D. (2006). Affect in fantasy play, emotion in memories and divergent thinking. *Creativity Research Journal, 18*, 347–354.

Russ, S. W., & Wallace, C. E. (2013). Pretend play and creative processes. *American Journal of Play, 6*, 136–148.

Sawyer, P. K. (1997). *Pretend play as improvisation.* Mahwah, NJ: Lawrence Erlbaum Associates.

Schacter, J., Thum, Y. M., & Zifkin, D. (2006). How much does creative teaching enhance elementary school students' achievement? *The Journal of Creative Behavior, 40*, 47–72.

Seja, A. L., & Russ, S. W. (1999). Children's fantasy play and emotional understanding. *Journal of Clinical Child Psychology, 28*, 269–277.

Sherratt, D. (2002). Developing pretend play in children with autism a case study. *Autism, 6*, 169–179.

Shirk, S., & Russell, R. (1996). *Change processes in child psychotherapy: Revitalizing treatment and research.* New York: Guilford Press.

Singer, D. G., & Rummo, J. (1973). Ideational creativity and behavioral style in kindergarten aged children. *Developmental Psychology, 8*, 154–161.

Singer, D. G., & Singer, J. L. (1990). *The house of make-believe: Children's play and the developing imagination.* Cambridge, MA: Harvard University Press.

Smilanski, S. (1968). *The effects of sociodramatic play on disadvantaged preschool children.* New York: Wiley.

Stagnitti, K., & Unsworth, C. (2000). The importance of pretend play in child development: An occupational therapy perspective. *The British Journal of Occupational Therapy, 63*, 121–127.

Stagnitti, K., Unsworth, C., & Rodger, S. (2000). Development of an assessment to identify play behaviours that discriminate between the play of typical preschoolers and preschoolers with pre-academic problems. *The Canadian Journal of Occupational Therapy, 67*, 291.

Sternberg, R. J., Kaufman, J. C., & Pretz, J. E. (2002). *The creativity conundrum.* New York: Psychology Press.

Ungerer, J. A., & Sigman, M. (1981). Symbolic play and language comprehension in autistic children. *Journal of the American Academy of Child Psychiatry, 20*, 318–337.

Wallace, C. E., & Russ, S. W. (2015). Pretend play, divergent thinking, and math achievement in girls: A longitudinal study. *Psychology of Aesthetics, Creativity, and the Arts.* 9(3), 296–305.

34 Creativity in Craft

Vlad P. Glăveanu

University of Bergen, Norway

Abstract

This chapter reviews research in the area of creativity and craft in psychology and connected disciplines. It stars by asking whether craft can be considered a domain and, in particular, if it is a creative one. Reflecting on the meaning of creativity in craftwork, it is argued both that a new definition of creativity is needed to capture aspects specific for this domain and that craft-like practices underpin creative activity in most other creative domains. Research on creative craft is presented in relation to its focus on creative actors, audiences, actions, artifacts, and affordances. Methodological issues associated with the study of craft are also reviewed and proposals made for a more comprehensive approach to craft creativity. In the end, four themes are abstracted from this domain and their relevance for the broader field of creativity studies is discussed.

Craft products are, arguably, ubiquitous; they can be found in virtually all homes, offices, and public spaces, serving either utilitarian or decorative functions, very often both. Pottery, woodcarving, jewelry, marquetry, metalwork, weaving, sewing, quilting, needlework, rug making, embroidery, knitting, calligraphy, book binding, egg decoration, ikebana, and floral design: all illustrate types of craft, many of them with ancient roots. Using wood, metal, clay, textiles, paper, stone, glass, plastic, and even trash, craftwork nowadays ranges from unique pieces carefully made by the hands of skilled artisans to the mass production of objects within industrial design. It is this diversity that poses a first challenge to scholars interested in the domain of craft. For as varied and widespread as craft products are, their recognition *as craft* (i.e., different from, and sometimes opposed to, art) is highly contingent on social and historical context. Moreover, one and the same general practice can have expressions that cross domain boundaries; take, for instance, the decoration of eggs, a common practice in many communities, particularly related to the celebration of Easter – is this traditional craft or decorative art? What about Fabergé eggs – art, craft, design, or all of them at once?

The dictionary offers us a first clue when it comes to defining crafts. As a noun, it generally designates objects made by hand; as a verb, exercising skill in the making of these objects.[1] This definition, resonating with lay understandings of the term, emphasizes thus the difference between the serial reproduction of objects and a traditional, non-mechanized way of making things. However, such a sharp

---

[1] From Oxford Dictionaries (www.oxforddictionaries.com/definition/english/craft)

distinction is problematic as most crafts nowadays involve a combination of resources, tools, and activities that employ both hand and mechanical production. To return to the example of decorated Easter eggs, while they are primarily made by hand, their making relies on industrial color pigments (unlike the small-scale production of natural colors within the family, now largely abandoned). Furthermore, today craftsmen increasingly use digital technologies in their work, a development that challenges the very notion of handiwork. In light of these observations it becomes more useful to operate with a set of general criteria rather than a specific definition of craft. The general features that apply to most types of crafts referred to in this chapter include: extensive use of manual labor, the importance of skills, their exercise through practice, the employment of specific material tools, the developmental role of apprenticeships, and reliance on tradition (Glăveanu, 2016, pp. 30–31). In this chapter, I argue for the addition of creativity to this set of defining features of craft.

In building this argument, I start by discussing why craft can be considered a domain and, specifically, a creative domain. Addressing old criticisms, I propose a broader view of craft as masterful performance, a position that underlines the important role played by craftwork within virtually any creative domain. Returning to the topic of creativity in craft, key studies in this area are reviewed in light of their contribution to our understanding of creative actors, audiences, actions, artifacts, and affordances. Main methodological approaches are considered next with a focus on how well equipped they are to capture the microgenetic aspects of craft creativity. Finally, some future directions in creativity research inspired by studies of craft will be presented. In outlining them, I hope not only to raise new questions about creativity (across domains) but also to encourage further explorations of craftwork, a domain that has been largely neglected in the past by creativity researchers (at least within psychology). As this chapter will come to show, craft is neither a "lesser" form of art nor a thing of the past, but a fundamental channel of creative expression at the level of person, community, and culture.

Craft as a Creative Domain

Before establishing whether craft can be considered a creative domain we need to reflect first on whether it qualifies as a domain to begin with. As mentioned in the introduction, there are a great number of human activities than fall under this category and, more than this, there is high variety between as well as within craft occupations. So, in this sense, if crafts can be considered a domain, then this domain is *far from unitary*. But this is arguably also the case for many other domains, for example the arts. And it is also the case that every domain of human activity evolves in time and should always be studied in view of historical time and geographical place. In the case of craft, for instance, one of the defining moments of its evolution into an "institutional" domain was at the turn of the twentieth century when the Arts and Crafts movement flourished in Europe and North America (see Crook, 2009, for a discussion of the relation between this movement and modernity). Before this time,

craftsmen had been traditionally organized in guilds whose existence was continuously threatened by the fast pace of industrialization. Developing a strong professional identity, even if as a reaction to external pressures, contributed greatly to
instituting crafts as a domain in its own right or, at least, in close proximity with
another, much more visible one – that of the arts.

The relation between arts and crafts and, more concretely, between artists and
craftsmen (or artisans) is complicated to say the least. Historically, these two fields
have a common origin: the practical activity of people aiming to add an aesthetic
dimension to their communal existence (Dewey, 1934). In time, however, the arts
transformed into a separate sphere from that of everyday life, leaving behind and, at
times, denying their craft origins. This is how a culture of art museums and galleries
developed, grounded in the possibility of distinguishing "real" and "valuable" art
from the more common and esthetically lacking outcomes of craftwork. When
craftsmen develop artistic pretentions, the space they are generally confined to is
that of "folk art," "outsider art," or "self-taught art" (Fine, 2004). Thus, an implicit
hierarchy is being constructed whereby the general domain of crafts remains subordinated to that of the arts. In this sense, Howard Becker (1978, p. 867) referred to
crafts as a *minor art-world*, particularly those that prioritize beauty alongside utility
and virtuoso skill. This feature is specific for what he calls artist-craftsmen (different
from ordinary craftsmen), a status attained in some craft occupations and not others
(e.g., plumbers) and by some artisans within the craft depending on how they view
and perform their practice (e.g., furniture making is a craft in which beauty is
prioritized by some producers but not all). Becker also notes in this context the
permeability of both art and craft-worlds, "in which what has been commonly
understood by practitioners and public to be a craft becomes redefined as an art or,
conversely, an art becomes redefined as a craft" (p. 863).

What is important to take from the above, for the purposes of our discussion, is the
fact that many crafts today, particularly artistic-crafts, are organized as creative
domains in a way similar to the arts. They enjoy special exhibition spaces, prizes,
a growing number of collectors, and associated educational programs. These
arrangements largely satisfy a common definition of domains in the psychology of
creativity advanced by Csikszentmihalyi (1988), in which domains are socially
instituted and the inclusion of new artifacts within a domain requires acceptance
by gatekeepers (such as museum curators, critics, etc.). At the same time, operating
with such a strict understanding of domains excludes all those everyday activities
performed by amateur craftsmen outside of any institutional arrangements. In other
words, it focuses on craft as discipline and less on craft as a process or practice
(Shiner, 2012) or as an embodied form of learning (Ings, 2015). Moreover, it makes
us less sensitive to the process of "institutionalization" of crafts, which is both
gradual and unequal, with some aspects being subjected to institutional evaluation
more than others. Returning to the example of eggs decorated for instance in
Romania, for instance, this practice has known, in the past two decades, a fast
process of institutionalization leading to the organization of museums, fairs, and
competitions (national and international). At the same time, the activity of numerous
craftsmen – or, rather in this case, craftswomen – in many rural areas of the country

is still "validated" by local social networks ranging from family members to customers. An extended notion of the craft domain is needed to account for both.

Beyond asking whether crafts are a creative domain or not it might be useful to explore what *kind* of creative domain they might be. Li (1997) proposed some time ago an interesting distinction between horizontal and vertical creative domains. The former are organized in ways that encourage individuals to always produce novelties; the latter are more traditional in the sense that they appreciate fidelity and continuity over time. If we take music as an example, some branches such an improvisational jazz would be better described as a horizontal (sub)domain, while others, such as classical music, as a vertical one. What is, by and large, the case of crafts? Li argued, based on his definition, that "modern Western painting exhibits more horizontal tendencies, traditional Chinese painting emphasizes vertical ones" (p. 110). Are all or most crafts described by a strict enforcement of norms and the rejection of (radical) novelty? This question is important for how we understand creative expression in this broadly defined domain. While the great variety of crafts practiced around the world makes it hard to generalize, it is safe to assume that craftwork is often associated with tradition rather than creativity. And tradition is commonly (mis)understood as a static body of knowledge and practices (see Negus & Pickering, 2004), at times the very antithesis of creativity! In contrast, an excessive focus in creativity research on novelty and originality (at least in the West; see Niu & Sternberg, 2006) doesn't often correspond to how craftsmen themselves understand the value of their work (Glăveanu & Tanggaard, 2014; Kozbelt & Durmysheva, 2007). Finally, prioritizing creative thinking obscures the fact that a lot of creativity in craft has much less to do with thinking (the conceptual aspect) than doing (embodied practice). If craft is a domain of creativity, what exactly is this creativity about?

The Meaning of Creativity in Craft

A common definition of creativity in psychology refers to it as the process that leads to the generation of novel/original and useful outcomes (Amabile, 1996). Although it is expected of most craft products to be, in some ways, useful, it is much more difficult to assess their degree of novelty and originality. This is the case for a number of reasons. First, crafts tend to draw on traditions of long duration and craftsmen often build their professional identity based on belonging to a tradition and continuing it. As such, radical departures from this tradition would lead to new and perhaps original products but not products that are valuable from the perspective of most craftsmen (think, for instance, how it would be to draw Christmas instead of Easter motifs on eggs in communities used to decorate them only for Easter). Second, there is a difference not usually acknowledged between the novelty of particular outcomes and the novelty of the practice itself. While it might well be the case that individual craft products are similar to each other, this doesn't mean that the craft as a whole doesn't use existing materials in an unusual way (e.g., glass etching whereby the possibility of scratching glass, usually a nuisance, is exploited in a creative manner). Last but not least, we are frequently making judgments about novelty based only on the final outcome and ignore the processes leading up to it. It is often the case that, although craftsmen might reach similar endpoints in their work (i.e., the same shape or pattern), they do so using variations of an established technique and constantly improvising along the way. Observing such *procedural or technical creativity* should be part of any comprehensive study of craft (a methodological issue I will return to later in the chapter).

Given the lack of in-depth research in this area, it might be easy to agree with Collingwood's (1938) view that craft is governed by "preconceived ideas," where "the craftsman knows what he wants to make before he makes it" (pp. 15–16). Postulating a direct link between idea and execution in craft further dismisses its creativity since, as noted by Amabile (1996), creative products come out of heuristic processes. Knowing in advance what, how, and when to do things undermines creative potential in craftwork. It also reflects an actor–observer difference in our understanding of craft. From the "outside," watching a skilled craftsman at work often gives the impression of attending a highly rehearsed, masterful performance. The movement is both elegant and precise, the artisan focused, the process perfectly controlled, and the outcome anticipated. This observer position however contradicts how craftwork is experienced from the "inside." It has been repeatedly documented that, even for those practices that are highly regulated and emphasize sameness, such as traditional dances, there is adaptation, freedom, and improvisation in both teaching (Dalidowicz, 2015) and execution (Hughes-Freeland, 2007). Once more, a phenomenological perspective is often missing from creativity studies.

The general distrust in the creative capabilities of craftsmen, such as that expressed by Collingwood has, however, a very long intellectual history. Its roots can be traced back to the philosophical distinction in Antiquity between knowing (*episteme*) and making or crafting (*techne*). The separation between abstract theory and technical ability might have been less strict for thinkers such as Plato and Aristotle (see Lehmann, 2012) but it certainly precipitated, in subsequent centuries, the division between "true" knowledge and mastering a technique. The separation between making and knowing can be observed to this day in the way education is organized (theoretical versus practical or vocational), research is classified (basic or applied), and creativity is conceived of (as thinking rather than doing). Indeed, the meaning of creativity in craft cannot be reduced simply to the cognitive part, as important as thinking is for the practice of any craft. Rather, creativity in this domain should be defined in terms of *making*, a process that encompasses cognition, affect, and behavior within meaningful action or activity (Glăveanu, 2013a, 2016). Creative craft doesn't result primarily in new or original ideas but in the *remaking* of cultural practices and traditions (a definition that resonates widely with Eastern conceptions of creativity, incidentally also cultural contexts where crafts have flourished for centuries). Craftwork, just as culture itself, is heterogeneous and dynamic, capable of adapting to new social and material circumstances. In this sense, thinking of tradition as a simple continuation of the past is misleading; every existing tradition is, in fact, a *neo-tradition* and, as such, should be both understood as the contemporary enactment of a historical practice.

However, even this broader view of craft is challenged by the wide use of repetition, including mechanical reproduction, by many artisans. If artifacts made a second time are never completely identical with the "original" (which, itself, is in fact a "copy" of something else), what can we say about the serial, industrial reproduction of craft products? Do they still renew craft culture in a creative manner? (See also the discussion of replication in Sternberg, Kaufman & Pretz, 2002.) Pye (1968) made a notable contribution to this debate when he differentiated between the workmanship of risk and that of certainty. In his own words:

> In the workmanship of certainty the result of every operation during the production has been predetermined and is outside the control of the operative once production starts. In the workmanship of risk the result of every operation during production is determined by the workman as he works and its outcome depends wholly or largely on his care, judgment and dexterity. (Pye, 1968, p. 52)

According to this distinction, Collingwood's accusation would apply only to the workmanship of certainty or the mass-production of craft. In contrast, hand-made craft is always open to failure and, as such, it requires a lot of creativity to solve problems on the spot, to imagine new possibilities, and turn accidents into opportunities. As Pye notes, in handicraft, the "workman admits to the work an element of the unaccountable and unstudied, of improvisation" (p. 31). Where does this leave industrial crafts (e.g., the mechanical production of carpets, jewelry, furniture)? Can there be any creativity involved in this type of practice? Recent scholarship on this topic argues against the view that things made in factories and things made by hand are polar opposites on the craft spectrum (Scarlett, 2011). In the end, conceiving the model to be duplicated involves a whole range of creative processes. Moreover, duplication fosters creative processes in terms of both use and interpretation (we can be reminded here of the inspiration drawn by pop art precisely from industrial reproduction). Finally, the use of replication raises an interesting question for creativity researchers concerning the meaning of a *copy* and the act of *copying*. Guth (2010) wrote, in this context, about the multiple modalities of the copy in traditional Japanese crafts:

> The copy carries out many kinds of cultural work in the context of Japanese crafts. While it sustains the authority of the past, those who make copies are not prisoners of that past. To represent the copy and copying as lacking individual expression and freedom of choice ignores the concrete material positioning of crafts makers as well as the various social and collective processes through which their creations are invested with value. . . . Copying should be understood as a form of production, interpretation and dissemination through which both practitioners and users construct meaningful places for themselves and others by creating a shared set of cultural values. It is a dynamic practice that makes tradition possible. Although they replicate something from the past, copies respond to new problems. In this sense, they are cultural forms that have a double temporality, speaking as much to history as to modernity. (p. 16)

What can we conclude, from the above, about creativity in craft? First of all, that such creativity needs to be understood in other terms than originality, divergent thinking, and radical change. In contrast, craft creativity is grounded in bodily engagement, improvisation, and constant adaptation to an ever-changing environment. Many would qualify these as little and mini-c creativity, sometimes as Pro-C (Beghetto & Kaufman, 2007), an illustration of personal or professional rather than historical, Big-C creativity. However, it is important to remember here that the practice of craft has deep social consequences not only for individuals but entire communities. These practices maintain and transform cultural identities as they distinguish between groups of craftsmen living within the same society. Even copying is an activity that plays multiple creative roles in craftwork. It leads to the generation of copies that valorize the best outcomes of craft and inspire future developments. As noted by Sennett (2008) in his seminal book *The Craftsman*, repetition in craftwork doesn't exclude but, on the contrary, cultivates anticipation, imagination, and rhythm. For example, repeating the same pattern on a new decorated egg involves, at every step, anticipation (how would this pattern look like in the end? Will it fit here as well?), imagination (would another pattern have worked as well? Are changes possible?), and rhythm (carried over from previous acts of decoration yet renewed by the practical challenges of drawing the motif on a new material support). More than this, Sennett points us to the fact that craftsmanship is much more than manual labor; it "names an enduring, basic human impulse, the desire to do a job well for its own sake" (p. 9). In this sense, craftwork is at the heart of creative activity in many other domains, from art and engineering to parenting and citizenship. Recognizing the role of craft in creativity moves us away from understanding it mainly in terms of *insight* (the creative idea) and helps us conceive it as *mastery* (creative making), a paradigmatic shift with broad implications for the psychology of creativity (for further details see Glăveanu, 2016). In order to explore the significance of this perspective it is necessary, however, to learn more about what characterizes creativity in craft and how this form of creativity can be studied, the topic of the next two sections; in the end, I will return to the issue of what we can learn more broadly about creativity by investigating craft.

Creativity and Craft: Research Themes and Main Findings

In this section I will discuss existing research on creativity and craft in psychology and related disciplines using the five As model as an analytical framework. This model, focused on the articulation between actors, audiences, actions, artifacts, and affordances in creative work (Glăveanu, 2013b), is arguably better equipped to capture the dynamic and relational aspect of creativity (compared to the four Ps of person, process, product, and press). One aspect that makes it particularly useful for an analysis of craft creativity is the fact that it postulates a *material* dimension to creative action represented by affordances (action possibilities). A quick overview of the literature on creativity and craft reflects not only the fact that research in this area is scarce, but also that existing studies concern themselves primarily with creative action rather than the creative person. This specificity might be due to the fact that craftwork, when compared to other domains, is more easily available for observation due to its concrete material outputs, well defined period of work, and, in general, the willingness of artisans to participate in research.

One of the few studies related to creative actors in craftwork raised the question of life-span creativity. Kozbelt and Durmysheva (2007) investigated Japanese ukiyo-e (pictures of the floating world) printmaking, a traditional art specific for the period 1670–1865. These woodblock prints and paintings depicting various subjects (landscapes, scenes from history and folk tales, people and occupations) greatly inspired European art, particularly through painters such as Degas, Manet, and van Gogh. Since this traditional art is well documented it was possible for the two researchers to review almost 2,000 illustrations from forty-four artists and collect data about their dates of birth and death as well as the date of many of their works. Compared to nineteenth- and twentieth-century French artists, they noticed that ukiyo-e printmakers peak slightly later and that the most widely reproduced prints were made by older individuals then in the case of European "old masters" and French modernists. Moreover, ukiyo-e artists show a positive relation between career peak and eminence, contrasting with the negative or null correlations found in Western samples of artists. Overall, this study points to a general tendency towards later-life achievement in the case of craftsmen, something that goes beyond East–West differences and should make us reflect on the different way in which creativity in craft is appreciated compared to the arts (for a discussion of age and creativity see Simonton, 1989).

An interesting addition to these findings comes from research that explores the meaning of craft for artisans, particularly its relation to well-being. Pöllänen (2013) analyzed in this context the written narratives of ninety-two textile craft makers aged 16 to 84. She found evidence of the fact that engaging in craft enhances well-being, by providing a sense of achievement and having a calming effect, and helps participants adjust to various life situations. The narratives included references to personal growth, the development of skill, control over one's body, feelings, and thoughts, and social and cultural awareness. Interestingly, the researcher found that craftsmen do not necessarily pursue creativity, at least intentionally, and their focus tends to be more on relaxation and coping with personal difficulties. This testifies to the multiple valences of craft and the fact that creativity is one among many other outcomes of this activity. It also points us to the value of analyzing actors' reflections regarding their own work.

Studies that focus on creative action in craft cover a range of aspects, from cognitive to social and material. The first category includes research by Junaidy, Nagai, and Ihsan (2013), which explored in-depth cognitive levels at the early stage of idea generation in a comparative analysis of craftsmen and designers. Four participants from Indonesia were included in the study, two craftsmen and two designers, all aged between 27 and 51. The method used was think-aloud protocols and verbalized thoughts which were analyzed using the concept network method (grounded in associative concept analysis). The main finding of the research was that craftsmen tend to activate low-weighted associative concepts with a smaller number of polysemous features (multiple meanings) compared to designers. This was taken to explain their concern for tangible issues such a proportion and shape; meanwhile, designers brought up other contextual elements, referring also to user preferences. While an interesting starting point, these findings open up new questions regarding the way craftsmen relate to materiality and their audiences. It also raises concerns over the ways think-aloud protocols might interfere with the participants' actions.

Yokochi and Okada (2005) offered a more in-depth analysis of the cognitive processes of a Suibokuga painter (a traditional Chinese ink painter). They used a case-study methodology including field observation, interviews, and a field experiment (more details are offered in the following section). The questions that animated this research referred to the process of image generation in the work of the artisan, the relation between current and past work, and that between creativity and bodily movement. What the researchers found was that the painter starts drawing with a local, not global, image in mind. The global image emerges gradually as several parts are made one by one. In this process, pictures are drawn in a fairly patterned way and any new lines create constraints that influence how the painter proceeds. Interestingly, the study also documented the fact that the participant sometimes exercises drawing lines by making them first in the air. These actions serve multiple functions such as positioning, rehearsal, and image generation. While closely documenting creative action as it unfolds in time, this study is, however, not equally informative about the broader social and cultural context of the artisan.

In an effort to capture the microgenetic aspects of craft (i.e., moment-to-moment changes in action) in their socio-material expression, I conducted an ample investigation of Easter egg decoration practices in northern Romania (Glăveanu, 2010, 2013a, 2013c). This study adopted a cultural psychological framework for the study of creativity that explores the inter-relation between creative action and creativity beliefs in a developmental perspective. The research used a combination of observation, including filmed observation (using subjective cameras/subcams, a technique discussed more at length in the next section), interview, and drawing tasks. More relevant here for understanding creative action in craft is the overall theoretical model which focused, following Dewey (1934), on the articulation in creative work between *doing* (acting on the world) and *undergoing* (being acted upon by the world). These action-perception loops, characteristic for creative activity, can be observed both in the general phases of decorating eggs and in the micro-processes involved in each one of them; these are phases and processes which typically alternate between immersion and detachment, engagement and reflection. By considering two main "forms" of undergoing, from the material support and from the social world, this schema allowed connecting, in research, ongoing action and artifacts with affordances and audiences (in this case represented primarily by collaborators and customers).

A study of seven egg decorators, all women with ages ranging from 8 to 41, evidenced three main phases of decoration: preparation, working on the egg, finish & use (Glăveanu, 2013a). These phases go beyond typical work sessions (the second phase) and also try to capture what happens before and after decoration takes place (accounting, for instance, for the many years of collecting motifs and exercising the craft). This broader perspective on a creator's activity is specific for cultural psychology, a discipline that favors the holistic and contextual study of creativity. Through these lenses, each general phase of decoration relates to specific forms of material and social undergoing, is informed by particular types of knowledge and procedures, and faces its own obstacles. For example, drawing the first motif on wax on the white surface of the egg is influenced by the shape and size of the egg (materiality), as well as informed by customers' taste and preferences (sociality). Knowledge of motifs and their meaning, alongside specific work procedures (for example, for segmenting the egg in pencil), are also important at this stage. Key challenges in drawing motifs refer to mistakes done in wax on the surface of the egg, wax and color that don't properly "catch on," etc. Importantly, the different stages of decoration don't follow each other in a linear manner. Except for some basic rules (e.g., applying colors from lighter to darkest), there is a lot of *flexibility* in how and when motifs are depicted on the egg. Subjective camera recordings documented such micro-moments of technical creativity (see Glăveanu & Lahlou, 2012) in two artisans drawing one and the same motif. Moreover, it captured the flexible movement between different actions and tasks in decoration which doesn't follow a typical sequence but, instead, is characterized by a back-and-forth dynamic and open to the influence of personal style. This research also revealed stylistic differences between experienced decorators and novices, including how novices exercise basic movements under the general guidance of more skillful peers.

Similar to the study of Yokochi and Okada (2005) and other explorations of creativity in art (e.g., Mace & Ward, 2002), this investigation of craft evidenced the fact that creative action unfolds at the interface between person and situation and depends equally on actor and artifact. As egg decorators often mention, "the decoration of the egg comes out while working," not before, and a constant question on their mind while decorating is "What else can I do here?"; in this sense, eggs are not "made," but "discovered" (Glăveanu, 2013a, p. 12). These observations and supporting interview quotes suggest the importance of materiality in craft and the fact that objects are invested by artisans with *agency*, being able to meet or resist the participant's actions and intentions. This observation resonates widely in similar research on folk traditions and, at the same time, contradicts the assumption that craftwork is mechanical and preconceived. For example, Mall (2007), studying *kōlam* patterns in South India (intricate designs made with rice powder on the floor at the entrance of houses and temples), reached a similar conclusion:

> The *kampi kōlam*'s capacity spontaneously to transform in directions different from those originally intended locates "creativity" somewhere between the intentions of the practitioner and this "self-generating" capacity of the *kōlam* form. Although most women tried hard not to be put in a position where they would have to test their wits against the *kōlam* (in having to "bring the pattern back"), they nevertheless agreed that this was the primary mechanism behind the generation of novel designs, and skilled women cultivated a receptiveness to this revelatory potential in the design's execution. (Mall, 2007, p. 70)

There are a few notable *processes* in craft making which contribute to its creativity. One of the main ones observed in egg decoration is creative combination. Indeed, different symbols, motifs, and patterns are constantly combined by artisans in ways that account for the size of the egg, its purpose, and the wishes of different "audiences." Even when trying to make similar or identical decorated eggs, folk artists recognize it is easier to change something than make an identical copy (which is virtually impossible in any case due to small differences in size, shape, the way color pigments "catch" on the egg, etc.). Subcamera recordings support the view that copying in this craft is more akin to a form of "translation," adapting motifs from one material support to another and, in the process, transforming them. The transmission of tradition involves, in this and many other similar cases, interpreting and appropriating norms, techniques, and patterns of decoration rather than reproducing them. This is what Sennett (2008, p. 11) referred to when noting that "the good craftsman, moreover, uses solutions to uncover new territory; problem solving and problem finding are intimately related in his or her mind" (p. 11). Nothing is already given in craft, despite its many constraints or, rather, *because* of these constraints. In their work, craftsmen need to improvise and be highly imaginative in order to produce artifacts that conform to a variety of demands: from customers, from tradition, and ultimately, imposed by themselves. Constrained freedom is a key feature of creativity in craft (see also Stokes, 2001).

Methodological Approaches

As noted above, there are only a handful of studies focused on creativity in craftwork. This can be partially explained by the fact that crafts are rarely associated with creativity, unlike the arts, a (mis)conception discussed at the beginning of the chapter. However, a second reason has to do with the numerous methodological difficulties faced by researchers interested in craft. First and foremost, a deeper understanding of craft requires dealing with a very complex universe of actors, traditions, and forms of personal engagement. Cooper and Allen (1999), in their research on women quilters in Texas and New Mexico at the turn of the last century, noted that, for their participants "the quilts seemed to be the format in which they had condensed much of personal, family, and community history" (pp. 18–19). How can these experiential and historical dimensions be added to creativity research methods primarily focused on evaluating products and personal traits? Second, even when conducting studies guided by more specific questions such as "How do artisans create their work?," researchers often find craftsmen unable or unwilling to talk about their process. Yokochi and Okada (2005) report that, when asked how they came up with certain ideas, some craftsmen said that new ideas and images suddenly fell from the sky (p. 241). While this might testify to the role of insight in craftwork, it does little to clarify what exactly happens during moments of inspiration. Lastly, it is difficult to use methods like think-aloud protocols (similar to Junaidy, Nagai & Ihsan, 2013) since verbalizing one's thoughts in the process of making, and in the case of highly embodied practices, is difficult and potentially distracting for the participants (Yokochi & Okada, 2005).

What is, then, the solution? Multi-method approaches are perhaps the most suitable. Cooper and Allen (1999), for example, used recordings, took extensive notes, and photographed the women while working, as well as their environment. While this ethnographic type of work has many benefits (chief among them the possibility of understanding the person and his/her work in cultural context), it also leads to a wealth of data that can become hard to analyze and report. Yokochi and Okada (2005) similarly used a combination of methods but focused on a single participant (Mr. K). They observed Mr. K's drawing activity, filmed it (with two different cameras), and interviewed the craftsmen afterwards about his process. Moreover, they developed an ingenious field experiment – they asked Mr. K to draw eight pictures created from fifteen random lines drawn by the researchers (and eight others without this constraint). The theme of the drawings was the same in both conditions (the four seasons, two pictures for each season). Interestingly, in this study the craftsman was shown videotape recordings of his work and was asked to remember what he paid attention to while drawing. As the two authors note, there are reliability concerns when it comes to using introspective reports, but this was the only way to interpret findings from behavioral data and field observations (pp. 253–254).

The key methodological difficulty in these cases is how to capture action as it takes place and, at the same time, understand it from the perspective of the creative actor without disturbing his or her activity. A potential solution to this dilemma is represented by the use of subcams or subjective cameras, first employed in creativity research in the study of egg decoration (Glăveanu, 2013a; Glăveanu & Lahlou, 2012). Part of a Subjective Evidence-Based Ethnography (SEBE), this technology involves audio and video recording the work of creators from *a first-person perspective* by placing a small camera at eye level (on a pair of glasses, a sun visor, etc.). The researchers afterwards review these recordings and get to formulate their own questions and hypotheses concerning the activity of the participant. Then, as part of SEBE, the researchers show the participant either the entire film or relevant parts for it and ask him or her to comment on what was happening at the time, stopping the video when necessary to allow for more explanations, and asking questions of relevance for them (e.g., questions about goals and intentions, feelings and thoughts at the time of working). One of the key benefits of this method is the fact that, when watching their activity from the same perspective as the one originally experienced in the situation, participants have a better chance at reactivating information about their psychological state at the moment of the recording. This capacity to *re-situate* oneself in the activity and thus access, in a more direct manner, the phenomenological quality of an experience after it took place (including days or even weeks afterwards) makes the use of subcams particularly relevant for studying creative action in craft and beyond this domain. The reason a craft such as egg decoration is especially suitable, however, is due to the fact that work on such small objects, constantly placed between the hands of the participants, would have been very hard if not impossible to record otherwise. While watching and commenting on the videos, the artisans not only got to verbalize implicit knowledge but also learnt about their own creative processes. This educational potential of SEBE adds to its use as a research method and can inspire further research on creativity and reflexivity (Glăveanu, 2015).

In the end, a few considerations on the evaluation of creativity in craft are needed. Most of the studies referred to here did not actually assess the level of creativity of craft products; instead, they focused on how creativity is expressed in craftwork. This, I suggest, is due to the fact that assessing the creativity of particular artifacts or comparing them against each other is not very informative in this domain. To begin with, as noted before, craft products are generally similar to each other, at least when made by members of the same community; at the same time, many craftsmen do not aim to be original in their work. Second, there are not many "expert" judges who can evaluate craft creativity. Conversely, almost everyone can appreciate skill and creativity in craft based on his or her experience. This raises an important methodological question: from whose perspective are we to evaluate creativity in craft after all?

The consensual assessment technique (CAT) proposed by Amabile (1996), and commonly used nowadays in creativity research, has the benefit of grounding the evaluation of creativity within its cultural and historical context. This context, nevertheless, is captured mainly by the consensus between judges. The assumption is that consensus is possible when it comes to creativity, even when judges are not given a definition of what creativity is. How does this take into account heterogeneity in creativity assessment? Returning to the example of creativity in Easter egg decoration, a study in which four groups of evaluators were used – artists, priests, folk specialists, and the artisans themselves – revealed significant qualitative differences in terms of how each group understood and appreciated the craft and its products (for details see Glăveanu, 2010). These differences can be explained by the fact that each group of evaluators represented a certain tradition relevant for this particular craft: religion, art, and anthropology. In addition, folk artists were given an opportunity to reflect on their own and other's creativity, something that is rare in creativity assessment. Importantly, responses were not recorded as creativity scores but participants were asked to present and justify their evaluations. This methodology, formalized as *multiple feedback* (Glăveanu, 2012a), shares with CAT an interest in the social constitution of creativity. However, it also differs radically from it in its focus on diversity within the social field of evaluation. Ultimately, it answers a different question than CAT: How do different communities of evaluators relevant for the artifacts being evaluated construct the meaning of creativity? Further applications of multiple feedback in the area of craft should start by reflecting carefully, in each case, on what these communities might be.

Creativity in Craft and Beyond

The chapter began by defining crafts as a domain of creativity. It then reflected on the particular meaning of creativity in this domain and argued, at the same time, that some dimensions of creativity are uniquely present in craft activities and that there is a craft element in most other creative domains. Why is this so?

Because the aspects most valorized in craft – bodily engagement, skilled work, informal apprenticeships, etc. – are, in fact, underpinning creative expression in domains as different as the arts, design, science and engineering, and so on. If they are not always highlighted in creativity research it is not because they are absent but due to the fact that creativity as a scientific field tends to emphasize the individual over the social, thinking over making, *episteme* over *techne*. In the end, I would like to briefly outline the kinds of questions that require further research in the area of creativity in craft; these are also topics we would find more often in creativity research if we were to take craft seriously.

(1) *Intentionality and accidents*. Is all creative action intentional action? What is the role of accidents and unexpected events in producing novelty? Craftwork illustrates very well the fact that intentions and goals are never fully set in advance. While it is the case that craftsmen start their work with a general idea in mind and are guided by the norms of a given tradition, the final artifact is defined as much by this idea as it is by small or big accidents along the way and the improvisation work needed to repair them and creatively exploit their consequences.

(2) *Materiality and habits*. Creativity, across domains, is a material and embodied practice. This applies even to the most intellectual occupations as it does to digital work. In all cases there is a material support and there are tools that aid creators in achieving their aims. This is all the more obvious in craft activities, in which artisans depend on a multitude of tools, both traditional and modern. Their use is exercised and turned into habit. Habit, however, is not the opposite of creativity but the very basis of improvisation and innovation (for a detailed discussion of this argument see Glăveanu, 2012b). What kind of habits foster creative action in different crafts?

(3) *Participation and apprenticeships*. Crafts are almost never taught in a formal manner; they are learned through encounters with others, through observing them and participating in the culture of one's family, community, and society. Guided participation and apprenticeships (Rogoff, 1995) are at the core of learning crafts and perfecting them. What is the role of informal learning and social interaction in the case of other creative domains?

(4) *Culture and style*. Craftwork grows out of culture and contributes to it. This contribution is not an exact replication of existing cultural elements; on the contrary, cultures adapt and evolve in part due to the creativity intrinsic to craft practices. What makes craftwork, at once, belong to a certain cultural tradition and continue it in more or less unique ways is the development of style. In crafts, style reflects both individuality and sharedness (Gowlland, 2009). It is an identity marker for the self as well as the group and, often, for an entire culture. How could we extend the notion of style beyond art and crafts into other creative domains seemingly "immune" to it, such as the sciences? What would style in the case of scientific work mean? How would it vary depending on discipline? Could style equally apply to the way audiences "consume" products from craft, science, or other creative domains?

Craft creativity is a very rich and yet barely explored area, at least in psychology. This chapter reviewed existing work on creativity and craft in both this and related disciplines. An argument was advanced that we need more research on creative craft and, equally, that we should learn from it more and use this knowledge to enrich the psychology of creativity both conceptually and methodologically. For centuries, the artist has been the undisputed prototype of creativity, often in opposition to and at the expense of the craftsman. Will we see a reversal of this position as our world becomes more connected, our creative expression more distributed, and our culture more open to mixing, remixing, and user-generated forms of participation?

References

Amabile, T. M. (1996). *Creativity in context*. Boulder, CO: Westview Press.

Becker, H. S. (1978). Arts and crafts. *American Journal of Sociology, 83*(4), 862–889.

Beghetto, R. A., & Kaufman, J. C. (2007). Toward a broader conception of creativity: A case for "mini-c" creativity. *Psychology of Aesthetics, Creativity, and the Arts, 1*, 73–79.

Collingwood, R. G. (1938). *The principles of art*. Oxford: Clarendon Press.

Cooper, P., & Allen, N. B. (1999). *The quilters: Women and domestic art, an oral history*. Lubbock: Texas Tech University Press.

Crook, T. (2009). Craft and the dialogics of modernity: The Arts and Crafts movement in late-Victorian and Edwardian England. *The Journal of Modern Craft, 2*(1), 17–32.

Csikszentmihalyi, M. (1988). Society, culture, and person: A systems view of creativity. In R. Sternberg (Ed.), *The nature of creativity: Contemporary psychological perspectives* (pp. 325–339). Cambridge: Cambridge University Press.

Dalidowicz, M. (2015). Crafting fidelity: pedagogical creativity in kathak dance. *Journal of the Royal Anthropological Institute, 21*, 838–854.

Dewey, J. (1934). *Art as experience*. New York: Penguin.

Fine, G. A. (2004). *Everyday genius: Self-taught art and the culture of authenticity*. Chicago: University of Chicago Press.

Glăveanu, V. P. (2010). Creativity in context: The ecology of creativity evaluations and practices in an artistic craft. *Psychological Studies, 55*(4), 339–350.

Glăveanu, V. P. (2012a). A multiple feedback methodology for the study of creativity evaluations. *Journal of Constructivist Psychology, 25*(4), 346–366.

Glăveanu, V. P. (2012b). Habitual creativity: Revisiting habit, reconceptualising creativity. *Review of General Psychology, 16*(1), 78–92.

Glăveanu, V. P. (2013a). Creativity and folk art: A study of creative action in traditional craft. *Psychology of Aesthetics, Creativity, and the Arts, 7*(2), 140–154.

Glăveanu, V. P. (2013b). Rewriting the language of creativity: The five A's framework. *Review of General Psychology, 17*(1), 69–81.

Glăveanu, V. P. (2013c). Creativity development in community contexts: The case of folk art. *Thinking Skills & Creativity, 9*, 152–164.

Glăveanu, V. P. (2015). Creativity as a sociocultural act. *Journal of Creative Behavior, 49*(3), 165–180.

Glăveanu, V. P. (2016). Craft. In V. P. Glăveanu, L. Tanggaard, & C. Wegener (Eds.), *Creativity – A new vocabulary* (pp. 28–35). London: Palgrave.

Glăveanu, V. P., & Lahlou, S. (2012). Through the creator's eyes: Using the subjective camera to study craft creativity. *Creativity Research Journal, 24*(2–3), 152–162.

Glăveanu, V. P., & Tanggaard, L. (2014). Creativity, identity, and representation: Towards a socio-cultural theory of creative identity. *New Ideas in Psychology, 34*, 12–21.

Gowlland, G. (2009). Style, skill and modernity in the Zisha pottery of China. *The Journal of Modern Craft, 2*(2), 129–141.

Guth, C. M. E. (2010). The multiple modalities of the copy in traditional Japanese crafts. *The Journal of Modern Craft, 3*(1), 7–18.

Hughes-Freeland, F. (2007). 'Tradition and the individual talent': T.S. Eliot for anthropologists. In E. Hallam & T. Ingold (Eds.), *Creativity and cultural improvisation* (pp. 207–222). Oxford: Berg.

Ings, W. (2015). Malleable thought: The role of craft thinking in practice-led graphic design. *International Journal of Art & Design Education, 34*(2), 180–191.

Junaidy, D. W., Nagai, Y., & Ihsan, M. (2013). Craftsmen versus designers: The difference of in-depth cognitive levels at the early stage of idea generation. In A. Chakrabarti, & R. V. Prakash (Eds.), *ICoRD'13, Lecture notes in mechanical engineering* (pp. 223–234). New Delhi: Springer.

Kozbelt, A., & Durmysheva, Y. (2007). Lifespan creativity in a non-Western artistic tradition: A study of Japanese ukiyo-e printmakers. *International Journal of Aging and Human Development, 65*(1), 23–51.

Lehmann, U. (2012). Making as knowing: Epistemology and technique in craft. *The Journal of Modern Craft, 5*(2), 149–164.

Li, J. (1997). Creativity in horizontal and vertical domains. *Creativity Research Journal, 10*(2–3), 107–132.

Mace, M. A., & Ward, T. (2002). Modeling the creative process: A grounded theory analysis of creativity in the domain of art making. *Creativity Research Journal, 14*, 179–192.

Mall, A. S. (2007). Structure, innovation and agency in pattern construction: The Kōlam of Southern India. In E. Hallam & T. Ingold (Eds.), *Creativity and cultural improvisation* (pp. 55–78). Oxford: Berg.

Negus, K., & Pickering, M. (2004). *Creativity, communication and cultural value.* London: Sage Publications.

Niu, W., & Sternberg, R. J. (2006). The philosophical roots of Western and Eastern conceptions of creativity. *Journal of Theoretical and Philosophical Psychology, 26*(1–2), 18–38.

Pöllänen, S. (2013). The meaning of craft: Craft makers' descriptions of craft as an occupation. *Scandinavian Journal of Occupational Therapy, 20*(3), 217–227.

Pye, D. (1968). *The nature and art of workmanship.* London: The Herbert Press.

Rogoff, B. (1995). Observing sociocultural activity on three planes: Participatory appropriation, guided participation, and apprenticeship. In J. V. Wertsch, P. del Rio & A. Alvarez (Eds.), *Sociocultural studies of mind* (pp. 139–164). Cambridge: Cambridge University Press.

Scarlett, S. F. (2011). The craft of industrial patternmaking. *The Journal of Modern Craft, 4*(1), 27–48.

Sennett, R. (2008). *The craftsman.* New Have: Yale University Press.

Shiner, L. (2012). "Blurred boundaries"? Rethinking the concept of craft and its relation to art and design. *Philosophy Compass, 7*(4), 230–244.

Simonton, D. K. (1989). Age and creative productivity: Nonlinear estimation of an information-processing model. *The International Journal of Aging & Human Development*, *29*(1), 23–37.

Sternberg, R. J., Kaufman, J. C., & Pretz, J. E. (2002). *The creativity conundrum: A propulsion model of kinds of creative contributions*. New York: Psychology Press.

Stokes, P. D. (2001). Variability, constraints, and creativity: Shedding light of Claude Monet. *American Psychologist*, *56*(4), 355–359.

Yokochi, S., & Okada, T. (2005). Creative cognitive process of art making: A field study of a traditional Chinese ink painter. *Creativity Research Journal*, *17*(2, 3), 241–255.

PART VII

Conclusion

35 Taking a Prospective Look at Creativity Domains

Molly Holinger

University of Connecticut

Vlad P. Glăveanu

University of Bergen

James C. Kaufman

University of Connecticut

John Baer

Rider University

Abstract

In this concluding chapter we take another look at the complex relationship between generality and specificity with the double aim of: (a) highlighting some of the main lines of argument developed across this Handbook, and (b) looking towards the future, in a prospective manner, to consider the transformation of creative domains, as well as its impact on the generality–specificity debate.

The study of creativity is inseparable from that of domains and disciplines. This statement may seem surprising given that most papers make claims about general creativity. Yet it is possible to argue that there is no creativity outside of specific contexts and situated activities. Even laboratory studies using domain-general measures of divergent thinking still collect data about a form of creative expression. For divergent thinking, the form is creative ideation, which is much more important for particular domains – in this case artistic (by emphasizing originality) and educational (by gathering data in a test manner, one that is likely to favor participants who benefited from schooling and, more generally, Western education).

There is, of course, the reverse argument. Creativity fascinates us precisely because it seems to transcend or, rather, conjoin together a variety of experiences. In this sense, being creative in the sphere of the sciences, arts, business, or everyday life can be characterized in similar ways by creators (such as, for instance, the notion of flow; Csikszentmihalyi, 1990) and perceived as such by outside observers. Although (for example) scientists, artists, and cooks use different tools and utilize different types of knowledge in their work, they might nonetheless engage in similar processes (e.g., experimentation, conceptual combination, analogical thinking).

Whereas these two facets of creativity – its domain generality and specificity – have often been understood as opposite, the present volume seeks new ways to conceptualize their relationship. In line with the basic assumptions of Amusement Park Theory (see Baer & Kaufman, 2005, Chapter 2 of this volume; Kaufman & Baer, 2004), each chapter is not only sensitive to the issue of generality and specificity but, most of all, to how these different facets may relate to each other and co-evolve over time.

In this concluding chapter we take another look at the complex relationship between generality and specificity with the double aim of: (a) highlighting some of the main lines of argument developed across this Handbook, and (b) looking towards the future, in a prospective manner, to consider the transformation of creative domains, as well as its impact on the generality–specificity debate. It is to be noted from the start that, although the variety of creativity domains included here is extensive, this volume did not intend to cover every potential discipline or practice associated with creativity. As noted in the Introduction, there are many emerging forms of creative expression that can and will, in time, add to the existing domains or constitute new ones (think, for instance, about creativity and the use of new technologies or social media). However, a guiding principle in putting together the list of chapters has been to include both "traditional" creativity domains, which have been intensively studied (e.g., visual art, music, play, dance, engineering, teaching, architecture, psychology) alongside less "traditional" domains of creativity (e.g., sports, craft, emotions, photography, animal creativity). Towards the end of this chapter, new questions will be raised concerning both the future of domains and creativity in the "domains of the future."

The Creativity Mosaic

The image of creativity emerging out of the contributions included in this Handbook is best described as dynamic and heterogeneous. Creating in each domain included here reflects its own mosaic of traits, processes, outcomes, and contexts, thereby contributing, in turn, to the big mosaic of creativity across domains. The metaphor of the mosaic is not accidental. It aims to capture both the plurality of themes reflected within each chapter as well as the multiple overlaps between these themes across chapters.

First, the discussion of domain-general and domain-specific aspects of creativity presents us with multiple positions, mostly aimed at striking a balance between these two poles. For instance, Beghetto (Chapter 30), approaches teaching creativity in the context of specific domains or "subjects areas" while, at the same time, emphasizing the importance of working with a view of what is beyond them. The chapter on engineering (Cropley, Cropley & Sandwith, Chapter 15 of this volume), explicitly mentions in relation to the generality – specificity debate that, for "as important as it is to articulate a unique perspective on creativity in engineering, it is also important to recognize how much is *not* different". The way in which creativity is defined in each chapter reflects well the importance of operating with more or less "classic" definitions (see Kaufman, 2016; Plucker, Beghetto & Dow, 2004), while nuancing the criteria of novelty and value, adding to them and, at times, challenging our conception of creativity from the perspective of particular domains. For example, Serafin and Dollinger (Chapter 8) specify that what is "useful" in photography relates, first and foremost, to eliciting emotional responses in viewers and impacting their understanding of life and art. Defining creativity becomes much more difficult in the case of animals (see Kaufman & O'Hearn, Chapter 27), adding an extra layer of complexity to the debate, with the lack of common terminology being one of the main obstacles in this area of research. In other cases, such as architecture (Vartanian, Chapter 7), the definition of creativity is closely associated with other concepts, for example aesthetics; whereas in the case of law (Mandel, Chapter 24), institutional constraints and norms take center stage, such as what is inscribed in copyright or patent law. In the end, Damian and Tou (Chapter 31) point to the fact that different cultures might emphasize different aspects of creativity, such as originality (in the West) and tradition and usefulness (in the East). The cultural level complexifies our understanding of domains since they are both embedded within a shared culture as well as carry their own, distinctive cultural characteristics. And it is not only national but also organizational culture that we should take into account (Mitchell & Reiter-Palmon, Chapter 20).

The metaphor of the mosaic applies also when considering the issue of assessment. In psychology, often, creativity assessment makes use of psychometric measures, expert judges, self-reported beliefs, or professional accomplishments, depending on the level of creativity under study (Kaufman & Beghetto, 2009). At the same time, there is increasing criticism of domain-general measures, most of which are based on divergent thinking (e.g., Thomson, Chapter 11; Cropley, Cropley, and Sandwith, Chapter 15). Such critiques are often matched by increased support for the use of expert or domain-specific ratings (e.g., Kaufman & Baer, 2012; Serafin & Dollinger, Chapter 8; Vartanian, Chapter 7). A focus on different domains reveals interesting, domain-tailored ways of evaluating creativity. In the case of photography, assessment can be based on the judgment of curators and juries (Serafin & Dollinger, Chapter 8), whereas in psychology, it would need to take into account the process of peer-review (Simonton, Chapter 14). An important question that emerges is whether it is easier to assess creativity in some domains compared to others. For example, in marketing, creativity can be more or less easily evaluated in terms of traditional criteria for performance (Taillard & Voyer, Chapter 19).

Another important issue relates to the call for improved domain-specific assessment of creativity (see, for instance, the chapters on emotions, Ivcevic, Bazhydai, Hoffmann, & Brackett, Chapter 29; teaching, Beghetto, Chapter 30; and sports, Memmert, Chapter 26). In this case, play might be a relatively rare example of a domain already benefiting from specific and nuanced forms of assessment (see Russ & Wallace, Chapter 33). Finally, some domains might not lend themselves to traditional assessments of creativity that highlight product novelty, but rather on measures of the work process itself. Such domains may stimulate novel methods for assessing creativity such as multiple feedback (such as in the domain of craft, see Glăveanu, Chapter 34) or new ways of eliciting creativity (motor creativity in dance, see Thomson, Chapter 11). Who should judge – and how – the creativity of different outcomes remains an open question and, more and more, we find calls for involving audiences, beneficiaries, or users in this process (Taillard & Voyer, Chapter 19).

In terms of personality and, more generally, the characteristics of the creative person, there is evidence of differences in personality traits both within and across domains. Szen-Ziemiańska, Lebuda, and Karwowski (Chapter 3) review existing studies and note many nuances. They point to the fact that, for example, neuroticism and extraversion seem to be associated with creativity, yet this association depends on the creativity domain, whereas extraversion appears to be related to creativity in a limited number of areas, particularly in everyday and entrepreneurial creativity. In addition, four of the Big Five personality traits – emotional stability, extraversion, openness, and conscientiousness – seem to correlate positively with leadership (Mitchell & Reiter-Palmon, Chapter 20). Even more interestingly, there is evidence suggesting that traits conducive for creativity in one domain might hinder creative expression in others (e.g., conscientiousness in sciences versus arts; Feist, 1998). The relation between creativity and mental health is also, to a great extent, domain-specific. For instance, mental illness seems to have a greater prevalence among artistic professions with writers being diagnosed with schizophrenia or bipolar disorder twice as often as non-writers (Oatley & Djikic, Chapter 5; see also different positions in Kaufman, 2014). The attributes of creative people are not only to be thought of as personal but as also being shaped by interactions with others. These interactions can model creative behaviors such as risk taking and openness to new ideas (Beghetto, Chapter 30).

A particular theme in the discussion about creative individuals is that of motivation. Motivation, particularly intrinsic motivation, is often considered to influence creativity regardless of domain (Amabile, 1996; Russ & Wallace, Chapter 33). People's motives are never uniformly intrinsic, of course, and one's motivation to be creative may easily shift from domain to domain (Kaufman & Baer, 2002). Finally, the possible interactions with both age and gender emerged in several chapters, such as Feist's (Chapter 12) discussion of the disproportionately low number of women in the physical sciences.

Other frequently mentioned topics, highly visible in the mosaic of creativity across domains, included expertise, education, well-being, and the relationship to society. Although receiving training in the domain and accumulating domain-specific (procedural and declarative) knowledge is certainly important, some domains (such as the sciences) are more likely to require more formal training than others (such as the arts, particularly crafts). In fact, crafts are almost never taught formally but learned through informal interactions and apprenticeships (Glăveanu, Chapter 34). Another difference between domains is visibility. Chapters in this book cover a wide scope, from the headlines that come with new scientific discoveries and technological advances to the everyday creativity found in the domain of emotions (Ivcevic, Bazhydai, Hoffmann & Brackett, Chapter 29). And yet it is precisely domains like emotions that help relate creativity with important topics such as psychological health and well-being. In fact, the theme of well-being was referred to in different chapters, particularly Forgeard and Elstein

(Chapter 32). There is some evidence suggesting that engaging in creative activity has a positive effect, even if not at all levels of creativity (see, for example, the case of everyday and professional writers in Oatley & Djikic, Chapter 5). When it comes to the role of audiences, there are domains in which collaboration is the norm and creativity is performative (such as acting, Goldstein & Levy, Chapter 9; and dance, Thomson, Chapter 11). However, relations to various audiences are present in any domain of creativity (Glăveanu, 2013). At times, as in marketing, they reverse roles and turn users into creators in their own right (Taillard & Voyer, Chapter 19).

Beyond the Generality–Specificity Debate

The debate between creativity as a domain-general versus domain-specific process is placed in the background of all the chapters included in this handbook. And yet contributors began from not an either/or position, but rather a dynamic, relational view of similarities and differences both within and across domains; referred to above as the creativity mosaic. Different chapters approached the mosaic differently. Simonton (Chapter 4), for example, makes a strong argument for generality by claiming that all creativity is combinatorial. In practice as well, domain generality might be assumed when dealing with creative work; intellectual property law, for example, takes a domain-general approach and does not have separate rules for different domains (Mandel, Chapter 24). However, among creativity researchers, there tends to be a general consensus concerning the importance of domains for creative expression.

To take a few examples, creativity in education is bound to the context of academic subject matter and its constraints (Beghetto, Chapter 30). Moreover, by adopting domain-specific lenses in teaching practices, creativity becomes more concrete, teachable, and easier to achieve. In marketing, an increasing use of technology gives the creative process a specific dynamic, simultaneously revealing untapped opportunities for creativity (Taillard & Voyer, Chapter 19); the same holds, certainly, for educational technologies (Peppler, Chapter 21). Most differences between creativity domains can be found, nonetheless, at the level of processes. Bonnardel and Bouchard (Chapter 22), distinguish between macro and micro-processes within design, a useful classification that can be considered more widely. As noted within their chapter, design thinking is perhaps one of the most specific models of the creative process coming out of this field, yet one that can and has been generalized effectively. Indeed, what may start off as domain-specific findings or models can end up inspiring research and practice in other, possibly distant, fields. The reverse also holds: domain-general models can be applied differently by researchers or practitioners within specific domains, or else only a small part of a model might be used (see, for example, the focus on illumination within the study of creative photography; see Serafin & Dollinger, Chapter 8).

In the end, one could think of the generality–specificity debate in creativity research as bringing together two tendencies: one towards *generalizing*, from one or two domains to many others, and one towards *specifying* or, in other words, making the general more concrete and nuanced, at the level of the domain and even of micro-domains (see Baer & Kaufman, 2005; Chapter 2). By discussing generalizing and specifying movements within creativity research we achieve a number of goals. First, we are likely to overcome the either/or logic that often makes the debate unproductive. Second, it allows us to consider less how creativity "is" and more how it "becomes" when we move our analytical focus up and down different levels of generality. It is thus not a question of whether a certain creative activity is the same or different from others but of how it *appears* to us when considering it in a narrower or wider context. Third, we can consider along these dynamic, temporal lines, what exactly it is that we can generalize and what should remain specific. For instance, findings about the creative process in particular domains might be difficult to generalize, whereas research methods may be "transferred" more easily to other forms of creative work.

Last but not least, an emphasis on generalizing and specifying can make us sensitive to what is placed at the intersection between domains and what exactly brings multiple domains together. For example, creators tend to interact with a variety of other people before, during, and after they create their work. This observation can be found in the arts (e.g., music, Kozbelt, Chapter 10; visual arts, Pelowski, Leder, & Tinio, Chapter 6), business (e.g., advertising, Kilgour, Chapter 18; entrepreneurship, Carayannis & Harvard, Chapter 23), and the sciences (e.g., biomedicine, Tan & Grigorenko, Chapter 13; computer science, Barnett & Romeike, Chapter 17; mathematics, Sak, Ayvaz, Bal-Sezerel, & Özdemir, Chapter 16), as well as in social and everyday life domains (e.g., the culinary domain, Horng & Lin, Chapter 25; therapy, Forgeard & Elstein, Chapter 32; violence and terrorism; Ligon, Sporer & Derrick, Chapter 28). Going in the direction of domain generality, we might think about what categories of interaction are important across domains (such as mentors, colleagues, gatekeepers, or the general public) and what kind of relations are established with them (such as collaborative or competitive). A focus on specificity takes us in the opposite direction of trying to understand unique audiences and relationships (ranging from people who enjoy the products of culinary creativity to the beneficiaries of new medical solutions in biomedicine). Being able to consider both these facets opens up the possibility of considering creators and their audiences as they participate in more than one domain and sometimes exchange roles in the process (think, for instance, about the roles of teachers and students when considered from the perspective of instruction versus using new technologies). In the end, these relational ways of understanding domains are a marker of today's hyper-connected societies and invite us to reflect on how they might evolve in the future.

Creativity and the Future of Domains

Just like our theories and models of creativity, domains are in a constant process of change. There is a reason why we wonder today, looking back in history, whether the term "Renaissance person" reflects a certain bygone reality (Kaufman, Baer, Beghetto, & Ivcevic, 2010). It is not only that we have, particularly in the last few decades, produced, accumulated, and shared more knowledge than an individual living in the age of Da Vinci could have imagined; the notion of domains of creativity is, itself, questioned. In a world dominated by digital technologies and unprecedented mobility, self-contained and well-defined domains are increasingly becoming a thing of the past. In exchange, multi-domain expertise becomes necessary (Szen-Ziemia ńska, Lebuda & Karwowski, Chapter 3), as well as the diversifying experiences of working in various fields and across various cultures (Damian & Tou, Chapter 31). It is not only our activity that changes but our understanding of domains and what it means to contribute to one or more. Domains are not disappearing. They are transforming and this transformation bears the mark of creativity.

There is ample evidence of this process within the pages of the present volume, which offers an overview of both traditional (such as those in the arts and sciences) and non-traditional domains of creativity (such as law, culinary, terrorism, and animal creativity). Further, the inclusion of chapters on such topics as emotions, crafts and play challenges a common view of domains as institutionalized, bounded fields. To take the example of emotions (see Ivcevic, Bazhydai, Hoffmann & Brackett, Chapter 29), their studies go beyond professional areas and enter the sphere of everyday life and of psychological experience. Similarly, researching the area of crafts and creativity (see Glăveanu, Chapter 34) reveals processes that go beyond a narrow definition of artisans and folk art. Indeed, there is craftsmanship in creative work beyond what is commonly recognized as craft. This discrepancy raises the issue of how we align our conceptions of domains with the multiple and fluid practices that constitute today's creative practices. Within "classic" domains, as well, our expectations can be violated, as when John Cage recorded silence as a song (see Kozbelt, Chapter 10). Is this music? Is it creativity? And, if so, what does it say about the domain of music and its contemporary expression?

Creativity in the Domains of the Future

If the future of domains is open to transformation, so too is creative expression. In fact, the ways in which we express our creativity today are bound to change in the not-so-distant future. Consider the advances in technology, the Internet, and social media and their impact on everything from interpersonal relations to the way we envision economy and society. It is often said that educators today need to realize that they are training children for areas of work that are probably not invented yet and preparing them to face problems that can't even be anticipated today. Creativity, as a twenty-first-century skill (Trilling & Fadel, 2009), is called upon to respond to such challenges and these responses will change domains, often in radical ways. A concrete example is *multiculturalism*. Considered to boost creativity (see Damian & Tou, Chapter 31), multiculturalism is itself developing into a societal domain of creativity – which can present both challenges and opportunities. From building highly creative and culturally diverse workgroups to rethinking national and cultural boundaries and identities, creativity in the area of multiculturalism can be expected to increase in visibility over the next decades.

Readers are invited thus to consider, in a prospective manner and based on the contributions included here, what creativity and creative domains could look like in the future. Similarly, will the generality–specificity debate continue to organize our discussion? One hypothesis is that this dichotomy will transform, leaving room to the more pragmatic question of how and when we can generalize findings and tools from one domain of activity to others or how domain general knowledge or approaches can help us intervene in applied domains. Another one is that domains of creativity will be studied developmentally. Csikszentmihalyi (1990) wrote of creativity in the domain of the future. This idea has never been timelier. The future as a domain of creative thinking and action is a *transversal concern*, mobilizing creative people and teams across the numerous domains and disciplines included within these pages. In studying each of them, the future-oriented directions needed for creative action must be considered and cultivated. Paradoxically, thus, it might not be what creators do today within and across domains that matters most but, rather, what they do thinking about tomorrow and the numerous, general *and* specific ways they find to anticipate and create the future that is of the essence.

References

Amabile, T. M. (1996). *Creativity in context: Update to "The Social Psychology of Creativity."* Boulder, CO: Westview Press.

Baer, J., & Kaufman, J. C. (2005). Bridging generality and specificity: The amusement park theoretical (APT) model of creativity. *Roeper Review, 27*, 158–163.

Csikszentmihalyi, M. (1990). *Flow: The psychology of optimal experience.* New York, NY: Harper & Row.

Feist, G. J. (1998). A meta-analysis of personality in scientific and artistic creativity. *Personality and Social Psychology Review, 2*, 290–309.

Glăveanu, V. P. (2013). Rewriting the language of creativity: The five A's framework. *Review of General Psychology, 17*, 69–81.

Kaufman, J. C. (Ed.). (2014). *Creativity and mental illness.* New York: Cambridge University Press.

Kaufman, J. C. (2016). *Creativity 101* (2nd edn.). New York: Springer.

Kaufman, J. C., & Baer, J. (2002). Could Steven Spielberg manage the Yankees?: Creative thinking in different domains. *Korean Journal of Thinking & Problem Solving, 12*, 5–15.

Kaufman, J. C., & Baer, J. (2004). The Amusement Park Theoretical (APT) Model of creativity. *Korean Journal of Thinking and Problem Solving, 14*, 15–25.

Kaufman, J. C., & Baer, J. (2012). Beyond new and appropriate: Who decides what is creative? *Creativity Research Journal, 24*, 83–91.

Kaufman, J. C., Beghetto, R. A., Baer, J., & Ivcevic, Z. (2010). Creativity polymathy: What Benjamin Franklin can teach your kindergartener. *Learning & Individual Differences, 20*, 380–387.

Kaufman, J. C., & Beghetto, R. A. (2009). Beyond big and little: The four c model of creativity. *Review of General Psychology, 13*(1), 1–12.

Trilling, B., & Fadel, C. (2009). *21st century skills: Learning for life in our times.* San Francisco: Jossey-Bass.

Index